NEW FRONTIERS OF PHILANTHROPY

NEW FRONTIERS OF
PHILANTHROPY

A Guide to the New Tools
and Actors Reshaping Global
Philanthropy and Social Investing

Lester M. Salamon, Editor

OXFORD
UNIVERSITY PRESS

OXFORD
UNIVERSITY PRESS

Oxford University Press is a department of the University of Oxford.
It furthers the University's objective of excellence in research, scholarship,
and education by publishing worldwide.

Oxford   New York
Auckland   Cape Town   Dar es Salaam   Hong Kong   Karachi
Kuala Lumpur   Madrid   Melbourne   Mexico City   Nairobi
New Delhi   Shanghai   Taipei   Toronto

With offices in
Argentina   Austria   Brazil   Chile   Czech Republic   France   Greece
Guatemala   Hungary   Italy   Japan   Poland   Portugal   Singapore
South Korea   Switzerland   Thailand   Turkey   Ukraine   Vietnam

Oxford is a registered trademark of Oxford University Press
in the UK and certain other countries.

Published in the United States of America by
Oxford University Press
198 Madison Avenue, New York, NY 10016

Library of Congress Cataloging-in-Publication Data

New frontiers of philanthropy : a guide to the new tools and actors reshaping global
philanthropy and social investing / edited by Lester M. Salamon.

pages cm

Includes bibliographical references and index.

ISBN 978–0–19–935754–3 (hardback : alk. paper)   1. Charities.
2. Investments—Moral and ethical aspects.   I. Salamon, Lester M.

HV40.N448 2014

361.7—dc23

2013043895

9 8 7 6 5 4 3 2 1
Printed in the United States of America
on acid-free paper

For Vanessa, Cas, Ben, Dominick, Zoe, and Zev,
May they grow up in a world in which the new frontiers of
philanthropy
Have helped to open opportunities and improve life chances
For all of the world's children.

There are moments in history when the needs of an age prompt lasting, promising innovation.

—Monitor Institute, 2009

CONTENTS

LIST OF FIGURES

LIST OF TABLES

LIST OF BOXES

FOREWORD

William Dietel

NEW FRONTIERS OF PHILANTHROPY IS the guidebook to the revolution that has been informing and shaping global philanthropy over the past decade. This collection of thoughtful and provocative essays is the first successful effort describing the new players and new tools that are reshaping global philanthropy. The intellectual Sherpa of this expedition into twenty-first-century philanthropy is Lester M. Salamon, who has been exploring this new world for more than 25 years and who has assembled an outstanding team of colleagues to introduce the reader to the most exciting, promising, and problematic new regions of global philanthropy.

The philanthropy of the twentieth century was a remarkable social phenomenon by any standard of measurement. By the beginning of the twenty-first century, however, its inadequacies, its restricted vision, and its organization inefficiencies were glaringly obvious. In spite of a spate of recent books extolling philanthropy's successes, especially those of foundations—the twentieth century's singular philanthropic institutional achievement—the foundation model has proven inadequate to meet the social and environmental challenges of the early twenty-first century. We need new financial capital, new intellectual capital, new institutional forms, and a fresh understanding of the dynamics of global problems and how the multifaceted tools of twenty-first-century philanthropy can be used most effectively in concert with government and for-profits to effect needed fundamental social and environmental change.

The economic and social challenges to humankind as we crossed into the twenty-first century required "a significant revolution" in philanthropy. Indeed, such a revolution appears to be underway at the frontiers of philanthropy and social investment. In his introduction to this important book, its editor states that "the world of philanthropy seems to be experiencing a 'Big Bang.'" New actors and new tools "for financing and promoting social and environmental objectives have become urgently needed."

Lester Salamon's introduction is a masterful essay that paints in broad strokes the revolution in philanthropy we are entering at a fast pace. His colleagues provide the details that inform the painting with its vibrancy and vitality. This may not be the best of times, it is certainly not the worst of times in spite of all our problems, but it promises to be one of the most exciting and demanding of times for everyone interested in a global civil society and an adventuresome philanthropic life.

Salamon and colleagues have described the changes being achieved by the new philanthropy as beyond grants, beyond foundations, beyond bequests, and beyond cash. The common imperative behind this shift is the search for "leverage," which they define as "the mechanism that allows limited energy to be translated into greater power." Its proponents hope that their new tools will go far beyond the current flow of charitable resources from foundations and individuals. They want to believe that they can open the spigots of charitable dollars and socially minded private investment capital on a mammoth scale. It is an ambitious goal, but the jury will be out for some time before we know whether it was a realizable objective.

This revolution has developed its own vocabulary that borders on the arcane, and, not surprisingly, while it has its ardent exponents, it also has vocal critics. The editor's objective is "to provide a clear and accessible road-map to the full range of important new developments taking place on the frontiers of philanthropy and social investments." The roadmap may not prove to be another GPS, but it is a well-conceived guide to these new developments as they are emerging. Social performance finance, albeit a matter of fascination to philanthropods, is still something of a mystery to many traditional philanthropists. This effort to "provide a more coherent guide for those who are contemplating entry into this territory" is much needed, for often the language of the converts suggests only epigones can truly understand the gospel. Salamon and company have rendered a valuable service to philanthropists of all kinds everywhere. Simply put, this is a vital book if one wants to understand what is happening in twenty-first-century philanthropy.

While Salamon is enthusiastic about the promise of this "significant revolution," he is careful to describe the considerable obstacles it still confronts. As of 2013, it is not clear whether many of the new role players and their exotic tools can surmount the barricades resistant to change. The task before the revolutionaries is sobering.

These essays inexorably lead to the fundamental question of whether or not these new ideas, players, tools, and organizations can inspire and inform and support the desire of the masses of humankind who wish to take an active part in deciding their own future. If the philanthropic revolution fails to empower fundamental change in the structures of economic and political power, what legacy does it leave a civil society in need of reformation? Will social-impact investing turn out to be another detour on the way to addressing the basic causes of economic and environmental injustice, or will it find ways to "leverage" the cause of advocacy for change?

In addition to new tools for leveraging private capital for social progress, humanity requires instruments of social and environmental change commensurate with the magnitude and profundity of the global problems that threaten the future of humankind. One of the fundamental problems is the inadequacy of the existing, traditional models of charity and philanthropy to respond fully to the magnitude of the capital needs of the global civil society.

The potential power of the new ideas and experiments outlined in this book may help solve the daunting risk capital needs we face. To cite a single example, mission-related investing only yesterday was regarded as fuzzy thinking, impractical, decades away from acceptance within the cautious, slow-moving upper reaches of the foundation community. Mission-related investing did not emerge from the Council of Foundations, Independent Sector, or the Philanthropy Roundtable. It was the carefully nurtured creature of a handful, literally, of foundations that courageously pioneered finding ways and means to bring all their financial assets to bear on their mission, not just their grant funds. One of the leaders of this revolutionary change was the F.B. Heron

Foundation, which today has 50 percent of its financial assets successfully invested in mission-related instruments.

Donor-advised funds were also an aberration only yesterday. Today they are a positive and successful challenge to the almost automatic creation of foundations for the superwealthy. The number of modest givers using donor-advised funds increases with every passing year, and the total of funds thus deployed shows an astonishing increase. The creative impulse behind the growth of DAFs has come not only from within philanthropy, but from corporate sponsors such as Fidelity, Vanguard, and Schwab, whose entry in the field boosted access and reduced costs for tens of thousands of potential donors. Giving circles and conversion foundations are also examples of new ways of thinking and acting philanthropically.

All too typically, the reaction of many traditionalists to the ideas and experiments in this book has been, at least initially, one of suspicion and resistance. The new philanthropists, particularly the so-called social entrepreneurs, however, have begun to seize the initiative and to question the static thinking of the philanthropic establishment. More important, the increase in the number of charitable donors globally who bypass the establishment in their thinking and action has increased markedly, and this phenomenon is part of the exciting story of twenty-first-century philanthropy outlined in the book.

It is also important to note that we are on the edge of vitally important changes in our understanding of why people act philanthropically, whether through charitable giving or larger concepts of social investment. Thanks to brain mapping and the neurological research made possible by the fMRI technology, we are finally beginning to understand how we learn and, equally important, why we act philanthropically. It is no longer a guessing game of best intentions and ad hoc explanations. Acting to help others is critical to our health and well-being as humans. Some have suggested that by midcentury we shall have developed a new understanding of what it means to be religious, and that belief will be trumped by the joy of service, including the giving of self, talents, and financial assets.

No book on global philanthropy and social investing can cover all aspects of this vast subject. It is important to note that those of us who have spent our lives in the civil society sector, whether on the donor or donee side, find it imperative to remind ourselves that no one has yet demonstrated that our work is more than one part of a much larger dynamic. Government and business, finance, and commerce are also essential parts of any effort to make the social system more just, equitable, and safe. Philanthropists continually need to remind themselves and the communities they serve that their contributions to a better world, however important, are modest in comparison to what government and for-profit activity can and do accomplish. This is meant, not as a criticism of philanthropy, but as a reminder that an informed sense of proportion is the best shield against philanthropic hubris.

Finally, whether social-impact investing is a "significant revolution" or just one more skirmish on the border of philanthropic evolution is for the historians to determine. Meanwhile the demand for fundamental systemic change in our economic and political systems gathers speed. Those with limited power to effect significant improvement in their lives will insist on being heard. It is not clear what role philanthropy, the old and the new, will play in this revolution. But what is clear is that this book, and the fundamental message it projects, is what has been needed to help keep philanthropy in the conversation.

PREFACE

Mario Morino

LESTER SALAMON AND HIS ENTIRE team of contributors have done a true service to all of those who care about solving the world's wicked problems. Combining front-line knowledge, academic rigor, and Salamonic wisdom, this volume is the definitive chronicle of the innovations that are infusing new life into the well-intentioned but often-staid world of philanthropy.

This book was an ambitious undertaking, far more onerous and time-consuming than the team anticipated. Many previous efforts have looked at individual constellations of innovative practices, such as venture philanthropy and impact investing. But no one previously has taken on the massive task of mapping the thousands of points of light that have emerged in recent years.

Throughout my career in the for-profit and nonprofit sectors, I have always believed that it was critically important to map innovative practices emerging on the periphery of an established field. Even when I've been racing (or stumbling) forward in building a new venture, I've had the good sense to team up with wise observers who could categorize the new practices, understand how they relate to one another, and develop some common definitions. This kind of painstaking mapping is a prerequisite for channeling energies, avoiding reinvention, and building a true field capable of solving—not just salving—wicked problems. I salute Salamon and colleagues for taking this on and working at it for years, stopping and starting several times to ensure they got it right.

The map they have drawn is exciting to behold. Even the most skeptical readers of *New Frontiers of Philanthropy* will come away with a clear sense that innovators around the world are ushering in a wealth of disruptive ideas and boundary-crossing models. In the words of Salamon, the world of social change is truly moving "beyond grants," "beyond foundations," "beyond bequests," and "beyond cash." I'm convinced these ideas and models go beyond flavor-of-the-month fads.

My colleagues and I at Venture Philanthropy Partners (VPP) have been a part of this revolution. But only a small part. While we have been working to expand the philanthropic toolkit to include the kind of strategic counsel and leadership support that the best venture capital and growth equity firms provide to their portfolio companies, many others have been working to expand and improve the social-change toolkit in different ways.

For example, the Bill and Melinda Gates Foundation, which is structured in many respects like a traditional foundation, has pioneered the use of new financing mechanisms that pull private pharmaceutical firms into solving big problems in a way that traditional grants could not. One creative "pull mechanism," called an "advance market commitment," provides binding assurances to pharmaceutical firms that if they succeed in developing specific vaccines desperately needed in the developing world, governments and philanthropic donors are committed to purchasing defined quantities at reasonable prices.

As is true with all types of innovation, social innovators pop up on the map, literally and figuratively, in surprising places. I learned in this volume that the world's first full-fledged social stock exchange is emerging in the diverse island nation of Mauritius, which has a GDP only a third as large as the Gates Foundation's coffers. If successful, Mauritius's Impact Exchange (iX) could make it much easier for companies with social and environmental missions to raise more capital, from more investors, more efficiently than they could in any other way.

Meanwhile in India, Mauritius's longtime friend and trading partner to the north, social innovators are catalyzing change on a massive scale. With clever incentives, they've mobilized private companies to provide health insurance to more than 60 million people living below the poverty line.

And yet these exciting developments do not represent evidence of pervasive, game-changing transformation throughout civil society. The reality is that the innovative practices highlighted here touch only a small minority of organizations, funders, and governments. In the words of a wise Swahili proverb, "To run is not necessarily to arrive."

I salute Salamon and the other contributors for avoiding wide-eyed boosterism. They balance their assessments of the new tools and new actors with clear-eyed analysis of the many challenges that remain. At this stage of analysis, there's always a temptation to aggregate the many points of light into a gleaming beacon of hope. But as the authors of this volume understand, overstatement often proves to be a disservice to the innovators and those they give their lives to serve. Hype works against a new movement by creating unrealistic expectations for what these innovations can produce. Over the medium and long term, it can cause donors and investors to flee rather than flock.

As promising as the new models are, they are still operating only at the periphery of civil society. More important, we must acknowledge that their on-the-ground results will be gated by a common challenge that is bigger than the money challenge. The single biggest constraint on social-change organizations is an acute shortage of great talent. As Salamon cautions, we can't just pay attention to the supply side of the social capital market. We must also address the demand side—that is, the entrepreneurs who need the capital to work their wonders.

Meaningful, measurable change simply doesn't happen without passionate leaders who are also highly competent managerially and have the good sense to build this competency in their teams. They recruit and develop talent that aligns with their organization's guiding principles and fits well into its culture. They bring a keen judgment that allows them to use the information they collect to stay focused, course-correct, and keep on improving. They have high emotional intelligence that allows them to understand the sensitivities and navigate the complex ecosystems in which they are working.

In the early years of VPP, I took the organization's leadership and staff to the offices of General Atlantic, LLC, a preeminent global growth-equity firm that invests to build great companies. In a discussion with one of the best executives I've had the pleasure of knowing, one member of the VPP team asked, "What's the most important thing you do to help the firms in which you invest?" He said simply, "Make sure the firm has a great CEO, and then make sure he or she has or gets a great number two. It's all about the people."

So as we address the world's biggest challenges, we can and must channel promising new streams of capital into mighty rivers that can power lasting change. But let's not rely on capital strategies alone. Let's make an equal commitment to make sure there are great social-change leaders available to make use of them. Great leaders who are intentional in defining their approaches. Great leaders who are rigorous in gauging their progress. Great leaders who are willing to admit mistakes. Great leaders who are capable of quickly adapting and improving. Great leaders who have an unrelenting passion for improving lives. These are the leaders who will do the most to expand the frontiers of what philanthropy is able to accomplish.

ACKNOWLEDGMENTS

IT HAS BEEN SAID THAT "it takes a village to raise a child." But, as any author knows, the same applies to raising a book. And that is certainly the case here. My debts in bringing this book and its separately published introduction, entitled *Leverage for Good,* to fruition have been enormous, and I gratefully acknowledge them here. They are owed to Rip Rapson, President of the Kresge Foundation, who early on recognized the niche that this book would fill and helped provide the support and encouragement that made them possible; to William Burckart, who assisted me in organizing the project, recruiting authors, maintaining contact, and managing the substantial paper flow that any project of this scope entails; to Luther Ragin, now at the Global Impact Investment Network (GIIN), who encouraged the effort and gave selflessly of his time to review most of the chapters and offer additional comments and advice; to the members of the Project Advisory Committee (listed in the Appendix at the back of this volume) for their enormously helpful comments and assistance at numerous points in the process; to David Erickson and his colleagues at the Federal Reserve Bank of San Francisco for providing meeting space at the Fed and other support and encouragement to our work; to Bill Dietel and Mario Morino, who agreed to write a foreword and preface, respectively, to introduce the work to the broader audiences it seeks to address and who provided inspiration along the way; to the authors of the separate chapters, incredibly thoughtful and dedicated professionals all, who spent what I am sure is far more hours than they ever imagined responding to my detailed comments and suggestions to get their chapters into a consistent form and make this complicated topic accessible to the broadest possible audience; to David McBride, the social sciences acquisition editor at Oxford, who skillfully moved the project through the complex Oxford review process; to Chelsea Newhouse at the Johns Hopkins Center for Civil Studies, who patiently and professionally handled the process of bringing the manuscript into conformance with the protocols and formats that Oxford procedures stipulate; and last, but by no means least, to my lovely wife, Lynda, who put up over an unforgivably long period with the inevitable distractedness and preoccupation that writing inevitably entails, and did so with enormous understanding and support.

Without taking away anything from the enormous assistance I received from all of these friends and colleagues, at the end of the day I recognize that responsibility for this final product, with whatever faults it might still have, belongs with me, and I accept it fully.

Lester M. Salamon
Annapolis, Maryland
September 21, 2013

ACKNOWLEDGMENTS

DIRECTORY OF PARTICIPANTS

Editor and Project Director

Lester M. Salamon is a Professor at The Johns Hopkins University and Director of the Johns Hopkins Center for Civil Society Studies. He previously served as the founding director of the Johns Hopkins Institute for Policy Studies, as the director of the Center for Governance and Management Research at the Urban Institute in Washington, DC, and as Deputy Associate Director of the US Office of Management and Budget. Dr. Salamon is an expert on the tools of government and has been a pioneer in the empirical study of the nonprofit sector in the United States and around the world. His book *America's Nonprofit Sector: A Primer* is the standard text used in college-level courses on the nonprofit sector in the United States. His *Partners in Public Service: Government and the Nonprofit Sector in the Modern Welfare State* won the 1996 ARNOVA Award for Distinguished Book in Nonprofit and Voluntary Action Research, and in 2012 was awarded the Aaron Wildavsky Enduring Contribution Award from the American Political Science Association. Dr. Salamon's recent books include *The Tools of Government: A Guide to the New Governance* (Oxford University Press, 2002); *Global Civil Society: Dimensions of the Nonprofit Sector* (Kumarian Press, 2004); *Rethinking Corporate Social Engagement: Lessons from Latin America* (Kumarian Press, 2010); *America's Nonprofit Sector: A Primer*, third edition (Foundation Center, 2012); and *The State of Nonprofit America*, second edition (Brookings Institution Press, 2012). Dr. Salamon received his B.A. degree in Economics and Policy Studies from Princeton University and his Ph.D. in Government from Harvard University. He served from 1998 to 2006 as the Chairman of the Board of the Chesapeake Community Foundation.

Project Coordinator

William Burckart is the Managing Director of Impact Economy (North America) LLC. Prior to this role, he managed special initiatives for the Johns Hopkins Center for Civil Society Studies, including the New Frontiers of Philanthropy, Philanthropication thru Privatization, and Nonprofit Value Proposition projects. He previously assisted Venture Philanthropy Partners in the seven-year assessment of its investment portfolio, worked in the United Kingdom Parliament, and served as an editor for *BizShanghai*. Mr. Burckart holds an M.A. in Public Policy from Johns Hopkins University and a B.A. in International Affairs from George Washington University.

Contributors

Elise Balboni recently rejoined Local Initiatives Support Corporation (LISC) as Chief Credit Officer after serving as a consultant for nonprofits and foundations in the area of charter school facility financing. Previously, she served as LISC's Vice President of Education Programs, where she had responsibility for oversight of the Educational Facilities Financing Center. Prior to joining LISC, she served as an Associate in municipal finance at CS First Boston and Cambridge Partners and as Budget Director for the Massachusetts Senate Committee on Ways and Means. Ms. Balboni received her B.A. from Harvard University and her M.B.A. from the Stanford Graduate School of Business.

Jessica Bearman works with philanthropic and other mission-based organizations, helping them become more effective and responsive to the communities that they serve. She is the author of *Drowning in Paperwork, Distracted from Purpose*, a study of grant-makers' application and reporting practices, as well as many supporting materials and workshops on this topic. As a consultant and in her prior role as deputy director of the New Ventures in Philanthropy, Ms. Bearman has written and spoken widely about new and established philanthropy and is the author of several studies of giving circles and shared giving, including *Giving Together, More Giving Together*, and *The Impact of Giving Together*.

Shari Berenbach's 30-year career ranges from international banking to microfinance in both the public and private sectors. She was recently named President and CEO of the US African Development Foundation after having served as Director of USAID's Microenterprise Development Office (2010–2012). From 1997 to 2010 she led the Calvert Foundation, an impact-investing pioneer. Earlier she worked for the International Finance Corporation, Citigroup, and Solomon Brothers. She has an M.B.A. in Finance from Columbia University, and graduate and undergraduate degrees from the University of California. Ms. Berenbach currently serves on the Calvert Foundation Board and the FASB Non-profit Advisory Committee.

Matthew Bishop is the US Business Editor and New York Bureau Chief of *The Economist*. He was previously the magazine's London-based Business Editor, and is also the author of "Essential Economics," the official *Economist* guide to economics. He is a member of the World Economic Forum's Global Agenda Council on the Role of Business. Mr. Bishop is coauthor with Michael Green of *Philanthrocapitalism: How Giving Can Save the World* (Bloomsbury, 2008) and *The Road from Ruin: How to Revive Capitalism and Put America Back on Top* (Crown, 2010).

Monica Brand is founder and Principal Director of Frontier Investments, a growth stage equity fund sponsored by ACCION International to invest in disruptive business models that catalyze breakthrough innovation in financial inclusion. Prior to assuming the role as fund manager, she launched and ran ACCION's Marketing and Product Development Unit and worked in Mexico with Compartamos Bank, the largest microfinance institution in Latin America. Before joining ACCION, she founded Anthuri Catalysts to help prepare potential portfolio companies for investment. She currently serves as an Adjunct Professor at the John Hopkins School of Advanced International Studies (SAIS), teaching a graduate-level course on impact investing. Ms. Brand received both an M.B.A. and an M.A. in Education from Stanford University and a B.A. magna cum laude in Economics from Williams College.

Craig Churchill, Team Leader of the International Labour Organization's Microinsurance Innovation Facility, based in Switzerland, is a pioneer and leader in the microinsurance field with over two decades of microfinance and microinsurance experience. He serves as the Chair of the Microinsurance Network and is on the governing body of the Access to Insurance Initiative. Mr. Churchill has authored and edited over 40 articles, papers, monographs, and training manuals on various microfinance topics. *Protecting the Poor: A Microinsurance Compendium,* volumes 1 (2006) and 2 (2012), which he edited, are the most authoritative books on the subject.

Rick Cohen, is an award-winning investigative journalist and the Washington-based national correspondent of *Nonprofit Quarterly* magazine. Prior to joining NPQ, he was executive director of the National Committee for Responsive Philanthropy, a national philanthropic watchdog. His experience includes serving as vice president of the Local Initiatives Support Corporation, vice president of the Enterprise Foundation, and director of Jersey City's Department of Housing and Economic Development. In addition to his regular columns in *Nonprofit Quarterly,* he has also written op-eds and feature pieces for a variety of other newspapers and journals including the *Washington Post,* the *Boston Globe,* the *Financial Times,* and numerous others.

Bill Dietel served as President of the Rockefeller Brothers Fund (RBF), 1975–1987. Prior to his time with RBF, he was Principal of the Emma Willard School, Assistant Dean and Assistant Professor at Amherst College, and an instructor of History at the University of Massachusetts. He has served on more than 25 nonprofit boards that include the New York Public Library, Public Radio International, Pierson Lovelace Foundation, Guidestar International, and the F.B. Heron Foundation. He founded Dietel Partners, a philanthropic advisory service in 2000. Mr. Dietel holds a Ph.D. from Yale University, a B.A. from Princeton University, and is a Phillips Exeter Academy graduate.

Michael Edwards is a Distinguished Senior Fellow at Demos in New York, and the editor of the web magazine *Transformation@openDemocracy.* He has worked for many different organizations including Oxfam, Save the Children, the World Bank, and the Ford Foundation, where he directed the Governance and Civil Society program from 1999 to 2008. His latest books include *Civil Society,* the *Oxford Handbook of Civil Society,* and *Small Change: Why Business Won't Save the World.* Mr. Edwards received the Gandhi, King Ikeda Award from Morehouse College in 2011. His website is http://www.futurepositive.org.

Angela M. Eikenberry is an associate professor in the School of Public Administration at the University of Nebraska at Omaha, where she also serves as the advisor for the nonprofit concentration in the M.P.A. program. Her main research interests include philanthropy and nonprofit organizations and their role in democratic governance. She has published articles in numerous academic journals and her research has been featured on NPR's *All Things Considered* and in the *Stanford Social Innovation Review.* Her book *Giving Circles: Philanthropy, Voluntary Association, Democracy* (Indiana University Press) won the CASE 2010 John Grenzebach Research Award for Outstanding Research in Philanthropy, Published Scholarship.

XXX DIRECTORY OF PARTICIPANTS

David J. Erickson is director of the Center for Community Development Investment at the Federal Reserve Bank of San Francisco and edits the Federal Reserve journal *Community Development Investment Review*. His research areas in the Community Development Department of the Federal Reserve include community development finance, affordable housing, economic development, and institutional changes that benefit low-income communities. He has been a leader in the collaboration between the Federal Reserve and the Robert Wood Johnson Foundation on bringing health together with community development. His publications include *The Housing Policy Revolution: Networks and Neighborhoods* (Urban Institute Press, 2009), and *Investing in What Works for America's Communities: Essays on People, Place, and Purpose* (Federal Reserve Bank of San Francisco and Low Income Investment Fund, 2012). Mr. Erickson holds a Ph.D. in history and a master's degree in public policy from the University of California, Berkeley, and an undergraduate degree from Dartmouth College.

Peter Frumkin is a Professor of Social Policy at the University of Pennsylvania, where he directs the Masters in Nonprofit Leadership program and the Center for High Impact Philanthropy. He is the author of *Strategic Giving, On Being Nonprofit, Serving Country and Community,* and other books and articles on philanthropy, nonprofit strategy, volunteering, and social entrepreneurship.

Katie Grace is Program Manager at the Initiative for Responsible Investment (IRI) at Harvard University, where she conducts research on public policy and impact investment, sustainable cities investment, and place-based frameworks for community development. She has authored or coauthored a number of works on impact investment, sustainable cities investment, and corporate social responsibility disclosure requirements, among other topics. Prior to coming to the IRI, she worked as a research analyst at the Tellus Institute. Ms. Grace graduated from Williams College with a B.A., cum laude, in Political Science and a Concentration in Leadership Studies.

Michael Green is the Executive Director of the Social Progress Imperative. He was formerly a senior official in the British Government, where he served three Secretaries of State for International Development as head of communications and managed the UK aid program to Russia and Ukraine. Mr. Green is coauthor with Matthew Bishop of *Philanthrocapitalism: How Giving Can Save the World* (Bloomsbury, 2008) and *The Road from Ruin: How to Revive Capitalism and Put America Back on Top* (Crown, 2010).

Lisa Hagerman is the Director of Programs at DBL Investors, a double-bottom-line venture capital firm in San Francisco. She was previously the Director of More for Mission at the Harvard Kennedy School, a research and advocacy initiative promoting mission investing, which she built into a network of over 90 foundations representing over $38 billion in total assets. She was previously a Vice President of Economic Innovation International. In addition, she has 10 years of banking experience, three of which were with Wells Fargo Bank in Government Relations and seven years with Citibank's Latin American Marketing Division. Dr. Hagerman holds a Visiting Research Associate position at Oxford University, School of Geography and the Environment. Ms. Hagerman received her bachelor of arts degree from Bucknell University, her M.A. in Political Science from the University of North

Carolina at Chapel Hill, and her doctorate in Economic Geography from Oxford University.

John Kohler is cofounder of Toniic, a syndication network of worldwide impact investors. He currently serves as an Executive Fellow and Director of Social Capital at Santa Clara University's Center for Science, Technology and Society, and has 20 years of executive-level experience at technology corporations including Hewlett Packard, Silicon Graphics and Convergent Technologies, Unisys, and Netscape Communications, the latter of which he served as one of the founding executives. Mr. Kohler is the author of a recent report entitled *Coordinating Impact Capital: A New Approach to Investing in Small and Growing Businesses* and currently serves on a number of boards and advisory bodies, including Redleaf Group, LucidMedia, PACT (an NGO based in Washington, DC), the UCLA Venture Capital Fund, the UCLA Sciences Board of Visitors, and the World Economic Forum. Mr. Kohler received his bachelor's degree concentrating in International Economics from UCLA and completed executive programs at Wharton and Stanford business schools.

Robert Kraybill is Managing Director at Impact Investment Exchange Asia (IIX) and a member of the Board at Shujog. He is a senior finance executive with over two decades of capital market experience as an investment banker (with Morgan Stanley, Credit Suisse, Wasserstein Perella, and Dresdner Kleinwort Wasserstein) and as a private equity investor (Marathon Asset Management). He has significant experience in emerging markets in Asia and came to the region as regional head of investment banking for Dresdner Kleinworth Wasserstein. More recently, he was head of Asian private equity for Marathon Asset Management. In addition to his work at IIX and Shujog, he is Senior Advisor to Asian Tiger Capital, a financial services boutique operating in Bangladesh, and has served as an Adjunct Professor in the M.B.A. program of Singapore Management University. Mr. Kraybill holds a B.A. from Princeton University, magna cum laude, and a J.D. from the University of Pennsylvania School of Law, summa cum laude.

Steve Lydenberg is Partner, Strategic Vision, of Domini Social Investments and Founding Director of the Initiative for Responsible Investment. He has been active in social research since 1975. He was a founder of KLD Research & Analytics, Inc. and served as its research director from 1990 to 2001. He has written numerous publications on issues of corporate social responsibility and responsible investing. Mr. Lydenberg holds a B.A. in English from Columbia College and an M.F.A. in theater arts from Cornell University, and holds the Chartered Financial Analyst designation and is a member of the Boston Security Analysts Society.

Maximilian Martin is the founder and Global Managing Director of Impact Economy and President of the Impact Pledge Foundation. He previously served as Founding Global Head and Managing Director of UBS Philanthropy Services, Head of Research at the Schwab Foundation, Senior Consultant with McKinsey & Company, instructor in Harvard's Department of Economics, and Fellow at the Center for Public Leadership, Harvard Kennedy School. Dr. Martin created the first university course on social entrepreneurship in Europe and holds an M.A. in anthropology from Indiana University, a M.P.A. from Harvard University, and a Ph.D. in economic anthropology from the University of Hamburg.

Norah McVeigh is Managing Director, Financial Services, at the Nonprofit Finance Fund, where she is responsible for NFF's investing products, including on and off balance sheet lending, New Market Tax Credits (NMTC), and credit enhancement. Her portfolio includes a $60 million loan portfolio, and a $231 million NMTC portfolio. She also develops and operationalizes new impact-investing products and key partnerships. Before joining NFF she worked at the Housing Development Fund in Stamford, Connecticut, and at International Voluntary Services. Ms. McVeigh holds an M.A. in Public and Private Management from the Yale School of Management and a B.S. from Georgetown University.

Mario Morino serves as chairman of the Morino Institute and cofounder and Chairman of Venture Philanthropy Partners. His career spans more than 45 years as entrepreneur, technologist, and civic and business leader. He also has a long history of civic engagement and philanthropy in the National Capital Region and northeast Ohio. Mr. Morino is the primary author of the book *Leap of Reason: Managing to Outcomes in an Era of Scarcity* (2011), which is informing efforts in more than 50 countries to increase the impact of nonprofits, foundations, and public-sector entities.

Alex Nicholls is the first tenured lecturer in social entrepreneurship appointed at the University of Oxford and was the first staff member of the Skoll Centre for Social Entrepreneurship in 2004. His research interests range across several key areas within social entrepreneurship and social innovation, including the nexus of relationships between accounting, accountability, and governance; public and social policy contexts; social investment; and fair trade. To date he has published more than 50 papers, chapters, and articles and four books. Most appear in a wide range of peer-reviewed journals and books, including four sole-authored papers in *Financial Times* Top 30 journals (with another under review and resubmit). His 2009 paper on social investment won the Best Paper Award (Entrepreneurship) at the British Academy of Management. In 2010, he edited a special edition of *Entrepreneurship, Theory and Practice* on social entrepreneurship—the first time a top-tier management journal had recognized the topic in this way. Dr. Nicholls is the General Editor of the Skoll Working Papers series and the Editor of the *Journal of Social Entrepreneurship*.

Lauren Peterson works at Abt Associates, where she supports activities designed to increase the use of risk management and financing strategies to improve access to quality healthcare by low-income households, and contributes to research on a variety of health finance topics in developing countries. Prior to joining Abt Associates, she worked for the International Labour Organization's Microinsurance Innovation Facility in Geneva, Switzerland. Ms. Peterson holds a bachelor's degree in Public Policy with highest honors from the University of North Carolina at Chapel Hill.

Luther M. Ragin Jr. is Chief Executive Officer of the Global Impact Investing Network. He was previously Vice President for Investments at the F.B. Heron Foundation and a William Henry Bloomberg Lecturer in Public Management at the Harvard Kennedy School.

Lisa Richter is cofounder and principal of GPS Capital Partners, a US-based consultancy assisting large and small foundations and institutional investors to design and execute impact investing strategy. GPS's services span asset classes, return expectations, geographies, and sectors, with a focus on increasing equitable access to opportunity. GPS network consultants have managed impact investment portfolios totaling some $4 billion within foundations, community development financial institutions, equity funds, and banks. Ms. Richter authored the *Grantmakers in Health Guide to Impact Investing* and coauthored *Equity Advancing Equity*, a guide to US community foundation impact investing; she frequently leads educational events on impact investing.

Julia Sass Rubin is an Associate Professor at the Edward J. Bloustein School of Planning and Public Policy at Rutgers University. She has written numerous journal articles and book chapters on developmental finance and advised a number of organizations on this topic, including the US Small Business Administration and the John D. and Catherine T. MacArthur Foundation. Ms. Sass Rubin earned her Ph.D. and M.A. from Harvard University, an M.B.A. with distinction from Harvard Business School, and an A.B. with honors from Harvard-Radcliffe College. She was a postdoctoral fellow at the Alfred A. Taubman Center for Public Policy at Brown University.

Shirley Sagawa is Senior Policy Advisor to America Forward, a policy coalition of social entrepreneurs, and serves as a Center for American Progress fellow, and an Adjunct Professor at the Georgetown Public Policy Institute. She is author of *The American Way to Change: How National Service and Volunteers Are Transforming America* (Jossey-Bass, 2010), and coauthor of *The Charismatic Organization* (Jossey-Bass, 2008) and *Common Interest, Common Good: Creating Value through Business and Social Sector Partnerships* (Harvard Business School Press). She served in the Obama transition and as a presidential appointee in the first Bush and Clinton administrations. Ms. Sagawa played major roles in developing the Social Innovation Fund, the Corporation for National and Community Service, and AmeriCorps. She began her career working for Senator Edward M. Kennedy and is a graduate of Smith College, the London School of Economics, and Harvard Law School.

Rod Schwartz is CEO of ClearlySo. His background in equity research, investment banking, and venture capital makes him an unconventional but authoritative writer on the social finance sector. Joining Wall Street in 1980, he rose to become the number one ranked financial services analyst at PaineWebber and then held senior management posts at Lehman Brothers and Paribas, before leaving the sector in 1997 to found the venture capital firm Catalyst. At Catalyst, he became passionate about innovative businesses that earn a living by trying to make the world a better place. A pioneer in this social investment marketplace, he transformed Catalyst into a social business consultancy and in 2008 launched ClearlySo, which raises investment for social entrepreneurs. Mr. Schwartz guest lectures on social finance at the Said Business School (Oxford) and other European universities and is a regular sector commentator. Former Chair of Shelter and JustGiving, he currently chairs The Green Thing and Spacehive. He holds an M.B.A. and B.A. from the University of Rochester.

Durreen Shahnaz is the Founder and Chairwoman of Impact Investment Exchange Asia (IIX), the Founder and Managing Director of Shujog, and an Adjunct Associate Professor at the Lee Kuan Yew School of Public Policy. In a career spanning over two decades, she has built a track record as a successful banker, media executive, and social entrepreneur. She began her professional career as an investment banker at Morgan Stanley (New York), followed by stints at Grameen Bank (Bangladesh), the World Bank (Washington, DC), and Merrill Lynch (Hong Kong). As a media executive, she headed up the Asia operations of Hearst Magazine International, Reader's Digest Asia, and Asia City Publishing. She also founded, ran, and sold oneNest, a social enterprise and global marketplace for handmade goods. She is a TED 2010 Fellow as well as an Asia Society 21 Fellow. Ms. Shahnaz he is an appointed member of the World Economic Forum's Global Agenda Council on Social Innovation for 2011 and is on the advisory board for CASE i3 at Duke's Fuqua School of Business. She is also the Social Entrepreneur in Residence for INSEAD's Social Entrepreneurship Catalyst Program. She holds a B.A. from Smith College, an M.B.A. from the Wharton School at the University of Pennsylvania, and an M.A. from the School for Advanced International Studies at Johns Hopkins University.

Vince Stehle is Executive Director of Media Impact Funders, an affinity group of foundation officials and philanthropists who support public interest media. Previously, he was a consultant with the John S. and James L. Knight Foundation. Before that, he was Program Director for Nonprofit Sector Support at the Surdna Foundation, a family foundation based in New York City. Prior to joining Surdna, he worked for 10 years as a reporter for the *Chronicle of Philanthropy*, where he covered a broad range of issues about the nonprofit sector. Mr. Stehle has served as Chairperson of Philanthropy New York (formerly the New York Regional Association of Grantmakers) and on the governing boards of VolunteerMatch and the Nonprofit Technology Network (NTEN). Currently he serves on the Board of Directors of the Center for Effective Philanthropy.

Mary Tingerthal is the Commissioner of the Minnesota Housing Finance Agency. She has worked in the field of social lending and investing for much of her career, including her service as Vice President of Capital Markets at Community Reinvestment Fund (CRF), where she pioneered the use of rated asset-backed securities backed by small business and affordable housing loans to attract over $100 million in investments from social and market investors. Ms. Tingerthal also served as President, Capital Markets Companies for the Housing Partnership Network, where she staffed the Charter School Financing Partnership.

Brian Trelstad is a Partner at Bridges Ventures, a leading developed market impact investment fund. Until January 2012, he was the Chief Investment Officer of Acumen Fund. Brian previously worked with McKinsey & Company and the Corporation for National Service. He has degrees from Harvard College, Stanford University's Graduate School of Business, and the University of California at Berkeley's Department of City and Regional Planning. Mr. Trelstad is a Henry Crown Fellow of the Aspen Institute and a Kauffman Fellow of the Center for Venture Education.

Melinda T. Tuan is an independent consultant who is passionate about helping philanthropic organizations be more effective. Previously, she cofounded REDF, a social venture fund that works with a portfolio of nonprofit organizations employing formerly homeless and very low-income individuals in market-based enterprises. She is recognized nationally for her work in high-engagement philanthropy, foundation effectiveness, nonprofit capacity-building, and evaluation. Ms. Tuan graduated from Harvard University magna cum laude with an A.B. in Social Studies focusing on urban poverty and homelessness and holds an M.B.A. and certificate in nonprofit management from the Stanford Graduate School of Business.

Drew von Glahn oversees the World Bank's Development Marketplace, a grant-based program that focuses on surfacing and supporting high-performing social enterprises working in developing countries. He has been a social entrepreneur himself, having been the cofounder and Managing Partner of Third Sector Capital Partners, a leading advisor for the social enterprise sector on such innovative financings as social-impact bonds and pay-for-success. Prior to Third Sector, he was the President and CEO of FEI Behavioral Health, the social venture subsidiary of the Alliance for Families and Children. Mr. von Glahn's background also includes senior positions in several global investment banks, including Credit Suisse and ING, where he gained invaluable experience in debt and equity markets and corporate finance.

Caroline Whistler is currently Partner for Advisory Services at Third Sector Capital Partners, where she leads client and government advisory engagements and develops customized PFS arrangements. She cofounded Third Sector Capital Partners with Drew von Glahn and George Overholser after completing a Fulbright Fellowship in Brazil researching nonprofit sustainability with Ashoka and Fundação Getulio Vargas University. Previously she worked at Nonprofit Finance Fund (NFF) Capital Partners, a leader in applying growth metrics and accountability to equity-like financing for high-performing nonprofits. While at NFF, Ms. Whistler structured growth capital campaigns, conducted economic feasibility analyses, and designed scenario planning tools to help raise millions in capital for nonprofits.

David Wood directs the Initiative for Responsible Investment's (IRI) research and field-building work on responsible investment across asset classes, and currently manages projects on RI strategy with pension fund trustees, mission investing by foundations, the changing landscape of community investing in the United States, and impact investing and public policy. The IRI is a project of the Hauser Institute for Civil Society at Harvard University. Prior to joining the IRI he taught the History of Ethics, including the History of Economic Thought and Human Rights, at Boston University. Mr. Wood holds a Ph.D. in History from the Johns Hopkins University, and serves on the Board of Directors of US SIF: The Forum for Sustainable and Responsible Investment.

PART I

INTRODUCTION

CHAPTER 1

THE REVOLUTION ON THE FRONTIERS OF PHILANTHROPY: AN INTRODUCTION

Lester M. Salamon

Overview: The Search for Leverage

On September 28, 2011, *Microfinance Africa*, a newsletter serving the microfinance industry on the African continent, reported news of an important, if unusual, development designed to help East Africa cope with the region's food shortage and resulting skyrocketing food prices. An unexpected consortium had come together to channel US$25 million to a series of small and medium-sized East African agricultural enterprises whose businesses could help link the region's smallholder farmers to improved production and marketing opportunities.* Although the US Agency for International Development was a party to this consortium, this was not your normal top-down, government-funded development project. Rather, USAID had teamed up with three foundations (the UK-based Gatsby Charitable Foundation, and the US-based Rockefeller and Gates foundations), a major US investment firm (J.P. Morgan Social Finance), and Pearl Capital Partners, a private, Kampala-based investment company dedicated to channeling private equity to smallholder agricultural enterprises in Africa.[1]

What may be most unusual about this deal in the current climate of development assistance, philanthropy, and finance, however, is that it is no longer unusual at all. Rather, it is an example of what students of the field have begun referring to as "yin-yang" deals, deals that bring together, as in Chinese thought, seemingly contrary forces that turn out to be uniquely capable of producing new life forms when taking advantage of their interdependencies.[2] In the present arrangement, USAID managed to stimulate the investment of $25 million into building a robust agribusiness sector in East Africa with only $1.5 million of its own money, and all of that in the form of technical assistance to small and medium-sized businesses funded out of President Obama's flagship Feed the Future initiative. The investment fund itself was assembled by combining a USAID guarantee of an $8 million loan from J.P. Morgan's Social Finance Unit that was further leveraged by $17 million in equity investments made by the three foundations, which functioned in this deal as "philanthropic banks" rather than traditional grantmaking charities.[3]

Sizable yin-yang deals of this sort are slowly becoming the new normal in efforts to combat the enormous social, economic, and environmental problems that confront our world at the present time. And none too soon. With the resources of both governments and traditional philanthropy barely growing or in decline, yet the problems of poverty, ill-health, and environmental degradation ballooning daily, it is increasingly clear that new models for financing and promoting social and environmental objectives have become urgently needed.

Fortunately, a significant revolution appears to be underway on the frontiers of philanthropy that is providing at least a partial, though still embryonic, response to this dilemma. The heart of this revolution is a massive explosion in the tools of philanthropy and social investment, in the instruments and institutions being deployed to mobilize private resources in support of social and environmental objectives. Where earlier, such support was limited to charitable grants and gifts made available directly by individuals or through charitable foundations and corporate giving programs, now a bewildering array of new instruments and institutions has surfaced to tap not simply traditional charitable resources but also private *investment capital*. Included are loans, loan guarantees, equity-like investments, barter arrangements, social stock exchanges, bonds, secondary markets, investment funds, and many more. Indeed, the world of philanthropy seems to be experiencing a Big Bang similar in kind, if not in exact form, to the one thought to have produced the planets and stars of our solar system.

> A significant revolution appears to be underway on the frontiers of philanthropy and social investment.

> A bewildering array of new instruments and institutions has surfaced to finance social-purpose activities.

Even a quick glance at the emerging landscape on the frontiers of contemporary philanthropy around the world yields a rich harvest of unfamiliar names and terms: Bovespa in Brazil; Social Capital Partners in Canada; Impact Investment Exchange in Singapore; Acumen Fund, Root Capital, and New Profit in the United States; Bridges Ventures, Big Society Capital, and NESTA in the UK; Blue Orchard in Switzerland; Aavishkaar International in India; Willow Impact Investors in Dubai; Calvert Foundation; the Schwab Charitable Fund; the Community Reinvestment Fund; community development financial institutions; TechSoup Global; conversion foundations; and many more (see Figure 1.1).

At the core of this enormous proliferation of entities lie four important processes of change. In particular, contemporary philanthropy is moving:

- **Beyond grants.** deploying a variety of new financial tools for promoting social purposes—loans, loan guarantees, equity-type investments, securitization, fixed-income instruments, and, most recently, social-impact bonds.
- **Beyond foundations.** creating a host of new actors as the institutional structures through which social-purpose finance is proceeding—capital aggregators, secondary markets, social stock exchanges, social enterprise brokers, internet portals, to name just a few.
- **Beyond bequests.** forming charitable or social-purpose capital pools not simply through the gifts of wealthy individuals, but also from the privatization of formerly public or quasi-public assets or the establishment of specialized social-purpose investment funds.
- **Beyond cash.** utilizing new barter arrangements and internet capabilities to facilitate the giving not just of money, but of a variety of in-kind

FIGURE 1.1
Philanthropy's "Big Bang"

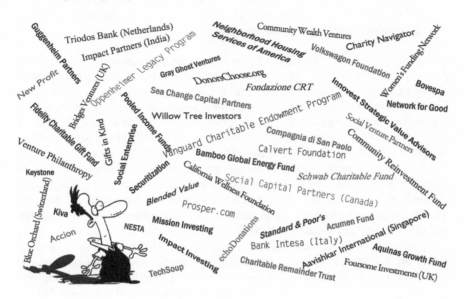

forms of assistance, whether it be volunteer time or computer hardware and software.

Behind these movements is a common imperative, usefully summarized in a single word: *leverage*. Leverage is the mechanism that allows limited energy to be translated into greater power. It is what allowed Archimedes to claim that, given a lever and a place to stand, he could "move the whole world."[4] In the philanthropic context it means finding a way to go beyond the limited flow of charitable resources generated by the earnings on foundation assets or the annual contributions of individuals to catalyze for social and environmental purposes some portion of the far more enormous private investment capital resident in banks, pension funds, insurance companies, mutual funds, and the accounts of high-net-worth individuals.[5]

> Leverage is the mechanism that allows limited energy to be translated into greater power.

The upshot is the emergence of a "new frontier" of philanthropy and social investing that differs from twentieth-century philanthropy in at least four ways. It is:

- **More diverse,** involving a wider variety of institutions, instruments, and sources of support
- **More entrepreneurial,** moving beyond "grant-making," the giving of resources, to capture the possibilities for greater leverage that comes from adopting an investment orientation, focusing more heavily on measurable results, and generating a blend of economic and social returns
- **More global,** engaging problems on an international scale and applying models developed in cross-national settings

- **More collaborative,** interacting explicitly not only with the broader civil society sector, but also with new social ventures serving the "bottom of the pyramid," as well as with a broad array of private financial institutions and government agencies

The result, as outlined in Table 1.1, is a new paradigm emerging on the frontiers of philanthropy and social investing. Where traditional philanthropy relied chiefly on individuals, foundations, and corporate philanthropy programs, the new frontiers of philanthropy engage a broad assortment of private financial institutions, including banks, pension funds, insurance companies, investment advisors, specialized investment funds, and foundations that function as philanthropic banks. Where traditional philanthropy concentrated mostly on operating income, the new frontiers concentrate far more heavily on investment capital, which funds long-term development. Where traditional philanthropy channels its assistance almost exclusively to nonprofit organizations, the new frontiers support as well a wide assortment of social enterprises, cooperatives, and other hybrid organizations. Where traditional philanthropy brings a charity perspective to its work, focusing exclusively, or at least chiefly, on social return, actors on the new frontiers of philanthropy bring an investment orientation, focusing on social and financial return and seeking to build self-sustaining systems that bring permanent solutions. Where traditional philanthropy mobilizes a relatively small share of its own resources, the new frontiers of philanthropy leverage the deeper reservoirs of resources resident in the private capital markets. And where traditional philanthropy tends to be satisfied with *output* measures, the new frontiers put greater emphasis on reliable *outcome* metrics.

> A new paradigm is emerging on the frontiers of philanthropy and social investment.

To be sure, these differences are hardly universal. What is more, the changes are far from fully developed. But neither are they trivial. Indeed, as reflected in Figure 1.2, a complex social-purpose finance ecosystem is emerging to channel funds from banks, pension funds, insurance companies, foundations, high-net-worth individuals, and others through a variety of social-impact investment organizations, support institutions, and new types of grantmakers, to

TABLE 1.1   THE NEW FRONTIERS OF PHILANTHROPY PARADIGM

Philanthropy = "The provision of private resources for social or environmental purposes."

Traditional Philanthropy	New Frontiers of Philanthropy
Foundations, individuals	Foundations + investors, investment firms
Operating income	Investment capital
Grants	Diverse financial instruments/capital tranches
Nonprofits	Nonprofits + social ventures
Social return	Social + financial return
Limited leverage	Expanded leverage
Output focus	Outcome focus/metrics

FIGURE 1.2
The New Frontiers of Philanthropy Ecosystem

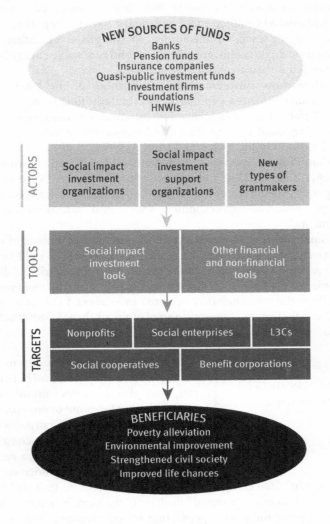

an increasingly diverse set of nonprofits, social ventures, social cooperatives, and related organizations to achieve poverty alleviation, environmental improvement, improved health and environment, strengthened civil society organizations, and improved life chances.

Microfinance, perhaps the earliest manifestation of this phenomenon of mobilizing private investment capital for social purposes, is now a mature $65 billion industry with its own trade association, research arm, network of "retail" outlets, secondary markets, and access to global capital markets through rated bond issues. And it is just getting started: recent estimates place its *potential* market north of $250 billion.[6]

But microfinance is just one component of the burgeoning financial ecosystem emerging on the new frontiers of philanthropy, broadly conceived. Hundreds of investment funds like the one featured in the African Agricultural Capital Fund vignette outlined above have surfaced around the world and found investors willing to take a chance on them.

- **Aavishkaar International**, for example, incorporated in Singapore but operating in India, raised an initial $18 million for an Indian microfinance investment fund in 2008. It then proceeded to assemble an additional $14 million more by January 2009 to support promising Indian micro, small, or medium-sized companies operating in the agriculture, dairy, healthcare, education, and renewable energy fields in rural or semiurban areas of the country.[7]
- **The Grassroots Business Fund**, an offshoot of the World Bank's International Finance Corporation, has similarly built a robust portfolio of $8.5 million in investments and technical assistance engagements supporting small and medium-sized businesses serving low-income populations in India, Africa, and Latin America.[8]
- **Bamboo Finance**, a commercial investment firm based in Switzerland, manages another $250 million of investments in a range of small companies providing access to affordable housing, healthcare, education, energy, livelihood opportunities, water, and sanitation on three continents.[9]
- **The Small Business Investment Funds**, initially an affiliate of CARE, the international development agency, has invested $378 million in 338 small and mid-sized companies across 22 emerging markets.[10] Indeed, according to author Lisa Richter in Chapter 2 of this volume, such socially and environmentally oriented investment funds may already number 3,000 around the world and may already have US$300 billion in assets under management.

> A commercial revolution appears to be underway around the world at the bottom of the pyramid.

For these investment funds to do their work, of course, they must find not only inves-*tors*, but also inves*tees*—promising enterprises, whether for-profit or nonprofit, serving social and environmental purposes in a way that yields revenue as well as social good. And finding them they are. Indeed, a commercial revolution appears to be under way around the world at what University of Michigan professor C. K. Prahalad brilliantly termed the "bottom of the pyramid," the base of the world's income scale, where the vast majority of the world's population lives.[11] Inventive entrepreneurs are finding ways to transform this population into avid consumers of solar panels, cell phones, eyeglasses, reusable sanitary napkins, and dozens of other basic commodities while also creating opportunities for them to become proprietors and wage earners in artisan shops, small-scale agribusinesses, and marketing ventures of various sorts. The result is evident in the appearance of firms such as Peru's Agrícola Viñasol (AVSA), an agricultural company created in 2001 as the commercial arm of a Peruvian NGO to help small farmers improve and market their fruit and vegetable products; or Jaipur Rugs, which works with 10,000 low-income weavers and spinners in India to upgrade their production methods, secure healthcare, and market their products; or Zara Solar, which has enabled thousands of low-income Tanzanian families to switch from polluting kerosene stoves to cheaper and cleaner solar-powered ones.[12] (For an illustration of the range of fields in which such social entrepreneurs have surfaced see Table 1.2.)

While the changes underway are inspiring and by no means trivial, however, they remain scattered and largely uncharted in any systematic fashion. Individual practitioners typically have a handle on one or another of the

TABLE 1.2 ACUMEN FUND INVESTMENTS, BY PORTFOLIO TYPE

Agriculture	**(Health con't)**
BASIX Krishi Samruddhi Limited (India)	Circ MedTech (Rwanda)
GADCO Coöperatief (Ghana)	DART (Kenya)
Global Easy Water Products (India)	Drishtee (India)
Gulu Agricultural Development Company (Uganda)	First Micro Insurance Agency Pakistan
Jassar Farms (Pakistan)	Insta Products (Kenya)
Juhudi Kilimo (Kenya)	LifeSpring (India)
Micro Drip (Pakistan)	Pagatech (Nigeria)
National Rural Support Program (Pakistan)	PVRI (India)
Microfinance Bank (Pakistan)	Sproxil (Nigeria)
Virtual City (Kenya)	UHEAL (Kenya)
Western Seed (Kenya)	VisionSpring (India)
	Voxiva (India)
Education	Ziqitza Health Care Limited (India)
Edubridge (India)	
Hippocampus Learning Centres (India)	**Housing**
	Kashf Foundation (Pakistan)
Energy	Jamii Bora (Kenya)
d.light design (India)	Kashf Foundation (Pakistan)
Husk Power Systems (India)	Kashf Holdings Private Limited (Pakistan)
Orb Energy (India)	Medeem (Ghana)
	Saiban (Pakistan)
HEALTH[a]	
A to Z Textile Mills (Tanzania)	**Water**
Botanical Extracts EPZ Limited (Kenya)	Ecotact (Kenya)
Books of Hope (Kenya)	GUARDIAN (India)
BroadReach (Kenya)	Pharmagen Healthcare Ltd (Pakistan)
	Spring Health (India)
	WaterHealth International (India)

[a] See Carmody et al., 2011, 66, for descriptions of these businesses.
Source of data: Acumen Fund homepage, accessed August 18, 2012, http://acumenfund.org.

relevant innovations, but the full scope of the changes has yet to be visualized, let alone pulled together and examined in a systematic way. Even the terminology used to depict these developments is in flux. Established terms such as "program-related investments" (PRIs), "mission investing," "market-rate investments," all of which tended to apply narrowly to foundations, have recently been superseded by the term "social-impact investing," which itself covers only a portion of the emerging field and involves its own significant ambiguities.[13]

> It is now necessary for these concepts to make the jump to broader strata of participants and observers.

What is more, much of the extant literature on these developments takes the form of quasi "gray material," available only in limited editions to a restricted audience. Largely lacking have been materials that can take the changes underway out to a broader audience and that can penetrate the sizable academic universe training nonprofit managers, social entrepreneurs, business leaders, bankers, investment managers, corporate social responsibility officers, and public policy experts. For the new approaches to philanthropy and social investing to achieve the impact of which they are capable, it will be necessary for these concepts to make the jump to broader strata of participants and observers. Even early innovators have come to recognize this point, arguing, as two of them recently put it, that the "challenge now is to bring this [impact investment] perspective from the fringe to the mainstream," which will require "a new generation of ... communicators" who can "absorb the lessons from visionary practice and communicate them effectively to much wider audiences."[14]

The Objective and Game Plan of This Volume

The objective of the book being introduced here is to do precisely this, to provide a clear and accessible roadmap to the full range of important new developments taking place on the frontiers of philanthropy and social investment as we have conceptualized them in order to broaden awareness of them, increase their credence and traction, and make it possible to maximize the benefits they can generate while acknowledging the limitations and challenges they also face.

It must be emphasized, however, that in exploring the "new frontiers" of philanthropy we are not in any way minimizing the critical role that traditional philanthropy continues to play, or the enormous contributions that existing philanthropic institutions continue to make. Indeed, as will become clear, the creation of the new frontiers has itself not only resulted in important part from groundwork laid by traditional philanthropic actors, but also opened an important new role for these traditional institutions to perform, a role that a number of them have come to recognize and seize.

> Three analytical distinctions shape the structure of this book.

To make sense of these developments, we have made three analytical distinctions that shape the structure of this book. First, the book draws a basic distinction between the *actors* that are surfacing in what I am calling the new frontiers of philanthropy, and the *tools* that these actors are utilizing. This distinction is dictated by the extraordinary explosion of activity in this new "philanthropic space" and the confusion that has consequently resulted in sorting out who is doing what. Since any particular actor can utilize a variety of tools, this distinction is crucial to clarifying what is going on.

Second, within each of these groupings I have attempted to identify a manageable set of distinctive categories into which to sort the enormous variety of both actors and tools that has surfaced, drawing, where possible, on existing capital-market typologies. Generally speaking, the actors are differentiated according to the functions they are performing. Thus, some are assembling or aggregating capital for deployment into social-purpose activities, others are providing secondary markets or exchanges to allow investors to enter or exit the space, and still others are prospecting for promising ventures or offering specialized technical assistance to such entities. To be sure, because this field is still in its infancy, the degree of specialization that has been attained remains limited, which means that a single actor may be performing a variety of roles or utilizing a multitude of tools (see Box 1.1).

Even so, it is impossible to make sense of this field without drawing some meaningful distinctions among the basic functions being performed (the actors)

BOX 1.1

CALVERT FOUNDATION: A MULTITASKING SOCIAL-
IMPACT INVESTMENT FIRM

The Calvert Foundation, launched in 1995, performs a variety of functions
in the social-impact investing arena. In particular, it

- Manages close to $200 million in social-impact investments
- Markets a Community Investment Note to generate capital from
  social investors
- Operates a registered investment advisory service

Created its own donor-advised fund, since spun off as a separate entity

Source: Personal interview, Shari Berenbach, April 29, 2013.

---

and the types of instruments being used (the
tools). As will become clear, this book identifies 11 more or less distinct types of such
actors and eight major types of "new" tools,
though we recognize that others may sort the
chaos differently and the dynamism at work
will likely yield additional types of both actors
and tools as the frontiers expand.

> A description of these new actors and
> tools would be incomplete without
> addressing the important crosscutting
> issues they face or without acknowl-
> edging the critical role that traditional
> philanthropy continues to play.

Finally, beyond the actors and tools there is
also a set of crosscutting issues that the new
frontiers of philanthropy have posed for the
evolution of this new arena of philanthropy and social investment. A description
of these new actors and tools would be incomplete without addressing these important crosscutting issues and some of the difficult dilemmas they pose for
the field.

Given this conceptual framework, the book's discussion falls naturally into
three major parts in addition to the present section carrying this introduction.
Part 2 thus examines the extraordinary array of new *actors* that have come to
populate "philanthropic space" broadly conceived. Included here are capital
aggregators, secondary markets, social stock exchanges, foundations as philanthropic banks, enterprise brokers, and several more. Each of the chapters in this
section takes up a particular class of *actor* and examines a common set of its
characteristics—the *defining features* of that actor, the major *variants* that nevertheless exist, the *rationale* for this type of actor, the *scale* of its activities, the basic
mechanics of the actor's operations, the *challenges* that each confronts, and the
track record this type of actor has achieved to date.

Part 3 then examines the various *tools* being deployed by these actors.
Many of these are tools that have functioned in the worlds of business and
government for decades but are just gaining acceptance in the worlds of philanthropy and social investment—tools like loans, loan guarantees, other
credit enhancements, equity investments, bonds, responsible investing and
purchasing, and securitization. Others are truly novelties, such as
"social-impact bonds," prizes, and crowd sourcing. In each case, the chapter

examines the basic character of the tool, the different variants of the tool, the rationale for its use, the scale of usage in the social and environmental fields, the basic mechanics, and the track record.

Finally, in Part 4 attention turns to some of the most significant *crosscutting issues* that these developments pose. Included here are the potential normative and distributional consequences of the shift of control over support for social and environmental purposes from governments and charitable institutions to private investment sources, whether there is a sufficient flow of adequate deals to absorb the newly available capital, the status of efforts to meet the field's demand for measurable social and environmental impacts, the likely future evolution of these new frontiers, and the policy measures needed to facilitate the expansion of these tools and actors in a responsible fashion.

Taken together, the result is the first comprehensive account of the new actors and tools operating on the frontiers of philanthropy—deepening the knowledge base from which to inform, educate, train, and responsibly promote this new mode of social-purpose activity.

> This chapter pursues four major tasks: descriptive, analytical, normative, and prescriptive.

The purpose of this initial chapter is to provide an overview of this new frontier and a synthesis of the book's principal messages. More specifically, the chapter pursues four major tasks:

- First, *descriptive*—to introduce readers to the major types of actors and tools that have taken shape on the new frontiers of philanthropy and identify some of their distinctive and novel features
- Second, *analytical*—to explain why this extraordinary proliferation of actors and tools is surfacing at this point in time, and hence, what the prospects are for its continued development
- Third, *normative*—to acknowledge some of the challenges and risks that these developments also bring with them and the steps that have so far been taken to address them
- Fourth, *prescriptive*—to identify the steps that are still needed to capture the substantial benefits these developments promise while avoiding the risks that they also pose

A Word about Terminology

Before turning to the first of these tasks, however, it is necessary to say a word about terminology. As already noted, the field of action covered by this volume is already a terminological wasteland, strewn with a substantial number of defeated or discarded terms. As one early adventurer on this frontier put it recently, "[When] I started working in this space in 2002 I was a PRI maker; then I became a social investor; mission investor was in there; and now I'm an impact investor; but [my work] has pretty much stayed the same."[15] Under the circumstances it is incumbent on us to be clear about how we are using certain crucial terms and why.

New Frontiers of Philanthropy

We begin, naturally enough, with the headline term we have used for the title of this book: "new frontiers of philanthropy." No doubt this term will encounter its own pushback from some quarters, and on two different grounds. In the first place, there are those who draw a sharp distinction between "philanthropy" and social-purpose "investing," viewing philanthropy as an old-fashioned term conjuring up Lady Bountiful images of paternalistic charity dispensed to homeless orphans—not quite the

> We use the term "philanthropy" in its most basic meaning: *that* is, as *the provision of private resources for social or environmental purposes.*

image sought by the new breed of investment-oriented, metrics-driven "philanthrocapitalists" and "impact investors."[16] What is more, there will be those who question whether the "new frontiers" are all that new. After all, as we note in Chapter 5, "Foundations as 'Philanthropic Banks,'" the use of nongrant forms of assistance to promote social purposes—the key feature of this type of actor—was pioneered more than 200 years ago by Benjamin Franklin, who established a charity that provided loans to indigent artisans.

Nevertheless, I am convinced that "new frontiers of philanthropy" is an apt description of the topic of this volume, certainly compared to any of the likely alternatives. For one thing, the phenomena that we include within the ambit of this volume embrace more than the new forms of social investing that have come to be known as "impact investing." Also included are such developments as responsible investing and purchasing, prizes, crowd sourcing, and various types of giving and investing collaboratives. Perhaps more centrally, we use the term "philanthropy" in its most basic and broadest meaning: that is, as *the provision of private resources for social or environmental purposes.*[17] The form in which these resources are delivered is thus not as crucial in this definition of philanthropy as the purpose towards which they are directed. In this sense, the social-purpose finance that is a principal focus of this book fits well within the field of philanthropy so conceived.

At the same time, while many of the phenomena covered here may not be new to the world, most are new to social and environmental purposes or are operating at a scale in this field that has not been seen before. Thus, for example, some forms of insurance, such as burial insurance, have been available to the poor for a long time. What is new is the marketing of microinsurance products by private, for-profit insurance companies to meet the health, crop, or disaster insurance needs of the poor at prices they can afford. Similarly, capacity-building has been available to nonprofit organizations for several decades. But instead of focusing on the traditional topics of board development, fundraising, and accounting systems, the new frontier of social-purpose capacity-building is focusing on scaling up promising ventures, establishing earned-income streams, and tapping into various forms of investment capital. Finally, even donor-advised funds, a relatively new form of charitable instrument, have been around for several decades in the United States. What is new is the emergence and rapid expansion of corporate-originated charitable funds offering donors the opportunity to operate their donor-advised funds through offshoots of the for-profit investment firms that manage their core investments.

All of these are developments that have attained meaningful scale in the past two decades, some in the past five years. But all of them involve the mobilization and distribution of private resources for social or environmental purposes, which is the essence of philanthropy.

Using the term "philanthropy" to depict these developments is not only technically correct, however. It also has the virtue of reminding us that, though these

> Using the term "philanthropy" also has the virtue of reminding us that, though these activities are expected to generate a profit, the fundamental objective remains "social" in the full dictionary meaning of that term.

activities are engaging private businesses and often utilizing forms of assistance that are expected to generate a financial return, the fundamental objective remains "social" in the full dictionary meaning of that term as "of or having to do with human beings living together as a group in a situation in which their dealings with one another affect their common welfare."[18] Only in this way will we avoid the peril that two early champions of these developments had in mind when they warned that the activities on the frontiers of philanthropy could be made "too easy" if the definition of social and environmental impact becomes "so loose and diluted," or, I would add, so muted, "as to be virtually meaningless."[19]

Social-Impact Investing

For this reason also, we have chosen to introduce a slight adjustment to the term of art that has been advanced in much of the available literature to depict what in many respects is the central beachhead on the new frontiers of philanthropy—namely, the mobilization of private investment capital for social and environmental purposes. That term is "impact investing." This term grew out of a series of meetings convened by the Rockefeller Foundation in the mid-2000s as part of its effort to rally private investment houses, and the private investment capital they help direct, into support for the burgeoning social enterprises emerging in both developed and developing countries around the world. Existing terms, such as "social investing," or "program-related investing," or "mission-related investing," or "socially responsible investing," were perceived as either too soft, or too closely associated with foundations and philanthropy, or too broad, or too passive to appeal to the hardheaded managers of private investment capital. What is more, they were perceived to be incapable of passing muster as a distinct "asset class" around which a new line of investment business could be organized.

> The term *impact investing* itself provides little clue about what the content of such "positive impact" is supposed to be.

To their credit, the inventors of the "impact investing" terminology came up with a brilliant solution that served this purpose well. The problem is that the solution may have served this purpose too well, opening the door to precisely the danger that the 2009 Monitor Institute Report warned against: that is, leaving the underlying concept "so loose and diluted" as to make it "virtually meaningless." Although advocates of impact investing regularly emphasize that impact investments are "investments intended to create positive impact beyond financial return,"[20] the term itself provides little clue about what the content of such "positive impact" is supposed to be or what the standard for recognizing its presence is. It thus implicitly puts the emphasis on the idea of investment return rather than on the idea of social and environmental benefit.

Nor does a recent book on impact investing by two leaders in the field do much to clarify the matter. There we learn that "all organizations, for-profit and nonprofit alike, create value that consists of economic, social, and environmental components. All investors, whether market rate, charitable, or some mix of the two, generate all three forms of value."[21] Indeed, one recent publication on the topic goes so far as to define the term "impact" in "impact investment" as "a meaningful change in economic, social, cultural, environmental and/or political conditions due to specific actions and behavioral changes by individuals, communities, and/or society as a whole."[22]

But if all organizations and all investors create "positive impact," and if the term "impact" in "impact investment" consists of *any* "meaningful change," regardless of its direction or content, how are we to differentiate "impact investors" from plain vanilla investors? The answer, it appears, hinges on "intention," particularly the intention of investees, and on the attention that investors pay to "the blended value returns" reflected in serious impact reporting.[23] But "intention" is notoriously difficult to assess and, as the 2009 Monitor report on impact investing acknowledges, there is "reason to be skeptical" about social- and environmental-impact measurement systems because "the existing financial markets and incentives create major pull toward 'greenwashing' and dilution of standards ... as asset managers seek to respond to growing client interest in impact investing without wanting to take on the long and difficult work of ensuring investment impact."[24] Already the field has developed a set of impact measures that are so numerous that they begin to resemble those prizes in grade-school contests designed to ensure that every child comes home a winner. No wonder some skeptics have begun to worry that the definition of "impact investing" is coming to resemble "a dog's breakfast,"[25] while others have insisted on adding an adjective like "community" in front of the term to clarify the impacts that the investments are expected to make.[26]

To avoid a similar charge of vagueness, our approach in this volume follows this latter course. Taking our cue from the observation of Bugg-Levine and Emerson that "impact investing for blended value unites the power of business with the purpose of philanthropy,"[27] we suggest that the term for depicting this phenomenon should give equal weight to both sides of this equation. Hence we use the term "social- and environmental-impact investing," or just "social-impact investing" for short, to refer to it in order to place equal emphasis on the financial and the social or environmental effects these investments are supposed to produce.[28]

Social Purpose

If we propose to attach the term "social" to the term being used more generally to depict a significant component of the activity on the new frontiers of philanthropy, it is obviously necessary to clarify what we have in mind by it. Fundamentally, therefore, this book takes social-impact investments to be investments that significantly seek to generate "social value," that is, to *promote the health, well-being, and quality of life of a population, particularly disadvantaged segments of that population; encourage the free expression of ideas; or foster tolerance.* Even so, opinions can differ about what truly counts as a "social-impact investment." For example, some observers consider an investment to serve a social purpose if it is made in a disadvantaged area, regardless of who the beneficiaries are, whereas others argue that "the fact that an investment is made in a poor country is not sufficient to qualify as an impact investment."[29]

For our purposes here, whether an investment can be judged to serve a social purpose can be determined by how it affects any of three crucial factors: first, the

> Whether an investment can be judged to serve a social purpose can be determined by how it affects any of three crucial factors.

population assisted by it, particularly whether it is a disadvantaged population in some significant sense; second, the *production process* it supports, particularly whether it explicitly involves the employment and training of a disadvantaged or excluded population or reduces the environmental impact of the production; and third, the *goods or services* produced, for example, whether they have inherent environmental advantages.

Investment Capital versus Operating Income

One other terminological distinction about which it will be important to be clear is that differentiating investment *capital* from *operating revenue* in any enterprise, whether for-profit or nonprofit Much of the discussion of the financing of social-purpose organizations, particularly that centered on nonprofit organizations, has focused on *operating revenue*, which is the income that organizations use to run their ongoing annual operations. This money typically comes in part from individual and foundation gifts, from government grants and contracts, and from fees for service.[30]

> Investment capital is in many senses the lifeblood of an organization.

The resources flowing to social-purpose organizations from most, though not all, of the actors on the new frontiers of philanthropy, however, are of a different sort. They take the form of *investment capital*, which is revenue that may contribute to operating income in the future, but fundamentally goes to build long-term organizational capacity and capabilities through the purchase of such things as equipment, facilities, skills, and strategic planning that are expected to serve the organization over the longer haul (see Box 1.2).

Investment capital, too, can come from many different sources and take many different forms. Some can even come from gifts, as when a wealthy patron gives a work of art to a museum or donates the resources to construct a building at a university. More commonly, however, investment capital comes in one or both of two other forms: (*a*) *debt*, that is, loans, or the proceeds of a bond sale, which

---

BOX 1.2

INVESTMENT CAPITAL VERSUS OPERATING REVENUE

Operating revenue allows an organisation to deliver defined outputs or outcomes. It covers day-to-day activities, regular service provision and ongoing projects. It often takes the form of payments for contracted services, grants and donations.

Investment capital provides finance to build an organisation's long-term capacity to achieve its social mission.

Source: UK Big Society Capital, http://www.bigsocietycapital.com/what-social-investment.

is a type of loan; or (*b*) *equity*, the purchase of an ownership, or equity, stake in an organization. In both cases, the providers of investment capital typically require something in return for their investment—payment of principal plus interest in the case of debt; and an ownership stake and payment of a share of whatever profits or surplus the investee might earn in the case of equities.

Investment capital is in many senses the lifeblood of an organization because it is what allows the organization to grow. However, investment capital has historically been hard for social-purpose organizations to secure. For one thing, if they are nonprofits, they cannot accept *equity investments*, perhaps the most attractive form of investment capital because it is essentially free. This is so because equity investors do not have to be paid back unless a firm earns a profit and pays dividends or its shares rise in price. But nonprofits are prohibited from paying dividends to their investors or owners and cannot sell shares of their ownership to outside investors. This makes them unable to tap equity investments without special arrangements. *Bond revenue* is also typically off the table for social-purpose organizations because, as will become clear below, it is hardly economical to issue bonds for denominations much below $50 million, a threshold that leaves all but the largest social-purpose organizations, such as universities and hospitals, waiting at the altar. This leaves *loans*, but due to the perceived riskiness of social-purpose revenue streams, social-purpose organizations often have to pay premium rates for the debt they take on. Reflecting this, a survey of US nonprofit human service, community development, and arts organizations conducted by the Johns Hopkins Nonprofit Listening Post Project found that 80–90 percent of surveyed organizations in these fields reported a need for investment capital to acquire technology, purchase or renovate facilities, or develop new programs, but fewer than 40 percent reported success in securing the needed capital (see Figure 1.3).[31]

FIGURE 1.3
US Nonprofit Capital Needs and Success in Securing Capital, 2006

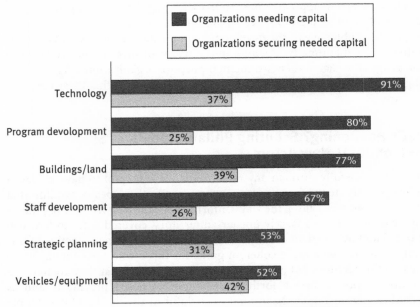

PERCENT OF ORGANIZATIONS

FIGURE 1.4
US Nonprofit Difficulty Accessing Investment Capital from Various Sources, 2006

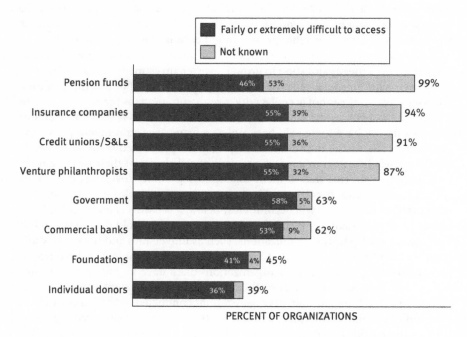

PERCENT OF ORGANIZATIONS

When asked what experiences they have recently had securing investment capital from various sources, moreover, over 90 percent of these organizations reported finding it either fairly or extremely difficult to access the major sources of investment capital in the US economy—pension funds, insurance companies, credit unions, and venture capitalists—or they simply had no experience or knowledge of how to approach these sources, leaving them dependent on commercial banks and foundations (see Figure 1.4).[32]

A principal objective of the developments that are the focus of this book is to remedy this dilemma by opening new streams of investment capital for a broad range of social and environmental purpose organizations. Against this background, it is therefore possible to turn now to look at what these developments are.

What's Happening? Scouting Philanthropy's New Frontier I: New Actors

To travel successfully through any new frontier, it is helpful to have at least a basic map of the terrain and some way to identify the types of wildlife that might be encountered along the way. Unfortunately, the new frontier of philanthropy has so far been a largely uncharted territory, covered with underbrush and populated by a variety of unfamiliar life-forms. A central objective of this volume is to provide a more coherent guide for those who are contemplating entry into this territory but need a bit more clarity about what they are likely to encounter before venturing forth. Accordingly, as noted previously and as reflected in Figure 1.5, we have found it helpful to divide the philanthropic frontier into two major regions: the region of the *actors* and the region of the *tools*. The region of the *actors* contains the many new institutions that have come to occupy what we have termed philanthropic space. Although there is enormous diversity among these actors, it is possible to discern some clustering into 11 more or less identifiable "tribes." Similarly, the region of the *tools* houses the instruments available to these actors to do their work. Eight types of such instruments are identified, ranging from loans and credit enhancements to new types of grants.

> Unfortunately, the new frontier of philanthropy has so far been a largely uncharted territory.

The purpose of this section and the one that follows is to provide a basic introduction to these various actors and tools to set the stage for the more in-depth examination provided in the balance of this volume. Because most visitors to this new frontier are likely to encounter the new actors in all their variety first, we begin in this section with them and then take up the new tools in the section that follows.

> The new frontier of philanthropy is already home to some remarkable life-forms.

What even the most cursory visit to the new frontier of philanthropy makes clear is that while this territory is hardly fully settled, neither is it totally uninhabited. To the contrary, it is already home to some remarkable life-forms.

As suggested in Figure 1.5, these life forms can be grouped into three types. The first are essentially new types of financial investment institutions that have

FIGURE 1.5
Actors and Tools on the New Frontiers of Philanthropy

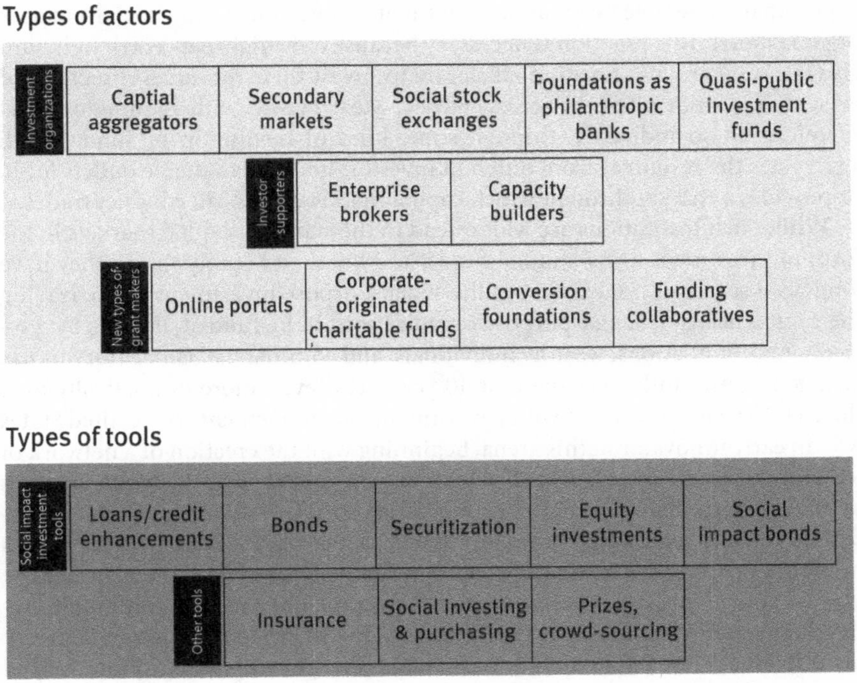

Types of actors

Investment organizations				
Capital aggregators	Secondary markets	Social stock exchanges	Foundations as philanthropic banks	Quasi-public investment funds

Investor supporters	
Enterprise brokers	Capacity builders

New types of grant makers			
Online portals	Corporate-originated charitable funds	Conversion foundations	Funding collaboratives

Types of tools

Social impact investment tools				
Loans/credit enhancements	Bonds	Securitization	Equity investments	Social impact bonds

Other tools		
Insurance	Social investing & purchasing	Prizes, crowd-sourcing

emerged to move capital within the newly emerging social-impact investment market. Included here are five types of entities with names quite different from those of traditional philanthropic institutions: they are "capital aggregators," secondary markets, social stock exchanges, quasi-public investment funds, and a special set of foundations functioning as "philanthropic banks." The second group consists of actors that supply various forms of support to these new social-impact financial institutions. Included here are "enterprise brokers," new types of "capacity builders," and a variety of supportive infrastructure organizations. Finally, there are a variety of other actors that remain focused on the more traditional philanthropic tool of grants but are doing so in novel ways. Included here are corporate-originated charitable funds, conversion foundations, online portals and exchanges, and funding collaboratives. Let us examine each of these groupings in more detail.

Social-Impact Investment Institutions

Given the emphasis that the new frontiers of philanthropy are putting on leveraging new sources of investment capital for social and environmental purposes, the natural starting point for a Cook's tour of this frontier region is with the new financial entities that have surfaced to tap and channel these sources. As noted previously, five broad types of new actors in particular deserve attention here.

> Easily one of the most crucial of the new actors on the frontiers of philanthropy is the set of capital aggregators.

Capital Aggregators

Easily among the most crucial of these actors are the social-impact *capital aggregators*. As profiled more fully in Chapter 2 of this volume, these are the organizations that assemble capital for ultimate investment in social-purpose organizations. This function is necessary because only high-net-worth individuals (HNWIs) are in a position efficiently to invest their resources directly, and even they do not often do so exclusively. Most people with money to invest therefore do so indirectly, through some kind of institution or fund, which aggregates the resources from different investors and finds suitable outlets for it, or provides a market through which capital market actors can conduct trades.

While such institutions are widespread in the standard capital markets in the form of investment firms, mutual funds, and bond and equity funds, they have long been scarce or nonexistent in the social-purpose investment arena, leaving the capital needs of social-purpose organizations to be funded, if at all, by governments, foundations, wealthy individuals, and commercial banks. But this has changed significantly over the past 40 years, and even more dramatically over the past 10 years, much of it with government encouragement. The United States was an early innovator in this arena, beginning with the creation of a network of federally financed community development corporations in the 1960s, a series of state-government-stimulated equity funds to promote job creation in distressed regions beginning in the late 1960s and into the 1970s and 1980s,[33] and a number of supportive federal tax and other policies designed to encourage the flow of private investment capital into low-income housing and community redevelopment.[34] With the invention and spread of microcredit through the work of individuals like Muhammad Yunus, and the growing recognition, helped along by C. K. Prahalad, of the "profits at the bottom of the pyramid," moreover, the number of capital aggregators focusing on social-purpose investments has accelerated.

As befits their varied origins, social-purpose capital aggregators come in many shapes and sizes and draw on a variety of sources of capital, including high-net-worth individuals, foundations, and increasingly in recent years, main-line financial institutions such as pension funds, insurance companies, and global financial service firms like J.P. Morgan Chase, Bank of America, Citibank, and UBS, all of which have been attracted by the opportunity to "do good while doing well" and begun to see in so-called social-impact investing a promising new "asset class."[35]

Not only do the sources of capital aggregated by these entities vary, but so do the forms in which they make it available to investees. Thus, some funds concentrate on loans or other forms of debt, while others specialize in providing equity in various forms to particular classes of ventures at various stages in their development, from early start-up to financing the leap to sustainability.

Most aggregators focus on a particular market niche or region. Thus, for example, ACCION International focuses on microfinance lending institutions in Third World countries. Reflecting the growth of this field, just one of ACCION's affiliates, Banco Compartamos in Mexico, raised $467 million in an initial public offering of stock in 2007, helping to boost the overall global microfinance industry to over $65 billion under management as of 2010.[36]

Then there are the more than 900 community development financial institutions in the United States focusing on distressed urban and rural communities, including more than 600 community development loan funds, 50 venture capital funds, 200 community development credit unions, and 85 community development banks. These institutions had $50 billion under management as of the end of 2013, generated through a wide assortment of investment instruments, including common or preferred stock in the CDFIs themselves, linked deposits, guarantees of CDFI loans to particular classes of borrowers, or subordinated loans to the CDFIs to strengthen the CDFIs' balance sheets and thus permit them to access other resources.[37]

Whatever their focus or range of investors, however, all social-impact capital aggregators function as middlemen in the social capital market, reaching out to investors willing to invest their capital in social-purpose activities and in turn locating promising social-purpose ventures in which to place it. Given the different risk and return appetites of investors, however, different capital aggregators can operate at different points in the social capital marketplace. Alternatively, they can assemble capital "stacks," or "structured investment products," like the one mentioned in the vignette that led off this chapter, with different layers, or "tranches," each with its own risk-return characteristics, and therefore each with its own potential class of investors.

> Social-impact capital aggregators function as middlemen in the social capital market.

Observers of the field have therefore begun drawing a distinction between "impact first" investors, who seek to maximize the social or environmental impact of their investments while maintaining a floor for financial return; and "finance first" investors, who seek to achieve a higher, risk-adjusted market rate of return while still meeting a threshold of social or environmental impact.[38] Where the respective financial and social-impact "floors" lie for these respective investors can therefore differ considerably. Thus, for *impact-first investors*, the impact threshold may be higher and the financial threshold lower than the respective thresholds for financial-first investors, and vice versa. This yields slightly different "sweet spots" for the different investors in the social-impact investment space, as shown in Figure 1.6.[39] Thus, quadrants B and C in Figure 1.6 may work for "impact first" investors, while quadrants and A and C are the available locations for "finance first" investors.

Not surprisingly, different types of social-impact capital aggregators will operate in these different zones. As a general rule, nonprofit social-impact capital aggregators tend to appeal to investors with an "impact first" orientation, frequently individuals or foundations. For their investors, the financial return threshold can be set below where for-profit investors might put it, and they might be willing to accept a higher ratio of risk to return. These investors are therefore highly prized for the kind of structured investment products described above because they will more willingly accept the first-loss grant or guarantee tranches on the bottom of such structured investments, thus absorbing much of

FIGURE 1.6
The Relative Domains of Impact-First and Finance-First Social-Impact Investors

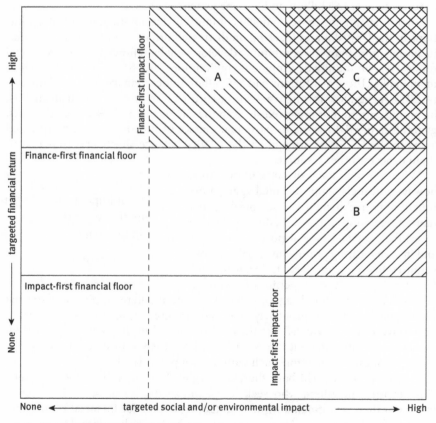

A = Domain of finance-first investors
B = Domain of impact-first investors
C = Domain of both finance-first and impact-first investors

the risk and making it possible for profit-oriented private investors to enter deals that would otherwise have little appeal to them.

Typical of this type of nonprofit social-purpose capital aggregator is Acumen Fund, a nonprofit capital aggregator founded in 2001 that has built a robust portfolio of investments supporting "entrepreneurs able to provide critical services [water, health, housing, and energy] at affordable prices to people earning less than four dollars a day" in eight countries of South Asia and East and West Africa—clearly an impact-first objective.[40] The organization goes after "philanthropic capital," which tends to be satisfied with lower return rates or merely return of principal, but still strives to make "disciplined investments intended to yield both financial and social returns" (see Box 1.3).

For-profit capital aggregators are more likely to set the financial return bar higher while still seeking meaningful social returns. Thus, for example, UK-based Bridges Ventures and Dubai-based Willow Impact Investors are both for-profit, social-impact capital aggregators that utilize a private-equity model, attracting funds from investors with more of a risk-adjusted market return expectation.[41]

Whatever their strategy, form, focus, or market niche, however, it seems clear that social-impact capital aggregators have mushroomed in number, size, and diversity over the past decade or more. One indicator of this is the 190 funds already listed on the ImpactBase website created by the Global Impact Investment Network (GIIN), a network of social-impact investors organized by the Rockefeller Foundation and several partners. In addition to the 190 funds listed, this site has attracted 730 accredited investor-subscribers.[42]

> Social-impact capital aggregators have mushroomed in number, size, and diversity over the past decade or more.

More generally, as already noted, Lisa Richter estimates in Chapter 2 of this volume that the number of capital aggregators may have reached 3,000 internationally, with $300 billion under management. Growth rates of funds under management have been dramatic, moreover. Global investments in clean energy thus grew from US$36 billion in 2004 to $155 billion in 2008 and, despite the financial crisis, still stood at $145 billion at the end of 2009.[43] Between 2004 and 2008, according to Richter, US CDFI investments grew at an annual compound rate of 10 percent a year, global microfinance investments by 20 percent a year, and global clean-technology investments by 30 to 40 percent a year.

Nor does it appear that this trend is weakening. One influential report prepared in 2009 by J.P. Morgan Social Finance estimated a global demand for social-impact investments over the ensuing decade ranging from $400.6 billion to nearly $1 trillion in just five fields (housing, rural water supply, maternal health, primary education, and financial services).[44]

What performance data are available on existing social-impact investments suggest, moreover, that investors may have incentives to meet this demand. Thus, for example, drawing on data generated by the CDFI Data Project and the Microfinance Information Exchange, Richter reports that net loss rates were under 1 percent for US CDFIs for the period 2000–2008, that they rose temporarily to 1.78 percent by the end of 2009, but even

> Capital aggregators are both expecting, and so far achieving, return rates on their social-impact investments in line with high-performing benchmark equity and debt indexes.

BOX 1.3
ACUMEN FUND MISSION STATEMENT

Changing the way the world tackles poverty

Our mission is to create a world beyond poverty by investing in social enterprises, emerging leaders, and breakthrough ideas.

Our vision is that one day every human being will have access to the critical goods and services they need—including affordable health, water, housing, energy, agricultural inputs and services—so that they can make decisions and choices for themselves and unleash their full human potential. This is where dignity starts—not just for the poor but for everyone on earth.

The Challenge. Tremendous wealth is being created in the world today thanks to globalization and the power of technology and markets. Yet there is a growing gap between rich and poor. Something must be done to extend the benefits of the global economy to the majority of the world's population that lives on less than four dollars a day.

Why Charity Alone isn't the Answer. Poor people seek dignity, not dependence. Traditional charity often meets immediate needs but too often fails to enable people to solve their own problems over the long term. Market-based approaches have the potential to grow when charitable dollars run out, and they must be a part of the solution to the big problem of poverty.

Why the Marketplace Alone isn't the Answer. Very low-income people are too often invisible to businesses and society. Businesses see no significant market opportunity and governments view low-income areas as having insufficient tax revenues to pay for basic services like clean water, healthcare, housing and energy. Building new models that provide these critical services at affordable price—in the face of high costs, poor distribution systems, dispersed customers, limited financing options and, at times, corruption—requires imaginative business solutions and partnerships supported by investors willing to take on a risk/return profile that is unacceptable to traditional financiers.

Changing the Development Paradigm. We believe that pioneering entrepreneurs will ultimately find the solutions to poverty. The entrepreneurs Acumen Fund supports are focused on offering critical services—water, health, housing, and energy—at affordable prices to people earning less than four dollars a day.

The key is patient capital. We use philanthropic capital to make disciplined investments—loans or equity, not grants—that yield both financial and social returns. Any financial returns we receive are recycled into new investments. Over time, we have refined the Acumen Fund investment model, built a world-class global team with offices in four countries, and learned what does and does not work in growing businesses that serve low-income people.

Source: Acumen Fund, "About Us," accessed August 12, 2012, http://www.acumenfund.org.

then remained below the 2.49 percent mortgage "charge-off" rate at regular, non-CDFI, federally insured US banks. Microfinance institutions similarly experience net loan loss rates under 1 percent. More generally, available evidence suggests that capital aggregators are both expecting, and so far achieving, return rates on their social-impact investments, both debt and equity, in line with high-performing benchmark equity and debt indexes, such as the S&P 500, Russell 2000 Growth, PIMCO Total Return, and J.P. Morgan Emerging Markets Bond.[45]

Secondary Markets

While capital aggregators are one important set of financial actors that have surfaced on the new frontiers of philanthropy, they are by no means the only one. A second set consists of social-impact *secondary markets*. These are institutions that purchase the loans originated by capital aggregators, refreshing the capital available to the capital aggregators so they can make additional loans. To do so, the secondary market institutions use a process called "securitization" to bundle the loans into packages and use them as collateral against which to issue bonds on the capital markets.[46]

> *Secondary market operators* have also sprung up in the social-purpose arena.

Secondary markets have long functioned in the regular capital markets, especially in the housing field. Readers familiar with US capital markets will recognize this as the function performed by the Federal National Mortgage Association, lovingly known as "Fannie Mae," originally established as a government corporation to purchase federally guaranteed home mortgages from the originating commercial banks and savings and loans.

This function did not develop in the social-impact investment arena until the late 1980s, however, with the establishment of the US-based Community Reinvestment Fund (CRF), created to support the growing low-income housing and community development market. As detailed by David Erickson in Chapter 3, CRF initially had to raise its capital through private placements of community development bonds. In 2004, however, it was finally able to issue a bond "rated" by one of the quasi-official rating agencies, Standard and Poor's, which allowed it to attract eight new institutional investors that had previously been unable to invest in CRF bonds because of investment guidelines that prevented them from investing in unrated securities. To date, CRF has purchased over $1.4 billion in community development loans from more than 150 lending organizations located in 46 of the country's 50 states.[47]

By demonstrating the power of securitization and secondary market purchases to inject fresh capital into social-impact investment markets, CRF has stimulated the emergence of additional secondary market institutions in different social-impact fields. For some of these, like CRF, secondary market transactions are their exclusive function, while for others the secondary market activity is an offshoot of a robust loan origination activity. This is the case, for example, with Habitat for Humanity International (HFHI), the well-known international nonprofit that mobilizes volunteers to help low-income families construct homes for themselves. To cover the costs of building supplies and equipment for the houses they help build, HFHI affiliates have approximately

$1.4 billion in mortgages outstanding to new homeowners. To allow the affiliates to continue their construction activities, HFHI has developed a secondary market operation called the FlexCAP program under which it purchases a portion of these loans from the affiliates using capital it generates from selling investors 7- or 10-year notes backed by the pledged mortgages. Habitat then pays off these notes from the principal and interest payments made by the homeowners. The program has a 100 percent repayment rate and has allowed HFHI to raise $107 million.[48]

Nor are these isolated examples. Partners for the Common Good (PCG), a CDFI founded in 1989 to serve Catholic institutions, recently raised $25.3 million to purchase home mortgages from its affiliates; Blue Orchard, a Swiss microfinance investment fund, raised nearly $200 million to purchase microfinance loans from 21 microfinance investment organizations around the world; and BRAC, the huge Bangladeshi nonprofit development organization, similarly recently raised $180 million in capital to purchase microfinance loans made by its affiliates.[49]

Social Stock Exchanges

A third type of innovation taking shape on the frontiers of philanthropy brings the concept of a stock exchange to the social- and environmental-impact investment arena. Social stock exchanges provide a more efficient way for social-impact investors to connect with social ventures seeking capital. Unlike social-impact capital aggregators and secondary-market operators, who must go through the trouble of searching out investors who share their social-impact/risk-return appetites and then market their investment products to them, social stock exchanges simply provide platforms through which dispersed investors can locate social investments in which they are interested. What is more, exchanges provide automatic assurance to such investors that they can exit the investments whenever this becomes necessary or desirable. Of course, for this to be possible, as Shahnaz, Kraybill, and Salamon note in Chapter 4 of this volume, the exchanges must develop listing rules, standard disclosure requirements for the listed entities, and trading mechanisms that are efficient, accurate, and fraud-proof.

> Social stock exchanges are a third class of organizations taking shape on the frontiers of philanthropy.

One of the earliest uses of this mechanism in the social-impact arena was in the environmental area. The Chicago Climate Exchange, created in 2003 in anticipation of the hoped-for passage of a "cap and trade" permit system for "carbon emission credits," allowed companies able to achieve emission reductions cheaply to secure tradable credits that they could sell through the exchange to companies for which emission reductions would be far more costly. Although the 2010 failure of cap-and-trade legislation in the US Congress caused a pullback for the Chicago Climate Exchange, the Kyoto Protocol, which came into effect in 2005, has allowed other emission-trading exchanges outside of the United States (which did not sign this Protocol) to expand well beyond what the Chicago exchange was handling. Thus, the European Climate Exchange, the world's largest, saw its volume expand from 94 million equivalent tons of carbon dioxide in 2005 to 5.3 billion equivalent tons in 2010, and it is only one of 10 such exchanges operating globally. According to the World Bank, overall carbon trading stood at US$142 billion as of 2010, though the global economic slow-down coupled with an overly generous supply of free credits in Europe has caused at least a temporary pullback in trading.[50]

The first social investment "exchange" outside of the climate arena emerged in 2003 in Brazil with the launch of the Bolsa de Valorous Socioambientais (BVSA), or Social and Environmental Investment Exchange, though this entity functions more like an online contribution platform such as the ones described in Chapter 8 of this volume than an actual investment vehicle. BVSA screens projects to de-termine their alignment with the UN Millennium Development Goals, but donors who "invest" in these projects are entitled only to social, but nor finan-cial, return.[51]

More ambitious, formalized private placement markets have now surfaced as well. These include Mission Markets in the United States, Impact Partners in Singapore, and Artha in India. More ambitious yet are several full-fledged social stock exchanges that are now nearing operational status in a number of locations around the world. These include Social Stock Exchange Ltd (SSE) in the UK, Impact Exchange (iX) in Mauritius, and the Impact Investment Exchange (IIX) in Singapore. The most fully developed at this point appears to be the Mauritius iX entity, which has received formal regulatory approval from the Stock Exchange of Mauritius (SEM) of rules for listing and trading qualified social- and environmental-purpose initiatives and social-impact investment funds within the SEM structure but under a separate SEM board. Further, iX Mauritius has now teamed up with the Singapore Impact Investment Exchange to work with the SEM to bring iX to a successful launch.

Quasi-Public Investment Funds

Public-sector organizations have also joined the march toward creating specialized social-impact capital investment programs and facilities. Prominent among these have been the entries by several of the multi-national development banks such as the World Bank and the Inter-American Development Bank. Unlike the capital aggre-gators described earlier, these institutions es-sentially pool *public sector* resources for social-impact purposes.

> Public-sector organizations have also joined the march toward creating specialized social-impact investment programs.

Thus, for example, the International Finance Corporation (IFC), an affiliate of the World Bank created to stimulate private business in developing countries, has recently added a social-impact investment initiative to its portfolio. As just one example, the IFC has funneled $481 million to 63 private school projects in developing countries aimed at supplementing grossly inadequate public school systems with low-cost private education options. In Kenya, for example, 23 pri-vate schools have received an average of $300,000 in loans each, and 113 others have received advisory support.[52]

The Inter-American Development Bank has similarly established a Multilateral Investment Fund (MIF) through which it has also actively entered the social-impact investment field. One recent investment, for example, involved a $25 million loan and $5 million in equity finance in Mexico's IGNIA Fund, which helped leverage a total of $102 million for investments in small and medium-sized enterprises serving those at the base of the pyramid.[53]

Nor are multinational development banks the only public-sector entities developing social-impact investment entities. The UK government has been especially active, and especially inventive, in channeling public, or quasi-public, resources into social-impact investment activity. This has included dedicating proceeds from the UK lottery to the creation of a "foundation of social innovation" called NESTA, and tapping the proceeds of long-dormant and unclaimed bank accounts to seed a sizable, quasi-public, social-impact investment fund called Big Society Capital that is expected to end up with assets approaching £400 million (US$600 million).[54]

Foundations as "Philanthropic Banks"

Finally, a number of charitable foundations have begun moving well beyond the traditional foundation reliance on grants as the chief, or only, form of financial assistance and begun functioning as virtual "philanthropic banks" or social investment funds. Some of these institutions are simply applying social, environmental, and corporate governance (ESG) screens to increased shares of their normal investment decision-making.[55] But a number of others are combining this type of investment screening with more active engagement in the social-impact investment market. This has involved going well beyond the traditional foundation reliance on the tool of grants and utilizing a much wider array of financial instruments—for example, loans, loan guarantees, equity investments, bonds, and bond guarantees. And it has also involved tapping not only their grant budgets but their core investment assets as well, thus challenging the long-standing foundation tradition of keeping separate their two major lines of "business": their "investment business," which has historically been expected to focus single-mindedly on responsibly maximizing investment income; and their "grant business," which has historically been expected to focus narrowly on dispensing some share of the resulting proceeds in the form of charitable grants.[56]

> A number of charitable foundations have begun functioning as virtual "philanthropic banks," tapping their core investment assets and going well beyond their traditional reliance on the tool of grants.

A broad array of foundations has begun moving in this direction, ranging from midsized institutions such as the KL Felicitas Foundation, the Babcock Foundation, the Wallace Global Fund, and the Educational Foundation of America to some of the nation's largest foundations, such as the Annie E. Casey Foundation, the Kellogg Foundation, the Kresge Foundation, and the Robert Wood Johnson Foundation, among others.[57] Thus, as detailed by Salamon and Burckart in Chapter 5 of this volume, the KL Felicitas Foundation, created by dot-com entrepreneur Charlie Kleisner and his wife, Lisa, has 78 percent of its core assets committed to social-impact investments. The H. B. Heron Foundation in New York, a pioneer in this arena, has 42 percent so invested and has announced a commitment to move this to 100 percent. Nor is this an exclusively US phenomenon. The Esmee Fairbarn Foundation in the UK and the Fondazione CRT in Italy have joined this parade as well, the latter creating a separate subsidiary, the Fondazione Sviluppo e Crescita (the Development and Growth Foundation) to get around Italian laws limiting the ability of foundations to use their assets in such leveraged ways to support for-profit enterprises.

This expanded foundation experimentation with novel forms of financing is not entirely new, of course. The 1969 US tax law that established the foundation "payout" requirement also opened the door for foundation use of an expanded array of financial instruments through what were called "program-related investments" (PRIs). However, PRIs were conceived as a form of grant funded out of a foundation's 5 percent grant budget. What is more, because of the administrative constraints placed on this vehicle and the general conservatism of foundation financial management, the number of PRI makers out of the more than 75,000 US foundations peaked at 133 in 2004 and dropped back to 120 as of 2007, the year before the US financial meltdown. While these tended to be fairly large institutions, moreover, the overall share of foundation assets devoted to such PRIs has never exceeded 1 percent.[58]

What the new breed of "foundations as philanthropic banks" is doing is reimagining the field by taking the PRI concept to a new level—breeching "the Chinese wall" between the program and investment sides of the foundation house, utilizing a much broader array of financial instruments, and consciously seeking greater leverage from their investments by using their funds to catalyze the flow of private investment capital into social-purpose activities.

Social-Impact Investment Support Institutions

To assist the capital aggregators, secondary markets, foundations as philanthropic banks, and quasi-public investment funds that have surfaced in this new social-impact capital market, a variety of types of service providers have also recently surfaced. Three of these in particular deserve special attention here: enterprise brokers, sustainability capacity builders, and new infrastructure organizations.

> A variety of new types of service providers have also recently surfaced to assist the capital aggregators.

Enterprise Brokers

One of the most significant of these support entities for the social-impact financial institutions are what might be called "enterprise brokers." Enterprise brokers are individuals or institutions that perform the crucial middleman function of helping capital aggregators identify promising ventures capable of delivering the desired combination of financial and social returns, and helping such ventures find their way to investors with the substantive and financial interests aligned with the ventures' activities and needs.

As described by Hagerman and Wood in Chapter 6 of this volume, the need for this function arises from the significant transaction costs that exist on both sides of the social-impact investment market as investors and social entrepreneurs search out partnerships that align their respective fields of activity, desired forms of investment, and risk and return profiles across a highly fragmented social-impact investment space. Also at work are the special difficulties of assessing risk in the social-impact arena given the uncertainties of new products being marketed by relatively untested social entrepreneurs to bottom-of-the-pyramid consumers whose market behavior has yet to be fully analyzed.

Capacity Builders

Another function that has expanded and assumed new forms with the growth of social ventures and social-impact investment is that of social-venture capacity builders. As noted earlier, capacity builders and technical assistance providers have operated in the nonprofit or social-purpose organization arena for decades. Indeed, nonprofit capacity builders in the United States have their own infrastructure organization called the Alliance for Nonprofit Management, a specialized organization called BoardSource to provide advice on the management of boards of directors, and a robust affinity group of foundation supporters known as Grantmakers for Effective Organizations (GEO).

> New *capacity builders* have emerged focusing on sustainability and scaling.

For the most part, however, these existing organizations and consultants have focused on standard organizational management topics such as fundraising, special events, board development, accounting systems, and human resource policies. What Melinda Tuan identifies as the "new capacity builders" in Chapter 7 of this volume have a considerably different focus. Their objective is organizational *sustainability* and *scaling*. They assist organizations to develop *earned-income strategies*, access the new, nongrant forms of capital now available, and measure social outcomes.

These new capacity builders fall into two broad groups, though there is extensive interaction between the two. One group takes its inspiration from a celebrated 1997 *Harvard Business Review* article that challenged foundations to act more like venture capitalists by taking a more active role in improving the management and operations of the organizations they support.[59] This has given rise to the field of "venture philanthropy" populated by organizations that provide a combination of funding and intensive, "high-engagement" technical assistance and organizational development that they either provide themselves or hire outside consultancies to deliver for them. Some of these organizations are traditional foundations like the Edna McConnell Clark Foundation, which has decided to pursue its mission of helping young people from low-income backgrounds become independent through a strategy of making very large grants to a limited number of promising organizations and pouring substantial capacity-building assistance into the grantee organizations to ensure their long-term sustainability (see Box 1.4).[60]

Others are regular public charities that have raised funds through other means and similarly use them to provide a combination of capacity-building assistance and funding to targeted ventures. Included here are organizations such as New Profit, the Roberts Enterprise Development Fund (REDF), Social Venture Partners (SVP), and Venture Philanthropy Partners (VPP). New Profit, for example, is a 47-person firm founded in 1998 that has raised money from nearly 50 individual and family philanthropists to provide in-depth technical and financial help to 27 promising social ventures that have in turn served over 1.4 million people across the United States.[61]

A second group of sustainability capacity builders are classic consultancies that have made a specialty of promoting organizational sustainability but do not

---

BOX 1.4
EDNA MCCONNELL CLARK FOUNDATION

HOW WE WORK

We believe that an effective and efficient way to meet the urgent needs of youth is to make large, long-term investments in nonprofit organizations whose programs have been proven to produce positive outcomes and that have the potential for growth. Our funding consists largely of support for business planning, capacity building and program evaluation, so that grant-ees can expand while maintaining the quality of their programs, make an impact on the life trajectories of more young people, and eventually become organizationally, programmatically and financially sustainable. Our goal is to help develop a growing pool of organizations that serve thousands more youth each year with proven programs.

Source: "How We Work," Edna McConnell Clark Foundation, accessed May 11, 2013, http://www.emcf.org/how-we-work/.

---

themselves provide financial assistance. Some of these are hired by venture phi-lanthropies to deliver the required technical assistance, while others are hired directly by emerging social enterprises or traditional nonprofits wanting to boost their revenues from earned income. Included here are the Bridgespan Group, a dedicated social-purpose consulting firm that grew out of the for-profit Bain Consulting firm; Community Wealth Ventures, a subsidiary of the antihunger organization Share our Strength that focuses on helping organizations develop earned-income strategies; and the Nonprofit Finance Fund, which helps organi-zations manage their balance sheets.

While venture philanthropy and social venture capacity builders more gener-ally emerged initially in the United States, they have spread far wider. The European Venture Philanthropy Association, for example, has attracted 127 in-dividual and organizational members that share five key features: they have capital to invest; they focus on providing long-term funding to social-purpose organizations, whether nonprofit or for-profit; they are primarily seeking a social, rather than a financial, return; and they take an active role in promoting the "core development" of the organizations they are supporting.[62] (See Box 1.5 for the operating characteristics of "venture philanthropy" as practiced by the members of EVPA.)

Yet another model for capacity-building in the emerging social venture and social-impact investing space is afforded by The Hub. Launched in London in 2005, The Hub is a network of 4,000 aspiring social entrepreneurs in some 31 chapters around the world, who meet to share experience, contacts, and ideas, and who share work spaces in which to nurture early- stage venture ideas. Separate Hub chapters are free to formulate their own approaches to capacity-building. Thus, for example, Hub Johannesburg runs a Hub Business Clinic that offers twice-monthly skills sessions for social entrepreneurs, while the Hub Bay Area recently launched Hub Ventures, a structured program that helps a select group of entrepreneurs develop their concepts through

---

BOX 1.5

SEVEN KEY CHARACTERISTICS OF EUROPEAN VENTURE PHILANTHROPY

---

1) **High engagement**—Hands-on relationships between the social enterprise or nonprofit management and the venture philanthropists.
2) **Organizational capacity-building**—Building the operational capacity of the portfolio organizations, by funding core operating costs rather than individual projects.
3) **Multiyear support**—Supporting a limited number of organizations for 3–5 years, then exiting when organizations supported are financially or operationally sustainable.
4) **Nonfinancial support**—Providing value-added services such as strategic planning to strengthen management.
5) **Involvement of networks**—Providing access to networks enables various and often complementing skill-sets and resources being made available to the investees.
6) **Tailored financing**—Using a range of financing mechanisms tailored to the needs of organizations supported.
7) **Performance measurement**—Placing emphasis on good business planning, measurable outcomes, achievement of milestones and financial accountability and transparency.

Source: European Venture Philanthropy Association, http://www.evpa.eu.com.

---

mentorship, workshops, and other technical assistance and then awards $75,000 in seed capital for those with the most promising concepts.[63]

Infrastructure Organizations

In addition to the entities described above, which all offer essentially "retail" assistance and support to social-impact investors, social entrepreneurs, or main-line nonprofit organizations in new ways, a substantial network of infrastructure organizations has also emerged to support the work of these operating entities at a more macro, or wholesale, level. These entities serve a number of crucial functions for the fields in which they operate: they connect the actors in the field to each other; they popularize and publicize the field and thereby attract newcomers and external support; and they legitimize and strengthen the practice.

> A substantial network of social-impact *infrastructure organizations* has also emerged.

The social-impact investing space has provided the most fertile ground for the growth of such infrastructure organizations, with separate entities emerging to service virtually every constituency, and every nook and cranny, of this rapidly developing field. Thus, for example, one of the earliest entrants was the Opportunity Finance Network, created in 1985 to support US community development financial institutions (CDFIs) in their mission of aiding "low-income, low-wealth, and other disadvantaged people and communities join the economic mainstream."[64] Now US CDFIs also have the Community Development Venture Capital Alliance and the National Federation of Community Development Credit Unions. Similarly, "sustainability investors" have the Aspen Network of Development Entrepreneurs (ANDE); socially motivated banks participate in the Global Alliance for Banking Values. Similarly, advocates of "responsible investing" have joined together in the Social Investment Forum (SIF) to promote adherence to the UN Principles for Responsible Investment (UNPRI), which calls on firms to adhere to responsible environmental, social, and corporate governance (ESG) standards.[65] CGAP, the Consultative Group to Assist the Poor, is a consortium of 33 donors with the common goal to advance access to financial services for the poor.[66] US foundation officials making active use of program-related investments (PRIs) formed the PRI Makers Network to share experiences, develop best practices, and attract other foundations into the fold. As interest grew in other ways to extend the mission-related activities of foundations as well (e.g., through screening endowment investments or strategically voting shares) a new organization emerged called More for Mission, initially headquartered at Boston College. Now these two have come together under the banner of the Mission Investors Exchange.[67] European foundations engaging in social-impact investing and high-engagement grantmaking have similarly felt the need for an infrastructure organization, and 130 of them have joined together, as noted earlier, in the European Venture Philanthropy Association. Microfinance investors have also found it useful to build infrastructure organizations to serve their particular needs, giving rise to the Microfinance Investment Exchange and the International Association of Microfinance Investors (IAMFI).

Notwithstanding this profusion of infrastructure organizations, a group of foundations, development agencies, and private financial institutions convened by the Rockefeller Foundation in a series of key gatherings in 2007 and 2008 came to the conclusion that a broader field-building effort was still needed that could bring these various separate initiatives together under a common umbrella and move the field beyond what one pair of authors termed "uncoordinated innovation."[68] The upshot was the launch in 2009 of yet another infrastructure organization called GIIN, the Global Impact Investing Network, but this time with substantial funding from the Rockefeller Foundation, J.P. Morgan, and the US Agency for International Development. GIIN was charged with the task of accelerating the development of the social-impact investing industry by creating critical infrastructure, improving practice, establishing a common language, and stimulating field-building research. To do so, it has established an "Investors' Council" made up of leading impact investors from around the world; created so-called Impact Reporting and Investment Standards (IRIS), a broad set of indicators through which social-impact investors can measure the social performance of their investments; established an online database of impact investment funds called "Impact Base" to facilitate collaboration among funds working in similar fields and geographies; and carried out a variety of outreach efforts to elevate the visibility of the field and encourage its expansion, including research designed to establish social-impact investing as an "asset class" with its own skill requirements, organizational structures, metrics, trade groups and educational offerings.[69]

New Types of Grantmaking Entities

While the previous new actors on the frontiers of philanthropy all focus on some aspect of social-impact investing involving nongrant forms of finance, other entities are bringing imaginative new approaches to mobilizing more traditional forms of charitable activity through such mechanisms as online portals, funding collaboratives, and corporate-originated charitable funds.

Online Portals and Exchanges

One of the more innovative of these are the entities making creative use of the new communications technologies to connect donors and investors directly to recipient organizations and ventures with an immediacy that has not been possible before. As described by Vince Stehle in Chapter 8 of this volume, a new class of *online portals or exchanges* has emerged to perform this function across a diverse array of charitable resources. These are not just internet service providers that happen to be used to transfer cash, commodities, and volunteering opportunities, however. Rather, they are organizations specific-ally structured to serve as transfer points be-tween donors and beneficiaries, often with the benefit of elaborate databases and se-curity systems. What is more, they have evolved to handle at least three different types of valued resources: (*a*) financial resources, including short-term cash and long-term investment capital; (*b*) commodi-ties, such as computer hardware and soft-ware, pharmaceuticals, and food; and (*c*) services, both paid and volunteer.

> A new breed of on-line portals has surfaced making creative use of the new communications technologies to connect donors and investors directly to recipient organizations.

As with so much of the activity on the new frontiers of philanthropy, these online portals have mushroomed in number and scale. One recent source identifies over 170 such entities handling charitable giving alone.[70] Just one of these, Network for Good, has generated an estimated half billion dollars of contributions to some 60,000 organizations from its inception in 2001 through early 2011. Kiva, a different type of entity, allows small-scale social entrepreneurs in faraway places to access loans funded through donations from socially oriented investors in the United States, western Europe, and elsewhere. From its founding in 2005 through 2012, Kiva has facilitated over $360 million in loans from over 835,000 individuals to nearly 885,000 social entrepreneurs, 82 percent of whom are women, and achieved a repayment rate of nearly 99 percent.[71]

TechSoup Global, another online portal, provides nonprofit organizations access not to cash, but to technology hardware and software contributions for a modest fee. Through late 2010, the organization had distributed 6.6 billion units of technology products to 133,000 organizations around the world.[72] VolunteerMatch performs a similar function for volunteers, operating a huge matchmaking operation to help individuals and businesses with volunteer pro-grams to connect potential volunteers with organizations that need their services. VolunteerMatch estimates that in 2010 alone its volunteer assignments generated social value worth more than $600 million if organizations had had to pay for the assistance they received from the organization's volunteer placements.[73]

To be sure, these online portals have not yet achieved a scale that rivals main-line contribution mechanisms. What is more, there is valid reason to ques-tion whether they are making a net addition to the resources being mobilized for charitable purposes. Nevertheless, as this set of actors has gained traction and visibility, they have prompted a wave of innovative newcomers to this field that together are injecting new vibrancy and immediacy into traditional charitable giving and volunteering. Among these relative newcomers are Care2.com, mobilizing social change advocates; Idealist.com, providing job postings in the social-purpose arena; Americares.com, delivering medical supplies; and DonorsChoose, providing assistance to schoolteachers.

Corporate-Originated Charitable Funds

Side by side with the emergence of for-profit social-purpose investment funds has been the appearance of another new set of entities—huge charitable funds originated by some of the country's largest for-profit investment companies, such as Fidelity Investments, Charles Schwab and Sons, and Vanguard. These funds have been set up to manage charitable funds for the investment clients of these firms as well as others. Thirty-two such corporate-originated charitable funds are now in operation in the United States alone, with assets of $12 billion, mostly in the form of some 88,000 "donor-advised funds." These are pools of charitable resources that are similar to minifoundations, allowing donors to receive charitable tax deductions on the full value of their contributions when they set up the funds, but then permitting them to direct contributions from the funds over their lifetimes.

> Though barely two decades old, corporate-originated charitable funds have already outdistanced community foundations in the number of donor-advised funds that they manage.

As examined by Rick Cohen in Chapter 9 of this volume, the first of these funds was founded only in 1991, but in 21 years it has already overtaken the scale of donor-advised funds managed by the country's largest community foundation, which has been in existence for nearly 100 years. By streamlining their back-office and investment functions through service contracts with their originating firms, these entities have posed a significant challenge not only to community foundations but potentially to the continued growth of foundations more generally. Taken together, the 32 corporate-originated funds already manage donor-advised fund assets roughly equivalent to those managed by the country's entire network of over 600 community foundations, which previously held a virtual monopoly on the management of such funds.[74] In the process they have helped to stimulate broader introduction of information-management technology and more sophisticated investment management in the charitable enterprise more generally.[75] While still focused heavily on grantmaking, moreover, these entities have begun to experiment with some of the broader financial instruments now penetrating the social investing arena generally.

Conversion Foundations

Yet another type of charitable institution that has made its appearance on the new frontiers of philanthropy is what has come to be called a "conversion foundation." Unlike classical independent foundations, which are normally formed out of the fortunes amassed by individual entrepreneurs, conversion foundations are formed out of the process of privatizing some public or quasi-public asset. The

> Over 500 conversion foundations have now been identified around the world.

asset in question can be a government-owned enterprise, a government-owned building or other property, specialized streams of revenue under government control (e.g., proceeds from state-run lotteries or sales of mineral rights), debt swaps, and conversions of quasi-public organizations such as nonprofits into for-profits.[76]

The emergence of this type of foundation can be traced in important part to the recent neoliberal push to privatize public, or quasi-public, institutions. While the proceeds of such transactions usually find their way into government budgets, or, in some celebrated occasions, into the pockets of politicians, it turns out that in a number of cases the proceeds are placed into existing or newly created foundations and form all or a portion of the assets of such institutions.

One of the earliest examples of this phenomenon was the creation of the Volkswagen Foundation out of the privatization of the Nazi Party–inspired, state-owned Volkswagen Company in the aftermath of the Second World War. The resulting foundation, created in 1960, has become one of the leading foundations in Europe, with assets of $3.5 billion dedicated to the promotion of German science. In the process, the Volkswagen Foundation has served as a role model or template for several other privatization transactions in Germany.[77]

But the Volkswagen case is hardly an isolated example: this alternative use of privatization proceeds has occurred far more frequently than has previously been recognized, yielding significant charitable endowments, some of them quite huge. Indeed, the present author has identified over 500 such "conversion foundations" around the world, with examples of each of the types of initial assets identified above. Thus, for example La Scala, the famous Milan opera hall, is an example of the transfer of a government-owned opera company and free use of its theater to a foundation set up to manage the opera company and raise additional support for it. The King Baudouin Foundation in Belgium provides an example of a foundation supported in significant part by a stream of revenue coming from a state-owned lottery. Debt swaps that give debtor nations relief from foreign debt in return for their placement of a corresponding amount of local currency into a charitable endowment have occurred in many parts of Latin America and in the case of the German-Polish Friendship Foundation; and the transformation of nonprofit organizations into for-profit firms during which all or a portion of the nonprofit's assets are vested in a charitable foundation has occurred with many nonprofit hospitals and health insurance nonprofits in the United States and with nonprofit or cooperative banks in Italy, Austria, New Zealand, and the United Kingdom.[78]

Not only is this phenomenon important in and of itself, but also it points to a possible avenue for the creation of meaningful charitable endowments in many less developed countries, where the private wealth to create sizable foundations is largely lacking, but where governments are in possession of sizable state-owned enterprises or valuable mineral rights whose sale could be used in part to create foundation-type philanthropic endowments dedicated to the health and welfare of local citizens.

Funding Collaboratives

Another intriguing development on the frontiers of philanthropy has been the spread of funding collaboratives, which offer both individuals and institutions a vehicle for collective grantmaking or social-purpose investing. Though they differ significantly in the types of participants they engage (e.g., individuals vs. organizations), the types of resources they jointly assemble or in-fluence (e.g., grants, loans, equity invest-

> At least 500 giving circles have been documented in the United States.

ments), and the types of recipients they support (e.g., individuals, nonprofits, social entrepreneurs, other organizations), these entities share the idea of pooling knowledge and resources, operating collectively, and thereby reducing costs and maximizing impact. They also serve the important social function of bringing like-minded individuals and organizations together around a common purpose.

As documented by Angela Eikenberry and Jessica Bearman in Chapter 10 of this volume, one of the most common types of these funding collaboratives is the "giving circle," a group of people who pool some share of their charitable resources together and decide collectively what organizations to support through grantmaking, voluntary assistance, or both. At least 500 such giving circles have been documented in the United States, but this probably understates the number of such groups. Some of these are general purpose in orientation, while others are "identity" or "diversity" focused. In addition to their important charitable role they also perform a social role, bringing together philanthropically inclined individuals in a geographic area and building important social bonds among them.

Similar groupings have now arisen to serve the growing field of social-impact investing. One of these, called Toniic, has built an exclusive global community of 42 social-impact investors seeking to place $100 million into global social enterprises. The network shares information about promis-ing ventures among its members, conducts collaborative due diligence reviews, and encourages members to invest in a coordinated fashion in iden-tified, promising ventures.[79]

The collaborative giving and investing bug has not only bitten individuals. It has also smitten organizations, which have come to recognize the need for col-lective action to address large problems. One of the earliest manifestations of this was the formation of what is now known as Living Cities, which grew out of a collaboration of six foundations determined to halt the deterioration of American cities. Now over 20 years old, this funding collaborative has blos-somed into a network of 22 foundations and financial institutions that have col-lectively invested nearly $1 billion in urban redevelopment projects in 22 US cities.[80] Investors Circle, another example of a funding collaborative, is a 20-year-old network of angel investors, foundations, and family funds that has stimulated the investment of $152 million in some 250 social ventures and funds dedicated to improving the environment, education, health, and community.[81]

A Teeming Subcontinent: Summing Up

In short, an explosion has occurred on the frontiers of philanthropy, a "Big Bang" that has unleashed a host of new actors eager to put their talents and energies into the search for new solutions to age-old problems, and who are finding new resources to finance their efforts. Some of these new actors are mining the supply side of the developing social investment market. Others are providing a variety of support services either to the financiers or to the entities they are generating resources to support. And still others are applying new technologies or new approaches to traditional grant-based philanthropic efforts. Whatever the form, however, the result is a burst of energy and innovation that has not been seen in philanthropic space at least since the time of Andrew Carnegie and John D. Rockefeller, if not yet quite since Jesus, Muhammad, and Maimonides.

> A withering array of new instruments is now being deployed in the social-purpose arena.

What's Happening? Scouting Philanthropy's New Frontier II: New Tools

This explosion of new actors has not, of course, taken place in a vacuum. Rather, it has been accompanied, and in some sense prompted, by an enormous proliferation of tools through which to pursue social and environmental objectives. These two developments thus go hand in hand. A revolution is therefore underway not only in the institutional forms functioning in "philanthropic space," broadly conceived, but also in the tools they are deploying to advance philanthropic objectives, supplementing the traditional tool of charitable grants and gifts with a withering array of new financial and nonfinancial instruments.

Many of these "new" tools are not new to the world, of course, as noted earlier. Rather, many of them, such as loans, equity investments, bonds, and securitization, have long pedigrees in the world of business finance, and increasingly in government as well.[82] What is new is their deployment in the world of philanthropy and social investment.

What makes these tools increasingly attractive in this new arena is their capacity for *leverage*, for bringing added resources into the social-purpose arena, particularly the kind and scale of resources controlled by banks, investment houses, pension funds, insurance companies, and high-net-worth individuals. A foundation or individual making a grant or gift, for example, typically generates social value equivalent only to the size of the grant or gift. But if that same foundation or individual uses its resources to guarantee a loan made by a commercial bank or pension fund, it can leverage far more resources than it puts at risk.

While many of the new tools being introduced into social-purpose activity are not new to the world, their deployment in this new arena has necessitated a variety of adjustments and modifications, many of them highly innovative if not yet fully legitimized or understood. Loans have therefore had to be supplemented with a variety of "credit enhancements" to induce risk-averse private investors to keep interest rates low enough for social-purpose organizations to afford. Equity investments have had to be modified to get around legal prohibitions on nonprofit distribution of profits. And new types of bonds have had to be invented to get around cumbersome "rating" provisions and ensure a flow of long-term, patient capital into promising social ventures.

While a full elaboration of the evolving shape of these new tools is the task for the chapters that follow, a brief overview of some of the central features of the major tools may help prepare readers for the fuller explications available in the balance of this book. As before, we differentiate between the relatively new *financial investment tools* such as loans and equities and other tools that make new use of *nonfinancial interventions* such as crowd sourcing or socially responsible investing and purchasing.

Social-Impact Financial Investment Tools

Loans

A useful starting point for the discussion of financial investment instruments is the tool of loans and its next of kin, "credit enhancements." Loans are by far the most common social-impact investment tool. When the US Congress opened the door for foundations to make so-called program-related investments

> Loans are by far the most common social-impact investment tool.

in the Tax Reform Act of 1969 and to count them as part of their required "payout requirement," it mostly had loans in mind. And not surprisingly, loans have remained the dominant form of PRIs, accounting in 2006–2007, the latest period for which data are available, for nearly 80 percent of all PRI transactions and over 85 percent of all PRI dollars.[83] Cooch and Kramer found a similar picture when they broadened the lens from PRIs to "mission investing" by US foundations more generally: of 520 such investments identified, 63 percent were loans and another 19 percent some other type of debt.[84] This picture has been further confirmed by an even broader study of 2,213 social-impact investments made by a pool of 52 investors. As shown in Table 1.3, as of 2011 these social-impact investors had $4.4 billion in social-impact investments outstanding, of which 75 percent of the deals and 62 percent of the assets ($2.7 billion in all) took the form of various types of debt.[85]

Loans are one form of *debt*. The basic concept of a loan is fairly straightforward: a lender provides cash (the principal) to a borrower, who is obligated to repay the cash, typically with interest, either over time or at an agreed-upon time in the future (the maturity date). Compared to other forms of debt, such as bonds (discussed below), loans tend to be smaller in size and shorter in maturity. But all forms of debt differ from the other major type of investment capital,

TABLE 1.3   ASSET CLASS OF SOCIAL-IMPACT INVESTMENTS

Instrument type	Number	%	Amount (USD, m)	%
Private debt	1,345	61%	2,296	52%
Bilateral loan agreement	152	7%	191	4%
Deposit	106	5%	70	2%
Guarantee	10	0%	73	2%
Equity-like debt	48	2%	78	2%
Public debt	1	0%	2	0%
Subtotal, debt	**1,662**	**75%**	**2,710**	**62%**
Private equity	548	25%	1,655	38%
Public equity	2	0%	10	0%
Subtotal, equity	**550**	**25%**	**1,665**	**38%**
Real assets (reported)	**1**	**0%**	**2**	**0%**
TOTAL	2,213	100%	4,377	100

Source: Yasemin Saltuk, Amit Bouri, and Giselle Leung, "Insight into the Impact Investment Market: An In-Depth Analysis of Investor Perspectives and Over 2,200 Transactions," J.P. Morgan Social Investment, December 14, 2011, 6, accessed June 12, 2013, http://www.thegiin.org/cgi-bin/iowa/download?row=334&field=gated_download_1.

equity, which involves a share of ownership and does not create an obligation for repayment unless the recipient entity earns a profit. Loans thus entail less risk than equities, but correspondingly typically involve less return.

As loans have come to be used in the social-impact arena, however, they have grown in complexity, as noted in more detail in Chapter 12 of this volume. Loans can thus be "secured," that is, backed up by some asset that the lender can seize if the loan is not repaid, or "unsecured." Real estate loans have therefore traditionally been the least risky because they are backed by tangible property. Social ventures frequently have little tangible property, however, which means that they are rarely in a position to offer security for their loans. J.P. Morgan's 2011 study of 2,213 social-impact investments cited earlier thus found that 60 percent of the debt investments were unsecured. Loans can also be "senior," or "subordinated." A senior loan has the first call on any payment or assets in case a borrower is unable to pay its loan obligations, whereas a subordinated loan is paid off only after other lenders or investors. For-profit providers of loans to social ventures tend to require a senior position to reduce their risk. Finally, loans can be "soft" or "hard." Soft loans are ones that offer flexible or lenient terms for repayment, usually at lower than market interest rates. Such flexible terms are typically needed by start-ups and even second-stage social ventures due to the frequent lack of tangible assets with which such ventures can secure their loans and the uncertain prospects for their businesses.

Credit Enhancements

Because of the relative riskiness of many social ventures, a variety of inducements have had to be added to loans in order to attract lenders and get them to accept the below-market rates that early-stage social ventures typically require. This was the case with the African Agricultural Capital Fund (AACP) deal cited at the outset of this chapter. In order to induce J.P. Morgan's Social Finance Unit to make an $8 million loan to this fund, the US Agency for International Development had to guarantee the loan, thus protecting J.P. Morgan against any loss.[86] Such guarantees are one type of inducement known as "credit enhancements." Credit enhancements are designed to alter the risk-return ratio sufficiently to allow private investors to participate in a deal despite their legal obligation to maximize profit for their shareholders. In other cases, foundations or other social investors with a "social impact first" orientation will provide grants, subordinated loans, or equity capital as the base of a funding "stack" to absorb any initial losses on an investment. In this way they protect private investors who hold more senior positions in an investment consortium, thereby encouraging the private investors to participate and lowering their return requirements. Thus, in one deal detailed by Nicholls and Schwartz in Chapter 21, Fair Finance, a UK microfinance lender, generated a £2 million loan from Société Générale and BNP Paribas that was underwritten by a £750,000 foundation grant and a £350,000 soft loan from Big Society Capital, the UK Government's social investment fund.

> Credit enhancements are designed to alter the risk-return ratio sufficiently to allow private investors to participate.

Fixed-Income Securities

Another group of debt instruments increasingly being used in the social-impact investing arena is *fixed-income securities*. These are essentially huge loans with longer maturities typically sold through underwriters or investment banks that then market them to various types of investors, including pension funds, insurance companies, and high-net-worth individuals. Given their size and highly indirect marketing, fixed-income securities are usually put through an elaborate *rating process* before they are offered to the investing public. Fixed-income financing is an enormous component of global capital markets with an estimated $95 trillion of outstanding debt at the end of 2010 despite the recent financial meltdown. They therefore have the capability to generate huge sums of capital for major undertakings.[87]

As described by Elise Balboni and Shari Berenbach in Chapter 13, the most common type of fixed-income security is a long-term *bond*, but shorter term *notes* are also used. Borrowers who raise funds through fixed-income securities enter into contracts to pay bondholders the amount borrowed on an agreed maturity date and to pay interest, known as the *coupon*, at regular intervals over the life of the bond. Bondholders, in turn, can sell the bonds to other investors if they choose to do so, with the price varying depending on the relation between the *coupon rate* on the bond and prevailing interest rates in the market.

Given their scale and complexity, fixed-income securities are used most commonly by fairly mature institutions with reliable streams of revenue capable of covering coupon payments. Among social-purpose organizations, universities and hospitals have been the heaviest users of fixed-income securities, often with the aid, in the United States, of a credit enhancement in the form of tax deductions for investors on the coupon payments they receive.

But innovative ways have been found to tap this lucrative tool to finance other social-purpose activities as well. At one end of the continuum of innovations is the International Finance Facility for Immunisation (IFFIm), an ambitious global effort to underwrite the production, distribution, and delivery of vaccines against polio, measles, tetanus, and other deadly diseases to 500 million children in 70 of the world's poorest countries. The financing of this effort has been pursued through bonds, but bonds that will ultimately be paid for through guarantees provided by several European governments and marketed by Goldman Sachs and Deutsche Bank. As the IFFIm website explains, "by issuing bonds in the capital markets" IFFIm "converts long-term government pledges into immediately available cash resources." The inaugural issue of IFFIm bonds in 2006 raised $1.7 billion, 1.7 times the original $1 billion goal, and $3.6 billion have so far been raised in toto.[88]

> Especially imaginative has been the Community Investment (CI) Note mechanism launched in 1995 by the Calvert Foundation.

Equally imaginative has been the Community Investment (CI) Note mechanism launched in 1995 by the Calvert Social Investment Foundation (Calvert Foundation), a community development finance institution headquartered in the United States, with support from the Ford, MacArthur, and Mott foundations. CI Notes are essentially mini-bonds, unrated, and sold directly to individual investors by Calvert Foundation, indirectly by brokers, and now online through a subsidiary of eBay. Investors can choose the term (1, 3, 5, 7, or 10 years) and the interest rate they would like to receive (0, 1, 2, or 3 percent).

The Calvert Foundation then invests the proceeds either in community-based intermediaries promoting affordable housing or inner-city development in the United States, or microfinance and fair-trade farmworker cooperatives internationally. To date, this innovative fixed-income instrument has generated $220 million of capital from 10,000 citizen-investors with losses below 1 percent—all of it offset by Calvert Foundation–provided reserves—thus ensuring timely payment of principal and interest to all investors.[89] Perhaps equally important, the Calvert experience has led a number of other social-purpose CDFIs and related institutions to launch their own unsecured and unrated retail note programs to raise capital for social-purpose initiatives.

Other examples of credit enhancements attached to bonds include the $30 million bond protection provided by the Bill and Melinda Gates Foundation that allowed KIPP Houston, a for-profit network of charter schools, to raise up to $300 million in tax-exempt bond proceeds from private investors for the expansion of its charter-schools network at no cost to the Gates Foundation. More generally, the US Treasury created a new CDFI Bond Guarantee Program in 2011 to assist CDFIs to finance their affordable housing and community development activities in the wake of the 2008 financial crisis.

Securitization

Closely related to the tool of bonds is an additional debt-related instrument known as *securitization*. Securitization is the mechanism that "secondary market" actors use to bundle individual mortgages or other debt instruments together for sale to investors in order to generate capital that primary lenders can use to make new loans. Like many of the other "new" tools entering the arena of social-purpose finance, securitization has long been used in the standard financial arena. Indeed, it was problems in the main line securitization field that produced the US financial crisis in 2008, as securitized mortgages turned out to be worth far less than advertised to unwitting investors, including some of the country's premier banks and investment houses. But securitization has entered the world of social-purpose finance as well, although the global financial crisis has put a chill on investors' willingness to buy the securities backed by social-purpose loans even though these loans have performed much better than the ones issued by main line for-profit lenders.

As explained more fully by Mary Tingerthal in Chapter 14 of this volume, securitization involves the assembly of hundreds or thousands of individual loans into packages for sale to so-called special purpose entities, which then issue bonds or other securities backed by the loans for sale to ultimate investors.[90] The loans securing the bonds can be home mortgages (mortgage-backed securities) or loans for various other purposes, such as car loans, credit card balances, or, in the social-purpose arena, loans to microenterprises or charter schools (asset-backed securities). The transactions involved in setting prices for the securities backed by these bundles of loans are naturally highly complex since estimates must be made of the riskiness and likely returns on the underlying loans given their maturities, interest rates, likelihood of being paid off, and the relation of all of this to general market conditions.

Given the uncertainties traditionally surrounding social-purpose investment, securitization made relatively slow progress in this field until relatively recently. Instead, secondary market actors in this investment arena had to rely on private placements and the creation of specially organized funding consortia rather than the established machinery available to market "rated" securities. In addition, they have had to secure various credit enhancements such as bond guarantees, and reserves against losses, from angel investors or philanthropic institutions.

In the early 2000s, however, secondary market operators in the housing and microfinance arenas finally succeeded in penetrating this highly lucrative vehicle for channeling significant resources into social-purpose activity. Thus, as noted in Chapter 3 of this volume, in 2004 the Community Reinvestment Fund (CRF), a US-based secondary market focusing on low-income housing and community development mortgages, managed to assemble and market the first "rated" bond backed by low-income housing and community development loans, allowing it to attract funds in the process from eight new institutional investors whose strict investing guidelines would have kept it out of the deal without the rating. CRF subsequently brought three other rated securitizations to market before the 2008 financial crisis cooled investor responses.

The global microfinance industry has also managed to find its way to the securitization tool. Blue Orchard, a Swiss microfinance investment fund brought the first microfinance security to market in 2004 and managed to raise $67 million, which was used to refresh the capital of microfinance investment intermediaries (MIIs) across the globe. Subsequently, at least nine other securitization deals for microfinance loans have been successfully closed, the most recent being the huge $180 million securitization successfully marketed by the Bangladesh Rural Advancement Committee (BRAC) in 2006. As of 2008, a total of $525 million had been raised through the securitization of microfinance loans globally, a sizable sum, though still only 12 percent of all outstanding MII investments.

Equity

Even more attractive to social-purpose organizations than securitization is the tool of equity investments. The loans that underlie securitizations must ultimately be paid back with interest, after all. Equity investments carry no such obligation. Equity investment usually takes the form of shares issued to an investor in exchange for capital. Unlike with debt, the organization has no legal obligation to repay the amount invested or to pay interest. Equity investors usually invest in organizations that they believe will grow. In return they expect to receive dividends paid out of the organization's earnings and/or capital gain on the sale of the organization or on selling their shares to other investors. But if the enterprise does not pay dividends or does not do well, the equity investor can lose its money. Equity investments thus carry the highest risk and therefore typically command the highest returns.

> Even more attractive to social-purpose organizations than securitization is the tool of equity investments.

Equity finance has historically been less commonly used than debt finance by social-purpose organizations. This is so in part, as noted earlier, because many social-purpose organizations are nonprofit in form and are legally prohibited from issuing ownership shares or distributing any profits they may earn. What is more, even for-profit social enterprises take considerable time to generate profits, making them unattractive to social-purpose investors. Even patient capital providers like foundations have been somewhat reluctant to make equity investments. Thus, the 2007 study of 52 US foundation mission investors by Cooch and Kramer found that only 14 percent of the 520 investments made by these institutions were equity investments. Although equities accounted for 45 percent of the investment dollars, moreover, the overwhelming majority of these were real estate deals where a tangible asset was involved.[91] More generally, a J.P. Morgan study of 52 social-impact investment funds, each with at least $25 million in assets under management, found in 2011 that equity investments accounted for only 25 percent of the 2,213 investments identified, though they accounted for 38 percent of the assets.[92]

Nevertheless, as Brand and Kohler show in Chapter 15 of this volume, the recent growth of social enterprises, many of which take the form of for-profits, cooperatives, or other hybrid forms, has opened the social-purpose field to a much more substantial use of equities and to the growth of a wide assortment of equity funds to provide them. Perhaps reflecting this, a more recent J.P. Morgan survey suggests some expansion in social-impact investor use of equity. According to this survey, over 80 percent of a sample of social-impact investors reported making some use of equity investments in 2012 compared to only 66 percent that reported using private debt instruments, though this recent study did not report the share of deals or finances that involved the equity tool.[93]

Much of this social-purpose equity investment takes the form of so-called private equity, that is, investments in firms that are not listed on regulated stock exchanges open to the public. Rather, the investments are handled privately, typically through equity *funds*, which have grown substantially in both numbers and assets in recent years. One estimate of the private equity fund market in the United States identifies 375 so-called socially responsible "alternative investment funds," that is, funds that invest in unlisted companies that incorporate environmental, social, and governance (ESG) criteria into their investment decisions. Taken together, these funds have close to $81 billion of assets under management, an increase of nearly 16 percent over the previous year. Of this total, roughly $34 billion are in private equity and venture capital funds and $44 billion in real estate funds, some portion of which also takes the form of equity investments.[94]

The Community Development Venture Capital Alliance (CDVCA), the trade association supporting one branch of this industry that focuses on supporting business development in lagging regions, describes its members' purpose as being to "provide equity capital to businesses in underinvested markets, seeking market-rate financial returns as well as the creation of good jobs, wealth, and entrepreneurial capacity."[95] Kentucky Highlands, one of the earliest of these funds, was originally formed in 1968 to stimulate growth and create employment opportunities in an economically depressed nine-county region of southeastern Kentucky but has since expanded its geographic focus and leveraged its original funding from the federal government by attracting bank capital stimulated by the Community Reinvestment Act. In 35 years, Kentucky Highlands's equity investments have helped 220 businesses generate $178 million in support, creating more than 9,900 jobs, and generating risk-adjusted market rates of returns to its investors.[96]

Equity finance through equity funds is hardly restricted to the United States and other developed markets, however. A considerable number of such funds has found it possible to undertake equity funding with meaningful returns in emerging markets as well. Thus, for-profit firms such as UK-based Bridges Ventures, Dubai-based Willow Impact Investors, and Singapore-based Aavishkaar International have established operations adhering fairly closely to a classical private equity model, raising money from investors expecting a market

---

BOX 1.6

AAVISHKAAR INTERNATIONAL

We at Aavishkaar have taken it upon ourselves to be the leaders of micro equity investments to create scalable small entrepreneurs with significant social impact.

[The] Aavishkaar I [Fund] was created to promote inclusive development in rural and semi-urban regions in India. The fund's mission was based on the premise that promising Micro, Small to Medium-sized enterprises (MSMEs) will help drive positive changes in the underserved regions of the country.... Aavishkaar I's capital [US$14 million] is fully deployed in 22 companies...operating across Agriculture, Dairy, Healthcare, Water and Sanitation, Technology for Development, Education and Renewable Energy sectors.

Source: Aavishkaar International, http://www.aavishkaar.in.

---

rate of return and finding promising ventures serving the "bottom of the pyramid" in which to invest (see Box 1.6).[97]

In addition to the private equity reaching ventures through equity funds, individual investors also make considerable amounts of equity investment in social-purpose ventures directly, often with the aid of angel investor or social entrepreneurial networks such as the Social Venture Network, Investors' Circle, the Slow Money Alliance, or Toniic. Investors' Circle, for example, is a network of 150 investors, donors, and family offices that has helped to place $150 million of investment in over 200 separate companies and networks addressing social and environmental objectives.[98]

As reflected in Chapter 15 by Monica Brand and John Kohler, private equity can itself take a variety of forms. "Standard equity" is typically used for more mature firms needing equity to scale up proven operations. Another type of equity, known as "quasi equity," discussed below, is more often used for early-stage firms needing greater leeway or for nonprofit social enterprises that are barred from sharing ownership with investors or distributing profits to owners and therefore are not able to access standard equity. Even standard equity takes a variety of forms, moreover, such as "common stock," "preferred stock," and "convertible preferred equity." These forms of so-called standard equity offer investors successively expanded ownership rights and privileged access to any gains that the firm may generate. The greater the uncertainties surrounding the enterprise, the more such rights and privileges will be demanded by equity investors.

Because equity provides no guarantee of return, equity investors, particularly private equity investors, that is, those investing in companies not listed on any public exchange, typically take great care in assessing enterprise capabilities and pinning down their rights to review enterprise decisions, often taking positions on enterprise boards. Complex "term sheets" are utilized to detail such things as the amounts and uses of the equity funds being provided, the valuation of the firm and its business model, the exact type of equity instrument being used, any decision rights granted to the investor, and incentives or controls placed on the owners or managers.

Beyond the capital promoting social-purpose activities through *private* equity funding, which typically focuses on early-stage or mezzanine finance, a third type of social-purpose equity investment has also grown enormously in recent years as a byproduct of the emergence of investment-screening mechanisms such as the UN Principles for Responsible Investment (PRI). These mechanisms apply socially and environmentally conscious investment criteria to *public* equity being sought by more mature firms through regulated stock exchanges. As detailed more fully in Chapter 18, some 230 pension funds and other investment institutions controlling over $25 trillion in assets have endorsed the UN PRI criteria. As of 2011, $3.3 trillion in investment assets were being managed under some form of responsible investment criteria in the United States, and the comparable figure in Europe as of 2011 was €6.8 trillion (close to US$9 trillion at 2012 exchange rates), with approximately one-third of these assets in Europe in equities.[99]

Quasi Equity

Powerful as equity finance is as a source of capital, it is not universally available for social-purpose activities. For one thing, many social enterprises are quite young. A survey of social enterprises conducted in the UK in 2011, for example, revealed that 54 percent of social enterprises were less than 10 years old, and 31 percent less than five years old. By comparison, the comparable percentages for all small businesses in the UK were 33 percent and 15 percent.[100] Given the amount of time it takes for an enterprise to become reliably profitable, this can deter equity investors. In addition, many social enterprises are nonprofit in legal form and are barred from issuing ownership shares to potential investors or distributing profits to them in the form of dividends. Finally, even where they are investing in for-profit firms, equity investors can worry about whether they will be able to find a market for their shares if they want to exit from an equity investment in a social venture.

> Quasi equity essentially gives investors returns that look like equity returns but without giving them ownership shares in the organization.

At the same time, all of these social-purpose ventures are in need of risk capital both to get started and to expand, and loans may not be appropriate if returns are not secure enough to meet loan repayments. Fortunately, a number of innovations have surfaced to cope with this challenge. One of these is the creation of "matched bargain markets" or full-fledged *social stock exchanges* as detailed above and more fully in Chapter 4 of this book. Such exchanges provide a reasonably reliable market through which investors can exit from social-purpose equity investments without costly transaction costs.[101] Another innovation is the use of structured finance instruments that pool different types of finance in a single deal, with equity investors buffered by other sources that provide grant funding or loans to absorb the initial risk of loss. Aavishkaar International, for example, reports that its investment instruments are generally "a mix of common equity and convertible debentures. When appropriate, we also use quasi-equity, preferred convertibles, preferred redeemable, mezzanine loans, royalties and other venture capital instruments. Flexibility in structuring of investments to help scale businesses while minimizing promoter's dilution is one of our major differentiators."[102]

BOX 1.7
QUASI EQUITY

"Sometimes debt financing is inappropriate for social sector organisations, especially in the high-risk start-up phase. Equally, equity investment may not be possible if the organisation is not structured to issue shares.

A quasi-equity investment allows an investor to benefit from the future revenues of an organisation through a royalty payment which is a fixed percentage of income. However the investor may gain nothing if the organisation does not perform. This is similar to a conventional equity investment, but does not require an organisation to issue shares. The share of future revenues that a quasi-equity investor receives is usually linked to income and not profit, as social sector organisations are often not structured to make profits for distribution.

Source: "What Is Social Investment," Big Society Capital, accessed June 12, 2013, http://www.bigsocietycapital.com/what-social-investment.

One of the more interesting developments in the field of social-purpose equity investing, however, is the expanded use of various forms of so-called quasi equity. As described more fully by Nicholls and Schwartz in Chapter 21, and by Brand and Kohler in Chapter 15, quasi equity essentially gives investors returns that look like equity returns but without giving them ownership shares in the organization (see Box 1.7). This is done by creating some form of debt contract or royalty arrangement that guarantees investors a share of revenue growth either for the organization as a whole or for a particular program. For example, HCT Group, a network of UK charities that provides transportation services for disadvantaged communities but also competes for commercial transportation contracts, used a quasi-equity instrument to generate £4 million (US$6.4 million at 2012 exchange rates) to purchase vehicles and facilities, but did so without diluting the nonprofit ownership structure of the organization.[103]

Social-Impact Bonds

Another innovative tool that has recently made its appearance in the social-purpose finance arena goes by the name of "social-impact bonds." As examined more fully in Chapter 16, social-impact bonds provide a way to finance preventive services that can ultimately save governments or other entities substantial sums over the long run but that typically have trouble attracting from governmental sources

> Social-impact bonds provide a way to finance preventive services by monetizing the future savings to government such services can generate.

the upfront capital needed to sustain themselves until such savings materialize. They do so by monetizing the future savings by attracting private investors willing to take the risk of financing the services in the short run in return for a guaranteed share of the savings in the event that the long-term savings materialize.

Here's how they work: a government agency recruits an intermediary that believes it knows how to structure a preventative human-service initiative that can save the government money once put in place, and who is willing to recruit private-sector funders who will cover the multiyear upfront costs. In return, the government pledges that if the intervention meets or exceeds its goals, the government will return the investors' original investment plus some return based on a sliding scale dependent on the degree of success the intervention achieves.

As this suggests, social-impact bonds (SIBs) are really not bonds in the true sense of the word, but rather, like quasi equity, a strange amalgam of equity and debt. Like equity, social-impact bonds only generate returns for their investors if the activities they support meet certain performance thresholds. If not, investors are at risk of losing their principal or ending up with no net return on their investment. Like bonds, however, SIBs have fixed terms and the upside return is capped.

The initial trial of this new tool is underway at Peterborough Prison in the UK. A British social investment fund called Social Finance raised £5 million (≈US$ 8 million) from 17 investors to fund a comprehensive rehabilitation program for first-time offenders leaving the Peterborough facility over a six-year period, with a promise from the UK government that it will pay back this investment with interest on a sliding scale if the intervention achieves a target reduction in the recidivism rate of the affected offenders compared to a control group.[104]

Already this idea has spread to the United States, where it goes by the name "pay-for-success." The first US adoption was announced in early August 2012 in New York City with a similar first-offender focus, but with capital advanced not mostly by charitable foundations, as in the UK example, but by the for-profit investment firm Goldman Sachs, which is investing $9.6 million in loan funds into the effort.[105]

Other New Tools

In addition to the social-impact investment tools newly available on the frontiers of philanthropy are a variety of other new instruments or approaches being deployed in the social and environmental action arenas. Three of these in particular also deserve attention here: microinsurance, socially responsible investing and purchasing, and new types of grants.

Microinsurance

Less exotic, but no less powerful, a new tool of philanthropy is microinsurance. Like many of the other new tools examined previously, there is nothing especially new about the tool of insurance. What is new is the creation of adaptations of the standard tool of insurance to make it accessible to the millions of people living almost totally exposed to multiple forms of risk at the bottom of the economic pyramid. As examined by Craig Churchill and Lauren Peterson in Chapter 17, recent estimates put the share of low-income people with insurance in the world's 100 poorest countries at less than 3 percent.[106] This means that over 97 percent of the populations in

> Recent estimates put the share of low-income people with insurance in the world's 100 poorest countries at less than 3 percent.

these countries remains exposed to any of a series of typical threats to their security—illness, drought, storms, floods, or death of a family member—that can drive them further into poverty or frustrate efforts to escape from it.

While many savings or insurance schemes, such as funeral insurance, have surfaced indigenously to help mitigate this exposure, these typically lack the crucial feature required for cost-effective and reliable insurance—namely, risk-pooling over a large enough group of people to reduce premiums to a low enough level to be affordable while providing enough protection to be worth the cost.

Fortunately, however, thanks to cooperation among national governments, international organizations such as the International Labour Organization, and private insurance companies, new "microinsurance" products have surfaced and begun to tap the bottom-of-the-pyramid market.[107] One estimate in 2010 put the number of people covered by microinsurance schemes globally at 135 million. But this just scratches the surface of the global need and is heavily concentrated in only a few countries. Indeed, a 2010 Swiss Re study estimates the number of people living on $1.25 to $4.00 a day who could afford small premiums but are not covered by conventional insurance to be in the neighborhood of 2.6 billion, with an additional 1.4 billion people living on less than $1.25 a day potentially reachable with the help of subsidies.[108]

As with so many other of the new tools being deployed on the frontiers of philanthropy, the limited penetration of insurance products into the bottom-of-the-pyramid market is a consequence of the delayed recognition on the part of for-profit insurance providers of the possibilities for profitable operations that this market offered. Also at work, however, have been the inherent complexities of the insurance product—the product must be marketed to huge numbers of people in order to be viable, mechanisms must be put in place to verify the occurrence of an insured loss and calculate its value, some way must be found to estimate the likelihood of such losses in advance so that premiums can be calculated, and the premiums must be kept low enough to be affordable by low-income clients.

Overcoming these barriers has required considerable innovation and teamwork on the part of governments, insurers, foundations, international organizations, and other actors with connections to those on the bottom of the pyramid. The innovations underway are already striking: a program in India that has mobilized private insurance companies to extend health insurance to some 63 million individuals living below the poverty line in 25 Indian states;[109] claim verification systems for crop insurance that index payments to weather conditions and for livestock that use radio-frequency identification devices; mobilization of microinsurance finance institutions, such as Prodem in Bolivia, or utility companies, such as CODENSA in Colombia, with significant links to the low-income populations of their countries, to market a variety of insurance products to their underserved customers. These innovations have been encouraged, and in turn disseminated, through a growing network of infrastructure organizations such as the Microinsurance Network, the ILO facility mentioned earlier, the Joint Learning Network for Universal Coverage, and the Munich Climate Insurance Initiative.[110]

Socially Responsible Investing and Purchasing

A rather different mechanism for achieving social and environmental purposes without the need of complex financial instruments takes the form of *socially responsible investing and purchasing*. Advocates of social-impact investing have

> Assets in Europe managed according to a socially responsible investment standard as of 2012 stood at 6.8 trillion euros, or close to US$9 trillion.

been somewhat dismissive of this route to social and environmental change, seeing it chiefly as a way to "minimize negative impact rather than proactively create positive social or environmental benefit."[111] But, in practice, this mechanism has gained considerable traction on the positive side of the ledger as well.

The key to socially responsible investing and purchasing is the mobilization of investors and consumers to pressure companies to operate in socially and environmentally responsible ways. As detailed more fully in Chapter 18 of this volume, this can be done through a variety of channels—promoting positive or negative investment *screens*, establishing investment *standards*, voting *shares* of stock in ways that encourage responsible corporate behavior, introducing *resolutions* for vote by shareholders, engaging corporate leaders in *dialogue, boycotting* undesirable products, or encouraging purchase of other products that meet various criteria, such as those relating to labor rights, health concerns, treatment of animals, sustainable forestry, or support for indigenous people.

Though hardly entirely new, socially responsible investment and purchasing expanded considerably in the 1990s and into the 2000s, as new technologies and increased corporate sensitivity to risks to their "reputational capital" gave added leverage to investors and consumers with social concerns on their minds. One important boost was the development in 2006 of the UN Principles of Responsible Investment, which established standards for responsible environmental, social, and governance behavior on the part of corporations. By 2012, as noted earlier, some 230 pension funds and other investment funds had endorsed these principles and pledged to follow them in their own investment activities.

Socially responsible investment has attracted particular interest in European investment circles. The European Sustainable Investment Forum (Eurosif), a network of 79 pension and investment funds and eight national affiliated SIFs, puts the scale of assets in Europe managed according to one or another type of socially responsible investment standard as of 2012 at 6.8 trillion euros, or close to US$9 trillion.[112] What is more, the growth of socially responsible investing appears to have outpaced the growth of overall investment on the continent in recent years, with four out of six responsible investment strategies growing by more than 35 percent per annum since 2009.[113] In the United States, the comparable figure is a sizable $3.3 trillion of assets managed under responsible investing guidelines.

Whether because of such socially responsible investment pressures or other factors, socially responsible investment reporting has become a staple of larger corporations globally. Institutions such as Instituto Ethos in Brazil have actively diffused this practice in their countries and regions, with over 600 firms in Brazil alone producing social responsibility reports showing their alignment with Ethos's demanding standards. As one observer put it: Ethos "officialized" CSR in Brazil, making it "the thing to do for corporations that wanted to be considered progressive and responsive to the country's enormous social problems."[114]

Side by side with the expansion of ethical investing has been an expansion of ethical purchasing. As Lydenberg and Grace report, the global market for organic food and beverages already totaled $23 billion as of 2007, and organic personal care sales in the United States alone totaled another $9 billion. As pressures mount on businesses to report on their social responsibility practices, they have joined consumers as socially responsible purchasers, utilizing their supply chain management to serve their social responsibility aspirations. Japanese, European, and some Latin American companies have been especially active in this fashion, as have their governments.

To be sure, while the growth of socially responsible investing and purchasing has been impressive, such practices still represent a tiny fraction of the activity in their respective domains. What is more, the evidence of actual financial impact of either tactic on the financial health or stock prices of companies remains scant.[115] Nevertheless, there is evidence that at least some companies are behaving as if it does make a difference, which may be all that counts.

Grants

While much of the buzz on the new frontiers of philanthropy has focused on nongrant forms of assistance on grounds that traditional grantmaking is not capable of achieving significant leverage, in fact some important innovations have recently appeared in the grant world as well. What is more, these innovations come on top of a variety of prior ways in which grantmaking has attempted to achieve greater leverage through such devices as start-up grants, matching grants, and pilot projects intended to demonstrate workable innovations that governments can subsequently take up.

> Some important innovations have recently appeared in the grant world as well.

One such recent innovation is the practice of "venture philanthropy" covered previously in this chapter, which combines big-bet grantmaking with intensive organizational capacity-building and close-in supervision. But another whole area of innovation involves various forms of competition pursued through prizes and crowd sourcing. As outlined in Chapter 19, this form of grantmaking constitutes "a breath of fresh air in the world of grants." Unlike traditional grants, which are essentially designed and managed by foundation program officers, competitions, prizes, and crowd sourcing begin from the premise that there is a market of ideas and that the best use of foundation resources is to tap into it as broadly as possible.

Some prizes are used after-the-fact to reward notable accomplishments in a field. Examples here include the Pulitzer Prizes for literature or the Nobel Prize. Increasingly, however, a different type of prize is emerging that takes the form of an open competition to provide a solution to a concrete problem. Examples here include the X Prize, which offers $10 million to the first team to achieve a specific goal, such as designing a private vehicle that could fly a pilot to the edge of outer space; or the Case Foundation's Make it Your Own Award, which allows citizens to vote on which of a number of community improvement organizations Case should reward with a $25,000 grant; or Toyota's Ideas for Good prize, which it gives to the person or organization that applies one of five categories of automotive technology developed by Toyota successfully in another field to solve a community or public problem.

According to a recent McKinsey and Company report, such prizes have mushroomed in recent decades. Almost $250 million in new prize money became available during the first decade of the twenty-first century, and the total funds available through large prizes more than tripled over that decade, surpassing $375 million. Indeed, McKinsey and Company estimates that the total prize sector could now be worth as much as $1 to $2 billion.[116]

Conclusion

In short, an enormous explosion is taking place in both the actors and the tools occupying the new frontiers of philanthropy. But how can we explain this phenomenon and what insights can such explanations offer into the durability of this phenomenon? It is to these more analytical questions that we must now turn.

Why Now?

From the evidence at hand, it appears that a number of underlying forces have been at work to produce the new frontiers of philanthropy at the present time. What is more, both demand and supply factors seem to have been at work.

The Demand Side of the New Social Capital Market

That a new frontier has formed in the world of philanthropy and social investment in recent years seems to be due, in the first instance, to a set of demand factors that have gained salience during this period. These factors take at least three different forms.

The New Inferno

> A gathering "perfect storm" of trends threatens our civilization.

In the first place, long-standing problems of poverty and inequality that continue to entrap large swaths of the world's population have recently been joined by serious environmental threats to form a modern version of Dante's inferno, with its multiple circles of human suffering. Today's counterpart to Virgil, who was Dante's guide through the nine circles of hell, is the environmentalist Lester Brown, whose *World on the Edge* paints as vivid a picture as did Dante's *Divine Comedy* of what awaits us if bad habits and current tendencies continue unabated.[117]

As Brown puts it: "A gathering 'perfect storm' of trends threatens to send civilization into economic and political chaos."[118] To Dante's imagined nine circles of hell Brown adds six terrifying trends.

First up in the catalog of sins in Brown's account is the depletion of the earth's water supply as a consequence of overdrilling by farmers and deforestation of large portions of the earth's land area. As a consequence, water tables are falling and wells going dry in some 20 countries, including the three that produce half of the world's grain—China, India, and the United States.

Water shortage, in turn, combines with overfarming, overgrazing, and expanding urbanization to yield the second devastating trend: loss of the earth's topsoil and ultimately of its inherent productivity, leading ultimately to desertification, when the earth becomes unable to support life. Desertification now affects 25 percent of the earth's land area and threatens the livelihood of more than 1 billion people, with two huge dust bowls forming in the Asian heartland and in central Africa, and with evidence of severe drought even in the American West.

These problems are in turn intensified by the third devastating trend: over-consumption of fossil fuels and the resulting warming of the earth, posing enormous threats to the food supply, generating more severe and more numerous weather emergencies, and displacing millions of people.

Those displaced by the rising seas, more destructive storms, and expanding deserts will then become part of a fourth devastating trend: a massive growth in the numbers of "environmental refugees," people forced from their homes by the devastating storms provoked by rising temperatures, by the advancing desert, by falling water tables, and by unregulated toxic wastes. This phenomenon is, in turn, being accentuated by a fifth distressing trend: rapid population growth, especially in the least prosperous regions of the world. This has produced what Brown terms a "demographic trap," as larger families produce poverty and poverty leads to larger families. At least 40 percent of the population in the world's 20 poorest countries are thus under 15. Large numbers of youngsters, especially young men, without decent employment opportunities, in turn become a prescription for disaffection, crime, and ultimately even insurgencies.

All of this is contributing to the sixth harmful trend: a striking rise in the number of failed states. And as states fail, further deterioration of the economic infrastructure of roads, power, water, and sanitation systems ensues, inviting further fragmentation of authority and the rise of rival armed gangs and cliques. Somalia, Chad, Sudan, the Congo, Afghanistan, and Iraq have moved fairly far down this road, and even highly populated countries like Pakistan and Nigeria have significant portions of their territories in "failed-state" status.

Taken together, this complex of miseries has massively expanded the need for serious attention to poverty alleviation and long-term solutions to food, water, health, and environmental crises.

Tapped-out Governmental and Charitable Resources

These interrelated environmental, economic, social, and political needs would be difficult to meet under any circumstances. But they are being confronted now by a world that has been experiencing enormous economic shocks, unsustainable governmental spending, and charitable resources that, while growing, do not come close to being able to deliver the resources needed to address the problems that exist. With the US debt now 107 percent of the country's gross domestic profit, and debt levels in France and Germany above the European Union's legislated upper limit of 60 percent of GDP, even the world's richest countries are in no position to take robust action to mitigate these global problems.[119] Indeed, most of them are in cutback mode with respect to some of the most crucial social and environmental protections for their own people, and this in the face of still escalating unemployment in many places.[120] And global charity, even generously estimated, is a very small fraction of what governments are able to spend. Even in the United States, philanthropy from all sources—individuals, foundations, and corporations—accounts for no more than 10 percent of the income of the country's nonprofit organizations, and a dramatically smaller share of overall government social welfare spending.[121]

The Rise of Social Entrepreneurs

A third set of demand factors that has contributed enormously to the developments outlined here has been the appearance of a new social force in the form of a growing army of so-called social entrepreneurs, "restless people," as journalist David Bornstein has styled them, who become almost possessed by imaginative new ideas to address major problems and who are "so relentless in the pursuit of their visions that they will not give up until they have spread their ideas *everywhere*."[122]

Why this development occurred when it did is hard to pin down with certainty, but probable culprits likely include the worldwide spread of education, creating sizable cadres of educated professionals in very unlikely places; the "global associational revolution" that led to a widespread surge of social-change-oriented nonprofit organizations, or "NGOs," able to engage some of these educated professionals;[123] the dot-com explosion with its inspiring message of technological innovation leading to dramatic changes in life-chances; and the networking possibilities created by the new communication technologies and by capacity-building organizations such as Ashoka, which has spent the past several decades identifying and fostering this new breed of actor on the *demand* side of the philanthropic marketplace. Whatever the cause, the result has been to create a mechanism to perform the critical function of translating almost incomprehensible human need into concrete, actionable solutions capable of yielding demonstrable results and attracting the attention of a new breed of socially conscious investors.[124]

Microcredit was the leading edge of this development, and its rapid growth into a $65 billion industry with its own network of microfinance investment funds in the 35 years leading up to 2010 has been a source of inspiration to many of these social entrepreneurs. Indeed, a veritable "fourth sector" has emerged around the world consisting of socially conscious individuals who have discovered novel ways to produce social value out of existing resources in ways that produce real change in the lives of disadvantaged people.[125] They are thus providing less expensive fresh water, eyeglasses, sanitary pads, housing, healthcare, solar panels, primary education, cell phones, and dozens of other products and services needed by disadvantaged consumers or made by them for sale in other markets.

These social entrepreneurs need capital in order to grow their businesses, and this need is enormous. According to one estimate, of the 365 to 445 million micro, small, or medium-sized firms in developing countries, 70 percent need outside funding but lack access to it.[126] These firms, which generate a third of the GDP and 45 percent of the employment in developing countries, have unmet demands for capital estimated to total $2.1 to $2.5 trillion. This estimate is similar to the estimate cited earlier of $400 billion to $1 trillion in potential demand for capital in businesses serving bottom-of-the-pyramid populations in just five fields (housing, water, maternal health, primary education, and microfinance).[127]

In short, the reality of an enormous number of people living on the edge of economic, environmental, physical, and social disaster, increasingly attracting the attention of innovative social entrepreneurs who are finding new ways to combine existing resources to produce low-cost products and services, but who are confronting constrained resource availability from both government and traditional private philanthropy, translates into a huge demand for the new tools and new actors that we have identified emerging on the new frontiers of philanthropy and social investment.

Supply-Side Factors

But the existence of a large and growing demand for investment capital and other forms of philanthropic innovation is not yet a guarantee that this demand will be met. To the contrary, the current mismatch between needs and resources, even though especially intense in recent years, is hardly a new development. By itself, therefore, it can hardly account for the striking recent emergence of the new actors and tools that we have documented. At best it is a necessary condition for these developments. But it is certainly not a sufficient one. For this latter, supply-side factors are needed as well. What is particularly unique about the present situation is that such factors have not only surfaced, but have mushroomed in the past decade or more. Why is this so?

First Responders and Incentivizers

One important factor, clearly, were the adventurous first responders to the capital needs of early social entrepreneurs, first in the developed Global North, and subsequently in the Global South. These early efforts established a surface plausibility for the idea that it might be possible to find imaginative and workable ideas for solving massive problems of inadequate housing, lagging services, and lack of employment opportunities within the communities experiencing these problems, and to do so in a way that, at a minimum, protected the principal of those providing the upfront capital and, in many cases, offered the prospect of a reasonable rate of financial return. This opened the possibility of attracting not just philanthropic capital, but also actual private investment capital, into such efforts.

Some of the earliest experience in attracting such capital into this type of venture occurred in the housing field in the United States. A crucial ingredient here was the series of incentives provided by government policymakers. This included the provisions in the 1969 tax act's payout requirements for charitable foundations authorizing foundations to make program-related investments (PRIs) in for-profit ventures, and to count these toward their required grantmaking obligations if they promoted valid foundation objectives. This was followed by a succession of other measures: by the Community Reinvestment Act (CRA) of 1977, which incentivized commercial banks to channel more of their lending into the disadvantaged communities from which they drew significant deposits; by the Low-Income Housing Tax Credit (LIHTC) of 1986, which provided tax credits for private investments in low-income housing; and by the Riegle Community Development and Regulatory Improvement Act of 1994, which fostered the network of community development finance institutions designed to help channel the funds from banks, insurance companies, and other institutions into valid, community-based housing and community development efforts.

Taken together, these policy steps helped to stimulate a significant flow of private investment capital into low-income housing and community development activity in disadvantaged neighborhoods across the country and to foster a cadre of professionals and institutions with experience tapping private investment resources for social-purpose activities.[128]

Institutions such as the Low Income Support Corporation (LISC) and the Enterprise Foundation emerged to link the providers of finance to the developers of low-income housing and community development projects.

Other early responders included the Calvert Foundation, created in 1988 by a consortium that included Calvert Investments, a socially responsible mutual fund company, and the Ford, MacArthur, and Mott foundations; and the Acumen Fund, established in 2001 with support from the Rockefeller Foundation. Both of these institutions are early examples of what we earlier termed social-impact capital aggregators, generating capital resources from institutional and individual social investors and channeling them to promising social ventures in the United States and around the world. The Calvert Foundation currently has nearly $200 million invested in 250 community organizations in all 50 US states and over 100 countries, while Acumen has generated $69 million in investment capital that it has committed to 63 social ventures in eight countries generating an estimated 55,000 jobs.[129]

Along with the network of community development finance institutions fostered in the United States and comparable early community development investment vehicles in other countries, these early responders not only generated important capital to finance developing social enterprises, but also generated something at least equally important: an initial track record of promising innovations and a set of experienced promoters of a new route out of poverty and disadvantage featuring what Acumen Fund describes as "imaginative business solutions" developed by "pioneering entrepreneurs" supported by "investors willing to take on a risk/return profile that is unacceptable to traditional financiers."[130] What is more, they served as prototypes for similar policy innovations in other countries, such as the 2002 Community Investment Tax Relief Scheme in the UK, which fostered a comparable set of community development investment vehicles in that country.

New Concepts: The Fortune at the Bottom of the Pyramid

> Ideas rule the world.—Plato

What gave thrust to the work of these first responders, however, was a second important supply-side development that arose, interestingly enough, in the realm of ideas. Indeed, proving once again the truth of Plato's observation that "ideas rule the world," one of the most significant causes of the revolution in the financing of social-purpose activities in recent years has been the reconceptualization that has occurred about the causes of poverty and how to overcome it. That reconceptualization was spearheaded by the microfinance industry, brought to wide public attention by Nobel laureate Muhammad Yunus, and generalized by C. K. Prahalad.

Microfinance is, in many respects, an old story, but it is a story that has been repeatedly forgotten since its first appearance in the Irish Loan Fund created by Jonathan Swift in the eighteenth century. As it resurfaced through small-scale lending experiments in Bangladesh and elsewhere in the 1970s, microfinance accomplished a fundamental conceptual breakthrough: it demonstrated that the poor represent a *resource* rather than a liability, and a resource that can generate growth and wealth if approached in the right way. In the case of microfinance, that approach took the form of recognizing in groups of uneducated, poverty-stricken, rural women eager to improve their life circumstances a resource in the form of peer pressure that could substitute for absent physical or financial collateral to secure small revolving loan funds through which each of the women in the group could, over time, establish some type of income-earning microenterprise that could propel them down the road toward economic self-sufficiency while enabling them to pay back the loan with interest.

What ultimately lifted this concept to take-off status was not only the significant international recognition provided through the work of Muhammad Yunus and his Grameen Bank, or the financial expansion provided by a number of early capital aggregators such as Accion and Kiva, but a book by a University of Michigan corporate strategy professor of Indian origin by the name of C. K. Prahalad. What Prahalad argued in his 2004 boldly titled book, *The Fortune at the Bottom of the Pyramid*, is that the phenomenon that gave rise to the success of microcredit was not restricted to small-scale lending to groups of rural residents, but rather applied to a wide range of products and services needed by people living in even the direst of poverty, and that such products and services could be delivered to these people at prices far more affordable than they were currently spending while still earning profits for investors.[131] This alchemy was possible, Prahalad showed, because of a "penalty" levied on bottom-of-the-pyramid (BoP) consumers as a result of the difficulties and dangers of delivering goods and services to the areas where they live, and the resulting lack of competition to drive prices down. BoP consumers thus end up paying more for the items they consume than do the better-off. Prahalad thus showed that, by designing products and distribution channels that can be accessed by people of limited means who have needs for a variety of products but often pay a premium price, clever entrepreneurs can take advantage of this "bottom-of-the-pyramid penalty" to improve the living conditions and economic prospects for BoP residents while covering their own costs and earning meaningful profits.

New Players, New Mindsets

The crystallization of the idea of a "fortunate at the bottom of the pyramid" happened to coincide, moreover, with a third crucial supply-side element: the appearance at the door of the philanthropic arena of a new set of actors that Matthew Bishop and Michael Green have dubbed "philanthrocapitalists"— generally young, dot-com millionaires and billionaires, who, having made vast riches relatively early in life, have turned to philanthropy as a way to give back and create value in a different sphere. Bill Gates is doubtless the living icon for this development with his bold decision to retire from his Microsoft day job, establish a large foundation, and turn his energies and intellect to solving the world's problems of poverty and ill-health. Jeffrey Skoll and Pierre Omidyar, founders of e-Bay and early supporters of the social venture phenomenon, are other examplars of this same phenomenon, as is Charly Kleisner, whose KL Felicitas Foundation is profiled in Chapter 5 of this book as a model of what a foundation that aspires to function as a philanthropic bank looks like.

This group of funders is driven by what Kleisner describes as a "deep responsibility to do something meaningful with the wealth we've created" but also a passion to bring the entrepreneurial style that had stood them in such stead in the world of business to their new social-purpose objectives.[132] Many of them are therefore not content with traditional philanthropy, or at least what they perceive to be traditional philanthropy, and have resolved to transform it, producing a philanthropy that is "'strategic,' 'market conscious,' 'impact oriented,' 'knowledge-based,' often 'high engagement,' and always driven by the goal of maximizing the 'leverage' of the donor's money."[133] As Bishop and Green put it: "As entrepreneurial 'philanthropreneurs,' they love to back social entrepreneurs who offer innovative solutions to society's problems" and are comfortable with, indeed insistent on, utilizing financing approaches that bring to the world of philanthropy some of the dynamism and leveraging possibilities characteristic of modern corporate finance.

But it is not only dot-com multimillionaires turned philanthrocapitalists who have gotten religion and resolved to turn their attention and their considerable talents and resources to confronting the world's problems. Demographers have identified similar sentiments in two entire new generational clusters— Generation X (those born between 1961 and 1981) and the millennials (those born between 1982 and 2001). Unlike their baby boomer parents, these genera- tions are populated disproportionately by people found to be seeking a better balance between work and other aspects of their lives, and to exhibit extraor- dinary enthusiasm and idealism.[134]

Whatever the truth of these demographic generalizations, there is strong evi- dence that significant numbers of a whole new generation of business school students and recent graduates have been bitten by the social enterprise and social-impact investing bug, eschewing careers that focus solely on maximizing earnings in place of bringing their business skills to activities with a significant social-purpose dimension. One clear manifestation of this is Net Impact, a 20-year-old organization of young professionals that describes itself as "a com- munity of more than 30,000 change-makers using our jobs to tackle the world's toughest problems, demonstrating that it's possible to make a *net impact* that benefits not just the bottom line—but people and the planet, too."[135] Characteristically enough in our globalized world, Net Impact is a global pres- ence, boasting 300 student and professional chapters worldwide.

Ironically enough, these sentiments seem to have received a significant boost from the 2008 global financial meltdown and ensuing recession. Suddenly, high-net-worth individuals across a broad front, as well as mom-and-pop inves- tors, had to come to terms with the almost overnight disappearance of substan- tial portions of their wealth. Whatever the economic impact of this realization, the psychological one seems to have been equally transformative for many. If wealth could disappear so quickly, perhaps accumulating it was not the highest goal one could have in one's life. Perhaps using at least some of it to do good in the world could produce more true value in the form of personal satisfaction, particularly if this could be done in a way that would at least preserve the prin- cipal and perhaps even generate a reasonable return.

How fully such sentiments surfaced in the aftermath of the financial crisis is difficult to determine at this point, but the spurt of interest in so-called social-impact investing among family offices and advisors to high-net-worth individuals in the wake of the crisis is certainly consistent with the belief that it played a role. What is more, chaos on Wall Street, the City, and other financial centers also produced more concrete contributions to the growing supply of social capital by releasing thousands of skilled financial experts, some voluntarily and some not so voluntarily, to consider alternative careers. And a number of these skilled professionals were sufficiently burned out by their high-pressure, quick-return, financial-industry experiences to crave opportunities to put their talents and knowledge to work in settings that yielded more personal satisfaction. Not surprisingly, a good number of them found their way into the expanding industry of social-impact capital aggregators.

Emblematic of this development is the career of Pasha Bakhtiar, a Swiss-born researcher who entered the world of traditional investment banking in 1998, earned an M.B.A., and seemed well on his way to a successful career in this lucrative field, even earning a "Rising Star in Wealth Management" award from Institutional Investor in 2007. But in 2010, in the wake of the global financial crisis, Bakhtiar turned his back on the world of traditional investment banking to cofound Willow Impact Investors, a social-impact investment firm that aggregates capital for investments in what it terms for-profit companies "committed to generating positive, sustainable, and demonstrable social and environmental impact while complying with a commercial imperative."[136]

Financial Crisis: Limited Alternative Investments

The financial crisis and ensuing recession contributed to the supply side of the social capital market in an even more direct way as well: it made social-impact investments look good by transforming them into some of the most profitable investments available. It did so, of course, not by boosting the returns on

> The financial crisis made social-impact investments look good.

social-impact investments but by deflating the returns on other types of investments. With global stock markets staggering, the financial industry experiencing rapid disintermediation, and interest rates on everything from US Treasuries to certificates of deposit plummeting to historic lows, social-impact investments that offered even 3–4 percent returns and default rates that looked like the gold standard next to previously prized junk bonds and derivatives emerged as some of the most attractive investment options available. And many of these problems persisted for more than four years. The year 2013 thus opened with money managers and investors complaining of suffering from "battered investor syndrome" as they looked out at money market accounts yielding barely a half of a percentage point of interest, two-year certificates of deposit under 1 percent, 10-year US Treasuries under 2 percent, and global stock markets barely back to where they had been five years earlier.[137] Doubtless some of the $4.4 billion in social-impact investments clocked in 2011, not to mention the $2.5 billion invested in 2010, was motivated at least in part by invidious comparisons with the returns available from more traditional investments, especially with respected investment firms such as J.P. Morgan reporting both expected and realized returns on social-impact investments in line with relevant market benchmarks.[138]

Infrastructure

Building on the contributions of these first responders and new converts has been a concerted effort to create an infrastructure to support the new frontiers of philanthropy. To be sure, as noted earlier, a robust set of infrastructure organizations had already surfaced in this arena by the turn of the twenty-first century. The Opportunity Finance Network, the Social Investment Forum (SIF), the Consultative Group to Assist the Poor (CGAP), the PRI Makers Network, More for Mission, the Microfinance Investment Exchange, and the International Association of Microfinance Investors (IAMFI) are just a few of the entities created in the past decade or two to promote the new actors and new tools surfacing in the social investing arena.

Notwithstanding this profusion of infrastructure organizations, however, a group of foundations, development agencies, and private financial institutions convened by the Rockefeller Foundation in a series of key gatherings in 2007 and 2008 came to the conclusion that a broader field-building effort was still needed that could bring these various separate initiatives together under a common umbrella and move the field beyond what one pair of authors termed "uncoordinated innovation."[139] The upshot was the launch in 2009 of yet another infrastructure organization called GIIN, the Global Impact Investing Network, but this time with substantial funding from the Rockefeller Foundation, J.P. Morgan, and the US Agency for International Development.

GIIN was charged with the task of accelerating the development of the social-impact investing industry by creating critical infrastructure, improving practice, establishing a common language, and stimulating field-building research. To do so, as noted earlier, it has established an "Investors' Council," created so-called Impact Reporting and Investment Standards (IRIS), established an online database of impact investment funds called "Impact Base," and carried out a variety of outreach efforts to elevate the visibility of the field and encourage its expansion.[140]

Technology

Finally, the appearance and growth of the new frontiers of philanthropy chronicled here has been significantly enhanced by the vast advances in communication technology over the past two decades. This technology has effectively made it possible to bring the supply of capital virtually to the doorstep of the social entrepreneurs in need of it, and for organizations such as the Calvert Foundation and Acumen Fund to assemble significant portfolios of investment capital from contributions with denominations as small as $20. In addition, the new technology has significantly reduced one of the major causes of the so-called bottom-of- the-pyramid penalty, access to BoP consumers. In the process, it has rendered a variety of BoP business models far more viable than they could otherwise ever have been. As Churchill and Peterson show in Chapter 17 of this volume, for example, technology is enabling providers of microinsurance to reach the BoP market on a mass basis thanks to the availability of mobile phones, smart cards, and new payment systems. Online giving and investment portals such as Kiva and Network for Good would similarly not have been possible were it not for the technological advances.

Summary

In short, there is reason to believe that the recent changes taking place on the frontiers of philanthropy are more than a passing fad. Some significant underlying forces have been at work to produce this development at this time. What is more, these forces are operating both on the demand side of this evolving market—creating a strong need for the changes that are underway—and on the supply side—stimulating the availability of both the talents and the finances to meet this need.

Some of these forces are admittedly ephemeral (one can hope, for example, that global markets will return at some point to a greater degree of normalcy). But others appear more durable—the new excitement about the BoP market, foundations' interest in expanding the leverage they can get out of their resources, the new attitudes and new actors taking an active role in social and environmental problem-solving, and the maturation of social-impact investments as an asset class. Indeed, some close observers are already envisioning the brave new world that lies ahead for these new-frontier developments. Thus, Maximilian Martin, in Chapter 23 of this volume, outlines four developing trends that he sees already taking shape—a shift from microfinance to microfinancial services, a shift from development finance to base-of-the-pyramid investing, a shift from relationship grantmaking to strategic monetization of future savings, and a shift from social entrepreneurship to "synthesized social businesses."

But none of this means that the road ahead for these developments is clear of obstacles. To the contrary, significant challenges remain. It is to these that we must therefore now turn.

Remaining Obstacles

The discussion to this point has painted an enormously positive picture of the potential consequences of the changes taking place on the frontiers of philanthropy and social investing. More than that, it has documented some underlying factors that appear to be driving these changes and giving them durability, thus enhancing the possibility that they can achieve the enormous breakthroughs they promise in the lives of millions of disadvantaged people throughout the world.

But no clear-eyed assessment of these developments can proceed very far without acknowledging the considerable obstacles that these developments also still confront. These obstacles take a number of forms, but five of them seem especially important to acknowledge and, ultimately, confront.

> No clear-eyed assessment of the new frontiers of philanthropy can proceed very far without acknowledging the considerable obstacles that still remain.

No Good Deed Goes Unpunished: Normative Implications of the New Frontiers

In the first place, it is important to recognize that the shift in the locus of decision-making responsibility for allocating social-purpose resources from charitable foundations and government program officers to private-sector investment managers, and the new investment focus and metrics-oriented emphasis that this will bring with it, does not come without distributional consequences. Simply put, there will be winners and losers resulting from this shift in the locus of responsibility, and in the criteria for allocating resources, in the social-purpose arena. And not all of these consequences will best serve the social-purpose objectives claimed for the new-frontier initiatives.

As Michael Edwards reminds us in Chapter 20, performance metrics give inherent advantages to some types of interventions over others, and these are not always the interventions with the greatest social impact. Impact measures, for example, tend to be short term in nature, rarely extending beyond a year or two. Significant social change, however, often takes five or 10 years. Do we really want to tie ourselves to assessment regimes that systematically disadvantage initiatives with the greatest chance of achieving long-run change?

In addition, the investment orientation and metrics emphasis of the new frontiers give an advantage to service activities—providing healthcare, or food, or electricity to people. But past experience has shown that some of the most profound improvements in the lives of disadvantaged people result not from the provision of particular services but from the elimination of unequal structures of power and barriers to opportunity, and these require vigorous advocacy efforts instead. This is the lesson, for example, of the American civil rights movement. Civil rights organizations were not in the business of providing housing, or needed healthcare, or education to the country's African American citizens. They could therefore hardly have had much appeal to social-impact investors fixated on these tangible manifestations of social impacts as the major criteria for success. But the truth is that their ultimate impact on the life-chances of millions upon millions of America's African-American citizens easily trumped that of any number of narrow service initiatives with strong two-, or even four-, year performance records. Fortunately, however, there were enlightened foundations and individual people of conscience willing to support the advocacy campaigns that opened the doors of opportunity through which tens of thousands of America's African-American citizens have been able to walk since then. Will all the hype and enthusiasm generated by the "new frontiers" phenomenon draw too much attention and resources away from the similar advocacy efforts still required elsewhere to break down oppressive structures of power and barriers to opportunity? Without confronting these dilemmas, the social-impact investment movement can easily find itself running afoul of the very social change impulses it is claiming to be advancing.

The Conundrum of Social-Impact Measurement

One way to protect against the risks of mission creep inevitably involved in pursuing social-purpose objectives through market means is to build in performance standards for the social-purpose objectives that are every bit as stringent as those for the financial objectives of such investments. To their credit, the promoters of the new social-impact investment movement recognized the need for such performance standards and have launched a variety of efforts to develop them. To date, however, these efforts remain what Brian Trelstad, a prominent leader in this field, concedes in Chapter 22 of this volume to be still "an elusive quest." Despite the compelling logic of the concept of "blended value," or blended return, embracing financial, social, and environmental elements, this concept remains merely a powerful metaphor since no tool yet exists to measure reliably the blended return on philanthropic investments, and certainly none that can compare the relative blended returns across a diverse set of interventions.

> The formulation of a reliable way to measure social impact remains, at best, a "work in progress."

Much of the work to date has focused on formulating a common taxonomy of potential social, environmental, and financial performance indicators. The most ambitious of these taxonomies is the Impact Reporting and Investment Standards (IRIS), supported by the Rockefeller Foundation and developed under the auspices of the Global Impact Investing Network. This taxonomy includes more than 400 indicators in terms of which social-impact investors can demonstrate the social and environmental, as well as financial, performance of their investments. As noted earlier, however, the dilemma is that with so many different indicators against which social performance can be demonstrated, the performance measurement system comes to resemble those grade-school drawing contests designed so that the number of prizes is large enough to send every child home a winner.

To get around this problem, the creators of IRIS have joined forces with B Lab, a nonprofit organization involved in identifying and promoting so-called benefit corporations, to create a rating system for social-impact investments and investors.[141] Called the Global Impact Investing Rating System, or GIIRS, this system rates companies in terms of their performance in four major areas—corporate governance, treatment of workers, impact on the environment, and role in the community, including patterns of supply-chain management and diversity of the workforce—giving companies a composite score based on answers to 50–120 weighted questions.[142] The system thus bears marked resemblance to the various corporate social responsibility reporting systems discussed in Chapter 18 of this volume.

While these developments are promising, most observers are in agreement with Trelstad in seeing the formulation of a reliable way to measure social impact to be what one author calls, at best, a "work in progress."[143] What is more, the take-up of nonfinancial performance measures remains limited among investors. Thornley and Dailey, writing in 2010, reported "limited evidence" of reporting on nonfinancial performance by most investors in their annual reports, with anecdotal reporting the most prevalent form of reporting by those who do report.[144] O'Donohue and coauthors found a similar dearth of serious nonfinancial performance reporting among a surveyed group of "impact investors," with only 2 percent using a third-party impact measurement system, and the rest using, at best, their own proprietary systems or the systems used by their investees.[145]

This is understandable enough given how complicated, expensive, and subjective nonfinancial performance measurement can be, but it could lead the field in the wrong direction. Many close observers of social-purpose activity endorse an approach to measuring the impact of this work that I have elsewhere termed "What would Google do?" And what Google would do is to focus on the user, to assess impact by asking the people who are meant to benefit from an investment.[146] Instead, prominent experts in the social-impact investing world have proposed what they term an "investor-centered" approach to building social-impact performance measurement systems. But this leaves the field of social-impact investing vulnerable to false claims of social impact and the potential for significant mission creep as standard financial performance measures come to trump more uncertain and costly nonfinancial ones. Indeed, there is already evidence of such pressures in the social enterprise field. Thus, a recent survey of 25 social ventures in the United States found that 22 experienced "significant conflicts" between their missions and the demands of corporate stakeholders, and that the two that were most successful financially reported deviating most significantly from their social mission by reducing the time devoted to advocacy, weeding out the most needy, and hence most costly, clients, and focusing on activities with the greatest revenue-generating potential.[147]

Still a Boutique Business

Quite apart from the challenge it faces in demonstrating its social-impact bona fides to skeptics, the social-impact investment movement has also not quite succeeded in making the "sale" to its primary audience: main-line institutional investors such as pension funds, insurance companies, sovereign wealth funds, and major corporations.[148] To be sure, important progress has been made, with an estimated $8.0 billion in new impact investments clocked in 2012 according to recent data assembled by J.P. Morgan Social Finance and GIIN, up from $4.4 billion in 2011, and $2.5 billion in 2010, with a projected increase to $9.1 billion in 2014.[149] What is more, new funding intermediaries are forming on an increasingly global scale, as the earlier discussion indicated.

Impressive as this progress is, however, it is well to remember that $8.0 billion is still well under 5/100th of 1 percent of the $14,442 billion of assets in US commercial banks, less than 1/10th of 1 percent of the $7,963 billion of assets in US mutual funds, and just slightly over 1/10th of 1 percent of the $6,080 billion of assets in US pension funds.[150] And that is just US capital markets. A World Economic Forum report issued in September 2013 confirms this basic point and identifies this limited penetration of social-impact investing into the world's mainstream capital markets as threatening to tag the social-impact investing movement as little more than "a hype," or passing fad.[151]

As Mary Tingerthal reports in Chapter 14 on securitization, advocates of low-income housing and community development finance, who have dreamed of tapping the highly promising tool of asset-backed securities to finance the revitalization of ailing communities, have so far found this dream "largely unrealized." Even in the field of international microfinance, which has attracted considerable private-sector funding, the ability to leverage resources by "securitizing" debt instruments remains in its infancy: only 12 percent of the $4.2 billion in debt instruments held by Microfinance Investment Intermediaries internationally, and less than 1 percent of total microcredit loans outstanding, have been assembled into debt instruments that can be sold to investors in order to refresh the makers of microfinance loans.

The subfield of "sustainable and responsible investing," which covers entities that apply some type of environmental, social, or governance criteria to their investments, has attained greater scale. The most recent data found $3.7 trillion of assets managed against such screens in the United States.[152] This is a much less active form of utilizing assets for social and environmental purposes, however. Even so, it still represents a fairly modest 2.6 percent of all financial assets in US financial institutions.

The reasons for this slow climb are not hard to discern and have been recognized from the outset. Among the factors well rehearsed in the literature are the relative immaturity of many social enterprises, the limited experience of many of the management teams, the novelty of some of the investment vehicles, and the enormous uncertainties surrounding the liquidity of the investments due to the lack of tested exit opportunities. Add to this the inevitable country risk factors, the exchange rate risk factors, the high transaction costs, and the

> Inefficiencies in the social-capital markets, skill deficits on the part of potential investees, and the sheer difficulty of BoP businesses conspire to limit investment demand.

lack of clear data on investment returns and it is easy to see why social finance remains today what Erickson in Chapter 3 calls a "boutique business," and why three-fourths of the respondents to a recent J.P. Morgan survey of impact investors concluded that this industry, while "growing," is nevertheless "still in its infancy."[153]

The Pesky Issue of Deal Flow

Another factor inhibiting the growth of the social-impact investment market arises not from the supply side of the market in the form of investor reticence, but from the demand side in the form of investee absence. How can this be so? After all, as research reported in Chapter 21 of this volume shows, of the estimated 365 to 445 million micro, small-, and medium-sized firms in developing countries, 70 percent need, but do not have, access to external funding, and this does not even include the informal enterprises so numerous in these countries. Why are these enterprises not pressing their claims for capital on the increasingly plentiful sources of it?

Broadly speaking, three main lines of explanation of this apparent paradox can be identified. The first such line of explanation focuses on inefficiencies in the social capital markets. Such markets have long been fragmented, disjointed, relatively small, and therefore difficult to access. Even with the new technologies, the geographical, physical, conceptual, and psychological distances between the 400 million small entrepreneurs in need of capital and the relative handful of social capital aggregators in a position to deploy it remains measured in light-years. Add to that the significant costs of due diligence and structuring transactions and it is easy to see why the flow of investible deals remains somewhat anemic despite the clear need.

The second line of explanation for why impact investors continue to identify a "shortage of quality investment opportunities" as one of the top two most serious challenges they face relates less to the inefficiencies of the market than to the skill deficits on the part of potential investees.[154] The entities involved in social-purpose activities are typically nonprofit organizations, small-scale mom-and-pop enterprises, faith-based charities, cooperatives, mutual societies, and courageous, individual social entrepreneurs. Few are schooled in the basics of finance. As outlined in a Venturesome report discussed in Chapter 20, many lack a clear understanding of the difference between operating income and investment capital, are unable to identify their own financial needs with precision, are unschooled in the different financial instruments available to them, and are unaware of how to assemble multiple sources of finance into manageable funding packages.[155] This lack of basic financial literacy leaves a yawning gulf between the seekers of capital, who tend to bring forward, at best, micro deals, and the potential providers of it, who are accustomed to operating at a scale orders of magnitude larger than this. And it is a gulf that those involved in building the social-impact investing industry have curiously neglected to address very coherently in their zeal to bring the new investors to the table first.[156]

It is perhaps the third line of explanation for the lagging deal flow in the social-impact investing market that is the most demanding, however. Simply put, there are too few deals because the BoP market, for all its promise, is an enormously difficult market in which to operate, and certainly in which to operate at a profit while adhering to meaningful social-purpose objectives. Harvey Koh and colleagues identify the situation well when they describe the "heavy

A "pioneer gap" confronts the social-purpose market, limiting the supply of investible deals able to absorb the pent-up supply of social-investment capital.

burden" that firms pioneering new business models in BoP environments regularly confront:

They must develop and refine their models the hard way, by trying them out in an unforgiving, low-margin marketplace. Inevitably they suffer failures and setbacks on the road to viability. Often they also have to invest heavily in educating customers about the possibilities of new "push" solutions and in developing unskilled suppliers and fragmented distribution channels to serve their requirements. Although excited by their novelty, investors are often rattled by the firms' risk profiles and are unimpressed by their financial returns, all the while suspecting that they might actually be savvy nonprofits masquerading as commercially viable models.[157]

Despite the optimistic assumptions about the enormous flow of resources poised to pour into promising bottom-of-the-pyramid businesses, the task of bringing such businesses to the point of attracting serious capital is a long and tortuous one. As Koh and his colleagues point out, it took the Grameen Bank 17 years to break even after its launch in 1976, and other trajectories have proven equally demanding. The Acumen Fund has had to filter through more than 5,000 companies over 10 years to find 65 promising enough to invest in, and this with a set of financial return expectations that is highly conservative by investment standards. Indeed, the average after-tax profit of Acumen's portfolio companies remains under water. And no wonder. Monitor Group research in India suggests that it takes 10 years for an inclusive social enterprise to achieve a scale sufficient to generate profitable operations.[158]

Given this situation, social-impact investors have shied away from the early financing of promising BoP businesses. But this creates a classic "free rider" problem: while all investors would benefit from joint support of promising businesses during their early, uncertain start-up phases, no particular investor can see it in its interest to do so for any particular promising business since once its concept is proved, multiple competitors will swoop into the market to benefit from the initial investment without sharing in the cost. The result is what Koh and colleagues term "the pioneer gap," the absence of funding to support the critical start-up phase of promising social ventures and the resulting lack of sufficient investible deals to absorb the pent-up supply of social investment capital.

Just as in other cases of such "market failures," what is needed in such circumstances is a nonmarket solution to the market imperfection. Traditionally, this role is played by government in cases of other so-called collective goods, such as national defense, and government can play a critical role here as well. The UK's Department for International Development, for example, provided crucial early-stage financing for the M-PESA mobile phone electronic payment system that has brought financial services for the first time to 9 million Kenyan residents. The US Agency for International Development provided similar assistance in the early development of clean-burning cooking stoves in Ghana.[159]

But given the political risks of choosing successful technologies or business models, responsibility for overcoming this particular market imperfection may more properly belong to the institutions we earlier referred to as "foundations as philanthropic banks," that is, foundations willing to tap their endowments as well as their grant budgets to leverage their resources for maximum impact on the causes they have chosen to advance. Koh and his colleagues refer to this as "enterprise philanthropy," but we might just as well refer to it colloquially as "PRIs on steroids." It essentially involves identifying highly promising BoP business propositions that have gotten beyond the initial proof of concept and helping them to validate the commercial viability of their products, prepare the market for their launch, and get them into initial operation in order to facilitate the eventual investment of private, return-seeking capital that can bring the resulting businesses to scale.[160] Such support can take the form of grants, but it might equally take the form of low-interest or no-interest loans, or noncontrolling equity.

Getting Beyond Comforting Assumptions

What the discussion above suggests is that those promoting, or operating on, the new frontiers of philanthropy may be approaching a moment of truth. Many of the developments identified here have been launched with enor-

> Three comforting assumptions about social-impact investing have now been significantly challenged.

mous fanfare and enormous hope. Long-standing tensions between doing good and doing well were miraculously being suspended; market rates of return were available from activities pursued with the intention of achieving social and environmental progress; private investment markets were available to replace government and private charities as the principal sources of social-purpose growth capital; and a new era of social-purpose finance was just around the corner.

These assertions have hardly been disproved. Indeed, the developments outlined in this chapter, and in this volume, retain considerable momentum and immense promise. Still, the field has achieved sufficient maturity to be able to acknowledge the hard slog that still lies ahead. In particular, three comforting assumptions that have helped to fuel the hype around social-impact investing, as well as some of the other innovations on the frontiers of philanthropy, have now been significantly challenged, if not completely refuted, and the resulting realities must now be confronted as the field moves into the next phase of its development.

Traditional Market Risk-Return Ratios?

In the first place, many of the return expectations broadcast in the early literature on social-impact investing seem overly optimistic and unsupported by the actual experience of the pioneers operating in the field. To be sure, there are powerful examples of BoP businesses that are producing significant social benefit while generating impressive market returns. But those businesses required years of painful incubation before they sprang into view as mature enterprises achieving the returns for which they are now celebrated in the literature. Yet this long and costly incubation is too often discounted or totally ignored, as are the dozens of other promising business offspring that never survived the embryo stage. While it may not be the case, as Kevin Starr has warned, that "there's really only one bottom line—it's either impact or profit, and the demands of investors can pull an organization away from the target population toward those able to pay more," the fact remains that enticing investors with the returns achieved by the handful of success stories can create expectations that can easily move the field in this direction.[161]

The solution here need not be to give up on the promise of social-impact investing and the mobilization of private investment capital for social and environmental purposes. Rather, the solution is to recognize the need for more complex financial packages in order to accommodate the financial return needs of private investors without ignoring the exceptional risk profiles facing most start-up businesses serving BoP markets.

A Substitute for Government?

> Unlocking capital for social-purpose activity turns out to require a crowbar.

This brings us to a second comforting assumption that has crept into the new frontiers of philanthropy mindset. This is the assumption that social-impact investing, the mobilization of private investment capital for social and environmental purposes, can significantly substitute for lagging governmental resources and involvement. To be sure, the ideology of privatism has a long lineage in American political thought, and particularly so in the philanthropic arena.[162] It should come as no surprise, therefore, that a potent theme in the "philanthrocapitalism" playbook is the suggestion that just as the private sector can "do it better than government" in running businesses and generating profits, so too it can do the same in advancing social and environmental objectives. Government is therefore not needed, or at least not needed as much, in this arena.

This assumption, too, however, finds little support in the evidence. If it takes a village to rear a child, it appears to take a virtual cabinet of government departments to generate even a small trickle of private investment capital into social-purpose activities. This, at any rate, is the experience in the one field of social-purpose investment in the United States that has attracted perhaps the most substantial, if still small, flow of such capital—that is, affordable housing and community development. To stimulate and sustain that flow of funds has required the joint actions of no fewer than seven government agencies: the US Congress, the Board of Governors of the Federal Reserve System (FRB), the Federal Deposit Insurance Corporation (FDIC), the Office of the Comptroller of the Currency (OCC), the Office of Thrift Supervision (OTS), the Internal Revenue Service, and the Community Development Financial Institutions Fund in the Department of the Treasury. These officials have responsibility for administering four different programs that have been needed to get private investment capital flowing into inner cities and affordable housing. As described earlier, these are the Community Reinvestment Act (CRA), incentivizing bank investments in distressed communities; the Low Income Housing Tax Credit, which offers tax credits to investors in low-income housing; the Community Development Financial Institution (CDFI) Fund, which supports the nationwide network of CDFIs; and the New Markets Tax Credit, which provides tax breaks to investors in distressed areas.

As we have seen, public-sector funding, or other forms of assistance, provided either directly or through multinational development banks, has been equally important in helping to nudge private-sector investors into participation in social-purpose efforts in other settings as well, including the UK and in much of the developing world. Unlocking capital for social-purpose activity turns out to require a crowbar and often the kind of muscle and resources that governments alone can wield. While no one can doubt the crucial role that private capital can, and is, playing, no one either can realistically expect the private sector to do it on its own.

Goodbye to Traditional Philanthropy?

Finally, from what has been said, it should be clear that the predictions of the imminent demise of traditional philanthropy that have accompanied the rise of social-impact investment in some quarters are as exaggerated as the ones that reached Mark Twain announcing his untimely death. As the discussion of the "pioneer gap" and the need for complex financing "tranches" make clear, the new world of social-impact investing requires the old world of traditional philanthropy in order to succeed. The one cannot easily function without the other.

This is not to say that traditional philanthropy can be maximally helpful if it continues to function in traditional ways. Rather, traditional philanthropy will have to change if it wishes to remain fully relevant in the new world of social-purpose finance that is emerging. It will need to function as a catalyst for more complicated funding consortia. It will need to partner with other types of funding institutions, both public and private. And it will need to learn how to combine its traditional tool of grants with other resources of its own, and with the resources of other types of institutions, to achieve the leverage needed to gain traction on the serious problems the world confronts. In philanthropy as well as in other spheres, the world of "either-or" must be replaced by the practice of "both-and."

Prescription: The Way Forward

From what has been reported here it should be clear that the new frontiers of philanthropy hold enormous promise for gaining meaningful traction on a wide range of social, economic, and environmental problems facing the world at the present time. To be sure, the solutions on offer from many of the new developments taking place on the frontiers of philanthropy and social investing may not be appropriate for all problems or all locations. One recent analysis suggested, for example, four key conditions that must be met for social-impact investment to work properly: (1) the issue or problem should be of a scale that makes it unlikely that either government or philanthropy will have the resources alone to address it; (2) there must be a viable market-based solution available or in reasonable prospect; (3) mainstream private investors should not already be heavily engaged; and (4) market-based solutions must be considered morally acceptable.[163] Clearly, not all of the globe's challenges, and perhaps not even the most severe of them, will meet these criteria. What is more, even those that do will stumble along the way because many of the new techniques have their own problems: their complexity deters many potential participants, standards for ensuring valid social outcomes are not fully developed, and investors with the patience to wait out the lengthy proof-of-concept phase of social-purpose investments may not be forthcoming.

> Despite limitations, there is sufficient promise to warrant further active encouragement.

Yet, despite these limitations, observers have identified a number of areas where these new actors and tools enjoy significant potential, and new such areas are being discovered on a regular basis. Included are such areas as housing, healthcare, education, utilities, agriculture, financial services, and insurance. In all of these, imaginative products such as low-cost solar panels, modular housing, cheap eyeglasses, reusable sanitary napkins, and clean-burning stoves are transforming lives while generating at least modest profits for investors and entrepreneurs. In short, despite the obstacles and limitations, there is sufficient promise in the developments taking place on the frontiers of philanthropy to warrant further active encouragement of them.

But what form should such encouragement take? Based on the discussion here, six steps seem especially worth pursuing.

Visualize

In the first place, there remains a significant need to enable more people to visualize and grasp the dramatic changes underway on what we have termed the "new frontiers of philanthropy." The developments portrayed in this book are diffuse and diverse. It is therefore all too easy for people to miss the forest for the trees, indeed to fail to comprehend that there is a substantial forest at all. Drawing a circle around these developments and finding a way to portray them coherently is thus the first step toward allowing the various stakeholders involved—individual investors, investment managers, financial institutions, social entrepreneurs, philanthropic institutions, nonprofit managers, and the general public—to appreciate the enormity of the changes and to begin to position themselves more actively in relation to them. Hopefully, this volume, with its systematic identification and analysis of a sizable range of the new actors and tools that are emerging, will contribute usefully to this visualization goal and to the action that will hopefully flow from it.

Publicize

Visualization is just a first step toward the broader awareness-raising needed to bring the message of the new frontiers to the various groups of stakeholders whose involvement holds the key to its promise. For this, a much more robust educational and field-broadening effort will be required.

> Despite a substantial investment of time and resources, this field remains well off the beaten path of main-line philanthropy and private investment, and virtually unknown to all but the most intrepid nonprofit explorers.

To be sure, some components of the new frontiers phenomenon have begun to achieve meaningful scale in terms of the numbers of institutions engaged. The Forum for Sustainable and Responsible Investing (US SIF Foundation) thus identified 443 institutional investors, 272 money managers, and over 1,000 community investment institutions such as community development financial institutions and credit unions in the United States alone that are applying various environmental, social, and corporate governance (ESG) criteria to their invest-ment analysis and portfolio selection as of the end of 2011, and 200 of these institutions filed or co-filed shareholder resolutions on these issues at publicly traded companies from 2010 through 2012.[164] But though impressive, these numbers are hardly overwhelming, especially given that the sustainable and re-sponsible investing movement had its start four decades ago and is a less demanding form of activity than the more direct forms of social-impact invest-ing identified in this volume. Especially striking is the limited involvement on the part of foundations, which are institutions with clear social objectives that could be advanced by the use of social, environmental, and good-corporate gov-ernance screens on their investment portfolios. Yet US SIF was able to identify only 95 out of the country's 76,545 foundations—a mere one-tenth of 1 percent of the foundations—that reported applying ESG criteria to their investments. And only $60.3 billion of the total $590.2 billion in foundation assets—or about 10 percent of the total—is definitively subject to such criteria as a consequence.[165]

Elsewhere, knowledge of the developments outlined here remains hit-or-miss at best, even among critical stakeholders, such as foundations, investment man-agers, pension funds, mutual fund firms, and nonprofit organizations across a broad array of fields. The social-impact investing component of this new develop-ment is particularly in need of broader communication and awareness-raising. As evidence of this, a 2013 survey by CFA Institute, the largest association of in-vestment professionals in the world, found that two-thirds of financial advisers surveyed confessed to being unaware of "impact investing."[166] In short, despite a substantial investment of time and resources, this field remains a distant subcon-tinent, well off the beaten path of main-line philanthropy and private investment, and virtually unknown to all but the most intrepid nonprofit explorers.

To overcome this, it will be necessary to take information on the new fron-tiers of philanthropy out to a broader strata of participants and observers, to bring knowledge of the new tools and actors "from the margins to the main-stream," as a recent World Economic Forum document recently put it.[167] This will require new materials that can penetrate the academic settings where the next generations of nonprofit executives, money managers, and foundation offi-cials are being trained, as well as new "mainstream messengers" capable of serving, as two prominent advocates of the field have recognized, as "the con-duits that can absorb the lessons from visionary practice and communicate them effectively to much wider audiences," a task that this book, and the field-broadening efforts that can flow from it, has set for itself, and that others will hopefully help it achieve.[168]

Incentivize

A third important encouragement needed is outright incentivization. A key conclusion of recent work assessing the early history of some of the emerging new forms of philanthropy and social investment is the continued im-portance of credit enhancements, regulatory requirements, tax breaks, and other forms of incentives for these new tools to live up to their promise of delivering meaningful social,

> The rhetoric of social-impact investing has come full circle in just a decade regarding the relative roles of the private market, government, and foundations.

economic, and environmental gains to disadvantaged populations and regions while still attracting the involvement of private investors. The long gestation period of microcredit, the "pioneer gap" facing most other BoP products before they become commercially viable, and the array of regulatory requirements, tax advantages, and grants that was required to stimulate a flow of private investment capital into affordable housing in the United States all speak volumes about the need to engage other actors beyond the private investors who have been the featured actors in the hype recently surrounding social-impact investment.

In a sense, the rhetoric of social-impact investing has come full circle over just the past half-decade. Initially promoting the new, market-based, social investment instruments as a way to fill in for lagging government and traditional philanthropic support of social and environmental problem-solving, advocates of these new, market-based instruments have recently come to the realization that government and institutional philanthropy are actually not only important, but "doubly important," to the success of the market-based approaches.[169] Increasingly needed are complex funding "stacks" that combine grants, unsecured loans, and various forms of guarantees, subsidies, and occasionally regulations provided by governments and charitable foundations in order to unleash the flow of private investment capital and to make complex undertakings possible.

For this to be possible, however, both governments and foundations will need to alter their current modus operandi. Governments in the United States and the UK have begun to do this, albeit only in selective spheres. Elsewhere, the environment for the new approaches outlined here is often more restrictive. Credit enhancements from external sources that lower the interest rate on loans to social entrepreneurs in India, for example, are disallowed by laws prohibiting external loans at rates below those offered by the Bank of India. Elsewhere, foundation support for for-profit businesses is prohibited or discouraged even if the businesses advance the social-purpose missions of the foundations, while laws permitting companies to seek a balance between social-purpose and profit are nonexistent in many places. Coherent efforts to eliminate legal and other impediments and institute positive incentives for the kinds of investment in social-purpose activities described here will thus be necessary, as Shirley Sagawa argues convincingly in Chapter 24 of this volume.

So, too, will be a willingness on the part of more foundations to join the ranks of foundations as "philanthropic banks," outlined in Chapter 5. They, too, will be needed to join the public-private investment consortia that the new actors and tools make possible, to tap into their full asset base, and to make use of a wider array of tools of action than traditional one-off grants.

Legitimize

For these incentives to be forthcoming, however, more progress will be needed in developing the social-impact performance standards that can fully legitimize government and foundation support for the new forms of social investment.

> If the field is serious about its nonfinancial performance indicators, it will need to broaden its approach.

Because they are utilizing market means and potentially generating market-rate returns to at least some of their investors, social-impact investing, as well as some of the other new forms of philanthropy and social-purpose activity, must be even more vigilant than traditional philanthropy about retaining public trust. Demonstrating their social-purpose bona fides will therefore be a perennial, and growing, challenge for such initiatives, particularly if the hoped-for return rates begin to materialize, a point that early supporters of these initiatives have clearly recognized.[170]

To date, however, the field has yet to produce what the pivotal 2009 Monitor report identified as a "standard-setting body that would help create a threshold for what would be considered a social-impact investment."[171] Although a standard-setting body has been established, its criteria tend to mirror broader corporate social responsibility criteria rather than targeted thresholds for what can be considered an impact investment. And while targeted impact measures have been identified, they are not attached to a standard-setting body establishing thresholds and are at any rate so numerous that almost any investment seems likely to be able to justify itself as a social impact one in terms of them.

If the field is serious about its nonfinancial performance indicators, it will need to broaden its approach. Instead of focusing its search on "investor-centered" indicators, as some have suggested, it will need to focus at least equal attention on indicators that are convincing to the two chief sources of the incentives these tools have proven to need in order to function effectively: government and private philanthropy. And this will likely involve some way to bring the constituencies of these investments more actively into the performance measurement picture, something that none of the extant performance systems does.

Capacitize

A fifth step needed to capture the promise resident in the new frontiers of philanthropy is to attend to the critical issue of deal flow. This will require more than visualizing and publicizing the new opportunities. Also required is serious training to build what one observer has called the "investment readiness" of actual or potential entrepreneurs.[172] Many of the personnel in position to access the new resources potentially available through the new frontiers of philanthropy are lacking the rudimentary financial knowledge to do so effectively. They are often managers of nonprofit organizations, community organizers, or microbusiness owners. Most of their experience is in the world of grant funding or small-scale bank lending. A fairly robust training effort is therefore required to prepare such organizations and personnel to generate deals that meet the market tests required for the new tools of social investment.

> A fairly robust training effort is required to attend to the critical issue of deal flow.

A report by the UK social investment fund Venturesome, for example, identified a broad range of issues facing social investees in the UK as they seek to negotiate the new financial environment in which they find themselves. As reflected in Box 1.8, these include some basic financial skills and basic financial awareness. Left unattended, they will continue to impede the realization of the promise that social-impact investing holds out.

As Maximilian Martin notes in Chapter 23 of this volume, a bold effort is needed to "synthesize" social entrepreneurs rather than wait passively for their emergence.

BOX 1.8

KEY GAPS IN KNOWLEDGE ON THE PART OF POTENTIAL
SOCIAL INVESTEES

---

(1) An inability to identify their own financial needs

(2) Lack of understanding of the difference between operating income
and capital

(3) Lack of awareness of the financial instruments available and the relative pros and cons of each

(4) Limited awareness of the different capital providers available to them

(5) Failure to recognize that grants are not free money, but rather involve significant costs

(6) Lack of confidence and knowledge to structure deals blending different investor appetites and instruments[173]

Actualize

Finally, at the end of the day, what is needed is the hard task of doing deals, of
scouting the terrain of promising social innovations, deciding which ones might
hold promise of becoming commercially viable while generating significant
social or environmental payoff, supporting them through the treacherous
proof-of-concept phase, assessing their realistic capital and managerial needs,
amassing the needed combination of financial and technical assistance, and
taking the resulting concepts to scale. Clearly, the transaction costs of this set of
tasks are enormous. It is no wonder, then, that a recent status report on the
social-impact investing "industry" identified "placing and managing capital" as
one of the six top challenges the field faces.[174]

This challenge will not likely be met by social-impact investors working on
their own. It will require consortia to come together to share intelligence, identify promising investment options, pool resources, spread risk, improve practice,
and reduce transaction costs. Some promising signs of such developments are
already in view. One intriguing example is the West Coast's Toniic consortium,
a group of social-impact investors that has come together for precisely this set of
purposes.[175] Still, some of the infrastructure identified by the Monitor Institute
in 2009 as needed to actualize the promise of social-impact investing, such as a
series of "industry-defining funds that can serve as beacons for how to address
specific social or environmental issues," or the placement of substantial risk
capital in "catalytic funding structures" that would be available to help incentivize a range of impact investments, have either not yet appeared or are still in
embryo.[176] Clearly, fully actualizing the promise of the new frontiers of philanthropy remains a work in progress, though a work that continues to attract talent
and energy.

Conclusion

Enormous challenges confront the global community at the present time. Failed states, international terrorism, global warming, persistent poverty, deforestation, water shortages, ill-health, food shortages, and youth unemployment are just some of the problems that exist.

The new tools and actors examined in this volume are not a panacea for solving these problems. Yet it is hard not to see them as one of the more promising developments in an otherwise dismal scenario of lagging resources and resolve. Though not without their problems, these developments hold the promise of bringing significant new resources into efforts to solve the world's problems of poverty, ill-health, and environmental degradation; of unleashing new energies and new sources of ingenuity for social and environmental problem-solving; of democratizing giving and social problem-solving, and of constructively leveraging new technologies and new attitudes about social responsibility to gain new traction on enduring human problems.

It is perhaps not surprising, therefore, that these developments have even found their way into the consciousness of an aging, now-retired, conservative pope, whose 2009 encyclical, *Caritas in Veritate,* pointedly acknowledged that "the traditionally valid distinction between profit-based companies and non-profit organizations can no longer do full justice to reality, or offer practical direction for the future."[177]

The new frontiers of philanthropy described in this book provide powerful support to this observation. But so, too, do they underline the pope's caution about the need to remain vigilant that the "new composite reality" that is emerging, while not excluding profit, makes sure that profit is used, as Benedict put it, as "a means for achieving human and social ends." This is the hope that the new frontiers of philanthropy holds out for us, and that this book seeks to advance. At a time of diminished resources, and diminished expectations, it is, for better or worse, one of the most promising hopes we have.

Notes

* Unless otherwise noted, dollar amounts reported are in US dollars.

1. "USAID and Impact Investors Capitalize New Equity Fund for East African Agribusiness," Microfinance Africa, accessed May 11, 2013, http://seedstock. com/2011/10/05/usaid-global-impact-investing-network-j oin-to-create-east-africa-agricultural-investment-fund/.

2. For a discussion of this term in the context of social-impact investing, see Jessica Freireich and Katherine Fulton, "Investing for Social and Environmental Impact: A Design for Catalyzing an Emerging Industry," Monitor Institute, January 2009, 33, accessed January 9, 2014, http://www.monitorinstitute.com/downloads/what-we-think/ impact-investing/Impact_Investing.pdf (cited hereafter as *2009 Monitor Report*).

3. For a fuller explication of this nontraditional mode of charitable foundation operation and some of the institutions pioneering it, see Chapter 5 of this volume.

4. Cited in John Tzetzes, *Book of Histories (Chiliades)*, trans. Francis R. Walton (Lipsiae, 1826), 2:129–30.

5. For comparison purposes, the assets held by US foundations as of 2010 totaled $618 billion, which yielded approximately $45 billion of charitable grants. By comparison, the assets in commercial banks in the United States totaled $14.4 trillion (nearly 25 times the foundation assets), in mutual funds $8.0 trillion, in insurance companies $6.6 trillion, and

in money market funds $2.8 trillion. By "leverage" here I do not mean loading mountains of debt on the balance sheets of charities, but rather using charitable resources to stimulate a greater flow of private investment capital into social and environmental purposes. The recent financial crisis is full of lessons about the dangers of overleveraging, but the philanthropic world is seriously underleveraged, which brings its own dangers in terms of leaving serious social and environmental problems to fester. Foundation data from the Foundation Center accessed at Foundation Center, "Highlights of Foundation Yearbook," Foundations Today Series (2011), accessed May 10, 2013, http://foundationcenter.org/ gainknowledge/research/pdf/fy2011_highlights.pdf; data on other institutions from the Federal Reserve as reported in the US Census Bureau, "Statistical Abstract of the United States, 2012," accessed May 10, 2013, http://www.census.gov/compendia/statab/cats/ banking_finance_insurance/financial_assets_and_liabilities.html.

6. Based on data generated by the International Association of Microfinance Investors, "Microfinance Investment," accessed May 11, 2013, http://www.iamfi.com/microfinance_ investment.html.

7. "About Us," Aavishkaar, accessed August 12, 2012, http://www.aavishkaar.in.

8. Grassroots Business Fund, "2011 Annual Report of the Grassroots Business Fund," accessed May 11, 2013, http://gbfund.org/sites/default/files/GBF_AR_2011.pdf.

9. "The Bamboo Finance Private Equity Group," Bamboo Finance, accessed May 11, 2013, www.bamboofinance.com.

10. Small Enterprise Assistance Fund (SEAF), "Our Impact," accessed June 6, 2013, http://seaf.com/index.php?option=com_content&view=article&id=36&Itemid=82&lang =en.

11. C. K. Prahalad, *The Fortune at the Bottom of the Pyramid: Eradicating Poverty through Profits* (Philadelphia: Wharton School Publishing, 2004).

12. Lucy Carmody, Benjamin McCarron, Jenny Blinch, and Allison Prevatt, *Impact Investing in Emerging Markets* (Singapore: Responsible Research, 2011), 102.

13. On some of the difficulties of the "impact investment" terminology, see below and Chapter 20 of this volume.

14. Antony Bugg-Levine and Jed Emerson, *Impact Investing: Transforming How We Make Money While Making a Difference* (San Francisco: Jossey-Bass, 2011), 151.

15. Christa Velasquez, "Advancing Social Impact Investment through Measurement," accessed May 11, 2013, http://www.frbsf.org/cdinvestments/conferences/social impact-investments/transcript/Velasquez_Panel_3.pdf.

16. As noted more fully below, the term "philanthrocapitalism" was coined by Matthew Bishop and Michael Green to depict a new class of dot-com billionaires like Bill Gates who have turned their attention to philanthropy. See Matthew Bishop and Michael Green, *Philanthrocapitalism: How The Rich Can Save the World* (New York: Bloomsbury, 2008). The terms "impact investment" and "impact investors" were coined by a group of philanthropists and investors assembled by the Rockefeller Foundation to consider how to expand the available pool of resources for social and environmental purpose activities.

17. This definition is consistent with *Webster's New World Dictionary,* which defines "philanthropy" as "a desire to help mankind"; and "philanthropic" as "interest in the general human welfare." Victoria Neufeldt, *Webster's New World Dictionary of American English*, 3rd College Edition (New York: Prentice Hall, 1991), 1014.

18. *Webster's New World Dictionary,* 1272.

19. Frieriech and Fulton, *2009 Monitor Report,* 6.

20. Nick O'Donohoe, Christina Leijonhufvud, Yasemin Saltuk, Antony Bugg-Levine, and Margot Brandenburg, "Impact Investments: An Emerging Asset Class," J.P. Morgan, November 29, 2010, 5, accessed January 7, 2014, http://www.rockefellerfoundation.org/ uploads/files/2b053b2b-8feb-46ea-adbd-f89068d59785-impact.pdf.

21. Bugg-Levine and Emerson, *Impact Investing*, 9.

22. Steven Godeke and Raúl Pomares with Albert V. Bruno, Pat Guerra, Charly Kleissner, and Hersh Shefrin, "Solutions for Impact Investors: From Strategy to Implementation," ed. Lisa Kleissner and Lauren Russell Geskos Rockefeller Philanthropy Advisors, November 2009, 10.

23. Bugg-Levine and Emerson, *Impact Investing*, 9.

24. Freireich and Fulton, *2009 Monitor Report*, 35–36.

25. Kevin Starr, "The Trouble with Impact Investing: P1," *Stanford Social Investment Review*, January 24, 2012, 22, accessed May 11, 2013, http://www.ssireview.org/blog/entry/the_trouble_with_impact_investing_part_1.

26. In a lead article in a recent edition of the Federal Reserve Bank of San Francisco's *Community Development Investment Review*, Thornley and Dailey thus call attention to their use of the term "community impact investing" rather than "impact investing" precisely in order to make clear that they are focusing on "low-income domestic markets and only to investments targeting social returns." Ben Thornley and Colby Dailey, "Building Scale in Community Impact Investing through Nonfinancial Performance Measurement," *Community Development Investment Review* 6.1 (2010): 3.

27. Bugg-Levine and Emerson, *Impact Investing*, xix.

28. This usage is also gaining ground in international circles. Thus, for example, the UK's new Big Society Capital institution refers to its field of activity as "social investment," which it defines as "the provision and use of capital to generate social as well as financial returns." See "Social Investment Is a Way of Using Capital to Generate Social Impact as Well as Some Financial Return for Investors," Big Society Capital, accessed May 11, 2013, http://www.bigsocietycapital.com/what-social-investment.

29. For the former position see, for example, Rob Schwartz, *Social Investment* (London: Clearly So, 2012). For the latter position see Friereich and Fulton, *2009 Monitor Report*, 14.

30. In the United States, the breakdown of these sources for the core nonprofit service and expressive organizations takes the following form: 10 percent from private philanthropy from all sources; 38 percent from government grants and payments; and 52 percent from private fees and payments. See Lester M. Salamon, *America's Nonprofit Sector: A Primer*, 3rd ed. (New York: Foundation Center, 2012), 39.

31. Lester M. Salamon and Stephanie Geller, "Investment Capital: The New Challenge for American Nonprofits," Listening Post Project Communiqué No. 5, Johns Hopkins Nonprofit Listening Post Project, 2006, 5, accessed July 29, 2013, http://ccss.jhu.edu/publications-findings?did=265.

32. Salamon and Geller, "Investment Capital," 8.

33. Included here were the Kentucky Highlands Investment Corporation (1968), the Massachusetts Capital Resource Company (1977), the Arkansas Capital Corporation (1985), and Kansas Venture Capital (1987), See "Kentucky Highlands Investment Corporation," Rural Housing and Economic Development Gateway, US Dept of Housing and Urban Development, accessed March 2, 2013, http://www.hud.gov/offices/cpd/economicdevelopment/programs/rhed/gateway/pdf/KentuckyHighlands.pdf; "Mass Capital, Company," Massachusetts Capital Resource Company, accessed May 11, 2013, http://www.masscapital.com/company/; "Company History & Information," Arkansas Capital Corporation Group, accessed May 11, 2013, http://arcapital.com/programs/our-history/; "Kansas Venture Capital, Inc. ("KVCI")," Kansas Venture Capital, accessed May 11, 2013, http://www.kvci.com/. I am indebted to Belden Daniels for references to these early entities.

34. These included programs such as the following: the Low Income Housing Tax Credit, which provides tax incentives for private investments in low-income housing; the 1977 Community Reinvestment Act, which made regulatory decisions on bank branching

contingent on demonstrations by banks that they were making investments in the same low-income neighborhoods from which they were extracting deposits; and tax and grant subsidies for so-called community development finance institutions, i.e., financial institutions with a primary mission of improving economic conditions for low-income individuals and communities. For more detailed discussions of these developments, see David Erickson, *The Housing Policy Revolution* (Washington, DC: Urban Institute Press, 2008); and Lean Benjamin, Julia Sass Rubin, and Sean Zielenbach, "Community Development Financial Institutions: Expanding Access to Capital in Under-served Markets," in *The Community Development Reader*, ed. James DeFilippis and Susan Saegert (New York: Routledge, 2008).

35. For a discussion of "impact investing" as an "asset class," see O'Donohoe et al., "Impact Investments," 6.

36. CGAP, "The History of Microfinance," prepared for CGAP UNCDF donor training, "The New Vision of Microfinance: Financial Services for the Poor," accessed June 11, 2013, http://www.slideshare.net/JosephSam/the-history-of-microfinance-cgap. Cited in Lisa Richter, "Capital Aggregators," in *New Frontiers of Philanthropy*, ed. Lester M. Salamon (New York: Oxford University Press, 2013).

37. "CDFI Data Project," Opportunity Finance Network, accessed February 13, 2014, http://www.opportunityfinance.net/industry/default.aspx?id=234; see also O'Donohoe et al., "Impact Investments," 80–81.

38. These concepts were first articulated by Freireich and Fulton, *2009 Monitor Report*, 32. See also Thornley and Dailey, "Nonfinancial Performance Measurement," 6.

39. This figure is adapted from one presented in Freireich and Fulton, *2009 Monitor Report*, 32. However, Freireich and Fulton assume that all social-impact investors have the same financial and social-impact expectations. In fact, however, there is reason to question this assumption, though the basic concept that some meaningful floor exists for both social and financial return for both sets of investors, and the many that fall in between, is a crucial defining one for the field.

40. "About Us," Acumen Fund, accessed August 18, 2012, http://acumen.org/.

41. Willow Impact Investors, for example, describes itself as pursuing "an investment strategy that seeks to generate market-rate returns or more, while investing in businesses that deliver tangible positive environmental impact or social benefit." The firm identifies as its "primary objective" to "deliver strong and sustainable financial returns for our investors while achieving maximum social and environmental impact." "Investment Policy," Willow Impact Investors, accessed March 2, 2013, http://www.willowimpact.com/about-us/company/investment-policy.html.

42. Adam Gromis, Impact Exchange manager, e-mail to author, September 4, 2012. See also Yasemin Saltuk, Amit Bouri, and Giselle Leung, "Insight into the Impact Investment Market: An In-Depth Analysis of Investor Perspectives and Over 2,200 Transactions," J.P. Morgan Social Investment, December 14, 2011, accessed January 8, 2014, http://www.thegiin.org/cgi-bin/iowa/download?row=334&field=gated_download_1, 8.

43. "Global Trends in Clean Energy Investment: Q4 2009 Clean Energy Fact Pack," New Energy Finance, accessed May 11, 2013, http://www.newenergyfinance.com.

44. O'Donohoe et al., "Impact Investments," 6.

45. Carmody et al., *Impact Investing in Emerging Markets*, 10; O'Donohoe et al., "Impact Investments," 34–35; Saltuk, Bouri, and Leung, "Insight into Impact Investment," 24–27.

46. For a discussion of the tool of "securitization," see Chapter 14 of this volume.

47. "Quick Facts," Community Reinvestment Fund, accessed September 1, 2012, http://www.crfusa.com/AboutCRF/Pages/QuickFacts.aspx.

48. "Flexible Capital Access Program (FlexCap): Investment Summary," Habitat for Humanity International, accessed May 11, 2013, https://www.missioninvestors.org/system/files/tools/Habitat%20for%20Humanity%27s%20FlexCAP%20summary.pdf.

49. "Fact Sheet," Blue Orchard, accessed May 11, 2013, http://www.blueorchard.com/jahia/webdav/site/blueorchard/shared/Publications%20and%20Resources/BlueOrchard%20Factsheets/0907_Fact%20sheet%202009_EN.pdf.

50. World Bank, "State and Trends of the Carbon Market," World Bank Group, 2011, 9, accessed May 11, 2013, http://siteresources.worldbank.org/intcarbonfinance/Resources. For a discussion of recent trends, including a 2013 refusal by the European Parliament to support a slowdown in the issuance of new permits in view of the drop in their price, see Stanley Reed and Mark Scott, "In Europe, Paid Permits for Pollution Are Fizzling," *New York Times*, April 22, 2013, B1.

51. Evan Weaver, "Marrying Cash and Change: Social 'Stock Markets' Spread Worldwide," *Christian Science Monitor,* August 30, 2012, http://www.csmonitor.com/World/Making-a-difference/Change-Agent/2012/0830/Marrying-cash-and-change-Social-stock-markets-spread-worldwide.

52. Carmody et al., *Impact Investing in Emerging Markets*, 60.

53. "The IDB Group: Your Partner for Impact Investing in Latin America and the Caribbean," IDB Group, accessed May 11, 2012, http://idbdocs.iadb.org/wsdocs/getdocument.aspx?docnum=36886146.

54. "About Us," NESTA, accessed May 11, 2013, http://www.nesta.org.uk/about_us; Robert Hutton, "Cameron Opens $1 Billion Big Society Bank to Fund Charities," Bloomberg, April 4, 2012, accessed May 11, 2013, http://www.bloomberg.com/news/2012-04-03/cameron-opens-1-billion-big-society-bank-to-fund-charities.html; "How We Are Funded," Big Society Capital, accessed May 11, 2013, http://www.bigsociety-capital.com/how-we-are-funded.

55. One recent estimate puts the amount of foundation assets subjected to such screens at some $60 billion in the United States, roughly 10 percent of all foundation assets, still a fairly small fraction of total foundation assets, but growing. US SIF, the Forum for Sustainable and Responsible Investment, "Report on Sustainable and Responsible Investing Trends in the United States: 2012," 2012, 54. For more detail on such "socially responsible investing," see Chapter 18 of this volume.

56. In the United States, for example, foundations are required by law to dispense at least 5 percent of the value of their assets in grants or related administrative costs in support of their approved charitable missions.

57. I am indebted to Thomas van Dyke and Shari Berenbach for identification of a number of these institutions.

58. Data on the number of foundations making PRIs and the share of qualifying distributions recently taking this form from Steven Lawrence, "Doing Good with Foundation Assets: An Updated Look at Program-Related Investments," in *The PRI Directory*, 3rd ed., ed. Foundation Center (New York: Foundation Center, 2010), xiii. Total number of private foundations in the United States from Foundation Center, *Foundation Yearbook, 2009* (New York: Foundation Center, 2010).

In an effort to promote greater use of the PRI mechanism, the Internal Revenue Service recently issued a proposed rule that would provide a broader array of examples of the types of activities that would satisfy the IRS restrictions on PRIs. Internal Revenue Service, "Notice of Proposed Rulemaking: Examples of Program-Related Investments REG-144267-11," in *Internal Revenue Bulletin: 2012-21*, May 21, 2012, accessed April 13, 2013, http://www.irs.gov/irb/2012-21_IRB/ar11.html.59 Christine Letts, William Ryan, and Allen Grossman, "Virtuous Capital: What Foundations can Learn from Venture Capitalists," *Harvard Business Review*, March–April 1997, 36–46.

60. Edna McConnell Clark Foundation "How We Work," accessed May 11, 2013, http://www.emcf.org/how-we-work/.

61. "About Us," New Profit, accessed May 11, 2013, http://newprofit.com/cgi-bin/iowa/about/9.html.

62. European Venture Philanthropy Association, *European Venture Philanthropy Directory 2010/11* (Brussels: European Venture Philanthropy Association, 2010), 15. Unlike their US counterparts, European venture philanthropy organizations combine the attributes of US venture philanthropies, which generally restrict themselves to grant funding, with what we have termed "foundations as philanthropic banks," which deploy a far wider array of financial instruments.

63. "About," The Hub, accessed October 20, 2012, http://www.the-hub.net/about.

64. "About," Opportunity Finance Network, accessed October 12, 2012, www.opportunityfinance.net/about.

65. "About Us," UN PRI, accessed October 20, 2012, http://www.unpri.org; "About Us," Social Investment Forum, accessed October 20, 2012, http://www.socialinvest.org.

66. "About Us," CGAP, accessed October 20, 2012, http://www.cgap.org/p/site/c/aboutus/.

67. "What's New in Mission Investing," Mission Investors Exchange, accessed October 20, 2012, http://www.moreformission.org; "About Mission Investors Exchange," Mission Investors Exchange, accessed October 20, 2012, https://www.missioninvestors.org/about-us; "The Origins of Mission Investors Exchange," Mission Investors Exchange, accessed October 20, 2012, http://www.missioninvestors.org/about-us/origins-mission-investors-exchange.

68. Freireich and Fulton, *2009 Monitor Report*, 12.

69. O'Donohoe et al., "Impact Investments," 17.

70. MarketsforGood, "Upgrading the Information Infrastructure for Social Change", Summer 2012, 11, accessed May 11, 2013, http://www.marketsforgood.org/wordpress/wp-content/uploads/2012/11/MarketsforGood_Information-Infrastructure_Fall-2012_.pdf.

71. "About," Kiva, accessed October 20, 2012, http://www.kiva.org/about/stats.

72. "TechSoup Global by the Numbers, Quarterly Report, October 2010," TechSoupGlobal, accessed May 11, 2013, http://www.techsoupglobal.org/press/selectcoverage.

73. "Our 2011 Annual Report Infographic," VolunteerMatch, accessed October 23, 2012, http://blogs.volunteermatch.org/engagingvolunteers/2012/06/25/our-2011-annual-report-infographic-the-story-of-you/.

74. "2011 Donor-Advised Fund Report," National Philanthropic Trust, accessed May 11, 2013, http://www.nptrust.org/images/uploads/2011%20Donor-Advised-Fund-Report%281%29.pdf.

75. Early critiques of the corporate-originated charitable funds centered on the fact that they were legally constituted as "public charities," as opposed to foundations, and thereby avoided the legal restrictions on foundations, including the restrictions requiring the payout of at least 5 percent of their assets each year as grants. As Cohen shows, however, the larger such funds have established internal procedures that encourage robust payout, and most of the funds have proved to have payout rates at least as high as those required of foundations.

76. This discussion draws heavily on Lester M. Salamon, "Privatization for the Social Good: A New Avenue for Global Foundation-Building," *The Privatization Barometer*, July 2010, 48–54; and Lester M. Salamon, *Philanthropication thru Privatization: Building Permanent Assets for Social Progress* (Milan: il Mulino, 2014). Available for download at: p-t-p.org.

77. Examples of these other foundations include Deutsche Bundesstiftung Umwelt, Stiftung Baden-Wurtemberg, and Stiftung Innovation (Rhineland-Palatinate).

78. In 1991, for example, Italy converted its 88 nonprofit and quasi-public savings banks into joint stock companies, but left ownership of all of the stock in the resulting joint stock banks in what used to be the charitable arms of the prior banks, creating 88 foundations. By the time the foundations were authorized to sell this stock in 1994, its value exceeded €24 billion (or US$31 billion at current exchange rates). Since then the assets of these "foundations of banking origin" have climbed further, producing a philanthropic revolution that has transformed Italy from a philanthropic backwater into one of the leading philanthropic nations in the world as measured by the per capita size of its philanthropic endowments. As of 2008, the combined assets of Italy's foundations of banking origin exceeded €50 billion, or some US$65 billion. Fondazione Cariplo and Compagnia di San Paolo, two of the largest of these foundations, both had assets in excess of €9 billion, or approximately US$12 billion, as of 2008, which put both of them ahead of such major US foundations as the Rockefeller Foundation ($3.1 billion in assets as of 2008), and the Ford Foundation, America's second largest ($9.1 billion in assets as of 2008). Data on US foundations from Foundation Center, *Foundation Yearbook: Facts and Figures on Private and Community Foundations, 2008 Edition* (New York: Foundation Center, 2008), 18. Data on Ford Foundation: "About," Ford Foundation, accessed February 6, 2010, http://www.fordfound.org/about. A virtually identical process occurred even earlier in New Zealand, when a series of New Zealand nonprofit banks were converted into stock companies, and the shares placed into a network of 12 community trusts. More recently, the purchase of a number of nonprofit health insurance organizations and hospitals by for-profit firms in the United States has led to the creation of almost 200 so-called health conversion foundations, including the $3.6 billion California Endowment. California Endowment, Form 990PF, 2012, accessed September 29, 2013, http://www.calendow.org/uploadedFiles/homepage/HeadeFooterMisc/03152013-TCE-99 0PF-3-31-2012.pdf.

79. "Global Gathering," Toniic, accessed October 19, 2012, http://toniicglobalgathering. eventbrite.com/.

80. "History," Living Cities, accessed October 19, 2012, http://www.livingcities.org/ about/history/.

81. "About," Angel Investors Network, accessed October 19, 2012, http://www. angelinvestors.net/about.

82. For an analysis of the use of varied tools of action, including varied financial tools of action, in the governmental sphere, see Lester M. Salamon, *The Tools of Government: A Guide to the New Governance* (New York: Oxford University Press, 2002).

83. Lawrence, "Doing Good," xvi.

84. Sarah Cooch and Mark Kramer with Fi Cheng, Adeeb Mahmud, Ben Marx, and Matthew Rehrig, "Compounding Impact: Mission Investing by US Foundations," FSG Social Impact Advisors, March 2007, 17, accessed January 7, 2014, http://www.fsg.org/ Portals/0/Uploads/Documents/PDF/Compounding_Impact.pdf?cpgn=WP%20DL%20 -%20Compounding%20Impact.

85. Saltuk, Bouri, and Leung, "Insight into Impact Investment," 11–12. Two years later, however, this same source reported that the share of impact investors surveyed who reported using a private equity instrument exceeded the share reporting use of debt by 83 percent to 66 percent, though no information was provided on the numbers of transactions of each type that these different investors made. See Yasemin Saltuk, Amit Bouri, Abhilash Mudaliar, and Min Pease, "Perspectives on Progress: The Impact Investor Survey," J.P. Morgan Social Finance, January 7, 2013, accessed January 8, 2014, http://www.

jpmorganchase.com/corporate/socialfinance/docu-
ment/207350_JPM_Perspectives_on_Progress_2013-01-07_1018749_ada.pdf, 9.

86. "USAID, Global Impact Investing Network Join to Create East Africa Agricultural
Investment Fund," SeedStock, accessed May 11, 2013, http://seedstock.com/2011/10/05/
usaid-global-impact-investing-network-join-to-create-east-africa-agricultural-
investment-fund/.

87. Financial Markets Series, "Bond Markets 2011," The City UK, 2011, 1, accessed May
11, 2013, http://www.thecityuk.com/assets/Uploads/BondMarkets2011.pdf.

88. "Bonds," IFFIm, accessed May 11, 2013, http://www.iffim.org/bonds/.

89. "Community Investment Note," Calvert Foundation, accessed May 11, 2013, http://
www.calvertfoundation.org/invest/how-to-invest/community-investment-note.

90. Some securitization transactions use a financial instrument called a collateralized
debt obligation (CDO) instead of a bond as the vehicle for raising capital from investors.
CDOs can be backed by a variety of types of loans and can be sold in "tranches" that carry
different maturities, interest rates, and risk associated with them.

91. Cooch and Kramer, "Compounding Impact," 17. A later study of 74
mission-investing foundations by the Foundation Center found half of these institutions
making mission-related equity investments, but mostly in publicly traded equities, though
a third reported making private equity investments of the sort typically available to small,
social enterprises. Steven Lawrence and Reina Mukai, "Key Facts on Mission Investing,"
Foundation Center, 2011, 3, accessed January 8, 2014, http://foundationcenter.org/
gainknowledge/research/pdf/keyfacts_missioninvesting2011.pdf.

92. Saltuk, Bouri, and Leung, "Insight into Impact Investment," 11.

93. Saltuk et al., "Perspectives on Progress," 9.

94. Joshua Humphreys, "Sustainability Trends in US Alternative Investment," US SIF
Foundation: The Forum for Sustainable and Responsible Investment, 2011, 3, accessed
October 19, 2012, http://www.investorscircle.net/accelsite/media/3195/Sustainability%20
Trends%20in%20US%20Alternative%20Investments%20Report.pdf.

95. This set of venture capital funds is supported by a trade association called the
Community Development Venture Capital Alliance (CDVCA)

96. "Equity Investments," Kentucky Highlands Investment Corporation, accessed
November 3, 2012, http://www.khic.org/equity.html. Another example of the same type
of fund is CEI Ventures, a for-profit subsidiary of a 26-year-old community development financial institution headquartered in Wiscasset, Maine, that makes equity
investments in promising companies providing quality jobs for low-income people in
northern New England. The firm's Coastal Ventures II fund raised $20 million from 30
institutional and individual investors for equity investments in companies that
"promote socially beneficial products and services, opportunities for women and
minorities, environmentally friendly business practices, and the enrichment of
distressed and rural communities." "Overview," CEI Ventures, accessed November 3,
2012, http://www.ceiventures.com/.

97. "About Us," Aavishkaar, accessed November 4, 2012, http://www.aavishkaar.in/
about-us/.

98. Humphreys, "Sustainability Trends."

99. US Social Investment Forum Foundation, "Sustainable and Responsible Investing
Trends," 11; Eurosif, "European SRI Study: 2012," Eurosif, 2012, 63, accessed May 11, 2013,
http://www.eurosif.org/research/eurosif-sri-study/sri-study-2012.

100. Social Enterprise UK, *Fightback Britain: A Report on the State of Social Enterprise
Survey 2011* (London: Social Enterprise UK, 2011), 15.

101. A "matched bargain market" is a private trading platform, typically handled by an
investment company, through which social-purpose investors can sell their shares to other

investors looking to enter a particular market. One example is that provided by the Ethical Property Company (EPC) in the UK. This social venture offers office space for social-purpose organizations in the UK. It finances its property acquisitions from equity capital raised from the sale of shares. Its shares are not sold on the London Stock Exchange or the Alternative Investment Market, however. Rather, its 1,357 shareholders bought their shares through a matched bargain market guided by Stocktrade, a division of the stock-broker firm of Brewin Dolphin Limited, which also handles all trades and is responsible for using all reasonable effort to match willing buyers and sellers both for EPC and other social ventures that have chosen to use this route to financing their operations as well. "How to Invest," Ethical Property, accessed November 4, 2012, http://www.ethicalproperty. co.uk/howtoinvest.php.

102. "Investment Approach," Aavishkaar, accessed November 4, 2012, http://www. aavishkaar.in/about-us/investment-approach/.

103. For information on the HCT Group, see "Welcome to HCT Group," HTC Group, accessed November 4, 2012, http://www.hctgroup.org.

104. The goal is to reduce the 60 percent recidivism rate for such offenders and thereby save the government millions of pounds. If the funded social sector organizations providing the wraparound rehabilitation services succeed in reducing one-year postrelease reconvictions by at least 7.5 percent among this population compared to a control group, then the investors will get their money back with 2.5 percent interest. If the performance exceeds this target, investors will be rewarded with a return higher than this, up to a maximum of 13 percent. Based on information available in: Social Finance, "A New Tool for Scaling Impact: How Social Impact Bonds can Mobilize Private Capital to Advance Social Good," 2012, accessed November 4, 2012, http://www.socialfinance.org.uk/ resources/social-finance/new-tool-scaling-impact-how-social impact-bonds-can-m obilize-private-capita; "Home," Social Finance, accessed November 4, 2012, http://www. socialfinance.uk/print9.TO ADVANCE S.

105. MDRC, a New York–based employment and training organization will manage the program and make payments to a set of nonprofit organizations that will carry out the program. For Goldman Sachs to break even on its payments to MDRC, the program will have to reduce recidivism on the part of program participants by 10 percent compared to a control group. Greater success will save the city more money and accrue a higher return for Goldman Sachs. "Mayor Bloomberg, Deputy Mayor Gibbs, and Corrections Commissioner Schriro Announce the Nation's First Social Impact Bond Program," City of New York, Office of the Mayor, accessed November 4, 2012, http://www.nyc.gov/html/ index.html.

106. Jim Roth, Denis Garand, and Stuart Rutherford, *The Landscape of Microinsurance in the World's 100 Poorest Countries* (Appleton, WI: Microinsurance Center, 2007).

107. On the International Labour Organization's Microinsurance Innovation Facility, see "Microinsurance Innovation Facility," International Labour Organization, accessed May 11, 2013, www.ilo.org/microinsurance.

108. Swiss Reinsurance Company *Microinsurance—Risk Protection for 4 Billion People* (Zurich: Swiss Re, 2010); Craig Churchill and Michael J. McCord, "Emerging Trends in Microinsurance," in *Protecting the Poor: A Microinsurance Compendium*, vol. 2, ed. Craig Churchill and Michal Matul (Geneva: International Labour Organization and Munich Re Foundation, 2012).

109. For a discussion of this and other innovations mentioned here, see Churchill and Matul, *Protecting the Poor*.

110. For further detail on these initiatives, see Chapter 17 of this volume.

111. O'Donohoe et al., "Impact Investments," 5.

112. Eurosif, "European SRI Study: 2012," 63. The seven distinct types of socially responsible investment mechanism identified by Eurosif include sustainability themed investment, best-in-class investment selection, norms-based screening, exclusion of holdings from investment universe; integration of ESG factors in financial analysis, engagement and voting on sustainability matters, and impact investment.

113. Eurosif, "European SRI Study: 2012," 7.

114. Quoted in Lester M. Salamon, *Rethnking Corporate Social Engagement: Lessons from Latin America* (Sterling, VA: Kumarian Press, 2010), 33.

115. See, for example, David Vogel, *The Market for Virtue: The Potential and Limits of Corporate Social Responsibility* (Washington, DC: Brookings Institution Press, 2005), 37.

116. McKinsey and Company, *And the Winner Is. . . Capturing the Promise of Philanthropic Prizes* (n.p.: McKinsey and Co., 2009), 16.

117. Lester Brown, *World on Edge: How to Prevent Environmental and Economic Collapse* (New York: Norton, 2011).

118. Brown, "World on Edge," PowerPoint presentation available at "Books," Earth Policy Institute, accessed April 14, 2013, http://www.earth-policy.org/books/wote.

119. Landon Thomas Jr., "As the Bailouts Continue in Europe, So Does the Flouting of Rules," *New York Times* November 29, 2012, B3.

120. David Jolly and Jack Ewing, "Unemployment in Euro Zone Reaches New High," *New York Times*, November 30, 2012, accessed May 11, 2013, http://www.nytimes.com/2012/12/01/business/global/daily-euro-zone-watch.html.

121. Salamon, *America's Nonprofit Sector*, 39.

122. David Bornstein, *How to Change the World: Social Entrepreneurs and the Power of New Ideas* (New York: Oxford University Press, 2004), 1.

123. Lester M. Salamon, "The Rise of the Nonprofit Sector," *Foreign Affairs* 73.4 (July–August 1994): 109–22.

124. See Bornstein, *How to Change the World*, for examples of such actors. On the "global associational revolution," see Salamon, "Rise of Nonprofit Sector."

125. See, for example, Carlos Borzaga and Jacques Defourny, *The Emergence of Social Enterprise* (New York: Routledge, 2001); Alex Nichols, *Social Entrepreneurship: New Models of Sustainable Social Change* (Oxford: Oxford University Press, 2006); Dennis R. Young, Lester M. Salamon, and Mary Clark Grinsfelder, "Commercialization, Social Ventures, and For-Profit Competition," in *The State of Nonprofit America*, 2nd ed., ed. Lester M. Salamon (Washington, DC: Urban Institute Press, 2012).

126. Peer Stein, Tony Goland, and Robert Schiff, *Two Trillion and Counting: Assessing the Credit Gap for Micro, Small, and Medium-Size Enterprises in the Developing World* (Washington, DC: International Finance Corporation and McKinsey & Company, 2010), 1.

127. O'Donohoe et al., "Impact Investments," 39.

128. Although, as Chapter 5 notes, only three-tenths of 1 percent of all foundations— less than 200 institutions in all out of more than 75,000—have made any PRI in a typical recent year, and only eight-tenths of 1 percent of foundation charitable distributions are taking this form, the fact remains that the PRI program created a significant cadre of foundations skilled in making charitable investments in low-income housing, community development, minority housing, and other social-purpose activities. Data on the number of foundations making PRIs and the share of qualifying distributions recently taking this form from Lawrence, "Doing Good," xiii. Total number of private foundations in the United States from Foundation Center, *Foundation Yearbook, 2009*. For further description of the revolution in housing policy that these initiatives fostered, see Erickson, *The Housing Policy Revolution*.

129. "Mission and History," Calvert Foundation, accessed January 2, 2013, http://www.calvertfoundation.org/index.php?option=com_content&view=article&id=66&Itemid=76;

"Acumen Fund Ten Year Report, 2001–2011," Acumen, 2011, 1, accessed January 2, 2013, http://www.acumenfund.org/uploads/assets/documents/Acumen%20Fund%20Ten%20 Year%20Report%202001%20-%202011a_3wcsNw56.pdf.

130. "About Us," Acumen Fund, accessed December 4, 2012, http://www.acumenfund. org/about-us.html.

131. Prahalad, *Fortune at the Bottom.*

132. Charly and Lisa Kleissner, and Raúl Pomares, personal interviews with author, March 26, 2010 and January 23, 2012.

133. Bishop and Green, *Philanthrocapitalism*, 6.

134. Atul Dighe, "Demographic and Technological Imperatives," in Salamon, *The State of Nonprofit America*; William Strauss and Neil Howe, *Millennials Rising: The Next Great Generation* (New York: Vantage, 2000).

135. "Home Page," Net Impact, accessed October 1, 2012, http://netimpact.org/.

136. "About Us: Our Team," Willow Impact Investors, accessed August 10, 2012, http:// www.willowimpact.com/about-us/.

137. Data on rates from *New York Times*, January 4, 2013, B8. "Battered investor syndrome" comment from Ed Yardeni, founder of Yardeni Research, as quoted in *New York Times*, January 2, 2013, B1.

138. O'Donohoe et al., "Impact Investments," 11, 31–34; Saltuk, Bouri, and Leung, "Insight into Impact Investment," 16–24.

139. "Investing for Social & Environmental Impact: A Design for Catalyzing an Emerging Industry," Monitor Institute, accessed May 11, 2013, http://www.monitorinstitute.com/impactinvesting/documents/InvestingforSocialandEnvImpact_FullReport_004. pdf.

140. O'Donohoe et al., "Impact Investments," 17.

141. "Benefit corporations" are businesses that meet especially demanding standards of corporate purpose, accountability, and transparency. B Lab provides a rating system for such corporations and awards a "B-corporation" label to companies that demonstrate adherence to one of a number of third-party rating systems for corporations. "About B-lab," B Lab, accessed February 5, 2013, http://www.benefitcorp.net/about-b-lab.

142. "How GIIRS Works," B Lab, accessed February 5, 2013, http://www.giirs.org/ about-giirs/how-giirs-works.

143. O'Donohoe et al., "Impact Investments," 72; E.T. Jackson and Associates, "Accelerating Impact: Achievements, Challenges and What's Next in Building the Impact Investing Industry," Rockefeller Foundation, 2012, xvi, accessed January 8, 2014, http://www. rockefellerfoundation.org/uploads/images/fda23ba9-ab7e-4c83-9218-24fdd79289cc.pdf.

144. Thornley and Dailey, "Nonfinancial Performance Measurement," 16.

145. O'Donohoe et al., "Impact Investments," 22. More recent data suggest some improvement in the penetration of nonfinancial impact measurement, though the phrasing of some survey questions makes it difficult to assess this development fully. Thus, a recent survey of impact investors found only 33 percent reporting that they considered "standardized impact metrics" "very important," though another 65 percent were willing to rate them "important" or "somewhat important." Similarly, only 30 percent of responding impact investors reported using "third-party ratings" for "all potential investments," though another 60 percent indicated that they use them "if available." Saltuk et al., "Perspectives on Progress," 16.

146. Lester M. Salamon, 2011, "What Would Google Do? Designing Appropriate Social Impact Measurement Systems," *Community Development Investment Review* 7.2 (December 2011): 43–47. Applied to the field of social-impact measurement, this approach has been termed "constituency voice" and developed formally by David Bonbright through an organization called Keystone. "Constituency Voice," Keystone, accessed February 9, 2013, http://www.keystoneaccountability.org/analysis/constituency.

147. SEEDCO, *The Limits of Social Enterprise* (New York: SEEDCO Policy Center, 2008).

148. E. T Jackson and Associates, "Accelerating Impact," xiii.

149. The $8.0 billion figure comes from a survey of 99 investors identified by the Global Impact Investment Network and J.P. Morgan Social Finance and reporting managing $US10 million or more of impact investment capital as of the end of 2012. The $4.4 billion and $2.5 billion figures come from a similar survey of 52 impact investment intermediaries undertaken by J.P. Morgan in late 2011. See Saltuk et al., "Perspectives on Progress," 3–4; and Saltuk, Bouri, and Leung, "Insight into Impact Investment," 5.

150. "Federal Reserve Statistical Release, Z.l, Flow of Funds Accounts of the United States, March 2011," Board of Governors of the Federal Reserve System, accessed May 11, 2013, http://www.federalreserve.gov.releases/z1/201000311.

151. Michael Drexler and Abigail Noble, preface to "From the Margins to the Mainstream: Assessment of the Impact Investment Sector and Opportunities to Engage Mainstream Investors," World Economic Forum, September 2013, accessed January 9, 2014, http://www3.weforum.org/docs/WEF_II_FromMarginsMainstream_Report_2013.pdf, 3.

152. US SIF Foundation, "Sustainable and Responsible Investing Trends," 11.

153. For discussions of factors limiting the growth of the social-impact investing industry, see Katie Hill, *Investor Perspectives on Social Enterprise Financing* (London: City of London, Big Lottery Fund, Clearly So, 2011); E. T. Jackson and Associates, "Accelerating Impact," xiv, 19–20. For J.P. Morgan survey results, see Saltuk, Bouri, and Leung, "Insight into Impact Investment," 5. Although continued progress was reported in a 2013 report by J.P. Morgan Social Impact, it was notable that the most the authors could claim was that 58 percent of the respondents to their survey were able to report that "more than a few investors" were "already designing an impact investment strategy" but that only 4 percent of respondents could report that "many investors" were doing so. Saltuk et al., "Perspectives on Progress," 18.

154. Saltuk, Bouri, and Leung, "Insight into Impact Investment," 4. A similar complaint surfaced in second place in a 2013 publication drawing on a similar survey. See Saltuk et al., "Perspectives on Progress," 9.

155. Venturesome, *Access to Capital: A Briefing Paper* (London: CAF Venturesome, 2011).

156. As E.T. Jackson and Associates put it gingerly in an assessment of the state of the impact-investing industry: "While the impact investing industry has, understandably, been focused largely on its supply side efforts to mobilize and place capital, its leading organizations have done relatively less work on actively developing the capacity of ventures to effectively prepare for capital infusion and to use it effectively." E.T. Jackson and Associates, "Accelerating Impact," xv.

157. Harvey Koh, Ashish Karamchandani, and Robert Katz, "From Blueprint to Scale: The Case for Philanthropy in Impact Investing," San Francisco: Monitor Group, April 2012, 10, accessed February 2, 2013, http://www.mim.monitor.com/downloads/Blueprint_To_Scale/From%20Blueprint%20to%20Scale%20-%20Case%20for%20Philanthropy%20in%20Impact%20Investing_Full%20report.pdf.

158. Koh, Karamchandani, and Katz, "From Blueprint to Scale," 4–6.

159. Koh, Karamchandani, and Katz, "From Blueprint to Scale," 15–16.

160. Koh, Karamchandani, and Katz, "From Blueprint to Scale," 18–19.

161. Starr, "Trouble with Impact Investing." See also Laura Hattendorf, "The Trouble with Impact Investing: P2," *Stanford Social Innovation Review* 14 (April 18, 2012): 14; Mary Tingerthal, "Securitization," Chapter 14, this volume.

162. See, for example, Lester M. Salamon, "Of Market Failure, Voluntary Failure, and Third-Party Government: Toward a Theory of Government-Nonprofit Relations in the Modern Welfare State," in Lester M. Salamon, *Partners in Public Service: Government-Nonprofit Relations in the Modern Welfare State* (Baltimore: Johns Hopkins University Press, 1995), 33–52.

163. Bugg-Levine and Emerson, *Impact Investing*, 90.

164. US SIF Foundation, "Sustainable and Responsible Investing Trends," 11.

165. US SIF Foundation, "Sustainable and Responsible Investing Trends," 54; "Highlights of Foundation Yearbook, 2011 Edition," Foundation Center, accessed February 10, 2013, http://foundationcenter.org/gainknowledge/research/pdf/fy2011_highlights.pdf.

166. Usman Hayat, "Do Investment Professionals Know about Impact Investing?" CFA Institute, July 2013, cited in World Economic Forum, *From Margins to Mainstream*, 5.

167. World Economic Forum, *From Margins to Mainstream*.

168. Bugg-Levine and Emerson, *Impact Investing*, 151.

169. E.T. Jackson and Associates, "Accelerating Impact," xviii; Freireich and Fulton, *2009 Monitor Report*, 47–48; Koh,, Karamchandani, and Katz, "From Blueprint to Scale," 7–9.

170. Freireich and Fulton, *2009 Monitor Report*, 47; O'Donohoe et al., "Impact Investments," 76; Ben Thornley, David Wood, Katie Grace, and Sarah Sullivant, *Impact Investing: A Framework for Policy Design and Analysis,* Pacific Community Ventures and the Initiative for Responsible Investment at Harvard University, January 2011., 15–16, Accessed September 10, 2013, http://hausercenter.org/iri/wp-content/uploads/2010/12/Impact-Investing-Policy_FULL-REPORT_FINAL.pdf UN Development Program, *Human Development Report* (New York: UN Development Program, 2011), v; Shirley Sagawa, "A Policy Agenda for the New Frontiers of Philanthropy," Chapter 24, this volume.

171. Freireich and Fulton, *2009 Monitor Report*, 47.

172. E.T. Jackson and Associates, "Accelerating Impact," 29.

173. Emilie Goodall and John Kingston, "Access to Capital: A Briefing Paper," CAF Venturesome, 2009, 4, accessed February 10, 2013, http://www.marmanie.com/cms/upload/file/CAF_Venturesome_Access_to_Capital_0909.pdf.

174. E.T. Jackson and Associates, "Accelerating Impact," 21–27.

175. "About: How It Works," Toniic, accessed February 24, 2013, http://toniic.com/about/how-it-works/.

176. Freireich and Fulton, *2009 Monitor Report*, 46.

177. *Encyclical Letter Caritas In Veritate, of the Supreme Pontiff, Benedict XVI, to the Bishops Priests and Deacons, Men And Women Religious, the Lay Faithful, and All People of Good Will, on Integral Human Development, in Charity and Truth*, para. 46, accessed May 5, 2011, http://www.vatican.va/holy_father/benedict_xvi/encyclicals/documents/hf_ben-xvi_enc_20090629_caritas-in-veritate_en.html.

Suggested Readings

Bugg-Levine, Antony and Jed Emerson. *Impact Investing: Transforming How We Make Money While Making a Difference*. San Francisco: Jossey-Bass, 2011.

Lucy Carmody, Benjamin McCarron, Jenny Blinch, and Allison Prevatt. *Impact Investing in Emerging Markets*. Singapore: Responsible Research, 2011.

Freireich, Jessica, and Kathryn Fulton. "Investing for Social and Environmental Impact: A Design for Catalyzing an Emerging Industry." Monitor Institute, January 2009.

Prahalad, C. K. *The Fortune at the Bottom of the Pyramid: Eradicating Poverty through Profits*. Philadelphia: Wharton School Publishing, 2004.

PART II

NEW ACTORS

CHAPTER 2

CAPITAL AGGREGATORS

Lisa Richter

THE CRANE ARTS BUILDING IS a red-brick structure whose four stories hum with creative activity. The former bath fixtures factory and horse stable now houses 39 artist workspaces and studios that have become important cultural destinations for artists and audiences. Temple University's Tyler School of Art offers fellowships there, providing artists with a stipend, access to the facilities, and gallery space. An active schedule of events featuring exhibitions, arts fundraisers, and performances draws people into the neighborhood and has spurred additional local development.

Not long ago, the building was one of many in disrepair that told a story of hard times for the area. Once the heart of Philadelphia's manufacturing industry, this area reported unemployment rates that reached more than double the US average and a poverty rate that was over 33 percent. Fortunately, however, the building was located in a community served by The Reinvestment Fund (TRF), a federally certified community development financial institution (CDFI) created in 1985 with a mission to transform neighborhoods and create opportunity for economically challenged families and communities.

Now, with over $700 million in assets under management, TRF has honed a strategy of "applying capital, insight and expertise at the point of impact—the location and moment where they can do the most good."[1] Its 25-year track record reflects skillful aggregation of public and private subsidy funds with flexible investment capital placed by socially motivated "impact investors," all of which leverage conventional capital for organizations and projects that could not attract such capital on their own. TRF's financing for quality affordable housing, public charter schools, child care, fresh food markets, and cultural institutions such as the Crane Arts project has helped to jump-start activity in both abandoned communities and emerging markets such as green energy.

Defining the Actor

Defining Features

TRF is an example of a "capital aggregator," an important type of institution to be involved in supporting low-income communities. Capital aggregators are a type of financial institution that serves the function of pooling capital to provide loans, equity, and other forms of financing to households, businesses, organizations, and projects, often with a geographic focus. Functionally speaking, capital aggregators are financial intermediaries or middlemen: they raise capital from investors and provide financing to a range of entities.

Social-impact investment capital aggregators, which are the focus of this chapter, perform this middleman role to finance activities that serve some social purpose, such as benefiting the poor, preserving the environment, or promoting social innovation. They raise capital from foundations and like-minded investors (social-impact investors, collectively) who seek some combination of social as well as financial return and often leverage these resources by using them to attract other, larger sources of capital to the sectors they serve. In addition, they typically combine their financing with capacity-building services for their investees and make efforts to influence public policy and capital markets by demonstrating the creditworthiness and efficacy of the projects, organizations, and populations they finance.[2]

Capital aggregators in the social-impact investing field differ from foundations, which essentially utilize their own assets to promote socially desirable objectives, typically without expectation of financial return. Social-impact capital aggregators, by contrast, typically mobilize others' resources, often aggregating resources from several different sources—private individuals, foundations, insurance companies, pension funds, government, and others, most of which require some measure of financial return. So, too, social-impact investment capital aggregators differ from "socially responsible investors" in that they tend to channel investment into currently underserved markets, whereas the socially responsible investors attempt to steer investments among firms in already well-served markets.[3] Finally, social-impact investment capital aggregators differ from venture philanthropy aggregators, which pool grant dollars to fund innovative social change through structures that adapt the accountability framework of the capital markets to track social—but not financial—return on investment.

Design Features and Major Variants

Social-impact capital aggregators can take many forms. These forms vary along four major dimensions: (a) the investees or target market being served; (b) the corporate structure of the aggregator; (c) the structure, form, and terms of the investments made; and (d) the investors from which the aggregators secure their capital. In each case, form follows function as defined by what is best suited to the underserved needs of the target market. The discussion below outlines the variations along each of these dimensions.

Target Market or Population

Most social-impact capital aggregators were founded for the purpose of providing capital to an underserved target market, which could be a geographic area, business sector, or population that otherwise lacks access to capital on reasonable terms. For example, an aggregator might pool-capital to invest in the small to medium-sized business sector across many developing economies, such as the Grassroots Business Fund, whose mission is to "help build and support High Impact Businesses that provide sustainable economic opportunities to millions of people living at the base of the economic pyramid."[4] Alternatively, an aggregator might invest in a range of community development organizations, including affordable housing developers, small business lenders, and social services providers, within a particular geographical area, such as Boston Community Capital.[5] Capital aggregators have also been known to focus on emerging social enterprise sectors, such as community health centers, charter schools, clean tech, and sustainable agriculture. An example is Primary Care Development Corporation, which extends loans to community health centers primarily in New York state.[6]

Corporate Structure

Capital aggregators can take any of a number of organizational forms (see Table 2.1). These range from familiar financial institutions, such as banks, credit unions, and venture capital funds, to more specialized loan funds and microfinance institutions. Such entities are organized under a range of legal forms—for-profit, nonprofit (nongovernmental or NGO), or cooperative. For example, Southern Bancorporation is a US, for-profit regulated bank holding company with a primary mission of community development in distressed rural areas of Arkansas and Mississippi. As a capital aggregator, its primary source of capital is the insured deposits that impact investors place in Southern's regulated bank subsidiaries, which these banks relend to local small businesses, NGOs, and households that otherwise lack access to credit.[7] Root Capital (further described below) is a nonprofit loan fund that lends to rural small businesses and cooperatives throughout the developing world.[8] Self-Help Credit Union is one of over 250 member-owned cooperative credit unions in the United States that focus their lending on low-income members and their communities.[9] While there is debate about the role that earning a profit should play in a capital aggregator's strategy, the for-profit structure can enable greater and more rapid access to capital with which to pursue a social or environmental mission, while at the same time putting such a mission focus in potential jeopardy.

Aggregators may operate multiple affiliates with different corporate structures under a coordinated, or holding company, structure. These may pool different types of grant and investment capital or execute complementary community development functions. Many aggregators operate both for-profit and nonprofit affiliates, called hybrid structures.[10] The nonprofit affiliates may attract grant and subsidized capital to provide financing, technical assistance, or other market-building services. For example, Pacific Community Ventures is a nonprofit organization that provides a range of business consulting and networking services to grow small businesses that create jobs for low-income individuals in Northern California.[11] It also provides social-impact tracking for venture capital funds that seek social as well as financial returns (the so-called double bottom line). Its for-profit affiliate, PCVFund, is a venture capital fund that invests in qualified growth businesses that work with the nonprofit affiliate.[12]

Capital aggregators include both regulated and unregulated institutions. Banks and credit unions are regulated depository institutions, which carry regulator-imposed requirements for capital, asset quality, management qualifications, earnings, liquidity, and sensitivity.[13] Government insurance for deposits accompanies this regulation, making it possible for banks and credit unions to offer investors risk-free savings and cash management accounts within certain limits.[14] While depository regulations may limit the flexibility of bank lending in some respects, the deposit insurance vastly expands the capacity of these institutions to attract low-cost funds for use in their investment activities.

TABLE 2.1 CAPITAL AGGREGATOR DESIGN FEATURES AND VARIANTS

Capital aggregator by asset class & organization type	Target market (investees)	Financing for the target market by asset class	Investors	Corporate form[a]	Expected financial return		
					N/A	Below-market	Market
Grants							
Venture philanthropy	High-performing nonprofit organizations with convincing plan to scale	Grant that serves as equity or growth capital	Foundations, other philanthropists	NGO/ unregulated	X		
Debt (Loans)							
Microlenders	Indigenous microlending organizations, microentrepreneurs	Loans for relending to microentrepreneurs, direct microloans. Bonds backed by securitized microloans.	Foundations, faith-based investors, banks, pension funds, multilateral organizations, individuals	Varies; may be NGO, for-profit, regulated. unregulated		X	X
Loan funds	Affordable housing organizations, nonprofit organizations, small businesses	Loans for relending to borrowers that cannot access affordable debt from conventional lenders	Foundations, faith-based investors, banks, individuals	NGO/ unregulated		X	
Bond funds	Community real estate projects, often financed with government guarantee; can include debt securitizations such as for housing, micro- or small business loans	Long-term, fixed interest rate debt for projects such as affordable housing or nonprofit facilities.	Foundations, faith-based investors, banks, pension funds.	For-profit / Regulated			X
Insured Deposits							
Banks	Small businesses, range of nonprofit and faith-based organizations, households	Loans for range of small business, nonprofit organization and household needs, often using government guarantees.	Foundations, faith-based investors, insurance companies, selected, socially motivated banks and individuals	For-profit/ regulated		X	X

Credit unions	Households; some micro- and small businesses	Loans for household and micro- or small business needs; may use government guarantees	Nonprofit, member-owned financial cooperative	Cooperative/ regulated		X
Private Equity						
Venture capital	Emerging companies with innovative product ideas	Equity capital and/or convertible debt for seed or early stage business launch	Foundations, universities, corporations; angels (individuals)	For-profit / may be regulated Less common: NGO	X	X
Growth funds	Expansion stage companies with tested products	Equity capital and/ or convertible or subordinated debt for business expansion	Foundations, universities, insurance companies, pension funds, selected, socially motivated banks	For-profit / may be regulated	X	X
Buyout funds	Established companies, to improve efficiency and profitability.	Equity capital and/ or convertible or subordinated debt for the purchase of businesses.	Foundations, universities, insurance companies, pension funds, selected, socially-motivated banks.	For-profit / May be regulated	X	
Real assets						
Commodities or commodity funds	Properties or commodities, or funds that purchase such assets	Equity for the purchase of physical assets, or ownership interests in partnerships that purchase such assets	Foundations, universities, insurance companies, pension funds, selected, socially motivated banks	For-profit / may be regulated	X	X

[a] Some capital aggregators can be structured as either NGOs or for-profit entities, and either regulated or unregulated. This includes loan funds, microfinance institutions, and venture or private equity funds.

Note: An X indicates which category of financial return the particular type of aggregator is seeking.

Other types of capital aggregators may or may not be regulated, depending upon the type of investing they will carry out, the number of investors, and other factors. While unregulated aggregators have greater flexibility in structuring and managing their loan and investment portfolios, high-performing entities increasingly subscribe to principles of self-regulation, investment discipline, and performance reporting promulgated by industry trade groups such as the Opportunity Finance Network for US-based CDFIs or the MIX Market for global microfinance institutions. Adherence to such principles is an important tenet of many efforts to expand social-impact investing as an industry.

Structure, Form, and Terms of Investments

Aggregators can use a variety of investment vehicles or asset classes, such as equity, loans, guarantees, deposits, or physical assets, to structure the investments they make in social-purpose activities. Each asset class is best suited to a particular function. Equity investments, for example, are best suited to fueling growth in for-profit businesses. From a legal standpoint, they convey an ownership interest to the investor and therefore cannot be used to finance traditional NGOs, which, as public charities, cannot offer private ownership stakes.

The investment terms, including the expected financial return, are described as market-rate or below market-rate on a risk-adjusted basis. Investment asset classes carry varying risk and associated expected return levels. In general, investors expect a higher return for investments that carry greater risk. The actual return on specific investments may over- or underperform expected returns or benchmarks for the asset class, however.[15]

Sources of Capital

Effective capital aggregators are skilled in combining public and private grants and other forms of credit enhancement to mitigate the risks of financing transactions that generate important social impact but fall outside conventional financial risk-return parameters. The investors from whom different capital aggregators secure their investment capital include a range of investor types with varying risk-return expectations. Many, such as pension funds, are subject to fiduciary responsibility guidelines that require them to seek market or near-market rates of return on a risk-adjusted basis. Others, however, are willing to accept below-market rates of return to accelerate or deepen social impact and may, in fact, have regulatory supports for doing so. This includes US private foundations, which are authorized to make program-related investments (PRIs) that can be counted toward the foundation's required annual charitable distribution requirement. The Tax Code of 1969 defines private foundation PRIs as investments that meet the following criteria:

- The primary purpose is to accomplish one or more of the foundation's exempt purposes.
- No significant purpose is the production of income or appreciation of property.
- No purpose is influencing legislation or taking part in political campaigns on behalf of candidates.[16]

Other types of foundations (such as community and corporate foundations) and social-impact investors, including faith-based investors, banks, and individuals, may make a portion of their investments on similar terms. Some adapt the "PRI" terminology, while others refer to these investments as "impact first" investments that prioritize social or environmental outcomes and accept a relatively low expected return on a risk-adjusted basis.[17]

The capital aggregator's ability to attract capital is often limited by geographic or sector priorities among investors. Thus, a US bank may invest only in capital aggregators that provide financing in its assessment area under the federal Community Reinvestment Act (CRA); a foundation may invest only in aggregators who provide financing in a programmatic area of interest, such as education.[18]

Some capital aggregators have developed specifically to fill such niche investors' interests. For example, the Arizona Multi-bank Community Development Corporation (CDC) was created specifically to enable a consortium of banks to fulfill their obligations under the CRA to invest a portion of their funds in low- to moderate-income areas from which they draw their deposits. Eligible borrowers include affordable housing, small business development, and nonprofit organizations operating in these areas. The Partners for the Common Good Loan Fund was created to aggregate capital from faith-based investors, including orders of women religious, to provide financing to social enterprises throughout the United States and abroad. Impact Community Capital in California was created to aggregate capital from insurance companies in order to invest in projects benefiting low- to moderate-income communities and populations.

Scope and Scale

Social capital aggregators have a rich history, stretching back to the fund created by the Irish author Jonathan Swift in the early 1700s to lend to the "industrious poor," tradesmen whose creditworthiness he evaluated by reputation and the ability to secure two guarantees.[19] Benjamin Franklin created a similar loan fund in the United States.[20] German farmers founded credit unions in the 1860s to finance unmet agricultural credit needs.[21] African Americans formed similar institutions as early as 1890 and more generally in the 1930s to provide credit to African American farmers in the South who otherwise lacked access to it.[22]

Overview

Despite these early precursors, it was not until the 1960s that more comprehensive efforts were launched to address the financial needs of the poor through the creation of new capital-aggregating institutions. But the field has grown considerably since then. Capital aggregators now operate throughout the world. Collectively, the assets under management of these institutions likely exceed $300 billion, including approximately $30 billion in US CDFI assets, over $65 billion in global microfinance assets, over $188 billion in clean-tech funds, approximately $20 billion in triple-bottom-line equity funds, and other social-impact investment capital aggregators that do not fall under these categories.[23]

While the growth has been significant, however, the field remains fragmented and limited in relation to the problems it is trying to address. Indeed, it is difficult to estimate the overall volume of global or US impact investments under management. Looking at US investors alone, components include, but are not limited to, foundation program-related investments; foundation market-rate impact investments; CRA-motivated bank lending; domestic pension and insurance fund economically targeted investments (ETIs), faith-based investments, as well as pension investments outside the United States, such as TIAA-CREF's investments in microenterprise.[24]

The range of these segments suggests the fragmentation of the marketplace. Each represents a set of variations in programmatic priorities (social objectives, investment themes, or sectors); geographic targeting; required investment size (from less than $10,000 per investment for small foundations to more than $150 million for large state pension funds); asset class (which informs investor preferences because of investors' need for diversification or liquidity management); and targeted rates of financial return.[25]

In addition to being fragmented, the social-impact investor marketplace remains small relative to both the capital needs of underserved communities and the assets under management in conventional capital markets. Most social-impact investor segments also lack systematic tracking. For some that are tracked, the reporting tends to be in the form of annual originations, versus sector assets under management. Thus, the Foundation Center reported $742 million in PRI originations between 2006 and 2007 ($371 million per year on average), based upon an analysis of 173 foundations that made at least one PRI of $10,000 or more in those same years. These originations represented less than 1 percent (0.8 percent) of the $91.9 billion of all charitable distributions by the foundations during the same time period, and just over one-tenth of 1 percent (0.11 percent) of US foundation estimated average aggregate assets of $648 billion for the same period.[26]

A more recent Foundation Center report found that about 14.1 percent of respondents to its January 2011 Foundation Giving Forecast Survey engage in some form of social-impact investing. Among these, approximately one-half hold PRIs with below market-rate risk-adjusted return expectations, 28 percent hold both PRIs and impact investments with market rates of risk-adjusted return, and 22 percent hold only social-impact investments with market rates of risk-adjusted return.[27] Although the survey suggests growing use of social-impact investing among foundations, it does not quantify foundation social-impact-investing assets outstanding. It also acknowledges persistent variations in how foundations track social-impact investments, with the result that reported market-rate holdings may include screened "socially responsible investments" that are generally excluded from the sector's totals by social-impact-investing analysts.

Available tracking reflects similar challenges in scale of social-impact-investing volume relative to conventional investing in other segments. For example, US federal regulatory agencies reported 2010 aggregate bank CRA loan originations of $40.3 billion (against an estimated $12 trillion in aggregate FDIC-insured banking assets at year-end 2010), and a 2007 report of US pension fund ETIs reported cumulative volume of $11 billion through 2007 (against estimated 2007 US aggregate pension assets of $15 trillion).[28]

Types of Capital Aggregators

Given this fragmentation, it is necessary to examine each of the different segments separately to gain a clear sense of the industry, both domestically in the United States and internationally. The following sections do so for some of the major industry segments.

Community Development Financial Institutions

In the United States, the emergence of socially oriented capital aggregators was significantly aided by the War on Poverty of the 1960s, which supported the creation of a network of community development corporations (CDCs) that could deploy capital in development projects in low-income communities. By the early 1970s, a new class of capital aggregator had emerged in the United States and abroad to provide credit to poor and excluded populations as part of a community development strategy. In the United States, these entities would later be called community development financial institutions, or CDFIs. They aggregated capital from socially motivated institutional and individual investors to reinvest in underserved urban and rural communities, often ethnic minority communities with high rates of poverty and disinvestment.[29]

From the outset, these institutions ranged in corporate form from regulated banks and credit unions to unregulated loan funds, venture capital funds, and microenterprise funds. The banks, credit unions and loan funds provided a range of debt; the insured depositories (banks and credit unions) provided debt and financial services (savings and payment services); and the venture capital funds provided equity and equity-like debt to communities and populations that were historically underserved. For example, Urban Partnership Bank (formerly ShoreBank), a development bank created in 1973 to serve the disinvested African American communities on Chicago's South Side, extended loans for homeownership and rental housing rehabilitation, small businesses, and community NGOs and churches, while also providing retail financial services.[30] The Lower East Side Peoples Federal Credit Union was organized in 1986 to mobilize local, nonpredatory savings accounts that support local personal, business, and housing loans.[31] Kentucky Highlands was created as a venture capital firm in 1972 to reduce poverty in rural Appalachia by developing substantial businesses to produce job opportunities for citizens, and developing or discovering entrepreneurs to lead these firms.[32]

By the early 1990s, CDFIs had established a track record of successful financing. They achieved a critical victory in 1994 when the Clinton administration created the Community Development Financial Institutions Fund (CDFI Fund), a federal agency under the US Department of Treasury to both certify and provide competitive financial awards to qualifying CDFIs. The CDFI Fund formally defined a CDFI as an organization that meets these criteria:

- Is a legal entity at the time of certification application
- Has a primary mission of promoting community development
- Is a financing entity
- Primarily serves one or more target markets
- Provides development (capacity-building) services in conjunction with its financing activities

- Maintains accountability to its defined target market
- Is a nongovernment entity and not under control of any government entity (tribal governments excluded).[33]

The CDFI Fund has contributed significantly to the growth of US capital aggregators that are certified as CDFIs. Many CDFI Fund award programs require private-sector matches or other investments. The CDFI Fund's Bank Enterprise Award program rewards insured depository institutions such as banks and savings and loans for making investments in CDFIs, and such investments also assist the banks in meeting their responsibilities under the CRA. Over the years, the CDFI Fund has added programs that further incentivize investment in CDFIs, including the New Markets Tax Credit program, which provides tax incentives for CDFIs and similar intermediaries to finance commercial and business projects in low- to moderate-income communities.[34] Other examples include the Capital Magnet program and the Healthy Food Financing Initiative.[35] In addition to benefiting from these programs managed by the CDFI Fund, CDFIs attract and deploy capital in conjunction with numerous other public-sector programs that provide credit enhancement or investor protection against loss, including the Low Income Housing Tax Credit, and programs of the US Small Business Administration, Department of Agriculture, Bureau of Indian Affairs, and Health Resources Service Administration.

As a result of both CDFI Fund investment, leveraging of public-sector credit enhancement programs, and the private-sector investments that this leveraged, CDFIs have attracted billions of dollars in new assets. They also gained recognition as effective partners to conventional financial institutions in meeting underserved capital, financial services, and capacity-building needs. As of January 31, 2012, there were 972 certified CDFIs in the United States, including banks, credit unions, loan funds, venture funds, and microenterprise organizations operating with a primary mission of community development in distressed and underserved markets.[36] As of December 31, 2008, the industry reported $29.4 billion in assets under management.[37]

Double- and Triple-Bottom-Line US Capital Aggregators

While the early capital aggregators typically attracted concessionary capital to finance community development initiatives, such as affordable housing and small business development, by the 1990s aggregators began to raise capital with broader double- (DBL) and triple-bottom-line (TBL) objectives, that is, with the goal of delivering market-rate financial returns, along with social and/or environmental benefits. Notable early examples were Calvert Ventures, which makes direct investments in companies "run by visionary entrepreneurs who have identified profitable ways of addressing society's needs."[38] Another example is Economic Innovation International (EII), which seeks to "produce risk-adjusted market rates of return for large, repeat institutional investors (the first bottom line) by partnering with community stakeholders to create measurable jobs, wealth and community revitalization for low-income residents in emerging markets (the second bottom line) and generate green development for the sustained health of the planet (the third bottom line)"; EII claims to have generated $150 billion in triple-bottom-line fund assets during its 40 years of existence.[39] The creation of trade associations such as Investors' Circle[40] helped to set the stage for the later emergence of numerous DBL and TBL funds in clean-tech, real estate, and other sectors.

International Capital Aggregators

A robust set of capital aggregators has also emerged internationally. Many of these evolved from informal savings and credit organizations that operated for centuries in the developing world. Formal models began to emerge as early as 1895 with the opening of entities such as the Indonesian People's Credit Banks (BPR) or the Bank Perkreditan Rakyat, which later became the largest microfinance system in Indonesia.[41]

The foundation for today's successful microfinance industry was laid in the 1960s and 1970s. ACCION International, one of the leaders in this field, was founded in 1961 in Caracas, Venezuela, to address poverty in Latin America's cities through microloans to the poor. Beginning in the 1970s, now well-known programs in South Asia began extending microloans to groups of borrowers with income-generating microbusinesses. Focused primarily on women borrowers, programs such as SEWA Bank (founded in 1973 by the Self-Employed Women's Association in India) and later the Grameen Bank, BRAC, ASA, and Proshika, combined lending with social and business supports, including some forced-savings programs.[42]

The emerging microcredit programs demonstrated excellent repayment rates among poor borrowers, particularly women. They also showed that the poor would pay the rates of interest needed for the lending programs to cover their costs. Through high repayment and cost-recovery interest rates, lenders began to achieve long-term sustainability and broad market penetration. To accelerate these trends, associations such as Women's World Banking and the Small Enterprise Education and Promotion (SEEP) Network promoted field learning, development of common reporting templates, and best practices.[43]

Impressed with the potential of microfinance as a poverty alleviation strategy, significant donor-led and investor-led initiatives emerged to formalize, strengthen, and scale the sector.[44] In 1995, a Consultative Group to Assist the Poor (CGAP) was created at the World Bank to support the development and evolution of the microfinance field.[45] That same year, Profund Internacional was created as the first venture capital fund dedicated to investing in microfinance.[46] This was followed in 1996, by the creation of MicroRate, the first microfinance rating agency, and in 1998, by the formation by Dexia and BlueOrchard, the first microfinance investment vehicles with market returns.[47] In 2002, CGAP created the Microfinance Information Exchange (MIX) with a broad goal of "strengthening the microfinance sector through objective data and analysis."[48] MIX has continued to promote transparency by gathering standardized reporting data from microfinance institutions (MFIs) around the world."[49]

This financial and technical support laid the groundwork for leading MFIs to develop sustainable commercial operations backed by global multinational and private investors. In 1992, ACCION International helped found BancoSol in Bolivia, the world's first commercial bank dedicated solely to microfinance. By 1997, BancoSol became the first microfinance institution to issue dividends to shareholders, and today it offers its more than 70,000 clients a range of financial services, including savings accounts, credit cards, and housing loans.[50] ACCION has replicated the BancoSol model through more than 15 ACCION-affiliated organizations that are now regulated financial institutions.[51] In 2007, one of these, Banco Compartamos of Mexico, raised $467 million in an initial public offering.

The microfinance sector continues to broaden its product offerings in response to the experience that permanent poverty alleviation calls for multifaceted interventions. The emerging financial-inclusion marketplace offers savings, insurance, payment services, and remittances, along with microcredit, in the hope that these products can stabilize families and set the stage for broader progress toward meeting the Millennium Development Goals for ending poverty by 2015.[52]

Accompanying the growth of microfinance in recent decades has been the emergence of specialized intermediaries serving the capital and information needs in the small and growing business sector (SGB), that is, small grassroots businesses such as coffee farmer cooperatives and artisan associations that are generally considered too small and risky for commercial banks but too large for microfinance.[53] Examples of such capital aggregators include Root Capital, the Acumen Fund, Bamboo Finance, and Bridges Ventures. Collectively, these and similar aggregators have raised and deployed hundreds of millions of dollars of capital to developing economies.

Additional capital aggregators in the form of so-called funds of funds have now emerged to invest in microfinance funds, SGB funds, and regulated depository institutions with a development focus. For example, Equator Capital Partners (formerly ShoreCap) raised an initial $22 million for investment in a portfolio of 15 regulated microfinance and small business banks in 15 countries, generating profitable exits or partial exits from eight institutions. These portfolio companies now represent over $3 billion in total assets, with more than $3.5 billion in cumulative development loans to over 1.8 million borrowers from 492 financial service outlets since Equator's original investment. Plans are underway for expansion into other countries.[54]

Rationale

The basic rationale for the existence of social-impact investment capital aggregators lies in certain "failures" or limitations of the conventional capital markets. Two of these limitations have been particularly salient. The first arises from risk-return calculation methodologies and preferences among conventional capital providers that create *gaps* in funding for certain classes of investees. The second arises from the high *transaction costs* facing potential investors willing to serve these classes of investees and the resulting need for some intermediary that can reduce these costs.

Overcoming Market Gaps

So far as the first of these market failures is concerned, social-impact investment capital aggregator types exist to fill credit, capital, financial service, and financial information needs of any individual, household, small business, or NGO that falls outside the risk-return parameters of conventional financial institutions. Conventional institutions typically avoid providing direct financing for these segments because they are perceived to carry too much risk or the transactions are too small to justify the transaction cost.

Historically, racial and gender discrimination were significant factors in the failure of conventional institutions to provide equitable access to financing, and such bias continues to adversely affect both the availability and the terms of financing in many settings. In addition, conventional lenders often avoid potential investees who may lack assets or credit history; have early-stage needs (such as the predevelopment phase of a real estate project); and depend on innovative approaches to problem-solving (which carry the risk of untested, new business lines). They may also avoid geographies that lack developed markets, the rule of law, or concentrated demand for investment or "deal flow" (including US rural areas).

Thus, examples of financing needs that have often been unmet by conventional financial institutions include the following:

- Any loan to any individual or owner of a business who is from an ethnic minority group, or in some geographies, any individual who is female[55]
- Loans to impoverished or low- to moderate-income individuals, households, and entrepreneurs, who may lack assets to secure a loan (collateral), a formal credit history or experience in accessing and using credit
- Loans in low- to moderate-income urban, rural, and reservation communities, which include communities of concentrated poverty and often, though not always, correspond to loans in communities of color[56]
- Loans to, and investments in, emerging segments, the capital structure or business model for which may be unfamiliar, such as charter schools in the United States and fair-trade agricultural cooperatives in developing markets
- Equity and equity-like investment in the range of urban and rural small businesses that have growth and job creation potential but are unlikely to grow to a scale that will meet the return expectations of commercial venture and private, equity-capital investors
- Small transactions in general, which coincide with the size range of most household, small business, or NGO loans in low- to moderate-income and rural communities

As described elsewhere in this chapter, capital aggregators succeed in providing financing to these underserved segments by combining their financing with financial and capacity-building services. In structuring their financing, aggregators combine subsidies, grants, and various forms of credit enhancement with investment capital to be able to prudently and cost-effectively deliver capital to small, emerging, and otherwise marginalized household and organizational investees.

In responding to these capital market gaps, capital aggregators have increasingly augmented traditional community development financing approaches by incorporating a more holistic approach that includes investments in human development (child care, education, workforce development, and criminal justice reform), family economic security (savings, insurance, and asset building), and "green" initiatives aimed at better positioning the poor to achieve health and financial security. Examples include mixed-income transit-oriented development; facilities for quality early child care, high-performing public charter schools, and other educational programs; social services-enriched housing; community health centers that incorporate environmental sensitivity; and innovative approaches to reducing recidivism among incarcerated individuals.

Such projects bring services, jobs, and strengthened social connections to low- to moderate-income communities and residents.

Reducing Transaction Costs

So far as the second market failure is concerned, the relatively small scale of many of the investees aided by capital aggregators, and the fragmented distribution of investors willing to make capital available to them, combine to make the market for linking these investors to these investees highly imperfect. Capital aggregators function to overcome this imperfection. They offer a cost-effective means for tapping the resources of social-impact investors— large, small, and with varied programmatic and geographic priorities—and making them available to a range of qualified yet underserved households and organizations in need of financing.

Capital aggregators' effectiveness in providing financing lowers the cost and risk for their investors, while providing a convenient, safe, and sound access point for households and organizations in need of financing who may lack any access to financing and financial services, or lack such access on nonpredatory terms.

Basic Mechanics

In order to operate effectively, a capital aggregator typically must carry out six basic tasks: (1) determine social and financial investment objectives; (2) generate capital from investors, which typically requires establishing credibility, determining an investment structure, and targeting potential investors; (3) identify suitable investees and structure the investments in them; (4) provide ancillary services to ensure success; (5) monitor and report to investors on investment performance; and (6) repay investors as agreed with expected returns. The discussion below describes these basic tasks in a bit more detail.

Determining Investment Objectives

In both the conventional and the philanthropic context, the capital aggregator's success is gauged by the degree to which it can raise investor capital, then deploy the capital in financing activities that meet or exceed investor financial return objectives.[57] In both contexts, achieving this success depends largely upon the capital aggregator's knowledge of the opportunities and risks in the sector in which it is investing.

In the philanthropic and social-impact investing context, capital aggregators take on the additional function of meeting social and environmental, and not just financial, investment objectives. This requires as rigorous a business plan to identify how the aggregator intends to achieve its planned social impact as is required for demonstrating how it plans to achieve its anticipated financial return.

Raising Capital

Once settled on investment and social objectives, the capital aggregator must set about raising the capital needed to fulfill these objectives. A key step is to produce evidence that it has the organizational capabilities, including a board of directors and management team with the skill, market knowledge, strategy, and organizational resources—including initial aggregation of capital—sufficient to meet investors' objectives.

Given the fact that capital aggregators typically serve markets that have previously received little investment, the aggregator must undertake a business plan to demonstrate the presence of qualified demand for financing and any other services, as well as the aggregator's strategy and competitive advantage for meeting that demand and the structure or mixture of capital (i.e., debt, equity, guarantees, as well as grants in some cases) it requires to do so.

Once that is set, the aggregator can determine the investment products with which it can raise a suitable amount and type of capital to fund its planned financing activities in the target market.

This includes structuring product offerings in asset classes with risk-adjusted return levels that match the financing needs and repayment capacity of the aggregator's target investees, while also including fees, shared financial gains, and/or a "spread" (the difference between the interest rate the aggregator pays for capital and the interest rate that it charges borrowers) to cover the aggregator's costs. The aggregator may seek to aggregate a so-called capital stack or structured financing pool that includes layers (also called tranches) of capital with different risk-return expectations. Typically, the stack includes a first-loss tranche, which is often grant-funded; one or more intermediate or subordinated debt tranches, which absorb any losses that exceed the amount of the first-loss tranche; and finally, a senior debt tranche, which absorbs only those losses that exceed the full amount of the first-loss tranche plus any intermediary layers. The aggregator may also create liquidity structures, such as lines of credit or secondary market arrangements to sell some of its loans as a means to generate cash for either additional financing activities or repaying investors.[58]

Upon structuring a capital offering, the aggregator must identify target investors and formulate strategies for marketing its investment products to them. Here capital aggregators face an investor marketplace that, while growing, remains fragmented and still relatively small in total assets under management, as reported in the "Scope and Scale" section above. While capital aggregators play a critical function in absorbing relatively large investments of capital that they can redeploy in much smaller investments at the community level, the variations in investor requirements can make it difficult to identify a critical mass of investors with aligned objectives. This poses significant challenges for the aggregator's task of identifying a sufficient number and size of investors whose priorities match its investment objectives.

Investing Capital

Ultimately, the success of a capital aggregator depends not simply on its success in raising capital. At least as important is its skill in finding suitable opportunities in which to invest the capital it raises. The aggregator's execution of the investing function will naturally vary according to its target market and strategy, such as, for example, whether it will provide small loans to microentrepreneurs, or facilities (building) loans to NGOs. Nevertheless, there are significant commonalities involving some key steps, including sourcing, performing due diligence, negotiating investment terms, closing investments, monitoring and reporting on investment performance, and repaying invested capital with expected returns—all of which must be consistent with the aggregator's loan or investment policy. Further detail on these functions is outlined below.

Sourcing

The sourcing function (also called deal pipeline development) calls upon the capital aggregator's market knowledge and networks of leaders within the target market to identify investment opportunities that offer both the greatest potential social impact and a reliable source of repayment with some agreed-upon level of financial return (yield).[59]

Due Diligence

Due diligence involves assessing the creditworthiness or repayment capacity of an organization or a proposed project. Depending upon the type of investment being considered, the due diligence process can be extremely rigorous and time-consuming, involving judgments about a prospective investee's capital adequacy, asset quality, management, earnings, liquidity, and sensitivity to interest rate and currency fluctuations, among other factors. This so-called CAMELS analysis is adapted from bank regulators, who developed it to evaluate the safety and soundness of banks. It is widely used to assess the creditworthiness of a range of financial institutions and other organizational types.

Additional due diligence judgments apply to particular types of organizations and projects. For example, due diligence on equity investments in growth businesses must review both the competitiveness of the firm's products or services and the adequacy of patent or other intellectual property rights documentation. Due diligence on construction projects must evaluate the sponsor's ability to secure local zoning or building code approvals, as well as any potential subsidies, such as US Low Income Housing Tax Credits or New Markets Tax Credits.

Closing the Investment

Care must also be taken in the process of negotiating and closing investment agreements to make certain that both social and financial objectives are documented. Investment documents may contain terms or covenants that restrict the use of proceeds to charitable purpose or call for best efforts to generate particular social outcomes, in addition to a range of financial performance requirements.

Providing Ancillary Services

In addition to offering capital, most aggregators also offer both financial and capacity-building ancillary services that build demand for their financing and strengthen investee skills and financial position. This also helps to manage the risk of inexperienced investees. For example, capital aggregators may offer or link their customers to providers of safe financial services, such as credit unions and other providers of savings and payment products, insurance, and access to any government benefits that may enhance financial stability, such as the Earned Income Tax Credits for low-income families in the United States. Such financial services are a particularly prominent component of capital aggregators supporting international microfinance, where access to savings and insurance are recognized as necessary buffers against economic shocks.[60]

In addition to financial services, capital aggregators offer a broad range of capacity-building services that they customize to their target investees. These services, too, help to mitigate the risk of providing financing to inexperienced investees. For small and growth businesses, aggregators may offer business planning and marketing assistance, capitalization planning, management assistance, mentoring, access to business networks and CEO forums, and specialized expertise and strategic advice.[61] Similar types of assistance are offered to NGOs and small microenterprises.

In addition to offering capacity-building services directly, many aggregators participate in networks that focus on building the capacity within their sectors and the impact-investing field generally. For example, many US CDFIs belong to the Opportunity Finance Network, a trade association whose mission is to "lead CDFIs and their partners to ensure that low-income, low-wealth, and other disadvantaged people and communities have access to affordable, responsible financial products and services."[62] Among global capital aggregators, many microfinance institutions participate in the MIX, SBG lenders and investors participate in the Aspen Network of Development Entrepreneurs (ANDE), and socially motivated banks participate in the Global Alliance for Banking Values.[63]

Monitoring and Reporting on Investment Performance

Investors increasingly demand in-depth reports on capital aggregator financial and social-impact performance. To generate these reports, the capital aggregator must monitor investee performance on a regular basis to provide the needed assurance to investors that its investments are achieving expected social and financial investment objectives. Typically, the capital aggregator gathers financial reporting data from its investees at least quarterly. It may more frequently monitor certain types of investments, such as real estate projects under construction, equity investments in growth companies, and microfinance borrowing groups. Quarterly portfolio monitoring compares the financial performance of investments to investment covenants, organizational budgets, past-period performance and, often, peer benchmarks. Social-impact investment capital aggregators have adapted many portfolio monitoring protocols for financial performance from the conventional investment arena, including risk-rating investment portfolios designed to assess the adequacy of loan loss reserves. Lenders generally use the risk ratings as a basis for calculating needed additions to their loan loss reserves. When circumstances cause a loan's odds of repayment to deteriorate, the capital aggregator typically intensifies the monitoring process, often requiring monthly financial reporting and regular telephone or other communications.

Capital aggregators that invest equity (versus debt) follow somewhat different procedures. Given the speculative nature particularly of venture investments, funds expect to lose approximately a third of their original investments, break even or achieve return of principal on a third, and make significant gains on a third. To hedge risk, they typically make their investments in stages, beginning with very small amounts and adding "follow-on" investments only when firms are meeting milestones or appear likely to do so with a capital infusion.

In addition to financial reporting, capital aggregators perform social-impact reporting. This is typically on an annual basis, although it may be more frequent.[64] Social metrics are as varied as the range of foundation, bank, and other impact investor mission, programmatic, and geographic interests. Thus, a foundation interested in increasing access to clean water in the developing world may require reports of water plants or pumps installed as a result of investment, as well as increase in the number of households with access. A bank with CRA obligations to lend in low- to moderate-income communities in the United States may require reports of affordable housing units built, small businesses financed, and net new jobs created by census tract within its assessment area.

In addition to reports on measurable outputs, impact investors frequently seek analyses of investment outcomes (changes in conditions in the target market), as well as impact (changes that would not have occurred "but for" the capital aggregator's investment). Such analyses are generally much more difficult and costly to prepare. As such, they remain an area for continued research and development of more efficient methods.[65]

Aggregators typically supply investors with annual reports, including audited financial statements and some form of social-impact reporting. Many capital aggregators have investors that are larger aggregators (funds of funds). The smaller capital aggregators must provide detailed quarterly financial reporting and at least annual social-impact reporting to their larger aggregator investors.

Repaying Invested Capital with Expected Returns

The final step in a capital aggregator's management of its investments is to repay investor principal (the original amount invested), as well as any yield (interest, dividends, or capital appreciation, net of fees).

As noted, capital aggregators structure the asset class, terms, and pricing of their investment products to match the form and cost of funds they need to pursue their social objectives. This produces variation in the form, time horizon, and certainty of the returns that capital aggregators deliver. For example, Triodos Bank in the Netherlands offers a range of deposit products that fuel its "More green, Less greed" lending programs throughout Europe and the developing world.[66] It typically pays interest over the life of the deposit, and returns investor principal upon demand (for fully liquid accounts) or at maturity (for term accounts). Current interest rates range from 0.10 percent to 3.75 percent, depending upon the deposit amount and term.[67]

Although the impact-investing industry continues to grow, many capital aggregators remain capital constrained. To deal with this problem, venture capital funds typically require "lock-up periods" (commitments) of at least five to seven years. For those that are capitalized with debt, the implication is that, if they repay their investors as agreed when their debt capital comes due, they may be required to reduce their financing activities. Often social-impact investors will renew their debt capital commitments in order to ensure continued financing by high-performing aggregators. However, this is a suboptimal solution. Additional capital is needed in the marketplace in order to ensure investor liquidity while also enabling high-performing aggregators to attract new investors and continue to grow.

Operational Challenges

Capital aggregators face a range of operational challenges. Broadly speaking, they can be grouped under five headings. First, capital aggregators operate within a fragmented impact-investing marketplace for which the organizing infrastructure is still under development. Second, aggregators are relatively small by capital markets standards, and focus on markets that are perceived to be risky. Third, the number and range of market-tested investment opportunities remains limited, and access to them highly imperfect. Fourth, the recent economic downturn has presented additional challenges, including the contraction of available capital sources, and some loss of investor confidence in financial innovation and complexity. Fifth, there is uncertainty about the regulatory environment and a need for updating certain enabling regulations, including the CRA. The discussion that follows elaborates on these key challenges.

Underdeveloped Infrastructure

Although the emerging social-impact investment marketplace continues to bring forth investors with a wide range of social and financial objectives on the supply or "buy" side, along with an equally wide range of organizations and projects seeking capital on the demand or "sell" side, the market infrastructure for organizing this growing, complex ecosystem of sources and uses of capital remains in the early stages of development. Current constraints and emerging developments include the following:

- Lack of accessible sources of information on potential investment opportunities, particularly for those that are not publicly traded. A number of web-based clearinghouses and exchanges for social-impact investing are under development, as described elsewhere in this volume, but these are still somewhat embryonic.[68]
- Lack of systematic financial and social performance data on social-impact investments, including those by the range of capital aggregators. Since capital aggregator investments are often privately held, readily accessible, public information on performance remains limited. In addition, most social-impact measurement is currently based upon outputs, whereas impact investors often seek further evidence of outcomes and impact that would not have occurred without impact investment. In the absence of such data, investors and investment advisors have difficulty both identifying investments that fit their social and financial criteria and making the case that particular investments are achieving either financial returns that are comparable to conventional investments, or social benefits that justify lower financial returns.[69]
- Lack of financial modeling and communications on potential social-impact investing returns that can persuasively make the case for moderate but stable returns on investments across asset classes. Such modeling could help to allay what some refer to as a "false dichotomy" that impact investors must trade off financial for social return.
- Lack of regulatory systems or enforcement with the flexibility to ensure the safety and soundness of financial institution operations

and protect consumers from predatory products, including protecting productive institutions whose intense mission focus on disadvantaged target markets may on rare occasions such as the recent economic crisis produce unusually high concentrations of risk.

- Limited understanding of the value proposition of capital aggregation among some philanthropic investors, who may choose to make direct versus capital aggregator investments based upon a belief that they can only achieve impact through direct relationships with the community-based organizations and entrepreneurs who are the end users of capital.

- Lack of a sufficient cadre of professionals who possess the requisite combination of mission orientation, market knowledge, and financial skill to manage the range of institutional functions that the expanding social investing industry requires. Graduate business schools are increasing their offerings in this area, but the supply or recruitment of talent remains constrained, particularly talent representative of the cultural diversity of the communities that social-impact investing aims to serve.

Small Scale and Perceived Riskiness of Potential Social-Impact Investments

Challenges related to the small scale and perceived risk associated with capital aggregator financing activities include the following:

- High transaction costs relative to the size of transactions in underserved markets. Cultivating qualified demand requires both extensive capacity-building and deal-structuring to incorporate credit enhancements, both of which add costs.

- Difficulty in attracting equity or equity-like capital that can enable capital aggregators to maintain strong balance sheets and net worth, while also leveraging capital to expand impact and provide investor liquidity.

- Fragmentation of the investor marketplace based upon varying geographic and programmatic priorities, which can make it difficult to raise capital in needed volumes.

Limited Qualified Deal Flow

Given capital aggregators' focus in underserved market segments and geographies, they frequently take on the related challenges of working with inexperienced investment prospects and cultivating latent demand among organizations or individuals who may not yet be aware of the benefits of obtaining financing to advance their goals. The implications for capital aggregators include these:

- Limitations in both the number and size of transactions that are investment-ready at any given moment

- Limited ability in many segments or geographies to aggregate demand for capital sufficient to absorb the large investment volumes that major institutional investors (e.g., large foundations and pension funds) typically seek to place

- A need for grant or other resources to support capacity-building efforts in order to prepare prospective investees for investment and cultivate latent demand for capital

Impact of the 2008 Financial Crisis

Although the 2008–9 financial crisis produced a questioning of core assumptions about how profit should be generated and risks managed in the conventional capital markets, and the economic stimulus produced an influx of funding for certain capital aggregator projects, the downturn also limited the scale and flexibility of many impact-investing capital sources. For example:

- Bank failures and consolidations tightened credit criteria at banks and other conventional institutions, and the reduction of corporate profits for a period of time limited the supply of capital to finance affordable housing, commercial real estate, and nonprofit facilities in low-income communities.
- Public-sector programs that provide the cash flow or credit enhancement for community-based health, human service, and other projects have been significantly reduced or are at risk of reduction.
- Investors demonstrated some skittishness about structured investment products in the aftermath of the subprime crisis, resulting in requirements for higher levels of credit enhancement.[70] While structured finance (capital stacks) got a bad name in that crisis, it remains an effective tool for capital aggregators seeking to extend financing to fundamentally creditworthy but underserved borrowers.

Constraints on Policy Supports for Capital Aggregators

The history of social-purpose capital aggregation in the United States makes clear the importance of public policy incentives such as the CDFI designation and awards, the regulatory provisions of the CRA, and tax credit programs such as the Low Income Housing Tax Credit and New Markets Tax Credit in promoting social-impact investing. In the aftermath of the financial crisis, a heightened focus on risk management and containing public-sector deficits, along with partisan debates on the appropriate role of financial regulation, threaten to limit both the policy supports and financial resources needed to spur continued development of this field, at least in the United States. For example, partisan forces in the United States have worked to undermine CRA by suggesting that its requirements for bank lending in low- to moderate-income areas precipitated the global financial crisis. This is doubly troubling in view of the fact that trends in the conventional financial services delivery system, such as the increasing popularity of online versus branch-based banking and the rise of nonbank financial-service companies, have convinced many advocates of the need for a revision and extension of the basic CRA requirements.[71] For example, many financial services customers in low- to moderate-income communities purchase services through mortgage and insurance companies, securities firms, large credit unions, and nondepository affiliates of banks.[72] Many advocates believe that some or all of these firms should be subjected to CRA or similar community reinvestment requirements. In the meantime, competing claims for public-sector financial resources and moves to eliminate special tax incentives created uncertainty regarding the reauthorization and funding of programs with a strong community investment track record, such as the New Markets Tax Credit. In the context of a policy framework organized around the concept of "too big to fail," some have argued for an alternative concept of "too important to fail" to guide treatment of key organizations that provide credit and financial services to otherwise underserved low- to moderate-income and minority communities.

Track Record and Overall Assessment

In the approximately 40 years during which capital aggregators have developed as formal financial institutions worldwide, they have amassed significant accomplishments:

- An estimated $300 billion in assets under management by over 3,000 capital aggregators worldwide, including US CDFIs, global microfinance institutions, global clean-tech funds, and other aggregators.
- An impressive track record of performance in basic financial terms:
  - Through 2008, capital aggregators achieved robust, consistent compound annual growth rates, including 10 percent for US CDFIs for the five years from 2004 to 2008, over 20 percent for global microfinance institutions during the same period, and reported rates in the range of 30 to 40 percent for clean tech.[73]
  - Loan performance has generally been strong: Net loss rates were under 1 percent for CDFIs for the period 2000 to 2008. While these escalated to 1.78 percent as of the end of 2009, they remained under the comparable charge-off rate of 2.49 percent at FDIC-insured banks and have since begun to come down.[74] Net loan losses at microfinance institutions at year end 2009 were 0.7 percent, which is in line with generally low historical loss rates for those microfinance institutions that self-report to the Microfinance Information Exchange over a period of years.[75]
- Strong indications of social impact, albeit through metrics that have yet to be standardized. For example:
  - The 495 CDFIs tracked in the CDFI Data Project invested $5.53 billion in fiscal year 2008, which financed and assisted businesses and microenterprises that created or maintained 35,624 jobs; financed the construction or renovation of 60,205 units of affordable housing; and provided 16,405 responsible mortgages to first-time and other homebuyers.[76]
  - In 2009, certified CDFI banks demonstrated so-called median Development Loan Intensity for housing loans in low-to moderate-income neighborhoods that was over 3.5 times greater than the median for all domestic banks, based upon federal Home Mortgage Disclosure Act data. CDFI banks demonstrated so-called median Development Deposit Intensity for deposits in low- to moderate-income neighborhoods that was over five times greater than the median score for all domestic banks, based upon FDIC data.[77]

- Microfinance institutions reached over 86 million borrowers with loans of an average size of $1,588; these institutions served 95.8 million voluntary savers.[78]

- A track record of continued innovation to better serve the financing and related needs of poor and vulnerable customers, as well as to support environmental sustainability at large. Such innovation has led capital aggregators to enhance their financing services with capacity-building and to incorporate environmental sustainability principles into their core business. It also enabled them to develop novel substitutes for conventional collateral, credit reports, and identity documentation. Going forward, the field is making increasing use of technology to both evaluate and transact business.
- A growing marketplace of impact investors and investment advisors interested in going beyond negative screens to generate proactive change and receptive to a range of reliable financial returns combined with measurable social returns. There has been continued growth of networks to serve these investors with information, training, and peer collaboration leading to co-investment.
- Ongoing and important efforts at industry self-regulation, as seen in the membership criteria of certain US CDFI associations (Opportunity Finance Network and Housing Partnership Network), voluntary performance reporting in several microfinance networks, and voluntary participation in such rating services as the CDFI Assessment and Rating Service (CARS) and MicroRate.

At the same time, as capital aggregators have developed, important operating challenges have emerged, as noted previously. Among the most important are these:

- Constrained ability to provide investor liquidity
- Continued need for subsidy to entice investors, support investee capacity-building, and continue development of the impact-investing market infrastructure
- Social-impact measurement protocols that remain largely individualized to particular capital aggregators, often as required by their investors, although efforts are underway to standardize and streamline an approach and to improve methods for capturing outcomes along with outputs
- A need for improved communications to make the case for social-impact investing generally and capital aggregators in particular

In the aftermath of a global financial crisis that called into question conventional wisdom regarding trade-offs between financial and social return, capital aggregators and the broader field of social-impact investing offer tested models for generating both financial and social returns. With continued effort to refine those models and build the supporting market infrastructure, the prospects for even better performance in the future are significant.

Notes

1. "Frequently-Asked Questions, The Reinvestment Fund," Reinvestment Fund, accessed October 2, 2012, http://www.trfund.com/about/faq.html.

2. For purposes of this chapter, I refer to "social-impact investing capital aggregators" simply as "capital aggregators." In particular instances where I highlight characteristics that are common to all types of capital aggregators, I refer to "capital aggregators in general." In those instances where I draw contrasts between social-impact investing and conventional capital aggregators, I refer to "conventional capital aggregators."

3. For a discussion of socially responsible investing, see Chapter 18 of this volume.

4. "About Us—Grassroots Business Fund," Grassroots Business Fund, accessed September 20, 2012, http://www.gbfund.org/about-us.

5. "Home—Boston Community Capital," Boston Community Capital, accessed September 20, 2012, www.bostoncommunitycapital.org.

6. "About Us—Primary Care Development Corporation," Primary Care Development Corporation, accessed September, 20, 2012, http://www.pcdc.org/about-us/.

7. "Mission—Southern Bancorp," Southern Bancorp, accessed September 20, 2012, https://banksouthern.com/mission/.

8. "About Us—Root Capital," Root Capital, accessed September 20, 2012, http://www.rootcapital.org/.

9. "Our Mission—Self-Help Credit Union," Self-Help Credit Union, accessed September 20, 2012, http://www.self-help.org/. The trade association of US Community Development Credit Unions is the National Association of Community Development Credit Unions, "Who We Are—National Federation of Community Development Credit Unions," National Federation of Community Development Credit Unions, accessed September 20, 2012, http://www.natfed.org/.

10. For a discussion of the range of new hybrid corporate forms emerging in the social purpose space, see Marc Lane, *Social Enterprise: Empowering Mission-Driven Entrepreneurs* (Chicago: American Bar Association Publishing, 2011).

11. "About Pacific Community Ventures," Pacific Community Ventures, accessed September 26, 2012, www.pacificcommunityventures.org/about.

12. "About—PCV Fund," Pacific Community Ventures, LLC, accessed September 26, 2012, www.pcvfund.com/about.asp.

13. Collectively, these aspects of bank management are referred to as CAMELS. They are used by banking regulators as the basis of safety and soundness evaluations, and are adapted by investors as the basis for evaluating a financing entity's creditworthiness. Jose A. Lucas, "Using CAMELS Ratings to Monitor Bank Conditions," *Federal Reserve Bank of San Francisco* 19 (1990), published July 11, 1999, http://www.frbsf.org/econrsrch/wklyltr/wklyltr99/el99-19.html; Sonia Saltzman and Darcy Salinger, "The Accion CAMEL, Technical Note," published September 1998, http://www.mixmarket.org/sites/default/files/medialibrary/10011.150/CAMEL.pdf; "CARS™ Brochure," CARS: Opportunity Finance Network, accessed September 25, 2012, http://www.carsratingsystem.net/pdfs/CARS™Brochure.pdf.

14. Investors can extend FDIC insurance in qualifying banks beyond the current government limit of $250,000 per depositor using the Certificate of Deposit Account Registry Service (CDARS). On a case-by-case basis, FDIC insurance of up to $50 million per qualifying bank may be available through CDARS. "CDARS Homepage," Promontory Interfinancial Network, accessed September 25, 2012, www.cdars.com.

15. For a more detailed discussion of the relationship between asset classes, risk levels, and expected rates of return, see Chapter 11 of this volume, "Overview: The New Tools of 'Philanthropy.'"

16. "Internal Revenue Manual–7.27.19 Taxable Expenditures of Private Foundations," Internal Revenue Service, accessed September, 25, 2012, http://www.irs.gov/irm/part7/irm_07027-019.html

17. Significantly, there is nothing in the PRI regulations that prevents a foundation or other investor from investing in 'a for-profit entity or realizing strong financial returns, provided that the primary purpose of the investment is charitable and no significant purpose is generation of income or appreciation of capital.

18. This 1977 federal law requires FDIC-insured depositories to make loans and provide other financial services throughout their service areas, including their low- to moderate-income communities. For further information, see the Community Reinvestment Act, Federal Financial Institutions Examination Council, last modified August 21, 2012, http://www.ffiec.gov/cra/.

19. Swift's model gave rise to an Irish industry of loan funds that operated for 200 years, initially with charitable and tax funding, but later by taking interest-bearing deposits in order to extend credit. The loan funds served an estimated 20 percent of Irish households at their peak, including women, who made up approximately one-quarter of borrowers. Ireland's Potato Famine of 1846–1848 decimated the population served by the loan funds, leading to their demise. Aidan Hollis, "Women and Microcredit in History: Gender in the Irish Loan Funds," in *Woman and Credit: Researching the Past, Reconfiguring the Future*, ed. G. Campbell, B. Lemire, and R. Pearson (Oxford: Berg Press, 2002), 73–89.

20. Ronnie Phillips, "Benjamin Franklin and the Invention of Microfinance," review of *Benjamin Franklin and the Invention of Microfinance* by Bruce Yenawine, *Economic History Association Book Reviews*, October 27, 2010, http://eh.net/book_reviews/benjamin-franklin-and-invention-microfinance.

21. "The History of Microfinance," Global Envision, published April 14, 2006, http://www.globalenvision.org/library/4/1051/.

22. Bruce Reynolds, "Black Farmers in America, 1865–2000: The Pursuit of Independent Farming and the Role of Cooperatives," Rural Business-Cooperative Service, US Department of Agriculture, RBS Research Report 194, published October 2003, http://www.rurdev.usda.gov/rbs/pub/RR194.pdf; "Coalition of Community Development Financial Institutions," accessed September 25, 2012, http://cdfi.org/index.php?page=info-1a.

23. "Providing Capital, Building Communities, Creating Impact: CDFI Data Project 2008," Community Development Financial Institutions, http://www.opportunityfinance.net/store/product.asp?pID=177; "Microfinance at a Glance—2010," Microfinance Information Exchange, accessed September 25, 2012, http://www.mixmarket.org; "Economic Innovation International Homepage," Economic Innovation International, accessed September 23, 2012, http://www.economic-innovation.com/; Ron Pernick, Clint Wilder, Trevor Winnie, and Sean Sosnovec, *Clean Energy Trends 2011*, Clean Edge, March 2011, http://www.cleanedge.com/reports/pdf/Trends2011.pdf.

24. Economically targeted investments (ETIs) are defined by the Department of Labor as investments selected for the economic benefits they create apart from their investment return to the employee benefit plan; "Interpretive Bulletin Relating to Investing in Economically Targeted Investments," EBSA Final Rules, US Department of Labor, published October 17, 2008, http://webapps.dol.gov/FederalRegister/HtmlDisplay.aspx?DocId=21631&AgencyId=8&DocumentType=2. A 2005 investment policy of one of the largest volume ETI investors, the California Public Employees' Retirement System, defined an ETI as "an investment which has collateral intent to assist in the improvement of both national and regional economies, and the economic well-being of the State of California ('the State'), its localities and residents. Economic stimulation includes job

creation, development, and savings; business creation; increases or improvement in the stock of affordable housing; and improvement of the infrastructure." See "California Public Employees' Retirement System Statement of Investment Policy for Economically Targeted Investment Program," CalPERS, accessed September 23, 2012, http://www.calpers.ca.gov/eip-docs/investments/policies/other/economically-targeted/eco-target-inv-prg.pdf; "J.P. Morgan, Omidyar-Tufts, TIAA-CREF: A Conversation with Prominent Microfinance Investors," Microlinks, USAID, accessed September 20, 2012, http://microlinks.kdid.org/events/jp-morgan-omidyar-tufts-tiaa-cref-conversation-prominent-microfinance-investors.

25. "Attachment 3, Equity Term Sheet," CalPERS, accessed September 25, 2012, http://www.calpers.ca.gov/eip-docs/about/board-cal-agenda/agendas/invest/201109/item07c-03.pdf.

26. Steven Lawrence, "Doing Good with Foundation Assets: An Updated Look at Program-Related Investments," The Foundation Center, accessed September 20, 2012, foundationcenter.org/gainknowledge/research/pdf/pri_2010.pdf; "Change in Foundation Assets Adjusted for Inflation, 1975–2009," The Foundation Center's Statistical Information Service, published February 2011, http://foundationcenter.org/findfunders/statistics/pdf/02_found_growth/2009/06_09.pdf.

27. "Key Facts on Mission Investing," The Foundation Center, published October 2011, http://foundationcenter.org/gainknowledge/research/pdf/keyfacts_missioninvesting2011.pdf.

28. "Community Reinvestment Act, National Aggregate Reports," Federal Financial Examination Council, accessed September 20, 2012, http://www.ffiec.gov/craadweb/national.aspx; $12 trillion in aggregate FDIC-insured banking assets figure does not include broad in-state targeted investments. See Lisa Hagerman, "More Than a Profit? Measuring the Social and Green Outcomes of Urban Investments," Harvard Law School Labor & Worklife Program, July 2007; Chris Brummer, Josh Friedman, Billy Lockyer, and Duncan Niederauer, "The Future of Wall Street and the Financial Industry," Milken Institute, presentation given on May 3, 2011, milkeninstitute.org/presentations/slides/2740GC11.pdf; "2008 Global Pension Assets Study," Watson Wyatt Worldwide, published January 2008, http://www.watsonwyatt.com/research/pdfs/200801-GPAS08.pdf.

29. "Coalition of Community Development Financial Institutions."

30. "Urban Partnership Bank—Foundations," Urban Partnership Bank, accessed September 20, 2012, https://www.upbnk.com/foundations.

31. "About Us—Lower East Side People's Federal Credit Union," Lower East Side People's Federal Credit Union, accessed September 20, 2012, https://lespeoples.org/about-us/25th-anniversary-gala/.

32. "About KHIC," Kentucky Highlands Investment Corporation, accessed September 25, 2012, http://www.khic.org/about.html.

33. The Community Development Financial Institutions (CDFI) Fund was established by the Riegle Community Development and Regulatory Improvement Act of 1994 to promote economic revitalization in low-income communities. "Community Development Financial Institutions Program," Community Development Financial Institutions Fund, last modified September 13, 2012, http://www.cdfifund.gov/what_we_do/programs_id.asp?programid=7.

34. "New Markets Tax Credit Program," Community Development Financial Institutions Fund, last modified September 23, 2012, http://cdfifund.gov/what_we_do/programs_id.asp?programID=5.

35. "Capital Magnet Fund," Community Development Financial Institutions Fund, last modified June 8, 2012, http://www.cdfifund.gov/what_we_do/

programs_id.asp?programID=11; "Financing Healthy Food Options," Community Development Financial Institutions Fund," last modified, May 5, 2012, http://www. cdfifund.gov/what_we_do/FinancingHealthyFoodOptions.asp?programID=13.

36. For listings of certified CDFIs by name, type, and state see "931 Certified Community Development Financial Institutions as of 11/30/2010," Community Development Institutions Fund, last modified December 14, 2010, http://www.cdfifund. gov/docs/certification/cdfi/CDFIList-ByType-11-30-10.pdf.

37. While there has been no sector-wide update of this data, OFN began to issue quarterly market conditions reports in 2008. Designed to report on how CDFIs were managing during the financial crisis, these reports cite the fact that significant numbers of CDFIs are capital constrained (25 percent as of second quarter, 2011), meaning that they could provide additional financing if they had additional capital. However, they do not cite a large decline in sector capital under management. Indeed, trend data show that 49 percent of respondents to OFN's quarterly market conditions survey saw an increase in capital liquidity year over year and 35 percent saw a decrease. See "CDFI Data Project, 2008," Opportunity Finance Network, accessed September 25, 2012, www.opportunityfinance.net/industry/default.aspx?id=236; http://www. opportunityfinance.net/store/downloads/CDFI_Market_Conditions_Q211_ Report%20I.pdf.

38. "Calvert Ventures," Akama: Open Business Directory, accessed September 20, 2012, http://www.akama.com/company/Calvert_Ventures_a2b442780462.html; "Economic Innovation International Homepage."

39. "Economic Innovation International Homepage."

40. "Investors' Circle," Investors' Circle affiliated with SJF Institute, accessed September 20, 2012, http://www.investorscircle.net/.

41. Much of this discussion of international microfinance is adapted from CGAP UNCDF Donor Training: "The History of Microfinance," Global Envision, accessed September 23, 2012, http://www.globalenvision.org/library/4/1051/.

42. "The History of Microfinance."

43. Founded in 1976, the mission of Women's World Banking is to "expand the economic assets, participation and power of low-income women and their house-holds by helping them access financial services, knowledge and markets." See "About WWB," Women's World Banking, accessed September 25, 2012, http://www.swwb. org/; founded in 1985, SEEP represents practitioners who believe that "sharing practical experiences within a trusting environment would result in improved microenterprise development practices." See "About Us—SEEP," Small Enterprise Education and Promotion Network, accessed September 20, 2012, http://www. seepnetwork.org/Pages/AboutUS.aspx.

44. Many of the new supports for microenterprise cited here are taken from Paul Cheng, ed., "The Impact Investor's Handbook: Lessons from the World of Microfinance," Charities Aid Foundation, Market Insight Series, February 2011, accessed September 20, 2012, http://www.cafonline.org/pdf/impact_investor_report_2011.pdf.

45. "About," Consultative Group to Assist the Poor, accessed August 15, 2013, http:// www.cgap.org/about.

46. "Profund Internacional," CGAP Microfinance Gateway, accessed October 2, 2012, http://www.microfinancegateway.org/p/site/m/template.rc/1.11.47720/.

47. Cheng, "Impact Investor's Handbook."

48. "Mix Market Homepage," Microfinance Information Exchange, accessed October 2, 2012, http://www.mixmarket.org.

49. "About MIX," Microfinance Information Exchange, accessed September 20, 2012, http://www.themix.org/about-mix/about-mix#ixzz1IVbCKQei.

50. Banco Sol declared cash dividends of $162,857, or.45 per share on 1996 earnings of $1.1 million. "BancoSol," Accion International, accessed September 20, 2012, http://www.accion.org/Page.aspx?pid=666.

51. CGAP, "The History of Microfinance," adapted from CGAP UNCDF Donor Training, accessed September 26, 2012, http://www.globalenvision.org/library/4/1051/.

52. United Nations, "Millennium Development Goals," accessed September 20, 2012, http://www.un.org/millenniumgoals/.

53. "About Us—Root Capital."

54. "Asian Development Bank Backs ShorCap II Fund with $10M," Microfinance Africa, published December 10, 2012, http://microfinanceafrica.net/tag/equator-capital-partners/.

55. Racial and gender bias have been drivers of both disinvestment and predatory lender targeting.

56. Reservation communities are a special case where sovereignty and land tenure issues create a need for customized transaction structures.

57. The ability to meet financial return expectations is particularly important among social-impact investors such as foundations and pension funds, which operate under fiduciary responsibility regulations. See discussion in following texts: Mark Kramer and Anne Stetson, "A Brief Guide to the Law of Mission Investing for U.S. Foundations," FSG Social Impact Advisors, accessed September 23, 2012, http://www.fsg.org/Portals/0/Uploads/Documents/PDF/The_Law_and_Mission_Investing_Brief.pdf; Lisa Richter, "Guide to Impact Investing," Grantmakers In Health, May 2011), http://www.gih.org/usr_doc/GIH_Guide_to_Impact_Investing_FINAL_May_2011.pdf; "Interpretive Bulletin Relating to Investing in Economically Targeted Investments"; and Craig Metrick, "The Line in the Sand: ESG Integration vs. Screening and 'Economically Targeted Investments,'" last modified July 11, 2012, http://www.mercer.com/articles/1407905.

58. For a discussion of secondary market operations, see Chapters 3 and 14 in this volume.

59. For further detail on this sourcing function, see Chapter 6, "Enterprise Brokers," in this volume.

60. Graham Wright, "The Power of Successful Market-Led Savings Mobilization, published April 19, 2011, http://microfinance.cgap.org/2011/04/19/the-power-of-successful-market-led-savings-mobilisation/. For further information on the tool of insurance, see Chapter 17 on insurance in this volume.

61. A number of these services are offered by Pacific Community Ventures' Business Advisory Services, "Development Investment Capital," Pacific Community Ventures, published May 2006, http://www.pacificcommunityventures.org/media/pdf/PCV-White-Paper-Development-Investment-Capital.pdf.

62. Individual CDFI types belong to sector-specific trade associations, such as the National Federation of Community Development Credit Unions, the National Community Investment Fund (CDFI bankers), and the Community Development Venture Capital Alliance. "Overview of Opportunity Finance Network," Opportunity Finance Network, accessed September 20, 2012, http://www.opportunityfinance.net/about/; "Who We Are—National Federation of Community Development Credit Unions"; "NCIF Homepage," National Community Investment Fund, accessed September 24, 2012, www.ncif.org; "About Us—CDVCA," Community Development Venture Capital Alliance, accessed September 25, 2012, www.cdvca.org.

63. "Microfinance Information Exchange Brochure," Microfinance Information Exchange, accessed September 26, 2012, http://www.themix.org/sites/default/files/

MIX%20Brochure.pdf; "About ANDE," Aspen Institute, accessed September 21, 2012, http://www.aspeninstitute.org/policy-work/aspen-network-development-entrepreneurs/about-ande; "Global Alliance for Banking on Values," Global Alliance for Banking on Values, accessed September 22, 2012, http://www.gabv.org.

64. US private foundations that make PRIs in for-profit entities must comply with Expenditure Responsibility, a regulation that requires documentation of a preinvestment assessment that PRI proceeds will be used for charitable purposes, followed by annual reports that describe and certify this charitable use.

65. For a discussion of the state-of-art of impact measurement, see Chapter 23 of this volume.

66. "Personal Savings Overview," Triodos Bank, accessed September 20, 2012, http://www.triodos.co.uk/en/personal/savings-overview/.

67. Ibid.

68. For further detail, see Chapters 1, 4, and 6, "The Revolution on the Frontiers of Philanthropy," "Social and Environmental Exchanges," and "Enterprise Brokers," respectively, in this volume.

69. The Global Impact Investing Reporting Index is one effort attempting to address this concern. See "Impact Reporting and Investment Standards," Global Impact Investing Network, accessed September 21, 2012, http://www.thegiin.org/cgi-bin/iowa/reporting/index.html. For further insight into the status of such measurement efforts, see Chapter 23, "The Elusive Quest for Impact," in this volume; Lester M. Salamon, "What Would Google Do? Designing Appropriate Social Impact Measurement Systems," *Community Development Investment Review* 7.2 (2011): 43–47; and Ben Thornley and Colby Dailey, "Building Scale in Community Impact Investing through Nonfinancial Performance Measurement," *Community Development Investment Review* 6.1 (2011): 1–46.

70. For further detail on the tool of "credit enhancements," see Chapter 12 of this volume, "Loans, Loan Guarantees, and Credit Enhancements."

71. Tom Feltner, "Over Community Objections, the Federal Reserve Approves Capital One Acquisition of ING," Woodstock Institute, published February 15, 2012, http://www.woodstockinst.org/blog/blog/over-community-objections,-the-federal-reserve-approves-capital-one-acquisition-of-ing/.

72. "Community Reinvestment Act," National Community Reinvestment Coalition, accessed September 26, 2012, http://www.ncrc.org/programs-issues/community-reinvestment.

73. Community Development Financial Institutions, "Providing Capital, Building Communities, Creating Impact," CDFI Data Project 2008; Microfinance Information Exchange, "Microfinance at a Glance—2010"; "Economic Innovation International Homepage"; Pernick et al., *Clean Energy Trends 2011*.

74. Pernick et al., *Clean Energy Trends 2011*; "Market Conditions," Opportunity Finance Network, accessed September 22, 2012, http://www.opportunityfinance.net/store/categories.asp?cID=29.

75. Opportunity Finance Network, "Market Conditions"; "2009, MFI Benchmarks," Microfinance Information Exchange, published October 2010, http://www.themix.org/publications/mix-microfinance-world/2010/10/2009-mfi-benchmarks.

76. Community Development Financial Institutions, "Providing Capital, Building Communities, Creating Impact," CDFI Data Project 2008.

77. National Community Investment Fund, *Too Important to Fail: The Impact of Community Development Banking Institutions: 2009 and Beyond* (Chicago: National Community Investment Fund, 2010), 7, accessed September 23, 2012, http://www.ncif.org/images/uploads/20101108_2009_ImpactReport_FINAL.pdf.

78. Microfinance Information Exchange, "Microfinance at a Glance—2010."

Suggested Readings

Bernholz, Lucy, and Lisa Richter. "Equity Advancing Equity: How Community Philanthropy Can Build Racial and Social Equity through Mission Investing." Blueprint Research & Design Inc. and GPS Capital Partners LLC, 2009. http://www.communityphilanthropy.org/downloads/Equity%20Advancing%20Equity%20Full%20Report.pdf.

Cheng, Paul, ed. "The Impact Investor's Handbook: Lessons from the World of Microfinance." Charities Aid Foundation, February 2011. http://www.cafonline.org/pdf/impact_investor_report_2011.pdf.

Godeke, Steven, and Doug Bauer. "Philanthropy's New Passing Gear: Mission-Related Investing. A Policy and Implementation Guide for Foundation Trustees." Rockefeller Philanthropy Advisors, 2008. http://rockpa.org/document.doc?id=16.

Richter, Lisa. "Guide to Impact Investing." Grantmakers in Health, May 2011. http://www.gih.org/usr_doc/GIH_Guide_to_Impact_Investing_FINAL_May_2011.pdf.

CHAPTER 3

SECONDARY MARKETS

David J. Erickson

SONDRA NELSON IS AN AFRICAN American elementary school teacher in Durham, North Carolina.[1] In the mid-1990s she applied for a loan to purchase a home but was turned down by a bank because she did not have a perfect credit history. Although she was current on her bills at the time of purchase, she had fallen behind on her student loan payments in the past, and that caused her credit score to drop to 635.

But fortunately, one of Ms. Nelson's coworkers told her about a special program that had been created by an organization called Self-Help, a community development financial institution (CDFI) with a commitment to providing access to capital to low-income borrowers to buy homes, start businesses, and build charter schools and other community facilities they needed.[2]

Self-Help had a long history of providing loans to borrowers like Sondra who were being turned down by traditional banks. In the past, Self-Help's home loan program was successful and profitable, but relatively small. In an effort to expand its reach, Self-Help decided to partner with Wachovia Bank, which had a much wider branch network than Self-Help had. In this partnership, Wachovia would make mortgage loans like the ones Self-Help made—responsible terms but with some leeway to borrowers who were not qualifying for standard mortgages. In essence, Self-Help began operating a "secondary market," buying "its kind of loan" from Wachovia, which acted as the loan originator. This was a win-win situation since Self-Help reached far more borrowers and Wachovia could operate somewhat outside its normal comfort zone knowing that Self-Help would purchase the loans from the bank.

In the course of the 1990s, Self-Help expanded this small secondary-market approach with the growth of partnering banks like Wachovia and by enlisting new bank partners. Thousands of hard-working North Carolinians, with situations similar to Sondra Nelson's, were consequently able to realize their goal of owning a home.

What is more, on the strength of the performance of this program, Self-Help North Carolina was able to convince the Ford Foundation to underwrite a nationwide extension of this program and to enlist Fannie Mae, the government-sponsored enterprise (GSE) established by Congress to purchase mortgage loans, to acquire loans that met Self-Help's standards even though they might fall outside of Fannie's standard underwriting guidelines.[3] This was only possible, however, because the Ford Foundation put up a $50 million loan loss reserve fund that allowed Self-Help to sell the mortgages to Fannie "with recourse," that is, with a right to collect the proceeds without the need to proceed to a foreclosure, a significant credit enhancement. Ford also provided funds to research the effects of the program, including ongoing interviews with borrowers to see how their lives changed after they received their mortgages. The program was also designed with a small risk premium fee collected by Self-Help to cover all loan losses and make the program self-sustaining.

All the players involved were necessary to make this much larger secondary market work: (1) banks and their extensive nationwide networks of branches, which originated the loans; (2) Self-Help as an intermediary that aggregated and pooled the loans; (3) the Ford Foundation with its credit-enhancing grant that gave Self-Help the financial strength to motivate Fannie Mae involvement; and (4) Fannie Mae to buy the mortgages. In this case, Fannie Mae became the secondary market for the low-income home loans, and without that participation, the Self-Help program would have been a small operation.

And the achievements of this secondary-market operation, known as the Community Advantage Program (CAP), have been anything but small. Before the program was put on hold because of the 2008 financial crisis and Fannie Mae's placement under government conservatorship, 39 mortgage lenders had participated in CAP, ranging from small, local institutions to very large national banks. The program had funded 51,000 home loans totaling $4.6 billion. And despite lending to a more vulnerable population and weathering the worst mortgage market in 70 years, Self-Help's risk premium fee has covered all charge-offs to date. Indeed, research conducted at the University of North Carolina, Chapel Hill, found that, for borrowers with similar characteristics, the estimated default risk for a 2004 conventional subprime loan is about four times that of a CAP loan.[4] This evidence suggests that a responsible loan product that is priced properly because it has a secondary market outlet is a win for both low-income borrowers and the institutions making and selling the mortgages.

At the same time, Self-Help had to price its loan products at market interest rates in order to make them marketable, and this has highlighted a dilemma facing social investors as they consider whether nonprofits and nongovernmental agencies with a deep commitment to mission should participate in larger structures, like secondary markets, that hold out the promise of scale but demand standardization and more market-rate pricing. The balance of this chapter takes up this question in the course of examining the existing world of secondary markets like Self-Help in the social investment arena, what the many variations of this actor look like, what some of the examples are, and how they advance social purposes.

Defining the Actor

Defining Features

In *Corporate Finance*, Ross, Westerfield, and Jaffee divide financial markets into two groups: *money markets*, which offer debt and pay off in the short term; and *capital markets*, which offer longer-term debt and equity.[5] The capital markets have greater capacity, cheaper money, and longer terms. So there is an incentive for financial institutions to take their assets (loans on businesses, real estate, or other purposes) and sell them in the capital markets as secondary market transactions for better rates and terms, thus freeing up capital for additional loans.

Of course, any discussion of secondary markets today takes place under the dark cloud of the financial market meltdown of 2008 and 2009, much of it caused by abuses of the secondary-market mechanism for investments such as mortgage-backed securities (MBSs). The mechanism of the secondary market did not cause the crisis of 2008–2009, however, since secondary markets operated successfully for decades prior to 2008, providing liquidity and growth capital for the money markets in a safe and responsible manner. What caused the crisis were abuses of the secondary-market mechanism, and it is the assumption here that a more regulated secondary market will re-emerge.

In the case of social finance, secondary-market actors perform the function of acquiring loans that are made by lending organizations such as banks, credit unions, microfinance institutions (MFIs), community development finance institutions (CDFIs), and similar institutions. These loans might range from a microfinance loan to a group of women using the proceeds to purchase a sewing machine in Bangladesh to a bank's construction loan for a charter school in a low-income neighborhood in Baltimore.

In essence, the secondary market operates as a resale market, as opposed to a primary market in which loans are originated by lenders.[6] In the secondary market, those who hold loans—the MFI's sewing machine loan or the bank's charter school loan—try to sell them to investors who want to purchase them. The purchaser gets the stream of future cash flow from the loan, and there often is some type of guarantee from the seller or a third party to protect against future defaults by the original borrower.

In the example above, for instance, Self-Help initially operated as a traditional lender where it originated single-family mortgages. Self-Help, however, quickly ran out of capital to make additional loans by simply lending the money it had on its balance sheet and then holding all those loans in its portfolio. In that scenario, Self-Help would have had to monitor the loans and process the payments (also known as servicing the loans) for their full terms (30 years in this case) and slowly build back its capital stock with borrowers' monthly mortgage payments. Instead, Self-Help innovated its approach, ultimately culminating in CAP. The loans were both fair to the borrower and attractive to an investor. In this case, it was Fannie Mae that purchased the loans. This arrangement was made possible in part because Self-Help was able to use the credit enhancement provided by the Ford Foundation. These loans also had a risk premium, or fee, to help guard against default. These two reserves served as a guarantee to the investor on future borrower performance. Once a loan such as Self-Help's CAP mortgage is sold, responsibility for collecting payments when due and otherwise servicing the loan, for a fee, may remain with the originating lender, Self-Help as the aggregator, or be assigned to another entity. In any case, these payments ultimately go to the investors to pay off what they spent for the loans, while the proceeds of the loan sale replenish the capital of the original lender. This allows the lender to make a new loan for a borrower like Sondra. In this way, social investors get access to additional resources while limiting the assets they must carry on their own balance sheets.[7]

Design Features and Major Variants

Self-Help's CAP is not, of course, the only secondary-market entity in the social investment arena. There are a number of others utilizing what are actually a variety of secondary-market approaches. Included here are entities that engage in whole loan sales, loan participation note sales, syndications, private place-ments, securitization, use of bonds, and many others. The following is a discus-sion of a few of the most common variations on achieving a secondary market for social finance loans.

Whole Loan Sales

Perhaps the most straightforward secondary-market transaction is a whole loan sale. In such a transaction, secondary investors take ownership positions in a single large loan or in a pool of smaller loans.[8]

Loan Participation Notes and Syndications

Variations on whole loan sales are loan participations and syndications. In both cases, it is an opportunity for multiple investors to participate as secondary-market investors, essentially purchasing a share of a single big loan or a pool of loans. Three good examples of this variation are the loan participa-tion model developed by Partners for the Common Good, ROC USA, and the loan syndication developed by Boston area foundations for an effort to build more affordable housing with social services for tenants who were formerly homeless.

Partners for the Common Good (PCG) is a CDFI founded in 1989 by the Christian Brothers Investment Services, an investment advisory and asset management firm for Catholic institutions. Although PCG used to originate its own loans, it saw an unmet need in creating a loan participation product, mod-eled in part on a long-standing and informal practice among community bank-ers who come together to share pieces of a loan that are too big for one bank.[9] In this case, PCG joins with other organizations not to originate loans, but to purchase loans originated by others. Here is how the arrangement works: In instances where PCG is in a two-partner participation, it typically purchases 50 percent of the loan that was originated by the initial lender. PCG purchases a smaller share in multiparty participations, and it shares collateral and fees on a proportional basis. Since 2004, PCG has originated 79 participation pur-chases with 31 lending partners totaling $25.3 million.[10]

ROC USA is another CDFI that maintains a loan participation program that provides funding for owners of manufactured homes to come together and buy their mobile home parks. Manufactured homes, often referred to as mobile homes, are often placed on land that is not owned by the homeowner. The homeowner runs the risk of steep rent increases or the cost of relocation when a park owner decides to sell the land. In addition, many home parks are not kept up to the minimum standards for health and safety. But it has been diffi-cult for owners to get the financing they need to turn their home sites into resident-owned communities (or "ROCs"). Since 1984, the New Hampshire Community Loan Fund, a CDFI, has helped establish 97 ROCs, which provide space for 5,400 manufactured homes.

In 2008, the loan fund launched an effort to take its model nationwide with the ROC USA, LLC, a coalition of four nonprofits—the New Hampshire Community Loan Fund, CFED, NCB Capital Impact, and NeighborWorks America. Much of the early funding to create this new entity came from the Ford Foundation.[11] Additional support came in various forms including grants, program-related investments (PRIs), and market-rate investments from the

Calvert Foundation, Fannie Mae, the CDFI Fund, Bank of America, Merrill Lynch, and other investors.[12]

The ROC USA financing model depends on a market-rate first mortgage being originated by its subsidiary, ROC USA Capital, at a higher than appraised value (110 percent). Secondary-market investors buy a portion of these loans but only up to between 75 and 85 percent of the appraised value. The difference is held by ROC USA Capital, which acts as a credit enhancement for the outside investors. An additional risk mitigant is the work ROC USA does to provide active asset management for loans to ensure that the communities are well run and maintained. The current loan portfolio is $18.8 million, where $14.8 is held by senior loan participants and $4 million is still held on ROC USA's balance sheet. Senior loan participants are often banks, state housing finance agencies, and CDFIs.[13]

Loan syndications build on the loan participation model. The syndicator acts almost as a broker between the originating lender (or lenders) and investors. The syndicator takes the loan (or pool of loans) and then coordinates a group of lenders to advance a portion of the total necessary funds. The originating lender often retains loan servicing and the relationship to the borrowers. The syndicator plays the role of go-between for the investors and the loan originator/servicer. The syndicator collects all the fees and arranges the sale of the loan assets to the investors.

There is also an approach that turns loans into asset-backed notes and sells them directly to investors as private placements. A great example of this variant is the Flexible Capital Access Program (FlexCAP) from Habitat for Humanity. Habitat is well known for its work in bringing volunteers together with potential homeowners to put "sweat equity" into the homes they build. This model has been extremely successful for Habitat for Humanity International (HFHI), which has affiliates across the United States and around the world. To date, HFHI has built 90,000 homes domestically, and another 370,000 homes internationally. And while the homes are built with donated labor and material, they still often have a mortgage to help cover the cost of development. These loans are always at zero interest, but are otherwise similar to conventional home mortgages. In the United States, Habitat affiliates hold an estimated $1.4 billion in mortgages.[14]

Rather than sit on those mortgages, Habitat developed the FlexCAP program to create a secondary market to free up more capital for its mission work. The idea is simple: participating affiliates decide which loans to put into the pool, although never more than 60 percent so they have other loans that can be substituted into the pool in the event a mortgage becomes delinquent.[15] HFHI, in turn, sells to investors 7- or 10-year notes that pay a return of around 5 percent and are backed by the pledged mortgages. Then HFHI sends the proceeds of the sales back to the affiliates as loans. The affiliates' payments on the loans are passed through a trustee, Wells Fargo Bank, as note payments to the investors. The bank holds the collateral and administers the payments to both the affiliates and the investors. The program has a 100 percent repayment rate.[16] To date, FlexCAP has raised $107 million, which provided funds for an estimated 3,300 additional Habitat homes.[17]

FlexCAP financing is building more homes, and also giving Habitat affiliates an ability to take advantage of opportunities, such as the drop in real estate prices. Consider the example of the Lakeland, Florida, Habitat's use of its FlexCAP loan. In April 2009, Lakeland Habitat received a $454,000 loan from the program. It used that money to purchase a 22-acre site for $325,000. This price was less than half of what it sold for in 2007, but even with the steep discount, the Lakeland Habitat could not get a loan to buy the land. Now the affiliate plans to develop 30 energy-efficient homes there that "will feature a community garden, farmers' market and playground."[18]

As successful as this program has been, it faced an uncertain future in 2008 when most of its investors, US banks, pulled out. Rather than shut the program down, Habitat looked to see "if there were other investors who were interested in stepping into the breach," according to Luther M. Ragin Jr., formerly vice president of investments at the F.B. Heron Foundation. Heron hosted a convening to see if other foundations might be interested in participating in FlexCAP. They also invited insurance companies, high-net-worth individuals, state housing finance agencies, and other investors. The following year, despite continuing trouble in financial markets, FlexCAP recorded its best year yet thanks to the new investors.

Securitization

On the secondary-market evolutionary scale, securitization may be at the top, since it has all the advantages of the variants discussed previously (sources of new capital, liquidity, risk spreading, etc.), but it also has the promise of scale because it is a mechanism that, in normal times, can handle a truly massive volume of product. As outlined more fully in Chapter 14 of this volume, securitization involves pooling loans and then selling investors shares of the pool as security. The securities can then be traded in tertiary markets without involving the initial issuer. It is important to note that securitization has historically been the dominant tool for the secondary market.

Securitization of domestic social finance loans in the United States was pioneered by the Community Reinvestment Fund (CRF). CRF got its start in 1989, and its growth through the 1990s represented a major advancement in the effort to create a vibrant secondary market for community development loans. CRF has purchased more than $1.2 billion in community development loans from over 150 lending organizations located in almost all the states in the country.[19]

Prior to the economic crisis, the most exciting development on the securitization front was the issuance of "rated" securities by CRF in 2004 and 2006. Previously CRF had been able to privately place hundreds of millions of dollars in community development loans, but this is often with a small number of socially motivated investors. By having its security rated by Standard and Poor's, however, it was able to attract new investors. For example, in CRF 17, issued in November 2004, the "first three tranches were rated AAA, which enabled eight new institutional investors with strict investing guidelines, including Northwest Mutual Life, to buy into the deal."[20]

CRF continued improving the process. In May 2006, CRF rolled out its second rated security, CRF 18, containing a number of credit enhancements, including "overcollateralization," that is, the value of the underlying assets exceeded the face value of the notes sold; "subordination," that is, where some socially motivated investors and the government were willing to be last in line for repayment in case of a default; and an interest reserve account, which provided the transaction with a rainy-day fund that could be tapped in an emergency (or seized by the investors in case of a default). In addition to all these credit enhancements, Standard and Poor's analyzed many years of Small Business Administration (SBA) small business performance data as proxy variables in order to develop an appropriate statistical risk model for estimating the risk of CRF 17 and 18.

Securitization is a fantastic secondary-market tool because it lends itself to creating a secondary market for a wide array of underlying assets. Thus, according to one authority:

> Virtually all forms of debt obligations and receivables have been securitized in the U.S.: residential mortgages; home equity loans; commercial loans; manufactured housing loans; timeshare loans; auto, truck, RV, aircraft and boat loans and leases; credit card receivables; trade receivables (just about any type, i.e., airline tickets, telecommunications receivables, toll road receipts); equipment loans and leases; small business loans; student loans; lottery winnings; legal fees from tobacco litigation; and record album receivables.[21]

The current turmoil in the credit markets has put a hold on using this tool, but with proper safeguards, it is likely to be reintroduced into the social capital market.

Bonds

Bonds are another promising vehicle to use in fostering a secondary market. State housing finance agencies can fund affordable housing mortgages (single and multifamily) with the proceeds of taxable and tax-exempt bonds, often with federal credit enhancements that lower long-term borrowing costs.

One program that holds tremendous promise, but has yet to be implemented, is the CDFI Bond Guarantee Program—authorized for up to $1 billion per year. The CDFI Bond Guarantee was authorized as part of the Small Business Jobs Act of 2010. It authorizes the CDFI Fund, a part of the US Treasury, to administer a program that offers a 100 percent federal guarantee for bonds that are used to benefit low-income individuals or communities.[22] The Treasury Department may guarantee up to 10 bonds per year, with each issue having a minimum of $100 million. The total cannot exceed $1 billion per year.[23] The program is short-lived, however, as it sunsets in 2014.

This source of capital, which could amount to billions of dollars, is an ideal instrument to jump-start the secondary market in domestic social finance. Such a jump is clearly needed. As one close observer of the social capital market put it: "We thought we were making progress before the crisis hit, but with that pace, given those transaction costs, it would be the next generation before significant sources of capital were available to the CDFI industry."[24]

At the same time, there is concern that the CDFI industry is too small to execute $1 billion in transactions a year. As one observer put it, there is a sense "that the dog caught the car. Now what?" But because the bonds are flexible and backed by the full faith and credit of the federal government, it means that the uses of the bonds are also flexible and transaction costs will be low. Too often, CDFIs have offered products that matched what funding streams were available to them, rather than what their borrowers really needed. This program will allow CDFIs to recapitalize by selling their existing loans into the bond pools and use the proceeds to innovate new lending products for the low-income communities they serve.[25]

There are other ways the government can play a role in promoting a secondary market. One strategy mentioned above is the use of government-sponsored enterprises, such as Fannie Mae. They have played a role as the secondary-market investor for social finance loans, as the Self-Help example above demonstrates. But since their fate is unclear, it is not certain they will play that role in the future.

Real Estate Investment Trusts

Another variation of the secondary market is a real estate investment trust (REIT). The Community Development Trust (CDT) was started by the Local Initiatives Support Corporation—a community development intermediary with considerable foundation backing—in 1998 to create a secondary market for mortgages on apartment buildings that served low-income tenants. A REIT is a corporate entity that invests in real estate. It thus does for real estate investments what a mutual fund does for investing in stocks. CDT uses the REIT structure to supply debt and equity capital from institutional investors, such as banks, pension funds, and insurance companies, to expand the amount of capital that goes into revitalizing low-income communities.

A driver of CDT's work is the Community Reinvestment Act, which motivates banks to make investments in the areas where they do business (their "assessment areas" in the parlance of the act).[26] To date, CDT has invested more than $750 million, primarily in multifamily affordable housing developments, in 40 states and regions. CDT's secondary-market Debt Program has helped to create and preserve close to 22,500 units of affordable housing in the United States.[27]

Monetizing Remittances and Other Future Flows

An interesting secondary-market variant in the international arena is the State Department's recently launched BRIDGE program. Along with its US and El Salvadoran and Honduran partners, BRIDGE will provide debt financing in these two Latin American countries backed by future remittances from the United States.[28] In explaining the program, Secretary of State Clinton said:

> Every year, millions—actually, tens of millions—of people around the world leave home to find work. They settle in countries where they think they have a better economic future, then they begin sending money back home. And they send it to their families for all kinds of purposes. Now, if they send these remittances through the formal financial system, they create huge funding flows that are orders of magnitude larger than any development assistance we can dream of. By harnessing the potential of remittances, BRIDGE will make it easier for communities in El Salvador and Honduras to get the financing they need to build roads and bridges, for example, to support entrepreneurs, to make loans, to bring more people into the financial system.[29]

In El Salvador, for example, the International Finance Corporation of the World Bank (the IFC) will "provide up to $30 million of debt financing to Fedecredito using an innovative funding approach that leverages the significant remittances of El Salvadorans working abroad to increase lending to micro-entrepreneurs and low-income people in the country."[30] Fedecredito is a cooperative owned by 55 El Salvadoran credit unions and workers banks. This financing structure—debt funding backed by future remittance flows—is the first of its kind that is focused on low-income clients, according to the IFC.[31]

Securitizing future flows of funds is not new in the international arena. It has its origins in sovereign banking crises in the past when borrowers in developing country were looking for ways to access capital on better terms than were available through their domestic banking systems. "In a typical future flow transaction, the borrowing entity (originator) in a developing country sells its future products (receivables) directly or indirectly to an offshore Special Purpose Vehicle (SPV), which issues the debt instrument," according to Suhas Ketkar and Dilip Ratha.[32] In this way, the SPV operates in a fashion similar to the Self-Help CAP program by providing capital upfront and getting paid back over time from the income stream.

New technology also is providing retail investors increased access to the secondary market.[33] New websites such as Prosper.com and LendingClub operate as true, but restricted, secondary markets that only allow the trading of securities backed by loans originated on the platform. But the technology also provides an avenue to implement all the variants discussed in this section—loan participations, syndications, securitizations, and so on. Most of the obstacles to the development of these online secondary-market platforms are regulatory and not technological.[34]

Finally, there are additional sites that act like secondary markets and will play an important role in getting the social finance industry "secondary market ready." These include online investment options such as Kiva and MicroPlace, which raise money to recapitalize microfinance institutions making loans to low-income entrepreneurs. They are not, therefore, secondary markets in the strict sense: They provide capital directly to the MFIs, and there is no formal connection to the underlying asset (i.e., a specific microfinance loan, or pool of loans). But by facilitating transactions between capital providers and lenders, they are pioneering the web tools that will be necessary to support online secondary-market activity in the future.[35]

Scope and Scale

Although the secondary markets became nearly moribund in the wake of the 2008 US financial crisis, the history leading up to 2008 proved that secondary markets could be used to provide outlets for the social finance industry, and the recovery from the 2008 crisis has revived confidence in their future. Getting to this point has involved a long journey, however.

Early efforts by community development lenders to access institutional capital did not get their start until the 1980s and early 1990s. The efforts were led by lender consortia such as Community Preservation Corporation (CPC) in New York City, Savings Associations Mortgage Company (SAMCO) and the California Community Reinvestment Corporation (CCRC) in California, and Community Investment Corporation (CIC) in Chicago.[36] These isolated regional efforts grew up alongside more national efforts to actually securitize specific types of loans, such as co-op loans securitized by a subsidiary of the National Cooperative Bank (NCB), or small business loans that were securitized with help from the Small Business Administration (SBA).[37]

NeighborWorks, a national network of affordable community development organizations, was also a significant player in the inchoate efforts to securitize community development loans. Its subsidiary, Neighborhood Housing Services of America (NHSA), started securitizing CDBG loans in 1974 and used a secondary market to replenish the revolving loan funds of local NeighborWorks organizations. Although NHSA purchased hundreds of millions of loans from local NeighborWorks organizations and their local lending partners, they discontinued this activity in 2009 in the wake of the financial crisis.[38]

As the discussion in the variants section above demonstrates, however, there have been many experiments to bring secondary-market operations to domestic social finance—even when the capital markets were effectively shut down.

International efforts to use secondary markets for social finance may have started later than domestic US efforts, but before the financial crisis, they made dramatic progress in a very short period of time. BlueOrchard issued the BlueOrchard Microfinance Securities 1 (BOMS1), the first collateralized debt obligation (CDO) for microfinance institutions in emerging markets in 2004.[39] A CDO is a security that is backed up by bonds or loans. In this case it was $40 million of microfinance loans, but the deal reopened a year later for an additional $67 million.[40] That first transaction carried a 100 percent guarantee to senior note holders provided by the US Overseas Private Investment Corporation (OPIC).[41]

Soon, however, investors became more comfortable with fewer protections. The Global Commercial Microfinance Consortium (GDMC) was structured by Deutsche Bank with only a partial guarantee structure.[42] "Unlike the BlueOrchard deal, senior investors in the Consortium took exposure to micro-borrowers and could potentially lose three-fourths of their invested capital," according to Asad Mahmood, managing director of Deutsche Bank Social Investment Funds. "These investors, therefore, had a vested interest in investigating and understanding the risks inherent in the asset class."[43] They also demonstrated that they did not require the 100 percent guarantee of earlier transactions.

Other microinvestment vehicles have followed, many of them based on the same model as GDMC. BlueOrchard Loans for Development 2006 (BOLD1) was arranged by Morgan Stanley and raised nearly $100 million as a collateralized loan obligation (CLO). It was backed by unsecured senior loans in 21 MFIs around the world.[44] BOLD2 in 2007 was the first microfinance CDO to be publicly rated and received the *Financial Times*' "Sustainable Deal of the Year" award in 2008.[45]

Some secondary-market transactions have grown in size, like the ProCredit Bank Bulgaria and Bangladesh Rural Advancement Committee (BRAC) securitization, the latter of which, undertaken in 2006, was the largest deal yet at $180 million (equivalent in Bangladeshi currency). The ICICI bank in India has made strides in developing a secondary market for Indian MFIs that also helps it meet new banking regulations.[46]

During the global financial crisis, investors' appetite for these types of investment vehicles dropped off dramatically. "Liquidity dried up almost overnight, with planned microfinance funds being pulled late in the marketing process," is how one investment report put it.[47]

It remains to be seen how the secondary market for social finance—both domestic and international—will respond to a return to more robust activity in the capital markets. But breakthroughs like the ones by CRF and BlueOrchard are likely to be a foundation on which to build.

Rationale

Perhaps the greatest rationale for developing a secondary market for social finance assets is the possibility of unlocking a flood of new capital from both retail and institutional investors who have indicated that they are interested in making investments in socially redeemable assets as long as there is a possibility for a reasonable rate of return. That such capital is available is increasingly becoming clear to experts in the field. Noting that "global pension plans alone represent $23 trillion in assets" and high-net-worth individuals another $39 trillion, Allison Duncan of Amplifier Strategies and Georgette Wong of Take Action! recently argued that social investing "represents the single biggest opportunity for capital to unleash the power of the private sector and of entrepreneurial innovation to solve some of society's toughest challenges."[48] A recent report by J.P. Morgan and the Rockefeller Foundation estimates that in five sectors (housing, rural water delivery, maternal health, primary education, and financial services), there is a social-impact investment potential for invested capital of $400 billion to $1 trillion over the next 10 years.[49] Similarly, a recent survey of 4,000 Americans concluded that there is a $120 billion demand from retail investors for social-impact investments, what is referred to as mission-related investments, or MRIs.[50] And this is above and beyond the resources in foundation endowments that could be invested in a way that both serves the foundation's mission and provides a return. Meantime, proven strategies for fighting poverty and improving communities are going starved for needed funds. As Tom Bledsoe, CEO of the Housing Partnership Network, has argued, the community development industry is "equity constrained" due to weaknesses in its funding model.[51] And other practitioners are reaching the same conclusion.[52]

The rationale for secondary markets in such a setting springs from at least four key contributions such markets offer. In particular, they (1) bring new sources of capital into a field, in this case connecting socially motivated investors to social enterprises; (2) generate the liquidity that investors frequently like to see before investing; (3) spread risk so investors know they are protected against the failure of any particular social enterprise or group of such enterprises in a particular geographic area or field; and finally, and perhaps most importantly, (4) organize the market in a way that allows for specialization and innovation on a scale that is needed to begin to turn the tide against poverty.

Connecting the huge, but largely untapped, world of socially motivated investors with the world of investable opportunities is a challenge. The current system of investing in intermediaries, who lend to the poor, is incapable of either effectively investing the needed volume of capital or attracting the volume in the first place because it lacks the ability to give investors what they want—steady, predictable investments with known risk parameters. While the investment market may total trillions of dollars of investable capital, to date, these investors have remained on the sidelines in large part because there is not sufficient standardized product in the marketplace to attract them. As a consequence, social finance today remains a boutique business.

Vibrant social finance secondary markets would give investors a lot of options in terms of what types of activities to invest in and a number of new options for how to do it (e.g., long or short term, large or small amounts, and with the ease of a keystroke in the way that the regular capital markets work today). It would create an environment in which investors all along a spectrum (government subsidy, philanthropy, CRA-motivated capital, socially motivated capital, market capital) could participate in social finance investment instead of being constrained by what too often seems simply a choice between market and charity. This is what is often referred to as the "capital stack." In the Self-Help vignette, for example, local banks, large national banks, a community development financial institution, a foundation, and a government-sponsored entity all participate in the same investment, but with very different roles and risk/return targets.

More sources of capital from more and different types of investors would create liquidity and flexibility in the social enterprise arena that is currently hemmed in by the narrow priorities of charities and governments. For example, most of the money spent on revitalizing low-income neighborhoods in the United States goes to building affordable housing, even though we know many communities have other higher priorities for improving their neighborhoods. The money goes to housing because that is what is subsidized by the federal government.

Secondary markets spread risk across a broad group of investors, which can attract additional capital into social-purpose investments. Much of the rationale for creating Fannie Mae (and later securitized mortgages) was that banks had a concentration of loans that left them vulnerable to real estate downturns in their local regions. Fannie Mae allowed banks to diversify their assets. Today, most social finance is often concentrated geographically or by industry and carries the same risk.

And this is not the only risk that is mitigated through a more complex social finance system brought about by a secondary market. As one recent analysis of community development financial institutions (CDFIs) notes: "Serving low-income local markets with limited resources means that, almost by definition, CDFIs cannot over time carry the uncertainties and the costs of credit risk, interest rate risk, servicing and other operating costs. With their smaller balance sheets and limited supplies of grant subsidy, CDFIs must place assets with entities that have the balance sheets, longevity, and efficiencies to produce the lowest interest rate available."[53] The secondary market introduces the option for the nonprofit or NGO to move a loan off its books as a way to limit its risk of the loan having trouble (e.g., difficulty in collecting payments or even default) at the same time it frees up internal resources to source more deals and serve more clients.

In the end, however, the value of a secondary market goes far beyond new sources of capital, liquidity, or spreading risk. In fact, a secondary market could have revolutionary potential to inspire a quantum leap in the evolution of antipoverty work in the United States and abroad. At root, more capital flowing through the system will increase the scale and scope of mission-related work, but as the growth continues, there will be a pressure for the entire system to change to handle the new activity. This change would force small nonprofits and NGOs, for example, to get out of a vertically integrated business model where they make a loan, hold it on their books, and service the loan repayment. Instead, these smaller groups might migrate to more of a broker role, capitalizing on their close relationships to the end users of capital and their knowledge of local conditions. This new network of institutions might feed loans to intermediaries that now are handling volume in the millions of dollars range. But if they were fed by a new network of brokers with product, and knew they had an outlet to sell that new product (once it was seasoned) to a secondary-market investor, the intermediaries might achieve volume in the billion-dollar or trillion-dollar range. Put differently, each node in the social finance network could specialize in what it does best, then grow in scale in response to increased capital flowing through the system. In essence, this is what Self-Help was able to achieve with CAP. What if there were similar systems in place for multifamily mortgages, small business and microcredit loans, and loans for community resources like schools, child care facilities, health clinics, and parks?[54]

What the development of a thicker and more sophisticated social finance network would also bring is a system that can finally focus on the needs of the end user, the customer. Today, the social finance network has a few products—affordable housing, money to start microbusinesses, and so forth—and uses those tools as a way to help low-income individuals and communities. But in some ways, this is a hammer constantly looking for a nail. What if the communities need products other than what the network provides? Having more flexible capital will allow the network to diversify its product line and "sense and respond" to what a low-income borrower, village, or neighborhood needs.[55]

Basic Mechanics

There are many good reasons to sell loans into a secondary market, as mentioned above, but it is not easy. It requires a number of players and has added complexity and uncertainty. As one long-time veteran of community development finance has put it:

> The vast majority of CDFIs are small and local, and, to the extent anything can be traditional in an industry barely twenty-five years old, traditional in the sense that they are structured as vertically integrated portfolio lenders heavily reliant on low-cost funding. The capital markets are huge, efficient, market-based, and global. Even the most sophisticated CDFIs find them difficult and often frustrating to access.[56]

So how does social finance sell its low-volume, customized assets into the high-volume secondary markets? It may be an oversimplification, but at a basic level, it is important to establish who are the sellers and who are the buyers. The next step is to figure out what these investors want to buy and what the sellers are willing to sell. This process is time-consuming and costly.

Consider the example of California Community Reinvestment Corporation (CCRC) and its sale of a pool of whole loans to Impact Community Capital, a consortium of insurance companies looking to make socially motivated investments. Their first loan sale closed in 2000 and included 12 loans that totaled $40 million.

"Selling loans is a lot like selling used cars," according to George Vine, CCRC's consultant on secondary-market sales. "The seller usually knows much more about the product than the buyer and the buyer is naturally suspicious about the seller's motivation for selling."[57] In order for the seller to overcome the buyer's concerns, the seller has to assemble all the data and information necessary to evaluate the loans and make an investment decision.

Before assembling the bid package, however, the seller must decide which loans to sell. A number of considerations go into this decision. It can depend on whether the seller is trying to maximize the price by selling the loans with the highest interest rates, or manage risk by diversifying geographic or borrower concentration, or it may be motivated by a short-term need for liquidity.

The bid package can go out to a small selection of potential buyers for their analysis. The buyers can be institutional investors such as banks, pension funds, or insurance companies. Or they can be individual retail investors working through an intermediary, such as an investment fund.

Once the seller picks the best bid from the group of investors, there is a period of buyer's due diligence that can be lengthy and involved, with site visits, additional inspections, follow-up reports, and legal arrangements that minimize the buyer's risks. As part of the due diligence process, the investor must make an assessment of loan-pool performance. This evaluation includes, but is not limited to, loan prepayment rate (what current loan balance might voluntarily prepay); default rate (how many loans will "go bad"); and loss severity (the default amount that is not recovered).[58]

It is best to have data on many loans that cover a long span of time. Armed with these data, the investor can build statistical models to get a clearer picture of future risks.[59] Data that go into these calculations include term and amortization of the loans, their interest rates and loan amounts, and specifics about the collateral. Data about the borrowers will include debt coverage ratios, loan-to-value ratios, and credit scores.[60]

Finally, there is a closing sale where the assets are formally transferred, with the risks for performance going forward to the buyer and the proceeds from the sale deposited with the seller. The relationship between buyer and seller does not necessarily end at that point, however. The seller can retain the loan-servicing function, for example, to preserve the relationship with the borrower. And there are often guarantees and other legal agreements that keep the two parties connected.[61]

It is important to acknowledge that engaging in a secondary-market transaction also requires loan sellers to reconsider their business models and how they do their work since it will impose many new restrictions on them. "The core of the decision to sell loans," according to one observer in the field, is "how to strike an appropriate balance between mission and loan liquidity."

> The secondary market values standardization in types of loans, loan terms, and loan documentation. Many [social finance institutions], however, value their ability to customize credit facilities to better meet their customers' needs. Standardization and customization stand in direct conflict; so too do the secondary-market values of large volumes and market risk-based pricing versus [social finance institution] values of local orientation and making difficult projects happen. These conflicts force [social finance institutions] into a delicate balancing act.[62]

This issue was also raised earlier in the Self-Help CAP example; to some degree using secondary markets requires social finance institutions to make a trade-off to sacrifice deep mission impact in order to achieve scale.

Operational Challenges

Although the concept is relatively straightforward, in practice there are many obstacles to creating and operating a secondary market—some inherent in developing any secondary market and others that might be unique to social finance loan pools. Seven such obstacles in particular confront the further development of secondary markets in the social-impact investment arena.

The "First Mover" Problem

To some degree, all pioneers of existing secondary markets had to find ways to standardize their lending practices and loan documents, collect and report consistent data, and overcome initial skepticism from the investor community.[63] In the case of single-family mortgages, for example, many specific factors bear on an individual home's value (location, quality of materials, design, etc.). It took years to establish a successful track record and create confidence in the investor community to believe pools of single-family mortgages could be turned into a secondary-market investment. This evolution would not have taken place without the careful management and credit enhancements from the federal government and Fannie Mae and Freddie Mac. As important as building investor confidence, however, was the role Fannie Mae and Freddie Mac played in establishing uniformity for applications and loan documents. They introduced the standard mortgage application in 1973 and followed with standard mortgage documents for all states in 1975.[64]

The creation of secondary markets for social finance loans faces all the challenges that the single-family mortgage market did (data, standardization, and interest from investors), but it has the added complications of low volume, thin spreads that make pricing difficult, and a business model that puts an emphasis on boutique loans with high levels of customer service that require intensive loan servicing. These characteristics do not lend themselves to the high volume that a secondary market requires.

One significant obstacle that must be overcome, therefore, is the identification of a mechanism through which to make the changes that are necessary to foster robust secondary markets. In the absence of a Fannie Mae, it is hard to imagine what entity would have had the power to mandate the necessary (and potentially painful) changes that were required in the housing field in the United States. Yet, in order to develop the social-impact secondary market further, participants will need the same kind of standardized legal documents, underwriting procedures, and data collection, and this will require greater coordination and system integration.

The Data and Information Gap

The key to attracting investors to the social-impact investment market is better pricing of investment products, but the key to better pricing is better data to enable the industry to turn uncertain investments into investments with known risks that can be priced fairly.

The volume of sales of securities derived from securitization in the regular capital markets generates a tremendous amount of data on prices and performance. This allows buyers and sellers to communicate more confidently about prices and risks. No such body of data or means of communication exists in the social capital market, however.[65] As the US Government Accountability Office noted in a recent report:

In contrast to other mortgage-backed and asset-backed securitizations, there is no comprehensive mechanism for sharing information with interested lenders, investors, and capital market intermediaries [in the social capital market]. Ad hoc networks, lender trade associations, and investor organizations do exist, but they do not provide updated and comprehensive data and information on a regular basis regarding loan volume. Neither do they provide a list of interested lenders, potential investors, securitization mechanisms, and credit enhancement providers.[66]

In the absence of these mechanisms, most secondary-market transactions in the social finance world have to follow a laborious journey to hunt down buyers, provide them with information, and negotiate conditions, guarantees, and terms for each transaction.

Developing Social Metrics

Another aspect of standardization that is often overlooked is the need to standardize the measurement of social benefit. In the social finance world, as Chapter 22 of this volume notes, there is both universal agreement on the need for better social outcome measurements and no consensus on how to meet that need. In the end, an effective way of measuring the social impact from institutional, retail, and government investments could change the way we look at both government and the market. A growing consciousness among consumers and investors about social and environmental issues is already changing the types of products and services that are available in the marketplace. Government, too, is seeking to change the ways it does business by providing more resources to programs that are proven to work and by directing funds away from programs that do not. Xavier De Souza Briggs, the former deputy director of the US Office of Management and Budget, captured this idea at a recent Federal Reserve Community Development conference where he explained that leaders in the federal government are trying to change "the DNA of the federal government" so that it can take more risks and reward investments that yield better social outcomes. That change—both in the market and for government—requires better data on, and better conceptualization of, social impact.

Organizational Capacity

Involvement in secondary-market transactions also imposes additional demands on social-purpose lenders. For example, it requires significant improvements in internal capacity to accumulate larger volumes of loans and to "warehouse" them. An organization needs more capital on its balance sheet to help manage the flow of loans.

A lender also needs new internal skill sets to manage the volume and exposure that managing a bigger balance sheet requires. With significantly more loans, more debt, and more borrowers, lenders will be exposed to more risks of nonperforming loans and to market risks such as a swiftly dropping market interest rates that could trigger a wave of prepayments.[67] Acquiring the skilled personnel and systems for handling these more complex management challenges is one of the major challenges facing the social investment field going forward.

Need for Credit Enhancement

In addition to substantial amounts of data and information that are easily shared, another element that is necessary for secondary-market operations is some combination of guarantees, reserves, collateral, or other credit-enhancing elements of the transaction. These mechanisms can be quite simple, as when a seller of loans simply agrees to swap out underperforming loans for ones that are doing well, as Habitat for Humanity does for its FlexCAP bond program. And the use of reserves is common, as in the case of Self-Help when it created a risk premium charge to its borrowers that funded a credit-enhancing reserve.

Foundations and government can provide credit enhancements as well, based on their creditworthiness. In the case of Self-Help's CAP program, a $50 million foundation grant provided the enhancement. And the charter school facilities bond program is made possible by a relatively modest credit enhancement from the US Department of Education. The CDFI bond program has a government guarantee as do many of the Small Business Administration (SBA) loan programs.[68]

Collateral, such as a home, can also be pledged as a credit enhancement, but this can be complicated. Allowing investors true claim on collateral might be a challenge for nonprofits and NGOs since it might be politically complicated to repossess assets from the world's poorest people. But as one observer has noted: "If you want people to have good housing, you have to be able to take it away from them. Because foreclosure is an option, homeowners can borrow at very low rates over a long term."[69]

Attracting Investors

There are many speculations about the massive latent demand for social finance assets, but this is still a theoretical proposition. What if you build it, and they don't come? In the social finance world, the underlying assets usually perform well, both domestically and internationally, but they do not get treated that way in the conventional finance marketplace. As one social investor put it recently, "We believe we have something tantamount to a 'AA' risk and we're not necessarily getting 'AA' pricing right now."[70]

Getting investors to try something new, especially those with regulatory restrictions such as pension funds, may require a host of changes in the incentive structure to help nurture social secondary markets in their early years.[71] This is similar to what was done for the home mortgage market in the mid-twentieth century. But to encourage the growth of the social finance secondary markets, there will probably need to be changes to the Employee Retirement Income Security Act of 1974 (ERISA), which guides the use of retirement funds, the Community Reinvestment Act of 1977, which governs bank lending and investment in low-income communities, and the Securities and Exchange Commission, which oversees the securities industry, along with many other rules and regulations.

Consider the example of creating online secondary markets for social finance that was discussed above. Currently a $647 million industry, online peer-to-peer lending is expected to grow to $5.8 billion by 2015, according to an industry leader.[72] But this industry is hampered by regulation that essentially treats someone who wants to lend a low-income borrower $100 to help her open her pet store the same as a Wall Street investor who must meet minimum qualifications of net worth and knowledge of the market in order to invest.

What is referred to as "suitability requirements," for example, can bar anyone with less than $100,000 in net worth from participating in peer-to-peer lending, which prices out the vast majority of potential retail investors. More importantly, it prices out the potential low-income investor who might be willing to take a chance in his or her neighborhood or village if a secondary-market vehicle existed for small investor participation. More than the money raised, this could be a consciousness-raising moment for communities all over the world. Almost anyone, anywhere, could make investments in themselves.

Mission Challenge

Finally, the rules of the road will have to be explicitly clear and guard against both the bad behavior—including outright fraud—that brought down the financial markets in 2008–2009 and a drift away from mission. The secondary market provides opportunities for specialization, but it also creates principal-agent problems and transaction costs. The social finance system must guard against losing the commitment to helping low-income borrowers at one end of the spectrum and also avoid falsely touting social-benefit claims to investors on the other end.

Track Record and Overall Assessment

As helpful as fully functional secondary markets are for social investors, it is safe to say that today they are underdeveloped and underutilized in this arena. The potential to leverage philanthropic dollars with this type of actor is enormous, however. As the discussion above demonstrates, the concept has been proven in multiple ways, with multiple asset classes. But many of these efforts appear to be one-offs or require very high amounts of subsidy to maintain them. And most of them depend on a functioning capital market to generate the scale of investment that seems possible.

This is not to say that there is not tremendous potential for this actor going forward. There has been substantial institution-building of public-purpose entities (community development corporations, community development financial institutions, nongovernmental organizations[NGOs], microfinance institutions, social enterprises, etc.) over the last 30 years that are now in a position to generate a critical mass of social investments.

It might be best to start with investments, product types, and asset classes with the best track record in terms of volume, data, and other preconditions necessary for success. The resulting infrastructure can then be extended to more asset classes going forward. This strategy would help build the latticework of the secondary-market field (the supporting institutions such as rating agencies, law firms, broker-dealers, etc.). It would also be an exercise in what one industry observer calls "baby steps," intermediate efforts to promote secondary markets.[73] In the end, a breakthrough seems inevitable since the network of socially motivated lenders has grown beyond traditional social finance strategies (e.g., government and foundation grants) and continues to knock on the door of the capital markets. It seems time to swing that door open.

Notes

1. Sondra Nelson is a composite example of a typical participant in a low-income mortgage loan program operated by Self-Help, a North Carolina community development finance institution. This composite was prepared by Allison Freeman and is based on panel survey data of CAP borrowers maintained by the University of North Carolina Center for Community Capital. Survey data and a description of the project are available at Center for Community Capital, "Good Business and Good Policy: Finding the Right Ways to Serve the Affordable Housing Market," University of North Carolina, Center for Community Capital, July 2009, accessed October 4, 2012, http://www.ccc.unc.edu/documents/CAP_Policy_Brief_July09.pdf.

2. "Access to Capital," Self-Help Credit Union, accessed October 4, 2012, http://www.self-help.org/about-us/policy-initiatives/access-to-capital.

3. The Center for Community Capitalism at the University of North Carolina at Chapel Hill has been studying the performance of these loans, which "could not otherwise be readily sold in the secondary market because of their perceived higher risks." These loans have "flexible underwriting and typically include one or more of the following features: low or no down payment, higher debt-to-income ratios, approval of borrowers with spotty credit records or no established credit, and waivers of private mortgage insurance and the usual requirement that a borrower have at least two months of loan payments available as a cash reserve at the time of closing." Michael A. Stegman, Roberto G. Quercia, and Walter R. Davis, "Sharing the Wealth through Homeownership: A Preliminary Exploration of the Price Appreciation Experiences of Low- and Moderate-Income Families Who Bought Homes under the Community Advantage Secondary Market Loan Program," Center for Community Capitalism, University of North Carolina, July 21, 2004, revised July 8, 2005, accessed October 4, 2012, http://www.ccc.unc.edu/documents/ccc-sharethewealth.pdf.

4. Roberto Quercia and Janneke Ratcliffe, with Michael A. Stegman, "The Community Reinvestment Act: Outstanding, and Needs to Improve," in *Revisiting the CRA: Perspectives on the Future of the Community Reinvestment Act*, ed. Prabal Chakrabarti, David Erickson, Ren S. Essene, Ian Galloway, and John Olson (San Francisco: Federal Reserve Banks of Boston and San Francisco, 2009), 51.

5. Stephen A. Ross, Randolph Westerfield, and Jeffrey Jaffe, *Corporate Finance* (New York: McGraw-Hill/Irwin, 2006).

6. The New York Stock Exchange, for example, is a secondary market. Investors trade securities of companies without the involvement of the issuing company. While stock markets are potentially the largest secondary markets, this article will explore a simpler version of this actor where the defining characteristic is the subsequent sale to an investor of a loan that had already been originated by a lender.

7. As one source puts it, access to a secondary market is "not only about gaining access to almost infinite amounts of money at very low cost, but also about minimizing the cost and the risk to the organization as a whole, while maximizing mission impact." See Charles Tansey, Michael Swack, Michael Tansey, and Vicky Stein, *Capital Markets, CDFIs, and Organizational Risk* (Durham: Carsey Institute at the University of New Hampshire, 2010), 261.

8. For much more detail of how a transaction like this is conducted, see the "Basic Mechanics" section below and Chapter 14 in this volume, on securitization.

9. Jeannine Jacokes, CEO of Partners for the Common Good, interview by the author, January 31, 2010.

10. Jeannine Jacokes, interview by the author, February 9, 2012.

11. "Foundations have been critical to ROC USA Capital's success to date," according to ROC USA Capital's managing director, Michael Sloss. "Both the Ford Foundation and the Calvert Foundation have made early PRIs to ROC USA Capital's balance sheet, providing critical liquidity to make the loans." Michael Sloss, e-mail to the author, February, 17, 2011.

12. "About Us," ROC USA, accessed October 4, 2012, http://www.rocusa.org/about-us/background/default.aspx.

13. Michael Sloss, "Aiding Resident Ownership in Manufactured-Home Communities: An Interview with ROC USA," interview by Kim Martin, PRI Makers Network, available at http://primakers.net/files/Aiding%20resident%20ownership%20in%20manufactured-%20An%20interview%20with%20ROC%20USA%20%28edited%20ms%2012-17-2010%29.pdf.

14. Habitat for Humanity International, "Flexible Capital Access Program (FlexCAP): Investment Summary," n.d., 1.

15. Luther Ragin, vice president of Investment at the F.B. Heron Foundation, which was an investor in the FlexCAP program, interview by the author, February 3, 2010.

16. Habitat for Humanity, "Flexible Capital Program (FlexCAP): Information Memorandum," June 30, 2010, 5.

17. Habitat for Humanity International, "FLexCAP: Investment Summary," 1.

18. Habitat for Humanity "FlexCAP: Information Memorandum," 20–21.

19. "Quick Facts," Community Reinvestment Fund, accessed October 4, 2012, http://www.crfusa.com/AboutCRF/Pages/QuickFacts.aspx. "CRF has begun to harness the power of markets to organize disparate development lenders," according to CRF president and CEO, Frank Altman. "The secondary market structure not only enables development lenders to tap the institutional capital markets, but it also fundamentally changes the ways in which these lenders view themselves. The participants in CRF's secondary market no longer view government grants as the sole source of capital in their development loans. They will be able to sell them to private investors and thereby diversify the sources of capital on which they rely to fund new economic development loans." Altman stressed that "we must increasingly regard federal assistance as a catalyst or incentive for private-sector investment." These efforts translate into finding "ways to improve the productivity of each dollar," he said. Frank Altman, testimony before the Subcommittee on Public Buildings and Economic Development—Committee on Transportation and Infrastructure, February 22, 1995, Washington, DC.

20. Elizabeth Wine, "Helping the Poor via the Capital Markets," *Investment Dealers' Digest*, February 28, 2005, http://www.highbeam.com/doc/1G1-129358437.html.

21. Timothy C. Leixner, "Securitization of Financial Assets," Institute of Higher Education Policy, 2007, accessed October 4, 2012, http://www.ihep.org/assets/files/gcfp-files/Securitization_of_Financial_Assets.pdf.

22. Investments must meet the definition of community or economic development used in the Riegle Community Development and Regulatory Improvement Act of 1994.

23. CDFI Fund, "Special Opportunities in the Community Development Financial Institutions Fund (CDFI Fund)," US Department of Treasury, CDFI Fund, n.d., accessed October 4, 2012, www.cdfifund.gov/who_we_are/SpecialOpportuniesAtCDFI.pdf.

24. Cathy Dolan, chief operating officer of the Opportunity Finance Network, interview by the author, December 1, 2010.

25. Dolan, interview.

26. For more detail on how CDT has structured its transactions, see Judd S. Levy and Kenya Purnell, "Case Study: The Community Development Trust Taps Wall Street Investors," *Community Development Investment Review* 2.1 (2006): 57–63.

27. David Sand, chief investment officer of CDT Advisors LLC, e-mail to the author, February 17, 2011.

28. The US partners include International Finance Corporation at the World Bank; the US Overseas Private Investment Corporation; USAID; and the Inter-American Development Bank.

29. Hilary Clinton, "Inclusive Finance: A Path to the MDGs Luncheon," speaking at the Helmsley Hotel, New York City, September 22, 2010, http://www.state.gov/secretary/rm/2010/09/147595.htm.

30. International Finance Corporation, "IFC's First Remittance-Secured Financing Enables Credit for El Salvador's Microenterprises, Lower-income People," press release, June 16, 2010, http://www.ifc.org/IFCExt/pressroom/IFCPressRoom.nsf/0/7703082F149 7FBD385257744005CA5F8.

31. International Finance Corporation, "IFC's First Remittance-Secured Financing."

32. Suhas Ketkar and Dilip Ratha, "Securitization of Future Flow Receivables: A Useful Tool for Developing Countries," *Finance and Development* 38.1 (2001), accessed October 4, 2012, http://www.imf.org/external/pubs/ft/fandd/2001/03/ketkar.htm.

33. Ian J. Galloway, "Peer-to-Peer Lending and Community Development Finance," Federal Reserve Bank of San Francisco, 2009.

34. US Government Accountability Office, "Person-to-Person Lending: New Regulatory Challenges Could Emerge as the Industry Grows," July 2011.

35. US Government Accountability Office, "Person-to-Person Lending."

36. US Government Accountability Office, "Housing Finance: Expanding Housing Finance: Expanding Capital for Affordable Multifamily Housing," October 28, 1993, 57, http://www.gao.gov/cgi-bin/getrpt?RCED-94-3.

37. Kenneth Temkin and Roger C. Kormendi, *An Exploration of a Secondary Market for Small Business Loans* (Washington, DC: Small Business Administration, 2003).

38. Brittany Dunn, "Neighborhood Housing Services of America Is Closing Shop," DSNews, June 11, 2010, http://www.dsnews.com/articles/neighborhood-housing-services-of-america-is-closing-shop-2010-06-11.

39. Blue Orchard, "How We Operate," http://www.blueorchard.com/jahia/Jahia/pid/358.

40. Blue Orchard, "How We Operate."

41. Asad Mahmood, "Microcredit and Capital Markets," in *Market Intelligence: Sustainable Banking; Risk, Reward, and the Future of Finance*, ed. Joti Mangat (London: Thomas Reuters, 2010).

42. Ajit Jain and Caroline Norton, "Microfinance: Where Do We Stand Today?" *MicroBanking Bulletin* 18 (Spring 2009): 9.

43. Mahmood, "Microfinance and Capital Markets," 6.

44. Ian Callaghan, Henry Gonzalez, Diane Maurice, and Christian Novak, "Microfinance: On the Road to Capital Market," *Journal of Applied Corporate Finance* 19.1 (2007): 120.

45. Blue Orchard, "How We Operate."

46. Mahmood, "Microfinance and Capital Markets," 8.

47. Jain and Norton, "Microfinance," 10.

48. Allison Duncan and Georgette Wong, "Social Metrics in Investing: The Future Depends on Financial Outperformance and Leadership," *Community Development Investment Review* 6.1 (2006): 60.

49. Nick O'Donohoe, Christina Leijonhufvud, Yasemin Saltuk, Antongy Bugg-Levine, and Margot Brandenburg, "Impact Investments: An Emerging Asset Class," J.P. Morgan, November 29, 2010, 6, accessed January 7, 2014, http://www.rockefellerfoundation.org/uploads/files/2b053b2b-8feb-46ea-a dbd-f89068d59785-impact.pdf.

50. Hope Consulting, "Money for Good: The U.S. Market Opportunity for Impact Investments and Charitable Gifts from Individual Donor and Investors," Hope Consulting, May 2010, 10, accessed October 4, 2012, http://www.hopeconsulting.us/pdf/Money%20for%20Good_Final.pdf.

51. David Erickson, "NeighborWorks America: Symposium Proceedings," Federal Reserve Bank of San Francisco, forthcoming.

52. David Erickson, "The Secondary Market for Community Development Loans: Conference Proceedings," *Community Development Investment Review* 2.2 (2006): 10.

53. Tansey et al., *Capital Markets*, 64.

54. For a discussion of how this bigger network could be an effective tool to revitalize low-income neighborhoods and regions in the United States, see David Erickson, *Housing Policy Revolution: Networks and Neighborhoods* (Washington, DC: Urban Institute Press, 2009).

55. I am in debt to Ellen Seidman for this idea.

56. Ellen Seidman, "Bridging the Information Gap between Capital Markets Investors and CDFIs," *Community Development Investment Review* 2.2 (2006): 36.

57. George Vine, "Selling Affordable Housing Loans in the Secondary Market," *Community Development Investment Review* 2.1 (2006): 50.

58. This summary is from Laura Choi, summarizing information from the National Credit Union Administration, in Laura Choi, "Creating a Marketplace: Information Exchange and the Secondary Market for Community Development Loans," Federal Reserve Bank of San Francisco, July 2007, 24.

59. As University of Michigan economist Robert Van Order said at a Federal Reserve conference on how to establish a secondary market for community development loans, "Without [good data], you're at risk of people who make the loans keeping the good ones and selling you the bad ones." Van Order noted that "understanding credit history and having a big database" gives investors some comfort that they are making good risk-return estimates. Erickson, "Secondary Market," 10.

60. Mary Tingerthal, "Turning Uncertainty into Risk," *Community Development Investment Review* 2.2 (2006): 25.

61. For another example of how loan pools are assembled and sold to secondary market investors, see John McCarthy, "Strategies for Selling Smaller Pools of Loans," *Community Development Investment Review* 2.1 (2006): 40.

62. Vine, "Selling Affordable Housing Loans," 54.

63. "First mover" is a concept well known in financial circles, as reflected in the following recent speech by Federal Reserve chairman Ben Bernanke: "The high costs of gathering information, together with the difficulty of keeping information proprietary, may have created a 'first-mover' problem, in which each financial institution has an incentive to let one of its competitors be the first to enter an underserved market. Without some coordination, the first-mover problem may result in no institution choosing to incur the costs of entry." See Ben S. Bernanke, "The Community Reinvestment Act: Its Evolution and New Challenges, last modified March 30, 2007, http://www.federalreserve.gov/newsevents/speech/bernanke20070330a.htm.

64. Denise DiPasquale and Jean L. Cummings, "Financing Multifamily Rental Housing: The Changing Role of Lenders and Investors," *Housing Policy Debate* 3.1 (1992): 22.

65. For an excellent treatment of the problem of connecting buyers and sellers with the information they need in the social finance market, and how technology might help solve the problem, see Choi, "Creating a Marketplace."

66. US General Accounting Office, "Community and Economic Development Loans: Securitization Faces Significant Barriers," October 2003, 24.

67. Wine, "Helping the Poor," 31.

68. For a fuller discussion of credit enhancements, see Chapter 12 of this volume.

69. Erickson, citing Van Order, in "Secondary Market, 10."

70. Cited in Erickson, "Secondary Market," 18.

71. "Pension funds have a fiduciary responsibility, which results in a bias against investments that are perceived as risky relative to alternative investments." DiPasquale and Cummings, "Financing Multifamily Rental Housing," 13. Public pensions are regulated by the Employee Retirement Income Security Act of 1974 (ERISA), and private pension funds have similar guidelines.

72. Galloway, "Peer-to-Peer Lending."

73. Jacokes, interview, 2012.

Suggested Readings

Erickson, David. "The Secondary Market for Community Development Loans: Conference Proceedings." *Community Development Investment Review* 2.2 (2006): 8–23. http://www.frbsf.org/community-development/files/investmentreview.pdf.

Seidman, Ellen. "Bridging the Information Gap between Capital Markets Investors and CDFIs." *Community Development Investment Review* 2.2 (2006): 36–39. http://www.frbsf.org/community-development/files/investmentreview.pdf.

United States General Accounting Office. "Community and Economic Development Loans: Securitization Faces Significant Barriers." GAO-04-21. October 2003.

Vine, George. "Selling Affordable Housing Loans in the Secondary Market." *Community Development Investment Review* 2.1 (2006): 49–56. http://www.frbsf.org/community-development/files/cdireviewvol2issue12006.pdf.

CHAPTER 4

SOCIAL AND ENVIRONMENTAL EXCHANGES

Durreen Shahnaz, Robert Kraybill, and
Lester M. Salamon

IT WAS A SAD DAY for founders Ben Cohen and Jerry Greenfield when Vermont-based ice cream-maker Ben and Jerry's was acquired by Unilever. Unable to raise enough capital to fend off the conglomerate, the founders had to accept Unilever's bid out of fiduciary duty to their shareholders, and no longer could they protect their "Profit, People, Planet" triple bottom line, where ice cream parlors often doubled as voter registration sites. Anita Roddick, founder of the Body Shop, had a similar experience. "One of the biggest mistakes I made was to go public and onto the stock market," she once confessed. "If I had had the knowledge then, and the patience [that I have now], I would not have.... Going public is really a way of saying that your financial bottom line is your motivator, and how you treat the community doesn't matter."[1] The Body Shop was bought by L'Oreal in 2006.

Acquisition by a larger conglomerate seems to be part of the life cycle of most successful social-impact businesses. Cereal maker Kashi was bought by Kellogg in 2000; Odwalla was acquired by Coca-Cola in 2001; organic chocolate maker Dagoba was acquired by Hershey's in 2006; Naked Juice was acquired by Pepsi in 2006; natural toothpaste-maker Tom's of Maine was acquired by Colgate-Palmolive in 2006; Silk Soymilk was bought by Dean Foods, and most of Silk's products are no longer organic. This trend suggests a common dilemma facing promising social ventures: lack of capital for scaling up to sustainable operations while preserving the primacy of mission.

Social stock exchanges, the focus of this chapter, represent one potentially important mechanism for resolving this dilemma. Such exchanges offer *businesses with a social and/or environmental mission* control over missions, a limit on speculation, and an investor base with an understanding of their social and environmental value. They provide requisite liquidity, exit paths, and price discovery for investors.

Defining the Actor

Defining Features

Social stock exchanges and climate exchanges are similar to exchanges operating in traditional financial markets in that they provide a market-type mechanism through which dispersed investors can buy and sell financial instruments

FIGURE 4.1
Social-Impact Investment Continuum: From Philanthropy to Social-Impact Investing

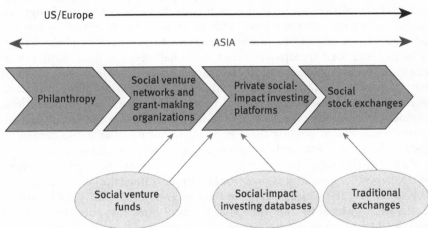

that deliver capital to the issuing firms. However, they differ from traditional financial exchanges because of their mission to promote the social and/or environmental aspects of the companies whose stock or other financial instruments are traded on them. These exchanges provide platforms enabling a large, dispersed group of investors with similar investing missions to invest in and trade financial instruments that promote social and environmental purposes while also achieving a financial return.

Social stock exchanges can be viewed as the end stage of social-impact investing.[2] As Figure 4.1 suggests, the social-impact investment continuum can be roughly classified into four broad categories: traditional philanthropy, social venture funds and platforms, private placement investment platforms, and social stock exchanges. Only the latter two can be appropriately considered to be social stock exchanges, though the latter is a more developed form.

Traditional philanthropy tends to involve individuals or particular institutions making decisions to support particular social-purpose organizations, typically with grants. Grant-based platforms arise when philanthropy moves from an individual decision-making process to a group-influenced activity through the formation of joint funds, networks, or "funding collaboratives," though typically still focusing on grants.[3] Private placement platforms provide a vehicle through which private investors who meet certain criteria prescribed by regulation can buy and sell securities directly for their own accounts rather than through brokers. Because of this character, they tend to be more limited in their participation than true social stock exchanges.

True social and environmental exchanges extend the basic concept of private placement platforms by providing broader marketplaces for public offerings and secondary trading of financial instruments of enterprises with a significant social or environmental mission. They serve as a marketplace for listing, trading, settlement, and clearing of shares and bonds issued by social enterprises and, in the case of environmental exchanges, for the trading of financial instruments that help firms offset the costs of achieving environmental goals. They thus provide a mechanism for listed companies to raise capital for social or environmental purposes through primary placements of securities and provide liquidity to investors through secondary trading of securities.

The term "social stock exchange" has been used in the past to refer to quite different entities that are not stock exchanges per se, but rather philanthropic grantmaking platforms. Their use of the terms "social stock exchange" or "social investment exchange" is not without basis, as they have applied many of the concepts of traditional financial markets to the field of philanthropy, including increased transparency and accountability. But their similarity to true social stock exchanges ends there. "Investments" in projects made through these philanthropic platforms are really donations, and are not returned to investors. Though each transaction is termed a "purchase" of "shares," these transactions currently take the form of donations. Moreover, the *social and environmental "shares"* sold by these entities are not negotiable and cannot be traded. The investment yields social impact only, not financial returns.

As for the climate exchanges, they have come to life and have grown tremendously in both scope and scale over the last 10 years since the launch of the first such exchange, the Chicago Climate Exchange, in 2003. This growth, which accelerated significantly after the Kyoto Protocol came into effect in 2005, has seen rapid increases in the number of such exchanges in operation, the regions of the world served by these exchanges, the types of contracts traded on the exchanges, and most significantly, the volume of transactions executed. In so doing, climate exchanges have demonstrated the benefits of utilizing an exchange mechanism in pursuit of social goals. Climate exchanges have proven their worth as mechanisms both for transparently establishing a market price for carbon and other greenhouse gases and for efficiently channeling private capital to address environmental issues. The success of these pioneers among social and environmental exchanges points to a potentially large role for other social and environmental exchanges, including the new breed of social stock exchanges, in addressing other social goals.

While there are significant differences between social stock exchanges and climate exchanges—and indeed significant variations among social stock exchanges and among climate exchanges—these actors all share the following defining features:

- Each provides a platform that brings together a large and dispersed group of investors.
- Each enables transactions to take place among investors (i.e., secondary trading) and in some cases also enables transactions between investors and entities seeking investment.
- Each offers investors the prospect of a financial return while also generating positive social or environmental impact.

An important implication of the last of these features is that these exchanges facilitate *investment* transactions rather than donations or grants. These exchanges are also distinguished from other actors in the social capital markets primarily by enabling secondary transactions among investors.[4]

To function, such exchanges typically require the following key ingredients:

- Listing rules that determine which instruments are available for trading and that require information relating to the financial and social/environmental characteristics of the investment to be disclosed in a standardized manner

- A fairly uniform set of financial instruments available for trading
- A set of rules for negotiation, trading, settlement, clearance, and governance, and a system of membership or some other mechanism for ensuring that those trading on the exchange abide by its rules

Design Features and Major Variants

While social and environmental exchanges all share common features, they also exhibit a wide range of variations. For the purposes of our discussion, we divide the field into its three main variants: (1) climate exchanges, (2) fully regulated social stock exchanges, and (3) private placement platforms. There are significant differences among these variants, and differences also occur within each major type. The most fundamental of these differences fall along four key axes: (1) the types of investment products that are traded; (2) the nature and extent of regulation; (3) the types of investors and other participants allowed to trade; and (4) the mechanism through which the exchanges contribute to the advancement of social and environmental goals. We will discuss each of these axes of variation in turn.

Products Traded

The most fundamental difference between climate exchanges and fully regulated social stock exchanges—and the source of many of the other differences between these two exchange mechanisms—is the type of investment product traded on the exchange. Climate exchanges enable trading in environmental rights, typically the right to emit a certain amount of carbon or other greenhouse gas during a certain time period. They thus resemble traditional commodities exchanges in many ways. They enable investors to buy and sell carbon credits and other environmental rights in a manner similar to how commodities exchanges enable the purchase and sale of physical commodities. Climate exchanges have evolved in response to "cap and trade" regimes (whether voluntary or imposed by government regulation) that seek to limit the emission of a pollutant through a mechanism that allocates a strictly limited, but transferable, quantity of emissions rights and requires that emitters hold sufficient rights to cover their emissions. Emitters not able to reduce their emissions below a given target must purchase emission rights, thus providing revenue for other emitters to install pollution equipment allowing them to reduce their emissions below their limits. In this way, the market in emission rights allows emission goals to be achieved in the most cost-effective way.

Fully regulated social stock exchanges are, by contrast, more closely related to traditional stock exchanges than to commodities exchanges. These exchanges, which are under development in various jurisdictions as of this writing, enable investors to purchase and trade securities issued by social enterprises[5] in the same way that traditional stock exchanges enable trading in securities issued by traditional companies. The exchange prescribes listing rules that set criteria for which securities are eligible to be listed. The primary distinction between traditional stock exchanges and fully regulated social stock exchanges is that the requirements for listing on the social stock exchanges will ensure that only securities issued by social enterprises (or, in some cases, funds investing in social enterprises) are listed. In many cases, these securities, whatever their form, will be issued by a social enterprise to a large, diverse group of investors in what is called a "primary offering" at the same time that they are listed for trading on the exchange and begin secondary trading, that is, trading among investors.

The range of products traded on social and environmental private placement markets both overlaps with, and is potentially broader than, those of the other variants. Depending on the market, these may include both environmental rights and securities issued by social enterprises and by funds, fisheries quotas, interests in private partnerships that invest in social enterprises, and securities of social enterprises that have not met the disclosure standards required for listing on a fully regulated social stock exchange. Like a fully regulated social stock exchange, these private placement markets may offer both primary investments into social enterprises as well as secondary trading of a wide array of instruments, though to a more limited market of investors. Secondary trading of certain instruments (particularly of shares and bonds of social enterprises) may be fairly liquid with a significant volume of transactions in any particular security. Secondary trading in other instruments (e.g., interests in private funds) may be much more limited.

Regulatory Status

Both climate exchanges and fully regulated social stock exchanges are heavily regulated, though under different regimes. In many jurisdictions, commodities exchanges and securities exchanges are regulated by separate bodies, and this regulatory division carries over to climate exchanges and social stock exchanges. Because of regulatory requirements designed to protect investors, social enterprises or funds that apply to list their shares on social stock exchanges are required to meet strict standards for disclosing information about their businesses, their financial results, and their social and environmental performance. The details of these regulations will naturally vary among different examples of these two exchange mechanisms, but the general characteristic of fairly extensive regulatory structures is likely to hold.

Because private placement markets are directly accessible only by those investors who are its members, all of whom must be sophisticated investors, the need for regulation to protect the investors is less extensive than in the climate exchanges or fully regulated social stock exchanges. Many of the unique features of private placement markets derive from this fundamental distinction, which leads on the one hand to lower regulatory compliance costs and on the other hand to lower liquidity due to a more limited universe of investors.

Investors/Market Participants

Most exchanges offer trading privileges to only a small group of members in order to enable the exchange to enforce its trading rules. As we have already seen, the members may be the ultimate investors—as in the private placement markets—or they may comprise a mix of market professionals and brokers—as is the case for the fully regulated platforms.

It is also useful to focus on the identity of the ultimate end users of the exchanges. In the case of climate exchanges, the end users are a mixture of emitters (who are required to hold emission permits sufficient to cover their actual emissions), promoters of carbon mitigation projects (who may have been issued emission credits as compensation for their mitigation efforts), market makers, brokers, and professional investors speculating on price movements in the rights traded. The natural buyers of carbon credits are those emitters who have not been allocated sufficient permits to cover their actual emissions. The natural sellers of credits are those emitters who have been allocated more credits than they need and promoters of mitigation projects that have earned credits through these projects.

In the case of social stock exchanges, the natural sellers of securities are social enterprises and social investment funds seeking to raise capital through primary issuance of securities. The natural buyers are social- and environmental-impact investors seeking to achieve social impact by providing financial resources to social enterprises, while also seeking to achieve some financial return. These impact investors are expected to include a combination of socially minded high-net-worth individuals, foundations seeking to make mission-aligned investments, certain socially responsible investment (SRI) funds, and public-sector institutional investors. For fully regulated social stock exchanges open to the general public, buyers may also include individual retail investors investing either directly or through social-purpose mutual funds.

Mechanism for Advancing Social/Environmental Goals

While both climate exchanges and social stock exchanges use an exchange mechanism to promote social purposes, they do so in slightly different ways. Climate exchanges are the byproduct of cap-and-trade regulatory regimes, which limit the amount of a certain pollutant that may be emitted in defined geographic areas and require that enterprises either make the needed mitigation investments to meet the standards imposed on them or purchase enough pollution permits to come into compliance without making the improvements. By providing a platform for the trading of the permits created by these systems, climate exchanges establish a transparent market price between the cost of abatement for the mitigating firm and the value of not having to invest in abatement for the polluting firm. The significance of this is twofold. First, by providing an efficient means of trading these permits at a price determined by the market, climate exchanges enable those emitters that can most easily reduce emissions to do so and sell their excess permits to those emitters for whom reduction would be more costly, thus allowing the required emissions reduction to be achieved in the most cost-effective way. Second, by awarding mitigation projects that meet certain criteria additional permits that can then be sold to emitters through climate exchanges, these exchanges provide a mechanism through which private capital is channeled to environmentally friendly mitigation projects, again making use of market pricing to ensure that the most efficient projects receive this funding.

Social stock exchanges also promote social purposes but without the spur of an external regulatory regime. Rather, they provide a way for socially motivated investors to assign value to different social enterprises and a mechanism through which dispersed investors can supply capital to these enterprises with the assurance, provided by the exchange's listing regulations, that the firms meet certain basic standards. Through primary offerings of securities to investors, social stock exchanges provide a direct mechanism through which capital can be channeled to social enterprises. By mandating disclosure of financial and social/environmental indicators, the exchanges give social-impact investors confidence that they have all of the information necessary to make informed investment decisions. By offering the prospect of liquidity, the exchanges increase the attractiveness of an investment to the investor, thereby enhancing the ability of social enterprises to raise capital.

Other Variations

In addition to the major variants noted above, there are numerous other differences within each type of exchange with respect to such things as the range of securities listed, the fields of activity, the exact details of regulatory regimes, and even the geographic locus of participating firms on both sides of the transactions. Similarly, exchanges are likely to vary in their organizational structure and in their social-impact reporting requirements. However, the major structural and conceptual differences outlined above are the most salient.

Scope and Scale

The arena of social and environmental exchanges is evolving rapidly, with the most established actors just barely a decade old and entire classes of entities (including the social stock exchanges) still in the early stages of development. This section will discuss the evolution of the sector to date including a brief discussion of the precursors to the entities operating today.

The Chicago Climate Exchange (CCX) was established in 2003 to facilitate trading in greenhouse gas emission credits among members—based primarily in North America—who committed, on a voluntary but legally binding basis, to reduce their emissions by 6 percent through 2010. The market served as a trading platform allowing members who were having difficulty meeting their reduction commitments to buy excess credits from other members who had exceeded their required reductions. Membership grew to over 450 members, including emitters with annual emissions of 680 million metric tons of CO_2 equivalent (tCO2-eq) as well as other parties desiring to buy or sell emission credits.[6] Volumes grew steadily, reaching 69.2 million tCO2-eq at their peak in 2008.[7]

The expansion of the CCX, however, was soon eclipsed by the rapid growth of similar exchanges that followed in its footsteps after the Kyoto Protocol came into effect in 2005, creating mandatory emissions caps covering most greenhouse gas emissions from 37 developed countries. That year saw the launch of the European Climate Exchange (ECX) and four other exchanges focused on trading the equivalent of compliance certificates for the European Union Emissions Trading Scheme ("EU ETS"), which was adopted by the European Union to aid in meeting its obligations under the Kyoto Protocol. The market for trading in EU ETS would quickly grow to be the largest market for carbon credits, and the ECX would grow to be the largest of the climate exchanges serving this new market.

The overall volume of trading in the carbon market—both on and off exchanges—was estimated at 8.7 billion tCO2-eq as of 2009, valued at over $143 billion.[8] To put this in perspective, the total volume of greenhouse gas emissions globally in 1990 was 39.4 billion tCO2-eq, so that the carbon market is now handling just over one-fifth of what global emissions stood at as of 1990.[9] Of the total trading volume, trading in EU ETS allowances accounted for over two-thirds, at 6.3 billion tCO2-eq as of 2009.[10] At the same time as overall trading volumes have increased, the share of such trading taking place on climate exchanges (as opposed to over the counter) has steadily increased—from less than 5 percent early in 2005 to over 50 percent by 2009.[11] As a result, the volume of contracts traded on climate exchanges has increased dramatically, with the volume on the largest exchange, the ECX, growing from 94 million tCO2-eq in 2005 to 5.3 billion tCO2-eq in 2010.[12]

While the CCX pioneered the market for climate exchanges, it ceased trading in 2010 after its holding company, Climate Exchange PLC (which also owned ECX), was acquired by Intercontinental Exchange (ICE). An explanation for the divergence in fortunes between the CCX and ECX may lie in the contrasting regulatory environments in the United States and the EU. The cap-and-trade system associated with the CCX operated on a wholly voluntary basis, with a view to preparing for the eventual introduction of a mandatory cap-and-trade system in the United States. However, as the likelihood of the United States adopting a mandatory cap-and-trade system diminished, the appeal of the CCX also declined, to a point where trading virtually came to a halt. By contrast, the legally mandated EU ETS system has ensured a steady demand for emissions permits from European emitters.

While trading in EU ETS allowances accounts for the majority of trading volume, the scope of the market continues to expand. From one exchange in 2003, there are now over 10 climate exchanges in operation, with several more in various stages of preparation. Climate exchanges have also begun to expand beyond the core European market, to Australia and Canada and even to developing countries such as China. In 2009, New Zealand became the first non-EU country to adopt a nationwide cap-and-trade system for emissions. Similar systems have been adopted by a number of regions within North America, most notably in the state of California. At the same time, after five consecutive years of robust growth, the World Bank reported that the total value of the global carbon market stalled in 2010 at $142 billion, a product of uncertainties over the post-2012 regulatory environment.[13] Still, as the evidence of climate change grows, regulatory systems to contain it seem likely to resume their spread. And as the experience in the EU demonstrates, as such systems spread, climate exchanges are likely to follow.

Whereas climate exchanges have taken the lead in demonstrating the applicability of the exchange model in the environmental sector, social stock exchanges and private placement markets are still in the development phase. Trading in securities issued by social enterprises has grown over time, but to date has occurred without the benefit of an established exchange. For example, in the UK, since as early as 1984 when Traidcraft, a UK charity that assists disadvantaged small producers in developing countries to benefit from trade, issued shares to a broad group of investors, there has been secondary trading in the shares of social enterprises.[14] Beginning in 2000, brokers focusing on the social sector, such as Brewin Dolphin, began to operate a market in shares of Traidcraft and other unlisted but widely held social enterprises.

A number of initiatives are now underway to create fully regulated social stock exchanges to bring added liquidity and transparency to these markets and encourage more widespread investment in social enterprises. In some cases these are starting out as private placement markets with the goal of evolving into true exchanges when the regulatory clearances are achieved. In other cases dual institutions are being set up. And in still others, the social stock exchange is designed to function in partnership with an established exchange.

Thus, for example, two initiatives to develop formalized private placement markets serving the social sector have recently been launched. These include Mission Markets, a deal origination platform and trading platform supporting the social and environmental capital markets launched in February 2011 in the United States; and Impact Partners, which is operated by Impact Investment Exchange (IIX), a Singapore-based enterprise that is also developing a fully regulated social stock exchange.[15] Both of these platforms allow social enterprises to raise capital in privately negotiated transactions from sophisticated impact investors. When fully operational, Mission Markets also expects to facilitate private trading in a wide range of environmental rights as well as securities issued by social enterprises. Impact Partners is a deal origination private placement platform created in March 2011 to connect social-impact investors with a select group of prescreened social enterprises in Asia. Similarly, in India, Artha has created a pilot deal origination platform with 94 invited "partners" focused on social-impact investment opportunities in that country.[16]

Efforts to establish full-fledged social stock exchanges are also underway. In the UK, Social Stock Exchange Ltd (SSE) is seeking to partner with an existing FSA-regulated stock exchange provider.[17] In Mauritius, in May 2011, the Stock Exchange of Mauritius (SEM) in cooperation with NeXii of South Africa received formal regulatory approval of rules for listing and trading qualified social- and environmental-purpose initiatives and impact investment funds. This initiative will operate under the supervision of a separate board of the Mauritius exchange and will be branded the Impact Exchange, or iX. In early 2013, IIX, the Singapore enterprise, and NeXii announced plans for IIX to assume NeXii's role in working with the SEM to bring the Impact Exchange of Mauritius to a successful launch later in the year. IIX intends to utilize the networks of issuers and intermediaries that it has built up through the operation of its private placement platform to support the first listings on the Mauritius Impact Exchange.

The appetite for this type of entity is also growing apace, as is the scale of the social-impact investment field generally. In the UK alone, public share issues for "ethical businesses" grew from a little over £4 million between 1991 and 1995 to more than £32 million between 2001 and 2005.[18] More generally, the potential social-impact investing market has been projected to be US$1 trillion over the next 10 years.[19] By comparison, the socially responsible investment market has been estimated at US$7 trillion today, up from nearly nothing 30 years ago, demonstrating the potential for rapid growth.[20] In short, while full-fledged social stock exchanges are not yet up and running as of this writing, the seeds for such exchanges have been firmly planted and considerable ferment is in the air.

Rationale

Stock exchanges have been in existence in the UK since at least 1694, when the English king William III first made government debt instruments transferable from one person to another, and even earlier in Amsterdam and fourteenth-century Bruges, in what is now Belgium.[21] Such exchanges facilitate the transfer of capital from those seeking to invest it to those with promising investment outlets.

If such exchanges are essential even in the regular capital markets, where firms are typically well known to investors, and financial institutions in command of capital are easily identifiable, they are even more critically needed in the still-emerging social and environmental capital markets, where investors are far more scattered and hard to identify and ventures much more obscure, embryonic, and untested. The rationales for exchanges in the social and environmental investment arena are quite similar to those that apply in the standard investment arena, with at least one important difference. Fundamentally, four such rationales can be identified: *first*, the reduction of transaction costs; *second*, the efficient allocation of capital; *third*, liquidity; and *fourth*, especially relevant to the social and environmental investment arena, protection of mission.

Reduction of Transaction Costs

Perhaps the most fundamental rationale for the existence of social and environmental exchanges is the opportunity they afford to reduce the transaction costs in linking potential investors with potential investees. Even with the emergence of a variety of capital aggregators, as detailed in Chapter 2 of this volume, the social and environmental capital market remains grossly underdeveloped, imposing considerable search costs on both investors and investees.

Consider the challenge facing an investor wishing to make a social-impact investment. The investor must first identify appropriate investment candidates either through a network of contacts or through relationships with advisory firms that specialize in raising capital for social enterprises. As Chapter 6 of this volume shows, however, such firms are still in the early development stage, and many investors, including institutional ones, are having to undertake the search process on their own. Assuming the investor identifies investment candidates, he or she must then perform due diligence on both the financial and social aspects of the social enterprise's business. This process will involve requesting, reviewing, and verifying information provided by and about the social enterprise. Only a relative handful of venture capital funds, foundations, and certain ultra-high-net-worth individuals are able to mount this kind of effort, and even the few collaborative investment groups such as Toniic, described in Chapter 10, are unable to handle these search functions at a scale needed to sustain this marketplace at a reasonable level.

The great advantage of a social stock exchange is that it can make the investment process simpler and more transparent and, therefore, less expensive and less risky. A properly functioning social stock exchange eases the investment process in a number of ways. It lowers investors' search costs by making it easier to identify social enterprise investment opportunities. It does this in part by ensuring that standardized information about each listed social enterprise is publicly available, and in part by centralizing the listing of social enterprises on a single platform so that they are not scattered among the thousands of traditional companies listed on mainstream financial exchanges. An exchange provides a centralized marketplace where investors can buy and sell a standardized financial instrument in an environment that encourages transparency as to the characteristics of the instrument traded and the prices paid. By creating platforms that bring together social enterprises seeking investment with impact investors aiming to direct investment to enterprises, and by systematizing the information flow between the two, social stock exchanges can substantially reduce the transaction costs of investing in social and environmental purposes and provide access to the broadest possible range of investors and the largest pool of investment capital. In the process, they substantially boost the flow of investment capital into social enterprises so that these enterprises can expand their operations and magnify their social impact.

This same transaction cost rationale operates as well in the case of environmental exchanges. Climate exchanges also make the process of trading permits much more efficient, reducing search costs and transaction costs dramatically. In the absence of an exchange, an emitter needing to buy permits would have to find an emitter willing to sell permits (directly or through a broker). The two parties to the trade would then have to negotiate and document the transaction. The existence of an exchange, which centralizes trading, eliminates the need to seek out a specific counterparty. The exchange also standardizes transactions, so there is no need to negotiate any terms (apart from price) or to create specialized documentation.

Efficient Allocation of Capital

A second crucial rationale for social and environmental exchanges results from their ability to promote the efficient allocation of capital. They do so by providing "price discovery," that is, information as to the price at which the market values a financial instrument, and hence an enterprise or activity. While this has obvious relevance in the standard business market, it has relevance as well in the social and environmental arena. Social- and environmental-impact investors are equally interested in the return on their investments, though they will likely measure this return in social and environmental terms as well as financial ones. An exchange can provide signals in the form of the prices social-impact investors are willing to pay for securities of various social enterprises about the relative value the investors place on the social returns they are getting from these ventures.

Though it applies as well to social stock exchanges, this attribute of exchange mechanisms is particularly evident in the operation of exchanges in the environmental arena. Cap-and-trade environmental regulatory systems exist to force polluters to internalize the costs of their activities by placing a price on the emission of carbon or another pollutant. The rationale for the entire system is that the cap will force emissions to be reduced in the aggregate. The addition of an exchange mechanism, by enabling the efficient trading of emission permits, makes it possible to achieve the reduction in the most cost-effective manner. Thus, if one emitter finds it very costly to reduce emissions while another finds it relatively inexpensive to do so, the first emitter can buy the permits it needs from the second emitter. By centralizing trading and making transparent the prices at which transactions take place, a climate exchange lets all parties see what is effectively the price of emitting a given amount of carbon. This very efficiently sends price signals that allow all emitters to plan effectively whether to reduce emissions themselves or purchase permits from others who can reduce emissions at lower cost. The aggregate net result of this efficient trading process is that the emissions reduction mandated by the cap can be achieved at the lowest overall cost.

Some cap-and-trade systems incorporate a further element, allowing additional emissions permits to be issued to projects that mitigate the effects of emissions. These projects would otherwise be outside of the regulatory cap-and-trade system—typically, they may be projects undertaken by entities not subject to the cap or in geographies not covered by the system. In many cases, these might be innovative projects designed to reduce emissions in less developed countries. In the European Union cap-and-trade system, these additional permits are called "Certified Emissions Reductions" (CERs) and are available to projects in developing countries that can demonstrably reduce greenhouse gas emissions. The incorporation of this element into the system has a dual role. First, it provides further scope for lowering the cost of reducing emissions—if it is less expensive for an emitter to fund projects that create CERs than to reduce emissions of its own business, the cost of complying with the cap can be reduced. Second, it provides funding for innovative environmental projects in developing countries that might otherwise not have been commercially viable. This is because project promoters can factor into their business plans the income to be earned by selling CERs. The price discovery mechanism that climate exchanges provide gives project promoters the information they need to make these decisions. And the efficiency that a centralized exchange brings to the trading system is a key element making it possible for creators of CERs to sell them to emitters who need them. Climate exchanges, therefore, serve to promote the efficient allocation of resources to environmentally beneficial projects in developing markets.

Liquidity

A third key rationale for the creation of social or environmental exchanges is the liquidity they offer to investors, that is, the ability they provide an investor to sell an investment with relative ease if and when the need to do so arises. In the absence of such an exchange, the investor must be prepared to commit its capital to an investment for at least a number of years, as there is likely to be no prospect of immediate liquidity. This further winnows the field of investors who can participate in this type of investment. The knowledge that one will have the ability to sell an investment when needed can make the investment substantially more attractive. The relative ease and lower cost of investing on a social stock exchange coupled with the prospect of liquidity offered by an exchange naturally opens up investment in social and environmental activities to a much wider range of investors—including all manner of institutions, individuals, and mutual funds—and makes investment in social enterprises much more attractive to investors.

Mission Protection

A final rationale for the creation of specialized social and environmental exchanges, as opposed to listing social and environmental enterprises on existing, traditional stock exchanges, is the protection such specialized exchanges afford to the missions of the social and environmental enterprises. This is a matter of enormous importance to social and environmental entrepreneurs for whom the protection of mission is fundamental.

Unlike raising capital on a traditional stock exchange, raising capital on a social stock exchange enables the social enterprise to access a group of investors whose investment objectives are aligned with the enterprise's social mission and who are familiar with and supportive of its business model. Many social enterprises that have considered listing on traditional stock exchanges have been deterred by the prospect of conceding ownership (and potentially control) to an investor base that may be indifferent, if not hostile, to the social enterprise's social mission. Moreover, these investors may be unfamiliar with the social enterprise's business model and have limited interest in investing in what is in many cases a small company relative to other companies listed on traditional stock exchanges. By contrast, the impact investors who will invest in securities listed on a social stock exchange will be supportive of the social enterprise's social mission and unlikely to push the social enterprise to sacrifice this mission in order to enhance its profitability. They are also much more likely to be familiar with the business models utilized by social enterprises and more comfortable with investing in relatively small companies. Furthermore, while the rules of a traditional stock exchange encourage companies to be run solely to maximize financial value for shareholders, the rules of social stock exchanges are expected to be crafted to enable social enterprises to enshrine and protect their social missions through a variety of mechanisms.

The existence of dedicated social and environmental exchanges can also be attractive to investors, making it easier for investors to verify that prospective investment opportunities will generate the desired social or environmental impact by requiring transparent reporting of listed entities' social aims and outcomes, which is not typically required of companies listed on traditional exchanges. The extensive reporting requirements and rigorous review that accompanies a listing on an exchange provides a degree of assurance to investors and relieves them to a large extent of the need to perform firsthand due diligence on the social enterprise's financial and social returns.

A Crucial Trade-off

There is, of course, a trade-off involved in making the investment process so much easier for the investor. Social enterprises seeking to list securities on a social stock exchange must make a significant commitment to disclose all material information about their financial results and social impact in a standardized format at the time of listing. This information is then vetted by a number of third parties, including auditing firms and the social enterprise's advisors before being publicly disclosed to potential investors. While this system of disclosure reduces cost significantly for investors, it does entail a significant commitment from the social enterprise—in terms of both management time and cost.

For the operator of a social stock exchange, the decision to operate a fully regulated exchange or a private placement marketplace is largely a matter of striking a balance between the benefits to the investor of access to complete information and the corresponding costs to the social enterprise of providing such rigorous disclosure. As compared to a fully regulated exchange, a private placement marketplace is likely to require a lesser degree of disclosure—in terms of both the amount of information that must be disclosed and the frequency with which it must be refreshed. This will lower costs to the social enterprises seeking to list on the exchange but will place greater risk and a greater burden to make independent investigations onto potential investors and will, therefore, limit somewhat the range of investors who will be interested in investing on the exchange and therefore the liquidity that the exchange can offer. A fully public market can ultimately offer the largest investor base and the greatest degree of liquidity, but it is subject to much more stringent regulation, which may limit the types of securities that may be traded as well as raise the costs to the issuer. The exact balance that is struck between the information required to be disclosed and the investor base that can be accessed may be a function of regulation in the jurisdiction in which the exchange operates, and will therefore vary from country to country.

Basic Mechanics

Like traditional stock exchanges (e.g., the New York Stock Exchange and NASDAQ in the United States, the London Stock Exchange in the UK, the Tokyo Stock Exchange in Japan, and the Bombay Stock Exchange in India), social stock exchanges serve as marketplaces for listing, trading, settlement, and clearance of shares, bonds, and other financial instruments issued by or for social enterprises or enterprises serving social and environmental purposes. As such, their basic mechanics mirror those of traditional stock exchanges, with the important difference of emphasizing social and environmental criteria in both their initial listing criteria and periodic reporting requirements. More specifically, six key steps are involved in establishing such an exchange, though the details involved in these steps will differ widely depending on the general regulatory structure for exchanges in the jurisdiction in which the exchange chooses to locate.

Organizational Structure: Freestanding or Modular?

An initial and quite fundamental decision in the design and operation of a social or environmental exchange is whether to establish it as a freestanding structure or to connect it in some fashion to an existing exchange from which it can borrow technology and operational procedures. The three most advanced social stock exchange developers as of this writing—IIX, the Social Stock Exchange in the UK, and NeXii—seem to have decided on the modular approach and are utilizing existing exchange infrastructure in partnership with traditional exchanges. This has the obvious advantages of accelerating the start-up process and reducing costs, but it brings with it the corresponding risk of causing uncertainties in the minds of social entrepreneurs about the exchange's ability to uphold its listees' commitments to their missions. Such exchanges need to make clear, therefore, their substantive autonomy even while benefiting from operational synergies. To address this, these social stock exchanges will each operate as separate boards of the traditional exchange with which they partner, with their own listing criteria and operational rules. The major environmental exchanges established to date—the Chicago Climate Exchange and the European Climate Exchange—have taken a different route, establishing stand-alone organizational entities, perhaps because their chief product differs substantially from counterpart products traded on other exchanges.

Determine Types of Securities Traded

Quite apart from whether a social or environmental exchange is freestanding or connected in some fashion to an established exchange, an early step is to identify the types of securities that will be traded. In the case of fully regulated social stock exchanges, these will likely be *shares* issued by for-profit social enterprises, *bonds* issued by either for-profit or not-for-profit social enterprises, and shares or bonds issued by funds that invest in for-profit or nonprofit social enterprises.[22] Such exchanges can handle both "primary offerings" to large groups of potential investors as well as "secondary trading" of existing shares or bonds.

As noted earlier, the securities traded on environmental exchanges are somewhat different, consisting of rights to pollute. Different exchanges can specialize in particular pollutants, such as carbon or other greenhouse gases and pollutants.

Various other features of these securities can also be specified. For example, certain social stock exchanges may limit listings to securities issued by social enterprises or funds operating in particular geographic regions or in particular fields (e.g., housing, community development, healthcare). Geographic limits are more common in environmental exchanges, though as noted, it has been possible to extend the reach of an environmental exchange focused on one region to pollution abatement in another region, as has been done with the European Climate Exchange's Certified Emissions Reductions program.

Establish Listing Rules

In addition to establishing the types of securities that can be listed, social and environmental exchanges must prescribe listing rules, which set the conditions under which securities will be allowed to list. More specifically, the listing rules set out (1) the initial requirements for the issuers; (2) the disclosure rules; and (3) the continuing obligations of the issuers.

The primary distinction between traditional stock exchanges and fully regulated social stock exchanges is that the requirements for listing on the social stock exchanges include social and environmental criteria and not simply financial ones. The exchanges must therefore develop specific social and environmental performance requirements that listing firms must meet, and disclosure requirements through which to demonstrate this performance. This is needed both to protect the social missions of the listed companies and to ensure transparency for the investors.

In addition to the initial listing requirements, exchanges must establish continuing requirements that issuers must meet and procedures for verifying fulfillment of these requirements. IIX, for example, envisions a social listing committee operating in parallel to the financially oriented listing committee of the marketplace operator with which it has formed a partnership, and meeting regularly to review ongoing compliance with social-impact and disclosure requirements.

Identify Membership Criteria and Rules

Stock exchanges typically have "members" who alone are eligible to trade on the exchange. Such members agree to abide by rules relating to such things as avoiding insider trading, agreeing to make a market in certain securities when wild fluctuations occur, and generally honoring purchase and sales commitments they make on behalf of their clients or customers.

Fully regulated social stock exchanges mirror this *broker-member* structure of traditional stock exchanges, with trading taking place between brokers (usually acting on behalf of clients) and other market members in securities that have been "listed" on the exchange. A crucial step in the development of social or environmental exchanges is therefore the development of criteria for such trading members, the specification of membership or licensing fees, the development of rules that will govern member activities, and, ultimately, the recruitment of these members. Social stock exchanges may choose to apply particularly stringent rules at the outset. For example, they may decide to limit membership to social-impact investors in the early years before extending membership to a broader array of investors or investment firms.

As noted previously, a number of early precursors of social stock exchanges have taken the form of social-impact private placement markets, which are essentially narrow bands of investors who handle a limited array of investments in carefully selected social ventures. Investors in these markets, access the market directly rather than through brokers or other intermediaries.

While retail investors may be the ultimate investors on social stock exchanges, they are unlikely to play an immediate role.[23] More likely will be the involvement of sophisticated individuals, institutional investors, and investment funds until the exchanges gain sufficient visibility and track record to reassure retail investors.

Establish Rules for Trading, Settlement, Clearance, and Governance

Another critical step involves developing the procedures for negotiating, trading, settlement, clearance, and governance of the exchange. These set in place the operational structure for all activity on the exchange. As referenced earlier, the relationship with existing exchange infrastructure and regulators will determine to a large degree how much design freedom the social exchange will enjoy in this process. For those exchanges that operate under the general umbrella of an existing exchange, the procedures will likely mirror those of the affiliated organization, except for the continued stress put on efforts to preserve the social mission of the listed enterprises. For freestanding exchanges, procedures must be established from scratch, though it is likely that borrowing from the traditional exchanges will be extensive.

Operational Challenges

Social stock exchanges are all still in the development stage as of this writing. Nevertheless, a number of operational challenges are already in evidence. These include regulatory issues, technological issues, user acceptance, and constraints on listing costs.

Regulatory Issues

Stock and commodity exchanges are subject to complex regulations about their internal governance and operations in order to protect the investing public from fraud or abuse. These regulations are primarily implemented and enforced by financial regulatory bodies in their country of operation, such as the Securities and Exchange Commission (SEC) in the United States, Securities Regulation Commission (CSRC) in China, the Financial Services Commission (FSC) in Mauritius, and the Financial Services Authority (FSA) in the UK.

Social stock exchanges must operate within the framework of these same regulations and must therefore overcome a number of regulatory challenges. First, the organization must secure a license to operate as an exchange in its market of operations. The licensing process is more rigorous and demanding for marketplaces open to the general investing public than for private marketplaces handling trades among a small group of informed institutions and individuals.

Second, the organization must devise listing rules that meet investors' and regulators' expectations for robust disclosure of financial and social results without being unduly burdensome on social enterprises that choose to list.

Third, the organization must develop exchange rules that protect investors' rights while also protecting social enterprises from the mission drift that may accompany shareholder primacy.

Finally, in the case of listings of foreign companies, the organization must overcome any regulatory hurdles unique to cross-border capital flows between the home countries of the exchange and the social enterprise. For instance, social enterprises in India must first list on Indian domestic exchanges before listing in foreign markets.

Technological Realities

Exchanges have grown increasingly complex in basic operational terms necessitating complex technological systems to facilitate quotation and matching of buy and sell orders, to clear and settle completed trades, to capture and disseminate trading data, and to ensure security and protect against fraud. This inevitably creates scale economies that make niche markets increasingly difficult to sustain. The result is to make it necessary to seek partnership arrangements to reduce the start-up costs and make initial operations feasible. Inevitably, however, such relationships can infringe on the operating autonomy of the social stock exchanges and confuse potential investors and investees alike. Great care therefore has to be taken in working out these partnership arrangements and in communicating the resulting arrangements to key stakeholders.

User Acceptance

Even once the regulatory hurdles are overcome and the technological issues resolved, significant challenges remain in attracting users to the exchange. This involves building the willingness and readiness of social enterprises to list and impact investors to transact on the exchange as well as gaining the acceptance of other members of the ecosystem.

The record of the Chicago Climate Exchange suggests that there are challenges on both the demand and supply sides to achieving the scale needed to sustain such exchanges. On the demand side, it remains to be seen whether there is a sufficiently large pool of social enterprises that are ready to seek capital from public markets, that have the ability to meet the required reporting and governance standards, and can be convinced of the value of listing with its attendant need for ongoing extensive reporting of financial and social outcomes, potential loss of control, and potential misalignment with investor interests. On the supply side, it similarly needs to be seen whether there is a sufficient quantity of social-impact investor resources to fuel a robust exchange and provide sufficient liquidity to reassure investors that if they get in, they can also get out if and when they want to. Social-impact investors may be unwilling to forgo the comfort level afforded by private placement markets for the initially greater uncertainties of regulated but still more indirect and untested social stock exchanges.

To overcome these problems, capacity-building aimed at emerging social ventures as well as extensive marketing and outreach to the broader social capital market ecosystem will be needed. This means gaining the acceptance of investment banks, brokers, research providers, rating agencies, law firms, private banks, and related stakeholders and opinion makers. This will doubtless require patience, time, and perseverance as well as plenty of start-up capital.

Ability to Keep Costs Sufficiently Low

Closely tied to acceptance on the part of social enterprises will be the costs of registration, listing, and trading. The costs of listing involve both the listing fees charged by the exchange and the professional fees associated with preparing for listing and conducting any associated capital-raising exercise. Of these two cost components, professional fees will typically account for the vast majority of the cost. A key driver of these costs is the regulatory regime applicable to listing. The more tightly regulated the listing process, the more expensive it will be to prepare the necessary listing materials. This factor may encourage social stock exchanges to avoid highly regulated jurisdictions with high costs of listing, at least until the sector has reached greater scale. A second key factor influencing the cost of preparing for listing will be the willingness of professional advisors to adapt their offerings for the social enterprise sector. The various social stock exchange operators have begun to forge a network of intermediaries to work with social enterprises. Similar to the way nominated advisors (in the UK) currently function on other stock exchanges, their role would be to bring social enterprises to market, perform due diligence, and ensure all listing and ongoing obligations are met. For instance, the Impact Exchange in Mauritius will require a nominated impact advisor to assist in preparing social enterprises for listing.[24]

Track Record

The track record for the most established social and environmental exchanges spans less than a decade, and others are not yet operational. Nevertheless, a number of observations can be made.

Perhaps the most encouraging sign of the potential for social stock exchanges has been the success of the environmental exchanges. In fewer than 10 years, environmental exchanges have grown from zero to 10 institutions with current annual transactions estimated at $142 billion. As exchanges, the climate exchanges have generally functioned extremely well, with high volumes, good liquidity, and acceptance from the financial community. This has created a useful precedent that gives a surface plausibility to the premise underlying efforts to create true social stock exchanges, with all of the challenges these entail.

To be sure, the success of the environmental exchanges in reducing carbon emissions is so far open to some question. The issuance of too many credits has resulted in low prices, which have proven to be a weak incentive to reduce emissions.[25] What is more, future prospects are almost entirely dependent on regulatory developments. The closing of the Chicago Climate Exchange with the collapse of hopes for a meaningful national cap-and-trade pollution control mechanism in the United States is an object lesson for those with overly Pollyannaish expectations. On the other hand, the establishment of a robust cap-and-trade system in America's most populous state, California, gives some assurance that this setback may ultimately prove temporary. More generally, signs point to the increasing reliance on cap-and-trade systems in the regulation of emissions globally, which suggests these mechanisms will grow in importance. In addition, over time, these systems may be expected to be applied to areas other than greenhouse gas emissions, leading to further expansions.

In the case of fully regulated social stock exchanges and less regulated private placement markets, the court is still out. Certainly, dedicated efforts are underway, spearheaded by entrepreneurial personnel and supported by at least a small group of farsighted investors. These embryonic institutions are forging important new collaborations that hold considerable promise for the future.

As the current trend of growth in social enterprise continues and the demand for social-impact investing expands, more traditional exchanges will embrace the features of social stock exchanges. The future prospects of both climate exchanges and social stock exchanges are encouraging because of the growing awareness on the part of both consumers and investors. Bringing people, planet, and profit together in capital markets is thus no longer a fantasy but a reality that is here to stay.

Notes

1. Anita Roddick, "A Dame of Big Ideas: The Sataya Interview with Anita Roddick," *Sataya Magazine*, January 2005, accessed July 31, 2013, http://www.satyamag.com/jan05/roddick.html.http://www.satyamag.com/jan05/roddick.html.

2. According to a recent J.P. Morgan and Rockefeller Foundation report titled "Impact Investments: An Emerging Asset Class," impact investment is defined as investments intended to create positive social impact beyond financial return. Nick O'Donohoe, Christina Leijonhufvud, Yasemin Saltuk, Antony Bugg-Levine, and Margot Brandenburg, "Impact Investments: An Emerging Asset Class," J.P. Morgan, November 29, 2010, accessed June 6, 2013, http://www.rockefellerfoundation.org/uploads/file s/2b053b2b-8feb-46ea-adbd-f89068d59785-impact.pdf.

3. For a discussion of such "funding collaboratives," see Chapter 10 of this volume.

4. A number of web-based peer-to-peer lending sites enable secondary transactions among lenders. However, this is true primarily of those sites used for profit-focused lending in developed markets rather than on socially driven lending to microentrepreneurs in developing markets.

5. Social enterprises may be mission-driven for-profit companies or market-oriented not-for-profit companies. For-profit social enterprises may issue debt or equity securities, while not-for-profit social enterprises are limited to issuing debt securities.

6. Marianne Lavalle, "A U.S. Cap-and-Trade Experiment to End," *National Geographic*, November 3, 2012, accessed June 6, 2013, http://news.nationalgeographic.com/news/news/energy/2010/11/101103-chicago-climate-exchange-cap-and-trade-election.

7. World Bank, "State and Trends of the Carbon Market 2010," 2010, 30, accessed November 12, 2012, http://siteresources.worldbank.org/INTCARBONFINANCE/Resources/StateAndTrend_LowRes.pdf.

8. World Bank, "State and Trends," 1.

9. H. Holger Rogner et al., introduction to *Climate Change 2007: Mitigation. Contribution of Working Group III to the Fourth Assessment Report of the*

Intergovernmental Panel on Climate Change, ed. B. Metz, O. R. Davidson, P. R. Bosch, R. Dave, and L. A. Meyer (New York: Cambridge University Press, 2007), accessed April 1, 2012, http://www.ipcc-wg3.de/assessment-reports/fourth-assessment-report/.files-ar4/Chapter01.pdf.

10. As of 2010, the EU ETS share had grown to 84 percent with the decline in growth of other markets. World Bank, "State and Trends of the Carbon Market," 2011, accessed November 12, 2012, http://siteresources.worldbank.org/INTCARBONFINANCE/Resources/StateAndTrend_LowRes.pdf.

11. World Bank, "State and Trends," 2011.

12. IntercontinentalExchange website: https://www.theice.com/homepage.jhtml.

13. World Bank, "State and Trends," 2011, 9.

14. Jamie Hartzell, "Creating an Ethical Stock Exchange," Skoll Center for Social Entrepreneurship Working Paper, Oxford University, August 2007, 1, Accessed April 1, 2012, http://www.sbs.ox.ac.uk/centres/skoll/research/Documents/Ethical%20Stock%20Exchange.pdf.

15. Two of the authors of this chapter are the founder and managing director of IIX.

16. "Artha Platform—Home," Artha Platform, accessed November 12, 2012, http://www.arthaplatform.com/.

17. "Home," Social Stock Exchange, accessed April 1, 2012, http://www.socialstockexchange.com/sse/?page_id=11.

18. Hartzell, "Creating an Ethical Stock Exchange," 8.

19. O'Donohoe et al., "Impact Investments."

20. Robeco and Booz & Co., "Responsible Investing: A Paradigm Shift," October 2008, accessed April 1, 2012, http://www.booz.com/global/home/what-we-think/reports-white-papers/article-display/responsible-investing-paradigm-shift.

21. Hartzell, "Creating an Ethical Stock Exchange," 1.

22. As in the traditional stock exchange, the major difference between shares and bonds is that shareholders are owners, whereas bondholders are lenders. Also, bonds tend to have a defined maturity (expiration date), whereas shares may be outstanding indefinitely. For a discussion of equities (shares), see Chapter 15 of this volume. For a discussion of bonds and other fixed-income securities, see Chapter 13.

23. There does seem to be an appetite from retail investors for social-impact investing, and initial research suggests that this demand will not cannibalize their annual philanthropic giving. Hope Consulting, "Money For Good," May 2010, accessed April 1, 2012, http://www.hopeconsulting.us/pdf/Money%20for%20Good_Final.pdf.

24. Anne Fields, "New Impact Investing Stock Exchange Is Making Steady Progress" *Forbes*, August 30, 2012, accessed June 6, 2013, http://www.forbes.com/sites/annefield/2012/08/30/new-impact-investing-stock-exchange-is-making-steady-progress/.

25. See, for example, Stanley Reed and Mark Scott, "In Europe, Paid Permits for Pollution Are Fizzling," *New York Times*, April 21, 2013, accessed June 6, 2013, http://www.nytimes.com/2013/04/22/business/energy-environment/europes-carbon-market-is-sputtering-as-prices-dive.html.

Suggested Readings

E.T. Jackson and Associates. "Accelerating Impact: Achievements, Challenges and What's Next in Building the Impact Investing Industry." Rockefeller Foundation, July 2012. http://www.rockefellerfoundation.org/uploads/images/fda23ba9-ab7e-4c83-9218-24fdd79289cc.pdf.

Hartzell, Jamie. "Creating an Ethical Stock Exchange." Skoll Centre for Social
    Entrepreneurship Working Paper. Said Business School, Oxford University, August
    2007. http://www.sbs.ox.ac.uk/centres/skoll/research/Documents/Ethical%20
    Stock%20Exchange.pdf.
Impact Investment Shujog Limited. "Impact Investors in Asia: Characteristics and
    Preferences for Investing in Social Enterprises in Asia and the Pacific. Asian
    Development Bank, 2011. http://www.adb.org/sites/default/files/impact-investors.
    pdf.
Knoepfel, Ivo, and David Imbert. "A Comparison of Leading Financial Centres'
    Positioning in the Field of Sustainable Finance." onValues Ltd, June 2012. http://
    hausercenter.org/ iri/wp-content/ uploads/ 2012/11/Comparison- of-leading-
    financial-centres- positioning- on-sustainable- finance_ June2012.pdf.

CHAPTER 5

FOUNDATIONS AS "PHILANTHROPIC BANKS"

Lester M. Salamon and William Burckart

DESPITE A 10-YEAR TRACK RECORD of high performance, Habitat for Humanity International (HFHI)'s innovative FlexCAP program, a "secondary market" type of operation that allowed the organization to recapitalize its affiliates with new mortgage money and thus to build additional new homes on a continuing basis,[1] ran headlong into the chaos created by the 2008 credit crisis. Simply put, commercial banks, the typical purchasers of the FlexCAP notes that allowed Habitat to buy mortgage loans from its affiliates, began to pull out of the program because they were increasingly concerned about their own capitalization in the face of the crisis and were no longer willing to make what they perceived as risky housing-related investments. HFHI, as a result, was ready to shut down the program, which would have severely limited HFHI housing construction at precisely the time when it was most desperately needed and land and other input prices were at their lowest.

Fortunately for HFHI, and for the thousands of families that depend on it, however, an unusual financial institution came to the organization's rescue. This institution was not a bank, or an insurance company, or a pension fund, or an investment house. It was a charitable foundation, but a new breed of this venerable type of institution—a foundation operating as a veritable "philanthropic bank."

US foundations, like their counterparts in many other parts of the world, ironically function much like classic private investment companies, investing their assets in stocks and bonds to maximize their financial returns and then using some or all of the resulting earnings to make charitable grants.[2] But in the late 1990s, the F.B. Heron Foundation, a New York charitable foundation focusing on child care, housing, and community and economic development, set out on a different course: to determine if a private foundation can "prudently make investments from its endowment that support its mission without jeopardizing the value of that endowment and, consequently, its ability to support that mission in the future."[3] To this end, F.B. Heron began experimenting with a wide range of alternative investment vehicles that could be deployed in support of its charitable mission—loans, loan guarantees, linked deposits, fixed-income instruments, and private equity—as well as with a wide assortment of investment partners, some of them for-profit entities.

As of the end of 2009, the Heron Foundation had over $110M in these types of nongrant activities under management, representing approximately 43 percent of the foundation's assets.[4] In the process, it has helped open a new chapter in foundation operations, one that a number of other foundations are now beginning to embrace as government budgets are cut, human needs continue to escalate, and the pressures to generate greater "leverage" from the limited foundation assets intensifies.[5]

Already involved with HFHI as an early investor in the FlexCAP program, Heron was a natural stop for HFHI personnel seeking a way to salvage the highly effective FlexCAP program from the ravages of the financial crisis. And Heron did not disappoint. Realizing that a traditional grant would not have attracted commercial investors to reinvest in the FlexCAP Program, Heron instead provided assistance in the form of a $3.5 million loan carrying a 5 percent interest in an effort to signal confidence in the underlying portfolio of assets HFHI was purchasing. In addition, it used its convening power to encourage other philanthropies and institutional investors to join in. And join in they did.

Defining the Actor

Defining Features

Heron is one of a growing breed of charitable foundations in the United States and around the world that are operating as "philanthropic banks," using substantial portions of their assets in creative ways to advance their missions and opening a variety of "windows" through which to dispense financial assistance—not just the old stand-by grant window, but also a loan window, a loan guarantee window, a linked deposits window, a fixed-income security window, and even a direct investment or equities window.

This is not an entirely new development, of course. Benjamin Franklin was this country's first "philanthropic banker," leaving 2,000 pounds sterling in a revolving loan fund dedicated to giving young artisans a start in life. "Philanthropy at five," the first recorded philanthropic investment circle, followed a hundred years later, its members financing ambitious low-income housing projects, some managed through "limited dividend corporations," and all determined to accomplish social good while achieving a 5 percent return on investment.[6]

In the wake of the Great Depression, however, institutionalized philanthropy lost sight of these early pioneers and defaulted to the presumably much safer course of building a veritable Chinese wall between the two wings of its house: an investment wing that was given the job of managing the organization's endowment in accord with prevailing "prudent man" trusteeship rules aimed at guaranteeing the best combination of financial return and preservation of capital possible; and a separate grantmaking wing that was given the job of dispensing a carefully controlled part of the resulting earnings in ways that served the organization's charitable mission consistent with the need to preserve the capital. Among smaller foundations that handle their investment function through external investment consulting professionals this tension is even more severe since such professionals are typically rewarded on the basis of narrow investment performance and often lack the mission commitments of foundation staff. It was not until the urban riots of the 1960s and the accompanying escalating concerns about poverty and equal opportunity demonstrated the urgent need to get more mileage out of foundation resources than this model allowed that a small group of forward-thinking leaders at the Taconic and Ford foundations found their way at least partly back to these early experiments and were emboldened to propose a different, more leveraged, way, to deploy foundation resources.

The upshot was the invention of the program-related investment, or PRI, the setting aside of a portion of a foundation's grant budget not for grants, but for loans or other vehicles of financial assistance that could stretch the foundation's resources by being paid back, with interest. The Ford Foundation, the first to initiate such a concept in 1968, put it this way in the statement announcing its decision to set aside $10 million—about one-third of 1 percent of its assets at the time—to finance such PRIs: "The Foundation does not have nearly enough cash to meet all the demands on its agenda, so the program-related investments should be a way to stretch limited funds, as well as attract the funds of others to good projects."[7]

With the passage of the Tax Reform Act of 1969, the legitimacy of such uses of foundation assets was enshrined in law, though with limitations. When the 1969 tax act embraced language cautioning private foundations against making any investment that could imperil their ability to generate funds needed to support their charitable activities, advocates of the PRI concept secured inclusion of Section 4944, authorizing private foundations to make "program-related investments" that may generate limited or no financial return. However, the law imposed some restrictive conditions, requiring:

- That the primary purpose of the investment be to accomplish one or more of the foundation's "exempt purposes"
- That no significant objective of the investment be the production of income or the appreciation of property
- That no purpose of the investment be to lobby, support, or oppose candidates for public office or to accomplish any of the other political purposes forbidden to private foundations[8]

Promising though the PRI mechanism was, however, it has experienced what can best be described as a slow climb. Constrained in part by IRS regulations, and in part by cautious foundation legal counsel who have encouraged institutions to seek specific IRS confirmation of the legality of each PRI deal, the take-up of the PRI mechanism has long been limited. Thus, based on the most recent data, fewer than three-tenths of 1 percent of all foundations—less than 200 institutions in all out of more than 75,000—have made any PRI in a typical recent year, and only eight-tenths of 1 percent of foundations' qualifying distributions are taking this form.[9] As one reflection of this, when a group of PRI-supporting foundations got together in April 2007 to establish a new affinity group to promote the concept of "mission investing," that is, using a foundation's investment assets, and not just its grants, to support its mission, they could not imagine naming it anything more ambitious than "2 percent for Mission," such were the constraints they perceived to be impeding the approach.[10]

What the new breed of "foundations as philanthropic banks" is doing is reimagining the field by taking the PRI concept to a new level. The director of mission-driven investments at the W.K. Kellogg Foundation seemed to reflect as much when he observed that "the Ford Foundation was the original impact investor, and those of us that have followed are building on their work and helping the field reach its potential."[11] While few have yet reached the position now staked out by the F.B. Heron Foundation, which recently declared its intention to commit 100 percent of its endowment to mission investments and to convert itself into a " 'foundation as enterprise' " whose "sole purpose" is "the effective deployment of philanthropic capital to achieve mission," using "all asset classes and all enterprise types" in the process,[12] a number are clearly moving in this direction. Indeed, the defining features of this new breed of foundation are clearly evident in the F.B. Heron declaration. Succinctly put, they involve the following:

- A clear commitment to breech more thoroughly the Chinese wall between the investment and program sides of foundation activity by *mobilizing substantial portions of the institution's investment assets* for programmatic purposes, whether these assets are managed internally or externally
- The utilization of a *much broader array of tools* to advance charitable missions, including not just grants, but also loans, loan guarantees, fixed-income instruments, linked deposits, equity-type investments, and the application of a wide assortment of positive and negative screens and active voting of proxies to ensure consistency of foundation investment activity with foundation missions
- The *conscious pursuit of greater leverage* in the use of foundation assets, focusing particularly on mobilizing the flow of private investment capital into social-purpose activities and using the convening power and social and intellectual capital of foundations to leverage philanthropic impact
- An *explicit investment focus*, seeking demonstrated social as well as financial returns backed up by meaningful metrics
- A willingness to be *agnostic with regard to the type of institutions* supported, including for-profits, nonprofits, and various hybrids so long as they are pursuing objectives in line with foundation charitable missions

To be sure, some of these commitments are evident in a wide array of foundations. As Chapter 19 shows, for example, many foundations have sought leverage even with their traditional grantmaking, experimenting with techniques such as pilot projects, matching grants, high-engagement grantmaking, competitions, and support for nonprofit ventures. But what is distinctive about what we are terming "foundations as philanthropic banks" is their embrace of all five, and particularly their heavy emphasis on the first two.

A Note on Terminology

Although we refer to such institutions as "foundations as philanthropic banks," we are aware that the term "bank" carries a variety of potentially misleading connotations if taken too literally, particularly in the wake of the recent banking difficulties. But we believe it captures well the notion of an institution offering financial help through a wide variety of financial instruments, and feel that pairing this term with "philanthropic" will help make clear that while the means being deployed are financial, the objective is still charitable and philanthropic.[13]

As noted in the introduction to this volume, a wide variety of terms has been used to refer to the transactions that such foundations might engage in: program-related investments (PRIs), mission-related investments (MRIs), impact investments, market-rate investments, below-market-rate investments, venture philanthropy, and likely others as well.[14] Several of these—such as mission-related investment—are used exclusively in connection with foundations, which causes confusion when foundations team up in these transactions with any of the other types of entities that have surfaced in the social-purpose investment arena, as other chapters of this volume have shown. We will therefore stick with the variant of the term that has recently gained popularity internationally—that is, "impact investment"—but that we have altered slightly throughout this volume to emphasize the type of impact that is of particular interest, namely social and environmental impact. Hence we refer to "social- and environmental-impact investment," or "social-impact investment" for short. Whatever the term, *the central defining feature of this mode of operation is the use of multiple instruments in addition to grants in order to leverage available resources to maximize social or environmental impact.*[15]

Design Features and Major Variants

While all foundations operating as philanthropic banks share the basic defining characteristics described above, there are a number of important variants of this model arising from differences in the way these institutions approach some key dimensions of their operations. Much of the available data on this mode of foundation operations has focused almost exclusively, however, on a fairly narrow range of actual activity, namely, that encompassed by foundation program-related investments. While some recent work has usefully extended the focus more broadly,[16] developments have been so rapid that we felt it imperative to undertake our own additional investigation to deepen our understanding of the "philanthropic bank" concept. Accordingly, we have undertaken in-depth case studies on nine foundations that seem to have moved fairly far down the road toward operating as philanthropic banks. Included, as noted in Table 5.1, were foundations that range in size from the $37.4 billion Bill and Melinda Gates Foundation to the $10.5 million KL Felicitas Foundation. Seven of the nine are US based, and two are based outside the United States. In terms of experience with social-impact investments, the earliest experimenter of the group included here was the Mary Reynolds Babcock Foundation in North Carolina, which entered this mode of operation as early as 1983; while the most recent entrant is the Bill and Melinda Gates Foundation, which made its first PRI in 2006 and its debut as a serious social-impact investor only in 2008, though it did so in a big way.[17]

In each of these foundations we conducted in-depth examinations of two to three actual investments selected to reveal how the foundation operated its mission-investment work. Altogether, 31 such cases were examined ranging across a broad spectrum of fields and types of assets.

Taken together, this work has highlighted five dimensions in terms of which the foundations functioning as philanthropic banks differ from each other: (1) the *share of resources* they devote to social-impact investments, (2) the *types of instruments* they deploy, (3) whether the *source of the capital they deploy* comes from program funds or endowment assets, (4) the *fields* in which they operate their investment activities, and (5) the balance they strike between reliance on *internal versus external staff* and *program versus investment personnel*. These dimensions are important because together they help to define

TABLE 5.1 CHARACTERISTICS OF NINE ILLUSTRATIVE FOUNDATIONS OPERATING AS PHILANTHROPIC BANKS

Foundation	Assets ($mns)	Location	Geographic service area	Major fields	Year founded	First PRI/MRI
Bill and Melinda Gates	$37,430.2	US West	Global	Health,poverty alleviation, education	1994	2006
W.K. Kellogg	$6,620.4	US Midwest	US,Latin America, South Africa	Economic security, education, health	1930	2007[a]
John D. and Catherine T. MacArthur	$5,737.3	US Midwest	Global	Community development	1970	1986
Fondazione CRT	$4,833.3	Northern Italy	Northern Italy	Housing, economic development	1991	2007
Annie E. Casey	$2,797.8	US Northeast	US	Education, child care, economic development	1948	1998
Esmee Fairbairn	$1,382.9	UK	UK	Arts, education, environment, social welfare	1961	1997
F.B. Heron	$253.7	US Northeast	US	Home ownership, enterprise development, child care	1992	1997
Mary Reynolds Babcock	$161.5	US Southeast	US Southeast	Community and economic development	1953	1983
KL Felicitas	$10.5	US West	Global	Social enterprise	2000	2000

[a] The W.K. Kellogg Foundation made three earlier PRIs in 1998, but did not launch a full-fledged Mission-Directed Investment Program until 2007, which is the date we have therefore noted here. See n. 17.

the *risk appetite* of the foundation, the balance it is comfortable striking between leveraging its resources for maximum impact now and preserving them for future activity tomorrow. Let us examine each of these dimensions in turn.

Share of Resources Devoted to Social-Impact Investing

According to our definition, foundations that operate as philanthropic banks devote a "meaningful share" of their resources to social- and environmental-impact investments. What constitutes a "meaningful share," however, is open to debate. As one benchmark, we can take the share of foundation assets that find their way into PRIs. In the most recent year for which data are available, that figure stood below one-tenth of 1 percent, a fairly low bar indeed.[18] In their more narrow study of 55 foundations that reported making "mission investments," including both market rate and below-market rate investments, Cooch and Kramer found that the average share of assets devoted to such investments stood at 2.6 percent, still fairly low, leading these authors to conclude that "most foundations are not yet harnessing the power of the vast majority of their assets for mission-related purposes."[19]

Among the nine foundations we examined in some depth, the record easily exceeds these benchmarks. As reflected in Table 5.2, the median share of assets

TABLE 5.2 EXTENT OF "PHILANTHROPIC BANK" ACTIVITY, NINE ILLUSTRATIVE FOUNDATIONS, BY TYPE

Type Foundation	Size class	Ratio of mission investments to:		Diversity of instruments[b]
		Assets	Grants[a]	
Mature				
KL Felicitas	Small	0.78	3.03	High
F.B. Heron	Small	0.42	1.26	High
Transitional				
Fondazione CRT	Large	0.089	N.A.	High
Mary Reynolds Babcock	Small	0.069	0.25	Mid
Annie E. Casey	Large	0.050	0.14	High
J.D. and C.T. MacArthur	Large	0.050	0.22	Low
Experimental				
Bill and Melinda Gates	Large	0.027	0.03	High
Esmee Fairbairn	Medium	0.023	0.16	Mid
W.K. Kellogg	Large	0.015	0.07	Low
Mean		**0.169**	**0.65**	
Median		**0.050**	**0.19**	

[a] Ratio of investments to grants estimated by dividing outstanding investments by five-year total of grants on the assumption that investments remained in force for an average of five years. Gates and Esmee Fairbairn estimates based on data provided on new social-impact investments as percentage of total grants in the given year. Grant Data from 990 forms and Foundation Center.

[b] Low = 1 to 3 different instruments; medium = 4 to 5 instruments; high = 6 or more instruments.

Sources: Author interviews, internal documents, 990 forms, and Foundation Center, "Foundation Growth and Giving Estimates," various years, accessed August 15, 2013, http://foundationcenter.org/gainknowledge/research/pdf/fgge11.pdf. All data and estimates are as of 2009–10, when the bulk of interviews were completed. Some features may have changed since then for some foundations.

devoted to social-impact investments among these foundations was 5 percent, and the average was nearly 17 percent. More impressively, calculated as a share of multiyear grants, these investments, on average, brought into the mission activity of these foundations an additional 65 percent of resources than were delivered in grants over the previous five years.[20]

These averages obscure a considerable degree of variation, however, in the relationship between the investment activity and both the assets and grant budgets of these foundations. In terms of the share of assets devoted to social-impact investments, the nine foundations varied from a high of 78 percent in the case of the KL Felicitas Foundation, a small Silicon Valley Foundation operated by dot.com entrepreneur Charly Kleissner and his wife, Lisa, to a low of 1.5 percent in the case of the W.K. Kellogg Foundation, a relative newcomer to the world of social-impact investing. In fact, it is possible to identify three relatively distinct clusters of foundations along the continuum of movement into the "philanthropic bank" mode of operation: first, a "mature" cluster made up of foundations that have committed well above 10 percent of their assets to social-impact investing, with the result that these social-purpose activities manage to outdistance their five-year grant budgets, in one case by three times; second, a "transitional" cluster made up of foundations that have committed 5 to 10 percent of their assets to social-impact investing, allowing them to boost the financial scale of their social-purpose activities by anywhere from 14 to 25 percent beyond what they spent on grants over the recent five-year period; and finally, an "experimental" group of foundations, several of which have made significant social-impact investment "bets," but in which these investments still comprise a fairly small share of their total assets, ranging from 1.5 percent in the case of the Kellogg Foundation to 2.7 percent in the case of the Bill and Melinda Gates Foundation, though given the scale of the Gates Foundation this still adds up to an impressive scale of investment activity. Put somewhat differently, a quarter of our sample of foundations are devoting over 50 percent of their assets to social-impact investments, another 50 percent are devoting between 5 and 10 percent of their assets to such investments, and the remaining fourth are in the experimental phase with less than 3 percent of their assets devoted to social-impact investment. Significantly, however, the foundations in this latter grouping are generally quite large institutions, so that 1 to 2 percent of their assets still constitutes a considerable scale of resources. In other words, if they are "experimenting" with social-impact investing, they are doing so at a scale that easily puts them ahead of the so-called mature group of institutions.[21]

Even this does not do full justice to the impact this foundation investment activity can have, however; for the real impact does not flow alone from the relation that the investment activities bear to foundation assets or grants. More important by far is the impact that comes from leveraging other sources of capital—from the $50 million loss reserve that the Ford Foundation provided to Self-Help North Carolina that ultimately allowed this secondary market for affordable housing loans to access $4.7 billion of private capital to refresh the capital of low-income housing finance organizations and thus allow them to extend new loans to some 51,000 low-income homeowners, or the $30 million partial guarantee that the Gates Foundation extended to the Kipp Charter School network in Houston that allowed it to access $300 million in bond financing at supportable rates for Charter School construction, or the $3.5 million loan that the F.B. Heron Foundation extended to Habitat for Humanity at the height of the recent financial crisis, which provided assurances to banks, insurance companies, and pension funds to continue their critical support to this important lifeline program. Measuring these leveraged impacts precisely is unquestionably difficult, but there is little question that they represent the real payoff from the new era in foundation social-purpose activity that this new breed of "foundations as philanthropic banks" is forging.

Asset Classes

One of the most striking features of foundations operating as philanthropic banks is the range of tools that they utilize. Indeed, a defining feature of such foundations is their active use of forms of financial assistance that go well beyond grants. Among just the 31 deals entered into by the nine institutions we examined in depth we found 15 different asset types in use, as noted in Table 5.3. These included senior loans, subordinated loans, convertible loans, bonds, bond guarantees, private equity investments, investments in venture capital funds, investments in equity fund of funds, and quasi-equity investments. Debt instruments (loans and fixed-income securities) were somewhat more common than equities (shares of stock), but what is striking is the sizable 42 percent of all the deals that did involve some form of social-purpose equity investment, a novel

TABLE 5.3 ASSET CLASSES OBSERVED IN SAMPLE PHILANTHROPIC BANK DEALS

Asset class	Deals	
	Number	%
Debt	**18**	**58.1%**
Loans	**14**	**45.2%**
1. Senior loan	1	3.2%
2. Subordinated loan	5	16.1%
3. Loan fund	4	12.9%
4. Loan guarantee	1	3.2%
5. Convertible loan	3	9.7%
Fixed-income securities	**4**	**12.9%**
6. Bond	1	3.2%
7. Bond guarantee	2	6.5%
8. Social impact bond	1	3.2%
Equity	**13**	**41.9%**
Real estate	**2**	**6.5%**
9. Real estate fund	2	6.5%
Public equity	**1**	**3.2%**
10. Public equity fund	1	3.2%
Private equity	**10**	**32.3%**
11. Direct private equity	4	12.9%
12. Private equity fund	2	6.5%
13. Venture capital fund	2	6.5%
14. Private equity fund of funds	1	3.2%
15. Quasi equity	1	3.2%
Total	**31**	**100.0%**

deployment of foundation assets. This is consistent with findings in the recent Foundation Center survey of 74 "mission-investing" foundations, though it is a considerably more extensive level of equity investment than that uncovered in the FSG study of 55 mission-investing foundations during an earlier period, suggesting a growing willingness of these "foundations as philanthropic banks" to experiment with a considerably more varied range of investment vehicles than the more basic loan vehicles that characterized the earlier PRI activity.[22]

Especially inventive in this regard has been Fondazione CRT of Italy. Operating through a specially constituted subsidiary, Fondazione Sviluppo e Crescita (the Development and Growth Foundation), the Fondazione manages investments in a closed-end real estate fund with social aims, operates a social housing initiative, owns nearly 50 percent of a microenterprise investment fund, owns 100 percent of a venture capital firm, is part owner of a microcredit firm extending loans to small businesses and families having difficulty accessing the traditional credit system, and operates a management company promoting technology transfer to foster high-tech firms in the Piedmont region of Italy.[23]

Even in their grant activity, moreover, foundations functioning as philanthropic banks are operating in novel ways, increasingly using grants to help seed complex structured investment arrangements entailing multiple *tranches*, or layers, of capital, with each tranche subordinate to the next. Grants typically take the "first-loss tranche" in these arrangements—that is, they absorb the risk of any initial losses on an investment up to the amount associated with the value of that tranche. Thus, for instance, the critical key to the success of the secondary market operation initiated by Self-Help, a community development financial institution based in North Carolina, to help investors in low-income housing recapitalize their lending programs was a $50 million Ford Foundation grant to Self-Help that has acted as a reserve against any potential losses on the loans originated by the participating lenders. The results have been staggering: the program has managed to purchase more than $4.7 billion in affordable mortgage loans, providing assistance to more than 51,000 families.[24]

While all foundations operating as philanthropic banks make extensive use of tools other than traditional grants, some significant variations exist among these foundations in terms of the extent of reliance on particular asset classes. Paradoxically, some of the earliest entrants into social-impact investing report the most risk-averse portfolios, whereas a number of the most recent entrants appear to have the highest risk tolerance. Thus, for example, the Mary Reynolds Babcock and MacArthur foundations, both of which began making social-impact investments in the early to mid-1980s, remain heavily invested in loans and fixed-income securities, mostly in real estate, and the same is true of the Annie E. Casey Foundation, which began making such investments in the latter 1990s.[25] By contrast, the two most recent entrants into social-impact investment among our nine target foundations—the W.K. Kellogg Foundation and the KL Felicitas Foundation—are heavily invested in equities, which generally involve greater risk.[26] This suggests that, increasingly, the timing of the launch of mission investing activities plays a role in the determination of asset mix. Early entrants entered the field when PRIs were the dominant modality of social-impact investing, and loans and fixed-income securities have long been the asset of choice for PRIs. As the field has matured, foundations have gained confidence to move into riskier asset classes, and the newcomers have followed this lead. Also likely important is the geographic focus of the foundation.

Place-based funders like the Mary Reynolds Babcock Foundation in North Carolina, for example, report facing challenges in finding sufficient deals in their target area that can absorb more sophisticated tools. This points up the need for attention to the demand side of the new social-impact marketplace and not just the supply side, a topic that is examined in the introduction to this volume and that is taken up more fully in Chapter 21.

Program- versus Endowment-Funded Investment

Another basis for differentiating philanthropic banks relates to the source of the resources used for their social-impact investing. This is of enormous significance since the resources available in the endowment are much greater than those available in any given year's grant budget. The problem is that orthodox interpretations of prevailing law on foundation asset management discourage foundation investment managers from being willing to tap endowment funds for social-impact investment. This orthodoxy has been fueled by a long-standing misunderstanding of prevailing law governing foundation investment behavior. Under both federal and state law, foundation managers are required to exercise "loyalty" and "care" in investing the foundation's assets. As we have seen, US Federal tax law, in Section 4944 of the Internal Revenue Code, further prohibits foundation directors from making "jeopardizing investments," that is, investments that might jeopardize the pursuit of the foundation's tax-exempt purposes. Furthermore, the impression that Congress intended to proscribe social-purpose investments from foundation endowments was ironically further solidified by inclusion in the federal tax law of the special exemption from the prohibition on jeopardizing investments for the whole class of investments known as "program-related investments," which, as noted earlier, can even be counted toward a foundation's required 5 percent payout so long as they are intended to advance the foundation's charitable purpose, are not primarily pursued to generate income, and are not undertaken to further a legislative or political purpose. By making a special exemption for this class of investments, Congress inadvertently fed the misimpression that the only mission-oriented investments that were permissible are those with a below-market return, that these were to be considered part of a foundation's grant budget and not part of its investment management, and that investments undertaken to pursue mission purposes, even when they came with an expectation of generating close to a market rates of return, were otherwise somehow suspect because their objective was not primarily the preservation and expansion of the foundation's asset pool.

In fact, however, none of these supposed limitations imposes very significant barriers to the ability of foundations to devote their investment assets to mission-related investment purposes. Writing in a well-known 1981 Council on Foundations *Handbook on Private Foundations*, author David Freeman put it this way: "Despite the admonition in Section 4944 against investments that jeopardize the carrying out of their purposes, foundations have considerable latitude in their investment alternatives," and more recent analysis has come to an identical conclusion.[27] The duty of loyalty and care fundamentally translates into a rule of prudence requiring reasonable care in choosing investments. And the prohibition against jeopardizing investments similarly boils down to exercising "ordinary business care under the facts and circumstances prevailing at the time of the investment."[28]

While many observers continue to distinguish between market-rate social-impact investments, which are typically made from endowment resources, and below-market rate social-impact investments, which are typically made from grant budgets and counted toward the payout requirement as PRIs, most of the foundations operating as philanthropic banks have, operationally at least, moved beyond this distinction and actively engage their endowment resources in their social-impact investing activity.[29] Thus, as shown in Table 5.4, six out of the nine foundations we categorized as substantial enough social-impact investors to be classified as "philanthropic banks" tap both their endowment and grant funds for these investments, and four of them rely mostly on their endowments. Because legal restrictions in Italy do not clearly permit foundations of banking origin to make equity investments, particularly from their endowments, and prohibit them from engaging in credit transactions, Fondazione CRT in Turin, Italy, has taken the innovative step of creating a separate entity to handle its social-impact investments, placing in it a portion of its programmatic resources each year.[30] Clearly, though, active utilization of endowment assets is one of the distinguishing features of foundations that are increasingly operating as philanthropic banks. In addition to giving them access to a much broader array of assets, it also relieves them of the case-by-case IRS review that foundations have typically felt obliged to undergo to qualify their PRIs as satisfying their payout requirement.[31]

Fields of Activity

While social-impact investments can be made in almost any field, some fields or types of activity are especially suited to this mode of operation. Included are activities with a reliable stream of revenue that can be counted on to pay back a loan or other investment, or activities involving acquisition of a tangible asset that can act as security for a fixed-income investment. Such situations are more likely to arise in some fields than in others. Reflecting this, even foundations

TABLE 5.4   SOURCE OF PHILANTHROPIC BANK CAPITAL

Type	Source of philanthropic bank capital		
Foundation	Mostly grants	Balance grants / endowment	Mostly endowment
Mature			
F.B. Heron			X
KL Felicitas			X
Transitional			
Fondazione CRT	X		
Mary Reynolds Babcock		X	
Annie E. Casey			X
MacArthur	X		
Experimental			
Esmee Fairbairn		X	
W.K. Kellogg			X
Bill and Melinda Gates	X		
Total	**3**	**2**	**4**

operating as mature philanthropic banks tend to focus their energies on particular fields. As noted in Table 5.5, the most common of these are housing and economic development, with six and five of our nine target foundations, respectively, operating in these fields. For instance, the Mary Reynolds Babcock Foundation has 100 percent of its social-impact investments in housing and community development. For the Annie E. Casey Foundation this figure is 70 percent, while at the Heron Foundation it is 40 percent. Interestingly, for Annie E. Casey, education and child care have received only 2 percent of the social-impact investment resources each, which is notable because this foundation focuses its grant activities on children and youth. Evidently there are limitations on the fields in which social-impact investments can most reliably be used. This means, of course, that not all foundations can be expected to engage in such investments. Thus, for example, the Mary Reynolds Babcock Foundation began using social-impact investments only when it shifted its focus from capacity-building for small, grassroots advocacy organizations and coalition-building across race and class—fields in which philanthropic bank approaches do not work well—to a strategy focused on having a more direct impact on poverty and helping people and communities build economic assets. As further evidence of this link between programmatic focus and utility of social-impact investments, although education has attracted investments from five of these organizations, most of the proceeds have gone towards the support of facilities for charter schools rather than for education programs per se.

This concentration of activity is even more striking when we examine the distribution of our 31 deals. Thus, as shown in Table 5.6, close to half of these 31 deals fall into the economic development category. This included the substantial number of investments in equity funds and may therefore be somewhat

TABLE 5.5   PRIMARY FIELDS AND STYLE OF PHILANTHROPIC BANK INVESTMENTS

Type	Fields				
Foundation	Housing and community development	Economic development	Education	Health	Field building
Mature					
F.B. Heron	X	X	X		X
KL Felicitas		X		X	X
Transitional					
Fondazione CRT	X	X			
Mary Reynolds Babcock	X				X
Annie E. Casey	X	X	X	X	X
MacArthur	X				X
Early Stage					
Esmee Fairbairn	X		X		
W.K. Kellogg		X	X	X	X
Bill and Melinda Gates			X	X	X
Total	6	5	5	4	7

TABLE 5.6 DISTRIBUTION OF PHILANTHROPIC BANK
DEALS AMONG FIELDS

Field	Deals	
	Number	%
Housing	7	22.6%
Economic development	15	48.4%
Education	3	9.7%
Health	3	9.7%
Environment	3	9.7%
Total	**31**	**100.0%**

misleading since these funds will ultimately channel the resources into various fields of activity. Another 20 percent of the deals focused on housing and community development. By contrast, health, education, and the environment were the focus of only 10 percent of the deals each.

Staffing

A final basis for differentiating philanthropic banks relates to the way the institutions staff their social-impact investment function. Generally speaking, as reported in Table 5.7, while making some use of external staff, all of these institutions engage internal staff in the management of their social-impact investment work. Interestingly, moreover, it is overwhelmingly specialized social-impact investment staff that have been brought in to handle this function, not regular investment staff. This may reflect the long-standing emphasis on investment return as the measure of performance for both internal and external investment staff. Interestingly, few of these foundations indicated extensive involvement of the program staffs in the social-impact investments. These findings suggest a growing professionalization and regularization of the social-impact investment work consistent with the maturation of these institutions as "philanthropic banks." This may explain the striking difference between these findings and those reported in previous studies. Thus, the Ford Foundation's 1991 retrospective on its PRI investments chronicles the integration of specialized PRI investment staff and regular program staff following the shift of the PRI function to the "program" side of the house in the early 1980s. Notes the report: "The years since this reorganization have led to greater integration between PRI and grant programs. . . PRI requests are reviewed by both grant and PRI staff."[32] A similar conclusion emerged from the FSG study, which covered the period 2001–2005. In that study, too, investment staff were not the main actors in the social-impact investment work. But it was the program staff who were identified as carrying the load in this period, not specialized social-impact investment staff and their outside advisors. One explanation for this different result may be that during the periods covered by these earlier reports most of the investments were still of the PRI variety, and therefore being made out of program funds, for which program staff would have responsibility. The increased use of endowment funds to capitalize social-impact investing by the more mature "philanthropic banks" has apparently brought a

TABLE 5.7 STAFFING OF PHILANTHROPIC BANK ACTIVITY

| Type | Staffing pattern | | | | | | | | Investment Style | | |
| | External staffing | | | Internal staffing | | | | | | | |
Foundation	Mostly external	Balance internal & external	Mostly internal	Mostly program	Mostly investment	Mostly special MRI staff	Balance program & investment	Balance program & special MRI	Mostly direct	Balance direct & indirect	Mostly indirect
Mature											
F.B. Heron			X			X				X	
KL Felicitas		X				X				X	
Transitional											
Fondazione CRT			X			X					X
M.R. Babcock	X						X				X
Annie E. Casey			X			X					X
MacArthur			X			X					X
Experimental											
Esmee Fairbairn			X			X				X	
W.K. Kellogg		X				X				X	
Bill & Melinda Gates			X					X	X		
Total	1	2	6	0	0	7	1	1	1	4	4

new type of staff into the picture, one that was not on the scene when the earlier study was done and not included in its identification of staffing options.[33]

Building specialized internal social-impact investment staff may not be an option for all foundations seeking to gain the leverage that operating as a philanthropic bank brings. And our data reveal an alternative option as well reflected in the operation of the Babcock Foundation's quite robust, but differently structured, social-impact investment operation. Recognizing its lack of capacity to structure and monitor individual deals in its targeted fields of operation, Babcock, a smaller, regionally focused foundation, has chosen to operate and invest in experienced intermediaries with track records for underwriting and monitoring social-impact investors. In short, they operate their social-impact investments much as they operate their overall endowment investors, by relying on outside professionals whose performance they monitor.

This mode of operation seems likely to become more widespread, moreover, as the social-capital market develops. As outlined in Chapter 2 of this volume, a significant growth has occurred in the number of capital aggregators, or investment funds, that have surfaced in the social-purpose investment arena, and these entities function as transmission belts between sources of funds and social enterprises in need of them. What is more, as noted in Chapter 6 of this volume, specialized "enterprise brokers" have also begun to surface—entities that focus not on aggregating capital but on vetting promising social-impact investment options in particular fields. These developments suggest that operating as philanthropic banks is not reserved only for large foundations with numerous staff but can be a workable mode of operation for foundations of many different sizes and levels of sophistication.

Indeed, while specialized social-impact investment staff have assumed the lead for social-impact investments at many of the foundations functioning as philanthropic banks, these foundations, too, nevertheless draw in external advisors or investment staff during the assessment of particular deals. For instance, the Esmee Fairbairn Foundation utilized outside counsel, both investment and legal, for two of the three deals examined here: one to leverage the financial insight of a co-investor and the other to clarify the legal liability of the foundation for the investment. The Kellogg Foundation similarly utilizes external advisors for particular types of assistance. In the three deals examined here this was not because the foundation lacked resident skills but rather because the increasing volume of direct deals simply necessitated an increase in capacity at the foundation. Kellogg indicated that outsourcing investment management costs the foundation, on average, 2 percent of mission investment earnings.[34]

In fact, only one of the institutions examined here makes most of its investments directly into the end users of its resources. The other eight make their investments into funds, or utilize some combination of direct investments and investments through such funds. As the social-purpose intermediary market matures, it seems likely that this avenue will become more popular for foundations, enabling them to keep their internal staffing limited while relying on the capital aggregators and enterprise brokers to perform a kind of middleman role, identifying promising ventures in various fields for an array of philanthropic banks and coordinating the due diligence and monitoring in ways that reduce the fixed costs to any one foundation.

Scope and Scale

Gauging the size of the universe of foundations functioning as philanthropic banks is complicated by the novelty of the phenomenon and the gross gaps in basic knowledge about this facet of foundation operations. What seems clear, however, is that the numbers are fairly small, but growing.

The only relatively complete data on nongrant forms of foundation assistance focus on program-related investments.[35] As already noted, those data make clear that even this highly limited form of nongrant activity engages a fairly small portion of the entire foundation universe. The number of PRI makers peaked at 133 in 2004 and dropped back to 120 as of 2007, the latest year for which data are available. This latter figure represented considerably less than two-tenths of 1 percent of the 75,187 foundations in existence as of that year.[36] Since some foundations make PRIs in one year but not another, it is likely that the actual universe of foundations that have ever made a PRI is higher than this. One estimate, based on the number of foundations that FSG initially identified for its survey from PRI records as having ever made a PRI, would put that number as not greater than 300, still only four-tenths of 1 percent of all foundations in existence as of 2007.[37]

PRI-making foundations are generally, but by no means exclusively, among the largest foundations, but the scale of PRIs is nevertheless dwarfed by the scale of both foundation assets and foundation grants. In particular, the $387.7 million in PRIs authorized in 2007 represented less than one-tenth of 1 percent of the $682.2 billion in foundation assets, and barely eight-tenths of 1 percent of foundation grants and other distributions. This limited scale likely results at least in part from the limitations on the PRI instrument resulting from the perceived need to secure IRS approval in order to justify treating the investments as eligible to earn payout requirement credits, a need that, as noted earlier, has been substantially reduced by recent, revised IRS guidance on permissible types of PRIs.

Data on the scale of foundations going beyond PRIs to utilize their endowments for social-impact investing are even more limited than the data on PRI makers. But some clues have recently become available. In the first place, of the 300 at least one-time PRI makers surveyed by FSG for its 2007 report, only 92 responded. Only 55 of these provided detail on their investments, however, and the overwhelming majority (82 percent) of these investments were loans, suggesting that they were really PRIs and not so-called market-rate investments made out of foundation endowments. This suggests a relatively small band of pioneering institutions engaged in endowment-based, social-impact investing as of 2005, the latest year on which the FSG researchers were able to collect data.

If this is the case, responses to questions asked about social-impact investing on the more recent 2011 Foundation Center annual survey of 1,200 foundations suggest that this pioneering band has gained significant adherents. Of the 1,200 foundations surveyed, 168, or 14 percent of the total, reported some type of social-impact investing in the year preceding the survey.[38] Of these, about half were exclusively PRI investors, suggesting that 7 percent of foundations may have experimented with non-PRI, endowment-based social-impact investments. Roughly half of these were clearly in the experimental phase of this practice, however, devoting 5 percent or less of their assets to such investment. This leaves 3.5 percent with the level of investment involvement that would qualify them to be considered "philanthropic banks." Since the Foundation Center data indicate that foundations with grant budgets in excess of $10 million are twice as likely as those with grant budgets under $10 million to engage in such endowment-based social-impact investment, we can roughly, and generously, set the upper limit on the number of foundations functioning in a fashion that begins to approach our model of a "philanthropic bank" at 75 institutions.[39]

Globally, the picture of social-impact investing among foundations is even less clear. In the first report on the European venture philanthropy industry released in late 2011, the European Venture Philanthropy Association (EVPA) reported that the 50 organizations responding to its survey had invested roughly 1 billion euros in venture philanthropy in Europe. However, the overwhelming majority of this (72 percent) took the form of high-engagement grantmaking, leaving only 28 percent, roughly 280 million euros, to be used for equity and quasi-equity investments (11 percent), debt (9 percent), guarantees (2 percent), and other types of investments (6 percent).[40]

While comparable data for other regions is unavailable, founders of the EVPA recently launched the Asian Venture Philanthropy Network (AVPN), suggesting that venture philanthropy is emerging in Asia as well. And outside the United States this term is being used to refer not just to its American concept—high-engagement grantmaking—but to what we here term social-impact investing as well. Our research indicates that such international experimentation is indeed occurring, with foundations such as Italy's Fondazione CRT and the UK's Esmee Fairbairn Foundation helping to lead the push for more leveraged forms of charitable financing. The case of Fondazione CRT is particularly noteworthy because, as noted above,[41] Italian law places constraints on the extent to which the foundations of banking origin in that country can directly engage in venture philanthropy management of nonprofit organizations, make loans, or utilize other financial instruments.

Rationale

The appearance of "foundations as philanthropic banks" may constitute a new chapter in the long history of organized philanthropy, but it also represents only the latest manifestation of a long-standing philanthropic impulse. As Peter Frumkin reminds us in Chapter 19 of this volume, philanthropy has long struggled to find ways to expand the impact of its work. From the scientific charity movement of the late nineteenth century to the more recent experimentation with pilot projects and the new techniques of high-engagement grantmaking, philanthropists have searched for ways to stretch the limited resources at their command to achieve the social objectives they have sought.

But even if philanthropic banking is but the latest manifestation of a deeply rooted philanthropic impulse, its appearance and growth at this point in time reflect a number of special factors and circumstances that combine to provide the rationale for this philanthropic innovation. Four of these factors in particular seem especially important.[42]

Get Off Your Assets

In the first place, the growing involvement of foundations in social-impact investment, including particularly investment of endowment assets, reflects a growing frustration on the part of many foundation leaders over the mismatch between the problems they are attempting to address and the grant dollars available to address them. With $682.2 billion in assets in their portfolios in 2007, the 5 percent minimum foundation payout requirement was only able to bring $44.4 billion in grant resources to the solution of societal problems. To put that into context, the total income of America's nonprofit service and expressive organizations in that year stood at $1.3 trillion, which means that foundations accounted, at most, for no more than 3 percent of US nonprofit revenues, and even that assumes that all foundation grants went for assistance to US nonprofits, and not to operating expenses or assistance to non-US organizations, which is certainly not the case.[43]

In a sense, foundations have been functioning like an army that goes into all-out battle leaving 95 percent of its troops and firepower back on the home front. With a growing realization of the enormity of national and international challenges and a begrudging recognition of the inability of governments to cope with them on its own, philanthropists have been compelled to look at new ways to squeeze social value out of the full resources at their command. What social-impact investing makes possible is to tap more of this firepower for mission-related purposes, and to do so in ways that often yield a reasonable financial return as well, refreshing the philanthropic corpus even while using it for mission-related purposes.

As noted earlier, this is the logic that led the Ford Foundation, in the wake of America's urban riots of the 1960s, to launch its PRI innovation and to justify this move on the grounds that "the foundation does not have nearly enough cash to meet all the demands on its agenda."[44] This logic is also what convinced the Annie E. Casey Foundation to launch a program of endowment-based social-impact investing in 1998. The foundation was already making grants at a rate of 8 percent of assets, well above the required 5 percent payout rate, but felt a need to accomplish more. Social investments provided the only way to achieve more without depleting its ability to sustain its activities.[45] And this is the logic that inspired the F.B. Heron Foundation in 1996 to become what in many respects has emerged as the "poster child" for the "foundations as philanthropic banks" movement.[46]

Leverage

The rationale for foundations functioning as philanthropic banks does not arise alone from the foundations' desire to tap into endowment assets to promote organizational missions, however. For all their scale, after all, foundations are hardly the largest agglomerations of investment capital in the American (or world) economy. The $682 billion in US foundation assets is barely one-fifth the size of the $3.0 trillion dollars in US money market funds, one-seventh the $5 trillion in US life insurance company assets, one-tenth the $6.4 trillion in US pension fund assets, and one-eleventh of the $7.8 trillion in US mutual fund assets.[47] The great opportunity opened up by the strategic use of foundation assets in social-impact investing is not only to tap the resources in foundation endowments, but rather to use these resources as well to expand the flow of resources from these much larger pools of investment capital into social and environmental purposes.

The template for such incentivization of private capital flows into social and environmental purposes was set in the 1970s thru the 1990s, when the

US federal government created a number of measures to encourage the flow of private investment capital into low-income housing. This included the Community Reinvestment Act, which created regulatory incentives for banks to help meet the credit needs of the low- and moderate-income communities from which they often derived deposits; the Low Income Housing Tax Credit, which provided tax credits for investors in low-income housing; and tax and grant support for the creation of a network of community development financial institutions (CDFIs). Taken together, these incentives unleashed a significant flow of new private capital into disadvantaged communities around the country.[48] One estimate puts the level of private investment channeled into low-income housing alone by the Low Income Housing Tax Credit between 1987 and 2006 at $6 billion per year, producing more than 115,000 low-income rental units annually.[49]

As the availability of public funds to incentivize the flow of private investment capital into social-purpose activities dries up, as now seems in prospect, foundations see an opportunity to bring some of their resources into the picture, as the Gates Foundation did by structuring a complex credit enhancement to help induce private investors to reduce the carrying cost of a major charter school bond issue, as described in Chapter 13 of this volume; or as the Heron Foundation did by providing a loan that reassured potential investors in the Habitat for Humanity vignette described at the outset of this chapter; or as the Ford Foundation did by providing a "first loss" reserve for Self-Help North Carolina's secondary market for low-income housing mortgages.

In these and other ways, foundations are encouraged to tap into their endowment assets not alone to "get off their own assets," but even more so to bring other pools of assets into the social-impact game.

New Players, New Mindsets: Supply-Side Factors

A third factor propelling the emergence of foundations as philanthropic banks comes from the supply side of the philanthropic marketplace—from the emergence of new cadres of philanthropists with mindsets different from those of their predecessors. Centrally important here has been the emergence of what Matthew Bishop and Michael Green have called "philanthrocapitalists," generally young, dot.com millionaires and billionaires, who, having made vast riches relatively early in life, are turning to philanthropy as a way to give back and create value in a different sphere. But many of these philanthrocapitalists are not content with traditional philanthropy, or at least what they perceive to be traditional philanthropy, and have resolved to transform it, producing a philanthropy that is "'strategic,' 'market conscious,' 'impact oriented,' 'knowledge-based,' often 'high engagement,' and always driven by the goal of maximizing the 'leverage' of the donor's money."[50] It is also a philanthropy that is comfortable with, indeed insistent on, utilizing financing approaches that bring to the world of philanthropy some of the dynamism and leveraging possibilities characteristic of modern corporate finance.

Jeffrey Skoll and Pierre Omidyar, founders of e-Bay, are prime exemplars of this phenomenon, but no one exemplifies it as fully as Charly Kleissner, who, with his wife, Lisa, has created in the KL Felicitas Foundation an institution that comes as close to functioning as a philanthropic bank or investment firm as any. A Silicon Valley entrepreneur with successful (and profitable) stints at Hewlett-Packard, Apple, and other Silicon Valley firms, Charly found himself with a sizable fortune and a partner who joined him in feeling what he describes as a "deep responsibility to do something meaningful with the wealth we've created." But Charly was not content with the traditional model of grant-based philanthropy. His passion was to bring the entrepreneurial style that had stood him in such stead in the world of business to his new social-purpose objectives. This involved developing an investment strategy, locating promising social ventures, creating an investment portfolio, and managing risks and returns—in short, functioning as a philanthropic bank, and enlisting others to move in the same direction.[51]

New Opportunities: The Demand Side

That these new philanthropists were able to put their new approach to philanthropy into operation and convince others to join them was, finally, facilitated by the emergence during the same period of a new set of actors on the *demand* side of the philanthropic marketplace: namely a robust array of social entrepreneurs who have set about establishing a new type of enterprise—the social venture—that pursues social purposes through market mechanisms, for example, by preparing former drug addicts for productive work not by giving them training but by establishing a catering business that trains them in an actual work setting. The classic example of this merger of market means and social ends has been the microfinance industry, which had blossomed into a $50 billion industry in the 35 years leading up to 2010 by providing small loans to some 100 million low-income people in countries throughout the world. To finance this enormous credit operation, microfinance investment funds have been created and have sought capital initially from private foundations, and ultimately from investment banks, insurance companies, and pension funds.

But microfinance is just the leading edge of a more massive global surge of social ventures and social entrepreneurs. Through the work of Ashoka and other change agents, a veritable "fourth sector" has emerged around the world consisting of socially conscious individuals who have discovered novel ways to produce social value out of existing resources in ways that produce real change in the lives of disadvantaged people.[52] This phenomenon has been fueled as well by the insights of C. K. Prahalad about the profits that can be made at the "bottom of the pyramid" by designing products and distribution channels that appeal to people of limited means who have needs for a variety of products but often pay a premium price because of inadequate or inappropriate packaging or distribution systems.[53]

These developments have brought new actors into the social-purpose space, actors who have great resonance for the new dot.com investors, as well as for a new business-school-savvy type of foundation program officer. Their worldview is consistent with the metrics-driven outlook of the new philanthropic actors and offers a greater promise of demonstrated effectiveness. They thus make far more possible than ever before the kind of leveraged finance and strategic use of charitable endowments that the new breed of foundation officials is seeking.

To be sure, these developments are not without their downsides, as Chapter 1 of this book has documented. The bright promise of microfinance, for example, has recently been dimmed by assertions that it exploits disadvantaged people by charging loan rates that, while well below prevailing rates in lagging regions, still seem exploitative by general international lending standards. Similarly, the flow of investible ventures has not kept pace with the scale of available investment resources, and significant mismatches remain between the time dimensions and return expectations of private investors and the scale-up prospects and profitability prospects for the ventures. Still, these may well be the normal growing pains of a still embryonic field rather than evidence some structural shortcoming of the emerging new model of social-purpose finance.

Basic Mechanics

Logically, the task of operating a foundation as a philanthropic bank should be easier than operating one as a traditional grantmaking foundation. After all, the traditional grantmaking foundation gives its money away with no hope of return. Since it gets no financial return it should logically take extra special pains to be sure its grants are achieving the maximum social return they can. By contrast, a foundation that operates as a philanthropic bank has the comfort of knowing that at least some of its funds can be returned so that it can use them over again if it did not get its hoped-for social return the first time around.

The flaw in this simple logic, of course, is that grant operations have the benefit of being judged against a single social goal whereas social-impact investments must be managed against dual social and financial objectives. And, at least for investments made out of foundation endowments as opposed to their grant budgets, the comparison group against which such investments are judged in their financial dimensions is not the foundation's array of grants but its array of other market-rate investments. What is more, even social-impact investments made out of the grants budget are likely to be considerably more complex in financial, if not programmatic, terms, necessitating a variety of added considerations and corresponding bodies of knowledge. For this reason, the enormously expanded leverage and impact that philanthropic banks can achieve comes at a price in terms of the added complexity, and, because of their frequently added scale, the added risk that their social-impact investments also brings with them. While care must be taken to avoid exaggerating the difficulties involved, as is often done, it is important to recognize the additional steps that such investments require beyond those normally involved in foundation grantmaking. Fundamentally, four such sets of tasks are involved, each of them involving a variety of steps.

Changing the Culture

In the first place, operating as a philanthropic bank requires a culture change on the part of foundations. As noted earlier, one of the prevailing orthodoxies of organized philanthropy has long been a belief that foundations are best served by erecting a Chinese wall between their two lines of business—grantmaking and investment management—with the latter aiming to maximize financial returns and the former attending to the distribution of all or a portion of the proceeds to advance the foundation's charitable mission. As we have seen, this orthodoxy has been firmly rooted in the historic "duty of care" assigned to managers of charitable trusts in the common-law tradition, and incorporated into positive law provisions such as that found in the 1969 US tax law's discouragement of "jeopardizing investments" in civil law countries. Even without these legal provisions, however, investment managers are typically judged against standards that reward performance and reputation on the basis of financial, and not social, returns achieved.

Notwithstanding the fact that respected authorities on foundation law have concluded that the legal restrictions on foundation investment require only "reasonable care" in making investment decisions,[54] such provisions, coupled with the performance incentives facing investment managers, have contributed to deeply ingrained beliefs about the need for sharp separation between the investment and grantmaking decisions of charitable institutions in order to protect charitable assets and ensure foundations' ability to serve their charitable missions into the future. Similar misgivings arise on the program side, moreover, where concerns about the added burdens of mastering complex financial dealings, unfamiliar balance sheets, and new asset classes combine with deeply ingrained beliefs on the part of some program officers that grants are more socially impactful than investments, impeding easy embrace of the new leveraged mode of operations.

An early task of those seeking to transform foundations into philanthropic banks is therefore to break through these cultural resistances. As one social-mission investment officer put it: "The hardest part of my job is not finding worthwhile investments or teaching program officers the difference between equities and loans; the hardest part is changing the culture."[55] And since cultures are highly resistant to change, this task requires considerable time and patience. Oftentimes, it also requires changes in leadership.

Given the influence that successful investment managers frequently enjoy among foundation board members, opposition from occupants of this position can often constitute an insurmountable obstacle. One leading foundation indicated that the actual enactment of a mission investment program had to await the departure of an unenthusiastic chief financial officer. An enthusiastic board champion can also be critical. The impetus for the F.B. Heron Foundation to become a beacon for the social-impact investing community came initially from the board, but it was usefully and forcefully promoted when William Dietel, the former president of the Rockefeller Brothers Fund, became board chair. Dietel challenged the board of this foundation to exercise "mission stewardship," which he asserted "challenges board members to do more than keep foundation assets from jeopardy. It asks board members to govern in a way that maximizes foundations' overall effectiveness."[56]

Top executive leadership can also be crucial. Doug Stamm at the Meyer Memorial Trust, Rip Rapson at the Kresge Foundation, and Sterling Speirn at Kellogg were all new chief executives whose openness to this new philanthropic-bank mode of operation was crucial in overcoming, if not totally erasing, these cultural barriers. But all three had to work hard to build board and staff support for the foundation role. At Kellogg, for example, even though new leadership had come on board and was supportive, the board was in the mood for new ideas, and the staff that introduced the concept had built up trust with the board, it took eight months and two further board meetings after the initial board conversation for the team to put together an implementation plan capable of winning board support, and even then what was authorized was an "action/learning exercise" with a time horizon of five to 10 years.[57]

Devising an Investment Policy and Strategy

As the Kellogg example above makes clear, one route to defusing resistance to the idea of social-impact investing is to develop an explicit strategy or policy that delineates the key features that will characterize this facet of foundation operations. This is particularly true given that the legal provisions that seem to limit such uses of foundation resources, at least in the common-law countries, essentially boil down to procedural standards. No category of assets is identified as a per se violation of the prohibition on "jeopardizing investments" in the United States, for example. Rather, penalties can only be incurred if it is determined that managers have "'failed to exercise ordinary business care and prudence, under the facts and circumstances prevailing at the time of making the investment."[58]

Significantly, our research found that all nine of the foundations we identified as at least experimental "philanthropic banks" had formulated some type of overarching strategy or policy to guide their social-impact investment activities. This distinguishes these "philanthropic banks" from the broader group of foundations engaged in either PRIs or market-rate social-impact investing. According to the recent Foundation Center survey of this broader group of foundations, fewer than half (46 percent) reported having a formal investment strategy or policy statement.[59] Formulating an explicit investment strategy is thus a sign that a foundation is considering social-impact investing to be a regular part of its portfolio of approaches and not simply an ad hoc, one-off event.

Indeed, the development of a formal social-impact investment strategy can be seen as an important turning point for a foundation. The case of the Mary Reynolds Babcock Foundation illustrates this point well. The Babcock Foundation began making PRIs in the early 1980s but found this instrument unsuited to the foundation's strategy at the time, which focused on advocacy and capacity-building activities for grassroots organizations, which lacked the revenue-generating models that the PRI tool required. Once the foundation shifted its strategy to having a more direct impact on community and economic development, it returned to the use of PRIs and mission investments and accompanied this shift with the development of a policy plan linking social-impact tools to the foundation's revised strategy.

Properly designed, a social-impact investment strategy would be approved by a foundation's board and would address a number of key features of the social-impact investment activities, including:

- The fields in which investments would be made
- The general approach to be used (e.g., investment screening, proxy voting, proactive investment)
- If proactive investment, the asset classes to be eligible for inclusion in the portfolio (e.g., linked deposits, various classes of debt, various classes of equities, etc.) and the asset mix to be sought
- Whether the investments will be funded out of the grant budget, the endowment, or some combination of the two; and, if the latter, in what proportions
- The scale of resources to be committed
- What internal staffing arrangements to establish for this set of activities
- Whether to deal directly with investees or work through various investment funds, and if some combination, in what proportions

- What criteria to apply to potential investments in terms of risk, rate of return, leverage possibilities, and other relevant factors[60]
- What decision process to use (board review of all investments? general board guidelines but board approval only for deals above a financial or risk threshold?)

Making Investments

Once a general game-plan is in place, a foundation is in a position to begin exploring actual investments.[61] This is a multistep process often extending over many months and can be pursued in a variety of ways depending on the foundation's size, appetite for risk, areas of focus, and other factors. The basic steps will typically involve the following, however.

Identifying a "Pipeline" of Investment Opportunities

An early first step in making social-impact investments is to identify an array of potential investment opportunities—organizations that potentially meet the foundation's criteria for investment in terms of field, asset class, risk level, and related factors. This step can be approached in a variety of ways. Some foundations do it the old-fashioned way: they wait for applicants to apply. Social ventures and nonprofit organizations seeking capital will likely have existing contacts with funders in their fields of action and will not be shy in seeking support. It can then be up to the foundation to decide whether a grant or some form of investment asset is the appropriate assistance vehicle to offer. The KIPP Houston deal outlined in Chapter 13 seems to have unfolded in this fashion. KIPP initially approached the Gates Foundation seeking a grant, and the idea for a guarantee-type mechanism evolved subsequently after discussions with foundation personnel and outside consultants.

Foundations operating in a relatively narrow range of fields and willing to operate through intermediaries can similarly rely on word-of-mouth clues from fellow investors in their field. Thus, for example, the Mary Reynolds Babcock Foundation, which focuses its investment activity on community development financial institutions, has been able to rely on grantee relationships and networking as opposed to broad industry landscaping efforts. Networking organizations such as the PRI Makers Network, which merged with the More for Mission project to form the Mission Investors Exchange, can be valuable in this process.

Increasingly, however, foundations functioning as true philanthropic banks are broadening and intensifying their search processes, especially as they go beyond investment in social-purpose investment *funds* and reach out directly to individual investees. As detailed more fully in Chapter 6, this has led to the emergence of a class of "enterprise brokers," solo operators or specialized social-impact investment teams within main-line investment firms, that specialize in identifying potential investees for more mature philanthropic bank-type foundations. More for Mission, an affinity group serving foundations interested in social-impact investment, has identified 30 such enterprise brokers. To help jump-start this industry, several foundations even joined forces to provide funding to bring one major US investment house, Cambridge

Associates, into the field. CA's social-impact investment team now boasts 17 advisors across five global offices.

Foundations interested in researching promising social ventures in their chosen fields of activity can access these enterprise brokers in a variety of ways—either tapping into known listings of promising ventures maintained by the enterprise brokers or hiring the firms to undertake specialized searches. One recent example of the latter strategy was the elaborate search that the Kellogg Foundation enlisted Imprint Capital Advisors, one of the new enterprise broker organizations, to undertake to help it identify promising social ventures doing innovative activities in the field of food and well-being.[62] Reaching out to a nationwide network of contacts, Imprint did a complete environmental scan and surfaced several hundred firms, which it then presented to Kellogg Foundation staff as the first step in a complex winnowing process.

One further modality for handling this investment pipeline development process is through an investment version of a funding collaborative, one of the new types of philanthropic actors examined in Chapter 10 of this volume. A good example of such a collaborative is Toniic, which styles itself as "an international impact investor network promoting a sustainable global economy by investing in entrepreneurs addressing the fundamental needs of people and planet."[63] Toniic functions as an investor collaborative, identifying promising ventures, vetting these with other investor-members, and sharing due diligence assessments.

Initial Assessment of Opportunities

Once a philanthropic bank has identified potential investment opportunities, it will typically engage in early discussions with stakeholders and conduct basic analysis to determine the viability of the potential investment. This involves the collection of both objective financial and organizational data and subjective assessments of stakeholder opinions or perspectives. Such data-gathering can be handled either by internal staff or external consultants.[64] For example, the Gates Foundation undertakes all the early-stage assessments for its investments internally and only uses external parties in cases where specialized experience is needed or when designing new financial mechanisms. An example of how the foundation's process unfolds can be seen in its investment in Inigral, a social media start-up that partners with universities to create online social networks that increase student engagement and student success. Since Inigral had an unproven business model, the decision to invest was based primarily on social rather than financial returns, which qualified this investment as a PRI. The social return goals of the foundation's investment in Inigral were (1) to further the foundation's understanding of how to promote student retention and college completion; (2) to learn more about the role of products like Inigral's in promoting social activity and peer support among students; and (3) to use this investment to learn about the challenges that early-stage companies face in achieving scale and navigating higher education procurement practices. In pursuance of this latter goal, the foundation conducted a sensitivity analysis (i.e., the process of assessing the risks associated with an investment based on different assumptions about expected returns). The foundation's primary concern here was to identify risk mitigants and perform financial modeling to ensure that subsequent financing rounds would support Inigral for a sufficient amount of time for the foundation to actually achieve the hoped-for social returns.

In contrast, the Kellogg Foundation utilizes a highly structured, data-driven, and highly selective process to cull the lists of potential investees identified by its consultant. In the case of the decision to invest in Revolution Foods, a provider of healthy meals to vulnerable children, for example, Kellogg staff worked closely with its consultant, Imprint Capital, to develop a data-rich algorithm with which to winnow the list of several hundred potential social-purpose food and nutrition organizations identified by Imprint down to one highly promising candidate.

Conduct of Due Diligence

Once a promising investment has been identified, a foundation must still carry out an in-depth due diligence review. This is a more intensive review of the financial and operational capabilities of a potential investee, examining such features as the capacity and tenure of executive leadership; the level of capitalization, debt, and cash flow; the organization's track record; and its legal structure and financial standing (e.g., to make sure there are not any outstanding liens against it).[65] In the case of the Heron Foundation loan to HFHI mentioned at the outset of this chapter, for example, both the Heron Foundation and a third-party consultant conducted comprehensive due diligence reviews, and this despite the fact that the foundation had previously provided grants to various HFHI affiliates over the years and was, as a result, generally familiar with the organization.[66] Similarly, when Kellogg invested in Southern Bancorp—a CDFI focused on increasing access to economic opportunity, financial literacy, and community development on the part of disadvantaged citizens—both Kellogg and an external consultant conducted due diligence reviews. This process included two two-day site visits by Kellogg and external consultants, numerous calls with senior management, in-person meetings with each subsidiary bank president and CEO within Southern Bancorp's network, meetings with board members, and reference calls. This process also included review of key documents, such as customer contracts, commercial arrangements, and existing creditor relationships, the company's charter and bylaws, board minutes for the last two years, and recent financial documents. In addition, existing loan documents spelling out the priority of various security interests and the levels of organizational collateral pledged were also reviewed.

The Annie E. Casey Foundation is equally rigorous in its approach to due diligence. When the foundation was interested in an investment in ACCION Texas, a microfinance lender focused on increasing access to community supports and economic opportunities for low-income families, its vetting included examining whether the investment furthered the foundation's mission, the potential impact of the investment on the foundation's program, the financial strength of the recipient organization, the strength of the organization's management, the geographic coverage of the organization, the ability of the investment to attract other investors, and the potential of the investment to promote replication of the supported model.

Determining the Appropriate Investment Tool or Set of Tools

As noted earlier in this chapter and elaborated throughout this volume, there is an increasingly broad spectrum of tools that philanthropic bank foundations can use to support a promising deal. These include loans, credit enhancements, linked deposits, fixed-income instruments, and equity, to name just a few. In addition, there is an increasingly broad array of social-impact investment entities, such as equity funds, loan funds, bond funds, and venture capital funds. Each of these tools has its own financial risk and return profiles and each offers different leverage possibilities. But each also has different skill requirements for investors. Enterprise brokers therefore often play a role in structuring the deal and selecting the appropriate tool.

A good illustration of this step is the decision of the Heron Foundation to utilize a loan to head off the discontinuation of Habitat for Humanity's FlexCAP spending program, as discussed at the beginning of this chapter. One factor that figured into the foundation's decision was the hope that a regular loan at a precrisis market rate would signal to other investors Heron's confidence in this program and thereby stimulate private-sector investors to extend loans as well. Similarly, when the KL Felicitas Foundation invested in Healthpoint Services—a provider of healthcare services to rural populations in India—it chose to use a convertible note (i.e., a debt instrument that can be converted into equity at a later date) because it was not ready to make full equity investments yet wanted to give the investee the opportunity to hold off return of principal for an extended period to provide this start-up an opportunity to develop its business before having to confront the need to repay the loan, and allowing it to make the refund in the form of stock in the company rather than hard cash. Such "patient capital" helps bridge the gap between being a start-up and being ready for the market.

Likewise, the Mary Reynolds Babcock Foundation provided a combination of grants and a loan to the Natural Capital Investment Fund (NCIF) with the aim of helping that institution grow to become a community development financial institution (CDFI) loan fund. The Babcock support consisted of an organizational development grant, a planning grant, a capital grant, and then finally a PRI loan. The investment was structured with staged commitments to incentivize responsible growth and help NCIF become investment-ready. The PRI ultimately helped expand the NCIF's capacity to lend, the size of its investments, and its geographic area of service.

Negotiating the Terms and Conditions of the Investment

The final step in arranging an investment is to negotiate the terms and conditions with the recipient. For loan, bond, or equity funds, these are often laid out in the fund's subscription documents, though foundations can often negotiate their exposure level in complex structured finance deals. Key issues that have to be pinned down at this phase, in addition to the basic investment tool, include factors such as the target rate of financial return, the expected measurable programmatic return, the time span of the investment, the level of risk exposure (e.g., whether the foundation's position is a senior position, which immunizes it in part from risk, or subordinated, meaning that it covers the initial losses if things turn sour), and the reporting and monitoring arrangements.[67]

Social-impact investments that seek market-rate financial returns involve especially demanding requirements at this stage due to the need to pin down the social-impact expectations. For instance, the MacArthur Foundation's private equity investment in Terra Capital, a venture capital firm focused on environmentally stable business models, carried a targeted financial return rate of 10 to 20 percent, a specified programmatic return expectation of increased business formation in a targeted geographic areas, a time span of 10 years, high exposure because the investment was in equity, and terms under which the foundation would receive both an annual report and quarterly reporting on financial and programmatic achievements.

Taking another approach, the Mary Reynolds Babcock Foundation's investment in a bond to help capitalize Community Capital Management, a community development financial institution, specified a financial rate of return (as with all the foundation's mission-related investments) based on the benchmark appropriate for this asset class (i.e., the Barclay's Capital Aggregate for bonds), which ranged from 4.7 to 6.3 percent over the last 10 years. The programmatic return was measured in units of affordable housing, mortgages, home ownership, and job creation. The time span was undefined because as long as the investment performed, it fit within the foundation's asset allocation strategy. This was considered a very low-risk deal with low exposure but still carried the expectation of quarterly financial reports and annual social-impact reports.

Managing Investments

The tasks associated with social-impact investing do not end when an investment is made. Every bit as important as the front-end setting of strategy, selection of investees, and structuring the investments are the monitoring and management tasks that follow on them. Two basic steps are involved here: first, monitoring performance; and second, intervening when necessary to remedy problems or to liquidate positions.

Monitoring Performance

Once an investment has been made, investees of philanthropic banks are required to report regularly on a number of critical features of the investments. As noted above, these include key financial indicators (i.e., cash on hand, levels of debt, and net worth), personnel (i.e., securing agreements to ensure that key staff members remain at the firm and/or that the foundation is alerted when key staff depart the firm), programmatic monitoring (i.e., confirmation that the agreed-upon social returns are being achieved), and organizational monitoring (i.e., keeping the foundation abreast of staff, executive, and board developments as well as organizational infrastructure issues).[68] Quarterly and annual reports or meetings on the financial performance of investments are nearly uniform across the foundations in our research. However, reporting on social performance tends to be less standardized, with the frequency and depth of monitoring and reporting highly specific to the individual foundation or deal.

For this reporting to be meaningful, however, the foundations have to review the reports as regularly and seriously as the investees generate them. For example, the Heron Foundation requires daily reports on its sizable investment in the US Community Investing Index, an index fund invested in large- and mid-cap companies that serve economically underserved populations. In addition to reviewing these reports, the foundation convenes a group of advisors for research recommendations every quarter. The Mary Reynolds Babcock Foundation receives quarterly financial and annual social-impact reports from the Natural Capital Investment Fund (NCIF). The foundation also has a grantee relationship with NCIF, which helps give it additional oversight and confidence in its investment. Moreover, officials from the office of the chief financial officer at the Gates Foundation meet with legal and program staff quarterly to review the portfolio-monitoring reports of all the program-related investments made by the foundation. On a yearly basis, valuation committee meetings are held to review portfolio performance and revise loss reserves when needed.

A key part of foundation monitoring of its social-impact investments is regular reporting to the foundation's board of directors. The board cochairs of the Bill and Melinda Gates Foundation, for example, are described as "very actively involved in approving and monitoring [the foundation's] investments" and "typically get sent a pipeline update of the deals on an annual basis."[69] This poses special difficulties in the case of the Fondazione CRT because a separate entity was set up by the foundation—the Fondazione Sviluppo e Crescita—to administer the foundation's social-impact investments. However, the staff of CRT is involved in the work of the subsidiary, and the board of CRT continuously monitors the activity that this entity undertakes.

From the evidence at hand, however, not all foundations involved in social-impact investing keep their boards regularly informed of progress, though periodic reports at two- or three-year intervals are not uncommon.[70] One possibly revealing indication that regular monitoring of investment performance may not be as rigorous as might be desired among the general pool of social-impact investors comes from the difficulty that FSG researchers encountered in collecting data on the financial performance of the loans made by its 55 study foundations. As the FSG researchers reported: "Due to a lack of data from most foundations, sufficient information was available to analyze only 18% of completed loans."[71]

Dealing with Floundering Investments

The whole point of careful monitoring is to spot problems before they escalate into serious dilemmas. Typically, a foundation has a few options at its disposal, including the ability to "call" its collateral (i.e., buy back the underlying real property, general liens, or cash collateral of a deal at a previously negotiated price), extend or accelerate the repayment period by restructuring the terms of the investment, or accept a default on a loan or a loss on an equity investment.[72]

Although our research revealed little evidence of floundering investments in need of significant restructuring, there were a number of instances where the length or size of investments had to be increased or interest rates adjusted to avoid more serious problems. However, some foundations have had to take more dramatic steps. For instance, the Mary Reynolds Babcock Foundation's investment in Gateway CDC, a community development corporation focused on low-income housing and business and community development initiatives, ran into problems when homeowners experienced problems paying back their mortgages. The foundation initially responded by doubling down on its 1992 initial loan of $100,000 with a $30,000 grant in 1993, and then upped the ante by providing a second $100,000 loan in 1995. Although the investee was able to make its required 4 percent interest payments for the first four years of its relationship with Babcock, it ultimately defaulted on the second loan. In retrospect, the foundation concluded that this deal would have been more appropriate as a grant than an investment given the income level at which the organization was directing its efforts. In the process, this deal convinced the foundation that it did not have the capacity to structure and monitor individual deals. Rather than withdraw from the use of investment tools, however, it was at this point that the foundation revised its PRI policies by deciding to invest only in experienced intermediaries with strong track records for underwriting and monitoring investments of the sort that the foundation wished to support.

Operational Challenges

The emergence of foundations as philanthropic banks raises a variety of challenges for both foundations and the organizations they are seeking to assist. While these challenges have tended to be exaggerated, they are nevertheless real and need to be confronted. In particular, at least four key challenges confront foundations seeking to operate as philanthropic banks. While grantmaking is hardly immune from these challenges, particularly given recent developments calling into question the "hands-off" attitude that has governed the management of grants and urging "high engagement" with grantees and greater attention to the impact of grantmaking,[73] the implications are still greater for the investment activities.

Legal Complications

In the first place, nongrant forms of assistance raise legal complications that typically do not arise in the operation of grant programs. These complications apply unevenly, moreover, to what in the United States are referred to as PRIs as contrasted with other social-impact investments.[74] Thus, for example, as noted earlier, to qualify for PRI status in the United States an investment cannot have the production of income or appreciation of property as its primary purpose, and the investment cannot be used to generate an "economic benefit beyond ordinary and usual compensation for services."[75] Because these judgments are difficult to make, foundations usually seek either a letter ruling from the IRS or an opinion letter from a lawyer prior to making such investments.[76] Thus, for example, before it felt justified in moving ahead with a PRI investment it was contemplating in Terra Capital Investors, a venture capital firm promoting socially responsible business practices, the MacArthur Foundation's legal team and PRI staff felt obliged to request a private letter ruling from the IRS since investments in venture capital funds had not previously been explicitly authorized as eligible for PRI use.[77] Such a letter can prove an investment was made in "good faith" in the event that issues with the investment arise, and can serve as an initial screen for whether or not actually to invest.[78] Further, when a foundation claims PRI status for an investment in a for-profit organization, it must be able to show that it exercises "expenditure responsibility" with respect to the transaction and that the ultimate purpose must be to accomplish one or more of the foundation's charitable purposes. This means tracking the funds from the time they leave the foundation to the time they reach their charitable destination.[79]

PRIs are also subject to the so-called self-dealing restrictions that apply to all foundation investments, which means they cannot be made to certain "disqualified persons," that is, persons with some substantial economic interest in the foundation.[80] Other requirements apply only to non-PRI social-impact investments, though in this case the restrictions are the same as those that apply to all other foundation investments. Thus, for example, for all non-PRI investments, foundations, and their officers and directors, are prohibited from owning more than 20 percent of a business enterprise.[81] Other social-impact investments are also subject to the restrictions mentioned earlier on "jeopardizing investments," that is, investments that jeopardize the foundation's ability to pursue its charitable mission. As we noted earlier, however, these latter restrictions can be met merely by exercising "reasonable care."

In some countries, the limitations on foundation investment activity are even more restrictive than these. Thus, as already noted, Italian law governing the important class of Italian foundations of banking origin prohibit these foundations from making loans or engaging in other credit activities, and create serious ambiguities about whether other forms of investment are permissible. Fondazione CRT consequently had to create and fund a separate affiliate through which to pursue its social-impact investing activities. Similarly, investment activities by foundations are also legally prohibited in India. This has led philanthropists in India to focus on high-engagement philanthropy in the form of capacity-building, giving circles, in-depth issue and industry analysis, and an industry forum for knowledge exchange. A similar situation exists in Japan, where foundations are obliged to hold their assets chiefly in government bonds, which significantly limits their ability to leverage their resources. Indeed, it limits their grantmaking as well since bond interest rates have been quite low in Japan over an extended period.

Beyond the restrictions on the permissible types of investments, other complications relate to the tax treatment of interest or principal repayments on foundation investments. In the United States, a PRI can count towards the 5 percent payout requirement for the foundation in the year in which the PRI is made. But principal repayments on PRIs count as negative distributions, which means that they must either be added to the investment assets of the foundation and therefore made subject to the excise tax foundations must pay on these assets, or added on top of the foundation's minimum 5 percent payout in the years that the principal repayments are made.[82] Like other investments, moreover, social-impact investing that yields substantial earnings in the form of interest or dividends can affect a foundation's payout since the payout requirement stipulates that a foundation must pay out the higher of *all earned income* or 5 percent of the market value of its assets.

While none of the foundations in our research indicated legal complications with any of the investments examined, a number of precautionary steps appear to have been taken with particular investments that ran peculiar risks. For example, when the Gates Foundation invested in Inigral as a PRI, the foundation built in the right to withdraw from the deal if Inigral failed to pursue its charitable purpose. Similarly, the MacArthur Foundation's investment in Nitliplan, a financial intermediary extending credit to small farmers and business people in postwar Nicaragua, required special public notice activities because it entailed a loan in a foreign country.

Skill Requirements

Knowledge of the law on foundation investments is not the only specialized body of knowledge required for use of nongrant forms of foundation assistance, however. Also required is knowledge of the often-arcane features of different asset classes and investment structures as well as skills in reading balance sheets, interpreting due process assessments, evaluating underwriting reports, and interpreting the risks of complex investment structures involving multiple investors. To be sure, these skills are not necessarily more demanding than those required to evaluate grant applications in complex program areas, particularly given new pressures to apply sophisticated outcome measures and random controlled trials. But the skills required for the broadened social-impact investment functions of the new breed of foundations as philanthropic banks have simply not been resident broadly in foundation program or investment staff, necessitating significant attention to staff capacity-building. What is more, at least some of the skill requirements are specific to particular investments. For instance, in the Heron/HFHI case, the Heron Foundation had already invested in the FlexCAP notes prior to 2008 through its community investment account. However, when the foundation invested in the US Community Investing Index fund it found that the investment advisors with the most experience with screened portfolios knew next to nothing about investing in low- to moderate-income communities.

Fortunately, a pool of individuals with experience in social-impact investing is slowly emerging, and foundations are supplementing internal staff with outside consultants and enterprise brokers with experience in the social-impact investment field. At the same time, foundations like the Kellogg Foundation have come to recognize the need for a hybrid model of skills, requiring both investment discipline *and* mission clarity. Since its program staff does not generally have the needed skills in business analysis, and the investment staff does not generally have the needed skills in assessing mission impact, Kellogg is working to foster cooperation between the programmatic and specialized social-investment staffs, augmenting these capabilities with external support when the foundation runs into bandwidth issues in terms of either time or specific expertise. This focus on cooperation seems to be an increasingly common dimension of foundation social-impact investing. For instance, the Gates Foundation uses a balance of program and specialist (PRI) staff, typically relying on the program team to monitor the programmatic aspects of its social-impact investments, whereas the special PRI, or social-impact investment, team focuses on monitoring financial performance.

Tensions between Program Staff and Investment Staff

How successful such coordination and cooperation can be, however, is still open to some question. As stated above, nongrant forms of assistance require two quite different sets of knowledge and skills: program knowledge and investment knowledge. These skills are rarely combined in the same person, requiring concerted efforts to achieve harmonious relationships between the two. Ideally, both sets of staff should therefore be involved in all aspects of the assistance process; however, this is frequently not the case. One relatively early study thus reported that "coordination between program and finance teams tends to be weak, with only about a quarter of foundations indicating that their program and finance staffs collaborate closely in managing mission investments."[83]

Our research supports this finding. Of the nine foundations we examined in depth, only two reported a balance between program and investment staff in handling social-impact investments, as shown in Table 5.7. As one leading foundation officer explained: "Beyond basic skill requirements, foundations need to be able to achieve a critical cultural shift from grantmaking to philanthropic banking and prepare themselves for engaging various issues as investors as opposed to grantmakers."[84]

Inadequate Supply of Qualified Ventures

A final challenge for foundations desiring to operate as philanthropic banks relates, ironically enough, to the adequacy of "deal flow," the availability of sufficient deals that can meet the exacting requirements of the investing foundations. Most nonprofits lack the financial acumen to access the new tools, and the number of social ventures with such skills is also limited.[85] As outlined more fully in Chapter 21, this suggests the need for a long-term capacity-building effort aimed at building the financial literacy of potential investees.

In the short run, several other options have surfaced. The Kellogg Foundation, as we have seen, has effectively enlisted the aid of one of the enterprise broker firms to press existing networks to come up with robust lists of potential investees in the foundation's chosen fields of operation. The HUB, a network of capacity-building facilities has emerged to provide "sheltered workshops" for aspiring social enterprises, and a number of other capacity-building consulting groups, such as New Profit, NeST, and Community Wealth Ventures, offer coaching and financial aid to promising ventures. Through Toniic, as we have seen, the KL Felicitas Foundation is building an investment collaborative for fellow social-impact investors. Alternatively, the Esmee Fairbairn Foundation indicated that some of its investment flow comes from the grantmaking side of its operations; however, this flow is limited because very few grantees fit the requirements for investment. For alternate investment flow, the foundation turns to its network of other investors in the field and receives direct enquiries from social entrepreneurs; but, despite this, it is finding that there are a limited number of good investment opportunities for long-term, patient capital.[86]

Track Record and Overall Assessment

The performance of philanthropic banks is difficult to determine with precision. One reason for this is the relative novelty of the field. Over half of the 82 foundations that the Foundation Center identified as makers of market-rate (i.e., non-PRI) social-impact investments, for example, have been making them for only five years or fewer, barely sufficient to cover the time span of a typical investment.[87] Although experience with PRIs extends over a longer time span, solid financial assessments of their performance are remarkably absent, evidence that PRIs are still viewed through a "grants lens" where recovery of principal is not a major consideration. Little data on repayment or rates of return are collected, therefore, in the Foundation Center's extensive PRI database.[88] FSG researchers were similarly frustrated in their efforts to gain an overview of the financial performance of the 55 foundations on which they gathered detailed financial data. For one thing, only 28 of these foundations reported "completed" loans. Significantly, 75 percent of these foundations achieved a zero default rate. However, as noted earlier, because of what FSG researchers reported as "incomplete records and lack of staff resources" the foundations were unable to provide any information on what share of the loan dollars were repaid and what share went into default.[89]

Despite these limitations, however, there is growing evidence, particularly among the foundations operating as philanthropic banks, that the new investment thrust is achieving its social objectives with little sacrifice of financial returns, especially given the recent chaos in the traditional capital markets. Part of this evidence comes from the Ford Foundation, the granddad of PRI investors. In a 1991 report on its PRI activity, Ford reported on the 229 program-related investments it made between 1968 and 1991. Of the $196 million in total investments, $71.3 million had been repaid and $17.2 million written off, for a default rate of 7.5 percent, with 55 percent of the total still outstanding. Since Ford scored these in comparison to its grant budget, which registered what could be considered a 100 percent financial default rate (since grants are not repaid at all), the Foundation took enough comfort, even in this early record, to continue making PRIs at a rate of $15 million annually, and to increase its set-aside of endowment resources for PRIs from an initial $10 million in 1968 to $130 million as of 1991.

More germane data are available from some of the more mature foundations operating as philanthropic banks that we examined in depth. Especially revealing, for example, is the record of the F.B. Heron Foundation. Reporting at the end of 2009, for example, following one of the most discouraging periods of financial tumult, Heron was able to report total returns on its assets for the prior three-, five- and seven-year periods that placed it "at or near the median of the BNY Mellon Mid-Large Foundation Total Fund Universe for those periods," even though the foundation had committed a striking 43 percent of its endowment assets to social-impact investments.[90] Other evidence of the performance of Heron's social-impact investments included the following:

- Of $20.9 million in PRI investments outstanding, the foundation reported only 1.6 percent of outstanding commitments delinquent and the remainder yielding a weighted interest of 3.6 percent, well above prevailing rates on 10-year Treasury notes.[91]
- The annualized total return since inception (June 2001) on the foundation's two separately managed fixed-income social-impact portfolios stood at 5.57 percent as of December 31, 2009, well within the range of its Barclays Capital US Aggregate benchmark.
- The annualized total return since inception (November 2005) on the foundation's externally managed public equity portfolio of companies with US Community Investing Index "best of class" rating on community investing criteria was −0.42 percent, which beat the S&P's worse −0.62 percent performance.
- The return rate on the foundation's linked deposits in 21 community development banks and nine low-income designated credit unions was an impressive 2.6 percent, compared to an 0.21 percent return for the Merrill Lynch three-month Treasury Bill Index.

In short, far from "paying a price" for its use of assets to promote its charitable objectives, this "philanthropic bank" was performing at least on a par with its commercial peers, and in many cases ahead of them, in financial performance while achieving important social objectives to boot.

While full detail is not available on the other philanthropic banks that we examined, the partial data available on them suggests a similar record. Thus, for example:

- The Annie E. Casey Foundation's investment in ACCION Texas discussed earlier—a loan with a target financial rate of return of 3 percent and a programmatic return of an increase in economic opportunities for low-income families in San Antonio—has achieved a return on investment of 3.3 percent, with similar results on the foundation's other debt investments. Comparable returns were reported for the foundation's three equity-fund investments. Although one will likely lose $1 million out of a $3 million investment, the returns of the remaining two funds will far exceed any loss on the other one.

- The Mary Reynolds Babcock Foundation reports high satisfaction with its social-impact investment activities. The foundation's investment in Community Capital Management (CCM)—a separately managed bond fund—achieved a return rate of 5.05 percent from August 1, 2005, to December 31, 2010, roughly equivalent to the benchmark for the foundation's fixed-income investments (the Barclay Capital Aggregate Index) while achieving a the foundation's programmatic goals of promoting affordable housing, home ownership, job creation, and job placement.

Beyond these financial data, perhaps the most encouraging indication of the performance of these emerging foundations as philanthropic banks is the planning they are doing for the future. Fundamentally, all of these institutions are bullish about the future of the course they have embarked on. To be sure, each has experienced failures, or at least deals that did not meet expectations. But each is also making a bet on both the wisdom and the feasibility of its new leveraged mode of activity. Indeed, both KL Felicitas and the F.B. Heron Foundation have decided to step up their social-impact investment game, seeking, as officials of the Felicitas Foundation put it, the "aggressive goal to move to 100 percent impact investments."[92]

Experimental philanthropic banks such as the Kellogg Foundation and Esmee Fairbairn are at a different point of evolution, seeking to transform committed funds into actual investments in a meaningful and responsible progression. In another sign of energy in the field, the Gates Foundation, not yet a transitional philanthropic bank foundation but one whose level of resources allocated to nongrant activities makes it a major player nonetheless, intends to orient its social-impact investing activity increasingly towards making big bets, using higher-risk equity vehicles and more complex financial transactions in the future.

Conclusion

In short, a new spirit is animating at least part of the foundation world at the present time, both in the United States and internationally. Foundations are coming to understand the limitations of traditional grantmaking as a vehicle for achieving substantial progress in addressing national and global problems. They are therefore searching for ways to extend their impact and leverage their resources.

One manifestation of this is the effort to get more results out of grants by becoming more self-conscious about measuring outcomes, and engaging more deeply with grantees. But another is the effort to go well beyond grants to utilize a sometimes dizzying array of other financial instruments—loans, loan guarantees, bonds, bond guarantees, equity investments, linked deposits, and many more—and to do so not just with the relatively small shares of total resources required to be devoted to grantmaking, but with the far more substantial shares of endowment assets typically held back to support that grantmaking into the future.

The upshot of this latter development is the emergence of a new model of a charitable foundation, one that resembles a charitable bank, with multiple windows capable of deploying a variety of financial instruments in support of the institution's charitable mission. Pioneered by a number of relatively small or modest-sized innovators, this model is now attracting a critical mass of main-line institutions.

This route to enhanced charitable impact is not without its challenges. As we have seen, it faces important legal obstacles, particularly internationally; requires substantial retooling of both foundation and grantee staff and operations; and, at the end of the day, may come up short in finding enough good "deals" in a short enough time to sustain the "buzz" that this new mode of operation has created.

Despite these obstacles, however, there is reason for at least muted optimism about the potentials this new mode of foundation operations holds. For one thing, the number of foundations dipping their toes into this investment arena has grown substantially in recent years. For another, a substantial cottage industry of enterprise brokers, capacity builders, capital aggregators, secondary markets, and support organizations has grown up around them, providing information, needed services, and moral support to help nurse reluctant players into the field, as the chapters in this volume show. And, as this chapter has demonstrated, the track record to date, while hardly without its setbacks, has clearly provided an impressive proof of concept. To be sure, not all foundations will travel this path, nor should they. But for those so inclined, the excitement promises to be palpable and the rewards substantial.

Notes

1. "FlexCAP: Helping Finance: Habitat's Mission," Online Partnerships: Federal Home Loan Bank of Atlanta, published fall 2010, http://corp.fhlbatl.com/PartnershipsFall10.aspx?id=2489.

2. In some countries, such as Japan, foundations are required to invest significant portions of their assets in government bonds or other worthy assets. Elsewhere, such as the United States, they are merely required to act "prudently" with their investment assets. The one big difference between foundations and classic investment banks, at least in the United States, is that foundations are required to devote at least 5 percent of their asset value each year to charitable support, a figure few private investment companies, or other corporations, come close to achieving.

3. Heron Foundation, *New Frontiers in Mission-Related Investing* (New York: F.B. Heron Foundation, 2004).

4. F.B. Heron Foundation, "Mission Investing at the F.B. Heron Foundation: Data Summary (As of December 31, 2009)," unpublished internal document.

5. For an early look at the F.B. Heron model, see Michael Swack, "Expanding Philanthropy: Mission-Related Investing at the F.B. Heron Foundation," Carey Institute, University of New Hampshire, 2009, accessed November 9, 2012, http://www.fbheron.org/documents/carsey_expanding_philanthropy_2009.pdf.

6. Ford Foundation, *Investing for Social Gain: Reflections on Two Decades of Program-Related Investments* (New York: Ford Foundation, 1991), http://www.fordfoundation.org/pdfs/library/Investing_For_Social_Gain.pdf, 5–6.

7. "New Options in the Philanthropic Process: A Ford Foundation Statement of Policy," quoted in Ford Foundation, *Investing in Social Change* (New York: Ford Foundation, 1968), 6.

8. This provision was also made necessary by two other features of the laws under which foundations operate. The first is the "duty of care" that the trustees of any endowed trust are obligated to uphold, which binds trustees to be prudent in the management of the assets given into their care. Investments in programs likely to put the assets at risk are thought to violate this duty no matter how worthy the programmatic objectives of the investment might be and are therefore barred as part of a foundation's investment activities. The second is the provision in the 1969 tax act requiring foundations to pay out as grants or other "qualifying distributions" 5 percent of their average assets each year. Without some specific authorization for "program-related investments" in the law, foundations would not be able to engage in such investments through their charitable programs either. For a detailed discussion of program-related investments, see Christie I. Baxter, *Program-Related Investments: A Technical Manual for Foundations* (New York: John Wiley & Sons, 1997), 2.

9. Data on the number of foundations making PRIs and the share of qualifying distributions recently taking this form from Steven Lawrence, "Doing Good with Foundation Assets: An Updated Look at Program-Related Investments," in Foundation Center, *The PRI Directory: Charitable Loans and Other Program-related Investments by Foundations*, 3rd ed. (New York: Foundation Center, 2009), xiii. Total number of private foundations in the United States from Foundation Center, *Foundation Yearbook, 2009* (New York: Foundation Center, 2010).

10. See "More for Mission: Home," More for Mission, accessed July 20, 2012, http://www.moreformission.org. This group was subsequently renamed More for Mission, and as of 2012 has merged with the PRI Makers Network to form Mission Investors Exchange. "About Us: Mission Investors," Mission Investors Exchange, accessed July 20, 2012, http://www.missioninvestors.org/about-us.

11. Tony Berkley, personal interview, September 20, 2013.

12. Clara Miller, "The World Has Changed and So Must We," based on excerpts from F.B. Heron's Strategy Document, F.B. Heron Foundation, published April 2012, http://www.missioninvestors.org/tools/world-has-changed-and-so-must-we.

13. A more precise term might be a "philanthropic investment firm," since banks may not engage in as wide an array of financial transactions as investment firms, but investment firms are likely to be far less familiar entities, even to readers of this volume. It therefore seemed wise to use the more familiar term to suggest the concept being emphasized.

14. "Market-rate investments" in the foundation arena are commonly treated as synonymous with "mission-related investments," and "below-market-rate investments" with PRIs.

15. The new instruments being deployed by foundations as philanthropic banks may be other than purely financial ones. For example, the Abell Foundation in Baltimore has consciously used legal action to promote solid public policy changes in support of inner-city youth. Personal interview with Robert Embry, Baltimore, 2010.

16. The Foundation Center began collecting systematic information on program-related investments in the early 1990s and had built a database of nearly 5,400 individual PRIs of $10,000 or more valued at a total of $3.8 billion as of 2009. For the most recent report on these data, see Lawrence, "Doing Good with Foundation Assets." A technical manual on PRIs was assembled in the 1990s and is available as Baxter, *Program-Related Investments*. More recent work has broadened the focus to include a broader array of investment types. Notable here are Sarah Cooch and Mark Kramer with

Fi Cheng, Adeeb Mahmud, Ben Marx, and Matthew Rehrig, "Compounding Impact: Mission Investing by US Foundations," FSG Social Impact Advisors, March 2007, accessed January 7, 2014, http://www.fsg-impact.org/ideas/pdf/Compounding%20 Impact(5).pdf, which gathered general information on "mission investing" policies of 92 foundations engaged in PRI activities, and investment data on 55 of these; and a special study on foundations that make market-rate mission-related investments carried out by the Foundation Center and issued as Steven Lawrence and Reina Mukai, "Key Facts on Mission Investing," Foundation Center, 2011, accessed January 7, 2014, http://foundationcenter.org/gainknowledge/research/pdf/keyfacts_missioninvesting2011.pdf.

17. As noted in the note to Table 5.1, the W.K. Kellogg Foundation made an initial foray into making program-related investments with three such investments in 1998, but did not make any subsequent PRIs until the foundation launched its Mission Driven Investment (MDI) program in 2007. This latter year therefore seemed the appropriate one to use to mark the real start of the foundation's "philanthropic bank" activity. Information based on Berkley, interview.

18. Data reporting PRIs totaling $387.7 million as of 2007, the latest full year for which data were available as of this writing, from Lawrence, "Doing Good with Foundation Assets," xiv. Data reporting total foundation assets of $682.2 billion as of 2007 from Foundation Center, *Foundation Yearbook: Facts and Figures on Private and Community Foundations, 2010* (New York: Foundation Center, 2010), x.

19. Cooch and Kramer, "Compounding Impact," 26.

20. We used the five-year total of grants on the assumption that mission investments have an average life span of five years. Comparing outstanding investments to a single year of grants would be misleading.

21. Interestingly, these proportions are virtually identical to ones that the Foundation Center found among a group of 82 foundations it surveyed that make "market-rate mission-related investments." According to the Foundation Center, just over a quarter of the 82 market-rate mission-related foundation investors it surveyed reported devoting over half of their assets to such investments, placing them squarely in our "mature philanthropic bank" category; about half reported devoting 5 percent or less of their assets to such investments, placing them close to our "transitional" grouping; and the remaining 20 percent reported devoting less than 1 percent of their assets to such investments, placing them just below our "experimental" grouping. Lawrence and Mukai, "Key Facts on Mission Investing," 2.

22. The Foundation Center data use the foundations as the unit of analysis rather than the deal and found that 50 percent of the 74 foundations reported some public equity investment and 32 percent some private equity investment, though there is likely overlap between these two figures. The FSG study examined 520 mission investments and found that debt instruments accounted for 82 percent of the total and equities for only 14 percent. In terms of the *amount* of investment recorded by the FSG researchers, however, the equity share is considerably higher at 45 percent, though most (36 percent) of this is in the form of real estate investments, which tend to involve far less risk. See Lawrence and Mukai, "Key Facts on Mission Investing," 3; and Cooch and Kramer, "Compounding Impact," 17. In addition to these essentially financial vehicles, social-impact investors also make use of various investment screens in their core foundation investment, but our research revealed that the foundations operating as philanthropic banks are more focused on proactive, direct investments than in the somewhat more passive activity of deploying screens on the more standard foundation investments.

23. Angelo Miglietta, "New Ideas and Experiences in Granting and Supporting Social Investment: The 'Strange' Case of Fondazione CRT and Its Network," unpublished paper, 2010.

24. "Self-Help Secondary Market," Self-Help Credit Union, accessed July 20, 2012, http://www.self-help.org/secondary-market. See Chapter 4 of this volume for more information on this program and other secondary market operations.

25. In the case of the Mary Reynolds Babcock Foundation, for example, 90 percent of its social-impact investments are in debt instruments, mostly fixed-income bonds and bond funds. In the case of the Annie E. Casey Foundation, this figure is close to 90 percent, though 40 percent of the assets are in subordinated loans, which have a higher risk exposure than general loan pools.

26. W.K. Kellogg has 37 percent of its social-impact investments in equities and KL Felicitas 45 percent, of which roughly half is in public equities and half in private equities.

27. David F. Freeman, *The Handbook on Private Foundations*, published for the Council on Foundations (Cabin John, MD: Seven Locks Press, 1981), 69; Mark Kramer and Anne Stetson, "A Brief Guide to the Law of Mission Investing for U.S. Foundations," FSG Social Impact Advisors, October 2008, accessed August 23, 2013, http://www.fsg.org/Portals/0/Uploads/Documents/PDF/The_Law_and_Mission_Investing_Brief.pdf, 1.

28. Bruce Hopkins, *The Law of Tax-Exempt Organizations*, 9th ed. (Hoboken, NJ: John Wiley & Sons, 2007), 380.

29. This distinction between below-market-rate investments (commonly used to depict PRIs) and "mission-related investments" has introduced some confusion into reporting on social-impact investing. Recent Foundation Center research has continued to distinguish fairly sharply between PRIs and market-rate investments. The FSG work cited earlier draws this distinction but does not divide the investment activity it reports along this dimension.

30. The law governing Italian foundations of banking origin (l. 153/1999, art. 8) is somewhat ambiguous about what these foundations can use their assets and income for. The law states that the foundations have to use their income (whatever it is) to cover their operating expenses, pay taxes on their earnings, set aside some compulsory reserves (in a percentage that is determined annually by the Treasury Ministry and was 20 percent of income for the year 2011), use at least 50 percent of the residual to make grants in so-called relevant sectors, pursue other statutory aims or set aside some more (noncompulsory) reserves, and pay grants that are determined by the law. Italian foundations cannot make loans (art. 3) or act in the credit market, which limits one whole class of financial transactions. Although in principle they can use their assets to make equity investments, the language speaking exclusively about grants and the requirement that they diversify their investments in order to get an "adequate income" (art. 7) put some constraints on this as well. Dr. Paolo Barbetta, personal interview, July 15, 2011.

In the case of Fondazione CRT, the initial capital for its separate entity, the Development and Growth Foundation, came from an exceptional surge in earnings in the mid-1990s. Subsequent capitalization of this entity has come out of the grants budget of the foundation. In 2009, for example, the foundation devoted nearly 42 percent of its grant budget to Fondazione Sviluppo e Cresceta, its investing subsidiary. Ashley Metz Cummings and Lisa Hehenberger, "Strategies for Foundations: When, Why and How to Use Venture Philanthropy," Alliance Publishing Trust, October 2010, accessed August 23, 2013, http://evpa.eu.com/wp-content/uploads/2011/06/EVPA-Knowledge-Centre_Strategies-for-Foundations.pdf, 30; Miglietta, "New Ideas and Experiences."

31. Recently issued IRS guidelines update the examples of permissible PRIs in ways that may relieve this obstacle to the broader use of PRIs by foundations. See "Examples of Program-Related Investments," 26 CFR Part 53, REG-144267-11, RIN 1545-BK76, published in *Federal Register*, vol. 77, No. 76 (April 19, 2012), Proposed Rules, 23429.

32. Ford Foundation, *Investing for Social Gain*, 4, 6.

33. This staffing pattern is not without its consequences in terms of the substance of social-impact investing. One of the foundations we examined in depth underwent a significant narrowing of its social-impact investment portfolio with a change in the personnel responsible for this function at the foundation. From all accounts, this shift had less to do with any shift in board strategy than with the expertise of the person managing the portfolio.

34. Thomas Reis, Kellogg Foundation, personal interview, May 10, 2010.

35. Lawrence, "Doing Good with Foundation Assets," xlv.

36. Data on the number of foundations and the size of foundation assets and qualifying distributions (grants plus administrative costs) from Foundation Center, *Foundation Yearbook, 2010*, 4.

37. Based on data in Cooch and Kramer, "Compounding Impact," 45.

38. Lawrence, "Key Facts on Mission Investing," 1.

39. This figure was derived by applying the 3.5 percent of foundations estimated to be devoting over 5 percent of their assets to social-impact investments to the 362 foundations with grant budgets of $10 million or more, and by applying a figure half as great to the 4,436 foundations with grant budgets between $1 million and $10 million.

40. European Venture Philanthropy Association, "European Venture Philanthropy Industry: Preliminary Results of First EVPA Survey," published November 16, 2011, http://evpa.eu.com/wp-content/uploads/2010/08/ VP-Industry-data_for-conference_FINAL.pdf, 13. The European Venture Philanthropy Association embraces foundations that engage in "high-engagement grantmaking" as well as those that utilize investment-type tools of social-impact investing. For a discussion of high-impact investing, see Chapter 7 of this volume.

41. See note 26 above.

42. For a more extensive discussion of these and other factors propelling the emergence of the "new frontiers of philanthropy," see Chapter 1 of this volume.

43. Data on foundation assets and grants from Foundation Center, *Foundation Yearbook, 2010*, 4. Data on nonprofit service and expressive organization revenue from Lester M. Salamon, *America's Nonprofit Sector: A Primer*, 2nd ed. (New York: Foundation Center, 2012), 30.

44. Ford Foundation, *Investing for Social Gain*, 6.

45. Christa Velasquez, personal interview, November 2010.

46. Swack, "Expanding Philanthropy."

47. Salamon, *America's Nonprofit Sector*, 49, based on Federal Reserve data available at http://www.federalreserve.gov/releases/z1/20090312.

48. See, for example, David J. Erickson, *The Housing Policy Revolution: Networks and Neighborhoods* (Washington, DC: Urban Institute, 2009).

49. Erickson, *Housing Policy Revolution*, 148–49.

50. Matthew Bishop and Michael Green, *Philanthrocapitalism: How the Rich Can Save the World* (New York: Bloomsbury Press, 2008), 6.

51. Charly and Lisa Kleissner, and Raúl Pomares, personal interviews, March 26, 2010, and January 23, 2012.

52. See, for example: David Bornstein, *How To Change the World: Social Entrepreneurs and the Power of New Ideas* (New York: Oxford University Press, 2004); Alex Nichols, ed., *Social Entrepreneurship: New Models of Sustainable Social Change* (Oxford: Oxford University Press, 2006); Dennis R. Young, Lester M. Salamon, and Mary Clark Grinsfelder, "Commercialization, Social Ventures, and For-Profit Competition," in *The State of Nonprofit America*, 2nd ed., ed. Lester M. Salamon (Washington, DC: Urban Institute Press, 2012).

53. C. K. Prahalad, *The Fortune at the Bottom of the Pyramid: Eradicating Poverty through Profits* (Philadelphia: Wharton School Publishing, 2004).

54. Freeman, *Handbook on Private Foundations*, 69. See also Kramer and Stetson, "Brief Guide," 1.

55. Kimberlee Cornett, telephone interview, January 27, 2012.

56. Quoted in Kramer and Stetson, "Brief Guide," 3.

57. Foundation investment staff indicated that the open, candid approach was crucial to receiving buy-in from the board, and similar work has been needed with the staff. Reis, interview.

58. IRS Regulation 53.2944-1(a)(2)(i), cited in Freeman, *Handbook on Private Foundations*, 69. See also Kramer and Stetson, "Brief Guide," 6. As discussed earlier, limitations may be more severe in some civil law countries, where entire classes of assets, such as loans in the case of Italian foundations of banking origin, are declared off limits. See discussion below on limitations for further information on this point.

59. Lawrence and Mukai, "Key Facts on Mission Investing," 2.

60. One illustrative strategy document identified the following criteria to apply to a potential social-impact investment: (1) whether it is in a "program area of special interest to the foundation"; (2) whether it allowed an organization to leverage financing from traditional financing sources; (3) whether it would establish a financing model that main-line financing institutions might be more likely to adopt in the future; (4) whether it would bring the beneficiary organization into contact with new financial resources; (5) whether it would build new skills, attitudes, and capacities into the recipient organization; (6) whether the beneficiary was an organization that the foundation wanted to establish a long-term relationship with; (7) whether the activity supported required a sizable upfront infusion of resources for which traditional grantmaking would not be appropriate; (8) whether there is a reasonable expectation that the investment can be repaid; (9) whether the level of risk is acceptable such that any loss or failure to recover the investment would be considered consistent with the programmatic objectives of the foundation. Cited in Baxter, *Program-Related Investments*, 41–42.

61. In the case of the Babcock Foundation, the sequencing of these steps was slightly different, as the foundation board consciously adopted a policy of "learning by doing" and formulated its policies as it gained experience with its early investments.

62. "Go: Investing for Impact—the Early Years," W.K. Kellogg Foundation, accessed July 20, 2012, http://mdi.wkkf.org/Our-Process-and-Tools/Inside-the-MDI-Process.aspx, 4; John Goldstein, Imprint Capital Advisors, personal interview, San Francisco, October 23, 2011; Reis, interview.

63. "Home," Toniic, accessed November 9, 2012, http://toniic.com/index.php/; Lisa Kleissner, personal interview, San Francisco, CA, October 23, 2011.

64. Neil Carlson, "Program-Related Investing Skills, Strategies for New PRI Funders," *Grantcraft*, 16, accessed July 20, 2012, http://www.grantcraft.org/index.cfm?fuseaction=Page.viewPage&pageID=821.

65. Carlson, "Program-Related Investing Skills," 16.

66. Heron Foundation, "HFHI Write-up & Checklist," unpublished internal document, 2008.

67. Carlson, "Program-Related Investing Skills," 16.

68. Carlson, "Program-Related Investing Skills."

69. Julie Sunderland, personal interview, Washington, DC, January 1, 2011.

70. Baxter, *Program-Related Investments*, 391–449.

71. Cooch and Kramer, "Compounding Impact," 25.

72. Carlson, "Program-Related Investing Skills," 16.

73. See, for example, Paul Brest and Hal Harvey, *Money Well Spent: A Strategic Plan for Smart Philanthropy* (New York: Bloomberg Press, 2008); and Thomas J. Tierney and Joel L. Fleishman, *Give Smart: Philanthropy That Gets Results* (New York: Public Affairs Press, 2011).

74. As noted earlier, the distinction here is between investments that do not seek a market-rate return and can be treated as fulfilling a foundation's payout requirement, and investments that, while serving mission purposes, may also generate market-rate returns.

75. Francie Brody, Kevin McQueen, Christa Velasquz, and John Weiser, "Current Practices in Program-Related Investing," Brody, Weiser, Burns, 2002, accessed November 9, 2012, http://www.brodyweiser.com/pdf/currentpracticesinpri.pdf, 1.

76. Carlson, "Program-Related Investing Skills," 4. As noted earlier, the Internal Revenue Service recently updated its guidance on permissible types of PRIs to help overcome this problem. See note 28 above.

77. Gregory Ratliff, "MacArthur PRI Portfolio Summary," internal memorandum, January 23, 2000, 10–11.

78. Carlson, "Program-Related Investing Skills," 4.

79. Baxter, *Program-Related Investments*, 88.

80. Baxter, *Program-Related Investments*, 89; Hopkins, *Law of Tax-Exempt Organizations*, 374–76.

81. Baxter, *Program-Related Investments*, 89. A number of exceptions exist to this "excess business holding" restriction in addition to that for PRIs. See Hopkins, *Law of Tax-Exempt Organizations*, 378–79.

82. Foundations are subject to an excess tax of 2 percent on their undistributed assets. To avoid a penalty excise tax on the repaid PRI, foundations must increase their qualifying distributions in the year the PRI is paid back by the amount of the repayment. Baxter, *Program-Related Investments*, 88; Brody et al., "Current Practices," 2.

83. Cooch and Kramer, "Compounding Impact," 4.

84. Sunderland, interview.

85. For a discussion of the capital literacy of a core set of US nonprofits, see Lester M. Salamon and Stephanie L. Geller, "Investment Capital: The New Challenge for American Nonprofits," Listening Post Project Communiqué No. 5, Johns Hopkins Center for Civil Society Studies, 2006, accessed July 29, 2013, http://ccss.jhu.edu/publications-findings?did=265; and Clara Miller, "The Looking Glass World of Nonprofit Money," *Nonprofit Quarterly*, March 1, 2005, accessed August 23, 2013, http://nonprofit-financefund.org/files/docs/2010/NPQSpring05.pdf.

86. Danyal Sattar, personal interview, June 29, 2011.

87. Lawrence and Mukai, "Key Facts on Mission Investing," 3.

88. Lawrence, "Doing Good with Foundation Assets," xiii–xix.

89. Cooch and Kramer, "Compounding Impact," 24.

90. F.B. Heron Foundation, "Mission Investing at the F.B. Heron Foundation: Data Summary," unpublished internal document, December 31, 2009.

91. The foundation did report that 14.6 percent of the remaining 98.4 percent of its PRI resources, though "performing," were on a "watch list."

92. Steven Godeke and Raúl Pomares with Albert V. Bruno, Pat Guerra, Charly Kleissner, and Hersh Shefrin, "Solutions for Impact Investors: From Strategy to Implementation," ed. Lisa Kleissner and Lauren Russell Geskos, Rockefeller Philanthropy Advisors, November 2009, accessed November 8, 2012, http://rockpa.org/document.doc?id=15, 46.

Suggested Readings

Baxter, Christie I. *Program-Related Investments: A Technical Manual for Foundations.* New York: John Wiley & Sons, 1997.

Cooch, Sarah, and Mark Kramer, with Fi Cheng, Adeeb Mahmud, Ben Marx, and Matthew Rehrig. "Compounding Impact: Mission Investing by U.S. Foundations." FSG Social Impact Advisors, 2007. http://www.fsg-impact.org/ideas/pdf/Compounding%20Impact(5).pdf.

Freeman, David F. *The Handbook on Private Foundations.* Published for Council on Foundations. Cabin John, MD: Seven Locks Press, 1981.

Lawrence, Steven, and Reina Mukai. "Key Facts on Mission Investing." Foundation Center, 2011. http://foundationcenter.org/gainknowledge/research/pdf/keyfacts_missioninvesting2011.pdf.

CHAPTER 6

ENTERPRISE BROKERS

Lisa Hagerman and David Wood

IN 2007 RAÚL POMARES, AN investment advisor then at Guggenheim Partners, was retained by the KL Felicitas Foundation, an innovative social investment fund interested in finding promising ventures that could yield both financial and ecological returns. Pomares became aware of Beartooth Capital, a private equity fund whose "business model deliberately focuses on the integrated goal of conserving important land and generating competitive financial returns" via limited development, ecosystem services, conservation easements, carbon sequestration projects, and other relatively innovative strategies aimed at preserving the land's natural value.[1]

Beartooth seemed potentially interesting to Felicitas's principals, and Pomares was asked to undertake a due diligence review. But due diligence in this case had to go beyond the typical analysis of the firm's quality of management, the depth of its project pipeline, and the credibility of its return projections. In addition to the normal baseline financial due diligence, Pomares also had to undertake a careful examination of the nature of Beartooth's idiosyncratic investment proposition, which proposed to monetize ranchland ecosystems with support from both ranch owners and conservation groups.[2] For this client, Pomares thus had to assess not just the financial viability of the investment, but also its credibility in achieving promised conservation and restoration objectives.

Defining the Actor

Defining Features

The broadened search and due diligence processes illustrated in the Guggenheim partners case have become standard features of the crucial "enterprise broker" function that has surfaced in the social-purpose investing arena. The key to this function is the linking of social and environmental investors to promising ventures that have the potential of delivering market returns along with associated social and environmental benefits.

As the vignette illustrates, this function can be more complex in the social- and environmental-impact investing field than in investment management more generally. It not only requires attention to a rigorous investment discipline, but also involves assessing the validity of the targeted social and environmental returns based on the investor's intent and asset allocation objectives.

This chapter will focus on the emerging entities that perform the intermediating role in sourcing deals and connecting investors with mission-oriented investment funds and with the ventures they are seeking to support. The defining feature of these entities is that they connect investors with particular social or environmentally focused investment opportunities. In the course of doing so, however, they also often assist investors in refining their investment focus in line with their responsible investment objectives. In both respects, these entities to some extent operate at the transactional level, helping *particular* investors identify and work with *particular* investees. As such, their work fulfills a role distinct from that of two related types of organizations that help support the work of such enterprise brokers: first, *social investment ratings firms*, which provide ratings systems, set standards, and conduct research into the measurement of social, environmental, and economic returns that can be used by enterprise brokers in developing investment portfolios for particular investors; and second, *social investment infrastructure organizations,* which are advocacy and information-sharing organizations that promote social investment and encourage investors to participate in it.[3] These latter organizations indirectly serve to link investors to enterprises by facilitating the flow of information and the development of networks that reduce the costs of transactions.

Enterprise brokers, the focus of this chapter, connect investors with social investment opportunities. These organizations tend to be for-profit entities helping institutional investors understand the landscape of mission investments across asset classes and issue areas. They may either advise their clients specifically on mission-related strategies (both below-market program-related investments [PRIs] and market-rate mission-related investments [MRIs]) or on broadly integrating environmental, social, and governance (ESG) factors into their investment management process.[4] The role of enterprise brokers is to work with social investors in designing a mission-related investment or strategy, and in some cases they may also manage and deploy assets on behalf of their clients. This chapter focuses primarily on the enterprise brokers and to a more limited extent on the social investment infrastructure organizations. The social investment ratings firms and the ratings they have formulated are the focus of Chapter 22 of this volume.

Design Features and Major Variants

The enterprise broker function is still embryonic in the social- and environmental-impact investing field. As a consequence, it is far from fully differentiated or institutionalized. Broadly speaking, participants in this arena differ along three basic dimensions: first, their degree of specialization; second, their organizational structure; and third, the range of services they offer.

Degree of Specialization

So far as the degree of specialization is concerned, some enterprise brokers are parts of organizations that provide a broad array of other traditional investment advisory services beyond those focusing on social or environmental-purpose organizations. They are mainstream investment management firms that also dedicate a small team of personnel to social- and environmental-impact investment activities. Examples here include Mercer Consulting, with a Responsible Investment team, Cambridge Associates, with a dedicated MRI team, and Evaluation Associates, with institutional clients having mission-related mandates. Others, however, specialize in social- or environmental-purpose organizations or both. Specialization can go well beyond this general social-purpose orientation, moreover, with differentiation possible in terms of (*a*) issue areas of key importance to the institutional investor (e.g., community development or land conservation); (*b*) asset classes (e.g., equities vs. fixed income); (*c*) types of recipient entities (e.g., for-profit firms, nonprofits, micro-enterprises); and (*d*) stages of venture development (e.g., start-up, "mezzanine" financing).

Organizational Structure

Enterprise brokers may take on several different forms. First, enterprise brokers can be solo practitioners offering individual consulting assistance to investors. In this case enterprise brokers provide specialized consulting services tailored to a specific mission or impact investor's objectives across issue area, geography, and asset allocation. For example, in some cases consultants may be directed by their clients to focus on issue areas such as supporting women entrepreneurs or clean-tech investments. Criterion Ventures, for instance, has developed a Women Effect Investment Initiative that works with investors to create a gender lens for investment strategies.[5]

Second, enterprise brokers can function within mainstream for-profit investment firms that include dedicated services to investors seeking social-purpose investments as either a major or subsidiary part of their operations. This is the pattern evident, for example, at the previously mentioned Cambridge Associates.

Finally, but to a lesser extent, enterprise brokers can operate within non-profit organizations committed to promoting social ventures both in the United States and abroad. For instance, offshore funds, such as the members of the Aspen Network for Development Entrepreneurs (ANDE), who focus on small and growing businesses, may serve the function of enterprise brokers in emerging markets.

Range of Services

Finally, important differences exist in the range of services that enterprise brokers offer. Some focus their work on the potential recipients of social investments, identifying portfolios of promising investments and marketing these to investors. Others offer a full range of services for the investors as well. They advise institutional investors, such as public-sector pension funds, on the practice of social- and environmental-impact investing, helping them choose among fields or activity and asset classes. They serve a variety of roles in connecting investors to investable opportunities in line with an investor's mission and geographic objectives. They may also advise at a broader strategic level to formulate mission-investing policies or craft general responsible investing language to include in investment policy statements (IPSs).[6] These consultants may also play a role in sourcing deals and connecting investors to opportunities that align with their mission and investment objectives.

Enterprise brokers vary in their approach to the client/consultant relationship, sometimes creating investment strategies and sourcing deals, and in some cases directly managing a pool of assets. Some brokers or investors opt for a carve-out approach, while others utilize an integrated approach. An example of a carve-out approach is the W.K. Kellogg Foundation's $100 million mission-driven investment program that seeks investments to align with the foundation's mission to propel vulnerable children out of poverty.[7] In this case, the foundation mission-investor chose to dedicate a small pool of assets to mission investing as a pilot program for the organization. An example of an integrated approach is that of the KL Felicitas Foundation, which defines its SMSI (Sustainability, Mission, Social Component Investment) strategy as one that covers its entire portfolio.[8] Mission investment consultants in both cases helped these foundations to design a customized strategy based on the particular foundation's unique financial and mission objectives.

Social Investment Infrastructure Organizations

Supporting the work of these enterprise brokers is an evolving network of "infrastructure organizations" that operate at more of a macro level. These organizations strive to expand the field by connecting mission-driven investors to each other, encouraging new investors to enter the field, and providing information resources of various sorts that help legitimize and strengthen the practice. A growing group of infrastructure bodies has emerged, reflecting the multitude of (at times competing) definitions and overlapping practices that have surfaced in the social investment industry. Different field-building organizations, or social investment infrastructure organizations, frame the multitude of definitions and practices from a viewpoint specific to their core constituents or investor circles (e.g., foundations, other institutional investors, venture philanthropists, social- and environmental-impact investor proponents).[9] Because these organizations operate quite differently from the enterprise brokers that are the principal focus of this chapter, we take them up here only as they impact the work of these entities at the center of the chapter's focus.

Scope and Scale

The "enterprise broker" community in the social- and environmental-impact investment arena remains highly embryonic, yet it has displayed striking growth in recent years It is now more common among midsized and larger investment firms to have an internal team or set of individuals who can respond to client requests about mission investing, and there are some firms, such as Mercer Investment Consulting in the environmental, social, and governance (ESG) space, that have made more robust commitments to the field. Indeed, More for Mission, an affinity group serving the foundation community, has developed a listing of over 30 mission investment consultants that fall within the categories of "Dedicated Mission-Related Investment Consultant/Advisor" or "Institutional Consultant/Advisor with a Dedicated Mission Related/ Responsible Investment Team."[10] These firms may serve a range of clients including high-net-worth individuals, family offices, foundations, consultants, wealth advisors, and institutional investors.

Included here are firms such as Imprint Capital, one of whose major clients is the Kellogg Foundation, with its $100 million carve-out program mentioned earlier. The firm's tagline is "Imprint Capital Advisors is an impact investment firm. We build and manage deeply customized mission investment portfolios for institutional investors."[11] As noted on the firm's website, the firm's services range from strategy development to portfolio execution to transaction structuring—applied across asset classes, interest rates, and return profiles. The breadth and depth of the firm's services range from strategy development to portfolio execution and management. It also offers a "help desk service" for investment advisors and mission investors and actively promotes social-impact investing through broad field-building work.[12]

GPS Capital Partners provides an example of an independent specialized consultant. The firm was founded in 2006 to assist foundations and other institutional investors design and implement investment strategies that enhance mission and public purpose goals. GPS Capital Partners focuses on the spectrum of mission investments—across both below-market program-related investments (PRIs) and market-rate mission-related investments (MRIs). Clients range from smaller family foundations to some of the nation's largest private foundations. GPS advises foundations across program areas ranging from healthy communities and healthcare to education and sustainable economic development. In 2011 the firm partnered with Grantmakers in Health to provide a resource guide for mission-related health investments.[13]

In another example, Economic Innovation International has for more than four decades been assisting clients in the United States and overseas to build mission-driven venture funds, mezzanine capital funds, private equity real estate funds, funds of funds, and long-term development banks. Since 1970, Economic Innovation and its partner firms, Strategic Development Solutions and First Infrastructure, have built more than $150 billion of equity and debt mission funds in 43 states and 21 countries of Asia, Africa, Europe, and Latin America. Economic Innovation helps clients identify the mission and market to be served, identify the fund manager, prepare legal documents, cultivate investors, close the fund, and assist in monitoring social returns. In 2007, the partners prepared a *Double Bottom Line Investors Handbook* funded by the Ford Foundation to assist clients seeking to build mission-driven private equity funds.[14]

Federal Street Advisors works with family foundations and family offices with a focus on social- and environmental-impact investing. The firm's website notes: "Once you tell us what you want to accomplish with your organization's assets, it is our job to determine the appropriate course of action."[15] The firm's management team includes a professional staff of eight with a specialized investment professional dedicated to foundation services. The firm assists institutional clients with investment policy statements, asset allocation, manager evaluation, manager search and evaluation, integration of environmental, social, and governance (ESG) factors, performance monitoring, and reviewing and reporting.[16]

Cambridge Associates provides an example of a mainstream consulting firm with a dedicated mission-related investing team. Cambridge Associates is unique in that its mission-related investing team was seeded with the support of three private foundations (Annie E. Casey Foundation, F.B. Heron Foundation, and Meyer Memorial Trust) with a deep interest in promoting the field of mission investing. The Cambridge Associates MRI team provides services ranging from overseeing a portfolio of investable opportunities across both the public and private markets by asset class and type of MRI strategy, to in some cases broadly advising on shareholder engagement (e.g., double-bottom-line real estate, social venture capital, clean tech, etc.). The firm's MRI Group includes 17 members across five global offices, and it has made available to the mission-investing foundation community access to its proprietary database of 286 managers (as of Q1 2011) across various asset classes and strategies such as: community investing, ESG investing, and double-bottom-line real estate.[17]

Another mainstream firm with a dedicated team is Mercer Investment Consulting, a leading investment consultant with assets in excess of $3.5 billion. Created in 2004, and focused on "Environmental, Social, and Governance (ESG)" issues, the dedicated mission-investing unit at Mercer includes 16 dedicated professionals in five offices worldwide who work directly with social- and environmental-impact investors to develop social- and environmental-impact investing strategies and implementation plans. The unit also produces research across social- and environmental-impact responsible investing issues such as a February 2011 report, "Climate Change Scenarios—Implications for Strategic Asset Allocation."[18]

Rationale

Mission investment consultants and advisors work with individual investors on crafting strategies and sourcing deals that meet mission investment goals. They take a more active role in applying the language and shared best practices that infrastructure organizations formulate. In many cases, their role is to reduce the market barriers that can prevent capital from flowing to the underserved markets. Such barriers include the transaction costs associated with investors being able to find the players and investment opportunities, inadequate risk management resulting from inadequate pooling and spreading of risk among investors, failures in pricing up to the associated risk, and market-prejudice and lack of information in seeing opportunities. These inefficiencies in the market can deter private-sector investment and simultaneously open up an opportunity for investment fund managers to profit by perfecting the market inefficiencies.

Enterprise brokers play a role in linking investors to investment opportunities that require additional due diligence and expertise. They are able to reduce the transaction costs by dedicating resources specifically to sourcing and due diligence on potential investees and fund managers—identifying opportunities with sufficient information and research to justify investment decisions. They bring specialist knowledge of the field, relationships with and analysis of funds and deals, and a familiarity with barriers to mission investment as experienced by specific investor peer groups. They may also use emerging tools in the industry, such as ratings and assessment tools at the company and fund level. In the process, enterprise brokers play a role in creating a social and environmental investment strategy and rebalancing portfolios as needed, creating a pipeline of investable opportunities evaluated by dedicated staff often according to specialist knowledge of particular social and environmental issues. Enterprise brokers may be selected by institutional investors based on their experience with similar clients (e.g., public-sector pension funds, foundations, both independent or family), their objectivity and lack of conflict of interest, and their competitive fees. Enterprise brokers fill a role in the field as institutional or individual investors may not be able to dedicate in-house resources to seek potential managers or investments in line with their mission investment objectives and institutional goals.

Basic Mechanics

Enterprise brokers may be viewed as intermediaries connecting mission-driven investors to investment vehicles. These brokers identify products that meet their clients' investment objectives and advise on how products may be incorporated into a broader responsible investment strategy. They may focus on a particular investment class or take an investment approach across a range of asset classes (e.g., cash, fixed income, public equities, private equities, infrastructure, commodities). While an enterprise broker's role can vary by type of organization and focus, it generally involves steps such as those outlined below.

Identification or Refinement of Investor's Investment Strategy in Line with Its Mission and Values

Enterprise brokers work with investors to assess their investment objectives based on their unique organizational goals. In doing so they may craft an investment policy statement specific to an investor's mission, programmatic objectives, and geographic interests or include broad responsible-investing language in the general investment policy statement.

Identification of Desired Balance of Asset Classes Based on an Investor's Risk-Return Characteristics

Enterprise brokers advise on an investment approach that seeks a portfolio composition that is consistent with an investor's risk appetite. A strategic asset allocation policy is determined in which the consultants set a target percentage for each asset class—across traditional and alternative investments.

Identification of Investor's Priority Investment Areas by Theme and Geography

Enterprise brokers help investors seek investment opportunities across mission and programmatic objectives. These themes can include environment (e.g. clean-tech), community development, education, sustainable agriculture, health, and the like across specific geographies and regions.

Manager Evaluation and Due Diligence to Meet Investor's Risk-Return Appetite and Social/Environmental Investment Objectives

For example, an enterprise broker may evaluate a range of fund managers across the spectrum of returns, social/environmental objectives, and asset class parameters (e.g., DBL Investors in venture capital, Community Capital Management in fixed income, and Trillium Asset Management in public equities). Enterprise brokers evaluate funds and investments by assessing the track record and management of a potential fund or venture. They evaluate such funds and investments on their ability to meet investors' social and environmental objectives and risk and return targets, typically using financial industry benchmarks (e.g., Barclays Aggregate Bond Index in fixed income).

Selection of Fund or Investment

In some cases enterprise brokers have discretion to select investments based on the criteria their clients have given them; in others, consultants report to staff, or a specific social and environmental investing subcommittee, or a board of trustees making the case for a particular fund or direct investment.

Performance Evaluation and Ongoing Monitoring

Enterprise brokers may assist with the continued evaluation of both the financial and the social/environmental returns against benchmarks. Reports are usually submitted on a quarterly basis.

Operational Challenges

Enterprise brokers face a number of operational challenges in fulfilling their mission. Some of these are shared by other types of organizations involved in the social-impact investment arena, and some are particularly applicable to enterprise brokers.

In particular, four such challenges deserve special attention here.

- *Identifying a core client base and continued demand for their services.* The field of social-impact investing remains nascent, with relatively few established players. Interest in the field does not necessarily translate into ongoing business relationships, and for many investors the goal is to develop capacity in existing relationships rather than create new ones, potentially diminishing the demand for social- and environmental-impact investing specialists.
- *Challenges in finding investable opportunities that tightly align with a client's unique mission and geographic targets.* Especially for market-rate investments, narrow mission fit is difficult to achieve, and is more likely to conflict with preexisting investment strategies and asset allocation policies. Though there are increasing numbers of investable options across asset classes, the pool remains relatively small in the context of the broader investment universe.
- *Obstacles in finding the needed analytical expertise.* Social-impact investments may have idiosyncratic investment propositions, and so require specialization either in specific sectors, or at least capacity to analyze and underwrite unfamiliar types of investments, both of which may create staffing challenges. In some institutions, the cost of developing social- and environmental-impact investing expertise may outweigh its benefits, if relatively few existing or potential clients are interested in the service. In addition, mission investors will require some demonstration of the social value of their portfolios, a task that may be unfamiliar and require substantial internal or external resources. Underwriting social benefit is not typically part of a traditional consultant's expertise.
- *Challenges on the part of larger firms in adapting to a relatively new strategy.* For the larger investment firms (e.g., Callan Associates, Towers Watson, Mercer, Wilshire Associates, etc.) that may seek to offer or expand services in social- and environmental-impact investing, there

are questions about the level of client interest and demand to warrant dedicated resources to expand services in this area. In addition, from the perspective of building their core business, there may be hesitation from senior management to lead the company in this direction.

Track Record and Overall Assessment

The mission investment space for foundations and the social- and environmental-impact investing space more generally have received increased attention in recent years, embracing new asset classes, types of investors, and social and environmental goals. The proliferation of infrastructure organizations, consultants, and advisory service firms is certainly a sign of interest and activity in the field. The work that these organizations undertake has also helped better define what social investment consists of, how the various activities under the responsible investment umbrella relate to each other, and, perhaps most importantly from the standpoint of the information brokers, how to make it easier to communicate the nature of the field to a broader audience.

But this is still very much a work in progress. As one sign, while in this chapter we have gathered these various groups under one umbrella, those stakeholders who self-define as social, responsible, mission, or impact investors may resist the idea that they are doing the same sort of investing. More importantly, the transition from theory to practice in all these areas may be painstakingly slow, as efforts by new investors to take up social investing run up against institutional and cultural barriers determined by long-standing relationships with traditional advisors and fund managers, skeptics who question social investing as a deviation from conventional investing theory, and so on. In this context, skeptics may view the proliferation of the information brokerage services described here as a result of hype, or a sign (in the case of the growth of specialist firms) of the marginal status of social- and environmental-impact investing in the broader investment community.

On balance, we believe this is a field that is still growing, and institutionalizing, with relatively impressive results given the barriers to carving out a new set of investment practices within the highly organized, and politically and economically powerful, conventional world of investment. The growth of niche market consultancies has helped catalyze product development, and the entrance of large traditional investment consultancies into the field has both helped legitimize and grown social investment in practice, given their larger client bases and longer-standing relationships with target investors. This particular phase of enterprise brokering in the social- and environmental-impact investment universe is particularly complex and uncertain. In the wake of the global financial crisis, investors have become more open to rethinking the nature of their investment practice, while simultaneously retreating to past practices as part of their increased risk aversion. The example of foundations is particularly instructive here. The process of rebalancing their portfolios, and, perhaps more importantly, of rethinking their grant budgets and other forms of support for grantees in need in the face of radically reduced resources, has limited their ability to take up mission investing at scale. At the same time, resource constraints, and a growing skepticism of financial engineering for its own sake, have made the topic of mission investing especially salient. If the field is to grow to scale in the medium term, it will be in large part due to the work of the enterprise brokers examined in this chapter, who provide many of the tools that can help transform the appealing idea of social-impact investing into an investable practice.

Notes

1. See "Beartooth Capital Homepage," Beartooth Capital, accessed October 11, 2012, http://www.beartoothcap.com.

2. See the evaluation that Pomares put together for the KL Felicitas Foundation here: Raul Pomares, "KKF-MRI Evaluator, Beartooth Capital," accessed October 11, 2012, http://www.klfelicitasfoundation.org/assets/finalpdfs/MRI_Evaluator/KFF_MRI_Evaluator_Beartooth_Capital_I_LP_V1.4_022108.pdf.

3. Measuring financial, social, and environmental returns is a central component in assessing investment return objectives, and ratings systems and advisory firms serve as tools for investors. Lisa Hagerman and Janneke Ratcliffe, "Increasing Access to Capital: Could Better Measurement of Social and Environmental Outcomes Entice More Institutional Investment Capital into Underserved Communities?" *Community Development Investment Review* 5.2 (2009): 43–64. Financial returns are typically measured against established benchmarks such as the Barclays Capital Aggregate Bond Index for fixed-income products, the NCREIF Property Index for equity real estate, the Thomson Financial Venture Economics Index for venture capital, or the S&P 500 for public equities. Measuring social and environmental returns remains a challenging task, with fewer established conventions for measurement than for financial returns, though there are a growing number of advisory firms and rating agencies helping mission investors assess the impact of their mission-investing portfolios. These organizations provide either a qualitative assessment of social and environmental returns on investment or in some cases a rating or score. Investment advisory firms may focus on a particular asset class, such as cash, fixed income, public equities, and private equity. These advisory service firms are either nonprofit or for-profit entities that serve a broad base of clients, both institutional investors and investment managers. For further detail on efforts to devise metrics with which to measure nonfinancial returns, see Chapter 23 in this volume.

4. For a definition of mission investing across both below-market PRIs (which can count towards the 5 percent payout for private foundations) and market-rate mission-related investments (MRIs), see "What Is Mission Investing," More for Mission, accessed October 11, 2012, http://www.moreformission.org/page/34/what-is-mission-investing.

5. "Women Effect Investments," Criterion Institute, accessed October 11, 2012, http://criterioninstitute.org/womeneffectinvestments/.

6. For examples of investment policy statements with general social- and environmental-impact investing language or a unique mission-investing policy statement see "Mission Investing Policy," More for Mission, accessed October 11, 2012, http://www.moreformission.org/page/11/mission-investing-policy. For approaches and strategies to social-impact investing see Steven Godeke and Raúl Pomares with Albert V. Bruno, Pat Guerra, Charly Kleissner, and Hersh Shefrin, "Solutions for Impact Investors: From Strategy to Implementation," ed. Lisa Kleissner and Lauren Russell Geskos, Rockefeller Philanthropy Advisors, November 2009, accessed October 11, 2012, http://www.community-wealth.org/_pdfs/articles-publications/pris/book-godeke-pomares-et-al.pdf.

7. "Pioneer Investors," Global Impact Investing Rating Systems, accessed October 11, 2012, http://giirs.org/for-investors/pioneer-investors.

8. "More for Mission: Current Practices and Trends in Mission Investing," More for Mission, published October 2009, http://www.missioninvestors.org/system/files/tools/2 009-survey-of-foundations-by-more-for-mission.pdf.

9. For example, the United Nations Principles for Responsible Investment (UNPRI) network is an international group of investment institutions representing over $18 trillion in assets that has adopted the term "responsible investing" to express its interest in promoting a set of investment standards that emphasize the environmental, social, and corporate governance (ESG) responsibilities of firms. This has spawned a US network called the Social Investment Forum (SIF) with a similar purpose. Foundations have tended to adopt the phrase "mission investing" to convey their approach to social investment and created their own network called "More for Mission," now based at Harvard University. PRI Makers Network also focuses on foundations but concentrates on a more narrow range of investment vehicles. The Global Impact Investing Network (GIIN), sponsored by the Rockefeller Foundation, uses the term "impact investing" and focuses on a broader range of private, for-profit investors. Smaller field-building organizations, with a narrower focus, are continually emerging and include organizations such as Confluence Philanthropy, with a focus on environmental sustainability, and Toniic, which focuses on angel investors, entrepreneurs, and enterprises. For further information on these various support organizations, see "Principles for Responsible Investment," UNEP Finance Initiative and UN Global Compact, accessed October 11, 2012, http://www.unpri.org; "Forum for Sustainable and Responsible Investment," US SIF, accessed October 11, 2012, http://www.socialinvest.org; "More for Mission—Home," accessed October 11, 2012, http://www.moreformission.org; "PRI Makers—About Us," PRI Makers, accessed October 10, 2012, http://www.primakers.net/about; "Confluence Philanthropy—Home," accessed October 11, 2012, http://www. confluencephilanthropy.org/; and "About Toniic," Toniic, accessed October 11, 2012, http://www.toniic.com/.

10. See the listing at "Consultants," More for Mission, accessed October 11, 2012, http://www.moreformission.org/page/12/consultants.

11. See "Imprint Capital—Home," accessed October 11, 2012, http://www.imprintcap. com/.

12. "Imprint Capital—Home."

13. See "Grantmakers in Health—Home," accessed October 11, 2012, http://www.gih. org/.

14. See "Economic Innovation International," Economic Innovation International, accessed October 11, 2012, http://www.economic-innovation.com/; "Strategic Development Solutions," Strategic Development Solutions Group, accessed October 11, 2012, http://www.sdsgroup.com/; "First Infrastructure— Home," First Infrastructure, accessed October 11, 2012, http://www.1stinfrastructure.com/

15. See "Federal Street Advisors—About Us," Federal Street Advisors, accessed October 11, 2012, http://www.federalstreet.com/.

16. "Federal Street Advisors—About Us."

17. See "Cambridge Associates—Mission Related Investing," accessed July 1, 2013, http://www.cambridgeassociates.com/foundations_endowments/working_together/specialized_expertise/mission_related_investing.html.

18. See "The Climate Change Report: The Impact of Climate Change on Strategic Asset Allocation," Mercer Consulting, accessed October 11, 2012, http://www.mercer.com/articles/1406410.

Suggested Readings

Godeke, Steven, and Raul Pomares. "Solutions for Impact Investors: From Strategy to Implementation." Rockefeller Philanthropy Advisors, 2009. http://www.rockpa.org/document.doc?id=15.

Hagerman, Lisa, and J. Ratcliffe. "Increasing Access to Capital: Could Better Measurement of Social and Environmental Outcomes Entice More Institutional Capital into Underserved Communities?" *Federal Reserve Bank of San Francisco Community Development Investment Review* 5.2 (2009): 43–64.

Hagerman, Lisa A., et al. "Investment Intermediaries in Economic Development: Linking Public Pension Funds to Urban Revitalization." *Community Development Investment Review of the Federal Reserve Bank of San Francisco* 3.1 (2007): 45–65.

Rockefeller Foundation et al. "Gateways to Impact Industry—Survey of Financial Advisors on Sustainable and Impact Investing." 2012. http://gatewaystoimpact.org/images/gatewaystoimpact.pdf.

Saltuk, Yasemin. "A Portfolio Approach to Impact Investment." J.P. Morgan Global Social Finance Research, October 2012. http://www.ignia.com.mx/bop/uploads/media/121001_A_Portfolio_Approach_to_Impact_Investment.pdf.

Wood, David, and Lisa A Hagerman. "Mission Investing and the Philanthropic Toolbox." *Policy and Society* 29.3 (2010): 257–68. http://www.sciencedirect.com/science/article/pii/S1449403510000251.

Wood, David, and Belinda Hoff. "Handbook on Responsible Investment across Asset Classes." Chestnut Hill: Boston College Institute for Responsible Investment, 2007. http://hausercenter.org/iri/wp-content/uploads/2010/05/IRI_Responsible_Investment_Handbook_2008_2nd_Ed.pdf.

CHAPTER 7

CAPACITY BUILDERS

Melinda T. Tuan

IN 1990, GEORGE R. ROBERTS, COFOUNDER of Kohlberg Kravis & Roberts (KKR), a leveraged buyout firm, founded the Homeless Economic Development Fund (HEDF), later renamed REDF (the Roberts Enterprise Development Fund). Roberts wanted to use his philanthropy to harness the power of the private market to address the issue of homelessness and achieve more impact through his philanthropic capital. That same year, Roberts and his colleagues came across a new social enterprise called Ashbury Images (AI), located in San Francisco's Haight-Ashbury district. With a social mission of providing employment for formerly homeless individuals, AI struggled to successfully employ a handful of target employees in its first year, in important part because it lacked a viable business plan for its silkscreen printing business, a network of individuals with the necessary skills to run the enterprise efficiently, access to potential customers, and financial capital to help the business grow.

Over the following 15 years, REDF forged an intensive partnership with AI to address the organizational challenges confronting this start-up social enterprise and its parent nonprofit, New Door Ventures. REDF provided investment capital in the form of unrestricted grants, capital grants, a bonus pool for AI managers, access to program-related investments, lines of credit and recoverable grants from REDF and other like-minded funders and creditors; ongoing business and strategic planning support; and human capital assistance through REDF's business networks, internships at AI for M.B.A. students and graduates, and recruitment of top talent for senior positions at AI and New Door.

In addition, with the assistance of BTW Consultants, an evaluation firm, REDF created an ongoing social outcome measurement system that tracked every new AI employee at six-month intervals over a two-year period across seven categories of expected social outcomes, including employment status, increased income, housing stability, and various other measures of success. REDF used these data to demonstrate that 91 percent of the individuals AI hired were still employed two years after starting at AI and that REDF achieved a positive social return on its charitable investments in AI.[1]

When the formal partnership between AI and REDF ended in 2005, their collaboration bore evidence of significant fruit. Over REDF's 15-year investment, AI employed over 115 formerly homeless and very-low-income individuals. In 2005, AI attracted over $2.4 million in sales, generated $84,310 in operating profit, and employed 16 individuals. New Door realized over 73 percent of its annual revenue in 2005 through AI and its other social enterprises, increasing its financial sustainability while enabling it to further meet its mission to provide employment and job training for at-risk youth in San Francisco.[2]

Defining the Actor

REDF is one example of a new type of capacity builder that has emerged in the philanthropic and social investment arena in the past 20 years. What fundamentally sets this new type of capacity builder apart from the numerous technical assistance providers that have operated in the nonprofit and social-purpose arena in the past is the range of skills and knowledge they seek to impart.

Defining Features

A simple definition of a capacity builder is a person or organization that assists another organization or individual in developing a set of skills that can improve its operation and performance. The nonprofit sector has attracted a variety of technical assistance providers and capacity builders for decades. For the most part, these organizations and individual consultants focused on imparting a core set of management skills related to areas such as board development, fund development, accounting systems, information technology, and human resource development.

While these topics remain important, what sets what we are calling the "new capacity builders" apart from their predecessors is their focus on a new set of topics, including especially: strategies for scaling up promising programs and organizations; talent recruitment; alternative financing mechanisms designed to produce financial sustainability, including earned-income activities, lines of credit and debt, program-related investments, and mission-related investments; and the measurement of social return on investment.

Design Features and Major Variants

This "new frontier of capacity-building" contains two broad categories of new capacity builders: (1) those that use a high-engagement mode of delivery accompanied by funding; and (2) those that focus on the new set of topics, but use more conventional, non-high-engagement means of delivery and intervention.

High-Engagement Capacity Builders

The first of these types of new capacity-building entities emerged in the late 1990s with an emphasis on applying venture capital practices to philanthropy. These practices include taking bigger risks, combining capacity-building with funding, investing large sums of money over longer time horizons, leveraging networks, and building the capacity of portfolio organizations through hands-on involvement in order to achieve scale, financial sustainability, and measurable results. Also known as "high engagement" funders or "venture philanthropy" funds, these new organizations employ a similar approach to REDF—providing large sums of often unrestricted funding alongside a suite of capacity-building activities over long periods of time to achieve measurable social impact. High-engagement funders can be differentiated from each other by their geographic focus (e.g., regional vs. national); issue area (e.g., youth development, economic opportunity); and how they deliver their capacity-building services, whether primarily through staff, volunteers, paid consultants, or a combination of these approaches. They can be further differentiated based on their sources of funding. In particular, some are private foundations that are funded out of their endowment(s), while others are independent nonprofit organizations that must raise their own operating budgets and charitable investment dollars from external sources, including foundations, corporations, individuals, and the government.

One example of a foundation that is a high-engagement capacity builder is the Edna McConnell Clark Foundation (EMCF), a private foundation based in New York City. In 2000, EMCF transformed itself into a high-engagement capacity builder by providing significant, long-term growth capital to a small portfolio of exemplary youth-serving organizations located across the country that had proven the effectiveness of their programs. Its investment goals are to help develop and expand a pool of organizations that can serve thousands of additional low-income youth each year. EMCF helps its portfolio members achieve organizational sustainability on a significant scale through its highly engaged approach to philanthropy and measures the success of its portfolio organizations across three areas: organizational strength, financial viability, and program quality and evaluation.

In contrast, New Profit, based in Boston Massachusetts, is a nonprofit organization that raises charitable funds from private foundations and individuals in order to support its diverse portfolio of innovative social entrepreneurs and their nonprofit organizations. These organizations address a wide range of issues including youth development, education, workforce development, public health, and the environment. Founded in 1998, New Profit invests significantly in each portfolio organization's visionary leadership and builds their capacity to use data and results to manage their organizations. New Profit's ultimate goal is to scale its portfolio organizations in order to achieve widespread social change. Other leading high-engagement, nonfoundation capacity builders working to scale organizations' social impact include REDF, the Robin Hood Foundation,[3] Social Venture Partners (SVP), and Venture Philanthropy Partners (VPP).

Specialty Capacity Builders

The second broad category of new capacity builders focus on the same array of new topics and issue areas as the high-engagement providers, but rely on more conventional modes of intervention such as training sessions and singular consulting engagements to deliver their capacity-building services. In addition, they tend not to bring financial resources into the organizations they help. These non-high-engagement capacity builders encompass a spectrum of consultants from solo practitioners to pro bono volunteers to for-profit global management consulting firms and independent nonprofit organizations. Most of the non-high-engagement capacity builders specialize in one or just a few of the new capacity-building topics, such as strategic planning for scaling, talent recruitment, earned-income strategies, alternative financing mechanisms, or social outcome measurement.

For example, the Bridgespan Group, the Monitor Group, and McKinsey & Company have developed specialized practices to help social-purpose organizations scale up their activities. The Bridgespan Group, a national nonprofit strategy consulting firm founded in 2000 by for-profit Bain and Company, has worked with each of the EMCF portfolio members on developing business plans to scale up their youth-serving organizations over time. Bridgespan's planning process not only maps out the stages of growth for the organization but also helps the organization realign its services and programming, including at times spinning off divisions that are not mission critical or financially self-sustaining, and increasing fee-for-service activities that generate net income for the organization.

In the area of talent development and recruitment, entities such as Commongood Careers and Bridgestar have emerged to help expanding social-purpose organizations identify and develop senior leadership. Commongood Careers was founded in 2005 in partnership with New Profit to enable innovative nonprofits to build strong organizations through recruitment, retention, and development of outstanding talent. Bridgestar is an initiative of the Bridgespan Group that provides talent search services, a nonprofit management job board, content, and tools designed to help nonprofit organizations build strong leadership teams and individuals to pursue career paths as nonprofit leaders.

Other capacity builders have emerged to help social-purpose organizations develop earned-income activities. One example is Community Wealth Partners (CWP), a for-profit subsidiary of the nonprofit Share Our Strength. CWP consults with nonprofit organizations on how to become more self-sustaining by generating revenue through business ventures and corporate partnerships, including social enterprises and social franchising. As the "new frontiers of philanthropy" outlined in this book have become more widespread and more widely used, other capacity builders have surfaced to help social-purpose organizations understand, identify, and access these alternative financing mechanisms. Key examples include organizations such as the Nonprofit Finance Fund, GPS Capital Partners, and Imprint Capital Advisors, all of which provide consulting assistance to nonprofits and foundations to assist them in securing, or in the case of foundations, providing, these new, or newly expanding, types of assistance.

Finally, in response to the new emphasis being placed on measuring the impact of social-purpose activities, other capacity builders have arisen to help social-purpose organizations respond to the new impact measurement expectations. BTW Consultants (BTW) is one example of such an entity. Founded in 1998, BTW provides applied research and evaluation consulting to nonprofit and philanthropic organizations in order to inform their organizational effectiveness. BTW served as a key partner to REDF in its efforts to design and implement its social outcome measurement system and social return on investment (SROI) framework. Other examples in this area include SVT Group, a leading, for-profit advisory firm that was founded in 2001 to further the adoption of SROI and other impact management standards; and the SROI Network in London, founded in 2008 to build the capacity of individuals and organizations to conduct SROI analyses throughout Europe.

Scope and Scale of New Capacity Builders

Although technical assistance providers to nonprofit organizations have been in existence for some time, the nonprofit and social-purpose capacity-building that is the focus of this chapter seems to have undergone a major boom since the mid-1990s.[4] As one indication of this, a Google search for "nonprofit capacity-building" nets over 2.7 million resources. Similarly, there has been a surge of degree and nondegree nonprofit management training programs at colleges and universities around the country. As of 2009, 168 US colleges or universities had graduate degree programs with a concentration in the management of nonprofit organizations in the United States alone, up from only 17 as recently as 1990, and similar developments are evident elsewhere.[5] Although these programs differ from the capacity builders that are our focus here, which deliver their services to individual organizations, their growth is also emblematic of the explosion of capacity-building entities and resources across the social sector.

Growth in Number of High-Engagement Capacity Builders

Both types of new capacity builders identified earlier have experienced substantial expansion. Prior to 1997, only a couple self-identified "high engagement" funders or "venture philanthropy" funds existed, including the New York City–based Robin Hood Foundation, which was founded in 1988, and Philanthropic Ventures Foundation in northern California, which was founded in 1991. With the dot.com boom and subsequent rise of fortunes of individuals engaged in entrepreneurial start-ups and venture capital, the number of venture philanthropy funds also increased dramatically. In 2001, a survey conducted by CWP (formerly known as Community Wealth Ventures) identified 37 different venture philanthropy organizations in the United States.[6] These venture philanthropy organizations were selected and profiled on the basis of their high level of engagement with grant recipients; their focus on building capacity in those organizations; and their primary objective of achieving a social return on investment rather than financial return.

While not all of these venture philanthropy organizations still exist, some of the earliest models, such as Social Venture Partners (SVP), have not only survived but have replicated nationally and internationally. Founded in 1997, SVP created a network of successful individuals in Seattle, Washington, who combined their money and professional skills with a passion for philanthropy to develop long-term partnerships with nonprofit organizations and strengthen their capacity for maximum impact. Since its founding, the SVP network has grown from a single organization in Seattle to over 32 different SVPs in cities around the world from Boston to Bangalore. The SVP Network Office, founded in 2001, supports the efforts of the growing number of SVPs and provides capacity-building assistance to cities that are interested in creating a SVP chapter in their local region. Similarly, a vibrant community of venture philanthropists has emerged in Europe, and is supported by a European Venture Philanthropy Association that boasts 150 members from over 20 countries.[7]

Growth in Number of Funding Sources for Capacity-Building

The growth in the number of high-engagement funders involved in capacity-building has been instrumental in growing the capacity-building field. This growth has been further stimulated in the United States by the development of a network of funders called Grantmakers for Effective Organizations (GEO), formed in 1998 to promote organizational effectiveness strategies and practices. By 2013, GEO's network had grown from eight original founders to include over 400 grantmaking organizations committed to building strong and effective nonprofit organizations. While these 400-plus GEO members represent a small fraction of the more than 75,000 private foundations in the United States, they include some of the largest and most influential foundations in the sector. In addition, the very existence of GEO has legitimized capacity-building as a field of practice among foundations. According to the Foundation Center, funding for technical assistance or capacity-building more than doubled from $95.8 million in 1998 to $196.9 million in 2008.[8] Also notable is the emergence of a network of foundations engaged in making program-related investments (PRIs), which are nongrant forms of financial assistance that qualify as part of a US foundation's 5 percent payout requirement as well as mission-related investments. Similar to GEO's growth and trajectory, the Mission Investors Exchange has been growing quickly, jumping from a handful of members at its founding in 2008 to over 200 foundation members in 2013, including many of the largest foundations in the sector.

Growth of Specialized Capacity Builders

Fueled in important part by this growth in support for capacity-building both from foundations and from individual organizations, there has been significant growth in the number and variety not only of high-engagement capacity builders, but also of more traditional, specialized providers. Many of these are solo consultants or small consultancy groups. A professional association called the Alliance for Nonprofit Management has formed to serve these individuals, and this association claimed over 180 members by 2011.[9] Similarly, virtually every major, international for-profit strategy consulting firm has launched a social sector practice. Additionally, in the few years since its founding in 2008, the SROI Network has expanded beyond the UK to 11 European countries, South America, Australia, Canada, the United States, Korea, and South Africa, with over 600 members working to build the capacity of individuals and organizations to conduct social return on investment analyses.[10]

Rationale

The new capacity builders have come into existence in the past two decades in response to a combination of demand and supply factors.

Demand Factors

On the demand side, the pressures giving rise to a new type of capacity-building in the social-purpose arena include the growing awareness of the limitations on government support of social and environmental problem-solving, the resulting growing pressures on nonprofits to develop financially sustainable business models, the increased pressures from government and funders for objective demonstrations of effectiveness in solving societal problems as a condition of continued funding, expanded for-profit presence in fields in which nonprofits operate, and the general enthusiasm for bringing market approaches to solving social and environmental problems. All of these factors have necessitated a different type of nonprofit management, and as a result a type of nonprofit manager and a different type of nonprofit capacity builder.

Twenty years ago, a nonprofit candidate with an M.B.A. on his or her resume would have been rejected as having irrelevant skills and attitudes to successfully manage a social service organization. Today, top-level positions at many nonprofit organizations require or highly prefer a candidate with an M.B.A., relevant experience in the private sector, or both, indicating a clear recognition of the types of skills necessary to effectively run rapidly growing organizations. Today's top candidates for C-level positions in leading nonprofit organizations must be able to manage the diversity and complexity of a nonprofit's multiple programs, provide rigorous financial reporting on a variety of sources of revenue, or bring professional marketing, development, or HR expertise, not to mention a passion for the mission of the organization and an ability to wear a multitude of hats.

In 2006, the Bridgespan Group released a report entitled "The Nonprofit Sector's Leadership Deficit," which examined the leadership requirements of nonprofit organizations with revenues greater than $250,000, excluding hospitals and institutions of higher education. Based on the trends and study results, Bridgespan concluded that between 2006 and 2016, these organizations will need to attract and develop nearly 80,000 new senior managers per year.[11] An updated version of this study conducted in 2008 confirmed the leadership deficit.[12]

Given the limited resources of the nonprofit sector, the challenges involved with recruiting the top talent necessary to lead growing organizations in meeting their missions are significant. Whereas most major executive search firms such as Spencer Stuart and Heidrick & Struggles have nonprofit practices, the fees earned on nonprofit searches are dwarfed by the profitability of other for-profit searches, making nonprofit executive searches less attractive services for them to provide. In addition, the fees of executive search firms are largely unaffordable to the majority of nonprofit organizations. All of these factors have created a need for a new breed of capacity builders able to equip nonprofit managers with the new skills demanded by this new environment.

Supply Side: Emergence of High-Engagement Capacity Builders

Fortunately, this demand for a new style of nonprofit and social-purpose capacity builders coincided with the emergence of a cadre of individuals and organizations willing, in fact eager, to fill this demand. The new high-engagement capacity builders have primarily been founded by individuals who amassed their wealth in the 1980s and 1990s through their business achievements. Most of these new funders came out of private equity, hedge funds, venture capital, high technology, and other entrepreneurial ventures, and were determined to apply the same hands-on involvement and rigor that brought them success in the private sector to their philanthropy to make a measurable difference. These high-engagement capacity builders sought out organizations that could benefit from the suite of services they had to offer to more effectively address social issues at a greater scale and impact. In partnership with the social-purpose organizations, the new economy donors implemented the capacity-building activities they had used successfully in the private sector, including hiring the best business-planning services; investing in talent recruitment and development; encouraging the implementation of earned-income activities and use of debt; and measuring their social returns.

For example, George R. Roberts created REDF because he saw the limitations of government in addressing social needs and wanted to employ private-sector business practices to address the problem of homelessness by funding and creating social-purpose enterprises. Mario Morino cofounded VPP because he wanted to improve the lives of children and youth of low-income families in the National Capital Region by backing select organizations that had the potential to scale and significantly increase their impact. Other new economy donors funded new high-engagement capacity builders such as New Profit, Robin Hood, and SVP—all with the aim of scaling and growing their portfolios of nonprofit organizations in order to achieve greater social impact.

Basic Mechanics of New Capacity Builders

While there is great variation among the entities engaged in capacity-building, the basic steps involved in their capacity-building work are similar. These steps include (1) identifying and assessing the capacity needs of an organization; (2) designing and delivering an appropriate method of building the identified capacity or suite of capacities; (3) designing and executing a measurement plan to track the results of the capacity-building; and (4) designing and executing an exit strategy.

Identifying and Assessing the Capacity-Building Needs of an Organization

Building the capacity of an organization involves, first, understanding where the organization's strengths are and which areas are in need of improvement. There are a couple of ways to identify an organization's capacity-building needs: (1) the organization, including its board and/or staff members, assesses what capacity-building it needs and looks for a resource to fill that need; or (2) a funder or external consultant identifies a particular capacity gap in the organization that needs to be addressed in order for the organization to fulfill its goals. Regardless of who initiates the capacity-building process, consultants are often engaged to assess the capacity needs of an organization using different types of tools and techniques. For capacity-building consultants with a focus on social outcomes, their assessment tools are typically focused on assessing the organization's capacity to measure the outputs, outcomes, and impact of its programs. In contrast, the strategy and management consulting firms tend to conduct more comprehensive capacity assessments using one or another variety of a SWOT (strengths, weaknesses, opportunities, threats) analysis.

One organizational capacity assessment tool, developed by McKinsey & Company for VPP, focuses on seven elements of organizational capacity: (1) aspirations, (2) strategy, (3) organizational skills, (4) human resources, (5) systems and infrastructure, (6) organizational structure, and (7) culture. A somewhat more detailed Organizational Capacity Assessment Tool utilized by Social Venture Partners (SVP) focuses on 10 key areas of organizational capacity: financial management; fund development; information technology; marketing and communications; program design and evaluation; human resources; mission, vision, strategy, and planning; legal affairs; leadership development; and board leadership. The tool helps SVP and the investee evaluate the organization's current capacity across these 10 areas and their subcategories by rating the organization against four possible levels of capacity. The tool also helps facilitate the process through which SVP and the investee establish their capacity-building goals in each of the relevant areas over the duration of the three- to five-year partnership (e.g., moving board leadership from a level in which the "board provides little direction, support or accountability to staff leadership" to a level in which the "board provides strong direction, support, and accountability to staff leadership").

The Bridgespan Group takes a different approach to identifying the capacity-building needs of an organization by analyzing each of its nonprofit client's programs against two measures: alignment with intended impact (e.g., how strong is the program's mission fit?) and financial margin (e.g., does the program generate net income for the organization?). Using data on net income generated on each program, total cost of each program, and an assessment of the degree to which the program contributes to the organization's mission, Bridgespan creates a two-by-two matrix depicting how the entire organizations' programs perform across these dimensions. As reflected in Figure 7.1, the visual results are compelling and help direct the organization's investment decisions, capacity-building efforts, and overall business planning regarding which programs should be invested in to maximize mission and net income growth, which programs might be kept primarily for income reasons, and which programs should be transitioned out of the organization.

Designing and Delivering an Appropriate Method of Building the Specific Capacity or Suite of Capacities Identified

The primary methods by which capacity-building services might be delivered to a social-purpose organization include paid consultants, volunteers, staff, or a combination of these options. Additionally, each of these methods can be distinguished by whether the capacity-building is conducted through education or training; short-term consulting projects on a one-off basis; longer-term strategy-related consulting projects; or ongoing high-engagement partnerships involving a variety of capacity-building activities.

High-engagement funders primarily deliver their capacity-building services through ongoing, long-term partnerships involving a suite of capacity-building

FIGURE 7.1
Mission Alignment versus Financial Margin

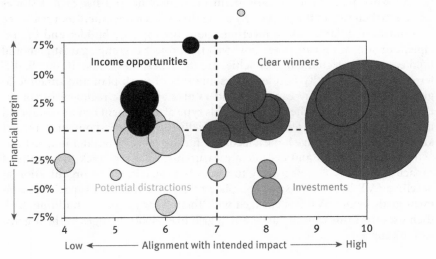

services, and they use a combination of paid consultants, internal staff, and volunteers. The Edna McConnell Clark Foundation, for example, relies exclusively on the Bridgespan Group to work with its portfolio grantees on developing long-term business plans. New Profit works with Monitor, and VPP engages a variety of consulting firms, including McKinsey and Monitor, as well as VPP staff and donors and volunteers to work with its grantees. In contrast, SVP relies primarily on its partner volunteers to provide capacity-building to its investees and supplements this with paid consultants on an as-needed basis. Some high-engagement funders engage in building the capacity of their portfolio organizations' boards of directors by joining the board or recruiting highly skilled professionals to join the board.

For high-engagement funders, whenever capacity-building is provided by consultants, an important consideration involves the method by which consultants are selected and compensated for the project. Some high-engagement funders choose to provide a grant to an organization to hire a capacity-building consultant. Others opt to pay consultants directly to provide the capacity-building services to their grantees. In both cases, the high-engagement funder may choose to designate a particular consultant; provide a list of recommended consultants; or provide minimal or no assistance in helping a grantee select an appropriate consultant. The pros and cons of these various options for both high-engagement funders and the non-high-engagement capacity-building consultants and organizations will be discussed further in the operational challenges section.

Designing and Executing a Measurement Plan to Track the Results of the Capacity-Building

There are several dimensions along which capacity builders measure the results of their capacity-building efforts, including tracking the progress and deliverables of the capacity-building activities; assessing the level of satisfaction of the capacity-building recipient with the services delivered; and measuring the incremental change in capacity in the organization pre- and post-capacity-building intervention.

In order to track the progress and deliverables, capacity builders can use a project work plan with a clearly delineated timeline and list of milestones related to each step of the project. By using this written document as a reference tool during regular check-in meetings, both the capacity builder and the recipient organization can assess how well the project is going against plan and hold each other accountable for achieving the milestones. Most, if not all, different types of capacity builders use some sort of work plan and timeline to guide their work. Many capacity builders also assess the recipient organization's satisfaction with their services. This type of assessment can be conducted using a paper or web-based survey; and ideally the survey respondents are kept anonymous to encourage honest feedback for the capacity builder in question.

In order to design and execute a measurement plan to track the results of capacity-building, it is necessary to assess the capacity of an organization at baseline. SVP has its investees complete their organizational capacity assessment grids before SVP has engaged with them in any capacity-building. SVP then uses the same capacity assessment grid to evaluate changes in the organization's capacity over time.

Designing and Executing an Exit Strategy

Designing and executing an exit strategy entails figuring out what will happen to the participating organizations after the capacity-building initiative is complete. The design and execution of exit strategies vary widely along the spectrum of capacity builders based on the nature of the capacity-building activity and their level of engagement with the recipient organization. Capacity builders that provide education or training as their method of building capacity do not tend to design formal exit strategies. Their exit typically involves the delivery of the product.

For capacity builders who engage in short-term consulting projects on a one-off basis there is also usually a clear and clean exit strategy from the beginning of the engagement. For example, the successful recruitment of a new hire for an organization is a very tangible closure to a talent recruitment firm's capacity-building efforts. For entities such as a nonprofit loan fund that uses debt to fund and build capacity, exit strategies involve a final financial transaction or series of transactions, such as the repayment of a loan, all of which must be spelled out in detail in legal and financial documents.

In contrast, high-engagement capacity builders tend to design more thorough and complicated exit strategies. Most high-engagement funders design their exit strategies based on the number of years of projected charitable investment; the social and financial performance of the organization; the quality of the relationship between the two entities; and a plan for the organization's sustainability beyond the high-engagement relationship. SVP, for example, uses a written memorandum of understanding between SVP and its investees that clearly lays out the expectations for the partnership over time. These expectations reference items such as the time frame for the relationship and the transition plan for outgoing investees.

Operational Challenges

There are many challenges facing capacity-building organizations as they work to improve the operations of social-purpose organizations. These challenges can be divided into four categories: (1) the limitations of capacity-building knowledge and experience; (2) the difficult dynamics of doing capacity-building work; (3) the insufficient capacity and capabilities of the capacity builders; and (4) the lack of social sector support for capacity builders. In this section we examine each of these categories of challenges in turn.

Limitations of Capacity-Building Knowledge and Experience

Gaps in knowledge impede capacity-building at each step of the process. These gaps include overly narrow approaches to identifying capacity needs; ineffective methods of building capacity; inappropriate, impractical, and inconsistent measurement plans; and unsuccessful exit strategies.

Overly Narrow Approaches to Identifying Capacity Needs

Properly diagnosing the capacity-building gap within an organization is the first step towards a successful capacity-building effort. Often, however, the true needs of the organization are not clear to the capacity builder. Sometimes, a capacity issue such as an organization's inability to generate timely, accurate financial reports is simply the tip of the iceberg. For example, it may be that the organization cannot generate accurate financial reports because its underlying financial accounting system was custom-designed by a staff person who has now left the organization and no one knows how to use it; or staff do not understand how to input and analyze financial data; or the organization does not have the appropriate hardware to run the necessary accounting software; or all of the above. The process of accurately assessing the capacity needs of an organization can be compared to pulling a loose thread from a sweater and realizing that the entire garment is unraveling.

The various versions of the McKinsey Capacity Assessment Grid being used by a number of high-engagement funders is a helpful way to more comprehensively and objectively assess an organization's fundamental capacity. However, for capacity builders focused on specific functional areas, such as talent recruitment or social outcome measurement, it can be challenging to assess the true need, as they lack a window into the related capacity issues in the rest of the organization. Often, a capacity builder engages in one particular project at the request of an organization or funder only to find that the particular capacity issue is just a symptom of a larger undiagnosed organizational issue.

Ineffective Methods of Building Capacity

Once a capacity builder has accurately identified and assessed the capacity-building needs of an organization, the next challenge is to determine the appropriate method(s) of delivering the capacity-building activities. For consultants, the method can be rather straightforward. Typically, a consultant or consulting firm contracts with an organization to provide a particular capacity-building service.

For high-engagement funders, however, given the inherent power imbalance between funder and recipient, there are many more complex dynamics and issues to consider in deciding what types of capacity-building to deliver and by what means. These issues include how to interface with the organization's board and leadership; for example, whether to take a board seat, whether and how to change board composition, whether and how to address poor leadership, and how to work with leadership during times of transition. There are no clear answers for how to select the most effective method of building capacity in these areas. Some high-engagement funders choose to take board seats, whereas others choose to exert influence through less formal relationships.

Other issues include whether to engage consultants versus staff versus volunteers to deliver the capacity-building services; who should select the consultants; and who should pay them. Regarding the method of payment, a report by the TCC Group recommends that funders make grants to nonprofits so they can hire consultants themselves, as opposed to making a grant to the consultant directly to provide the services.[13] In this way, the consultant is accountable to the nonprofit and there may be more incentive for the nonprofit to heed and implement the recommendations of the capacity builder if they are paying for the services themselves. The downside to this approach is there may be less accountability between the nonprofit and funder as a result of the way the funds flow.

Regarding use of consultants, staff, or volunteers, the approach varies by organization. When SVP began its work in 1997, it exclusively relied on partners to deliver capacity-building services. Over time, SVP learned that partners do not always have the skills investees needed, and in 2000 they began using a combination of partners and consultants to deliver the quality services their investees needed. Regarding the selection of consultant or capacity builder, the high-engagement funder may prefer to contract with a single provider to work with its entire portfolio. On the other hand, some organizations prefer to work with a variety of different consultants. This issue is an ongoing and unresolved source of tension for many high-engagement funders.

Inappropriate, Impractical, and Inconsistent Measurement Plans

The issue of whether and how to measure the impact of capacity-building and capacity builders is an enormous one in the sector. A fair amount of the debate can be attributed to the lack of meaningful, practical, and consistent methods of evaluating the effectiveness and impact of organizational capacity-building. While there are many qualitative case studies of successful organizations that have benefited from capacity-building, there are few, if any, widely accepted metrics for demonstrating the quantitative results of capacity-building. Paul Light observed in his book *Sustaining Nonprofit Performance*: "There is very little hard evidence that capacity-building produces a significant return on investment, not because capacity-building has a dismal record, but because it has almost no measurable record at all."[14] Paul Shoemaker, executive connector of SVP Seattle, added, "It is hard as heck to *truly* measure capacity building, but we have plenty of empirical, real world experience with nonprofits to verify the approach."[15]

In light of this reality, a few organizations, primarily high-engagement funders such as SVP, VPP, REDF, and EMCF, have been conducting ongoing evaluations of their capacity-building work to inform their own efforts, but little has been published to date. Despite the lack of measurable, quantitative results of capacity-building, the US government recently recognized the value of the high-engagement philanthropy approach in producing highly effective results for low-income communities. In 2009, the Corporation for National and Community Service (CNCS) launched the Social Innovation Fund (SIF) to expand social programs that have been proven effective in improving economic opportunity, healthy lives, and youth development. The SIF explicitly chose to invest in outstanding existing grantmaking "intermediaries" to select, fund, and build the capacity of high-impact community organizations to achieve its goals. Of the 11 inaugural intermediaries selected by the SIF in 2010, four are high-engagement funders, including EMCF, New Profit, REDF, and VPP.

Unsuccessful Exit Strategies

As noted earlier, properly exiting a capacity-building relationship can be very tricky. In an ideal world, the capacity builder has done its job well and left the organization in a much stronger position than before the capacity-building engagement and with the internal ability to address its capacity needs going forward. One of the most challenging aspects of an exit strategy for high-engagement funders is how the organization will fill the financial gap left after the relationship ends. High-engagement funders often represent a significant percentage of an organization or program's revenues. In the absence of a more rational nonprofit capital market, it is difficult to find other philanthropic sources of funding to "takeout" high-engagement grants.

Some high-engagement capacity-builders are trying to raise growth capital funds or attract federal dollars to replace their funding as part of their exit strategy for portfolio organizations. For example, in 2008, EMCF launched its Growth Capital Aggregation Pilot (GCAP) project, through which it raised $200 million for four of its highest-performing, long-standing portfolio organizations. EMCF president Nancy Roob stated in her June 2008 letter to the nonprofit community: "We launched this pilot initiative because we knew we could no longer 'go it alone' if we wanted to finance more effectively over the long run our most promising grantees.... Raising up-front growth capital and spending it down over several years while other reliable and renewable funding streams kick in should ensure that co-investors will be able to exit responsibly and effectively."[16]

Difficult Dynamics of Doing Capacity-Building Work

There are many relational dynamics involved in capacity-building work, including (1) the organization's level of trust with the capacity builder; (2) the potential power imbalances between the organization and capacity builder; (3) the organization's level of readiness to engage in a capacity-building effort; and (4) the degree of cultural "fit" between the two entities.

Lack of Trust

Often, capacity-building needs are identified when there is a crisis in the organization, sometimes involving an unexpected leadership change or financial shortfall. The relational dynamics involved in accurately identifying the capacity-building need can be especially challenging if the need has been identified by a funder of the organization or if financing a program is conditional upon the capacity improvement. In these cases, the capacity-building engagement may feel almost punitive.

Power Imbalances

More generally, with high-engagement funders, there are power imbalances in play that are inherent in any relationship between a funder and a grantee because the funder holds the money. These can be exacerbated when dealing with issues related to an organization's capacity to do its work well. A power imbalance also exists between non-high-engagement consultants and organizations, although in these cases the organization is the one with the power to fire the consultant, disagree with the findings, or not recommend the consultant to other potential clients. Trust and honesty are essential ingredients to successful capacity-building efforts, and they can be very hard to achieve in many situations.

Level of Readiness

An organization's readiness to engage in a capacity-building effort—at each step of the process—is another significant challenge. Some organizations may be resistant to having a capacity need identified; others may not be ready to act on the recommendations of a capacity-building effort. Sometimes the lack of readiness has to do with an organization's overall financial instability; other times it may have to do with the defensiveness of a leader within the organization. In order to address this issue of readiness, some capacity builders have developed tools and techniques for assessing organizational readiness for capacity-building. REDF, for example, instituted a process of working with potential portfolio organizations on a short-term capacity-building project, as well as in-depth financial and measurement systems reviews, in order to assess the organization's willingness and readiness to engage in a more comprehensive, long-term capacity-building partnership.

An additional factor contributing to organizational readiness is the potential lack of resources to carry the project through to completion. This latter point is less relevant for high-engagement funders, who typically provide the funding necessary for the capacity-building, although funders have been known to underestimate the true costs. It is, however, a significant issue for consultants who are hired directly by an organization and both parties find they have underestimated the time and resources required to successfully complete a capacity-building project.

Cultural Fit

Finally, the issue of cultural "fit" between the capacity builder and recipient organization can pose significant challenges. In any capacity-building initiative good communication, trust, and a positive relational dynamic are essential to success. Whether conversational style, personality, cultural beliefs or mores, these fit factors can be an asset or a hindrance to productive working relationships. In particular, some in the field have pointed to the incongruence between the limited number of nationally recognized capacity builders of color and the growing numbers of people of color working in the sector. To address this issue of culture in particular, some capacity builders have been working to increase the diversity among their staff and boards of directors. This added diversity will likely aid the capacity builders in better understanding how different cultures perceive and build organizational capacity.[17]

Insufficient Capacity and Capability of the Capacity Builders

The quality of capacity-building provided to organizations is only as good as the capacity and capability of the capacity builders. Many capacity builders face challenges related to their own ability and capacity to deliver the necessary resources and services to other organizations. These challenges include some of the same areas in which they work to build capacity: strategic planning for growth, talent recruitment and development, financial sustainability, and measuring the impact of their work. Nonfoundation, nonprofit capacity builders in particular must raise their own funds to be able to provide their services to other social-purpose organizations in a financially sustainable manner. All of the capacity builders are competing for top talent with the private sector, government, and each other. And as discussed earlier, the field has yet to develop standardized metrics for measuring changes in organizational performance, much less deal with the attribution issues related to those changes.

Lack of Social Sector Support for Capacity Builders

While most people in the field agree that strengthening an organization's ability to plan, grow, sustain, staff, govern, manage, and measure itself well is essential to enabling an organization to meet its social mission, the field has still not completely embraced the practice of capacity-building. GEO has been instrumental in raising awareness of the importance of capacity-building, yet there is still a long way to go in terms of institutionalizing capacity-building practices and priorities within foundations across the country. In the fall of 2002, when a number of foundations saw their endowments plummet, one of the first budget items to be downsized was capacity-building funding. For example, the David and Lucile Packard Foundation, which had been a leader and champion for organizational effectiveness (OE) in the field up to that point in time, reduced its organizational effectiveness budget significantly and dismantled its formal OE practice. While Packard continued to fund capacity-building for its grantees post-2002, its support was nowhere near its previous levels. Since 2002, no clear, well-established foundation leader has stepped in to champion the cause of capacity-building in the sector.[18]

The new Office of Social Innovation at the White House and the launch of the Social Innovation Fund are steps in the right direction in terms of raising the profile of capacity builders and incentivizing public and private support for the efforts of organizations that build the capacity of nonprofit organizations to scale their work and measure the impact of their efforts. Ultimately, more conclusive evidence of the positive social outcomes resulting from organizations' strengthened capacity may be needed to more fully engage the sector's support for capacity builders.

Track Record and Assessment

In many ways, capacity-building is still a cottage industry, without a set of broadly accepted and enforceable practice standards or ways to certify quality. In the absence of standards, it can be challenging to demonstrate the effectiveness of one capacity-building effort over another. Despite the significant growth of the capacity-building movement, only a handful of evaluations of the impact of capacity-building efforts have been conducted to date.

High-Engagement Capacity Builders

The continued growth in the number of high-engagement funders since 1990, despite two economic downturns, is one way to assess their track record. Their sustained existence may be an indication that this approach to building the capacity of nonprofit organizations has staying power.

Regarding more formal assessment of the new capacity builders, individual high-engagement funders have evaluated the impact of their work. In 2005, an evaluation of SVP's capacity-building activities with its investees concluded that, overall, the investees surveyed were satisfied with their SVP relationships and listed SVP's strengths as its focus on capacity-building, multiyear funding, great work from partners, and highly skilled staff. The investees reported that SVP had positively affected their reputation, especially with other foundations, and one investee noted, "It [our relationship with SVP] really has taken us to a new level, which is what we hoped for but we could not have pictured when we signed up."[19] Overall, the results of the survey suggested that SVP should not make any dramatic changes to its capacity-building approach to working with investees. While other high-engagement funders have not been as prolific as SVP in measuring and publishing the impact of their capacity-building efforts, periodic assessments conducted by other high-engagement funders such as EMCF, REDF, and VPP show similar positive results regarding their approaches to capacity-building over time.[20]

Capacity Builders Focusing on New Types of Capacity-Building Activities

To date, very little evaluation of the new non-high-engagement capacity-builders has been conducted. However, in 2008, the Center for Effective Philanthropy (CEP) conducted research regarding the types of capacity-building assistance foundation grantees received and how the grantees viewed this assistance.[21] CEP's research aimed to examine the prevalence of the practice of capacity-building in addition to grants, and whether organizations or programs receiving the capacity-building believed they had been strengthened as a result.

CEP's research findings showed that while foundation staff believe that assistance beyond the grant is important, they know little about the actual results of the assistance they provide. The majority of grantees of a typical large foundation received no assistance beyond the grant, and the 44 percent that did receive assistance generally received just two or three types of assistance. In addition, foundations engaged in providing just two or three types of assistance to grantees appeared to be ineffective. The study concluded that in order to make a meaningful difference to grantees, foundations need to make significant investments to provide the needed spectrum of assistance.[22] Most foundations are not equipped to provide a spectrum of assistance, as the study noted a typical foundation program officer manages a portfolio of 58 active grants.[23] This volume of active grants management precludes most foundation program officers from engaging in any capacity-building activities, much less a spectrum of activities. In addition, most foundation program officers are not trained to provide general strategic management advice or function-specific capacity-building assistance.

The Center for Effective Philanthropy's research on the effectiveness of foundation capacity-building activities suggested that many non-high-engagement capacity-building efforts have limited impact. As the report noted, "Despite the significant attention and energy—not to mention financial resources—foundations devote to providing assistance beyond the grant, much of it appears to be ineffective."[24] However, the report went on to say that it is possible to make a demonstrable difference if a foundation is able to address a range of needs of grantees that are well positioned to receive more in-depth involvement by a funder. In many ways, this study lends credence to the new high-engagement mode of capacity-building in the social sector.

Conclusion

A new type of capacity builder has thus emerged in the social-purpose field. Over the last two decades, these new capacity builders have brought a new emphasis on scaling promising programs; helping organizations achieve financial sustainability through the use of a wider toolkit of financial instruments and strategies; identifying new sources of talent; and developing social outcome measurement systems and metrics to demonstrate the value of their collective work. While each of these new capacity builders has established a track record and achieved some success in its efforts, the standouts among these new capacity builders appear to be the high-engagement capacity builders. In many ways, the high-engagement funders in particular seem to have been successful because they combine the resources and efforts of the variety of new capacity builders in their work with social-purpose organizations. Indeed, in his book *The Foundation: A Great American Secret,* author Joel Fleishman predicts that high-engagement philanthropy will eventually come to dominate philanthropy in the United States. He concludes his book by arguing that it is "steadily becoming obvious that charitable dollars disbursed by the methods and practices of venture philanthropy … significantly overachieve in impact the dollars spent the old-fashioned way."[25]

Notes

1. BTW Consultants, *GGCI Social Impact Report 2006: What a Difference a Job Makes. The Long-Term Impact of Enterprise Employment* (San Francisco, CA: REDF, 2006).

2. Tess Reynolds, e-mail to author, March 5, 2010.

3. Despite its name, the Robin Hood Foundation is a public charity, not a private foundation.

4. Shiree Teng, *Packard Foundation Organizational Effectiveness* (Los Altos, CA: David and Lucile Packard Foundation, 2010).

5. Roseanne Mirabella, "Nonprofit Management Education: Current Offerings in University-Based Programs," accessed May 14, 2012, http://academic.shu.edu/npo/. See also Roseanne Mirabella, "University-Based Educational Programs in Nonprofit Management and Philanthropic Studies: A 10-Year Review and Projections of Future Trends," *Nonprofit and Voluntary Sector Quarterly 36* (2007): 4.

6. Community Wealth Ventures, *Venture Philanthropy 2001: The Changing Landscape* (Washington, DC: Morino Institute, 2001), 30.

7. "EVPA—About Us," European Venture Philanthropy Association, accessed October 12, 2012, http://evpa.eu.com/about-us.

8. Steven Lawrence, director of research, Foundation Center, e-mail to author, March 30, 2010.

9. Jeanne Bell, Compasspoint Nonprofit Services / Alliance for Nonprofit Management, e-mail to author, August 11, 2011.

10. Tania Vera Burgos, SROI Network, e-mail to author, August 13, 2011.

11. Thomas J. Tierney, "The Nonprofit Sector's Leadership Deficit," Bridgespan Group, accessed October 12, 2012, http://www.bridgespan.org/nonprofit-leadership-deficit.aspx?resource=Articles.

12. David Sims, Katie Milway, and Carol Trager, "Finding New Leaders for America's Nonprofits," Bridgespan Group, 2009, accessed October 11, 2012, http://www.bridgespan.org/Publications-and-Tools/Hiring-Nonprofit-Leaders/Hiring-Strategy/Finding-Leaders-for-America-s-Nonprofits.aspx#.UHg_n1FnAxE.

13. Conservation Company, *Building the Capacity of Capacity Builders* (Philadelphia: Conservation Company, 2003), 80.

14. Paul Light, *Sustaining Nonprofit Performance: The Case for Capacity Building and the Evidence to Support It* (Washington, DC: Brookings Institution, 2004), 44.

15. Paul Shoemaker, SVP Seattle, e-mail to author, August 12, 2011.

16. Nancy Roob, "$120 Million in Growth Capital Secured to Advance Opportunities for Low-Income Youth," published June 2008, http://www.emcf.org/who/presidentspage/120millionsecured.htm.

17. Conservation Company, *Building the Capacity*, 79.

18. Shiree Teng, *Packard Foundation Organizational Effectiveness*.

19. Monica Ghosh, *Social Venture Partners 2005 Investee Feedback Survey: Summary Report* (Seattle: Social Venture Partners, 2005), 4.

20. Venture Philanthropy Partners, *Perception Matters: How VPP Is Learning from Its Stakeholders: The Results of the Chatham Group Perception Study* (Washington, DC: VP Partners, 2009).

21. Ellie Buteau, *More Than Money: Making a Difference with Assistance beyond the Grant* (Boston: Center for Effective Philanthropy, 2008).

22. Buteau, *More Than Money*, 5.

23. Buteau, *More Than Money*, 14.

24. Buteau, *More Than Money*, 14.

25. Joel L. Fleishman, *The Foundation. A Great American Secret: How Private Wealth Is Changing the World* (New York: Public Affairs, 2007), 279.

Suggested Readings

Center for Effective Philanthropy. *More Than Money: Making a Difference with Assistance beyond the Grant. Boston: Center for Effective Philanthropy, 2008.*

Grantmakers for Effective Organizations. *Funding Effectiveness: Lessons in Building Nonprofit Capacity.* San Francisco: John Wiley & Sons, 2004.

Light, Paul. *Sustaining Nonprofit Performance: The Case for Capacity Building and the Evidence to Support It.* Washington, DC: Brookings Institution, 2004.

CHAPTER 8

ONLINE PORTALS AND EXCHANGES

Vince Stehle

IN THE IMMEDIATE AFTERMATH OF Hurricane Katrina, people around the world were glued to their television sets watching in horror as the city of New Orleans and the Gulf Coast region were inundated in one of the worst natural disasters ever to strike the nation. But Hurricane Katrina was remarkable not only for the scope of its destruction, but also for the fundamental shift it sparked in charitable giving. For the first time, more than half of the contributions provided for disaster relief came in the form of online giving. And in particular, a new type of organization—the online portal—emerged as the generator of a significant portion of this online giving.

In the wake of Katrina, Network for Good, the leading philanthropic portal in the United States, received about $13 million in contributions—$3 million of it in one day—which it distributed to nearly 350 charities. Likewise, VolunteerMatch—a site that brings together individuals who want to volunteer and organizations that need volunteers—saw a huge spike in activity. Volunteer referrals in the month of September 2005 surged by 300 percent, resulting in a record 80,000 connections.

As always, a small handful of leading nonprofits attracted the lion's share of contributions and volunteers. The American Red Cross was the dominant recipient of all types of giving, both online and traditional. And the Red Cross even received a majority of support through Network for Good and VolunteerMatch.

But hundreds of other charities benefited from the giving and volunteering generated by both portals. Overall, the American Red Cross received 80 percent of disaster relief in response to Katrina. At Network for Good, the Red Cross received 60 percent of all contributions, and the remaining funds went to 343 other charities, reflecting the desire among many donors to support a broader array of causes when they are given greater information and a comprehensive choice. As just one example, for the first time animal welfare organizations saw tens of millions of disaster assistance dollars pour in to rescue the animals left homeless in the storm and in many cases to reunite them with their dislocated families.[1]

Though a dark moment in the country's history, the response to Katrina thus also marked an important milestone in philanthropy, demonstrating the growing potential of online portals to transform philanthropic giving. Even while they remained a small percentage of total online giving and an even smaller part of the overall philanthropic response, the rise of philanthropic portals demonstrated that people would respond to greater choice by giving to a broader array of nonprofit causes.

Defining the Actor

Defining Features

Information technology has revolutionized many aspects of nonprofit and philanthropic practice. Nowhere is this more evident than in the emergence of a new type of entity specializing in using the new information technologies to transfer philanthropic and social investment resources to individuals and organizations. We will refer to these entities as *online social-purpose portals and exchanges*. An online portal or exchange is an organization that uses the internet to provide individuals and organizations a way to engage in value transactions with a social or environmental purpose. Such transactions can involve the provision of any of three different types of resources: (*a*) financial resources for both current operations and longer-term investment; (*b*) commodities (e.g., computer hardware and software, pharmaceuticals, food); and (*c*) services (both paid and volunteer).

Online portals may be considered the quintessential actors on the new frontiers of philanthropy. For many other areas of philanthropic practice, new actors and methods result from a gradual evolution of practice and regulation. Online portals, however, could not have existed in an earlier time, before the rise of the internet and related digital information technologies. Only in the new networked economy of the digital age would it be possible to create such online portals and exchanges.

Online portals are not simply internet service providers that happen to be used to transfer cash or identify volunteer opportunities. Rather, they are organizations that specialize in the transfer of such socially valuable resources and that build databases and security systems to ensure that both donors and beneficiaries are properly vetted.

Major Variants

Although all online portals for charitable and social investment purposes share the basic feature of utilizing new communications technologies to transfer value for social purposes, they also differ along a number of dimensions. These include their organizational structure, the type of the resource they transfer, and the type of "customers" they engage on both the supply and demand side of the resource exchange.

So far as the structure is concerned, online portals are not "open-source" exchanges among scattered individuals. Rather, they are actual organizations with regularized processes. However, the organizational structure can be nonprofit or for-profit, although, as we shall see, many of the most successful ones appear to be nonprofit in basic organization.

Greater differentiation is evident in the type of resources that the portals exchange. As noted earlier, these can take the form of cash, commodities, or services. The cash assistance can take the form of operating income or investment capital. Similarly, a multitude of commodities can be transferred. Finally, services can be provided by either paid staff or volunteers. This has given rise to a considerable degree of proliferation of portals as new entities emerge to fit new market niches.

Online Cash Giving

Network for Good, the portal that figured prominently in the response to Hurricane Katrina, is illustrative of an internet portal engaged in provision of cash for operating support. Network for Good was launched soon after the attacks of September 11, 2001, at a time when there was an outpouring of emotional concern resulting in a spike in giving and volunteering throughout the nation. Network for Good was established as a nonprofit internet service with contributions from AOL Time Warner, Cisco Systems, and Yahoo! "The three partners, although competitive in the technology marketplace, have long shared an altruistic vision of their marketplace's role in philanthropy," said Network for Good CEO Bill Strathmann. "They see the Internet as a 'rocket booster' to fuel individual giving to charities and expand people's involvement in good causes."[2]

Over the years, Network for Good has gradually become the leading site that allows individuals to make a contribution to any charity in the United States, using the comprehensive database of charities provided by Guidestar.[3] In addition to raising more than $500 million in its first decade, Network for Good also provides access to thousands of volunteer opportunities in collaboration with VolunteerMatch, another online portal, as noted below.

Other examples of portals providing cash include Kiva, which connects people who want to support entrepreneurs in developing countries with small loans provided via microfinance institutions; and DonorsChoose, which enables donors to support individual public school teachers in obtaining resources that they would be unable to secure from cash-strapped public school budgets. From its founding in 2005 to 2011, Kiva has facilitated nearly $250 million in loans from almost 630,000 lenders who have in turn provided financing to over 635,000 entrepreneurs in more than 60 countries worldwide.[4] And since its inception in 2000 until 2012, DonorsChoose had obtained nearly $90 million in funding for over 217,000 projects serving over 5 million public school students nationwide.[5]

Product Donations

A second type of online social-purpose portal facilitates the exchange of products. Such portals obviously source their exchange differently from portals that facilitate the exchange of cash. Among other things, they deal directly with the producers of the commodities or products, which are typically corporations, rather than individuals. Illustrative of this second type of portal is TechSoup Global. TechSoup Global is an online portal that gives nonprofit organizations access to technology products and information about how best to use them. As of late 2010, TechSoup had distributed more than 6.6 million hardware and software products to more than 133,000 nonprofit organizations in 36 countries around the world, for a total savings of more than $2.2 billion.[6]

Good360 is a product distribution service that enables donations by large corporate partners from a wide range of industries to thousands of qualified nonprofit organizations according to whatever charitable criterion is set by the corporate contribution partners. From its founding in 1984 under the name

Gifts in Kind through 2012, Good360 had distributed more than $7 billion worth of products, including appliances, building supplies, and health and personal care goods from hundreds of corporate partners. Good360 distributes some of its inventory through community redistribution partners who help to break down large quantities of product into manageable portions for distribution to eligible charities on a regional basis. But much of the organization's inventory is distributed through an online exchange that enables nonprofit organizations to find products that they can then obtain by delivery from Good360 warehouses or directly through retail stores engaged in the distribution network.

Several other organizations operate large-scale product donation services, but most of them operate within a closed network of distribution partners, where supply and demand are limited to those groups capable of delivering mass quantities to needy individuals on a regular basis. Feeding America (formerly known as America's Second Harvest) distributes mass quantities of food from major corporate partners to its fixed network of food banks across the country. Americares provides pharmaceuticals, medical supplies, and other relief supplies to international relief and development organizations operating around the world. But neither of these organizations operates an open exchange where donors and recipients can directly connect to give or obtain products or services.

Provision of Services

A third type of online portal in the social-purpose arena focuses on the provision of services, whether by paid staff or volunteers. Thus, for example, Care2.com is probably the largest progressive social change community online, with nearly 16 million members and roughly 13 million unique users per month. Care2.com provides a range of services to individuals and nonprofits. Since 2001, one of Care2.com's most popular services has been the Petition Site, which has delivered more than 2 million petitions with more than 65 million signatures covering a broad range of topics, including animal rights, education, and the environment among many other concerns, to thousands of companies, politicians, and media outlets.

Another example of an internet portal offering services is Idealist.org. During most of its history, Idealist.org has been regarded first and foremost as a place for nonprofits and individuals to connect around job postings. The site also provides volunteer matching and a broader array of information about nonprofits and community service opportunities. As of the first quarter of 2011, Idealist.org featured more than 7,000 job opportunities and over 12,000 volunteer opportunities, along with other information from nearly 62,000 organizations.

Perhaps the leading example of an internet portal engaged in the exchange of services, however, is VolunteerMatch. Just as the internet has transformed the act of giving, so has it sparked a fundamental shift in volunteer recruiting. Many large charities now recruit volunteers directly from their own websites. And many more have turned to online services, like VolunteerMatch.

VolunteerMatch was established in 1998 to help everyone find a great place to volunteer. The basic idea was to create a central database that would hold the broadest selection of volunteer opportunities, giving every individual the widest selection to match his or her interests. For the individual, one has only to select a zip code and a general category of interest to find dozens or perhaps even hundreds of volunteer opportunities. For charities, it is now possible to cheaply and easily upload volunteer opportunities with highly specific selection criteria to ensure that volunteer applicants are properly qualified for the task.

This approach was designed both to make it easy for people to act upon their noble impulses and to increase participation by offering volunteer positions that most closely reflected their areas of interest. It was also believed that placing volunteers in activities that actually reflect their interests would lead to greater satisfaction among volunteers. Over the years, all of these objectives and assumptions would be validated as the organization grew from a scrappy Silicon Valley start-up, born in the basement of the Palo Alto Chamber of Commerce, to become the leading online volunteer recruitment service.

Scope and Scale

Online philanthropy of all types—gifts of cash, volunteering, and product donations—grew at a rapid rate over the entire decade from 2000 through 2010. The ePhilanthropy Foundation estimated online giving at about $500 million in 2000, rising to more than $4.5 billion in 2005.[7] Comprehensive data are hard to come by, but it appears that online giving saw robust growth even after the economic downturn in 2008. While the annual philanthropy compilation *Giving USA* saw overall giving decline from $314 billion to $307 billion from 2007 to 2008—the first drop in 20 years—an analysis of *Giving USA* data by the fund-raising consulting firm Blackbaud projected that online giving actually increased a substantial 44 percent to a total of $15.42 billion in 2008.[8]

Still, it must be noted that, even in a strong year, online philanthropy still represents only a small percentage of total charitable giving. More to the point, online social-purpose portals—internet sites and services that facilitate exchanges on behalf of large numbers of donors and beneficiaries—themselves make up only a small portion of online giving.

Nevertheless, these sites have achieved significant impact, and their growth from idea to full-blown implementation in roughly a decade is a remarkable achievement. At Network for Good alone, cumulative contributions from its inception in 2001 topped $500 million as of March 2011, swelled in important part by the outpouring of contributions triggered by the combination of the earthquake, tsunami, and nuclear crisis in Japan. Thus, in less than a decade, a single philanthropic portal—Network for Good—has been the conduit for more than half a billion dollars in support to more than 60,000 different non-profit organizations. Similarly, VolunteerMatch has delivered over 5 million volunteer referrals to more than 75,000 nonprofit organizations. And in 2010 alone, VolunteerMatch generated a social return in the form of volunteer referrals worth more than $600 million. TechSoup Global, for its part has delivered 6.6 million units of donated software and hardware products, and provided more than $2 billion in savings to more than 133,000 nonprofit organizations in 36 countries around the world since its launch in May 2000.[9]

The pace of growth of these actors has also been striking. For example, when Discountech was created as a product distribution division of TechSoup in 2002, the value of donated products was nearly $19 million. The following year, the value of product donations through TechSoup grew to almost $76 million, and by 2004 it had doubled to more than $151 million. By 2010, the value of TechSoup product donations exceeded $450 million.

There are many more websites that enable exchange-for-value transactions of all types. Very few have achieved a level of market share reflected among the examples cited here. Until now, most of the largest players in this field have been located in the United States, though there have been a few notable international exceptions. JustGiving is an online portal based in the United Kingdom that has facilitated contributions of more than 700 million pounds (US$1.09 billion) to more than 9,000 charities between its creation in 2001 and 2011.[10] And in India, GiveIndia provides a platform for individuals to support charities, delivering roughly 200 million rupees (US$4 million) to more than 270 registered charities in fiscal year 2011.

Rationale

How can we account for the appearance and rapid growth of these online portals in the philanthropic and social investing arena? Broadly speaking, two sets of factors appear to be at work: first, supply-side factors; and second, demand-side factors. Sorting out which came first is difficult, and it is probable that the two expanded in tandem as the supply-side factors opened opportunities that had formerly never been imagined and thereby triggered demand that was, at best, latent.

Supply-side Factors

The key to the supply-side factors were the rapid advances in new media technology over the past two decades that resulted in a vast expansion of information available to nonprofit managers and donors of all types. It was not long ago that information about nonprofit organizations was relatively scarce. Nonprofits were seldom covered in the mainstream press and they were not generally transparent and effective in communicating their activities to the widest audience. In one generation the availability of information has gone from scarcity to abundance, and the problem has shifted from a lack of information to information overload.

During the 1990s, the rise of the internet as a widespread information system began to revolutionize many fields of practice. And along with that sense of revolution there was a gold-rush mentality that led to a speculative stock boom and eventual crash that shook the foundations of the global economy. While the crash of the commercial internet sector may have dampened interest and confidence in technology services by and for nonprofits somewhat, in the long run it appears to have been a boon for several leading nonprofit internet services by making talent and equipment that had grown enormously expensive in the boom years suddenly plentiful and cheap for nonprofit groups.

Also important in opening the possibility of using the internet to transfer resources to charitable and social-purpose ends, at least in the United States, was the establishment of Guidestar, which collects the Form 990s that US nonprofits are required to file annually with the Internal Revenue Service and posts them on the World Wide Web, thus providing the critical database that allows the online portals to connect the providers of cash, commodities, and services to the social-purpose organizations in need of them. In addition to the information it draws from the 990 forms, Guidestar also provides every organization the opportunity to elaborate upon basic data with additional details about program objectives and impact. In addition to providing this data through its own website, Guidestar also powers other services—like Network for Good and VolunteerMatch—that seek to offer comprehensive information and services for every nonprofit organization.

Demand Factors

Although the establishment and growth of online portals for philanthropic and social-purpose activities would not have been possible without the supply of new online communications technologies, they also required a *demand* for such services. Social-purpose portals allow donors and investors to identify precisely which causes reflect their interests most closely and to choose the charity that most appeals to them. In some cases, they lower obstacles to giving by the general public. They also permit nonprofit institutions and other institutional actors to harness the internet to obtain goods and services efficiently and to promote their cause to the widest possible audience.

Research conducted by Network for Good provides evidence of the added value such portals provide, particularly in special circumstances and for specific demographic groups. A 2006 Network for Good study of giving during natural disasters, for example, found that the internet is ideally suited to facilitate giving in the wake of disasters by harnessing the impulse to give in seconds.[11] Media coverage of the 2004 Asian tsunamis drove web traffic that was 10 times the normal volume at Network for Good, and donations jumped six times normal volume, with even more dramatic results in the wake of Hurricane Katrina. Subsequent studies showed spikes in giving during the December holidays and particular penetration of online portals among younger demographic groups, with the median age of Network for Good donors being 38, compared to an average age of over 60 for traditional donors.[12]

In addition to tapping a different demographic, the online portals make it possible to respond to a broader array of donor and investor interests. Giving through Network for Good follows a classic long-tail distribution, with a small number of leading charities taking in about half of the donations, but thousands of smaller charities combining to make up the other half. This "long tail" phenomenon, described first by *Wired Magazine* editor Chris Anderson, suggests that the internet enables organizations like Network for Good to present the broadest possible array of options and that wider consumer choice will lead to a much more diffuse distribution of resources.[13] In addition, this research suggests that the online portals have responded to consumer demand for a more efficient market for charitable and social-investment activity, with organizations that work harder to tailor their messages being more successful in obtaining more and larger gifts.[14]

The first decade of the twenty-first century was thus a proving ground for new practices in online giving, investing, and volunteering. At the beginning of the decade, trends and possibilities were identified, aspirations were expressed and bold objectives were set. On the launch of Network for Good in November 2001, Steve Case, then chairman of AOL Time Warner said, "By combining the passion, expertise and grass-roots affiliations of our nonprofit partners and the reach, resources and Internet capabilities of our corporate founders, we will be able to make giving, volunteering and speaking out on issues as central a part of the Internet as shopping or getting e-mail."[15] By the end of the decade, online exchanges had demonstrated their viability. Only now that these services are widely available can their full impact be seen. As technology innovation expert Clay Shirky notes, "Communications tools don't get socially interesting until they get technologically boring."[16]

Basic Mechanics

Given the boundless nature of the internet, there are countless websites devoted to promoting giving and volunteering. But few of these services have achieved a level of usage that either justified their initial investment or for that matter sustained their continued operation. The Information Superhighway is littered with the wreckage of vehicles that were not able to operate with a high enough velocity or fueled with enough resources to operate for the long haul. In most categories of service, the vast bulk of internet traffic goes to a small number of leading websites. Online shopping is dominated by a few big sites like eBay and Amazon in the same way that the online news business is dominated by major media brands like CNN and the *New York Times*. These sites are sometimes referred to as category killers, in that they hold a competitive edge that makes it almost impossible for other firms to compete.

The same is true in online philanthropy, where a relative handful of major platforms dominate usage. According to a study done for the Hewlett Foundation in 2009, the top 10 online philanthropy platforms, including Guidestar, Network for Good, Care2.com, DonorsChoose, and Kiva, among others, account for about 80 percent of all traffic to the dozens of sites included in the study.[17] And although the internet is a global arena, online portals based in the United States dominate the field. Given this dynamic, it is critical for online philanthropy portals to achieve a leading position, or they will fail to achieve the critical mass of participation necessary to generate impact or sustainability.

Nonprofit organizations may instinctively resist the urge to achieve dominance through a winner-takes-all strategy. It may seem that this level of market dominance is inconsistent with nonprofit values and could keep smaller charities from benefiting equally in the networked economy. But this uneasiness is misguided because these nonprofit web portals are designed to deliver the benefits of dominance directly to all charities through a winner-shares-all strategy.

Philanthropic support has generally been difficult to obtain for this sort of activity. And there is little appetite for maintaining continued philanthropic support for these services once they have been established. In order to achieve a significant share of the market, online philanthropy portals thus need to develop investment and revenue strategies that enable them to grow quickly and continue to generate enough resources to maintain operations indefinitely. More specifically, five operational steps become crucial for the development and sustenance of such portals.

Identifying a Market Niche

In the first place, information portals must identify a promising market niche, a product or service that can garner the needed traffic required to support a viable portal. This can often happen serendipitously as a byproduct of other activities. This was the case with TechSoup, for example.

TechSoup began its life as CompuMentor, one of the nation's leading nonprofit technology assistance providers. Begun in 1987 as a service that connected computer industry professionals who wanted to help and nonprofits that needed specific guidance in technology, CompuMentor had, by 1999, evolved into a consulting service providing technical assistance throughout the state of California. Given the organization's focus on technology and deep connections in the information technology industry, it was only natural that CompuMentor began exploring ways to use the internet to deliver its knowledge and service to a wider group of clients and beneficiaries beyond its regional service area. At the same time, the organization had developed a fledgling social enterprise serving as a distribution agent for software companies that were willing to give away excess software packages.

CompuMentor launched its online information portal, which it cleverly called TechSoup, in May 2000. The organization decided to build up its software distribution program as a way to attract an audience for all of the helpful information it was going to provide. CompuMentor convinced its corporate partners, most notably Microsoft, to expand their software donation program through the new portal, in a special area that was initially called Discountech and was later renamed TechSoup Stock. The basic appeal for technology companies was that CompuMentor could vet eligible nonprofit organizations according to whatever criteria the companies set. In addition, the fact that TechSoup provided lots of tutorials and community boards where users could obtain helpful guidance in using the products meant that the companies could expect their products to be used correctly, without having to field lots of technical support calls. Soon several leading technology companies, including Cisco, Adobe, and Symantec, were providing millions of dollars of donated products through the TechSoup portal.

A similar evolution is apparent in the history of VolunteerMatch. As noted above VolunteerMatch started as a small experiment to promote a more coherent approach to matching volunteers to volunteering opportunities in the Silicon Valley region of California. The idea that this could become a national, and even international, volunteering portal was far from the minds of its early founders, but quickly became apparent as the popularity of the site took off.

Developing a Business Plan

Identifying a potential market niche is a necessary, but not sufficient, condition for launching a successful online portal. At least as important is a high degree of business planning to demonstrate viability to potential supporters and investors and to develop business strategies that will deliver adequate revenues for continued success. Each of the successful portals highlighted earlier devoted significant attention to business-planning efforts, often working with outside consultants to strengthen their operating plans. And two of them, VolunteerMatch and TechSoup Global, went on to win grand prize awards in the prestigious Business Plan Competition sponsored by the Yale School of Management and the Goldman Sachs Foundation.

From the outset, for example, CompuMentor undertook an unusual level of business planning for the development and implementation of TechSoup. Business planning was a requirement under the terms of the initial foundation grants it received to develop the TechSoup portal. But even after launch, CompuMentor continued to engage strategy advisors to hone its business plans.

A key feature of this business planning is the development of a revenue model that gives promise of generating enough income to sustain the portal once initial funding disappears. In the case of TechSoup, for example, this model rests on the collection of a small administrative fee for each product donation it processes. Thus, a popular product like Microsoft Office 2010 might cost a charity $23 at TechSoup, compared to the suggested retail price of $250 for the same product in the commercial marketplace. Although TechSoup's pricing represents a huge cost savings for participating charities, it has nevertheless been a healthy source of revenue for the organization. Indeed, based largely on the large volume of transactions carried out by its product donations program, TechSoup's annual operating budget has grown from about

$3 million in 2000, prior to the organization's expansion on the internet, to $27 million in 2010. Likewise, the number of employees has grown in the same time frame from 20 to 200. The ratios are striking. In a decade the organization has grown 10-fold on a business model that delivers high-quality technology products to charities at a huge discount from what they would pay on the open market.

VolunteerMatch formulated a somewhat different approach, focusing its revenue strategy not on individual volunteers or the nonprofit organizations hosting them, but on business enterprises needing help in managing their employee volunteer programs through specialized access to the VolunteerMatch database. VolunteerMatch learned that companies with tens of thousands of employees would be willing to spend tens of thousands of dollars each year for information technology tools that would help them manage their employee volunteer placements. By offering customized services for large-scale corporate clients, VolunteerMatch was able to generate fees that allowed it to become practically self-reliant financially.

Raising Start-up Capital

Armed with a convincing business plan, online portals can then approach potential funders for the critical start-up capital needed to transform an interesting idea into an operating reality. For Network for Good, this step was achieved relatively easily due to its origins as a partnership among three dominant technology companies—AOL Time Warner, Cisco Systems, and Yahoo! The portal also benefited from a partnership with Helping.org, an online resource created by the Benton Foundation with support from AOL Time Warner. Finally, Network for Good also took advantage of a range of other resources provided by its corporate founders. In addition to cash contributions, corporate partners also provided substantial support in the form of technology resources, as well as in-kind contributions of staff time, and significant strategic guidance from corporate executives serving on the Network for Good governing board. And by July 2002, Network for Good had become the backbone of President George W. Bush's national service initiative, USA Freedom Corps, which provided access to volunteer opportunities at 50,000 government and nonprofit volunteer organizations through a single internet search engine.

TechSoup similarly benefited from early contact with technology companies such as Microsoft, Cisco, Adobe, and Symantec, who were attracted, as noted above, by the combination of careful vetting of potential recipients of the firms' hardware and software and the tutorials and assistance the portal provided to users of its products. This translated into millions of dollars of donated products, which TechSoup was able to transform into hundreds of thousands of dollars of administrative fees.

VolunteerMatch had a somewhat more challenging time generating needed start-up capital. It did not have the backing of major media companies like AOL Time Warner and Microsoft to ensure its successful launch. Nor did it have the commitment of corporate technology resources to build a powerful internet service and or millions of dollars in software products to attract a large audience of clients. If it was going to achieve a dominant position in the marketplace, it was going to have to build an excellent service from scratch, and it would need philanthropic investors to buy into its strategy.

Fortunately, in 2000, VolunteerMatch was able to obtain support from a few key foundations, the Carnegie Corporation of New York, the Surdna Foundation, and Atlantic Philanthropies, which together provided a challenge grant of $2.5 million to serve as the nucleus of a campaign to raise $8 million in growth capital that would help VolunteerMatch develop a business plan and become a sustainable enterprise. These core funders, in turn, orchestrated an opportunity for VolunteerMatch leadership to present its case to a larger group of funders, which ultimately led to the generation of $9.4 million in growth capital. In the process, VolunteerMatch generated a quarterly reporting system that has allowed the organization to chart its impact and measure the social return on its investments.[18] A decade after its successful growth capital campaign, VolunteerMatch has delivered nearly 5.4 million volunteer referrals

Marketing

To succeed, online portals must connect to hundreds and thousands of users. While the magic of the internet can facilitate this, it can hardly guarantee it. Managers of the portals must therefore develop sophisticated marketing strategies and build sizable databases. Not only this, but they must also create systems that provide some guarantee against fraud and misrepresentation so that donors and investors can have some reasonable protection that their resources are going to good use.

Network for Good had perhaps the clearest head start in this area thanks to its initial corporate sponsors, who featured this portal prominently on their major media sites, like CNN and Yahoo! News. This relationship has been particularly important in the immediate aftermath of natural disasters, at a time when millions of people are paying close attention to events as they unfold and when they are most motivated to take action to help.

But Network for Good has not just coasted on the strength and assistance of its early backers. Rather, it has aggressively taken advantage of one of the major advantages of social-purpose portals—their ability to conduct market research, to obtain and analyze information about how their users behave that gives a far more detailed and timely account of what is happening in the marketplace. The interactive nature of the online exchange means that every transaction is easily tracked via client relationship management software and other resulting data that can be used for a variety of purposes: reporting back to grantmakers and other supporters to demonstrate the scale and quality of their impact, reporting internally for business planning and management purposes, and increasingly to identify and share market trends and other environmental data with the broader field.

Network for Good has also taken to heart one of the critical insights identified early in the internet revolution, that the interactive nature of marketing in a networked economy is fundamentally different from the traditional broadcast model. Marketing is now a conversation with the client, rather than a blast out to an undifferentiated mass audience.[19] Reflecting this, Network for Good also offers individuals and donors different ways of using its services. Individuals are able to make a gift to any organization that appears in the comprehensive Guidestar database of US charities. But Network for Good also invites and encourages charities to tailor their Network for Good web pages to better reflect the specific appeal of their cause. This customization has a significant impact on giving, particularly in cumulative giving over time. For example, donors who contributed to the generic pages presented directly out of the Network for Good portal gave an average gift of $163 in 2007, rising to $202 in 2009. For donors who contributed to customized pages designed by charities, beginning gifts were $187 and giving in 2009 rose to $279.[20] The basic message in this detail is that online giving is a relationship and the more intimate and personal the communications associated with the experience, the larger the contribution will be.

Active marketing also figures prominently in the basic mechanics of other online portals. One of the most successful portals in the area of public relations is DonorsChoose, which has been able to garner the passionate embrace of an impressive group of celebrities, including Oprah Winfrey and satirist Stephen Colbert, both of whom have used their broadcasts repeatedly to stimulate giving to DonorsChoose. For Kiva, one of the keys to the organization's success is the catalog of stories of entrepreneurs seeking loan support from Kiva lenders. The compelling stories of individuals—their needs and aspirations—are at the heart of the enterprise.

Continuous Reinvention

Operating as they do on the cutting edge of the new information technologies, online portals also have to build into their basic operations a continuous process of reinvention. TechSoup's predecessor, CompuMentor, recognized this explicitly in its submission to the 2003 Yale–Goldman Sachs Business Plan Competition, for which it won a grand prize. As CompuMentor stated in the preface to its submission, "Business planning is a dynamic, ongoing process that does not simply end with entry into a national business planning competition.... Nor does it end with the initial launch of the venture itself. Strategic thinking constantly evolves and adapts to the realities of the business and philanthropic environments surrounding each venture."

And now TechSoup is finding it necessary to put this insight into practice as the marketplace for computer products and services is shifting from physical and digital products that operate within an office or on a desktop computer toward a virtual marketplace where services are delivered to end users via "the cloud," requiring it to adjust its business model to adapt to the new market realities.

Similar adjustments have also had to be made by other online portals. For Kiva, the same thing that animates much of the interest among lenders—the stories of individual entrepreneurs in need—was also the source of some controversy. In the field of microcredit, Kiva operates as an aggregator of support that is delivered through intermediaries who vet specific entrepreneurs in the field. In 2009, a debate erupted over Kiva's model, suggesting that it was no different from the international child support charities of an earlier era that offered donors the illusion of being able to support a specific beneficiary, even though that was a false impression and in any event would have been a highly impractical model of relief aid.[21] To its credit, Kiva quickly acknowledged that the individual stories on its website are not meant to be viewed as representing direct recipients in a transaction. Now Kiva offers clear and simple explanations of how loan decisions are made and how they are represented to potential Kiva lenders.

Operational Challenges

While the online portals have had the advantage of riding a tidal wave of technological innovation, that wave has been known to throw other upstarts into empty backwaters. Indeed, a variety of operational challenges confront this emerging industry.

For one thing, not everyone is equally enamored of handling their social-purpose activities through impersonal web intermediaries. What is more, there are losers as well as winners from the activities of the portals. VolunteerMatch, for example, perceived this early in its development as an upstart enterprise in the conservative field of volunteer recruiting. Traditionally, volunteer recruiting efforts were carried out directly by charities and in some cases by local volunteer centers, an uneven patchwork of local service providers, few of which were operating with state-of-the-art information technology. Many of these organizations correctly saw a service like VolunteerMatch as a strong new competitor to their basic function. Like the daily newspaper that saw its classified ads disappear when craigslist.com came along, local volunteer centers saw themselves being dis-intermediated by a new service that could do the same thing digitally for the entire nation that each volunteer center was designed to accomplish on a much less efficient basis.

And even for successful online portals, the same trends in technology and society that helped propel them forward could also undermine their continued success. In commercial services the Darwinian order is perhaps more evident. Facebook may be the dominant force in social networking today, but only a few years ago MySpace was the market leader and before that Friendster was a major player connecting people digitally as they had never before been able to connect. The early market leaders were not able to consolidate and maintain their position and an upstart dislodged them.

Several online social-purpose portals and exchanges have grown to prominence over the past decade. And while they have not been displaced by competitors or other market dynamics, they will need to adapt to changing market forces going forward to survive and thrive.

Among the critical factors these organizations will need to contend with are the development of the mobile Web and the battle over keeping the internet open and freely accessible. TechSoup is thus not alone in facing the challenges arising from the shift from the computer to mobile devices. As consumers shift their attention to the mobile Web, online portals will need to adapt their services to enable more location-based services that can deliver information that is highly relevant to users wherever they are.

Equally important will be the regulatory regime governing access to the internet. From its inception, the internet has operated on a fundamental principal of network neutrality, where any individual user is able to obtain any piece of information freely available on the internet, without interference or discrimination from the internet service providers. Increasingly, large and powerful telecommunications companies are seeking greater leeway in delivering internet service. And ultimately these service providers may have the ability to favor one product or service over another, resulting in potential advantages and disadvantages for online portals.

Track Record and Overall Assessment

The development and growth of social-purpose portals and exchanges has resulted in potentially transformative change in the practice of philanthropy and nonprofit action. These new services have enabled individuals and organizations to engage in transactions that would scarcely have been possible a generation ago. And they have delivered significant resources to charitable causes in a manner that is more highly targeted than was previously possible.

At the same time, the total amount of resources flowing through these portals has not displaced the importance of traditional approaches to fundraising, product distribution, and service provision. They have not revolutionized nonprofits and philanthropy in the way that digital media have fundamentally changed journalism and the music industry. These new digital services are an important new source of financial support and are generally breeding innovation in the voluntary sector. They have yet to generate a fundamental reordering of resources and practice. But they are moving in that direction.

Notes

1. Cynthia Leonor Garza, "Katrina Images Spark Record Pet Charity Giving," *Houston Chronicle*, November 11, 2005, accessed October 13, 2012, http://www.chron.com/disp/story.mpl/special/05/katrina/3453906.html.

2. Katya Andresen, *Robin Hood Marketing: Stealing Corporate Savvy to Sell Just Causes* (San Francisco: Jossey-Bass, 2006), 217.

3. Guidestar is a database of US nonprofit organizations built up from the Form 990 returns that US charities with at least $25,000 in annual income are required to file with the US Internal Revenue Service.

4. "About Kiva, Statistics," Kiva Microfunds, accessed October 13, 2012, http://www.kiva.org/about/stats.

5. "Impact to Date," DonorsChoose, accessed October 13, 2012, http://www.donorschoose.org/about/impact.html.

6. TechSoup, "TechSoup Global by the Numbers, Quarterly Report October 2010," 2010, http://www.techsoupglobal.org/press/selectcoverage.

7. "Study Shows Online Donors Respond in Crisis Situations," Clifton Gunderson, *Nonprofit Insight Newsletter* 1 (2007), accessed October 12, 2012, http://www.clifton-gunderson.com/Content/K1C56KGA0X.pdf?Name ... pdf.

8. Steve McGlaughlin, "Giving USA Report for 2008 and Online Fundraising Estimates," Connections: A Blog by Steve McGlaughlin, Blackbaud, published June 10, 2009, http://forums.blackbaud.com/blogs/connections/archive/2009/06/10/giving-usa-report-for-2008-and-online-fundraising-estimates.aspx.

9. TechSoup, "TechSoup Global, 2010."

10. "JustGiving, Our Story," JustGiving, accessed October 13, 2012, http://www.justgiving.com/about-us/.

11. "Impulse on the Internet: How Crisis Compels Donors to Give Online," Network for Good, published September 2006, http://www.networkforgood.org/downloads/pdf/Whitepaper/20061009_crisis_compels_donors.pdf.

12. "The Young and the Generous: A Study of $100 million in Online Giving to 23,000 Charities," accessed October 13, 2012, http://www.fundraising123.org/files/The%20Young%20and%20The%20Generous%20A%20Network%20for%20Good%20Study.pdf.

13. Chris Anderson, "The Long Tail," *Wired*, October 2004.

14. "The Online Giving Study: A Call to Reinvent Donor Relationships," Network for Good, published December 2010, http://www.onlinegivingstudy.org/.

15. Network for Good, "Internet, Nonprofit Leaders Launch 'Network for Good' To Support Local and National Charities," news release, November 19, 2001. http://www.networkforgood.org/npo/about/press/pressreleases/2001/11-19.aspx.

16. Clay Shirky, *Here Comes Everybody: The Power of Organizing without Organizations* (London: Penguin, 2008), 105.

17. David Koken, "The Current State of Online Philanthropy," accessed November 2009, http://www.scribd.com/doc/24062122/Nonprofit-Marketplace-Report-D-Koken.

18. VolunteerMatch measures the social return on its receipts by calculating the number of new volunteers referred through the system in a given period, multiplying this average number of hours served, and then multiplying the result by the average hourly nonfarm wage rate.

19. As outlined first in the Cluetrain Manifesto in 2000, a central thesis of the internet revolution is that "companies that don't realize their markets are now networked person-to-person, getting smarter as a result and deeply joined in conversation, are missing their best opportunity," see "The Cluetrain Manifesto, 95 Theses," Cluetrain, accessed October 13, 2012, http://www.cluetrain.com.

20. "Online Giving Study 2010," Network for Good, accessed October 13, 2012, http://www.fundraising123.org/files/Community/Online_Giving_Study_2010R.pdf.

21. Stephanie Strom, "Confusion on Where Money Lent via Kiva Goes," *New York Times*, November 8, 2009.

Suggested Readings

Hart, Ted, James M. Greenfield, Steve MacLaughlin, and Philip H. Geier Jr. *Internet Management for Nonprofits: Strategies, Tools and Trade Secrets*. The AFP/Wiley Fund Development Series. New York: Wiley, 2010.

Kanter, Beth, and Katie Delahaye Paine. *Measuring the Networked Nonprofit: Using Data to Change the World*. San Francisco: Jossey-Bass, 2012.

Ross, Holly, Katrin Vercla, and Alison Levine, eds. *Managing Technology to Meet Your Mission: A Strategic Guide for Nonprofit Leaders*. San Francisco: Jossey-Bass, 2009.

CHAPTER 9

CORPORATE-ORIGINATED CHARITABLE FUNDS

Rick Cohen

JOHN BUTLER, A SMALL BUSINESS owner, had a stock that had greatly appreciated. His financial advisor told him that it had gone as far as it was going to go, but if he were to sell it, he would take a capital gains hit, maybe a 20 to 30 percent hit. At that time the Fidelity Gift Fund, one of the new corporate-originated charitable funds, had just cut its minimum contribution level from $10,000 down to $5,000. Butler's financial advisor pointed out that if he donated the stock to the Fidelity fund he would avoid the capital gains problem. As it turned out, Butler's financial advisor had Butler's stock holdings in a custodial account at Fidelity, so it was very easy for him to transfer the stock to a charitable gift fund at the Fidelity Gift Fund. Noted Butler: "So we opened up the account. We did it in about three or four clicks online, and in three or four days, we were supporting a variety of things. Our philanthropy is very much tied to the things we're committed to—supporting a library foundation and a public education foundation. Our Fidelity account is our philanthropic checkbook. Altogether for us, it cost 50 or 60 basis points, and that's worth it for us. We spent it down over the past couple of years, but made additional cash contributions to it. If we had done this any other way it would have been a lot more expensive, maybe 100 to 150 basis points, and would have taken longer."

This donor's story has been replicated by hundreds of thousands of his peers who have established charitable accounts with funds like those created by Fidelity, Schwab, Vanguard, and other investment firms. The corporate-originated charitable funds established by these firms constitute a "breakthrough innovation" in the charitable sector by making charitable giving faster, less expensive, and less cumbersome, particularly for donors of moderate or middle income or socioeconomic status. In doing so, their innovation has created a competitive yardstick that has compelled other major actors in philanthropy, particularly community foundations that attract and manage donor-advised funds, and smaller private foundations, many of which might be less costly were they reconstituted as donor-advised funds, to change their practices, cost structures, and in some cases institutional structures.

Such funds have proved to be especially attractive to donors who (1) are financially comfortable but not necessarily wealthy; (2) hold appreciated stock in which the income generated would be undone by the capital gains tax had the donor "cashed out"; (3) possess a reasonably certain philanthropic giving agenda that did not require much if any philanthropic advice; (4) are attracted by the ability to establish the account and begin making charitable donations quickly, with a low "entry" threshold and very low costs; (5) want access to choices for investing the charitable dollars in any of a large array of mutual funds; (6) are attracted by the sponsoring firm's ability to handle all of the paperwork of verifying the charitable eligibility of the recipients of the donations and handle all of the tax reporting documentation and reporting; and (7) appreciate the sponsor's ability to create easy-to-navigate online access to the donor's charitable account and his or her personal investments through the firm.

The emerging upside of the advent of corporate-originated charitable funds is the potential that this faster, less expensive, online mechanism for charitable giving will result in increased levels of charitable giving, perhaps overall, and certainly in the demographic of millions of investors with mutual fund investments.

Defining the Actor

Corporate-originated charitable funds are public charities established by some of the nation's largest mutual fund companies and financial services firms, such as Fidelity, Vanguard, and Schwab, that manage, invest, and make distributions from funds or accounts established by charitable donors. Their distinction from the multitude of other charitable institutions such as private foundations or combined giving organizations is that they can coordinate a donor's charitable giving with his or her personal and family investment-, income-, tax-, and estate-planning needs—and generally at a lower cost or fee than charged by other kinds of charitable institutions because of the scale and technological sophistication of their overall financial operations.

Such funds are just barely two decades old as of this writing. In 1991, Fidelity Investments created a fully charitable arm, the Fidelity Charitable Gift Fund, through which it has already attracted several billion dollars in charitable donor-advised funds. Not long afterward, Fidelity was joined by other mutual fund investment companies such as Vanguard and Schwab that also saw the benefit in sponsoring entities that would attract and manage the donor-advised funds of thousands of investors.

Today, there are approximately 25 corporate-originated charitable funds of some significance.[1] While Fidelity, Vanguard, and Schwab are much larger than the others in terms of assets, the sponsors of the others are well-known mutual fund companies and commercial banks, including Goldman Sachs, Citigroup, Bank of America, T. Rowe Price, the Oppenheimer Funds, Legg Mason, Raymond James, Franklin Templeton, and some specialized firms like the Calvert Social Investment Foundation, which restricts its investment options to socially responsible corporations, funds, and projects, and the National Philanthropic Trust, which besides its own gift fund provides "private label" services to others, essentially operating corporate-originated charitable funds for other investment firms under their names and identities.

Defining Features

The corporate-originated charitable funds are affiliated with financial services firms that are for-profit entities. As competitors, they do their utmost to establish their distinctiveness and differences, but there are some common characteristics:

Donor-Advised Funds

Although these entities offer an array of charitable investment options, including charitable remainder trusts and other alternatives described below, the *primary* charitable tool offered by these firms that has vaulted them into a significant position in philanthropy is the donor-advised fund. Donor-advised funds have been described as "the poor donor's foundation": they are charitable giving accounts established by donors at a public charity to support donors' charitable priorities and charitable beneficiaries, but without the need to establish a full-fledged foundation. The donor is eligible to receive an immediate charitable tax deduction for the full value of the initial donation up to 50 percent of the donor's adjusted gross income (AGI). In contrast, a donor's contribution to a private foundation is limited to a deduction of 30 percent of AGI.

Until the Pension Protection Act of 2006, there was no clear definition of exactly what constituted a donor-advised fund. But the act identified some basic characteristics. According to this act, a donor-advised fund operates as follows:

- It aggregates and manages donor-advised funds in separately identifiable donor accounts.
- The fund manager tracks contributions to and from the fund with specific reference to the donor who established and capitalized the fund.
- Despite the donor's involvement in the fund, the donation is owned and controlled by the sponsoring 501(c)(3) fund-managing organization.
- The donor or the donor's representative must reasonably expect to be able to provide advice to the managing entity regarding the investment of, and distributions from, the fund, although the advice is just that—advice or recommendations, while the ultimate decision-making control over the investment and distributions from the fund rests with the managing entity.

Additional Tools

While donor-advised funds are by far the primary tool that corporate-originated charitable funds have developed and refined, they are not the only tool that a donor might access in the arsenal offered by such organizations. Typically, the funds offer a variety of other charitable instruments:

- **Charitable remainder unitrusts (CRUTs) and charitable remainder annuity trusts (CRATs),** which allow donor-investors to establish an account in which the donor receives an annual payment, either a percentage of the account or a fixed dollar amount, for the donor-investor's life. After death, the remainder of the account is transferred to a designated charity or number of charities.
- **Charitable lead trusts**, which structure regular payments to charities during the life of the investor-owner. At his or her death, the remainder is transferred to the donor's beneficiaries as opposed to charities.
- **Pooled income funds**, which are pooled gifts that are invested together, with income from the fund distributed to the fund's participants and named charitable beneficiaries according to the investor-donor's share of the fund.

Although these other investment and charitable vehicles are available through the corporate-originated funds, the corporate funds do not specialize in them to the extent that other managers of donor-advised funds do. Thus, among the corporate-originated charitable funds, these other types of instruments account for only 6 percent of assets under management, compared to 80 percent among all managers of donor-advised funds tracked by the National Philanthropic Trust.[2] This is significant since donor-advised funds, which account for 94 percent of the assets of corporate-originated charitable funds, are entirely devoted to charity, whereas the assets and income of charitable trusts and pooled income funds are divided between the donor, who can benefit personally, and charities that might receive funding over time or at the death of the donors. This testifies to the charitable intent of the corporate-originated funds.

Public Charity Status

An early source of contention with the corporate-originated charitable funds concerned whether a commercial firm such as the originators of these funds should be permitted to operate a tax-exempt charitable fund. While the sponsors, so to speak, are commercial firms, the charitable funds are separate legal entities established as 501(c)(3) tax-exempt corporations approved by the US Internal Revenue Service. Although possessing capital comparable to some of the nation's largest foundations, these entities are so-called public charities in the meaning of US tax law, and not private foundations.[3] As such, they are exempt from the following special restrictions that apply to foundations:

- A tax of 1 or 2 percent on net investment income
- Specific penalty "excise taxes" for excess business holdings or investments that might jeopardize the foundation's tax exempt status
- Prohibitions against "self-dealing" and penalty excise taxes for violating those prohibitions
- The requirement to distribute an average of 5 percent of the aggregate fair market value of their investment assets each year in the form of charitable distributions
- A requirement that they must disclose the amount and recipients of their grant distributions

As independent public charities, the gift funds benefit from certain public charity protections beyond the exemption from the private foundation requirements, taxes, and fees noted above. As public charities, corporate-originated charitable funds do not have to disclose to the public the names of their donors and the amounts they have contributed, and they do not have to specifically identify the name, location, amount, and purpose of each grant they make.

In practice, the top corporate-originated charitable funds do much more than the law requires. While they maintain the confidentiality of the names of their donors, they do typically identify the names of all of the recipients of grants made by their funds. The 3,698-page Form 990 filed by Fidelity Charitable Gift Fund in 2008 is almost entirely a listing of the grants made through the fund. Many other public grantmaking charities such as community foundations disclose only limited parts of their grantmaking portfolio. Although exempt from mandatory payout rules that apply to foundations, most of the charitable gift funds maintain policies that require a composite or cumulative 5 percent payout.

Although they do not necessarily assess each individual donor-advised account they manage, the corporate-originated charitable funds monitor accounts to determine if they do show reasonable levels of activity and might contribute to the charitable fund's falling below the 5 percent payout threshold.

Relation to Financial Service Firms

The functional relationship with a financial services firm is also a distinctive feature of these funds, reflected not only in structural relationships, but in their modeling the low-cost and increasingly online dynamics of the parent firms.

The primary sponsors of these charitable funds are very large Fortune 500 mutual fund companies. Although they are not new, the number of these mutual funds mushroomed starting in the 1970s, with more than 8,000 mutual funds serving 264,499 investors in existence by the end of 2008. As of 2010, these funds had $10 trillion under management.

By creating charitable giving instruments accessible to mutual fund investors sponsored by their mutual fund investment companies, Fidelity and its peers make it easier and simpler for mutual fund investors to use a portion of their investments for charitable donations. The charitable gift funds access several functions or services provided by the financial services companies, through service contracts and fees. This includes particularly the online platforms that the companies have established for their mutual fund brokerages (although in each case, the sponsoring company has reportedly made significant additional investments in the online platforms to accommodate, fit, and support the charitable business) and an array of investment options from which donors to the gift funds can select for their accounts.

Operationally, how much does the financial company manage and control the charitable fund? In each instance, legally, the charitable fund is established as an "independent public charity," and their managers in interviews are quite adamant about underscoring and guarding that independence. So what, then, is the meaning of "affiliated" or any other synonym that might be applied to the relationship of the charitable fund and the corporate entity that created it?

Vanguard's website suggests the following: "A majority of the Program's Trustees are independent of Vanguard. Although Vanguard provides certain investment management and administrative services to the Program through a service agreement, the Vanguard Charitable Endowment Program is not a program or an activity of Vanguard." Three of the six named Vanguard trustees appear to be completely independent of Vanguard; of the three with Vanguard connections, one is a retired member of the Vanguard board, leaving two with current Vanguard relationships.

The operational description is similar at Schwab Charitable: "Schwab Charitable Fund is an entirely separate entity from The Charles Schwab Corporation and its affiliates. However, Charles Schwab and its affiliates provide certain investment management, administrative, and recordkeeping services to the Fund." The legal separation is further demonstrated by two operating components: an investor who wants to open a charitable account must make the application directly to Schwab Charitable rather than simply establishing or reprogramming investment funds from a Schwab brokerage account. The biographies of the six trustees governing Schwab Charitable indicate that only one, Charles Schwab himself, is directly connected with the financial services firm.

In a letter to the US Department of Treasury, Schwab Charitable's CEO, Kim Wright-Violich, explained the operating relationship as follows: "The Charitable Fund has entered into agreements with Schwab affiliates to perform administrative, record keeping and investment management services. Pursuant to the Charitable Fund's conflict of interest policy, the decisions to engage these entities were made by the independent members of the board. Services performed by the Schwab affiliates are provided at or below fair market value, and the Board carefully monitors these contracts and the fees to ensure they are fair to the charity."[4]

The independent charitable entities that are the charitable funds appear to maintain their functional autonomy by purchasing back administrative support and accessing their investment options by paying for the services through the fees they charge donors. In some cases, reportedly, the sponsoring firms invested in the charitable entities toward the creation of their online platforms and other elements of their business models, and these investments are being repaid over time. Nonetheless, in no case does it appear that the corporate entity is dictating to the separately incorporated 501(c)(3) charitable entity to the point where its autonomy and charitable status might be jeopardized.

Distinctions from Other Funds

In the past, corporate-originated charitable funds have been challenged on grounds that their relationship with commercial financial services firms undermines their legitimacy as charitably oriented national sponsors of donor-advised funds. Over time, however, other charities have developed or expanded their functions to include sponsorship of donor-advised funds and begun to emulate some of the charitable gift funds' innovations around cost and investment. Among the more prominent types of entities that have moved to create and sponsor donor-advised funds are universities, hospitals, faith-based organizations, and, in an appeal to moderate-sized charitable donors, even affiliates of the United Way. Appendix Table 9.A1 compares the corporate-originated charitable funds to community foundations and independent foundations along a number of dimensions, focusing particularly on the donor-advised funds.

From the point of view of the donor, a corporate-originated charitable fund performs most of the functions of a charitable foundation. The donor does not have to establish a corporation and file for private foundation status, establish an office, hire and supervise staff, hold board meetings, and file quarterly and annual forms with the Internal Revenue Service and relevant state government agencies. The "foundation" in the operation of a donor-advised fund absorbs all of the structural and programmatic elements that would normally be addressed through a foundation.

Corporate-originated charitable funds differ from community foundations in that they are fundamentally transactional. There is little or no interest in having the funds "sit" in accounts rather than being as quickly as possible given to charities. Community foundations, on the other hand, are fundamentally community institutions, often positioned as community problem-solvers, deploying both philanthropic capital and knowledgeable staff to address community issues. As a result, the community foundations are in a position to advise donors on how best to achieve their charitable objectives or look to get donors to make their donations "unrestricted," available to the community foundation itself to use as it determines rather than strictly following donors' charity-specific recommendations. Frequently, community foundations solicit donations to "field of interest" funds, for example, programs for youth, women's issues, or affordable housing, from which the foundation staff would then make grant decisions. That sort of programming requires a level of staffing that makes community foundation operating costs higher than those of the corporate-originated charitable funds.

There is no specific barrier that prevents any public charity from offering a donor-advised fund service, and many types of organizations have done so, as noted above. In nearly all cases, however, they are either topically, institutionally, or geographically restricted in their purposes. In addition, in almost all of these instances, the proportion of revenues and giving attributable to their donor-advised fund and related charitable instruments is tiny. For community foundations, donor-advised funds constituted 33.5 percent of their assets in 2007 but accounted for 62.1 percent of their grant distributions. For community foundations with more than $1 billion in assets, 73 percent of their grant distributions came from donor-advised funds. Because the corporate-originated charitable funds do not look to establish their own program fields, the vast majority of their distributions are attributable to donor-advised funds and other transactional charitable throughputs.

Major Variants

While all of the corporate-originated charitable funds share a number of common features, they also differ along a number of dimensions. Among the most salient of these differences are those related to their size, administrative cost structure, and investment options.

Size

Size is one of the major bases for differentiating the 21 or so largest corporate-originated charitable funds. Of these 21 funds, three stand out in terms of size, accounting between them for 77.3 percent of the $9.56 billion in assets that corporate-originated charitable funds held in donor-advised funds as of 2009. Of these three, the largest by far is the Fidelity Charitable Gift Fund. Created in 1991, the FCGF had $3.8 billion in assets under management as of fiscal year 2009, as shown in Table 9.1. Indeed, the Fidelity CGF became the nation's third largest public charity in 2008. Despite a sharp downturn in grantmaking by private foundations, community foundations, and individual charitable givers in general in 2009, the FCGF made 298,000 charitable gifts in 2009, a 1.8 percent increase over 2008, providing nearly $1 billion in support to 60,000 nonprofits.

The second largest corporate-originated charitable fund is the Schwab Charitable Fund, with assets of $1.832 billion in 2009, followed closely by Vanguard Charitable Endowment, which had become the twenty-fifth largest public charity by 2009, with $1.789 billion in assets under management.

While none of the remaining corporate-originated charitable funds comes close to these big three in terms of scale, they are hardly small operations. As shown in Table 9.1, the smallest manages more than $10 million in assets while several manage assets in the $200–$500 million range. Clearly, these institutions have caught on as vehicles for managing charitable assets.

TABLE 9.1 MAJOR CORPORATE-ORIGINATED CHARITABLE FUNDS, BY SIZE OF DONOR-ADVISED FUND ASSETS AND ANNUAL DAF GIVING, FISCAL YEAR 2009

Fund	Corporate originator	Total assets under management ($millions)	DAF assets under management ($millions)	DAF giving ($millions)	Number of DAFs
Fidelity Charitable Gift Fund	Fidelity Investments	$3,833	$3,783	$997.6	50,735
Schwab Charitable Fund	Charles Schwab Corp.	$1,832	$1,821	$412.4	11,474
Vanguard Charitable Endowment Program	Vanguard Group	$1,789	$1,779	$383.2	6,823
National Philanthropic Trust Donor Advised Fund	National Philanthropic Trust	$597.7	$550.6	$165.8	1,423
Citigroup Global Impact Funding Trust	Citigroup Philanthropic Services (Smith Barney)	$240.4	$240.4	$78.0	1,492
Bank of America Charitable Gift Fund	Bank of America	$233.1	$233.1	$23.4	n.a.
AYCO Charitable Foundation	AYCO Company	$222.7	$219.6	$86.7	2,262
Renaissance Charitable Gift Fund	Renaissance Inc.	$220.3	$209.6	$35.9	1,767
U.S. Charitable Gift Trust	Eaton Vance Distributors	$348.5	$159.2	$40.1	2,096
Raymond James Charitable Endowment Fund	Raymond James Trust Company	$104.8	$102.6	$17.6	902
Goldman Sachs Philanthropy Fund	Goldman Sachs & Co.	$100.5	$100.2	$23.7	385
Oppenheimer funds Legacy Program	Oppenheimer Funds Inc.	$80.3	$79.5	$12.7	1,378
Harris myCFO Charitable Giving Fund	Harris myCFO	$79.2	$77.4	$5.0	60
T. Rowe Price Program for Charitable Giving	T. Rowe Price Group	$52.6	$52.0	$12.4	1,439
Johnson Charitable Gift Fund	Johnson Investment Counsel	$34.0	$33.9	$4.7	190
AMG Charitable Gift Foundation	AMG National Trust Bank	$31.8	$31.4	$5.3	80
Calvert Giving Fund	Calvert Social Investment Foundation	$237.6	$28.7	$3.2	423
RSF Social Finance	RSF Social Finance	$122.9	$18.4	$2.6	93
American Gift Fund	American Gift Fund	$17.8	$15.1	$2.0	147
Heartland Charitable Trust	Heartland Financial	$13,8	$13.8	$1.1	79
LM Charitable Gift Trust	Legg Mason Inc	$6.6	$6.6	$1.0	49
Total		**$10,200**	**$9,556**	**$2,314**	**83,297**

Administrative Costs

The key innovation of the financial services firms was their ability to design and market a low-cost, technologically advanced mechanism for charitable giving. In large measure, that in and of itself is a significant advance in the world of charity, making charitable giving easier and less costly, potentially increasing the amount of charitable giving. As compared to private foundations and most community foundations, the transaction costs of establishing accounts in these charitable gift funds is quite low. At the same time, there are some differences among them. Thus, for example, with respect to administrative costs, which cover setting up the accounts, generating records and reports for the donors' tax purposes, verifying the charitable status of grant recipients, and making payments to the 501(c)(3) charities, Fidelity, Vanguard, and Schwab typically receive significant plaudits for their low-cost structures.[5] While the competitive funds appear to be striving to lower their costs, they are still significantly higher than the big three. Thus, for example, compared to the 0.60 percent rate paid by fund holders on the first $500,000 of assets in the Fidelity or Schwab funds, fund holders in the National Philanthropic Trust would pay 0.775 percent,[6] in the Goldman Sachs fund 0.70 percent,[7] and in the Bank of America fund 0.78 percent.[8]

Investment Options and Costs

In addition to variations in administrative costs, the various corporate-originated charitable funds have also evolved different investment options for their fund holders. At Fidelity, for example, there are four basic categories of investment options that vary with the risk appetite of the fund holders—a "legacy giving pool," a "lifetime giving pool," a "preservation giving pool," and a fourth option geared to large investors who by virtue of the size of their charitable funds are permitted to select outside financial advisors.

Schwab has taken a decidedly different route. For one thing, it has opened its donor-advised funds to management by registered investment advisors, thus allowing investors to have the same person manage their charitable fund as manages their other investments. This allows donors to invest in almost any vehicle and does not bind them to mutual funds, including mutual funds of the originating company, as is done in most of these funds. Schwab has also adopted an "open architecture" approach that allows fund managers to offer funds other than those of the originating investment firm. Fidelity, but not Vanguard, has adopted the first of these innovations, but others have yet to adopt the latter, at least as of this writing.[9]

Firms also vary somewhat in the charges they levy on accounts. Each mutual fund has its own management and operating expenses, and even these change depending on the net asset value of the fund. The composition of fees might include "loads" or commissions charged when buying or selling a fund, though Vanguard and Fidelity have a number of "no-load" funds that frequently do as well if not better than more expensive front-loaded or back-loaded funds.[10]

Schwab and others are also developing and offering socially responsible investment options, but the Calvert Social Investment Fund is entirely devoted to socially responsible investments. The "standard allocation" option for Calvert investors is a mix comprised of the Calvert Community Investment Note (a fixed rate of return investment in specific microlending, affordable housing, and community development projects and facilities), the Calvert Social Investment Fund Money Market Portfolio (money market investments selected to meet "the dual objectives of financial soundness and societal impact"), and the Calvert Social Investment Bond Portfolio (government and corporate bonds meeting social investment criteria). Other Calvert options give investors a variety of other social investment mixtures.[11]

Other Variations

Other features of these funds also differ somewhat, but not fundamentally. Thus, for example, the funds vary somewhat with respect to their minimum contributions, minimum grants, payout stipulations, and ancillary products. Since many of these relate to how these firms address the common features of the mechanics of this actor, we take them up in the mechanics section below.

Scope and Scale

Though barely two decades old, the corporate-originated charitable funds have already outdistanced community foundations in the number of donor-advised funds that they manage, and have come close to equaling them in the DAF assets they control. What is more, their growth trends suggest that they are likely to outdistance the community foundations in assets in the near future, although community foundations have recently enjoyed a growth spurt as well, at least in numbers of funds.

Thus, according to the authoritative annual research compiled by the National Philanthropic Trust, the size of the donor-advised fund market reached $29.96 billion held in 161,873 accounts as of 2010. Of these, more than 88,000 were held by so-called national charitable sponsors, mostly the corporate-originated charitable funds.[12] This was twice the 43,000 managed by community foundations (see Table 9.2).[13] But the assets held in DAFs by these two groups of institutions as of 2010 were roughly comparable—$12 billion in the national funds (mostly corporate-originated funds) and $12.6 billion in community foundations. What this makes clear, as shown in Table 9.2, is that the average fund size in the corporate-originated funds is well below that in the community foundations, suggesting that the corporate-originated funds are serving a less wealthy population, thus helping to extend institutional philanthropy to a broader portion of the population.

Donor-advised fund growth has been robust in recent years. Between 2006 and 2010—not a banner financial period given the economic crisis—the total number of donor-advised funds increased by nearly half, 48.2 percent, and the total asset value in such funds grew by 30.9 percent. In percentage terms, the community foundations achieved a higher growth rate between 2006 and 2010 (83 percent vs. 42 percent). But in terms of numbers, the national DAF sponsors, mostly corporate-originated funds, had the upper hand, adding over 26,000 funds, compared to 19,433 on the part of the community foundations. The national funds also gained ground on community foundations in terms of assets under management, growing their assets by $3.72 billion compared to the aggregate community foundations' $2.18 billion.

Even these figures may understate the scale that the corporate-originated charitable funds have achieved, however, because they compare approximately

25 charitable funds to more than 700 community foundations. The top three corporate-originated charitable funds thus easily exceed the top three community foundations in asset size by orders of magnitude. Indeed, the corporate-originated charitable funds rank among the largest public charities in the nation. Thus, as of 2011, in terms of aggregate private contributions, Fidelity Charitable ranked third (behind the United Way Worldwide and the Salvation Army), Schwab seventh, and Vanguard twenty-seventh. However, the other corporate-originated charitable funds identified here are also quite large, several ranking among the largest 400 charities in the nation.[14]

In addition to their development of accessible products, the impressive growth of the corporate-affiliated charitable funds can be attributed in important part to their association and origins with some of the nation's leading mutual fund companies. This has given them an immense marketing advantage. According to the Investment Company Institute, 44 percent of US households—51.6 million in absolute terms—owned mutual funds as of 2010, and most of these are middle income, precisely the clientele most likely to establish a donor-advised fund.[15] The fact that the primary sponsors of these charitable funds are major mutual fund companies with thousands of investor customers gives the charitable funds a large, accessible market of potential charitable donors to be leveraged. The two largest charitable funds are, in fact, associated with the two largest mutual fund companies, Vanguard Group and Fidelity, and each of these is a company with assets in excess of $1.2 trillion.[16]

As significant as the growth in the number and asset value of donor-advised funds is the grant funding that they distribute to other public charities. Indeed, although still trailing the community funds by 4.4 percent in total DAF assets as of 2010, the corporate-originated charitable funds exceeded the community foundation DAFs in grants by 55 percent, as Table 9.2 also shows. Indeed, the payout rate at the national donor-advised funds stood at 24 percent in 2010, compared to 14.7 percent among the community foundation funds.

The more rapid growth in total DAF assets managed by national funds, the significantly higher grants paid out by these DAFs, and their smaller average national fund DAF size are all significant factors. They indicate that the DAFs managed by national funds, predominantly corporate-originated charitable

TABLE 9.2 KEY COMPARATIVE CHARACTERISTICS OF DONOR-ADVISED FUNDS OF CORPORATE-ORIGINATED CHARITABLE FUNDS AND COMMUNITY FOUNDATIONS, 2006–2010

Year	National DAF sponsors			Community foundations		
	2006	2010	% Change	2006	2010	% Change
Institutions	38	32	−15.8%	72	267	270.8%
DAF accounts	62,212	88,428	42.1%	23,480	42,913	82.8%
Assets in DAF accounts	$8.27 B	$12.0 B	45.0%	$10.37 B	$12.6 B	21.0%
DAF grantmaking	$2.16 B *(2007)*	$2.86 B	32.4%	$2.24 B *(2007)*	$1.85 B	−17.4%
Average DAF account size	$153,531 *(2007)*	$135,556	−11.7%	$321,352 *(2007)*	$292,486	−9.0%

Data sources: National Philanthropic Trust, "Donor Advised Fund Market," November 2008; National Philanthropic Trust, "Donor Advised Fund Report 2011," accessed October 5, 2012, http://www.nptrust.org/images/uploads/2011%20 Donor-Advised-Fund-Report%281%29.pdf.

funds, are importantly democratizing charitable giving by providing midsized donors an opportunity to create charitable endowments that they can manage from their own living rooms or studies.

Rationale

In some sense it is no surprise that these charitable innovations were devised by the large investment firms. Fidelity and Vanguard are among the nation's largest financial services firms, both offering well over 100 investment fund options. Both were among the leaders in the growth of mutual funds in the 1980s and 1990s, with innovations such as no-load funds and low-cost "index funds." These funds offered relatively modest investors opportunities to choose investment vehicles and diversify their investments in ways that they could not have done simply and affordably otherwise. It was only natural for these firms, after creating a market in making stock market investment vehicles accessible to a wide range of investors, to see opportunities for creating philanthropic giving vehicles that also would be accessible to more than just highly affluent people.

The Fidelity Charitable Gift Fund received IRS approval as a public charity in 1991 and quickly entered the donor-advised fund market. In 1996, the IRS recognized the National Philanthropic Trust, and two years later approved the Vanguard fund. However, critics challenged the concept from the beginning, with some of the harshest criticism coming from the community foundation world, which was most threatened by the emergence of competitors linked to the for-profit world in the donor-advised fund market. As Earl Taylor of the Omaha Community Foundation put it in 2000, "They should never have received IRS approval in the first place. They have succeeded in having a tax exemption for investing in their for-profit accounts.. . . Why should taxpayers be assisting the for-profit Fidelity Investments program?"[17] Reflecting this, the Vanguard approval was accompanied by a set of criteria outlining a set of characteristics required of approved charities managing donor-advised funds. In Vanguard's case, this involved primarily the stipulation that the charitable fund be a full-fledged public charity with its own board and governance structure, not an activity or program of the Vanguard mutual fund company.

Given this criticism, it may be useful to reflect on the rationale for such corporate-originated charitable funds. Fundamentally, the rationale may be seen from two perspectives: the supply side (the financial services firms) and the demand side (latent and actual charitable donors).

From the point of view of the firms, a combination of business and altruistic considerations led to the creation of the corporate-originated charitable funds. Principal among these considerations were the following:

- The opportunity to retain the business of current investment fund holders by adding new products that would keep investors' charitable funds invested in the firms' mutual fund investment offerings
- The opportunity to attract new customers to the firms' investment products by reaching out to donors interested in establishing donor-advised funds and otherwise likely to establish such accounts with community foundations
- The likelihood that, thanks to their existing technologically sophisticated trading platforms and knowledge of investment vehicles,

they could provide more effective investment services at lower cost than their major competitors in the donor-advised market, namely community foundations

- The availability of a business model dedicated to making sophistical investment vehicles available and accessible to people who are not among the "superwealthy," precisely the model that was missing in the donor-advised fund field
- The opportunity to add to the reputations already enjoyed by several of these firms as philanthropically committed institutions by being associated with and sponsoring public charities that would end up distributing hundreds of millions of dollars annually to nonprofits
- A ready network through which to market the new product thanks to the tens of thousands of clients already invested in the firms' mutual funds, and who might be attracted to another product linked to the financial services firms
- The opportunity offered by organizing charitable funds as public charities to avoid many of the restrictions and costs associated with foundation status

But as the rapid growth of these corporate-originated charitable funds reveals, the advantages claimed by the institutions creating the funds were more than matched by the advantages felt by their customers. Specifically, the rationale for these funds from the point of view of donor-investors included the following considerations:

- The promise of higher returns than those available through other donor-advised fund managers thanks to the access to the wide array of sophisticated investment vehicles managed by highly respected investment management firms
- Lower administrative costs than those charged by other donor-advised fund sponsors, such as community foundations
- Lower barriers for establishing funds in terms of threshold size and upfront costs than alternatives at community foundations or private foundations
- Greater start-up and operating ease because the funds avoided the costs and hurdles of establishing separate private foundations and handled all of the paperwork of distributing gifts, and securing certification of charitable status to meet tax deductibility requirements
- Availability of a wide array of new tools such as the Better Business Bureau Wise Giving Alliance and internet sites such as Guidestar for learning about charities and giving donors the ability to choose
- The opportunity to enjoy these advantages while still having all the advantages that other donor-advised funds offered—that is, of making donations to the charitable funds and getting an immediate charitable deduction for the entire value of the contribution even though the funds would not be fully distributed to designated recipient charities potentially for some years, during which their value would increase

These firms did not invent donor-advised funds. They did, however, provide a distinctive business model for charitable giving that was a "no frills" alternative to establishing donor-advised funds at community foundations, a significantly less expensive mechanism for charitable giving than the community foundation and private foundation alternatives, a mechanism that would allow for the creation of charitable accounts and the distribution of charitable gifts to charities much more quickly than other alternatives, and a structure that was attractive and affordable to donors who were economically comfortable but did not enjoy hugely high net worth.

Basic Mechanics

The "actors" in this instrument of charitable giving—the corporate-originated charitable funds—are essentially passive players. They fundamentally go into action when a donor has cash, stock, or real estate to dedicate to charitable giving by the creation of a donor-advised fund at Fidelity, Vanguard, Schwab, or their competitors. At the same time, the funds have had to put in place crucial machinery and policies to govern their operations. Although the funds are competitive in what they offer to attract donors, there is some consistency in the steps they have had to take and the decisions they have had to make with respect to their donor-advised fund activities. Fundamentally, 10 steps are involved in establishing and managing a corporate-originated charitable fund.

1. Designing the Basic Operational Machinery

One of the great advantages that the corporate-originated charitable funds have brought to the charitable sector is their sophisticated technology for processing financial transactions. Establishing this technology and the systems it supports has thus been a crucial step in the development of these organizations. Most of the funds have shared in this development. As a consequence, each of the more successful corporate-originated charitable funds is known for the following:

- Sophisticated technological platforms so that nearly all of a donor's charitable giving can be conducted online
- Online access to donors' giving histories and charitable investment options, allowing for nearly real-time tracking of income and disbursements
- Rapid processing of charitable transactions so that grants to charities are achieved in days, sometimes hours, rather than weeks or months
- Extensive record-keeping by the funds on behalf of the donors, simplified by the fact that the donor takes a charitable tax deduction for the donation to the gift fund, not for each grant from a donor's fund made to a recipient charity

Thanks to this technology, the task of setting up and managing a donor-advised fund at one of the corporate-originated funds is fairly straightforward. Although many of the accounts at Fidelity, according to its CEO, are initiated by paper submissions, one of the increasing attractions to establishing accounts at the corporate-originated charitable funds is that much of the process can be done online. The online or download-and-print application forms are straightforward, but presume that the donor has considered several variables in the process.

Thus, for example, the Schwab application asks for the names and basic information about the donors that will be involved in the account, but also asks for the names of up to two "account nominators," individuals such as family members other than the donors, investment advisors, accountants, or others who are to be given the authority to recommend grants and investment choices independent of the donor. Since the funds become general assets of the charitable gift fund to be used for its grantmaking in the event a fund holder dies without identifying successors, funds typically[1] recommend that donors designate such successors or specify what should be done with their funds' assets upon their death.

2. Attracting Donors

Once the basic machinery is in place, the corporate donor-advised funds have had to market themselves to potential donors. Here the association with an originating investment firm provided an enormous advantage in the form of huge customer lists. Marketing materials also had to be developed to explain this new concept and donors made aware of their options. Although sometimes described as "checkbook philanthropy" because of their ease and simplicity, the charitable gift funds all recommend that potential donors think strategically about what they want to accomplish through their charitable giving. Unlike charitable donations made in response to individual charities or the United Way's solicitations, in the corporate-originated charitable funds, donors are establishing accounts of some size, from $5,000 to $25,000 as minimums, which implies a more strategic analysis of the donor's charitable mission;

3. Determining Minimum Fund Size

One of the basic issues each of the corporate-originated charitable funds has to settle is the minimum fund size to accept. Generally speaking, these funds have targeted midsized donors whose charitable assets might be sized well below that of many foundations. Among the three largest of these funds, Vanguard has the highest minimum threshold for establishing an account, $25,000, the same threshold as Goldman Sachs and Citigroup. A donor's additional deposits in a Vanguard account must be no lower than $5,000. Both of Vanguard's two large competitors, Fidelity Charitable and Schwab Charitable, lowered their minimum initial account sizes to $5,000. Additional contributions to a Schwab charitable account must be no less than $500, but Fidelity has eliminated any minimum increment size. The $5,000 threshold is replicated by Franklin Templeton and the Calvert Giving Fund. Most of the other corporate-originated charitable funds establish $10,000 minimum account sizes, with additional increments ranging from $500 to $1,000.

These irrevocable contributions to the charitable gift funds can be made in the form of cash, stock, or real estate, but there are different valuation and charitable tax deduction rules that apply to each.[18] While the charitable gift funds are independent of their parent financial services corporations, donors with both Fidelity and Vanguard brokerage accounts can make transfers to their firm's respective charitable fund more rapidly than by transferring from other accounts, one of the attractions of the corporate-originated funds linked to massive mutual fund companies like these. Brokerage account investment advisors can often play a helpful role in these decisions, including advising on tax considerations, another advantage that the charitable funds enjoy.[19]

4. Assisting Donors in Developing a Charitable Strategy or Mission

None of the charitable funds exerts pressure on donors to support particular issues or charities. However, most of the funds provide assistance to donors in thinking through their charitable strategy. For example, the Fidelity Fund's web page gives potential donors useful questions to consider that might shape the kind of charitable giving they might want to do through the gift fund, leading to a "giving mission statement" that includes the kinds of issues the donor might want to address, questions of geographic scope, and personal involvement (the latter specifically about whether the donor wants to be anonymous in his or her gifts). These questions remind the donor that charitable giving through donor-advised funds, charitable trusts, and other mechanisms of this sort, while at a scale much smaller than the nation's largest foundations, should nonetheless be a thoughtful, deliberative action. Among other things, donors are reminded that by law they can only *recommend* distributions from their DAF, and even then only to eligible public charities.

5. Establishing Investment Options

Donors to charitable gift funds can choose investment strategies for their charitable accounts. In the case of sizable DAFs, some of the gift funds have been willing to allow donors to work with a selected investment advisor, though one that the gift fund approves. For most donors, however, the choice must be made from among an array of options established by the fund. Typically, the funds establish choices from among the mutual funds of its originating firm. Thus, as noted earlier, Fidelity offers a choice of three major pools of assets. Schwab Charitable offers a menu of nine individual investment pools or three asset allocation pools. Many of the options can become extremely imaginative to attract donors and respond to donor interests and needs.[20] Schwab also provides a useful and comprehensible questionnaire that permits donors to think through their most appropriate investment options, ranging from "conservative" investment strategies that offer donors stability over growth, "balanced" strategies for donors with longer-term giving objectives, and "growth" strategies for donors interested in very long-term giving.

6. Setting Grant Policies and Options

Each of the funds has special requirements regarding minimum grant distribution sizes. The lowest grant minimum for distributions is Fidelity's. Donors can make grants as small as $50 from their accounts at Fidelity. Schwab is not far behind with a minimum grant size of $100. Much more typical are the $250 minimum grant sizes at Calvert, Bank of America, and most others, and the $500 minimum at Vanguard.

Besides the economic rationale of reducing the administrative costs per grant dollar expended, the argument for the larger grant minimums, as one representative of the funds suggested in an interview, is that the larger grant size encourages more "serious," thoughtful, deliberative grantmaking. In this sense, the corporate-originated charitable funds are trying to encourage truly *philanthropic* behavior, which requires research, analysis, and purpose, versus *charitable giving*, which is often more emotional and immediate.

Whether to reduce costs or encourage more serious philanthropic grantmaking, some of the funds limit the number of grants that can be made from accounts, particularly for smaller investors. Calvert's social investment fund limits the number of grants that can be made from a donor's fund to 12 per year if the fund is smaller than $25,000, but larger funds can make an unlimited number of grants during the calendar year. At T. Rowe Price, the cap on the number of charitable distributions per year is 10 for accounts of less than $250,000, 25 for accounts between $250,000 and $499,999, and up to 100 for accounts over $1,000,000. Generally, the donor need not predetermine the specific recipients or timing of grants, but rather can make grants at any time. It is also possible to predetermine a regular schedule of future grants to specific charities.[21] The charitable gift funds review charities designated for contributions, but these reviews are to determine eligibility, not the quality of the recipients. It is up to the donors or their designees to do the research for determining the desirability of assisting specific charities. Fidelity says that it can process new donations to designated charities within 10 business days, but donations to charities previously assisted can be processed (or regranted) online almost immediately.

7. Establishing Payout Policies

Unlike foundations, the corporate-originated charitable funds are not legally required to have a minimum level of grantmaking. Such provisions were put in place for independent foundations because of a tendency of some donors to use foundations as a way to avoid estate taxes while sitting on the resulting assets. Because part of the income earned from donor-advised fund investments can sometimes be dedicated to the general funds available to community foundations for their own unrestricted grantmaking, some community foundations do not allow donors to "spend out," that is, to entirely deplete, their accounts for some initial period of years.

This practice does not seem to be in place at the corporate-originated charitable funds, particularly the big three, which appear to be committed to maximizing, or at least not retarding, the outflow of capital from the donors' accounts. This may help account for the fairly high payout rates these funds are achieving, as noted previously. Indeed, several of these funds require that their aggregate charitable accounts distribute at least 5 percent of their asset value each year.[22] To enforce this policy, the funds retain the privilege of requesting grant recommendations from any of its DAFs that failed to achieve a 5 percent giving level over the previous five-year period.[23] By virtue of their history of high grants payouts (in Fidelity's case, averaging over 20 percent for several years), these funds do not appear in any danger of becoming warehouses for wealth. To the contrary, several of the funds impose minimum frequencies for grants. For example, Vanguard requires at least one grant from every charitable account every seven years, and can require additional grantmaking if the payout rate jeopardizes the 5 percent net payout that Vanguard has established for its entire program.

8. Offering Specialized Products and Functions

In addition to their investment and grantmaking functions, the corporate gift funds have also extended their activities into a variety of ancillary activities that have allowed them to function as more "full-service" charitable institutions.

Thus, for example, just as community foundations frequently engage their donors and their families in educational activities that encourage charitable giving as a family value, the corporate-originated charitable funds have adopted similar practices, creating opportunities for family members to engage children and grandchildren in the world of charity. Fidelity's survey on volunteering, released jointly with VolunteerMatch (a national nonprofit providing web-based mechanisms for volunteer recruitment), emphasizes the importance of volunteering for charitable giving. Similarly, Fidelity's Gift4Giving program allows donors with charitable accounts to set aside a portion of their funds as gifts to other individuals, in amounts as small as $50, for them to make charitable grants to IRS-qualified public charities. This obviously facilitates donors' introducing their family members to the experience of charitable giving, but it also potentially benefits Fidelity by introducing Gift4Giving recipients to the process of donor-advised funds and to the technological platform of the Fidelity program.[24]

Calvert's array of socially responsible investments is another mechanism for mobilizing the socially impactful benefits of otherwise passive investment of moneys designated for future charitable beneficiaries. Schwab has also received significant positive publicity for its offering donors a mechanism by which they can designate up to 10 percent of their Charitable Gift Account balance to be used as guarantee funds for microfinance loans in the developing world.[25]

Through these various ancillary activities, the corporate funds seem determined to demonstrate that the new mechanism for charitable giving that they have created is going to induce more charitable giving rather than simply the relocation of charitable giving from foundations or community foundations to corporate-originated funds.

9. Monitoring Investments and Distributions

Whether or not the donor establishes a fund through a paper submission or online, the corporate funds provide donors numerous ways in which to monitor their giving. By accessing his or her account, a donor can see his or her history of grantmaking by recipient charities, by fields of interest, and by time period. In addition, the donor can also monitor the performance of the investment of the funds and, once online, add to the charitable accounts in whatever minimums are established by the gift funds.

10. Keeping Records and Reporting

The funds provide donors with simple and clear records needed for tax payments. For example, Fidelity provides a confirmation of each contribution to the charitable gift fund, which serves as the donor's tax receipt since the tax deduction is for the contribution to the charitable gift fund, not for the "subgrants" made to specific charities. The fund also supplies donors with a completed IRS Form 8283 for noncash contributions over $500. Besides the information that the donor can see online, Fidelity sends donors quarterly summarized statements of their giving.

Operational Challenges

Following a 15-year period of enormous growth beginning with the launch of the Fidelity Charitable Gift Fund in 1991, corporate-originated charitable funds entered a period of testing beginning in 2006 and stretching through this writing. Three major challenges have confronted these organizations during this period, and at least two of them seem likely to persist into the foreseeable future.

Economic Recession

In the first place, the financial services industry with which the corporate-originated charitable funds are closely connected was hard hit by the economic crisis that began in 2008 and continues as of this writing. Investment company assets in mutual funds dropped from \$12.002 trillion in 2007 to \$9.604 trillion in 2008, and as of 2010, had climbed significantly, but still remained below their 2007 level, at only \$11.821 trillion.[26] The number of shareholder accounts in mutual funds was back up to 292,109 in 2010, almost as high as the prerecession 292,590.[27] Although by 2010 the mutual industry had recovered most of its former scale, continuing market volatility has kept investors on edge, and the industry facing continuing uncertainty.[28] Nonetheless, the mutual fund industry, while taking a huge hit in the recession along with the rest of the economy, seems to have come out of the recession ahead of other investment vehicles and to be on a trajectory of recovering the value it lost after 2007.

Financial Industry Regulatory Reform

While the three largest national mutual fund firms with connections to the corporate-originated charitable funds appear to have had no specific connection to the financial irregularities that led to the implosion of the mortgage markets, and the corporate-originated charitable funds themselves specifically did not contribute in any way to the nation's economic free-fall, new efforts to regulate or reregulate the financial sector have touched on investment firms as well as commercial lenders. In the February 2010 hearings of the Financial Crisis Inquiry Commission, witnesses called for a regulatory regime that "cover(s) the shell banking system and the investment banks and the money market mutual funds [and] the commercial banks," in part because of the trillions of dollars provided by mutual funds as financing to banks.[29] One legislative proposal considered during debates over the postcrisis banking regulation legislation would have subjected mutual funds to bank-like regulation and oversight concerning credit quality, risk management, and liquidity, even requiring mutual funds and their shareholders to contribute to a dissolution fund for failing financial institutions.

The legislation that was eventually passed in late 2010, the Wall Street Reform and Consumer Protection Act (the Dodd-Frank Act), surprisingly left mutual funds relatively untouched, however. In part, the legislation took aim at two behaviors of financial institutions that contributed to the nation's economic downturn, the practice by some banks of taking too much risk (or inducing borrowers or investors to take too much risk) and the excessive complexity of their lending and investment instruments. The mutual funds were not seen as having played significant roles in undermining the nation's economic stability and therefore do not appear to be much affected if at all by the provisions of Dodd-Frank directly. To the extent that mutual funds continue to avoid the excessive leverage and risk of the investment vehicles employed by Wall Street before the recession, they will for the moment sidestep the scope of the legislation. If, however, because of investment practices, the mutual funds come to be seen as a source of systemic risk, the lens of Dodd-Frank oversight could shift. Nonetheless, there is nothing specific to Dodd-Frank that targets the mutual funds, much less corporate-originated charitable funds, but Dodd-Frank's emphasis on consumer protection would be the appropriate watchword for the corporate charitable fund industry.

Charitable Regulation

Far more than the economic crisis itself or the regulatory fallout for financial firms resulting from it are the challenges that the corporate-originated charitable funds face from broader concerns that are affecting the charitable sector of which it is a part. Such concerns have been raised in recent years by staff and members of the Senate Finance Committee. For two years, the Senate Finance Committee under the leadership of Senator Charles Grassley (R-Iowa), with significant support from the then-minority leader of the committee, Senator Max Baucus (D-Montana), conducted several hearings concerning abuses in the charitable sector. While most of the headline cases concerned operating nonprofits such as the American Red Cross, the United Way, and the Nature Conservancy, there was significant attention to abuses among some donor-advised funds and DAF managers. More recently, the battle over the federal debt has raised even broader issues about the tax treatment of charitable contributions. These various efforts have raised three sets of potential challenges to the corporate-originated charitable funds.

Mandatory Minimum Payout from Donor-Advised Funds

As previously noted, as "public charities," the corporate-originated charitable funds are exempt from the requirement placed on private foundations to make so-called qualifying distributions annually equivalent to 5 percent of their net assets. As noted earlier, this provision was imposed in the 1969 tax act in response to evidence that some donors were claiming substantial tax deductions from establishing private foundations but then letting the foundations sit on the proceeds without distributing them to charities.

For charitable gift funds associated with corporate firms such as Fidelity, Vanguard, and Schwab, a mandatory payout requirement that would apply to the entire nonprofit entity, perhaps comparable to private foundations' 5 percent payout, would be easily attainable, as they typically display actual payouts three or four times that level, as already noted.[30]

However, not all donor-advised funds have such sterling records. Indeed, many community foundations place no payout requirements on the individual DAFs they own and control and sometimes discourage DAFs from spending down in their early years. What is more, even in the corporate-originated funds it is possible for some donors to "park" their assets in donor-advised funds, receiving the full value of a charitable deduction for doing so, while expending little or no moneys toward their charitable purpose. Currently, the high overall payouts or spend-downs of some donor-advised funds in a sponsoring organization can camouflage or mask what might be the negligible payouts of other funds in the organization's portfolio. One solution to this problem would be to enact mandatory payout requirements applicable to individual funds, as opposed to the overall charitable assets controlled by a fund manager such as Fidelity, Vanguard, Schwab, or a community foundation. The Pension Protection Act of 2006, which carried a number of responses to operational lapses on the part of nonprofits, originally included language concerning minimum payouts for DAFs, but that was dropped in the final legislation. However, the idea that there should be a DAF payout (or, if construed more broadly, a public charity minimum payout requirement) still receives attention and support in public policy circles.

Extending Other Private Foundation Restrictions to Donor-Advised Funds

In addition to the payout requirement, the Senate Finance Committee staff report and hearings surfaced a number of other areas of potential donor-advised fund abuse. In a "white paper" it prepared in advance of the hearings, the Finance Committee staff called attention to a number of such problems and made specific recommendations for reform.[31] In addition to requiring a mandatory 5 percent payout requirement for donor-advised funds, these recommendations proposed applying private foundation rules against self-dealing to public charities, so that self-dealing transactions (such as lending money or other credit, payment of unreasonable compensation, and the furnishing of goods and services) with disqualified persons (modified to include corporations and partnerships in addition to individuals) would be subject to punitive excise taxes.

The concerns that underlay these recommendations found expression in the testimony of at least one witness at the Senate Finance Committee hearing, who testified about DAF funds used to pay for donors' personal expenses, dubious grants through US nonprofits to potentially disqualified nondomestic organizations, and grants in support of donors' business interests.[32] All of these examples were drawn, however, from the operations of the National Heritage Foundation, a single national sponsor of donor-advised funds.[33] Still, the surfacing of these abuses has left behind a residue of concern about the operations of donor-advised funds, if not specifically about the corporate-originated funds. Indeed, in 2006, following the Finance Committee hearings, the Internal Revenue Service added charitable abuses to its list of "dirty dozen tax scams," and cited as an example a donor moving assets or income to a donor-advised fund, but maintaining control of the assets "without transferring a commensurate benefit to charity."[34]

TABLE 9.3   PAYOUT RATES OF NATIONALLY SPONSORED AND COMMUNITY FOUNDATION DONOR-ADVISED FUNDS, 2007–2010

Year	National DAF sponsor payout rate	Community foundation DAF payout rate	Payout rate of all DAFs
2007	16.7%	14.8%	16.5%
2008	17.9%	15.1%	17.6%
2009	19.9%	15.8%	18.6%
2010	19.3%	12.9%	17.1%

Source: National Philanthropic Trust, "Donor Advised Fund Report 2011," accessed October 5, 2012, http://www.nptrust.org/images/uploads/2011%20Donor-Advised-Fund-Report%281%29.pdf. Reproduced with permission.

The Pension Protection Act (PPA) of 2006 that resulted in part from this set of hearings consequently included a number of provisions affecting the donor-advised fund industry. In particular:

- For the first time in federal law, the legislation actually defined a donor-advised fund as "any fund or account, generally owned by and lodged in some other sponsoring organization, that is separately identified by reference to the contributions of the donor or donors who reasonably expect to possess and exercise advisory rights over the fund's charitable distributions."
- The PPA instructed the Internal Revenue Service to conduct a study of the appropriateness of the charitable deduction for donations to donor-advised funds and whether DAFs should be subject to a mandatory payout requirement.
- The legislation prohibited grants to individuals and to any organization if the grants were not for charitable purposes (subject to penalties on both the donor fund and the recipient organizations) and denied deductibility for grants to veterans organizations (501(c)(19) and (c)(23) organizations), fraternal organizations (501(c)(8) and (c)(10) organizations), and cemetery companies (501(c)(13) organizations).
- PPA also prohibited grants that would provide more than incidental benefits to donors, donor advisors, or related parties, established financial penalties for funds that make grants to provide prohibited benefits, and for fund managers who knowingly approve prohibited benefit grants.

Changing Charitable Deductibility

A third possible area of policy action of potential significance for the corporate-originated charitable funds concerns possible changes in the deductibility of charitable contributions. With increased concerns over the deficit bequeathed by the Iraq War, the Bush tax cuts, and the bank crisis and ensuing recession, intense efforts have been launched to find potential budget savings or ways to close what are thought to be tax loopholes. The Obama administration has proposed a capping of the charitable deduction for very wealthy people in successive federal budgets, though none of these proposals has passed so far.

A somewhat different proposal advanced by Congressman Xavier Becerra (D-California) would retain higher deductions only for charitable contributions to organizations that address issues of poverty or deprivation in American communities on grounds that only about 10 percent of all charitable contributions go to these purposes at present.[35] While the opposition to such proposals is considerable, particularly to those involving changes to the deductions for charitable contributions, there is reason to believe that some changes are possible and perhaps inevitable given the severity of the nation's fiscal problems and the political refusal to consider tax increases even on the most wealthy as a meaningful part of any solution. While it is difficult to predict what impact such charitable deduction limitations would have on ultimate charitable contributions, it is not impossible that they could slow the growth of the overall donor-advised fund market, and the corporate-originated funds within it.

Growth of Competition

In addition to the challenges arising from the economy and from public policy, the corporate-originated charitable funds may also be facing more robust competition from community foundations and other types of institutions that have witnessed the growth of the corporate-originated funds and decided to beef up their own operations. Community foundations and other sponsors of donor-advised funds have watched and learned from the corporate-originated funds' success in achieving cost efficiencies and providing investment choices that respond to donors' interests and needs. In recent years, the doors have been opening between the corporate funds and the community foundations for collaboration and partnerships, with the community foundations recognizing their "competitive advantage" in understanding and addressing local charitable needs and the national funds seeing their role in providing highly efficient one-stop-shopping services to donors who know generally how they want to deploy their charitable assets. Overall, the instrument of donor-advised funds is a growing field, whether developed by hospitals and universities, community foundations, or corporate-originated funds. Although at the outset of Fidelity and Vanguard some community foundations reacted with strident hostility to the prospect of what they perceived as competition from for-profit mutual fund companies, many have adjusted to the notion that there is room for both, responding to differently motivated donors, and even room for collaboration.

Overall Assessment

Have the corporate-originated charitable funds added anything distinctive or valuable to American philanthropy? Critics of the gift funds and of donor-advised funds in general suggest that DAF-supported grantmaking is little different than the charitable giving of individual donors, not adding up to an achievement of new social value in philanthropy. And some have even argued that the corporate funds have created negative effects by weakening other charitable institutions, such as community foundations.

To answer this question, it may be useful to break it into five parts focusing on the possible impact of the corporate-originated funds on (1) the amount of giving; (2) the efficiency of giving; (3) the involvement in giving; (4) the distribution of giving among fields; and (5) the avoidance of possible negative consequences resulting from the warehousing of philanthropic resources. While the verdict is clearly still out, it should be clear from the evidence already cited that the assessment on these funds overall must be generally quite positive. Let us review the evidence.

Have the Corporate-Originated Charitable Funds Increased Charitable Giving?

Despite the substantial philanthropic tradition of the Johnson family behind Fidelity and the Schwab history of philanthropy in the San Francisco Bay Area, it is by no means clear that eleemosynary motivations were the prime reason behind the creation of the original corporate-originated charitable funds. To the contrary, solid business reasons were also at work related to upselling, that is, providing an additional service to keep the investment business of their clients inside the firms.[36] Still, it is valid to ask whether the appearance of these funds has had any noticeable impact on the scale of charitable giving.

Observers suggest that it is impossible to determine whether the advent of the corporate-originated charitable funds has actually increased the overall amount of charitable giving (above and beyond the marginal potential increase through lower transactional costs). The charitable giving proportion of the US gross domestic product has not appreciably changed upward since the emergence of the corporate funds. One of the nation's philanthropic experts remarked that "the percentage of Americans who give stays pretty steady over time and the percentage of wealth [devoted to charitable giving] stays pretty steady over time, [so] it's possible that there's nothing [about the corporate-originated charitable funds] that has expanded the pie."

However, the CEO of the Fidelity Charitable Gift Fund, Sarah Libbey, told *Nonprofit Quarterly* in an interview that more than half of the fund's current donors were not clients of the investment side of the firm. External observers confirm that "due to their advertising resources, they probably have some donors who are using them only for the charitable giving fund" as opposed to the corporate sponsors' simply focusing on "keeping [existing] customers." That would indicate that at least in Fidelity's case, the firm is attracting people through the Charitable Gift Fund's own portal as opposed to simply mining current Fidelity investors for their charity or philanthropy business. But that could still be simply a displacement of charitable givers from other venues, for example, moving their donor-advised funds from community foundations or other sponsors to Fidelity. For example, one moderate donor described his experience with establishing an account at Vanguard, noting that, in his experience, it "would have taken longer at [the community foundation where he formerly had his donor-advised fund], a lot more expensive, taking three to five days, not online, and 100 to 150 basis points, while Vanguard would have been 30 to 40 basis points." Similarly, as noted below, some small foundations are disbanding and shifting their assets into donor-advised funds, but both examples would be charitable giving displaced from one venue to another, not necessarily a significant increase in charitable giving.

However, Libbey also reported that, based on surveys, 70 percent of Fidelity donors report increasing their personal giving as a result of having a fund at Fidelity, explaining, "When you establish a giving account (at Fidelity) and you have made the decision to transition from checkbook giving or sporadic giving because you've gotten an appeal in the mail...it becomes part of the household vernacular...the sheer fact of having an account is something that is creating good habits" in the form of increased levels of giving.[37] The anecdotal information provided by Fidelity would, if more generalizable throughout this subsector, suggest that the ease of giving that the corporate-originated charitable funds provide leads to increased levels of charitable giving.

Have the corporate-originated charitable funds "topped out," as one researcher asked? Notwithstanding the prolonged international recession, no one interviewed for this analysis suggested that the future for the corporate-originated charitable funds was not going to be a continued trajectory of growth. As one experienced researcher put it: "People might not have as much appreciated assets [during this recession], but [the corporate-originated charitable funds] make giving easier, and there's a lot more in the culture to make sure you do give, so there's going to be a market for people to put money in without a lot of folderol."

Have the Corporate-Originated Charitable Funds Increased the Efficiency of Charitable Giving?

As we have seen, the Fidelity proposal to become a sponsor of donor-advised funds initially prompted concern from the community foundation world, which until that point was by far the dominant player in the then still-fledgling donor-advised fund field. Although the Internal Revenue Service approved the applications of Fidelity, Vanguard, and other mutual fund firms as sponsors of donor-advised funds, the enmity of some community foundations to the well-heeled competition of these mammoth firms has been hard to break, though corporate-originated charitable fund adherents are not shy about reminding interlocutors that many community foundations were established by commercial banks and for a very long time were operated with as much if not more functional integration with their bank sponsors than the corporate-originated charitable funds have with their mutual fund sponsors.

In recent years, there has been begrudging acceptance of the fact that the corporate-originated funds are, as one Midwestern community foundation CEO put it, "fulfilling a [market] niche of price sensitivity. . . giving donors a transactional product for a very, very low price." More generally, there has been a recognition of the contribution the competition from these funds has made to community foundations. As one longtime philanthropic advisor put it: "Fidelity invested a lot of money in technology and simply beat the socks off the community foundations in terms of service." The result, according to this CEO, has been changes in the community foundation world in response to the corporate-originated charitable funds' sharply dropping fees and improving their technological platforms. The competition from the corporate-originated charitable funds has benefited community foundations, compelling them to change. According to one philanthropic advisor, "Many foundations have since caught up, making it easy to do things, to call someone on an 800 number, and to process checks and grants more quickly."

Nonetheless, most community foundations are aware that they cannot compete on price and technology simply because of the scale of the corporate-originated charitable funds. One independent competitor acknowledged that, because "the commercial funds have economies of scale, a small DAF here [will find it] impossible to do what Fidelity does at a cost comparable to Fidelity's." The community foundations cannot compete with the corporate-originated charitable funds on costs and investment, but they can offer donors with specific community interests an important charitable giving resource. As one community foundation CEO put it, "We're going through the analysis of what's the value proposition on our side; we understand and know the community really, really well." The impact may be an improvement in community foundation operations, leveraging their competitive advantage with donors interested in geographically specific charitable investments and often "field of interest" charitable concerns, while the corporate-originated charitable funds aim to increase charitable giving that is less geographically constrained.

Nor are these corporate-originated funds finished innovating. Even though managing philanthropic assets cannot possibly make the corporate-originated charitable funds the kinds of revenues or profits that the parent firms earn from their mutual fund investment activities, they are still related to highly profitable and profit-making companies and will, according to one observer, "innovate what they can offer [so long as they] stay true to the mission of making money."

Schwab's microlending guarantee program in partnership with the Grameen Foundation is one example of how corporate-originated charitable funds can design programmatic innovations that serve charitable objectives without undermining the core business model of providing a very inexpensive, online mechanism for conducting charitable grantmaking. The Calvert model of investing in socially responsible funds, reflected to some extent in increasing socially responsible options offered by Vanguard and Fidelity, is another. Fidelity's speed in making Haitian relief grants underscores what donors want from the such funds: "Fidelity discovered that there was a big universe of people who didn't want a lot of advice, but wanted to [be able to] act quickly."

Have the Corporate-Originated Funds Helped to Democratize Philanthropy?

Although the corporate-originated charitable funds indicate that they exist for the donor who has a strategy of grantmaking and a strong sense of charitable goals, the critique of the corporate-originated charitable funds is that they operate like charitable checkbooks, more "charitable" than "philanthropic." From the perspective of experts who have had extensive interactions with these funds, and in some cases staffed the funds of competitors of the big three, the corporate-originated funds are something like a foundation mechanism for donors who are not big enough to create full-fledged foundations. In their view, it "democratizes philanthropy," that is, it makes foundation-like grantmaking possible for self-directed donors who, at larger scales, would be foundation founders rather than the contributors to donor accounts at these firms or community foundations. A perspective on the leadership of the Fidelity program is that their intent was in part "to help make Fidelity customers and clients become more philanthropic."

Most observers suggest that it is no surprise that these charitable innovations were devised by the large investment firms. Fidelity and Vanguard are among the nation's largest financial services firms, offering a multitude of investment vehicles for investors, both offering well over 100 investment fund options. They were among the leaders of the growth of mutual funds in the 1980s and 1990s, with innovations such as no-load funds and low-cost "index funds." These funds offered relatively modest investors opportunities to choose investment vehicles and diversify their investments that they could not have had simply and affordably otherwise. It is a logical consequence, once we have seen a market in making stock market investment vehicles accessible to a wide income-range of investors, that these same firms would see opportunities for creating philanthropic giving vehicles that also would be accessible to more than just highly affluent people. The fact that the average size of the donor-advised funds at the corporate-originated funds is smaller than that of community foundations lends credence to this line of argument.

The checkbook metaphor is commonly used by observers of the corporate-originated funds, though not by the funds themselves, which emphasize the more thoughtful or strategic approach of their donors compared to most. One philanthropic advisor summarized the niche of these firms as appealing to an emerging reality of the character of American charitable donors, that "most Americans are local givers and they're not looking for any or needing any advice and direction, and thus for them, whatever way is cheapest or most convenient is going to work for them; the commercial providers [have provided] the equivalent of a philanthropic checking account.. . . For most of the people who use the donor-advised funds of the big three, their experience is only about convenience and cost, it's a commodity, and they're no more interested in an experience with their DAF than with their checking account."

For those donors who want a more tactile charitable experience, they can go to community foundations with geographically specific interest areas or choose specialized funds such as the Tides Foundation, which says its core business is donor-advised funds dedicated to promoting social change, or the various local and regional member funds of the Funding Exchange, such as the Liberty Hill Foundation in Los Angeles and the Appalachian Community Fund in Ohio.

Experience suggests that most smaller donors are not interested in paying the premium for advice, frequently knowing what they want to support with their charitable giving. One of the nation's philanthropic experts contended that "what Fidelity proved in 1991 is that donors in fact don't want any advice. [Fidelity] served a no-advice product and they hit it out of the ballpark." Many experts in the philanthropic advice world suggest, as one put it, that "the people who are willing to pay for donor advice are by and large very substantial givers, a quarter million dollars and above, focused on issues rather than institutions, and focused on issues beyond their local community." What the corporate-originated charitable funds offer in the way of advice is basically links that allow donors a "do-it-yourself" approach to advice.[38] The message is that donors should do their own research on the charities they might support with their giving.

Have the Corporate-Originated Charitable Funds Altered the Trajectory of Charitable Giving in Substantive Ways?

Quite apart from the scale, cost, and participation in giving, a further question arises about the possible impact of the corporate-originated charitable funds on the distribution of giving among fields or types of organizations. Although the gift funds classify their categories of giving differently than do other sources, most significantly Giving USA, it seems clear that giving through donor-advised funds reaches different types of recipients compared to general charitable giving. In particular, while religion receives the largest single share of overall giving (36.2 percent in 2009, for example) donor-advised fund giving de-emphasizes religion in favor of human services and education.

For example, among community foundation-managed donor-advised funds, education received 28.0 percent of all distributions, followed by human services with 27.1 percent, health with 2.5 percent, and the arts with 10.5 percent. Religion's share of DAF distributions through community foundations was a comparatively small 6.1 percent.

Overall, the tendency in DAF giving through national corporate-sponsored funds is also toward secular, human service charities rather than religious recipients, though the Vanguard Charitable Endowment's distributions, while highly focused on human services (51 percent of grants for human services and 16 parent for education) had a relatively larger 20 percent share flowing to religion than most of the other large corporate-originated funds.[39] With its emphasis on investing only in socially responsible corporations and funds, the

Calvert Social Investment Fund's distributions show a distinctive social justice dimension. A pie chart of Calvert's distributions supplied in January 2010 indicated religion receiving 9 percent of distributions, health 6 percent, education 10 percent, and "children and families" 9 percent, but Calvert's categories include 29 percent for "advocacy and social action" and 7 percent for "human rights."

Disaster relief has also been a favorite outlet for funding from the DAFs managed by the corporate-originated charitable funds. For example, the Fidelity Charitable Gift Fund was processing grant dollars for Haitian earthquake relief activities a little over two hours after the earthquake happened in Port-au-Prince, with a total of $13 million donated for earthquake relief as of March 2010.[40] Similarly, Vanguard launched a disaster relief program (the Sustainable Disaster-Recovery Fund) in 2007, with distributions to disaster relief agencies determined by the Vanguard staff, not by donor recommendations.[41]

As more scrutiny is directed toward the content of charitable giving in a time of prolonged economic stress and governmental funding cutbacks, the human service, disaster relief, and even social justice directions of national corporate-originated funds is noteworthy.

Do Corporate-Originated Charitable Funds Warehouse the Money?

Finally, how valid are the initial fears of some that the corporate-originated charitable funds would become warehouses where the wealthy could park their money and secure substantial tax benefits while contributing little to actual charitable support?

From the evidence presented already, it seems that this fear is largely unfounded. Payout rates at the corporate-originated funds have been robust, not laggard. As one private foundation executive noted, "I think the funds have demonstrated that they're doing their work efficiently and effectively, with a decent amount of transparency; they're not warehouses of wealth, but clearly the funds go in and they go out. People are very active with their giving." He suggested further that "they are very vibrant, nimble vehicles [as compared to] an endowed [foundation] fund."

Another dimension of charitable warehousing occurs when donor-advised funds provide inappropriate benefits to donors or their families. For several years, the Internal Revenue Service placed donor-advised funds on the list of "dirty dozen" tax scams. However, in recent years, donor-advised funds have been taken off the IRS list of problematic investments, and the IRS's own study of donor-advised funds, released in December 2011, gave DAFs not only a relatively clean bill of health in terms of abuses, but suggested for the moment that the high payout rates of DAFs did not necessitate the creation of a mandatory, foundation-like payout rate.[42]

Conclusion

In short, the corporate-originated charitable funds appear to have been, and continue to be, a useful innovation in the world of philanthropy. They have brought more people, more effectively, into charitable giving, channeled this giving into valid human service purposes, provided a reliable mechanism for responding to disasters, and done all of this while avoiding the obvious danger of becoming warehouses for wealth while providing tax benefits for the rich. The end result has been a significant "democratization" of philanthropy. The creation of national entities to manage charitable funds, linked to the ability to invest the funds in a wide variety of investment vehicles, makes philanthropic giving for moderate and middle income households, particularly those households that choose to itemize their tax deductions, relatively simple, flexible, affordable, and fast.

TABLE 9.A1 COMPARISONS BETWEEN CORPORATE-ORIGINATED CHARITABLE FUNDS AND OTHER CHARITABLE ORGANIZATIONS, CIRCA 2009

Characteristic	Corporate-originated charitable funds (donor-advised funds)	Community foundations	Private foundations
Number of operating entities	Of any significant size, only approximately 21	737	67,379 independent foundations plus 2,745 corporate as of 2008
Grantmaking	DAF grantmaking of 21 funds for fiscal 2009: $2.3 billion (42.9 percent attributable to Fidelity Charitable Gift Fund)	$4.1 billion (2009), est. $2.12 attributable to community foundations' DAF accounts	Independent foundations: $32.8 billion (2009); corporate foundations: $4.7 billion
Recommended minimum size of fund	Generally $5,000–$10,000, but others $25,000 (Vanguard, Goldman Sachs)	Typically $10,000 or higher	No specific size, but many consider foundations below $10 million uneconomic
Average size of donor-advised fund accounts (2009)	Fidelity $74,578; Schwab $158,713; Vanguard $260,721; ($111,920 for all corporate funds)	$284,000	Average independent foundation size: $7.1 million in 2009
Total DAF assets under management	$9.6 billion	$10.3 billion	
Start-up costs	None	None	All of the costs for creating a fully functional foundation, including staffing, office, etc.
Operating costs	Administrative fees below 60 basis points for the top three	Administrative fees of 150 basis points or higher	All operating costs of management, financial, audit, legal
Charitable tax deductibility of cash donations	Up to 50% of adjusted gross income	Up to 50% of adjusted gross income	Limited to 30% of adjusted gross income

(Continued)

TABLE 9.A1 (CONTINUED)

Characteristic	Corporate-originated charitable funds (donor-advised funds)	Community foundations	Private foundations
Charitable tax deductibility of appreciated stock	Fair market value up to 30% of adjusted gross income	Fair market value of up to 30% of adjusted gross income	Fair market value of up to 20% of adjusted gross income
Charitable tax deductibility of real estate and closely held stock	Fair market value up to 30% of adjusted gross income	Fair market value of up to 30% of adjusted gross income	Cost basis up to 20% of adjusted gross income
Payout requirement	None by statute, though funds typically hold to a minimum of 5% across the board	None by statute, policies vary	Annual minimum required payout of 5% of net assets (incl. admin costs)
Donor involvement and control in grantmaking	Donor recommends charities as beneficiaries, but decision is the charitable gift fund's; corporate-originated charitable fund verifies public charity status of recipient.	Donor may recommend charities as beneficiaries, but typically the community foundation promotes community issues and causes.	Donor establishes mission of the foundation, appoints initial board of directors, may or may not be involved in grantmaking over time.
Staff support in grantmaking	Advice in grantmaking relatively minimal; donors in need of advice typically seek outside philanthropic advisors; staff conduct due diligence reviews of recommended charities	Staff provide due diligence review of grantees recommended by donor, conduct research as needed or requested on specific nonprofits, provide advice and promotion on charitable issues, needs, and priorities in the community.	Foundation staff develop grantmaking policies, solicit and review potential grant recipients, monitor grants and collect reports, providing advice to foundation board of trustees, which makes ultimate grantmaking decisions.
Donor confidentiality	Fund may be "named" or not, at the donor's choosing, but donors' identities are not disclosed if so desired; distributions may also be kept confidential.	Fund may be "named" or not, at the donor's choosing, but donors' identities are not disclosed if so desired; distributions may also be kept confidential.	Detailed disclosures regarding grantmaking and, if relevant, any new contributions to the foundation by the donor(s), shown on Form 990PF

(Continued)

TABLE 9.A1 (CONTINUED)

Characteristic	Corporate-originated charitable funds (donor-advised funds)	Community foundations	Private foundations
Investments	Donor typically selects from a menu of approved investment options, mostly from the "parent" financial services firm, but some firms allow recommendations from investment advisors approved by the charitable fund sponsor.	Generally little or no donor control of investments; investments selected by foundation's investment advisors (sometimes donor can select from approved investment advisors); investment fees netted from yield	Investment policies the responsibility of the management of the foundation

Statistical sources: For the corporate-originated charitable funds' donor-advised funds, the *Chronicle of Philanthropy*'s Donor-Advised Funds Data, published in 2010, supplemented and verified by inspection of the funds' Form 990s; for the statistics on donor-advised funds sponsored by community foundations, the 2010 "Donor Advised Fund Report" of the National Philanthropic Trust, http://www.centerforgiving.org/LinkClick.aspx?fileticket=fVBnSOgx4x8%3d&tabid=85&mid=493; for independent and corporate foundations, the Foundation Center's Foundation Growth and Giving Estimates (2011 edition), http://foundationcenter.org/gainknowledge/research/pdf/fgge11.pdf.

Notes

1. The list of corporate-originated charitable funds is drawn from the author's review and analysis of lists and statistics compiled by the *Chronicle of Philanthropy*, the Investment Company Institute, and the Financial Services Roundtable, among others. The corporate-originated funds, always hovering around two dozen or so, are a component, albeit a large one, of what the National Philanthropic Trust classifies as "national charities" that sponsor donor-advised funds. Although the NPT research does not specifically identify the entities in this category, its most recent annual statistical report on DAFs counts 32, which it defines as follows: "A tax-exempt organization with national reach in fundraising and grantmaking. National charities include independent organizations, such as National Philanthropic Trust, and other charitable organizations affiliated with financial institutions." These latter likely include the two dozen or so corporate-originated charitable funds. Among the other national sponsors might be organizations such as the Tides Foundation (San Francisco), Rockefeller Philanthropic Advisors (New York), Charities Aid Foundation (Virginia), the Funding Exchange (New York), and the American Endowment Foundation (Ohio), all not directly originated or sponsored by, or affiliated with, a corporate financial services organization.

2. National Philanthropic Trust, "Donor Advised Fund Report 2011," accessed October 5, 2012, http://www.nptrust.org/images/uploads/2011%20Donor-Advised-Fund-Report%281%29.pdf.

3. According to Section 509(a) of the Internal Revenue Code, private foundations receive their funding from relatively few sources and typically rely on their investment earnings for their ongoing operational expenses. A public charity such as the Fidelity Charitable Gift Fund receives its support from the general public, that is, multiple sources, and does not receive more than one-third of its income from investment returns.

4. "Schwab Charitable Treasury," Schwab Charitable Fund, accessed August 8, 2012, http://www.schwabcharitable.org/pdf/Schwab_Charitable_Treasury.pdf.

5. All three of these organizations charge an initial 0.60 percent on the first $500,000 or $1 million of assets in an account, and smaller amounts for subsequent investments, but Vanguard is particularly aggressive in lowering fees for larger accounts, dropping them to 0.14 percent for the next $29 million and 0.04 percent for accounts between $30 million and $100 million. Kyle Bumpus, "Best Index Funds: Does Vanguard Still Rule the Roost?" Amateur Asset Allocator, published March 9, 2010, http://amateurassetallocator.com/2010/03/09/best-index-funds-does-vanguard-still-rule-the-roost.

6. Based on a blended rate of 0.85 percent for the first $250,000 and 0.70 for the next $250,000, as presented in the Charitable Administrative Fee table in "Donor-Advised Fund Program Guide," National Philanthropic Trust, accessed October 5, 2012, http://www.nptrust.org/images/uploads/DAF-NPT-FOR-DAFPG-0311.pdf.

7. "Goldman Sachs Philanthropy Fund Program Circular," Goldman Sachs, accessed October 5, 2012, https://gspf.goldman.com/gloria_static/DonorWebConfigs/gspf/1/forms/Program%20Circular.pdf.

8. Based on a blended rate of 0.90 percent on the first $100,000 and 0.75 percent on the next $400,000, as presented in "Bank of America Charitable Gift Fund Program Guidelines and Fees," Bank of America, accessed October 5, 2012, https://bankofamerica.npportal.org/portal/Policies.aspx#Fees. Among the other mutual fund companies, the one that offers the administrative fee structure most comparable to the big three is T. Rowe Price, whose T. Rowe Price Program for Charitable Giving has a fee structure that on paper looks competitive with Fidelity's, Vanguard's, and Schwab's. Fees there equal 0.50 percent for accounts up to $500,000, 0.39 percent for accounts between $500,000 and $1 million, 0.18 percent for accounts up for accounts up to $5 million, 0.10 percent up to $15 million, and 0.09 percent above $15 million. However, T. Rowe Price requires a larger initial fund investment of $10,000, as opposed to the $5,000 minimum of Fidelity and Schwab, requires a minimum $250 grant size compared to Fidelity's $50 and Schwab's $100, and imposes a limitation on the number of grants that a donor may issue without incurring additional fees (10 for accounts less than $250,000, 25 for accounts less than $500,000, 50 for accounts less than $1 million, and 100 for accounts over $1 million).

9. Kimberly Wright-Violich, correspondence with the author, August 30, 2011.

10. On average, the fees of mutual funds have been dropping in past years. According to the ICI, the average fees of stock funds dropped from 1.22 percent to 0.99 percent between 2003 and 2008, bond funds from 0.95 percent to 0.75 percent, and money market funds from 0.44 percent to 0.38 percent. These declines were reversed during the 2008–2009 recession, however, as a result of the one-third drop in fund values, which meant that the fixed costs had to be supported by a smaller amount of funds, boosting expense ratios of mutual funds, according to the market research firm Morningstar, roughly five to eight basis points for most domestic mutual funds and equity funds.

11. Thus, for example, the "balanced allocation" option adds the Calvert Social Investment Fund Enhanced Equity Portfolio (targeted to exceed the Russell 1000 index return rate) and the Calvert Capital Accumulation Fund (socially responsible mid-cap

stocks), geared toward greater principal growth; and a customized option includes access to Calvert's Global Impact Ventures (GIV) fund (with private debt and/or equity stakes in social enterprises, innovative nonprofits, and microfinance institutions). Among the GIV platform components are the Acumen Fund (mission focused on health, water, energy, and housing projects in India, Pakistan, Kenya, Tanzania, South Africa, and Egypt), Public Radio Fund investment notes (United States), the Renewal2 fund (investments in environmental innovation, organic and natural foods, green consumer products, and green building, largely in North America), and E+Co People and Planet Notes (capital and skills training to local entrepreneurs in developing countries with an emphasis on climate change mitigation).

12. The National Philanthropic Trust identifies 32 so-called national charitable sponsors. Included in this category are the dozen or so corporate-originated charitable funds of principal concern to us here along with a small number of other institutions that manage donor-advised funds but for which DAFs are likely not the major activity.

13. National Philanthropic Trust, "Donor-Advised Fund Report 2011." In addition to the 88,000 DAFs managed by the corporate-sponsored charitable funds and the 43,000 managed by community foundations, the remaining roughly 30,500 DAFs are managed by a variety of other "single-issue" sponsors, such as universities, hospitals, United Way, and other charitable institutions.

14. Thus, the National Philanthropic Trust ranks 55th, the Goldman Sachs Philanthropy Fund 156th, the Renaissance Charitable Foundation 232nd, the Ayco Charitable Foundation 314th, and the Bank of America Charitable Gift Fund 349th. "Philanthropy 400 Data," Chronicle of Philanthropy, data published for 2011, http://philanthropy.com/section/Philanthropy-400/237/.

15. "2011 Investment Company Fact Book," Investment Company Institute, accessed October 5, 2012, www.ici.org/pdf/2011_factbook.pdf, Figure 6.1.

16. "2012 Financial Services Fact Book," Insurance Information Institute and Financial Services Roundtable, accessed October 5, 2012, http://www.fsround.org/fsr/publications_and_research/files/2012FinancialFactBook.pdf, 159.

17. Mary Williams Walsh, "The Charitable Gift Fund Phenomenon: Is it a Boon for Nonprofits or a Ploy for Investors?" Grantsmanship Center, accessed October 5, 2012, http://www.tgci.com/magazine/The%20Charitable%20Gift%20Fund%20Phenomenon.pdf.

18. Cash and cash equivalents can be contributed by check, wire, or electronic funds transfer, giving the donor an immediate charitable tax deduction for the full value of the donation up to 50 percent of AGI. Publicly traded stock, mutual fund shares, and special assets such as real estate can all be used, though all must have been held for more than a year and are tax deductible for their fair market value up to 30 percent of the donor's AGI.

19. Kimberly Wright-Violich, former executive director of the Schwab Charitable Fund, personal correspondence with the author, August 30, 2011. As described in the vignette that opened this paper, one of the particularly attractive investment options is contributing securities with unrealized long-term capital gains. Were the donor to cash out such securities, he or she would be hit with a capital gains tax. By donating the securities with the unrealized capital gains directly to the charitable gift fund, the charity receives the full fair market value and the donor avoids the capital gains tax.

20. With Fidelity's Pooled Income Fund, for example, donors can donate cash or securities to the fund, take a partial charitable tax deduction, and for the lifetime of two designated income beneficiaries (for example, the donor and a spouse, although

the donors can name other persons, such as children or grandchildren) receive quarterly income payments generated from the fund's investments. At the death of the income beneficiaries, the value of the fund or trust is then distributed to up to 10 charitable beneficiaries. Schwab also offers donors an array of Charitable Remainder Trust options: Charitable Remainder Annuity Trusts that provide a fixed dollar payment to income beneficiaries, Charitable Remainder Unitrusts that pay out a fixed percentage of the annual valuation of the trust assets, and within the Unitrust structure, one that pays out the lesser of the trust's net income or a fixed percentage and another that changes the payout structure based on a predefined trigger event.

21. For example, Schwab operates an "Express Granting" system and Fidelity a structure of "scheduled grants" on a monthly, quarterly, semiannual, or annual basis.

22. Given the low administrative costs attendant to these funds, and the fact that the 5 percent "payout" requirement for the funds, like the comparable one for foundations, includes administrative costs, the payout requirement for the corporate-originated funds comes much closer to an all-grants payout than the 5 percent required qualifying distributions of private foundations.

23. Fidelity's policy on this matter reads as follows: "The Gift Fund's formal grant-making policy requires that minimum annual grants, on an overall basis, be greater than 5% of the Gift Fund's average net assets on a fiscal five-year rolling basis. If this requirement is not met in a fiscal year, the Gift Fund will ask for grant recommendations from Giving Accounts that have not had grant activity of at least 5% of the Giving Account's average net assets over the same five-year period."

24. "Inside Fidelity," Fidelity Investments, accessed August 2012, http://content. members.fidelity.com/Inside_Fidelity/fullStory/1,,7799,00.html.

25. The first phase of this program was targeted to generate $10 million in guarantees for more than 100,000 microloans through the Grameen Foundation. Donors' funds would be used as guarantees for 24- to 36-month periods, would not leave the donors' investment pools, and would only be drawn on to cover losses on the microloans beyond the reserves built into the financing by Grameen.

26. Investment Company Institute, "2011 Investment Company Fact Book."

27. Investment Company Institute, "2011 Investment Company Fact Book." By net assets, equity funds had increased from their recession low of $3.7 trillion in 2008 to $5.667 trillion in 2010, hybrid funds from $498.3 billion to $741.1 billion, and bond funds from $2.208 trillion to $2.608 trillion.

28. The volatility is evident in the persistent softness in mutual fund money market funds, both taxable funds that decreased from $2,917 trillion in 2009 to $2.474 trillion in 2010 and tax-exempt money market funds down from $398.3 billion in 2009 to $330 billion in 2010.

29. Financial Crisis Inquiry Commission, Hearing on day 1. Records of these hearings are available at http://fcic.law.stanford.edu.

30. "Donor Advised Funds Provide the Majority of Grant Funds Awarded by Community Foundations," Council of Foundations, published January 13, 2009, http:// www.cof.org/files/Documents/Research/08donoradvisedpaper.pdf. Between 2003 and 2007, based on the author's examination of their own grant distributions, Fidelity's payout was 23 percent, Calvert's 14 percent, Schwab's around 20 percent, and Vanguard's 21 percent, compared to an average payout of community foundations surveyed by the Council on Foundations of 13.1 percent and a median payout of 9 percent. Moreover, the most recent information available from the funds suggests that despite the vicissitudes in the markets and the economy, the payout rate of the charitable gift funds continues to be

high, including Fidelity's announcement that its payout rate continues to surpass 20 percent. More generally, payout rates for the national DAFs remained well above 15 percent between 2007 and 2010, while those for community foundations hovered around 15 percent before declining more sharply in 2010, as reflected in Table 9.3.

31. US Senate Committee on Finance, Charity Oversight and Reform, "Keeping Bad Things from Happening to Good Charities," congressional hearing on June 22, 2004, http://www.finance.senate.gov/hearings/hearing/download/?id=066c0319-b047-4 bcb-b985-d7834070346e.

32. Committee on Finance, Charity Oversight and Reform, "Keeping Bad Things from Happening."

33. MacNab's litany of National Heritage Foundation abuses earned the foundation investigations by the Internal Revenue Service, ultimately resulting in a $6.2 million judgment against the foundation in favor of donors who claimed to have been misled by the firm. In 2009, the National Heritage Foundation filed for Chapter 11 bankruptcy, essentially wiping out the $25 million invested in 9,000 donor-advised funds. Deborah L. Jacobs, "Charity Bankruptcy Leaves Many Donors in Distress," *New York Times,* November 11, 2009.

34. "IRS Announces the 'Dirty Dozen' Tax Scams for 2006," Internal Revenue Service, published February 7, 2006, http://www.irs.gov/uac/IRS-Announces-%E2%80%9CDirty-Dozen%E2%80%9D-Tax-Scams-for-2006.

35. Rick Cohen, "A Conversation with California Congressman Xavier Becerra," Cohen Report, published January 16, 2008, http://www.nonprofitquarterly.org/cohenrep ort/2008/01/16/a-conversation-with-california-congressman-xavier-becerra/.

36. As one interviewee put it, the firms "didn't want to say we can do 1 through 4 of your investment needs, but not number 5."

37. Rick Cohen, "Fidelity's Charitable Gift Fund Shows Well in Recession," *Nonprofit Quarterly,* March 15, 2010, http://www.nonprofitquarterly.org/index.php?option=com_content&view=article&id=1997:fidelitys-charitable-gift-fund-shows-well-in-recession &catid=153:web-articles.

38. For example, Vanguard's website button on education and resources for donors provides links to the Council on Foundations and the United Way of America for education and to Guidestar, the Better Business Bureau's Wise Giving Alliance, and the Independent Charities of America for evaluating potential charitable options and recipients. Fidelity gives its donors access to Guidestar's Guidestar Analyst Reports as a service of the Charitable Gift Fund. The reports cover some 200,000 charities, providing financial and narrative analyses, including benchmark measures for comparisons among nonprofits in specific groups and subsectors.

39. Vanguard Charitable, "Annual Report: Focus on Giving," published June 30, 2009, 7. By comparison, the Fidelity Charitable Gift Fund has an equally high proportional emphasis on giving to human services, 24.9 percent, and in education, 23.6 percent, but lower in distributions for religion—10.9 percent. "Learn about Charity," Fidelity Charitable, accessed August 2012, http://www.charitablegift.org/learn-about-charity/ difference.shtml.

40. Cohen, "Fidelity's Charitable Gift Fund."

41. "Special Fund Allows Tax-Free IRA Gifts," Vanguard Charitable Endowment Program, accessed October 5, 2012, https://www.vanguardcharitable.org/giving/news/ news_specialfundallowstaxfreeiragifts_11072007.html.

42. "Report to Congress on Supporting Organizations and Donor Advised Funds," Department of the Treasury, published December 2011, http://www.grassley.senate.gov/ about/upload/Report-to-Congress-Sup-Orgs-and-DAF-FINAL-12-5-11-2.pdf.

Suggested Readings

Cohen, Rick. "Making Charitable Money Flow: Mixed Results with Donor-Advised Funds." *Nonprofit Quarterly*, August 22, 2013. http://www.nonprofitquarterly.org/phi lanthropy/22829-making-charitable-money-flow-mixed-r esults-with-donor-advised-funds.html.

Cohen, Rick. "The Myths and Realities of Commercial Gift Funds." *Nonprofit Quarterly*, Fall 2010.

Cohen, Rick. "Overcoming Outmoded Skepticism: Seeing National Donor-advised Funds for What They Are." Nonprofit Quarterly, April 19, 2012. http://www. nonprofitquarterly.org/philanthropy/20178-overcoming-outmoded-skepticism-seein g-national-donor-advised-funds-for-what-they-are.html.

Cohen, Rick. "What a Donor Advised Fund CEO Advises for Nonprofits." *Nonprofit Quarterly*, October 18, 2010. http://www.nonprofitquarterly.org/index. php?option=com_content&view=article&id=6516:what-a-donor-advised-fund-ceo-a dvises-for-nonprofits&catid=153:features&Itemid=336.

Fidelity Charitable. "Fidelity Charitable Giving Report 2013." http://www. fidelitycharitable.org/docs/giving-report-2013.pdf.

National Philanthropic Trust. "2012 Donor-Advised Fund Report." http://www.nptrust. org/daf-report/market-overview.html.

CHAPTER 10

FUNDING COLLABORATIVES

Angela M. Eikenberry and Jessica Bearman

Most of the time the problems of the world seem overwhelming and
I struggle with feelings of helplessness and impotence that come from
knowing that I am only one person with limited time, resources, and power
to effect a change in the injustices and pain in the lives of women of the
world. Then I think of all of the Dining for Women members across the
country and the power that women united can wield, and I feel a
glimmer of hope.
—Marsha Wallace, founder of a network of giving circles called Dining for Women

FOR FUNDERS, COLLABORATING CAN SEEM difficult and contrary to business as usual. As Doug Nelson of the Casey Foundation notes, "Lots of foundations want their identity, their stamp, on ideas and grant transactions to be protected. They don't want to lose the brand identity of their grantmaking, or compromise their individual authority over the use of money. When you pool funds, you lose some of that authority, and for some foundations, that's an uncomfortable risk."[1] Yet Peter C. Goldmark, tenth president of the Rockefeller Foundation, realized in 1988 that redeveloping a distressed neighborhood in just one of America's poorest cities could cost billions of dollars over the span of several years. No single private funder had enough money to do this, let alone in several cities, over many years, and "on a scale that anyone would describe as solving the problem."[2] So he reached out to a handful of other foundation CEOs to form what was then an unprecedented funding pool. The result, unveiled in 1991, was a $62.5 million fund created by seven foundations (Rockefeller Foundation, the Lilly Endowment, the Pew Charitable Trusts, the John D. and Catherine T. MacArthur Foundation, the William and Flora Hewlett Foundation, the Knight Foundation, the Surdna Foundation) and a for-profit insurance company (Prudential Insurance Company of America). The group called itself the National Community Development Initiative, or NCDI and, later, Living Cities.

Living Cities is now a collaboration of 22 leading foundations and financial institutions that have collectively invested nearly $1 billion to improve the lives of low-income people in two dozen cities across the United States by building homes, stores, schools, child care centers, healthcare and job-training centers, and other community assets using a combination of grants, loans, loan guarantees, and equity investments.[3] Besides achieving *scale* and creating *synergies* among the various sectors and kinds of capital represented at the table, a driving purpose of Living Cities is *learning* about urban vitality and development. Each partner organization contributes funding and leadership to Living Cities. CEOs serve on the board of directors, and more than 80 senior staff take part in standing committees, which are responsible for setting the effort's pro-grammatic agenda. This level of engagement and collaboration is essential to Living Cities' success. As Living Cities president and CEO Ben Hecht noted: "No matter how heroic the efforts of one person or how much 'scale' one organiza-tion could achieve, it never would be enough. A new approach to social change had to be defined and nurtured."[4] It is only by pooling substantial resources, collective knowledge and expertise, and different types of political and finan-cial capital that philanthropy can begin to solve urban problems that have long been seen as intractable.

Defining Funding Collaboratives

Living Cities is an example of a trend emerging across the United States and elsewhere in which a group of individual or institutional donors and investors, who share a common interest, pool funds, knowledge, and other resources to support social-purpose activities, conduct collective research on potential ben-eficiaries, and often make joint or coordinated decisions about the use of resources. We refer to these groupings as "funding collaboratives." Such groups typically include a meaningful degree of social interaction over the uses of pooled resources and some mechanism for joint or coordinated decision-making in the allocation of these pooled resources. While taking myriad forms, they all emphasize information exchange and learning, networking, and engaged, lev-eraged, and strategic grantmaking or investing.

Defining Features

Funding collaboratives differ from both traditional and newer philanthropic models. For both individual and institutional donors and investors, these groups provide support, learning opportunities, and leveraged impact that nei-ther individuals nor institutions can get on their own through other mecha-nisms such as individual grantmaking, check writing, giving through donor advised funds, text-message giving, or mutual fund investing. Unlike newer models, including online giving portals such as Kiva and DonorsChoose, col-laboratives also tend to emphasize face-to-face dialogue and discussion among members and deeper learning opportunities.[5] Funding collaboratives represent a shift from the traditionally individualized process of grantmaking or invest-ing to one that is coordinated and collective, potentially permitting a scaling up of impact. Funding collaboratives are different from mission investment inter-mediaries and individual donor-advised funds in that they are not just pass-through organizations or aggregates of single entities—they are often more than the sum of their parts because they encourage new foci, strategies, and educational opportunities for funders and investors.

Design Features and Major Variants

While sharing certain common features, funding collaboratives also differ along two crucial dimensions: types of participants and types of resources. Collaboratives comprising individual donors have somewhat different modes of operation and purpose than those made up of institutions. Similarly, collab-oratives relying chiefly on grants and operate differently from those deploying a broader range of investment vehicles. Some collaboratives also function primarily as information exchanges in support of either grantmaking or investing but do not actually engage in collaborative or coordinated giving or investing. We include them here because they are often pre-grant, or pre-investment entities, preparing grantmakers or investors to make their individual decisions.

Beyond these basic dimensions, collaboratives also vary widely in terms of structure and formality, social purpose, affiliation status, funding beneficiary, and mechanism and intensity of interaction. For example, giving circles, which tend to engage individuals and to focus on grants to nonprofits, range from small, informal groups to large, more formally structured organizations; focus on various areas of support depending on the interests of the members; are sometimes affiliated with a host institution, such as a community foundation, and sometimes have their own legal and financial status and staff; and have varying levels and types of interaction among members around educational, social, or engagement-focused purposes.[6]

Given this level of diversity, it may be useful to clarify the broad categories of funding collaboratives that have surfaced in recent years. Given that funding collaboratives are fundamentally membership organizations, it is most convenient to sort them first in terms of the nature of their membership and then in terms of the types of resources they pool or coordinate. Within this general framework it is then possible to identify some of the other salient variations. We begin by looking at those whose members are individuals and then look at those that involve institutions.

Collaboratives of Individuals

The contemporary funding collaborative phenomenon among individuals has largely grown out of the desire of philanthropists, or potential philanthropists, to improve their ability to target and leverage their grantmaking efforts. Significant differences exist, however, among the groups that focus only on grantmaking and those that have turned their attention to broader forms of assistance such as loans, loan guarantees, or equities. Finally, on the periphery of this array of actors are groups that are principally information exchanges and that help participants choose their grantmaking and investment decisions but stop short of pooling or coordinating grantmaking and investing.

Grantmaking Collaboratives of Individuals. This type of funding collaborative is a group of individuals who agree to pool some portion of their philanthropic resources and make joint or group decisions about its allocation. Prominent among such collaboratives are what have come to be known as "giving circles." Giving circles are groups of individual donors who pool their money and other resources and decide together what areas and organizations to support through grantmaking and other voluntary assistance. They typically include social, educational, and engagement opportunities for members, often creating more engaged relationships with funding recipients, and tend to be small in size and locally based. Research based on an initial analysis of 184 giving circles identified three major "ideal" types based largely on the size and degree of integration: small groups, loose networks, and formal organizations.[7] See Box 10.1 for examples of each type.

Small giving circles consist of a small number of people who pool funds, typically in equal amounts, ranging from $50 to $5,000. In most small groups, leadership is shared and all members are involved in agenda-setting,

---

BOX 10.1
THREE TYPES OF GIVING CIRCLES

SMALL-GROUP GIVING CIRCLE: NEW RIVER VALLEY CHANGE NETWORK

The New River Valley Change Network, a group of about 12 individuals with varying backgrounds and experiences, meets once a month in members' homes and offices in Blacksburg, Virginia, to give away money they contribute to a fund held at the local community foundation. Each member donates about $10 a month or $100 a year to the fund. The members decide together, through a consensus decision-making process, where to give their money. The group occasionally invites community experts and activists to their meetings to find out about projects or organizations in need of funding. They prefer to fund small organizations and endeavors that might lead to social change.

LOOSE NETWORK GIVING CIRCLE: WASHINGTON WOMENADE AND DINING FOR WOMEN

Washington Womenade raises money by holding potluck dinners where attendees donate $35 to a fund that provides financial assistance to individuals who need help paying for prescriptions, utility bills, rent, food, and so on. Membership in the group is casual; "members" show up when they choose, and the focus of their time together is highly social, with some discussion at the events about funding recipients. In 2002, a *Real Simple* magazine story on Washington Womenade led to the creation of more than 40 unaffiliated Womenade groups across the country. This article also inspired Marsha Wallace to start Dining for Women, now a national network of more than 177 groups across the country in which women meet for dinner monthly and pool the funds they would have spent eating out to support internationally based grassroots programs helping women around the world.

FORMAL ORGANIZATION GIVING CIRCLE: SOCIAL VENTURE PARTNERS

Social Venture Partners (SVP) started in 1997 in Seattle and now has expanded to at least 25 SVP-type giving circles in the United States and Canada. SVP's major foci are educating members about philanthropy and community issues and creating long-term, engaged relationships with funding recipients. The annual contribution to the group is around $5,000. SVP also asks members to volunteer at the nonprofit agencies they fund, providing consulting and capacity-building support. SVP affiliates fund in various areas but often take a strong interest in issues related to youth and education.

discussion, and decision-making. Small-group giving circles often have a social and educational focus in addition to their grantmaking. The social aspect is emphasized through informal group interaction and discussions. The educational aspect is relatively informal, taking place through the grantmaking process, site visits, meetings with nonprofit staff, and information-sharing among group members. Some small groups have staff support (typically provided by a community foundation) to help with administration or fiscal management, and some ask members to volunteer at nonprofit organizations.

In loose network giving circles, a core group of people oversee the group's activities, including ongoing organizing, planning, and grant decision-making. They are surrounded by a loosely affiliated group of individuals who come together around specific events such as potluck dinners. There is typically no minimum fee to participate, but "members" are asked to bring a donation—often $25 to $35—to an event. Loose networks rarely have paid staff support; members praise these groups for their flexibility and organic nature, low overhead, and lack of bureaucracy. Unique to these types of giving circles is their frequent focus on giving money and in-kind gifts directly to individuals in need or doing good work. Grant decision-making often occurs in an ad hoc fashion in response to the needs of individuals. Loose network giving circles have proven to be especially popular among women and next-generation donors, perhaps because they are so flexible and informal. They are also easily replicated in new locations, as the success of Womenade and Dining for Women attests.

Formal giving circles have codified structures and decision-making processes, looking very much like traditional voluntary organizations, with a board, committees, and, often, professional staff support. They are larger—generally over 25 members—and the cost to participate tends to be higher than the other two types of giving circles—ranging from $365 to $10,000 annually. The grant decision-making process typically involves a committee that either makes grant decisions directly or recommends finalists for a full membership vote. These giving circles tend to have formal educational programming in addition to grantmaking and other informal educational opportunities. In addition, many formal organizations provide opportunities for members to volunteer with nonprofit organizations.

In addition to their variations in size, giving circles can also vary in terms of the basis for recruiting members. Because personal interaction plays such an important role in such individual collaboratives, many of them recruit on a geographic basis. However, one of the recent developments is the emergence of "identity"- or "diversity"-focused funds. Such funds emphasize leadership by, donors from, and giving to specific populations, including communities of color, women, and lesbian, gay, bisexual, transgender, and queer (LGBTQ) communities.[8] While some identity-based collaboratives involve individuals in organizational settings (e.g., Hispanics in Philanthropy), most are groupings of individuals sharing a distinctive identity. For example, AsiaNextGen is a small-group giving circle whose members donate at least $1,000 annually to a pooled donor-advised fund held at the Asian American Federation of New York. Its focus is to educate and empower needy Asian American grant recipients in the New York City region. Funding decisions and education about community issues are informed by guest speakers or workshops about philanthropy and issue areas, site visits to nonprofit organizations, group discussion, and connections to philanthropic networks.[9]

Another variant on the giving-circle model is offered by Sea Change Capital Partners. Founded by two former Goldman Sachs partners, Sea Change has been building a nationwide donor network of wealthy individuals and family foundations that can mobilize existing sources of funds to provide growth capital for entrepreneurial organizations. Unlike the common giving-circle arrangement, Sea Change partners do not meet and discuss potential grantees. Rather, they function as a virtual community of individuals who share predetermined charitable interests and who make pledges to organizations that Sea Change staff have vetted and identified as worthy of their collective charitable support.

Investment-Oriented Collaboratives of Individuals. Although funding collaboratives largely focus on grantmaking, consistent with the overall findings of this book about the proliferation of non-grant forms of philanthropy and social investment, collaboratives have spread to the social investment community as well. The result is the emergence of a number of individual funding collaboratives with an investment, instead of just a grantmaking, orientation. Such collaboratives, sometimes referred to as "angel investor networks," are groups of high-net-worth individuals who collaborate to invest for some combination of financial and social return in early- and second-stage social enterprises.[10] These groups provide members with an increased knowledge base of investment opportunities, the ability to leverage funds, and a short-cut to completion of due diligence scrutiny. Angel investors often invest on a regional basis and are interested in active and personal relationships with companies in which they invest.[11]

One example of an angel investment network that focuses on social-impact investing is First Light Ventures, a fund that "serves as an incubator and investment partner to seed-stage, for-profit social ventures."[12] Its "investment strategy is designed to accelerate the successful development of scalable and sustainable social enterprises that provide goods and services to low-income customers in emerging markets around the world."[13] The group is testing its "Village Capital" model, inspired by the village bank model used in microfinance, in four locations: San Francisco Bay Area, California (West Coast Village Capital); Boulder, Colorado (Unreasonable Village Capital); New Orleans, Louisiana (Idea Village Capital); and Mumbai, India (Dasra Village Capital). The San Francisco–based West Coast Village Capital gives participants the opportunity to network with other social entrepreneurs, collaboratively refine and strengthen their business models and pitches, and work together to evaluate each other's businesses as potential investments.

Information-Focused Collaboratives of Individuals. A number of individual-oriented funding collaboratives function in what might be termed the prefunding arena. These groups of individuals feature collaborative learning and engagement programs for current and future donors or investors, without collaborative grantmaking or investing.[14] Resource Generation, an example of such a donor learning group, promotes "innovative ways for young people with wealth to align their personal values and political vision with their financial resources."[15] Through conferences, one-on-one discussions, and group gatherings that feature educational programs, Resource Generation supports personal development, understanding of socioeconomics, and the development of social change philanthropy.[16] Currently, Resource Generation works with "over 750 young people with wealth across the country."[17] Other examples of individual-oriented donor learning groups include Changemakers,

Philanthropy Workshop West (TPW West), and the Global Philanthropists Circle.

As interest in social-impact investing has grown, information-oriented collaborations of individuals have formed in the social investment area as well. Such social investment learning networks disseminate knowledge, create awareness, and build support for mission-related or program-related investing among foundations, financial institutions, and investment funds. These groups might facilitate collaborative mission- or program-related investing, but this is not something that occurs through the group itself; rather, their focus is on information sharing.

One such collaborative is Toniic, a staffed network of West Coast philanthropists and social investor that provides its members with investing support through easy access to high-quality deals, and process support, education, and a peer group to share information. Toniic members invest out of their own accounts, but receive many of the advantages of the high-touch angel networks in traditional investment sectors.[18]

Collaboratives of Institutions

Although funding collaboratives are often groups of individuals, institutions have increasingly come to see the value of collaboration in order to leverage funds, share knowledge, and scale up impact. Significant developments are evident in the creation of institutional collaboratives of several different sorts.

Grantmaking Collaboratives of Institutions. One of the more significant developments in the world of institutional philanthropy is the emergence of true joint-funding arrangements among foundations and other institutions. This usually requires the creation or designation of an entity to assemble the resources and regrant them.[19] Similar to giving circles, members are often asked to make a specific level of financial commitment to the pool. In some, the whole collaborative membership or a subgroup of the collaborative makes funding decisions; in others, grantmaking is largely delegated to an intermediary. According to Ralph Hamilton, "Administrative and governance structures also differ widely, from 'virtual' organizations with pass-through fiscal agents, to fully elaborated grantmaking institutions."[20] For example, the Fund for New Citizens is a joint effort of more than 20 foundations hosted by the New York Community Trust and designed to help immigrants in New York City. Founded in 1987, the fund has made more than $14 million in grants to "strengthen immigrant-led organizations, challenge punitive immigration laws, promote pro-immigrant policies at the State and City levels, and other similar purposes.[21] Strive, a consortium of some 300 partner organizations that have come together to promote an ambitious agenda of education improvements in Cincinnati, operates in a similar fashion, as does Empresarios por la Educación (Businesses for Education), a network of over 100 Colombian corporations that have joined forces to promote a similarly ambitious agenda of systemic changes in that country's education system.[22]

Investment-Oriented Collaboratives of Institutions. A number of institutional collaboratives pool funds not just for grantmaking, but also through a variety of investment instruments. One example of such an institutional collaborative that pools together investment resources is Living Cities, discussed at the beginning of this chapter. Similarly, Investors' Circle, a network of over 225 angel investors, professional venture capitalists, foundations, family offices, and others, uses private capital to promote the transition to a sustainable economy. Started in 1992, it claims success in facilitating the flow of over $133 million into more than 200 companies and small funds addressing social and environmental issues.[23] Investors' Circle staff screen investment opportunities and coordinate individual members' investments. Investors' Circle also offers members opportunities to gather for in-depth discussions and networking conferences and retreats.

Information-Oriented Collaboratives of Institutions. Perhaps not surprisingly, the most common form of institutional collaborative is the type that focuses primarily on information exchange rather than the allocation of pooled resources. Such collaboratives provide organizational representatives the opportunity to exchange information, discuss common challenges, and build relationships that can help them in various aspects of their work, but they do not actually assemble and distribute resources collectively, which puts them on the outer fringe of the funding collaborative phenomenon that is the focus of this chapter. Some of these are rather informal and are nested in larger organizations such as regional associations of grantmakers. For example, the Green Funders Affinity Group, affiliated with the Association of Baltimore Area Grantmakers, "explores ways that funders can work together to advance the goals of community greening, sustainability and protecting our natural environment for present and future generations"[24] Its members gather informally at educational programs and meetings to share information. Sometimes these conversations evolve into joint funding, but that is not the primary purpose of such affinity groups.[25]

Other information-oriented institutional collaboratives, such as Grantmakers in the Arts, Grantmakers in Health, and Grantmakers for Effective Organizations, are more structured, with regular dues and core staff who organize conferences and other information-sharing activities. Grantmakers in Health, for example, describes itself as

> a nonprofit, educational organization dedicated to helping foundations and corporate giving programs improve the health of all people. Its mission is to foster communication and collaboration among grantmakers and others, and to help strengthen the grantmaking community's knowledge, skills, and effectiveness.[26]

Similarly, the Funders' Network on Smart Growth and Livable Communities defines itself as "a membership organization that helps grantmakers across North America advance strategies to create fair, prosperous, and sustainable regions and communities that offer everyone the chance for a good life."[27]

In addition to information-focused institutional collaboratives oriented around a particular subject matter such as health, the arts, or the environment, other such collaboratives are oriented around a particular geographical area. Perhaps the most well-known of these are the 34 regional associations of grantmakers (RAs) located across the United States. These associations have been credited with playing "key roles on state level policy matters, knowledge building, new donor development, and joint funding opportunities."[28]

As interest in social-impact investing has grown among foundations and for-profit investment firms, new information-oriented institutional collaborations have surfaced among these groups as well. Prominent examples of such groups include the More for Mission Campaign, PRI Makers Network, and the

Global Impact Investing Network (GIIN). The More for Mission Campaign is a network of foundations that are committed to mission investing within their organizations by providing a range of informational and institutional resources for investors. Mission investing aligns a foundation's financial investments with the mission of the organization. The "Mission's network includes 96 participating foundations that collectively represent approximately $39 billion in total assets."[29] Similarly, PRI Makers Network helps foundations expand their use of program-related investments (PRI) to achieve their philanthropic goals. They provide a forum for networking, professional development, collaboration, and outreach to funders. Members include more than 150 foundations, which pay dues based on their level of PRI activity. The Global Impact Investing Network is also an institutional collaborative that engages private investment firms in addition to foundations and is dedicated to increasing the effectiveness of social-impact investing to solve social and environment problems.

Scope and Scale of Funding Collaboratives

Although the urge to collaborate in generating funding for charitable purposes has had a long history in the United States and elsewhere, the modern funding collaborative movement started in the late 1940s when grantmakers in the southwestern region of the United States began organizing themselves into a regional association to share information, enhance their leadership capacity, and engage in collaborative partnerships.[30] This pattern of collaborative funding expanded to individuals in the 1990s, when giving circles and identity-focused funds began to form, partly because of an increase in shared giving among women, the emergence of new donors seeking engaging ways to give back to society, and the increasing desire of individuals to have a greater say in their charitable giving.[31] The result has been an unprecedented growth in collaboration across sectors and among individuals and organizations.[32]

It is impossible to estimate the numbers of funding collaborative with any accuracy given their grass-roots and collaborative nature. However, the literature indicates that many types of funding collaboratives have doubled or tripled in number over the past two decades. For example, in 2003, Grantmakers for Effective Organizations identified 325 funder networks across the United States. They showed an increase from the 23 identified in 1981, 57 in 1990, and 129 in 2000.[33] According to a survey of 151 of these funder networks, 33 percent (49) managed a pooled grantmaking fund. In addition, since the Forum of Regional Associations of Grantmakers began to track giving circles in 2004, the number identified has more than doubled, to well over 500 groups.[33] There is strong indication that many more exist and continue to be created. A recent study also shows that 355 identity-focused funds were active in the United States as of 2009.[34] There is some duplication and overlap with the data above, but all indicate a growth among funding collaboratives.

There is less information available for social-purpose investment collaboratives. Preston indicates that the number of all types of angel investor organizations in the United States increased from an estimated 10 groups in 1996 to about 200 groups in 2003. She does not discuss how many of these angel investment groups include a social-purpose focus.[35] Data are not available for other types of investment collaboratives.

These groups are located all over the United States and increasingly in other parts of the world. For example, giving circles are located in at least 44 states and the District of Columbia in the United States. They are also found in Australia, Canada, South Africa, and the United Kingdom. Individual and institutional investors and learning networks are both US and globally focused. The European Venture Philanthropy Association now boasts 130 members from 20 countries committed to high-engagement philanthropy and the use of nongrant forms of assistance.[36] Already mentioned above, groups like Toniic and First Light Ventures focus on global investments.

Funding collaboratives provide a large amount of money and human capital resources for social benefit. Jessica Bearman estimates that the giving circles included in one study alone had given more than $100 million over the course of their existence to a wide range of issue areas.[37] Rockefeller Philanthropy Advisors also estimates that total giving for identity-based collaboratives is about $200 million annually, mainly in the areas of education, economic empowerment, health, and arts and culture.[38] While there is some overlap in these data (as 43 identity-focused funds in their study are giving circles), the data give some indication of the financial impact of these groups. In addition, angel investments for 2003 added up to approximately $18.1 billion.[39] It is not possible to know how much of this was focused on social-purpose investing, however. While donor and investment learning groups do not necessarily bring financial resources to bear on social issues, they do enable members to share and leverage resources and knowledge. This is true for all funding collaboratives to some degree and is one of their primary benefits.

Rationale

The growth of funding collaboratives in recent years reflects at least three important motivations. The first is the growing complexity of modern social and environmental problems and the resulting loss of faith in the ability of government on its own to address them. This has necessitated more pooling of resources and more integrated approaches to addressing problems. As Geri Scott notes in the case of workforce intermediaries, there is a need to "unleash the power that comes from jointly committing resources to address a problem so immediate—and so large—that few, if any, funders could tackle it alone."[40] As noted earlier, funding collaboratives like Living Cities were also founded on this belief.[41]

A second motivation leading to the creation of funding collaboratives is the realization that improved knowledge is needed to make giving most effective. After decades of grantmaking and social investing, many of the same problems persist in our communities. It is no longer possible to assume that giving and investing strategies are necessarily the right ones and lead to good outcomes. Collaboratives offer opportunities for donors and investors to obtain the financial and other knowledge they need to make strategic contributions and investments and be able to measure their impact. Individual donors, for example, recognize that "giving money effectively is not easy."[42] Likewise, investors can collaborate to learn about and find investment opportunities and conduct due diligence.[43] Powell and coauthors argue that "when the knowledge base of an industry is both complex and expanding and the sources of expertise are widely dispersed, the locus of innovation will be found in networks of learning, rather than in individual firms."[44]

Finally, collaboratives serve a social function for participants, enabling like-minded donors and investors to network and form social bonds in a world driven by what sociologists see as an increasingly individualized and fragmented society. Individuals have reacted to this fragmentation in part by seeking out more engagement in community, but in ways that match their personal interests, that they can control, in the context of their hectic lives. Some individual donors want greater involvement or engagement in their philanthropy, while others want easier ways to give to the community. Funding collaboratives such as giving circles allow for both. Younger people also seem to be more interested in collaborating, perhaps as a result of the fragmented environment in which they have grown up.[45]

Basic Mechanics

There is no one right way to organize a funding collaborative, but there are certain tasks that all of them must address. These include identifying a champion, formulating a purpose and focus, creating a governance structure and process for decision-making, figuring out how to finance the group, and determining the group's relationship with the organizations it funds.[46]

Identifying a Champion

Funding collaboratives usually start because an individual or small group champions its initiation. For instance, Preston notes that a successful angel investment group must have a champion or group of champions to ensure its successful establishment and operation.[46] Likewise, giving circles generally rely on the energy and passion of a catalyst—an individual (or perhaps a small group) with the energy and commitment to develop and market the idea.[47]

Determining the Composition of the Group

A crucial early decision for a funding collaborative is to determine the size and composition of the group. Obviously, the larger and more diverse the size, the more difficult it is to reach decisions and create a supportive internal culture. At the same time, the larger the group, the greater the impact. This often creates tensions as groups develop, with early founders having to adjust to a more structure and less intimate mode of operation.

Formulating a Purpose

Decisions about group composition are closely related to decisions about group objectives. For some collaboratives, this is done through a relatively formal process. For example, Preston suggests that angel investor groups conduct community assessments to better understand the nature of the investment community and potential group members. This can involve assessing: potential angel investors in the region; prevalent industries in the region; the entrepreneurial pool in the region; the entrepreneurial infrastructure that supports, educates, and fosters entrepreneurs and new businesses; support services/teams available; and the follow-on funding available for later-stage financing.[48] The Insight Center for Community Economic Development also suggests that institutional funding collaboratives conduct marketing and feasibility assessments.[49] This involves meeting with potential partners to communicate the idea and getting their feedback as well as analyzing "key regional industries to determine priorities for investment that fit funders' interests."[50]

Other collaboratives are less formal. Giving circles typically do not enter into such systematic assessments but rely on members to identify common areas of interest, including issue areas, population served, geographic area, and so on. Sometimes, giving circles will also invite "experts" in the field to present information to the group or the giving circle will assign group members to investigate particular issues.

Creating a Governance Structure and Decision Process

The next step for most funding collaboratives is to determine the right organizational structure and decision process for the group in relation to these. While there are many effective models, groups' shapes and operations vary according to their responses to these types of questions:

- Should the group be managed by members or an administrator? For instance, giving circles tend to be member-led, but some do get administrative assistance from host organizations. Institutional funding collaboratives often rely upon the staff of one or more members, either on a permanent or rotating basis. Investment collaboratives often retain paid staff because of the extra complexity of the due diligence tasks involved.
- How should leadership be selected—through formal elections? On a volunteer basis? By consensus?
- What committee structures should be put in place to handle various functions, such as a grants or investment committee, a marketing committee, a membership committee, an education or program committee?
- What is the best or preferred legal structure? The current prevailing angel investor group structures include affiliation without formal structure, nonprofit corporation, limited liability company, for-profit corporation, subchapter S corporation, and limited liability partnership. Giving circles can be unincorporated, affiliated with a community foundation or other fiscal agent as a donor-advised fund, or become a nonprofit corporation.
- How should the group make grants or investments? As a group of pooled or pledged funds or as individuals based on group due diligence, individual assessment, or side-fund investments with individuals making additional investments? Will the group use a request for proposals process? What are the criteria for funding or investing?

Financing the Group

Decisions will need to be made early on, and subsequently revisited, concerning the contributions that will be expected of members of the group. Included here are responses to questions such as the following:

- Will contributions be mandatory or voluntary?
- Will there be different contribution levels depending on the interest and resources of different members?
- Will there be a minimum contribution level and, if so, how much?
- How will the group fund operating costs? Through dues, percentage of committed capital or pooled funds, sponsorships, events and programs, or other fees?

Determining the Relationship with Recipient Organizations

Collective giving groups also must decide what kind of relationship they would like to have with funding recipients. Do they want to be involved with the organizations funded in some way beyond the funding? In what ways can they offer assistance? As noted earlier, for example, Social Venture Partners provides considerable capacity-building assistance to its recipients, drawing on the talents of its members to do so. This obviously raises questions about the expectations for all involved in this partnership and necessitates attention to the time demands put upon funding recipients.[51]

Once grants or investments are made, members may want to evaluate the impact of the group's funding. They can examine the short-term and long-term goals of the group on a regular basis and assess what has been learned, what should be changed in the future, and what the next round of funding will look like in terms of time, calendar, and so on.

Operational Challenges

Funding collaboratives face several distinct operational challenges. These include maintaining harmony and consensus, sustaining long-term capacity, and matching the desires and resources of the group with the needs of the funding or investment recipient.

Generally, because funding collaboratives involve a group of people or institutions getting together to share information and resources and, often, make decisions together, there is a certain degree of complexity in maintaining group harmony and consensus. For example, collaborations among grantmakers can be challenged by organizational cultures that place a high value on independence, recognition, and leadership; there is still a desire in every foundation to make their own decisions and design their own criteria, even when striving to work together.[52] There are also inevitably interpersonal tensions and time constraints.[53] Yet, surprisingly, this issue does not come up in the literature as much as one would expect, perhaps because these groups also tend to be voluntary and individuals or institutions can exit if they are dissatisfied with the direction of the group. Many abandon a desire for complete consensus and, like some giving circles, create mechanisms to streamline decision-making through committees or voting processes.

Many funding collaboratives also seem to face a challenge in sustaining the capacity of the group over the long term. The commitment, time, and resources needed to sustain the group can be daunting, especially for funders with finite resources to give or for volunteers who maintain the group outside of their regular jobs or other commitments. For example, giving circles are initiated by passionate community leaders, who often carry the burden of managing and growing the circle for years. Eventually, though, they become fatigued. Giving circles struggle with developing structures for sustainability over time, including codified systems and for board succession and balancing this with the often informal or nonbureaucratic nature of the group. Similarly, giving circles can find it challenging to recruit new members. Both issues are, at least in part, a result of the volunteer nature of giving circles. Because members and leaders are often running the giving circle in their spare time, between work, family, and other obligations, it can be hard to attend to anything beyond immediate operational needs. A Grantmakers for Effective Organizations report also found that sustainability-related issues are the key challenges for funder groups, including expanding membership and enhancing organization and issue area funding and visibility.[54]

Some funding collaboratives also share a challenge when it comes to aligning their interests and passions with the real needs of partners and ensuring that they do not overwhelm funding recipients with their own priorities, processes, and "help." For instance, some giving circles have had difficulty finding the "best" organizations that have a real need for their help. Part of this is due to members' lack of time to search out organizations. Another problem is that the organizations giving circle members approach about funding, because they tend to be small and locally based, do not always seem to be ready for the help. Nonprofit managers admit that the giving circles focused on high engagement are not always a great fit for their organizations. Giving circles must navigate the tension between meeting nonprofit organizations' needs—such as funding for general operating costs or for needs that are not of special interest to members but are needed by nonprofit funding recipients—and meeting the needs of giving circle members (the social, self-help/mutual aid aspect of giving circles)—such as donor education and enabling members to engage in the community. In many cases, the donor education/member engagement aspect of the giving circle is the most dominant aspect and can put burdens on nonprofit funding recipients. For example, some giving circles, as a means to educate and engage members, expect nonprofits to accept volunteer help from members in addition to funding, even when the volunteer help is not necessarily needed or wanted. Along similar lines, institutional funding collaboratives face the danger of skewing the field in whatever area in which they focus —so thoroughly "dominating a field with one particular approach that support for other approaches on the margin dries up."[55]

Tensions can also easily arise between an investment group's desire for greater financial return on investment and a social entrepreneur's needs, mission, and vision. A detailed case study of a social enterprise in the United States, created by the Seedco Policy Center—Community Childcare Assistance, which closed in 2003 after failing to secure the contracts it needed to operate successfully—concluded that organizations "driven to meet a 'double bottom' line for customers and clients have far more typically led to frustration and failure, drawing attention and resources away from the organization's core work."[56]

Finally, many funding collaboratives, particularly giving circles, are created as an alternative to the more formalized forms of established philanthropy, providing collective structures in which individual voices contribute to the dynamic workings of the whole. However, as they grow larger, more organizationally complex, and more "sophisticated," with staff and experience, they may find themselves unintentionally recreating the lofty bureaucratic structures that participants sought to escape when they created these alternative vehicles for their giving.

Impact and Conclusions

There has not been a great deal of research on the impact of funding collaboratives. Rather, the primary focus of work in this area has been on mapping and providing advice for how to form and run collaboratives. What little research is available on their value is encouraging, however. A recent comprehensive study of giving circles, which included a survey and interviews of current and past members of giving circles as well as of nonmembers across the United States, found that giving circles influence members to give more, give more strategically, and give to a wider array and larger number of organizations.[57] Giving circle members are also highly engaged in the community, and giving circles increase members' knowledge about philanthropy, nonprofits, and the community. We assume that some of these benefits, especially knowledge growth, also result from other types of collaboratives. This research also shows that giving circles increase knowledge of, and support for, minority-focused organizations. Identity-focused collaboratives also reach deeper into communities than mainstream funders, leverage new resources for community-based and grass-roots grantees, attract diverse donors more successfully than other vehicles, and develop community leadership and capacity.[58]

Hopkins found that institutional funding collaboratives increase philanthropic efficiency, frame comprehensive solutions, share risk, improve philanthropic governance, enhance communications and knowledge management, and set directions for the foundation world.[59] Other studies emphasize the opportunity funding collaboratives create to learn about new grantmaking strategies, leverage philanthropic resources for greater impact, and increase focus and attention on critical issues.[60] Buhl points out that local institutional funding collaboratives "have the capacity to democratize local philanthropy by creating a balance of power, ideas, and strategies and helping to level the playing field between larger and smaller funders."[61] These local collaboratives are reversing an historical pattern in which national foundations ask local foundations to co-invest in national initiatives. In addition, as Scott has noted, collaboratives involving the participation of multiple institutions can take a broader perspective on community problems and efforts to resolve them. Such collaboratives "can step back from the minutia of individual [organization] grant reporting to measure effectiveness on a larger scale of community impact and systems reform through a multi-part initiative."[62]

Regarding investment-oriented collaboratives, research by Steven Carden and Olive Darragh found that financial return on social investments can generate returns similar to those of the S&P 500, indicating that financial returns do not have to suffer when investors pursue social and environmental objectives.[63] Over the 10-year period they examined, focusing on investments made through Investors' Circle, "a portfolio of investments defined as socially responsible generated returns of 8 to 14%."[64] This is lower than the rate typically earned by angel investors, but comparable to capital market returns. Social investments seem to be a financially viable option for funding collaboratives.

Among the various trends emerging in the new frontiers of philanthropy, funding collaboratives seem to be one of the more promising. There is every indication that funding collaboratives will continue to flourish in the United States and elsewhere. The growth of such collaboratives in the past two decades demonstrates the power of the drive to collaborate, and today's economic realities make collaboration all the more imperative. The recent addition of social-purpose investor collaboratives to giving collaboratives adds another dimension to the contributions collaboration can make by joining philanthropic assets with private investment resources to maximize social benefit. There are difficulties inherent in running and sustaining collaboratives, but their benefits—of leveraged resources, pooled knowledge, and coordinated activity—make these challenges pale by comparison.

Notes

1. Quoted in Tony Proscio, "Common Effort, Uncommon Wealth: Lessons from Living Cities on the Challenges and Opportunities of Collaboration in Philanthropy," Living Cities, accessed October 18, 2012, http://www.livingcities.org/knowledge/media/?id=42, 3.

2. Quoted in Proscio, "Common Effort, Uncommon Wealth," 1.

3. "History," Living Cities, accessed March 29, 2012, http://www.livingcities.org/about/history/.

4. Ben Hecht, "Revitalizing Struggling American Cities," *Stanford Social Innovation Review*, Fall 2007, 27.

5. For a discussion of online portals, see Chapter 8 in this volume.

6. Jessica E. Bearman, "More Giving Together: The Growth and Impact of Giving Circles and Shared Giving," Forum of Regional Associations of Grantmakers, 2007, accessed March 29, 2012, http://www.givingforum.org/s_forum/bin.asp?CID=611&DID=5316&DOC=FILE.PDF; Angela M. Eikenberry, *Giving Circles: Philanthropy, Voluntary Association, and Democracy* (Bloomington: Indiana University Press, 2009).

7. Eikenberry, *Giving Circles*.

8. Rockefeller Philanthropy Advisors, *Diversity Funds Inventory* (New York: Rockefeller Philanthropy Advisors, August 2009).

9. "AsiaNextGen Giving Circle Profile," Forum of Regional Associations of Grantmakers, 2008, accessed March 29, 2012, http://www.givingforum.org/s_forum/doc.asp?CID=4088&DID=8793.

10. Not all angel investor networks qualify as "funding intermediaries" as the term is used here since not all of them engage significantly in social-purpose investments.

11. Susan L. Preston, "Angel Investment Groups, Networks, and Funds: A Guidebook to Developing the Right Angel Organization for Your Community," Ewing Marion Kauffman Foundation, August 2004, accessed March 28, 2012, http://www.kauffman.org/entrepreneurship/angel-investment-guidebook.aspx.

12. Grayghost Ventures, accessed October 18, 2012, http://www.grayghostventures.com/firstlight.htm.

13. "First Light," Grayghost Ventures.

14. Lucy Bernholz, Kendall Guthrie, and Kaitlin McGaw, "Philanthropic Connections: Mapping the Landscape of U.S. Funder Networks," Forum of Regional Associations of Grantmakers, Spring 2003, accessed October 18, 2012, http://www.blueprintrd.com/text/rag.pdf, 5–6.

15. "Who We Are," Resource Generation, accessed October 19, 2012, http://www.resourcegeneration.org/Who/index.html.

16. John C. Urschel, "Coming out of the Green Closet: Wealth Discourse and the Construction of Social Change Philanthropies," in *Foundations for Social Change: Critical Perspectives on Philanthropy and Popular Movements*, ed. Daniel R. Faber and Deborah McCarthy (Lanham, MD: Rowman & Littlefield, 2005), 245–70.

17. "Who We Are," Resource Generation.

18. "About," Toniic, accessed October 18, 2012, http://toniic.com/index.php/about/.

19. Ralph Hamilton, "Moving Ideas and Money: Issues and Opportunities in Funder Funding Collaboration," Funders Network for Smart Growth and Livable Communities, February 27, 2002, accessed March 29, 2012, http://www.fundersnetwork.org/files/Moving_Ideas_and_Money_Paper_2002.pdf.

20. Hamilton, "Moving Ideas and Money."

21. "The Fund for New Citizens," New York Community Trust, accessed March 29, 2012, http://www.nycommunitytrust.org/AbouttheTrust/

FundingCollaborativesandotherSpecialProjects/TheFundforNewCitizens/tabid/397/Default.aspx.

22. John Kania and Mark Kramer, "Collective Impact," *Stanford Social Innovation Review,* Winter 2011, 36–41; Lester M. Salamon, *Rethinking Corporate Social Engagement: Lessons from Latin America* (Sterling, VA: Kumarian Press, 2010), 58.

23. "Our Role," Investors' Circle, accessed October 18, 2012, http://www.investor-scircle.net/about-us.

24. "Green Funders Affinity Group," Association of Baltimore Area Grantmakers, accessed October 19, 2012, http://www.abagrantmakers.org/?GreenFunders.

25. Alice C. Buhl, "Local Donor Collaboration: Lessons from Baltimore and Beyond," Association of Baltimore Area Grantmakers, 2004, accessed October 18, 2012, http://www.aecf.org/upload/publicationfiles/pb3622h802.pdf, 15.

26. "About GIH," Grantmakers in Health, accessed March 29, 2012, http://www.gih.org/info-url_nocat2663/info-url_nocat.htm?requesttimeout=500.

27. "About Us," Funders' Network for Smart Growth and Livable Communities, accessed October 18, 2012, http://www.fundersnetwork.org/index.php/about/.

28. Bernholz, Guthrie, and McGaw, "Philanthropic Connections," 5.

29. "About Us," More for Mission, accessed October 18, 2012, http://www.more-formission.org/page/15/about-us.

30. Bernholz, Guthrie, and McGaw, "Philanthropic Connections," 1.

31. Tracey A. Rutnik and Jessica Bearman, *Giving Together: A National Scan of Giving Circles and Shared Giving* (Washington, DC: Forum of Regional Associations of Grantmakers, 2005), 19.

32. Michael McGuire, "Collaborative Public Management: Assessing What We Know and How We Know It," *Public Administration Review* 66.1 (2006): 33–43; Walter W. Powell, Kenneth W. Koput, and Laurel Smith-Doerr, "Interorganizational Collaboration and the Locus of Innovation: Networks of Learning in Biotechnology," *Administrative Science Quarterly* 41.1 (1996): 116–45.

33. Angela M. Eikenberry and Jessica E. Bearman, *The Impact of Giving Together: Giving Circles' Influence on Members' Philanthropic and Civic Behaviors, Knowledge, and Attitudes* (Washington, DC: Forum of Regional Associations of Grantmakers, 2009); Rutnik and Bearman, *Giving Together,* 19.

34. Rockefeller Philanthropy Advisors, *Diversity Funds Inventory.*

35. Preston, "Angel Investment Groups."

36. "About Us," European Venture Philanthropy Association, accessed March 29, 2012, http://evpa.eu.com/.

37. Bearman, "More Giving Together."

38. Rockefeller Philanthropy Advisors, *Diversity Funds Inventory.*

39. Preston, "Angel Investment Groups," 11.

40. Geri Scott, *Funder Collaboratives: A Philanthropic Strategy for Supporting Workforce Intermediaries* (Boston: Jobs for the Future, March 2007), iii.

41. Hecht, "Revitalizing Struggling American Cities," 27.

42. Dan Siegel and Jenny Yancey, "Philanthropy's Forgotten Resource? Engaging the Individual Donor: The State of Donor Education Today and a Leadership Agenda for the Road Ahead," New Visions, 2003, accessed March 28, 2012, http://www.hewlett.org/uploads/files/PhilanthropysForgottenResource.pdf, 16.

43. Preston, "Angel Investment Groups."

44. Powell, Koput, and Smith-Doerr, "Interorganizational Collaboration," 116.

45. Cynthia Gibson, *Funder Collaboratives: Why and How Funders Work Together* (New York: Grantcraft, 2009), 3.

46. Preston, "Angel Investment Groups," 11.

47. Bearman, "More Giving Together."

48. Preston, "Angel Investment Groups."

49. "Starting a Regional Workforce Funders Collaborative," Insight Center for Economic Community Development, accessed March 28, 2012, http://www.insightcced. org/index.php?page=starting-collaborative#Step_1.

50. Insight Center for Economic Community Development, "Starting a Regional Workforce Funders Collaborative," paragraph 5.

51. Angela M. Eikenberry, "Fundraising in the New Philanthropy Environment: The Benefits and Challenges of Working with Giving Circles," *Nonprofit Management and Leadership* 19.2 (2008): 141–52.

52. Gibson, *Funder Collaboratives*.

53. Gibson, *Funder Collaboratives*.

54. Steven LaFrance, Andrew Robinson, Rick Green, and Nancy Latham, "Funding Networks in Action: Understanding Their Potential for Philanthropy," Grantmakers in Effective Organizations, accessed January 8, 2014, http://www.socialimpactexchange. org/sites/www.socialimpactexchange.org/files/publications/Funder%20networks%20 in%20action.pdf.

55. Hamilton, "Moving Ideas and Money," 18.

56. Seedco Policy Center, *The Limits of Social Enterprise: A Field Study and Case Analysis* (New York: Seedco Policy Center, June 2007), 1–2.

57. Eikenberry and Bearman, *Impact of Giving Together*.

58. Rockefeller Philanthropy Advisors, *Diversity Funds Inventory*.

59. Elwood M. Hopkins, *Collaborative Philanthropies: What Groups of Foundations Can Do That Individual Funders Cannot* (Lanham, MD: Lexington Books, 2005).

60. The Philanthropic Initiative, "Donor Collaboration: Power in Numbers," April 13, 2009, accessed March 29, 2012, http://www.tpi.org/resources/primer/donor_collaboration_power_in.aspx.

61. Buhl, "Local Donor Collaboration," iii.

62. Scott, *Funder Collaboratives*, 8.

63. Steven D. Carden and Olive Darragh, "A Halo for Angel Investors," *McKinsey Quarterly* 1 (2004): 6–8.

64. Carden and Darragh, "Halo for Angel Investors," 6.

Suggested Readings

Eikenberry, Angela M., and Jessica E. Bearman. "The Impact of Giving Together: Giving Circles' Influence on Members' Philanthropic and Civic Behaviors, Knowledge, and Attitudes." Forum of Regional Associations of Grantmakers, 2009. http://www. givingforum.org/s_forum/bin.asp?CID=611&DID=25090&DOC=FILE.PD.

Gibson, Cynthia. *Funder Collaboratives: Why and How Funders Work Together.* New York: Grantcraft, 2009.

Kania, John, and Mark Kramer. "Collective Impact." *Stanford Social Innovation Review*, Winter 2011, 36–41.

Philanthropic Initiative, The. "Donor Collaboration: Power in Numbers." Philanthropic Initiative, April 13, 2009. http://www.tpi.org/resources/primer/donor_collaboration_power_in.aspx.

Preston, Susan L. "Angel Investment Groups, Networks, and Funds: A Guidebook to Developing the Right Angel Organization for Your Community." Ewing Marion Kauffman Foundation, August 2004. http://www.kauffman.org/entrepreneurship/angel-investment-guidebook.aspx.

PART III

NEW TOOLS

CHAPTER 11

OVERVIEW: THE NEW TOOLS OF "PHILANTHROPY"

Luther M. Ragin Jr.

IN THE PAST DECADE WE have seen an increasing flow of new investment tools for promoting social and environmental objectives. These tools, like the ones highlighted in Part 3 of this volume, often span a variety of asset classes—from cash equivalents to private equity. Similarly, some are below-market in their return expectations, while others seek and achieve risk-adjusted market-rate returns.

The proliferation of these tools offers both an opportunity and a challenge to philanthropic leaders and private investors, both institutional and individual—an opportunity in that they offer an increasingly compelling case to broaden and diversify the "toolbox" used to achieve positive social and environmental impact. The very existence and reported productivity of these tools place two seminal questions at the fore of philanthropic and financial discourse: first, for philanthropists, is a grant always the best instrument for achieving impact? And for investors, is financial return the only type of return to seek through investments?

At the same time, these tools pose a challenge. Outside of the familiar terrain of grantmaking, are investors able to assess the social or environmental impact of investments? And can they distinguish the creation of *real* social value from mere packaging? Similarly, can social return be measured with the rigor needed to give comfort to investors that their resources are making a difference?

Why Now?

What has happened in the past decade that has presented philanthropy and investors with these new opportunities? What are some of the factors that have challenged the "conventional wisdom" that philanthropic objectives are best achieved when investment decisions are made independent of social considerations and that investment decisions should be driven by considerations of financial return alone? I believe there are at least five:

- First, the continuing shortfall in traditional philanthropic and governmental resources versus demonstrated social needs
- Second, the growing sophistication of nonprofit practitioners and social entrepreneurs, particularly those in high-performing

organizations, for whom scale and sustainability have become strategic and operational imperatives
- Third, the realization by both foundations and private investors that some investments can achieve satisfactory financial returns while promoting positive social and environmental goals
- Fourth, a wider awareness among philanthropists and investors of the use and value of a broader toolbox for social engagement
- Finally, and perhaps most important, the wider acceptance of a role for market-based solutions in addressing social challenges from community development to environmental stewardship to global poverty

The Paradox of the Conventional Wisdom

It is ironic, of course, that the conventional wisdom—embraced most strongly by the devotees of private markets—often precludes our integrating what we know about investments and markets into philanthropic practice in order to maximize the *total* return on investment dollars. Commitment to a "grants only" strategy under-resources nonprofits and other social enterprises and limits them to often unsustainable, subsidy-dependent business models.

The conventional wisdom is particularly notably behind philanthropy's famed "Chinese wall" (the traditional separation of investment and programs) where there is often an implicit belief, by both investment and program staff, that investment and markets have a limited role in solving social and environmental problems. The effect of such a mutually reinforcing belief system may be to suboptimize social effort and performance.

An alternative vision, reflected in the chapters that follow, seeks bolder experimentation and the consideration of a broader toolbox for impact. Some institutions that ran full gallop into illiquid alternative investments in the past decade, often with unhappy consequences, have slowly begun to appreciate that many social-oriented investments provide reliable and uncorrelated returns. Others discovered that the simple act of placing insured deposits in social-purpose banks or low-income-designated credit unions provided affordable credit to the poor while allowing the institutions themselves to rediscover that cash equivalents really do have a place in a balanced, diversified investment portfolio.

FIGURE 11.1
Impact-Investing Continuum

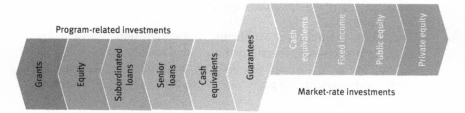

The Mission-Investing Continuum

The investment tools described here are not limited to any particular asset class or premised on any single rationale. But they suggest a fundamental question: can we accomplish greater social impact using a broader toolbox than we can through traditional philanthropy alone?

A useful tool for thinking about these issues is the social-impact-investing continuum first introduced by the F.B. Heron Foundation (see Figure 11.1). It organizes investment opportunities by asset class (e.g., cash equivalents, fixed income, public equity, private equity) and financial return (below-market and risk-adjusted market rate). The relative risks of various asset classes are recognized with the least risky asset classes arrayed toward the center of the continuum with greater financial risk reflected as one proceeds to the various ends of the continuum. Consequently, the continuum permits consideration of risk, return, and potential impact concurrently. By identifying the areas of the continuum where an investor believes it has the internal capacity and risk tolerance to invest, it permits a disciplined search for appropriate deal flow, consistent with asset class-specific performance benchmarks.

But are there sufficient "good" opportunities for prospective impact investors? In truth, the answer is there will never be enough opportunities, in a normative sense. But just as many investment tools in the chapters that follow did not exist 10 years ago, the landscape will continue to evolve with the breadth and quality of institutional demand.

Suffice it to say that today an investor committed to positive social or environmental change may find solid investment opportunities in a number of asset classes.

CHAPTER 12

LOANS, LOAN GUARANTEES, AND OTHER CREDIT ENHANCEMENTS*

Norah McVeigh and Julia Sass Rubin

IN 2007 FIRST BOOK WAS on a mission: giving children from low-income families the opportunity to read and own their first new books. Through the DC-based nonprofit's two programs—Book Bank, a centralized online system for publishers to donate books for distribution to disadvantaged kids, and Marketplace, an online bookstore that purchased books and resold them to community-based programs at deep discounts—it was reaching 1,000 programs serving low-income children. But First Book felt it could do more. If it expanded Marketplace, it could put more books in the hands of children faster and, equally important, it could generate net revenue that would reduce its dependence on grant funding (a time-consuming and unpredictable process). But expanding Marketplace would require $1.5 million for book inventory, a technology platform, and a marketing and outreach system. Where could the organization quickly find that kind of capital before others grabbed its Marketplace model?

As a nonprofit, First Book did not have access to equity, and securing grant funds from foundations could take several years. So the organization decided to borrow the money it needed. With a 10-year track record and a business plan in hand, the group obtained a $1.5 million loan from three lenders that supported the organization's social mission. The loan would be repaid from Marketplace sales, with payments scheduled so that they matched the anticipated revenue from the program.

Because First Book was counting on ambitious growth that was not assured, the lenders required that the organization create a debt service reserve by setting aside sufficient cash to make the first 12 months of loan payments. These funds, which would be put into a separate bank account, would serve as a "credit enhancement," or a way to improve the quality of First Book's creditworthiness in this transaction. Their purpose was to assure the lenders that their loans would be repaid in case Marketplace did not generate sufficient revenue to make the required payments.

In the end, Marketplace exceeded projections. By 2010, it was working with 6,000 programs and generating $6.5 million in revenue, years ahead of schedule, and First Book was able to repay the loan early. The organization's use of debt to address its timing issue—the gap between when it needed the funds to expand and when it could generate cash from sales or fundraising—shows how debt can sometimes meet a need for capital. And it underscores the positive role that debt and credit enhancement can play in helping nonprofit enterprises do their important work.

Borrowing money to achieve a desired end has been around for as long as humans have been doing business with one another. It also has been used for many years, by both individuals and governments, as an instrument of social benefit: to build homes, schools, roads, health clinics, bridges, and more. Congress even authorized the use of loans by foundations in the Tax Reform Act of 1969, which specifically allowed foundations to make so-called program-related investments (PRIs), generally in the form of loans, and treat them as equivalent to grants in meeting foundation "payout" requirements. Foundations such as Ford, Rockefeller, John D. and Catherine P. MacArthur, and F.B. Heron have made extensive use of PRI debt as a philanthropic tool. The complementary credit-enhancement tools have been around for just as long.

Today, there is a dizzying array of exotically named debt instruments—derivatives, actuarially priced debt pools, auction rate securities, and interest-rate swaps, to name just a few. The basic concept of debt, however, is quite simple: a lender provides cash to a borrower, with the expectation that the borrower will repay the cash at an agreed-upon time in the future. Used properly, credit can enable a host of activities that would otherwise be difficult, if not impossible. And, contrary to many people's assumptions, debt is extensively used by nonprofits to secure money for operations. In fact, debt levels among nonprofits are approximately the same as they are among for-profits of similar size.[1]

Despite their widespread use in the social sector, debt and credit enhancement remain widely misunderstood and frequently misused. Those in the social sector tend to use financial terminology imprecisely, and this is especially confusing with respect to loans. For example, both lenders and borrowers use terms such as "investment" to refer to different types of cash infusions made for purposes as diverse as buying a building, paying the salary of a fundraiser, and buying inventory; and in forms ranging from loans to grants to conventional equity. The key to the effective use of debt for social-sector leverage lies in understanding what the tool can and cannot do, how it works (and where it does not work), and when and how debt, whatever its source and purpose, can be employed to maximum advantage.

Defining the Tool

Debt comes in many different forms. In this chapter, we exclude from our discussion one class of debt instruments known as "bonds." Bonds are a form of loan. However, while most loans are held by the lender for their full term, the purchasers of bonds can actively trade them on a specialized market. Also, loans typically are issued for sums in the thousands, hundreds of thousands, or millions of dollars (or comparable sums in other currencies). While bonds can also be used for deals requiring millions of dollars, they often are issued in denominations in the billions or hundreds of billions of dollars. Bond issuances also have much more complex regulatory and legal restrictions. Because of these differences, this volume treats bonds in a separate chapter (Chapter 13).

To understand debt, it is important first to understand its terminology:

> A *loan* is a transaction in which one party with cash (the *lender*) allows another party (the *borrower*) to use its cash for a period of time—essentially renting out its cash. To compensate the lender for the use of its cash, the borrower pays *interest*. The cash being loaned is called *principal*. *Maturity* refers to the date on which the loan must be repaid.

Sometimes lenders require that a borrower strengthen its "credit" (its apparent ability to repay a loan), or the borrower wishes to obtain more favorable loan terms. The tool used to accomplish this is called a *credit enhancement*. It is typically needed when the actual or perceived financial condition of the project or the borrower, or the underlying market conditions, make it impossible for a borrower to obtain or handle debt financing without an enhancement. In some cases, a borrower might be able to get a loan, but the credit enhancement provides the lender with an incentive to offer more favorable rates and terms.

In the traditional market, higher-risk deals command higher interest rates, since lenders want to be paid for the risk they are taking. If a borrower can provide some form of credit enhancement, it can induce the lender to lower the interest rate or offer a longer term (repayment period) than the loan would otherwise warrant, making the loan more affordable for the borrower.

Credit enhancements can take the form of cash set aside to repay part of the loan, such as the *reserves* in the First Book example. They also can take the form of *loan guarantees*, which are agreements from other parties that they will repay the loan should the primary borrower default. Other common forms of credit enhancement include letters of credit, subordinate loans, and interest subsidies, all of which are discussed further in subsequent sections of this chapter.

Defining Features of Loans

As outlined elsewhere in this book, debt is one of three sources of capital available to social-sector organizations, *grants* and *equity* being the other two sources. Loans have several defining features that distinguish them from these other types of capital.

Lenders Expect Repayment

Unlike both grants and equity, a borrower is required to repay a loan to the provider of capital (the lender), regardless of whether or not the project that the lender financed was successful, and whether or not the financial condition of the borrower has improved or declined over the course of the loan. In fact, this expectation of repayment is a loan's most critical defining feature.

Borrowers Pay Lenders Interest and Fees

Lenders charge "rent" on the money they lend in the form of *interest*. Think about this as a *return* on *principal*, as opposed to a return *of* principal. Interest is typically calculated as a percentage of the principal and can vary, depending on the lender. A loan might be interest-free if the lender is willing to structure it that way, or it might be at market rate, or somewhere in between. The use of credit enhancements might reduce the interest rate the lender is seeking—in essence, providing the lender with additional assurances of repayment in exchange for a lower interest rate. In addition, some lenders charge the borrower application, origination, or commitment fees in a set dollar amount or *points* (a percentage of the face value of the loan), as a one-time charge for underwriting the loan.

Loans Are Documented

Agreed-upon loan terms are formalized in written legal documents that are binding on both the lender and the borrower. The number and complexity of the legal documents may vary, depending on the situation. The most important legal document is the *promissory note*, which memorializes the obligation of the borrower to repay the loan and typically includes the interest rate and the dates on which interest and principal payments are expected. The promissory note is frequently accompanied by a *loan agreement*, which details any other obligations, such as how the loan can be used, reporting obligations, financial restrictions, and any penalties for not adhering to the terms of the agreement.

Lenders Seek a "Second Way Out"

The lender not only expects the borrower to return principal and interest, it also may expect additional assurance that it can recoup its capital or "get out" of the loan. The borrower may be required to pledge other assets, such as real property, cash, or stocks, which will be taken by the lender in the event the borrower cannot repay the loan and defaults. Those assets, when they are pledged to back up a loan, are *collateral*. Collateral serves two purposes: First, it provides an incentive for a borrower to repay the loan, since the borrower risks losing its buildings or cash reserve in the event of a default. The borrower, therefore, has an incentive to take the loan more seriously than it might if the loan were not collateralized. Second, in the event the borrower cannot repay the loan, the lender can get its money back by taking possession of the collateral, selling it, and using the cash from the sale to satisfy the loan. In addition to collateral, a credit enhancement in the form of a loan guarantee or reserve can provide a "second way out" for the lender by requiring the loan guarantor to repay the obligation if the primary borrower defaults. Sometimes a lender will accept credit enhancement in place of collateral, and sometimes a lender will require both credit enhancement and collateral.

Nonpayment Has Consequences

In most cases, the consequences of nonpayment can be severe, and borrowers should be prepared for this possibility. Nonpayment results in late fees and higher interest rates and legal actions; borrowers can lose their collateral and be forced into bankruptcy. There are cases in which lenders forgo collection of a struggling loan because of the borrower's social mission, the cost to the lender of pursuing collection, or the lender's concern about potential public and media scrutiny of collection methods. However, most lenders will pursue all avenues to get repaid. When lenders do agree to forgive some of the loan, the borrower may still pay a price, as the damage to its reputation and credit history may hamper its future ability to raise funds.

Defining Features of Credit Enhancements

Credit enhancements have many of the same defining features as loans. Specifically, some types of credit enhancements require the borrower to pay interest and fees, as is the case with loans. This is especially the case when the enhancement takes the form of subordinate debt or guarantee. Subordinate debt (debt that is paid off after the other financial obligations of a defaulting organization have been satisfied) has an interest rate associated with it, while a guarantee usually has a fee. In some cases, the borrower also will be expected to cover the legal costs of negotiating and closing the credit enhancement.

As with debt, credit enhancements are evidenced through legal documents. The complexity of the documentation will vary, based on the type of credit enhancement. Guarantees frequently require one or two documents and subordinate debt a minimum of three (loan agreement, promissory note, and intercreditor agreement).

Providers of credit enhancement also may require a second way out. For example, the credit enhancement provider could ask the borrower to sign an agreement that requires the borrower to reimburse the provider for any losses incurred in case the borrower defaults on the loan. Depending on the financial condition of the borrower following a default, it might be difficult for the credit enhancement provider to recoup any of its losses. However, it could still choose to pursue legal measures to achieve reimbursement.

The most critical defining feature of a credit enhancement, however, is that it shifts the risk in the transaction from the lender to the credit enhancer. The provider of credit enhancement takes a less attractive or riskier position in the transaction vis-à-vis some other financing party, in order to induce the lender to make the loan.

Relation to Common Criteria

Risk

Lending is all about risk. But there are different types of risk. All loans carry financial and reputational risk to both the lender and the borrower. Loans to social-purpose entities also carry stewardship risk, which extends to parties beyond the lender and borrower.

A loan entails financial and reputational risks for the borrower, who may not be able to repay the loan and could lose valuable collateral and suffer reputational damage and a downgrade of its credit history, a key concern for its ability to obtain any future financing.

A loan also entails financial and reputational risks for the lender because the funds might not be repaid. The lender might not receive the interest payments it expects, and might even lose the principal if the borrower fails to repay the loan. If the loan is severely delinquent, the lender might have to spend additional funds to work out the problems with the borrower and to attempt recovery of some or all of the principal and interest. This could include taking possession of collateral and liquidating it or pursuing the loan guarantor to obtain payment. Unanticipated expenses might include legal costs, property expenses (if the lender forecloses and takes possession of real-estate collateral and must maintain it until it is sold), and the cost of loan work-out experts. Lastly, of course, there is "opportunity risk" because the lender, whose capital is tied up in a poorly performing loan, has forgone an investment with a better financial return.

Lenders also face the less tangible reputational risk of financing a project or organization that might turn out to be controversial, or possibly even involve criminal activity. In some instances there might be both financial and reputational repercussions for a lender—for instance, when a borrower claims "lender liability," saying the lender directed it to take certain actions that compromised its ability to repay the loan. In such a case, the lender might not only lose its principal and interest, it might be sued by the borrower as well.

While all lenders have a basic professional responsibility to avoid saddling borrowers with debt that is too burdensome, loans made for social purposes carry an additional stewardship responsibility to a larger constituency. For example, when the borrower is an organization that provides shelter and aid to victims of domestic violence, a loan that proves too challenging and ultimately financially damaging to the borrower might cause the organization to curtail programs or cease operations, a potential loss of vital services to vulnerable people. Such stewardship risk also carries reputational risk for the lender, from the negative publicity associated with curtailing or shutting down a provider of socially beneficial services.

While loans entail risk for the lender, that risk is still less severe than the risk involved in some other tools. For example, loans must be repaid even if an enterprise is not earning profits. Equity investments, however, may never be paid off if an enterprise loses money or goes out of business. In fact, in enterprises with both debt and equity, loan payments (interest and principal) will always be paid before any returns to equity holders. Grants, on the other hand, carry very limited financial or reputational risks, as they generally are not expected to be repaid.

Return

Lenders make money by providing loans that carry an interest rate. The riskier the loan, the higher the interest rate, which yields a higher return, to compensate for the greater risk that the loan funds will be lost. Riskier loans also cost the lender more in staff time spent trying to recoup the loans in case of default.

Examples of loans that carry higher financial returns as a result of higher-risk profiles include loans to subprime borrowers (borrowers with less than pristine credit); loans with longer terms (20 and 30 years) because it is harder for the lender to assess the state of the economy and the borrower's ability to repay that far into the future; and small unsecured lines of credit (including credit cards).

Typically the return on loans is lower, but more consistent, than the return on equity. Since equity providers take greater risks than lenders, they expect higher returns. For example, most loan interest rates in advanced market economies currently are 4 to 8 percent, while expected returns on equity investments are as high as 20 to 30 percent. This is also true for loans and equity investments made to social-purpose organizations. For example, a 2010 study of social-impact investing found that average returns expected for debt was 0 to 5 percent, whereas for equity it was 15 to 20 percent.[2] By definition, grants do not generate returns and usually do not have to be repaid.

In addition to generating financial returns, loans also may generate social benefits, such as jobs created as a result of a business expansion. Such benefits may be an overt objective or a byproduct of the loan. When the social impact is an objective for the lender, borrowers generally must produce and report social return metrics that, at a minimum, make it possible to connect financial investments to resulting social benefits.

These social benefits generally are framed as output measures (for example, how many children are vaccinated), changes from year to year (an increase in the number of children vaccinated), and outcome measures (a drop in the incidence of polio). The practice of seeking social as well as financial returns has been dubbed "double bottom line" lending. Projects that also have an environmental, or green, component often create the opportunity for "triple bottom line" returns.[3]

Leverage

In finance, "leverage" is a technique for multiplying gains. With loans, both financial and social gains are possible. From a financial perspective, debt is a means to achieve leverage when the debt allows the borrower to increase its assets, which in turn generates more net revenue. For example, a loan that helps a health center purchase computers and software to improve insurance and Medicaid billing—thus reducing time spent tracking down and collecting payments—can have the leverage of lowering expenses and increasing revenue.

Leverage also refers to the ability of one piece of financing to attract additional financing, or to fill a project gap. For instance, a borrower might be able to raise 80 percent of the funds needed to purchase a building through grants. The remaining 20 percent project gap could be provided by a grant from another source, an equity investment, or a loan, which enables the entire project to move forward. In this way, loans are similar to grants and equity in their ability to leverage.

There is a third type of leverage that relates to the ability to revolve the funds used from one project or investment to a second or a third. When loans are repaid or returns of equity are realized, those funds can then be used to make loans or equity investments in other deals. Grants do not offer this type of leverage since the funds generally are not returned.

Credit enhancements also increase leverage and can be the critical piece necessary to allow a project to go forward. Without the credit enhancement, the lender may not agree to provide the loan, so the borrower would not have the financing needed to build a building or expand a program.

For example, the Low Income Investment Fund (LIIF), a community development financial institution that lends primarily to nonprofits, partnered with the investor United Methodist Pension Fund to establish a guarantee of $260,000 as a credit enhancement for a $2.6 million loan to a New York City homeless shelter.[4] As Nancy Andrews, the head of LIIF, pointed out, "Given the AA credit enhancement ... LIIF induced even the most hard-boiled, profit-oriented firm on Wall Street to invest in a homeless shelter on Staten Island."[5]

Different forms of credit enhancements generate different levels of leverage. For example, a foundation can increase leverage by using subordinate debt rather than grant funds to fill a capital gap in a project. As the foundation's subordinated loan is repaid, it can recycle those funds to use for another project. A foundation can also increase leverage by using the assets on its balance sheet to guarantee a loan rather than using a grant, because the foundation does not have to restrict use of its assets during the duration of the guarantee, which enables them to be used for other purposes.

Another example of credit enhancement increasing leverage is the US Department of Education Credit Enhancement for Charter School Facilities program, which provides federal grants to serve as guarantees against charter school loan losses, reducing lenders' exposure in the event that a charter school defaults on its loans. The program played an important role in making charter school financing more available by providing $242 million in credit enhancements since 2001. This funding has supported or enabled "$2.71 billion in total financing for charter school facilities" and provided "approximately 8 percent of charter schools nationwide with access to financing to help them acquire, build, lease, or renovate school facilities."[6]

Ubiquity

Loans and credit enhancement have widespread applicability in the social sector. Loans can be used to acquire long-term assets, such as buildings, or fill short-term cash needs, such as bridging expected payments (receivables financing). They also can help facilitate "product or service diversification, expansion of existing service levels, investment to lower costs or raise productivity, quality improvements," or the ability to "take advantage of leverage."[7]

Analyses of IRS data in 1986 and in 2007 support the importance of debt, showing that 60 to 70 percent of nonprofits had some type of debt outstanding.[8] In fact, as of 2007, nonprofits had average debt-to-asset ratios comparable to those of US manufacturing firms, a sector that requires high levels of debt because of the need to purchase expensive equipment.[9]

Despite this high overall reliance on debt among nonprofits, its use varies widely among individual organizations, with some nonprofits taking on large amounts of debt while others use very little debt.[10] For example, IRS data revealed that debt-to-asset ratios for international youth development organizations averaged 12 percent, while for housing organizations they averaged 77 percent.[11]

This reflects significant variation in nonprofits' ability to access debt. As with for-profit organizations, successful nonprofit borrowers require access to a reliable flow of revenue sufficient to pay off the loan with interest, or the likelihood that the project or program that the loan is financing will lead to such a flow of revenue. This is most likely when the organization is funded by one or more reasonably secure government programs, serves clients directly able to pay for the organization's services, or enjoys steady access to charitable support. Not all social-purpose organizations are in this position.

Debt capital is also more accessible for medium- and large-sized nonprofits—such as universities, hospitals, museums, and large social-service agencies—that have access to credit from a variety of sources. Conventional lenders such as banks will more readily provide financing to these types of entities because of their track records, predictable revenue streams, available collateral, experienced boards and management teams, well-developed financial systems and reporting, and the size of their revenue and assets.

On the other hand, smaller nonprofits (typically those with annual expenses between $500,000 and $15 million) have more limited access to conventional credit because of their more modest assets and revenue, unpredictable revenue streams, limited collateral, and less specialized management. Social-purpose start-up organizations also have a hard time obtaining conventional loans as they lack the demonstrated track record that lenders frequently require.

A 2006 survey also suggests that many nonprofits may not be able to access the levels of debt that they require. The survey found significant unmet need for "investment capital ... the revenue needed to finance items intended to last more than a year," among human-service, community development, and arts nonprofits of all sizes and fields of activity.[12]

Operational Complexity

If debt is provided successfully, the principal and interest will be repaid, the credit enhancement will not be used, the programmatic aims will be achieved, and the costs of making the loans will be covered. However, all this requires knowledge or experience in underwriting and an understanding of the economics of the lending and credit enhancement business.

Underwriting, described more fully later in this chapter, is the lender's and credit enhancement provider's way of analyzing both the borrower and the market to determine whether the borrower can fulfill its obligations. At its most basic, this requires the ability to assess the financial wherewithal of the borrower and evaluate its position in the market and its prospects going forward. It also requires the ability to structure a loan and credit enhancement to meet the needs of the borrower and the requirements of the lender. Lenders and credit enhancement providers best positioned to be successful and bring benefit to borrowers also possess the following characteristics:

- Experience (a track record of successfully providing loans or credit enhancements), market knowledge, constructive dispassion, and ability to add value as a *business* advisor
- Deal sense: the ability to quickly grasp whether the borrower's financial need will be fulfilled by a loan or credit enhancement, and what structure is required to meet it
- Speed in decision-making, ability to deliver on promises, and clarity as to whether the lender's or credit enhancement provider's willingness to take risks and the products they offer are a good fit with the borrower's needs
- Efficiency with business aspects (closing, documentation, disbursement), and leadership among lenders and credit enhancement providers, if other parties are involved
- Understanding of the specific economic and policy context in which the borrower operates (for example, the role health clinics play in low-income communities, what alternatives exist in those communities for healthcare provision, and the economic viability of such clinics in light of the first two factors)

The successful provision of equity and grants also requires specialized expertise. Loans and equity both require the ability to assess if the enterprise can generate sufficient profits to enable repayment. However, equity has an additional layer of complexity, as it represents an ownership stake in the enterprise and, with that ownership, come rights or obligations. For example, equity owners may have a seat on the board of directors of the enterprise. They also may advise management of the enterprise on operations, something that lenders are actively discouraged from doing by the threat of lender liability.

Grant provision is less complex than debt or equity. While the grantmaker is certainly looking for its grant to produce positive results, the decision to make the grant carries fewer risks and therefore less need for a deep understanding of financial and market conditions and for lengthy documentation.

Social Implications

Loans and credit enhancements to social-purpose organizations provide three types of social benefits: (1) they fill financing gaps, enabling the borrowers to fulfill their social missions; (2) they help develop the social-purpose debt market for conventional lenders, making it easier for social-purpose organizations to obtain loans in the future; and (3) they allow lenders and credit enhancement providers to recycle capital and thereby spread the benefits further, as discussed in the leverage section of this chapter.

Filling financing gaps entails making debt available for activities or developments that are otherwise difficult to finance. As previously discussed, many nonprofits find it challenging to access debt from conventional lenders because they do not fit their lending criteria. This has necessitated the rise of a whole new set of "social purpose" lenders. Most notable among these in the United States are community development financial institutions (CDFIs), which are financial intermediaries that borrow capital from governments, foundations, and conventional financial institutions and relend it primarily to nonprofit organizations, as discussed in Chapter 2 of this volume.

CDFIs and other social-purpose lenders view the products they provide as not only filling immediate capital gaps, but also building a social-purpose debt market that eventually will become sufficiently profitable to attract more traditional sources of capital and loan products to the market. For example, CDFIs provided the initial facility and working capital financing for charter schools, as traditional lenders were hesitant to lend to them in the face of uncertainty over the charter-renewal process, heated political disputes, and the absence of a management track record. As the charter-school market has grown, conventional sources of capital have been attracted to the field, which now has access to bond financing and bank loans.

Design Features and Major Variants of Loans

As noted earlier, a dizzying array of loan products is now available, including senior debt, mezzanine debt, mortgage loans, bridge loans, balloon loans, bullet loans, permanent financing, and construction financing. Similarly, credit enhancements also take a wide array of forms, from various types of guarantees and reserves to different subordinations and interest subsidies. Distinguishing among these products can be confusing. However, debt options can generally be categorized in two ways: by the purpose or intended use of the loan; and by the structure of the loan. Similarly, credit enhancements can be categorized in terms of their type—funded or unfunded, and their structure.

Purpose of Loans

Loans are generally used to finance one of three primary activities or purposes: real estate, equipment acquisition, or working capital needs.

Real Estate Loans. Real estate related loans can be used at any stage of the project and for a variety of needs. Common uses of real estate loans are predevelopment financing to cover the upfront costs of a real estate project; acquisition loans, used to purchase land or buildings; and construction or renovation loans, used to cover the costs of construction or renovation.

Equipment Loans. Equipment loans, or term loans, are typically used to purchase equipment, such as computers and phone systems. They also can be used for other capital needs, such as the purchase of lighting for a theatre.

Working Capital Loans. Working capital loans are used to cover general operating expenses until expected revenue or income is realized or received. There are three primary types of working capital loans: bridge loans used to bridge payments, typically from a government agency or other funder; lines of credit to cover cyclical or regular delays in revenue; and financing to support the expansion of the organization or business.

Structure of Loans

The second way to distinguish loans is by structure: when and under what conditions the borrower can have access to the loan funds; when the borrower must make interest and principal payments; the term (duration) of the loan; what collateral requirements the lender has; and what type of interest rate the loan carries.

With regard to the first of these issues, some loans, such as acquisition or equipment loans, require or expect the borrower to take all of the loan funds at closing. Others permit the borrower to access the funds over time as they are needed (frequently referred to as the *draw* or *disbursement period*). For example, construction loans frequently have drawdown periods that allow the borrower to access funds to pay the contractor as it completes the project. Working capital lines of credit also have drawdown periods, so the borrower is only borrowing the amount that it needs, at the time that it needs it.

Another aspect of loan structure is the timing of when the borrower must make payments of interest and principal. Most loans require the borrower to begin paying interest immediately on the amount it has borrowed. Alternatively, the lender may allow the interest to accrue and either be added to the principal of the loan (*capitalized interest*) or paid in a lump sum, either during or after the completion of the loan period.

Some loans include a period of time during which only interest payments are required, with principal repayment beginning after that set period of time. Construction loans, predevelopment loans, and lines of credit are examples of these types of loans. Loan principal payments also have a schedule (how frequently and in what amounts the borrower has to make payments), and lenders usually strive to match the principal payments to when the borrower expects to have cash available to repay the loan.

Many loans have an amortization feature, meaning the borrower pays the principal in regular installments, over the duration of the loan. Loans may be self-amortizing, with regular payments of principal and interest that result in the loan being fully repaid at the end of its term. Equipment financing is an example of this type of loan in that it requires monthly or quarterly payments of principal (along with interest) over the life of the loan. Loans can also be partially amortized over time, but not completely paid off, with the remaining unpaid principal (called the balloon) due at the end of the loan term. For a loan with a five-year term and 15-year amortization, for example, approximately one-third of the principal will be paid by the end of five years, leaving two-thirds of the loan unpaid. Borrowers with partially amortizing loans must either raise or save enough cash to repay the loan, or, more commonly, seek out another lender to refinance the loan.

The term or duration of the loan is also a critical component. Generally loans are referred to as short term (anywhere from a few months to a couple of years), medium term (three to seven years), or long term (more than seven years). Construction loans and lines of credit are short term, typically 12 to 24 months. Equipment loans are medium term (three to five years), matching the useful life of the equipment purchased. Permanent financing is long-term (seven to 25 years), matching the useful life of the building purchased or built.

Loans are also structured with or without collateral. *Secured*, or *collateralized, loans* are loans for which the borrower has pledged an asset. If the borrower fails to repay the loan, the lender can take possession of the asset and liquidate it to repay the loan. One of the most commonly pledged assets is real estate, typically land or a building (in which case the loan is frequently referred to as a mortgage loan). Loans for which the borrower has not pledged any assets are called *unsecured loans*.

The final key aspect of loan structure is the type of interest rate charged. Loans have either fixed or floating interest rates. With fixed-rate loans, the interest rate is set at closing and does not change over the term of the loan. Floating- or adjustable-rate loans have interest rates that change when the base rate changes. The interest rate on floating-rate loans is typically based on one of two indices—the prime rate or the LIBOR rate—and when that base rate changes, the interest rate on the loan changes.[13] Loans also may have a rate "reset" feature whereby the rate is fixed for some period—typically three or five years—after which the lender has the opportunity to reset the rate.

Design Features and Major Variants of Credit Enhancements

Credit enhancements also come in different forms, depending on their purpose. Primary credit enhancements are guarantees, letters of credit, subordinate loans, reserves, interest subsidies, and tax incentives.

Guarantees are a common form of credit enhancement and consist of a promise by another entity to pay the principal, interest, or both, if the borrower is unable to make those payments. The guarantee's provider may be required to place some funds aside, to demonstrate that it has the funds available to honor the guarantee if necessary (considered a funded guarantee). Alternatively, the guarantee provider may be able to demonstrate sufficient resources to cover the guarantee by sharing its financial statements (an unfunded guarantee). The provider of the guarantee may or may not charge the borrower a fee for the guarantee.

Guarantees can be provided by individuals (board members, for example), a parent corporation, an affiliated entity, government agencies, or foundations. One of the longest running guarantee programs is the US Small Business Administration (SBA) guarantees for loans made by banks and other lenders to small businesses.[14] The existence of this program makes clear that nonprofits are not the only smaller economic entities needing credit enhancements to access and afford loans. The SBA program is only available to for-profit businesses, however, and no general purpose government guarantee program is available to nonprofits.

Over the last decade, nonprofits have therefore turned to foundations to guarantee social-purpose loans, and at least some foundations have responded, as detailed more fully in Chapter 5 of this volume. In 2011, for example, the Kresge Foundation adopted a policy allowing the foundation to make up to $50 million in loan guarantees. The foundation, which commits "a modest portion of its grant budget to provide for possible future calls on the guarantee," sees such guarantees as "a useful tool to meet a borrower's financing needs, leverage capital from other sources and preserve the foundation's assets."[15]

A second form of credit enhancement that is similar to guarantees is a letter of credit, an agreement from a bank or other type of financial institution guaranteeing payment if the borrower defaults. Letters of credit are often used in bond financing, with the bond purchaser requiring a letter of credit to support the bonds.

A third form of credit enhancement is the subordinated (mezzanine) loan, in which a lender agrees to provide a loan but to take a subordinate position behind another, typically conventional, lender (called the senior lender) when it comes to repayment of the debt. In the event the borrower lacks cash to make full debt payments, the senior lender receives its payments first and the subordinate lender receives payments only after the senior lender has been paid, thus absorbing all or part of the shortfall.

The subordinate lender in conventional transactions typically receives a higher interest rate than the senior lender, to reflect the higher risk of loss. Social-purpose lenders, however, may provide lower subordinate loan rates. This not only provides the senior lender with some protection, it also reduces the amount of interest the borrower might have otherwise paid, helping to increase the borrower's chance of successful repayment and further its social impact.

A fourth form of credit enhancement consists of reserves that are set aside to cover a portion of loan payments. Two common types of reserves are loan loss reserves and debt service reserves. Loan loss reserves are typically provided by third parties (e.g., foundations) in order to allow lenders to extend credit to borrowers that they otherwise would deem too risky. Debt service reserves are typically set up by the borrower, either with its own cash or, more commonly, by building the cost of the reserve into the total amount of the loan. Once the loan is made, the portion intended for the loan reserve is set aside to cover interest and principal payments, either during a specified period of time or any time that the borrower does not have the cash to make the required payments.

Interest subsidies are a fifth form of credit enhancement. Unlike guarantees and reserve accounts, which provide payments to a lender if the borrower is unable to repay the loan, interest subsidies lower a loan's interest rate, reducing a loan's risk by making it more affordable for the borrower. Interest subsidies frequently take the form of grants or similar funding. A recent US example is the qualified school construction bond (QSCB) program, created as part of the American Recovery and Reinvestment Act of 2009. QSCBs allow borrowing at minimal or no interest for the rehabilitation, repair, and equipping of schools, or to purchase land on which public schools will be built. Under the program, the federal government agrees to pay a certain amount of interest on behalf of the schools.[16]

The sixth form of credit enhancement is a tax incentive. There are various state and federal programs in the United States that provide tax incentives to spur investment in particular geographies or for particular types of projects. The Low Income Housing Tax Credit is a well-established program that provides tax incentives for investors to invest in affordable housing programs. Failure to comply with the program guidelines and requirements has tax consequences for the project developer and thus is seen as an incentive for the developer to meet its obligations, including loan repayments.

Patterns of Use

As discussed previously, although use of debt among nonprofits is high, access to debt capital is not uniform across the sector. Younger nonprofits and those with a smaller and less diversified asset base find it particularly challenging to obtain loans.[17] Nonprofits with a more inconsistent earning stream also are less likely to access debt because potential lenders perceive them as higher risk borrowers.[18] There also appears to be significant unmet need across the nonprofit sector, with organizations of various sizes and focus areas identifying difficulties accessing capital for items that will last more than a year.[19]

Another good measure of the overall demand for social-purpose loan capital is demand for capital to lend on the part of community development financial institutions (CDFIs), because of the key role that CDFIs play in financing nonprofits. Between 2006 and 2010 CDFIs saw their loans outstanding increase 54 percent from $2.58 billion to $3.98 billion.[20] According to a first-quarter 2011 survey of CDFIs, nearly 46 percent of respondents reported an increase in financing applications, and 48 percent reported an increase in loan originations over year-end 2010. Moreover, 67 percent of respondents expect demand for financing to continue growing.[21]

Demand for debt also increases in response to specific economic or policy changes. For example, in order to meet the Affordable Care Act's goal of serving 40 million additional patients within five years, US nonprofit community health centers, which are tasked with addressing a large portion of this demand, will have to invest $13.1 billion in physical, equipment, and technology infrastructure. Between 2005 and 2010, about a quarter (26 percent) of the centers' funding for such infrastructure projects was provided by debt, with grants and other cash and equity making up the rest. Assuming this pattern continues, the community health centers would have to raise approximately $3.5 million of debt over the next five years, a 230 percent increase on the $1.7 billion that they raised between 2006 and 2010.[22]

As demand for loans increases, so does the need for guarantees and other forms of credit enhancements, which have even more limited availability than capital for lending. For example, applications for the US Department of Education's Credit Enhancement for Charter School Facilities grant program has far exceeded the award amounts. In 2011 alone, $9.98 million in credit enhancement grant funds was made available, while the applications requested a total of $75.2 million.[23]

In addition to the broad reliance on debt among domestic nonprofits, it also is widely used in the international social investment field. A 2011 survey found that of the over 2,200 social investments reported, approximately 67 percent were in emerging markets across the world and approximately 75 percent used some form of debt as the investment vehicle, primarily in the form of un-secured loans.[24]

Tool Selection

Clearly, debt is an extremely important tool, with many benefits for borrowers and lenders. For borrowers, it typically provides the ability to access funds more quickly than if they applied for grants. And, by successfully borrowing and repaying loans, younger and smaller organizations can establish a credit track record that can enable them to access an even larger supply of capital. Furthermore, borrowers develop and hone a financial discipline that can serve them well in the long run, as well as a relationship with a knowledgeable financial partner who understands their business and can be helpful as they grow and evolve.

However, because debt comes with financial obligations and consequences, it is not appropriate for every social-purpose entity. While it takes less time to secure a loan than it does to get a grant, the borrower is likely to have to supply much more information to a lender than it would when applying for grants. Organizations that do not have the financial strength, the financial systems, and the information to accurately prepare and present financial information, assess and communicate their situation, and confidently manage their finances or reasonably plan for the future are ill-suited to borrowing funds, as are, of course, those with a history of nonpayment of debt.

Organizations that are unwilling to share information or contemplate problems or failures and develop requisite backup plans are generally not good candidates for debt given the regular communication expected by the lender and the long-term nature of the borrower-lender relationship. No plan ever gets implemented perfectly, and the borrower and lender must know that they can communicate and work together, whatever the circumstances.

Finally, debt only makes sense for organizations that enjoy access to a fairly reliable flow of resources, or can reasonably predict that such resources will result from the investment that the loan will make possible. In addition, access to loans typically requires the availability of some asset that can be used for collateral. Real estate is the most obvious such asset, which limits the use of loans to organizations involved in some type of real estate transaction, or with access to some other form of collateral, such as a guarantee from a foundation or other social-purpose entity.

Loans (like equity investments), frequently result in relationships with the social-purpose entity that are distinct from the grantee/grantor relationship, and for some lenders it can provide enormous satisfaction. By providing a loan, lenders enter into a relationship that frequently spans years and can yield both financial and programmatic results. A loan requires a lender to have a more robust relationship with an organization than a traditional grantmaker might. Whereas a grantmaker might focus on a single program, a lender is typically drawn into broader discussions concerning the entire organization, with special attention paid to the financial and economic aspects of the enterprise. Because the lender expects repayment, it must understand the underlying business dynamics of the organization and how the organization operates, in addition to its programmatic objectives.

Moreover, loans (again like equity investments) are typically in larger amounts than grants. Lenders thus have a larger impact on an organization than most grantmakers might. Because a lender is earning a financial return on the funds loaned, and expects to get the funds themselves repaid, it might be willing to place more funds with a single nonprofit group, in many cases enabling that borrower to undertake a larger program or project in a shorter period of time. In addition, because of the revolving nature of the capital—when the borrower pays back the loan, the lender can then relend the dollars to someone else, thus multiplying their impact in the market or community. Lastly, it is an opportunity for those who want to help increase access to debt for social-purpose organizations and are willing to step back as the market develops and becomes viable for more traditional sources of capital.

Socially motivated lenders that are interested in attracting other capital to the social-lending market should consider providing credit enhancement. This is a tool with tremendous potential and is particularly well suited for organizations, such as smaller foundations, that might want to use their balance sheet to provide guarantees without necessarily tying up cash.

On the other hand, loans and credit enhancement carry certain disadvantages for lenders. First, there is the possibility of loss. If the lender cannot tolerate loss, loans or credit enhancements are not appropriate tools for them to provide. The second disadvantage is cost. Operating a loan fund requires an ongoing commitment of resources that may not be feasible for everyone. Organizations that want to increase access to debt capital for nonprofits but have fewer resources to do so may want to consider lending to an existing community development financial institution, which can combine multiple sources of capital to fund the loans it makes to nonprofits.

Basic Mechanics

Financing with loans and credit enhancements happens in four phases: (1) identifying a credit need and alternatives to fill that need; (2) locating possible lenders and credit enhancement providers; (3) arranging the loan and credit enhancement (the due diligence, underwriting, and closing processes); and (4) managing the loan or credit enhancement after closing (making payments, reporting and working out any problems).

Identifying a Credit Need and Possible Solutions

Borrowers need debt financing when they have a need for more cash than they currently have on hand, or could reasonably expect to have in the near term, and equity and grants area not available or not cost-efficient to obtain.

The first step to obtaining debt financing is being able to specify the purpose, quantity, and timing of the financing need. An equally critical next step is identifying how the organization will generate the cash necessary to repay the loan. Proceeding with the loan process is only advisable if the borrower has a credible plan for repayment. If not, applying for a loan will be a futile use of resources.

Locating Lenders and Credit Enhancement Providers

Once the borrower has determined its financing needs, it can begin to identify and assess potential sources of that financing and whether it will need credit enhancement in order to secure that financing or obtain more attractive rates or terms. There are many potential sources of financing, as outlined in Chapters

1 and 2 of this volume. These include banks, foundations, and a variety of loan funds and intermediaries such as community development financial institutions, among others. Each of these lenders will have different areas of focus or priority, based on the type or purpose of the borrower, the size or stage of the borrowing the organization's development, and its location.

Lenders also have preferences for the types of products they provide and the size of loans they can make. Some are focused on real estate development and others on cash flow lending, or on financing technology. Certain lenders might also be restricted by the type of capital they have available to lend, with some having short-term capital and others long-term capital.

It can be a time-consuming process to identify the possible universe of lenders, and in some cases borrowers might seek the help of consultants in doing this. As the borrower investigates these options and identifies potential lenders, it also will be able to determine whether it will require credit enhancement to obtain the loan or to make its repayment more affordable. If credit enhancement is needed, either the lender may be able to connect the borrower with possible sources or the borrower will have to undertake a separate search for a provider. The universe of credit enhancement providers is likely smaller than for lenders. It typically consists of foundations, government programs, and individuals, such as board members of the borrower. One useful place to start might be with a foundation that has supported the organization in the part and that might be willing to offer a guarantee in lieu of, or in addition to, existing grant funding.

Arranging the Loans and Credit Enhancements

Moving from identifying sources of loans and credit enhancements to successfully obtaining a loan and credit enhancement entails five steps: due diligence; underwriting and structuring; getting approval; closing; and meeting the post-closing obligations.

Due Diligence

After a borrower and lender have reached an initial agreement that there is a potential match between the borrower's need and the lender's financing, they enter the due diligence and underwriting phase. During this step, which can take several weeks, months, or longer, the borrower provides information that helps the lender determine whether the borrower has the capacity to borrow and repay a loan. *Due diligence* is the process whereby the lender requests and the borrower provides key information about itself and its financing needs to the lender. *Underwriting* is the process whereby the lender analyzes that information to determine whether the borrower meets the lender's criteria.

During the underwriting process, the lender and borrower typically discuss and adjust the particular loan product and loan structure that will be provided. It is also during this part of the process that a lender will identify the need for collateral and the specific terms or conditions of the credit enhancement it requires. If a credit enhancement provider is considering the project, it will undertake a parallel due diligence and underwriting process, and the borrower will be working with that provider, as it is doing with the lender. In many cases, the borrower serves as the intermediary between the lender and the credit enhancement provider, sharing information and documents between them.

The extent of the due diligence process can vary depending on the purpose of a loan and the past relationship between the borrower, the lender, and the credit enhancer. Typical due diligence materials that a borrower will provide relate to its finances, management, and programs, and any issues related to the use and repayment of the loan.

A borrower's past and current financial performance is often an indicator of its future financial performance. To give the lender and credit enhancer a comprehensive understanding of its financials, the borrower usually will be required to submit three to five years of audited financial statements, the current year's budget, and the year-to-date financials for the current fiscal year. A borrower also can expect to provide information related to its history with debt and its current debt levels, as this will be an indication of whether the borrower can manage debt and whether it is taking on more debt than it can reasonably repay. Common information required includes terms, rates, conditions, and repayment performance on all existing loans. To demonstrate its ability to manage future debt payments, a borrower is frequently asked to provide financial projections, which can provide insight into its expected future financial condition. Typical financial projections look out one or two years at a minimum, and as far forward as five or 10 years, or until the expected repayment of the loan.

Because an organization's leadership is so critical to its success, lenders will ask for information that allows them to assess management's strengths and weaknesses. This usually includes organization charts, management resumes or bios, and key management's responsibilities. Understanding the role of the board and how it functions completes the leadership picture and helps identify any issues that may confront the organization. To obtain this information, lenders often will ask potential borrowers for a board list with bios and tenures, board committee lists, and minutes of the board or board-committee meetings.

The lender will want to place the loan and credit enhancement request in the context of the organization's history, track record, and plan for the future. Socially oriented lenders will be particularly interested in the borrower's mission statements, program descriptions, client profiles, and any results, impact measures, or awards.

If the loan is being used for a specific project—developing or launching a new program or product, expanding an existing program, or undertaking a facility project—borrowers will be asked for information about the project or program. This may include project team bios; project budgets (from inception to launch or opening); and sources and uses of capital for the project, to indicate how the borrower expects to fund the project, how this financing fits within the overall project budget, and whether there is a funding gap.

Frequently, much of this information is already summarized or put in context in an organization's *strategic plan* or *business plan*—a document that provides both a vision and a strategy for the organization, going forward. It provides the justification for a large program or project undertaking, and ensures that the organization has done the relevant market research and financial planning, and has identified and procured needed resources.

Underwriting

Once information is gathered, the process of underwriting begins. Lenders and credit enhancement providers will have underwriting standards—key criteria and basic thresholds—based on their specific financing parameters. Underwriting is the process by which a lender or credit enhancement provider determines whether a potential borrower meets its underwriting standards and is an acceptable credit risk. Typical underwriting criteria include thresholds for the number of years in operation (those that are interested in mature organizations might only consider borrowers that have been around for 10 or more years, whereas those interested in start-ups would have a much lower threshold); programmatic track record; management and board experience; annual revenue; operating results (surpluses or deficits); financial condition (balance sheet strength and an operating cushion of net assets); loan-to-value ratio (the ratio of the loan to the value of the collateral); and debt service coverage (the ratio of the debt payments to net income before depreciation and taxes). It is common for lenders and credit enhancement providers to have minimum or maximum thresholds or ranges within which they are comfortable providing capital.

The borrower's role in the underwriting process is to respond to questions clarifying or supplementing the information submitted in the due diligence process. There are dozens or even hundreds of questions that an underwriter might ask, but typically the underwriting process seeks answers to the following questions.

What Is the Nature of the Borrower's Enterprise or Business Model? In other words, what is the underlying economic and business proposition? Who are its clients and who pays for its services? (In the social sector, many times they are not the same.) Are there business or cash flow cycles? How do they earn money? How do they spend it? What is the borrower's market, its competition, the conditions in its industry, and are there any policy implications that might influence its underlying business model?

Is the Organization Financially Healthy? Has the borrower demonstrated an ability to control expenses, to break even, or to generate a surplus? Is it already carrying other liabilities and debt? Will it be able to handle additional debt? How predictable is its cash flow? Does it have a financial cushion of equity or net assets?

Is the Organization Well Managed? Whereas the mantra in real estate is "location, location, and location," the mantra in finance is "management, management, and management." A leadership team that can provide vision and balance it with an ability to make good financial decisions, especially when faced with economic or financial challenges, is critical for a viable organization. The financing providers also are likely to evaluate whether the organization has the appropriate number and level of staff for its size and complexity.

Is the Organization Effective with Respect to Its Mission and Able to Balance Mission with Financial Reality? How does it measure its effectiveness? How does it manage mission and financial trade-offs?

Has the Organization Undertaken Adequate Planning for the Project/ Product/Growth, and Does the Borrowing Request Make Sense? The level of planning should be relative to the size of the project, the complexity of the project, and the financial risk it represents. As projects move up the scale from small to large, simple to complex, and little to large risk, questions about financial plans, project teams, contingency, and backup scenarios become more relevant. A borrower's ability to discuss risk with those involved in the financing—in financial language—and its openness to the possibility that the project could fail, are an important sign of a strong borrower. The ability to make a compelling case for the social benefits the loan and credit enhancement will generate is also important in attracting the more socially focused lenders.

How Will the Loan Be Repaid? The borrower's ability to credibly address how and when it will generate excess cash (after paying its ongoing operating expenses) and in what amounts, will give confidence to any lender that the borrower will be able to meet its loan obligations. This is equally important to the provider of credit enhancement, which wants to be reassured that the borrower will be able to meet its obligations and the lender will not need to look to the credit enhancement for repayment.

A critical part of obtaining a loan and the accompanying credit enhancement is an unbiased analysis of the risks and the factors that mitigate those risks, including those specifically related to potential nonrepayment. Both the borrower and lender are interested in determining whether the loan might have other unintended consequences, such as saddling the organization with debt it cannot afford and forcing it to eliminate other programs to repay the loan. The process of assessing risks outlines the various points of vulnerability, whether they are within the borrower's control or not, that might impede repayment. Frequently they center on risk that the financial projections will not be met (expenses will be higher or revenue lower); key management or staff will leave; and political events will interfere. Outlining and discussing these possible risks, the likelihood of any of them happening, and how the borrower would anticipate responding in the event that they happen, contributes to a shared understanding of critical factors to assess during the underwriting process and to monitor once the loan has closed.

Typically, a smooth and successful underwriting process, whether it ends with a borrower obtaining a loan or credit enhancement or not, is characterized by having clear expectations about the process, open communication, and a commitment to responding in a timely manner. First, ensuring at the outset that the borrower, lender, and credit enhancer have a common understanding of the underwriting requirements, the time frame for making a decision, and the potential outcomes can avoid missteps during the process. Second, maintaining strong communication among the lender, the borrower, and the credit enhancer (if any) throughout the underwriting process keeps the process moving and allows any issues that might arise to be addressed quickly. Sharing updated information and any changes in plans establishes trust between the parties and saves time. Third, being able to provide information in a timely manner allows the lender and credit enhancement provider to move the request for financing forward on a reasonable timeframe.

Borrowers can expect the underwriting process to include conversations with the borrower's management and board and, frequently, site visits. Lenders and credit enhancement providers use site visits to affirm what has been provided in the due diligence documents, fill in gaps around issues that might be difficult to glean from written materials or a website, or identify possible risks, such as divergent priorities between board and management. In addition to speaking and meeting with the borrower, the lender and credit enhancement provider may want to speak to stakeholders—funders, other lenders, and industry leaders—for their perspectives on the organization and on industry trends.

Approval

After the underwriting is completed, the lender and credit enhancement provider typically prepare a written analysis and recommendations or credit memo. Most lenders and credit enhancers have an approval process that involves some approving body, whether an individual staff team or board reviewing and formally approving the written recommendation.

Closing and Documentation

After the loan or credit enhancement has been approved, the closing process begins. During this process, the borrower, lender, and, if applicable, credit enhancer document their agreement. Key documents generally include the promissory note, the loan agreement, and collateral documents.

The *promissory note* documents the obligation of the borrower to repay the loan, and typically includes the interest rate and the dates on which interest and principal payments are expected to be paid. The promissory note frequently is accompanied by a *loan agreement*, which is more detailed and includes any other obligations of the borrower. Examples of items typically found in a loan agreement include the purpose of the loan; conditions for closing on the loan (such as outstanding documents that must be provided); and conditions to access the loan funds.

The loan agreement also outlines the borrower's obligations and the lender's rights during the term of the loan. These include reporting requirements, performance benchmarks (all of which are frequently referred to as affirmative covenants), actions the borrower cannot take during the term of the loan (negative covenants), actions that would allow the lender to terminate the loan (events of default), and actions that the lender could take in the event of a default, including requiring repayment before the official repayment date (acceleration). Last, the collateral documents formalize the pledging of any of the borrower's assets as collateral for the loan, and the lender's rights to those assets in the event that the borrower is unable to meet the terms of the loan.

When credit enhancement is involved, the closing requires additional documents. For example, if the enhancement takes the form of subordinate debt, separate versions of the documents mentioned above will also be used to document the credit enhancement. Furthermore, an intercreditor agreement, which outlines the relationship between the senior and subordinate lender and the rights and obligations between these two parties, will also frequently be used. If the enhancement is a guarantee, a separate guarantee document will be required to specify the conditions under which the lender has a right to request payment from the credit enhancement provider. It is recommended that the borrower, lender, and credit enhancement provider involve legal counsel during the process, as these are legally binding obligations.

Postclosing Servicing and Monitoring

After the loan has closed, the work is far from over; in fact, this is when a large part of the lender's work—the servicing and monitoring of the loan—begins. At its most basic, the lender will bill and collect interest and principal payments and monitor any other issues affecting the borrower and the loan. These include late payments, changes in management, and delays in the project timeline. The borrower must meet its obligations under the loan agreements, including making timely payments and providing the required reports. While all of this is generally straightforward, there can be changes or events that require more active engagement by the parties.

Key to ensuring a smooth relationship during the life of the loan and credit enhancement is maintaining a good relationship among the borrower, lender, and credit enhancement provider. Typically the loan agreement and the credit enhancement documents will outline specific financial and programmatic reporting requirements. These reports are used by the lender and credit enhancement provider to gain insight into the organization, its financial health, and its program or project plans. The reports also are a tool to help identify any areas that might pose repayment risk, any new risks that materialize, and any items that might require amendments to the loan documents. In addition to the paper reports, regular phone calls and visits maintain contact between the lender, the credit enhancement provider, and the borrower and help to uncover any concerns. It is the responsibility of the borrower to alert the lender and credit enhancement provider to potential problems. The earlier the borrower informs the lender, the easier it is to resolve any potential problems.

When borrowers are unable to meet the obligations and conditions of the loan agreement, most lenders will seek some form of restructuring before turning to more serious workout options. Restructuring includes amending the terms of the loan so that the borrower can meet its obligations. Amendments might entail ways of reducing the borrower's cash flow burden either for short-term relief or more permanent relief. These include reducing interest rates, allowing interest-only payments, and extending the term or amortization of the loan. In many cases, restructuring can provide the breathing room for the borrower to make changes in order to continue to operate.

Loan restructures are not undertaken lightly. They require the lender to re-underwrite the loan to assess what went wrong, the amount of financial relief required, and the probability that the contemplated restructure will be successful at allowing the borrower to repay the loan. The borrower must provide updated information about its financial situation, including updated projections and assessments of alternative solutions, and engage in many conversations and meetings with the lender to reach a viable solution.

When problems are more significant or more complex, lenders move into more serious workout efforts and the borrower faces severe consequences. The amount of the unpaid loan, the complexity of the loan, and the lender's available resources will drive the scope of the workout effort. It usually will include calling upon any credit enhancement provided, foreclosing on collateral, or negotiating a settlement whereby a portion of the debt is repaid. In all of these cases, the situation is serious for the borrower, the lender, and any credit enhancement providers. In addition to the financial stress of nonpayment and the legal fees incurred, workout efforts are a distraction for a borrower's staff, diverting senior management from ongoing work, and, ultimately, putting services and clients at risk.

The terms of the credit enhancement determine when and to what degree the credit enhancement comes into play. The lender might call upon the credit enhancement provider when the first payment is missed. Alternatively, the credit enhancement can only be called upon as a last resort, when all avenues of restructure and collection have been exhausted. By having some credit enhancement, borrowers are able to reduce the amount of financial repercussions that result from nonpayment of the debt. However, even when the credit enhancement can cover some or all of the borrower's financial obligations, the reputational consequences of default remain.

Operational Complexities

Loans and credit enhancement are attractive financing options for many organizations; however, their use has several operating implications for the borrower. One of the key challenges is having the *appropriate staff* with the necessary skills to undertake the borrowing process. Using debt and credit enhancement requires financial planning acumen to identify and quantify the need, determine the organization's ability to repay any debt, produce the due diligence documents (for example, the business plan if required), negotiate the terms of the loan and credit enhancement, create regular financial reports, and manage through any problems that arise. All of this requires a certain level of financial experience and expertise. It is also time-consuming, and the borrower must be able to dedicate the necessary staff time to the process. Depending on the complexity of the transaction and the work involved, some organizations have staff in their finance or accounting departments with the relevant experience and capacity, while others might consider augmenting in-house staff with consultants or other temporary support. Along with the finance-related resources, borrowers also require access to legal expertise to review and negotiate the documents.

Borrowing also requires organizations to have the *systems necessary to produce regular and timely reports and information.* For instance, if a borrower is seeking a cash flow loan, the lender might request monthly cash flow reports, requiring the borrower to have a financial tracking and reporting system capable of generating such reports. If the borrower is using the loan for a real estate project, the lender might require detailed reports on how the construction process is progressing and how the funds are being used. Some social-purpose lenders also request social-impact reports, detailing how the work of the organization is affecting its clients.

A third operating challenge is *the process to identify appropriate lenders and credit enhancement providers.* Finding lenders that provide the type of financing that a borrower is seeking can be a time-consuming process. While there are lenders and credit enhancement providers in many markets, it can be difficult to connect to ones that serve a borrower's specific geography, service area, and type of loan or credit enhancement on affordable terms and with conditions that the borrower can meet. For many borrowers, this entails talking to commercial banks and researching lenders with a particular focus on the social or mission-driven market, such as foundations, community development financial institutions, or possibly board members or other high-net-worth individuals.

A fourth operational challenge inherent in taking on debt is *managing cash flow* in order to ensure that there is sufficient cash to make the loan payments on the schedule agreed to in the loan documents. Managing cash is part of managing any business or organization. Having the cash necessary to meet payroll, make rent payments, and pay other bills is part of daily operations. By borrowing, an organization is taking on one more cash obligation, and failure to meet that obligation has serious consequences. When cash is tight, borrowers sometimes must prioritize among obligations, paying one bill before another, and managing the consequences. Since not having sufficient cash to make a loan payment can put the loan in default and jeopardize the organization, successfully planning and managing cash needs is particularly important.

In general, loans and credit enhancement are useful tools that can be used to help organizations fulfill their missions. However, they can require additional resources and capacity to acquire and manage.

Track Record

Debt is necessary for all types of organizations, including nonprofits. Not only is it a viable means for organizations to expand or grow, but too little debt, in relation to total assets, can lead to capital starvation and sluggish growth.[25]

Nonprofits and other social-purpose organizations have a strong track record managing debt. A study based on 1986 IRS data found that the use of debt by a majority of tax-filing nonprofits was productive for those organizations; and a 2007 study of $2.3 billion in mission investments by 92 US foundations found that the default rate for nonprofit loan recipients (9.5 percent) was actually lower than that for the for-profit ones (19.4 percent).[26]

Even in the midst of the financial crisis, social-purpose loans more than held their own. For example, as of the end of 2009, the F.B. Heron Foundation had a default rate of less than 1 percent on its $38 million program-related investments portfolio. The portfolio consisted primarily of senior debt to nonprofits (60 percent), with subordinated debt and equity investments making up the rest.[27]

Heron's PRI portfolio had an intentionally discounted 3.8 percent rate of return. As Luther Ragin, Heron's chief investment officer at the time, pointed out, however, "3.8%, though below market, is a lot better than the minus 20% that some asset classes returned" during the recession.[28] In fact, during the economically challenging years of "2001, 2002, and 2008, PRIs were among the best-performing assets in foundations' portfolios."[29]

The performance of community development financial institutions, which lend primarily to social-purpose organizations, also attests to nonprofit organizations' ability to manage debt. A 2007–2009 study of a cohort of CDFIs found that they experienced only a modest deterioration in their loan portfolio, even during these peak recessionary years.[30]

Despite the consistently strong demand for debt by social-purpose organizations, there is only limited research examining how such organizations are using debt and credit enhancement, and what kinds of debt and credit enhancement would be most beneficial to support the sector's ongoing growth. Current research of this sort could help identify gaps in the availability of debt and credit enhancements and attract additional sources of capital to rectify those gaps, ensuring that social-purpose organizations have the capital they need to fulfill their objectives.

Notes

* The authors wish to express their appreciation to Clara Miller, who made significant contributions to an earlier draft of this chapter.

1. Robert J. Yetman, "Borrowing and Debt," in *Financing Nonprofits: Putting Theory into Practice*, ed. Dennis R. Young (Lanham, MD: AltaMira Press, 2007), 243–70.

2. Nick O'Donohoe, Christina Leijonhufvud, Yasemin Saltuk, Antony Bugg-Levine, and Margot Brandenburg, "Impact Investments: An Emerging Asset Class," J.P. Morgan, November 29, 2010, accessed January 7, 2014, http://www.jpmorgan.com/cm/cs?pagename=JPM/DirectDoc&urlname= impact_investments_nov2010.pdf, 10.

3. For a discussion of efforts to establish such performance metrics, see Chapter 22 of this volume.

4. See Chapter 2 for additional discussion of community development financial institutions.

5. Nancy O. Andrews, "Taking Capital for Social Purposes to a New Level," *Community Development Investment Review* 2011:71.

6. Credit Enhancement for Charter School Facilities Program, accessed June 18, 2013, http://www2.ed.gov/programs/charterfacilities/performance.html.

7. Howard P. Tuckman and Cyril F. Chang, "How Well Is Debt Managed by Nonprofits?" *Nonprofit Management & Leadership* 3.4 (1993): 349.

8. Tuckman and Chang, "How Well Is Debt Managed"; Robert J. Yetman, "Borrowing and Debt."

9. Tuckman and Chang, "How Well Is Debt Managed"; Yetman, "Borrowing and Debt."

10. Tuckman and Chang, "How Well Is Debt Managed."

11. Yetman, "Borrowing and Debt."

12. Lester M. Salamon and Stephanie L. Geller, "Investment Capital: The New Challenge for American Nonprofits," Listening Post Project Communiqué No. 5, Johns Hopkins Center for Civil Society Studies, 2006, 2, accessed July 29, 2013, http://ccss.jhu.edu/publications-findings?did=265.

13. The prime rate is the rate at which banks will lend to their lowest-risk customers. It is published daily in the *Wall Street Journal*. The prime rate is determined by using the Fed Funds Target Rate as set by the Federal Reserve at regular meetings, which are held approximately eight times a year, and adding a markup to that rate. The Federal Funds Target rate was 8.25 percent in January 1990 and 0.25 percent in 2012. Accessed June 17, 2013, http://www.newyorkfed.org/markets/statistics/dlyrates/fedrate.html. While the markup can vary, it has typically been around 3 percent. The LIBO Rate or LIBOR is the London Interbank Offered Rate and is the interest rate at which banks can borrow funds from other banks in the London interbank market. It is fixed on a daily basis and is an average of banks' interbank deposit rates for loans with maturities of one night to one year. The LIBOR for three-month loans in 2013 was approximately 0.27 percent. Accessed June 17, 2013, http://www.global-rates.com/interest-rates/libor/american-dollar/usd-libor-interest-rate-3-months.aspx.

14. The US Small Business Administration's (SBA) 7a program provides loan guarantees for small business loans made by approved banks and other types of lenders. In the event of default, the SBA is willing to reimburse up to 85 percent of the loss that the lender would otherwise sustain. The SBA also has a loan guarantee program for revolving lines of credit. Accessed June 18, 2013, http://www.sba.gov/content/7a-te rms-conditions.

15. Kresge Foundation, "Social Investment Practice Brochure," accessed June 10, 2013, http://www.kresge.org/sites/default/files/Brochure-socialinvestment.pdf.

16. National Charter School Resource Center, "March 2013 Newsletter: Charter Schools and Qualified School Construction Bonds," accessed June 17, 2013, http://www. charterschoolcenter.org/newsletter/march-2013-charter-schools-and-qua lified-school-construction-bonds.

17. Woods Bowman, "The Uniqueness of Nonprofit Finance and the Decision to Borrow," *Nonprofit Management & Leadership* 12.3 (2002): 293–311; Wenli Yan, Dwight V. Denison, and J. S. Butler, "Revenue Structure and Nonprofit Borrowing," *Public Finance Review* 37.1 (January 2009): 47–67.

18. Bowman, "Uniqueness of Nonprofit Finance."

19. Salamon and Geller, "Investment Capital."

20. Paige Chapel, Tess Colby, and Jon Schwartz, "Community Development Loan Funds," Altrushares Securities and CARS, September 2012, accessed July 13, 2013, http://altrushare.com/pdf/CDLF_Sept2012.pdf.

21. Opportunity Finance Network, "CDFI Market Conditions: First Quarter 2011," Opportunity Finance Network, June 2011, 1, accessed July 12, 2013, http://www.opportunityfinance.net/store/downloads/CDFI_Market_Conditions_Q111_Report_I.pdf.

22. Capital Link, "Capital Plans and Needs of Health Centers: A National Perspective," Capital Link, June 2012, 1–2.

23. Personal correspondence with Stefan Huh, director of the US Department of Education's Charter Schools Program, June 19, 2013.

24. Yasemin Saltuk, Amit Bouri, and Giselle Leung, "Insight into the Impact Investment Market: An In-Depth Analysis of Investor Perspectives and Over 2,200 Transactions," J.P. Morgan Social Finance Research, December 14, 2011, accessed June 12, 2013, http://www.thegiin.org/cgi-bin/iowa/download?row=334&field=gated_download_1.

25. Yan, Denison, and Butler, "Revenue Structure"; Bowman, "Uniqueness of Nonprofit Finance."

26. Tuckman, "How Well Is Debt Managed?"

27. Luther M. Ragin Jr., "Program-Related Investments in Practice," *Vermont Law Review* 35 (2010): 54.

28. Ragin, "Program-Related Investments in Practice."

29. Ragin, "Program-Related Investments in Practice."

30. Portfolio in arrears increased from 3.6 percent to 4.5 percent, while charge-offs grew from.15 percent to 0.25 percent. Community Development Financial Institutions, "The Financial Crisis and CDFIs: A Brief Look at 2007–2009 CIIS Data," March 1, 2011, accessed June 23, 2013, http://www.cdfifund.gov/impact_we_make/research/CDFI%20Crisis%20Trend%202007-2009%20Presentation.pdf.

Suggested Readings

Rubin, Julia Sass, ed. *Financing Low Income Communities: Models, Obstacles, and Future Directions.* New York: Russell Sage Foundation, 2007.

Seidman, Karl. *Economic Development Finance.* Thousand Oaks, CA: Sage, 2005.

Young, Dennis R., ed. *Financing Nonprofits: Putting Theory into Practice.* Lanham, MD: AltaMira Press, 2007.

CHAPTER 13

FIXED-INCOME SECURITIES

Elise Balboni and Shari Berenbach

IN EARLY 2009, KIPP HOUSTON, a high-quality charter school network in Houston, faced a large-scale version of the facilities dilemma confronting virtually all charter schools. Since its founding in 1994 as one of the flagship college preparatory charter schools in KIPP (Knowledge is Power Program) network, it had grown to 15 schools serving 4,500 students. At that time, 90 percent of its middle school graduates had matriculated to college, and the wait-list demand was more than double its capacity. KIPP Houston needed financing to develop the requisite educational facilities to increase enrollment further from 4,500 to 11,500 students.

Given its wait list and the surging parent demand for its academic program, administrators were confident that KIPP Houston would have the enrollment and the accompanying per pupil operating revenue from public federal, state, and local sources to pay for both the academic program and the facilities to house its students. However, the upheaval in the capital markets triggered by the subprime mortgage crisis in 2008 made credit unaffordable. The increases were particularly severe for smaller, lower-rated borrowers of tax-exempt debt, such as charter schools. Historically, charter schools had purchased bond insurance to obtain reasonable interest rates. However, the insurance companies' losses on various mortgage investments essentially led to their collapse, and there was no source of credit enhancement to help make charter school borrowing affordable. Charter school bond issuance declined from a high of 71 offerings in 2007 to only three in the first few months of 2009, and interest rates rose from lows of 5 percent to highs of over 9 percent.

Into this vacuum stepped the Bill and Melinda Gates Foundation in late 2009 by providing a $30 million guarantee to help secure $300 million in tax-exempt bond issuance to further high-quality public charter school expansion in Houston. This guarantee was the foundation's first US investment as part of an initiative announced earlier in 2009 that committed a total of $400 million in program-related investments over a two-year period to deepen the impact of the foundation's work through non-traditional means. It ultimately allowed KIPP Houston to close in November 2009 on an initial $67 million tax-exempt bond issue with overall borrowing costs of roughly 6 percent, the first significant charter school bond transaction sold in the United States since the credit tightening began in 2008.[1]

Defining the Tool

The KIPP Houston charter school transaction illustrates the use of bond financing for social-purpose activities. Bonds constitute one form of what are known as "fixed-income securities." Such securities are financial instruments that provide capital to an organization with a periodic return to the investor and repayment of the amount lent. Such securities differ from loans, which also provide capital with interest and capital repayment, in that loans are custom-crafted arrangements, usually between a borrower and a single financial institution that acts as lender. By contrast, bonds and other fixed-income securities typically involve much larger transactions in which an intermediary, like an investment bank, secures capital from a variety of sources by selling them a financial instrument that can be transferred easily. Because of this scale and the engagement of multiple institutions and investors, bonds also involve a variety of regulatory features that do not typically apply to loans.[2]

Defining Features

More specifically, fixed-income instruments are debt instruments in which the borrower enters into a contract with lenders to repay principal on a specific maturity date, and to pay interest, known as the *coupon*, at fixed intervals. Unlike stockholders, who have an equity, or ownership, stake in a company, fixed-income investors have a creditor stake, which means that they are lenders with a first claim on repayment of their principal and interest but no claim on corporate profits or assets beyond those committed in the contract. Fixed-income instruments provide corporate, government, and nonprofit borrowers with funds to finance long-term capital investments or current operating expenditures.

Fixed-income securities can be bought and sold and have a value that fluctuates. When they are first offered, or issued, in the primary market, they are generally sold to an underwriter, an investment bank, or a syndicate of investment banks, which resells them to investors. Alternatively, these "new" issue securities can be sold through private placements, in which they are sold directly to investors or "placed" with such investors through a placement agent. For nonprofit borrowers, there may be mission-driven investors, such as foundations or donors, willing to provide low-cost capital via a private placement. Fixed-income securities can then be resold on the secondary market. Unlike stocks, which are sold on centralized exchanges, bonds and other fixed-income securities trade in decentralized, dealer-based markets. Dealers vary in which types of securities they buy and sell and in their pricing. The extent of the secondary market for a particular instrument affects liquidity, the ease and cost at which it can be traded, and hence the price it can bring.

The interest rate an issuer pays for its borrowing is dependent on the issuer's creditworthiness, current market interest rates, and the term of the borrowing. Creditworthiness is a measure of the likeliness of full and timely interest and principal payments. Investors use a number of measures to assess creditworthiness, including general financial strength measures and criteria unique to particular sectors. Creditworthiness is often evaluated by independent specialized companies, known as rating agencies. An issuer can hire a rating agency to assign its bond offering a credit rating, which investors use in making their decisions. A weaker credit rating represents higher risk for investors and correspondingly higher interest rates. High-yield, or junk, bonds are fixed-income instruments deemed to be extremely risky, with high default risk and correspondingly higher interest rates necessary to attract investors.

The principal, par, or face value of a bond is the amount the borrower must repay to investors at maturity. When a bond is issued or resold, it can sell at a price that differs from its par value. A bond that sells at less than par is sold at a *discount*, and a bond that sells at more than par sells at a *premium*. The yield to investors is the rate of return on the bond. It can vary from the stated interest rate, or *coupon rate*, if the price at which the bond is sold differs from par. As market interest rates change, the price of the bond adjusts to equalize the bond's return to that of other investments in the market, with the yield and the price of a bond inversely related. When interest rates rise, bond prices fall, so that the overall yield or return to the investor will be comparable to other investments. The current yield is the annual yield based on the current market price for the bond. It is computed by dividing the annual coupon interest by the current price of the bond and does not take into account any other cash flows that will affect the investors' return. The *yield to maturity* for a bond is the rate of return the investor receives by holding a bond until it matures, taking into account both coupon payments and principal repayments.

The relationship between yield and maturities of bonds of the same credit quality is known as the *yield curve*. Generally, the yield curve is upward sloping; the longer the term, the higher the interest rate (see Figure 13.1). This is because the market expects a rise in general interest rates or because there is more risk associated with a longer time horizon. The steepness of the curve can vary. For example, it can be steep in the early years, with large differences in interest rates between bonds with one- versus three-year maturities, or it can be flatter, with fairly constant marginal increases between different maturities. There have been periods of exception to the generally upward sloping structure, when yield curves have been inverted (downward sloping) or flat. For example, in periods of high interest rates, the market anticipates declining interest rates further out in the future, thus leading to an inverted yield curve.

FIGURE 13.1
Typical Upward-Sloping Yield Curve

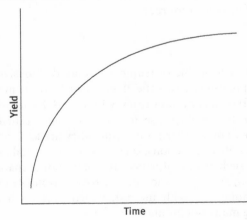

Relation to Common Criteria

Risk Level

Fixed-income products, such as bonds, are generally considered low-risk instruments. Risk levels vary based on the credit strength of the borrower and the structure of the security, which is often measured by a credit rating provided by independent rating agencies. Investment grade bonds, those with ratings of triple-B or higher, are considered relatively low risk. Unrated or high-yield bonds can have significant speculative elements and provide a correspondingly higher return.

Type and Level of Return

Compared to equities, which provide access to dividends and ownership stakes, financial return is typically modest for bonds and is based on risks assessed by investors or evaluated by rating agencies through determination of the credit rating. Investors in bonds and other fixed-income securities are generally seeking a constant and secure return on their investment. Interest is paid at fixed intervals, and the principal amount borrowed is repaid on a specified date. Returns vary with the maturity, or tenor, of the instrument, with instruments with longer maturities generally paying higher interest rates reflective of the higher risk associated with holding an asset over a longer time period, among other factors. Investors often require a premium for purchasing unrated fixed-income products. Some philanthropies or social investors, however, may intentionally elect below market financial return relative to the risk. Returns required for high-yield or junk bonds may be very high, reflecting the speculative nature of their repayment.

Degree of Leverage

Typically, fixed-income products have relatively low debt-to-equity ratios and, hence, provide relatively low levels of risk and return to investors. On the other hand, from a philanthropic perspective, bond guarantees such as that provided by the Gates Foundation in the example cited earlier offer enormous leverage. By offering a guarantee of a bond issue, the Gates Foundation was able to help stimulate the flow of millions of private investment capital into a social-purpose activity at below market rates without expending any of its own resources.

Ubiquity

Bonds and other fixed-income instruments are used extensively by both governments and corporations across the globe. The US government is among the largest issuers of fixed-income securities, with over $17 trillion outstanding as of this writing. In the nonprofit sector, fixed-income securities are broadly employed as a source of long-term financing. They are less commonly used to finance non-real-estate transactions, such as working capital, or in other international markets, such as microfinance. To obtain bond financing on reasonable terms, however, an organization must have a reasonable prospect of being able to repay bondholders with interest, which requires a reliable income stream, something many nonprofits do not have.

Skill Requirements

The issuance and trading of fixed-income securities, like other securities, is governed by extensive legal and regulatory requirements. In the United States, for example, fixed-income securities fall under the regulatory authority of the US Securities and Exchange Commission (SEC) and other regulatory and rule-making bodies designed to protect investors from potential fraud. As such, issuing and placing bonds typically requires the involvement of a host of professionals. There are firms that specialize in the legal and financial intricacies of bond issuance, which can assist organizations in the structuring and execution of their offerings. For example, in the case of the KIPP Houston bond offering discussed earlier, Vinson & Elkins served as bond counsel, RBC Capital Markets served as underwriter, and Coastal Securities served as financial advisor. There is also a need for significant board and management engagement to oversee the activities of these various professionals and develop a structure that best meets the organization's financing needs.

Social Implications

Fixed-income products have been used in a broad range of social-impact areas—from education (universities, private schools, charter schools), health (hospitals, clinics), economic revitalization (urban renewal, rural business, and industry), affordable housing, community facilities, and transit-oriented development, among other areas. While bond financing has been used in many sectors, this class of financing is typically limited to mature, well-developed institutions with the potential to generate reliable, consistent earnings (often associated with established government contracts). As such, start-up ventures without firmly committed revenue streams will have a harder time utilizing this form of financing.

Design Features and Major Variants

Although fixed-income securities are most often associated with the financing of corporations and governmental entities at various levels, they are also increasingly being used to finance nonprofits and other social-purpose organizations. Fixed-income securities share a number of crucial features; however, they also differ along a number of dimensions. The most significant of these are the type of instrument, the eligible uses, the issuer, tax status, maturity, interest or "coupon" rate, coupon dates, call provisions, credit enhancements, and reserve funds. Let us examine each of these in turn.

Type of Instrument

The most common fixed-income instrument is a long-term *bond*. Debt securities with shorter maturities are known as *notes*. While bonds generally constitute a debt obligation of an issuer, other fixed-income instruments—commonly referred to as "securitizations"—are "collateralized" or combined into dedicated pools of assets segregated into a distinct legal corporate shell or special purpose vehicle. Holders of such securities may look for repayment only from the instruments held by the special purpose vehicle. Examples include mortgage-backed securities and other asset-backed securities, which are secured by a specific revenue stream, such as credit card receivables, home equity loans, or automobile loans. (For further detail on "securitization," see Chapter 14 in this volume.)

Eligible Uses

Eligible uses of bond proceeds in the United States are defined by the Securities and Exchange Commission. Different uses are associated with different types of fixed-income securities. Notes are generally used to finance shorter-term working capital or cash flow needs, whereas bonds are generally employed to finance longer-term capital expenditures such as acquisition, renovation or construction of land, buildings, and equipment. Bond financing can also be used to refinance shorter-term commercial loans used for such purposes or to reimburse prior capital expenditures, subject to certain requirements. Proceeds can also be employed to pay costs of issuance, to fund debt service reserve funds, and to pay interest due during the construction period of a project that the issuer borrows in order to make debt service payments until the project is complete and revenue is generated.

Issuer

The issuer is the legal entity, whether corporate, governmental, or nonprofit, that registers or sells the fixed-income securities in order to raise capital. In most cases, the issuer is also the ultimate borrower or "obligor." However, in certain cases, the issuer serves solely as an intermediary, borrowing funds from investors and relending them to the end beneficiary and obligor. This is called "conduit issuance" (Figure 13.2). In such conduit issuance, the obligor's credit, rather than the issuer's, is still the basis for the offering, and its financial strength and the structure of the offering are the determinants of the interest rates investors will require. The obligor has the legal and economic obligation to make debt service payments to the issuer, who in turn pays investors.

In addition to direct issuance, nonprofits and other social-purpose organizations may have a choice of public or quasi-public conduit issuers that they can access for issuance of their debt on a tax-exempt basis. Most states have several statewide authorities that serve as conduit issuers either generally or for targeted sectors, such as education, healthcare, housing, or economic development. In addition, many states have regional industrial development authorities or other more locally based issuers who serve nonprofit organizations and other businesses within their specific geographies.

FIGURE 13.2
Conduit Bond Issuance

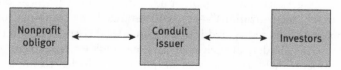

Tax Status

Bonds may be classified as taxable or tax-exempt. Interest on Treasury securities is taxable, as is the interest on most corporate debt. Bondholders pay taxes on the income earned on these investments. Municipal debt that is issued by states, cities, counties, and other local governmental entities to finance public capital improvements or other activities that satisfy a public purpose is generally exempt from federal taxation—the interest paid to investors is excluded from federal taxes—and can be issued without limit. In addition, the federal government allows federal tax-exemption for certain private activity bonds that benefit private projects or activities that also serve a public purpose (e.g., bonds for nonprofit hospitals, low-income housing). Federal tax law caps the volume of private activity bonds that individual states can issue, with the volume cap determined annually based on Internal Revenue Service and Census Bureau data.

In most states, interest from federally tax-exempt issues is also exempt from state and local taxation. Tax-exempt municipal bonds are broadly classified as either general obligation (GO) bonds or revenue bonds. GO bonds are secured by the full faith and taxing power of the issuing government and are considered the strongest of all tax-supported debt structures. Revenue bonds are secured by a defined revenue stream, such as municipal utility fees, gas taxes, tolls, or, in the case of charter schools, per pupil revenues.

Municipal issuers may also issue taxable securities for certain activities that do not provide a benefit to the general public, such as local sports facilities. Some states have adopted debt limits or management policies, through their state constitution, other legislative action, or administrative order, that restrict the amount and type of debt that can be issued.

Nonprofits or other social enterprises can benefit from lower-cost tax-exempt debt by issuing through a public or quasi-public conduit that issues debt on its behalf and relends the proceeds to the nonprofit. The nonprofit has responsibility for interest and principal payments, with the government entity acting solely as an intermediary, or conduit, in order to confer tax-exempt status to the borrowing.

Because the income investors receive from tax-exempt issues is free from federal income taxes and from state and local taxation in certain states, investors are willing to receive a lower interest rate on this debt to achieve the same after-tax return as taxable debt. The amount of this difference, or spread, varies over time, depending on broader economic and market factors. Through tax exemption, federal and municipal governments essentially pay a share of the interest expense for the project by forgoing the tax revenue they would have received.

Maturity

The maturity, or term, of a bond is the number of years during which the borrower agrees to meet the conditions of the offering, and the maturity date is the date by which the borrower has to repay in full the principal amount of the bond. Bond maturities vary greatly and should be correlated to the useful life of the asset being financed and any resulting cash flows stemming from that asset. Bonds typically mature between one and 30 years—though bonds with less than five years' maturity are less common, and it is possible to find bonds with maturities of 50 years or longer.

Municipal issuers generally strive to achieve level debt service payments for their offerings. They employ serial bonds and term bonds within a single offering to achieve level debt service. Serial bonds mature serially, or chronologically, generally over the first five to 10 years of the issuance. Term bonds mature later in the issuance, aggregating several years' principal repayment into a single maturity date, with required sinking fund payments normally required over the life of the bonds.

Coupon

The coupon is the periodic interest payment the issuer pays to investors during the life of the bond. The coupon rate is the interest rate at which the issuer calculates interest payments based on the face or principal amount of the bond. The interest rate utilized to calculate the coupon can be fixed at issuance for the life of the bond (fixed rate), or it can vary over a bond's term (floating rate or variable rate). In variable-rate bonds, the interest rate is set on certain designated dates in the future based on specific market indices, such as LIBOR (London Interbank Offered Rate), plus a predetermined spread to the index. There are also zero coupon bonds, which do not pay periodic interest over the life of the bond. Rather, the investor receives the interest payment at the bond's maturity, which can be beneficial from a cash flow perspective.

Coupon Dates

Coupon dates are the dates on which the issuer makes a periodic payment to bondholders. Coupon payments are generally made semiannually for bonds issued in the United States, with the exception of most mortgage-backed and asset-backed securities, in which payment is made monthly. In contrast, bonds issued in some European markets, and all Eurobonds, have annual coupon payments.[3] Coupon dates can vary based on the timing of the offering and the timing of the cash flows that serve as the source of repayment for the bonds.

Call Provisions

Some bonds give the issuer the right to repay or retire the bond before the final maturity date. This call right is attractive for borrowers. It gives them the ability to refinance their debt should interest rates fall or to pay off costly debt with surplus cash from operations. Conversely, it is detrimental to investors. As such, callable bonds generally pay higher interest rates than noncallable bonds. There is normally a period of call protection, a certain number of years from when a bond is first issued, during which it cannot be called. There may also be a call premium associated with early retirement. Generally, this premium will decrease according to a specified schedule until a particular date when the bonds can be called at par. Some public offerings include a make-whole call provision designed to provide investors with protection against reinvestment risk should the bond be called.[4]

Debt Service Reserve Fund

Bonds normally include a debt service reserve fund (DSRF) that is tapped to make debt service payments to investors should the borrower fail to make timely payments. The DSRF is generally funded with bond proceeds. At maturity, the DSRF is returned to the borrower or used to make the final debt service payment to the extent it has not been drawn upon.

Credit Enhancement

In order to achieve higher credit ratings and lower interest rates, many borrowers utilize credit enhancement to further secure their bond offerings, as was the case for the KIPP Houston bond issuance discussed in the vignette that opened this chapter. Credit enhancement can involve the substitution of a stronger third party's credit, as in the case of bond insurance, letters of credit or other third-party guarantees, or specific collateral pledged for repayment, as in the case of additional debt service reserves structured into the bond issue.

In third-party substitutions, investors look to the creditworthiness of the insurer, bank, or philanthropy that is providing the enhancement rather than to the strength of the underlying borrower. To the extent the borrower pays for this substitution, it should compare the cost of the credit enhancement with the interest savings realized from the superior rating of the third party. Bond insurance is typically used for long-term fixed-rate issues in which the insurer provides a 100 percent guarantee of principal and interest payments for the term of the bond in exchange for an upfront premium payment. Letters of credit are generally used for variable-rate issuances since the letter of credit typically has a term of one to five years during which a bank or other financial institution guarantees debt service payments in exchange for a letter of credit fee.

The tax-exempt bond market is primarily an investment grade market because of the credit strength of municipal borrowers based on their taxing authority. Historically, many lower-rated borrowers of tax-exempt debt purchased insurance or some other form of credit enhancement in order to access the market on favorable terms. However, the collapse of the municipal bond insurers in 2008 due to their losses on collateralized debt obligations and other structured financial products related to the subprime mortgage crisis forced tax-exempt borrowers to look to other sources for credit enhancement for their offerings.

When bond insurance is not a viable option, nonprofit or social-enterprise issuers have turned to philanthropic and government sources of credit enhancement. National or local foundations can provide full or partial guarantees for bond issues of nonprofit or social-enterprise organizations whose missions they support. In the case of a full guarantee, the foundation provides a 100 percent guarantee of the debt, which it can do through an unfunded guarantee, or balance sheet pledge. The foundation can also provide a partial, or limited, guarantee that provides investors protection for losses up to a certain amount, such as 20 percent of the par amount of the bonds, also on an unfunded basis. This was the case in the charter school bond issue described earlier in which the Bill and Melinda Gates Foundation provided a $10 million guarantee for a $67 million bond issue. Alternatively, philanthropies can provide funds for additional debt service reserves that can be tapped beyond the one-year debt service reserve typically funded with bond proceeds at closing. Federal and state programs may also be available to provide credit enhancement for nonprofit bond issuance. For example, the federal Credit Enhancement for Charter School Facilities Program awards grants to public and nonprofit entities that may be used as additional security for bond financing, in addition to other types of debt.

Patterns of Use

Overview

The outstanding global fixed-income market was estimated at $95 trillion at the end of 2010.[5] According to the Securities Industry and Financial Markets Association (SIFMA), as shown in Table 13.1, the United States had approximately $36 trillion in fixed-income issuance outstanding as of year-end 2010, representing 38 percent of the worldwide total. The US market consisted of $8.9 million in Treasuries and an additional $2.5 trillion in Federal Agency securities, accounting for 32 percent of the US total. Mortgage-related debt, including mortgages backed by Ginnie Mae, Fannie Mae, and Freddie Mac, as well as collateralized mortgage obligations (CMOs) and commercial mortgage-backed securities, accounted for $8.5 trillion, or 24 percent of the US total. Corporate, at $7.5 trillion, represented the next largest category, at 21 percent of the total. Debt issued by municipal issuers, including conduit debt issued on behalf of nonprofit borrowers, ranked next, with total outstanding of $3.8 trillion, or 11 percent of the total. Asset-backed securities comprised of auto, credit card, home equity, manufacturing, and student loans represented the smallest sector at just over $2 trillion.[6]

Fixed-income securities are primarily purchased by institutional investors, such as pension funds, insurance companies, banks, corporations, and mutual funds. Direct holding of fixed-income instruments by individuals is relatively limited, although municipal securities have had a greater retail market than corporate bonds or Treasuries.

TABLE 13.1   US FIXED-INCOME MARKETS

Fixed-income market	Trillions Outstanding
Treasury	$8.853
Federal agency securities	$2.539
Mortgage related	$8.516
Corporate	$7.511
Municipal	$3.796
Money market	$2.867
Asset-backed	$2.034
Total	$36.115

Source: Securities Industry and Financial Markets Association, "U.S. Bond Market Outstanding," December 15, 2011, 1, http://www.sifma.org/research/statistics.aspx.

Many types of social-purpose organizations have issued fixed-income instruments, including the following:

- Education (charter schools, private schools, universities)
- Health (hospitals, clinics, assisted living)
- Culture (museums, theaters, arts institutions, broadcasting stations)
- Recreation (YMCAs, community swimming pools, community centers)
- Housing (multifamily, special needs housing)
- Urban redevelopment

The securities for these different sectors are evaluated in terms of credit criteria unique to the particular sectors. Certain sectors have had greater success accessing the municipal market, either because of their size, the reliability of their revenue streams, or their longevity. For example, according to *The Bond Buyer's 2010 in Statistics*, the healthcare sector issued $31.2 billion in long-term bonds and colleges and universities issued $14.5 billion, representing 7 percent and 3 percent, respectively, of all municipal issuances.[7] Charter schools, on the other hand, are a relatively new sector, with 2010 issuance of $935 million, representing only 0.2 percent of total 2010 municipal issuance.[8]

As *capital seekers*, social-purpose organizations may consider bonds an attractive financing source that can provide long-term capital on favorable terms. Alternatively, such organizations may have endowments or some other form of investable assets. They may hold a significant share of their endowed assets in investment grade instruments as a store of wealth. In this capacity, such nonprofits may also be *capital providers*.

Endowed foundations are usually *capital providers* that invest in fixed-income instruments as part of a diversified portfolio of investments. On the program side, foundations may serve as credit enhancement providers, or guarantors, thereby enabling social-purpose organizations to access the fixed-income markets on attractive terms.

Illustrative Uses of Bonds for Social-Purpose Activities

While the full scale of usage of bonds for social-purpose activities is difficult to estimate with precision, a number of innovative examples have surfaced in recent years and deserve mention as illustrations of the potential of this tool.

Habitat for Humanity: Linda Mae/FlexCAP Bonds

Habitat for Humanity chapters across the country have helped low-income individuals gain access to single-family homes. While practices for individual chapters can vary, the typical approach involves land that is either donated or acquired at a discount; volunteers to help construct single-family homes; and distribution of the homes with zero-interest, 30-year mortgages issued by the Habitat chapters. This means that the assets of Habitat chapters may be tied up for 30 years and are not available for recycling to other families. To create liquidity for participating chapters, Habitat for Humanity International launched its Linda Mae Bond Program in 1997, initially named after Linda Fuller, Habitat's cofounder, and later redubbed FlexCAP Bonds. FlexCAP bonds are typically overcollateralized, that is, the total value of mortgages pledged as collateral exceeds the face value of the bond. Additional measures have been adopted to decrease the perception of risk for investors. If a pledged mortgage becomes delinquent, the Habitat affiliate is required to substitute a performing mortgage, of equal or greater value, for the delinquent mortgage. This requirement stabilizes the value of the collateral held by investors. These bonds are also unusual in that the payment of interest to investors is not linked to the interest earned on the mortgages. Since the underlying mortgages are interest free, bond coupon payments on the FlexCAP bonds are funded through donations and contributions to the Habitat chapters. The first issue in 1997 involved $6.5 million in mortgages. Since then, Habitat has raised over $100 million through the sale of bonds resulting in the financing of more than 3,700 homes.[9] Major purchasers included: Chase Manhattan Bank, MetLife, PMI Mortgage Insurance, and Prudential Insurance Co., among others.

International Finance Facility for Immunisation

The International Finance Facility for Immunisation is a global endeavor to finance the production and distribution of vaccines and to accelerate their distribution to populations around the globe with a goal of reaching 500 million children and ultimately saving 10 million lives. Bond proceeds, raised through the sale of bonds on the capital markets, have been used to finance the production, acquisition, and distribution of vaccinations for polio, measles, tetanus, yellow fever, hepatitis B, HIV/AIDS, and other common diseases. The governments of the United Kingdom, France, Italy, Spain, Sweden, and Norway are guaranteeing repayment of the bonds. The $1 billion inaugural issue in 2006, managed by Goldman Sachs and Deutsch Bank, was 1.7 times oversubscribed.[10] The triple-A-rated instrument was bought by the pope, the archbishop of Canterbury, central banks, fund managers, corporations, and insurance companies, as well as individual retail investors. The bond proceeds are managed by the GAVI Alliance, a public-private partnership that funds immunizations and other health-related efforts in 70 of the world's poorest countries. GAVI coordinates among the drug companies that produce vaccinations, international agencies, and host country health ministries involved in vaccine distribution. Since its launch in 2006, the program has raised over $3.6 billion.[11]

Community Capital Management and Access Capital Strategies Bond Funds

While this chapter has concentrated on individual bond instruments, in the late 1990s two fixed-income funds were launched, in part to help banks meet the requirements of the Community Reinvestment Act (CRA). This federal law requires banks to invest a portion of their assets in disadvantaged communities from which they draw part of their deposits. The first, Boston-based Access Capital Strategies Community Investment Fund, was formed in 1997 and was acquired by RBC Capital Markets in 2008. The second, Florida-based Community Capital Management, was launched in 1998. These intermediate-term bond funds hold rated instruments, primarily Fannie Mae– or Freddie Mac–issued mortgage-backed securities and taxable municipal instruments. The funds are able to target capital to specific localities and to report on the use of proceeds, enabling participating banks to include such investments within their overall community reinvestment activities. Today, both funds are available for sale to institutions, banks, foundations, high-net-worth individuals, and retail investors. Returns have generally met or surpassed returns defined by industry benchmarks, and these funds have grown substantially as a consequence. As of May 31, 2012, the CRA Qualified Investment Fund, managed by Community Capital Management, had $1.3 billion in assets under management and at year-end 2012 Access Capital Community Investment Fund had $610 million under management.[12]

Calvert Community Investment Notes

The Calvert Community Investment (CI) Note is a fixed-income product that is backed by the Calvert Foundation, a certified community development financial institution (CDFI). The CI notes were launched in 1995 with support from the Ford, MacArthur, and Mott foundations, initially intending to serve as a means through which individual investors could place capital into CDFIs. Over time, impact areas were expanded such that CI note capital now is lent to a mix of high-impact community-based intermediaries to finance affordable housing, small business loans, and community facilities in the United States. Internationally, funds are used as a source of loan capital for microfinance and as bridge financing for fair-trade farmworker cooperatives. Interest earned on the loans to borrowers covers the interest obligation to investors and the majority of operating expenses of the foundation (with the remainder raised through grants and donations). This taxable, unrated, medium-term note program is available through a continuous offering. Investors can select the term (1, 3, 5, 7, or 10 years) and the rate (0, 1, 2, or 3 percent). The CI notes are sold directly by the Calvert Foundation, indirectly by brokers and financial planners, and online via a web-based broker-dealer MicroPlace, a wholly owned subsidiary of eBay. Minimum investments of $1,000 apply unless the note is purchased online, in which case minimums drop to $20. By year-end 2010 the Calvert Foundation had nearly $220 million in CI notes outstanding, raised from more than 10,000 investors, with proceeds distributed to over 220 borrowers in the United States and around the globe. In over 15 years, cumulative portfolio losses remained below 2 percent and have been more than offset by foundation reserves, ensuring that all investors have received timely principal and interest payments.[13]

Other CDFI Investor Note Programs. While the Calvert Community Investment Note program is the single largest retail note program, it is not alone. Since the mid-1970s, community development financial institutions and other classes of loan funds have raised capital through the sale of notes to individuals and institutions in their communities. Institutions like the Reinvestment Fund (Philadelphia), Boston Community Capital, New Hampshire Community Loan Fund, the Northern California Community Loan Fund, and the Enterprise Community Loan Fund are among the many CDFIs that actively raise loan capital through the sale of investor notes. CDFIs typically issue notes backed by the financial resources of the institution. The notes are unsecured, without specific collateral available for investors if there were to be a default. Investors are typically individuals supportive of the organization. Faith-based institutions, such as religious orders, religious pension funds, and others are also important investors, as are local foundations. According to the Opportunity Finance Network, a CDFI trade association, the capital raised from individuals, local philanthropy, and the faith community has become an important source of capital. Such investor notes, while offering a fixed return, typically do not have a rating or the other more complete legal documentation usually associated with bond offerings. While historically very few of these programs have resulted in investor losses, these notes are not available for sale through broker-dealers, require special custodians, and, if problems were to arise, offer investors limited protection.

Tool Selection: When Does Bond Financing Make Sense?

Advantages

Nonprofits and other social-purpose organizations can undertake bond issuance on either a taxable or tax-exempt basis. Generally, if eligible and available, tax-exempt issuance will have lower borrowing costs because of the higher interest rates generally associated with taxable debt. However, there are a number of alternatives to tax-exempt bond issuance that organizations can employ to meet their financing needs, including conventional loans and federal tax credit financing in certain cases. Organizations should compare these alternatives, as well as any other government or private funding or financing programs, and determine which one best meets their unique needs. Generally, tax-exempt bond financing entails the following advantages compared to commercial debt:

- Rates will typically be lower, since commercial loans are made at taxable rates.
- Terms will also generally be longer and more flexible.
- Commercial loans tend to have shorter maturities, and thus subject the borrower to reinvestment risk.
- Commercial loans also tend to be more restrictive in terms of loan-to-value requirements than the bond market, which focuses on cash flow and debt service coverage to a greater extent.

Limitations

Nonprofit and other social-purpose organizations have successfully accessed the fixed-income markets for their financing needs. While hospitals and universities were the first to benefit from long-term tax-exempt issuance at scale, there has been a significant expansion in the types of social-purpose organizations that can access the market. The suitability of bonds or notes as an attractive financing tool depends upon a number of factors, however, and this option may therefore not be appropriate in all cases. Of particular concern are issues such as the following.

Scale

Given the total costs associated with bond or note issuance, individual offerings tend to be relatively large. A small offering would be $10 million or less, while minimum offerings of $50 or $100 million are common. In most instances, it is really only larger nonprofits that are well positioned to issue bonds or notes.

Predictable Cash Flow Streams

Bond and note issuers need to have a well-defined and reliable cash flow stream that enables them to meet their bond payments regularly. Predicable earning streams may come from a third party, such as a governmental entity. Alternatively, earnings may come from customers, such as student tuition payments or patient or insurance medical payments.

Asset Quality

While ultimately it is the cash flow stream that is used to repay principal and pay interest, bond underwriters and investors also typically analyze the value of any underlying real estate collateral. Such collateral serves as a backstop for their investment in the event that cash flow does not materialize as predicted.

Institutional Credibility

At its most basic level, a bond is a commitment of an institution to honor its long-term commitment to repay investors the proceeds raised through the sale of the bond. While bondholders look first to the cash flow that will be used to repay the loan and to the credibility of the bond trustee and other backstop mechanisms, it is fundamentally the credibility of the borrowing organization that matters. Will the institution be in existence 30 years in the future and have the capacity to meet its long-term obligations?

Involvement of Public Entity

Most nonprofit bond issues are likely to involve a public entity that serves as conduit issuer in order to confer tax-exempt status to the offering. While in some instances larger nonprofits will issue taxable bonds directly without engagement of a public entity, this is likely to be the exception because of the interest rate benefit of issuing on a tax-exempt basis. For that reason, access to such a public entity can be an important criterion for successful issuance.

Potential Ratings

A social-purpose organization's cost of funds for its bond issue is closely linked to the credit rating—with a higher rating indicating lower risk and resulting in a lower cost of funds. Organizations considering bond issuance need to consider first whether or not the instrument can be structured to provide an attractive rating. Otherwise, borrowing costs can be prohibitive. There are, however, certain exceptions, such as Calvert Foundation CI notes and the FlexCAP bonds, which are unrated instruments bearing affordable interest rates. Social investors have demonstrated an appetite for purchasing such unrated instruments and a willingness to receive yields below risk-adjusted levels.

Source of Credit Enhancement

In the current market, nonprofits and other social-purpose organizations that are perceived to be higher risk by the rating agencies and investors may also need some form of credit enhancement for their offerings in the absence of socially minded investors willing to provide below-market-rate capital. The market penalty in terms of interest rates has been historically high for borrowers with ratings below the A grade. Such enhancement could take the form of partial guarantees or additional cash reserves, as in the case of the limited guarantee provided by the Bill and Melinda Gates Foundation for the KIPP Houston transaction highlighted in the beginning of this chapter. Sources of enhancement are more limited since the collapse of the municipal insurers and can be difficult to secure. However, there are both public and private sources of credit enhancement specific to different sectors.

Opportunity Costs

Issuing a bond involves significant time on the part of an organization's board and management that may be put to better use. Does the organization have the required expertise, and is it prepared to make the necessary commitment to see the effort through to completion? Is it the best use of the organization's management resources? Even investor note programs require significant legal engagement to produce a prospectus and to file with the respective state securities agencies. They also require substantial time.

Before jumping into a bond issuance, organizations should closely examine other alternative sources of funds. In the United States, for example, certain federal tax credit programs offer attractive financing. A range of nonprofits can access the New Markets Tax Credit program, which seeks to stimulate development in low-income neighborhoods. Charter schools can access the qualified school construction bond and qualified zone academy bond programs. These tax credit programs, and others like them, often provide financing at low interest rates or contribute equity to the project through monetization of the tax credits. Allocation for these programs is limited, so acquisition is not automatic. Each of the programs also has certain limitations regarding eligibility based on location and uses of proceeds, which may further restrict their use.

Issuance Costs

With the host of professionals associated with issuing fixed-income securities, it is understandable that it is a costly endeavor. Borrowers typically fund these costs out of bond proceeds, subject to a cap of 2 percent of the tax-exempt issue amount. In cases where issuance costs exceed this cap, such as smaller bond offerings or particularly complex offerings, the borrower can add a taxable series of bonds to cover the additional expense.

Issuance costs include legal fees for bond and underwriter's counsel, rating agency fees, and trustee fees, as well as fees paid to the underwriter. Underwriters serve as intermediaries between the issuer and the capital markets and assume financial risk in the period between purchase and sale. Underwriters are compensated for this risk by the difference between the purchase price they pay to the issuer for the securities and the price at which they are sold to investors, called the gross spread or underwriter's discount.

Because many of the fees are fairly fixed in nature, smaller bond issues may not be economically feasible. While $1 million in legal fees may only marginally increase the borrowing cost on a $100 million bond issue; it would be prohibitively expensive on a $5 million issue. Other fees, such as the underwriter's discount, vary based on the par amount of the offering. As such, the banks that earn these discounts are incentivized to serve the larger offerings that earn higher revenues.

Basic Mechanics for Issuing Bonds

The process of bond issuance is a lengthy one. For frequent issuers, it may only take three or four months, but for new issuers, or for particularly complex offerings, it can take significantly longer, more than a year in some cases.

One important reason for the lengthy time that bond issuances take is the regulatory provisions under which bond financing occurs in most countries. In the United States, for example, the Securities and Exchange Commission has regulatory authority over the issuance, sale, and trading of corporate securities. Municipal securities were exempted from the registration requirements of the Securities Act of 1933 and the reporting requirements of the Securities Exchange Act of 1934; however, they were not exempted from antifraud provisions.[14] These provisions require that information provided in a securities offering or subsequent disclosure reporting not misstate or omit material information that could impact an investor's decision-making.

The Securities Act Amendment of 1975 required brokers and dealers of municipal securities to register with the SEC. In addition, it created the Municipal Securities Rulemaking Board (MSRB), an industry self-regulating body, which is subject to SEC oversight. The MSRB has responsibility for development of rules governing the activities of brokers and dealers in municipal securities, which are enforced by the SEC and other regulatory agencies, though the 1975 act did not require municipal issuers to comply with the registration or reporting requirements governing corporate securities.

Rule 15c2-12, originally adopted by the SEC in 1989 and amended in 1995, however, indirectly governs registration and disclosure of municipal securities today by imposing certain requirements on municipal underwriters. Thus, this rule requires underwriters to obtain and review an official statement from issuers for all offerings greater than $1 million and to distribute the offering document to investors within set time periods. Rule 15c2-12 also prohibits underwriters from dealing in securities of issuers that do not agree to provide continuing disclosure over the life of the offering, including annual financial information and occurrence of certain material events. These registration and disclosure requirements apply to all municipal issues except those sold in denominations of $100,000 or more that meet certain additional requirements.[15]

There are numerous legal and financial documents involved in debt issuance. The diagram in Figure 13.3 depicts the main documents utilized in bond transactions together with the relevant parties.[16] There are also borrower and issuer resolutions required to authorize the issuance.

Against the backdrop of these regulations and document requirements, bond issuance involves its own "twelve-step" program.[17] These steps include the following.

Step 1. Identify Discrete Purpose for Raising Capital through Bond Issuance

The first step in any bond issuance is to address certain fundamental questions. What is the proposed purpose of the bond issuance? How much is needed?

FIGURE 13.3
Legal Documents Typically Required in a Bond Transaction

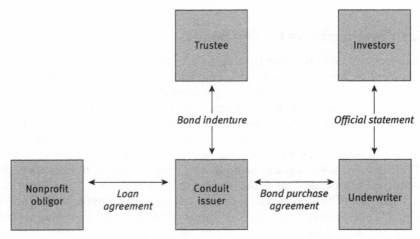

How does the issuance fit into the organization's long-term capital planning? What revenue will be generated to meet interest payments and eventual principal repayment? How certain is the projected revenue stream—is this derived from long-term government contracts or less consistent fundraising activities? Can the organization support debt service given other long-term financing needs?

Nonprofit borrowers often employ a financial advisor to assist them in answering these questions. The scope of services provided by financial advisors varies; however, they typically include evaluation of the borrower's capital plan, assistance in selecting underwriters, interaction with rating agencies and investors, review of legal and offering documents, and review of bond pricing and allocation.[18] Coastal Securities served as financial advisor in the KIPP Houston transaction highlighted at the beginning of this chapter.

Step 2. Build Internal Consensus within Board and Other Governing Agencies

A bond issue represents a significant, long-term commitment on behalf of a nonprofit organization. Therefore, a critical step in launching the issuance process is to assure agreement among various levels of the nonprofit's governance structure and among diverse stakeholders.

Step 3. Consult Underwriter, Bond Counsel, and Other Required Professionals

Since outside professionals are essential advisors and service providers in bond issuance, it is critical to consult outside expertise early on in the formulation process. In addition to financial advisors, underwriters, bond counsel, and other counsel may provide early-stage advice as well as make recommendations regarding debt structures that will result in the lowest overall borrowing costs. They also play important roles in developing the numerous legal and financial documents involved in debt issuance and in marketing the bonds.

Underwriters serve as intermediaries between borrowers and bond investors, initially advancing the capital and then selling the bonds to investors. Underwriters can be selected informally based on past relationships and reputation or more formally through a request for proposals (RFP) in which structuring ideas, past experience, and cost are compared. In the KIPP Houston transaction, RBC Capital Markets served as the lead underwriter and helped structure and market the issue. Other underwriters participated in sale of the issue, including First Southwest Company, BC Ziegler, Jefferies, Stifel Nicolaus, and the GMS Group.

Bond counsel, typically a specialized law firm, plays an integral role in the issuance of municipal securities by providing a formal opinion that the bonds are legal, valid, and binding obligations of the issuer and that interest on the bonds is exempt from federal income taxes and from state and local taxes, where applicable. Bond counsel is typically retained by the issuer and may assist the issuer with preparation or review of authorizing resolutions, trust indentures, official statements, validation proceedings, and litigation. Vinson & Elkins served as bond counsel on the KIPP Houston transaction.

Bond issuance may also entail the expertise of other counsel, including underwriter's counsel, disclosure counsel, and borrower's counsel. Underwriter's counsel is an attorney or law firm that has been retained by the underwriter to perform a due diligence review of the obligor and to prepare the bond purchase agreement between the issuer and the underwriter and in some cases the official statement. Underwriter's counsel provides certification that all material information has been disclosed. An issuer can retain disclosure counsel to provide advice on disclosure obligations and to prepare the official statement and continuing disclosure agreement. Alternatively, underwriter's counsel or bond counsel can assume these roles. In conduit issuance, borrower's counsel represents the borrower (as opposed to the issuer), advising the borrower on any provisions of the documents to which it is a party. In transactions involving nonprofit borrowers, borrower's counsel will render an opinion regarding the organization's tax-exempt status, its standing under state law, and the validity of the procedural authorizations for issuance.[19]

Step 4. Line Up External Support, If Needed

Most nonprofit bonds are issued under the auspices of a public entity with the authority to issue bonds on a tax-exempt basis. Typically, the nonprofit already has relationships with municipal or county government, the housing, educational, or transportation authority, or other public entity that may be available to serve as conduit issuer. There may also be a need for a third-party guarantor, such as a foundation or other institution committed to the success of the initiative. The guarantor should be involved early in the process in order to incorporate the type and structure of its guarantee into the documents.

Step 5. Prepare the Indenture and Loan Agreement

Bond counsel prepares and circulates the terms of the indenture and loan agreement that define the flow of funds and relative responsibilities among the issuing public authority and the nonprofit borrower.

Bonds are issued pursuant to an indenture or trust agreement between the issuer and the trustee, on behalf of bondholders. The indenture defines the terms of the offering, including interest rates, coupon dates, maturity dates, representations, and covenants. It also establishes the rights of investors and the remedies they can take in the event of default. The trustee represents the interest of the bondholders and monitors issuer compliance with the terms of the indenture. The indenture is typically summarized in the bond offering documents.

The issuer loans the bond proceeds to the nonprofit borrower pursuant to a loan agreement between the nonprofit organization and the issuer. The loan agreement includes repayment terms and the security for the loan. The issuer assigns most of its rights to the trustee as security for the bondholders, with its rights and responsibilities primarily restricted to receipt and distribution of payments.

Step 6. Develop Official Statement and Financial Plan

As the requisite elements of the bond issue and structure are addressed, the nonprofit borrower works with the underwriter, underwriter's counsel, and disclosure and borrower counsel, where applicable, to prepare an official statement that discloses the relevant financial and credit information for the borrower and the project.[20]

In a public offering, the issuer sells the bonds to an underwriter according to the terms of a bond purchase agreement, which is drafted by underwriter's counsel. In the case of conduit issuance, the bond purchase agreement is approved by the nonprofit borrower.

Step 7. Draft Documents to Be Reviewed by Rating Agency

In order to expand the number of investors for its bond offering, nonprofit borrowers may pay an independent, specialized company, or rating agency, to provide a credit rating for its issue. In the United States, nationally recognized statistical rating organizations (NRSROs) are rating agencies that are registered with the Securities and Exchange Commission. Ratings provided by NRSRO are used by both investors and regulators and affect the eligible investments and capital requirements of banks and other financial institutions. The SEC has certified 10 NRSROs, including three well-known in the United States—Fitch Ratings (Fitch), Moody's Investors Service (Moody's), and Standard & Poor's (S&P). The 2009 KIPP Houston issue was rated by Fitch and S&P.

When documents are in substantially final form, they are circulated to the applicable rating agencies so that they can assess the credit quality of the bond issuance. These agencies provide independent evaluations of the creditworthiness by providing credit ratings on scales ranging from highest to lowest quality, with different scales for short-term and long-term issuances. Each of the three agencies has its own system of ratings, although they are similar both in form and in the risk profiles corresponding to the different grades. The long-term rating scales use letter grades, with a highest rating of AAA from S&P and Fitch and Aaa from Moody's. The scales also use "notches" within grades, "+" and "−" in the case of S&P and Fitch and numbers ranging between 1 and 3 for Moody's. Credit ratings in the triple-B category or above are considered investment grade, while those falling below are referred to as non-investment grade, high-yield, or junk.

Step 8. Obtain Approval for Bond Issuance through Board Resolution

Once the organization is prepared to issue the bond, it must have a resolution from its board specifically authorizing the organization to take on the debt.

Step 9. Obtain Issuer Approval

Nonprofits that issue through a governmental conduit issuer must also obtain that entity's approval for the issuance.

Step 10. Market the Instrument to Investors

Typically, the underwriter is responsible for marketing the instrument by making the preliminary official statement available to potential investors. Marketing investor notes is generally a more informal process where the issuer sells its notes to supporters.

Step 11. Arrange Bond Pricing and Closing

When a bond is first offered for sale, it is presented with "indicative pricing." Since prices are determined by market interest rates, the maturity, and the perceived market risk, the final price is determined on the day of sale based on demand for the issue. Sale occurs when the bond purchase agreement between the issuer and underwriter is executed, and closing occurs with the delivery of the bonds to the underwriter in exchange for the purchase price together with delivery of the final executed bond documents.

Step 12. Service the Bond

Once the bond is closed and the nonprofit receives the proceeds to carry out its project, there is a third-party administrator or bond trustee that services the bonds. This trustee collects principal and interest payments from the nonprofit borrower and redistributes them to investors according to a set timetable, the debt service schedule.

Trustees are banking institutions selected by issuers to perform the administrative duties required by the terms of the bond indenture, including creation and maintenance of separate accounts, making payments to bondholders, and providing periodic financial statements. In addition to this administrative role, trustees act in a fiduciary capacity to protect the rights of bondholders. Trustees monitor the borrower's compliance with covenants included in the bond indenture, and in the event of default, they are empowered to take actions deemed reasonable and prudent to protect the rights of bondholders. Amegy Bank National Association serves as bond trustee for the KIPP Houston 2009 bond offering.

Operational Challenges

There are a number of operational challenges for fixed-income borrowers, some of which have already been mentioned.

Lengthy Process

As already noted, issuing a bond is an extensive, time-consuming process. It is not uncommon for a bond issue to take from six to 18 months between initial consultation with outside advisors and the final execution of the offering. Many social-purpose borrowers fail to appreciate this aspect of fixed-income issuance. They begin the process too late, are consistently behind schedule, and find that it can be very hard to catch up. Such miscalculations can have adverse effects on the organization's programmatic services, such as a school that does not complete construction in time for the beginning of the school year because of financing delays.

Complex Legal and Financial Undertakings

Fixed-income issuance requires board and management expertise to help the organization navigate through the issuance process and any long-term constraints the organization may have for its financing generally. In-house expertise is generally required to translate financials from formats required by auditors to those preferred by investors, which typically differ. Issuance also normally requires the assembling of a reliable team to research financing options and successfully issue the debt. Some social-purpose organizations may have long-standing relationships with such specialists; however, not all do and not all can afford them. The resulting costs of issuance can be prohibitively expensive for smaller issues.

Restrictive Covenants

Bond issuances generally include a number of covenants, or promises, that the borrower makes regarding its finances, its programmatic operations, and ongoing reporting or disclosure. These covenants can restrict a social-purpose organization's future operations and growth. For example, most issues include an additional bonds test, whereby the borrower is prohibited from issuing new bonds that are secured by the same assets or revenues unless certain benchmarks are met, such as a specific debt service coverage ratio. Covenants can also entail significant ongoing reporting, both financial and programmatic, which can burden already strained administrative capacities.

Capital Availability

While social-purpose borrowers are generally gaining access to the public capital markets, not all sectors have experienced the same level of market development. Shorter track records and lack of data on both issuance and performance restrict the investor pool in certain sectors, such as the charter school sector. These smaller investor pools tend to result in higher borrowing costs, which are based on limited demand rather than risk assessment. As a result, borrowing through such underdeveloped markets can sometimes be expensive. While nonprofit issuers in the past turned to insurance to help overcome these constraints, they must now turn to philanthropic sources to bridge any perceived credit gap.

Because of these challenges, fixed-income issuance is best suited for well-capitalized organizations with sophisticated boards of directors and the potential to generate the revenues for repayment. Such financing can be an effective tool for raising significant sums of long-term capital for large projects at attractive interest rates.

Track Record and Overall Assessment

The issuance of bonds for social purposes has been a staple of the financial markets and remains an important tool for nonprofits and other social-purpose organizations seeking to raise large amounts of long-term capital on attractive terms. While most nonprofit fixed-income securities have benefited large institutions, such as hospitals and universities, there are an increasing number of innovative strategies involving different classes of social-purpose organizations.

Some of the most promising innovations have included the use of guarantees by philanthropic institutions. By making available the credit quality of their own balance sheets, philanthropies are able to leverage significantly more capital from the public financial markets than they could make directly available. The Bill and Melinda Gates Foundation, the Heron Foundation, the MacArthur Foundation, and the Walton Family Foundation have been philanthropic leaders, coupling public and private resources to achieve significant scale. As outlined more fully in Chapter 5 of this volume, they are functioning as "philanthropic banks" or investment funds.

Other recent innovations include new kinds of assets financed with bonds—community development bond funds that target proceeds in response to investor requirements and retail note offerings made available to the general public with holdings of as little as $20. While most bond and note offerings continue to be rated by the established rating agencies, there are a growing number of instruments that are unrated and a growing number of social investors seeking to invest and accepting returns below their conventional benchmarks in exchange for social impact.

Issuing a bond is a multifaceted process that calls upon all levels of the organization, public support, engagement of public or philanthropic agencies, professional expertise, access to investors, and third-party servicers. While issuance is an extensive process that may require a year or more to fully execute, there are few comparable options to tap the same scale of financing on as attractive terms.

Fixed-income instruments are an important component of philanthropy—meeting a critical need for social-purpose organizations seeking capital, nonprofits managing endowments, foundations aiming to support established grantees, and foundations managing their own endowed assets.

In the world of bonds and fixed-income instruments, there is something for almost everyone!

Notes

1. Participating in this deal, in addition to the Gates Foundation, were affected charter schools and the Local Initiatives Support Corporation (LISC), a nonprofit community development organization, which together committed a matching $30 million in first-loss funds to the Houston program. The guarantees, including the foundation's guarantee, were made to a separate guarantee entity, PHILO (Public,

High-Impact, Low-Income, Open Enrollment) Houston, which in turn provides a guarantee to bondholders. The initial offering was oversubscribed by investors by three times.

2. For a discussion of loans, loan guarantees, and credit enhancements, see Chapter 12 of this volume.

3. Frank Fabozzi, Michael Ferri, and Steven Mann, "Overview of the Types and Features of Fixed Income Securities," in *The Handbook of Fixed Income Securities*, ed. Frank Fabozzi (New York: McGraw-Hill, 2005), 5.

4. Frank Fabozzi, Richard Wilson, and Richard Todd, "Corporate Bonds," in Fabozzi, *Handbook of Fixed Income Securities*, 320–22.

5. Financial Markets Series, "Bond Markets," The City UK, 2011, accessed June 13, 2012, http://www.thecityuk.com/assets/Uploads/BondMarkets2011.pdf, 1.

6. Securities Industry and Financial Markets Association, "U.S. Bond Market Outstanding," December 15, 2011, accessed January 8, 2014, http://www.sifma.org/research/statistics.aspx, 1.

7. "2010 in Statistics," *Bond Buyer*, February 14, 2011, 3A.

8. Local Initiatives Support Corporation, *Charter School Bond Issuance: A Complete History* (New York: Local Initiatives Support Corporation, Educational Facilities Financing Center, 2011), 5.

9. "Partnerships On-Line," Federal Home Loan Bank of Atlanta, accessed October 2010; "Habitat FlexCap Program," last modified October 9, 2012, http://www.habitat.org/newsroom/2012archive/10_9_2012_ImpactAssets.aspx.

10. "Bond Issuances," IFFIm, accessed January 13, 2010, http://www.iff-immunisation.org/bond issuances.html.

11. "Bonds," IFFIm, accessed October 18, 2012, http://www.iffim.org/bonds/.

12. "CRA Qualified Investment Fund Annual Report," Community Capital Management, May 31, 2012, http://www.crafund.com/general.php?category=CRA-Investors; "Access Capital Community Investment Fund," RBC Global Asset Management, accessed December 31, 2012, http://us.rbcgam.com/mutual-funds/fixed-income-funds/fg-4/fsg-7/fid-15/individual/overview/access-capital-community-investment-fund.fs.

13. "Calvert Foundation—Home," Calvert Foundation, accessed October 18, 2012, http://www.calvertfoundation.org.

14. Eugene Clark-Herrera and Darrin Glymph, *Charter Schools: Borrowing with Tax Exempt Bonds* (San Francisco: Orrick, Herrington & Sutcliffe, 2009), 42, 31.

15. Sylvan Feldstein, Frank Fabozzi, and Patrick Kennedy, "Municipal Bonds," in Fabozzi, *Handbook of Fixed Income Securities*, 280–82.

16. Clark-Herrera and Glymph, *Charter Schools*, 42.

17. Roger Davis and Alexandra Davis, *Nonprofit Corporations Borrowing with Tax Exempt Bonds* (San Francisco: Orrick, Herrington & Sutcliffe, 2001), 35–37.

18. William Wood, "Role of the Financial Advisor," in *The Handbook of Municipal Bonds*, ed. Sylvan Feldstein and Frank Fabozzi (Hoboken, NJ: John Wiley & Sons, 2008), 47.

19. Clark-Herrera and Glymph, *Charter Schools*, 49.

20. The official statement is the primary disclosure and offering document used for marketing municipal bonds to investors. A preliminary official statement (POS) is drafted and used for soliciting investors before financing terms are final. The final official statement (OS) is printed after sale of the bonds and contains the final bond terms, including principal amounts, coupon rates, yields, and maturities. The document contains information about the issuer, the borrower's finances and operations, the project that is being financed, the structure and terms of the bonds,

the security and sources of repayment for the borrowing, including any credit enhancement, and the credit rating. The official statement also identifies the professional participants involved in the offering, including underwriters and counsel, and includes as attachments the borrower's most recent audited financial statements and key bond documents.

Suggested Reading

Clark-Herrera, Eugene, and Maria C. Sazon. *Public Charter Schools: Borrowing with Tax Exempt Bonds.* 2nd ed. San Francisco: Orrick, Herrington & Sutcliffe LLP, 2012.

Fabozzi, Frank, ed. *The Handbook of Fixed Income Securities.* New York: McGraw-Hill, 2005.

CHAPTER 14

SECURITIZATION

Mary Tingerthal

LOS ANGELES LDC IS A certified community development financial institution that makes loans to start-ups, midsize businesses, and nonprofit organizations in distressed neighborhoods throughout Los Angeles. Though the performance of its loan portfolio had been good, by early 2004 the organization's access to capital to fund additional loans was quickly becoming constrained to the point that the organization was planning to turn away borrowers who needed their specialized lending and advisory services to grow their businesses. Fortunately, Michael Banner, president and CEO of Los Angeles LDC, had met Frank Altman, CEO of the Community Reinvestment Fund, USA (CRF), during 1992 when Altman had come to Los Angeles right after the Rodney King–related LA riots to share his solution for improving access to capital for mission-driven lenders. Altman's idea was to use his organization as a "secondary market" that would assemble the loans that such lenders were holding, sell bonds secured by these pooled loans, and return the proceeds to the lenders so they could originate additional loans, a process that Altman described as "securitization." Banner understood the securitization strategy and promised to work with CRF to assemble small-business loans that Los Angeles LDC was holding in order to enable Altman to sell them to Wall Street and other investors. As he began to exhaust his organization's available capital in 2004, Banner decided to contact Altman, and, after a review of the loan portfolio, Altman reported his willingness to include a $237,000 Los Angeles LDC small-business loan in the $51.1 million loan pool he was assembling, making Los Angeles LDC one of 38 mission-driven lending institutions to be included in the first CRF secondary market transaction to be formally rated by bond-rating agencies. In November 2004, CRF brought securities backed by these loans to market, reaping $46.1 million in bond proceeds, most of which went back to the 38 mission-driven lending institutions in 29 states, including Los Angeles LDC, refreshing their capital bases and empowering them to make additional loans to disadvantaged businesses and persons.

The experience of Los Angeles LDC and CRF in packaging a bundle of social investment loans and selling bonds backed by them to investors in order to replenish the capital needed by social investment loan originators illustrates the power of securitization, and the liquidity it provides, enabling the alternative community development lending market to maximize its impact. The 2004 CRF-17 bond offering was the first of four such "rated" asset-backed securities transactions that CRF had brought to market before the height of the global financial crisis, and CRF is just one of what are now a number of secondary market organizations helping to package social investments, as outlined more fully in Chapter 3 of this volume.

The CRF-17 story also highlights the two special features of the securitization phenomenon as it has begun to take shape in the social-purpose investment arena: first, the emergence of entities like CRF, which assemble loans from many relatively small social investment loan originators that often lack the scale to make securitization feasible on their own; and second, the importance of "social investors" willing to accept below-market financial returns, often in conjunction with market-rate investments, to make securitization feasible in the social-investment field. In CRF's case, this latter function was accomplished with program-related investments (PRIs) from the Ford, F.B. Heron, and MacArthur foundations, a large social investment from Prudential Social Investments, equity equivalent investments (EQ2s) from several banks, including US Bank and Wells Fargo, and a line of credit from US Bank. These social investors performed a number of crucial roles in the CRF example, from providing long-term capital that CRF used as working capital for its operations to helping to underwrite the line of credit that CRF secured in order to allow CRF to acquire sufficient loans for a cost-effective securitization.

Defining the Tool

Securitization is the process by which a secondary market organization or loan originator pools various types of loans—home mortgages, car loans, or credit card debt, for example—bundles the loans together in packages, sells bonds or other types of financial instruments backed by the loans to investors, and returns the proceeds to the originators of the loans so they can make additional loans.

The financial instruments used to bundle debt instruments are known as *securities*. These securities, which are bought and sold in financial markets, can take a variety of forms—bonds, debentures, notes, shares (stocks), and warrants.

The principal and interest on the loans underlying the bonds is paid to the investors on a regular basis, though the method varies based on the type of bond or other security. Loans backed by mortgages are known as mortgage-backed securities, while those backed by other types of loans are known as asset-backed securities.

Another term closely associated with securitization is *structured finance*. Structured finance is based on the principle that assets such as mortgage loans can be sold more effectively in the capital markets if they are "structurally isolated" and bundled together with like assets, rather than being sold with different types of assets. This structural isolation also protects the investor from any losses that might occur in the event of a bankruptcy of the originator or secondary market organization.[1]

Defining Features of the Tool

As described above, the financing instruments that will be discussed in this chapter are asset-backed securities and mortgage-backed securities. Since mortgage loans are also a type of asset, the term *asset-backed security* is often used in this chapter to refer more generically to both mortgage-backed and asset-backed securities. The process of creating these financing instruments is called *securitization* or *structured finance.* As both the instruments themselves and the process of creating them are essential to understanding the tool, the chapter will discuss both. (Because asset-backed securities are a subset of fixed-income securities, the reader can also refer to many of the defining features outlined in Chapter 13 of this volume focusing on fixed-income securities).

Asset-backed securities are financial instruments that are typically created by either an originator—a company that makes loans to individuals or companies—or a secondary market organization—a company that bundles loans made by multiple originators. Without securitization, an originator would typically raise capital through the sale of stock, through corporate borrowing, or, in the case of some social originators, through grants and donations, and then lend that capital to individual borrowers.

When creating an asset-backed security, the originator or secondary market organization takes the loans that are assets on its balance sheet and sells them to a separate legal entity, called a special purpose entity, in return for cash. This special purpose entity obtains the cash to buy the assets by selling bonds to investors that entitle the holders of those bonds to the future cash flows of the underlying assets. Because the assets are sold to the special purpose entity, the holders of the new asset-backed bonds have no exposure to the financial health of the originator or secondary market organization, and, most importantly, they have no exposure if the originator or secondary market organization goes bankrupt. Conversely, the asset-backed bondholders can be repaid only from the cash generated by the underlying assets, so if the individual borrowers default and fail to pay, the asset-backed bondholders face the risk of losing some of their investment. There are several devices used within the structure of asset-backed securities to protect bondholders from the risk of default that will be discussed in more detail later in the chapter.

The term *cash flow* is one that is used frequently in this chapter because it is a concept that is central to securitization. Cash flow means the amount of cash received by a lender from a borrower over the period of time that a loan is outstanding. For example, if a lender makes a $120 loan to a borrower at a 0 percent interest rate for a period of 12 months, the lender will receive cash flow from that loan of $10 per month. Because lenders charge interest for most loans, most cash flows involve payments of interest due and a repayment of the principal amount of the loan. The specific terms for how a lender will require that a particular loan be repaid are set forth in a *promissory note.* When cash flows are being prepared for an asset-backed security, the originator will enter the cash flows for each individual loan into a database and a computer application will aggregate the cash flows of all the underlying loans.

Relation to Common Criteria

Risk Level

Risk levels of asset-backed securities vary based on the credit quality of the underlying assets, the structure of the overall security offering, and the characteristics of the particular bond offered to investors. In a typical asset-backed security offering, bonds are offered at several different levels of risk that are determined by the likelihood that the investors will receive the cash flow to which they are entitled by the bond documents. Asset-backed security offerings are typically rated by at least one of the independent rating agencies, and may offer several series (or classes) of bonds with ratings ranging from AAA (highest rated and least risky) to "Not Rated" (most risky). Investors will typically expect to receive a higher yield for bonds that have a lower rating.

Asset-backed securities that are independently rated are subject to a highly regulated level of disclosure and transparency that is intended to be consistent among the issuers of securities. Prospective investors in asset-backed securities are entitled to a high level of access to information about the underlying assets, the originators and secondary market organization, and the other key parties to the transaction. Thus investors in asset-backed securities can mitigate their investment risk by fully utilizing this access to information and subjecting it to their credit analysis protocols.

Type and Level of Return

Investors in asset-backed securities typically receive monthly interest payments based on the outstanding principal balance of the bonds they own. The rate of interest paid (or yield) is partially dependent on the term of the securities. Chapter 13 in this volume, on fixed-income securities, contains a discussion about the relationship between yield (interest rate) and maturity, but, as a general rule, the longer the maturity, the higher the yield.

With respect to the payment of principal, most asset-backed securities are structured as "sequential pay" bonds. This means that the holders of different series of bonds will receive principal payments sequentially. For example, in the CRF-17 transaction discussed in the vignette above, the first set of bondholders was scheduled to receive all of the principal payments received from the underlying assets for a period of approximately 21 months, at which time their bonds would be paid off in full. Then the second set of bondholders was scheduled to receive all of the principal payments for the next 19 months, and so on through five different series of bondholders, with the final bondholders in a rated series scheduled to receive their final payment after eight years.

Investors who own bonds in the set that receives the first principal payments receive the lowest rate of interest, both because their bonds have a short maturity and because they have the lowest risk. In the CRF-17 transaction, the investors in the first series received a yield of 2.78 percent, while the investors in the last rated series received a yield of 8.60 percent. The weighted average yield for the entire security was 4.94 percent.[2]

Degree of Leverage

The degree of leverage that an originator or secondary market organization can obtain by issuing asset-backed securities will depend on the quality and the cash flow characteristics of the underlying assets. In order to determine how much cash an originator or secondary market organization can receive from the special purpose entity in return for its assets, it must compile a combined analysis of the cash flows of the underlying assets. This is typically done with the assistance of an investment banker. These cash flows, which will be used to pay both the expenses of the transaction and the investors, are then analyzed to determine the dollar amount of bonds that can be supported by the projected cash flows of the underlying assets. The combined cash flows are also subjected to a series of stress tests that are prescribed by the independent rating agencies to determine the ratings that are assigned to each different class of bonds. The stress tests include different assumptions about the number and dollar amount of loans that might default; the times at which those projected defaults might occur; and the severity of the loss that would be incurred as a result of default.

As an example of the degree of leverage achieved, in the CRF-17 transaction, CRF sold approximately $51.1 million in loans to the special purpose entity and the special purpose entity sold bonds to third-party investors totaling approximately $43.3 million, with CRF purchasing $2.8 million in remaining bonds (for a total of $46.1 million) and retaining a $5 million residual interest in the loans. Therefore, CRF achieved a leverage ratio of 6.5 to 1, based on the $7.8 million in equity that CRF retained compared to the total amount of loans funded.[3]

Ubiquity

Even in the wake of the recent financial crisis, asset-backed and mortgage-backed securities are still broadly used across the globe. At the peak in 2008, US asset-backed securities outstanding stood at $2.6 trillion and US mortgage-backed securities outstanding stood at $9.2 trillion. As of 2011, the levels were still $2.1 trillion and $8.9 trillion respectively.[4] However, the use of asset-backed and mortgage-backed securities for social purposes has been more restrained. For example, in the field of international microfinance, in the mid-2000s microfinance investment intermediaries (MIIs) developed transactions using a type of indirect asset-backed security known as a collateralized debt obligation (CDO) and brought 10 such transactions to market, but no new transactions have been completed in recent years. Similarly, the Community Reinvestment Fund brought four rated securitizations to market in the mid-2000s, but has not brought a new issue to market since 2008.

Almost any asset with a predictable cash flow can be securitized. As indicated in Chapter 3, on secondary markets, actual examples have included such esoteric items as fees from tobacco lawsuit settlements and record album receivables. The major asset categories tracked by the Securities Industry and Financial Markets Association (SIFMA) include automobile loans, credit card receivables, equipment loans, home equity loans, manufactured housing loans, student loans, commercial mortgage loans, residential mortgage loans, and other.[5] Loans originated for social purposes that might fit into these categories include loans for charter school or healthcare facilities, microfinance loans, and loans for alternative energy equipment.

Skill Requirement

For the originator or secondary market organization, the skill level required to assemble and issue asset-backed securities is at the extreme high end of difficulty, requiring the assistance of investment bankers, securities attorneys, and specialized accountants, as well as specialized financial partners such as trustees and special servicers.

For the investor, the due diligence required to properly analyze the underlying assets and the structure of the transaction will generally require the assistance of professionals with experience in evaluating fixed-income investments. However, because of the independent rating and highly prescribed structuring and disclosure rules that govern securities, the analysis can be more straightforward than analyzing the risk of a direct or syndicated loan to a non-profit corporation.

Social Implications

In the wake of the recent economic crisis, it would be easy to conclude that, given the degree to which asset-backed and mortgage-backed securities have been discredited, there will be little future use of this tool for social purposes. However, efforts are underway to restore the global securitization market under new rules and guidelines that will hopefully restore credibility to this important tool for bringing capital efficiently to markets that need it. As the authors of a recent textbook entitled *Elements of Structured Finance* note:

> Structured finance paradoxically may be the most optimistic, human-centered form of finance.... Any capital that can be conserved through this process can be redeployed to the frontier of innovation, and to improvements in the delivery of social services, and support for the arts and other things that enable us to adapt to our changing world, without reducing our current wealth.[6]

Many endeavors that generate social value could benefit from better access to efficiently priced capital since they are capital intensive. Some of these, such as affordable housing, have enjoyed relatively efficient means of accessing the capital markets through tools such as long-term tax-exempt bonds and securitization through Fannie Mae and Freddie Mac. Large nonprofit educational and healthcare institutions have also enjoyed relatively efficient access to long-term capital through the sale of tax-exempt bonds for the financing of their facilities. However, smaller organizations, such as charter schools and neighborhood health clinics, which are often the ones that serve the lowest-income communities, have not enjoyed similar efficient access to capital.

Design Features and Major Variants

In discussing the ways in which asset-backed securities may vary, it is important to remember the most basic element that defines these securities—the specific aggregate cash flows generated by the underlying assets. The word "structured" in the term *structured finance* fundamentally refers to the manner in which the cash is distributed to investors. Both the strength and weakness of structured finance is that, within certain legal and accounting parameters, issuers of asset-backed securities can set up almost any set of rules by which investors will receive their payments from the cash flow of the underlying assets. This means that an investor in asset-backed securities will use an investment analysis that includes assessments of reliability of the cash flow (credit risk); reliability of backup sources of cash in the event cash flows from the assets are interrupted (credit enhancement risk); the severity of loss in the event that one of the underlying borrowers does default and it is necessary to seize and then sell the collateral (risk of loss); and the likelihood that the asset will produce cash flows for as long as projected (duration risk).

Against this backdrop, it is possible to differentiate variants of the securitization tool along four major dimensions: (1) the type of asset being securitized; (2) the type of aggregator involved; (3) the type of investor being targeted;

and (4) the type of credit enhancement, if any, being employed. Let us examine each of these in turn.

Types of Assets

As discussed above, virtually any type of asset that produces a predictable cash flow can be packaged into an asset-backed or mortgage-backed security. The characteristics of the assets will shape the characteristics of the asset-backed security, however, because the cash flows of the individual loans are aggregated to form the cash flows for the security. For example, Table 14.1 outlines typical characteristics of acquisition loans (loans used to acquire property for future development) that might be generated by a community development financial institution (CDFI) lending to a nonprofit developer.

Compare this to loans that might be generated by a nonprofit lender providing a permanent mortgage loan for a housing development using Low Income Housing Tax Credits, as also shown in Table 14.1.[7]

A pool of such acquisition loans would produce aggregate cash flows very different from those produced by a pool of such permanent loans. Historically, it has been more typical to create asset-backed securities from loans with characteristics similar to those of the permanent loan described than from those with characteristics of the acquisition loans described. While the mainstream capital markets have produced asset-backed securities for shorter-term assets like auto loans (with a typical term of three to four years) these have been done by finance companies that can produce very large volumes of such loans that can easily support the expense of creating an asset-backed security.

Types of Loan Aggregators

As discussed earlier, securitization is not limited to loans as underlying assets, but loans are certainly the most typical assets to be securitized. Therefore the

TABLE 14.1   ILLUSTRATIVE CHARACTERISTICS OF TWO CLASSES OF ASSETS ASSEMBLED INTO ASSET-BACKED SECURITIES

	Type of Asset	
Loan characteristic	Acquisition loan	Permanent development loan
Term	3–4 years, with possible extension	30 years, often with repayment prohibition for first 10 years
Payment type	Monthly interest-only payments, with balloon payment upon permanent financing	Monthly payments of interest and principal until repaid
Interest type	Variable, based on index rate	Fixed
Loan-to-value ratio	90 percent	40 percent
Typical loan size	$500,000 to $2 million	$3 million to $10 million

Source: Opportunity Finance Network. *Inside the Membership: 2009 Statistical Highlights from the OFN Membership* (Philadelphia: Opportunity Finance Network, 2010).

most common party to use securitization is a company that is in the business of lending, often referred to as a loan originator. Any type of lending organization can choose to use securitization as a method of raising capital—banks, credit unions, community development financial institutions, insurance companies, and microfinance institutions. Most lenders that choose to raise capital by selling assets from their balance sheet will do so by working with established *secondary market players* such as Fannie Mae and Freddie Mac for US residential mortgages, microfinance investment intermediaries (MIIs), or, as in the case of CRF, specialized social investment secondary market organizations, rather than choosing to issue securities directly.

In determining whether securitization is a useful tool for its business, a loan originator or secondary market organization will need to assess whether its business will generate a sufficient volume of the type of loans it wishes to securitize in a short enough period of time to justify the expense of the securitization and to successfully manage the risks of aggregating the loans (these risks will be more fully discussed in the "Basic Mechanics" section of this chapter). To justify the expense of a direct securitization, it is generally felt that an originator must be able to generate a minimum pool of $50 million in loans in a period of one year or less, with a pool of at least $100 million in loans being even more desirable.

It is this need to generate a large volume of loans in a short period of time that has led to the development of aggregators or secondary market organizations in the field of securitization. Fannie Mae and Freddie Mac are the best examples of aggregators. They buy loans from thousands of mortgage originators across the country and generate mortgage-backed securities on a continuous basis. The Community Reinvestment Fund is also an example of an aggregator or secondary market organization. As noted above, the asset pool for the CRF-17 transaction included 128 loans originated by 38 individual direct originators from across the country.[8]

In the international microfinance field, securitization has been done largely through the issuance of collateralized debt obligations (CDOs) issued by microfinance investment intermediaries (MIIs). These MIIs make loans to microfinance institutions (MFIs), and the MFIs pledge the repayments from a pool of microloans to repay their loans from the MII. The MIIs then combine several of these loans to MFIs into CDOs and sell securities to third-party investors. Typically the MIIs will sell securities in total amounts much less than the amount of the underlying loans to the MFIs, thus retaining a substantial amount of the risk of repayment.

Types of Investors

Securitizations differ not only in terms of the types of assets and asset aggregators involved, but also in terms of the types of investors engaged. In fact, one of the primary reasons that securitization is such a powerful tool is that it allows the issuer to structure the payment of cash from the underlying assets in ways that meet the different needs of multiple types of investors. There are two primary dimensions along which investors can be differentiated—term and risk appetite—and securitization provides a way to manage both of these dimensions and therefore to engage investors with different attitudes towards both.

Term is the simplest concept to describe. As discussed in Chapter 13, a fundamental underpinning of fixed-income investing, including asset-backed securities, is the concept of the yield curve, which measures the difference between the interest rate that must be paid to investors on short-term as compared to long-term investments. These rates differ because the longer that investors commit to having their money outstanding, the more they want to charge for it. The amount of difference between the interest rate charged for a short-term security (for example, one month) and the longest security (for example, 30 years) will change from time to time, based on investors' expectations about interest rates and on current monetary policy. When expectations for future inflation are high, the difference will be large and the yield curve is said to be "steep." When expectations for future inflation are low, the difference will be small and the yield curve is said to be "flat." The yield curve for US Treasury securities is considered to be the "riskless" yield curve and is typically used as the baseline against which interest rates for many other fixed-income securities are compared. At the time that the CRF-17 transaction was completed in 2004, for example, the "riskless" yield curve ranged from 1.98 percent for one-month securities to 5.22 percent for 30-year securities.[9]

As described earlier, the "sequential pay" security is used to attract multiple investors to a security by providing investments with different expected terms, based on when they will receive principal payments. In the CRF-17 transaction, the five rated investor classes were expected to have the terms with the resulting interest rates shown in Table 14.2.

It is important to note that term is not the only factor that determined the interest rates shown in Table 14.2, but it does demonstrate that the longer an investor must wait for the repayment of its investment, the higher the interest rate it will expect. The column titled "Spread to Yield Curve" shows the additional yield that the investor required in excess of the "riskless" curve, and demonstrates that other risk factors are being taken into account in the longer classes.

This brings us to another major factor that differentiates various classes of investors—the perceived risk of the class in which they are investing. As Table 14.2 shows, the ratings assigned to the different classes of securities by Standard & Poor's in the CRF-17 transaction ranged from AAA to B. Classes A-1, A-2, and A-3 are all rated AAA, so the only thing that differentiates these classes is the time period during which they will receive their principal payments and be paid off in full. As Table 14.2 shows, the difference in the spread to the US Treasury yield curve among these classes is only slightly different (only 0.30 percent difference from shortest to longest). However, the Class C securities are

TABLE 14.2 INTEREST RATES PAID ON VARIOUS CLASSES OF CRF-17 SECURITIES AND COMPARISON TO YIELD CURVE ON US TREASURY SECURITIES

Class of security	Period to receive principal payments	Interest rate	Spread-to-yield curve	S&P rating
A-1	Month 1 to Month 21	2.77%	.40%	AAA
A-2	Month 21 to Month 40	3.59%	.50%	AAA
A-3	Month 40 to Month 57	4.21%	.70%	AAA
B	Month 57 to Month 73	5.72%	1.95%	A
C	Month 73 to Month 90	8.45%	4.50%	B

Source: Piper Jaffray & Co., "Final Pricing Curve for CRF-17," working paper, November 2004.

rated B by Standard and Poor's, which means that they have a much higher risk of losing money in the event that the underlying loans perform worse than projected. In this case, the investor needed 4.50 percent more than it would expect on the "riskless" yield curve to take on this added risk. Investors in the higher-rated classes are often referred to as senior investors, and investors in the lower-rated classes are often referred to as subordinate investors. Securities offerings structured with multiple classes of investors are often referred to as senior/subordinate structures.

Types of Credit Enhancement

A final basis for differentiating securitization transactions has to do with the existence and nature of so-called *credit enhancements* attached to the loans or the securities. Credit enhancement refers to features of an asset-backed security that reduce the risk to the investor. There are two major types of credit enhancement that are used in connection with asset-backed securities—*loan-level credit enhancement* and *pool-level credit enhancement*. Both types may be utilized within a single security.

Loan-level credit enhancement provides protection at the loan level in the event that a particular borrower fails to pay his or her loan. There are two primary forms of loan-level credit enhancement—loan guarantees and mortgage insurance. Loan guarantees protect lenders against loss in the event a borrower defaults on a loan. Such guarantees are most often provided by government entities such as the Small Business Administration and the Federal Housing Administration in the United States. When the loan is originated, it must meet certain prescribed eligibility and underwriting standards to qualify for the guarantee. Once the guarantee is issued for a given loan, it stays with the loan regardless of who the owner of the loan asset might become. In the event of default by the borrower, the owner of the loan must file for payment under the guarantee. Guarantees under various programs differ in terms of the steps that the owner of the loan must take prior to filing the claim, the amount of the guarantee (some are capped at a particular percentage of the loan), and the amount of time lag before payment is received under the guarantee. If asset-backed securities contain loans with guarantees, the details of the guarantee and the claims process for the guarantee are described in the disclosure materials for the securities.

Mortgage insurance operates in a manner similar to that of guarantees, but mortgage insurance is typically provided by private companies that are licensed and regulated under insurance law. These companies typically pay a "top loss" payment in the event that a loan defaults. Mortgage insurance has historically been used by borrowers who were unable to meet the requirement to provide a 20 percent down payment when purchasing a house. The borrower would often provide a 5 percent down payment and then purchase mortgage insurance, usually paying both an upfront and monthly insurance premium, and the mortgage insurer would pay a claim to the lender for the difference between 5 percent and 20 percent in the event that the borrower defaulted. During the recent financial crisis, many mortgage insurance companies failed and left investors in mortgage-backed securities without the loan-level credit enhancement that they thought they had to protect their investments.

Pool-level credit enhancement is provided at the level of the asset-backed security rather than at the loan level. Most often pool-level credit enhancement is designed to protect against an interruption of cash flow to the investors. For example, consider a case where an unguaranteed loan defaults and the borrower gives up the property that served as collateral for the loan to the lender. The lender sells the property and realizes enough cash from the sale to pay off the loan in full, including accrued interest. In this case, the investor does not incur a loss, but it is likely that it took the lender 12 to 18 months to sell the property and obtain the cash. Most investors do not want to take the risk of having their cash flow interrupted, so they look to some sort of credit enhancement at the pool level to reduce their risk of such an interruption.

Pool-level credit enhancement can take several forms, and a single asset-backed security may include more than one type. The simplest is a loan loss reserve, which is a pool of cash that is deposited with the trustee, and which the trustee uses to make payments to the investors in the event that there is not enough cash from the underlying loan payments on a given distribution date. A senior/subordinate bond structure also provides a pool-level form of credit enhancement. In such a structure, there are certain subordinate investors who agree that they will not receive their interest or principal payments in the event that there is insufficient cash to pay all investors. In the example above, these subordinate investors would likely benefit from the eventual recovery of the cash from the sale of the property, but their cash flow would be subject to interruption. Yet another form of pool-level credit enhancement is pool insurance. In this case, the originator structures the cash flows of the security to include a monthly premium payment to a third-party insurance company. In the event that cash flow is interrupted, the pool insurer steps in to make the payments and then has a claim on future proceeds from the disposition of defaulted loans. As with mortgage insurers, many pool insurers failed during the recent financial crisis, leaving investors without the protection they had anticipated.

Patterns of Use

Securitization is still a major tool of the capital markets. Even in the wake of the global financial crisis, the combined total of asset-backed, commercial mortgage and residential mortgage securities outstanding in the United States at the end of 2011 was $11.0 trillion, with securitized assets in Europe adding another $2.7 trillion. Even though the rate of issuing new securities has dropped dramatically from the peaks of the mid-2000s, in 2010, new residential mortgage securities in the US topped $1.7 trillion, new asset-backed securities totaled more than $107 billion, and new European securitizations totaled more than $551 billion.[10]

The ubiquity of this tool in the regular capital markets has led many to believe that it could be a powerful tool to draw capital to the social investment markets. In June, 2006, John Olson, Director of the Center for Community Development Investments at the San Francisco Federal Reserve wrote in an issue of the *Community Development Investment Review* dedicated to the exploration of securitization and other secondary market techniques:

"Frequently, the capital that is used to revitalize communities comes from mission-driven investors motivated by regulation, the fear of regulation, religious beliefs, or social justice. As any CDFI can tell you, the amount of capital available in this sphere is finite, and the competition over accessing these sources of capital can be fierce. A persistent dream of community development organizations has been to broaden the universe of investors, and ultimately access the institutional capital markets. The amount of capital available in these institutional markets is, for all practical purposes, and especially for community development purposes, infinite."[11]

Unfortunately, as of 2011, this dream remains largely unrealized.

By comparison to the size of the US Securitization market ($1.8 trillion), at the end of 2009 the Opportunity Finance Network (a US trade group that supports Community Development Financial Institutions (CDFIs)) reported that, among the 148 CDFIs responding to its annual lending survey, the outstanding balance of all loans on their balance sheets stood at only $5.2 billion, with almost none of these loans having been securitized.[12] Among CDFIs, Community Reinvestment Fund is the only organization to have brought rated asset-backed securities to market directly. The combined total of rated asset-backed securities brought to market by CRF is approximately $200 million. During the past decade, CDFIs have used numerous other structured financial transactions to attract capital to the community development sector, most notably financing structures utilizing the New Markets Tax Credit (NMTC) program, which has generated nearly $30 billion in community development investments since its inception in 2001.[13] The NMTC provides US corporations with income tax credits in return for their investment of capital into qualified businesses, including non-profit businesses, which are located in low income census tracts. The development of the NMTC program may well have replaced much of the need for CDFIs to use securitization as a strategy to raise capital, as they have used NMTC transactions to finance community facilities including charter schools and other educational facilities, community health centers, child care centers and facilities for many operating non-profits. The NMTC program is due to expire in 2012, so unless the US Congress takes action to extend it, no new allocations of NMTC will be available after 2012.

Perhaps another reason that direct securitization has not been used frequently by social lenders in the United States is that large parts of the potential social markets are already served by government structures that utilize securitization or techniques similar to securitization. For example, the US Small Business Administration offers loans to small businesses that are secured by their business real estate under its Section 504 program. With this program, which provided financing totaling an average of more than $5 billion each year for the past 5 years, the loans are originated by non-profit organizations known as certified development companies (CDCs). Much like a securitization program, the SBA funds these loans on a monthly basis, aggregates the loans into pools, and then issues SBA debentures equal to the amount of the pool. The SBA then uses the payments received from the borrowers to pay off the investors in the SBA debentures.[14]

In the field of affordable housing, capital has generally been available for first-time homebuyers and affordable rental housing through programs financed by state and local housing finance agencies through the sale of tax-exempt mortgage revenue bonds. These programs operate in a manner similar to mortgage-backed securities. In addition, until the financial crisis, Fannie Mae and Freddie Mac have provided outlets to social lenders such as Self-Help Credit Union for highly targeted single family mortgage programs (as described in the "Secondary Markets" chapter). Since the financial crisis,

Fannie Mae and Freddie Mac have provided the primary secondary market for single-family mortgages and loans for affordable rental properties.

The new CDFI Bond Guarantee Program authorized by the US Congress in 2010, described in Chapter 3 on secondary markets, offers perhaps the best opportunity to bring securities to market that are backed by social assets originated by CDFIs. By providing a guarantee issued by the US Treasury, this program could provide sufficient credit enhancement to make the issuance of asset-backed securities a cost-effective solution.[15]

A similar story of limited use of securitization can be found in the field of international microfinance. In its 2011 report, the International Association of Microfinance Investors (IAMFI) estimated that the global volume of microcredit loans outstanding at the end of 2010 was $65 billion, up from $12 billion in 2004. Much of the growth in this industry is attributed to the successful attraction of market-based capital to supplement philanthropic support, but the transformation of many MFIs (microfinance institutions) from nonprofit organizations into regulated entities in order to tap commercial sources of capital has also played a role. Still, of the $4.2 billion in debt investments held by microfinance investment intermediaries, only $521 million, or about 12 percent, was in the form of collateralized debt obligations (CDOs), which are a form of indirect asset-backed securitization. This represents only 12 percent of the outstanding MII investments and less than 1 percent of the total microcredit loans outstanding. Thus, even in a field of social finance that has an impressive record of attracting market capital in recent years, only a small percentage is attributable to securitization.[16]

The Consultative Group to Assist the Poor (CGAP) has reported that the average deal size for the lending organizations participating in the microfinance CDOs was about US$4 million and that 61 percent of the investors were institutional investors and 26 percent were development finance institutions. CGAP also reported that 93 percent of structured finance deals were done in Latin America and the Caribbean, eastern Europe, and central Asia.[17]

Tool Selection

Securitization offers a powerful vehicle for attracting capital to support many activities that generate large and regular payments of cash—ranging from payments of a few rupees a week from hundreds of small Indian entrepreneurs paying off their business microloans to payments of millions of dollars a year from American developers paying off their mortgage loans on large affordable housing projects. The power of securitization is that the technique relies on the skill of highly knowledgeable originators who know how to make good credit risk decisions about a particular group of borrowers. These originators then turn to a secondary market organization to bundle similar loans together to make them into an attractive investment (in terms of size, risk diversification, ease of investment, etc.) for large institutional and social investors. The job of the secondary market organization as the intermediary between the originators (who represent the needs of their borrowers) and the investors is to understand the needs of both and to structure the security in a way that allows capital to flow from investors to the borrowers.

At the same time, securitization in the social investment field is limited by the fact that it can only be used for social activities that generate enough revenue to make regular loan payments. This simple fact can make it difficult for social lenders to aggregate sufficient numbers of loans for securitization because these lenders usually lend to low-income persons directly or to organizations that serve low-income persons or communities. For example, it is known in the affordable housing field that if a developer wants to produce a housing development where the rents are affordable to households with incomes of no more than 30 percent of the median income, it will be virtually impossible for that development to make payments on a loan. This is because, at $15,000 annual income (which is 30 percent of the national median income of $50,000), an affordable monthly rent for that household is $375 (which is 30 percent of the household's monthly income of $1,250). The owner of the development will need all of the $375 to cover operating expenses, property taxes, and utilities and would have no revenue remaining to pay debt service. This is illustrative of many activities that serve low-income families—housing, child care, healthcare. Unless there is some level of government or philanthropic subsidy available, it is often impossible to serve social mission through lending. Many CDFIs and nonprofit developers have become expert at the complex task of structuring financing programs that take advantage of various government subsidy programs in order to meet community needs. In the international microfinance market, this issue has been addressed in part through an increase in direct equity and debt investing in microfinance institutions, and through the use of indirect asset-backed securities (pools of loans to the microfinance institutions that are, in turn, backed by the loans to the borrowers).[18]

With this basic premise in mind, it is most important that securitization be employed as a tool only in those portions of the social-lending spectrum where there is a large, steady stream of borrowing needs that are not met by another portion of the market. The field of CDFIs in the United States has struggled to find a class of assets that is needed by their borrowers on a consistent basis and that is also suitable for securitization. As discussed above, capital for permanent loans in the affordable housing sector is reasonably well provided by the established secondary markets of Fannie Mae, Freddie Mac, and the state and local housing finance agencies. As a result, much of the lending for affordable housing that is done by CDFIs is often for shorter-term acquisition or construction loans. Such loans tend to be less suitable for securitization because their short terms make them very suitable to hold on a CDFI's balance sheet. As discussed previously, financial consultants recommend that the minimum size for a securitization to be cost effective is $50 million. The average CDFI participating in the Opportunity Finance Network's 2009 lending survey originated only $11.4 million in loans that year.[19]

In 2006, the Housing Partnership Network[20] conducted a detailed survey of 10 of the largest CDFIs to determine if there were classes of assets that the CDFIs would prefer not to hold on their balance sheets and for which there was not a well-developed secondary market. The survey was conducted to determine if several CDFIs working together could generate enough loan volume to support the issuance of an asset-backed security. The survey resulted in identifying charter school facilities loans as the one class of assets where it appeared that there would be sufficient volume of loans suitable for securitization. Five of the CDFIs that participated in the survey subsequently formed the Charter School Financing Partnership LLC (CSFP) in 2007 and jointly applied for, and were awarded, a $15 million grant by the US Department of Education to be used to provide credit enhancement for a security backed by charter school facilities loans. CSFP intended to generate up to $150 million in capital by assembling a pool of 15 to 20 loans to charter schools located throughout the United States and then issuing a collateralized debt obligation (CDO) that utilized the $15 million grant as credit enhancement for the pool. The group reached the point of having a commitment and detailed term sheet from a major international bank to provide a temporary financing facility needed to accumulate the loans before they could be securitized. However, in the midst of the worst of the financial crisis, the market for CDOs collapsed in January 2008 and the commitment was withdrawn.[21] The CSFP continued to try to access the securitization market with a pooled credit enhancement approach through the middle of 2010 without success, as the rating agencies, in the wake of the financial crisis, demonstrated no willingness to look at assets that were not considered to be mainstream. CSFP finally sought and received permission from the Education Department to use the credit enhancement dollars, together with funds received by CSFP from a major foundation, to provide credit enhancement for individual charter schools issuing tax-exempt bonds to finance their facilities.[22]

As described more fully in Chapter 3 on secondary markets, the launch in 2012 of the new CDFI Bond Guarantee Program, which provides a 100 percent federal guarantee for up to $1 billion in bond transactions per year, holds the promise of changing this funding landscape for loans to low-income individuals and communities, at least on a temporary basis, though the future of this program remains unclear as of this writing.[23] Securitization is a tool that only works effectively at large scale, and there are significant barriers to the effective application of this tool to generate more capital for social purposes. However, the ability of the international microfinance market to attract private capital and the new CDFI Bond Guarantee Program may point to a new start for effective use of securitization in the social sector. More generally, the need and potential applicability of securitization may be far more widespread internationally, where the need for capital is greater than in the United States, and where the alternative availability of direct financing of social-purpose activities is far less fully developed.

Basic Mechanics

Securitization is an extremely powerful financial tool that can be used to bring additional capital to the social sector, but it is also highly complex, works only at a large scale, and requires a very deliberate business strategy. This section will identify the steps that must be taken to achieve a successful application of the securitization tool, using the Community Reinvestment Fund and the CRF-17 transaction as examples. More specifically, the discussion here focuses on ten such major steps.

Step 1. Assess the Business Case

The most basic premise driving the use of securitization is the existence of a large and continuous need for capital by a set of borrowers that an organization wishes to serve. This need for capital can come from the desire to free up capital currently invested in loan assets or from a steady stream of newly originated future loan assets.

Whether securitization makes business sense or not is by no means certain. As noted earlier, one of the primary benefits of securitization is a reduction in the cost of financing for assets. Paradoxically, this basic premise may be difficult to achieve because much social lending in the United States has been accomplished to date through the use of capital that does not require market rates of return, such as foundation grants and capital grants from the CDFI Fund Financial Assistance award program. Many of these social lenders have used this capital to lend to borrowers that would have trouble obtaining loans from the traditional sources of capital and have made the loans at rates that are lower than the market would require. As a result, if they try to sell the loans to be part of a securitization, they will often find that they must sell them at a discount because the interest rates are too low to attract investors. This suggests the need to make a number of judgments before even starting down the road toward implementing the securitization tool. Among these judgments are the following:

- Determining whether the loan product that is the target of the securitization will produce enough loan volume that the balance sheet of the organization originating the loans will not be sufficient to provide enough capital to meet the loan demand. If the balance sheet of the organization is large enough to fund all of the demand for loans, then securitization may not be needed.
- Determining whether the loans carry an interest rate sufficient to attract investors. As noted above, many social-purpose loans have subsidized interest rates that may paradoxically make them unattractive to potential investors.
- Finally, determining whether to build a business practice that allows the securitizer to access a standard securitization platform like Fannie Mae and Freddie Mac mortgage-backed securities, as the Self-Help Credit Union described in Chapter 3 did; or whether it wants to access the securitization market directly as was done by CRF with the CRF-17 transaction. For both of these options the organization will need much of the same operational capacity and expertise, but additional skills and capacity are needed when accessing the market directly. These include the business techniques and resources needed to successfully aggregate loans, package and sell the resulting securities, and then manage the post-securitization activities. As securitization expert Doug Winn put it in a recent article: "Much has been said about the challenges of selling pools of loans into the capital markets via securitization or other techniques. In our experience, the actual sale is often the least difficult part of the process.... The belief at our firm is that the process leading up to the sale is often more challenging than the sale itself."[24]

Step 2. Engage Professionals to Assist in Setting Up Operations

To design a successful loan product that will be suitable for securitization and that will generate the financial results that the organization is projecting, it is necessary to engage in a bit of "reverse engineering." An experienced financial consultant can assist the organization by providing models of securitization cash flows that are similar to those that it hopes to generate once the loan assets have been acquired. If the organization starts with where it wants to end up, it will need to understand crucial details about how to design the underwriting criteria and terms of the loans; how to price the loans on an ongoing basis; what financial resources are needed to support the aggregation of enough loans to securitize; and how the organization will manage the various risks that it will encounter along the way. Because securitization operates at a relatively large scale, even small errors in assumptions can result in a failed business model.

Step 3. Determine How to Fill All the Critical Roles That the Organization Will Need

The organization will likely have a number of roles that it will want to fill with members of its own staff, such as the origination and purchasing of loans and coordination of the securitization process. The organization will also need skills on its internal financial management and accounting team that can handle the particular tasks brought on by securitization. Loan servicing is also a critical element, both before and after securitization. A strong capability for information and data management is essential. It is likely that the organization will want to assemble a team of contractors that can provide specialized securitization skills, including legal counsel, an investment banker, and an outside accounting firm that is familiar with securitization accounting. Some highly specialized skills, such as hedging interest rate risk (as described below) on loans that are being aggregated for securitization, can be arranged on an ongoing contract basis that integrates with the organization's financial team.

Step 4. Develop the Financial Capability to Accumulate Loans

The securitizer will need to have the financial capacity to accumulate enough loans to securitize over a period of months. This will allow the organization to originate or purchase loans on an ongoing basis as borrowers need to borrow. Most organizations that intend to securitize do not have enough of their own equity capital to finance these loan fundings, so they arrange a short-term revolving line of credit called a "warehouse" line. This allows the organization to pledge a loan that it has funded as collateral for the amount borrowed under the warehouse line. Typically the organization can borrow no more than 80 percent of the value of each loan, so an organization that intends to aggregate $100 million worth of loans would need at least $20 million of its own capital to fund the balance of the loan, and most of that capital will need to be in the form of equity or net worth. If loans are being sold into a standardized securitization platform like Fannie Mae mortgage-backed securities, capital requirements for a warehouse line may be lower because the risk of repayment to the warehouse lender is lower than with a private securitization.

Step 5. Manage the Risks

There are three new risks that an organization will face if it chooses to securitize—pricing risk, interest rate risk, and risks around managing the balance sheet. While all lending organizations face a certain degree of risk in pricing their loan products, the *pricing risk* is far greater when an organization's exit strategy is tied to the larger capital markets. It is essential to develop a protocol for pricing that takes into account all of the expenses of securitization as well as the expenses of loan origination and servicing. It is further critical to have a model that takes into account ongoing changes in the securitization marketplace that affect the spreads over the "riskless" yield curve. This is related to, but separate from, the risk of changes in interest rates.

Managing *interest rate risk* is the second risk-related task. As discussed previously, the value of a fixed rate loan can go down if interest rates go up during the time that an investor owns a loan. For that reason, most organizations that aggregate loans for securitization will put in place an interest rate risk management or "hedging" program. In financial terms, a "hedge" refers to an investment in a financial instrument, the value of which can be expected to move in the opposite direction of an asset that the organization wants to hold. If the hedge investment is properly selected, when market interest rates increase, the hedge instrument increases in value, offsetting the loss on the underlying loans. However, if market rates decrease, the value of the organization's loans increases and its hedge instrument declines in value. Interest rate risk management requires daily attention from a specialist either on the organization's finance team or through a contract with a third-party professional. An effective hedging program also requires very good up-to-date data on the value of the underlying loans and requires a link to the system where the individual loans are being serviced.

Because the aggregation of loans will cause the size of the organization's balance sheet to fluctuate—growing during a period of aggregation and then shrinking when the loans are securitized—it can often be difficult to manage covenant restrictions that the organization may have with other lenders. It is important for the organization to have a strong capacity to forecast its balance sheet in order to determine if it is at risk of violating financial covenants as the balance sheet grows. Securitization is also the subject of numerous complex accounting rules, especially in the wake of the recent financial crisis.

Step 6. Accumulate the Loans

An organization that uses securitization must be fundamentally concerned with the soundness of the loans it is assembling. This means that it must be concerned about the interest rate spread on each loan it assembles. When an organization uses securitization to raise capital for its lending activity, the consequences of falling short on its production plan can have serious consequences for the organization. For example, a warehouse line of credit may contain a requirement that it be repaid in full at least once every year (this provision is known as a "cleanup" call). If the organization has not accumulated enough loans to go to market with a security within that period, the organization will be in default on its loan. All of the lending processes and policies must be designed and managed in close alignment with the requirements of the securitization process.

Step 7. Collect and Analyze Good Data

Since the fundamental underpinning of securitization is the ability to accurately reflect and project the cash flows of many individual loans, it is critical that the organization develop a robust system for capturing data on each of the loans and updating the data as the borrower makes loan payments. This will require a strong linkage with the systems being used to service the loans on an ongoing basis, whether the loans are being serviced by the originator or by a third-party company. This data system will need to be "real time" so that it can support critical processes such as hedging and pricing as described above. It is also necessary to capture a considerable amount of data that reflect the nature and credit quality of the loans. This will include data such as loan-to-value ratio, debt-to-income ratio, type of collateral securing the loan, type of borrower (for example, the business type code for small-business loans), and location of the borrower. If the organization is an aggregator and the loans were originated by multiple originators, information about the originators will also be necessary. Much of this data will be needed to complete the multiple data tables that are a required part of the disclosures to investors in the security offering statement.

Step 8. Assemble the Security

Once the organization has accumulated a sufficient number and dollar amount of loans to form a security, it needs to commence the process of creating the security and bringing it to market. If the organization has taken the steps outlined above during the time that the loans are being accumulated, the organization will have a good sense of when it would ideally like to bring the security to market. Because successful pricing and hedging strategies are quite time sensitive, planning for the next securitization literally begins as soon as a previous securitization is finished. With that in mind, the intense period of bringing a security to market commences about three to four months prior to the date on which the organization wants to close the security.

The first task is to assemble a list of the closed and committed loans that the organization intends to include in the security. The list will include key information about each loan, including outstanding principal balance as of a common date, interest rate, loan term, loan-to-value ratio, location, origination date, maturity date, and type of collateral securing the loan. This list will help the securitization team to determine the size of the securitization and to perform some initial analysis of the loan pool.

The second task is to assemble the securitization team—key staff from the organization (usually including a securitization coordinator and finance and servicing staff), securities attorney, financial consultant, and investment banker. The team will also need to select a trustee to administer the security, a servicer to collect the payments from the borrowers and remit them to the trustee, and, potentially, a special servicer to handle severely troubled loans. This team reviews the initial loan pool data and develops a timetable for completing the securitization.

The third task is to prepare the security. There are four major threads of work that occur simultaneously to carry out this task:

- *Preparing the cash flows, structuring the transaction, and working with the rating agencies.* This process is led by the investment banker. As discussed previously, the key dynamics of a securitization are driven by the cash flows. During this period there will be multiple iterations of the cash flows as the data from the pool of loans are more thoroughly analyzed. The organization may choose to remove certain loans from the pool because their characteristics cause problems within the cash flows. The investment banker provides preliminary feedback obtained by its trading desk from potential investors that may help to shape exactly how the various classes of securities are structured. Once the investment banker, the financial consultant, and the organization have agreed on the structure and the loans to be included, the cash flows are submitted to the rating agency for its initial review. This initial review may result in some further adjustments to the loan pool and the structure. The rating agency will also prescribe the parameters of the stress tests that the investment banker will run on the cash flows. These stress tests tell the rating agency how well the pool of loans is projected to perform under certain assumptions: how many loans might default; the timing of the defaults; and how much of the loan will be recovered following the default. From these "stress runs" the rating agency will determine the dollar amount of bonds that can be assigned to each rating class.

- *Preparing the legal documents.* This process is led by the securities attorney. There are four key documents that define the securities transaction—the sale and servicing agreement, the notes or bonds, the indenture, and the private placement memorandum. All of these documents must follow a general format prescribed by the US Securities and Exchange Commission or comparable body in other settings, including particular disclosures about the loans, the originator, the servicer, and the structure of the transaction.

  The private placement memorandum (PPM) is a summary document that provides information about the characteristics of the loan pool; summarizes the key terms of the notes or bonds, the indenture, and the sale and servicing agreement; provides information about the notes or bonds being offered; provides numerous tables that describe the individual loans; and contains many required disclosures about the transaction. This is the primary document used by the investment bankers to sell the securities to the investors. A preliminary version of the PPM is provided to investors prior to the sale and pricing of the securities, and a final version is provided to investors at closing. Because the PPM is a summary of the entire transaction, all of the other simultaneous processes described here contribute to the content of the PPM and therefore must be final before the PPM can be published. The preliminary PPM generally needs to be in the hands of investors at least a week before the investment banker prices the securities and takes orders for them. The closing of the transaction generally occurs within one to two weeks following the pricing date.

  The attorney is also responsible for forming the new special purpose entity to which the originator will sell the loans and which will issue the securities. The attorney takes special steps to ensure that the entity is "bankruptcy remote"—meaning that the investors will be isolated from any potential bankruptcy of the originator or secondary market organization. The attorney will issue a legal opinion prior to closing that assures investors of this factor.

- *Preparing the loan data.* This process is led by the securitization coordinator, working in close cooperation with the servicer. Because the borrowers are typically making monthly payments and new loans are often being added to the pool until fairly late in the process, the loan data are subject to change during the period that the security is being assembled. The coordinator is in constant contact with the investment banker to provide them with the information needed to produce the securitization cash flows, and absolute accuracy of the data is critical.

- **Preparing the physical loan files for due diligence and the collateral files for transfer to the trustee.** This process is led by the securitization coordinator. Since, under the terms of the PPM, the investors have the right to inspect the loan files for the underlying loans in the security, it is critical that the loan documentation be in good order. The rating agencies also have the right to review the loan files.

At the same time, the coordinator works to prepare the collateral files that will be transferred to the trustee at the time of the security closing, which assures investors they have full control of the underlying loans.

Step 9. Sell and Close the Security

As described above, the investment banker has the responsibility to market the securities to prospective investors. This will typically involve some initial "testing of the waters" with potential investors, the determination of a final offer price, and the opening of bids. By the close of the offering period, the specific investors and the pricing of each class of securities is set.

Following the pricing and order period, the investment banker reruns all of the cash flows with the actual rates at which the securities were sold. Up until this point all of the cash flow runs have used hypothetical pricing. It is at this point that the originator will know whether the securitization has produced positive financial results. The final cash flows are reviewed by the rating agency and they affirm their ratings. The cash flows are also submitted to the trustee so that it can set up its systems for administration of the securities. Based on the final cash flows, all of the financial information and disclosure tables that appear in the PPM and other legal documents are finalized.

On the day of the closing, all final documents are signed, investors remit their cash to the investment banker, and investors receive documentation for the securities they have purchased. The cash is then used to pay down the warehouse line of credit and to pay expenses of the securitization, with the remainder of the cash going to the originator.

Step 10. Manage the Securities

Once the securitization is completed, the ongoing management of the underlying pool of loans is primarily the work of the servicer. If the servicer is the same company as the originator, there is little change for the borrowers. If the loans are transferred to another servicer, a series of notices must be provided to the borrowers informing them of the change and notifying them about where they should send future payments. There is also extensive work for the servicing companies around the transfer of data and loan files to ensure that the loans are properly set up on the new servicer's system.

For the servicer, the loans must be identified in their systems as being a part of the security, and all loan payments received from the borrowers collected and remitted to the trustee on a monthly basis. All of this activity is governed by the terms of the sale and servicing agreement. The trustee works under the strict instructions of the notes or bonds, the indenture, and the sale and servicing agreement to distribute the cash it receives from the servicer to all of the parties entitled to receive payment. The key set of rules for the distribution of cash is set forth in the "flow of funds" section of the documents, also sometimes referred to as the "waterfall" of payments. Generally the first item in the "waterfall" is the payment of fees to the trustee and the servicer, followed by payments to the holders of the securities in the order of their seniority (i.e., Class A receives payment first, Class B receives payment second—and so on until there is no cash remaining). Depending on the type of credit enhancement used in the structure, the "waterfall" generally contains rules for when and how such sources of credit enhancement must be tapped and which of the security holders are entitled to funds from those sources.

Some sale and servicing agreements require that the servicer make up the difference between the amount received from borrowers and the amount expected by the trustee based on the cash flow model. This means that if a borrower makes its payment after the remittance date, the servicer is obligated to advance the difference from its own account. This obligation to advance generally continues until the loan is 90 days delinquent, at which point it moves into a process called special servicing, where the servicer typically begins the process of foreclosure or workout. Since special servicing requires specialized skills, some sale and servicing agreements require that the loans be transferred to a designated special servicer at this point in time.

It is at this point in the process that the sale and servicing agreement will contain instructions for what actions must be taken by the servicer or the special servicer to attempt to recover the maximum amount from the borrower or the borrower's collateral on behalf of the investors. Servicers often have very little flexibility within the terms of the sale and servicing agreement to take alternative actions without the express approval of the investors. This has been a major point of contention during the recent foreclosure crisis in the United States, as sale and servicing agreements might obligate the servicer to take a borrower's property through foreclosure even though it believes that a workout may be a better solution for both the investor and the borrower.

Operational Challenges

As the previous discussion suggested, there are numerous operational challenges to the use of securitization in connection with social investment. The following are some of the largest and most difficult challenges.

Lack of Sufficient Loan Volume to Utilize Securitization Effectively

As discussed previously, financial consultants recommend that the minimum size for a securitization to be cost effective is $50 million. Add to this the fact that this loan volume must be reasonably similar in type and term. The average CDFI participating in the Opportunity Finance Network's 2009 lending survey originated only $11.4 million in loans that year. This suggests that successful securitization may require an aggregator, such as the model demonstrated by the Community Reinvestment Fund, to consolidate the loan originations of multiple social lenders. Such aggregation is allowed for in the new CDFI Bond Guarantee program in the United States. The need for large volumes of loans that are reasonably similar to each other also suggests the need to develop standard loan origination and underwriting parameters, similar to those established by Fannie Mae and Freddie Mac in the housing field.

Shifts in Interest Rates and Credit Spreads

Securitization carries with it the risk of making and aggregating loans for an uncertain future. The originator faces the risk of changes in market interest rates as well as changes in "credit spreads"—the additional yield that investors will require to compensate for changes in the "riskless" yield curve. Hedging strategies have been reasonably well developed to mitigate the risk of interest rate changes, but these strategies must be managed by knowledgeable professionals. To manage the risk of changes in credit spreads, the originator must constantly monitor the securities marketplace and be willing to make changes to their loan-pricing strategy as these changes occur.

Management of Multiple Risks during the Period of Loan Accumulation

The need to aggregate loans from multiple originators will generally cause most secondary market organizations to need a warehouse line of credit. Because most of these lines of credit have one-year renewal clauses, failure to aggregate sufficient loans for securitization within that one-year period could cause the secondary market organization to default on its warehouse line. Another risk of defaulting on a warehouse line can arise if market conditions prevent the issuance of a securitization. This happened to many mortgage bankers during the height of the recent financial crisis when very little securitization of any kind was occurring. Some secondary market organizations, including Community Reinvestment Fund, were fortunate enough to have their warehouse lenders provide extensions, while others were forced into default and are now no longer in business.

Complexity of the Process

As outlined in the "Basic Mechanics" section above, securitization requires numerous simultaneous steps involving sophisticated expertise from both the staff of the secondary market organization and third-party professionals. Successful securitization also requires strong technology support to produce the constantly changing loan-level data that are essential to constructing the aggregate cash flows on which securitization is based. In addition, this complexity must be managed within tight time constraints in order to achieve the financial objectives of the secondary market organization and to avoid a default on the warehouse line.

Accounting Issues

As a result of the recent financial crisis and the failure of numerous lending organizations that utilized securitization, the stringency of the accounting regimen surrounding securitization has increased. The complexity and confusion surrounding the standards adopted by the Financial Accounting Standards Board (FASB) regarding asset-backed securities is extreme. The new standards focus on several key concepts. The first key principle is to determine whether a "true sale" has occurred between the secondary market organization and the special purpose entity that issues the securities (governed mostly by Financial Accounting Standard [FAS] 140). This is important because if it is later determined that the transaction was not a true sale, the investors may have lost the protection against bankruptcy of the secondary market organization that they sought and the secondary market organization may find the assets back on its own balance sheet.

A second principle is to determine more clearly the "fair value" of the assets being sold to the special purpose entity (governed mostly by FAS 157). This is particularly important for the secondary market organization to determine if the securitization has been profitable. A third key principle is the need to verify the value of debt securities on the books of the investors on an ongoing basis (governed mostly by FAS 115). This is important for all investors but is particularly critical for a secondary market organization that purchases subordinate securities during a securitization transaction because subordinate securities are subject to the greatest level of volatility in value (because they carry the greatest risk). The ownership of these securities by the secondary market organization can therefore cause major swings in its balance sheet and income statement.[25]

Upfront Expense to Aggregate Assets and Package a Security

Secondary market organizations that use securitization generally realize the bulk of the income from a securitization only when the securitization is complete. Therefore the originator needs sufficient working capital to pay operating expenses and many of the expenses of the securitization itself in advance of the securitization closing. This can cause a strain for many organizations, especially if they experience a time delay in bringing the security to market.

Track Record and Overall Assessment

The US Congress chartered Fannie Mae and Freddie Mac in 1968 and 1970, respectively, as private shareholder companies with the mission to "provide liquidity, stability and affordability to the U.S. housing and mortgage markets."[26] Congress also created the Government National Mortgage Association, commonly known as Ginnie Mae, in 1968 to serve as a guarantor for mortgage-backed securities that serve low- and moderate-income families who qualify for government-insured mortgages such as those issued by the Federal Housing Administration (FHA) and the Veterans' Administration (VA). The Ginnie Mae mission is "to expand affordable housing in America by linking global capital markets to the nation's housing markets."[27] In many ways we can point to this time as the beginning of the use of securitization for social purposes—providing long-term, fixed-rate mortgages for low- and moderate-income homeowners and for affordable rental properties in the United States.

For more than three decades, from 1970 to the mid-2000s, Fannie Mae, Freddie Mac, and Ginnie Mae securities were used to provide mortgage lenders with the capital that allowed them to continue making home mortgages to homeowners in the United States. Although there were criticisms of Fannie

Mae and Freddie Mac during this period, homeowners enjoyed very inexpensive mortgages (usually with interest rates just 0.25 percent over the "riskless" US Treasury rates) and homeowner mortgage defaults remained very low.

With the passage of the US Tax Reform Act of 1986, a new type of investment vehicle called the Real Estate Mortgage Investment Conduit (REMIC) made it much easier for private companies, in addition to Fannie Mae and Freddie Mac, to create and issue mortgage-backed securities. Many of these companies were formed to securitize "jumbo" or "nonconforming" mortgage loans—loans that were larger than the maximum mortgage amount set by Congress for Fannie Mae and Freddie Mac (around $170,000 at the time that the REMIC law was passed). In the 1990s many of these companies also began to make and securitize mortgages for borrowers that could not meet all of the standards of Fannie Mae and Freddie Mac, and these became known as "Alternative A" or "Alt-A"—meaning that they were "A" quality mortgages but could not meet the documentation standards required by Fannie Mae and Freddie Mac. They also began to offer "subprime" mortgages for borrowers whose credit was too poor to qualify for a "prime" mortgage from Fannie Mae or Freddie Mac.

In the decade beginning in 2000, the US mortgage markets began a frenzy of subprime lending and securitization that would culminate in the global financial crisis of 2008. Private issuers of mortgage-backed securities enjoyed unprecedented access to capital from around the globe, as investors and rating agencies looked at a 30-year track record of low mortgage defaults and rising home prices in most markets in the United States and felt that all mortgage-backed securities were a safe bet. Following the crash in 2008, much has been written about the dubious structured finance techniques, incompetent ratings by the major credit rating agencies, and fraudulent lending practices that allowed hundreds of thousands of mortgages to be made to homeowners who could not afford them.[28] Numerous global financial companies that had specialized in mortgage-backed securities—Bear Stearns, Lehman Brothers, Merrill Lynch, GMAC Residential Funding Corporation—went out of business. Fannie Mae and Freddie Mac, which also got swept up in the subprime frenzy, went under government receivership, having invested in many subprime mortgage-backed securities.

Against this backdrop it might be easy to conclude that securitization is a tool that will not see much use in the future world of social investing. But steps have since been taken to revive this tool. Internationally, the International Monetary Fund (IMF) and the International Organization of Securities Commissions (IOSCO) have published numerous discussion documents aimed at reforming securitization practices in all markets.[29] Of particular interest for the microfinance market, the Emerging Markets committee of the IOSCO has proposed a series of best practices for securitization in emerging markets, including more stringent standards for risk retention, stronger standards for disclosure and transparency of financial information, simplification of securitization products, and linkage between compensation to the securitizer and the long-term performance of the securities.[30] In the United States, as part of its efforts to stabilize the US housing markets, the Federal Reserve has invested billions of dollars in Fannie Mae and Freddie Mac securities since 2010 in order to the restore the faith of other investors in this critical market. All of this activity seems to indicate that lenders and investors continue to see securitization as a critically important tool for linking the need for long-term mortgages with investors seeking sound investments. And a look at the numbers shows that in

2010 in the United States $1.7 trillion in mortgage-backed securities were issued, along with $107 billion in asset-backed securities.

At the same time, there is little doubt that through its excesses of the mid-2000s, the securitization industry severely damaged the trust of investors in the soundness of asset-backed and mortgage-backed securities. Most of the securitization being done in 2011 was possible only because of explicit government guarantees, including an explicit agreement by the US Treasury to provide Fannie Mae and Freddie Mac sufficient capital to make up any deficiencies in net worth that might occur through the end of 2012.[31] It seems certain, nevertheless, that securitization will continue to be an important tool of the global capital markets, though it is uncertain how far this tool will extend beyond the markets that are perceived to be very safe, especially in the near future. It is likely that, in the next several years, any securitization of assets that support social purposes (outside the mainstream of residential mortgages) will need far more external credit support than was required prior to the global financial crisis. Passage of the CDFI Bond Guarantee Program in 2010 thus came at an especially propitious time, creating the opportunity to inject much-needed capital into the low-income housing and community development field in the United States. The initial tranche of support provided under this program came in late September 2013 with the award of an initial $325 million in bond guarantees to a series of four CDFIs.[32] Though this program is scheduled to end in 2014, hopes are high that the success of the initial round will convince Congress to extend the program.

Beyond this, the Community Reinvestment Fund demonstrated that securitization is a tool that can be effectively used to attract private capital to support loans to affordable housing as well as small businesses, including nonprofit businesses such as charter schools and healthcare facilities. The CRF story also demonstrated the importance of having social investors support this type of securitization. Social investors performed a number of crucial roles in the CRF example: (1) they provided long-term capital in the form of grants, program-related investments (PRIs), and equity-equivalent investments (EQ2s) that CRF used as working capital for its operations; (2) they provided short-term subordinate investments in CRF's warehouse line of credit helped induce conventional lenders to expand the size of the warehouse line and allow CRF to aggregate sufficient loans for a cost-effective securitization; and (3) they invested in securities issued by CRF, including highly rated classes (where investments were made as mission-related investments) and subordinate and unrated classes of securities (where investments were made as social investments). CDFIs and social investors would be wise to study the lessons learned from the CRF experience to chart the new course for attracting private market capital to social investing needs.

Another part of the field that warrants additional study is international microfinance. This is a field that attracted many social investors in the mid-2000s and has changed quite dramatically over the past 10 years. The first use of structured finance in the microfinance sector occurred only in 2004–5 by BlueOrchard Partnership with OPIC (Overseas Private Investment Corporation) and Developing World Markets.[33] Seven more microfinance CDO transactions were completed by 2008, but no additional securitized transactions have been brought to market since then.

As with all financial markets, the microfinance market has faced increased default levels, but in a report released early in 2011, the International

Association of Microfinance Investors (IAMFI) indicated that approximately 6 percent of debt investments in microfinance have required restructuring, compared to a global corporate default rate on noninvestment grade debt in 2009 of 9.7 percent.[34] This same report outlined detailed steps that the microfinance industry is taking to address the concerns of investors and to ensure a continued flow of capital to the sector. These steps include improving loan documentation to make documents more universally acceptable and enforceable, improving due diligence on loans and originators, developing better loan loss policies, and increasing attention to risk management practices. The IAMFI estimates that there is a $265 billion funding gap in the microfinance sector to meet existing demand, suggesting a market for securitization in this field.[35]

An equally challenging issue for the microfinance sector is a growing debate about the compatibility of market capital with the mission of helping the poor. Recent criticism of large microfinance institutions has led to public backlash in some countries. In an article titled "Lies, Hype, and Profit: The Truth about Microfinance," published in January 2011, Kentaro Toyama, a leading researcher on international development, noted the tendency of microfinance intermediaries to reach out to "formal investors" in order to extend microfinance's reach, but warned that "capitalist institutions have their dark side, too. Accepting such investments puts microcredit banks in the hands of shareholders whose primary goal is profit." In determining whether the investment is "good or bad," he suggests, "a well-considered balance is key."[36] What seems clear is that efforts to attract private capital into these markets will require the continued involvement of social investors as well.[37]

Conclusion

Securitization is a powerful and highly complex tool that has been used over the past 40 years to link trillions of dollars in investment capital with the borrowing needs of hundreds of millions of individuals and businesses. Prior to the global financial crisis, lenders with a social purpose began to tap this gigantic market, both directly and through established secondary market securitization platforms, to bring needed capital to low-income individuals and communities. Since the financial crisis, such access has been difficult, if not impossible. Lenders, investors, and regulators are already at work reforming the securitization markets to guard against the abuses that led to the global financial crisis. If social lenders and investors seeking to increase access to capital for low-income individuals and communities see value in having access to the securitization tool to attract more private capital in the future, they must be at the table articulating these needs as the reforms are taking shape. Much is to be gained if they succeed.

Notes

1. Frank J. Fabozzi, Henry A. Davis, and Moorad Choudry, *Introduction to Structured Finance* (Hoboken, NJ: Wiley, 2006), 3.

2. Piper Jaffray & Co., "Private Placement Memorandum for CRF-17 LLC," October 19, 2004.

3. Piper Jaffray & Co., "Private Placement Memorandum."

4. "US Mortgage-Related Outstanding," SIFMA, published January 31, 2011, http://www.sifma.org/research/statistics.aspx.

5. "US ABS Outstanding," SIFA, accessed May 1, 2011, http://www.sifma.org/research/statistics.aspx.

6. Ann Rutledge and Sylvain Raynes, *Elements of Structured Finance* (Oxford: Oxford University Press, 2010), 4.

7. "Resources: About LIHTC," Novogradac & Co, accessed May 1, 2011, http://www.novoco.com/low_income_housing/resources/program_summary.php.

8. Piper Jaffray & Co., "Private Placement Memorandum."

9. Piper Jaffray & Co., "Pricing Final Curve for CRF-17," unpublished work paper, November 2004.

10. "European Structured Finance Issuance," SIFMA, accessed April 11, 2011, http://www.sifma.org/research/statistics.aspx; "US ABS Issuance," SIFMA, accessed April 1, 2011, http://www.sifma.org/research/statistics.aspx; "US Mortgage-Related Issuance," SIFMA, accessed April 4, 2011, http://www.sifma.org/research/statistics.aspx.

11. John Olson, foreword to *Community Development Investment Review*, June 2006.

12. Opportunity Finance Network, *Inside the Membership: 2009 Statistical Highlights from the OFN Membership* (Philadelphia: Opportunity Finance Network, 2010).

13. "Reources: Reports and Research: CDFI Fund: NMTC Projects Finance through 2009," Novogradac & Co., September 21, 2010, http://www.novoco.com/new_markets/resources/reports.php.

14. "504 Loan Approval Statistics," National Association of Development Companies, accessed May 1, 2012, http://www.nadco.org/i4a/pages/index.cfm?pageid=3558.

15. "CDFI Federally Guaranteed Bond Summary of Terms," Opportunity Finance Network, accessed February 1, 2012, http://www.opportunityfinance.net/uploadedfiles/Policy/Bond/CDFI-Bond-Terms.pdf.

16. "Microfinance Investment," International Association of Microfinance Investors, accessed May 1, 2012, http://www.iamfi.com/microfinance_investment.html.

17. "Microfinance Investment," International Association of Microfinance Investors.

18. "Microfinance Investment," International Association of Microfinance Investors.

19. Opportunity Finance Network, *Inside the Membership*.

20. "The Network," Housing Partnership Network, accessed May 1, 2011, http://housingpartnership.net/network/.

21. New CDO issuances fell from a high of more than $750 billion in 2006 to $26 billion in 2010.

22. "Enterprises: Charter School Financing: Business Approach," Housing Partnership Network, accessed May 1, 2011, http://housingpartnership.net/enterprises/charter-school-financing/business-approach/.

23. "CDFI Federally Guaranteed Bond Summary of Terms," Opportunity Finance Network, accessed February 1, 2012, http://www.opportunityfinance.net/uploadedfiles/Policy/Bond/CDFI-Bond-Terms.pdf.

24. Doug Winn, "Growing Pains," *Community Development Investment Review* 2006:29–33.

25. Rutledge and Raynes, *Elements of Structured Finance*, 18.

26. "About Fannie Mae," Fannie Mae, accessed May 1, 2011, http://www.fanniemae.com/kb/index?page=home&c=aboutus; "About Freddie Mac," Freddie Mac, accessed May 1, 2011, http://www.freddiemac.com/corporate/company_profile/.

27. "About Ginnie Mae: History of Ginnie Mae," Ginnie Mae, accessed May 1, 2011, http://ginniemae.gov/about/history.asp?subTitle=About.

28. Michael Lewis, *The Big Short* (New York: Norton, 2010).

29. International Monetary Fund, "Restarting Securitization Markets: Policy Proposals and Pitfalls," *Global Financial Stabilization Reports* 2009:109–10.

30. Emerging Markets Committee of the International Organization of Securities, *Securitization and Securitized Debt Instruments in Emerging Markets Final Report* (IOSCO, 2010), 10–14.

31. "About Fannie Mae."

32. The four CDFI awarded guarantees were Clearinghouse CDFI, Enterprise Community Loan Fund, Inc., The Community Development Trust, LP and Local Initiatives Support Corporation. The three organizations chosen to issue the bonds as the Qualified Issuers were the Community Reinvestment Fund, Opportunity Finance Network, and TriSail Funding Corporation. Accessed February 11, 2014. http://www.dfifund.gov/news_events/CDFI-2013-41-Treasury_Announces_325%20 Million_Community_Development_Bonds_Financing_Low-Income_Areas_Nationwide.asp

33. "Microfinance Investment," International Association of Microfinance Investors.

34. International Association of Microfinance Investors, *Charting the Course: Best Practices and Tools for Voluntary Debt Restructurings in Microfinance* (New York: International Association of Microfinance Investors, 2011), 1.

35. "Microfinance Investment," International Association of Microfinance Investors.

36. Kentaro Toyama, "Lies, Hype, and Profit: The Truth about Microfinance," *The Atlantic*, January 28, 2011, http://www.theatlantic.com/business/archive/2011/01/lies-hype-and-profit-the-truth-about-microfinance/70405/.

37. "Microfinance Investment," International Association of Microfinance Investors.

Suggested Readings

Lewis, Michael. *The Big Short*. New York: Norton, 2010.

Federal Reserve Bank of San Francisco. "Secondary Markets for Community Development Loans." *Community Development Investment Review*, Special Issue, 2.1 (June 2006). http://www.frbsf.org/community-development/publications/community-development-investment-review/2006/june/secondary-markets-community-development-loans.

CHAPTER 15

PRIVATE EQUITY INVESTMENTS

Monica Brand and John Kohler

ZOONA IS A MOBILE PAYMENTS business with a vision of transforming the way people and organizations pay for purchases across Africa by reducing reliance on cash. The vast majority of financial transactions in Africa are done with cash, in a people- and paper-intensive way. In countries like Zambia (Zoona's core market) over 80 percent of adult income-earning people have no bank account ("the unbanked"). A further 50 percent are unconnected to modern communication technology. At the heart of Zoona's business is a payment platform that enables organizations from all sectors to transact business electronically with unbanked and remote consumers. Zoona's interoperable payment platform is backed by a proprietary technology and a countrywide network of agents that act as cash access points for end users.

To support its vision of a cashless Africa, Zoona needed to finance a business model that was both deeply rooted in the countries where it operates and able to scale seamlessly across borders to serve organizational clients with a pan-African footprint. As an early-stage company, Zoona's first years of operation were "funded" by the cash and "sweat equity" of its founders, the CEO and the CFO who joined subsequently, and their friends and families. Given the company's aspirations, they knew they needed more plentiful sources of capital. But as a company that was still unprofitable—even if partly because of its growth and expansion into new geographies and product lines—its choices were limited. Traditional debt or fixed-income investors typically require positive cash flow to service loan payments. Equity funding—which earns a return based on the appreciation in value of a company—is a better financing fit for a high-growth company with strong future prospects but limited current cash flow. That said, there are challenges in providing venture capital—equity to early-stage enterprises—in lesser developed markets (like Zambia) and for new business models (like mobile transactions).

Fortunately, Zoona was able to solve its immediate funding problem thanks to the emergence of a new breed of social-purpose equity finance organization (i.e., social-impact investors) using a variety of standard and hybrid forms of equity finance. Specifically, to finance its early stage of growth, Zoona secured business assistance and funding from the Grassroots Business Fund through a convertible note, an equity-like instrument that has elements of both debt and equity—a fixed, though delayed, repayment combined with an opportunity to convert into actual shares when and if the business begins to turn a profit. Later, Sarona Risk Capital Fund helped the company refinance this "starter capital" with a bridge loan—interim financing that replaces existing debt, allowing the user to meet its current obligations and provide immediate cash flow in anticipation of a future round of typically equity financing.[1]

This quasi equity, coming at a crucial time for Zoona and in a form the company could handle, helped create an "investable" company. The company was thus ultimately in a position to approach institutional funders for its first round of preferred equity funding, which it secured from Omidyar Network and Accion Frontier Investments. As part of their US$3 million investment, Omidyar and Accion Frontier took seats on Zoona's board of directors, established consent rights on key business decisions, and became very involved with the company's business. Sarona converted its bridge loan to equity, and it also became part of the Series A financing with a board observer seat. This staged use of equity had important implications for the growth and development of the company.

Defining the Tool

Equity is an investment tool through which the investor buys an ownership stake in a company and thereby secures a "share" in any dividends or capital gains that the business might generate in the future. If the company fails to attract buyers of its equity for a higher price than originally offered or is unable to generate excess profits for the payment of dividends, equity investors receive little or no profit on their investment. Worse yet, if the company declines in value or goes bankrupt, equity investors stand to lose most or all of their investment. An equity investor trades off the more certain returns that debt investors enjoy in exchange for the expectation of higher returns—either in the form of greater value appreciation (capital gains) or a share of the revenue streams of a company (dividends). In addition, private equity holders, that is, those who invest in companies whose shares are not listed on a regular stock exchange, in return for bearing the risk of illiquidity or uncertain repayment that this involves will often take seats on the board, have required consent rights over certain critical decisions of the company, and invest nonfinancial resources (talent recruitment, business development, strategic advice) to help the company grow and succeed.[2] As the vignette on Zoona above suggests, companies accept such increased investor control because the repayment of equity capital is tied to performance: *nothing is owed to the investor unless the company begins to earn a profit or the investor's ownership shares rise in value and can be sold.* In this way, equity can align incentives of managers and investors.

Defining Features

With equity, the rate of return is based on the performance of the company. Aside from whatever dividends they might earn, equity holders typically recover their investment only when they "exit"—sell their shareholdings to other investors or when the assets of the firm are liquidated and proceeds distributed once the firm's other obligations, including those to debt holders, are satisfied. This monetization via a liquidity event is unlike debt or fixed income, where rate of return is defined in advance. In addition, an equity holder's claim on the assets of a company is subordinate to that of debt holders, who are paid off first in the case of bankruptcy or liquidation.

Relation to Common Criteria

As outlined below, equity can be compared to other asset classes along a number of dimensions.

Risk

Equity investing is, in general, a high-risk, high-return proposition. Early-stage equity holders take on much higher risk in the hopes of the greater return they can receive if a company does well. Unlike debt, where eight or nine out of 10 companies will repay principal plus interest, early-stage equity investors typically expect the majority of their investments to provide little or no return with the earned profits from one or two "home run" investments compensating for the rest. The analogy is much like a pharmaceutical company that invests tremendous resources developing a variety of drugs with the anticipation that only one or two blockbusters will help them recoup the R&D expense of the ones that fail.

Equity investors can invest at varying stages of a company's growth trajectory. Equity is often used where the enterprise is in an early stage of development and unable to secure debt financing or to provide growth stage capital after a company has already proven that its business model actually works. The high reward nature of equity investing justifies its high risk and associated low hit rate when investing at this early stage.

Whether the social dimension of social-impact investing adds or mitigates risk for equity-backed companies is debated. On one hand, the unproven nature of the businesses (social enterprises) involved and, in some cases, the less developed state of markets (emerging) in which social-impact investors are operating create additional risk. On the other hand, social enterprises operating in these underserved markets often face less competition, which create first-mover advantages, that is, gains by being the initial, significant occupant of a market segment. In addition, the customer loyalty and mission-driven commitment to ethical business practices can create additional value for equity investors in social enterprises.

Return

Equity investing holds the potential for both high social and financial returns, especially for social enterprises pursuing disruptive innovation in high-growth markets where the potential for upside growth is strong. Indeed, some claim that "investing for impact in developing countries may offer better profits and more stable growth as compared to traditional investments in more advanced economies."[3] To date, evidence of investors that have realized market-rate returns from social enterprises—businesses seeking social and environmental as well as financial returns—is limited to certain impact sectors (like financial inclusion and clean energy) or investments within more developed markets (such as Bridges Ventures in the UK, which has successfully exited a few of its portfolio holdings).[4] Most of the impact investors interviewed for this book, however, claimed that it is too early to make a judgment as to whether commercial equity-like returns are more broadly achievable in social-impact investing. Some likened the state of social-impact investing to where the venture capital field was in the 1970s—"just the beginning."[5] At a minimum, equity investments in the social-impact arena that are managed towards an exit should achieve greater return than social bond investors. Without a financial exit, equity social-impact investing becomes an expensive form of philanthropy.

Leverage

It is very common in social-impact investing to use a range of debt and equity structures together as a company evolves and business needs and available financing change. Equity is critical to attract debt capital, as most debt agreements will stipulate maximum debt-to- equity ratios or minimum capital requirements, or both, and most debt providers require some minimum capital base or equity before they will lend. Initially, equity investors typically want their capital used to fund growth and expansion rather than service debt providers.[6] Over time as a company grows, equity holders will use debt to propel higher revenue and value creation without diluting the ownership percentage of existing equity investors. Thus, equity and quasi equity can play an important role absorbing losses as a company improves its cash-generating ability—making a company more attractive to more risk-adverse debt providers.

Ubiquity

Equity is a versatile investment tool that can be used in a breadth of fields and across markets. Its application in emerging and frontier markets[7] has less of a track record because of the (1) undeveloped or fragmented nature of the markets in such areas; (2) consequent extension of time frames to mature a business or realize a liquidity event; and (3) founder tendency to look at business partly as a role in society or family legacy. These realities (described more fully below in the "Operational Challenges" section) explain why there are not more equity transactions in emerging market, social-impact investing.

However, the use of equity and quasi equity as a new tool in social-purpose capital is on the rise. In J.P. Morgan's most recent survey of social-impact investors (which had nearly doubled its participation over the previous year), 83 percent state they use private equity.[8] A number of factors are contributing to this increase in use: the growing sophistication of social enterprises, the continued development of emerging and frontier markets, the rise of social-impact investing, and the involvement of new private-sector players—such as family offices, institutional investors, commercial financial institutions, and high-net-worth individuals. Equally interesting is that the majority of these investors consider equity a critical component of their toolkit, even though many social-impact investors invest with debt because of the associated liquidity and lower risk.

This increased use of equity is consistent with an improved market outlook, as evidenced by both capital committed and attitude towards prospects by social-impact investors.[9] Their willingness to commit more capital reflects the general progress expressed by the majority of investors surveyed across different dimensions of market growth, including pipeline, impact measurement, co-investor collaboration, data availability, intermediaries, and availability of complementary sources of capital.[10] In addition, a vast majority of respondents (78 percent) in a J.P. Morgan survey of impact investors stated a preference for growth-stage businesses, for which equity and quasi-equity is particularly well suited.[11]

Skill Requirements

Equity investing requires a diverse set of financial, business, and technical skills. Much like venture capital in Western markets, social-purpose equity investing has been an "apprenticeship" business where one learns by doing. There is no one "classic" background for social-impact investing. The field is composed of a diverse mix of development professionals including investors from the traditional banking, venture capital, and private equity arenas, management consultants, lawyers, successful entrepreneurs that want to give back, financial advisors, and other well-intentioned professionals wanting to leverage their skills in more impactful ways. Equity tools have become more complex in social enterprise environments because of (1) their application in diverse circumstances, (2) the incorporation of debt-like characteristics, (3) accommodations necessary for different regulatory and market environments, and (4) the hybrid nature of social-purpose entities. Industry interviews suggest the following key predictors of successful impact fund managers:

- Equity investment experience (structuring transactions, realizing exits)
- Background living in, working in, or connecting to the geography in question
- Relevant operational or sector expertise in the area of investment
- Social orientation and emotional intelligence (including the ability to align interests with entrepreneurs and build relationships across developing industries)

Design Features and Major Variants

As an instrument, equity can accommodate multiple investors with varying types of capital all participating in a single financing round (*vertical capital aggregation*) while also providing a structure for successive rounds of capital investment coinciding with the phases of an enterprise's growth (*phased financing*). Within the spectrum of social-impact capital providers, investors using a variety of investment structures may appear at different times along the growth phases of a start-up. The coordination of successive rounds of this type of phased financing approach is termed *horizontal capital aggregation* and can include philanthropic grants, program-related investments, quasi equity, and commercial debt.

As suggested earlier, equity funding can be divided into two broad categories. The first is *standard equity*. This is the type of equity that involves basic purchase of ownership shares of a company with the accompanying rights of ownership and receipt of a share of the profits. The second type, increasingly used in the field of social-impact investing, is called *quasi equity* because it incorporates some elements of standard equity but not all. For example, standard equity cannot be used to finance nonprofit organizations because, by law, such organizations cannot issue ownership shares or distribute profits to owners. Accordingly, quasi equity provides alternatives to both ownership and profit distribution. Both standard equity and quasi equity can take different forms, however. In the two subsections that follow we examine some of these forms, focusing first on standard equity and then looking at quasi equity.

Standard Equity

When an enterprise sells an equity stake to investors as a means of raising growth capital, it is making a very important promise: in return for the risk and illiquidity of such a financing, the enterprise will use the proceeds to dramatically grow the underlying value of its equity and reward equity holders for their early support by providing a resale opportunity that recognizes a significant step-up in value. Because investment capital used to purchase equity will not be returned for a pronounced period of time, many provisions of the financing transaction seek to provide investors voice in critical business decisions and anticipate problems that could occur during an extended holding period. Consequently these consent rights, protective provisions, or economic defenses become an important part of equity financing and account for the existence of a number of variations of the standard equity tool. We introduce some of these variations below.

- *Common stock:* The most basic form of equity investment, common stock, is a security that represents ownership in a company. Owners of common stock have a claim on any dividends a company generates, can participate in shareholder meetings, and get some say in the structure and decisions of the business. The influence of common stock holders on a company is minimal for most shareholders unless they own a significant percentage.

  In some social-impact investments, all of the stock issued to founders, employees, and investors is the same (usually common stock), but the company enters into an investor rights agreement that vests very strong control provisions to the board member representing the investor(s).

- *Preferred stock:* Preferred stock owners are typically entitled to a stronger vote in company affairs (via protective provisions and consent rights on important business decisions, such as mergers and acquisitions and executive compensation), higher potential dividend payments, and greater rights to company assets than common stock owners in case of liquidation. Most importantly, preferred stock carries a "liquidity preference," which allows preferred stock owners to get their cash out before other equity holders during an exit event. Most preferred stock is convertible, which means that it can be turned into common stock to enjoy full upside growth potential or liquidated ahead of common shares at a predetermined preferential price—usually one or two times the investment amount.[12]

  Most social-impact investors will use a preferred stock instrument, which wraps special economic provisions and decision rights (*consents*) within a certain series or class of stock. There are several reasons for taking this approach. First, because preferred equity investors come later in a company's growth, they are often not buying enough of the company to hold a controlling interest on the decision-making of the company. Consequently, they need certain "protective provisions" to safeguard their economic stake against adverse actions by the company. These "protective provisions" often include oversight on the issuance of new shares, on new and significant obligations of the company, and on mergers, acquisitions, assumption of debt, and the approval of new financing. Finally, because there is usually no recovery of investment until a successful exit event, protective economic provisions (*liquidation preferences*) are needed so that investors can be paid some or all of their original investment ahead of other equity holders.

- *Convertible preferred equity.* This form of standard equity is used where risk is high and company management is unable to attract sufficient financing elsewhere. This commonly used instrument allows the investor to either take a fixed liquidation preference (such as two times the amount invested) or convert to common stock if there is a successful liquidity event. Thus, the investor is protected on the downside and given some preference to returns on the upside in the event of even a modest success.
- *Warrants:* Warrants offer the right to purchase common stock at a specific price within a predetermined time period, usually five to 10 years. If the stock is not purchased or the exercise period lapses, then the warrant becomes worthless.

Quasi Equity

Quasi-equity instruments can be used where (1) enterprise maturity is too early to justify a full equity financing round; (2) the company is between rounds of equity financing; (3) upside acceleration in valuation is uncertain, but cash operations seem strong; or (4) the enterprise is a nonprofit organization or co-operative barred from distributing profit or issuing shares that grant voting rights on the basis of money invested rather than one person, one vote. These financing structures are often called "quasi equity" either because the instrument intends to roll into an equity structure or because it contains other equity-like provisions. Examples of these quasi-equity instruments—which combine elements of debt and equity—include the following:

- *Convertible notes.* Convertible notes are debt instruments designed to convert to equity at a discount to the subsequent round of equity financing. Convertible notes are the most common form of quasi equity. Many early-stage social-impact investors use this structure when an early-stage social enterprise needs equity-like financing but cannot support the weight and amount of a true Series A preferred round. Specifically, the preinvestment valuation a social enterprise start-up can command is so small that accepting equity financing would imply the owners diluting themselves dramatically and giving an equity investor a great deal of control. This solution to bridge the gap between the "bid" (what investors are willing to pay) and the "ask" (what the entrepreneurs think the early-stage social enterprise is worth) does not properly align incentives. Instead, many equity impact investors use convertible notes to help prepare promising enterprises for a full round of equity investment and build sufficient value to allow a significant follow-on equity raise without heavily diluting the founders. At the outset, this debt-like structure typically has a fixed term and interest rate. However, these notes typically have a clause that allows the investor to convert to equity at a discounted share price, inclusive of imputed interest, when a qualified equity financing occurs in the future.[13]

- **Royalty or revenue share payments.** Some organizations have begun using royalty-type payments in order to get around the challenges of equity financing in social-impact investing (finding suitable exits, convincing social entrepreneurs or family members to share control, prohibitions on nonprofit distribution of "profits" to equity investors in the form of dividends, etc). These are also called "revenue share" payments because the investor typically gets a percentage of top-line revenue over and above a predetermined threshold, which ensures sufficient cash to allow the company to thrive and grow. Such payments have been used in developed markets and are applicable in illiquid or still nascent emerging markets. A minor equity or warrant component (an option to buy stock at a certain price within a certain time frame) is typical in these structures as a way to "sweeten" the pot, though this does not work with nonprofits. Most royalty-based financing is structured like a loan, with interest and a fixed payment term, but with some participation in revenue growth if the business performs well, to enhance return.[14] Some royalty financing is entirely variable, whereby the company pays a percentage of revenue or profit up to a certain multiple (typically two to five times the investment) but only when there is cash flow available.[15]

- **Earn-outs.** Also referred to as a "structured exit," an earn-out is a contractual provision stating that the seller of a business is to obtain additional future compensation based on the business achieving certain future financial goals.[16] Earn-outs are often used in later-stage transactions, including mergers and acquisitions, when there is a significant gap in valuation expectations between the company (the seller) and the investor (the buyer). An earn-out provision is a way of structuring an investment so that the entrepreneur receives more than the investor's offer only if the business achieves a financial or business milestone. The financial goals are usually stated as a percentage of gross sales or earnings. Business milestones can include number of customers or number of products sold.[17]

- **Demand dividends.** A demand dividend is a fairly new form of financing that relies on strong cash flow of the enterprise but only requires payment when the investee is capable of paying. The structure is reflective of the longer cash flow cycles in frontier economies and is achieved through arrangements that involve periodic payments (quarterly vs. monthly) as a function of available business cash flow (e.g., 20–30 percent of EBITDA) up to a specific, predefined cap.[18] If cash flow is insufficient, payment rolls over to the next period without penalty, with some interest accruing.

    In the case of such demand dividend arrangements tied to revenue or free cash flow, a forecast and calculation model submitted as part of the financing would set the rules by which these payments are calculated. Any deviation from the forecast or method would require the express consent of the issuer. In the case of the demand dividend, the financing mechanism is replaceable at any time with another source of financing before or at the end of the prescribed term, with part of the new proceeds going to pay off the original obligation. In this way, a "phased" financing is also achieved.

Which type of quasi equity or conventional equity is most appropriate depends on the growth stage of the enterprise and the characteristics of its planned financing. As explained earlier in the Zoona example, bridge notes are most useful when providing urgently needed capital while a pending financing is being finalized. Similarly, convertible notes are a way of financing a young company even before it is ready to command its first round of equity investment. Seed stage or angel investors use this tool when a start-up needs capital but has built only a small amount of preinvestment value. The investment goes in as debt but with the intention to convert it to equity when a formal round of equity financing is pulled together. This formal round is usually anticipated within 12 months, and issuers of the note are more protected than equity holders in case of failure. Many impact investors, such as Village Capital, Grassroots Business Fund, and Accion Venture Lab, also use convertible notes to supply an exciting social enterprise with financing while it is still building sufficient value for a follow-on equity round.

Patterns of Use

Several important trends are evident in the use of private equity for social-impact investment purposes.

More Investors

New players are entering the social-impact investing space, and they have the potential to reshape the industry. Specifically, a recent survey conducted jointly by J.P. Morgan and the Global Impact Investment Network (GIIN) recorded increased activities from family offices and high-net-worth individuals, which were top investor categories (first or second) across target return profiles, particularly in equity investing.[19] These private investors have been joined by a variety of institutional players, including pension funds (TIAA-CREF), endowments (Kellogg, Tufts), and banks (J.P. Morgan, US Trust). These actors bring not only a larger resource base to equity investing but also new rigor. Responsibility, efficiency, and financial attractiveness were listed by these actors as top motivations for making social-impact investments.[20]

Examples of this shift from public to private funds in social-impact investing are very clear. When Accion Investments launched its first equity fund in 2002, the majority of the investors were development finance institutions. During its 10-year trajectory (which involved a recapitalization and restructuring to expand into new geographies), its equity investor base became primarily comprised of private institutional investors. This shift is reflective of increased interest among private institutional investors in the impact-investing space, and increasing proof that financial and social returns can be achieved simultaneously. Other leading equity microfinance investment vehicles as well as new financial inclusion funds like LeapFrog Investments have been able to tap significant amounts of private capital.

Some investors interviewed for this chapter attribute the reported increased use of equity in social-impact investing as a result of a bandwagon effect. Specifically, some claim that this "new" interest could be existing equity investors reclassifying their work as "social-impact" since it is popular with so-called limited partners, or LPs, that is, investors in funds. As one Silicon Valley technology investor now involved in the social-impact investing field put it, "It's a bit like adding '.com' to your name in 1999." Some call this relabeling "greenwashing" by "impact imposters" wanting to capitalize on the growing interest in social impact. The authors of this chapter would rather view the field as broad-based and discriminating, with different motivations and impact focus.

Increased Sector and Market Focus

Many social-impact equity investors are focusing on a particular sector or geography, consistent with the tendency in social-impact investing to focus on a particular target market (the base of the pyramid, the unbanked, the emerging middle class) or cause (renewable energy, clean water, financial inclusion, affordable healthcare, etc.). Empirical research on emerging market private equity funds conducted by the International Finance Corporation (IFC) (validated separately by other investigations)[21] reflects a positive correlation between the financial performance of equity funds with strong market ties (a fund manager that is locally based or is staffed by local nationals) and a substantive value add (either through a sector focus or strong operational skills).

This trend of increased sector and market focus makes sense in the use of equity. Equity works best with fast-growing companies operating in large markets with limited competition. Growth can come from disruptive technologies, innovative business models, or the application of an existing technology (or the transfer of a successful business model) into an underserved market. Depth of expertise—either by sector or by geography—can help equity investors to promote growth and return, given the power of networks and knowledge for deal flow, for understanding legal and regulatory constraints, and for achieving exits. In addition, being a "place-based" investor might actually make it easier to take advantage of low labor rates or other competitive advantages available to first movers.[22]

More Incubators for Social Enterprises Looking for Equity Capital

The increased use of equity among impact investors unfortunately is not closing the demand gap among social entrepreneurs. One possible reason is the strong presence of financial-first impact investors looking for growth-oriented companies that do not fit the profile of many social enterprises, which are mission focused (e.g., trying to improve access to potable water or promote sustainable energy) and are seeking profits but not necessarily aggressive growth. In other words, as depicted in Figure 15.1, there is a mismatch between what the suppliers of capital are looking for and what the builders of enterprises are providing.[23] The heart of the problem is that most of the available capital is looking for enterprises near the top of this pyramid—that is, more established businesses with high growth potential. Patient capital for the unmet demand at the base of the enterprise pyramid is harder to come by.

As noted elsewhere in this volume, a number of "incubators" and accelerators have been formed—like Toniic, Hub Ventures, Global Social Business Incubator, Start up Leadership—to service these early-stage businesses to help them become "investment ready."[24] Though it is still too early to determine how

FIGURE 15.1
Equity Investing Ecosystem

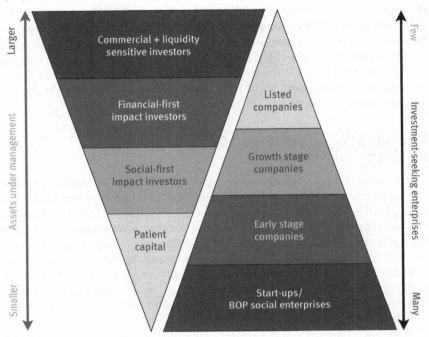

well these incubators are closing the supply-demand gap for equity capital, it is not clear that it can be closed.

Increased Use of Quasi Equity

More players are exploring creative combinations of debt and equity so that adept financial structuring can better address this gap and align incentives and interests of investors and social enterprises. A J.P. Morgan survey of impact investors found that 44 percent use "equity-like" debt structures, such as mezzanine capital, deeply subordinated debt, or a debt instrument with potential profit participation (convertible debt, warrants, royalties, debt with equity kickers).[25] Use of royalties—which combine monthly or quarterly income streams with a revenue or profit share "sweetener"—are on the rise because they help de-risk transactions while achieving strong returns.[26] "They are also attractive because of the greater liquidity expectations among fund investors (LPs), who are concerned about how they get their money back."[27] Other investors suggested interest in royalties and demand dividends from the company's perspective because there is less or no dilution of ownership and no pressure to sell: the instruments are self-extinguishing so an exit or liquidity event "becomes a process, not an event."[28]

The appeal to both investors and companies of structured finance is evident in the social-impact space. Microfinance investment vehicles have used blended finance since its early days. Profund—the first ever third-party fund in microfinance—used a variety of quasi-equity tools: (1) preferred shares with a minimum dividend (could defer and accumulate whenever there was cash available) and an "equity kicker" based on earnings; (2) subordinated loans, often with a set redemption (typically at some sort of multiple of book value of the microfinance institution, which would grow over time).[29] In addition, a few SME funds in Africa—including GroFin, Jacana Partners, and Business Partners Africa—are using structured payouts combined with options for upside growth.[30] In these cases, payout is tied to a revenue forecast or a specific percentage of profits with an option for upside and prestructured exits. Equity variants, as discussed here, are often at the core of structured exit financing and are increasingly being used.

Expanded Role of Subsidized Capital and Technical Assistance

Many social-impact investors have explored smart uses of subsidy as a precursor to equity, given the aforementioned challenges of using traditional equity instruments with early-stage social enterprises and the need for nonfinancial support. Philanthropy or in-kind support is at times critical, given the nascent nature of many social enterprise models and the underdeveloped state of the markets in which they operate. Firms pioneering new business models or markets face particular challenges on the journey to viability and scale. A recent Monitor Group/Acumen Fund report suggests that philanthropy can help close this "pioneer gap" and unlock the potential of social-impact investing.[31]

Some social-impact equity investors use subsidized capital as a complement to equity investments for driving continued R&D and innovation in portfolio companies, facilitating knowledge transfer, experimenting around disruptive models to reach new customer segments, helping early-stage companies become investment-ready and impact measurement. For example, LeapFrog Investments, the world's first microinsurance private equity fund, hired an associate director of mobile financial services through its grant-funded sister vehicle, LeapFrog Labs, to drive mobile-based innovation in portfolio companies to more rapidly expand access to otherwise disconnected customers. Similarly, Accion's Frontier Investments, a growth stage equity fund targeting innovative models for the unbanked, is complemented by its affiliate, Venture Lab, which targets similar social enterprises in the prerevenue or proof-of-concept phase and is sponsored by the nonprofit, Accion. Other social-impact investors, like Omidyar Network and Grassroots Business Fund, have legal structures that allow them to use both grants and equity investments to support their portfolio companies.[32] In short, there are multiple ways to combine equity investment with grant funding to overcome the challenges facing early-stage firms in underdeveloped markets.

That said, comingling subsidy with for-profit, commercial funds has downsides. First, such blending can complicate calculations of returns in the measurement of fund performance—a challenge for a new private investor trying to understand the risk-return profile of social-impact investing. Second, subsidizing an industry for too long can stifle competitiveness and business growth. Last, there can be moral and even legal challenges associated with subsidizing returns for investors with philanthropic capital. Even so, the persistent gap between the supply of equity-like capital and the demand by social enterprises requires creative thinking around new approaches and tools.

Tool Selection

Equity is enormously important for any business, but particularly for early-stage businesses. While equity is ubiquitously used for public company capitalization, it is also often the only choice for early-stage growth companies. Early-stage companies have few, if any, financing options available from traditional sources of debt financing. Early-stage companies usually cannot meet the cash, profit, depository, and operating requirements of traditional debt. Because of these limitations, they are deemed to be very risky investments. Consequently, equity investors are seen as capital "partners" who bring risk capital to the table, without which the idea would never get off the ground. It is even more beneficial if this financing partner can bring sector experience, contacts, strategic partner introductions, or access to human capital to the equation. If the company does not do well, the equity investor risks losing its entire investment and the entrepreneur will owe the investor nothing.

Choosing the right form of equity financing for a social-impact investment depends on a number of factors. Of primary importance is the type of exit the enterprise intends to achieve, which in turn is influenced by a company's growth stage, financing needs, and nature of the business. Also important are the market conditions—are there local private equity firms, an actively traded stock exchange, or companies with strategic interest in that country? Last, the liquidity preference of the social-impact investor and how it values *reliability* of the return versus the magnitude of the return will impact the tool's selection.

Table 15.1 describes the enabling conditions where equity or quasi equity best applies. Equity financing is typically targeted at the subset of businesses that have high growth potential, but quasi equity can extend the range to early-stage companies operating in more challenging market settings or for entrepreneurs with more limited growth ambitions.

TABLE 15.1   ENABLING CONDITIONS FOR EQUITY OR QUASI EQUITY

Dimension	Standard private equity	Quasi equity/other instruments
Geography/market	Well-developed capital markets and investment activity; functioning economies; lower friction business environments; attractive to strategics	Less developed markets with headwinds, ambiguous rule of law or enforcement, corruption, inflation; restrictions on import/export and/or profit repatriation; monetary policy + infrastructure challenges
Sector	Large addressable market; low penetration which allows for first mover advantages, rapid growth and scale	Limited or fragmented market, thin margins, slow or low growth potential
Entrepreneur proclivity	Interested in building a large, successful company.	Interested in remaining local/limited scale or maintaining personal or familial involvement.
Business	Attractive margins; developed distribution; access to qualified management and employees	Potential for sustainable, steady revenue; limited access to qualified employees
Investor priority	Prioritize potential for upside	Prioritize predictability of returns

Basic Mechanics

As is clear from the numerous examples in this chapter, "equity" is a broadly defined term that encapsulates a variety of investment activity. Consequently, there is no uniformity in how equity investment tools are deployed. That said, there are similar approaches used by most equity investors given the critical importance of shared vision, incentive alignment, and stakeholder relationships in successful equity investments. This section will present the basic mechanics involved in deploying equity by walking through the standard process of identifying, analyzing, negotiating, and managing an equity investment. It will also provide a thorough look at the standard components of an equity term sheet, the legal document that summarizes the proposed conditions of an equity investment.

Step 1. Identifying Promising Investments and Assessing Fit

A first step in deploying private equity is to identify promising investments and assess the fit with the particular orientation of the investor. This step involves several more or less distinct tasks.

Screening

The initial task in identifying promising investments is to screen what is available. Impact investors screen for meaningful social or environmental impact—usually with operations in areas where the greatest impact can be achieved. They then look for business sustainability and growth potential. Financial first investors also may screen for specific sectors, but will also filter out companies that do not meet a specific growth trajectory and return potential. All social-impact investors using equity will evaluate the core fundamentals of the business:

- *Management and stakeholders.* Is the management team flexible and open to working with investors? Are they nimble and open to shifting direction when market data invalidate initial business model approaches? Do they have relevant skills and experience to contribute to the business?
- *Business and revenue model.* Has the company demonstrated it has a product that people want and will pay for? Can the revenues sustain the cost—both at a unit economic level and at scale? Does the company have a defensible competitive advantage that is sustainable? Does it track key performance indicators that help management understand how the business is performing?
- *Addressable market.* Does the company have a large untapped group of clients that are potential customers for its product? Is it growing? How heavily competed is that market?
- *Enabling environment.* Is the macroeconomic and regulatory environment facing the company hospitable? Is it stable? Is there strong rule of law? Infrastructure?
- *Financials/capital structure.* How much revenue has the company earned? How quickly is it spending or "burning" cash? What percentage

of the company does the management own, to ensure good alignment with the incoming equity investors? Is the management's stake based on "sweat" (the effort management has put into building the company) and cash (actual money management has invested)?

- ***Exit.*** What are the likely paths for an equity investor to sell its shares? Merger, acquisition, or sale to a strategic investor? "Secondary" sale to another equity investor? Initial public offering (IPO)? Buy-back by management? Other options? An equity investor's return is driven by the timing and success of an exit or liquidity event.

Achieving Alignment

Equity investing is a time-intensive process that involves close collaboration. If there is not positive rapport and mutual respect between investors and entrepreneurs, the investment will likely not go well. As one social-impact equity investor interviewed put it, "The skills required from equity investors are about soft skills—how to align the interests of both entrepreneurs and capital providers."[33] This alignment is especially important with respect to the timing and need for exits, discussed below, as well as the notion of accountability and respect for contracts implicit in equity deal structures. Translating the "realities of the south-east to the terminology and standards of the north-west" often requires empathy and creativity.[34] Typically, equity investors will use a one- to two-page investment prescreen or deal memo that summarizes the basic aspects of the investment opportunity, including company overview, business/revenue model, management/sponsors, source/syndicate, addressable market, competitive advantage, financials, capital structure, and exit.

Step 2. Determining Investment Readiness

The receptivity of an entrepreneur to the kind of changes required to take on formal equity capital is an important indicator of investment readiness. Many of the changes have been discussed in this chapter, including sharing decision-making, restricting some uses of capital and professionalizing operations (i.e., compliance with local tax and legal authorities). But investment readiness also requires the development of a persuasive business model validated through a due diligence assessment.

Business Model Review

A company that takes on equity has presumably determined the target market it hopes to serve, its core value proposition, and basic business or revenue model. This scale-up plan is critical for the company to achieve the return expectations of an equity investor. The company also should have a concrete idea of how much money it wants to raise, a planned use of funds, operational and financial projections, and milestones the company plans to achieve as a result of the proposed equity infusion. The most prepared companies will be able to explain the unit economics of its business (costs and revenue per customer or per transaction) and speak to the size of the company's addressable market.

Attention to these factors differentiates business concepts from investment-ready companies. Often this information—collected via phone interviews or presented in investment memos, pitch decks, or financial models—will be the basis for a desk appraisal by the investor. A desk appraisal involves a summary of all information that can be collected remotely to conduct a preliminary assessment of the investment opportunity and to draft investment terms subject to on-site review. This step is important because of the costs and emotional commitment involved in traveling to visit the company's operations, meeting the managers and employees face to face, and discussing the rough terms of an equity investment. These elements are described in step 3 below.

Conducting Due Diligence

Due diligence refers to the activities undertaken to verify information gathered on an investment opportunity and the process of compiling missing data required to structure an investment. Due diligence typically involves on-site field-based work whereby the investor will visit company operations, check references of the management team, speak to actual and potential customers, and review (often audited) financial statements and key performance indicators. The due diligence process is very important to determine how transparent and thorough the management team has been in providing an accurate picture of the company's present status as well as its prospects. It is also an important way to gauge intangible aspects of the business, like organizational culture, employee morale, and the establishment of, and adherence to, standard operating procedures.

Diligence activities can be shared by investors in a syndicate or outsourced to local service providers on the ground (like local accounting or legal firms). Some investors will "piggyback" on diligence efforts undertaken by co-investors or will decide that the size of the investment only justifies a more cursory effort. Other investors will prepare a term sheet as a precondition for on-site field diligence. Either way, field diligence represents a serious commitment of time and resources and is typically done only for companies with a high likelihood of receiving an investment.

Step 3. Negotiating the Investment and Preparing the Term Sheet

A term sheet is a summary of conditions under which an investor will provide capital for a specific transaction. Term sheets are legally nonbinding, except for certain clauses such as confidentiality and "no-shop" clauses, which serve to "freeze the deal" for the investor while definitive funding documents are being finalized. "No-shop" means that the company cannot continue to find a better financing deal once it has signed the term sheet. Once a term sheet is signed, the parties are expected to make a "good faith" effort to move to financing. Below is a summary of the major components of a term sheet.

Amount and Use of Funds

The first part of the term sheet describes the total amount to be raised (number of shares times the price per share) and the use(s) of funds. The raised amount requested by the management team is set in light of company needs, while the investor evaluates if the proposed investment amount would best be invested up front as a lump sum or divided into tranches based on the future achievement of specific milestones or business goals. The use of funds (or "proceeds of the investment") is described generically and might include prohibited uses, such as paying off debt or repurchasing the shares of founding shareholders.

Valuation

The two basic components of valuation include the "premoney" and "postmoney" valuation. Premoney valuation is the price of the company at the time of the investment. The postmoney valuation is simply the premoney valuation plus the proposed investment amount. The determination of premoney valuation is more an art than a science in equity investing. In addition, it is difficult to capture the public good aspect of social enterprises using traditional valuation approaches, such as reliance on comparables, computing net present value, or applying the types of return targets used by venture capitalists.[35] This problem is particularly true in social-impact investing, where data on comparable transactions are either nonexistent or hard to come by. Alternative approaches and variants avoid some of these valuation conundrums. For example, some impact investors might add "goodwill" or other intangible value to a company in anticipation of a competitive advantage, improved employee retention, or strong customer loyalty engendered by a social enterprise. The difficulty of capturing these positive externalities accurately in valuation explains the continued need for development finance institutions and other public entities as investors in social-impact funds.

Type of Security

The type of security is the specific investment instrument being proposed in the term sheet. Investors typically request preferred equity, which has more rights and protections. Founders and angel investors typically receive common equity. "Convertible preferred" equity, which is often used in social-impact investing, provides the investor some of the privileges of preferred equity (to protect against the risk of investing in an untested concept) while allowing the optionality to convert into common shares if the company does well.

Preferential Rights

Preferred stock will often have specific rights and privileges associated with it. As discussed earlier, these preferential rights are compensation for the risk the equity investor is taking on and the greater amounts preferred equity holders typically invest. Among the most common preferences are (a) *liquidation preferences* allowing preferred shareholders to be paid off on special terms in case of a liquidity event (where a substantial proportion of the company is sold); (b) access to *dividend payments* forgone during early years of a company's development; *redemption rights*, which require a company to redeem an investor's shares at a preestablished price and within a specific time frame (typically five to seven years after initial investment) if a liquidity event has not happened; and *antidilution clauses*, which protect investors in the event a future financing is raised at the same or lower price than the previous financing.

Management Incentives and Controls

Stock options and management incentives are an important part of manager remuneration in an equity-backed company because they align incentives of management and the investor shareholders. These can take a number of forms.

- *Founder shares.* Typically, founders and management will own equity in the company because of cash they have infused to get the company off the ground plus "sweat equity" for their noncash contributions. It is important that the founders, managers, and other "key persons" to the business have strong equity participation, thereby linking these critical contributors more closely to the company's overall performance. For this reason, many equity investors will require a "lock-up" of founder-manager shares, which means they are prohibited from selling their shares for a fixed period of time.[36] In addition, equity investors will often require that founder-managers' ownership stake vest over time, typically three to four years. What this means is that founder-managers do not own their full percentage share allocation until a certain period of time has passed. Lock-ups and vesting create disincentives for managers to leave the company or sell their shares.
- *Employee stock option pools (ESOPs).* In developed countries, where equity markets are liquid and better understood, ESOPs can represent as much as 20 percent of the capital structure of a firm. In developing countries, where the number of high-profile IPOs is fewer and the understanding of, and experience with, equity is more limited, ESOP pools are usually in the high single digits, up to 10 percent. Although setting aside ESOPs can be dilutive to equity investors, most enlightened equity holders will establish equity incentives for managers and key employees so that they are rewarded the same way investors are—by building the business, increasing its value over time, and finding an exit.
- *Board composition and rights.* Another way equity investors align interests and balance decision-making with founder-managers is through board composition and rights. Typically, equity investment implies that new investors will take a seat on the board along with founder-managers. Ideally, one or two seats will be set aside for independent directors who have no affiliation with management or any shareholder. Independent board seats provide opportunities to bring in relevant expertise to help the company grow.

Shareholder Rights

To compensate for the greater risk they are assuming with their investment, equity holders will often be granted specific shareholder rights. In addition to a board seat and information rights (e.g., periodic performance indicators and financial statements), major or preferred shareholders often request certain consent rights. As outlined earlier, these "protective provisions" require investor approval over key business decisions such as mergers and acquisitions; hiring, firing, and remuneration of the CEO or other key persons; future issuances of equity; and changes to the shareholder agreement or business line.

These provisions are particularly important to social-impact investors, as they allow them to have a say in ensuring the mission-relatedness of core business activities. In addition, major and preferred shareholders are usually guaranteed pro rata participation in future equity rounds and a right of first refusal (ROFR), which allows the equity holder to match any offer made to purchase stock in the company by an outside third-party investor. These rights are very important to equity holders, as they allow them to reinvest in promising companies.

Exit Options

Given the importance of liquidity events to realizing an equity investor's return, most equity investments include mechanisms to facilitate an exit. Equity investors will often establish a timeline for finding an exit, encouraging equity shareholders to start a formal process of looking for buyers for their shares or selling their shares by a certain date. "Tag-along rights" allow minority shareholders to sell their shares along with a majority shareholder (at least a pro rata portion). Conversely, "drag-along rights" enable larger shareholders or groups of shareholders (usually a supermajority) to force minority shareholders to sell their shares alongside the majority selling shareholders, thereby avoiding problems associated with holdout investors. Given the challenges of realizing exits in emerging markets and nascent industries, more equity investors are exploring "self-liquidating" structures such as redemption rights (forced buy-back), earn-outs, or demand dividends, as noted earlier.

Step 4. Managing the Investment

How an equity investor manages the investment after the term sheet is signed and legal agreements are executed is as important as, if not more important than, how the deal is structured. Many equity investors establish 100-day plans to help ensure their capital is put to productive, high-impact uses. They will establish metrics, set budgets, and develop dashboards to track key performance indicators and formats for board meetings. Often an equity investor will become part of an executive committee of the board that works with management to support strategic decision-making and build operational capacity. Equity investors can serve as technical advisors and professional mentors to senior management, to help the company grow successfully. The critical areas equity investors involve themselves in reflect the most common board committees created when formal institutional capital is invested:

- *Talent/remuneration.* People are critical to company success and are always top priority for equity investors. Equity investors will get involved in identifying and recruiting new management talent as well as retaining and rewarding top performers through proper remuneration (including performance based bonuses or equity participation via employee stock option plans).
- *Audit/risk.* Because they are not receiving periodic payments that help demonstrate the health of a company, equity investors will typically set up an audit committee to periodically review the financial situation of the company. The focus includes the income statement (understanding trends in revenue growth, expense management, and ultimately profitability), cash flow management (which is critical for a company in

early or growth phase), and capital structure (using the right mix of debt and equity to help scale the business). This committee might also look at operational and technology risk, depending on the nature of the company.

In general, equity investors become actively engaged in the board and look for ways to support the company beyond capital, given that the investors' fate is now closely tied to that of the company.

Operational Challenges

Private equity investors know that they are investing in imperfect companies. That is the point. Social entrepreneurs seek growth capital from investors who understand that sustained profitability is months, if not years, away and that several other operational challenges are immediately in front of the enterprise. These challenges include rounding out the management team, establishing sales and distribution channels, or lowering production costs to maintain competitiveness within the market. These traditional challenges to equity investing are compounded when social elements are incorporated. Some of the main challenges are detailed below.

Lack of an Enabling Environment

Many companies operating in underdeveloped or frontier markets striving to have environmental and social impact often face additional "headwinds" to success that are endemic to the specific geographies in which they operate. Several such barriers often exist, as discussed below.

Regulatory Barriers

Local regulatory behavior can often present roadblocks to success. In several cases where photovoltaic price points now allow solutions for the energy poor, government subsidies on kerosene or outright tariffs on the importation of solar panels prevent market growth. The implication for attracting social-impact investment for companies offering alternative energy solutions in those environments is clear—don't invest until the risk of market price manipulation is contained. Lowering the cost of kerosene and other fossil fuels is a widespread practice and removing them to provide room for alternative sources of energy is both complex and politically charged.[37]

Inappropriate Monetary and Fiscal Policy

Monetary policy also plays a big role in the successful use of equity for social-impact investing. Because equity investments are capital injections made for many years and made into companies that promise high growth in their underlying value, sensitivity to currency exchange rates or outright devaluation is quite high.[38] In addition, tax and monetary policies that make it difficult to repatriate gains after monetizing an equity investment discourage investors from entering these markets. As explained earlier, returns for equity investors primarily depend on achieving a sale of their equity interest at some time in the future, rather than periodic payments along the way. Monetary policy that impedes equity investment or lengthens the time equity investors are required to wait to "exit" their positions is also a significant inhibitor, effectively reducing the effective return on investors' equity investments.

Corruption

Markets where corruption exists as a normal course of business and regulatory interaction pose real difficulties for social-impact investors and their portfolio companies. Company management is operating in an environment where a "level playing field" does not exist and the best-priced product or service may not win market share or large contracts. Delays in needed approvals from government authorities can be very hurtful to growth and the performance of companies, against which equity returns are based. Impact investors from, for example, the United States and the United Kingdom must also comply with the Foreign Corrupt Practices Act in their fiduciary, governance, and business oversight. As co-owners of the business and as fiduciaries, impact investors must guide company management to avoid participating in corrupt practices.

Limited Market Development

Equity investors realize a return on their investment when their shares are purchased or converted to cash. However, for many social enterprises and in many frontier markets, the exit options are less available for a variety of reasons, including small or fragmented markets, market failures (like information asymmetries), and inefficient or poorly developed capital markets (which make IPOs very challenging). Even well-positioned social enterprises with good cash generation can be challenging equity investment candidates because of the limited number of ways to monetize this value and provide a positive liquidity event for investors.[39] That said, leading industry players cite evidence that exit markets have become stronger in certain emerging and frontier countries—like Turkey, for example.[40]

Lack of Alignment between Investor Preferences and Enterprise Profiles

The expectations and preferences of investors are not always well aligned with enterprise profiles and desires, which make conventional equity use challenging in the social sector. This can take several forms.

Nature of Business/Growth Potential

Conventional venture capital equity investors target returns of five to 10 times their total cash investment. These returns are typically generated through growth and multiplying the underlying value of the invested enterprise. This type of enterprise growth is largely driven by disruptive technology, breakthrough innovation, and massive market adoption. Social enterprises are generally addressing basic gaps in access or infrastructure (e.g., water, health, financial services, energy). Many of these solutions have a local or regional scope and cannot promise the same explosive and broad growth in underlying company valuation. In addition, some social enterprises have legal restrictions (like nonprofits, which cannot distribute profits) or governance structures that can be punitive to growth.

Motivation of Founders and Families

In traditional equity, founding entrepreneurs sometimes have difficulty sharing decision-making and other controls that equity investors commonly request. This aversion to sharing control can be even stronger with a family-run business or social entrepreneurs, who can have fervent beliefs about how their companies should be run beyond turning a profit. There is also often a strong mission element, cultural norms, or family interests that influence the company's pursuits other than profit maximization and exit. In addition, entrepreneurs in emerging markets might enjoy the social status that goes with their position as head of an enterprise. This can be hard to relinquish if the business outgrows their capabilities, a situation not uncommon among fast-growing enterprises. In addition, relationships and family connections are critically important in frontier economies. As a result, many entrepreneurs start companies with family well-being and generational ownership—not market domination or quick exits—in mind. Encouragingly, there is evidence in certain emerging and frontier markets—like India and Kenya, for example—where a new generation of managers, some educated in Western markets, are adopting a "creator" versus "king" approach to scaling, building value, and exiting enterprises.[41]

Investor Governance Expectations

In a 2009 survey of over a thousand limited-partner investors worldwide, Groh and Liechtenstein concluded that the two most important criteria for capital allocation in emerging markets are investor protection/corporate governance provisions and the availability of skilled employees and management.[42] Not surprisingly, social-impact investors often demand protective provisions and special investor consents when using equity. Unfortunately, these controls can actually work against efficiency in decision-making and run afoul of founder inclinations. An efficient balance should exist between the day-to-day management of the company, periodic board oversight, and special carve-outs granted to investors.

Valuation Challenges

A social enterprise still developing a product and service (ideation or proof-of-concept phase) often cannot support a meaningful estimation of value now or in the foreseeable future. In traditional venture capital, this situation is ideal, as the investor can purchase a meaningful stake in the company for relatively small amounts of capital in the hopes of achieving outsized returns over reasonable time periods (five to seven years). Many social enterprises—especially those operating in emerging, frontier, or depressed markets—take longer to mature because of market dynamics (e.g., instability that disrupts business development or causes currency fluctuations), limited nonfinancial resources and infrastructure, delays in business development, and slow customer adoption. These delays have a strong drag on investor return because of the time value of money, that is, the fact that money now is worth more than money later.

Valuations are further complicated by uncertainties about the size and growth trajectory of investees in frontier markets. Equity investors need to be very clear about the stage of development and length of time it will take a prospective investment to exit, but such clarity is hard to establish. Long time horizons allow private equity investors to wait until a suitable time to exit and to have the time for strategic and operational changes to pay off, but they also increase the risk of other adverse external events. In a survey of 46 impact funds, Santa Clara's Center for Science, Technology and Society found that 50 percent of equity investors who originally projected an investment time horizon of three to five years are now expecting 7- to 13-year holding periods on those same small and early-stage investments.[43]

Long investment holding periods create another challenge: access to new capital. In a September 2013 report published by the World Economic Forum, several barriers were identified that prevented mainstream investment capital from participating in the impact sector. Among the findings were concerns over illiquidity, long investment holding periods, and limited track record of exits. Financial advisors and fund managers who direct investments for institutional investors (such as pension funds, sovereign wealth funds, and insurance companies) will predominately judge the deployment of capital along a risk adjusted yield curve. This means that investments with larger perceived risk will necessitate a higher yield. The lack of steady, high-yielding results from the social-impact sector thus far is keeping interested but hesitant fund managers on the sidelines. Additionally, the lack of a track record makes it difficult for existing impact fund managers to raise follow-on funds from existing investors, let alone attract new investment capital from more mainstream sources. The World Economic Forum report points to a number of structural and policy changes that could help assuage concerns over liquidity and long equity holding periods.[44]

Track Record

Because of its broad use, equity is a well-honed investment instrument that has delivered rewards for many investors. Typically, investors will have one or two spectacular investments that make up for the mediocre performers or outright write-offs in their portfolio. On balance, private equity markets have delivered returns to investors—both in developed and in emerging markets.

The story is decidedly more mixed in social-impact investing, though it is still early days. J.P. Morgan's 2011 survey of 52 impact investors noted "a lack of track record of successful investments" as the most significant challenge to growth of the industry.[45] Interestingly, a follow-up study two years later of nearly 100 impact investors revealed that 77 percent target "market rate returns" and that 64 percent actually "had at least one, if not many, investments significantly outperform in this way."[46]

There have been several celebrated equity exits reported by a variety of social-impact investing funds. Interestingly, the use of equity where the probability of exits is highest—in later-stage companies, in industries with established track records, and in more developed countries—has begun to be taken over by private, commercially oriented sector actors. For example, strong financial returns have led traditional commercial investors into Compartamos, SKS, and many other microfinance institutions.[47] In addition, clean tech has *overdelivered* on exits relative to its level of funding.[48] The picture is markedly different for earlier-stage companies operating in new industries and in frontier markets. Through interviews with social-impact sector participants, some clear dynamics affecting the chance of realizing liquidity from an equity-based impact investment have become clear. The further an investor ranged from late-stage companies in developed markets to early-stage enterprises in frontier markets, the more liquidity became uncertain and the more evidence of exits was difficult to obtain.

Some of this shift away from liquidity events has been intentional. Omidyar Network splits its social-impact investing between grants and investments. Moreover, as a sole investor fund, it is not constrained by a specific timeline the way most traditional "limited life" funds are. As CEO Matt Bannick commented, "We used to talk about 'risk-adjusted returns,' but have backed off that standard because (1) they are not possible in certain markets, and (2) sector building is critical. We *will* invest in companies that generate below-market adjusted returns if it helps develop an overall market."[49]

To manage through increased risk of return, social-impact investors have used several strategies to deliver significant social impact *and* financial return. In general, these approaches can be grouped in a few specific categories:

- *Sector- or geographically focused equity investing.* There are specific sectors like microfinance, financial inclusion, and environmental sustainability that have consistently delivered above-average returns for investors. Successful microfinance equity funds include Developing World Market, ProCredit, MicroVest, Elevar, Accion Investments, and others that take responsible finance seriously and have performed in the top quartile of emerging market funds for the relevant vintage years. In the environmental and sustainability arena, there are a number of solid exits in the conservation, recycling, and real estate areas cited by funds such as SJF Ventures (which focuses on resource efficiency and sustainability with representative investments that have been acquired or gone public at interesting exit multiples);[50] DBL (double bottom line) Investors, whose cofounder, Nancy Pfund, cites as some of her best impact exits Tesla (electric cars), and SolarCity (providing solar energy systems to homes and businesses); Beartooth Capital (which buys and refurbishes exceptional properties while creating financial, conservation, and community value); and Sarona Asset Management, a private equity fund–of-funds manager, which recently analyzed the performance of 13 value-focused investment vehicles with vintages from 2002 to 2007. The portfolios were comprised of 123 companies managed by 10 large funds across Africa, Asia, and Latin America. The net internal rate of return (including unrealized positions) was roughly 20 percent, with almost all targeting specific geographies and one-fifth of the portfolio companies coming from the telecom and technology sectors.

- *Established equity markets.* Funds like Huntington Capital and Bridges UK invest in more established markets like the United States and Europe, targeting conventional businesses addressing underserved markets. For example, Huntington Capital, a California-based fund that invests in "growth opportunities in underserved markets," lists successful exits for companies like Earthlite (massage tables) and Terra-Kleen (ground contamination solutions). Bridges UK boasts a number of successful exits from portfolio companies operating in underserved markets such as The Gym, which serves inner city populations with a no-frills, minimal commitment model; or Pure Washrooms, which installs and services washroom equipment in commercial premises of depressed areas.[51] For Bridges, the impact theme is "investing in deprived areas to stimulate the local economy and create jobs."[52] SJF Ventures and DBL Investors are both US-focused.

- *Relevant manager profile, base, and experience.* Recent research by potential investors in emerging market fund managers shows that equity investing in developing markets can have both social and financial impact. The International Finance Corporation (IFC), the private-sector investing arm of the World Bank, analyzed its portfolio of 150 fund investments between 2000 and 2009 and calculated that the return on its private equity funds (excluding real estate, debt, and listed equity funds) was 18.1 percent, comparable to the top quartiles of fund performance cited by Cambridge Associate Indices over the same period.[53] Even more interesting were the characteristics of the leading performers in the top decile. More than previous track record or frontier focus, the differentiating factor in fund quality was the manager's skill set. Specifically, managers who (1) have a local presence and employ local nationals, (2) offer value-addition capacity through past experience in running or advising companies, and (3) have private equity experience (who know how to work "back from exit to initial investment") were positively correlated with those funds that delivered superior financial returns.[54]

Cases of successful exits are still limited, given the stage of development of this social-impact-investing sector. Indeed, the equity track record as a social-*impact* investment tool is quite shallow. This is not surprising in view of the fact that the average reported holding period for an equity impact investment is longer than the term *impact investing* has been in use.

Still, equity success *can* be demonstrated. The number of examples depends on where you draw the line of what *is* social impact. For example, many in the emerging market private equity community would argue that their commercially oriented work has tremendous impact on the markets they serve—be it in terms of job creation, technology transfer, industry building, infrastructure development, or overall prosperity gained by the local communities.

The Global Impact Investment Network (GIIN) has formed a repository of impact investment funds called ImpactBase. Of the funds included so far, 23 private equity or venture capital funds that are focusing on risk-adjusted market-rate returns reported at least one exit—reportedly from equity. Combined, the 23 funds report a total of 119 investments exited and, as of this writing, controlled "committed capital" totaling US$1.16 billion. Ten of the funds reported four or more exits.

Many of these funds are engaged in the microfinance sector. Others are active in developed markets and work with companies that have a sustainable or environmental mission. Active for over 20 years, the Small Enterprise Assistance Fund (SEAF) provides an example of investment success in using equity for social, environmental, and developmental progress. It has made over 260 investments and has disclosed 184 exits where equity was involved. Of those, 87 were management buyouts, one was an IPO, and 42 were sales to strategic or financial buyers. SEAF's portfolio success is attributable to long years working in the field and a focus on SMEs that are operating in emerging economies (eastern and central Europe, China, India, Peru, and Colombia).

Shifting our focus to less developed economies and smaller enterprises brings more reports of social impact than of equity exits, though again it is premature to make definitive conclusions. A conversation with a manager from Bamboo Finance is representative of other interviews the authors had with leading impact investors. Bamboo decided to broaden its initial focus on microfinance to improving the quality of life for the local populations, beyond jobs (e.g., health improvement and housing). In addition, Bamboo wanted to trigger a "systems" change in the status quo, so that, for example, local poor populations could have the same or better repayment rates for certain services and that the banks would not "red-line" these neighborhoods. Return on most of the equity investments were yet to be realized, though they were promising.

Summary

In conclusion, equity is a valuable and efficient investment tool for social-impact investors. Its applicability is most clearly seen in growth-stage industries—especially those later-stage enterprises in more developed or emerging economies run by fund managers with relevant sector and geography expertise. For those social-impact investors venturing into frontier economies and impoverished communities, it is important to consider alternative quasi-equity structures that incorporate some element of fixed income and downside protection against risks and challenges inherent in these types of investments. It is also important for investors to be precise in explaining what part of the equity investing spectrum they are operating in, especially when making claims to "do well while doing good." This discipline in approach and communication will help ensure the social-impact industry delivers on its exciting promise and potential.

Notes

1. Bridge loans typically provide an investor the option to convert into shares at the next equity round and thus can be considered "quasi equity."

2. In general, private equity is considered longer-term and more illiquid than *listed* equities—companies traded on an exchange. Innovations in social stock exchanges are discussed in Chapter 4 of this volume.

3. Lucy Carmody, Benjamin McCarron, Jenny Blinch, and Allison Prevatt, *Impact Investing in Emerging Markets* (Singapore: Responsible Research, 2011), 11.

4. The distinction between *realized* and "paper" returns refers to actual cash outflows or distributions to investors in contrast to appreciation recognized "on the books" according to international financial reporting standards. "IFRS Resources," IFRS, accessed September 12, 2013, http://www.ifrs.com. Bridges Ventures is a fund manager in the UK, dedicated to using an *impact*-driven investment approach to create superior returns for both investors and society.

5. Interview with Sir Ronald Cohen, founder of Bridges UK, social-impact bonds, and Big Society Capital, February 7, 2013.

6. Equity protective provisions will often place limits over increased indebtedness.

7. "Frontier markets" is an economic term that was coined by International Finance Corporation's Farida Khambata in 1992 to describe a subset of emerging markets.

Frontier markets are investable but have lower market capitalization and liquidity than the more developed emerging markets. Frontier equity markets are typically pursued by investors seeking high, long-term returns and low correlations with other markets.

8. Yasemin Saltuk, "A Portfolio Approach to Impact Investment: A Practical Guide to Building, Analyzing, and Managing a Portfolio of Impact Investments," J.P. Morgan Global Social Finance Research, 2012, accessed January 8, 2014, http://www.ignia.com.mx/bop/uploads/media/121001_A_Portfolio_Approach_to_Impact_Investment.pdf, 8–9.

9. The 51 equity fund managers surveyed in 2012 raised US$3.5 billion, with the median per manager at US$21 million, and in 2013, they target US$5.7 billion with the median per manager at US$60 million. Saltuk, "Portfolio Approach," 19.

10. Saltuk, "Portfolio Approach," 10.

11. Saltuk, "Portfolio Approach," 8.

12. Participating preferred shares allow the investor to earn the liquidation preference and then participate in the upside on a pro rata basis with common shareholders. Because of the "double return," liquidation preferences are often capped.

13. Bridge loans are often used to cover cash flow gaps facing a company during an equity raise. They are typically simpler in structure and shorter in expected duration than promissory notes, but can also be converted to equity rather than paid out.

14. Scott Austin, "Entrepreneurs Going the Royalty Route Use a Share of Revenue to Pay Back Loans," *Wall Street Journal*, December 10, 2010, http://online.wsj.com/article/SB10001424052748704679204575646940403312602.html.

15. Arthur Fox, "Godfather of Royalty-Based Finance, on What VCs Are Missing," interview of Andy Sack, cofounder of Cypress Growth Capital, PE Hub, June 11, 2010, http://www.pehub.com/2010/06/11/arthur-fox-the-godfather-of-royalty-based-finance-on-what-vcs-are-missing.

16. "Terms: Earnout," Investopedia, accessed September 16, 2013, http://www.investopedia.com/terms/e/earnout.asp.

17. Investors structure earn-outs based on desired return and company forecast, with accelerated payment over time to give themselves desired IRR. Though both royalty financing and earn-outs return capital to investors based on a company's performance, there are differences regarding the accounting treatment during a liquidity event and how structured the exit is in earn-out vs. source: "How to Structure an Earn-out," Inc.com, accessed September 16, 2013, http://www.inc.com/guides/earn-out-structuring.html.

18. EBITDA—earnings before interest, taxes, depreciation, and amortization—is often used as a proxy for cash flow for early-stage companies.

19. Saltuk, "Portfolio Approach," 19.

20. Saltuk, "Portfolio Approach," 20.

21. David Wilton, *Characteristics of Successful GPs in Emerging Markets* (Washington, DC: Emerging Market Private Equity Association, October 2010), 5. The authors of "Coordinating Impact Capital" come to similar conclusions about the value of market and sector focus, as does the research done by Sarona Asset Management on successful emerging market private equity investors. Interview with Vivina Berla, senior partner, Sarona Asset Management, May 16, 2013.

22. Interview with Nick O'Donohue, CEO of Big Society Capital, March 19, 2013.

23. For a description of small- and medium-sized firms, see International Finance Corporation, "Interpretation Note on Small and Medium Enterprises and Environmental and Social Risk Management," International Finance Corporation, World Bank Group, January 1, 2012, http://www.ifc.org/wps/wcm/connect/

de7d92804a29ffe9ae04af8969adcc27/InterpretationNote_SME_2012. pdf?MOD=AJPERES.

24. See Chapter 7 of this volume.

25. Saltuk, "Portfolio Approach," 8–9.

26. Interview with Jonathan Tower, founder and partner of Arctaris Ventures, which provides royalty financing to small and medium enterprises, June 19, 2013.

27. Tower, interview.

28. Derek Anderson, "Clayton Christensen Talks Venture Capital, Crowd Funding, and How to Measure Your Life," Tech Crunch, April 4, 2013, http:// techcrunch.com/2013/04/06/clayton-christensen-talks-venture-capital-cr owd-funding-and-how-to-measure-your-life. Clay Christensen is the author of *The Innovator's Dilemma: When New Technologies Cause Great Firms to Fail*—a book about disruptive innovation.

29. Interview with Alex Silva, founder and CEO of Profund, Omtrix, and a variety of other social-impact-investing vehicles, February 15, 2013.

30. Interview with Simon Desjardin, Shell Foundation, April 8, 2013.

31. Harvey Koh, Ashish Karamchandani, and Robert Katz, "From Blueprint to Scale: The Case for Philanthropy in Impact Investing," Monitor Group, April 2012, accessed September 16, 2013, http://www.mim.monitor.com/downloads/Blueprint_To_ Scale/From%20Blueprint%20to%20Scale%20-%20Case%20for%20Philanthropy%20 in%20Impact%20Investing_Full%20report.pdf.

32. For other examples of the use of grants to supplement equity investments, see Saltuk, "Portfolio Approach," 10–11.

33. Interview with Vivina Berla, senior partner, Sarona Asset Management, May 3, 2013.

34. Berla, interview.

35. Social-impact investors use common approaches to valuation in equity investing such as the use of "comparables" (analyzing revenue or earnings multiples of companies with similar business lines, growth, or capital structures), discounted cash flow to determine net present value, or the "venture capital method," which translates a calculated terminal value into a required percentage ownership based on the investor's target rate of return. For further discussion of these valuation methods, see Josh Lerner and John Willinge, *A Note on Valuation in Private Equity Settings* (Boston: Harvard Business School Publishing, 2002), 1–8.

36. Some investors will allow founders to liquidate a small percentage of their holdings for personal cash flow needs.

37. Benedict Clements et al., "Case Studies on Energy Subsidy Reform: Lessons and Implications," International Monetary Fund, January 28, 2013, accessed September 16, 2013, http://www.imf.org/external/np/pp/eng/2013/012813a.pdf.

38. Central banks of emerging countries at times artificially suppress the value of the local currency to encourage exports, as part of a broader development strategy. Currency devaluation can make liquidation of equity financing done in hard currency difficult.

39. Saltuk, "Portfolio Approach," 22.

40. Interview with Gerhard Pries, managing partner and chief executive officer, Sarona Asset Management, February 11, 2013.

41. Pries, interview.

42. Alexander P. Groh, Heinrich Liechtenstein, and Miguel A. Canela, "International Allocation Determinants of Institutional Investments in Venture Capital and Private Equity Limited Partnerships," IESE Business School, February 2009, accessed September 15, 2013, http://www.iese.edu/research/pdfs/DI-0726-E.pdf.

43. John Kohler, Thane Kreiner, and Jessica Sawhney, "Coordinating Impact Capital: A New Approach to Investing in Small and Growing Businesses," Aspen Network of Development Entrepreneurs, July 2011, accessed September 15, 2013, http://www.scu.edu/socialbenefit/resources/upload/Coordinating-Impact-Capital.pdf.

44. World Economic Forum, *From the Margins to the Mainstream: Assessment of the Impact Investment Sector and Opportunities to Engage Mainstream Investors* (Davos: World Economic Forum, September 2013).

45. Yasemin Saltuk, Amit Bouri, and Giselle Leung, "Insight into the Impact Investment Market: An In-Depth Analysis of Investor Perspectives and Over 2,200 Transactions," J.P. Morgan Social Investment, December 14, 2011, accessed September 14, 2013, http://www.thegiin.org/cgi-bin/iowa/download?row=334&field=gated_download_1, 6–7.

46. Yasmin Saltuk, "Perspectives on Progress: The Impact Investor Survey," J.P. Morgan Social Finance, January 7, 2013, 4, accessed January 8, 2014, http://www.jpmorganchase.com/corporate/socialfinance/document/207350_JPM_Perspectives_on_Progress_2013-01-07_1018749_ada.pdf.

47. Tarun Khanna and Jayant Sinha, "The Microfinance Catalyst, October 4, 2011, accessed January 8, 2014, http://www.project-syndicate.org/commentary/the-microfinance-catalyst.

48. Matthew M. Nordan, "The State of Cleantech Venture Capital 2011," 8, http://mntempblog.files.wordpress.com/2011/12/the-state-of-cleantech-venture-capital-2011.pdf.

49. Interview with Matt Bannick, CEO Omidyar Network, February 12, 2013.

50. "Portfolio," SJF Ventures, accessed May 12, 2013, http://www.sjfventures.com/portfolio.

51. Interview with Michelle Gidens, managing partner, Bridges Ventures, March 7, 2012.

52. "Portfolio Exits," Bridges Ventures, accessed September 14, 2013, http://www.bridgesventures.com/node/177.

53. Wilton, *Characteristics of Successful GPs*, 4.

54. "Experienced PE professionals know what sells, know how to develop (and agree with the majority) on plans and milestones that will move the company towards that exit window, and know how to work with company management to execute the plan and exit within the target time frame." Wilton, *Characteristics of Successful GPs*, 6.

Suggested Readings

Bannick, Matt, and Paula Goldman. "Priming the Pump: The Case for a Sector Based Approach to Impact Investing." Omidyar Network, September 2012. http://www.ignia.com.mx/bop/uploads/media/Priming_the_Pump.pdf.

Drexler, Michael, et al. "From the Margins to the Mainstream: Assessment of the Impact Investment Sector and Opportunities to Engage Mainstream Investors." World Economic Forum, September 2013. http://www3.weforum.org/docs/WEF_II_FromMarginsMainstream_Report_2013.pdf.

Rangan, V. Kasturi, Sarah Appleby, and Laura Moon. "The Promise of Impact Investing." Harvard Business School Working Paper N9-521-045. November 4, 2011.

Saltuk, Yasemin, Amit Bouri, Abhilash Mudaliar, and Min Pease. "Perspectives on Progress: The Impact Investor Survey." J.P. Morgan Global Social Finance, January 7, 2013. http://www.jpmorganchase.com/corporate/socialfinance/document/207350_JPM_Perspectives_on_Progress_2013-01-07_1018749_ada.pdf.

CHAPTER 16

SOCIAL-IMPACT BONDS/ PAY-FOR-SUCCESS FINANCING

Drew von Glahn and Caroline Whistler

ANGIE RODRIQUEZ, DIRECTOR OF DEVELOPMENT for Roca, a nonprofit service organization based in Chelsea, Massachusetts, had just finished describing to the board how Roca's Intervention Model has been applied to East Boston's most disconnected youth. She spoke of drug dealers, high school dropouts, and those who are frequently trapped between prison and the streets in a destructive, costly cycle for both the young person and the surrounding communities until Roca intervenes.

Angie tells the story of Roca eloquently, for it was her story too. She is a graduate of the streets of Chelsea, the Latin gangs, and ultimately of the Roca program. She watched her brother be murdered, yet that did not stop her self-destructive behavior. It took the perseverance of Molly Baldwin, the founder and executive director of Roca, for Angie to redirect her life and ultimately escape the potential scenarios that were offered to her at age 13—crime, drugs, teen pregnancy, jail. Over the past years Roca had refined its program that re-engages Massachusetts' most disconnected young people—the Intervention Model for High-Risk Youth.[1] Under the board's guidance, Roca had shown its ability to replicate its model by expanding its services outside the Greater Boston area.

However, despite years of documenting compelling evidence of its impact, Roca's ability to scale its model was highly constrained. This was the result of a common set of problems for nonprofit social service providers. The first is the persistent dilemma of obtaining reliable, long-term funding. The second is the challenge of traditional government procurement processes, which seek low-bid service delivery rather than a joint commitment to invest in initiatives that have sustained outcomes. Grant funding was time-consuming and particular, and a great deal of management's energy had been invested in fundraising, with little certainty about attracting reliable resources. Meanwhile, government officials, with little ability to measure the real impact of the services they procured, inconsistently supported or referred disconnected young people to successful programs such as the Roca Intervention Model. Instead, the commonwealth funded more prison beds and other remedial services that are an expensive way to achieve unsatisfactory social outcomes.

Molly joined in the discussion as she reviewed with the board an alternative that was under consideration by the Massachusetts Department of Administration and Finance. The commonwealth was considering piloting a new initiative called social innovation financing (SIF). As contemplated by the state, SIF would be a variation on performance-based contracting for social services that mobilizes private investment capital to support expansions of social programs. Aside from its innovative use of upfront private investment capital, the key "twist" from more traditional procurement was to use defined social outcomes—not just service delivery—as the trigger to repay the private capital—an approach frequently referred to as "pay-for-success" (PFS) in the United States, a derivation of the "social-impact bonds" (SIB) model originally developed in the UK.

The Commonwealth of Massachusetts had released dual requests for responses (RFR) to implement this initiative—one for service providers to deliver outcome-based services and another for intermediary organizations to structure and provide the required financing to fund the contract. Ultimately, Roca was attracted to the potential of accessing repeatable and scalable private capital backed by a government pledge to reimburse the funders based on proof of success. Second, Roca would be able use the evaluation and monitoring requirements of the PFS to document and build upon its strong evidence-based business model. On August 1, 2012, Roca became the first lead service provider selected through a competitive social innovation financing procurement in the United States. As this chapter went to print, the first competitively bid, statewide pay-for–success/social innovation financing program was being finalized to scale Roca's operations and use government money to pay for outcomes, not outputs.[2]

Defining the Tool

Pay-for-success financing is a public-private partnership tool that combines performance-based contracting and private financing. By joining the two, governments are better able to align the procurement of, and payment for, services with the achievement of targeted social outcomes.

In the first component, pay-for-performance contracting, the government contracts with a lead contractor to implement a preventative intervention to address a social problem, often to reduce consumption of costly remedial services, with agreed-upon targeted outcomes that result in government payments only if success is achieved. Government contracts that are based upon achievement of outcomes are not new, yet the concept is nascent in the human services arena. And even for those social sector organizations that want to participate in this type of government payment structure, performance-based contracting poses a difficult proposition.

The second key component of pay-for-success contracts is that a third party funds the upfront operating capital required for the program. Tapping into private capital has three benefits: (1) it provides the necessary monies to ensure sufficient operational capital to launch and support the initiatives, (2) it transfers the risk of nonperformance from service providers to investors, and (3) it creates a level of transparency that provides a feedback loop that allows stakeholders to continuously assess the impact of the program. Should a provider, such as Roca, achieve the agreed-upon social outcomes, the state pays the project, and by extension repays the investors, the principal plus a risk premium. Under the PFS contract, third-party investors take on Roca's performance risk and can lose money if the program is ineffective. The state thereby reduces its financial risk, providing greater willingness by the public sector to either pilot high-potential opportunities or scale proven programs to achieve a wider social impact.

As this chapter delves further into the structure, mechanics, applications, and related considerations of pay-for-success financing, it is important to clarify the relevant terminology. The term "social-impact bond" (SIB) that is widely used to refer to this approach in the UK is misleading. Despite phrasing that implies that SIBs are bonds, in fact they are not bonds in the traditional capital market sense. As discussed in Chapter 13 of this volume, in traditional capital markets, "bonds" are financial debt instruments that require specific legal documentation, are regulated by government authorities, and are often evaluated by independent rating agencies. This combination allows bonds to be easily traded and often owned by retail investors (either directly or through managed funds). "Bonds" are very attractive financial instruments when (1) it is believed that there is a large volume of financings, and (2) the risk can be well measured. Both of these criteria are challenged in the initial application of PFS. Therefore, because of the newness of PFS financings, it is unlikely that the early-stage transactions will warrant the costs and time considerations associated with documenting and registering bonds.

Given these realities, for the reader's ease, when discussing the tool that combines the application of performance contracting and financing linked to third-party funders, we will use the terminology *pay-for-success financing* (PFS financing).

Defining Features

As an innovative tool, pay-for-success financing is highly flexible and open to multiple constructs. Variations of PFS financing are being developed across the globe with projects launched in the UK, the United States, and Australia, with pilots and nascent discussions underway in many other countries—including developing economies. These initiatives have the following in common:

1. They establish a public-private partnership to address intractable social problems.
2. They contract for measurable social outcomes.
3. They implement preventative interventions.
4. They transfer performance risk to third-party funders.
5. They align risk-based capital efficiently.
6. They establish transparency and a performance-based feedback loop.

Let us examine these defining features in turn.

Establish a Public-Private Partnership

PFS financing is a public-private impact collaborative that involves the joint action of government, private investors, and nonprofit or for-profit service providers. Each of these actors brings specific resources to the initiative. As a partnership, their individual priorities need to be aligned around a common objective—and in the case of PFS financing they coalesce around providing financial returns based on improved social outcomes.

Contract for Measurable Social Outcomes

Pay-for-success contracting is predicated on the measurement of social outcomes rather than the quantity or type of services provided. In that respect, it differs from much traditional social service contracting, which tends to focus on measuring outputs (e.g., how many individuals are served, how many "beds" are made available to the homeless, how many attended a job training workshop, etc.) rather than outcomes (e.g., the number of young men who have obtained and maintained employment, or the number of homeless individuals who successfully moved their lives forward in supportive housing arrangements).

Implement Preventative Interventions

PFS financing is framed around preventative interventions that target specific social outcomes, often reductions in the use of remedial services such as prisons, hospitals, shelters, or nursing homes. PFS financing provides a low-risk opportunity for government to test whether an intervention is effective, before allocating increased resources to the program. An additional attraction is that often these preventative programs drive fiscal savings for government along with improved outcomes.

Implementing preventative initiatives can be complex. In order to achieve the desired outcomes, in certain situations the PFS may require the service provision of multiple organizations, each delivering a specialized service that provides complementary and highly integrated solutions. To ensure coordination of services, a single organization may oversee the program delivery. This organization, often referred to as an "intermediary," acts as the lead contractor. The lead contractor provides oversight of the PFS contract and manages the coordination of services towards a common targeted solution.

Transfer Performance Risk to Third-Party Investors

Addressing challenging social outcomes and achieving targeted outcomes at a predetermined cost structure involves significant risks. This "performance risk" has been one of the binding constraints in testing or scaling new initiatives. Governments, with tight budgets, often lack the fiscal and political ability to direct funding towards preventative programs, even if research has shown that these investments will "pay off" in terms of savings in remedial services. As one state government official observed, state budgets largely fund "deep end" mandatory social needs, what is often called the safety net. As these mandatory programs continue to grow, particularly in times of fiscal constraints, the budget for prevention often shrinks.

In traditional performance-based contracting, it is the government contract-holder that bears either the majority, or at least a substantial portion, of the performance risk, the risk of having to cover costs if sufficient performance is not forthcoming. While many nonprofit CEOs are confident in their ability to achieve targeted social outcomes, as prudent managers of their organizations they are appropriately hesitant to carry this risk, particularly if they have not been subjected to rigorous evaluation in the past. This is a fundamental challenge in the design of nonprofit tax status, which limits, or at least discourages, the provision of equity-like resources that are available to for-profit companies. Nonprofits, lacking such a capital cushion, are limited in their risk-taking capacity.

Pay-for-success financing attempts to overcome this limited capacity of both government and service providers to absorb risk by having third-party funders take on the performance risk. This transfer offers an opportunity to prove to the government in real time that an intervention can produce valuable social outcomes and potentially relieve demand for mandatory services. If an intervention is successful under a PFS financing, government can redeploy its limited resources in a more informed and effective manner. This may eventually increase and rebalance public expenditures towards lower-cost preventative initiatives.

Align Risk-Based Capital Efficiently

Because of government's willingness to reward projects for success, a broad array of funding sources is anticipated to come forward to finance PFS contracts. At the outset, traditional philanthropic foundations will likely participate in the initial financings in order to absorb the risk of developing the "proof of concept" of the PFS financing tool. As evidence emerges that this form of financing can be efficiently structured and performance risk can be assessed, additional sources of capital will become available.

PFS financing is already attracting investors beyond the philanthropic foundations. For example, the recent PFS financing in New York City involved a community reinvestment act (CRA) loan of $9.6 million. The initiative funds an intervention to reduce recidivism of former inmates of the Riker's Island correctional facility.[3] The performance risk is 75 percent covered by a $7.2 million credit enhancement in the form of a loan guarantee from the Bloomberg Foundation., while the remaining 25 percent of the performance risk will be borne directly by the investors. By building upon known financing techniques, the PFS financing can be adapted to customized situations. Equally, PFS financing can eventually be structured along standardized financing templates that will allow broad replication and can attract a wider pool of funders and investors.

Establish Transparency and a Performance-Based Feedback Loop

Private investors are putting in the upfront money. Since their return will depend on the level of success in achieving specified outcomes, they will insist on clear and measurable definitions of metrics with all parties. Investors will require the ability to efficiently monitor results. What is more, government agencies that must ultimately pay the bill are equally interested in seeing evidence of progress, and will only pay once performance is rigorously measured and documented. PFS financing therefore requires a high level of transparency among government, investors, lead contractors, and the providers of services. It will require the design and implementation of evaluation methodologies that provide timely, cost-effective, and rigorous analysis.

Relation to Common Criteria

Like all tools of social action and social investment, the pay-for-success financing model must balance the key considerations of risk, return rates, and "best" applicability. In addition, as the social investing sector continues its path to-wards mainstreaming, those constructing PFS financing programs must be mindful of the limitations and potential for unintended consequences of the tool. In this section we examine how PFS financing compares to other tools in terms of these and other common issues.

Breadth of Application

Risk-based financing for the social sector is not new. Affordable housing financ-ing has become a well-established means of supporting improved living condi-tions for those of limited income. In addition, philanthropic foundations have used program-related investments (PRIs) to support the development of the-aters, museums, healthcare facilities, and real estate projects with an economic development focus. Yet most of these have been "asset based" or infrastructure financings. By providing the mortgage on these properties as collateral, these financings are able to provide strong risk mitigants for the funders.

What has been missing is scalable financing to support innovative social service interventions—initiatives that are service-based in nature and therefore lack the tangible assets or other forms of recourse for lenders as a means of mitigating risk. PFS financing seeks to use data and measurable outcomes, not tangible assets, to provide risk mitigation, and therefore access to funding for the social service sector. Where there are outcomes that can be well defined and measured, in a cost-efficient manner, the parties are able to build a PFS contract around a common shared value proposition and repayment mechanism.

Areas of application for PFS financing are driven by social, economic, and political priorities. If a local government is committed to achieving a given social outcome, PFS financing may offer access to upfront resources that incen-tivize public investment in such goals. Structurally, PFS contracts can be applied to a wide range of issue areas and to programs at various stages of de-velopment. In the human services arena, programmatic applications include health, social services, workforce development, and education. PFS financing can additionally be developed to address other societal concerns such as the environment and sustainable practices in energy, agriculture, and natural resources.

Programs funded through PFS financing can range from well-established interventions to highly innovative initiatives and integrated services from a multiprovider collaboration. If there is a government priority to address an existing social problem, it will be up to the investors to determine the degree of confidence they have in a given intervention's ability to achieve the desired out-comes. As discussed later in this chapter, given the flexibility of PFS financing, various approaches and constructs can be applied to allow government and investors to pursue a diversity of social outcomes and priorities. The more un-certain the outcome, however, the higher the performance risk of the project and the greater the risk premium investors will be likely to demand.

Fiscal Cost-Benefit Proposition

A general requirement to apply the PFS tool is that a successful program will result in fiscal savings to government. Many government entities are interested in the PFS tool primarily because of the potential fiscal savings it can produce. In fiscally constrained times, the cost savings argument becomes an even more important justification for the structuring work PFS demands. As noted earlier, in the case of Roca, Massachusetts determined that at least one-third of the youth aging out of the Department of Youth Services or juvenile probation have a high propensity to be incarcerated within a year of leaving. From a cost-benefit perspective, the full cost of Roca's four-year intervention model is less than one year of incarceration costs, and therefore an attractive financial and social proposition for the state. In its initial applications, the PFS will be predicated on achieving savings in existing government remedial services. By reducing or even eliminating the need for such "deep end" programs, savings will accrue, and a government success payment that returns capital to investors is justifiable. Governments will make similar fiscal cost assessments in determining the applicability of a PFS construct. But this means that PFS will only be workable, initially, in fields, and jurisdictions, where costly, deep-end programs are in operation. Where such programs do not exist, the savings will be nonexistent and the PFS mechanism may not initially work.

Risk Considerations

In pay-for-success financing, investors finance the lead contractor/intermediary, who in turn orchestrates payment to service providers until evaluation of outcomes determines repayment by government. It is the investors, therefore, that bear the majority of the performance risk—and by extension, the risk of not recovering their investment. Under this approach, the government becomes a facilitating partner, rather than the principal risk taker with taxpayer resources.

The risk of repayment to investors is based principally upon two key factors: (1) the performance risk associated with the likelihood that the lead contractor will meet the social outcome goals at an agreed upon cost; and (2) the payment risk associated with the likelihood that the government agency will make the contracted payment. We return to this point below.

Rates of Return

In the UK social-impact bond, a 7.5 percent reduction in the recidivism rate allowed for a return of principal as well as a nominal risk premium return for the investors. The rate of return increases on a sliding scale as the performance exceeds the 7.5 percent reduction, with the rate of return capped at 13 percent.[4]

Given the nascent stage of the PFS financing concept in the United States, parameters for pricing are still being developed. The initial projects under consideration have been indicating rates of return in the mid to high single digits with a sliding scale increase in returns should the PFS exceed base expectations. These early indications suggest that financing rates may not reflect the traditional capital market rates. This is due to several factors. One is the "social" aspect of the investment and the long-standing belief that funding social needs should be based largely on altruism. This "return versus mission" debate will most likely bias the rates lower than comparable capital markets constructs.[5] The second factor is the traditional capital markets pricing dynamic of supply and demand. Over the past half-decade there has been an increasing focus on civic minded investing. In 2010 Hope Consulting estimated that there is $120 billion in monies seeking social-impact-investing opportunities.[6] However, to date there are few places to invest such monies, resulting in an imbalance that favors lower pricing as investors compete for the investment opportunities.

The third consideration is the above-mentioned underdeveloped understanding of the risk factors related to achieving the targeted social outcomes. In the traditional capital markets, rates of return are influenced by the perceived risk considerations and the assessment of the program's capacity to achieve the required repayment terms. Since in a PFS financing investors will not have tangible collateral, their primary risk consideration in a PFS contract is the performance of the lead contractor. It will take a number of PFS financing issuances to begin to review and assess how these risk factors play out.

Until more applicable capital availability and risk/reward benchmarks can be achieved, early-stage financing rates in the United States will most likely be framed around certain proxies. These could include the following:

1. Benchmarks analogous to current program-related investment rates
2. The current rate of returns associated with CRA loans
3. The local government's current borrowing rates for its own general debt obligations
4. Financing rates for recent publicly supported infrastructure project financings (renewable energy, water and power, highway, etc.)

Degree of Leverage

Within the context of PFS financings, the leverage discussion has three distinct components: (1) the ability of government to achieve savings that are at a multiple to their cost of the program, (2) the ability of philanthropic-minded funders to maximize their resources, and (3) the level of debt financing versus equity, or equity-like, cushion in the capital structure of a PFS.

First, a central attraction of PFS financing for government is the belief that investments in preventative programs will not only yield greater impact, but will actually be cheaper in the long run than continuing to fund remedial services. Rigorous cost-benefit analyses are a critical component of any PFS financing structure to confirm if government savings are in fact a multiple compared to the cost of a proposed intervention.

Regarding the second leverage consideration, there is one simple fact in the philanthropic world—a grant is a 100 percent principal loss. There is no return of the investment, no ability to redeploy the monies. After the grant is spent, new resources will need to be located to continue to fund social programs. In PFS financing, there is the opportunity for socially minded investors to receive their principal plus a premium. These monies can be reallocated to the program or invested in other initiatives.

As to the makeup of the program's capital financing construct, there is the potential for numerous approaches. In the UK pilot, there was just one level of debt capital with numerous investors providing the funds and obtaining similar investment rights. As the PFS financing model evolves, it is anticipated that different layers of capital may come into play; senior debt, junior/subordinated debt, and equity/equity-like capital. This layering, common in the traditional capital markets, will allow the parties to structure the investments to align the varying expectations of performance with investor risk appetite. In addition, it is expected that in the early stages of the PFS, there will be a requirement for "first loss" philanthropic capital embedded in the transactions. These monies will act like equity, yet not offer the level of returns traditionally associated with equity risk taking. This will provide the senior lenders an equity-like cushion—which may be necessary until there is greater experience with the performance of the lead contractor and service providers.

Skill Requirements

There is a clear learning curve for all parties in the development and implementation of PFS financing. While the actual financial tool in itself will not necessarily call for development of new or unique skills, each party will need to reorient its traditional ways of interacting—as well as have an increased awareness of each other's operational requirements. Today, most social programs are designed around service delivery outputs such as number of individuals attending a workforce training. In PFS financing, providers will be accountable for the actual outcomes of the services rendered—such as retained employment or reduced recidivism. The resulting "managing to outcomes" will have a very material impact on how staff's jobs are defined and organizational performance is managed.

Government agencies will need to be more flexible in pay-for-success contracting structures, allowing lead contractors to better manage to outcomes instead of focusing on prescriptive services requirements. Also, to most effectively evaluate the outcomes, governments will need to put greater focus—and resources—on how their own administrative data can track the achievement of the targeted social priorities. Government will also have to understand the risk-return considerations facing external investors and the premiums they will have to pay in response. Meanwhile, investors will need to understand the operational risks associated with the intended interventions and the performance capabilities of the lead contractor. And last, evaluators will need to move away from highly controlled assessment environments to more dynamic measurement tools that build off of government administrative data.

Design Features and Major Variants

There are a number of options for how PFS financing is designed and implemented. In this section we examine four different bases for such variation relating to (1) how the process is managed; (2) how performance is measured; (3) what the field of operation is; and (4) what stage of development the project is in.

Lead Contractor Entity and Role

In the first place, it is anticipated that there will be a number of variant approaches to managing to outcomes. One of these is the establishment of a *lead contractor* or intermediary to coordinate service delivery. This was the case, for example, in the UK pilot, where a new intermediary organization, One Source, was established.[7] One Source selects, subcontracts, and coordinates the services that management believes are necessary to achieve the outcomes agreed with the government. One Source implemented a shared data management system among the key service providers—allowing each provider to supply input and obtain outcome data. It is One Source that is held accountable for the achievement of the targeted outcomes.

In the United States and internationally, it is anticipated that various forms of the lead contractor role will develop. In many cases, rather than establishing new entities for each PFS financing transaction, existing intermediary organizations with the programmatic capacity and evaluation expertise may opt to be the lead contractor and subcontract the services. Additionally, there exist well-established service providers, who have the operational, financial, and administrative capacity to act in the role of lead contractor. Many such organizations are already managing multiprovider integrated services.

The type of lead contractor chosen will be influenced by the role that the government is seeking from such an intermediary. In the case of juvenile justice in Massachusetts, the state chose Roca as the principal service provider because it had in place an evidence-based program with a strong track record of measuring and achieving outcomes, but decided to partner Roca with a consortium intermediary to assist in project management, capital raising, and financial oversight. Roca retains control over its model design, target population, and service delivery.[8] In the case of homelessness mitigation in Massachusetts, the state chose a consortium of existing actors to provide the intermediary role.[9]

A third variation in the management of the PFS financing role is the potential for specialized management companies to develop over time. Just as in other sectors like renewable energy, these nationally based organizations may be able to hire and staff local teams to provide the role of lead contractor for individual projects, while leveraging their large-scale management expertise and resources infrastructure. Similar business practices have been applied in the commercial real estate market for many years.

A major consideration in the design and selection of an intermediary organization is the fact that delivery—and oversight of delivery—must be highly localized. To effectively manage to successful outcomes, such organizations will need to have strong understanding of the local communities—their needs, resources, and political environment.

Performance Measurement Methodologies and Counterfactuals

Another area in which PFS financing will see variation will be in its design and application of evaluation methodologies. In the social services field, evaluation experts often insist on highly structured randomized controlled trials (RCTs) to determine outcomes resulting from a particular programmatic innovation. But RCTs have drawbacks. In order for the results of RCTs to be considered credible, for example, service providers often have to refrain from modifying their programs during the life of the evaluation. RCTs are also often highly customized and therefore expensive to design, manage, and evaluate. In addition, RCTs are not designed to provide cost-benefit assessments—a key requirement of government in determining the value of a PFS program.

To overcome the limitations of RCTs, PFS financing models will look to make greater use of evaluation methodologies that are based on government administrative data. As this data is already being processed by government agencies, it is readily available on a continuous basis and at negligible costs. The presence of this data may, in some cases, enable low-cost RCTs or other rigorous quasi-experimental designs, at least where administrative agencies keep track not only of PFS program participants but also other recipients of government treatment or assistance.[10]

An ongoing evaluation approach means that service providers are not only able to report on their impact, but also can use the information to manage and modify their service delivery. In the case of the Massachusetts juvenile justice PFS financing, administrative data from the Department of Youth Services, Probation, and Corrections will be used both to follow the target population on a randomized basis and to track recidivism outcomes for the treatment and control group in a randomized controlled trial design.[11]

Field of Operation

The programmatic application of the PFS financing tool can vary widely. Initiatives under active consideration at present include the following:

- *Juvenile justice/aging out programs.* Several interventions have shown that home- or community-based treatment of juvenile offenders instead of residential treatment can lower recidivism. Government reduces the cost of nights spent in residential custody.
- *Homelessness.* Programs that target and prevent chronic homelessness, often heavy causes of Medicaid spending, have the potential to reduce costs. Programs that divert families from shelters can also save monies in state-provided emergency assistance and child welfare.
- *School turnaround.* Some providers can increase graduation rates significantly for low-income school districts. Schools benefit from increased average daily attendance allowances, and states may see reductions in criminal justice and safety net expenses.
- *Early childhood education/literacy.* School districts are beginning to link universal prekindergarten interventions to the reduction in special education expenses and first- and second-grade repeat rates. Wraparound interventions exist to continue positive outcomes and savings to education and justice systems throughout academic careers.
- *Sustainable housing.* Initiatives providing supportive housing for low-income individuals or frequent users of hospitals can result in lower incidences of environmentally induced asthma and other health issues, reducing Medicaid consumption.
- *Workforce development.* Evidence has shown that intensive training and apprenticeship programs can successfully redirect at-risk young adults into well-paying careers. Government benefits from higher income taxes and lower criminal justice and safety net expenses.
- *Transitional care.* Specially trained medical staff can work with the elderly, before and after discharge, to ensure a successful transition to home care. Care results in improved health outcomes, reducing costs for Medicaid and Medicare.

In addition, the issues for which PFS may be applicable in developing economies can be materially different from those for which it may work best in developed countries. For example, a working group led by the Center for Global Development and UK-based Social Finance identified the following potential applications of PFS in low-income countries: antiretroviral treatment as prevention of HIV and TB in Swaziland; reduction of Rhodesian sleeping sickness in Uganda; the low-cost private school sector in Pakistan; access to quality secondary education in Uganda; SME pipeline generation and value creation; and energy efficiency implementation.[12]

Stage of Development

PFS financing should be viewed as principally an innovative financing tool. As such, we anticipate that the early transactions will be based on well-established—and documented—intervention programs. From the government's perspective, the primary focus will be on better understanding the financing tool and how to structure cost-effective public-private partnerships for social services in order to move forward with evidence-based contracting. Investor initial focus will be on the performance capability of the lead contractor to deliver the targeted outcomes, and on programs that have demonstrated efficacy such as in the Roca example cited earlier.

Programs such as those of Nurse Family Partnership (NFP) are strong candidates for an early PFS financing. For over 30 years, NFP has provided perinatal coaching and support to first-time mothers living in poverty. Rigorous RCTs have been applied to review the program, confirming its impact in improving the health of infants. Despite its documented success in improving the health outcomes of the newborns and achieving other social benefits, the organization believes it is serving less than a quarter of young mothers who would benefit from its services. In Los Angeles, NFP currently serves 1,000 young mothers annually, just one-sixth of the first-time mothers living in poverty.[13] NFP has the management expertise and experience to replicate its model—what is missing is the willingness and financial capacity for local governments to implement NFP's program at scale.

Over time, as familiarity with the tool broadens, and the procedures for its implementation and operation become established, we anticipate that PFS financings will begin to be applied to emerging interventions, such as the Vera Guardianship program in New York City. The Guardianship operates on about a $1 million annual budget to provide services designed to allow low-income elderly individuals remain in their homes rather than being placed in nursing facilities, or in many cases left in hospitals.[14] While the Guardianship Program, launched in 2005, has tracked improvements in the lives of the individuals with whom it works as well as savings from reducing the need for high-cost hospital stays and nursing facilities, it has not had a gold-plated RCT to confirm its outcomes. Vera's Guardianship program therefore represents a PFS that would be higher on the risk profile than NFP. Hence the traditional capital markets would likely require a higher rate of return on this program than on an NFP-based project.

Financing Structure

The PFS financing model seeks to replicate the established practices of traditional capital markets in which financings are structured and aligned to meet the operational funding requirements, expected repayment period, and programmatic risk profile of the particular transaction. The same forms of capital used to finance wind turbine farms, solar generating facilities, highways, and other major capital investments—such as senior debt, mezzanine debt, and equity capital—can be applied to PFS financing. In the Peterborough pilot, the monies were invested as limited partnership (LP) interests, a well-established form of providing risk capital to projects that provides investors an opportunity to share in any returns an enterprise may earn. The pending Massachusetts programs look to both debt and equity, and it is expected that several other capital market practices will be applied in structuring the funding of PFS transactions over time. For example:

- *Types of debt.* While the term "bond" is embedded in the early nomenclature of SIB financing, the form of debt financing available for this tool is quite broad. In the initial stages, the debt component of PFS financings will be more customized and may follow the constructs applied in the financing of renewable energy and affordable housing projects. Unlike financial security instruments that are registered with regulatory agencies—which allows broad public investor participation—the debt will be "privately placed" with professional investors who can cope with the uncertainty surrounding this new tool, the need to tailor financing to the specific circumstances of each PFS application, and the likelihood that amendments will be needed as circumstances change. As the PFS financing tool evolves and matures, it will become better able to tap into the broader investor universe, and the term "bond" may become applicable.

- *Syndicate structure.* To accommodate the various sources of capital, PFS financing can apply a syndication construct. In this arrangement a lead investor (or a small representative group) takes the initiative to engage with the government and lead contractor to develop a PFS contract and its associated funding construct. After developing preliminary terms for the financing, the lead investor(s) approaches a broad group of potential investors to determine their interest in participating in the financing. The investors will agree to one set of financing documents, each investor having pro rata decision rights based on its proportional commitment of the total financing.

- *Capital layering and risk tiering.* The traditional capital markets have come to appreciate that there are investor capital pools that have different risk appetites, and it is expected that the PFS financing market will be no different. Some investors will want a very safe investment and will be willing to take lower returns. Other investors may be comfortable with risk and therefore will be willing to take a lower security ranking in the funding. These investors may seek to negotiate higher returns for such a subordinated credit position.

In order to accommodate these different levels of risk appetite, the transaction can be structured such that investor repayments are based on different performance levels. In the case of the Peterborough financing, all investors were treated equally. However, in the case of juvenile justice in Massachusetts, the intermediary entity, Youth Service, is considering multiple sources of capital, with different tiers of risk. One tier, a senior debt tranche, will have first claims on any repayment. The second tranche, a quasi-equity layer of capital, will have subordinated claims on performance. If Roca meets 100 percent of its targets, all of the investors will be repaid principal and interest. However, if Roca achieves a lower level of performance, the senior tranche investors will receive the payments first, and the equity level will only receive payments once the senior debt is fully repaid.

Patterns of Use

The first social-impact bond was launched in September 2010 for the Peterborough prison recidivism program in the UK. Since then, numerous countries, including the United States, Australia, Canada, Israel, and Colombia have issued PFS financings or have begun earnest explorations into the construct's ability to combine known program and management approaches with established capital financing techniques.

In the United States developments have progressed steadily. Following the publication of an article on the Center for American Progress's website in March 2011,[15] exploration of pay-for-success financing has occurred at the federal, state, county, and local levels. At the federal level, the Federal Office of Management and Budget (OMB) held a convening of interested parties to explore the application of the pay-for-success concept in July 2011, and has initiated several solicitations to states and local governments calling for PFS financing under Department of Labor and Department of Justice Second Chance Act funding. A request for upwards of $500 million in funding for pay-for-success programs and incentive funds was included in the president's FY 2014 budget.[16]

Six states—Massachusetts, Minnesota, New York, New Jersey, South Carolina, and Illinois—have formally begun procurement processes to initiate pay-for-success financings. The priority in Massachusetts is chronic homelessness and services for young people aging out of state youth and probation services. The commonwealth is currently negotiating final contracts with winning bidders on its request for responses. The Massachusetts legislature has set aside up to $50 million for PFS contract payments. Minnesota has released requests for information from parties interested in participating in its "human capital performance bond,"[17] a government-issued bond that proposes to use bond revenue to pay service providers based on outcomes. New York State has released a broad request for information soliciting ideas and potential interventions for pay-for-success programs.

At the local government level, New York City formally launched the first US social-impact bond in August 2012 to finance an effort to reduce recidivism among former convicts in the Riker's Island penitentiary. The city has also launched a request for expressions of interest for other suggested intervention areas. Cuyahoga County, the largest county government in Ohio, has also launched a broad request for proposals for pay-for-success initiatives.

Globally, the PFS financing concept also continues to attract attention. In Australia, the government of New South Wales issued a request for proposals for two priority areas: reducing demand for foster care (out-of-home care) and a justice program similar to that of the Peterborough pilot. In its request for proposals, the government recognized that once an application was accepted, given the complexity and the dependence upon outcomes, further negotiations regarding the outcomes would be anticipated. In Canada, the Canadian Task Force on Social Finance included specific recommendations for social-impact bonds in the one-year update on its 2011 report "Mobilizing Private Capital for Public Good."[18]

Interest in the pay-for-success financing concept is rapidly evolving into experimentation on the part of innovative governments and those encouraged by federal procurement incentives. The examples above promise to be the tip of the iceberg of government entities developing social innovation financing projects. In addition, there is emerging interest to construct PFS-type financing in developing countries. In June 2013, the Development Impact Bond (DIB) Working Group included discussion of six options for using a derivative of the PFS concept in its consultative draft document.[19] Yet the operation of the PFS model in these settings may differ from its operation in more developed settings since these countries lack the fiscal resources to be the ultimate payer of DIB financings. But this could be the new role for development assistance. In lieu of the cash-starved governments paying for performance, development assistance and philanthropic organizations could step in and apply their development aid monies to the repayment of successful DIBs. The result would be the agencies focusing their resources on programs that are demonstrating positive outcomes—a better alternative than the traditional construct of development aid.

Tool Selection: The Rationale

The fundamental rationale for pay-for-success financing rests on several overriding considerations: first, the recognition that there continue to be social problems that current initiatives are not resolving; second, the difficulty in obtaining the financing to implement and scale up preventative approaches to social problems; third, the fiscal benefit of achieving alignment between funding and demonstrated positive outcomes; and last, the need to establish the necessary transparency to ensure that government is funding "what works."

High-Priority Social Needs

PFS financing will be most successful if applied where there is a social priority and a fiscal consideration that is relevant to government agencies and their local constituents. Given their outcome-focused approach, PFS financings can be well applied to what have been intractable social dilemmas—ones that if not addressed will lead to increasing social problems and concomitant fiscal outlays. A preventative program delivered via PFS provides government with a real and measurable solution—one that has the opportunity to subdue the escalating social and budgetary expenditures and produce meaningful changes in the lives of citizens. Particularly in cases of incarceration, lengthy hospital stays, nursing homes, and other forms of government-funded residential treatment, the costs of not investing in prevention are enormous, both for the government's resources and, in many cases, for individuals' health and well-being.

The Prevention Focus

The majority of the available public resources for social programs goes into treating the symptoms of social ills rather than into preventing them from occurring. Thus, first offenders too often commit a second crime, leading to expensive, long-term incarcerations, or homeless people are offered nightly shelters and food but not supportive housing, job training, and psychiatric counseling. PFS financing provides new capital to design, execute, and scale preventative interventions, ones that attack the causes of social ills rather than manage their consequences. Such interventions require long-term operating capital, which is rarely available from other sources. Traditionally, providers rely upon philanthropic contributions or government cost-reimbursement contracts. These funding streams are sporadic, subscale, or highly uncertain and as such limit the organization's ability to invest in replication and the development of sustainable intervention models. In addition, these sources often limit the funding to direct service delivery, which leaves a service provider without sufficient funds to cover the costs associated with properly managing and supporting the service delivery as well as restricting the funding of the organization's research and development—a necessary investment to continuously strengthen outcomes.

Aligning Metrics to Funding

For this preventative focus to work, however, a second important feature of the PFS financing mechanism is required, which in turn drives the ability of government to tap "investment capital." That is the use of affordable, concrete metrics that indicate progress toward the desired prevention objective. Historically, this connection between funding and demonstrated outcomes has been limited in social programming,[20] leaving government trapped in funding cycles with programs that are ineffective or have unknown outcomes.[21] Causes for social problems are complex, and therefore the requirement to measure "real impact" is equally demanding.

Previously, without data, investors had no capacity to structure risk-based financing that could drive long-term fiscal savings. There was no satisfactory means of measuring a credible value-proposition for government—one that provides the incentive to incur debt obligations. With measurable outcomes and cost-effective data and evaluation mechanisms, government can set terms with funders that appropriately align its fiscal and social objectives with those of the investors.

Transparency and Capacity for Dynamic Program Management

Government programs are largely designed in a prescriptive manner such that the contracts focus on "how" services are provided. In addition, the contracts are directly between government agencies and service providers. Several unintended consequences occur. As government executives are compelled to embed highly defined operational parameters for the service providers, any deviation from the prescribed terms requires time-consuming negotiations. In such an environment, program designs can remain in place for extended periods, limiting a provider's ability to adapt programs based on real-time learning.

Thus, a third ingredient of PFS financing is the implementation of highly transparent contracts that allow all parties to see performance trends, and thus to understand the need to adjust services to better achieve the targeted outcomes. Providers are able to manage to results rather than be constrained by established procedures. The PFS contract necessitates dynamic management—using available data to continuously improve outcomes. Because PFS financing ties ultimate reimbursement of investors to demonstrated performance, it makes investment in rigorous information-gathering and evaluation a pivotal requirement for third-party investors rather than an optional add-on. The financiers require ongoing availability of metrics, increasing the requirement for transparency, which ensures that the providers are constantly measuring and adjusting programs to strengthen their performance.

With a focus on prevention, alignment of risk capital with outcomes, and dynamic program management, PFS financing provides a framework for staying focused on real and measurable solutions to critical social challenges.

Basic Mechanics

PFS financings build upon a staged process that requires each project to undertake the following steps:

1. Contract with government for performance-based payments
2. Obtain financing
3. Implement preventative interventions
4. Evaluate impact and leverage feedback loop to achieve desired outcomes
5. Repay investors or reinvest in the project upon success

Figure 16.1 depicts the relationship among the key players involved in this tool and the discussion below examines each step in turn.

Step 1. Establishing the Government Procurement Contract

The first step in implementing a PFS financing is for government to initiate a procurement contract indicating a willingness to be the ultimate payer for successful outcomes achieved. Government commitment ensures investors that they will receive payments based upon achievement of performance criteria or other milestones being met in accordance with the agreement or contract. These payments may serve as a combination of return of principal to the investors plus an agreed-upon risk premium. An essential component of the government contract is multiyear contingent contracting, where the government commits today to future payments. From a procurement perspective, the following considerations are especially important:

FIGURE 16.1

Relationships among Key Players in a Pay-for-Success Project

1. Ensuring a competitive and transparent process in selecting the lead contractor and intervention
2. Ensuring that there will be sufficient funds to launch and support the PFS financing over a determined time period
3. Establishing assurances that government funds will be available for future-year conditional payouts
4. Achieving acceptable cost-benefit outcomes for taxpayers
5. Implementing a contract that is sufficiently flexible while incorporating adequate safeguards for the individuals receiving the proposed services

Transparent and Informed Procurement Process

PFS financing is a collaborative engagement requiring an open dialogue among the key stakeholders early in the process. The need for open dialogue must be balanced with government's conventional "competitive bid" processes. In order to facilitate the necessary dialogue, governments in the early PFS implementations have taken a staged approach, with some form of information solicitation through an initial request for information (RFI), which may lead to informal discussions with respondents. The purpose of this stage is for government to gain insight into the local priorities, capabilities, and resources of service organizations, intermediary agencies, and philanthropic investors so that when it does issue a formal procurement request it can be confident of quality responses.

Simultaneously during this period conversations take place among government agencies and departments. These internal discussions are used to (1) establish public sector priorities, (2) determine the cost and benefit of potential initiatives, (3) assess availability of administrative data and targetable populations, and (4) create a coordinated process to manage PFS financing initiatives across multiple government agencies. State governments, for instance, recognizing the potential to apply PFS financing across numerous programmatic areas, have taken to establishing one team to spearhead the PFS financing opportunity, leveraging the knowledge gained through the information solicitation process to ensure a coordinated and efficient management of multiple PFS financings. These teams incorporate the respective agencies, bringing together deep sector expertise (i.e., health, education, youth services, etc.) and finance and treasury skills.

These multistakeholder discussions are critical. A key premise of PFS financing is that governments will move away from prescriptive contracts in which each government agency dictates the method of service delivery for its particular services. Rather, it is expected that the lead contractors will commit to certain outcomes, but retain the flexibility to manage the type(s) of interventions and to manage the service provider(s). Responsibility for the design and structure of service delivery therefore shifts in large part to the lead contractor, who must design a delivery system that provides investors with the confidence that the PFS contract can meet the government objectives in a cost-effective manner. Yet this transition from traditional contract management must still be managed through existing procurement processes.

After an initial RFI or information-gathering process, governments move to a second phase—a competitive request for responses (RFR) stage. Given the newness of PFS, these requests for responses differ from traditional request for

TABLE 16.1   CRITERIA SET FOR SERVICE PROVIDERS AND INTERMEDIARIES IN MASSACHUSETTS PFS SOLICITATIONS

Criteria for	
Service providers	**Social innovation financing intermediaries**
Likelihood that the organization and program model will deliver its stated outcomes, as well as the magnitude of such outcomes	Likelihood that the proposal will successfully achieve its stated outcomes
Expertise with juvenile justice and youth services and experience working collaboratively with innovative service providers	The strength of the existing evidence base for assessing likely program impact
Ability to monitor success and measure outcomes, including counterfactuals	The cost effectiveness of the proposed delivery model in achieving the RFR objectives
Ability to assemble, manage, and oversee service provider organizations in order to achieve targeted outcomes	Ability to monitor success and measure outcomes, including counterfactuals
Ability to raise funding for service delivery operations as required	Extent to which the program establishes safeguards against harm for the target population
Demonstrated willingness and capability to collaborate effectively with state government organizations, service providers, and other entities	

proposals (RFPs) in that at this stage, selected parties essentially earn the "right to negotiate" with the government entity to construct final programmatic designs and contracts.[22]

In Massachusetts, the Executive Office of Administration and Finance (EOAF) issued two separate RFRs for juvenile justice, one for service providers and one for intermediaries. The state sought programmatic design—and associated budgets—from potential service providers. From intermediary respondents, the state sought proposals regarding programmatic management and governance, as well as a financing structure. Table 16.1 lists the criteria the state set for selecting providers and social innovation financing intermediaries.

Ensuring Sufficient Financing to Cover Program Costs

Over the decades, those involved in social services have come to accept that government and philanthropic supporters do not fund the full cost of delivering a program. Corners are cut, pay is low for highly qualified staff, little money is made available for appropriate infrastructure, technology is often antiquated, and funds are not made available for research and development and experimentation. This is unique to the social sector. Successful businesses, while being cost conscious, recognize the need for human capital talent, appropriate investment in technology and supporting infrastructure, and the ability to continuously test their and improve their business models. Investors require that the organizations that they fund have the sufficient resources to fulfill their commitments and succeed.

Along these lines, PFS investors will require that the initiative be appropriately funded. This will necessitate extensive operational due diligence to determine the cost of delivering services at scale. Investors will require financial modeling that forecasts the amount and timing of expenditures. In addition, they will be mindful that the program needs monies to cover the appropriate supporting infrastructure.[23] From the government perspective, they, too, want to be confident that the program has the capacity to be successful and that the intermediary has arranged sufficient capital.

Establishing Government's Commitment to Pay

PFS financings create an interesting challenge for government budgets. Most budgets are annual appropriations, which require the current sitting government's approval and the actual expenditure of the appropriated monies in the current fiscal year. In the case of PFS financings, there is need for *multiyear contingent commitments* by government. The service contract signed by an agency would obligate the government to make payments upon successful completion of the terms of the contract—regardless of the timing of the payment. Funders need to be confident that the government's legal commitment to make the payout ranks along with any authorized contractual obligation.

A number of options are available for handling these commitments. One option is to appropriate the full potential government commitment in the fiscal year in which the contract is signed, place the money in some form of escrow account, and pay it out on successful completion of the project or deposit it back into government coffers if the project fails to meet its objectives. Other options involve appropriations spread out over the expected life of the contract but held in some type of holding or trust account pending successful progress or accomplishment of project objectives. Either way, governments will need to obtain clear appropriations and implement funding constructs that will establish investor confidence that success payments will be honored.

Validating Government's Cost-Benefit Equation

A key consideration for government agencies (and all stakeholders) will be the fiscal impact of a PFS financing. Given the current constrained fiscal times, many governments will not be in a position to implement PFS financing projects if they cannot demonstrate the ability to either achieve cost savings or at least be cost neutral compared to existing expenditures. From an annual fiscal management perspective, traditional government cost analysis looks at the marginal costs savings (lower fiscal expenditures due to the costs specifically associated with an individual or a cohort of beneficiaries). This becomes challenging in that many government costs are fixed, and it will take material changes in the structure of the social safety net to achieve cash savings due to the investments in preventative interventions. However, this is not a reason for government to dismiss PFS financing.

Over time, as a program is scaled, government may be able to associate fixed cost savings from the efficacy of a program (e.g., closure of a prison wing in the case of recidivism programs or a homeless shelter in a homelessness prevention program.). In the early phases of the tool, government agencies will need to balance the political and fiscal challenges of achieving marginal savings in the short term with the expectation that there will be prospects of realizing fiscal impact over the long term.[24] Openness to apply PFS financings will come from governments that consider the project as a multiyear investment, which over time will lead to a reduction in fiscal expenditures and improved societal benefits, such as the ultimate shuttering of a prison and the economic—and human—benefit of a productive individual versus a convict.

Flexible Contract Structure

Following the procurement process, successful intermediary and service provider bidders are selected to negotiate with the state for final contracts. Traditional governmental procurement contracts focus on process and procedures. PFS financings require that the lead contractor have the flexibility to manage the initiatives in order to achieve the target outcomes—making adjustments as experience and learning dictate. At the same time, the government entity must reserve the right to ensure safeguards for the individuals served. It is expected that each PFS contract will define how much flexibility the lead contractor has to orchestrate service delivery depending on the needs of the negotiating parties. These negotiations will need to consider the investor's confidence that the contract provides the lead contractor the ability to manage effectively in order to achieve the targeted outcomes.

Step 2. Obtaining Financing

To implement the financing construct for PFS financings, the key players will be government, the lead contractor intermediary, investors, legal counsel, data and evaluation experts, and advisory firms specialized in structuring innovative social financings.

The mechanics of the financing construct will center around two key documents. The first will be the pay-for-success contract between government and the lead contractor. The second will be a parallel financing agreement between the lead contractor and investors. Hence, as shown in Figure 16.2, investors will not have a direct financial claim on a government agency.

FIGURE 16.2
Contract Arrangements for a Typical PFS Undertaking

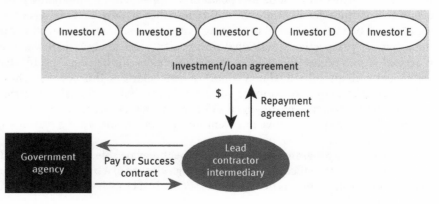

In addition, in order to limit the legal obligations of the intermediary, the intermediary's commitment to repay the investors is based upon receipt of performance payments from the government. To the extent that the performance targets are not met, no payments are required of the government, and the lead contractor is not obligated (or able) to make payment to the investors.

In traditional philanthropic grants that support nonprofit organizations, each individual funder enters into a direct agreement with an organization, each having its own set of conditions, disbursement terms, and monitoring requirements. Among the "innovations" that PFS will bring to the social sector, it is anticipated that PFS financings will offer the opportunity to utilize the capital markets approach of collaborative investing, or syndicated capital. In this approach, one or more funders take the lead in constructing the key funding and repayment terms. They work with the lead contractor, government agencies, and the independent evaluator to structure the arrangements. Prior to finalizing the various agreements, the lead investors approach a broader group of potential investors. This "road show" or "syndication" process introduces the investors to the potential program and the associated financing—reviewing its merits and investment considerations.

In this approach, each investor makes its commitment to fund the project, with the funding being made available to the lead contractor intermediary. Its commitment provides the investor a proportional interest in the investment vehicle and its decision rights. Once terms are agreed upon and sufficient capital is committed to the PFS financing, the intermediary enters into financing arrangements with the different investors. These can take several forms depending on the exact mix of debt, equity, quasi equity, and risk and return positions in the deal.

Establishing the Investment Entity

While PFS financing discussions generally refer to a "lead contractor" or "intermediary" organization, in most cases a new independent legal entity (a special purpose vehicle that could be a limited liability company [LLC] or nonprofit subsidiary, for example) will be formed to enter into contracts with the government and investors.[25] This approach is analogous to other forms of project finance such as building a renewable energy facility or affordable housing development. The investment entity becomes the counterparty for the performance commitment under the government service delivery contract, as well as for debt repayment obligations to investors. Establishing this as an independent legal entity protects the nonprofit service providers from additional legal risks.

Rights of Funders

As the funders bear the majority risk of nonperformance, they may retain the right to replace the service providers as determined in the financing agreement with the intermediary. In addition, the contracts will outline funder rights of remediation and oversight. For example, in the event of cost overruns, it will be the funder's prerogative to either inject additional capital to ensure that the lead contractor has sufficient resources to meet the targeted outcomes, or to wind down the project. In the event that there are multiple funders, as discussed previously, each funder will have a proportional right to approve changes in the financing agreement. In the event of major issues such as replacing the lead contractor or winding down the program, special majorities of the funders may be required.

Step 3. Establishing and Managing the Program Delivery

As discussed, both government and funders will seek a more dynamic, outcomes-focused program management role for the project, with the service delivery coordinated through an intermediary lead contractor. This moves the burden of managing to the desired social outcomes to the intermediary and investors. As the lead contractor designs and implements its proposed model, it will look to address the following:

- Build the program off of a known intervention that has demonstrated capacity to address the government's specific social outcomes target
- Address the key challenges in replicating and scaling to meet the specific situation; determine if the program design is best served by having multiple interventions and service providers or one strong service provider
- Select service provider organizations whose team has the experience to manage to the targeted social outcomes
- Implement performance-based incentive payments to align service provider, lead contractor, and investor interest
- Establish a multiyear budget ensuring that resource requirements are sufficiently funded and care is not denied for those who have begun services in the event that the project is terminated

Once the procurement contract is in place, and funds are made available by investors, the lead contractor is in a position to finance the service providers. Figure 16.3 provides a pictorial representation of the structure put in place in

FIGURE 16.3
Massachusetts PFS Organizational Structure

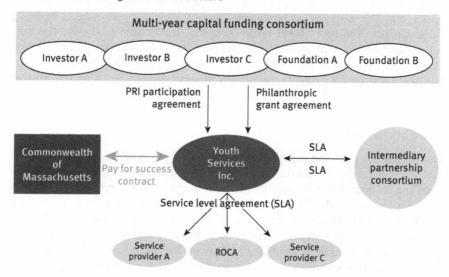

the case of the Massachusetts PFS, with Youth Services in the position of intermediary and Roca as the principal service provider.

In this role, YSI will manage the PFS program delivery, and maintain direct interaction with both the government and investors over the life of the contract.

Step 4. Ensuring Impact

The heart of PFS financing is the confidence that social impact will be achieved. Outcomes are the central determinant of payments from government and returns of capital to investors. The focus on outcomes requires the upfront articulation of well-designed evaluation methodologies in pay-for-success contracts, and the application of these methodologies with fidelity throughout the program implementation. While the "gold standard" random control trials may not always be appropriate, designs will need to establish comparative baselines and counterfactuals in the government contracts, and define clear referral processes and outcome metrics to be followed throughout the contract term.

By incorporating appropriate evaluation design components, including particularly adequate controls, the independent evaluators will be able to measure whether a particular PFS initiative achieved the outcomes or if results were due to other external factors (e.g., for recidivism separating out the effect on the population due to a change in judicial procedures, or general improvement in a regional hiring environment, etc.). Achievement of agreed-upon outcomes can then initiate payments from government to the lead contractor, and from lead contractor to investors.

Beyond establishing and monitoring benchmarks for program efficacy—the evaluation methodology acts as a management tool and feedback loop to identify needed midcourse corrections (e.g., to provide an additional service, alter the case management staffing ratio, modify the intervention to address a documented shortfall, etc.).[26]

Step 5. Repaying Investors

The PFS financing construct permits a wide range of options for structuring principal repayments and investment returns. Armed with the data from independent evaluators, the parties will be able to verify whether the success payments should be disbursed. These metrics can be set at various milestone points and are outlined in the initial contractual agreements.[27]

Based on the contract terms between the lead contractor and investors, the amounts paid out by the government may be repaid in either installments or a lump-sum payment at maturity of the financing contract. The repayment can be measured against a single benchmark tracked periodically, or it could be based on annual performance targets.

There are several considerations when establishing investor repayment and return mechanics. We anticipate models will be developed in which investors will receive proportional return of their capital investment based on the percentage of targets achieved. This will avoid the "all or nothing" performance hurdle, and reward the investors for improved social outcomes, albeit not at the fully desired level.

A final consideration for all parties will be whether or not to continue to support successful programs. Designs may develop in which the original investors, particularly philanthropic ones, agree to reinvest a portion of their initial capital to continue to support the program or fund a further scale-up of successful interventions

Operational Challenges

Challenges confronting the PFS financing concept fall into three main baskets: first, that the effort to attract private capital will lead inevitably to a loss of focus on the social objectives of the PFS model; second, that the natural learning obstacles of an innovation such as PFS financing may lead to highly visible mistakes that doom the experiment before it can truly gain its footing; and third, that a number of the tool's systemic features will turn out to be difficult to implement. These latter challenges include such concerns as the government's capability to make good on its long-term commitments of support, the willingness of lead agencies to take on the enormous effort that the PFS tool requires and the ability to rigorously test for impact.

Risk That Profit Concerns Will Trump Social Ones

The PFS financing model is predicated on the belief that private investors will be willing to make significant bets on achieving meaningful social objectives through social change interventions and that governments will pay for this. While this is a hopeful proposition, the jury is certainly still out on its validity. The danger is real, therefore, that the effort to attract private-sector funding may lead to a weakening of the commitment to the social goals of these experiments, or that pressures will be great to engage in "creaming" of target groups, or choosing to focus on the least difficult cases in order to show the greatest results for a given level of cost, especially given the difficulties of measuring social progress and allocating possible causes of observed progress.

Already concerns have been raised that PFS financing is taking precious dollars away from needed treatment programs to finance complex and costly experiments that will benefit wealthy investors and high-priced financial consultants. What is more, the technique can be faulted for seeming to justify government cutbacks by implying that nothing the government is doing works and only by turning to management consultants can complex social issues be "solved."

Natural Start-up Challenges

The second group of challenges facing the PFS financing tool relate to its nature as an early-stage innovation confronted with many of the start-up problems facing any new innovation. As one observer has noted, PFS financings face a steep learning curve as governments struggle to understand the complex new implementation structures, the role of intermediary/lead contractor becomes clear, and an investor base is created that is comfortable with this new "asset class."[28] It took over two years to structure and negotiate the Peterborough SIB. In the United States, for the juvenile justice initiative in Massachusetts it is estimated that the implementation of PFS financing will take a similar time-frame to execute. Inevitably, with so much hype surrounding the PFS concept, there is the danger that early missteps can turn Pollyannaish enthusiasm into excessive negativism in the minds of at least some observers. There is therefore a need to caution against overpromising what this innovation can accomplish and how fast it can demonstrate results. In the meantime, supporters can take comfort in the hope that each of these start-up challenges will diminish as experience expands and processes and procedures become familiar.

Systemic Impediments

Finally, it is necessary to acknowledge several very real systemic hurdles to the establishment of a robust public/private, impact-oriented collaborative such as PFS financings. These hurdles can be bracketed in five categories: (1) government sector engagement challenges; (2) evaluation challenges; (3) transition to an outcome-based business model by the lead contractor and nonprofits; (4) establishment of a collaborative working partnership among government, intermediaries, investors, and subcontracting nonprofit organizations; and (5) development of risk-based funding and capital layering.

Government Sector Engagement

The adoption of PFS financing will challenge a number of existing business practices of government. Hence, to move PFS financings forward the most important factor is senior-level government sponsorship. Public-sector leaders will need to be able to envision and articulate the benefits of a public/private collaboration towards social outcomes. Without such leadership, the necessary collaboration among different government agencies will not develop, and one cannot hope to initiate a government PFS financing.

Depending upon the locale and the social goals being pursued, the specific public sector barriers may include (1) lack of political will to undertake a complex innovation to address complex social problems; (2) constraints in procurement and contract management procedures; (3) availability and quality of administrative data; (4) government funding streams that create impenetrable operational silos among government entities, agencies, and departments; and (5) uncertainties about whether governments will really make good on their pledges to reimburse investors and provide the agreed bonuses for successful accomplishment.

Experience to date has shown that the willingness of government executives to engage in discussions to determine the potential benefits of a PFS financing cannot be taken for granted. It is clear that leadership needs to perceive the benefits—or at least recognize that the status quo is not a viable long-term solution. Government executives also need to be confident that their constituents can appreciate the long-term gains, fiscally and for society.

Constraints embedded in the procurement and contract management practices constitute another initial hurdle for government. Particularly in its early stages, PFS financings will challenge the existing regulatory environment and associated operational silos of government. Many social problems cross over the borders of multiple government agencies. To address homelessness, for example, will require engagement of local or regional housing, healthcare and mental health agencies, as well as public safety. There is then the need to coordinate among federal (HUD), state (Medicaid), and local governments, all of which may benefit financially if impact is achieved.

Additionally, budget departments are often mandated to reduce the cost of services, not procure more effective programs. However, to implement a new programmatic approach such as PFS, budget departments need to quantify the fiscal savings over other—less effective—social services. Governments will also need to accept multiyear contingent contracting with social service providers and surrender significant operational discretion to outside intermediaries. The promise of PFS financing may not be enough to overcome these procurement and contract management challenges.

The third practical consideration for government is definition of "successful" outcome metrics and the presence of administrative databases to measure them. Government budget agencies may seek to have the outcome metrics defined in fiscal terms, to include, for example, the achievement of specific fiscal savings in the definition of "successful outcomes." The challenge for service providers and investors is that success in achieving measureable social outcomes may not lead to immediate fiscal savings. Providers do not have influence on the operational management of the government, and hence it will be the responsibility of government to take the necessary budget and fiscal management decisions based on improved social outcomes. In the case of the Peterborough pilot, for example, a material reduction in the re-arrest rate of offenders may not lead to fiscal savings if the governmental authorities choose not to close prison facilities. Governments will therefore need to use social outcomes as the key measure of success and commit to managing budget and safety net programs based on the reduced need that results.

Logistically, government entities will also need to ensure that they have reliable and cost-effective databases in place to track social outcomes as defined in the PFS contract. Without the ability to track outcomes on an ongoing basis, the underlying payment-for-performance structure of PFS financing quickly unwinds. Especially important are databases that track all participants in a targeted government initiative against nonparticipating control groups so that comparisons can be made between those treated by the PFS intervention and those not.

A fourth challenge arises from the fact that the fiscal benefit to government may not always lie within the same government entity that is achieving the social benefit. In this case, the question that arises is "Who pays upon success?" Government funding streams are complex and often multilayered. In the United States, many programs are funded by dollars that come from a combination of federal, state, and local fiscal resources. If a county undertakes an initiative to reduce recidivism within its population, the fiscal savings of such preventative programs will over time be generated through the reduction of prison costs, which are largely state-funded expenditures. On the other hand, short-term incarceration of arrested youth (preadjudication) is often funded locally by counties. To address this concern in the case of the Massachusetts PFS financing, the commonwealth targeted youth programs in which the safety net support services are largely paid out of state resources. To develop PFS financings for only those initiatives that have single funding streams would materially limit the opportunity, however. Alternatives will be required—and this may require waivers by governments and budgetary mechanisms that bridge these funding streams, allowing local governments to apply state and federal funding to repay successful PFS financings.[29]

Finally, a major concern in structuring the PFS financing is related to the government's ultimate willingness to make required payments and reimburse investors, with premium bonuses, for successful outcomes, particularly if these outcomes do not become apparent until long after the governments that made the initial promises have left office. As noted earlier, there are a variety of mechanisms that can be put in place that can help ensure that the resources will be available when the time to pay arrives. In the case of Massachusetts the state legislature approved the funding, which provided confidence to investors. However, until some actual experience with governments meeting these obligations is achieved, skepticism will be warranted, especially in the current climate of sequestrations, mandatory furloughs, contract cancellations, and local government bankruptcies.

Commitment to Rigorous and Cost-Effective Evaluation

As noted earlier, random control trials (RCTs) can be quite expensive. The Nurse Family Partnership RCTs reportedly cost well into the millions of dollars. Such costs are prohibitive for a PFS implementation. In addition, as noted earlier, such controlled trials are often highly inflexible by design, which is inconsistent with the need for PFS contractors to adjust and manage on a dynamic basis. Over the past decade, governments have increasingly tapped the data that is a natural concurrence with public management. That said, even when data are there, governments and research organizations will need to invest time to make such data accessible for use in evaluation methodologies, a significant challenge given disclosure limitations for microdata on human subjects.

Even when accessible government databases exist, evaluation challenges remain. Social interventions are complex, and therefore attributing causality can be highly challenging and easily challenged. The reality is that no matter how rigorous an evaluation methodology, there may be external factors that affect the ultimate success of a PFS financing. Given this reality, PFS constructs are not a panacea that will be able to provide 100 percent certainty a program caused a particular outcome. If multiple providers are involved in treating the same individuals, it will become increasingly difficult to attribute success to any one intervention. Add to this the obvious pressures on governments, service providers, and investors to demonstrate "success," and the challenges to evaluation design and credibility become readily apparent. It is therefore up to all of the project parties, and particularly the intermediary and evaluator, to prioritize rigorous measurement of social outcomes as a means of determining whether impact was achieved or not.

Transitioning Provider Business Models to Outcome-Based and Collaborative Working Partnerships

PFS financing can be used to test new innovations—or new combinations of programs—but it is anticipated that early projects will most often be applied to replicating and scaling programs that have demonstrated some level of evidence-based outcomes and ability to achieve targeted impact goals. While government is ceding a majority of the performance risk of PFS financing to private investors, all parties are still keen to achieve measurable improvements in the lives of the targeted individuals. Therefore, PFS financing will prioritize innovations with a reasonable level of documented efficacy.

However, while many organizations claim to be evidence-based, few manage their operations based on outcome metrics. Staff is frequently monitored based on "how many individuals are served," and not on "how the life situations of target individuals have improved." In order to adjust to this transition, non-profits will need to reposition their business practices

Under PFS financing, the responsibility for ensuring that service providers incorporate effective outcome-oriented management models falls on the lead contractor. It is this entity that will be required to monitor and assess the performance of the various organizations that provide subcontracted services, to shape the business practices of subcontracting service providers, and to terminate relationships with underperforming organizations.

Establishing Collaborative Public-Private Partnerships

PFS financings bring a new contractual relationship among government and private organizations and investors. In structuring a PFS financing, each party will need to manage its own risks and benefits. As the application of PFS financing spreads, both geographically and across sectors, governments will have a steep learning curve. In order to balance the competing priorities, the process will benefit from the engagement of intermediaries to facilitate the discussions. In addition, a strong partnership will leverage a lead contractor that brings both sector expertise and a strong understanding of the local context. The operational and reputational risks placed upon the lead contractor are real. Lead contractors will need to be confident that they have clear understanding and agreements with government and investors. Without such thorough review of their operational, financial, and reputational risks, it will be difficult to recruit skilled organizations to perform this very necessary role.

Implementing Complex Financings

PFS financing is an innovative financing tool. While the financing components of PFS contracting have been applied in other sectors, they are a new application for the preventative social service arena. Addressing the risk/reward requirements of investors will require multiple layers of risk capital. In particular, during its early phase, as the concept is refined and the risks can be assessed, it is anticipated that philanthropic funders will provide an equity-like cushion with low rate-of-return expectations. The bulk of the operating capital will be from traditional lenders, ESG funds, community development financial institutions, and philanthropic program-related investment (PRI) sources. Each of these parties will have differing terms, return expectations, drawdown and repayment requirements, and oversight rights. Tying these requirements to a preventative social service delivery program will require a learning curve for all parties, and a common commitment to adhere to the maxim of "keeping it simple" while still structuring financings that are fully commercially priced.

Track Record and Overall Assessment

As PFS financing is in an early stage of design and implementation, there are no investor return data with which to measure success. However, in just a short period of time the review and initial investigation into PFS financing has grown at a rapid rate.

Over the near term, the success of PFS financings will be determined by three key metrics:

1. *Traction on development of PFS financing opportunities and actual launch of PFS projects.* The volume and diversity of launched PFS financings and implementation of pilots in multiple locations will be critical to develop the breadth and scope of use of the tool. Early pilots in New York City and Massachusetts offer encouraging signs of interest, with New York State, Cuyahoga County. and others following suit in 2013. Federal government solicitations and incentives will also be essential for broadening the base of participation in the PFS concept. So, too, will evidence of interest in other countries, including recent pilots in Australia, the UK, and Israel.

2. *Change in the dialogue of stakeholders.* PFS financings are a public/private collaboration, one that can allow a repositioning of a number of the entrenched perspectives that each stakeholder carries. An early indicator of progress will be establishment of the necessary dialogue and the willingness of the key constituents to allocate the time and resources necessary to address the design and implementation challenges highlighted in this chapter.

3. *Early-stage ability to demonstrate outcomes.* The opportunity for the development of PFS financings is quite real. Yet until the early stage pilots begin to demonstrate positive social outcomes under the allocated budgets, it would not be surprising for many governments to sit on the sidelines. Budget realities demand increased accountability, and recent steady progress by the nonprofit and philanthropic sectors toward evidence-based interventions create the environment for innovation. However, PFS is ultimately about moving to the achievement of improved social outcomes, and until these can be demonstrated, naturally cautious government agencies may not face pressures to innovate.

With all of these reasons for caution, as of September 2013, over a dozen states and counties in the United States were at varying stages of analysis and implementation of PFS financing initiatives. Assuming these concerns can be addressed, Figure 16.4 could well be the potential trajectory of the PFS financing tool.

Conclusion

As of this writing, there have been numerous advances in the discussion and implementation of PFS financings. In the case of Roca, Molly Baldwin and her team have proceeded with the Massachusetts state government to develop a working PFS model. Internationally, Safeena Husain of Educate Girls is looking at piloting a small PFS financing around her organization's community-based education program to increase engagement of young women in the Indian public school system. For both of these organizations, this is no great infatuation with the "latest innovation." Rather, both Molly and Safeena see the imperative of moving forward with evidence-based program designs. Continents apart, they see that the future is about accelerating the impact for those less fortunate through programs that focus on—and measure—outcomes.

FIGURE 16.4
Possible PFS Trajectory, 2012–2020

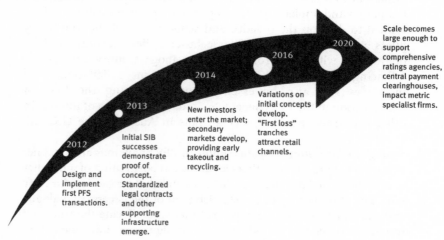

In a world where philanthropy is consistently challenged to take risks and facilitate the discovery of programs that work, pay-for-success financing is a new and potentially powerful tool. The structure allows service providers to tap new sources of capital, government to invest more dollars in preventative programming, and investors to seek financial returns while achieving increased social impact. From a government perspective, as one state health and human services official put it, PFS offers her an opportunity to "rebalance" her budget from high-cost "deep-end" safety net services to lower-cost preventative services. If successful, pay-for-success financings may help usher in transformative performance-based social services in the United States and around the world and restructure important parts of development assistance in the process.

Notes

1. Roca has a well-developed cognitive-restructuring and skill development intervention ("the Roca Intervention Model") that works with young men involved in the criminal justice system over two to four years to transform their lives and move them toward the outcomes of economic independence (i.e., successfully keeping a job) and living out of harm's way (i.e., staying out of prison).

2. As of August 2013, the Massachusetts Juvenile Justice Project was finalizing terms and conditions of the PFS contract and financing structure, with plans to implement the pilot in the fall of 2013.

3. City of New York, Office of the Mayor, "Mayor Bloomberg, Deputy Mayor Gibbs and Corrections Commissioner Schriro Announce Nation's First Social Impact Bond Program," published August 2, 2012, http://www.nyc.gov/html/om/html/2012b/pr285-12.html.

4. Vibeka Mair, "Peterborough Social Impact Bond Has Slashed Reoffending Rates Says MoJ," Civil Society.co.uk, accessed September 30, 3013, http://www.civilsociety.co.uk/finance/news/content/15384/peterborough_social_impact_bond_has_slashed_reoffending_rates_says_moj.

5. This trend can be seen in the current rate differential of the World Bank's own bond issuances and that of its Green Bonds. The latter are bonds that carry the same

World Bank credit, yet the investor's funds have been applied to specific environmentally friendly activities. The Green Bonds tend to trade at a slightly lower yield than the general debt of the World Bank.

6. Hope Consulting, "Money for Good," Hope Consulting, May 2010, accessed September 30, 2013, http://hopeconsulting.us/pdf/Money%20for%20Good_Final.pdf.

7. Emily Bolton, Suzanne Ashman, and Sarah Henderson, "Social Impact Bonds: The One* Service, One Year On," Social Finance, November 2011, accessed September 30, 2013, http://socialfinanceus.org/sites/socialfinanceus.org/files/sf_peterborough_one__year_on.pdf.

8. Massachusetts Executive Office of Administration and Finance, "Massachusetts First State in the Nation to Announce Initial Successful Bidders for 'Pay for Success' Contracts," published August 1, 2012, accessed September 30, 2013, http://www.mass.gov/anf/press-releases/fy2013/massachusetts-first-state-in-the-nation-to-announce-ini.html.

9. This consortium includes the Massachusetts Housing and Shelter Alliance (MHSA) and the United Way of Massachusetts Bay and Merrimac Valley. Neither of these organizations is a direct operator of service programs or shelter facilities, yet each has strong capabilities to oversee and coordinate multiple service delivery organizations, structure the necessary financing, and coordinate the required programmatic evaluations.

10. Coalition for Evidence Based Policy, "Rigorous Program Evaluations on a Budget," Coalition for Evidence Based Policy, March 2012, accessed September 29, 2013, http://coalition4evidence.org/wp-content/uploads/Rigorous-Program-Evaluations-o n-a-Budget-March-2012.pdf.

11. Massachusetts will also employ a difference-of-differences approach, comparing the results of the treatment population to results for similar populations in other areas of Massachusetts.

12. Center for Global Development and Social Finance, "Development Impact Bond Working Group Report Consultation Draft," Center for Global Development and Social Finance, June 2013, accessed September 29, 2013, http://www.cgdev.org/sites/default/files/DIB_WG_REPORT.pdf.

13. "Nurse-Family Partnership Program," LA County Maternal, Child, & Adolescent Health, accessed September 30, 2013, http://publichealth.lacounty.gov/mch/nfp/nfp.htm.

14. Vera Institute of Justice, "Guardianship Practice: A Six Year Perspective," Guardianship Project Issue Brief, Vera Institute of Justice, December 2011, accessed September 30, 2013, http://www.vera.org/sites/default/files/resources/downloads/Guardianship-Practice-a-Six-Year-Perspective.pdf.

15. Jeffrey Liebman, "Social Impact Bonds: A Promising New Financing Model to Accelerate Social Innovation and Improve Government Performance," Center for American Progress, published February 9, 2011, http://www.americanprogress.org/issues/open-government/report/2011/02/09/9050/social-impact-bonds/.

16. United States Office of Management and Budget, "The President's Budget for Fiscal Year 2014," accessed September 29, 2013, http://www.whitehouse.gov//omb/budget.

17. As defined by Steve Rothschild of Invest in Outcomes, Human Capital Performance Bonds (HUCAP) are state AA "annual appropriation" bonds that fund high-performing human services. "Home," Invest in Outcomes, accessed September 28, 2013, http://investinoutcomes.org/.

18. Canadian Task Force on Social Finance, "Mobilizing Capital for the Public Good: Measuring Progress during Year One," SocialFinance.ca, December 2011, accessed September 30, 2013, http://socialfinance.ca/uploads/documents/TFSF_ProgressReport_YearOne.pdf.

19. Center for Global Development, "Development Impact Bond."

20. One recent study of federal programs for youth found, for example, that of 10 large federally funded youth-serving social programs, only one, Early Head Start,

actually produced measurable social impact. See Jon Baron and Isabel Sawhill, *Federal Programs for Youth: More of the Same Won't Work* (Washington, DC: Coalition for Evidence-Based Policy, 2010).

21. Jon Baron, "Applying Evidence to Social Programs," *New York Times*, November 29, 2012, http://economix.blogs.nytimes.com/2012/11/29/applying-evidence-to-social-programs/?_r=0.

22. In the case of Massachusetts, the commonwealth used the learnings from the RFI process to select two priority social areas: (1) at-risk youth exiting juvenile probation and state youth services that have demonstrated high probability to end up in the adult prison system and (2) individual chronic homelessness. Executive Office for Administration and Finanace, "Request for Response: Social Innovation Financing for Youth—Intermediaries," Commonwealth of Massachusetts, January 18, 2012. http://hkssiblab.files.wordpress.com/2012/11/ma-rfr-youth-intermediaries.pdf.

23. One of the first investments under the Peterborough program by One Source was to finance the investment in database management tools. This enables the various service providers to have real-time data in order to more effectively monitor and manage their programs.

24. As an example, the Peterborough project targeted a 10 percent reduction in recidivism among 3,000 prisoners. At the scale of this program alone, it is unlikely that prisons will be closed, which is where the bulk of the government's expenditures lie.

25. In Peterborough, the parties agreed to establish One Source, Ltd.

26. In the Peterborough pilot, the investors funded the establishment of a shared database among providers. In addition, funds have been specifically allocated to innovation—which would have been of limited value if they did not have the data management tools to track the impact of these innovations. This feedback loop is essential for understanding the social benefit of the program and for ensuring financial success of the project through performance-based success payments.

27. In the Peterborough pilot, investors are repaid if an average 10 percent reduction in recidivism is achieved over a defined period of time. If such a metric is not achieved, investors receive no payments. Should this minimum target be achieved, investors receive both their return of initial capital and a margin.

28. Lenny Roth, "Social Impact Bonds," New South Wales Parliamentary Library Research Service, eBrief 17/2011, December 2011.

29. Government entities, including the federal government and New York State, are already directly addressing this issue in their procurements and demonstrating a willingness to engage in intergovernmental cost savings.

Suggested Readings

Center for Global Development and Social Finance. "Development Impact Bond Working Group Report Consultation Draft." Center for Global Development and Social Finance, June 2013. http://www.cgdev.org/sites/default/files/DIB_WG_REPORT.pdf.

Liebman, Jeffrey. "Social Impact Bonds: A Promising New Financing Model to Accelerate Social Innovation and Improve Government Performance." Center for American Progress, February 9, 2011. http://www.americanprogress.org/issues/open-government/report/2011/02/09/9050/social-impact-bonds/.

Third Sector Capital Partners. "Case Study: Preparing for a Pay for Success Opportunity." Third Sector Capital Partners, March 2012. http://www.thirdsectorcap.org/wp-content/uploads/2013/04/Third-Sector_Roca_Preparing-for-Pay-for-Success-in-MA.pdf.

CHAPTER 17

INSURANCE

Craig Churchill and Lauren Peterson

MONICA KIRUNGURU'S HUSBAND WAS AN outgoing man and a prominent member of his small community. The couple lived together on a farm near Mount Kenya, where they worked hard to support their seven children and five grandchildren. In August 2009, Monica's husband was admitted to the hospital. One month later, he died.

Coping with the emotional shock that accompanies the death of a life partner can be staggeringly difficult. Coping with the financial shock at the same time, however, can make the situation seem impossible. Typically, a Kenyan woman in Monica's circumstances would have two options to cover the hospital and funeral expenses: take out a high-interest emergency loan, or approach friends and family for money.

Monica was lucky. When her husband was admitted to the hospital, she was informed that he had bought health and life insurance. The policy paid out US$330 to cover hospital bills, a weekly stipend of US$25 for the family's living expenses during hospitalization (Monica used this money to continue paying the children's school fees), and US$400 toward the funeral, which was attended by over 1,000 people. She is now learning how to run the farm on her own, grateful not to be in debt.[1]

Monica's story illustrates the powerful difference that insurance can make in the lives of low-income persons around the world. Regrettably, her story is the exception among poor households struck by crises: less than 3 percent of the low-income people in the world's 100 poorest countries benefit from insurance.[2]

This lack of protection is especially problematic because low-income households are disproportionately vulnerable to risks and economic shocks. They live in risky environments, exposed to numerous perils, including illness, accidental death and disability, and loss of property due to theft or fire, agricultural losses, and disasters of both the natural and man-made varieties. Not only do these risks result in substantial financial losses, but vulnerable households also suffer from ongoing uncertainty about whether and when a loss might occur. Because of this perpetual apprehension, the poor are less likely to take advantage of income-generating opportunities that might help them to escape the vicious cycle of poverty.

While the poor are more vulnerable to risk than the rest of the population, they are in the unfortunate position of being least able to cope when a crisis does occur. Each year approximately 100 million people are so financially devastated by out-of-pocket payments for health services that they fall below the poverty line.[3] When a family member becomes ill, 26 percent of households in low- and middle-income countries resort to selling assets or borrowing money to cover healthcare expenses.[4] Indeed, uninsured risk is a significant cause of poverty.[5]

Although poor households often have informal means to manage risk, their coping methods generally provide insufficient protection. These risk-management strategies, such as spreading financial and human resources across several income-generating activities, often result in low returns. Informal risk-coping mechanisms, such as participation in rotating savings and credit associations (ROSCAs) and burial societies, tend to cover only a small portion of the loss, so the poor have to patch together support from a variety of sources. Plus, informal risk protection does not stand up well against catastrophic risks that affect entire communities, where neighbors are not in a position to help each other. Nor can it withstand a series of perils; before the household has a chance to fully recover from one crisis, it is struck again by another.

Perceptions that the low-income market cannot be insured are being challenged. The poor are becoming seen as a vast untapped market that aggregates substantial financial resources and has great need, facing many of the same risks that are routinely insured in higher income segments. Ironically, many of today's large insurance companies have their roots in mutual insurance schemes and industrial life assurance that targeted the working poor. But the insurance industry has evolved to the point that it is barely relevant to the majority of the world's population. Therefore, microinsurance can be described as a "back to basics" campaign for insurers to focus on the risk-management needs of vulnerable people, and to help them manage those risks through the solidarity of risk pooling.

By helping these households manage risk, insurance can assist them to maintain a sense of financial confidence in the face of significant vulnerability. If governments, donors, development agencies, and other stakeholders are serious about combating poverty, insurance has to be one of the weapons in their arsenal. This can be accomplished through the engagement of the insurance companies to serve the poor, or by providing a mechanism to extend social protection to workers outside the formal economy, or preferably both.

While this chapter explains several insurance solutions to enable low-income households to manage risk, it goes into detail about the potential of microinsurance and the engagement of the private sector to serve the low-income market and create effective, sustainable insurance services that reduce the vulnerability of the poor. As microinsurance approaches the frontiers of what is possible on a market (or quasi-market) basis, it could make a powerful impact in enabling the poor to have viable, affordable options to protect their lives, health, and hard-earned assets.

By leveraging the expertise of the private sector, microinsurance has considerable promise—but it remains far from living up to its potential. The first section of this chapter defines insurance and discusses how it relates to the new frontiers of philanthropy examined in this volume. Subsequent sections explore the patterns of microinsurance use, the rationale for selecting this tool, its basic mechanics, and its operational challenges. The chapter concludes with an overall assessment of the performance and future of microinsurance.

Defining the Tool

Defining Features

Insurance is a financial instrument that relies on risk pooling, which allows large groups of insured entities to share the losses resulting from the occurrence of an uncommon event. The insured entities—such as persons, businesses, households, communities, or even countries—are therefore protected from risk in exchange for a fee known as a premium. The premium amount is determined by an estimation of the frequency and severity of the event occurring. For insurance to work, seven characteristics must be met: (1) a large population is exposed to the same risk to create a risk pool; (2) policyholders must have limited control over the occurrence of the insured event; (3) the population exposed to the risk must have an insurable interest, which means that they would experience a loss if the event occurs; (4) mechanisms must be in place to verify the occurrence of a loss and identify its cause and value; (5) losses cannot be so catastrophic that a significant portion of the risk pool is affected at the same time; (6) there has to be a way to calculate the expected loss and chance of loss; and (7) the premiums must be affordable.[6]

Often people use the term "insurance" loosely to refer to general risk prevention and management techniques. For example, savings set aside for emergency purposes might be referred to as an insurance fund. A more precise definition of insurance involves this risk-pooling element whereby those in the risk pool who do not suffer a loss during a particular period essentially pay for the losses experienced by others. Thus, at a household level, when a loss occurs, insurance allows the beneficiaries to receive more complete compensation for their loss than they could have provided on their own. Insurance therefore reduces vulnerability as households replace the uncertain prospect of large losses with the certainty of making small, regular premium payments. Yet this risk-pooling function means that insurance is a much more complicated financial service than alternatives, such as savings or credit.

Relation to Common Criteria

Insurance generally compares favorably to other new tools of philanthropy and social investment along a number of criteria, primarily because it has a distinct function.

Risk Level

For investors or philanthropists interested in supporting microinsurance, it is important to recognize that this is a relatively new tool in the social-purpose arena where the actors involved are often learning by doing. As a result, microinsurance is on a steep learning curve, regularly taking two steps forward and one step back. Other philanthropic tools that are well tested and more mature may be less risky investments, but can they provide the same benefits as insurance? Can they enable low-income households to manage their own risks more efficiently? Indeed, insurance plays a unique role in assisting the working poor to manage risks, which warrants greater risk-taking by philanthropists.

In comparison to traditional insurance, microinsurance requires a fundamentally different approach. If insurers try to serve the poor by just tweaking their existing products and distribution models to make them relevant for the low-income market, they are unlikely to find success. Some insurers that serve low-income households do so through their corporate social responsibility (CSR) activities, and do not yet take microinsurance seriously as a business opportunity. Consequently, they are not making the investments needed for microinsurance to be successful, which reinforces their expectation that it does not generate sufficient returns. To overcome this self-fulfilling prophecy, it is important to collaborate with insurance executives who believe that the bottom of the pyramid (BOP) has potential, and who are willing to innovate and take a patient approach. There is evidence that some commercial insurers are making progress. A Microinsurance Network study showed that in 2011 at least 33 of the world's 50 largest commercial insurance companies offered microinsurance, but in 2005 only eight of them had relevant products—so there has been significant expansion in recent years.[7]

The risk level also depends on the capacity of the insurer, and whether it already has a good idea how to manage its core business, including basic insurance risks, such as adverse selection, moral hazards, and outright fraud (see Box 17.1). Just because a company has an insurance license does not mean that it is particularly well managed. Additionally, sufficient data may not yet exist to estimate the risks involved in insuring low-income populations. Applying risk experience pertaining to better-off individuals to the poor may provide a misleading basis for estimating claims.

Degree of Leverage

Microinsurance lies at the intersection between social protection and financial inclusion—both of which are key items on the agenda of the G20. For some risks, and for some market segments, microinsurance is viable, even profitable, as discussed in more detail below. In such cases, efforts to support the expansion of microinsurance can leverage the infrastructure and expertise of the entire insurance industry. Alternatively, in circumstances where microinsurance supports the expansion of social protection to workers in the informal economy, for example through public-private partnerships, then it is able to exploit the commitment of policymakers and government infrastructure, such as health facilities.

Insurance can also be used to increase access to productive investment. One of the reasons why lenders do not lend, or investors do not invest, is because of potential risks involved with a particular project. For example, rural banks often do not like to lend for agricultural purposes. However, if insurance were available to the bank for certain risks, like drought, then banks would be more willing to lend, resulting in greater agricultural productivity.

As a new instrument, it is important to also acknowledge the important role of donors, which are actively involved in helping microinsurance live up to its full potential by stimulating innovation and experimentation, attracting reluctant players into the market through seed funding, enhancing regulatory environments, and analyzing findings, managing knowledge, and disseminating results. The last point is important because knowledge management enables donors to accelerate the evolution of microinsurance. Through donor-supported knowledge sharing activities, microinsurers become exposed to lessons learned and successful innovations that can shorten the learning curve.

BOX 17.1

MANAGING RISKS: CONTROLLING ADVERSE SELECTION, FRAUD, AND MORAL HAZARD

Adverse selection is the tendency of persons who are likely to experience the event to purchase insurance. For example, with health insurance, adverse selection occurs when people who know they need health care apply for and obtain coverage. Adverse selection also occurs when people with a low chance of suffering the insured event opt out because insurance provides them with poor value for their money. This situation can have a destabilizing effect on an insurance system—if only people expecting to need health care receive insurance, then the risk pooling mechanism cannot work. To control adverse selection, insurers may screen risks. The process of screening prospective policyholders, also known as *underwriting*, is intended to control the risks that enter the risk pool. Through the underwriting process, high-risk individuals may be excluded or charged more.

Two other means of controlling adverse selection, which are common in microinsurance, are *exclusions* and *waiting periods*. A health insurance policy, for example, might have an exclusion for pre-existing conditions— health problems that the person had before purchasing the policy. With life insurance, a waiting period of a month or two between the time when policyholders begin paying premiums and when the coverage is applicable reduces the risk that someone who is about to die will purchase a policy.

With adverse selection, individuals are pursuing a perfectly sensible— and legal—path of self-interest. They opt in or out according to their assessment of their risk profile and the relative value of insurance. In contrast, *fraud* arises from deliberate misrepresentation by the client to the insurer. Examples of fraud include claiming that an insured event has happened when it has not, claiming benefits for people or properties that are not insured, or providing false answers to the insurer's screening questions. One way to manage fraud is by using claims verification methods, such as checking that the claim event has actually happened to the people or properties that were actually insured.

Moral hazard occurs when the insurance protection creates incentives for individuals to cause the insured event. With life insurance, for example, there may be circumstances when policyholders commit suicide so that their beneficiaries would receive some money; or the beneficiary could even murder the insured to receive the benefit. Moral hazard also applies to circumstances where insurance creates incentives for policyholders to behave in reckless or undesirable ways that increase the likelihood that the insured event will occur. For example, insurance for livestock might discourage policyholders from vaccinating or seeking appropriate medical treatment for their animals. Moral hazard is managed through exclusions that remove the financial gain from the undesirable action. For example, most insurance policies do not pay benefits if the injury, disability, or death is self-inflicted. *Co-payments* for health insurance policies and *deductibles* for property insurance also help control moral hazard.

Source: Craig Churchill, Dominic Liber, Michael J. McCord, and Jim Roth, *Making Insurance Work for Microfinance Institutions: A Technical Guide to Developing and Delivering Microinsurance* (Geneva: Social Finance Programme, International Labour Organization, 2003).

Type and Level of Return Available

Financial returns. Can microinsurance make a positive contribution to an insurance company's bottom line? Some conclusions can be gleaned from the case studies published by the ILO on behalf of the Consultative Group to Assist the Poor (CGAP) Working Group on Microinsurance (now the Microinsurance Network). For example, based on an analysis of AIG Uganda, which provides a group personal accident product to more than 20 microfinance institutions (MFIs), a 2005 study demonstrated that microinsurance can be a profitable line of business for commercial insurers, particularly for a basic product that is mandatory for all borrowers. In this case, of the premiums collected by the insurer in 2003, 32 percent were returned to policyholders in the form of claims—this is the claims ratio. As a result, on its microinsurance product, the insurer had a net profit between 18 and 23 percent.[8] Similarly, the credit life product offered by Madison Insurance in collaboration with four MFIs in Zambia had claims ratios below 50 percent, well below in most cases. So as long as the insurer could keep its administrative costs below 50 percent of premiums—which is not hard for a mandatory product, although the data was not available from the study—then it too was generating significant profits from microinsurance.[9]

For other products, the results are less clear-cut. One study predicted that endowment policies, which combine savings and insurance, such as the ones sold by Tata-AIG in India, would break even in three to four years if the insurer experiences continued high growth rates and high levels of persistency.[10] At Delta Life in Bangladesh, which also offers endowment policies, the insurer presumed that its microinsurance products were profitable, even though administrative cost ratios were high at close to 50 percent, because the claim ratio was below 10 percent, which provides poor value to policyholders.[11] Since these are voluntary insurance products sold on an individual basis, they are naturally much more expensive to distribute and service than the mandatory group policies.

A more recent study reached similar conclusions based on an analysis of five insurance companies serving the low-income market.[12] Where products are mandatory, or bundled with other financial or nonfinancial services as a member benefit, they can indeed be viable or self-sustaining. But they often do not provide particularly good value to low-income consumers who may not be fully aware of the benefits. Group-based products are much more likely to be viable than voluntary products sold to individuals or households.

The profitability of microinsurance also depends on the type of risk covered. According to Swiss Re, the greatest market potential is for life microinsurance, which includes credit life, funeral coverage, savings, and pension products.[13] Other products, especially health insurance, are difficult to provide on a sustainable basis because of the limited purchasing power of the poor, yet are in high demand. Agriculture insurance, including crop, livestock, and weather-based microinsurance, has strong growth prospects and is expected to be further leveraged as an effective way to deal with the agricultural risks and the repercussions of climate change. For both health and agriculture insurance to be sustainable, however, subsidized premiums may be required to provide value to low-income households.

Ultimately, the financial return available from investments in microinsurance will depend on the robustness of the market for this product, and the evidence to date is somewhat mixed. Insurance schemes for the poor have to find a way of balancing three competing objectives: (1) providing *coverage* to meet the needs of the target population; (2) minimizing operating *costs* for the insurer; and (3) minimizing the *price* (including the transaction costs for the clients) to enhance affordability and accessibility. These represent difficult choices that are best answered by involving those who ultimately benefit from the coverage to choose between them.

Social returns. Social investors are not just interested in the financial return, but also in the social return, and here insurance offers substantial promise, though the evidence available is limited. At the household level, the potential contribution of microinsurance to breaking the cycle of poverty has both protective and productive roles. On the protective side, insurance can protect policyholders from the financial consequences of various risks, including illness and death. If a risk is insured, the poor can cope more efficiently when they experience large losses. Regular payments of small premiums are easier to afford than the large immediate expenses that accompany crises, and therefore serve an important consumption-smoothing function.

On the productive side, insurance can be a means through which the poor can amass a lump sum of savings, for example through a long-term life insurance policy that allows them to build assets. Alternatively, insurance can help unlock access to productive inputs such as credit. There is also the peace-of-mind effect whereby the poor may feel less compelled to set aside as much contingency saving "under the mattress" if they are insured, and therefore they may make larger investments, possibly in higher-risk, higher-return activities.

While intuitive and backed by anecdotal evidence, rigorous research to demonstrate that insurance achieves these intended social returns largely remains outstanding. There are a number of impact studies on health insurance in Africa and Asia that illustrate the positive impact with regard to reducing out-of-pocket health expenditure and increasing the utilization of healthcare services. Knowledge on other impacts and the impact of other products is limited, although a raft of additional studies are underway.[14]

Beyond the household, insurance also has an impact at a community or macroeconomic level. Various studies have demonstrated a causal link between the development of the insurance industry in general and national economic development.[15] This is accomplished in part by supporting entrepreneurial activity. For example, by enabling businesses to operate with less volatility, insurance can promote economic stability. Since insurers and reinsurers have an incentive to reduce claims, they contribute to development by promoting risk reduction measures. Insurance can be used to manage certain risks faced by creditors and borrowers more efficiently than other financial instruments, thereby facilitating access to credit and stimulating entrepreneurial effort. Insurance also facilitates investment in higher-risk, higher-return business opportunities by helping measure and manage high-risk exposures. Investment in higher-return activities in turn contributes to higher productivity and economic growth.

More broadly within the economy, by mobilizing long-term savings, insurers are an important source of long-term finance that can be invested in initiatives such as infrastructure improvements, as well as acting as a significant stimulator for the development of debt and equity markets. As prominent investors in equity markets, insurers can compel listed companies to adopt stronger corporate governance measures and greater transparency. In summary, according to Brainard, "The net result of well-functioning insurance

markets should be better pricing of risk, greater efficiency in the overall allocation of capital and mix of economic activities, and higher productivity."[16]

An important item missing from the literature thus far is the possible specific contribution of microinsurance to the deepening and strengthening of the
insurance industry in general. Insurance industries in developed countries
were largely built on a strong foundation along retail lines, perhaps with roots
that can be traced back to friendly societies or industrial life assurance. The
insurance sectors in many emerging and developing economies evolved in the
second half of the twentieth century, and focused largely on corporate clients,
with little effort made to build the infrastructure required for retail or personal
lines. Since many countries have missed out on this initial stage of insurance
development and leapfrogged to more sophisticated lines, the insurance sectors
may be thin and not well developed. Microinsurance, however, can provide
them with an opportunity to rebuild from the bottom up and create a foundation of retail insurance, and ultimately make a stronger contribution to the
country's general economic development.

Skill Requirements

Although commonly grouped with savings and credit, insurance is a much
more complicated tool. It requires specific actuarial expertise to assess frequency and severity of risks, and often involves long-term commitments such
as life insurance or pensions. The logic behind the efforts from development
agencies to entice insurers into the low-income market largely stems from the
fact that they already have the technical insurance expertise, and the assumption that it is easier to enable them to adapt their skills to the reality of the
low-income market, rather than to assist development experts to build their
own insurance skills. An important area for philanthropic investment to support the emergence of microinsurance would be the development of more
microinsurance experts, particularly those from developing countries.

Ubiquity

The interdisciplinary nature of microinsurance may help to facilitate market
expansion. In the realms of public policy and international development,
microinsurance is interesting because of its potential to support many different
efforts. Few agencies have microinsurance departments. Instead, insurance is a
subtheme that cuts across various domains, including health and social protection, agricultural and livestock development, climate change and disaster management, microfinance, and small enterprise and cooperative development. As
a result, more types of organizations are becoming involved in microinsurance.

Major Variants

Although all insurance shares the common features identified in the previous
section, there are a number of variants of the insurance tool. Four bases of differentiation are especially worth noting. One differentiates insurance in terms
of whether it is offered on a market basis, as a supplement to a government
social protection system, or somewhere in between. The second is based on the
nature of the contract, whether it is for individuals, families, an affinity group,
or a meso-level coverage. The third feature differentiates insurance products in

terms of whether coverage is voluntary or mandatory. A fourth differentiates insurance products according to the type of risk insured against, including life, health, agriculture, and disaster coverage.

Between the Market and the State

A first basis for differentiating microinsurance schemes relate to whether they function on a market basis or as supplements to government social protections. Essentially, who is paying the premium, the policyholder, the government, or is there a cost-sharing arrangement? In developing countries, where government social protection benefits such as health insurance are available, they typically cater to formal sector workers, particularly civil servants, and rarely reach workers in the informal economy. To extend social protection schemes to excluded segments of the population, some governments are collaborating with the insurance industry through public-private partnerships (PPPs). In addition, countries are generally unable to provide comprehensive social protection systems against all relevant risks faced by each and every household. Thus, there are many possible applications for microinsurance as a substitute for, alternative to, or supplement to a government scheme, as illustrated in Figure 17.1.[17]

FIGURE 17.1
Possible Roles of Microinsurance in Relation to Public Social Protections

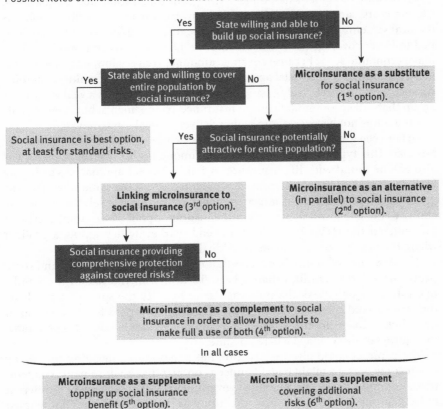

In the absence of formal social protection, microinsurance responds to an urgent need, though it should not absolve governments of their responsibilities. Nevertheless, it is most effective as a supplement to government schemes that facilitate a redistributive effect. Microinsurance can create delivery mechanisms to extend government programs (and subsidies) to the informal economy, and in so doing integrate the informal and formal social protection systems. For example, the emerging national health insurance schemes in Ghana, Rwanda, and the Philippines involve mutual or community insurance schemes as distribution channels.

Variations in the Type of Contract

The second variation is the type of contract that is offered. The most common contract type is for groups, so that the insurance scheme covers many people under one master policy. The group policyholder decides what type of coverage to buy for the members of the group. The policyholder is responsible for enrolling members, collecting premiums, disseminating certificates of insurance and product information, and assisting members to file claims. For efficiency and equity purposes, pricing is usually done on a community basis, so all group members pay the same premium.

At the other end of the spectrum are individual insurance contracts. Individual microinsurance is possible, but it requires a high participation rate among the potential target market to attain desirable financial results. Compared to group coverage, individual insurance can cost more than twice as much because of higher sales, underwriting, administration, and claims costs. Claims costs can be reduced through more rigorous underwriting, such as medical screening (since the bad risks are identified and filtered out or are limited to lower coverage). For microinsurance, however, this screening may not make economic sense because coverage amounts are very low, and moreover it may run counter to the social agenda. Therein lies the crux of making microinsurance work. It is relatively easy if the targeted population is a well-organized group that can accommodate group insurance arrangements, but is quite challenging if it is not because of the higher delivery and claims costs.

In between group and individual insurance contracts are schemes that cover families. This type of contract is common among health insurance plans, but also can be found with life insurance. A family benefit approach, which may include spouses, dependents, and even parents, carries the same advantages as group coverage in terms of larger numbers, lower adverse selection, and the ability to include low-risk persons in the insurance pool. For example, African Life entered the HIV/AIDS-ridden low-end market by developing a product where the family, rather than an individual, was the insured unit.

The downside of family benefits is that not everyone has a family, and some people have larger families than others. To deal with the size of the family, microinsurers either ask the policyholder to identify the specific dependents that are covered by the policy or they offer different prices for different sized households. To ensure that women and children are not left out, it is preferable to require family coverage where possible.

The contract could also be structured at a meso-level, meaning that many low-income persons might benefit under a contract that is with a bank, cooperative, a community, or even a national government. This arrangement is different from a group contract because the ultimate beneficiaries are not named explicitly, and the responsibility lies with the meso-level entity as to how it might use the benefits. For example, in the Philippines the cooperative insurer CLIMBS has a meso-level contract, underwritten by Munich Re, which pays benefits in the event of typhoons. CLIMBS then pays lump sums to its member cooperatives, which they offer to their members as low-interest loans for rebuilding lost assets. Meso-level contracts are therefore an efficient way of benefiting the poor, usually in the case of disasters, without contracting them directly.

Mandatory versus Voluntary Insurance

A third distinction among microinsurance products concerns whether the purchase is mandatory or voluntary. Mandatory or automatic insurance is often linked to other financial services such as credit or savings products whereby a borrower or saver automatically receives insurance coverage as well, or is obliged to take out a policy. Mandatory coverage can be particularly beneficial for insurers because it reduces adverse selection and fraud, lowers administrative costs, and improves claims ratios. Automatic microinsurance also includes coverage given for free, as a member benefit or loyalty incentive, such as the basic term life by Compartamos, an MFI in Mexico, which covers nearly 3 million persons, and the personal accident policy provided by IFFCO-Tokio with the sale of fertilizer, covering 3.5 million Indian farmers.

While mandatory products are often more affordable for clients, the clients may not fully understand the benefits or perceive value in the insurance product. Voluntary insurance products are available for both individuals and groups. Clients may have more options and perceive greater value in voluntary coverage, but schemes are often more expensive because of higher risks.

Variations in the Type of Risk Covered

Variations in the insurance tool also relate to the type of risk against which protection is provided. As shown in Table 17.1,[18] demand research consistently identifies illness, the death of a breadwinner, and theft and fire as the risks

TABLE 17.1   PRIORITY RISKS IN SELECTED COUNTRIES

Country	Priority risk
Uganda	Illness, death, disability, property loss, risk of loan
Malawi	Fear of death, especially in relation to HIV/AIDS, food insecurity, illness, education
Philippines	Death, old age, illness
Vietnam	Illness, natural disaster, accidents, illness/death of livestock
Indonesia	Illness, children's education, poor harvest
Lao P.D.R.	Illness, livestock disease, death
Georgia	Illness, business losses, theft, death of family member, retirement income
Ukraine	Illness, disability, theft
Bolivia	Illness, death, property loss including crop loss in rural areas

Source: Monique Cohen and Jennifer Sebstad, "The Demand for Microinsurance," in *Protecting the Poor: A Microinsurance Compendium*, ed. Craig Churchill (Geneva: International Labour Organization and Munich Re Foundation, 2006). http://www.microinsurancenetwork.org/publication/fichier/ProtectingthepoorAmicroinsurancecompendiumFullBook.pdf.

against which individuals most need protection, and in rural areas there is significant demand for agriculture insurance. Beyond that, natural disasters raise additional types of risk.

However, often the products in the greatest demand are the most difficult to design and thus the least available. This irony can be seen more clearly by examining select forms of insurance in more detail.

Health. In most countries, the greatest demand for insurance by the low-income market is for health coverage. However, health coverage is also among the most difficult products to provide. Health insurance, micro or not, is plagued by problems of adverse selection, moral hazard, fraud, and overusage, not just by the policyholders but by healthcare providers, pharmacies, and system administrators as well. For the products to be affordable to low-income households in the absence of subsidies, benefits must be rationed.[19] The primary innovation has been to restrict coverage to low-frequency, high-cost events such as hospitalization. In situations where the healthcare costs are not high compared to the opportunity costs of being away from one's work if hospitalized, then microinsurance benefits may instead pay per diem benefits and transportation costs. This type of "hospital cash" coverage has the advantage of not involving the healthcare provider, and therefore avoiding potential fraud or overcharging.

By focusing on inpatient care, however, insurance may encourage policyholders to delay treatment, which could ultimately increase the costs of care. So how can inpatient and outpatient coverage be viable for the poor? Subsidies would be the right answer, but where they are not available some organizations are experimenting with health savings accounts for outpatient and preventative care, combined with insurance for hospitalization. While it is too early to know if it is possible to strike an effective balance between the two, the concept is promising.

Health products that respond appropriately to client needs will help to generate demand among the poor. The key strategy to achieve this goal is to involve policyholders or prospective clients in the process of making hard choices between benefits and price. The poor cannot afford comprehensive coverage, so which benefits are they most willing to pay for, and how much are they willing to pay? Tools that can enable clients to see the trade-offs and voice their preferences—such as CHAT (Choosing Health Plans All Together) developed by the Microinsurance Academy in India—can contribute towards achieving appropriate product design.

Life. The prevalence of life microinsurance, particularly credit life, suggests that this is an excellent entry point for insurance companies interested in serving the low-income market, especially if it provides other benefits besides simply covering outstanding loans (see Box 17.2). But if insurers do not expand their product menu and offer better-value products to the mass market, they risk losing the trust of policyholders. One way life products might evolve is to include a savings component, building value over time, which would be an attractive proposition because policyholders would have something to show for their premium payments if they do not have a claim for the risk coverage. However, typical endowment or whole life policies do not provide good value, as a high percentage of premiums are used to cover sales commissions and the insurer's costs, and they are particularly poor value if the policy lapses because the policyholder had difficulty keeping up with the premium payments.

BOX 17.2

CREDIT LIFE AS A COMPETITIVE ADVANTAGE IN
CAMBODIA

Cambodia has a relatively high microfinance penetration and significant competition among MFIs. One MFI, Visionfund, uses its credit life product to promote its loan products because the outstanding debt is waived if the borrower dies. In addition, there are funeral benefits for the borrower, spouse, and children. "Insurance" is never mentioned in its promotional materials or in interactions with borrowers. The premium is "invisible" since it is embedded in the interest rate. Credit life is regarded as highly valuable by this successful MFI because it has given the organization an important competitive edge.

Source: John Wipf, Eamon Kelly, and Michael J. McCord, "Improving Credit Life Microinsurance," in *Protecting the Poor: A Microinsurance Compendium*, vol. 2, ed. Craig Churchill and Michal Matul (Geneva: International Labour Organization and Munich Re Foundation, 2012).

To overcome this problem, UAB Vie, a life insurance company in Burkina Faso, delivers insurance through its own low-cost agent network. The product, Cauri d'or, offers life and disability coverage to 14,500 informal sector entrepreneurs, such as those selling goods at market stalls in urban areas. Its success depends mostly on mirroring methods used by traditional *tontiniers*, who offer informal contractual daily savings schemes and take a monthly commission that equals the value of one day of gathered savings. Cauri d'or contributions are collected every day and are as low as 150 CFA (US$0.35) with terms varying from one month to five years. The insurance benefit is twice the value of the total contributions.

Funeral insurance is a term life insurance policy where the benefit is used to cover funeral expenses. The benefit can be in the form of a funeral service, a cash benefit that can be used to help pay for a funeral, or a combination of the two. Outside credit life insurance, funeral insurance is perhaps the most prevalent form of microinsurance in Africa. In fact, the funeral service channel may drive demand, distribution, and underwriting of funeral insurance.[20] The link to the funeral service creates a tangible benefit for insurance that engenders trust. Increasingly, insurers are starting to focus on ways to provide better value by adding elements beyond pure funeral coverage. In this way, funeral insurance is evolving into life insurance that can form the basis for asset accumulation and intergenerational transfers.

Agriculture and livestock. Another popular form of microinsurance covers agricultural risks. Perhaps the most significant innovation here is the emergence of index coverage, for example for rainfall. Historically, multiperil crop insurance has been fraught with adverse selection, moral hazard, and fraud problems, not to mention the high costs associated with claims adjustment. To overcome these issues, index insurance has emerged as a possible alternative since the claim is based on an objective and verifiable indicator—such as the lack or excess of rain in a specific period of time—which is not subject to the influence of individual farmers. Index insurance pilots have been launched in many countries, including Malawi, Ethiopia, Kenya, and India, although there have been teething pains. In particular, the lack of weather data makes it difficult to design and price the product, and the weather stations need to be close to the farmers, so that their losses closely correlate with the index, and the farmers accept the results.

Despite significant investments, the take-up of index products has been low. Besides educating farmers on the benefits of insurance, insurers are recognizing a need for further product enhancements. Technological advances in remote sensing as well as better availability of weather and agriculture data could lead to the next wave of index contracts that combine weather, area yield, and remotely sensed vegetative growth based on satellite images in order to design optimal contracts. Still, insurers have only been able to achieve significant scale in India, where the government is paying part of the premium so it is more affordable to farmers.

Livestock insurance is also challenged by moral hazard and fraud problems. The claims experience of the Indian insurer IFFCO-Tokio for cows and buffaloes was five deaths per hundred, whereas the actual mortality rate should be closer to three per hundred, suggesting that 40 percent of its claims were fraudulent. Typical controls in livestock insurance include the involvement of a veterinarian to verify the health of the animal and to tag the ear for identification. If the animal dies, the ear is cut and submitted to the insurer as part of the claims process. Judging from IFFCO-Tokio's experience, there are a fair number of Indian cattle with missing ears, and the vets are often complicit in the duplicity. To overcome this problem, the insurer experimented with radio frequency identification devices (RFIDs) that are injected into the animals instead of tagging. In the period from August 2008 to March 2010, almost 15,000 cattle were insured. The resulting claims ratio (42 per cent), which is less than a fifth of the claims ratio with traditional ear tags, suggests that the new technology is working.[21]

Interestingly, index insurance innovations are also being applied to livestock risks. International Livestock Research Institute (ILRI) has developed an index product for pastoralists in semiarid areas in northern Kenya to mitigate drought risks that severely affect their revenues from animal breeding, their only source of income. The product is underwritten by UAP Insurance and delivered by Equity Bank, Kenya's largest bank for the low-income market. The index livestock insurance contract is based on the normalized difference vegetation index (NDVI), which uses data remotely sensed from satellites to assess if the livestock's grazing area is sufficiently green.

Disaster. Natural disasters are particularly devastating for low-income households and can sink a vulnerable family into extreme poverty. Following the 2004 tsunami in Southeast Asia, the Asian Development Bank estimated that the number of poor persons increased in India by 645,000, in Sri Lanka by 250,000, and in Indonesia by more than 1,000,000.[22] In the immediate aftermath of the tsunami, a television journalist interviewed a shopkeeper on the Sri Lankan coast. The woman had nothing left of her shop and no obvious resources to help her reopen her business. The woman said, "I have lost everything, and I had no insurance. If I had insurance, it would be easier to start again."[23]

When a disaster occurs, local and global relief agencies launch donation campaigns to raise funds and provide support, which often take a long time to reach the intended beneficiaries. Other natural disasters attributed to global climate change, such as droughts and flash floods, are occurring with greater frequency over widespread areas, making aid an impractical and unsustainable solution. However if insurance is available for these risks, then it could be possible for payouts to be made quickly and provide assistance in a sustainable manner as shown in Boxes 17.3 and 17.4. While disaster insurance is at a meso rather than micro level, it is an interesting way that insurance can be used to support relief efforts.

Composite Products

In most jurisdictions, insurance companies have to have separate licenses to offer life and nonlife products (the latter also known as general, short-term, and property and casualty insurance). Yet low-income households need protection against a variety of risks. If the microinsurer is going to the effort of reaching low-income people, there is justification to include various benefits as long as the product remains simple and includes coverage that the poor really want. Composite products, which may include life and general insurance components that can even be underwritten by different companies, enable microinsurers to cost-effectively provide more comprehensive coverage that responds to the diverse needs of the target group. It is important, however, to avoid including unnecessary benefits that are "window dressing" to make the product look better for marketing purposes but are not really beneficial to policyholders.

In Kenya, the Cooperative Insurance Company (CIC) offers its Bima Ya Jamii (Insurance for the Family) to rural households through savings and credit cooperatives (SACCOs). This composite product provides inpatient health, accidental death and disability, funeral, and loss-of-income benefits,

---

BOX 17.3

CARIBBEAN CATASTROPHE RISK INSURANCE FACILITY (CCRIF)

Following the huge losses resulting from Hurricane Ivan in 2004, the Caribbean Community Heads of Government, with the help of the World Bank, developed a risk transfer program for member countries to mitigate the effects of natural disasters. Started in 2007, CCRIF insured its 16 member countries, many of which are quite small, against earthquakes, hurricanes, and excess rainfall. Based on historical data, country risk profiles were created, which influence a country's premium. Once a predefined level of shaking, wind speed, or amount of rain is reached, payout occurs within 14 days. In 2010, payouts included US$7.75 million for the earthquake in Haiti, US$12.8 million for Hurricane Tomas, and US$4.2 million for Hurricane Earl.

Source: Thomas Loster and Dirk Reinhard, "Climate Change and Microinsurance," in *Protecting the Poor: A Microinsurance Compendium*, vol. 2, ed. Craig Churchill and Michal Matul (Geneva: International Labour Organization and Munich Re Foundation, 2012).

BOX 17.4

DROUGHT IN ETHIOPIA

More than 13 million people in Ethiopia rely on sacks of grain and cans of cooking oil from the United Nations World Food Program (WFP) to avoid starvation. As cycles of drought and flash flooding escalate, the number of individuals reliant on donations continues to increase. The WFP is already supporting 100 million people in 75 countries, and with growing populations and diminishing resources, the program is not sustainable.

After Ethiopia's 2003 drought, WFP decided to develop a more reliable solution. The program, developed in partnership with Oxfam America, uses the WFP work-for-food safety net, but adds insurance to the mix. Farmers work on forestry, soil management, and irrigation projects after the harvest is over. For their work, they receive an insurance policy that will offer coverage in the event of a drought. Oxfam, with financial help from its partners, subsidizes the payment.

To measure rainfall, Oxfam uses satellite data. Local farmers are also given marked cylinders to mount on a stick, so that they can check the rainfall as well, which builds trust. So far the satellite data has proven accurate and people are buying the insurance—in 2010, a fifth of all those eligible enrolled.

Source: Tina Rosenberg, "To Survive Famine, Will Work for Insurance," *New York Times*, May 12, 2011.

---

with the health component underwritten by the government's National Hospital Insurance Fund (NHIF). Consequently, CIC is enabling NHIF to extend benefits to workers in the informal economy and in rural areas that the government scheme would otherwise not be able to reach.

Some providers have come up with enhanced versions of composite products that still give a choice to clients. Zurich Brazil has developed a product proposition called "Pick 4 a Dollar," which combines four types of insurance that can be purchased individually or in combination: personal accident, unemployment, daily hospital indemnity, and household property. In theory, products like this one should provide a superior value because clients can choose their optimal coverage. However, the jury is still out. Insights from behavioral economics show that choice overload might be an obstacle for consumers in their purchasing decisions. Simplicity is important. Products that provide various coverage options or opt-out/opt-in features can be so complicated that potential customers do not buy them.[24]

Patterns of Use

While obstacles to the spread of microinsurance are significant and daunting, they can be overcome, and they are being overcome, by a number of formal and informal insurers around the world that are developing new techniques to reach a vast underserved market, with different approaches in different regions.

A 2010 global study conducted by the insurance giant Lloyds estimated 135 million low-income people are covered by microinsurance schemes.[25] In 2012, back-of-the-envelope estimates suggest that the sector is approaching 500 million risks covered, with 60 percent of that outreach coming from India alone.[26] This huge increase comes from several factors including a broader definition of microinsurance, additional schemes that were identified, and robust growth. Yet the scope for continued growth remains. A 2010 report by Swiss Re suggests that insurers can reach 2.6 billion low-income persons who could afford small premiums but are not reached by the conventional insurance market. And an additional 1.4 billion people living on less than $1.25 per day could be reached with the help of subsidies or government support.[27]

This section considers three different dimensions to the patterns of use, including regional differences, the role of new technology, and the involvement of new stakeholders and consortia.

Regional Differences

Microinsurance has evolved quite differently depending on the region, with significant imbalances in outreach. In a 2006 study, 85 percent of the insured were in Asia, 10 percent were in Latin America, and 5 percent were in Africa. While that distribution has not changed dramatically, different developments are contributing to the expansion in each region.[28]

India: The World's Microinsurance Incubator and Laboratory

The Indian insurance industry is widely seen as the global leader in microinsurance innovation. One study estimated that by 2010, 300 million low-income persons were covered under state-supported mass health insurance schemes in India. In addition, 163 million poor persons had life, agriculture, or livestock insurance, often partly subsidized by the government. While these numbers may be optimistic, it is still reasonable to estimate that 60 percent of all persons covered by microinsurance live in India.[29]

A number of factors account for this leadership position.[30] For one thing, because of its sizable low-income population, India has offered insurers the possibility to generate economies of scale. Supportive public policies have also played a role. When the insurance industry was opened to private companies in 1999, one of the stipulations was that the companies devote a percentage of their portfolios to the rural and social sectors. Some insurers decided that if they had to serve these markets, they needed to try new approaches, and therefore they have innovated with product design, distribution, and consumer education efforts. These pioneers have also enjoyed the added advantage of working with a sophisticated network of intermediaries—nongovernmental organizations (NGOs), MFIs, self-help groups, cooperatives, and other aggregators, which are often positively disposed to insurance.

Finally, despite rapid growth and innovation by private insurance companies, the Indian microinsurance market is still dominated by public companies that are subsidized and have a mandate to assist the poor. Indian governments have also been willing to subsidize some products for low-income households, therefore making insurance more affordable. Particular preference is given to the agriculture and livestock sectors. In the extension of health coverage to populations below the poverty line (BPL), the government has contracted with insurance companies, both public and private, to manage Rashtriya Swasthya Bima Yojna (RSBY), a hospitalization scheme for the poor (see Box 17.5). The convergence of these factors all in one very large country creates a dynamic environment for the development of microinsurance.

The Mass Market in Latin America

Microinsurance in Latin America has developed in two complementary ways. The region's high penetration of microfinance institutions (MFIs) has created awareness about the potential of the low-income market and has encouraged customers to demand financial products that match their needs in countries like Bolivia, Ecuador, and Peru. At the same time, competition for insurance market shares in countries like Mexico, Chile, Brazil, and Colombia has led

---

BOX 17.5

**RSBY: HEALTH MICROINSURANCE FOR
THE POOREST IN INDIA**

With the objective of providing health insurance to BPL households, the Government of India in 2008 launched the RSBY initiative, which is a healthcare financing model making use of public-private partnerships (PPPs). The model leverages government financing, legislation and private sector expertise to improve the poor's access to healthcare services.

The scheme provides cashless health insurance coverage to BPL families who gain access to more than 700 in-patient medical procedures for a nominal registration fee. Health insurance providers are selected after a competitive bidding process. With their smart cards, individuals can use the health service facilities in any of the empanelled hospitals (both public and private) across India.

By the end of 2010, RSBY had been launched in 340 districts in 25 states, with 23 million active cards, insuring approximately 63 million individuals living below the poverty line. The successful implementation on such a scale can be attributed to the partnership the scheme has forged with eight insurers and 16 third-party administrators (TPAs)

In the first year, RSBY had a 2.4 percent incidence rate, which is lower than one might have expected since the previously uninsured target population would presumably have had a pent-up demand for healthcare services. Utilization rates are higher when cards are issued promptly. Villages that have at least one claim have a higher percentage of cards activated within the first 20 days of enrollment. To improve enrollment as well as usage, the scheme may need to engage in direct contracts with TPAs, instead of only contracting the insurers. A direct relationship with TPAs may improve performance monitoring and avoid multiple levels of sub-contracting of enrollment activities by TPAs.

Source: Janice Angove and Nashelo Tande, "Is Microinsurance a Profitable Business for Insurance Companies?" in *Protecting the Poor: A Microinsurance Compendium*, vol. 2, ed. Craig Churchill and Michal Matul (Geneva: International Labour Organization and Munich Re Foundation, 2012).

BOX 17.6

COLLABORATING WITH A UTILITY COMPANY IN COLOMBIA

In response to increased competition, CODENSA, the largest electricity distribution company in Colombia, has developed a customer loyalty program to strengthen its customer base. A core component of the strategy is to offer alternative, non-electricity products, including insurance, which can be paid through the electricity bill. With this objective, CODENSA entered into a partnership with Mapfre Insurance in 2003, and currently offers five products: life, personal accident, funeral, home, and vehicle insurance. As an equal partner with a significant investment in the project's success, CODENSA is committed to maximizing profitability and developing an effective microinsurance business model. Thanks to aligned interests and good project management, the project has enabled more than 300,000 families to manage risk more efficiently by paying insurance premiums together with their electricity bill.

Source: Anja Smith, Herman Smit, and Doubell Chamberlain, "Beyond Sales: New Frontiers in Microinsurance Distribution," in *Protecting the Poor: A Microinsurance Compendium*, vol. 2, ed. Craig Churchill and Michal Matul (Geneva: International Labour Organization and Munich Re Foundation, 2012).

---

insurance companies to explore the potential of the mass market. Volumes in Latin America, which are approximately 45 to 50 million risks, also come from a broader definition of microinsurance that includes the upper poor and lower middle class.[31]

A challenge for the insurance industry in Latin America is to go beyond MFIs and to implement alternative distribution channels to reach the low-income market. In countries like Colombia and Brazil, this move has been an important driver for microinsurance development, including partnerships with utility companies (see Box 17.6) and affinity groups like cooperatives and trade unions. More recently migrant workers associations, retailers, cell phone operators, and government conditional transfer programs are adding insurance services to their portfolios. These distributors often reach new markets and provide more efficient ways of collecting premiums than traditional insurance agents and brokers.

Africa: Moving beyond Funeral Insurance

Over the last 10 years, insurance has developed into a widely recognized financial intervention to help Africa's low-income populations to manage their financial risks. Based on data from more than 260 providers, a study by the ILO shows that microinsurance is growing and expanding throughout Africa. Over 14 million low-income people in Africa were covered by insurance at the end of 2008, which reflects a more than 80 percent increase from 2005. This is substantial growth by any standard. Of these, South Africa alone, where funeral insurance is pervasive, covers 8.2 million low-income persons, or almost

FIGURE 17.2
Microinsurance Outreach in Africa by Product Line

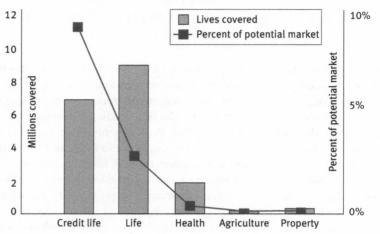

56 percent of the total number in Africa. The total microinsurance premiums received in 2008 amount to US$257 million, out of which regulated insurers collected 88 percent.[32]

Africa remains dominated by life insurance (see Figure 17.2). Health products, which are often cited in demand studies as the greatest need, only cover about 0.3 percent of the low-income population, with property and agriculture covering negligible percentages of the potential market. Despite the promising growth in recent years, additional effort is needed to develop health, agriculture, and property coverage, all significantly needed by the low-income market.

New Technologies

One of the major drivers in the growth of microinsurance has been the involvement of technology, which has the potential to help solve several major challenges. Historically, insurance has been a paper-based sector, with marketing brochures, application and claims forms, and policy documents. To streamline systems and lower costs, microinsurance needs to move beyond paper, and technology can make that possible. Increasingly, information and communication technology can be used for efficient, paperless administrative processes, thereby decreasing costs on a per client basis.[33]

Technology can enable microinsurance providers to reach the low-income market more effectively. Through mobile phones, smart cards, and new payment systems, it is streamlining the process of enrolling clients and collecting premiums. For example, in 2010, Trustco Mobile in Zimbabwe introduced life insurance as a loyalty incentive in partnership with EcoLife and First Mutual Life Assurance, and within one year it covered 1.6 million subscribers. In Ghana, the specialized microinsurance intermediary MicroEnsure and a mobile phone company, Tigo, launched Tigo Family Care in 2011, and it is growing by more than 4,500 new lives insured per day.[34]

From the customer's perspective, the process of accessing insurance and its benefits can be intimidating. Microinsurance has to reduce the barriers and make it easy to understand the coverage, enroll, pay premiums, and submit claims. In this regard, technology can provide a big boost, lowering customers' transaction costs, making it easier for them to get their questions answered, and receiving their claims faster.

New Coalitions and Stakeholders

Besides new technologies, microinsurance expansion and innovation has been supported by several general initiatives that have emerged in recent years.

The ILO's Microinsurance Innovation Facility, established in 2008 with support from the Bill and Melinda Gates Foundation, strives to stimulate the development of better insurance coverage for more low-income households by providing innovation grants and capacity-building support, conducting research, and disseminating lessons learned. The facility collaborates with diverse stakeholders to promote inclusive markets, including insurers, delivery channels, insurance industry actors, and researchers. The facility works with more than 50 organizations throughout Africa, Asia, and Latin America that are experimenting with new approaches to provide valuable insurance to the working poor; these experiences are then carefully documented and widely disseminated.[35]

The Microinsurance Network[36] is another vehicle seeking to improve the supply and demand for insurance services for low-income persons. A member-based network of multilateral agencies, insurance companies, technical assistance providers, policymakers, and academics, this network provides a platform for information sharing and stakeholder coordination to promote the development and proliferation of insurance products for low-income households.

Investors also have an important role to play in promoting inclusive insurance markets, as they can create a bridge between the capital markets and organizations extending insurance to low-income households. The only investment fund that specializes in microinsurance is LeapFrog, created in 2009 with investments from both social and commercial sources of capital to invest in financial services businesses that target the low-income market, with a particular interest in companies that provide insurance in Africa and Asia.[37] For example, LeapFrog invested in AllLife in South Africa, the only insurer of people living with HIV/AIDS in the country. AllLife has become a distinctive and profitable business model that has benefited the investor, the insurer, and the policyholders. The client base grew by 200 percent last year, and the company reports an average of 15 percent improvement in clients' health.[38]

Insurers themselves are the biggest investors in microinsurance, and multinational insurers and brokers are well positioned to support the development and expansion of insurance for the poor to replicate their successes across jurisdictions. For example, Aon Affinity, a subsidiary of Aon, reports covering 12 million mostly low-income people through mass-market schemes in six Latin American countries that access the client bases and use the payment systems of electricity, telephone, and water companies. Brokers Marsh and Guy Carpenter are involved in government schemes in India covering tens of millions of low-income persons, and now they are taking those experiences to other jurisdictions. In 2010, Allianz covered six million low-income persons in eight countries, while Zurich had 2.3 million policies covering "emerging consumers" in seven countries, up from 1.8 million in 2009.[39]

One promising field of joint action is the area of health insurance. Many organizations and initiatives currently provide policy assistance to expand health coverage to low-income households, including the Health Insurance Fund, Gesellschaft für Internationale Zusammenarbeit (GIZ), ILO, the World Health Organization, USAID, the World Bank, Partners for Health, and many others. To meet the demand for cross-learning, a diverse group of countries, including India, Ghana, Indonesia, the Philippines, Thailand, and Viet Nam, and several development partners have initiated a learning platform for countries implementing demand-side financing reforms to achieve universal health coverage. This platform, the Joint Learning Network for Universal Coverage, is creating a cohort of country-level practitioners and a series of tools for cross-country learning and problem-solving, and is promoting the dissemination of information to stakeholders throughout the world.[40]

Another area in which considerable joint exploration is underway concerns insurance for disaster relief in the context of climate change. The Munich Climate Insurance Initiative[41] was formed by insurers, climate change experts, NGOs, and policy researchers to find solutions to risks related to climate change. The group seeks to develop insurance solutions to help manage the impact of climate change and support pilot projects to develop products to better address the needs of clients and insurers as natural disasters occur with greater frequency on a wider scale.

Tool Selection

Insurance, per se, is not inherently a philanthropic tool, but microinsurance, by bringing insurance principles to disadvantaged populations, certainly qualifies given the definition of philanthropy embodied in this volume. As for microfinance, a compelling argument for supporting the emergence of microinsurance is that, for some products and for some target groups, it can be a sustainable development intervention, delivering significant benefits to the poor without needing ongoing donor support—although it does require assistance to cover start-up costs and the additional innovations required to push the frontier toward better client value.

The Provider Perspective

Since the vast majority of the population in developing countries lacks insurance coverage, there is enormous potential for insurers if they have the will to serve the low-income market and can figure out how to do so effectively. This "new market" perspective has been best articulated by C. K. Prahalad in *Fortune at the Bottom of the Pyramid*.[42] Prahalad's analysis draws examples from various industries, including construction, financial services, consumer goods, and healthcare. Based on case studies of successful innovations, Prahalad identifies common principles to be considered when innovating for the bottom of the pyramid (BOP). Although he does not analyze insurance, Prahalad's principles are remarkably applicable to the provision of microinsurance.

In particular, when serving the BOP, the basis for return on investment is volume. Even if the per unit profit is minuscule, when it is multiplied across a huge number of sales, the return can become attractive. This attribute is a perfect fit for insurance given the law of large numbers, which predicts that actual claims experience should run much closer to the projected claims when the risk pool is large, as it can be in microinsurance. When projections can be estimated with a high degree of confidence, then the product pricing does not have to include a large margin for error, making it more affordable to the poor. Prahalad also makes a strong case for (1) utilizing technology to enhance the efficiency of managing large volumes of small transactions; and (2) making significant investments in educating the market in order to create a demand—both of which are essential for the successful uptake of insurance by the poor.

As Prahalad's thinking filters through the insurance industry, many companies are looking seriously at the low-income market. Yet to serve the working poor, insurers have to think differently—about customers' needs, product design, delivery systems, and business models. Insurance companies and their partners are beginning to explore such new approaches, especially when the results from vanguard insurers show that it is possible to provide microinsurance profitably.

The Consumer Perspective

Microinsurance also makes considerable sense from the clients' perspective. This becomes particularly clear when compared with how credit or savings would perform in a similar situation. If a person faced with the same risk of illness or injury resulting in a US$3,000 loss were to rely on savings, the person would need to "put US$60 a year under the mattress for fifty years and finally achieve (near the end of life) the protection that would otherwise have been available every year by buying the above insurance plan for US$0.60 a year (for a total lifetime premium of only US$30.00)."[43] If the same person were to take out a US$3,000 loan to cover medical expenses, he or she would need to repay more than US$250 per year over 40 years to pay off the loan. In this case, insurance is clearly the most economical protection for a low-income household.

Insurance is not a useful tool, however, for inexpensive, frequent risks or for events that are within the control of the insured. This is one of the complications with health insurance, for example. While it is relatively easy to provide insurance for hospitalization—an infrequent event that can be very expensive—it is harder to cover outpatient or primary care that is likely to result in losses for the vast majority of persons in the risk pool. As a result, health insurance that covers inpatient and outpatient expenses tends to be more structured as a prepayment mechanism for primary care and risk pooling for hospitalization.

In general, credit is ill-suited for larger losses, such as expensive healthcare shocks and catastrophic events. Protection against these losses requires other forms of social protection, disaster assistance, or public support.[44] Emergency loans might be relevant for small losses, especially if borrowers still have a source of income that will allow them to repay the loan. Roth, McCord, and Liber suggest ensuring access to multiple sources of credit in an emergency as another risk-management strategy.[45] However, they also acknowledge the limitations. Clients in the middle of repaying one loan may not be allowed to borrow extra funds from the same source and could be at risk of assuming more debt than they can handle.[46] Defaulting on the loan is rarely perceived as a viable option. The poor generally go to great lengths to maintain their access to microcredit, if only to be assured access to a lump sum in future times of need.[47]

Drawing on savings is less expensive than using credit as a risk management strategy. However, a savings strategy is also only relevant for small losses, as poor households have difficulty amassing the funds required to manage risks adequately. In addition, those who have savings are reluctant to draw on them as they attempt to preserve them for earmarked purposes, such school fees or investing in a business.[48] Studies in Tanzania[49] and Bolivia[50] found that many people with significant savings prefer to borrow rather than draw on these savings when faced with an unexpected demand.

Self-insurance, which does not have a risk-pooling mechanism, is a common risk-management strategy for people at all income levels. Borrowing from family and friends is another widespread approach to meet unanticipated shocks.[51] However, the amount of money from friends and family is usually small and may not be readily available, especially when others experience the same crisis. This source of support also often comes with expectations of reciprocation, which can create longer-term financial worry. If income dips, households may be forced to take children out of school and put them to work, sell assets, or go even further into debt.[52] Depletion of productive assets is a last resort as it undermines the household's productive base and capacity to generate future income.

Consequently, insurance is a superior form of risk management than these alternatives for large losses, but in fact should be coordinated with savings, credit, and self-insurance for more complete risk management protection.

Basic Mechanics

This section first considers the product development process for microinsurance. It then illustrates how microinsurance differs from traditional insurance by responding to the characteristics of the target population, and it describes the players in the microinsurance value chain.

The Product Development Process

Product design for microinsurance follows the same basic rules as conventional insurance: the insurer needs to establish demand from the market, determine the risks that can be insured, and devise risk-management processes for ensuring the product's viability.

Market Research

The product design process begins with market research, which involves four basic steps: (1) defining the target market; (2) identifying what risks potential policyholders face and need to insure (and which risks are insurable); (3) determining which product features are important to the target market; and (4) establishing how much potential policyholders are willing and able to pay. Once the product has been launched, insurers should continue to conduct market research to ensure that the services are relevant and valued by the customers.[53]

Pricing

Proper pricing is also crucial for the long-term viability of a product. Pricing specialists for mainstream and microinsurance products should improve the premium over time through an iterative process that includes gathering and analyzing data on the target population, setting assumptions, calculating a premium, monitoring and evaluating the product experience, and refining the premium and product as necessary to optimize viability and client value.[54]

TABLE 17.2   KEY INSURANCE PERFORMANCE INDICATORS

Indicator	Calculation	Range for good financial value	Interpretation from consumer perspective
Incurred expense ratio	Incurred expenses/ earned premium	Below 25%	This ratio measures the efficiency of the product. The more efficient it is, the more valuable it can be if the savings on expenses are used to reduce the premium rate rather than increase profit.
Incurred claims ratio	Incurred claims/ earned premium	Around 60%	Shows how valuable the product is. A "high" ratio, in the absence of fraud and adverse selection, means the price of coverage is relatively "low" (the value is "high").
Net income ratio	Net income/earned premium	Not more than 10%	Shows how profitable the product is. Profit can be reduced by lowering the premium rate and thus increasing value for money.

Source: John Wipf and Denis Garand, "Performance Indicators for Microinsurance: A Handbook for Microinsurance Practitioners," 2nd ed., ADA asbl, October 2010, accessed January 10, 2014, http://www.micro-insurancenetwork.org/publication/fichier/KPI_MI_Handbook_v2_EN.pdf.

An important aspect of client value is the amount and type of coverage one can buy for a given price. As explained by Wipf, an actuary determines this by calculating the average expected claim, which is then loaded with administrative expenses and a margin for error to derive the premium rate.[55] A similar measure, the incurred claims ratio, can be calculated retrospectively on the basis of claims experience. This ratio is the proportion of premiums paid back to the collective insured in the form of insurance benefits. In the absence of adverse selection and fraud, a high ratio signifies good value for money. Related measures are the incurred expense ratio, which indicates how much premium is used to manage and administer the product, and the net income ratio, which shows how profitable the product is for the insurer. With these ratios, one can quantify value for clients, as illustrated in Table 17.2.[56]

Underwriting

After developing and pricing a product, the next step is to determine if a potential client's risk is worth taking, and if so, at what price. This is the underwriting process, where the necessary data and information on the client are gathered. Depending on the design of the insurance product, this may include personal data, information on the state of health, and preexisting conditions that may be excluded from coverage.[57] For traditional insurance, this might be done through a medical exam or an on-site inspection of a building. Such approaches are not viable for microinsurance, and therefore most products are pre-underwritten so that applicants that meet the eligibility criteria automatically receive coverage.

Marketing

When designed properly, insurance can be a valuable financial tool. However, even with a strong product, an insurance scheme can fail without an effective marketing campaign. The first step in designing a marketing strategy is to determine the target audience and their income levels. After identifying the target market, the next step is to determine the main messages that the insurer wants to convey. This is accomplished by considering the anti-insurance arguments that the target audience might have, and then designing messages to counter those arguments. For the low-income market in particular, four main marketing messages emerge: protection, solidarity, optimism, and trust.[58]

Paying Claims

Finally, paying a claim—delivering on a promise—is arguably the most important opportunity to reinforce the value of insurance. This should not be seen as innovative, yet in many countries insurers are notorious for being quick to take the policyholder's money and slow to pay it out. The best marketing opportunity for an insurer, the best way to change the opinion of a lukewarm and skeptical market, the best way to demonstrate its trustworthiness, is to pay claims. At least insurers should take great pains to avoid rejecting claims, for example, by keeping the product simple, making sure policyholders are crystal clear about what is and is not covered, and requiring only the most basic claims documentation.

Taking Account of the Characteristics of the Low-Income Market

There is nothing magical about the term "microinsurance." The popular insurance provided by financial cooperatives for many years could be called microinsurance where the members of those cooperatives are poor. The mass-market insurance delivered by insurers through affinity groups—such as the members of unions or the customers of retailers or utility companies—could qualify as well. Nevertheless, the term "microinsurance" is used here because it emphasizes the importance of understanding the needs, preferences, and characteristics of this target group: the low-income household, the working poor, the underserved.

Regardless of how one defines microinsurance, product design and access are key differentiators. The focus on simplicity and accessibility, and the efficiency of processes, separates microinsurance from traditional insurance. For example, insurance with a complex application form and numerous exclusions may not qualify as microinsurance, even if premiums are low and the product is intended for the low-income market. The following key characteristics summarize how insurance for the poor may differ from conventional insurance:

- *Relevant to the risks of low-income households.* Coverage should be linked to the greatest areas of vulnerability for low-income households, but often what is currently available from insurers does not really address the needs of the poor.
- *As inclusive as possible.* While insurance companies tend to exclude high-risk persons, microinsurance schemes strive to be inclusive. Since

the sums insured are small, the costs of identifying high-risk persons, such as those with preexisting illnesses, may be higher than the benefits of excluding them in the first place. Many exclusions can be just administrative nuisances that undermine efficiency rather than important controls for insurance risks.

- *Affordable premiums.* Microinsurance has to be affordable; otherwise the poor will not enroll in the scheme. Various strategies can help, including having small benefit packages, spreading premiums over time to correspond with the household's cash flow, and supplementing premiums with subsidies from governments or donors.
- *Clearly defined and simple rules and restrictions.* Insurance contracts are generally full of complex conditions and conditional benefits, written in legalese. Although the rationale for the fine print may be consumer protection, if the consumers do not understand what is written, its very purpose is defeated. Moreover, its content can give the insurance company an excuse not to pay a claim.
- *Easily accessible claims documentation requirements.* The process for accessing conventional insurance benefits can be so arduous that it discourages all but the most persistent claimants. While controls have to be in place to avoid paying fraudulent claims, for microinsurance to earn the trust of a reluctant market, it has to be easy for low-income households to submit legitimate claims.

In developing microinsurance products, affordability and product design features must be considered together. The product design must strike a balance among meeting clients' needs and preferences, providing appropriate benefits, applying low premium rates, and achieving sustainability or targeted profitability.

Designing the Delivery System: The Microinsurance Value Chain

Microinsurance can be delivered through a range of institutional arrangements, with different players assuming various functions in the insurance process illustrated in Figure 17.3. For microinsurance, the roles and responsibilities

FIGURE 17.3
Innovation Throughout the Distribution Process

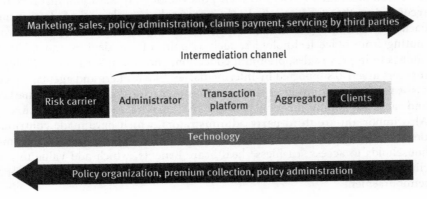

for these various aspects of the process can be quite different than for conventional insurance.

Risk Carriers and Enablers

A first set of actors in the microinsurance field are the risk carriers. In microinsurance, there are two primary types of risk carriers: (1) community-based and mutual insurers managing the insurance risk of their members; and (2) commercial insurers adjusting products and processes to cover the insurable risks of the low-income market. Community-based and mutual insurers should have an advantage over commercial companies because they are already familiar with the low-income market. The proximity of mutuals to their members often enhances their understanding of the needs of low-income persons, facilitates claim settlements, and tends to increase trust from the policyholders and reduces fraud. Even with these advantages, however, most mutuals do not appear to constitute an effective means to reach millions of low-income households, as they are limited by membership, governance, capacity, small capital reserves, and regulation. Although they are still common in some regions, they are being displaced in many countries by the entry of commercial insurers into the low-income market. While commercial insurers lack important advantages enjoyed by locally based mutuals, some have managed to compensate for their deficiencies through partnerships, technology, and other means. This group of insurers is well positioned to achieve massive scale, although it remains to be seen whether their products will provide value to the poor.

As the microinsurance industry continues to grow and becomes more complex, the need for reinsurance, actuarial assistance, and technological innovation has increased. Insurers in many cases have needed not only the reinsurers' financial safety net, but also their expertise in navigating the risks of more complex products. Reinsurance is particularly relevant for disaster products and index-based insurance.

Enablers and Intermediaries

Because this is a relatively new field, many microinsurers have relied on actuaries and consultants to provide advice and guidance to help design better products and systems, improve data capture and analysis, and provide improved insurance services to their policyholders. In addition, insurers are recognizing the need to efficiently process huge volumes of data using back-office technology with the support of technology suppliers, while promoting front-office technologies, such as point-of-sale devices and mobiles phones to improve sales, premium collection, and claims settlement. Finally, insurers are also supported by intermediaries, like brokers and agents, which assist by designing products that are appropriate for the low-income market and facilitate communication between risk carriers and delivery channels. Also important are third-party administrators, which have made contributions to the expansion of health microinsurance by enabling low-income households to access "cashless" healthcare benefits, which add value to the client by avoiding having to pay the healthcare costs upfront and waiting for a reimbursement.

Delivery Channels

Experience thus far suggests that an organization that already has financial transactions with the poor, and has their trust, could be a prospective aggregator or delivery channel. The rationale for insurers to use delivery channels is threefold. First, insurers can gain credibility by exploiting the relationship that the channel has with low-income households. Second, because of the small premium, it is difficult for a full-time agent to generate sufficient commission to sustain a livelihood. Consequently, many channels do other things as their main business, such as providing loans or selling groceries, with insurance commission providing a supplementary income. Third, the microinsurance business model has a greater chance of success if risk carriers can quickly achieve scale, which they can do by working in partnership with a delivery channel that already aggregates large numbers of low-income persons.

Operational Challenges

Microinsurance is not easy. Otherwise insurance companies would already be serving the low-income market and would not need philanthropic assistance to correct market imperfections. To understand clearly how to develop new business models for microinsurance, it is necessary to assess why mainstream insurance does not reach the poor. Although most of these issues have been mentioned above, this section summarizes the key challenges impeding the development of more inclusive insurance markets, focusing particularly on the negative opinions many low-income potential customers have about insurance, that challenge of affordability, the distribution challenges, getting providers to understand the low-income population's needs, the special challenge of renewals, and the obstacles created by regulatory provisions.

Prevailing over Negative Perceptions

A major challenge facing the microinsurance field is educating low-income persons and overcoming their bias against insurance. Besides not being able to afford the premiums, many are skeptical about paying for an intangible product with future benefits that may never be claimed—and they are often not too trusting of insurers. Creating awareness about the value of insurance is time-consuming and costly. A demand study conducted in Zambia[59] clearly revealed that insurance would not be a high priority for many persons, as indicated in the following quotes:

- "I think insurance is for people with a lot of money."
- "For now, I would rather work towards increasing my income, asset base, and livelihood, only then can I think of insurance."
- "I find it difficult to save because of the meager profits I make from my business ... this money used for insurance can be used for other things."

The microinsurance industry is nascent, and the information and experience on real demand—where people purchase and renew insurance policies voluntarily—is limited. For this reason, it is critical that anyone considering bringing insurance to the market expend the effort to confirm that the target market really wants the product.

What is more, preferences for insurance differ from place to place. Demand research shows that generalizing across countries is risky. A "one size fits all" approach does not typically consider differences in gender, location, or life-cycle position of the policyholder.[60] For example, in Nepal[61] and Indonesia[62] there is limited demand for life and funeral insurance, as funeral expenses are kept at a level that the family can afford. In contrast, life and funeral insurance are very much in demand in Uganda[63] and South Africa.[64] In both countries, there are high levels of expenditure on the rites associated with funerals; meanwhile, traditional systems of community support have been under stress, especially in regions affected by HIV/AIDS.

There is certainly a need to develop techniques to convey the usefulness of insurance to an illiterate or uneducated market. Some organizations rely on unconventional communication methods, such as street theater and soap opera-style videos. Efforts to sell insurance to the poor will be more effective if they are preceded by a financial education campaign that helps poor persons understand how insurance works, what it can and cannot accomplish, and how it complements other financial services. Communication and education efforts have to be done on an ongoing basis through a variety of different channels to create the foundation for an insurance culture. In many developed countries, it took generations before people commonly turned to insurance to address their risk-management needs.[65]

Besides financial education, microinsurers need to have a strong brand presence in low-income communities, with a reputation for being a reliable partner. Good branding goes beyond having nice billboards. In South Africa, Old Mutual's branding initiatives in rural areas include engaging with the local infrastructure, such as burial societies, village structures, and traditional leadership. The Imbizo program, an initiative of Old Mutual and its sister companies, Nedbank and Mutual & Federal, delivers a full spectrum of financial services using a community-based approach. The model links agents with community workers who facilitate sales, client servicing, and product refinement to meet local needs. Old Mutual employs and works closely with community members, organizes large gatherings with local authorities, and provides education sessions. In this way, microinsurance is integrated with corporate social responsibility efforts to show target communities that the company cares about social development.

Enhancing Affordability

Poverty limits the number of financial obligations that a person can take on. Experience from an MFI-linked insurance scheme in Nepal suggests that many poor households find the burden of an insurance premium on top of a loan repayment to be a strain.[66] Policyholders who already had health insurance were unwilling to pay a second premium for voluntary life insurance.[67] However, the mandatory nature of many microinsurance products makes it difficult to predict the true demand (and willingness to pay) among poor households for voluntary insurance at different premium levels.

To meet the needs of households with limited financial resources, insurance providers should structure payments so that premiums match the policyholders' cash flow. For example, Opportunity International in Albania had an insurance product fail not because the terms and pricing were unacceptable, but because the premium had to be paid in advance. The upfront payment requirements were not in line with the potential policyholders' cash flow.[68]

One potential solution is to link insurance to other financial services. Of CIC's Bima ya Jamii policies, 90 percent are bought with loan financing from savings and credit cooperatives (SACCOs). Linking insurance to credit has drawbacks, however. Clients who pay premiums on credit feel less ownership of the borrowed funds, so are less aware of the value they receive from insurance. Clients paying with credit might also buy policies that are beyond their repayment capacity.

Using remittances to pay for premiums is convenient for some poor households. Seguros Futuro, a cooperative insurer in El Salvador, developed a product to protect remittance recipients in the event of the death of the migrant worker. Clients are individuals who use cooperatives or Seguros Futuro's service points to collect remittances from family members who immigrated, mainly to North America. Another example of building on migration comes from the Philippines, where Pioneer Life targets the families of migrant workers who are part of a migrants' association at churches and schools. Pioneer provides a flexible endowment product that helps migrant families to save a part of transferred funds.

Another way to release liquidity constraints is to subsidize premiums. This approach is mostly used for health and agriculture products. The Indian government already subsidizes agriculture and livestock insurance. Some donors and governments are experimenting with temporary subsidies for health insurance to entice demand. The Health Insurance Fund, backed by the Dutch government, provides two-year subsidies for its health schemes in Nigeria to allow the poor to develop an appreciation for insurance. The rationale is that clients will see the value and continue to pay for coverage once the subsidies are removed. Permanent subsidies are also targeted at poorer classes in several countries. Indeed, it is hard to imagine valuable health insurance products for the poor without subsidies.

Extending Distribution

Distribution—how to get insurance to the poor—is a particular challenge since insurers' traditional approaches through brokers and agents will not be particularly effective. Insurers may be interested in targeting the low-income market, but it can be a real challenge to access poor communities, educate them on the value of insurance, and gain their trust. Furthermore, reaching economies of scale quickly is essential to making microinsurance sustainable. As discussed above, the emergence of technology such as mobile phones, smart cards, and effective payment systems may be an important step to overcoming this challenge.

Group and mandatory policies are another solution to this dilemma, but this approach may not make a significant contribution to building an insurance culture among the poor. For insurance to be demand-driven and truly reflect the needs of the poor, products should be voluntary. So finding distribution channels that can help insurers access clients, sell products, and administer policies is truly critical for long-term success.

Educating Insurers

Insurance professionals are usually unfamiliar with the needs and concerns of the poor. Similarly, corporate culture and incentives encourage salespersons to focus on larger policies and more profitable clients. As a consequence, the products typically available from insurers are not designed to meet the characteristics of the low-income market, particularly the irregular cash flows of households with breadwinners working in the informal economy. Other key product design challenges include inappropriate insured amounts, complex exclusions, and indecipherable policy language, all of which conspire against effectively serving the poor.

Although many insurers seem to be getting actively involved in microinsurance, it does not mean that they are all successful. Microinsurance champions within an insurance company often have challenges in convincing colleagues to share their enthusiasm. Support may be encouraged by demonstrating the size of the potential market, highlighting competitor successes, illustrating the social dimension of microinsurance, and exhibiting the learning and innovation opportunities. While this tactic can win the hearts and even the minds of colleagues, ultimately it is necessary to have positive results. Consequently, it is useful for an insurance company to establish a microinsurance department that has sufficient financial and technical resources. It is also necessary for that department to have some space and independence so it can go about its business differently than do the insurer's core operations. Finally, the department should have targets in the medium to long term, because if managers are expecting quick results, they are likely to be disappointed.[69]

Retaining Policyholders

Renewals are just as important as sales, yet many microinsurance schemes have experienced problems retaining policyholders. For schemes with voluntary participation, low renewal rates often indicate client dissatisfaction, possibly due to poor communication, unacceptable product value, unsatisfactory claims payment, and so on. Low renewal rates over extended periods will increase costs per unit of insurance since the fixed costs of the program must be distributed over fewer insured persons, which dampens participation and persistency even more since high expenses result in reduced product value.[70]

For clients who do not file a claim, it can be hard to see the benefits of microinsurance coverage, especially in the context of low insurance literacy. In a world of many temptations and limited resources, it is hard to maintain the discipline to renew policies while other goods and services provide more immediate rewards. To overcome this challenge, some schemes are extending value-added benefits to nonclaimants. For health insurance, for example, health camps, free checkups, counseling visits, mosquito nets, and other preventive measures make insurance products more tangible for low-income households and can help to increase renewals.

Customer care can still be improved in microinsurance. It is a natural extension of branding and marketing, as it builds trust, increases client satisfaction, and further explains key product functionalities to clients on a continuous basis. The latter is particularly important, as many practitioners have learned the hard way that providing too much information during a first contact does not yield satisfactory results. In many cases, customer care might be a key mechanism to keep clients happy and ensure they renew their policies. It is useful to remember that, in most cases, "word of mouth" is the most powerful marketing channel. Given that bad news travels faster than good news, any major mistakes by microinsurers can have lasting negative effects on the viability of microinsurance in a community.

Overcoming Regulatory Challenges

Another obstacle to the expansion of microinsurance is the regulatory environment in which insurers operate. Regulators are primarily concerned with ensuring financial stability, and they may perceive anything that is new or innovative as a potential threat. Consequently, efforts to stimulate financial inclusion can be perceived as in conflict with the maintenance of financial stability.

To overcome this problem, the global standard-setting body for insurance, the International Association of Insurance Supervisors (IAIS), together with international agencies, created the Access to Insurance Initiative to encourage insurance supervisors to put in place regulatory and policy measures conducive to the development of products, delivery mechanisms, and consumer protections appropriate for low-income clients without undermining stability.[71] Based on country studies carried out with the support of the Initiative and in collaboration with insurance supervisors, experts are studying how to follow a principled approach, instead of a rules approach, whereby proportionality can be used to develop a regulatory and supervisory framework that will better promote access to insurance in different economic and cultural settings. For example, products with small sums insured over short terms are less risky than long-term products for large amounts, and therefore do not warrant the same rigorous regulatory requirements. Chatterjee suggests that a proportionate approach will require steps to strengthen the capacity of supervisors so that they can make greater use of regulatory judgment to identify opportunities and problems early. It will also require moving away from the one-size-fits-all regulatory strategy and enhancing dialogue with stakeholders to stimulate innovation by the industry.[72]

Track Record and Overall Assessment

The volume and diversity of innovation taking place to extend insurance to low-income households in developing countries is certainly encouraging. What is more, it seems clear that those who are covered by insurance for certain risks are better off than they would have been if they were not covered when the risk occurs. However, while anecdotal evidence about the benefits of insurance, like the vignette at the beginning of this chapter, is bountiful, results from rigorous academic studies regarding the impact of insurance have thus far been inconclusive.

A review of academic research by Radermacher, McGowan, and Dercon finds that most impact studies have been conducted on health insurance, while knowledge of the impact of other types of insurance remains limited.[73] Recent studies do offer evidence that microinsurance provides some financial protection and suggests positive change through insurance. For example, Jütting detected a 45 to 50 percent decrease in out-of-pocket spending among the policyholders of four Senegalese *mutuelles*, or community-based mutual health insurance organizations, in comparison to nonmembers after controlling for other factors.[74] Schneider and Diop (2001) calculated that members of 54 community-based Rwandan health schemes spent a significant 76.5 percent less than nonmembers to address episodes of illness involving professional care visits.[75] However, the majority of the available evidence focuses on the reduction of out-of-pocket expenses.[76] The field lacks sufficient evidence on whether microinsurance provides more equitable access to services, and available evidence comes to contradictory conclusions.

More research is thus needed to understand the impact of microinsurance in a coherent manner. Such studies are not only of academic interest; they can provide important guidance for the sector's development and efficient use of donor and investor funds. It is also likely that microinsurance services must mature more, and provide greater value to the insured, before the impact of insurance to protect incomes and assets can be demonstrated convincingly.

There is thus a need to push the frontier of microinsurance further. The industry must continue to improve products to provide better value to the poor. When cost structures and commissions devour the majority of the premiums, it is impossible to return sufficient benefits to low-income households. Greater attention must be given to enhancing efficiencies so that products can provide better value. In fact, some companies that have ventured into microinsurance have done so in part to learn how to become more efficient, so that the lessons from microinsurance will benefit their conventional lines of business.

Great expectations are placed on the potential of technology to address some of these challenges. Technology can improve the microinsurance business because of the information-processing nature of the sector. Besides upgrading their management information systems, microinsurers must take advantage of ways to improve efficiency and reduce errors and fraud, through the use of smart cards, mobile phones, e-money, point-of-sale devices, biometrics, the internet, and wireless communications, among others. It is important to note, however, that technology will not fix a problematic product. Indeed organizations struggling with customer retention challenges cannot be significantly aided by technology solutions. At the end of the day, insurers and their partners need to make sure that they have products that are relevant for the market and distributed through a channel that is convenient for the poor, while fostering the trust of the low-income market in insurance and insurers.

Conclusion

The future success of microinsurance depends on achieving prudent, profitable, and continuous growth and development. What will be the development life cycle for microinsurance? How long will it be? At the moment, microinsurance is at an early stage of development, perhaps a toddler or a preschooler. But it is maturing quickly, requiring careful oversight to ensure that the interests of poor consumers are carefully protected.

The catastrophic risks of climate change, HIV/AIDS, and others still to come will have an important and dramatic impact on the provision of all insurance, and especially on microinsurance. Low-income people are typically the most impaired by catastrophic events. Since their incomes are low, they live in high-risk areas where others will not live. They take risks that make them more susceptible to diseases, and have a lower ability to cope when catastrophes do occur. Insurers and reinsurers need to recognize the effect of catastrophic risks on the low-income market and work to develop efficient mechanisms to help the poor prepare for these risks and recover after they occur.

Based on the experiences of microfinance, where self-promotion of the industry and its leaders has exceeded the results on the ground, it is important that the value of insurance as a tool to advance a development agenda not be overstated. Indeed, this tool has significant potential, but it has not demonstrated anything yet. To live up to its potential, it will be necessary to follow up on some of the key issues identified above, including consumer education, distribution, product design, and attracting more expertise to solve emerging challenges.

To insure the poor, customers, regulators, policymakers, insurers, social organizations, and philanthropists must work together with a common purpose:

- **Insurers** must strive to understand the low-income customer's changing needs and adapt products and services accordingly, continually improving the cost-benefit ratio for clients.

- **Regulators** must promote a development agenda for inclusive insurance markets, finding the right balance between protecting consumers and expanding access.
- **Policymakers** need to create an enabling environment that includes the necessary infrastructure for providing microinsurance.
- **Social organizations,** including employers and workers' organizations, cooperatives, NGOs, and other associations, need to organize workers in the informal economy to press for access to social protection or other types of microinsurance.
- **Philanthropists,** be they aid agencies, private foundations, or interested individuals, have a key role to play to support efforts to solve the remaining microinsurance challenges, and ensure that the lessons learned are widely shared.
- Lastly, the **billions of poor people** who do not have a formal way of coping with risk must respond positively to the efforts of providers and regulators to promote a culture of insurance and its capability to provide financial freedom, security, and well-being.

By itself, microinsurance will not put a major dent in poverty. However, if risk protection is effectively coupled with efforts to enhance productivity, the combination can make great strides toward alleviating poverty. Microinsurance will have succeeded when it is no longer needed. As the former chair of Delta Life, Monzurur Rahman, said, "We want to see the day when there is no more microinsurance, just insurance."

Notes

1. *Small Premiums, Long-Term Benefit: Why Poor Women Need Microinsurance* (Geneva: Microinsurance Innovation Facility, International Labour Organization, 2010).

2. Jim Roth, Michael J. McCord, and Dominic Liber, *The Landscape of Microinsurance in the World's 100 Poorest Countries* (Appleton, WI: Microinsurance Centre, 2007).

3. Ke Xu, David B. Evans, Guido Carrin, Ana Mylena Aguilar-Rivera, et al., "Protecting Households from Catastrophic Spending," *Health Affairs* 26.4 (2007): 972–83.

4. Margaret E. Kruk, Emily Goldmann, and Sandro Galea, "Borrowing and Selling to Pay for Health Care in Low- and Middle-Income Countries," *Health Affairs* 28.4 (2009): 1056–66.

5. Stefan Deacon and Martina Kirchberger, "Literature Review on Microinsurance," Microinsurance Paper Series No. 1, ILO Social Finance Programme, 2008.

6. George E. Redja, *The Principles of Risk Management and Insurance* (Boston: Pearson, 1998).

7. Marie-Amandine Coydon and Véronique Molitor, *Commercial Insurers in Microinsurance* (Luxembourg: Microinsurance Network, 2011).

8. Michael J. McCord, Felipe Botero, and Janet S. McCord, *AIG Uganda, A Member of the American International Group of Companies* (Geneva: Social Finance Programme, International Labour Organization, 2005).

9. Lemmy Manje and Craig Churchill, "The Demand for Risk-Managing Financial Services in Low-Income Communities: Evidence from Zambia," Social Finance Programme Working Paper No. 31, International Labour Organization, 2002, http://www.ilo.org/wcmsp5/groups/public/---ed_emp/documents/publication/wcms_117979.pdf.

10. Jim Roth and Vijay Athreye, *TATA-AIG Life Insurance Company Ltd. India* (Geneva: Social Finance Programme, International Labour Organization, 2005).

11. Michael J. McCord and Craig Churchill, *Delta Life, Bangladesh* (Geneva: Social Finance Programme, International Labour Organization, 2005).

12. Janice Angove and Nashelo Tande, "Is Microinsurance a Profitable Business for Insurance Companies?" in *Protecting the Poor: A Microinsurance Compendium*, vol. 2, ed. Craig Churchill and Michal Matul (Geneva: International Labour Organization and Munich Re Foundation Foundation, 2012).

13. Swiss Reinsurance Company Economic Research and Consulting, *Microinsurance: Risk Protection for 4 Billion People* (Zurich: Swiss Re Sigma, 2010).

14. Ralf Radermacher, Heidi McGowan, and Stefan Dercon, "What Is the Impact of Microinsurance?" in Churchill and Matul, *Protecting the Poor.*

15. For example, see Marco Arena, "Does Insurance Market Activity Promote Economic Growth? A Cross-Country Study for Industrialized and Developing Countries," World Bank Policy Research Working Paper 4098, 2006; and Peter Haiss and Kjell Sumegí, "The Relationship between Insurance and Economic Growth in Europe: A Theoretical and Empirical Analysis," *Empirica* 35.4 (2008): 405–31.

16. For more details on the impact of insurance development on economic development, see *Assessment on How Strengthening the Insurance Industry in Developing Countries Contributes to Economic Growth* (Washington, DC: USAID, 2006); Lael Brainard, "What Is the Role of Insurance in Economic Development?" Zurich Government and Industry Thought Leadership Series No. 2, 2008; and Harold Skipper, *Foreign Insurers in Emerging Markets: Issues and Concerns* (Washington, DC: International Insurance Foundation, 1997).

17. Yvonne Deblon and Markus Loewe, "The Potential of Microinsurance for Social Protection," in Churchill and Matul, *Protecting the Poor.*

18. Monique Cohen and Jennifer Sebstad, "The Demand for Microinsurance," in Churchill and Matul, *Protecting the Poor.*

19. Ralf Radermacher, Iddo Dror, and Gerry Noble, "Challenges and Strategies to Extend Health Insurance to the Poor," in Churchill and Matul, *Protecting the Poor.*

20. Christine Hougaard and Doubell Chamberlain, "Funeral Insurance," in Churchill and Matul, *Protecting the Poor.*

21. Anupama Sharma and Andrew Mude, "Livestock Insurance: Helping Vulnerable Livestock Keepers Manage Their Risk," in Churchill and Matul, *Protecting the Poor.*

22. *An Initial Assessment of the Impact of the Earthquake and Tsunami of December 26, 2004 on South and Southeast Asia* (Manila: Asian Development Bank, 2005).

23. Michael J. McCord and Monique Cohen, *Microinsurance Disasters: Steps to Take to Mitigate Risks Next Time* (Washington, DC: Microfinance Opportunities, 2005).

24. Aparna Dalal and Jonathan Morduch, "The Psychology of Microinsurance: Small Changes Can Make a Surprising Difference," in Churchill and Matul, *Protecting the Poor.*

25. Lloyds, "Insurance in Developing Countries: Exploring Opportunities in Microinsurance" Lloyds 360 Risk Insight, 2010, accessed January 10, 2014, http://www.microfinancegateway.org/gm/document-1.9.40798/Insurance%20in%20developing.pdf.

26. Craig Churchill and Michael J. McCord, "Emerging Trends in Microinsurance," in Churchill and Matul, *Protecting the Poor.*

27. Swiss Reinsurance Company Economic Research and Consulting, *Microinsurance.*

28. Churchill and McCord, "Emerging Trends in Microinsurance."

29. Churchill and McCord, "Emerging Trends in Microinsurance."

30. Rupalee Ruchismita and Craig Churchill, "Microinsurance Development in India," in Churchill and Matul, *Protecting the Poor.*

31. Churchill and McCord, "Emerging Trends in Microinsurance."

32. Michal Matul, Michael J. McCord, Caroline Phily, and Job Harms, *The Landscape of Microinsurance in Africa* (Geneva: Microinsurance Innovation Facility, International Labour Organization, 2010).

33. For more details see Anja Smith, Eric Gerelle, Michiel Berende, and Grieve Chelwa, "The Technology Revolution in Microinsurance," in Churchill and Matul, *Protecting the Poor.*

34. Churchill and McCord, "Emerging Trends in Microinsurance."

35. For more information see "Microinsurance Innovation Facility," International Labour Organization, accessed June 12, 2012, www.ilo.org/microinsurance.

36. The Microinsurance Network was originally established in 2002 as the CGAP Working Group on Microinsurance. For more information see the Microinsurance Network website: "Microinsurance Network—Home," Microinsurance Network, accessed October 19, 2012, http://www.microinsurancenetwork.org/.

37. For more information see the LeapFrog Investments website: "LeapFrog Investments—Home," Leapfrog Investments, accessed October 19, 2012, www.leapfroginvest.com.

38. "AllLife Portfolio," LeapFrog Investments, last modified 2011, http://www.leapfroginvest.com/PortfolioCompanyAllLife.

39. Churchill and McCord, "Emerging Trends in Microinsurance."

40. For more information see the Results for Development Institute website: "Joint Learning Network for Universal Health Coverage," Results for Development Institute, accessed October 19, 2012, www.resultsfordevelopment.org/projects/joint-learning-network-universal-health-coverage.

41. For more information see the Munich Climate Insurance Initiative website: "Munich Climate Insurance Initiative—Home," MCII, accessed October 18, 2012, http://www.climate-insurance.org/front_content.php?idcat=858.

42. C. K. Prahalad, *The Fortune at the Bottom of the Pyramid: Eradicating Poverty through Profits* (Upper Saddle River, NJ: Wharton School Publishing, 2004).

43. David Dror and Christian Jacquier, "Microinsurance: Extending Health Insurance to the Excluded," *International Social Security Association Review* 52.1 (1999): 71–97.

44. Paul B. Siegel, Jeffrey Alwang, and Sudharshan Canagarajah, *Viewing Microinsurance as a Social Risk Management Instrument* (Washington, DC: Social Protection Unit, World Bank, 2001).

45. Roth, McCord, and Liber, *Landscape of Microinsurance in Poorest Countries.*

46. Jim Roth, Denis Garand, and Stuart Rutherford, "Long-Term Savings and Insurance," in Churchill and Matul, *Protecting the Poor.*

47. Jennifer Sebstad and Monique Cohen, *Microinsurance: Risk Management and Poverty* (Washington, DC: Consultative Group to Assist the Poor, 2001).

48. Sebstad and Cohen, *Microinsurance.*

49. Altemius Millinga, *Assessing the Demand for Microinsurance in Tanzania* (Nairobi: MicroSave-Africa, 2002).

50. Carmen Velasco and Andrea del Grando, "Resultados del Market Research para La Programa Financiera," ProMujer, June 2004.

51. Cohen and Sebstad, "The Demand for Microinsurance."

52. Cohen and Sebstad, "The Demand for Microinsurance."

53. John Wipf, Domnic Liber, and Craig Churchill, "Product Design and Insurance Risk Management," in Churchill and Matul, *Protecting the Poor.*

54. Denis Garand, Clémence Tatin-Jaleran, Donna Swiderek, and Mary Yang, "Pricing of Microinsurance Products," in Churchill and Matul, *Protecting the Poor.*

55. John Wipf, Eamon Kelly, and Michael J. McCord, "Improving Credit Life Microinsurance," in Churchill and Matul, *Protecting the Poor.*

56. Wipf, Kelly, and McCord, "Improving Credit Life Microinsurance."

57. Radermacher, McGowan, and Dercon, "What Is the Impact."

58. Craig Churchill and Monique Cohen, "Marketing Microinsurance," in Churchill and Matul, *Protecting the Poor.*

59. Manje and Churchill, "The Demand for Risk-Managing Financial Services."

60. Cohen and Sebstad, "The Demand for Microinsurance."

61. Nav Raj Simkhada, Sushila Guatam, Mira Mishra, et al., *Research on Risk and Vulnerability of Rural Women in Nepal* (Kathmandu: Center for MicroFinance, 2000).

62. Michael J. McCord, Gabriele Ramm, and Elizabeth McGuinness, *Microinsurance Demand and Market Prospects: Indonesia* (Geneva: United Nations Development Programme, Gesellschaft für Technische Zusammenarbeit, Allianz Group, 2005).

63. Grace Sebageni, *Assessing Demand for Microinsurance in Uganda* (Nairobi: MicroSave Africa, 2003).

64. Hennie Bester, Doubell Chamberlain, Ryan Hawthorne, et al., *Making Insurance Markets Work for the Poor in South Africa, Botswana, Namibia, Lesotho and Swaziland— Scoping Study* (Johannesburg: Genesis Analytics, 2004).

65. Iddo Dror, Aparna Dalal, and Michal Matul, *Emerging Practices in Consumer Education on Risk Management and Insurance* (Geneva: Microinsurance Innovation Facility, International Labour Organization, 2010).

66. Cohen and Sebstad, "The Demand for Microinsurance."

67. *Fifth Semi-Annual Report on Pilot Testing of Microinsurance Services to Poor Clients of MFIs in Nepal* (Kathmandu: Center for MicroFinance, February 2005).

68. Richard Leftley, *An Overview of Insurance Product Design within the Opportunity International Network* (Oak Brook, IL: Technical Services Division, Opportunity International, 2002).

69. Janice Angove, Martin Herrndorf, and Brandon Mathews, "Teaching Elephants to Dance: Experiences of Commercial Insurers in Low-Income Markets," in Churchill and Matul, *Protecting the Poor.*

70. Denis Garand and John Wipf, "Risk and Financial Management," in Churchill and Matul, *Protecting the Poor.*

71. For more information see the Access to Insurance website: "Access to Insurance," Access to Insurance Initiative, accessed October 18, 2012, http://www.access-to-insurance.org/.

72. Arup Chatterjee, "Access to Insurance and Financial Sector Regulation," in Churchill and Matul, *Protecting the Poor.*

73. Radermacher, McGowan, and Dercon, "What Is the Impact."

74. Johannes P. Jütting, "Do Community-Based Health Insurance Schemes Improve Poor People's Access to Health Care?" *World Development* 32.2 (2004): 273–88.

75. Pia Schneider and François Diop, *Synopsis of Results on the Impact of Community-Based Health Insurance on Financial Accessibility to Health Care in Rwanda* (Washington, DC: World Bank, 2001).

76. Radermacher, McGowan, and Dercon, "What Is the Impact."

Suggested Reading

Churchill, Craig, ed. 2006. *Protecting the Poor: A Microinsurance Compendium.* Geneva: International Labour Organization and Munich Re Foundation.

Churchill, Craig, and Michal Matul, eds. 2012. *Protecting the Poor: A Microinsurance Compendium.* Vol. 2. Geneva: International Labour Organization and Munich Re Foundation.

Lloyds. "Insurance in Developing Countries: Exploring Opportunities in Microinsurance." Lloyds 360 Risk Insight, 2010. http://www.microfinancegateway.org/gm/document-1.9.40798/Insurance%20in%20developing.pdf

Roth, Jim, Michael J. McCord, and Dominic Liber. *The Landscape of Microinsurance In the World's 100 Poorest Countries.* Appleton, WI: Microinsurance Centre, 2007.

Swiss Reinsurance Company Economic Research and Consulting. *Microinsurance: Risk Protection for 4 Billion People.* 2010. Zurich: Swiss Re Sigma.

SOCIALLY RESPONSIBLE INVESTING AND PURCHASING

Steve Lydenberg and Katie Grace

IN SEPTEMBER 2007, A COALITION of 22 state officials, environmental groups, pension funds, money management firms, and institutional investors with $1.5 trillion in assets petitioned the Securities and Exchange Commission, demanding that this regulatory body require more complete disclosure by corporations of data relating to their practices and policies on global warming and climate change. They argued that these data were crucial to investment decisions and that by failing to recognize their relevance to the financial markets and society, corporations and regulators were failing in their duties. Additional petitions from this coalition followed in 2008 and 2009 and its coordinator Ceres joined with others in publishing a 2009 report demonstrating that many of the largest S&P 500 companies—including those with the most at stake in responding to the risks and opportunities from climate change—were providing only limited climate risk-related information to investors.[1] Finally, in January 2010, the Securities and Exchange Commission issued guidance for the first time to US corporations on their obligations to publicly report their exposure to climate change risks and its materiality to their operations. Investors and society were, at last, better able to understand how companies were, or were not, responding to this emerging issue of global importance.[2]

This campaign on climate change disclosure is just one example of a growing strategy for improving the quality of life for people throughout the world through the use of market pressures on businesses. Such initiatives as socially responsible investing and purchasing have been used by investors and consumers to communicate their concerns and interests to businesses via the routine practices of investing in stocks and buying products. Over the years, these tools have been used in investment initiatives such as the South Africa divestment campaign that helped bring an end to the apartheid legal system and in consumer boycotts that prompted Nike and Gap to take firmer action against unfair labor practices on the part of their suppliers in Asia and Latin America.

Defining the Tool

Defining Features

The fundamental premise of socially responsible investment and consuming is that all investment and purchasing decisions have social and environmental implications and that, at certain times, these implications rise to a level of concern that can appropriately prompt action. Through their effects on the bottom line or on the reputation of the firm, these market-based activities can communicate on social and environmental issues to the corporations that dominate our markets and have a profound influence on the quality of our daily lives. These choices by investors and consumers also have the virtue of raising for broad public debate important issues where action in public policy realms is also needed. Together these two approaches can make substantial contributions to ongoing discussions of many of the most important issues of our day and have the potential to influence both corporations and government as they contend with the complexities of the social and environmental challenges that our increasingly populous and prosperous world faces. However, while these tools have the ability to provoke broad, societal debates around important issues and in many cases have succeeded in changing corporate behavior, raising public awareness and promoting steps toward a more just and sustainable society, their success to date has been largely anecdotal, and it remains to be seen if they can produce fundamental systemic change.

Responsible investing and purchasing share a common strategy—the use of market pressures to achieve social and environmental benefits by altering the behavior of firms. They both take advantage of the growing corporate concerns about their "reputational capital" and their brand image in a globally competitive consumer marketplace, as well as increasing interest in the role that corporations play in promoting healthy, sustainable societies. Responsible investors and purchasers have created an orderly, market-based means for communication between corporations and society on such issues as the environment, energy, labor and human rights, militarism, and social justice, in sharp contrast to the days when demonstrations in the streets, boycotts, strikes, draconian regulation, and high-profile lawsuits were the primary vehicles through which society communicated with corporations on such issues.

Design Features and Major Variants

Although responsible investing and purchasing share a common strategy, they utilize different tactics. The structural difference in their tactics has important implications for the parties they engage and the means they employ.

Responsible Investing

Responsible investing seeks to affect corporate behavior by investing in, or divesting from, corporate securities—often called "screening" or "standard setting"—and by actively exercising proxy voting rights accorded investors by virtue of their ownership of corporate stock—commonly referred to as shareholder "engagement" or "activism." Since the 1970s, when responsible investment emerged in its modern form, many names have been applied to this discipline—socially responsible investing, ethical investing, sustainable investing, triple-bottom-line investing, social-impact investing, and best-of-class investing, among others. These different names reflect in part responsible investors' different motivations and strategies. Some seek to avoid investments they consider objectionable. Others view promoting positive social and environmental change by corporations as part of their mission as investors. Still others believe that incorporating social and environmental analysis into investment decision-making will boost financial returns.[3]

These approaches are not necessarily mutually exclusive and often coexist. A single responsible investor concerned about climate change, for example, might avoid coal companies, not wishing to profit from the worst of the carbon emitters; seek out wind power companies on the grounds that they will outperform financially; and work to persuade the oil companies in their portfolios to invest more heavily in research and development on alternatives to fossil fuels. Similarly, an investor concerned about human rights and economic development might shun companies doing business in Sudan or Burma given those countries' records of human rights abuses, invest or make deposits in microfinance institutions working to bring financial services to the poor around the world, and enter into dialogue with internet companies about their policies on censorship and protection of personal privacy.

Two primary mechanisms are available to responsible investors. The first is *screening* or *standard setting*, in which individual investors or organizations establish social screens to guide investment decisions, discouraging investment in some firms (negative screens) and encouraging investment in others (positive screens). The second is shareholder *engagement* or *activism*, in which shareholders introduce resolutions at corporate annual meetings, actively vote their shares, or engage in dialogue privately with corporations as individual investors or groups around specific issues of concern.

While responsible investment has historically been most often associated with public equities, it has applications in other asset classes as well. In the asset class of cash, for example, responsible investors may make deposits in community development financial institutions—including banks, credit unions, and loan funds serving the unbanked poor. In real estate, responsible investors may invest in green buildings, brownfield redevelopment, urban infill projects, and labor-friendly and transit-oriented development. In venture capital, they may seek out opportunities to support the development of clean technologies and alternative sources of energy.

Whatever the asset class and whatever the approach, the goal of responsible investment is ultimately the same—to assure that investments produce not only positive financial results, but are also aligned with the broader interests of society in creating a just and sustainable world.

Responsible Purchasing

Whereas responsible investing operates through the financial markets and has the potential to affect companies' capital needs, responsible purchasing—also referred to as ethical or preferential purchasing—operates through the consumer marketplace and has the potential to affect companies' revenues. Cowe and Williams define ethical consumers as "people who are influenced by environmental or ethical considerations when choosing products and services."[4]

The sheer volume of consumer purchases is astounding, accounting in the United States for more than two-thirds of total spending.[5] By choosing to purchase one product over another, a buyer signals his or her preference and, at least implicitly, expresses personal values and beliefs. These choices can be made on the basis of traditional concerns such as price, quality, brand name, or style. But as noted more fully below, consumers are increasingly taking social and environmental concerns into account when purchasing products, including labor rights, health concerns, cruelty to animals, sustainable forestry, and support for local economies.

Three broad groups of consumers engage in ethical purchasing: individuals, corporations, and governments. Each group uses different approaches and varying levels of impact and engagement.

The definition of an ethical product can vary from consumer to consumer, depending upon the values that the individual consumer or institution holds. These ethical considerations may be broad and all-encompassing, or they may be narrow and issue-specific. Consumers engaging in ethical purchasing may do so for reasons of self-interest, such as buying organic food for improved health, for reasons of conscience arising from internal ethics or ideas of justice, or to promote broader social and environmental goals.

Relation to Common Criteria

Risk

Compared to many of the other tools explored in this volume, responsible investing and purchasing carry fewer risks.

The items purchased or avoided by individual responsible consumers—the broadest base of participants—tend to be small in scale and have numerous available substitutes. This means that this variant of the tool can potentially be used by a broader clientele than responsible investing. Nevertheless, complexities in the gathering of information and the conveying of the most relevant data to individual consumers complicate this process. For example, the complexity of modern supply chains can make it difficult for consumers to identify the most appropriate target when it comes to labor abuses. Still, ethical purchasing is probably the easiest and safest way of expressing ethical concerns, as the downside risk is minimal.

The primary perceived risk of responsible investment relates to financial returns. The perception among many mainstream financial professionals—and often among those coming to the field for the first time—is that integrating social and environmental factors into investment decision-making necessarily hurts returns. As noted more fully below, however, the preponderance of academic studies of professionally managed responsible investment vehicles to date suggests that no such cost to returns necessarily exists. In addition, responsible investors who choose an engagement-only approach can maintain their traditional investment policies, whatever they may be, and consequentially run virtually no additional financial risk relative to their peers.

Type and Level of Return

Various academic studies show that returns from responsible investments are at or slightly above comparable investments, although others have shown a cost. For example, a review of 31 socially screened mutual funds from 1990 to 1998 by Meir Statman found that on average they outperformed their unscreened peers, but not by a statistically significant margin.[6] Similarly, a review of 80 academic studies on the links between corporate social responsibility and financial performance published in 2001 noted that 58 percent of the studies found a positive relationship to performance, 24 percent found no relationship, 19 percent found a mixed relationship, and only 5 percent found a negative relationship.[7]

David Vogel, in his book *The Market for Virtue*, has described the perennial debate about responsible investment and financial returns as follows:

> While there continues to be debate over whether the use of negative screens by virtually all SRI funds increases risk or lowers return (or both), or alternatively, whether socially screened investments are less volatile and result in higher returns, the consensus of the more than 100 studies of social investment funds and their strategies is that the [effect of screens on] risk-adjusted returns of a carefully constructed socially screened portfolio is zero. In other words, share returns are neither harmed nor helped by including social criteria in stock selection.[8]

Apart from the question of financial returns, both responsible investing and responsible purchasing are premised on the notion that they can generate "social returns." However, social returns are difficult to identify and measure and it is often difficult to draw a causal connection between positive social and environmental actions taken by corporations and specific responsible investing or purchasing initiatives.

Individual consumers, in conjunction with grass-roots activists, have had anecdotal success in shaping corporate decisions and market standards. For example, in the case of dolphin-safe tuna, a national boycott of StarKist—the world's largest canned tuna producer—was successful in pushing that company to declare in 1990 that it would stop purchasing, processing, and selling tuna caught by intentional chasing and netting of dolphins. Under similar boycott pressure and industry competition, Bumblebee and Chicken of the Sea followed StarKist's lead shortly after.[9] Similarly, in the 1990s Nike came under intense pressure from church groups and students at universities with Nike licensing contracts over human rights violations in their contract factories abroad. Well-publicized protests against Nike encouraged the company to institute new supply-chain management policies and a comprehensive corporate responsibility policy to address labor issues.[10]

Large-scale consumers such as corporations or governments can function as market-makers, supporting markets for ethical products. For example, the US government's General Service Administration has played an important role in building the green real estate market, and the Japanese government has a policy of giving preference in its purchasing to companies with strong environmental records. Often government preferential procurement goes hand in hand with soft regulations that support social programs such as minority-supplier development in the United States.

Degree of Leverage

Responsible investing and purchasing use markets to promote public debates around particular issues or firms and encourage incremental change in corporations through moral suasion. Their ability to make voices heard in debates about issues of long-term, broad concern has increased in recent years with the growing participation of large institutional investors in responsible investing and the influence of large civil society movements and concerned governments in responsible purchasing.

Ubiquity

Responsible investing and purchasing can be used in investment or purchase situations anywhere where an equivalent, more responsible alternative is available. As an increasing number of consumer and financial products position themselves as having a social return, the number of these opportunities continues to grow.

For example, architects and developers in the real estate world are increasingly stressing environmentally friendly design and construction. This presents a growing range of options for responsible investors in real estate. Similarly, the number of products for which organic and fair-trade alternatives are available for consumers continues to grow. Conversely, however, demand is as important as supply here, and consumers and investors will utilize ethical purchasing and investing only to the degree that they place a value on the ethical "content" of the product, as opposed to its price/returns, quality, and availability. Theoretically, there is no reason why responsible investment or purchasing should not ultimately be applicable to all investment and purchasing situations.

Skill Requirement

Responsible investment requires considerable skill to be applied successfully, including both specialized knowledge of social and environmental issues and solid understanding of investment techniques and the financial implications of screening and engagement.

Responsible purchasing requires a high level of understanding of social and environmental issues as well as corporate decision-making processes. Products can convey their ethical attributes via labels that designate them as organic, fair trade, local, energy-efficient, recycled, or any of a host of other categories. The availability and accessibility of this information at the point of purchase facilitates responsible purchasing. However, only a limited amount of information can be conveyed on each product label. With the number of sustainable product labels skyrocketing, consumers can have a difficult time sorting out their meaning and seeing past "greenwashing"—unsubstantiated claims to environmentally positive attributes or processes. For corporate and governmental consumers, ethical purchasing often requires the creation, support, and monitoring of new markets and suppliers, a potentially Herculean task for procurement officers. Ultimately, for ethical purchasing to succeed, it requires an engaged, informed, and concerned consumer. Ensuring that consumers have the information they need to make informed decisions has thus been a challenge for promoters of ethical products.

Social Implications

Responsible investment and purchasing have the potential to promote public debates and influence behavior and public policy on many of the most important issues of our time relating to the intersection of corporations and society. That potential can be seen in the progress that these movements have made in such areas as corporate labor practices in supply chains and the availability of organic food and fair-trade products. However, the ability of investing and consuming to produce fundamental, systemic change in the management of corporations and the societal benefit of products they offer has yet to be fully realized.

Patterns of Use

Both responsible investing and ethical purchasing are increasingly used worldwide to effect change, and saw dramatic upticks in the 1990s and 2000s in areas such as microfinance, organic and local food, and corporate social responsibility reporting.

Since the emergence of responsible investment in its modern form in the United States in the early 1970s, this discipline has evolved within the mainstream financial community from a quaint curiosity, or an object of outright hostility, to a practice that enjoys considerable credibility among many institutional investors around the world.

Prior to 1970, various religious organizations refused to invest in so-called sin stocks—primarily those associated with tobacco, gambling, and alcohol. But the burgeoning social concerns and activism of the late 1960s relating to issues such as militarism, the environment, and civil rights brought a new breed of socially responsible investors to the fore. Saul Alinsky's civil rights group FIGHT crashed the Eastman Kodak annual meeting in Flemington, New Jersey, in 1967. Ralph Nader's Campaign GM filed one of the first shareholder resolutions on social issues in 1970 demanding greater diversity on GM's board of directors. This period also witnessed the founding of the first socially responsible investment (SRI) mutual funds—for example, Pax World Fund founded by Methodist ministers with an antiwar focus. Throughout the 1970s, the filing of shareholder resolutions, often by religious organizations working through the Interfaith Center on Corporate Responsibility, was the most prominent—and frequently confrontational—manifestation of responsible investment.[11]

The 1980s saw the responsible investment movement take root in the United Kingdom,[12] grow in size and scope in the United States as more SRI funds were established, and gain a degree of legitimacy among institutional investors as reflected in the South Africa divestment movement. By the late 1980s, pension funds of scores of states and cities across the United States—including those of the states of Massachusetts, New York, New Jersey, and Wisconsin and the cities of Los Angeles, San Francisco, and New York—with hundreds of billions of dollars in assets had divested fully or partially of investments in companies with ties to South Africa. In the 1990s, responsible investment became truly international with the strong entry of European investors and the introduction of the vocabulary of "sustainability" into the market. Ten years into the twenty-first century, responsible investment has now spread to Asia and the Islamic world and established itself as a viable option for some of the world's largest institutional investors. Major insurance and money management firms in Europe, including F&C Investments and Aviva in the United Kingdom, Robeco and SNS REAAL in the Netherlands, and Société Générale in France, among others, made substantial commitments to responsible investment.[13] Emblematic of its current status is the emergence of the UN Principles for Responsible Investment. Launched in 2006 with the mission of integrating environmental, social, and governance issues into investments across all asset classes, by 2011 the PRI had attracted endorsements from some 230 pension funds and others with over $25 trillion under management around the world.[14]

As of 2010, some $3 trillion in assets were estimated to be managed under one form or another of responsible investment strategies in the United States.[15] The comparable figure for responsible investment assets under management in Europe in 2009 was €5 trillion.[16] Some of the largest pension funds in the world, such as those of Norway and France, along with pension fund managers such as APG and PGGM in the Netherlands and Hermes in the United Kingdom, have imposed social and environmental screens on their stocks, taken up engagement with corporate managers, and increasingly applied responsible investment principles to their investments in other asset classes.[17] In addition, other responsible investment innovations around products such as microfinance have become widely implemented around the world.

By 2009, some 3,300 corporations worldwide had taken up the practice of publishing corporate social responsibility reports—up from approximately 25 in 1992.[18] At that time the governments of France and Sweden had effectively mandated the publication by major corporations of CSR data along with their financial statements, and socially responsible or environmental stock indexes were offered on a number of worldwide stock exchanges including the Johannesburg Stock Exchange and Brazil's BM&F Bovespa.

Ethical purchasing has its roots in the nineteenth century but has also increased substantially in recent years.[19] Indeed, some writers see the current individual ethical purchasing movement as another wave of consumer activism, following in the footsteps of the Industrial Revolution era's human and labor rights movement and the 1930s consumer protection movement following the Great Depression.[20]

In the first decade of the twenty-first century, the highest proportion of ethical consumption took place primarily in developed countries. The UK's Cooperative Bank has reported that the market for ethical products by individual consumers in the country nearly tripled in under 10 years from £13.5 billion in 1999 to £36 billion in 2008. The areas of strongest growth have been in fair-trade-certified products, ethical food and drink, green home-related expenditure, and ethical finance.[21]

In 2007, the global market for organic food and beverages was estimated at $23 billion, more than doubling since 2002. In 2007, food and beverage sales in the United States made up 82 percent of total retail sales of ethical products, compared to 41 percent in the UK.[22] In that same year, organic personal care product sales in the United States totaled $9 billion, making up 15 percent of the entire personal care market.[23] Green building, energy efficient products, and green household cleaners are also growing in market share.

Product sustainability labels, a major component of sustainable consumption, have increased substantially. Thousands of product labels exist worldwide—some for particular product lines, some for particular issues, and they can be specific and rigorous or broad and lax. New organizations are being created constantly to address perceived holes in the information marketplace, but concerted efforts to coordinate among the often disjointed and overlapping existing labels are largely lacking. As of 2010, efforts to provide consumers with easily accessible information on the ethical attributes of products were moving from physical books like the *Shopping for a Better World* guide to social media and networking applications such as GoodGuide.

The adoption of ethical and sustainable consumption practices in business-to-business transactions has become a part of the wider movement of corporate social responsibility. Because ethical consumers have increasingly placed the responsibility for the sustainability of every process and activity leading to the sale of a product on the corporation distributing the product, corporations have been forced to evaluate and improve (when necessary) the policies and practices of their extended supply chains, requiring them to make additional expenditures and human resource commitments in order to create and enforce ethical codes of conduct.

Ethical sourcing has evolved differently in different regions. Japanese and European corporations have been relatively quick to pick up on the importance of ethical supply chain management. In general, US corporations have been slower to move, most often only at the behest of consumers and the threat of lost business.[24] In addition, US companies are more likely to see CSR as philanthropy and an aspect of corporate governance, while European and Japanese companies tend to take a more fundamental and holistic approach, applying corporate social responsibility tenets throughout their entire business.

Government procurement has also come to be used increasingly as a policy tool, though there are deep historical roots in government's use of procurement to promote societal goals such as employment for disabled soldiers, support for local businesses, fair wages, and status equality through preferential treatment for minority- and women-owned businesses.[25] Although the use of procurement policies to support particular social or environmental goals is relatively common in most governments, some rely on this tactic more than others. European countries, Japan, South Africa, Malaysia, and the United States have been particularly noted for their use of this tool. In recent years, climate change has received top billing on the international agenda, and many countries have implemented green procurement requirements, including Japan and the United States (Executive Order 13101 under President Clinton). Also notable are local initiatives on labor issues such as San Francisco's antisweatshop procurement policy, a policy that nine states, 41 cities, and 15 counties in the United States had adopted variations of as of January 2010.[26]

While the growth of responsible investing and purchasing has been impressive, it is important to put this growth into context, particularly in the wake of the financial and economic crisis of 2007–2011, which saw a decline in ethical purchases as purchasing power decreased and showed that the dominant forces in the financial community remained subject to abusive and societally detrimental investment practices. Although responsible investment can claim some substantive accomplishments, fundamental and systemic change in the financial community remains to be achieved. Similarly, while the growth of the organic food and beverage market has been impressive, it still represents less than 1 percent of the global retail food market, which was estimated in 2009 at about $4 trillion.[27] Observers of responsible purchasing have identified what they call the "30:3 syndrome," that is, the frequently observed fact that 30 percent of consumers profess to have ethical purchasing intentions while only 3 percent of purchases are in fact of ethical products.[28]

One of the biggest unresolved questions is whether substantial numbers of consumers in the major developing countries—Brazil, Russia, India, and China—will make ethical considerations part of their purchasing decisions.

Tool Selection

The basic premise of the responsible investing and purchasing tool is that all investments and purchases have societal and environmental implications that need to be taken into account. What is more, this tool offers the potential of especially cost-effective change—that is, by changing the behavior of the firms that produce negative societal and environmental consequences, and thereby reducing such consequences at their source rather than intervening later to offset their negative impacts.

This approach has gained added momentum in recent years as various trends are increasing the receptivity of corporations to the kinds of pressures that responsible investing and purchasing bring to bear. These include the globalization of markets, the rise of transnational corporations, rise of single-issue pressure groups, technological advances that make it harder to shield improper corporate practices from view, market power shifts towards consumers, effective marketing campaigns, and the larger corporate accountability movement—all of which have made corporations increasingly vulnerable and heightened their concerns about their "reputational capital."[29] This has coincided with the globalization of finance, the growing recognition of corporations' worldwide influence, dissatisfaction with short-termism in the financial markets, and a greater understanding of the societal and environmental impacts implicit in investment decision-making. All the forms of ethical consumption and investing have been shaped by these trends, and the increase in ethical consumption has increased the availability of ethical products and in turn broadened awareness of ethical concerns.

Particularly important for responsible investment's growth and increasing legitimacy has been the support of governments—and especially European governments—for the concept. In one sense, responsible investment—and its sister concept of corporate social responsibility (CSR)—can be seen from a European point of view as a form of soft regulation taken up by governments there as a means of indirectly directing corporations previously owned by the government toward the public good.

What form responsible investing and purchasing takes, however, depends on a number of factors. For responsible investors, it depends on whether the investor is an individual or an institution, whether the investor is experienced and comfortable with responsible investment techniques, whether and how deep the investor's concern runs on a particular issue, and whether the governmental or regulatory structures within which the investor is operating support responsible investment.

The primary impediment to responsible investment for individual investors is the fact that it takes knowledge, experience, and time to either select stocks or other investments according to social and environmental criteria and to engage with corporations or other purveyors of investment products to promote specific change. As a consequence, retail investors tend to work through intermediaries—publicly traded mutual funds with SRI screens—or, in the case of high-net-worth individuals, through private banks or money managers who offer customized responsible investment services.

Individual or retail investors also tend to care more about standard setting than engagement, since selection of stocks is a direct expression of their beliefs, while their voice is relatively small and consequently weak through the vehicle of direct engagement. Intermediaries such as mutual funds have the ability to bring expertise in standard setting and the pooling of assets for engagement to the table. In choosing to use these intermediaries, however, investors are dependent on the intermediaries' decisions on standards and choice of engagement campaigns.

For institutional investors entering the responsible investment field, engagement, as opposed to screening, is an attractive first step. Because no restrictions need be placed on investment choices, it sidesteps the question of whether standard setting will hurt financial performance.

For institutional investors with an explicit social-purpose mission such as foundations, environmental or community organizations, academic institutions, or hospitals, the more explicit their mission, the more likely the institution is to adopt responsible investment techniques. The deeper specific social or environmental concerns run for responsible investors, the more likely they are to want "not to profit from" a particular activity, which will push them toward standard setting. An animal rights organization, for example, is likely to want to screen out pharmaceutical companies that test on animals rather than simply to engage with them on the issue. Finally, institutional investors are likely to adopt responsible investment when government explicitly or implicitly endorses the concept. The entry of the $400 billion Norwegian national pension fund into the responsible investment sphere—it is now a leading responsible investor among pension funds—was initially prompted by an act of that country's parliament. Some of the largest money management companies in the United Kingdom—Aviva and F&C Asset Management, for example—strongly committed themselves to the field at a time when Tony Blair's government was strongly promoting the concept of corporate social responsibility.

Whether or not ethical purchasing is a useful and constructive tool also depends on a variety of factors. Perhaps the most important of these is the specific environment in which the purchases are made. One facet of this is the nature and size of the company that is making the product, and its predisposition to stakeholder and sustainability concerns. Also important are the presence of an activism campaign against the company, the frequency and volume of the purchases, and the amount of related publicity, among other factors.

For individual consumers, the success of responsible purchasing is heavily dependent on the engagement of other individual consumers. With hundreds of billions of dollars of products being sold every year, one person's decision to buy only 100 percent organic cotton apparel is likely to be subsumed in the sheer volume of purchases. If a group of consumers are all making the same decision and voicing their reasons for doing so publicly, it is more likely that corporations will pay attention. Ethical purchasing thus gains momentum through increased participation. The situation differs for government purchasers. As large volume purchasers, they have the potential to make markets for ethical goods by increasing demand substantially and engaging with contracted suppliers. For governments, as for individuals, price also often matters. A slight price premium for an ethical product multiplied across huge orders can make the cost differential substantial. Government procurement is effectively a form of soft regulation with less impact than that of a tool such as legislation. Still, government procurement can shape demand for products and implicitly promote policies that might be difficult to pass through legislature.

For corporate consumers, unlike government procurers or individuals, the costs of not engaging in ethical purchasing can be high, in terms of both risk and reputation management.[30]

Companies with highly visible brand names in labor-intensive industries such as apparel, footwear, toys, and sports equipment have been often targeted by activists and negatively affected by refusal to engage in ethical contracting.[31] The challenges of ethical purchasing and the threat of damaged reputations vary by industry, but the benefits of adopting ethical purchasing codes and supply chain management policies are relevant across all sectors.[32] Corporations' decisions on how to respond to ethical consumer campaigns are not always simple. For example, a company criticized for contracting with a supplier with poor labor policies may have concerns about cutting off its contract entirely and depriving the entire workforce of jobs. Instead, it may decide to engage with the supplier, hoping to improve its practices while continuing to face criticism.

Basic Mechanics

Responsible investing and purchasing both involve two broad sets of activities: first, the development of standards against which investing and purchasing decisions can be made; and second, the choice of implementing approach for applying these standards. The discussion below outlines these two broad sets of activities and the variations each can entail.

Standard Setting

Both responsible investing and purchasing begin with the articulation of standards against which investment and purchasing decisions can be made. Standard setting for responsible investors, for example, can be done before, after, or simultaneously with financial analysis and stock selection. Several types of standards can be employed in responsible investing. These include (*a*) the best-of-class approach; (*b*) the setting of absolute standards; and (*c*) decisions based on overall assessments or judgment.

Best-of-class standards divide investment opportunities into peer groups, score them on a broad range of sustainability factors, rank them, and then select for investment the highest scoring from each peer group—in the case of stock selection, this would mean the highest ranking corporations from each industry. The Switzerland-based SAM Group, for example, uses a best-of-class approach in creating the Dow Jones Sustainability Index, selecting the companies that score in the top 10 percent for their industry based on a variety of economic, environmental, and social sustainability indicators.[33]

By contrast, the FTSE4Good Indexes, working with the UK-based research firm EIRIS, sets *absolute standards* in such areas as the environment and human rights that all companies must meet in order to be included in their sustainability indexes. Unless a company passes that particular threshold, it is not eligible for investment, no matter what its industry.

A more broad-based approach that relies more on *judgment* than scores or specific thresholds is taken by other responsible investors, such as Domini Social Investments in the United States. Here, consideration is given to a combination of the strength of a company's stakeholder relations—that is, with employees, customers, suppliers, communities, and the environment—and the alignment of a company's business model with the creation of a just and sustainable society. An overall judgment is then formed on the appropriateness of the investment opportunity, with some industries excluded entirely, and others either underweighted or overweighted depending on their business alignment and the strength of specific companies' stakeholder relations.[34]

Individual consumers who engage in ethical purchasing tend to be holistic in their conception and application of ethics to what they buy, although many choose to focus on a single issue, such as child labor or organic agriculture. For many governments, ethical procurement is done on an issue-by-issue basis—for example, favoring environmentally friendly products or giving preference to minority-owned businesses. Instead of taking a holistic view of a supplier, governments tend to focus on specific issues that they consider to be of particular importance and suited for advancement via purchasing decisions. In their responsible purchasing programs, corporations may set their own ethical standards, but tend also to be responsive to the opinions of their stakeholders.

A variety of product labels, each of which has its own standards, assists responsible purchasers in the standard-setting process. A consumer may pick a product based on its label—that is, USDA organic, dolphin safe, FSC certified—which informs the consumer that the product has met a certain standard.

Implementing Standards

Once standards are set for responsible investment or purchasing decisions, several options are available for applying them.

Screening

One such option is screening, which involves either positive or negative decisions to invest in or purchase, or avoid investing in or purchasing, particular firms or products.

In responsible investment, one procedure is for researchers skilled in the application of social and environmental standards to review a large universe of stocks or other prospective investments against a set of criteria, separating out those that pass from those that fail. A list of qualified investments is then passed on to financial professionals who determine the relative attractiveness of the potential investments based solely on price. Conversely, financial experts can, according to their investment discipline and the financial goals of the investment product, select a list of qualifying investments that are then screened by experts in social and environmental standards. A third approach, favored by an increasing number of institutional investors and organizations, such as the Principles for Responsible Investment, involves a single investment professional, or team of professionals, combining both social and financial expertise and selecting investments by incorporating all factors simultaneously into their assessment of the attractiveness of an investment's current price. All three approaches are used within the financial world today.

As with responsible investing, responsible purchasing screens can be applied either positively—to buy a product—or negatively—not to buy a product or service. The latter can be called a boycott if done intentionally by groups of consumers.[35] For individuals, the application of screens manifests itself in daily decisions made at the supermarket or in stores. For corporations and governments, which purchase large quantities of products frequently, ethical purchasing depends on corporate contracts with suppliers and government procurement policies.

Individual consumer purchasing is a particularly visible manifestation of ethical purchasing. Individual ethical consumers are often motivated by issues of global reach, respond to the calls of single-issue activist organizations, and focus on highly recognizable corporate brand names such as Nike or Kimberly-Clark.[36] Most often, individual ethical purchasing focuses on everyday products such as groceries and paper towels where the environmental or social returns are easily identifiable and cost differential is minimal, rather than large infrequent purchases.[37]

Individual ethical purchasing is also facilitated when products display trusted, detailed information such as EnergyStar-certified appliances, which are endorsed by the Environmental Protection Agency, commonly available in stores, and visibly marked with the well-publicized EnergyStar label.

Corporate social responsibility ratings, reports, and product labels have attempted to make the identification process easier for consumers. However, the proliferation of these labels and reports can flood the market with so much information that it becomes difficult to identify what is most relevant and can increase confusion about which information to trust.

Ethical corporate purchasing is primarily accomplished through the use of supplier or vendor ratings, rankings, or requirements. Globalization and the growing use of external suppliers has shaped the development of ethical purchasing by corporations in that corporations no longer have direct control over every aspect of their supply chain. Consumer activism that holds retailers responsible for the actions of their third-party suppliers has forced corporations to include the creation of an "ethical supply chain" in their more broadly defined corporate social responsibility efforts.[38] As corporations often have long-term relationships with their suppliers, corporations engaging in ethical procurement will often rely on vendors to adhere to a company-created code of conduct written into contracts. Companies may or may not monitor compliance, and even those that do generally do not have, or provide for, the resources that allow for effective auditing of all suppliers. Corporate ethical purchasing is also a way of driving CSR down to smaller companies, encouraging the proliferation of ethical behavior. This extension of CSR can have a profound impact globally by improving the performance of a wide range of businesses.

Government ethical procurement is primarily dependent on procurement policies, subject to executive orders, top-down decision-making, and contracting requirements. Government procurement has generally not been a target of activism, as such activity is a slow, indirect, and often undetected route towards aligning corporate behavior with the principles of a just and sustainable society.

Engagement

The second mechanism through which responsible investing and purchasing is implemented is *engagement*. In the purchasing arena, consumers have relatively few convenient opportunities for communicating with specific companies on their individual purchasing decisions. However, when acting together in the form of formal boycotts against particular companies, products, or entire industries (for example the boycott of grapes in the 1970s to support the United Farm Workers), or conversely when acting informally together to support a type of product (for example, the trend toward purchasing of fair-trade coffee that began in the 1990s), their voice can be clearly heard. Grassroots campaigns around particular products or brands provoke public discussions about the role of products and corporations in society, and encourage public engagement regarding issues of sustainability.

In the responsible investing field several well-established mechanisms for engagement are available. Most directly, responsible investors can use their ownership of stock, and the voting rights that comes with it, to vote in support of, or opposition to, shareholder-sponsored resolutions on social and environmental issues for which stockowner votes are needed. Through this means, shareholders communicate effectively not only with corporate management, but with other shareholders in the corporation as well.

Responsible investors can also introduce their own resolutions on social and environmental issues for consideration at stockholder meetings. The regulatory framework in the United States and Canada makes the filing of shareholder resolutions easier than in other countries. In the United States, any shareholder who holds more than $2,000 in company stock for more than a year can file a resolution that will appear on the corporate proxy and be voted on by all shareholders. If companies contest the appropriateness of these resolutions (for example, asserting it is inappropriate because it is an item of ordinary business), the Securities and Exchange Commission rules on whether or not the company must include it. Filers must attend the company's annual meeting in person to present the resolution. Filing shareholder resolutions can be a time-consuming process. Many of the social and environmental resolutions filed each year are coordinated by groups such as the Interfaith Center on Corporate Responsibility and Ceres. Filers include faith-based organizations, public and private pension funds, foundations, unions, mutual funds, and concerned individuals, among others. Responsible investors file several hundred resolutions relating to the social and environmental conduct of US corporations each year, as well as an even greater number of resolutions related to the proper governance of these corporations.

The most frequent form of engagement, however, consists of less formal dialogue with corporations. This can run the gamut from simple and straightforward inquiries to clarify companies' policies or practices on an environmental issue to more complicated and politically challenging discussions on labor conditions at suppliers in emerging markets. Increasingly, responsible investors tend to communicate on complex issues in coalitions. Coalitions have the advantage of assuring the company of the widespread interest in the issue and of saving the company from having to deal with multiple investors on the same issue. For example the Carbon Disclosure Project is a coalition of some 475 institutional investors with assets of more than $50 trillion under management, which has been urging corporations to disclose their carbon footprint over the past several years.[39]

While standard setting and engagement can be viewed as alternative tactics, they can in fact be effectively used in tandem. As the economist Albert Hirschman has pointed out, a combination of voice (engagement) and exit (divestment or boycott) can be particularly effective. Either one used without keeping the other option open can lose its force. A shareholder's voice in engagement without the threat of divestment becomes weakened, but once shareholders have divested, they lose their ability to communicate directly with corporate management.[40]

Operational Challenges

Successful implementation of responsible investing and purchasing faces multiple challenges. Broadly speaking, they can be grouped under four headings.

Identifying Irresponsible Behavior or Products

Identifying corporations or products that can be clearly considered irresponsible or responsible is increasingly difficult. The multitude of individual products and the numerous social and environmental parameters on which they can be considered—not to mention the rapidity with which product content, production, and names can change—make for a potentially confusing landscape for the responsible consumer and investor. What is more, a company might be viewed as irresponsible overall, while one of its products is a top social and environmental performer in a particular category, or vice versa.

Demonstrating Effectiveness

Typically, neither responsible investing nor responsible purchasing can easily demonstrate a direct causal relationship between its actions and positive corporate change, nor can either measure the effectiveness of its initiatives through cost-benefit analyses. Measurements of effectiveness therefore must remain either anecdotal (for example, Gap began monitoring labor conditions at its overseas suppliers in response to stakeholder pressure and continues to involve these stakeholders in its monitoring activities) or general (for example, the number of corporate social responsibility reports issued by corporations has grown from virtually none in 1990 to over 4,000 in 2010 thanks in large part to pressure from the responsible investment community).

Lack of Coordination

Third, despite their similarities, responsible investing and purchasing remain largely separate strategies for influencing corporate behavior. Products subject to negative screens may be produced by companies approved by investors for their generally positive corporate performance, and vice versa. This can blur the influence of both approaches, confuse advocates, and provide grist for critics' mills.

Lack of Academic Recognition and Coherent Theory

Finally, neither responsible investing nor responsible purchasing has yet to be incorporated into academic training. One reason for this is that neither approach has yet formulated a coherent theory to guide its operations. By contrast, the world of contemporary finance has an elaborate theoretical framework within which it operates—generally known as modern portfolio theory (MPT). Although a number of the foundations on which MPT has been built, such as the efficient market hypothesis, have been severely shaken by the financial crises of 2007–2011, it is unlikely that responsible investment can make serious inroads into the financial community until it can offer an alternative theoretical framework of similar scope.

Track Record and Overall Assessment

Both responsible investing and responsible purchasing have attained a degree of acceptance in the decades from 1970 through 2010. Responsible investment, however, has not yet resulted in fundamental changes in the global financial industry, its products, or the rules by which investors play. Nor has responsible purchasing changed the drivers of the consumer marketplace, where price or style considerations continue to dominate, rather than considerations of social and environmental impact. Responsible investment was not able to prevent the global financial crisis of 2007–2011, one of the worst of the previous 70 years. Responsible consuming was not able to prevent an ever-expanding global epidemic of obesity or sharply rising greenhouse gas emissions during the first decade of the twenty-first century.

These two movements stand at a crossroads. Both have displayed a capability to encourage long-term thinking and heightened sensitivity to the environmental, health, and social consequences of economic activities and choices. Yet both are far from achieving dominance in their respective arenas.

Three ways forward are possible at this crucial juncture. Responsible investing and purchasing may simply fade away, once popular fads unable to alter mainstream behavior in either consuming or investing. Second, they may persist as niche markets, accepted as legitimate practices for distinct, but limited, numbers of investors and consumers. Finally, the mainstream could change, adopting the basic premise of the responsible investing and purchasing schools of thought—that all investments and purchases have societal and environmental implications that need to be taken into account.

For the third option to become a reality, much work needs to be done. Hopefully, the progress outlined here and the impediments to further progress also identified can point the way to such an outcome and help us achieve a world in which both consumers and investors realize the social and environmental implications of their decisions and act systematically on that knowledge.

Notes

1. Beth Young, Celine Suarez, and Kimberly Gladman, "Climate Risk Disclosure in SEC Filings," Ceres, June 2009, http://www.ceres.org/resources/reports/climate-r isk-disclosure-2009.

2. See Ceres press releases dated September 18, 2007, June 12, 2009, and January 27, 2010, available at http://www.ceres.org/press/press-releases.

3. For background on socially responsible investment, see Amy Domini, *Socially Responsible Investment: Making a Difference and Making Money* (Chicago: Dearborn Trade, 2000); and Amy Domini, Peter Kinder, and Steve Lydenberg, eds., *The Social Investment Almanac: A Comprehensive Guide to Socially Responsible Investing* (New York: Henry Holt, 1992).

4. Roger Cowe and Simon Williams, *Who Are the Ethical Consumers?* (London: Cooperative Bank, 2000), 4.

5. Meir Statman, "Socially Responsible Mutual Funds," *Financial Analysts Journal* 56.3 (May–June 2000): 30–39.

6. Joshua David Margolis and James Patrick Walsh, *People and Profits? The Search for a Link between a Company's Social and Financial Performance* (Hillsdale, NJ: Erlbaum, 2001), 10–11.

7. David Vogel, *The Market for Virtue: The Potential and Limits of Corporate Social Responsibility* (Washington, DC: Brookings Institution Press, 2005), 37.

8. "Dolphin-Safe Campaign," Greenpeace Foundation, accessed November 1, 2012, http://www.greenpeacefoundation.org/action/campInfo.cfm?campId=4.

9. "Social Responsibility: The Nike Story," Branding Strategy Insider, July 25, 2008, http://www.brandingstrategyinsider.com/2008/07/social-responsi.html.

10. See David Vogel, *Lobbying the Corporation* (New York: Basic Books, 1978) for an excellent account of the early days of shareholder activism and its effect on corporations.

11. For example, the Stewardship Funds was established during this period by the UK Society of Friends.

12. See Céline Louche and Steve Lydenberg, "Social Investing," in *Finance Ethics: Critical Issues in Theory and Practice*, ed. John Boatright (Hoboken, NJ John Wiley & Sons, 2010) for a detailed summary of the history and practice of responsible investment.

13. "About Us," UN Principles for Responsible Investment, accessed November 1, 2012, http://www.unpri.org/about/.

14. "Report on Socially Responsible Investing Trends in the United States, 2010," US SIF, accessed November 1, 2012, http://ussif.org/resources/pubs/trends/documents/2010TrendsES.pdf.

15. "European SRI Study 2010," Eurosif, accessed November 1, 2012, http://www.eurosif.org/research/eurosif-sri-study/2010.

16. "APG—Home," APG, accessed November 1, 2012, http://www.apg.nl/apgsite/pages/english/; "About PGGM," accessed November 1, 2012, http://www.pggm.nl/about_pggm/; "Hermes—Home," Hermes, accessed November 1, 2012, http://www.hermes.co.uk/.

17. "Corporate Register," Corporate Register, accessed November 1, 2012, http://www.corporateregister.com/.

18. Pat Auger and Timothy M. Devinney, "Do What Consumers Say Matter? The Misalignment of Preferences with Unconstrained Ethical Intentions," *Journal of Business Ethics* 76 (2007): 362. See also Cowe and Williams, *Who Are the Ethical Consumers?*; Rob Harrison, "Pressure Groups, Campaigns and Consumers," in Harrison, *The Ethical Consumer*; Alex Nicholls and Charlotte Opal, *Fair Trade: Market-Driven Ethical Consumption* (London: Sage, 2004); Sean Sheehan, "Responsible Purchasing Network Trends 2009: The 'State' of Sustainable Procurement," Center for a New American Dream, accessed November 1, 2012, http://www.responsiblepurchasing.org/publications/trends2009_naspo.pdf.

19. Yiannis Gabriel and Tim Lang, *The Unmanageable Consumer: Contemporary Consumption and Its Fragmentation* (London: Sage, 2006).

20. *Ten Years of Ethical Consumerism: 1999–2008* (London: Co-operative Bank, 2009).

21. "Ethical Consumers and Corporate Responsibilities," January 2007, quoted in Emma Conroy, "Conscientious Consumerism Pushes Sales of Ethical Products to an All-Time High," ReportBuyer, May 23, 2007, http://www.reportbuyer.com/blog/conscientious-consumerism-pushes-sales-of-ethical-products-to-an-all-time-high/; "Ethical Consumerism Report 2008," Co-operative Bank, 2008, accessed November 1, 2012, http://www.goodwithmoney.co.uk/assets/Uploads/Documents/ECR_2008_Web.pdf.

22. "OASIS Seal—Home," OASIS, accessed November 1, 2012, www.oasisseal.org.

23. Dale Neef, *The Supply Chain Imperative* (New York: AMACOM, 2004), 7.

24. Christopher McCrudden, *Buying Social Justice* (Oxford: Oxford University Press, 2007).

25. "Policy List," Sweat Free, accessed November 1, 2012, http://www.sweatfree.org/policieslist.

26. "Global Food Markets: Global Food Industry Structure," USDA Economic Research Service, accessed November 1, 2012, http://www.ers.usda.gov/Briefing/GlobalFoodMarkets/Industry.htm.

27. Cowe and Williams, *Who Are the Ethical Consumers?* 5.

28. Neef, *The Supply Chain Imperative*, 6.

29. Harrison, *The Ethical Consumer*, 56.

30. Virginia Haufler, *Public Role for the Private Sector: Industry Self-Regulation in a Global Economy* (Washington, DC: Carnegie Endowment for International Peace, 2001), 58.

31. Michael J. Maloni and Michael E. Brown, "Corporate Social Responsibility in the Supply Chain: An Application in the Food Industry," *Journal of Business Ethics* 68.1 (2006): 35.

32. "Dow Jones Sustainability Indexes," Down Jones with SAM, accessed November 1, 2012, http://www.sustainability-index.com/.

33. "FTSE4Good Index Series," FTSE, accessed November 1, 2012, http://www.ftse.com/Indices/FTSE4Good_Index_Series/index.jsp

34. "Domini—Home," Domini Social Investments, accessed November 1, 2012, http://domini.com/.

35. Harrison, *The Ethical Consumer*, 102.

36. Harrison, *The Ethical Consumer*, 56.

37. Allen White, "Consumption, Commerce and Citizenship: Transforming Markets to Drive Sustainability," *People 4 Earth*, September 2009, 12–13; "Finding the Green in Today's Shoppers," Deloitte and the Grocery Manufacturers Association, accessed November 1, 2012, http://www.deloitte.com/dtt/cda/doc/content/US_CP_GMADeloitteGreenShopperStudy_2009.pdf.

38. Neef, *The Supply Chain Imperative*, 4.

39. "Carbon Disclosure Project—Home," Carbon Disclosure Project, accessed November 1, 2012, https://www.cdproject.net/en-US/Pages/HomePage.aspx. See also *Building Sustainable Communities through Multi-party Collaboration* (New York: Interfaith Center on Corporate Responsibility, 2011) for an extensive discussion of how dialogue and coalitions can lead to collaborative initiatives between corporations and stakeholders.

40. Albert Hirschman, *Exit, Voice and Loyalty: Responses to Decline in Firms, Organizations, and States* (Cambridge: Harvard University Press, 1970).

Suggested Readings

Harrison, Rob, Terry Newholm, and Deirdre Shaw, eds. *The Ethical Consumer.* London: Sage Publications, 2005.

Louche, Celine, and Steve Lydenberg. *Dilemmas in Responsible Investment.* Sheffield: Greenleaf Publishing, 2011.

CHAPTER 19

NEW FORMS OF GRANTMAKING: COMPETITIONS, PRIZES, AND CROWD SOURCING

Peter Frumkin

PEPSI LAUNCHED ITS "REFRESH" CAMPAIGN when it decided that there might be a better use for the $20 million it spends each year on Super Bowl advertising.[1] Trying something new, Pepsi launched a campaign that invited nonprofit organizations of all shapes and sizes to present an idea for funding. Unlike normal corporate grantmaking, the decider would not be a distribution committee or a foundation director. Instead, Pepsi left the decision to the public. Its web-based competition gives the public the final say in who gets the money and challenges nonprofits to mobilize their communities in support of their grant requests. Pepsi Refresh is a competition that is open when it comes to the topic of the idea or innovation that can be entered into the competition, though it does spell out six very broad categories ranging from health to arts to the planet. Pepsi created a toolkit to help applicants navigate the process. It contains tips on turning an idea into a reality. It encourages nonprofit leaders and entrepreneurs to consult with their local communities to understand what might be particularly useful and timely. Awards range from as little as $5,000 all the way up to $250,000, and can go to aspiring social entrepreneurs, small organizations, or large established nonprofits.

The Pepsi process starts each month, with submissions accepted during the first two weeks or until 1,000 ideas are submitted, whichever comes first. Submissions are screened by the staff to ensure they are legal and safe, and approved projects are then posted and are ready to be voted on for a month. Pepsi describes its goals as follows: "We're looking for projects that are beneficial, achievable, constructive, and 'shovel-ready' (meaning it can be finished within 12 months of funding)."[2] The competition is designed to harness the wisdom of communities and also to encourage social networking, as organizations spread the word about their projects when seeking to mobilize votes.

Pepsi's model is not unique. Each year, new competitions, challenges, and prizes are announced as the search for talent and innovation continues. In this chapter, we review the rise of open, participatory, competition-based philanthropy aimed at identifying and rewarding a small number of winners. The use of challenges is one of a number of important innovations increasingly making their appearance in the field of grantmaking. While the basic practice of grantmaking remains intact in thousands of private foundations, new entrants to the field of philanthropy, including especially individual donors and corporations, are experimenting with new ways of transacting philanthropy. What all of the innovative uses of grants share in common is an intention to *leverage* philanthropic resources. When trying to go beyond traditional grantmaking, the goal is almost always to find ways to maximize social impact through process innovation in philanthropy. Over time, funders have tried a series of smaller, more tactical moves designed to increase the impact of their work.[3] These developments, including the use of matching grants, pilot project grants, and other variants to traditional charitable gifts, represent incremental changes within grantmaking. They are made with the goal of ratcheting up performance, sustainability, and accountability within the field through a more strategic approach to funding. Several of these, such as high-engagement grantmaking and the use of grants as credit enhancements for loans and bonds by foundations acting as "philanthropic banks," are treated elsewhere in this volume.[4] In this chapter we focus on competitions, prizes, and crowd-sourcing efforts. After defining the core innovation in these new practices, we compare and contrast them to the more common grantmaking tactics that the field has seen in recent decades.

Defining the Tool

Competitions, prizes, and crowd sourcing are a breath of fresh air in the world of grants. These tools differ in several important ways from traditional grants. Grants are gifts of money in support of organizations and programs, and often are the end result of a multistage grantmaking process that begins with an inquiry and ends when successful with decision to provide support. Grants have been around for a very long time, and there is nothing particularly new about them, at least in terms of the way they are most commonly practiced today. While there have been some modifications to the grantmaking process and in the underlying tactics used by donors to get impact, the end product remains a cash transfer from donor to recipient. The use of philanthropic competitions and challenges and the tapping of the wisdom of the crowd in selecting grantees introduces a new, more open dynamic to philanthropy and also changes giving from a transaction based on a promise to do good work to one more based on participation, decentralized decision-making, peer benchmarking, and the delivery of proven results.

Defining Features

Grants made as a result of competitions are different from traditional grants in several significant ways. First, competitions tend to be *open* to anyone and seek to maximize *participation*. Many foundation grantmakers set up barriers to applying for grants in the form of strict guidelines and the need for the preliminary submission of a letter of inquiry. In fact, competitions seek to break down these institutional barriers and focus on the "top of the funnel," not the bottom. This means that competitions are interested in drawing in as many applicants as possible and *democratizing* the grants process by making it transparent and open. A McKinsey report on the rise of prizes noted: "A core power of prizes derives from their openness: their ability to attract diverse talent, generate unexpected approaches, and reveal unusual perspectives in the face of a problem or challenge."[5]

Competitions tend to be clearer about selection criteria than traditional grantmakers. In most of the supporting materials around competitions there is almost always a statement of the judging criteria (and often a scoring rubric for entries), who the judges will be, and how the whole process will unfold. This is markedly different from the often opaque ways of foundation grantmakers, where the proposal review standards are rarely stated clearly and the relative control over the grantmaking decision—often split between staff and board—can be a source of confusion and frustration for applicants who hear one thing during a site visit and quite another in the letter that arrives from the funder months later.

The *speed* of competition also differentiates this as a tool for grantmaking. There are deadlines and time frames around almost all the competitions. This means that grants will be made on a specific date no matter what. In traditional institutional philanthropy, while there are board meetings and deadlines associated with getting a grant considered at any given board meeting, there is nothing to stop a foundation from pushing a proposal back from one meeting to another. Sometimes the docket is full, while in other instances questions that require clarification will push an application from one board meeting to the next. With competitions, the *deadline* drives the process forward and toward a date-defined conclusion.

Competitions also implicitly embrace the idea that there is a market of ideas and programs and that drawing attention to a problem—and the need for a solution—is inherently valuable and likely to expand the number of entrants into the marketplace of solutions. The McKinsey report observed: "Prizes attract diverse groups of experts, practitioners, and laypeople—regardless of formal credentials—to attempt to solve difficult problems, dramatically expanding the pool of potential solvers and lower the cost of attempting or recognizing solutions."[6]

Unlike traditional grantmaking, which focuses on getting funds to worthy organizations to do valuable community work, competitions are typically interested in something broader: drawing attention to an issue and highlighting the work of s small number of innovators and change-makers. In this sense, competitions are more public than old-school grantmaking in that the competition is the subject of advertising and public relations campaigns, and the winner is also celebrated at the end of the selection process. The McKinsey report commented on this fact: "Well designed prizes carry a strong element of theater that makes them newsworthy and media friendly. This messaging and brand-building potential is attractive to corporations looking to burnish their image or wealthy donors seeking to signal their arrival."[7] The report also noted that leverage can be the end result of this kind of publicity, leading others to consider working on a problem or funding a solution: "Prizes highlight and elevate superlative behaviors, ideas, and achievements in order to motivate, guide, and inspire others. Identifying excellence remains the cornerstone of many prizes—the essence of their power to produce change."[8]

Design Features and Major Variants

While all competitions embody these central features, not all uses of the competition form of grantmaking are identical. To the contrary, competitions are like ink blot tests in that they have been interpreted many different ways in terms of their intended impact. Indeed, among activities that embody competitions, several different variants can be distinguished. Two of the most salient of these are *prizes* and *crowd sourcing*.

Prizes

While they share much in common, there is a difference in method between competitions and prizes. Competitions start out challenging a field to come up with a solution to a public problem or to prove an effectiveness advantage in comparison with other organizations. Prizes, on the other hand, usually do not seek out new approaches but rather reward efforts already made by individuals and organizations. From the Field Medal in Mathematics to the Pulitzer Prizes to the Nobel Peace Prize, the underlying model is simple and straightforward. In order to identify, draw attention to, and encourage excellence in mathematics, writing, and humanitarianism, the three prizes mentioned here all seek to find the best work being done by individuals around the world. Those who are nominated for prizes may send in samples of their work or resumes, but most often they do nothing but wait for a decision from the jury. In contrast to challenges and competitions where there is pressure, prizes are fundamentally closed processes designed to reward and affirm the importance of particular contributions within a well-defined domain. While there are some prizes like the MacArthur Prize Fellowships, which are awarded based on creativity and which are agnostic as to field, most prizes try to direct attention to what constitutes excellence and lasting contributions within domains.[9]

Crowd Sourcing

Crowd sourcing is also a small variation on the competition model. It is an approach to problem-solving that seeks to harness the wisdom of the masses and to direct it toward the completion of specific tasks. Sometimes using social networks to spread the word, crowd sourcing represents an attempt to spread the word of a problem that needs to be solved and then to sort through all responses while looking for insights and usable knowledge. In the business world, Eli Lily and DuPont have used crowd sourcing to solve complex engineering problems, while Netflix has used it to improve the algorithm behind its system of recommending movies based on members' past selections.

One challenge to this model is that it can appear exploitative in that cash prizes are not always waiting at the end of the process. The masses are encouraged to step forward with solutions, but when they do, most receive nothing in return for the efforts the challenge has elicited. There are also concerns that this model of outsourcing innovation can lead to the diminishment of internal operational capacity, especially if an army of outsiders are being used to replace traditional decision-making processes within organizations.

When voting is included in the challenge process and the decision is actually put in the hands of the community, the competition process takes on an even more open and democratic feel. Not only is there an open invitation to solve a problem, but the most important decision of all—namely, who wins—is left in the hands of the community. This move resembles strangely enough an idea in grantmaking that had some popularity in the 1970s, when alternative funds tried to invert the power relationship between funders and recipients by having community members and nonprofit leaders make distribution decisions on behalf of these alternative funds.[10] By abdicating from the role of grantee selection and by placing the most important decision in the hands of the public, competitions with a voting component are thumbing their nose at the philanthropic profession and taking the decision out of the hands of trained foundation experts.

Voting is different from seeking community input or seeking input through the use of advisory bodies. The entire grantmaking decision is put in the hands of the voting public in some challenges, and entrants then seek to mobilize support through the use of social media. The main reason why competitions consider giving up all this power and placing it in the hands of the public lies in the fact that often the solution of the problem at hand may not be known and not the subject of expert review. In such cases, there is a belief that the masses may actually possess some collective wisdom when it comes to recognizing a social innovation or solution to a public problem.

Relation to Common Criteria

How do grants used for competitions, prizes, and crowd sourcing compare to the other "new tools" of philanthropy and social investing examined in this book? Let us look at some of the common criteria for judging these tools.

Risk

Prizes and competitions are not without risks. One of the most obvious risks associated with running a competition with a defined prize or award is that money must be given away whether or not a compelling solution has been proposed. One way to mitigate this risk is to have a range of prizes ranging from small to medium to large in order to allow for some discretion in matching the award to the merit of the proposal. Still, competitions commit a funder to making an award before seeing the applicant pool.

Another risk is related to publicity. Since competitions are high profile and can attract considerable media attention, at least compared to traditional foundation grantmaking, there is some risk that foolish and controversial solutions may be presented for consideration, and that winners may or may not deliver down the road on their promises. And while regular grant recipients often do fail, they tend to do so quietly. Not so with the winners of major competitions, where the media has been engaged before and during the selection process. Once the award is made the media will want to know what happened to the award funds and whether the pathbreaking idea or program bore fruit.

Another common concern about fairness and avoiding corruption arises when participation and voting become part of the design of the grant competition. It is often hard to rule out the possibility that multiple votes will be cast through electronic means by individuals or groups of persons working in concert. While many of the online voting systems have protections against ballot box stuffing, there is always a risk that the system will be compromised by a diligent cheater. This is a major risk because it not only undermines the openness and transparency claim of a competition but also casts doubt on the wisdom of the entire idea of seeking the wisdom of the masses. If the process of selecting winners appears compromised, the legitimacy derived from democratic and participatory principles disappears quickly and cannot be recovered very easily in the future.

Level of Return and Leverage

The social return of competitions and prizes is not inherently different from that of traditional grants, though the abundant presence of media coverage may create some special opportunities. In addition, by virtue of their focus on new ideas and innovations, competitions and prizes tend to involve bets that have potentially large returns—if the innovation actually works and if it can be brought to scale through replication. Competitions may also generate large returns because the amount of money devoted to supporting winners is typically larger than the run-of-the-mill grant from a foundation.

Ubiquity

Competitions can and have been used to promote an extraordinarily broad array of purposes, from basic scientific research on the human genome all the way to solutions to inner-city poverty, and everything in between. Some competitions do not specify a field at all and simply call for breakthrough ideas no matter in what areas they might be. This very ubiquity may point up one of the drawbacks of competitions and prizes, however: while they represent a powerful vehicle for stretching the bounds of knowledge and action, they implicitly discredit or downplay ideas that have already been discovered but are going starved for funds because they lack the sparkle that inventing something new seems to hold. And there are plenty of these ideas around as well.

Skill Requirements

Managing successful competitions requires a different and broader skill set than the one needed to manage a traditional grantmaking process. The most obvious requirement is a knack for publicity and marketing. Without a good number of entries, competitions cannot succeed in the quest to broaden the range of solutions to a public problem. In foundations, not only is there little marketing of grant opportunities, there is often a sense that applications from not vetted organizations applying over the transom only create more rejections and paperwork. In competitions there is a sense in which the number of entries is a sign of success, at least when it comes to engaging the public and drawing attention to a problem. Not so with foundation grantmaking processes. Another skill that is useful in the context of designing and overseeing a grant competition is a comfort with technology. Most of the new breed of philanthropic competitions involve at a minimum online submissions and sometimes complex online voting systems. While some of these technical requirements can be contracted out, there is still a tendency for competitions and challenges to be technology-heavy in their execution, with the best ones having very sophisticated web presences.

Patterns of Use

The rise of competitions in the philanthropic sector has been steep and undeniable. From 1970 to 2010 the total value of prizes awarded over $100,000—which are a subset of competitions since they may or may not be open to submissions—has increased from under $30 million to over $300 million. The raw number of prizes has increased 15-fold over this period.[11] At the same time, the

sheer number of attempts to incentivize and promote the resolution of a specified problem has risen as well. The ubiquity of competitions has been driven by
the actions of many large companies, including Pepsi, Toyota, Dell, and others
that have set forward challenges and engaged the public directly. These competitions have been supported in some cases by major media buys and advertising
campaigns designed to bring attention to the opportunity. As a consequence of
this broad media exposure, the idea of competitions aimed at solving community and social problems is now widely known and understood as a way of pursuing social impact.

While competitions have become popular vehicles in the United States, their
use abroad appears less developed. In many countries in Europe and Latin
America, philanthropy may now be institutionalized and more sophisticated,
but the idea of turning over decision-making to the crowd remains a stretch.
Culturally, the idea of a jury of experts awarding prizes is an internationally
accepted practice ranging from the Balzan Prizes in the humanities and sciences in Switzerland to the Man Booker Prize in literature in Great Britain.
Competition is a more American inclination, but in Europe it is gaining trac-
tion in the form of new competitions like ones announced by Rolex Awards for
Enterprise and Schwab Foundation Social Entrepreneur of the Year
Competition.

Tool Selection

The fundamental rationale for the use of prizes and competitions derives from
their openness and consequent ability to attract diverse talent and stimulate
novel approaches to long-standing problems. They thus tap into a broader
market of ideas than is typically available through the grant process, where
knowledge of potentially available support is often not effectively communicated. More generally, the McKinsey report on prizes identified six main objectives that prizes are especially equipped to achieve, and these apply more
generally to the broader array of competitions under consideration here.[12]
Included are the following:

- *Focus attention on an issue.* Competitions can be used to focus attention
  on a social problem, a technological hurdle that needs to be overcome, or
  a major issue of the day that the public does not yet understand.
- *Highlight best practices.* Winners of competitions get attention, and
  this creates an opportunity to define best practices. In the nonprofit
  context, this is a powerful function since evidence of impact is often
  less than perfect and there are many different service models for every
  human problem imaginable.
- *Strengthen community.* Competitions have the capacity to build
  communities of practice and expertise by focusing energy and talent in
  one particular area for a sustained period of time. When they focus a
  practice community on a problem, competitions can breed new forms
  of social capital and cooperation.
- *Increase participation.* Sometimes a problem is neglected because it is
  too difficult to solve or because there is no natural funding constituency
  for it. This is where competitions can enter and stir up enthusiasm and
  engagement. By getting large numbers of people to take part in a

collective problem-solving exercise, increased participation can be a goal in itself that can have powerful spillover effects.

- *Stimulate a market.* Competitions can convert latent demand into real demand by creating markets and a race for a solution. While there may not be a market for cheap space flights, for example, a competition can draw out both producers and consumers and construct a new market.
- *Problem-solving through innovation.* One of the most frequent goals of competitions is the production of new ideas and social innovations. While there may be many existing ideas and programs already in existence, there is little doubt that innovation remains a powerful draw.

Basic Mechanics

Given the range and diversity of the application of grants for competitions, prizes, and crowd sourcing, no single set of steps can easily capture the operational mechanics of this type of grant use. A more useful approach might therefore be to sketch some recent examples to suggest the diverse ways in which various types of actors have deployed these basic types of grants. We therefore consider four additional competitions: one hosted by a newly formed private foundation, another by a foundation committed to finding solutions to pressing scientific challenges, a third developed by a car company focused on technology innovation, and a fourth pioneered by a foundation operating in more traditional fields of philanthropy.

Crowd Sourcing for Innovations

From $60 million in wealth created through biotech investing, a new small private foundation was formed recently in California. The foundation set out to find a small number of big, breakthrough ideas that it could support and thereby avoid the traditional model of a small family foundation where money is spread widely and thinly across many organizations. In short, it sought to uncover the next microcredit movement, a social innovation that could scale and have major impact around the world.

To accomplish this goal, the foundation thought about doing what many new foundations do, namely put out a call for proposals and wait and see what comes in the mail. Instead, the foundation partnered with InnoCentive, an organization that specializes in framing problems and then inviting people from around the world to propose solutions. Why believe an open competition might generate innovation? "Central to our process," says InnoCentive, "is challenge-based problem-solving, where diversity of thought yields better outcomes every time. More minds working on a problem increases the probability that winning solutions will be found and found quickly."[13] This was a philosophy that the foundation founder found credible enough to guide his first steps into the world of philanthropy.

The RFP that the foundation posted on the InnoCentive website began as follows:

Most philanthropic giving is structured around particular problems or issue areas. Consequently, initiatives that fall outside popular issue silos usually experience difficulties in attracting funding. In such a funding environment, researchers and practitioners are often limited in their ability to pursue unpopular innovations. The Seeker for this Challenge is a foundation that seeks to identify one or a few unorthodox philanthropic investments with the potential to generate extraordinary returns to society. The foundation is interested in concentrating its capital in opportunities that have little access to alternative sources of funding. The foundation believes that such opportunities, that are both extraordinary and devoid of funding, are exceedingly rare and, consequently, difficult to identify. By posting this Challenge, the Seeker hopes to unearth one or a few such extraordinary opportunities. The foundation may invest up to $100,000 initially, and a total of up to $1,000,000 in the very best ones.[14]

In laying out the criteria that would be used to judge the entries, the foundation identified four key requirements: (1) potential for a transformational impact on the lives of the world's most disadvantaged people; (2) improbability of attracting funding elsewhere due to its risky and unorthodox approach; (3) ability to attract funding after initial foundation investment; and (4) opportunity to fund something new that is not on philanthropy's list of usual suspects.

Beyond these four criteria, the foundation put no restrictions on the nature of the ideas it would consider, though it indicated that the funding of academic studies was not a priority nor was the production of "reports." Much more of interest was the support of "neglected areas of innovation, including neglected science." Given the donor's scientific bent, this was a reflection of his belief that "the return on investment to society from a scientific breakthrough, or from the emergence of an entirely new field of inquiry, can be extraordinary."[15]

With the call for innovation by this donor being very broad, the foundation wanted to set out some examples of projects to which it would have been glad to have been an early funder. It came up with three such examples:

- The conception and adoption of Oral Rehydration Therapy (ORT), a simple and cheap treatment for dehydration associated with diarrhea, especially where intravenous solutions are unavailable. The breakthrough resulted from the demonstration of an astonishing 90 percent reduction in mortality in 3,000 cholera patients in a Bangladeshi refugee camp in India in 1971. *The Lancet* described ORT as one of the most important medical advances of the twentieth century, saving millions of children's lives every year.
- The Commonwealth Fund's experimental research grant to Dr. Georgios Papanikolaou for the scientific proof of principle of the Pap smear cancer screen. This funding was unavailable elsewhere.
- The Aravind Eye Hospital in India invested $300,000 to develop a low-cost intraocular lens (IOL) for use in cataract surgeries. The price of IOLs was reduced from $50–$150 to $2, making it viable for millions of people.[16]

To apply for the award, the foundation asked for each "solver" to submit a two-to five-page proposal, including a description of the innovation, a case for why it is needed, an explanation of why other sources of funding are unlikely to be obtained, a profile of the people who are behind the innovation, and a budget. Not knowing what would come in through the challenge and whether any of the ideas would be worthy of major funding, the foundation noted that implementation funding was not guaranteed for any submissions. To ensure that solvers do not think that the net was simply being cast without the intention to actually make an award, especially given the high bar that was set, the funder promised a guaranteed award of $5,000 to be paid to the best submission with smaller prizes of $2,500 to two additional submissions. This competition was judged by the foundation's donor and his assistant, with no public input on the selection process.

Open Competition for Solutions to Concrete Challenges: The XPRIZE

As another example, in 1995, Peter Diamandis announced the XPRIZE and immediately got worldwide attention. The challenge was to design a private vehicle capable of flying a pilot to 100 kilometers in altitude or just to the edge of space. Competition entrants would need to launch a reusable manned spacecraft into space twice within two weeks to demonstrate that they had solved the challenge of making space flight accessible. The main rationale for the XPRIZE was to stimulate the formation of a private-sector space industry that would challenge the work of NASA and the government and show that spaceflight could be possible for private citizens and companies. By building up a private space industry, Diamandis hoped to eventually create a new form of space tourism that would broaden public participation in space exploration. The competition also sought to stimulate individuals to innovate and solve technical problems in a fresh way. To drive innovation, a prize of $10 million was offered.

The prize was claimed in 2004 by the Tier One project directed by Burt Rutan and financed by Microsoft cofounder Paul Allen, using an experimental aircraft called SpaceShipOne that looked like a hybrid between a rocket and plane. While Rutan and Allen claimed the prize money, they ended up investing more than $100 million in their spacecraft, demonstrating that the competition did indeed leverage private investment in the quest to meet the challenge set by the XPRIZE.[17]

Since this first challenge, the XPRIZE Foundation has gone on to design and operate other competitions and challenges. Because its challenges tend to be focused on solving a scientific or technical challenge, there is no voting within the competition about who deserves the prize. Once the challenge has been met and certified, the prize money is delivered without further deliberation or assessment. The process is described by the foundation as follows: "An X PRIZE is a $10 million+ award given to the first team to achieve a specific goal, set by the X PRIZE Foundation, which has the potential to benefit humanity. Rather than awarding money to honor past achievements or directly funding research, an X PRIZE incites innovation by tapping into our competitive and entrepreneurial spirits."[18] Subsequent XPRIZES have been offered for a car that gets 100 miles per gallon of gasoline, for faster and cheaper systems for human genone sequencing, and for breakthrough technology when it comes to oil spill cleanups. The X PRIZE Foundation has argued that its approach, with a tight focus on specific scientific challenges, is unique and powerful in the leverage that it creates: "There are many types of competitions and awards around the world, but an X PRIZE is in a class by itself. What sets us apart from other non-profit organizations is our ability to frame a challenge and incentivize a solution in a way that our efforts and funds are multiplied exponentially by the teams who strive to compete and win the prize"[19]

Stimulating Participation and Engagement

The Case Foundation has its own approach that focuses on the voting element and less on the competition aspect. Through its Make It Your Own Awards, the foundation provides grants of $25,000 to four different organizations among 20 that are profiled on its web site. The idea of voting was appealing from the perspective of encouraging civic engagement and participation. The foundation explains its rationale as follows: "The Make It Your Own Awards is all about people coming together to take responsibility for the challenges facing their communities, something each of these finalists, in their own way and specific to the needs and styles of their community, have done. We're proud to lift up these stories and share them. Now it's up to the online community to choose who comes out on top."[20]

Competitive Applications of New Technology

In yet another example, Toyota has used the competition form to translate its automotive technology to other domains. Ideas for Good is a challenge to apply one of five categories of automotive technology to other fields and to solve in the process a community or public problem. The process involved soliciting ideas from the public, judging them using a panel of "gurus" and voting by the public, then awarding prizes (Toyota cars) to the winners. Toyota described the process and the rationale for the Ideas for Good effort in broad terms: " Big ideas are bigger than cars. Toyota has proved this time and time again by sharing our big inventions with the world outside of cars. Everybody has a few good ideas, and Toyota wants to help make some of them a reality. So we're sharing some of our most innovative technologies with you in the hope that you'll share your good ideas to improve the world."[21] Toyota's competition is a variant on the open subject and open voting model, in that it has some technological focus and a mix of expert judging and public input through a web voting system.

The Dell Social Innovation Challenge is an example of both the use of a challenge to identify solutions to complex problems around the world and participation in the form of voting on the best ideas by anyone willing to register and review the ideas presented by student innovators. The challenge is open to any and all full-time students at colleges and universities around the world. It aims to attract young problem solvers who are willing to bring fresh solutions forward to issues as broad as rural development, global health, renewable energy, education, and a host of other issues. One of the features of the Dell Challenge is that it encourages voting by the public on which ideas have the most promise and which therefore deserve the advance in the competition, which culminates in the awarding of over $100,000 in prizes. Students who enter use their social networks to mobilize support, and the wisdom of the crowd is checked by a more formal judging process that draws on the talents of a team of experts in social innovation and change.[22]

Operational Challenges

Competitions raise a number of difficult operational issues for grantmakers committed to this approach of locating and supporting people and projects. First, competitions are unpredictable. It is hard to know how many entries will be received, what their quality will be, and whether any of the entries will be deserving of winning.

Second, competitions and challenges precommit the donor to making an award before seeing the applications or entries. This means that money will need to be awarded even if the pool of applications is not what the grantmaker would have hoped for.

Third, when running a competition there are added administrative burdens when it comes to advertising and marketing the event. This can push a grantmaker away from simply giving funds away into new operational domains that may or may not be familiar.

Fourth, once a competition is announced there is the difficulty of responding to what are always a large number of questions about eligibility and judging criteria. For some donors, these questions will feel similar to those posed in relation to traditional grant guidelines. For others, the amount of curiosity and the level of demand for precompetition advice may be a surprising burden.

Fifth, there is often a need with competitions to assemble an outside jury or judging panel that will assess the entries and select a winner. This can pose new administrative and organizing demands on the grantmaker's staff, who must now coordinate the work of this external body.

Sixth, there are always complaints and challenges to the legitimacy and fairness of competitions. Because they are so public and because they propose to find the best and most deserving entries, there will always those who feel they have been wrongly denied recognition. While all grantmakers face occasional questioning about their decision-making, the public nature of open competitions increases the external scrutiny of the entire awards process.

Seventh and finally, there is the challenge of knowing whether the competition was effective in achieving its goals. Measuring performance in philanthropy is always hard. With competitions it is no different. There is no obvious answer to whether the number of entries is a critical or irrelevant output measure of competitions. Nor is there clarity about whether the ultimate social impact achieved by the winner of a competition can be meaningfully attributed to the receipt of the award. In all these ways and many others, running a competition raises many deep and complex operational challenges.

Track Record and Overall Assessment

How well have competitions and prizes fulfilled their claims of offering a more effective way to promote social change and achieve other philanthropic objectives? Unfortunately, systematic assessments that might make it possible to answer this question with anything approaching definitiveness are not available. What it is possible to do, however, is to compare the record of prizes and competitions to the variety of other attempts that have been made over the years to improve the performance of philanthropy. From this perspective it is possible to view the turn to competitions and prizes not as a sharp departure from philanthropy's past, but rather the latest chapter in philanthropy's long-standing search for innovations that can serve one overarching objective: how to increase the leverage of philanthropy, or put differently, amplify the impact of grants.[23] By leverage, donors usually mean a way of maximizing the impact of their contributions, ideally by creating significant activity or change with the modest use of grant dollars. Leverage can be created with new funds or additional resources of any kind drawn to a project as a result of one funder's decision to offer support. Creating leverage requires turning grants from closed-ended commitments into catalytic forces leading to greater productive work. Finding ways to achieve such results is important in philanthropy because the amount of money available to most funders is limited, especially when compared to the scope of human problems awaiting attention. The novelty and significance of competitions and crowd sourcing can therefore best be assessed when compared to other attempts to inject more leverage into philanthropy. Some aspects of the new voter-driven competitions actually connect directly and indirectly to prominent tactics for producing philanthropic leverage that have emerged over time in mainstream grantmaking.

I focus here on how competitions perform in comparison to several prominent grantmaking tactics that have been thought to increase the ability of foundations to achieve change and impact. These existing tactics can be divided into two main groups. The first group focuses on changes in grant technique and methodology (start-up grants, project grants; short-term grants, matching grants, large grants, grants driven by proactive RFPs), while the second looks for leverage through the specification of certain grantmaking targets or classes of recipients (funding for organizations overseas, support for commercial ventures within nonprofits, seeding interorganizational collaborations, working with organizations that will accept high donor engagement). Competitions tap into some and eschew other of these leverage ideas that exist in the broader grantmaking field.

Comparison to Other Leverage-Creating Grantmaking Techniques

Start-up Grants and Pilot Funding

To increase their impact, some foundations believe that nonprofits need to be coaxed into experimenting, innovating, and expanding. To encourage organizations along these lines, funders often seek out proposals for activities that represent a new activity or a strategic expansion of services, rather than a long-existing activity. This theory of leverage is particularly popular in the foundation world, in which newness is a critical ingredient to any successful proposal. Foundations want to employ their funds in ways that encourage change, and one way to do so is to favor grant requests for activities that are not currently ongoing. Of course, for nonprofits, the emphasis on novelty, innovation, and expansion can be problematic, especially when maintaining existing activities can, in itself, be a challenging proposition. This theory of leverage has led to a set of clever countermoves within the nonprofit community, moves designed to repackage existing activities in ways to make them appear novel. To the extent that such strategic gaming is going on, the effectiveness of funding new initiatives is diminished because it saps considerable energy from nonprofits and makes the donor-donee relationship more dysfunctional.

Philanthropic leverage has also come to be associated with the funding of pilot programs, which are intended as models that government and other private funders can replicate and take to scale. The lure of pilot or demonstration programs is that they do not start and end with specific funded activities, but instead hold forth the promise of having lives of their own. By attaching the term "pilot" to an initiative, funders can, without much cost, express a desire to see their efforts evaluated, recognized, and expanded if they turn out to be successful. The main drawback with this theory of leverage is that all too often it is just that, a theory. Few projects ever get replicated and the moniker "pilot project" has come to be attached to just about any new project. Nonprofit organizations have also wised up to the name game. Many proposals are described as pilots in order to excite funders and play into their desire for leverage. The gap between the rhetoric and the reality of pilot and demonstration programs is best seen in the huge number of pilot efforts that are routinely announced, and the paucity of replication efforts that funders have embraced.

Competitions represent a clear continuation of the trend toward the support of new initiatives over existing ones. Many of the competitions are oriented toward start-up entities, sometimes proposed by students and new social entrepreneurs. The attraction to new organizations stems from the fact that competitions start from the premise that problems have solutions and that many problems require new solutions. Rather than fund organizations that have been doing one thing for years, competitions typically look for a good idea that has yet to be fully and broadly implemented.

Project Grants

Competitions focused on social innovation directly buy into the credo that leverage may be gained by increasing control and focus. One way control is established is through the narrow circumscribing of purposes for which grants can be used. Many donors seek to target their giving to specific programs or projects within organizations, believing that these constraints make accountability, reporting, and assessment easier. With competitions the same logic obtains. Winners are required to condense their requests down to a single innovative idea or project idea, that can be stated quickly and clearly. These ideas, not broad missions or appeals for general support, are then funded or not funded. By focusing grants on projects, donors are able to pick and support specific activities within an organization's portfolio of programs. Because of the greater accountability that is possible when the terms and purposes of a grant are focused on specific activities, donors generally believe that project giving is particularly effective. For nonprofits, the rise of project grants has been a mixed blessing. It has allowed proposals to be narrowly targeted and encouraged detailed planning. However, it has made the securing of unrestricted general operating support increasingly difficult. As more and more funders have sought leverage through project giving, some nonprofits have complained about the difficulty of sustaining core activities.[24] Competitions usually do not try to solve the general operating challenge of existing organizations and in fact may actually complicate it by funding new initiatives and new ideas in the face of many proven program models that are already in existence. Prizes, on the other hand, often give unconditional support to individuals with the hope of enabling them to continue their artistic or scientific work.

Short-Term Grants

Most awards are one-time gifts that are designed to get something started, not sustain it over a long period of time. This is a model that resonates clearly with the motto "Get in and get out" of many large institutional funders. Long-term financial commitments have become less and less popular as donors have developed a theory of leverage related to the length of philanthropic support.

By not getting involved with recipients for more than three to five years, many institutional donors attempt to "seed" activities, then move on to other efforts. Short-term support allows funders to direct money to a larger number of organizations and in the process increase the overall reach of their grantmaking. The assumption behind this approach is that shorter commitments counter the tendency of nonprofits to grow dependent on a single funder. By limiting giving to a few years, donors communicate to nonprofits that they need to plan on achieving a diversified and flexible system for generating revenues. Again, this theory of leverage has posed problems for nonprofits in that seed funding terminates before replacement funds are located, leading to funding crises at inopportune times. Competitions make no promise of long-term support but instead reward promising ideas with often one-time infusions of capital. After the award is given, the sponsors of competitions want to see results, not the repeated request for additional funding.

Matching Grants

One of the most obvious ways to create leverage is to make the receipt of a grant contingent on an organization's ability to raise additional funds. Matching grants can take many forms. They can require a one-to-one match, a three-to-one match, a five-to-one match, or any other ratio desired by the funder. Often matching grants are a critical part of large annual fund drives at major cultural institutions. Solicitations are made to individual contributors with the assurance that every dollar contributed will be matched and made to go further. For some donors, the existence of a matching program makes donating funds more appealing. Matching grant programs are premised on the idea that philanthropy can catalyze further giving by offering an incentive that increases the impact of additional fund raising. Competitions and crowd sourcing tap into the idea of matching grants by being high profile and requiring mobilizing of outside parties. While competitions like Pepsi Refresh force nonprofits to mobilize voters, not donors, the logic of matching grants still pervades the model. Grants are given only when other supporters are mobilized for the cause in question.

On the surface, these contingent grants look like carrots dangled in front of nonprofits that cannot help but motivate them. There are at least two main problems with this approach to leverage building, however: first, matching grants often reinforce behavior that would have occurred even without the introduction of the funds. That is, it can be very hard to establish that the presence of a matching grant actually led to greater levels of giving by others or that other donors were attracted to giving because of a match being available. Ironically, if a challenge is met by a nonprofit, this may be evidence that an organization already possesses the breadth of support and fundraising capacity needed to mobilize significant amounts of funds, and that a matching grant simply added to sources that would have been received with or without the presence of the offer. Second, while they are intended to stimulate the mobilization of resources, matching grants can actually impose significant costs and burdens on nonprofits. Soon after the receipt of a matching gift, nonprofits must scramble for contributors willing to make gifts that will be eligible for the match, which can lead to new fundraising expenses, create a sense of false urgency, and distract the organization from its regular pattern of activity and long-term agenda. Competitions try to overcome these limitations of traditional matching grants by using the power of public attention to draw in other support for their cause or issue, not a demand that funds be raised on top of the award funds.

Large Grants

With their large awards often topping $1 million (and sometimes rising to $25 million), competitions aim to avoid what donors call "spray and pray grant-making" in favor of a concentrated approach with a small number of winners and many, many losers. This aspect of the model connects directly to the move in mainstream philanthropy to making a smaller number of very large grants. Suspicious of the impact of small grants spread widely across a large number of recipients, many foundations have sought leverage by making fewer but larger grants. The goal of such a strategy is to move away from disjointed and dissipated gift giving toward an approach that puts significant resources behind selected initiatives. The larger the grant, the larger the stakes become. For donors wanting to achieve leverage, concentrating giving on a few large initiatives has at times been difficult, given expectations among recipients and the difficulty of rejecting many requests in order to accept a few. After all, making a small consolation grant has long been a way of avoiding both tough choices and alienating community groups. Beyond the politics of saying no many times in order to say yes a few times, an important question that this theory of leverage raises is whether recipient organizations have the capacity to absorb large commitments of funds all at once, or whether large grants need to be built up over time in order not to overwhelm the capacity of smaller recipient organizations. Competitions use the promise of large awards to draw in entries and to shine the spotlight on the issue they seek to address. They also provide large enough grants to allow new projects to launch and go to scale.

Grants Driven by Proactive RFPs

Competitions are grounded in the idea of setting forward a call for solutions and not sitting passively waiting for a project to apply for support. Some mainstream grantmakers also refuse to sit quietly in their office for the mail to arrive each day with ever more requests for grants. While there is never a shortage of demands on donors, often the proposals that arrive over the transom disappoint, in terms of either subject matter or sheer coherence. As a result, donors have begun taking a more proactive stance when it comes to soliciting grant proposals. This sometimes involves contacting specific nonprofit organizations and encouraging the submission of the proposals, particularly if the donor has had a positive grantmaking relationship with the organization in the past. Other times, proactive donors simply open the door more widely through the creation of a request for proposals (RFP) that is advertised and open to any organization willing to deliver a proposal meeting the guidelines. RFPs spell out in great detail what the donor wants to accomplish and how the program should be carried out.[25] There is at least one aspect of the leverage achieved through RFPs and other proactive approaches that is controversial: It appears to be based on the assumption that the donor knows more about how to solve a given social problem than the service delivery community in the field. Given the pressure to be responsive, listen to needs, and "fund from the bottom up," RFPs and other proactive "top-down" approaches can ruffle some feathers.

Some large donors have taken the proactive approach to a different level and sought to stimulate competition among a small number of very large potential recipients. Larry Ellison, the founder of Oracle and one of the richest men in the world, announced that he would make a $150 million gift to fund an institute focusing on the connection between technology, society, and politics. Rather than go directly to one institution or to set out an open-ended request for proposals, Ellison approached Stanford University and Harvard University and played the two institutions off each other, making them vie for the funds. The idea is that competition for funds may be helpful to some extent, if it forces institutions to present their very best proposals and ideas, knowing that someone else will receive the funds if they fall short. Other big donors to higher education have taken a similar tact, seeking out a limited set of institutions for a specific project. Donor Patrick J. Mc Govern Jr., the founder of International Data Group, gave the Massachusetts Institute of Technology $350 million for an institute to study the brain, after giving six other potential host institutions the chance to make their case. While these are not formal competitions, they do use the model of the RFP or a specified desired goal as the driving point for grantmaking. In this way, there is a clear overlap between RFP grantmaking and the mounting of challenges.

Comparison to Other Leverage-Creating Grantmaking Targets

Overseas Funding

Geography can be a major factor in determining how much leverage is possible, particularly for American donors. A grant of $3,000 in New York might allow an education group to pay rent for a few weeks or cover the cost of one staff person's salary and benefits for a week. However, the same $3,000 when donated in Bangladesh or South Africa can make a huge difference in terms of the way people live and the assistance it can make possible. Thus, one way to achieve leverage in philanthropy is to choose a geographical location for philanthropy that allows a maximum amount of buying power for the donor. While it would be wrong to let buying power alone determine the area in which one chose to give, geography does become a more and more significant factor, particularly for small donors. It is a factor that needs to be weighed along with all the others in order to ensure that philanthropic resources are not only being spent, but used productively and meaningfully.

Competitions tend to be open to international entries and to the possibility that awards will go further in the developing world. Several grant competitions are open to students and young social entrepreneurs. Dell Social Innovation Challenge and the Global Social Venture Competition operated by the University of California, Berkeley, have had many finalists whose projects serve clients in developing countries around the world.

Support for Nonprofit Collaborations, Not Isolated Work

One of the earliest principles of Victorian charity was to make all necessary services available to the poor in one place. This place was often a settlement house in which poor immigrant families could turn for assistance with their problems, be they educational, financial, or social. Over time, as many parts of the nonprofit sector have become increasingly dominated by professionals, boundaries between service delivery fields have emerged, making integrated programs harder to find. Some foundations in recent years have seen a possibility for leverage through a return to these earliest philanthropic ideas about one-stop shopping for services—albeit now presented in the more fashionable language of collaboration and program integration.[26] The fostering of collaboration among nonprofit organizations is appealing because the specialization of nonprofit services has made navigating the system increasingly difficult for many clients. To encourage collaboration, some foundations give preference to grant requests that include plans for cross agency coordination. Leverage is achieved by reducing the redundancy and isolation of providers, and thereby improving the effectiveness of the entire service delivery system.

Competitions sometimes encourage collaborations by either requiring entries to describe their partners or by explicitly including collaborations as an element of their assessment rubrics. But at their most, challenges, and especially prizes, focus on the lone individual whose creativity and insight is celebrated.

Funding of Commercial Ventures within Nonprofits

One of the most important changes in the nonprofit sector in recent decades has been the rise of earned income as a source of agency finance. Competitions often require sustainability plans, and earned income is often at the heart of any such plan. Unlike contributed income, revenues from fees and ventures have no strings attached, and for that reason are attractive to many organizations. At the same time, funders have become aware of the entrepreneurial skills present in some nonprofits and have responded with an approach to building leverage that targets the commercial impulse of nonprofits. A growing number of donors now make grants to help nonprofits start or expand commercial ventures. While these activities are often substantially related to the mission of the nonprofit, at times they are unrelated. By supporting a nonprofit's ability to generate a stream of commercial income, funders see significant leverage.[27] Philanthropic funds are not only converted into one-time programmatic activities, but instead they are used to build income-producing capacity that will continue long after the grant funds are gone. For nonprofits, an emphasis on commercial revenues is both potentially liberating and distracting. Running successful ventures demands staff time and resources. Still, the availability of philanthropic funds to build capacity to move away from a dependence on contributed income is a potentially empowering proposition.

The desire of competitions to see their awards catalyze long-term social impact has led to an emphasis on earned-income strategies as a sign of sustainability. Thus, in Pepsi Refresh and other similar award programs aimed at finding high-performing nonprofit organizations, the commercial turn in nonprofits—far from being a distraction from mission—is encouraged as a sign of fiscal responsibility and long-term sustainability.

Support for Organizations Accepting High Engagement by Donors

Philanthropy has traditionally been driven by detailed paperwork and a certain hands-off etiquette. Grantmaking starts with the submission of elaborate proposals by nonprofits, which are read and reviewed by donors. Site visits and meetings may occur during the grantmaking process, especially if additional information is needed to arrive at a fair decision. Once the grant decision is reached and a check is mailed to the recipient, donors and recipients rarely speak again for a year or until the period of the grant is over and a report is due.

Sensing that this low level of engagement may not be optimal, some individual donors and foundations have begun to experiment with higher-engagement grantmaking.[28] Based on a theory of leverage that holds that donors have something more than money to contribute to nonprofits, donors have been trying to reshape donor-recipient relations in order to construct active, consultative relationships that start before proposal review, that build during program implementation, and that extend after the grant cycle is over.[29] High-engagement grantmaking requires that the donor have skills (managerial, legal, accounting, or other) useful to nonprofits and that recipients are open to receiving this nonmonetary input. Not all relationships can or should aim toward a high-engagement model, especially if the amount of funds involved is relatively modest. However, in cases where the financial commitment is high and where the skills needed are present, this model of engagement can be an appealing alternative.

One of the most misunderstood aspects of the high-engagement approach to leverage is that it often masks a donor's honest interest in making a personal connection to the causes that the donor supports. In this sense, the collaboration, consulting, and coaching that often goes on between donor and recipient on programmatic matters may not increase impact and produce leverage, but rather only increases the quality and meaningfulness of the donor's philanthropic experience. While it may have started out as a grantmaking tool that could increase effectiveness, high engagement has at times become an instrument to increase donor participation and to deepen the donor's satisfaction with giving. Even if giving can be confounded by personal needs and not organizational imperatives, donors can and do contribute more than money to nonprofit organizations. The problem arises when the motives of the donor are neither about increasing the effectiveness nor even about satisfying psychic needs for a deeper connection. In some cases, high engagement is actually a product of a lack of trust between giver and recipient. In such cases, assistance begins to blend into oversight, and consultation turns into micromanagement. The idea of donor engagement as a tool for increasing leverage has some hidden pitfalls and dangers that must be attended to before this tool can be embraced enthusiastically.

Competitions tend to have a split identity when it comes to engagement. There is often little help given to nonprofits seeking to win a competition during the application window. One reason is that donors hesitate to choose favorites or undermine the impartiality and fairness of the judging process. After a competition award has been granted, however, there is often an offer of help that comes with it. In many cases, the competition model comes from a commitment that organizations need to battle it out in the market for funding. Once that contest is over, there is some commitment by the operators of competitions to work with the winner and to share the business skills and insights of the competition operator.

As these comparisons show, the move to competitions, prizes, and crowd sourcing may be new, but it does have antecedents in the recent history of philanthropy, which has sought to find new and better ways to deliver grant funds.

In many ways, the rise of a more open and participatory approach to giving represents the latest theory of leverage. The bet that these new challenge and competition driven funders are making is simple enough: By engaging large numbers of people with a challenge, the hope is that new ideas and innovations in the resolution of complex problems will emerge faster than through traditional grantmaking practice.

Conclusion

Competitions, prizes, and broad attempts at crowd sourcing are interesting variations in the world of grantmaking. They represent a practical alternative for a field concerned at once with transparency and effectiveness. When challenges are open to all to enter, a central critique of philanthropy is overcome, namely that it is elitist and closed to outsiders. This is a significant improvement for the field. Challenges and crowd-sourcing efforts in philanthropy represent an admission that all answers do not reside with funders and a more humble approach to philanthropy centered on listening to the ideas of experts in the field. In this way, the most important aspect of these endeavors is that they declare that breakthroughs and innovations needed in the nonprofit sector are best found with an open agenda and a call to those in the field to come forward with solutions. The announcement of competitions and the tapping of broad swaths of the public is the ultimate antidote to the defensive and inward focus of professional philanthropy today. The increased professionalization of foundations over the past half-century has led to increased hiring from within the field and the codification of norms of grantmaking practice, and the construction of expert knowledge about effective philanthropy,[30] all of which have limited the ability of grantmakers to listen to voices outside the field.

The big unanswered question is whether awards made through these methods are in fact "better" and more effective than grants made the old-fashioned way through applications to funders for support. Given the absence of reliable and commensurable performance data in the nonprofit sector, this is a question that cannot be answered definitively. What is certain, however, is that pluralism and openness are powerful and valuable concepts that cannot help but strengthen the field of philanthropy over the long run.

Notes

1. A history of Pepsi Refresh can be found at "Pepsi Refresh Project," Pepsi Co., accessed July 20, 2012, http://www.refresheverything.com/

2. "Pepsi Refresh Project."

3. See Peter Frumkin, *Strategic Giving* (Chicago: University of Chicago Press, 2006), where a detailed discussion of the concept of philanthropic leverage can be found.

4. On high-engagement grantmaking, see Chapter 7 of this volume, "Capacity Builders." On grants as credit enhancements for loans and bonds, see Chapter 12, "Loans, Loan Guarantees, and Other Credit Enhancements," and Chapter 13, "Fixed-Income Securities." On foundations as "philanthropic banks," see Chapter 5.

5. Jonathan Bays, Tony Goland, and Joe Newsum, "Using Prizes to Spur Innovation," *McKinsey Quarterly*, July 2009.

6. McKinsey, "And the Winner Is. . . Capturing the Promise of Philanthropic Prizes," McKinsey & Co. Report, 2009.

7. McKinsey, "And the Winner Is."

8. McKinsey, "And the Winner Is."

9. On the MacArthur Foundation's fellowships, see "Frequently Asked Questions," MacArthur Foundation, accessed July 20, 2012, http://www.macfound.org/fellows-faq/ which describes the selection process and the underlying logic of this program started by renegade family member J. Roderick MacArthur.

10. Susan Ostrander, *Money for Change* (Philadelphia: Temple University Press, 1997).

11. McKinsey, "And the Winner Is."

12. McKinsey, "And the Winner Is."

13. "About Innocentive," InnoCentive, accessed July 20, 2012, http://www.innocentive.com/about-innocentive.

14. InnoCentive describes its work: "InnoCentive is the open innovation and crowdsourcing pioneer that enables organizations to solve their key problems by connecting them to diverse sources of innovation including employees, customers, partners, and the world's largest problem solving marketplace." See "About InnoCentive."

15. "About InnoCentive."

16. "About InnoCentive."

17. "X PRIZE," X PRIZE Foundation, accessed July 20, 2012, http://www.xprize.org/.

18. "X PRIZE."

19. "X PRIZE."

20. "About the Case Foundation," Case Foundation, accessed July 20, 2012, http://www.casefoundation.org/.

21. See Toyota's description and rationale for its program at "Ideas for Good," Toyota, accessed July 20, 2012, http://www.toyota.com/ideas-for-good.

22. "Dell Social Innovation Challenge," Dell and RGK Center for Philanthropy and Community Service, accessed July 20, 2012, http://www.dellchallenge.org/.

23. Paul Brest and Hal Harvey, *Money Well Spent* (New York: Bloomberg Press, 2008).

24. While the general trend in philanthropy has been toward greater restrictions on the use of grants, a counterargument has emerged that holds that general operating support is in fact the most strategic and effective way to deliver funding. See Paul Brest, "Smart Money," *Stanford Social Innovation Review*, Winter 2003, 44–53.

25. For cases of proactive grantmaking, see Joel L. Fleishman, *The Foundation* (New York: Public Affairs, 2007).

26. For a discussion of the power of collaboration in philanthropy see Lucy Bernholz, *Creating Philanthropic Capital Markets* (Hoboken, NJ: Wiley, 2004).

27. Leslie R. Crutchfield, John V. Kania, and Mark R. Kramer, *Do More Than Give: The Six Practices of Donors Who Change the World* (San Francisco: Jossey-Bass, 2011).

28. A discussion of the ways donors interact with grantees can be found in Thomas J. Tierney and Joel L. Fleishman, *Give Smart* (New York: Public Affairs, 2011).

29. Christine W. Letts, William Ryan, and Allen Grossman, "Virtuous Capital: What Foundations Can Learn from Venture Capitalists," *Harvard Business Review*, March–April 1997, 36–46.

30. Peter Frumkin, "The Long Recoil from Regulation: Private Philanthropic Foundations and the Tax Reform Act of 1969," *American Review of Public Administration* 28.3 (1998): 266.

Suggested Readings

Frumkin, Peter. *Strategic Giving.* Chicago: University of Chicago Press, 2006.

McKinsey and Co. "And the Winner Is. . . Capturing the Promise of Philanthropic Prizes." 2009.

PART IV

CROSSCUTTING ISSUES

CHAPTER 20

WHO GAINS, WHO LOSES?

Distributional Impacts of the New Frontiers of Philanthropy

Michael Edwards, Matthew Bishop, and Michael Green

Part A: Who Loses?

Michael Edwards

The assumption of much contemporary discourse about philanthropy is that market mechanisms will allocate private resources for the public good more efficiently and effectively than personal judgment, mutual solidarity, or democratic decision-making. However, for reasons that are explained in this chapter, the assumption that the objectives of philanthropy overlap extensively with the objectives of private investors is largely unfounded, and therefore is unlikely to deliver the benefits that are claimed for it. The use of market-oriented mechanisms may even damage the health and strength of civil society and thereby reduce the long-term social and political impact of voluntary citizen action, though there should also be some gains in the provision of socially and environmentally useful goods and services to lower-income groups. In implicitly endorsing efforts now underway to stimulate a greater flow of private investment capital into social and environmental problem-solving, this book opens the door to real, if unintended, risks to the objectives it seeks to accomplish. Therefore, great caution is required in pushing the frontiers of philanthropy further in this direction.

It is important to note that there is nothing new in conceptualizing philanthropy in terms of returns on investment and the use of detailed metrics and other instruments that necessarily accompany this approach. "Program-related investments" were invented at the Ford Foundation in the late 1960s and have been used with increasing frequency ever since, but crucially they were seen as a complement to other approaches based on grant-funding with fewer pre-specifications, not as a replacement for them, to be used only in particular circumstances where financial returns could be generated without significant trade-offs against social impact.[1] Indeed, philanthropy was valued precisely because of its ability to fund organizations and activities that did not make such returns and whose success could not be measured by short-term standard metrics, and therefore failed to attract support from other sources of revenue despite their important contributions to society. In this sense, grant- and investment-based approaches to philanthropy are no more in competition with each other than screwdrivers and hammers in a toolkit, which is why many business-oriented donors with substantial philanthropic experience (like George Soros) avoid the use of market mechanisms in their support for civil society, democracy, and human rights while utilizing them in their work on microfinance, microenterprise development, and other areas where quantifiable returns can be expected.

The problem comes when these different approaches to philanthropy are misapplied in practice, or when one particular approach so dominates the others that the *tools* of business and measurement (like planning and learning, which are neutral) are conflated with the *ideologies* of technocracy and the market (like competition and rates of return, which are not). Given the excitement that surrounds market-based approaches, there is a danger that this is what is happening today, with the result that equally valuable alternatives like membership contributions and social justice philanthropy will be displaced and delegitimized, leaving large areas of work unsupported or underfunded. The "distributional impacts" of such a trend are likely to be both serious and negative, though they are impossible to prove because the available evidence is so limited. In 10 or 20 years time one hopes that the research base will have evolved sufficiently to make more substantive conclusions possible, but for now the most useful approach may be to examine the logic behind too heavy an embrace of market-based tools and contrast their assumptions with what we know about the drivers of social change.

The "Marketization" of Philanthropy

Proponents of leveraging private investment resources for philanthropic purposes assume that it is possible to allocate resources efficiently among nonprofit actors based on measurable, objective, comparable, and reliable indicators of their value. Little by way of theory has been produced to support this assumption with the exception of the "theory of blended value," which states that all organizations produce value of different kinds (financial, social, and environmental), and that these different kinds of value can be consciously manipulated in order to alter the proportion of total output or value added they represent.[2] This much is true, but the theory says little about the conflicts and trade-offs that may arise between these different kinds of value, and it assumes a high level of equivalence between the actors, mechanisms, and conditions that produce them—in other words, it assumes that civil society and the market operate in the same or very similar ways.

This is a nonsensical proposition to those who see civil society as the realm of nonmarket social, cultural, and political action—a classic "category mistake" in philosophical terms.[3] But even when restricted to the world of nonprofit or hybrid organizations that seek to provide goods and services to low-income and other disadvantaged groups, the leveraging approach makes a number of leaps of logic that need to be interrogated. There are at least three sets of issues here: theoretical, methodological, and practical.

Theoretical Issues

The first set of issues concerns the theoretical incompatibility of different definitions of value and efficiency. Social goods are "incommensurable," meaning that they have no common measure of value, unlike profits, prices, and financial returns in economics, or the conventional measurement of efficiency in terms of maximizing output for as little input as possible. By contrast, nonprofits operate with full commitment to their missions even when they incur extra costs, and decisions in philanthropy are based on different views of what is "valuable" that are rooted in beliefs, preferences, ideologies, and experiences, screening out some interpretations and priorities and privileging others.[4]

For progressives, for example, support to groups that push for government intervention in health and education will produce returns that, if successful, would be considered negative by conservatives. Federated groups like the Girl Scouts of America have chapters that would be considered cost-inefficient from an accountant's point of view because they have too few members, but nevertheless are highly valued in their communities. And different problems, or different approaches to resolving them, may be of equal value in terms of social impact, but still be valued differently by different donors, as in the case of nonprofits that provide direct workforce training services to immigrants, those that advocate for an increase in the minimum wage from which immigrant workers would benefit, and those that focus on building up strong immigrant associations to fight for their rights. These three organizations are not in competition with each other in the market sense because their work is coequal, interwoven, and mutually supportive, even though parts of the philanthropic community may choose to concentrate on one rather than the others.

In addition, what some would factor into the equation as a cost would be measured as a benefit by others. Take, for example, the amount of time devoted by nonprofits to the messy processes of democratic debate and decision-making. According to Bronfman and Solomon, "efficient" nonprofits start and finish meetings on time "just like a business," but effective community organizations take whatever time it takes to bring different voices to the table and negotiate consensus, so this is a marker of high, not low, performance.[5] It is because of these normative differences that most nonprofits—unlike most firms—are "nonsubstitutable," because affiliations are based on loyalty, identity, and familiarity, not on the price and quality of the goods and services provided. This contradicts the principle of "exit" that provides one of the keys to the efficiency of the market model—the willingness to switch allegiances continuously between suppliers. It is unlikely that members of the National Association for the Advancement of Colored People will cross over to the Puerto Rican Legal Defense Fund if they feel dissatisfied.

Donors who are passionate about reducing domestic violence do not switch their investments to sustainable development when someone shows them that one has a "higher rate of return" or "more measurable results" than the other. In civil society, "doing your best" is more important than "being the best," which is a meaningless designation because of the differences described above. A better analogy is to an "ecosystem," not a market, in which a huge diversity of organizations interact with each other in ways that are organic rather than predictable and controllable. So the calculation of returns, including social returns, is a normative and political issue: resource allocation in philanthropy is an exercise in power and judgment, not a result of the market's "invisible hand."

Measurement Issues

If there is no agreement on what constitutes "social value," it follows that there are no universal measures of the social return on investment (SROI) that can be used to allocate resources between different nonprofit organizations.[6] The practice of measuring SROIs has advanced considerably in recent years, but not in a way that removes basic questions about accuracy, attribution, and aggregation. Most such measures are rough proxies for processes, capacities, and values that cannot be quantified, including empowerment, tolerance, authenticity, solidarity, and caring; crude aggregations that bundle together different indicators for different kinds of impact; or estimates of the financial value of those aspects of social impact that can be monetized, such as jobs created, which are measures of linear impact (more outputs from existing systems) not indicators of system transformation. None of these measures is robust or reliable enough to guide the allocation of resources in a philanthropic marketplace because every indicator has to be appropriate to the context—they cannot be generalized, nor therefore deployed in cross-organizational comparisons.[7] "The reason the non-profit sector exists at all is because it can fund and invest in social issues that the for-profit market cannot touch because they can't be measured. The non-profit market is not designed to be 'efficient' that way. Yet we're applying the same efficiency metrics to both sectors."[8]

Take, for example, the field of education reform, which has attracted large amounts of philanthropic investment. Some see standardized test scores in mathematics and English as a satisfactory measure of both educational achievement and value-added performance, a metric that is strong enough to dismiss individual teachers and close schools that fail to perform. Others reach the opposite conclusion, citing evidence that such measures are biased against African American and Latino children, omit crucial attributes of a rounded education such as civics and the humanities, and fail to control for poverty and other external factors that are crucial in determining success.[9] But because testing is much easier than measuring this broader constellation of factors, it becomes accepted as the mechanism by which resources are allocated—potentially a very dangerous conclusion.

The temptation to reduce complexity to a single number or small set of numbers is especially strong among those who want to rank nonprofits in order to redirect investment, but this is only possible with a vastly reduced conceptualization of what is meant by "social" impact. Many investors use this term to describe a *part* of society defined in terms of target groups for assistance, such as disadvantaged or lower-income families. But there are much deeper forces that impinge on social impact that are often ignored, such as social structure, power relations, patterns of collective action, and strategies for social and political mobilization, and it is these forces that historically have underpinned large-scale progress for just these groups. One example is PULSE, a system developed by the Acumen Fund that provides a common framework of financial and nonfinancial metrics that are supposed to cover social and environmental impact, yet (apart from a mention of board diversity and a few other indicators covering the composition of beneficiary populations) there is little that is social or relational about them at all—just a long list of quantitative indicators that describe the numbers of people served, their demographics, and the amounts of money that are spent on different activities.[10]

Even if one could agree on better social measures, they could not reliably be used to support one organization over others because they say little about what is causing the changes that are signaled. Social impact is an amalgam of interactions among different institutions and their environments that cannot be attributed to one organization in isolation from the others. This is the central failing of measurement models like "randomized control trials," which are much in vogue in philanthropy. They can record what is happening along certain observable dimensions with a high degree of accuracy, but they cannot explain why it is happening or how the same interventions would work in other settings, thereby undermining the claims to scalability and replication that are central to the market thesis.[11] And even if the attribution problem could be solved, nonprofits would continue to engage in the kind of data manipulation and exaggeration efforts that have plagued other attempts to link resource allocation with quantified failure and success. "Campbell's Law" remains in force: "The more any quantitative social indicator is used for social decision-making, the more subject it will be to corruption pressures and the more apt it will be to distort and corrupt the social processes it is intended to monitor."[12] Of course, none of this means that measuring social impact is impossible or undesirable—merely that great care must be taken in using such measures to allocate resources to nonprofits on a comparative basis, since so few of these measures are sufficiently reliable or robust. Therefore, the goal of measurement in this field is to share and to learn, not to rank and reward.

Practical Issues

Third, there are some obvious practical issues that arise from, and interfere with, the introduction of market-based tools into philanthropy. First and foremost are the time and opportunity costs of constructing data-collection and reporting systems for nonprofits that are strong enough to estimate performance and returns on investment. These are considerable, especially at the levels of sophistication required to deal with the methodological problems identified above, and the costs involved are particularly onerous for smaller organizations, or for nonprofits (often community- or grassroots-based) that lack the capacity and experience to satisfy donor requirements. The nonprofit sector is already full of complaints from organizations that spend an increasing amount of scarce staff time collecting data for monitoring and evaluation that they suspect is rarely used, and which has no influence over impact or performance.

In addition, the timescales required to measure the deeper dimensions of social impact—the structural and systemic changes that really matter—are generally too long to feed back into decisions over resource allocation by investment-minded philanthropists, who typically work on a three- to five-year cycle. Decisions therefore tend to be made too early, especially given the unpredictability of nonprofit work, which means that failure now may translate into success later on, and vice versa. And by emphasizing and publicizing a reductive version of returns and results, donors may increase the likelihood that nonprofit service-providers will be taken over by for-profit entities that see an opportunity for making quick financial gains, as in the case of microcredit organizations such as Compartamos in Mexico and SKS in India.[13]

Finally, research suggests that relatively few philanthropists are inclined to adopt the investment-based approach, with its emphasis on metrics and competition. There is a great deal of noise about this movement and some high-profile adherents, but most donors and even many social-purpose investors seem to prefer a more traditional, "warmer" style of giving in which non-market values predominate, such as loyalty and personal conviction, with a good amount of mutual learning thrown in.[14]

These difficulties raise important warning flags for those who are eager to attract private investment capital into social and environmental problem-solving.

Too complete an embrace of these market mechanisms and their attendant decision-making processes may well reallocate resources, but not according to any objectively comparable notion of impact, performance, value, effectiveness, or efficiency. And if only a limited range of organizations, strategies, and types of social impact can be measured, then social capital markets, stock exchanges, and the like will push resources to a subsector of nonprofits regardless of their real contribution to society. The overall result might be to reward nonprofits for superficial results and penalize those whose work is most important to long-term social change, especially those who do not "speak the language" of investment-based philanthropy or who cannot meet its demands. This is likely to have significant consequences for the question of "who gains and who loses" from philanthropy.

Distributional Impacts

The actual impact of these trends on the distribution of costs and benefits in society could be positive, negative, or neutral, depending on how widely they are adopted, and whether donors and investors use them sensitively or crudely. We lack the evidence to make these determinations at the present, but assuming that market-based approaches continue to penetrate to the mainstream of giving and social investment and are used with a high degree of formality and rigor, what effects might they have on the ability of civil society to promote social change?

The Type and Scale of Benefits Provided

The most obvious concern is that resources will migrate away from nonprofits that are doing important and effective work that has large distributional effects but that cannot generate a financial return on investment, or that produce social returns that cannot readily be measured, or that can be measured but nevertheless remain unpopular with investment-minded donors. Examples include community organizing, social movements and other forms of collective action by the poor, advocacy (especially if it involves protest and other forms of radical challenge), organizations that hold businesses accountable for their actions, and volunteer-led groups that provide care, solidarity, and other services in nonmarket settings. In these areas, nonprofits have little to trade or sell, and they tend to be less enthusiastic about the added burdens of information-gathering and interaction that venture philanthropy imposes. By contrast, the delivery of direct social and economic services by nonprofits would likely receive an increasing supply of resources, even though (in most cases) its impact on the underlying drivers of social change is fairly limited. This would seem to be confirmed by the spending patterns of those foundations and donor-advised funds that already follow a market-based approach, which tend to concentrate on organizations that strengthen individual economic assets and access to jobs and training, health and educational provision (including the development of new drugs and vaccines), housing, workforce development, microfinance, and microenterprise development. These activities will have some positive distributional consequences for those who benefit from them directly, but they are unlikely to change the "rules of the game" in ways that bring benefits to entire communities and populations through, for example, government-mandated improvements in the social functioning of private markets, increased salary levels and working conditions across the board, or strengthening the capacity of marginalized groups to fight for their rights.

A second problem is that the introduction of the market-based approach can lead to "mission drift" inside individual nonprofit organizations as they are pulled in different directions, with more and more pressure to deliver returns and results of the kind that are required by investors. This is a common conclusion from studies of nonprofit service-provision and social enterprise. For example, a recent survey of 25 such ventures in the United States by SEEDCO showed that 22 had significant conflicts between mission and the demands of corporate stakeholders, and that the two examples that were most successful in financial terms deviated most from their social mission—reducing time and resources spent on advocacy, weeding out clients who were more difficult to serve because of their higher per capita cost, and focusing on activities with the greatest revenue-generating potential.[15] In nonprofits that attempt to combine service delivery with the deeper elements of social change (an increasingly popular approach), such pressures can also make it more difficult to find and maintain the synergies that need to be developed between different strategies. They can also lead to the exclusion of certain social groups as nonprofits begin to mirror patterns of inequality that exist in the wider society, a problem that has already been identified in the UK social enterprise sector, for example, in which ethnic minorities are underrepresented.[16]

Third, even when successful, the small scale of nonprofit service delivery as compared to need (even in countries like the United States and UK, where large amounts of public resources are channeled through this sector) means that many people remain unprotected, a shortfall that is unlikely to be made up even if philanthropy continues to expand. Focusing resources on direct service-provision creates a "patchwork quilt" in place of the guarantees that can be obtained by building up the bargaining power of civil society in relation to the state. This point is very important. If one examines the roles that have been played by different institutions in reducing poverty, inequality, and discrimination in widely varying contexts across the world, three conclusions stand out. First, large-scale government action has been essential since only governments have the power to redistribute wealth and opportunities on the necessary scale—think of the East Asian "miracle" after World War II, America's New Deal and Great Society reforms, and the rise of the European welfare state.[17] Second, a strong and independent civil society has been crucial in all of these experiences in terms of pressuring government to play its role effectively, consolidate social contracts in support of pro-poor reforms, and act as a counterweight to the interests of business and the market. Third, the biggest welfare gains have come from substantive reforms in the economy, not simply from enabling more people to participate in systems that exist already, because those systems encourage downward pressures on wages and working conditions and the migration of jobs to lower-cost centers of production.

The common denominator of these experiences is that politics and power relations, not markets, have been the prime determinants of the structural changes that produce the largest distributional effects, yet it is the social and political role of civil society that is least suited to market-based approaches to philanthropy because it is so messy, unpredictable, and contested. It is not possible to correct for this problem by investing more heavily in nonprofit service-provision, so unless more of the new philanthropy and social investment finds its way to organizations that pursue work in each of the three areas described above, its impact on the drivers of social change will continue to be small. It is worth remembering that inequality in the United States has reached its highest level since records began, despite a year-on-year expansion in philanthropy and the arrival of new donors, investors, and approaches. For many years, there has been tension between radical and neoliberal interpretations of civil society, with the former seeing it is the social, cultural, and political ground from which to challenge the status quo and build new alternatives, and the latter as the service-providing not-for-profit sector necessitated by "market failure." This debate has been drawn into sharper relief by the rise of market-based approaches to philanthropy that heavily favor the latter interpretation, but the distributional effects of weakening the social and political capacities of civil society may be severe.

The Health and Strength of Civil Society

Civil society works best when its ecosystems are healthy and diverse, yet we know that these ecosystems have been eroded and distorted in many countries over the last 20 years. Diversity is declining as norms of good practice converge around a certain vision of professionalism, and resources are concentrated in organizations that can "speak the language" of their funders and deal with their demands for data and reports. Distance is increasing between nonprofits and the constituencies on whose behalf they are supposed to work, reorienting accountability upwards to donors and government regulators instead of downwards to the grass roots. Technocracy has transformed mediating institutions that once served as civic meeting grounds—like locally grounded schools, labor unions, congregations, and nonprofits—into service delivery operations. Alliances have become more difficult to sustain as competitive pressures increase. The public sphere has been fractured by privatization and the decline of consensus politics. Cross-class, federated membership associations have become much rarer, and the nonprofits that have replaced them function less effectively as training grounds for democracy and citizenship, and as conduits for popular pressure from below. As a result, the achievements of US civil society after World War II in securing progressive social legislation like the GI Bill of 1944, or in forming successful social movements that changed the landscape of America in the decades that followed, are much more difficult to replicate today.[18]

Clearly, these trends resulted from long historical processes in which philanthropy played a fairly minor role, but the rise of market-based approaches to funding the civil society of today may exacerbate them by applying a different and damaging logic to questions of impact and performance. Many social investors see nonprofits as another form of business rather than as communities of citizens who come together to solve problems using distinct logics of their own. These logics produce results that are often surprising to those trained in standard business practices because "social movements are most effective when they are purest, most radical, and most disorganized," a conclusion reached by researchers at Stanford University from a sample of 12,000 nonprofit groups.[19] The most successful were the *least* business-like because they had to be able to capture and channel the energy and passion of their staff and supporters in creative ways, and they put internal democracy and accountability ahead of technocratic strategic planning, impact evaluation, and management information systems.

As more and more nonprofits are encouraged to "behave more like a business"—calculating returns on their investment, designing complex metrics, presenting themselves as competing charity brands, and internalizing other aspects of market behavior—their effectiveness as civil society actors may actually decrease. There may also be a trend towards monopoly or oligopoly (as in financial markets), when resources are attracted to a small number of larger organizations that can outcompete, or simply outmuscle and outadvertise, their counterparts. There is already a belief among market-oriented philanthropists that there are "too many" nonprofits and that mergers should be encouraged, which may be true in some areas of service delivery but is not true in terms of civil society's social and political role, where many more groups are needed.

In addition, market-based approaches may dilute the "gift relationships" that are the essence of civil society—the reciprocity, intrinsic valuation and voluntary, "other-directed" behavior that differs radically from the transactional relationships and instrumental approach to results that underpin a focus on "returns on investment." As a report from five UK charities concludes, "A strong focus on financial success is associated with lower empathy, more manipulative tendencies, a higher preference for social inequality and hierarchy, greater prejudice towards people who are different, and less concern about environmental problems. Studies also suggest that when people are placed in resource dilemma games, they tend to be less generous and to act in a more competitive and environmentally-damaging way if they have been implicitly reminded of concerns about financial success."[20] This not an encouraging vision for the future of civic action.

The danger is that these trends will undermine civil society's transformative potential by reducing the ability or willingness of citizens' groups to hold public and private power accountable for its actions, generate alternative ideas and policy positions, push for fundamental changes in the structures of power, represent a different, nonmarket set of values and motivations, and organize collective action on the scale required to force through shifts in politics, social relations, and economics. Civil society will become a subset of the market, not a counterweight to the market's influence or a source of alternative values and priorities.

The Changing Balance of Power in Society and How It Affects Society's Capacity to Solve Social Problems

These problems are exacerbated by the control-orientation and impatience of many investment-minded donors and the power imbalances that tend to grow between donors and recipients as the field of philanthropy becomes more technocratic. Accustomed to the disciplines of supply-chain management and strict control over inputs, processes, and outputs; driven by the desire to solve problems quickly (and within their lifetimes), and convinced of the virtues of "efficient" (top-down) decision-making that may have served them well in their corporate persona, many of the new philanthropists and social investors are suspicious of democratic procedures and negotiated solutions to the problems they want to solve. Such imbalances are especially important because they give donors the ability to determine the outcomes of the normative and ideological contests over efficiency, effectiveness, and impact in the nonprofit sector that were described above, and more broadly, to decide which problems should be selected for attention and how they should be addressed. In effect, this gives them the power to govern the resolution of public policy dilemmas without clear accountability structures, at least to the public who are supposed to benefit from these endeavors, further accelerating the transfer of power and responsibility from the public to the private realm that characterizes contemporary capitalist societies. Yet there is no evidence that these trends lead to more effective problem-solving, or to problem-solving with distributional consequences that are more positive. Indeed, the literature on marketization in health, education, water, and other public goods suggests the opposite conclusion.

A key question for philanthropy in the future, therefore, is whether it will focus on resolving public policy problems directly as an actor in itself, or whether it will concentrate on building broadly distributed capacities for problem-solving across the wider population. The market-based approach tends to favor the former of these two approaches in order to zero in on specific problems and solutions, though it also prioritizes "leverage" over other institutions and sources of support for the solutions that are favored by the donors— like charter schools as the driving force of school reform, or place-based interventions like the Harlem Children's Zone. The latter approach is more democratic and arguably more effective in the longer run, because it creates a greater diversity of solutions appropriate for different contexts and builds stronger constituencies to put them into practice, but it is obviously less controllable and less amenable to the demands of standardized programming. In essence, the choice lies between philanthropy as a control system and philanthropy as a support system for broad-based participation in social change. No democratic society has been successful, however, in addressing poverty and inequality by inhibiting the ability of its citizens to undertake collective action on their own terms. The strength of the poor lies not in their individual assets but in their numbers, made effective through democratic political processes and the strength of representative pro-poor associations of the kind that are currently being defunded by investment-based philanthropy.

Conclusion

Among nonprofit organizations that provide the same goods and services under competitive conditions, market-based "philanthropy" and the effort to mobilize private investment capital to help solve social and environmental problems should yield some useful results, and disadvantaged social groups will receive some material benefits as a consequence. But the distributional consequences of this approach are likely to be small, because it has relatively little purchase over the drivers of social transformation. As one approach among many to funding social change its expansion makes sense, but as a generalized approach to philanthropy the market-based approach owes more to excitement and ideology than to evidence or logic. Unless this distinction is acknowledged, the trend towards marketization is likely to reduce attention to the poor, drive out support for advocacy and community organizing, and shift power out of the hands of citizens and those in need and into the hands of technocratic elites.

The "frontiers of philanthropy" are not located in any one of these approaches to the exclusion of the others, but in developing a funding system that matches and supports the diversity of the civil society ecosystem—with grants and investments, measured and spontaneous activities, and focused and distributed approaches to social problem-solving.[21] Such a system would recognize that important innovations are taking place in all parts of the philanthropic universe—in social justice philanthropy, "horizontal" philanthropy, foundations owned and governed by their beneficiaries, the fast and flexible approach of groups like the Philanthropic Ventures Foundation, and the revival of noncommercial, member-based financing, among many others.[22] None of these innovations deploys the methods of the market, but all of them have much to offer to the philanthropic landscape of the future. Recognizing their value will strengthen philanthropy and help to spread its benefits across the population much more widely, effectively, and fairly. At the very least, the market-based approach must be applied with greater rigor, clarity, specificity, sophistication, and caution as part of this wider suite of instruments. If so, we might all gain as a result.

Part B: Who Gains?

Matthew Bishop and Michael Green

"The problem of our age is the proper administration of wealth, that the ties of brotherhood may still bind together the rich and poor in harmonious relationship."[23] Andrew Carnegie, in his 1889 essay "Wealth," was writing about the challenges facing the industrial world of the nineteenth century, as rapid industrialization brought incredible wealth and disruptive social change to America. But he could equally have been writing about the world in the twenty-first century, where globalization has lifted more people out of poverty than at any time in history but at a cost in terms of equality and environmental sustainability.

We believe that the "new frontiers of philanthropy" described in this book, from first-loss guarantees for nonprofits to social-impact bonds and social stock exchanges, form part of a wider movement in philanthropy and in business that is rising to this challenge, a movement that we call "philanthrocapitalism."[24] While this movement takes some inspiration from Carnegie and his peers in earlier "golden ages" of philanthropy, the growing interest in new frontiers reflects a recognition that the world today differs in important ways from that of the late nineteenth century. Ultimately, the philanthropy of Carnegie's day was not sufficient to meet the challenges of his era. Thus, to have any hope of success in this time of bigger business and bigger government, significant innovation is required.

We will argue that the philanthrocapitalism movement, using new frontier approaches, is likely to be a substantial and long-lived force. The testing years of economic crisis have been survived with these underlying trends in far better shape than most people imagined possible back in the miserable last months of 2008. Provided the philanthropists and business leaders who are driving it remain focused on achieving what they like to refer to as "impact," it is on course to be a powerful source of innovation in addressing the big problems facing society. Nevertheless, it will not be able to achieve its full potential alone, only in partnership with the other institutions of modern society—the degree of whose cooperation, we believe, remains uncertain.

We will also argue that much of today's criticism of philanthrocapitalism is based on two fallacies. One is a misunderstanding of capitalism, assuming it to be necessarily short-termist, exploitative, and harmful to civil society (rather than sometimes so, usually as a result of some combination of ethical lapses, irrational exuberance, inadequate governance, and poorly designed or enforced regulation). The other is a misunderstanding of the role of the new frontiers within philanthrocapitalism, which assumes these approaches to be alternatives to giving, rather than, as most of the leading practitioners see it, complementing grant-making as part of a portfolio of philanthropically motivated activities.

Inevitably, there will be winners and losers as a result of the development of philanthropy's new frontiers—though we contend that if developed properly, the winners will be society as a whole, while the losers primarily will be organizations that are currently poorly run or no longer (if ever) well designed for their social purpose. On the other hand, as well as the uncertainty over the readiness of the existing social ecosystem to evolve, it remains to be seen if today's philanthropists have the dedication, self-discipline, and managerial talent needed to push the new frontiers to their full potential. Should they fail to do so, the nature of the winners and losers will be hard to predict and, from society's point of view, their impact could be significantly less beneficial, maybe even negative.

So far, however, we are encouraged overall by the philanthrocapitalism movement's seriousness of purpose and effectiveness of execution, both on its new frontiers and at its grant-making heart, and thus see plenty of reasons for optimism.

The New Frontiers in the Age of Philanthrocapitalism

The concept of "philanthrocapitalism" was proposed by Matthew Bishop in an extended article for *The Economist* in February 2006 and formed the basis for the book *Philanthrocapitalism*, which was released in 2008.[25] Though sometimes treated, inaccurately, as synonymous with terms such as "venture philanthropy," philanthrocapitalism is a broader concept that encompasses not just the application of modern business techniques to giving but also the effort by a new generation of entrepreneurial philanthropists and business leaders to drive social and environmental progress by changing how business and government operate.

The defining feature of philanthrocapitalism is not, as its critics suggest, a determination to replace traditional grant-making or the democratic processes of civil society with so-called market-based solutions, but rather its laser-like focus on achieving "impact." From Bill Gates on down the wealth ladder, those philanthropists who are leading the exploration of the new frontiers are doing so not out of some simplistic faith in a capitalistic ideology but in the pragmatic belief that deploying a range of tools on the basis of their effectiveness in achieving specific goals is more likely to help solve the world's biggest problems than relying solely on traditional grant-making.

The concept of new frontiers in philanthropy speaks to an evolution in the way that philanthropic capital is used in the quest for impact. For instance, a growing number of today's leading philanthropists no longer make a sharp philosophical distinction between making money and giving it away. E-Bay founder Pierre Omidyar has set up his philanthropic organization, Omidyar Network, not as a traditional grant-making foundation but as an entity that can apply the appropriate sort of capital to the problem in hand—sometimes grants, sometimes for-profit investments, from loans to equity. He has already had some success in encouraging for-profit microfinance as a way to extend financial access to many more poor people than could be reached by relying on nonprofit microfinance funded by grants alone.

Bill Gates made his initial commitment to global public health out of a conviction that pharmaceutical companies had neglected the diseases of the poor because they lacked the financial incentive to do otherwise; he would therefore use his fortune to, in effect, give poor people the purchasing power needed to secure Big Pharma's best efforts. In so doing, he displayed a clear recognition of the limits of market capitalism alongside a belief that the profit motive can be harnessed for good. Since then, his foundation has experimented with a range of new frontier ideas for doing this. At the same time, the foundation, along with other leading philanthrocapitalists, has become increasingly aware of the need to change how government works, if its goals are to be achieved. For instance, it partnered with Eli Broad, a self-described venture philanthropist, to try to change America's education policies.

The interest shown by philanthrocapitalists in new frontier innovations reflects their growing awareness of the limitations, left to itself, of traditional philanthropy. Underlying this focus on various forms of partnership, collaboration with, or "leveraging" of other institutions is a recognition that philanthropy will never be big enough to solve the world's toughest problems if it acts alone. There is little left of the hubris of the Victorian era and early twentieth century, when some leading philanthropists saw no need for the state in the social arena—a delusion that was laid bare by the failure of a Rockefeller-led coalition of philanthropists to resolve America's unemployment crisis in the 1930s. The Bill and Melinda Gates Foundation may be the biggest philanthropic foundation the world has yet seen, but its founder describes it as a "tiny organization" compared with the scale of problems it is taking on, and stresses that success will only be possible if the foundation can recruit others in all sectors of society to work alongside it.

At the same time, potential partners for philanthropy are seeing the need to break out of their sectoral silos and collaborate. Some in government realize that it cannot do everything, and in particular that government tends to be poor at innovation. In business, there is a growing recognition that partnering with nonprofits can create what Harvard University professor Michael Porter calls "shared value."[26] (Nonprofits may bring greater trust and an earlier identification of a social problem and potential solutions to it; business brings assets such as capital, expertise in global logistics, and how to market to the broader population.) In this emerging new division of labor, philanthropy's potential strengths include the ability to take an unusually long-term perspective, and to back unusually risky ideas—traits seen most famously in the decades-long Rockefeller-led efforts that helped save arguably a billion lives through the Green Revolution in Asia.

If this movement succeeds, not least through its harnessing of new frontier approaches, it will benefit society enormously, by helping to solve problems currently beyond us. But will it succeed?

Fad or Force?

While some of the early innovation on new frontiers was done by long-established philanthropies—the Ford Foundation pioneered "program-related investments," and a Rockefeller coined the phrase "venture philanthropy"—the driving force has been the emergence of a new generation of entrepreneurial philanthropists and business leaders willing to think differently. The question is: will this new army of philanthropists be up to the job of nurturing these new ideas to fruition?

After the 2008 financial crisis some critics feared the worst. Commentators such as British social innovation guru Geoff Mulgan predicted that the end of the golden age of capitalism would also snuff out philanthrocapitalism.[27] Such pessimism about the fortunes of the wealthy and their interest in giving has proven misguided as the billionaire philanthropy movement of which Bill Gates and Warren Buffett are the poster children has gone from strength to strength. Indeed, the two men have started along the road to what may become a formal, organized movement, winning new converts through their "Giving Pledge" campaign launched in 2010 to challenge America's billionaires to promise publicly to give away at least half their wealth. As of this writing, 81 of America's billionaires has signed on. In part, this is a tribute to the determination of the new generation of philanthrocapitalists to stick to the task. It is also testimony to the ability of the rich to better protect themselves from the downturn. As we predicted in the *Chronicle of Philanthropy* in October 2008, "no group will survive this crisis better than the very rich" and "this could be the greatest opportunity for acquiring assets in a generation and that will help the rich to build even bigger fortunes."[28] At the last count *Forbes* estimated that, after the number fell sharply in 2009, the world had around 1,426 billionaires in 2013, more than ever.[29]

Strikingly, at the first two annual gatherings of Giving Pledge signatories, new frontier approaches topped the agenda and were the subject of follow-up meetings. In 2011, the hot topic was the use of social media to advance social causes. In 2012, it was how to use their investments for good through impact-investing strategies. In the developing world, the rapid growth in the number of superrich is also creating an interest in how to play a more positive role in society, though in many cultures publicly declaring an intention to give away most of the family fortune is not applauded as it is in America.[30] There is anecdotal evidence that in such cultures some of the new frontier approaches that do not involve full-blown giving have greater appeal.

There are good reasons to expect the global supply of philanthropic capital, and socially directed business capital, to continue to grow over the coming decades, especially if a track record of success is developed that others will want to share in. This progress may be hampered, however, by the growing public skepticism toward the rich in general and to their efforts to explore philanthropy's new frontiers in particular. This mood swing was symbolized by the popular, Twitter-powered, global "#occupy" movement that sprang up in the summer of 2011. But the fact that #occupy made some telling points, especially about the failure of the wealth creation of recent decades sufficiently to benefit ordinary people, does not make the critics of philanthrocapitalism and new frontier philanthropy right.

Philanthrocapitalism and Its Critics

The most fundamental critique of philanthrocapitalism is that it is a contradiction in terms—an argument that was most colorfully expressed by the Marxist philosopher Slavoj Žižek in a discussion of the philanthropy of Bill Gates and George Soros in the *London Review of Books* in 2006:[31]

There is a chocolate-flavoured laxative available on the shelves of US stores which is publicised with the paradoxical injunction: Do you have constipation? Eat more of this chocolate!—i.e. eat more of something that itself causes constipation. The structure of the chocolate laxative can be discerned throughout today's ideological landscape; it is what makes a figure like Soros so objectionable. He stands for ruthless financial exploitation combined with its counter-agent, humanitarian worry about the catastrophic social consequences of the unbridled market economy. Soros's daily routine is a lie embodied: half of his working time is devoted to financial speculation, the other half to 'humanitarian' activities (financing cultural and democratic activities in post-Communist countries, writing essays and books) which work against the effects of his own speculations.

In other words, for Žižek a contradiction is hardwired into the concept of philanthrocapitalism: within his Marxist framework profit is always a product of exploitation of labor value, hence it is impossible, within this framework, for a capitalist to be anything but an exploiter.

This may seem an extreme, marginal critique, yet it seems to influence several critics of philanthrocapitalism and the new frontier approaches. Michael Edwards, for example, argues that "systemic change has to address the question of how property is owned and controlled, and how resources and opportunities are distributed throughout society." This is "the 'means of production' question that takes us back to Marx, and not just Adam Smith."[32] In a similar vein, Kavita Ramdas, reflecting on a meeting between Gates and Buffett and a group of Indian billionaires to promote the Giving Pledge, argues that "far too few in this elite club are willing to ask themselves hard questions about a model of economic growth that has made their phenomenal acquisition of wealth possible in a nation where more than 800 million people still languish in poverty."[33]

We do not dispute that the capitalist system can be improved to serve society better, but we find little useful in this fundamentalist critique. In *The Road from Ruin* we argue that before the crisis of 2008, capitalism worshipped short-term success measured by quarterly profits and daily increases in stock prices.[34] Now a new improved capitalism needs to emerge from the ruins of the old, which if it is sustainably to bring about a more prosperous world, must focus instead on long-term measures of success. Philanthrocapitalism is a capitalism that recognizes that it must be socially and environmentally sustainable. This new thinking is not necessarily a rejection of Milton Friedman's view that the only social responsibility of business is to maximize profits but rather a growing realization that a more constructive attitude to solving society's problems may increase business profits over the long term.[35] This is a revolution in how to value our institutions that was first heralded as "blended value" by Jed Emerson nearly a decade ago and christened more recently by Michael Porter as "shared value."[36]

For Michael Edwards, the idea that the winners of capitalism can or will be part of a process to transform our economic system is "akin to the man who tries to pull himself out of a swamp by his own hair."[37] This is a criticism that applies to all philanthropy by the rich, of course, though Edwards is particularly critical of some of the new frontier approaches that explicitly try to learn from or import techniques or values from the capitalist system. Instead, he argues, it is the countervailing power of civil society that must drive the reform (or overthrow?) of capitalism, and solve society's problems. "Civil society and the market are not just different—they pull in opposite directions," he argues.[38]

We share his view that civil society is crucial, as do philanthrocapitalists such as Bill Gates, George Soros, and Jeff Skoll, who are using their philanthropy to build up civil society with the goal of making it a more effective partner in solving society's problems. But to properly reflect what is happening today the definition of civil society needs to be broadened from the widely held but narrow version used by Edwards.

Civil society is different from the market, he believes, because its richness and diversity is a good in its own right, not in terms of the results it delivers. Better, he argues, to think of civil society as an ecosystem where diversity itself is precious, rather than a market of competitors. This framing puts philanthrocapitalism and the market-based tools of the new frontiers in contradiction to civil society. By treating civil society and nonprofit as synonyms, for-profit organizations, by definition, have no role in civil society. "No great social cause was mobilized through the market in the twentieth century," Edwards asserts. There is no space in Edwards's system for capitalism to play a positive civic role. Philanthrocapitalism has been assumed to be negative from the outset.

We believe that this argument is fundamentally flawed in two ways. First, it is based on a romantic view of the inherent goodness of nonprofit organizations. Edwards stresses the characteristics of mutuality, cooperation, and collective action as key features of this sector. This, indeed, is often the case. Yet we should not be dewy-eyed. Nonprofit organizations are not always champions of freedom and justice. For instance, Sheri Berman's article " Civil Society and the Collapse of the Weimar Republic" (which has been nicknamed "Bowling with Hitler") is a reminder that civic institutions, which she argues played a key role in strengthening Nazism's grip in Germany, can be double edged.[39]

Second, more fundamentally, Edwards's framing ignores the way that for-profit organizations create social or civic value. It is private business that, for example, has driven the explosive growth in cellular phones in Africa over the last decade, which has had a massive role in the economic and political empowerment of citizens. The International Center for Research on Women has similarly identified the motor scooter, created and disseminated by for-profit businesses, as one of the top innovations that has empowered women in recent years.[40] Profit and social value are not necessarily in contradiction. Indeed, profit may even contribute to strengthening civil society, as the Africa Media Development Initiative led by the BBC showed when it highlighted the importance of commercial success as a crucial part of developing a robust and independent media in Africa.[41]

The new frontiers of philanthropy, which are based on market tools and capitalist institutional models, may therefore demand a re-evaluation of how we understand and define civil society. Rather than falling into the business bad/ civil society good dichotomy, we should rather think of both for-profit and nonprofit organizations as part of civil society. They are just different forms of organization that generate economic and social value in different ways. The new frontiers are important because they are exploring tools to maximize both types of value.

For the new frontiers of philanthropy to make a positive contribution to our world, we need a shift in the conversation. This means dropping the idea that profit is necessarily exploitative and the presumption that civil society is exclusively about nonprofit organizations. Instead, we need a more pragmatic conversation about what works, which is the "impact" conversation being led by philanthrocapitalists. To do that we need better ways of measuring social as well as financial returns. This too is dogged with controversy.

Measure for Measure

The new frontier idea of measuring the performance of nonprofit organizations is resisted by, among others, Edwards, who argues that the social sector has no single unit of value, unlike the business world, which uses measures such as profit to compare businesses operating across countries and across sectors. "Markets work because they stick to a clear financial bottom line, use a simple mechanism to achieve it (competition), and require a relatively small number of conditions to make that mechanism work," he argues.[42] As a result, Edwards does not hold out much hope that "social return on investment" and similar methodologies will ever come up with an answer to the "bottom line" measurement question.

If the impact of civil society cannot be effectively measured but donors and social investors insist on metrics to allocate resources, Edwards warns, there is a significant risk of misallocation of resources. In particular, he suggests that there may be a reallocation of philanthropic capital to short-term service-delivery interventions, away from long-term social mobilization and advocacy (a critique echoed by Ramdas). This would be with good reason the stuff of nightmares for groups working in these "at risk" sectors, if it were true. But there are at least three problems with Edwards's argument.

First, where is the evidence that new frontiers approaches are actually displacing investments in social mobilization and advocacy? Ted Turner, when asked how he judges the impact of his $1 billion pledge to support the United Nations that kicked off the philanthrocapitalism revolution in 1997, replied, unempirically, "I just feel it is stronger."[43] Though grant-based interventions to support advocacy lie outside the scope of the new frontiers covered by this volume, public mobilization and advocacy are integral to what many philanthrocapitalists are doing, in recognition of the fact that influencing public policy may be the ultimate leverage.

Second, rejecting metrics out of hand leads to a Lake Wobegon world, where every child (and, presumably, every nonprofit) assumes itself and is assumed to be "above average." We find this both implausible and morally dubious, since it ultimately means abrogating responsibility for asking tough questions about how scarce philanthropic resources are used. Rather than taking a Panglossian view that the nonprofit sector cannot be improved upon, better measurement is an opportunity to make scarce philanthropic capital work harder. Selecting the right metrics is crucial, and a wrong choice can have nasty consequences, but this ought not to be beyond us. Less effective organizations will lose out, but that is not a good reason to defend the status quo.

Third, Edwards's argument is based on a caricature of how markets operate and flawed assumptions about what measurement means. He sees markets largely in terms of spot markets, like the high-volume, rapid-turnover trading that takes place in currencies or commodities. This is just one type of market. There are also markets for very long-term investments like infrastructure. Markets are not by definition short term. Nor do markets necessarily rely on single-point measures of performance such as quarterly profits or the stock price, which may be poor indicators of a business's long-term performance.

Metrics are simply tools to help us understand how an organization is performing and not an excuse to drop detailed analysis. This is one of the hard lessons of the financial crisis, where banks and other financial institutions relied too heavily on credit ratings and short-term profit measures. The challenge for all institutions, for-profit and nonprofit alike, is to find better measures of performance and for funders (as investors or donors) to take their stewardship responsibilities more seriously. This is not an argument against measurement per se, but a challenge to do better.

Whether talking about societies, corporations, or nonprofits we are, ultimately, what we measure. The wrong measurement tools—from quarterly profits to gross domestic product—create distortions in the choices we make. Rather than rejecting measurement out of hand, the crucial debate ahead is how we can improve measurement to incentivize the pursuit of sustainable well-being.

Who Governs?

Yet even if new frontiers approaches are net positive for society, some worry that this comes with a cost to society in terms of democratic accountability. "Giving is becoming governance," argues Robin Rogers, highlighting the growing impact that mega-rich donors have on the policy process by funding lobbying and social movements.[44] Ed Skloot warns that the Gates Foundation is so powerful it may "distort" the agenda on issues like global health.[45] Diane Ravitch has been leading a campaign against what she calls the "billionaire boys' club" of donors.[46]

These are questions that have more to do with traditional grant-making rather than the new frontiers. We have addressed these at length elsewhere and would emphasize the importance of transparency in giving and diversity of donors to mitigate this risk.[47] The issue for new frontiers is that, if these approaches can leverage new resources at scale, what are the implications for the role of the state?

The potential upside is that philanthropy is able both to help government spend its money more effectively and to reduce demands on the taxpayer, both desirable goals given the perilous state of most countries' public finances. One of the most promising new frontier ideas is the "social-impact bond," which is being pioneered by the British government and is being imitated by other governments including the US federal government (where they are known as "pay-for-success" bonds). As examined more fully in chapter 16 of this volume, the idea is to attract private capital (for-profit and philanthropic) to invest in solving deep-rooted problems that are soaking up public money, with the prospect of repayment by the public sector with interest if the intervention succeeds. The first example, launched in 2010, aims to reduce reoffending by released prisoners, which costs the British government millions of pounds a year. This goes beyond a standard public-private partnership, which is expected to provide the same service as the state but more cheaply. The social-impact bond aims to reward better social outcomes and not merely cut costs. The taxpayer is meant to be a winner from this process either way: in the event of failure it costs nothing; in the case of success the savings to government more than compensate for the cost of the payout.

That, of course, is the theory. How widely such tools can be applied and whether serious for-profit capital would be willing to invest in these instruments remain to be seen. The profit element of social-impact bonds also courts controversy among those who adhere to the idea that the very existence of profit must mean that someone is being ripped off.[48]

In other types of public funding of new frontiers approaches, such as a tax break for social investment, there would be a direct, upfront cost to the taxpayer. This cost has to be taken into account when evaluating the social utility of the new frontier approach in question. The gains and losses will vary on a case-by-case basis.

An even more distant risk is a concern that if new frontiers approaches reach sufficient scale, private organizations rather than public bodies could become responsible for the delivery of significant parts of a nation's welfare infrastructure such as schools or social housing, with an attendant loss in public accountability. We believe that this shift may be less significant than it seems, as the likeliest outcome would be for the state to shift from provider of services to a role as regulator and enforcer of standards—a shift that might even increase democratic accountability given the obvious conflicts of interest when the state is both provider and regulator.

Competence and a New Social Contract

We believe that we are at a crucial stage in the definition of a new global social contract for the twenty-first century that will define for a generation the relationship not just between the rich and the rest—as the Occupy Wall Street movement put it, the 1 percent and the 99 percent—but also between capitalism and society. The Giving Pledge has the potential to be a key part of the answer to the question of how the superwealthy should relate to society as a whole. It remains to be seen how a commitment to philanthropy will sit alongside obligations for the rich to contribute through the taxation system.

One factor likely to determine public opinion of philanthropy, especially as its tax-privileged status makes it a sort of outsourced form of public spending, is not how much is given, but how well it is given. The focus on impact, the hallmark of the philanthrocapitalist approach, is a driver of the quest for new tools for effective giving. Whether these tools of the new frontier work will play an important role in determining what sort of social contract emerges between the rich and the rest, including the extent to which inequality is allowed to continue to widen and the degree of progressivity demanded in the tax system.

One of the great uncertainties is whether the new generation of philanthrocapitalists will have the commitment to see the job through—especially as this is, at least in philanthropy if not business, a voluntary endeavor that might be easily discouraged if the going gets tough.

Another great uncertainty is whether they have the necessary competence. Succeeding in business is one thing, especially given its tolerance for command and control and unorthodox personalities, provided they deliver results. Partnering across sectors is another matter, requiring high emotional intelligence. And the problems are harder. As Warren Buffett famously put it, "In business you go after the low-hanging fruit. Giving money away effectively is far harder." A particularly tough challenge will be to develop an integrated "capital curve" for funding good ideas for social change, equivalent to the capital curve in business that describes how a company can be funded from initial start-up seed capital to an eventual flotation on the public stock markets. As we have argued elsewhere, in the world of social innovation, there are big gaps on the capital curve, especially when it comes to scaling up a nonprofit once it approaches medium size, and in managing the transition from non-profit to for profit.[49]

Not least because exploring the new frontiers will be risky, there will need to be a candor about failure that is rare in traditional philanthropy. "If you try a bunch of things, you often learn more from failure than from success," mused technology billionaire Elon Musk in an interview for *The Economist* after meeting with other Giving Pledge signatories in May 2012. His commercial ventures in space exploration, solar energy, and electric cars were "not picked because I thought they were the highest return on investment," he admits. Rather, he thinks that sustainable long-term success comes from using for-profit investments to solve big problems facing humanity. Musk teaches a crucial lesson for the success of the new frontiers—risk-taking means embracing and acknowledging failure, as a feedback loop for learning, as well as success.[50]

The philanthropy world struggles to talk about failure—not least because it tends to inspire negative headlines and criticism from those who are skeptical about the rich and their giving. Indeed, though the Giving Pledgers spent much of that meeting talking about failure, it was all done in private. This needs to change. Ironically, one of Bill Gates' biggest contributions to philanthropy may be that his wealth and prominence means that he has both raised the profile of giving and drawn criticism in a way that no one else could. Gates has also shown a welcome desire to disagree with, as well as learn from, his critics.

Candor about failure will be needed not least because developing the new frontiers is risky. Indeed, there is a danger that philanthrocapitalists will be too risk averse. Take impact investing for example. Research published by J.P. Morgan in 2010 claimed that there is now a potential $1 trillion pool of capital looking for what the bank calls "impact investments" that offer investors a combination of both financial and social or environmental return.[51] Well, maybe. But currently, for all the talk, only a tiny fraction of that sum is impact invested, apparently because of the risk aversion of those controlling the money.

Insufficient thought was given to the risks when philanthrocapitalists such as Omidyar Network encouraged the shift from charitable to for-profit micro-credit in India. They were right about the logic of the case for doing so: there is a business model that can attract far more money to lend to the poor than would ever be able to be reaped from charity. Yet in the rush to develop these new frontier models, insufficient thought was given, in some cases at least, to whether the microcredit industry had the capacity to grow so fast (such as in terms of the available supply of competent loan officers), or whether customers properly understood the financial products they were being sold. Thus, when Indian farmers in Uttar Pradesh committed suicide in 2010, blaming excessive debt borrowed from microcredit lenders, the newly public for-profit SKS Microfinance could not escape a share of the blame.[52]

To its critics, this was evidence of the folly of the for-profit new frontier of philanthropy. In our view, it was evidence of sloppy thinking, a deadly wake-up call and lesson to be learned if the potential to harness the profit motive to serve the "bottom of the pyramid" in other sectors, from water supply to education, is to be fulfilled.

It is not just the level of competence and commitment of the philanthrocapi-talists that remains unknown. The same applies to their potential partners. Governments have started to experiment with the new frontiers, from Barack Obama's White House Office for Social Innovation to David Cameron's Big

Society Capital and pioneering social-impact bond. Yet the scale of these initiatives to date is tiny. The danger is that the risk aversion of those in government, with re-election on their minds, will far exceed that of philanthropists. Businesses, too, may nod to Michael Porter's shared value, but limit their actions to what can be funded from the corporate social responsibility budget rather than put the new approach at the heart of their core business strategy. As for nonprofits, many have viewed with suspicion the new breed of philanthrocapitalists, with their emphasis on efficiency and results, and they may be tempted to resist them rather than partner.

In sum, then, we believe the new frontiers, as part of philanthrocapitalism, have the potential to make society as a whole a big winner, while creating only those losers who deserve to lose. Yet that happy result is far from inevitable. It will depend, not least, on the ability of all our institutions to evolve and adapt to make the most of the opportunity presented by the new multisectoral partnership approach to solving the world's biggest problems.

Notes

1. Ford Foundation, *Investing for Social Gain: Reflections on Two Decades of Social Investments* (New York: Ford Foundation, 1991).

2. Jed Emerson, "The Blended Value Proposition: Integrating Social and Financial Returns," *California Management Review* 45.4 (2003): 35–51.

3. Michael Edwards, *Civil Society* (Cambridge: Polity Press, 2009).

4. Peter Frumkin, *Strategic Philanthropy: The Art and Science of Giving* (Chicago: University of Chicago Press, 2006).

5. Charles Bronfman and Jeffrey Solomon, *The Art of Giving: Where the Soul Meets a Business Plan* (San Francisco: Jossey-Bass, 2009).

6. Geoff Mulgan, "Measuring Social Value," *Stanford Social Innovation Review*, Summer 2010, 38–43.

7. Alnoor Ebrahim and V. Kasturi Rangan, "The Limits of Nonprofit Impact: A Contingency Framework for Measuring Social Performance," Harvard Business School Working Paper 10-099, 2010.

8. Paul Shoemaker, cited in Michael Edwards, *Small Change: Why Business Won't Save the World* (San Francisco: Berrett-Koehler, 2010), 78.

9. Diane Ravitch, *The Death and Life of the Great American School System* (New York: Basic Books, 2010).

10. Acumen Fund, "Impact Reporting and Investment Standards," 2009, http://iris-standards.org.

11. Angus Deaton, "Instruments, Randomization and Learning about Development," Princeton University Program in Development Studies, Research Paper 269, 2010.

12. Donald T. Campbell, "Assessing the Impact of Planned Social Change," Public Affairs Center, Dartmouth College, Occasional Paper No. 8, December 1976, 49, accessed January 9, 2014, https://www.globalhivmeinfo.org/CapacityBuilding/Occasional%20Papers/08%20Assessing%20the%20Impact%20of%20Planned%20Social%20Change.pdf.

13. Edwards, *Small Change*, 41.

14. "All Donors Care about Impact," Tactical Philanthropy, June 2010, accessed November 29, 2012, http://www.tacticalphilanthropy.com/2010/06/all-donors-care-about-impact.

15. SEEDCO, *The Limits of Social Enterprise* (New York: SEEDCO Policy Center, 2008).

16. Leandro Sepulveda, Stephen Syrett, and Sara Calvo, "Social Enterprise and Ethnic Minorities," Third Sector Research Center Working Paper 48, 2010.

17. Robert Wade, *Governing the State: Economic Theory and the Role of Government in East Asian Industrialization* (Princeton: Princeton University Press, 2003).

18. Theda Skocpol, *Diminished Democracy: From Membership to Management in American Civic Life* (Oklahoma City: University of Oklahoma Press, 2003).

19. Alana Conner and Keith Epstein, "Harnessing Purity and Pragmatism," *Stanford Social Innovation Review*, Fall 2007, 65.

20. WWF-UK, *Common Cause: The Case for Working with Our Values* (London: WWF-UK, 2010), 8.

21. Lucy Bernholz, "Why Jumo, Facebook and the Rest Won't Change Everything," *The Guardian*, December 2, 2010.

22. For more information on these approaches see the following: Bill Somerville, *Grassroots Philanthropy: Field Notes of a Maverick Grant-Maker* (San Francisco: Heyday Press, 2008); Albert Ruesga and Dianne Puntenney, *Social Justice Philanthropy: An Initial Framework for Positioning This Work* (New York: Working Group on Philanthropy for Social Justice and Peace, 2010); and Susan Wilkinson-Maposa, Alan Fowler, Ceri Oliver-Evans, and Chao F. N. Mulenga, *The Poor Philanthropist: How and Why the Poor Help Each Other* (Cape Town: University of Cape Town Graduate School of Business, 2009).

23. Andrew Carnegie, "Wealth," *North American Review* 391 (June 1889): 653.

24. Matthew Bishop and Michael Green, *Philanthrocapitalism: How the Rich Can Save the World* (New York: Bloomsbury, 2008).

25. Matthew Bishop, "The Birth of Philanthrocapitalism," *The Economist*, February 23, 2006.

26. Michael E. Porter and Mark R. Kramer, "Creating Shared Value," *Harvard Business Review Magazine*, January 2011, accessed October 12, 2012, http://hbr.org/2011/01/the-big-idea-creating-shared-value.

27. Geoff Mulgan, "After Capitalism," *Prospect*, April 26, 2009, 157–70.

28. Matthew Bishop, "Philanthrocapitalism on Trial," *Chronicle of Philanthropy*, October 30, 2008.

29. Luisa Kroll, "Inside the 2013 Billionaires List: Facts and Figures," *Forbes*, March 25, 2013, accessed August 2, 2013, http://www.forbes.com/sites/luisakroll/2013/03/04/inside-the-2013-billionaires-list-facts-and-figures/.

30. Devin Banerjee, "Will an Indian billionaire Take the Pledge?" Wall Street Journal India Blog, August 9, 2010, accessed October 10, 2012, http://blogs.wsj.com/wealth/2010/08/09/will-an-indian-billionaire-take-the-pledge/.

31. Slavoj Žižek, "Nobody Has to Be Vile," *London Review of Books* 28.7 (2006): 10.

32. Michael Edwards. *Just Another Emperor? The Myths and Realities of Philanthrocapitalism* (New York: Demos, 2008).

33. Kavita Ramdas, "Philanthrocapitalism Is Not Social Change Philanthropy," Stanford Social Innovation Review Blog, December 15, 2011, accessed October 10, 2012, http://www.ssireview.org/point_counterpoint/philanthrocapitalism.

34. Matthew Bishop and Michael Green, *The Road from Ruin: How to Revive Capitalism and Put America Back on Top* (New York: Crown, 2010).

35. Milton Friedman, "The Social Responsibility of Business Is to Increase Its Profits," *New York Times Magazine*, September 13, 1970.

36. Emerson, "Blended Value Proposition."

37. Edwards, *Just Another Emperor?*

38. Edwards, *Just Another Emperor?*

39. Shari Berman, "Civil Society and the Collapse of the Weimar Republic," *World Politics* 49.3 (1997): 401–29.

40. International Center for Research on Women, *Bridging the Gender Divide: How Technology Can Advance Women Economically* (Washington, DC: International Center for Research on Women, 2010).

41. BBC World Service Trust, "African Media Development Initiative: Research Summary Report," 2006, http://downloads.bbc.co.uk/worldservice/trust/pdf/AMDI/AMDI_summary_Report.pdf.

42. Edwards, *Just Another Emperor?*, 57.

43. Bishop and Green, *Philanthrocapitalism*, 99.

44. Robin Rogers, "The Hidden Costs of Million-Dollar Donations," *Washington Post*, December 30, 2011, http://www.washingtonpost.com/opinions/the-hidden-costs-of-million-dollar-donations/2011/12/20/gIQAzpC1QP_story.html.

45. Edward Skloot, "The Gated Community," *Alliance*, September 1, 2011, http://www.alliancemagazine.org/en/content/gated-community.

46. Ravitch, *Death and Life*.

47. Bishop and Green, *Philanthrocapitalism*.

48. Polly Toynbee, "Who's in the Market for Sub-prime Behaviour Bonds?" *The Guardian*, July 4, 2011, http://www.guardian.co.uk/commentisfree/2011/jul/04/sub-prime-behaviour-bonds-fools-gold.

49. Matthew Bishop and Michael Green, "The Capital Curve for a Better World," *Innovations* 5.1 (2010): 25–33.

50. Matthew Bishop, "Elon Musk and the Giving Pledge: Space, Electric Cars and Philanthropy," *The Economist Online* video, 5:52, May 18, 2012, http://www.economist.com/blogs/babbage/2012/05/elon-musk-and-giving-pledge.

51. Nick O'Donohoe, Christina Leijonhufvud, Yasemin Saltuk, Antony Bugg-Levine, and Margot Brandenburg, "Impact Investments: An Emerging Asset Class," J.P. Morgan, November 29, 2010, accessed October 12, 2012, http://www.jpmorgan.com/cm/cs?pagename=JPM/DirectDoc&urlname= impact_investments_nov2010.pdf.

52. Yoolim Lee and Ruth David, "Suicides in India Revealing How Men Made a Mess of Microcredit," *Bloomberg Markets Magazine*, December 28, 2010.

Suggested Readings

Part A

Edwards, Michael. *Civil Society* (Cambridge: Polity Press, 2009).

Edwards, Michael. *Small Change: Why Business Won't Save the World* (San Francisco: Berrett-Koehler, 2010).

Frumkin, Peter. *Strategic Philanthropy: The Art and Science of Giving* (Chicago: University of Chicago Press, 2006).

Part B

Bishop, Matthew. *"The Birth of Philanthrocapitalism." The Economist*, February 23, 2006.

Bishop, Matthew, and Michael Green. *Philanthrocapitalism: How the Rich Can Save the World*. New York: Bloomsbury, 2008.

Edwards, Michael. *Just Another Emperor? The Myths and Realities of Philanthrocapitalism*. New York: Demos, 2008.

CHAPTER 21

THE DEMAND SIDE OF THE SOCIAL INVESTMENT MARKETPLACE

Alex Nicholls and Rod Schwartz

HACKNEY COMMUNITY TRANSPORT (HCT) IS a community enterprise, owned by a UK charity, which provides transport services to communities in East London, Yorkshire, and elsewhere in the UK. The company is profitable, has cash in the bank, over £25 million of turnover, and has been operating since 1982. It is widely seen as a model social enterprise.[1]

As a provider of bus services it has a need to purchase and finance buses, which are a large single expense. These are then used to operate on routes subject to contracts won normally in competitive tenders run by local authorities. Historically, HCT has funded these purchases through banks on a lease-finance basis, where the buses themselves—combined with HCT's excellent positive cash flows—provide security. HCT became increasingly concerned about its reliance on the banking system (interestingly, its fears predated any banking crisis) and also wondered if it could reduce financing costs.

After a lengthy process, it was eventually able to avail itself of £4 million of social finance.[2] This was divided roughly 50/50 between a straight five-year loan and a quasi-equity instrument, the returns on which were tied to HCT's revenue growth. The full £4 million would not have been raised without the inclusion of £2 million of a quasi-equity instrument because the lead investors, who were confident about the business' prospects, sought a higher return than debt would offer, and were comfortable tying this to revenue growth. This was a landmark transaction for several reasons. First, its size—at £4 million this was significant in the social investment sector in the UK. Second, its cost—HCT probably saved half of what it would have had to pay an investment bank for the transaction. Third, the blend of investors—they were a combination of institutional social investors (led by Bridges Ventures, through its Social Entrepreneur's Fund) and individual investors, organized via Rathbone Greenbank.

Hackney Community Transport's story is illustrative of an important global trend—the emergence of social-purpose organizations of various types that have achieved the scale and sophistication to access complex social finance resources either on their own or with the assistance of a variety of intermediaries. This is the crucial "other side" of the emerging social-impact investment market chronicled in the previous chapters of this book, and one that many enthusiasts for social-impact investing fear may be woefully underdeveloped. Indeed, many of those who see in the growth of social investing a way to reform capitalism in the aftermath of the 2008 global financial crisis consider the real challenge to building a robust social capital market to be not an insufficient supply of social investment capital but an insufficient supply of investment-ready deals.[3]

The purpose of this chapter is to evaluate this concern, to analyze and assess the level of demand for social investment. Specifically, it seeks to outline the structure and dynamics of the demand side of the social capital market; to critique some of the recent attempts to assess demand; to suggest methodologies for quantifying the scope and trajectories of the demand-side; and to conclude with reflections on key issues and barriers confronting demand-side players. To do so, the next section sets out key terms and definitions around the demand for social investment. After this, the sources of capital for social investment are considered, and this leads into a fuller assessment of how to measure the demand for social investment, acknowledging existing data and their limitations. A brief section detailing demand-side perspectives on the financial instruments available for social investment follows this discussion. The chapter concludes with a summary of key points and some observations on key issues in generating social investment demand going forward.

This chapter aims to capture global trends and structures, but an important caveat is that the bulk of existing research on social investment has a strong northern hemisphere/Anglo-Saxon investor focus and that this will—inevitably—produce a bias in what follows here. The research to date on social investment has been particularly driven by two factors. First, since 2000, the UK government has been the most active player globally in developing a domestic social investment market using fiscal, regulatory, and legal interventions as well as over £1 billion of direct investment.[4] This has generated a considerable attendant (mostly gray) literature. Second, since 2009, there has been a concerted effort—pioneered by the Rockefeller Foundation and J.P. Morgan—to foster the concept of "impact investing" among a predominantly US investor base.[5] The result has been a significant body of analysis designed to encourage US investors and fund managers to engage with a new set of investment models and opportunities at the "bottom of the pyramid."[6][7] While the actual flows of capital into impact investing remain small, the term has still gained considerable traction in the social investment space.

Social Investment Defined

In this chapter, social investment is taken to represent all flows of capital that are allocated to individuals, organizations, or projects that either demonstrate a primary strategic focus on generating social or environmental value for the public good (for example, work integration social enterprises) or that have such outcomes as a primary consequence of their action (for example, green tech firms). Furthermore, investment here is used to draw a distinction between operating revenue that effectively purchases/commissions goods and services (i.e., government service contracts, many foundation grants) and investment capital that builds capacity, capabilities, and assets in investee organizations and enables future expansion.[8] Social value creation is best understood in terms of the outputs and impacts of organizational action identified as "social" or "environmental" in terms of normative (and often localized) assessments of their positive effects across five dimensions:

- *Geography and demography.* Who the target market or beneficiaries are and where they are located, for example a project working in a deprived area or within disenfranchised populations

- *Organizational processes.* How value is created within an organization for key stakeholders and beneficiaries, for example work integration social enterprises that aim to bring excluded groups into the labor market
- *Goods and services produced.* How mission objectives are achieved in terms of outputs, for example providing care services or low-cost irrigation pumps
- *Sector.* In which category of economic activity the organization fits, for example health, education, clean/green technology, clean water[9]
- *Financial or organizational structure.* Who appropriates the value created, for example mutual or cooperative enterprises or dividend-capped or asset-locked legal forms (such as UK community interest companies—CICs)[10]

The investees on the demand side include social enterprises, charities, cooperatives, social businesses, and hybrid organizations combining elements of the state, the private sector, and the civil society sector engaging in social innovation.[11] Many social investees have been in existence for a long time, for example faith-based charities and cooperatives and mutual societies. However, over the past 20 years there has also been significant institutional innovation around social investment with the emergence, in many countries, of a growing social entrepreneurship or social enterprise sector.[12] This new sector has attracted considerable interest from governments, private-sector firms, and civil society organizations alike and has been characterized by new legal forms (Type 1 and Type 2 Social Co-operatives in Italy; the community interest company in the UK; the L3C form in the United Stats), operational fields (community development finance; housing associations), and whole markets (carbon exchanges; REDD).[13]

Of particular importance in terms of conceptualizing capital allocation in social investment is a separation of value creation and value appropriation.[14] In conventional finance, the owner of invested capital expects to benefit from an appropriate, risk-adjusted proportion of the resultant value created. This provides one of the underpinning logics of pure market theory extrapolated from Adam Smith's original conception of the "invisible hand" of the rational, utility maximizing *homo oeconomicus.* However, in social investment, the expectations of the owner of capital invested are typically more complex with respect to value appropriation. For example: a philanthropist might judge an investment by the value created for a beneficiary not for herself; a dedicated social investment fund may be seeking a blend of financial value returned to investors and social value for another party; finally, a commercial investor may be seeking only a "conventional" financial return while still creating social value for others, for example by buying equity in a microfinance company.

Sources of Capital for Social Investment

Before elaborating on the question of demand for investment, we need to have some understanding of how the investment process operates. For all practical purposes all investing begins with the money coming from individuals, whose funds are either directly invested or invested via financial intermediaries. Direct investing is very much for the minority, however, as most individuals believe that regulated financial intermediaries offer a more efficient way to secure their savings than could be achieved by acting on their own. The major exception to this are high-net-worth individuals (HNWIs) who invest at such a scale that direct investment can make financial sense. These HNWIs might do so via financial intermediaries, as will most individuals, or through "private banks," which offer dedicated—often bespoke—services. Some HNWIs even set up family offices of their own, which function as mini-intermediaries whose sole client may be an individual or their families. These offices make direct investments or invest via other financial intermediaries.

Individuals invest their savings through intermediaries in two basic forms— they do so via deposits, or through funds. Deposits are straightforward, and remain as liabilities of the depository system—via banks, building societies— each with different governmental degrees of guarantees and support, depending on their nature and amount. These are then loaned on to other individuals, businesses, governments, or other agencies in an attempt to secure a higher return over the rate paid by banks to the depositors, leaving them with a "spread" to cover costs and losses and, hopefully, earn a profit.

The other major category of individual investments can be classified as funds. These are regulated pools of financial assets, which are invested in debt, equity, and other instruments and asset classes, all in the pursuit of returns that are as high as possible subject to the specific mandate of the fund. For example, a fund set up to invest in high-quality government bonds should have a much more conservative portfolio than a venture capital fund, investing in early-stage businesses. Two special types of funds that receive large portions of individual monies are pension funds and insurance funds. They are set up for a specific and clearly outlined purpose, and invest accordingly. Such funds seek to maximize returns subject to the parameters of their fund documents, and may invest directly in assets designed to comply with these terms and offer attractive terms. Such assets might include other funds as well as directly into the securities or obligations issued by companies or governments. Pension funds are designed to build wealth for use in retirement, and frequently offer a fiscally advantageous form of capital building. Insurance funds will sometimes also contain fiscal advantages, but seek simultaneously to protect the policyholder against some predefined risk (poor health, disability, or one's heirs against the death of the policyholder).

In addition to these specialized funds there are many other types of funds, all designed to offer investors varying combinations of risk and return as well as exposure to different asset classes. For example, funds might offer exposure to high-quality equities, junk (low-grade) bonds, private equity opportunities, commodities, or internationally diversified portfolios.

There are two other primary ways individual money finds its way into the financial markets, and then potentially on into social investing, directly and via intermediaries. First, charitable donations and legacies constitute an important source of capital for the Third Sector. In the UK alone there are assumed to be £60–£80 billion of endowment assets available for grant-making or investment, which represent the accumulated grants of charitable donors past and present and the subsequent income from those donations.[15] In the United States this figure is estimated at £324 billion.[16]

Individuals also indirectly "make investments" via the taxes they pay. A portion of government spending is subsequently invested into public goods, other assets, or even into social investment funds themselves. The UK government has been a global leader in capitalizing the social investment market with over a £1 billion of taxpayer money, 2001–2011. The monies supporting similar schemes exist also in North America, Australasia, Asia, and, at the supra-national level, in the United Nations and European Union. All these funds deployed by governments or their operatives inevitably begin with individuals in one form or another. For example, the European Financial Stability Fund—and the funds at the disposal of the European Central Bank—emanate from taxes on individuals or government's ability to borrow in anticipation of being repaid from future taxation.

The Demand for Social Investment

Key Issues in Gauging the Demand for Social Investment

Several issues need to be considered in order to calculate the demand for social investment capital. The first is to set out what is meant here by the demand side. In this chapter, demand represents the capital sought by all potential investees seeking to generate social or environmental value for the public good.[17] This demand is not necessarily the same as actual investment, except where a market equilibrium can be said to exist. It seems intuitively obvious that innate demand will always be larger than actual capital flows,[18] but this may not actually be the case. Moreover, "demand" here does not equal the demand for capital by social investment intermediaries or brokers—although this will inevitably be part of the total. As will be discussed further below, an explicit focus on the end investee's financial needs, or at least its desires, presents significant methodological problems in terms of quantification, since existing data on the demand for social investment typically focuses on the opportunities for potential investors.[19]

Apart from the methodological problems mentioned above, there are a series of other complexities and logical issues that need to be taken into account before considering and assessing the actual demand for social investment. The first of these has to do with the very nature of what is meant by demand and supply. Typically, the supply of capital refers to those sums that might be invested, or could be invested, by organizations with capital to invest. However, as in mainstream markets, it is impossible to quantify supply without reference to price; where price can be taken as meaning assessments of perceived returns. Thus, without at least some discussion of price the concept of supply of capital is meaningless, since there is—theoretically at least—no limit to the supply of investment capital that could be made available if the price were deemed to be right.

Quantifying demand is also problematic. As with definitions of supply, it is clear that at lower prices—meaning lower interest rates—more money will be borrowed, and that if equity capital were available in abundance at high prices, meaning at higher company valuation multiples, the demand for it would soar as well. Categorical statements can only be made about demand and supply in equilibrium, namely where the financial markets clear at a given price. Nevertheless, despite these serious caveats, several attempts at quantifying the demand-side opportunity for social investment have been made and these are reviewed next.

Existing Estimates

In a pioneering study supported by Monitor consultants, Freireich and Fulton suggested that social investment—categorized here as "impact investment"—could grow to represent about 1 percent of all professionally managed assets making this market worth £310 billion globally over the next 10 years.[20] Of these, the most developed sector was suggested to be microfinance, with global microcredit volumes growing rapidly from £2.5 billion in 2001 to $25 billion in 2010.[21] The successful initial public offering of 30 percent of Compartamos—a Mexican microfinance institution—in 2007 realized £290 million and demonstrated the potential for highly attractive returns on investment.

J.P. Morgan Chase—supported by the Rockefeller Foundation—pioneered research into the impact investment market. O'Donohoe and coauthors and Saltuk endeavored to assess demand from social investees.[22] In the first report, the authors analyzed potential demand for social or impact investment in the developing world. This aimed to establish impact investment as a new asset class within portfolios, similar to equities or property. In doing so the authors believed that greater institutional resources would be committed to social investment. The report suggested that in the next 10 years the level of investable demand in the markets they identified would be approximately $1 trillion. In the second report, a more detailed analysis was undertaken of the investment intentions of the largest, predominantly US-based, investment institutions.

With respect to the sectoral structure of social investment demand, O'Donohoe and coauthors identified seven demand markets within the survey of impact investing:

- Basic Needs
  - Agriculture
  - Water
  - Housing
- Basic services
  - Education
  - Health
  - Energyo Financial services[23]

Their analysis suggested that, to date, the majority of impact investments have been made in housing ($790 million; 31.8 percent of total investment to date) and microfinance ($661 million; 26.6 percent). Projected future demand for impact investment was estimated as potentially reaching $1 trillion in the "bottom of the pyramid" markets found in developing countries. The report suggested projected demand by sector as affordable urban housing ($214 billion–$786 billion); microfinance ($176 billion); clean water for rural communities ($5.4 billion–$13 billion); primary education ($4.8 billion–$10 billion); maternal health ($0.4 billion–$2 billion).

This research supports an earlier analysis carried out by Campanale with respect to social investment opportunities for the £50 billion of UK charitable assets that were otherwise invested in profit-maximizing mainstream stocks that had no clear social or environmental objectives.[24] The sectors identified here were health (22.5 percent of the suggested total portfolio); efficiency and productivity (15 percent); sustainable transport (12.5 percent); cleaner energy (10 percent); water management (10 percent); learning and education (10 percent); environmental services (5 percent); safety (5 percent); quality of life (5 percent); social property and finance (5 percent). Brown and Norman suggested that in the UK in 2010–11 actual social investment was spread across a wider variety of sectors, with only housing (12 percent of total investment) and social care (10 percent) accounting for significant individual proportions of the whole.[25] Other sectors included social enterprises; community investment; health and well-being; education and training; religious institutions; employment support; sport and leisure; arts and culture; criminal justice; financial inclusion; human rights.

Finally, in terms of geographical spread, O'Donohoe and coauthors' findings suggested that the majority of impact investments up to 2010 had been made in the United States and Canada ($1,381 million: 55.7 percent of total investment) followed by Latin America ($223: 9 percent).[26] The report projected over a $1 trillion of demand in developing countries going forward. This contrasts with the historical data in the UK, where as we previously mentioned, only £165 million in social investment was identified in 2011, outside of government spending.[27] Elsewhere, research on the Asian impact investment market suggested that there is a demand opportunity of between $52 billion and $158 billion by 2020 concentrated in primary education (up to $50 billion), rural elderly care (up to $50 billion), and affordable housing (up to $33 billion).[28]

In the UK, Brown and Norman collected data from the largest social investors and estimated that £165 million had been invested in UK social enterprises in 2010.[29] However, it seems likely that this figure represents a significant undercalculation because of several factors:

- The sample, even of committed social investors, was not sufficiently comprehensive. For example the Co-op Bank, a major lender to the social economy, does not appear to have participated in the survey.
- Mainstream lenders and investors—such as Royal Bank of Scotland— were also excluded from the survey despite a number investing regularly in social businesses and enterprises.
- The substantial and growing number of HNWIs who are supporting the social business and enterprise sector were also excluded.
- Approximately 70 percent of the figure of £165 million was made in the form of fixed interest investments. A portion of those would have represented bonds or other forms of long-term investment to support development of the social enterprise. However, a significant portion may simply have consisted of short-term bank debt. This would mean the level of social *investment* was actually lower.

Another approach to estimating demand can be based upon categories of investment risk. In this respect, social investments are typically categorized in much the same way as conventional organizations, namely by life cycle (albeit often with a "social" risk premium). Thus, start-ups are considered riskier than well-established organizations. However, this may be a misleading comparison since many apparently established social enterprises and charities have long been dependent on intrinsically unstable sources of funding in terms of grants or government contracts. In addition, the social enterprise sector remains immature, with many more small organizations and recent start-ups than large players at scale—so perceptions of the riskiness of social investment may also be skewed by this factor too.[30] Joy, de Las Casas, and Rickey suggested that the social investee market needed a range of life-cycle financing:

- *Short- to medium-term working capital:* this is often needed to prepare for tendering for government contracts and to bridge gaps in the flow of other income/investment.

- *Stand-by facilities and underwriting/guarantees:* social enterprises often struggle to achieve and maintain a profit at small scale and are, therefore, perceived as too high risk for investment.
- *Medium-term growth and development capital:* there is a big gap in terms of high-risk capital in the £20,000–£250,000 range. Two-thirds of all social investment in 2010 were micro-grants of £5,000 or less.[31]
- *Long-term asset funding (i.e., property):* this provides collateral to leverage subsequent investment.[32]

Furthermore, conceptualizing risk in social investment is highly problematic per se since it does not typically relate directly to calculations of expected financial return alone, as it does in conventional finance. How to calculate *blended* social and economic risk and return profiles for social investments remains a matter for speculation rather than of established practice.[33] This is the case not only because blended metrics and accounting techniques have yet to become institutionalized, but also because the relationship between social investment and blended value creation may well be mediated by contextual factors far more complex than is the case for mainstream firms (for example, operating in less lucrative markets shunned by profit-maximizing firms). Moreover, the data for such an analysis simply do not exist. Thus, although it is interesting, we do not believe this approach will be fruitful.

Available historical data suggested the following market sizes. O'Donohoe and coauthors calculated that impact investment deals in the United States, for example totaled $2,481 million in 2010 (1,105 actual deals) spread across a range of demand-side sectors dominated by investments in housing $790 million (31.8 percent of total) and microfinance $661 million (26.6 percent); 65 percent of the deals were under $1 million.[34] This influential report also estimated the demand for impact investment over the next 10 years as between $400.6 billion and $987 billion, representing a profit "opportunity" of between $183 and $667 billion.[35] This demand was predicted chiefly in housing ($214–$786 billion) and microfinance ($176 billion) with the bottom-of-the-pyramid (BoP) market estimated at potentially reaching $8 trillion annually.[36] Such figures are supported by research elsewhere that suggests that, as another example, the demand for investment by social enterprises working in the clean water and sanitation sector in Asia alone will be £7 billion to £21 billion by 2020.[37] In contrast, total UK social investment in 2010 has been estimated at only between £165 million and £190 million.[38]

Sectoral Insights

This chapter suggests that a sectoral approach is likely to be the most appropriate approach to calculating social investment demand. However, it is also proposed here that a focus on emerging market issues alone will inevitably understate the actual market size and opportunity. Social investment also includes more mature areas of investment that have already become part of the mainstream and for which relatively good data are readily available, notably clean technology and community and mutual investment.

Clean Technology

Clean energy investment offers the potential for high financial returns to investors while also benefiting the environment. Historically, the growth of this sector has been driven largely by the attractiveness of its returns to mainstream investors rather than by its environmental impacts. Despite a dip in 2009, the overall global trend in clean energy investments over the past 10 years has been strongly positive. According to New Energy Finance, global clean energy investments (including direct investment in research and development, technology, and equipment) grew from £22 billion in 2004 to £90 billion in 2009.[39] Among the many funds interested in clean energy are Generation Investment Management, which integrates sustainability into its equity analysis and which closed a £400 million Climate Solutions Fund in 2008, and Mission Point Capital Partners, who have a £210 million fund focused on solutions that contribute to a low-carbon economy. Again, as was the case with SRI and impact investment (of which green tech could be seen as a subset), accessing green tech investment is largely limited to the demand-side investees that can offer access to publicly traded shares. An exception to this is the global carbon trading market, which has also been growing rapidly. The market was estimated to be worth £77 billion by the end of 2008.[40]

Community and Mutual Investment

Community investment refers to the provision of financial services to underserved communities and includes banks, credit unions, and loan funds. It has proved influential in the United States and, more recently, in Europe. In the United States, the Community Reinvestment Act (CRA), originally passed in 1977, provided incentives to increase investment in poor communities such that, in 2007, £16 billion was invested as a result of the CRA. In the UK, the Community Investment Tax Relief scheme (CITR) was introduced in 2002 (by the social investment task force) as a tax incentive to investors in community development finance institutions (CDFIs). The total CITR relief is worth up to 25 percent of the total investment. By 2007, CITR had generated between £53 and £58 million in new investments in CDFIs.[41] CDFIs lend and invest in deprived areas that cannot access mainstream finance. In the UK in 2010 CDFIs lent a record £200 million, up 77 percent from the previous reporting period. In the same period, the value of CDFI loan applications rose to £437 million (from £360 million previously) such that the UK CDFI loan portfolio stood at £531 million as of March 2010. CDFIs also helped their customers leverage an additional £100 million from other mainstream sources.

In 2008, UK cooperatives and mutual societies had revenues of more than £98 billion and assets of over £572 billion.[42] In continental Europe, over 240,000 cooperatives were economically active in 2005 working in many sectors, particularly agriculture, financial intermediation, retailing and housing, and as workers' cooperatives in the industrial, building, and service sectors. These cooperatives provide direct employment to 3.7 million people and have 143 million members.[43] Credit unions—localized mutual finance organizations—represent an important intersection between CDFIs and cooperatives. In 2010, 52,945 credit unions operated in 100 countries. Credit unions had 188 million members with total savings of $1.23 trillion, loans of $960 billion, reserves of $131 billion, and assets of $1.46 trillion.[44] Credit unions are particularly active in developing countries, with more than 22,000 in Asia and over 17,000 in Africa (2010). At a global level, in 2008, cooperatives and mutuals were responsible for an aggregate turnover of £700 billion, with estimated assets of over £3 trillion.[45] These figures suggest that mutual investment may be the largest single segment of the social investment market globally. Mutuals also demonstrate how the demand-side for social investment can be capitalized without recourse to mainstream funds or secondary investment markets.

In addition, microfinance has become a well-institutionalized sector over the past 20 years. Microlending and, increasingly, other financial services to the poor such as microsavings and microinsurance have grown from a series of small pilot projects in Bangladesh to being a multi-million-dollar sector some parts of which (when securitized) are now traded by mainstream financial institutions. As such, microfinance represents a core element of the existing impact-investing market and is considered further below.

This section has demonstrated that there is already a range of data from which calculations of the size and scope of the demand for social investment might be inferred. However, it is also the case that there are significant methodological limitations here. This suggests that the need for additional work. A best-practice approach to addressing this need and calculating demand more effectively might usefully proceed as follows:

- Identify all of the sectors of an economy where social businesses and enterprises might have a significant presence. In most markets, and certainly in most developed markets, there is no need to limit this only to sectors addressing basic needs and basic services. Many other sectors of the economy may have social businesses and enterprises active within them.
- Collect data on the size of each sector based on available national statistics such as GDP.
- Consider the growth potential in each sector over time: such forecasts are widely available from brokerage firm industry notes, and there is often a general consensus about growth rates.
- Engage social enterprise experts and practitioners in a given country to use published research, survey data, and common sense to estimate the share of each industry sector represented by social businesses and enterprises and to forecast whether this share will increase or decrease over time and at what rate.
- Analyze and assess what are the capital needs, on average, for companies operating in each sector. Use standard financial ratios such as assets or equity to turnover, equity to assets, or debt to equity.
- Apply the estimated market share of social businesses and enterprises to the whole sector and derive the investment capital needed at present and in the future.
- Summarize conclusions into an overall estimate of likely demand for social investment by country.

Financial Instruments from a Demand-Side Perspective

This section briefly reviews the range of financial instruments available for social investment from the perspective of investees. It aims to explore how each offers different opportunities and challenges for demand-side actors seeking capital. This is partly a function of the level of market development of each instrument—for example, equity remains of limited value in social investment because of the lack of established secondary markets or exchanges.

Grants

Historically, government, foundation, and other charitable grants have been the main form of capital flows into the social economy, aside from government spending. However, as was noted above, such funding has often taken the form of consumption rather than investment: that is, grants are used to fund operating income for specific programs or mission-related outcomes rather than to build the capacity of grantee organizations to improve their performance or scale their activities. In recent years the effectiveness and efficiency of such funding has increasingly been questioned, with two consequences: first, the rise of engaged or "venture" philanthropy that attempts to use venture capital approaches to grant-making; second, the emergence of social enterprises that eschew grant funding and seek to earn income from commercial markets.

Nevertheless, grant funding remains very important in terms of the demand side of social investment, particularly in terms of start-up capital for new social ventures that cannot access conventional bank funding. Grants also have the advantage, of course, of being nonrepayable, which is important for organizations that are unlikely ever to achieve profitability. However, grants also have drawbacks, notably that they are often short term and can be inflexible and narrowly programmatic. Moreover, as foundation assets have decreased because of the collapse of global stock markets and government debt has grown, grants have become increasingly difficult and competitive to access. Finally, raising grants can also be expensive and foundation reporting requirements onerous and time-consuming.

Debt

Social investees normally have five basic debt options: personal credit cards; personal bank overdrafts; mortgage finance; commercial loans from banks at market rates; and commercial and semicommercial loans from government and other social investors. Semicommercial loans typically offer nonmarket interest rates, long repayment periods, and repayment "holidays" that suspend interest—and, sometimes, principal—repayments for set periods. Indeed, Joy, de Las Casas, and Ricke noted that the majority of social investment demand in the UK to date was for "soft" or patient (i.e., long term) capital at semicommercial rates.[46]

Debt has the advantage that it can often be quicker to obtain than grants (assuming that the investee has collateral assets or healthy cash flows) and terms can be flexible (short, medium, or long term) and are open to renegotiation over time. Debt is useful in bridging funding gaps and helping build for growth and scale. Debt contracts also typically attract fewer reporting requirements than grants and offer greater autonomy. On the other hand, investees outside of profitable social enterprises may not be able to access mainstream debt since it must repaid with interest and security may be needed that could put assets at risk in the case of default.

Microlending attempts to address this market failure for the uncollateralized individual or small organization. In the process it has established microfinance as a new and growing sector within mainstream finance that represents the most significant social investment market globally. Microlending, which has grown most strongly in developing markets, offers small-scale entrepreneurs the first step towards bank finance and, ultimately, access to capital markets. Stein, Goland, and Schiff suggested that of the 365 to 445 million micro, small, or medium-sized firms in developing countries, 70 percent need, but do not have access to, external financing.[47] These firms are thought to generate 33 percent of GDP and 45 percent of employment in the analyzed developing countries—a figure that is even greater if informal organizations are also included. It is calculated that their unmet demand for debt credit is equal to $2.1 to $2.5 trillion, or 14 percent of total developing country GDP.

Quasi Equity

Quasi equity is becoming common in the social enterprise and investment arena, but is rare in the conventional world. Its essence is to give investors returns that look like equity returns, with the feature of being tied to the organization's underlying performance. This is typically done as some form of debt contract since quasi equity is typically offered by organizations that cannot generally issue standard equity shares, for example a charity or other organization that is unable to grant investors any control over the organization's mission or operations. However, to secure investment capital for high-risk projects such organizations need to offer satisfactory returns to the investor. This is often done by tying the returns to the revenue growth of the firm as a whole, or an individual project. In this way investors get equity-like returns, but without having any of the special rights associated with owning common shares. Social enterprises gain access to risk capital for vital developmental projects or general corporate finance. HCT Group (see above), a large UK social enterprise, was unable to issue equity and utilized a quasi-equity instrument to unlock £4 million of social investment.

Equity

Companies issue shares to investors who share in the risk and governance of the company as well as the upside. Shareholders own a stake in the company, normally a function of the percentage of outstanding shares they own. In most circumstances their voting interest in the company is equivalent to their proportion of total shares. Nevertheless, because of the nature of voting behavior and power dynamics, a 20 percent stake in a company is more than 20 times as powerful as a 1 percent stake. From the standpoint of preference in the event of liquidation, equity shareholders rank behind all other claimants (staff, the tax collector, creditors, trade counterparties, etc.)—they are a "residual claimant" after all others have been paid off.

The main advantage to being a shareholder, in addition to voting rights, comes from receipt of dividends and a percentage ownership of "the upside." In the event of an exit, or "realization event," shareholders are paid a portion of the price received for the company, normally equivalent to their share of the equity. Such exit events might include a sale to another company, a sale of all or a portion of the shares to another investor, or a listing on a stock market. For social enterprises or businesses offering common shares, a trade sale is the most likely form of exit. Some social enterprises, like the Ethical Property Company (EPC), are not seeking any ultimate exit event but have tried to create liquidity for their shares through open market mechanisms. They and other UK ethical firms see their shares trade on "matched bargain" markets, such as the one provided by a stock-brokerage firm.[48] EPC shareholders are able to sell their shares to other interested investors should they want to fully realize their investment. The difference between what they paid and what they realize represents a capital gain or loss. In addition, equity shareholders in EPC receive a regular annual dividend. This payment is another way for equity shareholders to earn a return on their investment.

For the most part, equity in social investment is very similar, if not identical, to equity as an investment in mainstream companies. The main differences lie in the governance arrangements of the company. These might restrict the freedom of the board in some way in order to ensure the continuance of the social mission, or provide for a certain percentage of any surpluses to be invested socially or retained by the company, or a myriad of other socially oriented limitations such as a "golden share" that prevents a takeover.

Issuing public equity has the advantage of raising potentially large amounts of capital on a permanent basis without the need for repayment. However, the investee must give up some ownership and control when issuing equity, and this is often either unattractive (for fear of mission drift) or impossible (because of legal limitations) for many social organizations. The continued absence of any established "social" stock markets—despite several important current initiatives in the UK, Brazil, South Africa, and Singapore—and the resultant lack of liquidity in social equity is also a major challenge to growing this form of social investment. Partly as a consequence of this, O'Donohoe and coauthors suggested that US impact investment to date has been dominated by private debt ($921 million: 37.1 percent of the total invested) and private equity ($836 million: 33.7 percent).[49] Research by IIX Asia suggests that this is also true of Asia, but that quasi equity / mezzanine finance and guarantees are also important.[50]

Structured Finance

Structured finance is what is often, perhaps rightly, blamed for the credit crisis of the past few years. Investment products were individually tailored to meet the specific needs of investors and issuers. Much has been written about how this simple idea had disastrous consequences for global finance, and it is not the purpose of this chapter to explore this further. However, the same principles apply in social finance as in conventional finance. Structured finance is a necessary and vital innovation where the mainstream markets are unable to get the needs of investors and issuers to meet. As a result a specialized investment product is individually developed to meet the needs of all.

In the social finance sector this is frequently the case where different types or classes of investors have different return or social-impact objectives. A government investor may have strong social-impact objectives, but be far more tolerant of lower returns, higher risk, or longer payback periods. A purely financial investor may be very keen to participate, but unwilling to sacrifice at all from the efficient market frontier, where risk and market return are balanced by market forces and may be indifferent to social impact. A third very broad group is the growing coterie of social investors who might be willing to consider a host of trade-offs, although each investor may have different trade-offs, and even greatly varying social impacts they seek. The "social financier" seeks to balance and combine all these in a single structured finance product that essentially tries to give everyone what they want, or at least enough of it so the deal goes ahead. Such transactions will be essential to move the investee markets forward. However, because of their individualized nature, they are costly and inefficient to arrange.

Guarantees can play an important part in making structured finance projects move along.[51] The presence of one entity willing to guarantee all or even a portion of the project's risk can be enormously valuable to break any logjam. Frequently governments or large grant-making organizations may have the capacity to underwrite a portion of the risk of a project and thereby catalyze a far larger investment than may otherwise have been the case. For example, in 2011, Fair Finance—a UK based microlender—raised a £2 million loan from Société Générale and BNP Paribas that was underwritten by £750,000 of philanthropic patient capital and a £350,000 soft loan from Big Society Capital, the social investment fund set up by the UK government. Moreover, such creative thinking can result in entirely new financial products. An example is the social-impact bond (SIB) deal structure in the UK.[52] The SIB aims to leverage private investment to address urgent issues of importance to the state (starting with crime and youth reoffending) structured so that the state provides the return on the private investment from some of the public expenditure savings that result from the impact of the external investment.[53]

Additional Demand-Side Barriers

While the focus in this chapter has been primarily on the financial demands of investees in the social economy, there are a range of other demand-side needs that are also critical in terms of the future growth of the social investment sector as a whole. For example, a report commissioned by the UK's Big Society Bank (now Big Society Capital) identified five crucial roles for market intermediaries in terms of supporting the needs of investees:

- To provide finance
- To provide access to people, networks, and expertise
- To provide market access and distribution (matchmaking)
- To provide support for innovation and start-ups
- To provide investment monitoring and performance information to investors[54]

This broader view of the demand side is particularly important to foster and grow this emerging investee market space—something well recognized in the engaged or "venture" philanthropy model, for example.[55]

Hill suggested that there are no easy solutions to achieving a rapid acceleration in social enterprise investment, but a series of interlinked issues and reforms.[56] However, the report identified the perceived lack of investable deal as a key problem. Another key observation was that investors perceive the level of risk in investing in the social sector to be far too high, relative to the prospective returns. In this respect, risk is seen in a very broad sense and encompasses the following:

- *Investment risk:* the relative immaturity of many social enterprises
- *Team risk:* the inexperience of management teams in this sector
- *Product risk:* short history of many of the financial vehicles proposed
- *Liquidity and exit risk:* untested or unavailable exit routes due to the novelty of the marketplace and absence of developed secondary markets

This report argued that policy initiatives could increase the level of return to investors or the likelihood of receiving such a return. For example, government or foundation capital could be used as risk capital—taking the first loss—to secure mainstream investor interest for new social-impact investment funds. Yet, despite the efforts of an interventionist government for over a decade, Evenett and Richter identified seven persistent challenges on the demand side of the social investment market place in the UK:

- *Fragmentation of capital supply and the absence of joined up and plural finance options.* There is a need for more collaboration and co-investment in the sector as well as more players in the market to build competition. Furthermore, pooling demand-side investment opportunities could bring in players for whom the market is currently too small.
- *Need for more bespoke business support* with deeply embedded cultural and technical issues that need addressing.
- *Lack of universally agreed metrics for social outcomes and no single "silver bullet" solution to this.* A pernicious consequence of this lack of accounting standards is high due diligence costs per deal and, therefore, high perceived risks in social investments.
- *Lack of clear market signals:* the mix of instruments in social investment noted above (i.e., including grants, soft loans, etc.) makes this a complex and difficult market for potential new entrants.
- *Restrictive regulatory and legislative environment for foundation assets* is restrictive.
- *Insufficient investor incentives such as tax breaks or government guarantees* (though more creative structured finance deals can address this).
- *Need for better deal brokering to address illiquidity of the secondary marketplace for social investment.*[57]

The Big Society Capital project may act as a catalyst for the development of funds to support social enterprise development in the UK. Indeed, Big Society Capital itself may be one of the most significant facilitative steps in accelerating the development of the social investment marketplace and is, at the time of writing, the most ambitious effort in this regard undertaken by any nation.

There is also a significant need for building better financial literacy on the demand side in terms of investment models, opportunities, and financial instruments. As a report from Venturesome noted, social investees need to address a range of issues in terms of their own financial expertise before they can make the most effective use of the emergent social investment market-place.[58] Of particular significance is educating the demand side to recalibrating expectations of the relationship between risk and return in terms of accessing nongrant funding. Overall, the report suggested that investees should undertake the following efforts:

- Identify their own financial needs more thoroughly
- Be aware of all available finance mechanisms and instruments and their pros and cons (and risks)
- Be aware of the different capital providers available to them and their requirements

- Have confidence to seek new finance from multiple sources and to structure deals blending investors with multiple risk and return profiles
- Distinguish between income and capital in both their accounting and investment plans
- Understand that grants are not free money (the can cost up to 15–25 percent of the capital raised: more than three times the typical cost of raising equity)

While both these reports focused solely on the UK demand side, their analysis and recommendations have universal currency for social economy investees. Another set of issues for the demand side concern life-cycle investment. While there is a fair availability of early-stage capital in developed markets, there continues to be a lack of mezzanine or growth capital for smaller organizations in the social economy. Traditionally this has been addressed by mutual finance, but it is also an opportunity for alternative public offerings and the development of social stock exchanges. Larger-scale demand is being addressed to some extent by the private debt and equity seen in impact investment.

Conclusions

This chapter has considered the demand side of social investment globally. Given the paucity of data on the demand side itself, much of what has been discussed has had to be inferred from existing material. Accordingly, this work has attempted both a synthesis of key reports in the field and a new analysis of the important issues. It has set out definitions, delineated the sources of capital available to investees, and attempted to provide some indications of the approximate size and scale of key sectors of the investee market. The chapter has also set out a new methodology by which more effective demand-side calculations may be made going forward. In addition, it has addressed the range of financial instruments from the investee perspective.

As has been made clear here, there are many challenges remaining for demand-side investees to access social investment. However, there may be positive outcomes from such challenges in terms of "toughening up" the social entrepreneur, and thereby assisting in making the social enterprise itself more durable over time. There may also be benefits in terms of driving innovation by necessity. For example, as was demonstrated above, in the course of seeking new funding, EPC not only raised money, but hit upon a new way of raising money via an alternative public offering of shares. This model of an ethical share issue was taken up in the UK by Cafédirect (a fair-trade coffee company) and has presented social enterprises on the demand side with a new path to capital. It may also enable other successful social enterprises to undertake exits without forfeiting their ethical underpinnings. Moreover, tens of thousands of UK retail investors have now become aware of the option to act as social investors, and an emerging infrastructure is coming into place to meet the needs of such businesses (such as the Social Stock Exchange, ClearlySo, and IIX Asia). Another example of social investment innovation driven by necessity has been the rise of mobile banking, particularly in Africa. Originating in the MPESA joint venture between the UK's Vodafone and Safaricom in Kenya (which was also part-funded by the UK government's Department of Foreign and International

Development), mobile banking allows the poor unbanked population of developing countries to store and exchange money safely and securely via their mobile phone. In this case, the demand side has been consumers of financial services themselves.

This chapter has taken many of the conventions of mainstream finance as holding true for social investment. For example, the assumption has been made that securitizing social investments and creating secondary markets for them would help develop the market further in a positive way. However, some caution may be needed in terms of such normative judgments. The collapse in 2010 of Shorebank—a venerable and prominent US CDFI—provided a timely reminder that social investment that conforms to the mainstream model of banking also becomes vulnerable to all the downside issues of mainstream finance. Indeed, this crisis prompted some to cast the Community Reinvestment Act as the start of the subprime crisis.[59]

In the same way, the normative framing of the demand side of social investment along the mainstream model may also prove problematic, not least because it ignores important issues of the reform of the institutional power structures around the supply and demand of capital.[60] Addressing this imbalance was at the heart of the original mutual movement. As modern states retrench following the effective nationalization of private-sector financial liabilities following the 2008 banking crisis, perhaps now is a good time to recast the demand side of social investment as not only investees seeking others' funds, but as a change agent in rethinking broader financial structures and relationships across the entire global economy.[61] Such, at any rate, is the promise now in the air.

Notes

1. Jonathan Guthrie, "'Social Loan' for Cause-Based Groups," *Financial Times*, February 21, 2010, http://www.ft.com/intl/cms/s/0/41e6c628-1f11-11df-9584-00144feab49a.html#axzz2Xo4ZfNGe.

2. In the interest of full disclosure, it should be noted that Catalyst Fund Management and Research, a company controlled by Rodney Schwartz, one of the authors of this chapter, acted in a corporate finance capacity for the HCT Group on this deal.

3. For example, see Geoff Mulgan, "After Capitalism," *Prospect*, April 26, 2009, 157–70; Michael Porter and Mark Kramer, "Creating Shared Value," *Harvard Business Review*, November 2011, 121–30; Colin Crouch, *The Strange Non-death of Neo-liberalism* (Malden, MA: Polity Press, 2011); Umair Haque, *The New Capitalist Manifesto* (Boston: Harvard Business Review Press, 2011).

4. Alex Nicholls, "The Institutionalization of Social Investment: The Interplay of Investment Logics and Investor Rationalities," *Journal of Social Entrepreneurship* 1.1 (2010): 70–100.

5. Jed Emerson and Antony Bugg-Levine, *Impact Investing: Transforming How We Make Money While Making a Difference* (New York: Jossey-Bass, 2011).

6. C. K. Prahalad, *The Fortune at the Bottom of the Pyramid: Eradicating Poverty through Profits* (Upper Saddle River, NJ: Wharton Business School Press, 2006).

7. According to Hammond et al., there are 4 billion bottom-of-the-pyramid (BoP) consumers globally—defined as all those with annual incomes below £2,000 in local purchasing power. Despite being poor, together they have substantial purchasing power, constituting a £3 trillion global consumer market that is growing fast in certain sectors. For example, between 2000 and 2005 the number of mobile subscribers in developing

countries grew more than fivefold to nearly 1.4 billion. There are, however, large variations across regions, with Asia (including the Middle East) having the largest market of 2.9 billion people, compared with eastern Europe's 254 million people. Sector markets also range widely in size and development, including water (roughly £13 billion); health (£98 billion); transportation (£111 billion); housing (£206 billion); energy (£269 billion); food (£1.8 trillion). It seems clear that there is significant investment potential in firms that serve BoP markets and that these constitute an important demand-side market. Allen L. Hammond, William J. Kramer, Robert S. Katz, Julia T. Tran, and Courtland Walkeer, "The Next 4 Billion: Market Size and Business Strategy at the Base of the Pyramid," World Resources Institute, March 2007, accessed January 9, 2014, http://www.wri.org/sites/default/files/pdf/n4b_full_text_lowrez.pdf.

8. An argument could be made that *all* social investment is purchasing an outcomes benefit in the sense that the investor "consumes" psychological and lifestyle benefits from her investment in addition to any financial returns. However, this subtle parse will be set aside here in favor of a more conventional understanding of purchasing/consumption versus investment.

9. The impact-investing "asset class" is partly defined by its seven main sectoral foci, namely investments in (developing country) agriculture, water, housing, education, health, energy, financial services. See Nick O'Donohoe, Christina Leijonhufvud, Yasemin Saltuk, Antony Bugg-Levine, and Margot Brandenburg, "Impact Investments: An Emerging Asset Class," J.P. Morgan and Rockefeller Foundation, November 29, 2010, accessed January 7, 2014, http://www.rockefellerfoundation.org/uploads/files/2b053b2b-8feb-46ea-adbd-f89068d59785-impact.pdf.

10. Rodney Schwartz, *Social Investment* (London: ClearlySo, forthcoming).

11. Alex Nicholls and Alex Murdock, eds., *Social Innovation: Blurring Boundaries to Reconfigure Markets* (New York: Palgrave Macmillan, 2011).

12. See David Bornstein, *How to Change the World: Social Entrepreneurs and the Power of New Ideas* (Oxford: Oxford University Press, 2004); Alex Nicholls, "What Is the Future of Social Enterprise in Ethical Markets?" Office of the Third Sector, 2007, http://webarchive.nationalarchives.gov.uk/+/http:/www.cabinetoffice.gov.uk/media/cabinetoffice/third_sector/assets/future_social_enterprise_ethical_markets.pdf; and Rodney Schwartz, "Social Business," in *Sustainable Investing: The Art of Long Term Performance*, ed. Cary Krosinsky and Nick Robins (London: Earthscan, 2008) 137–48.

13. More than 6,000 CICs had been registered in the UK by the end of 2011.

14. Filipe M. Santos, "A Positive Theory of Social Entrepreneurship," *Journal of Business Ethics* 111.3 (2012): 335–51; Nicholls, "Institutionalization of Social Investment."

15. Nicholls, "Institutionalization of Social Investment."

16. Nicholls, "Institutionalization of Social Investment."

17. Marthe Nyssens, *Social Enterprise* (London: Palgrave Macmillan, 2006).

18. However, while in conventional finance it is often the case that there will always be more demand than supply and that the key challenge is, therefore, to identify and shape the best deals from a larger field of investment opportunities, with respect to social investment some data suggest that there may be fewer investable deals than there is already available social investment capital. For example, while UK social investment capital allocated in 2010 was £190 million, one social investment fund—the Social Investment Business—had more than £500 million of requests for funding in the year to March 2010. See Cynthia Shanmugalingam, Jack Graham, Simon Tucker, and Geoff Mulgan, "Growing Social Ventures," NESTA and the Young Foundation, 2011, accessed January 9, 2014, http://www.nesta.org.uk/sites/default/files/growing_social_ventures.pdf.

19. O'Donohoe et al., "Impact Investments."

20. Jessica Freireich and Katherine Fulton, "Investing for Social and Environmental Impact: A Design for Catalyzing an Emerging Industry," Monitor Group, January 2009, http://www.monitorinstitute.com/downloads/what-we-think/impact-investing/Impact_Investing.pdf.

21. Deutsche Bank Research. "Microfinance: An Emerging Investment Opportunity," Deutsche Bank, December 19, 2007, http://www.dbresearch.com/PROD/DBR_INTERNET_EN-PROD/PROD0000000000219174.pdf.

Maximilian Martin, "Managing Philanthropy after the Downturn: What Is Ahead for Social Investment?" in *Viewpoint 2010*, ed. Maximilian Martin and Andreas Ernst (Geneva: IJ Partners, 2010), 11–21.

22. O'Donohoe et al., "Impact Investments"; Yasemin Saltuk, "Insight into the Impact Investment Market: An In-Depth Analysis of Investor Perspectives and Over 2,200 Transactions," J.P. Morgan Social Finance Research, December 14, 2011, 6, accessed June 12, 2013, http://www.thegiin.org/cgi-bin/iowa/download?row=334&field=gated_download_1.

23. O'Donohoe et al., "Impact Investments."

24. Mark Campanale, *Mission Related Investing and Charities* (London: Henderson Global Investors, 2005).

25. Adrian Brown and Will Norman, "Lighting the Touchpaper: Growing the Market for Social Investment in England," Boston Consulting Group and the Young Foundation, November 2011, accessed January 9, 2014, http://youngfoundation.org/publications/lighting-the-touchpaper-growing-the-market-for-social-investment-in-england/.

26. O'Donohoe et al., "Impact Investments."

27. Brown and Norman, "Lighting the Touchpaper."

28. Cynthia Chua, Abhinav Gupta, Vivian Hsu, Justin Jimenez, and Yvonne Li, "Beyond the Margin: Redirecting Asia's Capitalism," Advantage Ventures, 2011, http://www.avantageventures.com/sitedocs/av_report_final_full_screen_version.pdf.

29. Brown and Norman, "Lighting the Touchpaper."

30. According to the Social Enterprise Coalition (now Social Enterprise UK), in 2009, 30 percent of the UK social enterprises that it surveyed were less than five years old with a median turnover of only £175,000.

31. Shanmugalingam et al., "Growing Social Ventures."

32. Iona Joy, Lucy de Las Casas, and Benedict Rickey, "Understanding the Demand for and Supply of Social Finance: Research to Inform the Big Society Bank," New Philanthropy Capital and NESTA, 2011, accessed January 9, 2014, http://www.nesta.org.uk/library/documents/BSFFUnderstandingthedemandprint.pdf.

33. Jed Emerson, "The Blended Value Proposition: Integrating Social and Financial Returns," *California Management Review* 45.5 (2003): 35–51.

34. O'Donohoe et al., "Impact Investments."

35. This is consistent with Freireich and Fulton, "Investing for Social and Environmental Impact," who suggested that the market for impact investment would grow to $500 billion in the next five to 10 years.

36. This has been calculated as 4 billion consumers each earning $2,000 per year.

37. Chua et al., "Beyond the Margin."

38. Brown and Norman, "Lighting the Touchpaper"; Cabinet Office, "Growing the Social Investment Market: A Vision and Strategy," Cabinet Office, February 2011, https://www.gov.uk/government/uploads/system/uploads/attachment_data/file/61185/404970_SocialInvestmentMarket_acc.pdf.

39. New Energy Finance, *Global Trends in Clean Energy Finance Q4 2009 Fact Pack* (London: New Energy Finance, 2009).

40. "Global Carbon Market Shrinks in Q3, but Activity in North America and in the International Credit Market Sees Continued Growth," New Energy Finance press release, 2009, http://about.bnef.com/press-releases/global-carbon-market-shrinks-in-q3-but-activity-in-north-america-and-in-the-international-credit-market-sees-continued-growth/.

41. Community Development Finance Association, "CDFA: Annual Review 2007," Community Development Finance Association, June 2007, http://www.cdfa.org.uk/wp-content/uploads/2011/02/Annual-Review-07-Final.pdf.

42. Mutuo, *The Mutuals Yearbook 2009* (London: Mutuo, 2009).

43. The largest 300 cooperatives in the world generated $1.6 trillion in revenue in 2008 and employed over 1 billion people. See International Cooperative Alliance, "Global 300 Report, 2010," ICA, 2010, accessed January 9, 2014, http://ica.coop/sites/default/files/attachments/Global300%20Report%202011.pdf; Rafael Chavez Avila and José Luis Monzón Campos, "The Social Economy in the European Union," CIRIEC Working Paper, February 2008; and Jacques Defourny and Marthe Nyssens, "Social Enterprise in Europe: Recent Trends and Developments," EMES Working Paper No. 08/01 (2008), accessed January 9, 2014, http://www.emes.net/what-we-do/publications/working-papers/social-enterprise-in-europe-recent-trends-and-developments/.

44. World Council of Credit Unions, *Statistical Report 2010* (London: World Council of Credit Unions, 2011).

45. Nicholls, "Institutionalization of Social Investment."

46. Joy, de Las Casas, and Rickey, "Understanding the Demand."

47. Peer Stein, Tony Goland, and Robert Schiff, *Two Trillion and Counting: Assessing the Credit Gap for Micro, Small, and Medium-Sized Enterprises in the Developing World* (Washington, DC: IFC and McKinsey and Company, 2010).

48. Globally there is a range of organizations focussed on building key trading platforms to link investors and investees more effectively. For example: Social Stock Exchange (London); Sitawi (Brazil); Aavishkaar (India); CiYuan incubator (China); NeXii (South Africa with Stock Exchange of Mauritius); IIX Asia (Singapore). For further detail on such exchanges, see chapter 4 in this volume.

49. O'Donohoe et al., "Impact Investments."

50. Impact Investment Shujog, "Impact Investors in Asia: Characteristics and Preferences for Investing in Social Enterprises in Asia and the Pacific," Impact Investment Shujog and Asian Development Bank, 2011, accessed January 9, 2014, http://evpa.eu.com/wp-content/uploads/2011/05/Impact-investors-in-Asia.pdf.

51. For further detail on guarantees and other "credit enhancements," see chapter 12, this volume.

52. Social Finance, "Social Impact Bonds: Rethinking Finance for Social Outcomes," Social Finance, August 2009, accessed January 9, 2014, http://www.oregon.gov/gov/docs/OEIB/SocImpactBonds.pdf.

53. For further detail on social impact bonds, see chapter 16, this volume.

54. Shanmugalingam et al., "Growing Social Ventures."

55. Rob John, "The Evolution of High Engagement Philanthropy in Europe," Skoll Centre for Social Entrepreneurship Working Paper, June 2006, accessed January 9, 2014, http://evpa.eu.com/wp-content/uploads/2010/10/Skoll-Centre-VP-Venture-Philanthropy-The-Evolution-of-High-Engagement-Philanthropy-in-Europe.pdf.

56. Katie Hill, Investor Perspectives on Social Enterprise Financing," City of London, Big Lottery Fund, and ClearlySo, July 2011, accessed January 9, 2014, http://www.corpoflondon.com/NR/rdonlyres/1FC8B9A1-6DE2-4

95F-9284-C3CC1CFB706D/0/BC_RS_InvestorPerspectivesonSocialInvestment_forweb.pdf.

57. Rupert Evenett and Karl H. Richter, *Making Good in Social-Impact Investment: Opportunities in an Emerging Asset Class* (London: Social Investment Business and The City UK, 2011).

58. Venturesome, "Access to Capital: A Briefing Paper," CAF Venturesome, September 2009, http://evpa.eu.com/wp-content/uploads/2010/11/CAF-Venturesome-Access-to-Capital-20094.pdf.

59. "Small Enough to Fail: The Sorry End to a Bold Banking Experiment," *The Economist*, August 28, 2010.

60. Nicholls, "Institutionalization of Social Investment."

61. Crouch, *Strange Non-death*.

Suggested Readings

Nicholls, Alex, ed. *Social Entrepreneurship: New Models of Sustainable Social Change.* Paperback edition, with new preface. New York: Oxford University Press, 2008.

Nicholls, Alex, and Alex Murdock, eds. *Social Innovation: Blurring Boundaries to Reconfigure Markets.* New York: Palgrave Macmillan, 2011.

Nicholls, Alex, R. Paton, and J. Emerson, eds. *Social Finance.* New York: Oxford University Press, 2014 (forthcoming).

CHAPTER 22

THE ELUSIVE QUEST FOR IMPACT: THE EVOLVING PRACTICE OF SOCIAL-IMPACT MEASUREMENT

Brian Trelstad

TURNAROUND COURIERS IS A TORONTO-BASED bicycle courier business that exclusively recruits at-risk youth from shelters and youth service agencies to be bicycle couriers and administrative staff.[1] Launched in 2002, its goal is to "create a successful courier company while at the same time enabling at-risk youth to gain the experience, confidence and financial means necessary to maintain stable housing and eventually enter the job market."[2] With supportive coaching and management from TurnAround Couriers, young people are given the chance to launch a career through which they can ultimately work and live independently from government social services.

Rhode Yowert is one of TurnAround's success stories. A single mother who left home at age 16, Rhode had been living on welfare and was worried about her son's future. With the support of TurnAround Couriers, she is now fully employed and is considering new career options in emergency services.[3] In six years, TurnAround Couriers has trained 100 young people like Rhode. Eighty percent of those have made the transition into stable housing, more permanent employment, or have sought additional education.

TurnAround Couriers estimates that for $181,618—in a combination of up-front investment and cumulative operating losses over the six years through 2008—they have been able to save the national and provincial government $432,158 through a combination of reduced social service spending and additional payroll taxes generated by TurnAround's new employees.[4]

Viewed through conventional financial accounting, TurnAround Couriers would be judged a failure. Financially speaking, TurnAround booked a cumulative loss in its first six years of operation. However, social-impact investing practitioners have begun talking about a second bottom line, which measures the social value created by an investment. When this social value is added to the traditional single bottom line of a firm's net income, it produces a more complete understanding of the business's "blended value" as both a financial and social enterprise.[5] TurnAround Couriers calculates its social bottom line as $7,451 per employee per year of their employment. After some simple arithmetic, TurnAround reports that the social return of $432,158 on its $181,618 investment (SROI)[6] amounts to more than 200 percent.[7]

On first blush, a savvy investor might think that a return of more than 200 percent is pretty attractive. But as one thinks about it, should one really trust self-reported data from TurnAround Couriers? Isn't it in their interest to tell a compelling story using the data at their disposal? And might there be a selection bias among the young people they hire? To understand the impact more completely, shouldn't we know more about what happened to the youth at risk whom they *don't* work with? Maybe those nonclients (the control group) are also moving off of government assistance, perhaps even faster or more sustainably than those who work as TurnAround's bike couriers. And how does TurnAround's work compare with similar social enterprises in Canada, such as Renaissance Quebec, which reported SROI of 399 percent based on employing disadvantaged people in recycling clothing and consumer goods. Or perhaps Inner City Renovations, delivering an impressive SROI of 52 percent by training people in the building trades?

TurnAround Couriers and the other two social enterprises are supported, in part, by Social Capital Partners (SCP), a nonprofit venture philanthropy fund in Toronto that believes that market forces can help solve problems of underemployment for disadvantaged populations. To be clear, Social Capital Partners does not claim that SROI can answer these and many other questions, but they do use the methodology as a way to clarify and communicate the social value of the social businesses that they support for both internal and external purposes. In a presentation entitled *Why SROI?* SCP notes that "all [social enterprises] need a compelling story, and SROI analysis/reporting tells that story."[8]

SROI does just that: it tells a story. It creates a helpful framework and offers a set of managerial tools that allows program managers to better understand the logic models of social value creation in their investments or ventures. It tells a story about what is happening, but it does not capture and generate data that can allow an independent assessment of social investment opportunities or their social impact. SROI is not alone; it is one among many blended-value and double- or triple-bottom-line[9] assessment tools that hold promise of offering an objective way to assess the full social and economic benefit of alternative investments in terms that resemble those of standard investment metrics. Yet while holding enormous potential, these tools are still far from being able to deliver fully on this promise of being able to evaluate and compare the social impact of a grant or investment within or across social-impact investing portfolios.

This chapter traces the recent history and current state of practice of double-bottom-line measurement tools like SROI. While practitioners have made considerable progress towards developing and using tools to measure both financial and social (or environmental) returns, there is still a considerable gap between the rhetoric and the reality of what these tools can consistently offer. The field has not yet developed independent measurement tools that can offer funders reliable ways of measuring a blended return on their philanthropic initiatives, but there are new efforts underway that may well change this over the coming years.

Background: The Move towards Measurement

Early Origins

Social return on investment is one of many new tools that have been developed to evaluate the blended value proposition.[10] But the "blended value proposition" is hardly the first approach to have been developed to assess the consequences of social and environmental programs. To the contrary, the inventors of the blended value approach drew inspiration from two long-standing conceptual antecedents. The first was a simple and well-established tool in the evaluation of public and nonprofit interventions that focused on the impact value chain; the second was traditional cost-benefit analysis used primarily by federal and state governments in the United States, and by program evaluators hired by them.

The impact evaluation chain framework that dominated the evaluation of government programs and their nonprofit counterparts from the 1960s through at least the early 1990s differentiated four dimensions of programmatic interventions—inputs, outputs, outcomes, and impacts—as outlined in Figure 22.1. Inputs are the items needed to make a program operational, such as personnel, funding, intellectual property, and volunteer hours. These inputs, when combined, generate a set of outputs, or clearly measureable units of activity: students tutored, patients treated, acres put into conservancy, at-risk youth hired as bicycle couriers. Outputs, however, may or may not lead to the desired results. To determine whether they do, it is necessary to take an additional view and examine outcomes, or "the broader changes or benefits resulting from a program, as measured against its goals."[11] In the case of TurnAround Couriers, this would be the percentage of at-risk youth who move away from dependence on social services towards independent living, full-time employment, or additional education.

Even this is not the end of the road, however, because it is still necessary to establish the link between the program and the outcome, since the outcome could have resulted from some external cause, such as a general improvement in the economy. For this it is necessary to assess not just outcomes but programmatic *impact*. Impact is the difference between what would have happened if a program did not exist and what happened as a result of the programmatic efforts.

Impact, however, is incredibly hard to prove. It is comparatively easy to track outputs (number of couriers hired) and it is within reach to study outcomes (surveys of the income levels or housing stability of TurnAround's formerly at-risk employees, for example). But to prove impact, you need to define the counterfactual, or what would have happened to the program beneficiaries

FIGURE 22.1
Impact Chain

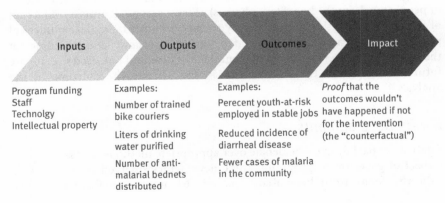

without the intervention, and prove that the intervention leads to a statistically significant difference.

To develop a proper counterfactual, an organization needs to design a randomized control trial or a rigorous, quasi-experimental study that can compare the outcomes of a randomly assigned treatment group (those receiving the services) against a randomly assigned control group (those that do not).[12] Such trials are often costly to conduct correctly, however, as they require large investments of time, expertise, and field workers, especially for impacts supposed to survive over an extended period. The widespread tendency in the field, therefore, was often to stop well short of establishing impacts, and in many cases to focus just on the easily measured outputs.

A second methodological starting point was *cost-benefit analysis*. Cost benefit analysis looks at the combination of qualitative and quantitative benefits and compares them with a program's costs. Cost-benefit analysis (also referred to as benefit-cost analysis) was introduced in the United States with the Flood Control Act of 1936, which sought to establish as federal policy that the benefits of any federal intervention should outweigh the costs of the intervention.[13]

Unlike traditional return-on-investment analysis used in the private sector, cost-benefit analysis seeks to quantify the public benefits that accrue to a wide array of individuals or institutions beyond those who directly pay for the program. For example, a road improvement or canal-dredging program funded by a state may generate broader benefits to households, businesses, and even jurisdictions beyond those financing the work. The idea that one can calculate a broader public benefit to compare with the costs of a program is central to the logic of double- and triple-bottom-line approaches to evaluating impact, including SROI.

By the early 1990s, cost-benefit analysis had been adapted in the nonprofit sector as "cost-effectiveness analysis." In the 1993 book *Cost Effectiveness in the Nonprofit Sector*, Gerald Schmaedick of TechnoServe defined cost-effectiveness analysis as "a rigorous system which tracks the costs of an activity or program and records the results, or at least indicators of the results, then compares the two in terms that permit an evaluation of whether the results justify the costs."[14]

While cost-benefit analysis and cost-effectiveness analysis responded to what Schmaedick saw as "a notable surge in the demand that programs be cost-effective" over the preceding decade, there were significant limits to the methodology. Robert Dorfman's 1996 article "Why Benefit-Cost Analysis Is Widely Disregarded and What to Do about It" summarized some of the prevailing concerns about cost-benefit analysis: first, it fails to define the universe of people to whom the benefits (or harms) accrue; second, it aims to reduce all of the analysis to a single unit, namely money; and third, the false numerical precision fails to capture inherent and inevitable uncertainty and inaccuracy in the estimates.[15] Other critics pointed out that the discount rate used to compare future benefits with today's cost can in fact dictate the outcome of the analysis.[16]

Recent Developments

Against the backdrop of the debate over appropriate methods for assessing the impact of government programs, three new factors emerged in the 1990s to shift the focus from benefit-cost analysis to more of a finance-oriented return-on-investment methodology. What's more, pressures mounted to apply this approach not just to government programs but to philanthropic grants and, ultimately, to the new class of social investments on the "frontiers of philanthropy" that is the focus of this book.

The first of these factors was the revolution in information technology that exploded in the 1990s. This radically lower costs and enhanced capacities of technology allowed nonprofits to make low-cost but significant investments in internal data management that produced meaningful shifts both within nonprofits and in the philanthropic environment more generally. Internally, many nonprofits implemented new business information systems that enabled significant changes in how they managed themselves. A 2001 study conducted by Princeton Survey Associates found that 84 percent of executives at human and social service organizations believed that information technology had profoundly shaped their service delivery and administrative functions over the prior five years.[17]

While most of the spending focused on routine information and communication systems such as websites, intranets, and e-mail services, some IT spending by nonprofits focused on collecting better program data with the intention of sharing impact with donors. As noted more fully below, the Roberts Enterprise Development Fund (REDF) built the OASIS (Ongoing Assessment of Social ImpactS)[18] program to capture information about each client of the 10 social service organizations in REDF's portfolio for two years after the clients' completion of job-training programs.

Externally, as the Internet changed the information landscape, a number of start-up efforts set their sights on transforming philanthropy with information services and online giving portals.[19] Guidestar, founded in 1994 and formally launched in 1996, laid the foundation for philanthropic information transparency by publishing the Form 990 tax returns required of all nonprofits with $25,000 or more of income in the United States. Guidestar's searchable clearinghouse enabled donors to look quickly at the financial performance of the country's largest charities, investigating everything from how much money was spent on fundraising and administration to what salaries were paid to the top five employees and how much cash the nonprofit had in the bank. This led, in turn, to the launch in the late 1990s and early 2000s of a series of organizations established to rate charities. However, the three leading rating organizations at the time—Give Wise, Charity Watch, and Charity Navigator—focused on the concept of philanthropic efficiency as reflected by low overhead ratios or low relative spending on non-program-related areas like fundraising and administration and therefore did little to answer the question of program effectiveness.[20]

Another consequence of the information revolution and the dot-com boom it gave rise to was the emergence of a crop of suddenly superwealthy Internet entrepreneurs, venture capitalists, private equity managers, and investment bankers, some of whom decided to bring at least a portion of their newfound wealth to bear on solving social and environmental problems, but resolved to do so in a new way that was consistent with the way they made their business decisions—that is, with the help of key performance indicators or enterprise level dashboards. These entrepreneurs formed part of a new class of so-called venture philanthropists, who resolved to bring the techniques of venture capital to the operation of philanthropy. As outlined in a seminal article in the *Harvard Business Review*, key features of the venture philanthropy approach included using a portfolio strategy to manage the risk across a range of philanthropic initiatives, investing in organizational capacity, offering nonfinancial assistance for growing organizations, and thinking clearly about performance measures, or "clear objectives that give the investors and the start-up managers a focus for their working relationship."[21] *Business Week* heralded this "The New Face of Philanthropy" in a cover story in December 2002, noted that new donors "demand results.... Recipients are often required to meet milestone goals ... and to produce measureable results—or risk losing their funding."[22]

Venture philanthropy continued to evolve into the new millennium. Early venture philanthropists sometimes established foundations alongside their for-profit companies, while others encouraged longtime philanthropic donors and grantees to adopt business principles, including performance measures. More recently, the focus on philanthropy and grant support of nonprofit organizations has given way to experimentation with a much broader array of financial instruments, such as loans, loan guarantees, and even equity shares; and to market-based solutions to social and environmental problems. The language of "venture philanthropy" has thus given way to a new vocabulary of "philanthrocapitalism" and "social-impact investing."[23] What all of these approaches share, however, is the challenge of measuring the social and environmental good being generated by these activities and then comparing it to the amount of capital invested, whether through a for-profit or a nonprofit structure.

Finally, these two developments—the new information technology and the emerging cadre of "venture philanthropists" and "philanthrocapitalists"— came together with a third force: a new breed of social entrepreneurs, dynamic and innovative change agents committed to blending traditional philanthropy with market mechanisms and operating through new types of quasi-nonprofit, quasi-profit social enterprises. Inspired by the calls to create blended value through ventures that can do well and do good and frustrated by the operations of traditional nonprofits, these social entrepreneurs resonated with the blunt talk of the philanthrocapitalists and the emphasis on metrics and helped to accelerate the new metrics paradigm by adopting and experimenting with a range of tools and techniques for tracking and communicating the social impact of their work to a new breed of donor-investors, using new technologies.

The Emergence of SROI and the Balanced Scorecard

Social Return on Investment

Among these tools and techniques, two in particular stand out, at least as metaphors if not yet as fully developed and broadly utilized standards. The first of these is the *social return on investment* framework (SROI) developed in San Francisco in 1997 by the staff of the Roberts Enterprise Development Fund (REDF). REDF was founded by the legendary private equity investor George Roberts and led by Jed Emerson, a charismatic and intellectually creative social worker from the Bay Area. REDF made grants to nonprofits that operated revenue-generating businesses that trained and employed low-income and formerly homeless individuals. Its staff believed that the investee organizations were making a difference, but "we couldn't tell whether our work—and the work of our portfolio agencies—was improving the lives of the people we all intended to help."[24]

Combining the impact chain and cost-benefit analysis with the principles of corporate finance, the SROI framework essentially looks at the cash flows of an enterprise to calculate the organization's economic value, and then calculates the social-purpose value, or "the direct, demonstrable cost savings and revenue contributions that are associated with individuals' employment in a social-purpose enterprise."[25] This social-purpose value can include an increase in income taxes generated by new employment or reduced spending on public assistance (i.e., homeless shelters or drug treatment programs) that the employees may no longer need now that they have a steady income and support. The combination of the enterprise value and the social-purpose value, net of any debt, can be compared with the program's costs to calculate a "social return on investment."

One of the SROI reports that REDF published in 1999 looked at Rubicon Bakery. As of 1998, REDF had granted $1,806,919 to Rubicon Bakery, which targets certain at-risk populations (e.g., the homeless, mentally ill, ex-convicts), provides them with workforce training services and employment, and tracks a range of social and economic indicators to understand the social impact of the investment of these services.[26]

After the first year, Rubicon Bakery, with REDF, published a comprehensive SROI report that showed that in 1999, Rubicon had sales of $761,000 and social subsidies of $178,000 for total revenues of $940,000. In the same year, Rubicon had enterprise expenses (the costs of running the bakery) of $910,000 and social expenses (the costs of providing additional services to at-risk employees) of $134,000 for total expenses of $1,044,000. The net margin was then a loss of 11 percent.[27]

On the social impact side, Rubicon services were estimated to save the government $16,807 in social service spending per each of the 18 target employees and generate $2,911 in new payroll taxes per employee per year through higher earnings. To track the outcomes of the individual employees of Rubicon and their other grantees, REDF developed a management information system (MIS) called OASIS (Ongoing Assessment of Social Impacts). The system collected indicators like wages, job retention, job promotion, housing stability, and involvement in the criminal justice system on each employee of each portfolio company at six-month intervals for two years.[28] Using the data collected through OASIS, REDF was able to more accurately estimate the savings realized and taxes generated from the employees trained by its businesses.

Despite the abundance of data and compelling analysis, REDF did not calculate a percentage-based social return on investment for this grant. It did calculate the blended value of the enterprise—a combination of the business's enterprise value, estimated at $10 million, and the social-purpose value, estimated at $19 million. The blended value of $29 million, when compared with the $1.8 million grant to Rubicon implied a return of 16 times the investment. Projections in the 1999 report called for the company to turn an operating profit and to increase the number of target employees, amortizing social expenses and leading to higher profitability and enduring social impact over time.

Unfortunately, REDF did not published SROI calculations subsequent to the 1999 analysis, although it did release a "Social Impact Report" in 2005, which details some of the longer-term observations around target employee income and savings to government, but lacks the enterprise-level data comparable to what was reported in 1999.[29]

Since Rubicon Bakery and Turnaround Couriers both deliver comparable social service programs to similarly disadvantaged populations, it would be tempting to ask which delivers the higher social return on investment. How should a prospective donor to either organization assess which of these two portfolio companies is doing a more effective job at employing disadvantaged populations? Unfortunately, the lack of a standard approach in their applications of the SROI framework, and the absence of data in the REDF case, make it difficult to evaluate performance over time and generate a comparative assessment of the two businesses.

Despite its shortcomings, the investment that REDF made in pioneering the SROI framework and in building OASIS reshaped the field of impact assessment in venture philanthropy. Its publications and transparency about what worked and what did not inspired a number of other venture philanthropy and social enterprise funds to attempt to replicate the SROI methodology. And the work continues to this day, with the SROI Network, a global network of practitioners who are promulgating standards on the SROI methodology and continuing to promote greater proficiency in the practice. The original intent of SROI was never (and is still not) to generate a single social performance number, but rather to foster a discipline that shares the quantitative assumptions about social value that can complement qualitative reporting in assessing program performance.

The REDF staff, including Emerson and his colleagues Melinda Tuan and Cynthia Gair, built a toolkit for others to use, but they were also clear about the limits of the methodology: it was expensive and time-consuming, it made somewhat imprecise estimates about the costs and benefits, it overestimated the attribution of cost savings to the social enterprise, and it lacked true industry comparables. Given some of the inherent methodological limits and Emerson's departure, the REDF staff stopped generating SROI reports in 2000, focusing instead on trying to learn what was happening in the individual employees' lives "without monetizing the outcomes or comparing these to their associated costs."[30]

Balanced Scorecard

At about the same time that SROI was being pioneered in the late 1990s, the balanced scorecard emerged as another complementary tool used by venture philanthropy funds to help demonstrate the blended value of a social enterprise.

Derived from the work of Harvard Business School Professor Robert Kaplan and his colleague David Norton, the balanced scorecard offered a strategic framework, clear thinking about mission and beneficiaries, and a mix of financial, operating, and social measures specific to each business that, if widely adopted, according to its creators will bring "a more efficient marketplace that rewards effectiveness, thereby bringing bigger benefits to society."[31]

In their original article, Kaplan and Norton describe the four required perspectives of a balanced scorecard, about which information is collected: customer, internal, innovation, and financial. That is to say, an effective organization must manage itself using a constant stream of feedback—and the requisite readjustments—based on feedback on each of the four areas. Social benefit organizations quickly jumped on board, using the balanced scorecard to manage themselves to the expectations of their beneficiaries, stakeholders, and internal efficiency goals.

New Profit, a venture philanthropy fund based in Boston, is one of the major champions of the balanced scorecard approach, requiring its grantees to use the tool. According to Kelly Fitzsimmons, a partner at New Profit: "The scorecard will align all our stakeholders for creating social innovation and social returns. That means the boards, investors, fund managers, foundations, and social entrepreneurs can bring all their resources to bear in the right way for strategic applications."[32]

One of the more prominent examples of the balanced scorecard approach is New Profit's portfolio company JumpStart, an organization that pairs college students with children in preschool to provide individualized tutoring focused on developing literacy and social skills needed to succeed in school.[33] JumpStart's balanced scorecard reports financial measures like revenue growth; operational measures like staff vacancy rates and number of university partners contributing students; and social-impact measures including gains in numbers of children enrolled in the program and gains on school readiness measures. Most of the data in the balanced scorecard is collected and managed by JumpStart itself, so it lacks the objective rigor needed to determine "impact." JumpStart does complement this ongoing performance management system with more rigorous longitudinal studies of student performance against a comparison group, conducted by independent researchers.[34] In the 2003 study by Daniel-Echols and Ziang, for instance, a "randomized, experimentally designed study was implemented at Boston and New York City Jumpstart sites beginning in the 1999–2000 program year. Children in Head Start programs only were randomized into Jumpstart or the comparison group. Significant Jumpstart group advantages were found for tested story and print concepts and letter and word identification at the end of year 1 and for observed language and literacy at the end of year 2; nearly significant Jumpstart group advantages were found for observed initiative skills at the end of years 1 and 2, observed social relations at the end of year 3, and vocabulary at the end of year 3."

According to the Harvard Business School case that details JumpStart's use of the tool, devising and rolling out the balanced scorecard was not without its challenges. "Building the capability within the management team to understand what measures mean and how to manage by those numbers is a significant challenge for JumpStart," one JumpStart board member confided.[35]

Like social return on investment, the balanced scorecard approach brought new analytical rigor to the practice of doing good. Both approaches emphasize the need to carefully track inputs, outputs, and outcomes and make sometimes difficult decisions based on data presented in managers' dashboards. Of course, each approach is not without its downsides, as discussed here.

Perhaps because of these difficulties, progress in coming to closure around a set of metrics for measuring the impact of social-impact investing has been far slower than many have hoped. Thus, a survey of 40 of the leading venture philanthropy organizations in the United States carried out in 2002 by Venture Philanthropy Partners revealed that 17, or nearly half, had not developed a performance measurement system, while only three had developed and were using a consistent framework like SROI or the balanced scorecard.[36]

A more recent 2010 survey of 10 leading mission investing firms found that all 10 had developed performance management systems, but only four were using the SROI framework. These include REDF, which has called for a modification in SROI; Social Finance in the UK; Social Capital Partners in Toronto; and New Philanthropy Capital in London. But as discussed above, all of these are using SROI in a way that precludes easy comparison among investments for the potential donor. The rest of the venture philanthropy funds reviewed, including Acumen Fund, New Schools, New Profit, Sea Change Capital, Venture Philanthropy Partners, Robin Hood, and Bridges Ventures in London have all developed their own customized systems to evaluate the social impact of their programs' investments.[37]

The Future of Impact Assessment

The venture philanthropy and social-impact investing communities have thus come a long way since the impact measurement movement began in earnest in the 1990s. What is more, the expectations to demonstrate quantifiable impact continue to rise. This was reflected powerfully in the 2009 launch of the Obama administration's Social Innovation Fund, which promised to establish "a new way of doing business for the federal government" by creating "a catalog of proven approaches that can be replicated in communities across the country."[38]

But as the previous sections have noted, we are a long way from being able to measure double- and triple-bottom-line investments in a way that organizations often claim they can. That the systems being deployed are still largely customized to each fund and are not interoperable is problematic for a field that claims it can demonstrate double- or triple-bottom-line returns across asset classes and fields of endeavor. And these systems are still focused primarily on counting outputs and making performance more transparent; they are still not equipped to place a value on the relative value of different outputs like a stable job or an access to affordable healthcare.

What therefore is needed to move this field forward? Perhaps the best way to understand this question is to depict a bit more systematically where things stand and what gaps need to be filled. For this purpose it is useful to draw a distinction between the nature of the evidence used in communicating impact (anecdotal vs. empirical) and the entities responsible for generating the evidence (subjective vs. objective).

By anecdotal evidence, we mean stories or case studies; by empirical evidence, we mean more quantitative data gained through observation or experimentation. By subjective, we mean information or data collected by people involved with the process or with a stake in a program's outcomes; by objective, we mean research conducted by independent third parties with a professional obligation to conduct research and not serve a client.

This suggests a two-by-two graph along the lines of Figure 22.2. The bottom left quadrant contains approaches that rely on essentially anecdotal evidence conveyed by persons with a stake in the outcomes. The material resulting from such approaches can be broadly characterized as "marketing materials." The upper right quadrant contains approaches that rely on empirical evidence generated by persons with no stake in the outcome. This is the domain of true "Impact Assessment." In between are two useful but partial steps along the path to true impact assessment. One of them taps empirical data but relies on subjective observers with a stake in the outcome. Done well, this can still be effective for what we have termed "Performance Management." The other relies on anecdotes, but anecdotes assembled by objective observers. This is the domain of "News and Case Studies."

FIGURE 22.2
Array of Impact Tools

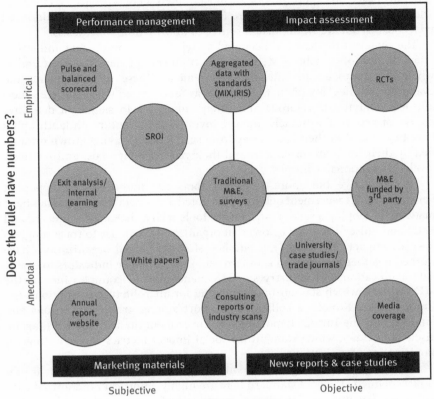

As discussed above, the field has made considerable progress moving from the bottom left-hand corner of this chart, characterized by individual anecdotes told by persons affiliated with the organization providing a service, towards more rigorous evidence-based methods. This is not to say that the marketing materials in stories like those about Rhode Yowert, the former welfare recipient now thriving as a bike messenger with TurnAround Couriers, or self-published white papers have no place in the field. To the contrary, they can put a human face on the more dry statistics or synthesize emerging trends in ways that more traditional research might not be able to. Internally authored white papers, in which a Social Capital Partner's portfolio manager might reflect on best practices the firm has developed, are important sources of new ideas, which prompt conversations. But they are *not* evidence of impact.

Practitioner-focused trade journals like the *Stanford Social Innovation Review* and *Innovations* are a step in the direction of more reliable assessments of what works and what does not when it comes to building high-impact social enterprises, but the question is how representative or reliable the anecdotes they report are. To achieve greater objectivity, one can move further to the right on the spectrum of "news reports and case studies" to materials generated by the media, university professors, or consulting firms. These analyses, sometimes private and sometimes public, are important sources of objective input, but are generally limited by their anecdotal nature. Consulting reports and business school case studies on the impact investing space, for example, are generally based on expert interviews and a limited set of self-selected customer and employee interviews. These are far less rigorous than their randomized trial cousins, but are an important source of information nonetheless.

The center of the figure is occupied by self-funded monitoring and evaluation studies (often called "M&E" by practitioners), perhaps the most underwhelming approach to impact measurement. These "measurement and evaluation studies" are often as expensive as randomized trials, but are generally less analytically rigorous and rarely conclusive to suggest a definitive course of action. Fortunately, impact investors and venture philanthropists have begun to shift their focus away from such studies, having grown unsatisfied by their inherent limitations and their relatively high cost and relatively low level of actionable insight.

Less objective but more empirical tools are found in the upper-left Performance Measurement quadrant. As noted, considerable progress has been made in developing a set of management tools such as balanced scorecard and SROI and Pulse (discussed below) that organizations can use to track progress towards impact. Promisingly, a number of social benefit organizations have worked together to develop a standard set of performance indicators to enable data aggregation and industry standard benchmarks. Examples include the MIX Market, which standardizes reporting for microfinance institutions; the Cultural Data Project, a collaborative effort among arts organizations and funders; and the Impact Reporting and Investment Standards (IRIS) (again, discussed below), which standardize social-impact metrics across a range of participating organizations.

Finally, in the upper right quadrant there is true impact assessment, as previously defined. The gold standard here are highly empirical randomized control trials. Fortunately, a considerable amount of experimentation has taken place in this space in recent years to broaden the use of randomized and quasi-random impact assessments.[39] Nevertheless, given its costs, this approach is generally unattainable for all but a small handful of priority initiatives backed by deep-pocketed donors.

With the bottom left helpful but not terribly rigorous while the upper right is rigorous but incredibly difficult (and expensive) to put into action, most of the action is concentrated in the intermediate areas. Fortunately, important progress has been made here, and other initiatives continue to bubble up in the field. Four relatively recent developments in particular deserve attention here.

Pulse

First is a new generation of web-based performance management tools like Pulse, created by the Acumen Fund and Google.org. Pulse is a portfolio data management tool that allows a philanthropic organization (a foundation, a social investment fund, or even a multisite nonprofit) to track the social, environmental, and financial performance of each of its enterprises over time and against their original plans.[40] Pulse is an example of a highly quantitative approach (with room for important qualitative commentary such as monthly reports) that enables consistent, periodic measures that "take the pulse" of an organization and allow donors or investors to track progress and intervene before problems arise. Pulse is similar in concept to the balanced scorecard, using internally generated data to inform management, in real time, about how their portfolio is performing.[41]

IRIS

Second, Pulse is part of a growing ecosystem of data standards designed to permit comparisons across organizations. The most fully developed of these is the Impact Reporting and Investment Standards (IRIS). A project of the Global Impact Investors Network (GIIN), with funding from the Rockefeller Foundation and the US Agency for International Development, IRIS has produced a consolidated set of reporting metrics in a wide assortment of fields, from microfinance to sustainable agriculture to renewable energy, that can introduce some standardization in the definition of various types of impacts.[42]

Even something as simple as a job can have multiple dimensions (full-time vs. part-time, permanent vs. seasonal, with benefits vs. without benefits). Beyond this, it has been difficult to weight achievements across fields adequately—how does the value of putting a former drug addict to work in a regular job compare with the value of sparing a youngster a case of malaria? More importantly, the IRIS standards, once adopted by foundations or fund managers, can enable data aggregation and cross-portfolio benchmarking to enable meaningful comparisons of social performance. A beta effort in the summer of 2011, with data collected from 450 social enterprises and seven social investors, demonstrated the power of new technologies and information standards to produce benchmarks that can enhance comparability of performance across funds.

B Lab

Third, using more consistent information standards, new ratings organizations are emerging that seek to generate simple, easy-to-understand social and environmental scores. The Global Impact Investing Rating System (GIIRS), managed by B Lab, has taken the additional step of ranking various performance standards and rating potential social enterprises and nonprofits in terms of their adherence to the most favorably ranked of these standards. This makes it less likely that every entity will be able to find some set of indicators in a large laundry list of possible IRIS- or MIX-type indicators in terms of which it can appear to earn an A in terms of its social impact.[43] Only in this way will it be possible for investors to differentiate truly promising from less promising social investments. In addition to the rating system, B Lab maintains a Standards Advisory Council, an independent body of nine experts in social and environmental sustainability that help B Lab score enterprises in terms of its key indicators.[44] These higher data standards and ratings systems may also play a critical role in enabling "social stock markets" to emerge and function.[45]

Constituent Voice

Finally, a fourth innovation is a set of instruments for bringing the voice of beneficiaries and their perception of impact or social value into the impact measurement equation. This voice has been strangely missing in all of the concern over demonstrating impact to investors, but it is ultimately fundamental. Under the leadership of David Bonbright, founder of the UK-based organization Keystone, social investors are now surveying their investees, and the enterprises themselves are asking their beneficiaries for feedback on the level and quality of perceived social impact delivered. Large companies in the United States and Europe largely ignored customer feedback into the 1960s, but the emergence of independent consumer satisfaction data (e.g., JD Power and Associates, *Consumer Reports*) has had a significant impact on product quality and profitability, as Fred Reichheld, the guru of customer loyalty strategies, has forcefully argued.[46] Bonbright points out that if this is the case in the private business sector, it might be even more true in the social sector, where social value creation may be even more closely linked to beneficiary satisfaction. Other efforts, like the Oxford Poverty and Human Development Initiative and the Grameen Foundation's Progress out of Poverty Index, rigorously measure the experiences of the poor—both qualitatively and quantitatively—in order to measure the impact of antipoverty policies on the people they target: the beneficiaries.[47] Ultimately, the impact of any intervention should be relevant—and important—to those that intervention seeks to benefit, and these efforts are at the leading edge of the push for greater accountability throughout the system.

The Chain of Accountability

This point about the role of program beneficiaries in impact measurement systems underlines a broader point about this entire field: Private investors seeking both a financial and a social return are not the only stakeholders of social ventures. Rather, there are multiple stakeholders for impact investments, and the stakes of the different stakeholders may differ significantly. This is particularly true when public resources are involved in the financing of social purposes—either directly in the form of grants, contracts, loans, loan guarantees or tax subsidies; or indirectly in the form of charitable tax deductions for individuals or foundations. The priorities of impact investors are therefore not the only ones that need to be served by impact measurement systems.

Rather, any particular social venture is likely to be embedded in a *chain of accountability*, a substantial array of stakeholders, each with its own preferred blend of impacts. As depicted in Figure 22.3, this chain could include private investors seeking various combinations of market and social return, private

FIGURE 22.3
Questions to be Informed by Data at Each Link in the Chain of Accountability

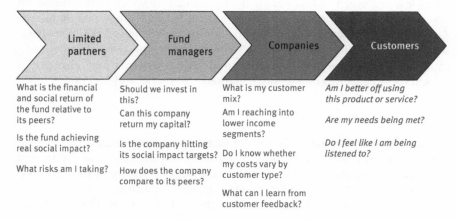

Limited partners	Fund managers	Companies	Customers
What is the financial and social return of the fund relative to its peers?	Should we invest in this?	What is my customer mix?	*Am I better off using this product or service?*
Is the fund achieving real social impact?	Can this company return my capital?	Am I reaching into lower income segments?	*Are my needs being met?*
What risks am I taking?	Is the company hitting its social impact targets?	Do I know whether my costs vary by customer type?	*Do I feel like I am being listened to?*
	How does the company compare to its peers?	What can I learn from customer feedback?	

foundations primarily interested in social return though perhaps with some return of capital, social entrepreneurs fundamentally committed to the social or environmental purpose and the respect of their peers, government officials interested in long-term solutions to serious problems and the potentials for using promising experiments as levers to push for system change, and program beneficiaries interested in gaining the long-term benefits that the program promises.

The chain metaphor is critical in realizing two fundamental points: first, just as a chain is only as strong as its weakest link, the information flows about social impact are only as strong as the weakest link along the chain of account-ability. If a program does not collect data as rigorously or frequently as REDF did using its OASIS system, it is very hard to report to donors on beneficiary outcomes. If companies do not track relevant and easy to measure performance measures, as JumpStart uses in its balanced scorecard, it will have a hard time reporting to donors or investors satisfactorily. Second, it is essential to under-stand that at each step in the chain different incentives and strategies might lead to different impact orientations. For example, an investor who cares more about social impact than financial returns, and who invests money in a blended value fund that makes venture-capital-style investments into social businesses, may be rudely disappointed by the social returns if the fund he has invested in com-pensates its portfolio managers solely on the basis of financial performance. Some funds like Core Innovations, which invest in businesses that make finan-cial services available to low-income consumers in the United States, are experi-menting with social-impact incentives that seek to strengthen the alignment between investor, manager, and company operator to deliver the blended return.

In reality, the "chain" is much more like a "network of accountability," less linear and more interconnected, but the fundamental point about information integrity and the potential for misalignment collectively pose an important warning for the impact investing community: one should not be overly fixated on the private investor community, or any link in the chain or node in the net-work, in designing impact measures. Too narrow a set of impact measures can actually cause harms by advantaging one set of stakeholders over others and thereby sacrificing significant support for promising ventures.[48] What is more, the nonprofit and for-profit ventures that are the recipients of social invest-ments may have functions beyond the delivery of services to a limited set of clients: they may (and perhaps should) have an objective of systems change that may entail extra costs that may appear to lower their SROI as traditionally mea-sured but produce vastly more important social changes in the long run, a point made powerfully in chapter 20 of this volume.

Conclusion: The Future of Moving to "Impact"

In short, the most advanced organizations in the social-impact arena are start-ing to deploy a range of tools, from the qualitative to the quantitative, and from the subjective to the objective, at different points along the chain of account-ability, and triangulating among them to understand whether and how their social investments are leading to absolute change. These tools—and the data they generate or analyze—are also making it possible to differentiate compara-tive performance among social enterprises.

Despite considerable progress, however, we are still a long way from being able to measure and compare systemic social change across a range of distinct interventions. More troubling by far, even these nascent efforts are starting to encounter considerable headwinds of resistance. Thus, Mario Morino, one of the United States' most prominent venture philanthropists, recently reported his concern that "the vast majority of funders and nonprofits are achieving, at best, marginal benefit from their efforts to implement outcomes thinking" and "may actually risk producing adverse effects on nonprofits and those they serve."[49] Other observers have reminded the field that "while metrics are critical and have their place, they're only one piece of the puzzle."[50]

This skepticism is echoed all around the web of accountability. At Acumen Fund, we heard our own investees ask us why they should bother to harmonize metrics. They still have to fill out multiple reports for multiple funders with little consistency among the forms. Some also complain that while they send in more data than they think is necessary, they never hear back from portfolio managers what they think the data mean or what we are learning from them. At the intermediary level, a few have recognized the collective action problem inherent in the adoption of consistent tools and standards: until funds are regulated or these become industry standards, there seems to be little incentive to spend more on measurement or to share data more broadly than necessary. And at the foundation or donor level, there is still skepticism that enterprises can deploy these tools effectively or that the data generated from them will inform donor strategy. Finally, and perhaps most critically, there is the fear that the elevation of the quantifiable metrics into performance standards may inadvertently reward organizations that are more productive in generating short-term results, but less effective in driving towards long-term systems change.

Most distressing of all, there is evidence that donors do not actually seem to care much about metrics. A 2004 article in the *Stanford Social Innovation Review* found little support for a focus on performance measurement systems among a group of high-net-worth individuals, many of whom expressed outright skepticism about the cost of implementing impact measures and the validity of their results, and these results were confirmed by two more recent studies by the Center for High Impact Philanthropy and Hope Consulting.[51]

These findings certainly seem borne out by the experience of JumpStart. Perhaps most frustrating to the staff was the missing link between the demonstration of performance and the ability to raise grant capital. "The connection between JumpStart's success at demonstrating impact and its ability to fundraise are at best tenuous," claimed JumpStart CEO Aaron Lieberman in the Harvard case study. "We double every single year, we get better impact measurements, and still no one ever comes back to us and says, 'Hey, you guys are doing great, we want to give more.'"[52]

This disappointing level of demand for impact measures among investors may, in turn, explain another gap in the field: the failure to develop a vibrant market of "enterprise brokers" and investment advisors to help donors and mission investors make philanthropic decisions in the same way that investment firms advise regular market investors. This is beginning to change, highlighted by leading-edge firms such as Imprint Capital, Arabella Advisors, and Tactical Philanthropy, but it is still early days.[53]

That we can't yet answer the big "So what?" question, however, does not mean that the incremental steps taken towards transparency, data collection, and aggregation are not important for performance improvements in the sector.

Performance management, metrics, and data-driven decision-making are bound to be more effective when more objective and empirical data are collected as close to the end of the chain of accountability as possible. These data, whether captured as part of the ongoing operations of a business or a social enterprise, through episodic consumer or beneficiary surveys, or as part of a rigorous, controlled experiment by social scientists, will move the sector toward improved performance. Organizations that invest in the systems to understand the impact of their services and who take performance measurement seriously should, over time, be in a better position to spot problems, observe trends, and improve the quality and effectiveness of their services. Enough social enterprises and venture philanthropies have made the investment, from use of SROI to deployment of Pulse to the adoption of the IRIS standards, that expectations have changed for how well an organization should be able to report on its social performance.

Ultimately, the value of measurement systems is that they enable staff to communicate and share information consistently over time, from the end users through the front-line program staff up to the board and management (and occasionally to the ever-widening circle of donors who care). Managers are able to spot performance problems, make program improvements, and discover success stories in a well-conceived and easy-to-manage system. Whether it is the balanced scorecard or SROI or the use of Pulse, metrics enable clear thinking about what the organization is trying to achieve, and what measures are needed to ensure programs are on track—and they can warn management when effectiveness begins to slip. Whether particular investors make use of the resulting measures or not, when significant amounts of public funding or even indirect public incentives are being directed to invest in and scale up "innovative ideas that work," it is incumbent on all stakeholders to measure and communicate, to the best of their ability, at a reasonable cost, the evidence of their program's impact.

Notes

1. The author would like to acknowledge the contributions of Acumen Fund Portfolio Manager Rob Katz and former summer associate Michael McCreless in the research and writing of this chapter.

2. "About TurnAround Couriers," TurnAround Couriers, accessed November 12, 2012, http://www.turnaroundcouriers.com/about/.

3. Laurie Monserbraaten, "Helping Youth Cycle Away from Poverty," *Toronto Star*, January 1, 2009, A3, accessed November 12, 2012, http://www.turnaroundcouriers.com/media/Jan_TorStar_09.pdf.

4. Analysis based on "TurnAround Couriers Social Return on Investment Report," TurnAround Couriers for the years 2004 to 2008 and the six-year review 2002–2008, accessed June 17, 2011, http://www.turnaroundcouriers.com/about/social-audits.

5. This is also known as double-bottom-line accounting.

6. Throughout this chapter, SROI will stand for social return on investment. SROI allows analysts to measure nonfinancial value (i.e., environmental and social value) relative to investment.

7. SROI calculation based on summary cost savings divided by total investment amount: Total Cost Savings to Society over 6 Years / Total Investment Required over 6 Years ($432,158 / $181,618) = 2.38 or 238 percent. Via "Turn Around Couriers 2008

report," accessed November 12, 2012, http://www.turnaroundcouriers.com/wp-content/uploads/2009/04/TAC_SROI_Report_Year_6.ppt.

8. "Why SROI?" Social Capital Partners, March 2009, http://socialcapitalpartners.ca/images/uploads/docs/Why_SROI_March_2009.ppt.

9. Double-bottom-line accounting factors in social impact along with financial impact; triple-bottom-line accounting adds environmental impact along to the first two.

10. The blended value proposition states that all organizations, whether for-profit or not, create value that consists of economic, social, and environmental value components—and that investors (whether market-rate, charitable, or some mix of the two) simultaneously generate all three forms of value through providing capital to organizations. The outcome of all this activity is value creation. Since that value is itself nondivisible, value is (by definition) a blend of these three elements. See "About Blended Value," Blended Value, accessed November 12, 2012, http://www.blendedvalue.org/about/.

11. "Evaluation in Philanthropy: Perspectives from the Field," Council on Foundations and Grantmakers for Effective Organizations, December 2009, http://www.geofunders.org/publications.aspx.

12. The Abdul Latif Jameel Poverty Action Lab at the Massachusetts Institute of Technology is a leading practitioner of randomized control trials, also known as randomized impact evaluations. For more, visit "What Is Randomization?" Poverty Action Lab, accessed November 12, 2012, http://www.povertyactionlab.org/methodology/what-randomization.

13. Robert Dorfman, *Measuring Benefits of Government Investments* (Washington, DC: Brookings Institution Press, 1965).

14. Gerald Schmaedick, ed., *Cost-Effectiveness in the Nonprofit Sector: Methods and Examples from Leading Organizations* (Westport, CT: Quorum Books, 1993), 4.

15. Robert Dorfman and Michael H. Rothkopf, "Why Benefit-Cost Analysis Is Widely Disregarded and What to Do about It," *Interfaces* 26.5 (1996): 1–6.

16. Paul R. Portney, "Benefit-Cost Analysis," in *The Concise Encyclopedia of Economics 2008* (Indianapolis, IN: Library of Economics and Liberty), accessed November 12, 2012, http://www.econlib.org/library/Enc/BenefitCostAnalysis.html.

17. "Wired, Willing and Ready: Nonprofit Human Service Organizations' Adoption of Information Technology," Princeton Survey Research Associates, Independent Sector, December 2001, http://www.independentsector.org/pdfs/wiredwillingready.pdf.

18. "An Information OASIS," Roberts Enterprise Development Fund, accessed October 10, 2012, http://www.redf.org/learn-from-redf/publications/121.

19. Holly Hall, "A Brave New World of Giving: Rapid Rise of On-line 'Portals' Raises Big Questions for Charities," *Chronicle of Philanthropy*, June 15, 2000.

20. Stephanie Lowell, Brian Trelstad, and William Meehan, "The Ratings Game: Evaluating the Three Groups That Rate the Charities," *Stanford Social Innovation Review*, Summer 2005, 39–45. A more recent set of online efforts, such as Greatnonprofits, Philanthropedia, and Givewell, are using expert analysis and the wisdom of the crowds to provide more insight into program effectiveness. It is still too early to tell whether these start-ups will succeed in driving donors towards more effective organizations, but they are promising experiments.

21. Christine Letts, William Ryan, and Allen Grossman, "Virtuous Capital: What Foundations Can Learn from Venture Capitalists," *Harvard Business Review* 75.2 (1995): 36–44.

22. John A. Byrne, "The New Face of Philanthropy," *Business Week*, December 2, 2002, http://www.businessweek.com/magazine/content/02_48/b3810001.htm.

23. Matthew Bishop and Michael Green, *Philanthrocapitalism: How Giving Can Save the World* (New York: Bloomsbury Press, 2009).

24. Cynthia Gair, "A Report from the Good Ship SROI," REDF, accessed November 12, 2012, http://www.socialreturns.org/docs/good_ship_sroi_gair.pdf.

25. Gair, "Good Ship SROI," 6.

26. "Rubicon Bakery SROI Report," REDF, accessed October 12, 2012, http://www.redf.org/system/files/%2820%29+SROI+Report+-+Rubicon+Bakery.pdf.

27. "Rubicon Bakery SROI Report," REDF.

28. Fay Twersky and Jed Emerson, "Webtrack and Beyond: Documenting the Impact of Social Purpose Enterprises: Profile of a Management Information System," in *REDF Box Set: Social Purpose Enterprises and Venture Philanthropy in the New Millennium* (San Francisco: REDF, 1999), accessed November 12, 2012, http://community-wealth.com/_pdfs/articles-publications/social/report-redf99-2.pdf.

29. "Social Impact Report," REDF, accessed November 12, 2012, http://www.redf.org/learn-from-redf/publications/122.

30. Melinda Tuan, "Measuring and/or Estimating Social Value Creation: Insights into Eight Integrated Cost Approaches," Bill and Melinda Gates Foundation Impact Planning and Improvement Working Paper, December 2008, accessed November 12, 2012, http://www.gatesfoundation.org/learning/documents/wwl-report-measuring-estimating-social-value-creation.pdf.

31. Robert S. Kaplan, *On Balance: The Balanced Scorecard and Nonprofit Organizations* (Boston: Harvard Business School Publishing, 2002).

32. "New Profit Inc: Governing the Nonprofit Enterprise," Harvard Business School, Case 9-100-052, July 2001, 8.

33. Allen Grossman and Arthur McCaffrey, *JumpStart* (Boston: Harvard Business School Publishing, 2001).

34. M. Daniel-Echols and Z. Xiang, "2000–2003 Follow-up Study of JumpStart Children," High Scope Educational Research Foundation, 2003; and D. Elson, L. Johns, and J. Petrie, "JumpStart's Service Learning Initiative: Enhanced Outcomes for At-Risk Children," in *From Passion to Objectivity: International and Cross-Disciplinary Perspectives on Service Learning Research*, ed. Shelly Billig and Sherril B. Gelmon (Charlotte, NC: Information Age Publishing, 2007), 65–87. For more information on both studies, and JumpStart's rigorous research agenda, see "JumpStart's Research," JumpStart, accessed October 2, 2012, http://www.jstart.org/site/DocServer/JumpStart_s_Research.pdf?docID=6321.

35. Grossman and McCaffrey, *JumpStart*, 11.

36. "Venture Philanthropy 2002: Advancing Nonprofit Performance through High-Engagement Grantmaking," Venture Philanthropy Partners, accessed October 21, 2012, http://www.vppartners.org/sites/default/files/reports/full_rpt_0.pdf.

37. Information according to author's research of listed organizations' websites completed in 2010.

38. Social Innovation Fund: Supporting Community Solutions," Corporation for National and Community Service, accessed October 20, 2012, http://www.nationalservice.gov/about/serveamerica/innovation.asp.

39. The Foundation Center's excellent TRASI (Tools and Resources for Assessing Social Impact) database is a very comprehensive collection of many methodologies. "Tools and Resources for Assessing Social Impact," Foundation Center, accessed October 21, 2012, http://trasi.foundationcenter.org/.

40. Pulse is a social measurement tool that we developed at Acumen Fund in partnership with Google.org, with support from the Skoll Foundation, the Lodestar Foundation, the W.K. Kellogg Foundation, and the Salesforce.com Foundation.

41. I have written previously on the approaches that Acumen Fund takes in measuring and managing the performance of its social investment portfolio. See Brian Trelstad,

"Simple Measures for Social Enterprises," *Innovations* 3.3 (Summer 2008), accessed October 21, 2012, http://www.mitpressjournals.org/doi/pdfplus/10.1162/itgg.2008.3.3.105.

42. "Impact Reporting and Investment Standards," GIIN, accessed November 12, 2012, http://iris.thegiin.org/.

43. The need to avoid this trap was emphasized in Lester M. Salamon, "What Would Google Do? Designing Appropriate Social Impact Measurement Systems," *Community Development Investment Review* 7.2 (2011): 43–47 and elaborated in chapter 1 of this volume.

44. "B Corporation: Homepage," B Corporation, accessed November 12, 2012, http://www.bcorporation.net.

45. Several nascent efforts are underway to create social stock exchanges that match social investors with investment opportunities. For a discussion of these efforts, see chapter 4 of this volume. Since these "social stock markets" are more about creating trading platforms for social investors than about measuring the impact of the enterprises being traded, this chapter will not explore them further.

46. Fred Reichheld, *The Ultimate Question: For Opening the Door to Good Profits and True Growth* (Boston: Harvard Business School Publishing, 2006). While Reichheld argues that consumer satisfaction data have impacted product quality and company profitability, there are those who argue that correlation does not imply causality; that being said, the argument is strong and generally logical.

47. The Oxford Poverty and Human Development Initiative's mission is to reduce poverty by ensuring that policy is grounded in people's experiences and values. More at "Oxford Poverty and Human Development Initiative: Homepage," Oxford University, accessed November 12, 2012, http://www.ophi.org.uk/. The Progress out of Poverty Index measures poverty levels of groups and individuals. Using the PPI, microfinance institutions can better determine their clients' needs, which programs are most effective, how quickly clients leave poverty, and what helps them to move out of poverty faster. More at "Progress out of Poverty," Grameen Foundation, accessed November 12, 2012, http://progressoutofpoverty.org/.

48. Salamon, "What Would Google Do?" See also the discussion in chapter 1 of this volume.

49. Mario Marino, "Social Outcomes: Missing the Forest for the Trees," Venture Philanthropy Partners, 2010, accessed November 2011, http://www.vppartners.org/learning/papers-and-perspectives/chairmans-corner/social-outcomes-missing-forest-trees.

50. Cynthia Gibson and William Deitel, "What Do Donors Want?" *Nonprofit Quarterly*, September 2010.

51. Katie Cunningham and Marc Ricks, "Why Measure? Nonprofits Use Metrics to Show That They Are Efficient. But What If Donors Don't Care?" *Stanford Social Innovation Review*, Summer 2004, 2, 1; Kathleen Noonan and Katharina Rosqueta, " 'I'm Not Rockefeller': 33 High Net Worth Philanthropists Discuss Their Approach to Giving," Center for High Impact Philanthropy, University of Pennsylvania, September 2008, http://www.impact.upenn.edu/images/uploads/UPenn_CHIP_HNWP_Study.pdf; Hope Consulting "Money for Good: The US Market Opportunity for Impact Investments and Charitable Gifts from Individual Donor and Investors," published May 2010, http://www.hopeconsulting.us/wordpress/wp-content/uploads/2013/03/MFG1-Full_July-2010.pdf.

52. Grossman and McCaffrey, *JumpStart*.

53. On the emergence of "enterprise brokers" in the social-impact investing field, see chapter 6 of this volume.

Suggested Readings

Ebrahim, Alnoor, and Kasturi Rangan. "The Limits of Nonprofit Impact." Working paper, Harvard Business School, 2010.

Trelstad, Brian. "Simple Measures for Social Enterprise." *Innovations* 3.3 (Summer 2008): 105–18.

CHAPTER 23

THE NEW FRONTIERS OF PHILANTHROPY IN GLOBAL PERSPECTIVE

Maximilian Martin

A Field in Transition

On March 18, 2010, the then UK justice secretary Jack Straw announced the world's first social-impact bond pilot.[1] Based on a contingent return model, it aims to mobilize up to 5 million British pounds for several specialized charities that work with the Peterborough prison in Cambridgeshire, England. The charities will provide a range of mentoring, education, and social support services for 3,000 male prisoners who have been sentenced to less than a year in jail. The UK justice secretary argued, "It's the short-term prisoners who have the highest propensity to reoffend. This bond will help to moderate increases in the prison population and produce a benefit for society." The chief executive of the St. Giles Trust, one of the specialized charities that will deliver services at Peterborough, described the bond as a "funding revolution."

The model is straightforward: the investors will receive a dividend from the government only if the program achieves a reduction greater than 7.5 percent in reoffending among the prisoners covered by the program, who are measured against an equivalent control group on the police national computer. The returns are contingent on success: the more money UK state agencies save through the program, the higher the return paid to bond investors, rising to a maximum of 13 percent, with payments made during years six and eight. If successful, the pilot has high replication potential because of the program's estimated effectiveness and the scale of the reoffending problem. Every GBP invested in a St. Giles Trust project to support prison leavers saves the government GBP 10; the UK National Audit Office estimates that reoffending by the 60,000 prisoners serving sentences shorter than 12 months is costing the UK up to GBP 10 billion a year.[2]

For global philanthropy, the social-impact bond represents an illustrative example of the fundamental changes under way in the field.[3] There are three reasons: first, the bond's innovative contingent return model; second, the execution partnership between a private social sector organization and a government agency in the provision of a core public good, safety; and finally, the role of social entrepreneurship in the initial conceptualization—the original idea for the scheme came from a social entrepreneurship organization, Ashoka, whose former head of social finance, Arthur Wood, first formulated the contingent return idea in 2006.[4] The UK social-impact bond will be run jointly by the UK Ministry of Justice and Social Finance, an ethical investment organization founded by private equity veteran Sir Ronald Cohen in 2007 with the stated objective of developing an effective social investment market in the UK.

Furthermore, the story of the social-impact bond provides an entry point to some of the changes underway in the field of global philanthropy. Around the world, philanthropy—defined, as suggested in chapter 1 of this volume, as the provision of private resources for social purposes, in the form both of grants and, increasingly, of "social" or "social-impact" investments generating a financial as well as a social return—has significantly expanded in scale and visibility in the past decade. Up until the recent great recession, there was even a widespread, contagious enthusiasm about a new golden era of philanthropy, and some of the newer forms of philanthropy may even have gained greater traction in the wake of this recession.

Because of their political independence, capacity to engage in the long term, and ability to pursue social change objectives in multiple jurisdictions, philanthropic foundations can, in principle, be highly effective change agents. However, to achieve large-scale impact, they need to leverage their resources extremely well: in the United States, the country with the world's best-endowed foundation landscape, philanthropy accounts for just about 10 percent of non-profit revenue, and foundations account for just over 10 percent of that, in total 1.3 percent of nonprofit revenue.[5] The concern for resource leverage is especially pronounced in the structures set up by entrepreneurial philanthropists around the world, who are often highly ambitious and sophisticated. They ask how they can maximize the catalytic effect of their philanthropy and how social enterprise and market-based mechanisms can be tapped as additional conduits for social change.

To understand the philanthropic field's logic of action, it helps to bring Kurt Lewin's and Pierre Bourdieu's notion of a "field" to bear on the analysis.[6] Social interaction inevitably takes place in some context, and this holds true for philanthropy as well. Thinking of it as field foregrounds its multiple dimensions and its semiautonomous nature. Trends in global philanthropy are broadly related to trends in other domains, but do not mirror them mechanically.[7] Based on the interplay between their location in a social network and their outlook on life, individuals and institutions occupy specific positions in a given field.[8] Over time, the specific positions they carve out crystallize in a field-specific logic of action, and actors' actions translate into a field's history. While not fully insulated from the dynamics in other fields, a field's specific history might differ considerably from overall historic developments.

This chapter will look at the current transformation of global philanthropy, its underlying logic of action and frontiers. Fields such as global philanthropy are governed by "rules of the game":[9] actors who do not master these rules will not be able to make meaningful interventions. To make sense, one must act according to the field's "logic of action." Thinking about global philanthropy as a field reminds us that the relevant parties are historical actors, constrained by the spirit of their times, and benefiting from the work done by previous generations. This chapter seeks to identify and analyze the four main fault lines which will influence the next decades of global philanthropy. All are related to what we can refer to as "the market revolution in global philanthropy." As global philanthropy moves beyond grant-making into investment approaches that produce social as well as financial returns, this accelerates the mainstreaming of a variety of niche activities that marry effectiveness, social impact, and market mechanisms.

In the next section, the chapter first discusses the general shift away from inefficient social capital markets, where resource allocation is relationship-driven, to a more value-driven allocation, as highlighted in the case of the social-impact bond above. Grants are expensive to raise and tend to be restricted to funding current service provision. Transaction costs in grant funding tend to be stifling, in addition to requiring an excessive time commitment to fundraising from the top leadership of the grantee organizations. As a result, nonprofit organizations enjoy insufficient flexibility to adapt, change, and invest in their workforce or infrastructure.[10] The section analyzes the constraints and the need for an increasingly efficient social capital market.

Subsequently, the chapter examines four frontiers in global philanthropy, starting with the shift from social entrepreneurship to synthesized social business. Social entrepreneurship is one of today's key frontiers in global philanthropy. Social entrepreneurs typically use market mechanisms to deliver a good or a service in a highly effective fashion to a marginalized or poor population that would not have the same level of access to the good or service otherwise. The section examines the experience of Ashoka: Innovators for the Public, and Aravind Eye Hospital in India. It argues that social entrepreneurship is becoming increasingly supply-constrained and will therefore begin to enter a new phase where organizational design features in addition to charismatic individuals will serve as guarantors of sustaining a socially entrepreneurial mission in scale, a phenomenon referred to as "synthesized social business."

The chapter then examines a second frontier of global philanthropy, microfinance and its shift to a broader paradigm of microfinancial services. With approximately 2.5 billion people from low-income countries and many of the 2.7 billion people from middle-income countries still underserved by the conventional financial services industry, microfinance is an important theater of the market revolution in philanthropy, deploying market mechanisms for the empowerment of the economically active poor. The section reviews how the microfinance field has successfully gone through different stages, leading to the emergence of a new asset class and a US$25 billion market with roughly 100 million borrowers, a potential demand of 500 million borrowers and a market size of US$250 billion, and looks at the current transition from a focus on credit to microfinancial services.

The chapter's next section looks at the third frontier of global philanthropy, namely the shift from development assistance to base-of-the-pyramid investing. At the core of the argument are the implications of the recent reconceptualization of the developing world as the so-called base of the pyramid (BoP). BoP refers to a gigantic market with four billion people and pent-up demand for a whole range of goods and services in areas such as education, health, housing, and sanitation. Shifting from development assistance to base-of-the-pyramid investing assumes that a joint deployment of capital, professional expertise, and technology and the local presence of a commercial investor with a global network can unlock significant economic and social benefits. The section examines the cases of Aureos Capital in the UK and Ignia Ventures in Mexico.

Subsequently, the chapter discusses global philanthropy's fourth frontier, the transition from classical grant-making to a strategic monetization of future savings. Grants remain the core business of philanthropy today, and many of the fundamental challenges humanity faces in the twenty-first century cannot be tackled by markets alone. Free markets do not internalize externalities such as environmental destruction or negative public health impacts on populations that are not working in the formal sector. Private or public subsidies are required. In some cases, they should be temporary, and directed toward establishing functioning marketplaces. In other cases, concerning pure public goods, subsidies are required on a permanent basis to achieve a given social objective. The section maps the strategic use of capital markets to monetize grant commitments in one of three cases: (1) whenever addressing a problem now is cheaper than addressing it in the future when a grant commitment is actually paid out, (2) when new marketplaces need to be constructed, or (3) when the most efficient solution provider is not a government agency. The Global Alliance for Vaccines and Immunization (GAVI), the World Sanitation Financing Facility (WSFF), and the social-impact bond are discussed to highlight the different changes underway.

The chapter's final section resumes the argument, situates the trends observed in the context of the recent great recession, and asks where global philanthropy is headed. Thinkers like William Petty, Adam Smith, and John Stuart Mill argued for centuries for the large-scale provision of public goods by governments, which only became a reality with the rise of the welfare state in the industrialized world in the twentieth century. The concept of public goods is now omnipresent in framing policy discussions. But given the state of public finances around the world and the suboptimal innovation orientation of the publicsector,awindowofopportunityhasopenedupforaphilanthropy-facilitated provision of public goods on a massive scale through market-based solutions. There is no practical reason why the techniques and concepts of investment banking and capital markets cannot be applied to solving some of the most pressing social challenges of the twenty-first century. The implications of the recent financial crisis are likely to accelerate the transformation of the field of global philanthropy.

From Inefficient Social Capital Markets to Value-Driven Allocation

As a secular trend, philanthropy is gradually moving away from a relationship-driven allocation of capital toward a value-driven one. This is changing the logic of the philanthropic field and will create an increasingly efficient social capital market over time.

The majority of charitable foundations operate on relatively small budgets. Moreover, similar to grant-seeking civil society organizations, grant-making organizations follow a wide range of theories of change and impact assessment, allowing for little standardization of processes and potential for efficiency gain across organizations. Foundations operate in a fragmented resource allocation system with high search and capital allocation costs. Not only does an individual or organization looking to participate in the philanthropic sector face a bewildering array of players; in many countries the processes of nonprofit registration are also complex, tax incentives discouraging, and sector regulations cumbersome. In short, the social capital market is not fully efficient. In addition to the sheer transaction cost of allocating philanthropic capital, proponents of the "inefficient market hypothesis" also note that too little value-driven allocation takes place in philanthropy. The majority of grant-making is currently not based on nonprofit performance, but is instead highly relationship-driven. Therefore, philanthropists and social investors do not necessarily reward better performers with additional resources. Putting a cost to this structural inefficiency, one study of the US nonprofit sector put the combined costs of grant-making and fundraising as high as 22 percent to 43 percent, that is, 10 times higher when compared to a cost of 2 percent to 4 percent of allocating capital in the stock market.[11] Compared to capital allocation processes in public markets, the "social capital market" looks disappointingly inefficient: transaction costs are too high, information flows insufficiently robust to reward performance, and investor preferences often overly influenced by relationship considerations. To be fair, it is more difficult to measure performance in the absence of a single profit measure; moreover the metrics in the for-profit sector are also becoming more complex as they increasingly need to track companies' performance against triple–bottom-line expectations, as is explored in chapter 22.

As a symptom of the social capital market's inefficiency, nonprofit leaders typically spend vast amounts of time on fundraising rather than on the continuous improvement of the work of the organizations they lead. This even holds true for organizational models that are considered to be especially innovative and effective, as in the case of social entrepreneurs. For example, a recent global survey among 109 social entrepreneurs by UK strategy consultancy and think tank SustainAbility revealed a lack of efficient capital allocation processes in this segment of global philanthropy as well: 72 percent of the social entrepreneurs interviewed considered accessing capital to be the main obstacle to growth, next to marketing and the further professionalization of their organizations.[12]

Given the sheer magnitude of social and environmental needs that global philanthropy seeks to address, the high transaction costs of grant financing can leave philanthropists frustrated as they seek to make a difference. But while there has never been a broad constituency for efficiency and effectiveness in the history of philanthropy, two interesting developments are likely to enable philanthropies to achieve greater impact in the decades to come.

First, a substantial portion of giving is likely to continue to be relationship-driven in the foreseeable future—but its proportion will nevertheless diminish substantially over the next decades. The relative importance of philanthropic capital seeking high demonstrated social returns is increasing. Some observers even argue that we are on the verge of a new social movement led by the wealthy. UK journalist Matthew Bishop and former UK development aid official Michael Green have termed this phenomenon "philanthrocapitalism."[13] In this view, the subset of philanthropy that seeks to provide transformational solutions to the issues it takes up has entered a qualitatively new phase in human history. Propelled by motivated business and celebrity philanthropists such as Bill Gates, Bono, Richard Branson, Angelina Jolie, and George Soros, it has become a veritable movement.

Second, global philanthropy is not only becoming more results-oriented with the grants it allocates, but it has also entered a healthy period of experimentation by blending social and financial returns, as previous chapters of this book have shown. This mirrors trends in mainstream investing, where globalization and geopolitical events increasingly drive capital towards underattended populations, and emerging market investments are becoming more relevant. Philanthropy now also experiments with for-profit models that create opportunities to do good and well at the same time. In terms of the gradual unfolding of a new approach, there is a parallel with ethical funds, sustainable investments, and socially responsible ventures. Commonly aggregated under the umbrella term "socially responsible investments" (SRI), such investments went through a long phase of uncoordinated innovation, but have finally seen substantive growth in recent years, and are now becoming a part of the mainstream in the investment space. What is more, this has become far more than an American phenomenon: over €5 trillion in SRI assets under management now exist in Europe.[14] As is the general case of a maturing industry, the number of actors has multiplied, forming a cluster. In Europe alone, there were an estimated 375 SRI funds in October 2007, and even if some went under, the postcrisis SRI industry is still sizable.[15]

As the equivalent of SRI penetrates the foundation world, what does this mean? There are multiple concepts for doing good and well at the same time. Over the years, the approach has therefore come to be referred to under different labels. The concepts of blended-value investing, mission investing, and impact investing all are based on a shared core idea: to invest (a part of) a foundation endowment or some philanthropic asset to achieve both financial and social returns. Conceptually, this is highly attractive. If a charitable foundation looks holistically at expenditure and investment policies as complementary ways to further its mission, it can generate greater social impact. In addition to distributing 2 percent to 5 percent of assets every year, a foundation could also invest some part of the other 95 percent to 98 percent of its assets in investments furthering its mission, provided it can do so without sacrificing the financial returns on endowment assets that are required to finance payouts in perpetuity.[16]

While the idea is intellectually straightforward, however, it has so far not been adopted widely in the global philanthropic community, in spite of multiple attempts by practitioners to advocate a unified view of investment policy and payouts. The foundational concept is elegant and clear, and at some point, one of the initiatives should succeed.[17]

As global philanthropy gradually moves from inefficient social capital markets to value-driven allocation, the examples of substantial innovation are multiplying. New allocation processes are coming on stream. They use investment mechanisms to steer capital toward pressing social and environmental issues more efficiently. If and how quickly these approaches will become mainstream is literally the sector's trillion-dollar-question, but if anything, the great recession of 2008–2009 has accelerated the pace. Over the long term, the emergence of an impact investing industry (whatever its ultimate name might be) can be considered to be a reasonably certain outcome, reducing the inefficiency of social capital markets and increasing the role of value-driven allocation. The remainder of the chapter analyzes developments in the four key theaters of this emergent industry: social entrepreneurship, microfinance, base-of-the-pyramid investing, and strategic monetization of future savings. Jointly, they will transform the philanthropic field in fundamental ways in the coming decades.

From Social Entrepreneurship to Synthesized Social Business

Social entrepreneurship is one of the key frontiers in global philanthropy. Though referred to extensively as a concept, there is no single definition of the subject. Defined as finding ways to combine existing resources in novel ways that yield added social value, social entrepreneurship is a perennial phenomenon: throughout human history, there have been people who have found innovative ways to fulfill social needs. As understood today, social entrepreneurs typically use market mechanisms to deliver a good or a service in a highly effective fashion to a marginalized or poor population that would not have the same level of access to the good or service otherwise.

As a concept, social entrepreneurship began to be theorized in the 1980s, based on the work of Bill Drayton, the founder of the pioneering institution of social entrepreneurship, Ashoka. Social entrepreneurship was widely discussed in the media for the first time in the 1990s. Subsequently, an increasing number of individuals and organizations began to devote their attention to elaborating some aspect of social entrepreneurship. In 2010, there were several thousand social entrepreneurs organized in global networks, and many more individuals and organizations who referred to themselves as social entrepreneurs or social enterprises. A sense emerged that social entrepreneurship might be the key ingredient to a new social contract for the twenty-first century.

When assessing the promise of social entrepreneurship, it is important to understand that no matter how effective, bottom-up evolution takes time. Typically, a social entrepreneurial approach results from trial and error rather than top-down planning. Successful social entrepreneurs combine lessons from the world of business and the world of civil society, and benefit from the global exchange of expertise and access to networks.

Take the emblematic example of providing low-cost cataract eye operations at the Aravind Eye Hospital in India. Focused on providing affordable, sustainable and equitable eye care in order to treat preventable blindness, Dr. Vanketaswamy (often simply referred to as "Dr. V."), set up the hospital in 1976. Both deeply spiritual and extraordinarily focused on efficiency, he reminded his staff constantly, "If McDonald's can deliver affordable hamburgers to the common person everywhere in the world, why can't we deliver eye care to everyone who needs it?" Keeping costs in check was one necessary condition to achieve scale. In the 1980s, David Green, then a fundraiser for the Seva Foundation in the United States, successfully secured from US manufacturers thousands of free intraocular lenses (IOLs) needed to perform cataract operations at low cost at the Aravind Eye Hospital in India.[18] Free lenses provided a core input necessary to scale the number of eye operations while keeping costs in check. Moreover, the Aravind Eye Hospital succeeded in redesigning the surgery process along the lines of scientific management, creating a low-cost eye operation value chain with standardized, quality outcomes.[19]

When Aravind's in-kind donation stream of IOLs dried up in the late 1980s because of a change in industry dynamics, the high cost of IOLs in the market, in excess of US$125, became a constraint for operating at scale. In response, David Green helped to establish a nonprofit organization, Aurolab, as the manufacturing division of Aravind Eye Hospital. In a remarkable exercise in technology transfer, Aurolab managed to manufacture high-quality IOLs at affordable prices—about US$5 a pair. Since 1992, Aurolab has supplied over 5 million lenses to its customers in India and over 120 other countries worldwide. Charging higher prices to wealthier patients made cross-subsidies to the poor possible. In 2009, Aravind treated about two-thirds of its patients for free. Every patient receives the same quality cataract operation, but patients who are treated for free are placed in considerably more spartan accommodations than paying patients. Given its low cost base and secure access to core components, the Aravind cataract operation business is fundamentally profitable. Once the Aravind Eye Care system ran smoothly, David Green began to consult to other eye care systems around the world. Learning from the Aravind experience has enabled approximately 250 eye care programs globally to become profitable since 2000, while offering quality services to the wealthy and the poor alike.[20]

Over the past 30 years, several social entrepreneurs have managed to create social businesses such as Aravind. They are financially sustainable and even profitable, though they tend to redistribute a large part of their profits through subsidized pricing to poorer client segments who cannot afford the good or service. This has led social entrepreneurs to take steps to further scale and replicate such initiatives. Properly run and scaled, such programs generate sufficient cash flow to support debt financing at manageable levels of risk, assuming suitable financial instruments can be created. One illustrative example of such an instrument was the Eye Fund, a US$20 million debt fund providing loans and guarantees to support the development of affordable eye care for the world's poor, created through a partnership among Ashoka, the world's leading network of social entrepreneurs, the International Agency for the Prevention of Blindness (IAPB), and Deutsche Bank.

Accompanying the growth of individual social entrepreneurs, and in some senses contributing to it, has been the creation of a sizable infrastructure of support organizations. Included here is Ashoka, the pioneering social entrepreneurship recruitment and support organization founded by American Bill Drayton in 1980;[21] the Schwab Foundation for Social Entrepreneurship, created in Switzerland in 1998 by Klaus Schwab, the founder and president of the World Economic Forum, and his wife Hilde; the Skoll Foundation, based in Palo Alto, California, founded in 1999 by Jeff Skoll, the first president of eBay; and university-based programs of research and education at such prestigious institutions as Harvard Business School (Social Enterprise Initiative, 1993), the University of Geneva, Switzerland (2003), IESE Business School in Barcelona, and the Said Business School at Oxford University (2004). Governments have also entered the field. For example, in the UK, the Millennium Commission granted an endowment to the Millennium Awards Trust in 2002 to fund the activities of UnLtd, Foundation for Social Entrepreneurs, a UK registered charity. Indeed, nonprofit and philanthropic leaders across a broad front have incorporated the social entrepreneurship label into their work as social entrepreneurship has been "mainstreamed" and integrated into global consciousness.

Still, one of the key questions going forward is how to fund social entrepreneurs efficiently. While the nonprofit sector is large and growing, it continues to be highly fragmented—for social entrepreneurs and more classical nonprofits alike. This holds back investment by raising costs and complexity. Consider that of 200,000 nonprofits founded in the United States between 1970 and 2003, only 144 had reached revenues in excess of US$50 million by 2003.[22] Fragmentation may lower the entry barrier for innovation, but it imposes higher transaction costs and renders expansion more difficult. Compare the due diligence and portfolio management of a US$100 million debt or equity investment vehicle that makes 100 portfolio investments of US$1 million each to a more standard private equity investment vehicle of the same size where the average investment is US$10 million. Assuming a typical private equity screening ratio of 100 opportunities for every investment made, the first vehicle would have to find, screen, and monitor 10,000 opportunities, whereas the latter has to find, screen, and monitor only 1,000. Moreover, in terms of effort-reward ratio, it is typically harder for social businesses to achieve full financial viability than for purely commercial ventures.

In the 2010s we are about to reach a point where the relative supply of high-performing individual social entrepreneurs will lag behind the demand for such talent. Simply put: there are not that many "Dr. Vs/Aravinds" who can be scaled further even if additional finance is available. As a rule of thumb, one can find about one additional Ashoka-quality social entrepreneur per annum per 10 million inhabitants. This means that we could in principle source 680 new social entrepreneurs per annum given a current global population of 6.8 billion.

One solution to this dilemma is to create institutions and incentive structures that reward social entrepreneurial behavior and thereby obtain both more companies and individual entrants in the space. We can refer to this approach as "synthesized social business."

A synthesized social business can be defined as a business venture whose social purpose is built into the holding structure of the company. For example, a philanthropic foundation could acquire a significant ownership stake and special voting rights in a company with the mission to make the good or service available to as many people as possible around the world. This setup would commit the company to pursue a "social" business strategy that focuses on higher volumes and lower margins, or a tiered pricing strategy that utilizes profits from wealthier consumers to subsidize services for less favored parts of society, as in the case of Aravind. The entity is considered a "synthesized" social business because the impulse to behave as a social business follows from the structure and business model of the company as opposed to the ethical commitment of the individuals who have founded or lead the company. Consider the case of TOMSShoes, a US footwear company that also operates a nonprofit subsidiary, Friends of TOMS. Assuming that there are over 1 billion people at risk for soil-transmitted diseases around the world that could be prevented with shoes, the company has redesigned its value chain in such a way that for every pair of shoes bought, another pair of shoes is given to a child in need; TOMS has positioned its one-for-one model as the central marketing theme of the company, and already inspired other companies to experiment with the same model (which is ultimately comparable to the Aravind eye care model, where paying patients subsidize those who cannot afford a cataract operation).[23]

Another facet of "synthesizing" more social enterprises consists of structural measures to raise the supply of would-be social entrepreneurs. One promising channel is "insemination" at the university level. Business schools around the world develop management talent on a massive scale, so it is currently much less scarce than social entrepreneurship talent. Given the interest of students around the world in the topic, the latter is growing fast, but from a low base. Steps can be taken to accelerate this process. For example, in 2010, Ashoka University conducted the first-ever Faculty Institute at Marquette University in Milwaukee. Taking a train-the-trainer approach, the institute trains senior faculty in the design and delivery of effective courses on social entrepreneurship, with the goal of raising the supply and quality of social entrepreneurship education at the university in question, which in turn should raise the supply of would-be social entrepreneurs.

Finally, developing a synthesized social business is often a particularly interesting option when technology and intellectual property are involved. With 185,000 patents issued by the US Patent and Trademark Office alone in 2008, developing just 1 percent of them through the formula of synthesized social business, and assuming that only one in every 10 new ventures will succeed, would nevertheless add another 20 percent capacity to the intrinsic social enterprise pipeline every year, and thus help to further close the supply gap for impact investments.[24]

From Microfinance to Microfinancial Services

Approximately 2.5 billion people in low-income countries and many of the 2.7 billion people in middle-income countries remain underserved by the conventional financial services industry.[25] Microfinance is an especially pertinent example of deploying market mechanisms for social change for two reasons: first, because the microfinance experience shows that the profit-motive and social impact do not necessarily conflict with one another, and second, because over the past three decades, the microfinance field has successfully gone through the different stages that the emerging impact investing industry is likely to go through over a shorter period of time.

Defined as the provision of finance to individuals with a low income, microfinance refers to financial services at the base of the economic pyramid that broaden access to capital. With a current market of US$25 billion, roughly 100 million borrowers, a potential demand of 500 million borrowers, and a market size of US$250 billion, it is one of the frontiers of philanthropy in the decades ahead, and an enormous capital allocation and social-impact opportunity.

Microfinance is now transitioning from a focus on credit to microfinancial services. In addition to microcredit, microfinance also includes microsavings, microinsurance, remittances, and other financial innovations. In a nutshell, microfinance provides different forms of access to capital for the economically active poor, with the objective of economic empowerment and poverty alleviation.

Microcredit portfolios share four characteristics. First, the target clients are low-income borrowers: typically, self-employed persons or owners of microbusinesses in the informal sector, rather than salaried workers. Second, the average loan size is small and often much less than €10,000 in Europe and central Asia, and US$7,500 elsewhere. Third, while more expensive than the provision of credit to wealthier segments of the population, microfinance is much cheaper than the unsecured credit provided by the loan sharks that have traditionally served the informal sector. Moreover, it takes place in an institutionalized, legal context rather than the context of organized crime and violence. Finally, microfinance uses alternative lending techniques. Operating with little or no conventional collateral, it deploys group lending and other techniques instead. In a group-lending model, individual members of a borrowing group can only access credit if the other members of the group meet their repayment obligations. This creates a strong degree of group-monitoring and lowers the due diligence and repayment enforcement costs for the lender. Group lending rolls over part of the risk to the group and keeps costs to the microfinance institution (MFI) down. Group lending is therefore generally considered to be more scalable than individual loans to the poor. However, practitioners sometimes argue that the group-centric approach produces average rather than excellent empowerment outcomes: borrowing group members do not necessarily accept that one of its members is a more successful microentrepreneur or has a better business idea, and therefore can and should deploy a much higher loan-to-project-revenue multiple (for example, 10:1). From a control perspective, there are also risks resulting from the fact that the MFI does not know all of its clients individually, and has few means to assess phenomena such as overindebtedness resulting from multiple loans from different MFIs active in a shared client franchise. There is general agreement that group lending is especially attractive where transaction costs are prohibitively high, as in rural areas.

Microfinance is not, of course, entirely new. Early examples include the nineteenth-century European credit cooperative movement stimulated by the work of Friedrich Wilhelm Raiffaisen, and the community-oriented pawnshops that Franciscan monks founded as early as the fifteenth century.[26] In fact, group lending was already well established in Bangladesh when Muhammad Yunus began his lending experiments to the poor in 1976, which led to the establishment of the Grameen Bank in 1980.[27]

But as a global movement and an emergent asset class, microfinance is a recent phenomenon. Similar to the founders of Acción and Banco Sol in Latin America in the 1970s, Muhammad Yunus made a difference because he found ways to *scale* microfinance, facilitating the emergence of a global movement that succeeded in turning microfinance into an investable proposition. Given the key role of access to capital in development, the ability to scale up microfinance at the grass-roots level will be one of the key factors determining the success of global philanthropy in the first half of the twenty-first century.

Similar to the case of social entrepreneurship discussed previously, the development of microfinance has taken time and holds lessons for other fields of philanthropy and impact investing. In the 1980s, microfinance was mainly seen as a highly effective tool for economic empowerment and poverty alleviation. The anecdotal life stories of the empowered individuals graduating from poverty took center stage. There was a sense that all that was missing was global scale. In the following decade, the microfinance industry grew and the financial profitability of banking for the poor came to the fore. The pendulum began to swing toward the other end of the spectrum, viewing microfinance mainly as a commercial investment proposition. During the 2000s, microfinance started to be positioned as a veritable asset class for investors, evidenced by the fast growth of many investment funds, and downplaying the nonprofit origins of the field.

Consider, for example the case of Banco Compartamos, a Mexican microfinance bank that currently serves 2 million clients, with a total active loan portfolio of 10 billion Mexican pesos (US$850 million) at the end of the first quarter of 2011, and a return on average equity of 31.8 percent.[28] Though started as a grant-funded nonprofit, by the time Banco Compartamos went public on the Mexican stock exchange in 2007, in a secondary offering of 30 percent of its shares, priced at US$468 million, it was already a highly profitable operation, making loans to the poor and boasting a rate of return on equity (ROE) of 56 percent.[29]

Following the growth of microfinance lending institutions, a range of microfinance investment vehicles (MIVs) emerged. Development institutions and the consulting firms to whom they outsourced fieldwork were the first to discover the financial potential of microbanking. Credit turned out to be a product that was relatively easy to replicate and adapt. Unlike other development projects, microbanking projects could lead to solvent and sustainable businesses. Properly run, a microfinance institution manages a highly diversified client pool and a revenue stream with many thousand payments every week. And the smaller the business, the larger the potential for economies of scale and the higher the margin: a microentrepreneur with sales revenues of two US dollars a day who is working on fixed costs of 50 to 100 cents is a representative example. Production and sales can often easily be doubled or tripled by lending a few hundred US dollars for working capital or fixed assets. However, making loans of such small size is very costly and labor intensive. Making the numbers work requires attention to operating efficiency.

Over time, public-sector seed investors succeeded in attracting interest from the private sector. To invest in microfinance institutions, the first ever for-profit investment fund was set up in 1998 and distributed through private banks in Geneva, Switzerland. In the early 2000s, many specialized fund management boutiques and fund advisers emerged. Ten years later, investors had a choice between a wide variety of microfinance investment funds offered both by specialized boutiques and global banks. In 2009, there were over 100 microfinance investment vehicles, and their growth has by and large not been adversely affected by the financial crisis. According to the latest CGAP (Consultative Group to Assist the Poor, World Bank) 2009 survey, MIV assets grew to over US$6.6 billion in a decade.[30] Investors include asset managers, socially responsible investment (SRI) funds, family offices, retail clients, and institutional investors such as pension funds. Well-known brands include BlueOrchard Finance and Symbiotics in Geneva, responsAbility Social Investment Services in Zurich, Triple Jump in the Netherlands, MicroVest in Washington, and Developing World Markets in New York. Building tailored products for specific groups of investors, the specialized boutiques are the most common point of investment entry for international private investors in microfinance today.

As the decade progresses, investors will face even more choice in the possible pathways through which to invest in microfinance: direct equity investments through banks and private equity funds; specialized microfinance investment funds offered by such institutions as Deutsche Bank and Credit Suisse; wholesale lending and guarantee schemes through which lenders place funds in institutions such as Société Géneral and BNP Paribas for onward lending to microenterprises; guarantee funds such as the International Guarantee Fund in Geneva, designed to mitigate country and currency risk; secondary market funds that invest in packages of microfinance loans; and direct peer-to-peer investment platforms such as Kiva or MYC4, which offer individual investors the opportunity to invest in social ventures screened by local partners.

Scaling what is already a big market will be the challenge ahead, and the future of microfinance consists of a broader shift toward microfinancial services. The 2009 Micro-Credit Survey acknowledges over 3,552 microfinance institutions reporting over 154 million microenterprise clients worldwide, of which over 106 million are among the poorest.[31] While the Micro-Credit Survey does not survey all of the financial services for the poor worldwide, it gives a good overview of the sector. Assuming an average loan of US$500 to $1,000, the current market size is at US$75 to $150 billion, suggesting a 30 percent annual growth of the industry over the past 10 years, when market size was estimated at US$15 to $30 billion. However, the underlying market demand is much bigger. Estimates indicate that there are at least 500 million microentrepreneurs worldwide. Each would require on average at least US$500 per annum to sustain his or her family and activities, yielding a target market of at least US$250 billion. Thus, about 10 percent to 20 percent of market demand is currently being met. From an investment perspective, about 250 MFIs around the world are currently commercially self-sustainable and interesting targets for foreign investors.

In 2010, the microfinance industry entered a crisis of confidence resulting from two developments: (1) overindebtedness of some clients, which in turn led to suicides in cases when clients were unable to meet their obligations, and (2) the controversy surrounding Muhammad Yunus's forced departure from the Grameen Bank.[32] With respect to overindebtedness, the case of previously fast-growing SKS Microfinance Limited in India received particular media attention, and many microfinance specialists sought to regain social investor confidence by repositioning microfinance more explicitly in the framework of "impact investing" or "microfinance plus" (understood as more quality and impact-focused microfinance).[33]

Before the financial crisis, the balance sheets of many MFIs were growing at an average rate of 25 percent to 50 percent per annum. Most of these institutions capture savings locally and are at least partially owned by local investors. Once the crisis of confidence is overcome, and as the decade progresses, we can expect a further development of the microfinance industry along the following three vectors. Together, they will complete the industry's shift from microfinance to microfinancial services.

First, as MFIs look for opportunities to grow their business, they will gradually cover all segments of the unbanked, from micro to small to medium entrepreneurs. Policy making entities in microfinance, such as CGAP, have therefore broadened the scope and array of microfinance, its definition and constituents and shifted from microcredit to microfinance, and now to the concept of "inclusive financial services." This expansion can also be referred to as "vertical growth": additional segments of the unbanked are gradually being integrated vertically into the financial services market: micro, small, and medium income-generating borrowers and enterprises, from vulnerable nonpoor to the extreme poor. Building microfinancial services renders the industry more heterogeneous. It means that microfinance investors now pursue segments as diverse as small village banking nonprofit MFIs, and small and medium enterprise (SME) finance commercial banks. Moreover, microfinance institutions are now also present in the industrialized world (e.g., Street UK).

A second industry trend is similarly a consequence of microfinance institutions' quest for scale. Following the evolving financial product needs of the micro, small, and medium entrepreneurs to improve their living standards, MFIs have already moved from microcredit into microsavings, microinsurance, and microremittances. Referred to as "horizontal growth," many providers of microfinance now transition from a single product offering such as microenterprise loans to a general offering framework of microfinancial services covering the entire span of daily needs and correspondent capital requirements, from microhousing to microutilities, microenergy, microinsurance, and so on. The 2010s will see further product development providing access to capital to finance needs as diverse as housing, food, energy, health, education, and water and sanitation, among others. Moreover, more and more microfinance institutions outside of the Latin American and South Asian regions where the current microfinance model took off first now regionalize and globalize.

Overall, structural microfinance industry change and increasingly sophisticated investment tools to allocate capital efficiently and price risk will give the sector more and more of a business rather than a philanthropy feel. When Muhammad Yunus and the Grameen Bank received the Nobel Peace Prize in 2006, there was still a widespread sense that microfinance was a panacea to succeed where classical development interventions failed. Since then, the pendulum has swung into the opposite direction. Criticism of the industry has grown. Examples in India and elsewhere have shown how counterproductive to the stated goal of economic empowerment and poverty alleviation an overheating microfinance market with excessive liquidity and competition can be.

The case of Compartamos in Mexico is instructive in this regard. As the company's profitability rose, questions were raised as to what constitutes a "fair" profit when providing financial services to the poor. Grameen Bank founder Muhammad Yunus famously argued that he feared that microfinance had been twisted to benefit investors, rather than the poor: "When you discuss microcredit, don't bring Compartamos into it," he suggested. "Microcredit was created to fight the money lender, not to become the money lender."[34]

This suggests the likely emergence of a third stream of developments, as the mainstreaming of microfinance ironically brings increased attention to the corporate social responsibility of MFIs. Codes of conduct for all stakeholders in the value chain will become more central, and in some cases required by MIVs. For example, Symbiotics, a leading Geneva-based microfinance investment platform that serves as portfolio manager or advisor to more than 10 microfinance funds and syndicates debt, has developed a social responsibility rating that is taken into account when making investment decisions. The Symbiotics screening examines the following seven dimensions: social governance; labor climate; contribution to financial inclusion; fair treatment of clients; diversity and quality of products; social responsibility towards the community; and environmental policy.[35] But the sector ultimately needs a widely shared social performance assessment methodology.

As the decade unfolds, we can expect the social impact of microfinance to be assessed in an increasingly realistic fashion. Far from a magic solution to poverty, microfinance can nevertheless be an extremely powerful tool to enable the economically active poor to raise their daily living standards and graduate from poverty over time. Given the remaining pent-up demand for capital among the poor, and the noticeable emergence of a veritable industry with the corresponding skill sets and an expanding product shelf, microfinance investments will continue to see amazing growth in the decades ahead, and can be expected to gradually fulfill the ambition of inclusive financial services around the world.

From Development Assistance to Base-of-the-Pyramid Investments

Next to social entrepreneurship and microfinance, global philanthropy's third frontier consists of the implications of the recent reconceptualization of the developing world as the so-called base of the pyramid (also "bottom of the pyramid," BoP). BoP refers to a gigantic market with four billion people and pent-up demand for a whole range of goods and services in areas such as education, health, housing, and sanitation.[36] The effectiveness of official development aid channeled through indigenous governments has come in for serious questioning in recent years; not only has this given rise to interesting experimentation with other forms of assistance, but it has also been a key driver in directing attention to the notion of the BoP.[37]

Shifting from development assistance to base-of-the-pyramid investing is based on the premise that a joint deployment of capital, professional expertise, technology, and the local presence of a commercial investor with a global network can unlock significant economic and social benefits. The units of analysis are no longer specific countries, but individuals—consumers—who have so far accessed goods and services at a significant disadvantage, both as consumers of basic goods and services, and as producers within some value chain, accessing, for example, credit, equipment, or logistics.

Global philanthropy and social investing have become involved in the mainstreaming of BoP investing, and this trend can be expected to continue. It is a direct consequence of the success of microfinance in providing capital to the economically active poor and their microbusinesses, as discussed in the previous section. Microfinance has demonstrated that market mechanisms can provide social and economic benefits to individuals in the lower income strata around the world, as well as attractive financial returns to investors. However, microfinance focuses on the economically active poor who often operate in the informal sector. It can therefore only provide a partial solution to address the pent-up demand among the poor for health, education, and basic goods and services, which requires a formal sector response in scale. Similar to microfinance, base-of-the-pyramid investing is bound to transform the boundaries and methodology of global philanthropy, and will provide new answers as well as raise uncomfortable questions in the process.

"Fair" levels of profit taking will be one question. Given the sheer scale of unmet needs and the aggregate purchasing power of the poor, base-of-the-pyramid markets can be expected to provide significant wealth creation opportunities for investors. These markets display several characteristics that cause and perpetuate disadvantaged access for the poor. Global philanthropy and social investing involvement should be assessed in terms of their contribution to removing these barriers. Key factors include entry barriers, lack of information, imperfect competition, insufficient vesting of property rights, as well as high search, transaction, and switching costs. As a result, business value propositions that serve the poor are often suboptimal. Poor consumers typically pay a "poverty premium," that is, prices for the goods and services they consume are often substantially higher than in conventional markets. This provides an opportunity for innovative investors willing to provide alternative, better-value propositions. Those who can overcome the structural hurdles to provide affordable goods and services at scale can both reap substantial profits and economically empower the poor. As some of these investments mature and the magnitudes of realistic financial returns become clearer, this will add another angle to the question of what would be a fair profit when serving the poor through a market-based solution.

A second question will relate to the proper role of philanthropy in base-of-the-pyramid investing. Global philanthropy increasingly recognizes that small, medium, and large enterprises with adapted value propositions for the BoP target segment will play a key role in meeting demand in the next decades. But the development of such firms is hampered in most of the developing economies by the underprovision of risk capital for small- and mid-cap enterprises. One role for global philanthropy and social investing is therefore the provision of such risk capital.

While we currently witness the early days of BoP investing, over time investments at the base of the pyramid are nevertheless likely to become another emergent asset class that will draw interest from commercial capital market players, and the rate of change seems to be faster than in the history of the microfinance industry. Analogous to the developments discussed in the previous section, where microfinance investment vehicles began to emerge in the late nineties, dedicated BoP investment vehicles (BIVs) were beginning to be created 10 years later. Similar to the MIVs, which would have had no microfinance institutions to invest in if there had not been philanthropic money and development assistance to get them off the ground, grant funding of base-of-the-pyramid companies at some point in their life cycle is similarly essential. As a rule of thumb, proof of concept needs grant money, whereas scaling up requires commercial money.

There is an increasing recognition among philanthropic and multilateral actors that grants cannot do the job in isolation from investment capital. Without facilitation, investment capital is often unwilling to go into the riskier or less conventional markets where the need is greatest, namely sub-Saharan Africa and developing countries that do not have large domestic markets or are not yet middle-income economies. BIVs therefore often operate in partnership or with the assistance of philanthropically minded or multilateral players who want to draw commercial capital into the development equation and are happy to establish joint capital pools. The original grant pool can be enlarged via investment arrangements that combine investors and philanthropists into consortia or funds, taking into consideration their different risk tolerance, return objectives, and expertise sets. Going forward, the joint capital pool approach where philanthropic organizations, official development agencies, and businesses collaborate to jointly develop a solution that neither of them could orchestrate on their own will become much more widespread. To illustrate this trend, consider two examples. First, let us look at the field of public health in Africa. Healthcare in sub-Saharan Africa is characterized by substantial access shortages for low-income populations, quality shortfalls, and excessive cost. Challenges include a shortage of physicians, nurses, and other health workers, too few and overcrowded public facilities, a sense of low-quality care in public hospitals and clinics, management and medical training gaps in health facilities, and compulsory fee-for-service payments at most public facilities irrespective of income level. To allow access to even public care, gatekeepers frequently impose side payments upon everyone, including the poor. Moreover, insurance schemes are insufficient, and a majority of healthcare expenditures are private and often funded out of pocket. While Africans need affordable and accessible quality healthcare, the public sector has neither the resources nor the expertise to provide a full-scale solution. A hallmark International Finance Corporation (IFC) study, *The Business of Health in Africa*, finds that 60 percent of healthcare financing in Africa comes from private sources and about 50 percent of total health expenditure goes to private providers.[38]

Given the limitations inherent in public-sector and donor-led approaches, innovative donors consider an investment approach promising for three reasons: there is already substantial demand for private-sector healthcare; there are profitable private-sector business models that could be scaled; and the healthcare sector is currently underserved by investment capital. However, simply throwing investment capital at the issue is unlikely to yield the intended results. Success requires mobilizing serious expertise in healthcare financing, healthcare training, medical and pharmaceutical manufacturing, and telemedicine, paired with the ability to mobilize production facilities, distribution systems, and networks to reach underserved and low-income groups.

Based on this view, the IFC, the African Development Bank, Deutsche Investitions- und Entwicklungsgesellschaft (DEG) and the Bill and Melinda Gates Foundation decided in 2007 to develop a commercial for-profit investment vehicle focusing on health in Africa. The objective was straightforward: to enable low-income Africans to gain increased access to affordable quality health services by backing healthcare companies in sub-Saharan Africa and helping them scale and professionalize their operations, while also providing investors with attractive long-term financial returns.

After an initial feasibility study and an extended deliberation period, the sponsors decided to create a dedicated Africa Health fund, to be managed by Aureos Capital, a UK-based private equity fund management company that was set up in 2001. Aureos specializes in investing in small to medium-sized businesses in emerging markets through multiple funds. Originally set up by CDC, the UK Government's Development Finance Institution, Aureos was bought out by its management in 2005. Investors in the Aureos funds are CDC, Norfund, FMO (the Netherlands' entrepreneurial development bank), and over 70 other institutional investors including international finance institutions, commercial banks, pension funds, funds-of-funds, high-net-worth individuals, family offices, and foundations.[39]

After more than three years of gestation, the Africa Health Fund was launched in June 2009 with initial commitments of US$57 million and a specified target to raise a total of US$100 million, with a final close in 2010. Fund investments focus on opportunities to increase the efficiency of the African health market. In June 2009, the fund made its first investment, acquiring a stake in the Nairobi Women's Hospital (NWH) in Kenya for US$2.7 million. NWH provides healthcare services for women and children, focusing on providing inpatient, outpatient, and specialized services for women, including antenatal, gynecology, obstetrics, breast cancer detection, and surgery, as well as operating East Africa's first Gender Violence Recovery Center. According to Aureos, the investment in NWH will help fund a management buyout, as well as the expansion of facilities such as clinics, beds, ambulances, and operating theaters in the East Africa region. At the time the investment was made, Davinder Sikand, regional managing partner of Aureos in Africa, argued: "The provision of capital to SMEs operating in the health sector in conjunction with professional private equity support will certainly increase the efficiency of the African health market. This will benefit sections of the population that previously had asymmetrical or no access to vital healthcare."[40] In a nutshell, the BoP investment approach is much more bottom-up than the development assistance framework that seeks to lift entire countries out of poverty. BoP investing is ultimately about increasing the efficiency of companies and industries, gearing them to provide affordable yet quality goods and services to the poor, and thereby achieving positive social impact.

BoP investing can also unlock value in middle-income economies. Consider the example of Ignia Ventures, a venture capital investment firm based in Monterrey, Mexico.[41] Ignia focuses on the bottom of the pyramid in Latin America, defined as 360 million out of the region's 550 million people who earn less than US$3,000 per year. Aggregating their purchasing power, the market is estimated at US$510 billion, of which US$130 billion is in Mexico alone, roughly covering 70 percent of the population. Ignia models its understanding of the needs of BoP clients based on the principals' experience in microfinance in Latin America, which was gathered through their involvement in the establishment of Banco Compartamos and other MFIs. The fund was set up to apply this expertise to BoP sectors outside the microfinance sector, including basic utilities, education, healthcare, and housing. To provide effective responses to the enormously underserved needs of low-income populations, both as consumers and as active participants in productive value chains, Ignia raised a US$102 million venture fund that seeks to empower entrepreneurship, generate social impact, and create attractive financial returns for its investors. To create value for its investors, Ignia follows a buy-and-build strategy. It looks for 25 percent to 100 percent equity stakes that support the founding and expansion of high-growth social enterprises that serve the base of the socioeconomic pyramid in Latin America. The fund seeks to invest in common or preferred stock of companies, in some cases structuring its investments as subordinated debt with warrants or convertible debt, in a range from US$2 million to US$11 million per company, typically in staged disbursements. One of the fund's first investments was Primedic, formerly known as Transparencia Médica, a provider of healthcare services in Monterrey, Mexico, that operated three clinics and one radiological imaging facility in 2009.[42] Primedic provides access to unlimited primary healthcare and selected medical technology services and specialists through an innovative membership program that is affordable to urban individuals and families who earn less than US$3,500 per person per year.

In the Mexican context, this is an interesting contribution that highlights how complementary entrepreneurial and classical "development" approaches can be. The Mexican government is aiming for universal health coverage by further expanding Seguro Popular, a government medical insurance program designed for low-income individuals in the informal sector or unemployed.[43] But near universal government medical coverage notwithstanding, 54 percent of the country's health spending was out of pocket in 2008, representing a US$27 billion market. This level of out-of-pocket spending results from the de facto high transaction costs "free" government medical insurance imposes, for example, long lead times due to inability to set up appointments, transportation costs due to lack of proximity of facilities, and on-site delays that negatively impact economically active individuals. The Ignia experience suggests that business solutions can indeed play a meaningful role in complementing more traditional development and social policy approaches, as well as grant-based philanthropy.

Viewed against the background of a general shift away from top-down classical development interventions toward more bottom-up or industry-focused entrepreneurial investment approaches, global philanthropy can be expected to play an important role in obtaining balance.

A key to the contribution BIVs will make to global philanthropy's social-impact agenda will be the right balance between profits and impact.

Although the BoP investment vehicles have the feel of venture capital and private equity funds to them, philanthropy nevertheless plays a catalytic role in facilitating their emergence and can help shape their social-impact agenda. There are three reasons. First, on a stand-alone basis, commercial investors would judge BoP investment opportunities purely on the basis of risk-adjusted financial returns; as a result, many investments that are both profitable and have a high social impact would not pass muster. This assigns an important enabling role to social or philanthropic capital. For example, a charitable foundation may be willing to provide subordinated debt at a relatively low interest rate to a commercial investment vehicle that invests in such healthcare companies, whereas a purely commercially minded investor might not. Second, by remaining engaged, global philanthropy can precisely help to ensure that BoP investments deliver both social and economic returns. Global philanthropy thus plays a crucial role with respect to standard setting in terms of reporting and social-impact measurement.[44] Finally, impact investments in BoP investment vehicles can represent an excellent way for philanthropies to invest a portion of their endowments in direct support of their charitable mission while also achieving a financial return.

From Classical Grant-Making to Strategic Monetization of Future Savings

The three frontiers of global philanthropy discussed previously all involved the combination of business methods and markets with philanthropic objectives focusing on the public good. Social entrepreneurship, microfinance, and base-of-the-pyramid investing all are important trends that will transform the way future generations will think about and conduct philanthropy. Nevertheless, many of the fundamental challenges humanity faces in the twenty-first century cannot be tackled by markets alone. For example, free markets do not internalize externalities such as environmental destruction or negative public health impacts on populations that are not working in the formal sector. To address these and other challenges, private or public subsidies are required, but given today's strains on both philanthropic and public resources, it is difficult to imagine where these subsidies will come from without a major shift in social finance. What this suggests is the need for a fourth innovation in social finance: namely, a way to monetize future savings in public or philanthropic resources, creating a stream of resources to address problems in the present, before they become severe, and thus avert heavier costs later.

To illustrate this point, consider the fourth United Nations Millennium Development Goal (MDG): the reduction of the mortality rate of children under age five by two-thirds by 2015. Immunization programs are a key element of a strategy to achieve this MDG, yet successful and comprehensive immunization remains a challenge. The World Health Organization (WHO) estimates that 24 million infants were not reached by the DTP3 vaccine in 2003 and are not vaccinated against common childhood diseases including diphtheria, tetanus, hepatitis B, yellow fever, measles, and polio.[45] The previous year, an estimated two million children under the age of five died of vaccine-preventable diseases around the world. Many more fall sick, miss school, and become part of the vicious cycle that links poor health to continued poverty in adulthood.

Immunization is a clear example where prevention through vaccines is much cheaper than treatment of disease. To address the needs for vaccines and immunization in the world's poorest countries with a per capita gross national income of less than US$1,000, the GAVI Alliance was created in 1999 with an initial grant from the Bill and Melinda Gates Foundation. GAVI is a public-private partnership between multiple agencies (WHO, UNICEF, the World Bank, industry representatives, the GAVI Fund, and donor and recipient governments). It channels funding to support the introduction of new vaccines as well as immunization programs for existing but underused vaccines. The scale of GAVI's buying and distribution power enables it to secure much lower prices for vaccines, which are then supplied to poor nations at a fraction of their cost. Other areas of activity include strengthening health systems, infrastructure, and education. GAVI has implemented an innovative performance-based grants program that rewards countries for increasing immunization coverage. Since 2000 it has committed more than US$1.6 billion to more than 70 of the world's poorest countries. GAVI's first 10 years are credited with having helped avert five million future deaths with GAVI-funded vaccines reaching more than 250 million children in the poorest parts of the world.[46]

GAVI is an interesting example not just because of the scale of its work, but also because of the innovative use of financing mechanisms. To lower the total cost of achieving the MDG in a context of finite resources, GAVI was able to borrow against future government grant pledges, with the aid of an entity called the International Finance Facility for Immunisation (IFFIm). Established in 2006, the IFFIm operates by raising capital from the international capital markets by borrowing against future grant pledges. At establishment, France, Italy, Norway, Spain, Sweden, and the UK each provided binding donor commitments to the IFFIm totaling US$4 billion, with Brazil and South Africa later committing additional funds.[47] Given the grant pledges of donor governments and IFFIm's association with the World Bank, IFFIm was able to raise capital on commercial terms with an AAA credit rating, using the same distribution channels to institutional and retail investors as any other AAA-rated bond. In November 2006, the IFFIm released its first bond issue (5 IFFIM 11, SWX), to raise US$1 billion through notes at 5 percent interest due on November 14, 2011, based on the donor government grant pledges. Interest is payable annually, and the notes received the highest credit rating (AAA) from all three major credit rating agencies (Fitch, Moody's, and S&P). The WHO estimates that IFFIm's resources could lead to the vaccination of more than 500 million people over the next 10 years, with the objective of preventing the deaths of 5 million children and 5 million adults via the usage of new and underutilized vaccines, targeted immunization campaigns, and the strengthening of health and immunization services in GAVI's target countries. The release and successful closure of this issue allowed IFFIm to monetize future donor grant commitments by raising commercial capital against donor government pledges.

The bond program to support GAVI is a significant innovation, enabling the deployment of capital for a cause now, when it is cheaper to address the problem, rather than later, when the cost will be higher. There is no reason why one cannot apply such innovative finance mechanisms to any grant-funded issue that involves externalities and intertemporal benefits. The previous discussion shows that the strategic monetization of future savings is not merely an exercise in financial engineering for donor governments operating under budget constraints: wherever prevention today plus the cost of a capital markets borrowing operation against future commitments is cheaper than treatment in the future in real terms, it makes sense to monetize commitments as in the case of GAVI.

There is a second facet worth highlighting. Grants can also kick-start transformational solutions to a wide range of social issues by constructing new hybrid subsidy-marketplaces. Let us look at another example, equally derived from the Millennium Development Goals: the domain of sanitation. The Millennium Development Goals set a target of reducing by half the 2.5 billion people without sanitation by 2015. Lack of access to basic sanitation causes widespread water-borne diseases with significant adverse socioeconomic implications. This affects people's health, their environment, and their ability to work, and has a negative impact on their community and the country's economy. According to the World Health Organization, 1.87 million people die every year from diarrhea and other water-related diseases, of which 80 percent are children between six months and five years of age.[48] Conservatively estimated, addressing this challenge requires at least US$10 billion every year. Seeing that large externalities are involved, where every US dollar spent on sanitation unlocks health and other benefits of US$3–$34, a structure similar to the IFFIm could in principle be deployed at some point to finance the scaling of global sanitation solutions. Unlike in the case of vaccines, however, there is no organized marketplace yet. It needs to be built first, and engineered to have supply meet demand at a reasonable price. To study and design market-based solutions for sanitation, the former head of Ashoka's Social Financial Services unit, Arthur Wood, set up the World Sanitation Financing Facility (WSFF) in Geneva in 2009, with the goal of getting money to the market of 2.5 billion people who do not have a toilet.[49] By identifying the market for sanitation products and services, matching demand and supply and ensuring that essential public funding is optimally used to support innovation through a streamlined capital flow, WSFF seeks to respond to the challenge of accessing finance or business attention. It aims to find alternatives to the standard transaction-cost-intensive fashion, discussed earlier, in which capital is allocated in the social capital market. To achieve this, the World Sanitation Financing Facility positions itself as a convener and agenda-setter that brings together people to realize the opportunities of the sanitation market, develop infrastructure, and provide access to finance for entrepreneurs and customers in need. To render its insights actionable, the WSFF has defined three work streams. First, it provides a platform for participants to brainstorm and pool expertise to generate practical solutions for financing sanitation at scale. Second, it identifies the sanitation market and various business lines and models for commercial investment. This work stream seeks to uncover and understand the best ideas across geographies and market segments so that financial products can be designed to support these businesses, both locally and at scale. Finally, the WSFF assists in financial innovation and a streamlined capital flow from public funders or banks and corporations to entrepreneurs and 2.5 billion potential customers. As of October 2009, approximately 30 organizations were represented in the WSFF, each committed to the objectives of the WSFF and recognizing that new thinking is required to contribute to the Millennium Development Goal target of halving the proportion of people without access to basic sanitation in 2015 and achieving universal sanitation coverage. WSFF estimates the total sanitation market to be over US$80 billion over 10 years, unlocking an additional US$685 billion of social externalities.

In addition to frontloading funding through capital market operations monetizing government pledges, as in the case of GAVI, or deploying grants to construct hybrid marketplaces, as in the case of WSFF, a third innovative approach consists of providing performance-based contingent returns, as was discussed in the introduction. This approach is especially attractive where more localized challenges, rather than big global issues such as health or sanitation, are addressed by means of the monetization of future savings through capital markets instruments. Consider again the issue of prison reoffenders that was discussed at the outset of the chapter.[50] Locking up people is costly, and prison places cost the UK taxpayer well over GBP 213 million a year. Thus, one might think that efforts are undertaken to keep the reoffending rate in check. But UK adults on short sentences astonishingly have traditionally received no formal support to help them to successfully reintegrate into their community, and reintegration routinely fails. Given its interventions, activities, experience with marginalized communities, and local knowledge, the nonprofit sector is in principle ideally positioned to address many of today's social challenges, provided it can finance itself more efficiently. This is the key goal behind Social Finance, the sponsor of the social-impact bond: the organization wants to enable the nonprofit sector to respond better to society's changing needs by providing access to a variety of investment instruments. Social-impact bonds provide a mechanism for private investors to invest funds into nonprofit organizations that deliver formal support on some issue where prevention costs less than treatment. Investors then receive success-based financial returns to the extent that the social-impact targets are met or exceeded. There is no reason why this model could not be applied to monetizing future savings on a range of social issues in all countries where government and the political process are sufficiently competent and trusted to reallocate public subsidies based on social performance. Since the launch of the first social-impact bond pilot in the UK, its applicability has been analyzed in Germany and Italy, while the Obama administration has earmarked US$100 million for experimentation with "pay-for-success" bonds for fiscal year 2012.[51]

As the examples of the IFFIm, the World Sanitation Financing Facility, and the social-impact bond demonstrate, important innovations are underway where future grant pledges or government savings are monetized today. The pilots are being closely watched in the philanthropic community. While the volumes that these solutions allocate are still minuscule in the global context of philanthropy, they hold the promise of such tremendous efficiency gains that they could provide a disruptive impetus well beyond the field of philanthropy, also influencing the fields of public finance and development assistance over the next decade. Next to social entrepreneurship, microfinance, and base-of-the-pyramid investing, strategic monetization of future savings is the fourth frontier of global philanthropy.

Conclusion: Lessons from the Great Recession—Global Philanthropy, *Quo Vadis?*

In short, given a general desire to make globalization work for everyone in the twenty-first century, and how to keep the planet inhabitable for future generations, this chapter, and indeed this entire book, have argued that an invaluable window of opportunity has opened up for global philanthropy to create greater impact, and that new forms of designing, financing, and running social change initiatives will drive progress. Global philanthropy is undergoing a market revolution that will lead to a more thoughtful and effective use of financial resources for social change. Social entrepreneurship, microfinance, base-of-the pyramid investing, and the strategic monetization of future savings are four cutting-edge theaters of this market revolution. Grant-making will not disappear, but market tools will provide a key ingredient to delivering philanthropic impact at scale. They are the new frontiers of global philanthropy, alongside the many unconquered old frontiers such as how to make partnerships work, measure impact, or be truly strategic rather than just claiming to be.

The recent financial crisis will end up accelerating this revolution. Philanthropy is at a reflexive moment. Prior to the crisis, there was some self-congratulation in the field and a sense of a new Gilded Age—the equivalent of Nobel Laureate Albert Michelson's (1852–1931) famous statement that "all that remains to do in physics is fill in the sixth decimal place." We know the next chapter in the story of classical physics. Rather than confirming the classical paradigm, the search for the sixth decimal place led to the emergence of quantum theory.

Calling into question some of the established wisdom about philanthropy, this chapter on the future of global philanthropy has similarly argued that four secular trends are transforming the field of global philanthropy in fundamental ways. Today, these trends are far from representing the hegemonic mechanism of how philanthropic capital is allocated. But they are already helping to reorient practice, and eventually will become center stage.

As we focus on the long view, it is now time to look at the likely transition path. How is the recent experience of the great recession that followed from the 2008 financial crisis likely to impact the diffusion and mainstreaming of the four trends?

To answer this question, it is useful to remember what has recently occurred. In 2009, the world economy re-emerged from its deepest recession since World War II. At a time of rising social needs, the recession and the resulting tightening of private resources triggered a major adjustment for global philanthropy. In the United States, about two-thirds of foundations reduced their payouts in 2009 and 460 foundations were wiped out, losing 80 percent or more of their endowment assets.[52] There is no comprehensive data set specifying the total number of foundation failures around the world, but there were numerous cases that grabbed the headlines. In Israel, for example, the philanthropy sector was hit hard by the 2008 collapse of Bernard Madoff's wealth management business, which was really an enormous Ponzi scheme that defrauded investors of billions of US dollars. For many charities associated with Jewish causes, whose funders had been Madoff's clients, the largest investor fraud attributed to an individual so far meant a total loss of assets.[53]

The great recession also had a high cost in terms of views taken for granted in global philanthropy. Deeply held assumptions were called into question, and several sacred cows fell from their pedestals. Take the much-admired large "superendowments" that had implicitly been seen as a benchmark in the investment community: they were not spared either. For example, the world's largest university endowment, at Harvard University, was reported to have lost at least 22 percent of its asset value between July and October 2008; the actual loss might have been even higher once illiquid investments in real estate and private equity had been properly valued.[54] The Yale Endowment was reported to be down from US$22.9 billion in June 2008 to

US$16.3 billion one year later, that is, minus 29 percent in the fiscal year 2008–2009.[55]

Private wealth, a key source of new gifts, was affected as well. Given their exposure to higher-risk financial products that tend to deliver greater-than-average returns when economies expand, but produced hefty losses in 2008, ultra-high-net-worth individuals' wealth shrunk by 23.9 percent in 2008, and relegated a large number of them down into the "mid-tier million-aire" bracket.[56]

Given the magnitude of the downward adjustment in asset values, philan-thropies around the world had to think hard about which expenditure streams they cared about the most. The sector entered a period of soul searching; doom-sayers found willing audiences around the world.

During the recession, many foundations considered adjusting expenditure downward and switching expenditures toward their most productive use.[57] For example, many foundations sought to contain their operating costs by imple-menting hiring and salary freezes or cutting travel budgets. In the UK, 29 per-cent of charities laid off staff.[58] With respect to non-operating expenditures, the picture was mixed; in the wake of a greatly increased demand for their services, many foundations chose to behave in a countercyclical fashion. A survey of the US Foundation Center anticipated that 50 percent of foundations would main-tain their expenditures for giving in 2010 compared to 2009, and 17 percent would increase them.[59] Some foundations also engaged in innovative approaches to support their grantees, removing restrictions on the deployment of funding or even using parts of their endowment in support of their grantees, for example via low- or zero-interest loans, or emergency lines of credit.

Rather than viewing the implications of the great recession merely as a narrow exercise in operational cost-cutting and a pro- or countercyclical choice on project expenditures, we need to look at its more far-reaching implications for the future of the field. The great recession affected the field's *habitus*, that is, its encoded views about how philanthropy should be done and is done in prac-tice. While it led to substantial short- and medium-term adjustment pain, it also proffered three valuable lessons for the future.

First, it highlighted the importance of understanding risk. Substantial losses can significantly erode the capacity of a foundation to support programs. The most immediate impact of a slowdown, recession, or stock market crash is felt on a foundation's endowment. Financial returns of the endowment are often the only method of grant support for charitable foundations. New gifts may not be forthcoming as readily in a recessionary environment. Suffering through the crisis, philanthropies all of a sudden understood how careful they had to be about the financial risks they took. They needed to balance the desire to obtain high financial returns to fund expenditures with the fiduciary duty of main-taining the real asset value of the endowment to be able to operate in perpetuity, and steer clear of catastrophic tail risks that could wipe out the entire endow-ment. The new focus on managing catastrophic downside was quite a departure from endowments' scramble for participating in the alternative investments game in order to capture higher financial returns that characterized the early 2000s run-up to the financial crisis. Going forward, a lower tolerance for risk raises questions about how to create impact—there is less money to be spent, so it must be spent more wisely.

Second, the great recession confirmed the fundamental importance of phil-anthropy, and its robustness. In countries where reliable data are available, the historical record for charitable giving during economic downturns is reassuring. In the United States, giving has not dropped for more than two years in a row since the early 1970s; once economic growth resumed, philanthropy quickly made up what it lost, and returned to a path of growth.[60] Evidence from other countries confirms that recession-correlated drops in giving are typically neither sudden, nor large, nor permanent. What is more, giving by foundations has held up even better during recessions. According to a study by the Foundation Center, US foundation philanthropy actually increased slightly each year in four economic downturns since 1980, even after correcting for inflation.[61] This observation broadly resonates with experiences in other parts of the world.

The third lesson has the most transformative implications for philanthropy. Given greater resource scarcity at a time of growing needs, the development of the field of impact investments (or social finance, social investments, mission-related investments, depending on the reader's preferred wording) will accelerate as a result of the great recession. Defined as for-profit social investments that create demonstrable social impact as well as financial returns for investors, such impact investments held up fairly well during the downturn, unlike traditional investments held in foundation endowments. For example, the performance of roughly US$25 billion in microfinance assets remained positive in 2008. In fact, one can even argue that the crisis has created takeoff conditions for the impact-investing field and its key areas of social entrepreneurship, microfinance, base-of-the pyramid investing, and monetization of future savings. Impact investments are forecast to grow to US$500 billion to 1 trillion by the end of the 2010s.[62] To sum it up, we can expect frontier philanthropy to gain market share over the 2010s at the expense of traditional philanthropy precisely because of the combined impact of reduced or more impact-oriented personal net worth and lower foundation asset values. Financial innovation will create exciting new opportunities to leverage philanthropic resources.

In the next decades, a more effectiveness and efficiency-minded approach to social change will become the norm rather than the exception. Over the course of the decade, inspiring examples of transformational social entrepreneurs and social businesses, microfinance investment vehicles and microfinance institutions, base-of-the-pyramid investment vehicles and their portfolio companies, as well as mechanisms such as the International Financing Facility for Immunization or the social-impact bond, will all move from the creative frontier of global philanthropy to its core. This is good news. Humanity has a lot of problems to solve in the decades that lie ahead; in retrospect, the recent financial crisis may have been a watershed point. In the process, the philanthropic field will undergo a fundamental transformation. But as the rules of the game in philanthropy and the *habitus* of giving adapt to the realities of human civilization in the twenty-first century, global philanthropy will continue to enact the first principles that render our existence on this planet human: caring for others, sharing resources, and the desire to be recognized in historical time and make a difference.

Notes

1. Helen Warrell, "Bond Offers Return for Lower Offending," *Financial Times*, March 19, 2010, http://www.ft.com/cms/s/0/d9dca292-32f6-11df-bf5f-00144feabdc0.html.

2. Frontier Economics, "Released Prisoner Support Programme Shown to Reduce Re-offending Rates," news release published March 15, 2010, http://www.frontier-economics.com/europe/en/news/894/.

3. For a fuller discussion of the operation of social impact bonds, or "pay-for-success" financing as it is called in the United States, see Chapter 16 of this volume.

4. For a discussion of the general context, see, for example, Arthur Wood and Maximilian Martin, "Market-Based Solutions for Financing Philanthropy," *Viewpoints* (UBS Philanthropy Services), 2006, 58–63, accessed October 26, 2012, http://www.impacteconomy.com/node/174. See also Social Finance, "Social Finance Welcomes the Government's Initiative to Pilot Social Impact Bonds as Announced in Their Policy Paper 'Putting the Frontline First: Smarter Government' Launched Today by the Prime Minister," press release published December 7, 2009, http://www.socialfinance.org.uk/downloads/press_releases/Press%20Release%20SIB%20Dec%2009%20FINAL.pdf.

5. Lester M. Salamon, *America's Nonprofit Sector: A Primer.* 3rd edition (New York: Foundation Center, 2012), 39, 49.

6. See Kurt Lewin, *Field Theory in Social Science: Selected Theoretical Papers*, ed. Dorwin Cartwright (Westport, CT: Greenwood Press, 1976).

7. For a discussion of the emerging social entrepreneurship field, see, for example, Maximilian Martin, "Surveying Social Entrepreneurship: Toward an Empirical Analysis of the Performance Revolution in the Social Sector," working paper of the Center for Public Leadership, University of St. Gallen, 2004, accessed October 26, 2012, http://www.impacteconomy.com/node/175.

8. Bourdieu elaborates these positions as a function of *habitus* and capital. For a discussion, see Pierre Bourdieu, *Outline of a Theory of Practice*, trans. Richard Nice (Cambridge: Cambridge University Press, 1977), 159–83. Bourdieu's concept of social fields is partially inspired by Kurt Lewin's vector psychology. It "refers to both the totality of actors and organizations involved in an arena of social or cultural production and the dynamic relationships among them." In social psychology, Kurt Lewin's field theory was highly influential (see, for example, Lewin, *Field Theory* for a collection of articles).

9. Collective misrecognition and conflict are central to Bourdieu's notion of the dynamics that shape social fields. To grasp the characteristics of a social field, consider the concept of a field in a game (Pierre Bourdieu, *The Logic of Practice*, trans. Richard Nice [Cambridge: Cambridge University Press, 1977], 67): "In a game, the field (the pitch or board on which it is played, the rules, the outcome, at stake, etc.) is clearly seen for what it is, an arbitrary social construct, an artifact whose arbitrariness and artificiality are underlined by everything that defines its autonomy—explicit and specific rules, strictly delimited and extra-ordinary time and space.. . . By contrast, in the social fields, which are the product of a long, slow process of autonomization,. . . one does not embark on the game by a conscious act, one is born into the game, with the game; and the relation of investment, *illusio*, investment, is made more total and unconditional by the fact that it is unaware of what it is. As Claudel puts it, 'connaître, c'est naître avec,' to know is to be born with, and the long dialectical process, often described as 'vocation,' through which the various fields provide themselves with agents equipped with the *habitus* needed to make them work, is to the learning of a game very much as the acquisition of the mother tongue is to the learning of a foreign language."

10. See United Kingdom, Cabinet Office, Office of the Third Sector, *Social Investment Wholesale Bank: A Consultation on the Functions and Design*, July 2009, 16, http://www.cabinetoffice.gov.uk/media/224319/13528%20social%20bank%20web%20bookmarked.pdf; William F. Meehan, Derek Kilmer, and Maisie O'Flanagan, "Investing in Society,"

Stanford Social Innovation Review 1.4 (Spring 2004): 35, http://www.ssireview.org/articles/entry/investing_in_society.

11. Meehan, Kilmer, and O'Flanagan, "Investing in Society."

12. SustainAbility, "Growing Opportunity," news release published March 28, 2007, http://www.sustainability.com/aboutsustainability/article_previous.asp?id=938.

13. Michael Bishop and Matthew Green, *Philanthrocapitalism: How the Rich Can Save the World* (New York: Bloomsbury Press, 2008).

14. Data from SiRI Company (2007), quoted in Munich RE, "Munich Re Shares as a Sustainable Investment (2008)," accessed October 26, 2012, http://www.munichre.com/sustainability/en/economy/munich_re_share/; Eurosif, "European SRI Study 2010," rev. ed., November 2010, 7, http://www.eurosif.org/research/eurosif-sri-study/2010.

15. Antoinette Hunziker-Ebneter and Oliver Karius, Forma Futura Invest AG, "Sustainable Investment to Enhance the Sustainable Quality of Life," presentation at the Oikos Anniversary Conference, St. Gallen, Switzerland, October 2007, http://www.oikos-international.org/fileadmin/oikos-International/Resources/071017_OIKOS_Presentation_Forma_Futura_long.pdf; see Lorraine Cushnie, "SRI Funds Hit by Market Turmoil," *Investment Week*, November 13, 2009, http://www.investmentweek.co.uk/investment-week/news/1562065/sri-funds-hit-market-turmoil.

16. See Maximilian Martin, "F4F—Finance for Foundations," SSRN, published June 25, 2007, http://ssrn.com/abstract=1322388.

17. The most recent high-profile effort in global philanthropy to invest financial assets for social and financial returns is the Global Impact Investing Network (GIIN). The GIIN was conceived in October 2007 and in June 2008 in Bellagio, Italy, where the Rockefeller Foundation gathered a small group of investors to discuss how to solve social and environmental challenges with greater efficiency. At the second meeting, a group of 40 international investors was organized under the framework of several initiatives. The work streams included the creation of a global network of impact investors, the development of a standardized metrics framework to assess the social and environmental impact of such investments, and a special working group of investors focusing on sustainable agriculture in sub-Saharan Africa. In 2009, the GIIN was then formally constituted as an independent organization with US 501(c)(3) charitable status under the fiscal sponsorship of US nonprofit strategy firm Rockefeller Philanthropy Advisors (RPA). The initiative initially forecast the emergence of a US$500 billion impact-investing industry over the next five to 10 years, later raised to a US$1 trillion forecast. See Jessica Freireich and Katherine Fulton, "Investing for Social and Environmental Impact," Monitor Institute, January 2009, accessed October 26, 2012, http://www.monitorinstitute.com/downloads/what-we-think/impact-investing/Impact_Investing.pdf; Nick O'Donohoe, Christina Leijonhufvud, Yasemin Saltuk, Antony Bugg-Levine, and Margot Brandenburg, "Impact Investments: An Emerging Asset Class," J.P. Morgan, November 29, 2010, accessed October 26, 2012, http://www.jpmorgan.com/cm/cs?pagename=JPM/DirectDoc&urlname= impact_investments_nov2010.pdf.

18. See "Aravind Eye Care System Home," accessed October 25, 2012, http://www.aravind.org; "Aurolab Home," accessed October 26, 2012, http://www.aurolab.com.

19. See Frederick W. Taylor, *The Principles of Scientific Management* (New York: Norton, 1967).

20. In the Middle East, David Green was introduced to ophthalmologist Akef El Maghraby in Egypt; together they developed what became the largest eye care program in the Middle East, the El-Maghraby Eye and Ear Hospitals and Centers.

21. For details see "Ashoka Home," Ashoka, accessed October 26, 2012, http://www.ashoka.org. Ashoka pioneered the stimulation of social entrepreneurship. Transferring

strategy consulting's performance principles to the social sector, Drayton set up an organization to encourage entrepreneurship as a driver for social change. Founded in 1980, the organization expanded in 30 years to more than 60 countries. Today, Ashoka has over 2,500 social entrepreneurs in more than 70 countries in its portfolio.

22. William Foster and Gail Fine, "How Nonprofits Get Really Big," *Stanford Social Innovation Review* 5.2 (Spring 2007): 46–55, accessed October 26, 2012, http://www. ssireview.org/articles/entry/how_nonprofits_get_really_big/.

23. See "Homepage," TOMS, accessed October 26, 2012, http://www.toms.com/.

24. See US Patent and Trademark Office, Patent Technology and Monitoring Team (PTMT), "U.S. Patent Statistics Chart Calendar Years 1963–2009," accessed October 26, 2012, http://www.uspto.gov/web/offices/ac/ido/oeip/taf/us_stat.htm.

25. Stephen Timewell, "Microfinance Gains Momentum," *The Banker*, February 2, 2005, 82.

26. See Jonathan Murdoch, "The Microfinance Promise," *Journal of Economic Literature* 37 (December 1999): 1573–74, accessed October 26, 2012, http://www.nyu. edu/projects/morduch/documents/microfinance/Microfinance_Promise.pdf; Henry W. Wolff, *People's Banks: A Record of Social and Economic Success* (London: P.S. King & Son, 1910), 23.

27. In the 1880s, the British colonial government of Madras in south India looked to the German experience for solutions to address poverty in India, and credit cooperatives soon took off. They reached 9 million members in 1946, but eventually lost steam. See Maximilian Martin, "Surveying Social Entrepreneurship," Viewpoints (UBS Philanthropy Services), 2004, accessed October 27, 2012, http://www.impacteconomy. com/node/177.

28. See "Compartamos Banco," Compartamos Banco, accessed October 26, 2012, http://www.compartamos.com/wps/portal.

29. Banco Compartamos traces its origins to a microfinance initiative called Compartamos AC, a nonprofit organization dedicated to social issues in Mexico launched in the poor areas of the states of Chiapas and Oaxaca. In the late nineties, Compartamos AC collaborated with Acción International, a US nonprofit organization focused on stimulating microfinance globally, in order to establish a commercial, regulated microfinance company in Mexico. In 2000, Compartamos received the respective license and established SOFOL Compartamos, a single-purpose finance company devoted to microfinance. Now set up as a commercial enterprise rather than a grant-funded nonprofit, Compartamos experienced amazing growth. From 2001 to 2006, its portfolio of active clients grew at a compounded annual growth rate (CAGR) of 46 percent, and its loan portfolio in US dollars even faster, at a CAGR of 60 percent. What was once a subsidy-funded operation had become highly profitable: 2001–2006 net income grew at a CAGR of 67 percent. In 2006, SOFOL Compartamos was finally granted a full banking license, becoming Banco Compartamos, and clearing the path for the initial public offering that would value the company at US$1.5 billion.

30. Consultative Group to Assist the Poor, *Financial Access 2009* (Washington, DC: Consultative Group to Assist the Poor and World Bank, 2009), 54.

31. Sam Daley-Harris, "State of the Microcredit Summit Campaign Report," Microcredit Summit Campaign, 2009, accessed October 26, 2012, https://promujer.org/ empowerment/dynamic/our_publications_5_Pdf_EN_SOCR2009%20English.pdf.

32. See Muhammad Yunus, "Letter from Nobel Laureate Professor Muhammad Yunus Addressed to Grameen Bank Members on His Departure from Grameen Bank," accessed October 26, 2012, http://www.grameen-info.org/index.php?option=com_conte nt&task=view&id=1043&Itemid=0.

33. Amy Kazmin, "Microfinance: Small Loan, Big Snag," *Financial Times*, December 1, 2010, http://www.ft.com/cms/s/0/a3edfeba-fd85-11df-a049-00144feab49a.html.

34. "Online Extra: Yunus Blasts Compartamos," *Bloomberg Businessweek*, December 13, 2007, http://www.businessweek.com/magazine/content/07_52/b4064045920958.htm.

35. See "Home," Symbiotics, accessed October 26, 2012, http://www.symbiotics.ch/en/index.asp.

36. The term "bottom of the pyramid" was first used by US president Franklin D. Roosevelt in 1932 in his radio address "The Forgotten Man." In the context of the Great Depression, he had the bottom of the US economic pyramid in mind. In 1998, C. K. Prahalad and Stuart L. Hart generalized the term to refer to the bottom of the economic pyramid in a global perspective, defined as 4 billion people living on less than two US dollars a day. For a discussion, see C. K. Prahalad, *The Fortune at the Bottom of the Pyramid* (Upper Saddle River, NJ: Pearson Prentice Hall, 2006) and Stuart L. Hart, *Capitalism at the Crossroads* (Upper Saddle River, NJ: Pearson Prentice Hall, 2007).

37. Today, it is used interchangeably with "base of the pyramid." See also UN General Assembly, Twenty-Fifth Session, Official Records, "Resolutions Adopted by the General Assembly," 1970, accessed October 26, 2012, http://www.un.org/documents/ga/res/25/ares25.htm; Anup Shah, "Official Global Foreign Aid Shortfall: $4 Trillion," *Global Issues*, April 25, 2010, http://www.globalissues.org/article/593/official-global-foreign-aid-shortfall-over-4-trillion; William Easterly, *The Elusive Quest for Growth: Economists' Adventures and Misadventures in the Tropics* (Cambridge: MIT Press, 2001); Dambisa Moyo, *Dead Aid* (New York: Farrar, Straus and Giroux, 2009). For the original critique of development, see James Ferguson, *The Anti-politics Machine* (Minneapolis: University of Minnesota Press, 1994); and Arturo Escobar, *Encountering Development* (Princeton, NJ: Princeton University Press, 1995); as well as Maximilian Martin, "The Deconstruction of Development: A Critical Overview," *Entwicklungsethnologie* 7.1 (1998): 40–59, http://www.impacteconomy.com/node/178.

38. See World Bank, International Finance Corporation, "The Business of Health in Africa: Partnering with the Private Sector to Improve People's Lives," International Finance Corporation, 2007, accessed October 26, 2012, http://www.unido.org/fileadmin/user_media/Services/PSD/BEP/IFC_HealthinAfrica_Final.pdf.

39. With its many country offices, a development mission, and business and investment approach, Aureos has the feel of a mini-IFC focusing on emerging markets; see "Home," Aureos Capital, accessed October 26, 2012, http://www.aureos.com.

40. See "Home," Nairobi Women's Hospital, accessed October 26, 2012, http://www.nwch.co.ke.

41. See "Home," IGNIA, accessed October 26, 2012, http://www.ignia.com.mx; Michael Chu, "Commercial Returns at the Base of the Pyramid," *Innovations* 2.1–2 (2007): 115.

42. Primedic was founded in 2000 by Dr. Paulino Decanini, an internationally recognized doctor who has been in public health and a practicing surgeon for over 15 years. See "Home," Transparencia Medica, accessed October 26, 2012, http://www.transparenciamedica.com/.

43. OECD, "Economic Survey of Mexico 2009: Achieving Higher Performance: Enhancing Spending Efficiency in Health and Education," July 30, 2009, http://www.oecd.org/document/48/0,3343,en_33873108_33873610_43394096_1_1_1_1,00.html. Also in OECD, *OECD Economic Surveys: Mexico*, July 30, 2009, 16.

44. For example, the Global Impact Investing Network, which was mentioned above, is seeking to accelerate the emergence of an impact-investing industry; a key element of this effort is its initiative on impact reporting and investing standards (IRIS). See

"Frequently Asked Questions," IRIS, accessed October 26, 2012, http://iris-standards. org/faq. For a related discussion, see the chapter 22 in this volume.

45. See World Health Organization, "Immunization against Diseases of Public Health Importance," Fact Sheet no. 288, March 2005, http://www.who.int/mediacentre/ factsheets/fs288/.

46. Julian Lob-Levyt, "GAVI Celebrates 10th Anniversary, Welcomes New 'Decade of Vaccines,'" statement released on January 29, 2010, http://www.gavial-liance.org/library/news/statements/2010/gavi-celebrates-10th-anniversar y,-welcomes-new-decade-of-vaccines; World Health Organization, UNICEF, and World Bank, *State of the World's Vaccines and Immunization*, 3rd ed. (Geneva: World Health Organization, 2009), 123; Kate Kelland, "Donors Asked for $4.3 Billion for Vaccines for Poor," Reuters, March 15, 2010, http://www.reuters.com/article/ idUSTRE62E1CD20100315.

47. Fitch Ratings, "Credit Analysis Report, International Finance Facility for Immunisation," September 2006.

48. World Health Organization, "Estimating Child Mortality Due to Diarrhea in Developing Countries," *Bulletin of the World Health Organization* 86.9 (September 2008), accessed October 26, 2012, http://www.scielosp.org/scielo.php?script=sci_arttext &pid=S0042-96862008000900015&lng=en&nrm=iso.

49. Arthur Wood, "Bottom-up and Top-down: A Sanitation Offer the Commercial Sector Cannot Resist?" presentation during World Water Week, Stockholm, August 17, 2009, http://www.worldwaterweek.org/documents/WWW_PDF/2009/monday/K11/ Presentation_2009_Stockholm_.pdf.

50. See Social Finance, "Social Impact Bonds: Rethinking Finance for Social Outcomes," 2009, http://www.socialfinance.org.uk/sites/default/files/SIB_report_ web.pdf; and Emily Bolton and Louise Savell, "Towards a New Social Economy: Blended Value Creation through Social Impacts Bonds," Social Finance, 2010, http://www.socialfinance.org.uk/sites/default/files/Towards_A_New_Social_ Economy_web.pdf.

51. See "Paying for Success," White House Office of Management and Budget, accessed October 26, 2012, http://www.whitehouse.gov/omb/factsheet/ paying-for-success.

52. Maximilian Martin, "Managing Philanthropy after the Downturn: What Is Ahead for Social Investment?" Viewpoints (UBS Philanthropy Services), 2010, accessed October 26, 2012, http://www.impacteconomy.com/node/91.

53. According to the *Financial Times* several charities faced closure. The Robert L. Lappin Foundation, which financed trips to Israel for Jewish students, said it would shut after losing its entire US$7 million endowment. The Chais Family Foundation, which gives US$12.5 million a year to Jewish causes in Israel, the former Soviet Union, and eastern Europe, also stated it would close. See Deborah Brewster, "Charities Face Winding Down," *Financial Times*, December 17, 2008, http://www.ft.com/cms/s/0/31 685748-cc6b-11dd-9c43-000077b07658.html; Vita Becker, "Charity Project Counts Cost of Alleged Fraud," *Financial Times*, December 16, 2008, http://www.ft.com/cms/s/0/80 7170de-cbb4-11dd-ba02-000077b07658.html.

54. "Ivory-Towering Infernos," *The Economist*, December 11, 2008, http://www. economist.com/node/12778077.

55. Geraldine Fabrikant, "Yale's Endowment Drops 13.4%," *New York Times*, December 18, 2008, http://opa.yale.edu/news/article.aspx?id=6899#.

56. See Capgemini and Merrill Lynch Wealth Management, "World Wealth Report," 2009, accessed October 26, 2012, http://www.ml.com/media/113831.pdf, 4.

57. See Maximilian Martin, "Managing Philanthropy in a Downturn," Viewpoints (UBS Philanthropy Services, 2009, accessed October 26, 2012, http://www.impacteconomy.com/node/81, 110-126.

58. See Charities Aid Foundation, "Charity Donations Fall as Demand for Their Services Grows," news release published September 14, 2008, http://www.cafonline.org/default.aspx?page=16118.

59. Steven Lawrence, "Foundations' Year-End Outlook for Giving and the Sector," Foundation Center, November 2009, accessed October 26, 2012, http://foundationcenter.org/gainknowledge/research/pdf/researchadvisory_economy_200911.pdf; for example, the Bill and Melinda Gates Foundation endowment, down from US$ 39 billion on January 1, 2008 to US$ 34.17 billion as of September 30, 2009, maintained spending at close to 10 percent of the endowment in 2009; see Eric Nee, "Q&A with Jeff Raikes," *Stanford Social Innovation Review* 8.1 (Winter 2010), accessed October 26, 2012, http://www.ssireview.org/articles/entry/qa_jeff_raikes/; Bill and Melinda Gates Foundation, "Foundation Fact Sheet," accessed October 26, 2012, http://www.gatesfoundation.org/about/Pages/foundation-fact-sheet.aspx.

60. Leslie Lenkowsky, "Nonprofit World Could Emerge Stronger from Economic Crisis," *Chronicle of Philanthropy*, October 30, 2008, http://philanthropy.com/article/article-content/57012/.

61. Foundation Center, *Foundation Yearbook* (New York: Foundation Center, 2008).

62. Freireich and Fulton, "Investing for Social and Environmental Impact," 4; and O'Donohoe et al., "Impact Investments."

Suggested Readings

Bourdieu, Pierre. *The Logic of Practice*. Trans. Richard Nice. Stanford: Stanford University Press, 1990.

Bourdieu, Pierre. *Outline of a Theory of Practice*. Trans. Richard Nice. Cambridge: Cambridge University Press, 1977.

Easterly, William. *The Elusive Quest for Growth: Economists' Adventures and Misadventures in the Tropics*. Cambridge: MIT Press, 2001.

Freireich, Jessica, and Katherine Fulton. "Investing for Social and Environmental Impact." Monitor Institute, January 2009. http://www.monitorinstitute.com/downloads/what-we-think/impact-investing/Impact_Investing.pdf.

Giddens, Anthony. *The Consequences of Modernity*. Stanford: Stanford University Press, 1990.

Giddens, Anthony. *The Constitution of Society: Outline of the Theory of Structuration*. Berkeley: University of California Press, 1984.

Hart, Stuart. *Capitalism at the Crossroads*. New York: Prentice Hall, 2005.

Kramer, Mark, and Sarah Cooch. "Investing for Impact: Managing and Measuring Proactive Social Investments." FSG Social Impact Advisors, 2008. http://www.fsg-impact.org/ideas/item/287.

Lewin, Kurt. "Field Theory and Experiment in Social Psychology: Concepts and Methods." *American Journal of Sociology* 44.6 (1939): 868–96.

Lewin, Kurt. *Field Theory in Social Science: Selected Theoretical Papers*. Ed. Dorwin Cartwright. Westport, CT: Greenwood Press, 1976.

MacDonald, Norine, and Luc Tayart de Borms. *Global Philanthropy*. Brussels: Mercator Fund, 2010.

MacDonald, Norine, and Luc Tayart de Borms. *Philanthropy in Europe: A Rich Past, a Promising Future*. Brussels: Mercator Fund, 2008.

O'Donohoe, Nick, Christina Leijonhufvud, Yasemin Saltuk, Antony Bugg-Levine, and Margot Brandenburg. "Impact Investments: An Emerging Asset Class." J.P. Morgan, November 29, 2010. http://www.rockefellerfoundation.org/uploads/files/2b053b2b-8 feb-46ea-adbd-f89068d59785-impact.pdf.

Prahalad, C. K. *The Fortune at the Bottom of the Pyramid: Eradicating Poverty through Profits.* Philadelphia: Wharton School Publishing, 2004.

Salamon, Lester M., Helmut K. Anheier, Regina List, Stefan Toepler, and S. Wojciech Sokolowski and Associates. *Global Civil Society: Dimensions of the Nonprofit Sector.* Vol. 1, Baltimore: Johns Hopkins Center for Civil Society Studies, 1999; Vol. 2, Bloomfield, CT: Kumarian Press, 2004.

Salamon, Lester M., S. Wojciech Sokolowski, and Regina List. *Global Civil Society: An Overview.* Baltimore: Johns Hopkins Center for Civil Society Studies, 2003.

Tayart de Borms, Luc. *Foundations: Creating Impact in a Globalised World.* New York: Wiley, 2005.

Yunus, Muhammad. *Banker to the Poor: Micro-lending and the Battle against World Poverty.* New York: Public Affairs, 2003.

CHAPTER 24

A POLICY AGENDA FOR THE NEW FRONTIERS OF PHILANTHROPY

Shirley Sagawa

ACCESS TO CAPITAL HAS LONG been a challenge for low-income communities and the businesses that serve them. Efforts to create a viable capital market serve these neighborhoods over the last century in the United States have included self-help credit pools created by immigrants, African American communities, and others, as well as community development corporations launched with federal funds from the "War on Poverty." In the 1970s, these incipient community development financial institutions (CDFIs) expanded their funding by seeking private investment and accessing new federal business-development loan funds. Nonetheless, CDFIs grew only incrementally through the 1970s and 1980s.

But this all changed beginning in the 1990s. By early 2013, as a consequence, more than 1, 000 CDFIs could be found operating in the United States, blanketing every state and the District of Columbia, serving both rural and urban communities, and responsible for generating $24 billion of equity and debt investments into low-income communities in the United States.

What produced this change was not any spontaneous surge of private investment capital into low-income communities. Rather, the stimulus that opened the door for this expansion of CDFI access to investment capital was a series of changes in government policy. In particular, two government policy innovations were largely responsible: first, the creation in 1994 of the CDFI Fund, a government agency that provides funding to CDFIs through a competitive application process; and second, a revision of regulations under the Community Reinvestment Act (CRA), an earlier act that had created strong incentives for commercial banks to make investment in the communities from which they draw their deposits. In 1995, CRA regulations were revised to recognize explicitly that loans and investments in CDFIs qualified as eligible CRA activities.[1] Thanks in part to this revision, it is estimated that for every $1 of government aid to CDFI entities, $20 is invested in low-income communities.[2]

The CDFI example described above illustrates ways in which government policy can accelerate the growth of certain new philanthropic forms", or, in this case, eliminate barriers that are impeding their growth. While much of the impetus for the emergence of the new frontiers of philanthropy has originated from the private sector, government continues to have an important role in stimulating private-sector involvement and eliminating barriers to its full development.

Four of these barriers in particular seem especially worthy of attention: first, regulatory barriers that limit the ability of nonprofit organizations to engage the new frontiers of philanthropy; second, the limited availability of investment capital with the risk and return profiles suitable to finance many social-purpose activities; third, imperfections in the markets for social-purpose investment; and finally, the significant lack of skills and experience with many of the new tools of philanthropy among nonprofit and philanthropic institutions.

This chapter discusses these main barriers to the growth of new forms of philanthropy and explores how government policy might help in overcoming them. Although the focus here is on policies in the United States, many of the barriers exist in other countries as well, though greater progress has been made in overcoming them in some other countries, most notably the UK.[3]

Regulatory Barriers

The tax code has been the principal vehicle through which government influences philanthropy in the United States. It does so by defining the entities that are exempt from paying taxes and able to receive tax-exempt donations. Traditional philanthropy fits easily within this framework. However, the decision to seek or not to seek tax-exempt status effectively limits access to many forms of capital. The current nonprofit/for-profit designation in fact may create an artificial choice for organizations that embrace the charitable, religious, educational, literary, scientific, and other purposes of nonprofit organizations while pursuing business activities that might well yield substantial returns. The implications of this decision as well as possible policy solutions are discussed below.

For-Profit and Nonprofit Differential Access to Investment Capital

Organizations, whether they are nonprofit or for-profit, require investment capital to start up and grow. Sometimes they have need of buildings or other costly assets, necessitating access to financing. At times they may need loans to tide them over or secure an opportunity.

However, whether an organization is for-profit or not-for-profit determines what type of capital it may access. While a nonprofit organization may receive tax-exempt donations, its inability to distribute profits implicitly limits its access to equity and other forms of investment capital. Nonprofit organizations are also restricted in the types of earned income they may generate, particularly if it is unrelated to their missions.[4] They may also find it difficult to obtain loans if they lack collateral or credit history, and may have to close their doors or depend on volunteer labor when times are lean. When rapid increases in demand or innovations call for capital expenditures, nonprofit organizations are at a disadvantage relative to for-profit companies, which can issue stock or obtain other funding more easily.[5]

On the other hand, the decision to operate as a for-profit company may also be limiting. A for-profit business, even one with a social mission, loses access to donated philanthropic capital, many government grants, and volunteer assistance. It also risks legal challenges from equity investors or regulators if the organization places social benefits over financial returns.

While some differential access to capital is necessary, and even desirable, it also has negative impacts. And rather than evening the playing field, government policies may in fact exacerbate the differences. For example, while many government programs and government-supported enterprises provide credit enhancement, loan guarantees, or other means to draw capital into defined markets, few of these incentives are available to nonprofit organizations. For example, the Small Business Administration's 7a program provides loan guarantees to approved banks to make loans to qualified entities to expand, acquire, or start a small business. But such loans are not available to nonprofits. Nonprofits are also ineligible for other SBA loan programs, such as the Microloan program, which offers loans to young or growing small businesses; or America's Recovery Capital Loan Program (ARC), enacted as part of the Recovery and Reconstruction Act to provide short-term relief for viable small businesses facing immediate financial hardship. Opening any of these programs to nonprofit organizations or establishing similar programs to serve such organizations would influence the flow of investment by lessening the risk entailed as well as the cost. Nonprofit organizations often need such support in order to undertake capital projects or capitalize potential earned-income opportunities.

The federal government has provided tax exemptions for state government bonds issued to support capital projects or nonprofit hospitals and educational institutions, but these are generally available only to very large institutions.[6] One recent model that could be extended to other types of nonprofits is the Credit Enhancement for Charter School Facilities program. Charter schools are public schools operated independently of the local school board, often with an educational philosophy different from other schools in the system. In many cases, they are nonprofit organizations that raise funding to supplement public dollars. Inadequate facilities are a challenge for many charter schools, which often do not receive facilities support from school districts and are usually unable to issue bonds backed by property taxes. As these nonprofit organizations seek loans, they often have only per-pupil school district revenue to point to as an asset and because charters must be renewed every three to five years, some lending institutions view them as a long-term lending risk. Under the federal credit enhancement program, charter schools compete for grants that will be deposited in reserve accounts that enable the schools to obtain better rates and terms on market-based financing to acquire, construct, or renovate facilities.

This type of support could be expanded to other nonprofit organizations that are similarly situated in their needs for facilities and likelihood of future fee-for-service or other earned-income streams, such as child care centers, nursing homes, or performing arts organizations. Evidence suggests that the need is great. For example, the Johns Hopkins University Nonprofit Listening Post Project conducted a nationwide survey in 2009 to discover the scope of stalled "shovel-ready" infrastructure projects at the nation's nonprofits (not including hospitals and universities).[7] Researchers found that nationwide, $166 billion worth of community infrastructure projects were ready to go if funding were available, including projects sponsored by museums, community and economic development organizations, and elderly housing and service organizations. The survey found that more than 1, 000 specific shovel-ready projects had been stalled by the credit crisis, representing some $10.6 billion of infrastructure investments. A credit enhancement program modeled on the Charter School Credit Enhancement Program or a loan guarantee program might open up new investment for nonprofit organizations for any or all of these purposes.

Uncertainty Due to Lack of or Limited Regulatory Framework

As new forms of philanthropy are invented, it often takes years for policymakers to develop rules that govern such activity. In some ways, this may be advantageous, allowing for creative giving and investing strategies to emerge and evolve. But in other ways, the lack of basic consumer protections and concern that transactions may be disallowed or invite legal action may inhibit their adoption.

For example, "program-related investments, " in which private foundations are permitted to invest in earned-income enterprises that advance the foundation's charitable objectives, were authorized in the Tax Reform Act of 1969.[8] But, as discussed more fully in chapter 5 of this volume, this tool has yet to become used widely, despite its advantages. In particular, fewer than 0.2 percent of all foundations use PRIs, and this is due in important part to the complexity of such arrangements, which make them difficult to administer.[9] For example, there is no uniform process in place to confirm that a foundation's proposed investment complies with PRI regulations, making it necessary to request an opinion from counsel or a private letter ruling from the IRS for each transaction, a costly process.[10] Recently, IRS issued a proposed regulation clarifying the range of transactions that it would consider eligible for PRI designation, but this regulations came 43 years after passage of the PRI legislation.

A new corporate form, the L3C, a "low-profit limited liability company, " is designed to get around some of the difficulties with PRIs and thereby open up new potentials for philanthropic investments that offer a return.[11] L3Cs are for-profit entities that by law have socially beneficial purposes. They are similar to the community interest companies authorized in the UK in 2004, a change that has resulted in 4, 000 double bottom-line businesses receiving the designation.[12]

As for-profit entities, L3Cs may attract a broad range of investors. However, their unique structure would allow different classes of investors to assume different levels of risk, with foundations assuming the most risk, thereby incentivizing other investors to participate. The L3C "brand" informs investors that the primary purpose of the organization is social benefit, not financial return, thereby relieving the organization of the threat of shareholder or regulatory suits challenging management for failing to pursue profit maximization.[13] At the same time, because of their legal obligation to pursue charitable or social-purpose objectives, L3C's relieve foundations of the legal fees and organizational costs associated with demonstrating that investments in L3Cs fulfill the legal requirement that PRIs go to entities pursuing a primarily charitable purpose. As such, the L3C form should eliminate the need for IRS private letter rulings on projected to qualify investments in L3Cs as PRIs.

As of mid-2011, nine states and two federal jurisdictions had adopted the L3C form. Under the full faith and credit clause of the Constitution, an L3C registered in any of these states can operate in any other state. However, as of mid-2012, the IRS had not adopted regulations regarding this new corporate form, even though the April 2012 IRS proposed regulations on PRIs added other new examples that broaden the investments that qualify as PRIs. As a result, program-related investments by foundations in these for-profit organizations must still be individually reviewed by the IRS. Federal legislation to expedite IRS review of L3Cs has been suggested to greatly streamline the process for making PRIs and substantially reduce the costs foundations incur.[14] Either way, it will be necessary to create for L3Cs something akin to the accountability system that has grown up around nonprofit organizations, which allows the public to view nonprofit tax forms and both the IRS and state attorneys general to police nonprofit activities.

While a half-century ago, the lines between for-profit and nonprofit organizations—and their access to capital—were clearly defined, today they have become increasingly blurred with the emergence of the L3C and similar hybrid forms, the movement of traditional for-profit companies to become socially responsible businesses, and the tendency of nonprofit organizations to increase their earned income through both related and unrelated business ventures. As a result, a broader range of philanthropic capital forms has been created and more are likely to emerge as the field continues to evolve. Some will be accommodated under existing law, while others, like the L3C, require new government action. However, even where new forms are legally authorized, systems for transparency, accountability, and other consumer protections have, in most cases, not yet been developed, which may inhibit the adoption of these new organizational forms as well as the availability of investment capital to support them.

Limited Investment Capital

While government funds are by definition not philanthropic capital, government spending may impact a nonprofit organization's ability to access certain forms of philanthropic support and the choices that private-sector funders make. Typically, government may increase access to investment capital in two ways: by developing the supply of capital through co-investment (incorporating investment rules and requirements) or directing capital, by influencing procurement decisions through taxes, subsidies, reporting requirements, and intermediation.[15]

Government Direct Spending as Incentive/Disincentive

Most forms of government spending leave little room for new—or traditional—forms of philanthropy. Public programs may inadvertently discourage private-sector investment by providing close to full funding for a program without a required match, making it difficult for organizations that receive substantial public-sector support to develop significant capacity for fundraising and leaving them dependent on public funds and highly vulnerable to dips in public budgets. Even more common is the situation with many voucher programs, such as Medicare and Medicaid, which fail to cover the full costs of the services, making it necessary for organizations to use their philanthropic support simply to make up the difference, leaving little left over to finance capital needs.[16] Finally, while some programs may require matching funds from nonfederal or nongovernmental sources, in such cases private funders are expected to support the choices of government regarding which organizations receive support.

Social Innovation Funds

Fortunately, some forms of government funding avoid these limitations. One such form is the Social Innovation Fund enacted through the Edward M. Kennedy Serve America Act. This program, intended to scale up proven innovative programs, turns the traditional "match" on its head by providing government grants to match the funding choices of "social innovation funds" operated by "existing grant-making institutions," such as foundations, state service commissions, or local governments. Resources provided are intended to serve as investment capital, not operating funds, to enable high-impact organizations to grow. Eligible social innovation funds must have a track record of operating consistent with the best practices of venture philanthropy. For example, they must have experience making substantial, multiyear grants, providing management assistance to grantees, and operating systems of data-driven decision-making and research. These grantees, in turn, make subgrants to nonprofit organizations to expand or replicate proven initiatives or support promising new initiatives in low-income communities.

In this way, the federal government encourages both a specific form of new philanthropy (venture philanthropy) and embarks on a new model for government funding in which public dollars support private choices, rather than vice versa. Though funded at a relatively modest level, as of 2012, the SIF had made $137.5 million in grants to 20 grant-making organizations that partnered with 130 additional funders to generate a total of $350 million in capital. If successful, this model could be expanded to engage more grant-makers, or similar funds could be created in other agencies focusing on specific public problems. Alternatively, a cross-agency fund could be created as an independent public or private entity, with board representation from relevant agency heads. A supported network of social investment funds could influence private philanthropy to make investments in organizations that get results, fuel innovation, and address the inequities of philanthropic asset distribution that leave vast parts of the country underresourced.[17]

New investment funds could also support the earned-income ventures of nonprofits. Much as the SBA has helped to finance the growth of small businesses, putting more than $30 billion into the hands of small business owners through its venture capital program, a venture fund could provide businesses operating with a social purpose or nonprofit social enterprises similar access to investment capital.

Other countries have employed similar tools to build for-profit companies deemed important to public interests. For example, the United Kingdom's Enterprise Capital Funds (ECFs) were created to provide investment capital to early-stage small businesses considered important to job growth and the economy. These privately managed funds, whose assets total more than £1 billion, use public funds to leverage private investment, with government investing up to £2 for every £1 of private investment. Government money is provided at rates of interest similar to those applicable to other government bonds, and successful investments also return a share of profits to the government.[18] In some cases, ECFs are focused on specific industries, such as the Sustainable Technology Growth Fund, a £30m fund launched in March 2007 to provide investment and expertise to UK technology businesses, particularly those that reduce natural resource usage, improve energy efficiencies, or reduce waste.[19] An even more ambitious UK initiative, the Big Society Capital fund, was authorized in 2012 by the Financial Services Authority (FSA) to help the social sector innovate, expand services, and develop better solutions to social problems. Capitalized with £400 million in funding from dormant bank accounts as well as £200 million in investments from major banks and regulated by the FSA, the fund will provide affordable finance opportunities to social enterprises as well as charities.

While it is too soon to tell whether the Enterprise Capital Fund or Big Society Capital will achieve their intended impacts, at least one UK expert, relying on the experience of angel investors in North America, suggests that the Enterprise Capital Funds may return funds to the Treasury, or at least be cost neutral.[20] The United States could be well advised to follow this UK example of extending or expanding government investments in funds to grow businesses that serve the public interest, whether they are operated by for-profit or nonprofit organizations—a policy tool with potential to leverage private funds for public purposes.

Social-Impact Bonds

As covered more extensively in chapter 16 of this volume, social-impact bonds represent another way to utilize public funds to mobilize private resources in support of social purposes. Developed initially in the UK, social-impact bonds enable government resources to be leveraged only after a private investor has supported specific prevention and early interventions that bring about an identified outcome for a target population that results in cost savings to the government. For example, private investors might support a program to reduce recidivism by youth offenders, who would be tracked over a period of three years. At the end of three years, the government would pay the private investors a return on their investment if the supported program actually reduces recidivism and therefore saves the government money in prison costs and other public costs relating to crime. The more effective the program and savings to government, the more investors get paid.[21]

This model has three advantages: (1) more funds are available for prevention and early intervention efforts that government often does not fund adequately; (2) government, hence taxpayers, only end up paying for effective programs that save taxpayers money; and (3) private investors have a financial incentive to ensure their programs are as effective as possible, as their return on investment is dependent upon it. Social-impact bonds address a major disincentive for evidence-based government spending—often the savings that result from a preventive intervention do not accrue to the entity that makes the investment. They also offer the potential to advance the frontiers of philanthropy by creating a mechanism for philanthropic investors to recoup their investment if it proves successful.

Tax Incentives

Tax policy can also be used to influence the availability and form of philanthropic investments, and a variety of innovations have recently been undertaken at both the national and the state level in the United States. While most of these have focused on incentivizing grant-based charitable giving, some have encouraged the use of more leveraged forms of support of the sort examined in this book.

For example, at the federal level, tax credits have incentivized taxpayers to make financial investments in specific types of businesses that benefit low-income communities, such as housing or business development. One example is the federal New Markets Tax Credit, enacted as part of the Community Renewal Tax Relief Act of 2000. Investors under this program may receive a credit against their federal income tax for making "qualified equity investments" in designated community development entities (CDEs) that use these funds to invest in low-income communities.[22] The New Markets Tax Credit may be claimed against an aggregate amount of $23 billion of investments over the life of the program. Research by the Government Accountability Office in 2007 found that this credit has been effective in increasing private investment in low-income communities.[23]

Similar tax benefits are available through the Low Income Housing Tax Credit (LIHTC), a dollar-for-dollar tax credit for affordable housing investments. The LIHTC provides funding for the development costs of low-income housing by allowing a taxpayer (usually the members of the partnership that owns the housing) to take a federal tax credit equal to a large percentage of the cost incurred for development of the low-income units in a rental housing project. LIHTC credits account for the majority of all affordable rental housing created in the United States today.

Other countries have adopted similar tax mechanisms to increase investment in socially beneficial businesses. For example, Australia's National Rental Affordability Scheme provides a tax credit, or cash payment in the case of tax-exempt nonprofit builders, for construction of property that will be rented at least 20 percent below market rate. The Netherlands' Green Funds Scheme provides tax incentives to investors of all sizes who invest in funds that finance low-profit environmental projects with the potential to be self-sustaining, such as sustainable housing, agriculture, and wind energy. Since the program's implementation in 1995, nearly a quarter million individuals have invested nearly 7 billion euros in green funds, financing more than 5,000 projects.[24]

US tax credits to stimulate other "new frontiers" investment could take advantage of the growing network of intermediaries, who have developed highly sophisticated systems for identifying promising solutions to community programs and taking them to scale. The use of a tax credit rather than appropriated funding to help finance these organizations offers greater potential for scale and sustainability, creates less bureaucracy, and puts the decisions for investment in specific organizations in the hands of these intermediaries instead of the government.[25]

Social-Purpose Investment Capital Markets

Another challenge for philanthropists and social-purpose organizations alike is the lack of an efficient capital market for social-purpose activities. Social-purpose organizations, including those that are innovative and highly effective, often spend substantial resources identifying and securing financial resources, and most remain at a suboptimum scale. At the same time, many providers of capital either support only those organizations they already know or spend significant resources sorting through large numbers of potential investments. Markets that both expand available resources and make the connection of investors and donors to social-purpose organizations more efficient are emerging in the United States and elsewhere. Government policy can play a highly useful role in creating, incentivizing, and supporting these markets.

Systems to Connect Investors to Organizations

Over the last decade, several trends have converged to make it easier for investors to identify appropriate social-purpose organizations. Technology has made it possible for information to be easily shared and transaction costs minimized. Increasingly sophisticated outcome measurement and other strategies to measure return on investment have made comparisons across organizations possible, at least along some dimensions, as outlined more fully in chapter 22 of this volume.[26] The adoption of business practices and models among innovative nonprofits, along with the increasing number of social entrepreneurs who choose to start for-profit businesses rather than nonprofit organizations, have opened the door to the adoption of business models for investment transactions in both sectors.

As outlined more fully in previous chapters, these models take many forms. For example, Kiva provides an online service enabling individuals to lend small amounts to individuals participating in microfinance projects around the world. Venture philanthropy funds, such as New Profit and the Acumen Fund, invite "investors" to support portfolios of organizations that expert staff have selected using criteria largely derived from the business sector. Charity rating systems, such as Charity Navigator and New Philanthropy Capital, assess nonprofit organizations in manners similar to mutual fund rating systems. In Brazil, a designated national authority was established to oversee the complex process of project approval, validation, registration, and monitoring of clean development projects in which industrialized nations could invest as a way to offset their emissions, typically at a lower cost than reducing their own emissions.[27] And as detailed in chapter 4, "social stock exchanges" have surfaced in a variety of global locales to provide a trading platform through which investors can invest in particular social-purpose enterprises.

While most of these efforts operate outside of the public sector, government might accelerate their growth and adoption in a variety of ways. Government leaders may use the bully pulpit to enhance their visibility and credibility. Because the infrastructure for these systems can be costly and difficult to support through philanthropic sources, public subsidies of exchanges might promote their growth and sustainability. The government might create, operate, or subsidize the creation of systems to assess potential investments, in much the way that the Brazilian government has supported a system to validate clean development projects, and the UK government has subsidized a social stock exchange through its Big Society Capital initiative with the hope that it will one day become an FSA-authorized exchange. Finally, if such systems attain substantial scale, a regulatory system could be warranted to protect and inform investors, much as the IRS governs nonprofits and the SEC oversees traditional stock exchanges in the United States.

Tradeable Tax Credits

Another proposal for a market-based system to expand the financial resources of social-purpose organizations is modeled on "cap and trade" systems to combat global warming. Through such systems, a central authority (usually a governmental body) sets a cap on the amount of a pollutant that may be emitted. The "cap" is allocated or sold to firms in the form of emissions permits that represent the right to discharge a specific volume of the specified pollutant. Firms are required to hold a number of permits (or credits) equivalent to their emissions. Firms that need to increase their volume of emissions must buy permits from those who require fewer permits, thereby engaging in a "trade." In effect, the buyer is paying a charge for polluting, while the seller is being rewarded for having reduced emissions. As noted in chapter 4 of this book, there are active "cap and trade" programs in place in various jurisdictions around the world, including the European Union Emission Trading Scheme designed to reduce greenhouse gases that may lead to climate change.[28]

A similar concept has been put forward in the UK to reward corporate social responsibility by awarding tradable tax credits to socially responsible businesses. Such mechanisms could also be designed to promote job creation. While nonprofit and low-profit organizations (such as LC3s) derive minimal benefit from tax credits because they pay little or no taxes, if they received tradable tax credits based on new hires, they could benefit from selling the credits to businesses that could make use of them.[29]

Limited Capacity

For new forms of philanthropy to grow, both investors and social-purpose organizations must have the necessary human capital and knowledge to participate. For example, many new forms of philanthropy require knowledge of finance and capital markets, rarely found among foundation personnel or nonprofit staff. Similarly, an organization seeking to develop an income-generating business venture—whether it will result in related or unrelated business income—requires staff with business skills not typically found among nonprofit employees. Venture philanthropists usually require the nonprofit organizations they support to have the capacity to measure outcomes and use data in a variety of sophisticated ways, and to possess other management capabilities that are the exception not the rule in the nonprofit sector. In fact, the lack of expertise, capacity, and relationships may well be a bigger barrier to accessing "new frontier" philanthropy sources than the availability of capital itself.

Unfortunately, government at all levels has done little to expand the capacity of nonprofit organizations, even for more traditional forms of giving. This is all the more surprising in view of the fact that nonprofits are responsible for delivering a substantial share of publicly funded services so that the effectiveness of government programs is significantly dependent on the effectiveness of its third-party implementers.[30] Yet neither at the federal level, nor in most states, is any agency tasked with monitoring, supporting, or advocating for the health and effectiveness of the nonprofit and philanthropic sector. As a result, few US government officials, in any branch or level of government, are knowledgeable about these organizations and the way that policy affects them, in sharp contrast to other countries, including Canada, Australia, and the UK, that have established government offices responsible for advancing nongovernmental organizations. The cabinet-level Office for Civil Society in the UK, for example, focuses on making it easier to run a charity, social enterprise, or voluntary organization; getting more resources into the sector; strengthening its independence and resilience; and making it easier for sector organizations to work with the state.

Bully Pulpit

Because awareness is an important aspect of promoting new forms of philanthropy, the bully pulpit can serve as a useful tool. Presidents, governors, and other public leaders have, on occasion, used their public platform, convening power, and other strategies to raise awareness of specific philanthropic forms.

For example, when President Clinton hosted the first White House Conference on Philanthropy, he called for programs to increase youth philanthropy, recognized contributions by communities of color, which may not come in the forms that are widely acknowledged, and highlighted new forms of giving to build awareness. President George W Bush, building on his father's encouragement of service through his "Thousand Points of Light" volunteer recognition initiative, launched a campaign to enlist professionals to contribute a total of one billion hours of pro bono service. President Obama embraced social innovation, creating the first White House Office of Social Innovation and Civic Participation and hosting numerous events to highlight the social innovation agenda, including the Social Innovation Fund.

State governments have also undertaken initiatives designed to influence philanthropic choices. For example, in the fall of 2006, then-Lieutenant Governor Mitch Landrieu founded the Louisiana Office of Social Entrepreneurship dedicated to promoting partnerships that combine "business principles with a passion for social impact." In Texas, the Center for Social Impact is a nonprofit organization with a direct connection to state government, including a governor-appointed executive director. The Texas Social Innovation Initiative enables nonprofit organizations with proven, results-based programs to receive statewide recognition for being innovative models and thereby attract increased resources.[31] Efforts such as these not only build awareness and visibility; they also create legitimacy for innovations, easing their adoption. However, these initiatives may have limited impact without additional support and resources to promote adoption of the innovations they champion.

Government-Supported Capacity-Building Assistance

Both public and private funding for training and technical assistance to build the capacity of both nonprofit organizations and philanthropists is extremely limited. Most federal grants limit nonprogrammatic activities (such as administrative or fundraising activities) to a small share of the grant. Yet there are promising examples that could usefully be built upon.

For example, the Compassion Capital Fund at the Department of Health and Human Services proposed by the George W. Bush administration as part of its faith-based initiative provided grants to expand and strengthen the ability of faith-based organizations to provide social services to low-income communities. Similarly, the modest Nonprofit Capacity Building Program, authorized by the Edward M. Kennedy Serve America Act, provided support to help small and midsize community-based nonprofits develop performance management systems. Various government programs provide training and technical assistance for nonprofit management functions. However, none of these programs operates on a scale to have a substantial impact,[32] and none focuses on helping organizations to access nontraditional philanthropic support. Nor do any of these programs target philanthropic organizations to broaden their awareness and ability to provide alternative forms of support to organizations. Increasing funding through any of these programs, or authorizing new funding to build the capacity of organizations and private-sector funders, might pay significant dividends, as might increasing the share of a grant that may be used for administrative functions.

National Service

One of the largest and longest US federal investments in nonprofit capacity has been the VISTA program, now part of AmeriCorps, which offers full-time volunteers to help antipoverty organizations increase their impact and sustainability. Programs such as VISTA and AmeriCorps could include a special focus on engaging skilled volunteers who can help nonprofit organizations access a broader range of philanthropic opportunities. The Edward M. Kennedy Act authorized a substantial increase in national service programs, including those that will increase the ability of nonprofit organizations to engage volunteer help. This increase could be targeted to enhance this purpose.

For example, the VISTA model could be expanded to enable high-growth/high-impact organizations to access larger groups of VISTAs. VISTAs may help to raise money, recruit and supervise volunteers, develop partnerships, and undertake other activities that extend the impact and sustainability of eligible nonprofits. However, the number of VISTAs has been limited by slow growth in appropriations[33] and the typical placement mechanism (federal employees approve the organizations that may sponsor VISTAs). A "VISTA Growth Fund" could enable the VISTA program to increase substantially by encouraging the placement of large numbers of VISTAs with high-growth national and regional organizations while continuing small-group and individual placements with grass-roots organizations, particularly those in rural communities where the program has been particularly effective.

Advocates have called for the next phase of governmental support for service to take AmeriCorps or similar full-time service programs to a level that will enable anyone who wants to serve to participate. Some estimate that one million positions would meet this demand and constitute a form of "universal national service."[34] This expansion of national service would have significant implications for the nonprofit sector and open extensive new opportunities to increase the capacity of organizations to access the new frontiers of philanthropy.

Other countries have adopted such universal national service, in many cases as an outgrowth of efforts to create an alternative to mandatory military service. In such cases, individuals who are exempt from military service or are conscientious objectors typically provide civilian service through NGOs or local government agencies. Some countries have designed their programs to address important needs. For example, in Germany, young men who are conscientious objectors as well as participants in the Volunteer Social Year, a youth service program for those seeking careers in social services, provide assistance to the growing population of older Germans. In Israel, exempt young adults (including Orthodox Jews, Muslims, and Christians) serve in children's programs, including schools, health clinics, and child care centers. Some countries have used full-time service to meet the needs of remote areas; for example, Mexico's Servicio Social requires students to serve for six months in areas lacking services, while the National Youth Service Corps of Nigeria, a one-year commitment for college graduates, sends teachers, engineers, doctors, pharmacists, and accountants to serve outside their home states in an effort to promote ethnic tolerance.[35]

An SBA for the Nonprofit Sector

A major reason for the weakness underlying federal policy for the nonprofit sector is the lack of expertise within the government itself. Both federal and state governments have, for the most part, paid little attention to the capacity of the sector that delivers most of its programming. No agency advocates for the sector, measures its health, ensures that it weathers economic downturns or natural disasters, or manages a system to distribute resources to improve and assist it. As a result, few officials know much about the sector, its needs, and its potential. These deficiencies affect the government's ability to address even traditional aspects of nonprofit and philanthropic organizations.

Policymakers seeking to increase new forms of philanthropy could do so by designating an entity within the federal government to support and build the capacity of nonprofits in much the way that it has supported small businesses. While providing minimal assistance to nonprofit organizations, the federal government has invested billions of dollars to support the capacity, growth, market development, and research and development functions of for-profit businesses.

For example, the Small Business Administration is a $600 million agency whose mission is to "maintain and strengthen the nation's economy by aiding, counseling, assisting and protecting the interests of small businesses and by helping families and businesses recover from national disasters." In furtherance of this mission, the SBA provides training and technical assistance to small business owners and entrepreneurs; manages a volunteer network available to help small businesses; provides loans and other financial assistance; helps small businesses with disaster recovery; reaches out to special groups, including women and minorities; and helps small businesses obtain and manage government contracts.

An alternative model is the National Academy of Public Administration (NAPA), an independent, nonprofit, and nonpartisan organization established in 1967 to assist government leaders in building more effective, efficient, accountable, and transparent organizations. Chartered by Congress to provide nonpartisan expert advice, the academy engages over 700 fellows—including former cabinet officers, members of Congress, governors, mayors, and state legislators, as well as prominent scholars, business executives, and public administrators. The academy helps the federal government address management challenges through in-depth studies and analyses, advisory services and technical assistance, congressional testimony, forums and conferences, and online stakeholder engagement. Under contracts with government agencies, some of which are directed by Congress, as well as grants from private foundations, the National Academy of Public Administration provides insights on key public management issues, as well as advisory services to government agencies.

The federal government might create a "Small Business Administration" or "National Academy" specifically for the nonprofit sector. Like small businesses, nonprofits range in size and sophistication, access to capital, and capacity to engage with the public sector, and have many of the needs addressed by the SBA and NAPA. An administration or academy for the nonprofit sector would not have to be a new agency. These functions could be housed within another agency, such as the Corporation for National and Community Service or even the SBA itself, or supported through a private-sector entity chartered by the federal government.[36] Legislation to create a federal council on the nonprofit sector, along with an interagency task force and support for research and data collection, has already been developed and could provide an interim step or even a potential permanent solution to the challenges discussed in this section.[37]

Conclusion

Much of the policy that shapes philanthropic organizations today emerged in response to "new frontiers" of an earlier time. This process of private-sector innovation and corresponding government action has resulted in an evolving framework that will continue to be reshaped as new philanthropic instruments and priorities emerge. While government engagement in the private sphere of philanthropy should not be undertaken absent a compelling purpose, neither should policymakers ignore the unintentional barriers created by policy, as well as the potential of new philanthropic forms and the ways that government can encourage them. As tightening budgets make it ever more urgent to find new ways to tap the power of private investment, new frontiers of government policy are needed to tap the potential of new philanthropy.

Notes

1. CDFI Coalition, "What Are CDFIs?," accessed February 9, 2013, http://www.cdfi.org/about-cdfis/what-are-cdfis/.

2. D. Fabiani, "CDFIs Leverage CDFI Program Awards Nearly $20 to $1!," Office of Financial Strategies and Research, CDFI Fund, Department of the Treasury, accessed February 9, 2013, http://www.cdfifund.gov/impact_we_make/Leverage.pdf.

3. Thornley et al., suggest a policy framework through which government action may influence impact investing either directly or indirectly. It may intervene by increasing the amount of capital for development (supply development); increasing the availability or strengthening the capacity of capital recipients (demand development); or adjusting the terms of trade, market norms, or prices (directing capital). Ben Thornley, David Wood, Katie Grace, and Sarah Sullivant, Impact Investing, a Framework for Policy Design and Analysis, Pacific Community Ventures and the Initiative for Responsible Investment at Harvard University, January 2011.

4. Nonprofit organizations may pursue earned income in accordance with their missions without incurring taxes or risking their tax-exempt status. They may also operate unrelated businesses, directly or through for-profit subsidiaries, in certain circumstances. The Revenue Act of 1950, in response to concerns that nonprofits were competing unfairly with business, imposed an "unrelated business income tax" (UBIT) requiring nonprofit organizations to pay tax on any income derived from a "trade or business" that was "regularly carried on" and not "substantially related" to the organization's exempt purposes.

5. Lester M. Salamon, *The Resilient Sector: The State of Nonprofit America*, (Washington, D.C.: Brookings Institution Press, 2003), 24.

6. Other government strategies to support nonprofit construction have included the Hill-Burton Act, which since 1946 has financed hospital construction, and tax-exempt state bonds for nonprofit facilities.

7. Lester M. Salamon, Stephanie L. Geller, Kasey L. Spence, and Wojciech Sokolowski, "'Shovel-Ready' but Stalled: Nonprofit Infrastructure Projects Ready for Economic Recovery Support," Listening Post Project Communiqué No. 12, Johns Hopkins Nonprofit Listening Post Project, 2009, accessed January 8, 2014, http://ccss.jhu.edu/publications-findings?did=257.

8. "Specifically, the category of PRIs is an exception to the jeopardizing investment rule of Section 4944 of the Internal Revenue Code ("IRC"). Section 4944 prohibits a private foundation from making any investment in a manner 'as to jeopardize the carrying out of any of its exempt purposes.' In plain English this means that Congress does not want a private foundation to make poor investments that jeopardize the charitable assets of a foundation." Jonathan C. Lewis and Robert A. Wexler, "Mission Investing in Microfinance: A Program Related Investment (PRI) Primer and Toolkit," Microcredit Enterprises, July 2007, 14, http://www.community-wealth.org/_pdfs/tools/pris/tool-microcredit-ent-pri.pdf.

9. Of the nation's more than 75,000 grant-making foundations, the Foundation Center has tracked 173 private and community foundations that made at least one PRI of $10,000 or more in 2006 or 2007. Steven Lawrence, "Doing Good with Foundation Assets," Foundation Center, 2010, 1, accessed August 22, 2011, http://foundationcenter.org/gainknowledge/research/pdf/pri_directory_excerpt.pdf.

10. Council on Foundations, "The Program-Related Investment Promotion Act of 2008: A Proposal for Encouraging Charitable Investments," accessed at http://www.cof.org/files/Documents/Conferences/LegislativeandRegulatory06.pdf. See also chapter 5 of this volume for further detail on PRIs.

11. Another type of "hybrid organization," benefit corporations, has the dual purpose of creating general public benefit by creating value for its stakeholders—such as the community, local and global environment, employees, suppliers, and customers—and creating a profit for shareholders. Therefore benefit corporations may be shielded from lawsuits by shareholders who argue the corporation has diluted their stock by putting general social value over profit. As of 2012, seven states had created benefit corporations as a legal form.

12. Italy, Spain, and France have enacted similar legal forms. Ben Thornley, David Wood, Katie Grace, and Sarah Sullivant, "Case Study 6: Community Interest Companies," Impact Investing, a Framework for Policy Design and Analysis, Pacific Community Ventures and the Initiative for Responsible Investment at Harvard University, January 2011.

13. Legal requirements to maximize value for shareholders are derived from many sources, including state corporate laws and SEC rules. Robert Hinkley, "How Corporate Law Inhibits Social Responsibility," Business Ethics Corporate Social Responsibility Report, January–February 2002, http://www.commondreams.org/views02/0119-04.htm. While many have argued that the profit maximization requirement does not preclude actions to benefit society more broadly (such as making charitable contributions or operating in a manner that takes into consideration the public interest), this matter is far from settled. See, e.g., Ian B. Lee, "Corporate Law, Profit Maximization and the Responsible Shareholder," *Stanford Journal of Law, Business & Finance*, March 2005, http://ssrn.com/abstract=692862; Julia A. Nelson, "Does Profit-Seeking Rule Out Love: Evidence (or Not) from Economics and the Law," prepared for the Symposium "For Love or Money," September 2010, http://ase.tufts.edu/gdae/Pubs/wp/10-06ProfitSeekingAndLove.pdf; Einer Elhauge, "Sacrificing Corporate Profits in

the Public Interest," prepared for Environmental Protection and the Social Responsibility of Firms, December 6, 2003, http://www.hks.harvard.edu/m-rcbg/Events/Papers/RPP_2-12-04_Elhauge.pdf.

14. The Philanthropic Facilitation Act, developed by Americans for Community Development.

15. Thornley et al., "Impact Investing."

16. "Medicaid Reimbursement in School-Based Health Centers: State Association and Provider Perspectives, a Report of the National Assembly on School-Based Health Care," June 2000, http://ww2.nasbhc.org/RoadMap/Public/Funding_IB_MedicaidReimbursement.pdf. For example, Medicare and Medicaid reimbursement rates below the cost of delivering care have been cited as factors associated with the financial distress of nonprofit hospitals. Tae Hyun Kim, "Factors Associated with Financial Distress of Nonprofit Hospitals," *Health Care Manager* 29.1 (January–March 2010): 52–62.

17. While it is too soon to know the impact of the Social Innovation Fund, critics have raised concerns about its fit with rural areas, which may have limited access to philanthropic support that would enable them to access SIF resources. Alternative vehicles may be needed to build the capacity of rural areas to participate. One proposal, the Rural Philanthropy Growth Act, would use federal funds to seed community foundations in rural communities.

18. Enterprise Capital Fund Guidance for Applicants, Third Round, April 2008, http://www.bis.gov.uk/files/file45483.pdf.

19. Green Economy Initiative, Enterprise Capital Fund—Sustainable Technology Growth Fund, accessed September 19, 2011, http://greeneconomyinitiative.com/news/186/ARTICLE/1307/2009-01-02.html.

20. "At the risk of using evidence in the US as a proxy for the UK market, the Government could see a healthy return from this initiative or at least achieve its 'cost neutral' objective. The largest study on the financial returns of angel investors in North America, published in November 2007 by the Kauffman Foundation, shows investors participating in organized groups achieved an average 27 percent internal rate of return on their investments. Overall, angel investors experienced exits that generated 2.6 times their invested capital in 3.5 years from investment to exit. This return compares favorably to that of other private equity investments, including those of early-stage venture capital. Seven percent of exits generated returns above 10 times their initial investment." John Crickett, "Enterprise Capital Funds: Are They Working?" Business Opportunities and Ideas Blog, November 30, 2007, http://www.businessopportunitiesan-dideas.com/508/enterprise-capital-funds-are-they-working; "Angel Investors in Groups Achieve Investment Returns in Line with Other Types of Equity Deals," November 12, 2007, http://www.kauffman.org/Details.aspx%5C?id=1032.

21. Jeffrey B. Liebman, "Social Impact Bonds, A Promising New Financing Model to Accelerate Social Innovation and Improve Government Performance," Center for American Progress, February 2011.

22. To be certified as a CDE able to award New Market Tax Credits, an organization must

- be a domestic corporation or partnership at the time of the certification application;
- demonstrate a primary a mission of serving, or providing investment capital for, low-income communities or low-income persons; and
- maintain accountability to residents of low-income communities through representation on a governing board of or advisory board to the entity.

The credit provided to the investor totals 39 percent of the cost of the investment and is claimed over a seven-year period.

23. "Tax Policy: New Markets Tax Credit Appears to Increase Investment by Investors in Low-Income Communities, but Opportunities Exist to Better Monitor Compliance," Government Accountability Office, January 2007, http://www.community-wealth.org/_pdfs/articles-publications/cdfis/report-brostek-et-al.pdf.

24. Ben Thornley, David Wood, Katie Grace, and Sarah Sullivant, "Case Study 7: Green Funds Scheme," Impact Investing, a Framework for Policy Design and Analysis, Insight at Pacific Community Ventures and the Initiative for Responsible Investment at Harvard University, January 2011.

25. Such a tax credit could operate in a manner similar to the federal New Markets Tax Credit. Certified entities, such as those that have experience with social-impact investments, high-engagement grant-making that involves substantial multiyear grants, PRI investments, and the provision of additional resources to grantees, such as pro bono professional services, would receive the authority to issue to their individual and corporate donors the opportunity to claim the credit. Specific amounts could be designated for the achievement of specific goals, such as increased economic opportunity or improved education outcomes. In this way, the credit would incentivize funders to become increasingly outcome-focused and support the scaling of high-quality organizations with proven programs.

26. Examples include social return on investment. See, for example, chapter 21 of this volume; and Jed Emerson, Jay Wachowicz, and Suzi Chun, "Social Return on Investment (SROI): Exploring Aspects of Value Creation," Harvard Business School, Working Knowledge for Business Leaders, January 29, 2001, http://hbswk.hbs.edu/archive/1957.html; cost-benefit analysis as utilized by the Washington State Institute for Public Policy, "Benefits and Costs of Prevention and Early Intervention Programs for Youth," September 17, 2004, http://www.wsipp.wa.gov/rptfiles/04-07-3901.pdf; common outcome measurements, proposed by the Urban Institute, "Building a Common Outcome Framework to Measure Nonprofit Performance," September 2006, http://www.urban.org/UploadedPDF/411404_Nonprofit_Performance.pdf; and other nonfinancial performance measurement tools discussed in Ben Thornley and Colby Dailey, "Building Scale in Community Impact Investing through Nonfinancial Performance Measurement," *Community Development Investment Review*, accessed January 9, 2014, http://www.frbsf.org/publications/community/review/vol6_issue1/Thornley_Dailey.pdf.

27. "Emissions Trading," Wikipedia, accessed October 18, 2012, http://en.wikipedia.org/w/index.php?title=Emissions_trading&oldid=518386997; Ben Thornley, David Wood, Katie Grace, and Sarah Sullivant, "Case Study 5: Clean Development Mechanism (CDM)," Impact Investing, a Framework for Policy Design and Analysis, Pacific Community Ventures and the Initiative for Responsible Investment at Harvard University, January 2011, http://www.pacificcommunityventures.org/insight/impactinvesting/report/05-Clean_Development_Mechanism.pdf.

28. Ben Thornley, David Wood, Katie Grace, and Sarah Sullivant, "Executive Summary," Impact Investing, a Framework for Policy Design and Analysis, Pacific Community Ventures and the Initiative for Responsible Investment at Harvard University, January 2011.

29. This idea was proposed by Lester Salamon, "Tradeable Tax Credits," *Chronicle of Philanthropy*, February 10, 2010, http://ccss.jhu.edu/tradeable-tax-credits-a-chronicle-of-philanthropy-op-ed-by-lester-salamon.

30. See: Lester M. Salamon, *Partners in Public Service: Government-Nonprofit Relations in the Modern Welfare State* (Baltimore: Johns Hopkins University Press, 1995).

31. Andrew Wolk, "Advancing Social Entrepreneurship, Recommendations for Policymakers and Government Agencies," Aspen Institute and Root Cause, April 2008.

32. In FY2011, the Corporation for National and Community Service's Nonprofit Capacity Building Fund received $1 million. The Nonprofit Capacity Building portion of the Strengthening Communities Fund (the successor to the Compassion Capital Fund) received $34 million from the Recovery Act stimulus bill in 2009 but received no regular appropriations in FY2011.

33. In FY2011, approximately 8,000 VISTAs were supported with $100 million in federal appropriations.

34. Michael Brown, AnnMaura Connolly, Alan Khazei, Wendy Kopp, Michelle Nunn, Gregg Petersmeyer, Shirley Sagawa, and Harris Wofford, "A Call to National Service," *American Interest* 3.3 (January–February 2008).

35. Colleen Buhrer, "Service as a Strategy: Addressing Critical National Needs," Innovations in Civic Participation, November 2008; Jeninne Lee-St. John, "How Others Serve," *Time*, August 30, 2007.

36. Examples of publicly chartered nonprofits include the American Red Cross, the National Trust for Historic Preservation, the National Academy of Public Administration, and NeighborWorks America.

37. See The Nonprofit Sector and Community Solutions Act, introduced by Representative Betty McCollum (D-MN), June 16, 2010.

Suggested Readings

Miller, Clara. "The Equity Capital Gap." *Stanford Social Innovation Review*, Summer 2008, 41–45. http://community-wealth.org/_pdfs/articles-publications/pris/article-miller.pdf.

Sagawa, Shirley. *The American Way to Change: How National Service and Volunteers Are Transforming America*. San Francisco: Jossey-Bass, 2010.

Thorley, Ben, David Wood, Katie Grace, and Sarah Sullivant. "Impact Investing: A Framework for Policy Design and Analysis." Pacific Community Ventures and the Initiative for Responsible Investment at Harvard University, January 2011.

Wolk, Andrew, "Social Entrepreneurship and Government: A New Breed of Entrepreneurs Developing Solutions to Social Problems." In *The Small Business Economy: A Report to the President*. Small Business Administration, Office of Advocacy, 2007. Accessible at publicinnovators.com.

APPENDIX

New Frontiers of Philanthropy Project Advisory Committee

Frank Altman
President and Chief Executive Officer, Community Reinvestment Fund

Doug Bauer
Executive Director, The Clark Foundation

Shari Berenbach
President and Chief Executive Officer, US African Development Foundation

Lucy Bernholz
Founder and President (*former*), Blueprint Research & Design

Stuart Davidson
Managing Partner, Labrador Ventures

Christopher L. Davis
President, Money Management Institute

William Dietel
Managing Partner, Dietel Partners

David Erickson
Director, Center for Community Development Investments, Federal Reserve Bank of San Francisco

Marc J. Lane
Founder, Marc J. Lane Wealth Group

Maximilian Martin
Founder and Global Managing Director, Impact Economy

Clara Miller
President, F.B. Heron Foundation

Mario Morino
Cofounder and Chairman, Venture Philanthropy Partners

Luther Ragin
President and Chief Executive Officer, Global Impact Investing Network

Lisa Richter
Principal, GPS Capital Partners

Jack Sim

Founder, World Toilet Organization

Greg Stanton
Founder, Wall Street Without Walls

Vince Stehle
Executive Director, Media Impact Funders

Luc Tayart De Borms
Managing Director, King Baudoin Foundation

Mechai Viravaidya
Founder, Condoms & Cabbages

Kimberly Wright-Violich
President (*former*), Schwab Charitable Fund

GLOSSARY

Lester M. Salamon

adverse selection. A situation in which sellers of a product or an investment have more information than the buyers, or vice versa, leading one or the other to lose money.

bond. A particularly large type of fixed-income security, usually subjected to a *rating* process by a rating agency to provide assurance to potential investors ("rated bonds"), though unrated bonds, or *notes*, are also used, especially in the social-impact investment universe.

capacity builder. A person or organization that assists another organization or individual in developing a set of skills that can improve its operation and performance.

capital aggregator. An institution that assembles capital from multiple sources and channels it into ventures of various sorts.

capital stack. An arrangement in which different layers, or "tranches," of investment capital, each with its own risk-return characteristics, and therefore each with its own potential class of investors, are combined, or pooled together, in a deal. Also referred to as "structured financing."

collateral. Any form of asset used as security for a loan to be surrendered to lenders in whole or in part if the loan cannot be repaid.

collateralized debt obligation (CDO). A security, or pledge to pay someone, that is backed up by bonds or loans.

community development finance institution. One of a network of approximately 900 community development loan funds, venture capital funds, credit unions, and community development banks in the United States that focus on investing in distressed urban and rural communities and have been designated by the US government as eligible to receive support from the federal government's CDFI support fund.

conduit. An entity, such as a governmental unit, that issues a bond on behalf of the ultimate borrower, or obligor, in order to secure a more favorable interest rate or provide tax or other relief on behalf of the ultimate recipient of the proceeds.

conversion foundation. A charitable foundation formed out of the process of privatizing some public or quasi-public asset, such as a government-owned enterprise, a government-owned building or other property, specialized streams of revenue under government control (e.g., lotteries), or the conversion of a nonprofit into a for-profit company.

convertible note. A debt instrument that can be converted into equity at a later date.

corporate-originated charitable fund. A public charity established by a mutual fund company or financial services firm through which donors can manage, invest, and make distributions from charitable funds or accounts that they set up within the charity, usually utilizing the vehicle of a donor-advised fund.

coupon rate. The stated interest rate paid by borrowers to bondholders, which may differ from the actual *yield* depending on the price that bonds are sold for over time.

credit enhancement. A special inducement such as a guarantee or reserve fund added to loans in order to attract lenders into what are perceived as risky investments.

debt. Any of a number of forms of investment, such as loans, bonds, or mortgages, that convey to investors a claim on repayment of both the original "principal" amount of the investment plus "interest," i.e., a percentage of the original investment, either over time or at an agreed-upon time in the future (the maturity date).

donor-advised fund. A pool of charitable resources that donors deposit for management in community foundations, corporate-originated charitable funds, or other nonprofit institutions, for which the donors receive the full value of their charitable tax deduction at the time of deposit and out of which they make charitable contributions to eligible nonprofit organizations over a period of years.

economically targeted investment (ETI). An investment that a regulated pension fund in the United States is permitted to make in an enterprise that contributes to economic development even though the expected return to the pension fund is below that expected from other investments.

enterprise broker. An individual or institution that performs the critical middleman function of helping social-purpose investors identify promising ventures capable of meeting their investment objectives.

equity investment. An investment that gives an investor an ownership share of an enterprise and hence a claim on a portion of any profits the enterprise generates, as well as the opportunity to sell these shares for a profit at a later date.

finance-first investor. An investor that seeks to achieve a risk-adjusted market rate of return on its investments while still meeting a threshold of social or environmental impact.

fixed-income security. A huge loan with generally long maturity, typically marketed through underwriters or investment banks to various types of investors, including pension funds, insurance companies, and high-net-worth individuals, each of which will take on a portion of the investment.

foundation as philanthropic bank. A foundation that makes use of its assets and not just its grant budget for program-related purposes and that utilizes an assortment of nongrant forms of assistance to achieve greater leverage than is possible with grants alone.

funding collaborative. A network that offers groups of either individual or institutional donors and investors vehicles for collective grantmaking or social-purpose investing.

fund of funds. An investment fund that contains a number of separate funds, each with its own risk and return focus, making it easier to assemble complex funding stacks for particular deals.

greenwashing/impact-washing. An unsubstantiated claim to environmentally or socially impactful outcomes.

impact-first investor. An investor that seeks to maximize the social or environmental impact of its investments while still meeting a threshold of financial return.

initial public offering (IPO). The initial sale of stock in a company whose stock is being listed for sale on a regulated stock exchange.

investment capital. Revenue that fundamentally goes to build long-term organizational capacity and capabilities through the purchase of such things as equipment, facilities, skills, and strategic planning that are expected to generate annual operating revenue for the organization over the longer haul.

liquidity. Funds available for deployment or investment.

liquidity preference. A right extended to preferred stock owners that allows them to get their cash out of an investment before other equity holders in the event of a liquidation or other exit event.

limited liability company (LLC). A flexible form of enterprise that blends elements of partnership and corporate structures, providing limited liability to its owners without the cumbersome regulatory provisions applicable to corporations.

maturity. The date on which a loan must be repaid.

microfinance investment vehicle (MIV). An investment fund serving as the conduit for capital flowing into microfinance investment institutions for ultimate distribution to microenterprise entrepreneurs.

moral hazard. The risk that a party to a transaction has not entered into the contract in good faith, has provided misleading information about its assets, liabilities, or credit capacity, or has an incentive to take unusual risks in an attempt to profit before the other party learns the real facts.

mortgage-backed security. A bond or other fixed-income security backed by home mortgages.

online portals and exchanges. Organizations that make use of the internet to facilitate direct provision of cash, commodities, and/or services (paid and volunteer) to recipient social-purpose organizations.

operating income. The income organizations use to run their ongoing annual operations.

par. The "face value" of a bond, representing the amount that the borrower must repay to investors at maturity.

preferred stock. Equity shares that entitle their owners to a stronger voice in company affairs (via protective provisions and consent rights on important business decisions), higher potential dividend payments, and greater rights to company assets than common stock owners in case of liquidation.

points. Application, origination, or commitment fees calculated as a percentage of the face value of a loan that lenders often charge as a one-time fee for underwriting the loan.

price discovery. Information as to the price at which the market values a financial instrument.

principal. The amount borrowed through a loan.

private equity. An equity investment that is made in a company that is not listed on a regular public stock exchange.

private placement platform. A mechanism through which private investors who meet certain criteria prescribed by regulation can buy and sell securities directly for their own accounts rather than through brokers or publicly accessible markets.

program-related investment (PRI). Support that foundations in the United States are permitted to count toward their required minimum distribution, but that they can provide in the form of loans, equity, or other nongrant financial instruments to for-profit as well as nonprofit organizations so long as the support does not have a commercial purpose and is in furtherance of the foundation's general charitable mission.

promissory note. The legal document typically used to formalize the obligation of a borrower to repay a loan and to record the interest rate the borrower has agreed to pay, the dates on which interest and principal payments are to be made, the penalties in the event of delinquencies in these payments, and the collateral the borrower is putting up in the event of failure to pay on time.

public equity. An equity investment that is made through a registered public stock exchange.

quasi equity. A form of equity investment that allows an investor to benefit from the future revenues of an organization through a royalty payment geared to income rather than a share of any profits earned and that often conveys some advisory role in the management of the organization but not an ownership share.

rated security. A bond that is rated as creditworthy by one of the quasi-official bond rating agencies, such as Standard and Poor's.

resale market. An institution that is involved in reselling financial instruments or other items that have been issued and sold by other entities.

risk-adjusted market rate of return. Financial return, or earnings, on investments equivalent to those available in the market for investments with similar risk exposure for the investor.

secondary market. A financial institution that raises capital through the issuance of bonds and uses it to purchase the loans originated by primary lenders, refreshing the capital available to these lenders so they can make additional primary loans.

secured debt. Debt that is backed by some asset that the lender can seize if a loan is not repaid.

securitization. A financial process that involves assembling bundles of loans (e.g., mortgage loans) into packages and using them as collateral against which to issue bonds on the capital markets, with the proceeds of the bond sales going to pay for the purchase of the bundles of loans.

senior debt/loan. A loan or other debt that has a first call on payment or collateral in the event a borrower is unable to pay its debt obligations.

sequential-pay bond. A bond that pays the holders of different series in a given bond issuance in sequence, with the holders of the bonds in the first set paid off before those in subsequent sets.

servicing. The process of collecting payments on loans, keeping track of delinquencies, sending reminders to borrowers, and initiating foreclosures or other steps to secure payment.

social stock exchange. A regulated trading platform through which dispersed social-purpose investors can locate and invest in social-purpose enterprises and through which social-purpose enterprises can secure capital they need to expand and grow.

soft loan. A loan with flexible terms intended to permit start-up firms time to become profitable.

structured finance. See *capital stack* above.

subordinated debt/loan. A loan or other debt that is paid off only after other lenders or investors are paid, in the event a borrower is unable to pay its full obligations.

syndication. The process of enlisting multiple funders in an investment tranche such as a bond sale.

triple- (double-) bottom-line investment. An investment that seeks significant returns along three (or two) different dimensions: financial, social, and environmental.

underwriting. The process whereby a lender analyzes the information provided by a borrower as part of the due process review to determine whether the borrower meets the lender's criteria for making a loan in terms of years of operation, track record, management and board experience, annual revenue, financial condition, loan-to-value ratio, and debt service coverage.

unsecured debt. Debt that is not backed by a particular asset (collateral) that could be seized in the event a loan is not repaid.

venture capitalist or fund. An individual or organization that makes typically equity, or equity-like, investments in start-up or early-stage for-profit companies and secures significant roles in the management of the companies in an effort to maximize the returns on its investment.

venture philanthropy. A form of foundation operation under which sizable grants are made to a small number of organizations with which the foundation works intensely not only to support programs but also to upgrade management and general operations.

warrant. An investment vehicle that offers an investor the right to purchase common stock at a specific price within a predetermined time period, usually five to 10 years.

yield curve. A curve that expresses the relationship between the interest rate that must be paid to investors on short-term as compared to long-term investments, with the yield curve generally sloping upward since yields are generally higher on longer-term investments than shorter-term ones.

BIBLIOGRAPHY

Aavishkaar. "About Us." http://www.aavishkaar.in/about-us.

Aavishkaar. "Investment Approach." http://www.aavishkaar.in/about-us/investment-approach.

Abdul Latif Jameel Poverty Action Lab, Massachusetts Institute of Technology. "What Is Randomization?" http://www.povertyactionlab.org/methodology/what-randomization.

Accion International. "BancoSol." http://www.accion.org/Page.aspx?pid=666.

Acumen Fund. "About Us." http://www.acumenfund.org/about-us.html.

Acumen Fund. "Acumen Fund Ten Year Report, 2001–2011." 2011. http://www.acumenfund.org/uploads/assets/documents/Acumen%20Fund%20Ten%20Year%20Report%202001%20-%202011a_3wcsNw56.pdf.

Acumen Fund. "Impact Reporting and Investment Standards." 2009. http://iris-standards.org.

Advantage Ventures. "Beyond the Margin: Redirecting Asia's Capitalism." Hong Kong: Advantage Ventures, 2011. http://www.avantageventures.com/sitedocs/av_report_final_full_screen_version.pdf.

Akama: Open Business Directory. "Calvert Ventures." http://www.akama.com/company/Calvert_Ventures_a2b442780462.html.

Altman, Frank. Testimony before the Subcommittee on Public Buildings and Economic Development, Committee on Transportation and Infrastructure, US House of Representatives, February 22, 1995.

Anderson, Chris. "The Long Tail." *Wired*, October 2004.

Anderson, Derek. "Clayton Christensen Talks Venture Capital Crowd Funding and How To Measure your Life." Tech Crunch, April 6, 2013. http://techcrunch.com/2013/04/06/clayton-christensen-talks-venture-capital-crowd-funding-and-how-to-measure-your-life/.

Andresen, Katya. *Robin Hood Marketing: Stealing Corporate Savvy to Sell Just Causes*. San Francisco: Jossey-Bass, 2006.

Andrews, Nancy O. "Taking Capital for Social Purposes to a New Level." *Community Development Investment Review* 2.1 (2006): 69–71. http://www.frbsf.org/community-development/files/cdireviewvol2issue12006.pdf.

Angel Investors Network. "About." http://www.angelinvestors.net/about.

Angove, Janice, Martin Herrndorf, and Brandon Mathews. "Teaching Elephants to Dance: Experiences of Commercial Insurers in Low-Income Markets." In *Protecting the Poor: A Microinsurance Compendium*, vol. 2, ed. Craig Churchill and Michal Matul. Geneva: International Labour Organization and Munich Re Foundation, 2012.

Angove, Janice, and Nacelle Tande. "Is Microinsurance a Profitable Business for Insurance Companies?" In *Protecting the Poor: A Microinsurance Compendium*, vol. 2, ed. Craig Churchill and Michal Matul. Geneva: International Labour Organization and Munich Re Foundation, 2012.

APG. "APG—Home." http://www.apg.nl/apgsite/pages/english.

Aravind. "Aravind Eye Care System Home." http://www.aravind.org.

Arena, Marco." Does Insurance Market Activity Promote Economic Growth? A Cross-Country Study for Industrialized and Developing Countries." World Bank Policy Research Working Paper 4098, 2006.

Arkansas Capital Corporation Group. "Company History & Information." http://arcapital.com/programs/our-history/.

Artha Platform. "Artha Platform—Home." http://www.arthaplatform.com/.

Asad Mahmood. "Microcredit and Capital Markets." In *Market Intelligence: Sustainable Banking; Risk, Reward and the Future of Finance*, ed. Joti Mangat. London: Thomas Reuters, 2010.

Ashoka. "Home." http://www.ashoka.org.

Asian Development Bank. *An Initial Assessment of the Impact of the Earthquake and Tsunami of December 26, 2004 on South and Southeast Asia*. Manila: Asian Development Bank, 2005.

Aspen Institute. "About ANDE." http://www.aspeninstitute.org/policy-work/aspen-network-development-entrepreneurs/about-ande.

Association of Baltimore Area Grantmakers. "Green Funders Affinity Group." http://www.abagrantmakers.org/?GreenFunders.

Auger, Pat, and Timothy M. Devinney. "Do What Consumers Say Matter? The Misalignment of Preferences with Unconstrained Ethical Intentions." *Journal of Business Ethics* 76 (2007): 362.

Aureos Capital. "Home." http://www.aureos.com.

Aurolab. "Home." http://www.aurolab.com.

Austin, Scott. "Entrepreneurs Going the Royalty Route Use a Share of Revenue to Pay Back Loans." *Wall Street Journal*, December 10, 2010.

B Corporation. "B Corporation: Homepage." http://www.bcorporation.net.

Bamboo Finance. "The Bamboo Finance Private Equity Group." www.bamboofinance.com.

Banerjee, Devin. "Will an Indian Billionaire Take the Pledge?" Wall Street Journal India Blog, August 9, 2010. http://blogs.wsj.com/wealth/2010/08/09/will-an-indian-billionaire-take-the-pledge/.

Bank of America. "Bank of America Charitable Gift Fund Program Guidelines and Fees." https://bankofamerica.npportal.org/portal/Policies.aspx#Fees.

Bannick, Matt, and Paula Goldman. "Priming the Pump: The Case for a Sector Based Approach to Impact Investing." Omidyar Network, September 2012. http://www.ignia.com.mx/bop/uploads/media/Priming_the_Pump.pdf.

Baron, Jon. "Applying Evidence to Social Programs." *New York Times*, November 29, 2012. http://economix.blogs.nytimes.com/2012/11/29/applying-evidence-to-social-programs/?_r=0.

Baron, Jon, and Isabel Sawhill. *Federal Programs for Youth: More of the Same Won't Work*. Washington, DC: Coalition for Evidence-Based Policy, 2010.

Baxter, Christie I. *Program-Related Investments: A Technical Manual for Foundations*. New York: John Wiley & Sons, 1997.

Bays, Jonathan, Tony Goland, and Joe Newsum. "Using Prizes to Spur Innovation." *McKinsey Quarterly*, July 2009. http://www.mckinsey.com/insights/innovation/using_prizes_to_spur_innovation.

BBC World Service Trust. "African Media Development Initiative: Research Summary Report." BBC World Service Trust, 2006. http://downloads.bbc.co.uk/worldservice/trust/pdf/AMDI/AMDI_summary_Report.pdf.

Bearman, Jessica. "More Giving Together: The Growth and Impact of Giving Circles and Shared Giving." Forum of Regional Associations of Grantmakers, 2007. http://www.givingforum.org/s_forum/bin.asp?CID=611&DID=5316&DOC=FILE.PDF.

Beartooth Capital. "Beartooth Capital Homepage." http://www.beartoothcap.com.

Becker, Vita. "Charity Project Counts Cost of Alleged Fraud." *Financial Times*, December 16, 2008. http://www.ft.com/cms/s/0/807170de-cbb4-11dd-ba02-000077b07658.html.

Benjamin, Lean, Julia Sass Rubin, and Sean Zielenbach. "Community Development Financial Institutions: Expanding Access to Capital in Under-served Markets." In *The Community Development Reader*, ed. James DeFilippis and Susan Saegert. New York: Routledge, 2008.

Berman, Shari. "Civil Society and the Collapse of the Weimar Republic." *World Politics* 49.3 (1997): 401–29.

Bernanke, Ben. "The Community Reinvestment Act: Its Evolution and New Challenges." Last modified March 30, 2007. http://www.federalreserve.gov/newsevents/speech/bernanke20070330a.htm.

Bernholz, Lucy. *Creating Philanthropic Capital Markets*. Hoboken, NJ: Wiley, 2004.

Bernholz, Lucy. "Why Jumo, Facebook and the Rest Won't Change Everything." *The Guardian*, December 2, 2010. http://www.theguardian.com/voluntary-sector-network/2010/dec/02/online-philanthropy-networks.

Bernholz, Lucy, Kendall Guthrie, and Kaitlin McGaw. "Philanthropic Connections: Mapping the Landscape of U.S. Funder Networks." Forum of Regional Associations of Grantmakers, Spring 2003, 5–6. http://www.blueprintrd.com/text/rag.pdf.

Bernholz, Lucy, and Lisa Richter. "Advancing Equity: How Community Philanthropy Can Build Racial and Social Equity through Mission Investing." Blueprint Research & Design and GPS Capital Partners, 2009. http://www.communityphilanthropy.org/downloads/Equity%20Advancing%20Equity%20Full%20Report.pdf.

Bester, Hennie, Doubell Chamberlain, and Christine Hougaard. "Making Insurance Markets Work for the Poor: Policy, Regulation and Supervision: Evidence from Five Country Case Studies." Cenfri, 2008. http://cenfri.org/documents/microinsurance/2008/Cross-country_Impact%20of%20regulation%20on%20microinsurance%20development_2008.pdf.

Bester, Hennie, Doubell Chamberlain, Ryan Hawthorne, Stephan Malherbe, and Richard Walker. "Making Insurance Markets Work for the Poor in South Africa, Botswana, Namibia, Lesotho and Swaziland—Scoping Study." Genesis Analytics, 2004.

Big Society Capital. "How We are Funded." http://www.bigsocietycapital.com/how-we-are-funded.

Big Society Capital. "Social Investment Is a Way of Using Capital to Generate Social Impact as well as Some Financial Return for Investors." http://www.bigsocietycapital.com/what-social-investment.

Bill and Melinda Gates Foundation. "Foundation Fact Sheet." http://www.gatesfoundation.org/about/Pages/foundation-fact-sheet.aspx.

Bishop, Matthew. "The Birth of Philanthrocapitalism." *The Economist*, February 23, 2006.

Bishop, Matthew. "Elon Musk and the Giving Pledge: Space, Electric Cars and Philanthropy." *The Economist Online*, video, 5:52, May 18, 2012. http://www.economist.com/blogs/babbage/2012/05/elon-musk-and-giving-pledge.

Bishop, Matthew. "Philanthrocapitalism on Trial." *Chronicle of Philanthropy*, October 30, 2008. http://philanthropy.com/article/Philanthrocapitalism-on-Trial/57010.

Bishop, Matthew, and Michael Green. "The Capital Curve for a Better World." *Innovations* 5.1 (2010): 25–33.

Bishop, Matthew, and Michael Green. *Philanthrocapitalism: How Giving Can Save the World*. New York: Bloomsbury Press, 2009.

Bishop, Matthew, and Michael Green. *The Road from Ruin: How to Revive Capitalism and Put America Back on Top*. New York: Crown, 2010.

Bishop, Matthew, and Michael Green. *Philanthrocapitalism: How the Rich Can Save the World*. New York: Bloomsbury Press, 2008.

B-Lab. "About B-lab." http://www.benefitcorp.net/about-b-lab.

B-Lab. "How GIIRS Works." http://www.giirs.org/about-giirs/how-giirs-works.

Blended Value. "About Blended Value." http://www.blendedvalue.org/about/.

Bloomberg Businessweek. "Online Extra: Yunus Blasts Compartamos." *Bloomberg Businessweek*, December 13, 2007, http://www.businessweek.com/magazine/content/07_52/b4064045920958.htm.

Blue Orchard. "Fact Sheet." http://www.blueorchard.com/jahia/webdav/site/blueorchard/shared/Publications%20and%20Resources/BlueOrchard%20Factsheets/0907_Fact%20sheet%202009_EN.pdf.

Blue Orchard. "How We Operate." http://www.blueorchard.com/jahia/Jahia/pid/358.

Board of Governors of the Federal Reserve System. "Federal Reserve Statistical Release, Z.l, Flow of Funds Accounts of the United States, March 2011." http://www.federalreserve.gov.releases/z1/201000311.

Bolton, Emily, Suzanne Ashman, and Sarah Henderson. "Social Impact Bonds: The One* Service, One Year On." London: Social Finance, November 2011. http://socialfinanceus.org/sites/socialfinanceus.org/files/sf_peterborough_one__year_on.pdf.

Bolton, Emily, and Louise Savell. "Towards a New Social Economy: Blended Value Creation through Social Impacts Bonds." Social Finance, 2010. http://www.socialfinance.org.uk/sites/default/files/Towards_A_New_Social_Economy_web.pdf.

Bond Buyer, The. "2010 in Statistics." Published February 14, 2011. http://www.bondbuyer.com/pdfs/2010yrend.pdf.

Bornstein, David. *How to Change the World: Social Entrepreneurs and the Power of New Ideas*. New York: Oxford University Press, 2004.

Borzaga, Carlos, and Jacques Defourny. *The Emergence of Social Enterprise*. New York: Routledge, 2001.

Boston Community Capital. "Home." http://www.bostoncommunitycapital.org.

Bourdieu, Pierre. *The Logic of Practice*. Trans. Richard Nice. Stanford: Stanford University Press, 1990.

Bourdieu, Pierre. *Outline of a Theory of Practice*. Trans. Richard Nice. Cambridge: Cambridge University Press, 1977.

Bowman, Woods. "The Uniqueness of Nonprofit Finance and the Decision to Borrow." *Nonprofit Management & Leadership* 12.3 (2002): 293–311.

Brainard, Lael. "What Is the Role of Insurance in Economic Development?" Zurich Government and Industry Thought Leadership Series No. 2. Zurich Financial Services Limited, 2008.

Branding Strategy Insider. "Social Responsibility: The Nike Story." July 25, 2008. http://www.brandingstrategyinsider.com/2008/07/social-responsi.html.

Brest, Paul. "Smart Money." *Stanford Social Innovation Review*, 2.1 (Winter 2003): 44–53.

Brest, Paul, and Hal Harvey. *Money Well Spent: A Strategic Plan for Smart Philanthropy*. New York: Bloomberg Press, 2008.

Brewster, Deborah. "Charities Face Winding Down." *Financial Times*, December 17, 2008. http://www.ft.com/cms/s/0/31685748-cc6b-11dd-9c43-000077b07658.html.

Bridges Ventures. "Portfolio Exits." http://www.bridgesventures.com/node/177.

Brody, Francie, Kevin McQueen, Christa Velasquz, and John Weiser. "Current Practices in Program-Related Investing." Brody, Weiser, Burns, 2002. http://www.brodyweiser.com/pdf/currentpracticesinpri.pdf.

Bronfman, Charles, and Jeffrey Solomon. *The Art of Giving: Where the Soul Meets a Business Plan*. San Francisco: Jossey-Bass, 2009.

Brown, Adrian, and Will Norman. "Lighting the Touchpaper: Growing the Market for Social Investment in England." Boston Consulting Group and Young Foundation, 2011.http://youngfoundation.org/publications/lighting-the-touchpaper-growing-the-market-for-social-investment-in-england/.

Brown, Lester. *World on Edge: How to Prevent Environmental and Economic Collapse*. New York: Norton, 2011.

Brown, Michael, AnnMaura Connolly, Alan Khazei, Wendy Kopp, Michelle Nunn, Gregg Petersmeyer, Shirley Sagawa, and Harris Wofford. "A Call to National Service." *American Interest* 3.3 (January–February 2008).

Brummer, Chris, Josh Friedman, Billy Lockyer, and Duncan Niederauer. "The Future of Wall Street and the Financial Industry." Paper presented at the Milken Institute, May 3, 2011. http://milkeninstitute.org/presentations/slides/2740GC11.pdf.

BTW Consultants. *GGCI Social Impact Report 2006: What a Difference a Job Makes. The Long-Term Impact of Enterprise Employment*. San Francisco: REDF, 2006.

Bugg-Levine, Antony, and Jed Emerson. *Impact Investing: Transforming How We Make Money While Making a Difference*. San Francisco: Jossey-Bass, 2011.

Buhl, Alice C. "Local Donor Collaboration: Lessons from Baltimore and Beyond." Association of Baltimore Area Grantmakers, 2004. http://www.aecf.org/upload/publicationfiles/pb3622h802.pdf, 15.

Buhrer, Colleen. "Service as a Strategy: Addressing Critical National Needs." Innovations in Civic Participation. November 2008.

Bumpus, Kyle. "Best Index Funds: Does Vanguard Still Rule the Roost?" Amateur Asset Allocator, published March 9, 2010. http://amateurassetallocator.com/2010/03/09/best-index-funds-does-vanguard-still-rule-the-roost.

Buteau, Ellie. *More Than Money: Making a Difference with Assistance beyond the Grant*. Boston: Center for Effective Philanthropy, 2008.

Byrne, John A. "The New Face of Philanthropy." *Business Week*, December 2, 2002. http://www.businessweek.com/magazine/content/02_48/b3810001.htm.

Cabinet Office. "Growing the Social Investment Market: A Vision and Strategy." Cabinet Office, February 2011. https://www.gov.uk/government/uploads/system/uploads/attachment_data/file/61185/404970_SocialInvestmentMarket_acc.pdf.

California Wellness Foundation. "Financial Statements." http://www.calwellness.org/assets/docs/annual_report/TCWF_FS_2008.pdf.

Callaghan, Ian, Henry Gonzalez, Diane Maurice, and Christian Novak. "Microfinance—On the Road to Capital Market." *Journal of Applied Corporate Finance* 19.1 (2007): 120.

CalPERS. "Attachment 3, Equity Term Sheet." http://www.calpers.ca.gov/eip-docs/about/board-cal-agenda/agendas/invest/201109/item07c-03.pdf.

CalPERS. "California Public Employees' Retirement System Statement of Investment Policy for Economically Targeted Investment Program." http://www.calpers.ca.gov/eip-docs/investments/policies/other/economically-targeted/eco-target-inv-prg.pdf.

Calvert Foundation. "Calvert Foundation—Home." http://www.calvertfoundation.org.

Calvert Foundation. "Community Investment Note." http://www.calvertfoundation.org/invest/how-to-invest/community-investment-note.

Calvert Foundation. "Mission and History." http://www.calvertfoundation.org/index.php?option=com_content&view=article&id=66&Itemid=76.

Cambridge Associates. "Mission Related Investing." http://www.cambridgeassociates.com/foundations_endowments/working_together/specialized_expertise/mission_related_investing.html.

Campanale, Mark. *Mission Related Investing and Charities*. London: Henderson Global Investors, 2005.

Canadian Task Force on Social Finance. "Mobilizing Capital for the Public Good: Measuring Progress during Year One." SocialFinance.ca, December 2011.

Capgemini and Merrill Lynch Wealth Management. "World Wealth Report." 2009. http://www.ml.com/media/113831.pdf.

Capital Link. "Capital Plans and Needs of Health Centers: A National Perspective." June 2012.

Carbon Disclosure Project. "Carbon Disclosure Project—Home." https://www.cdproject.net/en-US/Pages/HomePage.aspx.

Carden, Steven, and Olive Darragh. "A Halo for Angel Investors." *McKinsey Quarterly* 1 (2004).

Carlson, Neil. "Program-Related Investing Skills, Strategies for New PRI Funders." Grantcraft, 16. http://www.grantcraft.org/index.cfm?fuseaction=Page.viewPage&pageID=821.

Carmody, Lucy, Benjamin McCarron, Jenny Blinch, and Allison Prevatt. *Impact Investing in Emerging Markets*. Singapore: Responsible Research, May 2011.

Carnegie, Andrew. "Wealth." *North American Review* 391 (June 1889): 653–64.

CARS™: Opportunity Finance Network. "CARS™ Brochure." http://www.carsratingsystem.net/pdfs/CARS™Brochure.pdf.

Case Foundation. "About the Case Foundation." http://www.casefoundation.org/.

CDFI Fund. "Special Opportunities in the Community Development Financial Institutions Fund." US Department of Treasury, CDFI Fund, n.d. http://www.cdfifund.gov/who_we_are/SpecialOpportuniesAtCDFI.pdf.

CEI Ventures. "Overview." http://www.ceiventures.com.

Center for Global Development and Social Finance. "Development Impact Bond Working Group Report Consultation Draft." June 2013. http://www.cgdev.org/sites/default/files/DIB_WG_REPORT.pdf.

Center for MicroFinance. *Fifth Semi-annual Report on Pilot Testing of Microinsurance Services to Poor Clients of MFIs in Nepal*. Kathmandu: Center for MicroFinance, 2005.

CGAP. "About Us." http://www.cgap.org/p/site/c/aboutus/.

CGAP Microfinance Gateway. "Profund Internacional." http://www.microfinancegateway.org/p/site/m/template.rc/1.11.47720/.

Chapel, Paige, Tess Colby, and Jon Schwartz. "Community Development Loan Funds." Sector Landscape and Financial Analysis, Altrushares Securities and CARS, September 2012. http://altrushare.com/pdf/CDLF_Sept2012.pdf.

Charities Aid Foundation. "Charity Donations Fall as Demand for Their Services Grows." Charities Aid Foundation news release, September 14, 2008. http://www.cafonline.org/default.aspx?page=16118.

Chatterjee, Arup. "Access to Insurance and Financial Sector Regulation." In *Protecting the Poor: A Microinsurance Compendium*, vol. 2, ed. Craig Churchill and Michal Matul. Geneva: International Labour Organization and Munich Re Foundation, 2012.

Chavez Avila, Rafael, and José Luis Monzón Campos. "The Social Economy in the European Union." CIRIEC Working Paper, 2008.

Cheng, Paul, ed. "The Impact Investor's Handbook: Lessons from the World of Microfinance." Charities Aid Foundation, Market Insight Series, February 2011. http://www.cafonline.org/pdf/impact_investor_report_2011.pdf.

Choi, Laura. "Creating a Marketplace: Information Exchange and the Secondary Market for Community Development Loans." Federal Reserve Bank of San Francisco Working Paper 2007-01, July 2007. http://www.frbsf.org/community-development/files/wp07-011.pdf.

Chronicle of Philanthropy. "Philanthropy 400 Data." Published for 2011. http://philanthropy.com/section/Philanthropy-400/237/.

Chu, Michael. "Commercial Returns at the Base of the Pyramid." *Innovations* 2.1–2 (2007), 115–146. DOI:10.1162/itgg.2007.2.1-2.115.

Churchill, Craig, and Monique Cohen. "Marketing Microinsurance." In *Protecting the Poor: A Microinsurance Compendium*, ed. Craig Churchill. Geneva: International Labour Organization and Munich Re Foundation, 2006.

Churchill, Craig, Dominic Liber, Michael J. McCord, and Jim Roth. *Making Insurance Work for Microfinance Institutions: A Technical Guide to Developing and Delivering Microinsurance*. Geneva: Social Finance Programme, International Labour Organization, 2003.

Churchill, Craig, and Michael J. McCord. "Emerging Trends in Microinsurance." In *Protecting the Poor: A Microinsurance Compendium*, vol. 2, ed. Craig Churchill and Michal Matul. Geneva: International Labor Organization and Munich Re Foundation, 2012.

City of New York, Office of the Mayor. "Mayor Bloomberg, Deputy Mayor Gibbs, and Corrections Commissioner Schriro Announce the Nation's First Social Impact Bond Program." Published August 2, 2012. http://www.nyc.gov.

Clark, Catherine, Jed Emerson, Julia Balandina, Robert Katz, Katherine Milligan, Robert Ruttmann, and Brian Trelstad. *Investing for Impact: How Social Entrepreneurship Is Redefining the Meaning of Return*. Zurich: Credit Suisse, January 2012.

Clark-Herrera, Eugene, and Darrin Glymph, *Charter Schools: Borrowing with Tax Exempt Bonds*. San Francisco: Orrick, Herrington & Sutcliffe, 2009.

Clements, Benedict, et al. "Case Studies on Energy Subsidy Reform: Lessons and Implications." International Monetary Fund, January 28, 2013. http://www.imf.org/external/np/pp/eng/2013/012813a.pdf.

Clifton Gunderson. "Study Shows Online Donors Respond in Crisis Situations." *Nonprofit Insight Newsletter* 1 (2007). http://www.cliftongunderson.com/Content/K1C56KGA0X.pdf?Name.pdf.

Clinton, Hillary. "Inclusive Finance: A Path to the MDGs Luncheon." Speech at the Helmsley Hotel, New York City. September 22, 2010. http://www.state.gov/secretary/rm/2010/09/147595.htm.

Cluetrain. "The Cluetrain Manifesto, 95 Theses." http://www.cluetrain.com.

Coalition for Evidence Based Policy. "Rigorous Program Evaluations on a Budget." March 2012. http://coalition4evidence.org/wp-content/uploads/Rigorous-Program-Evaluations-on-a-Budget-March-2012.pdf.

Coalition of Community Development Financial Institutions. "About the CDFI Coalition." http://cdfi.org/index.php?page=info-1a.

Cohen, Monique, and Jennifer Sebstad. "The Demand for Microinsurance." In *Protecting the Poor: A Microinsurance Compendium*, ed. Craig Churchill. Geneva: International Labour Organization and Munich Re Foundation, 2006.

Cohen, Rick. "A Conversation with California Congressman Xavier Becerra." The Cohen Report, January 16, 2008. http://www.nonprofitquarterly.org/cohenreport/2008/01/16/a-conversation-with-california-congressman-xavier-becerra/.

Cohen, Rick. "Fidelity's Charitable Gift Fund Shows Well in Recession." *Nonprofit Quarterly*, March 15, 2010. http://www.nonprofitquarterly.org/index.php?option=com_content&view=article&id=1997.

Cohen, Rick. "Making Charitable Money Flow: Mixed Results with Donor-Advised Funds." *Nonprofit Quarterly*, August 22, 2013. http://www.nonprofitquarterly.org/philanthropy/22829-making-charitable-money-flow-mixed-results-with-donor-advised-funds.html.

Community Capital Management. *CRA Qualified Investment Fund Annual Report*. Published May 31, 2012. http://www.crafund.com/general.php?category=CRA-Investors.

Community Development Finance Association. "CDFA: Annual Review 2007." Published June 2007. http://www.cdfa.org.uk/wp-content/uploads/2011/02/Annual-Review-07-Final.pdf.

Community Development Financial Institutions Fund. "Capital Magnet Fund." Last modified June 8, 2012. http://www.cdfifund.gov/what_we_do/programs_id.asp?programID=11.

Community Development Financial Institutions Fund. "Community Development Financial Institutions Program." Last modified September 13, 2012. http://www.cdfifund.gov/what_we_do/programs_id.asp?programid=7.

Community Development Financial Institutions Fund. "The Financial Crisis and CDFIs: A Brief Look at 2007–2009 CIIS Data." March 1, 2011. http://www.cdfifund.gov/impact_we_make/research/CDFI%20Crisis%20Trend%202007-2009%20Presentation.pdf.

Community Development Financial Institutions Fund. "Financing Healthy Food Options." Last modified May 5, 2012. http://www.cdfifund.gov/what_we_do/FinancingHealthyFoodOptions.asp?programID=13.

Community Development Financial Institutions Fund. "New Markets Tax Credit Program." Last modified September 23, 2012. http://cdfifund.gov/what_we_do/programs_id.asp?programID=5.

Community Development Financial Institutions. "Providing Capital, Building Communities, Creating Impact: CDFI Data Project 2008." http://www.opportunityfinance.net/store/product.asp?pID=177.

Community Development Institutions Fund. "931 Certified Community Development Financial Institutions as of 11/30/2010." Last modified December 14, 2010. http://www.cdfifund.gov/docs/certification/cdfi/CDFIList-ByType-11-30-10.pdf.

Community Development Venture Capital Alliance. "About Us—CDVCA." http//www.cdvca.org.

Community Reinvestment Fund. "Quick Facts." http://www.crfusa.com/AboutCRF/Pages/QuickFacts.aspx.

Community Wealth Ventures. *Venture Philanthropy 2001: The Changing Landscape.* Washington, DC: Morino Institute, 2001.

Compartamos Banco. "Compartamos Banco." http://www.compartamos.com/wps/portal.

Confluence Philanthropy. "Home." http://www.confluencephilanthropy.org/.

Conner, Alana, and Keith Epstein. "Harnessing Purity and Pragmatism." *Stanford Social Innovation Review* 5.4 (Fall 2007): 61–65.

Conroy, Emma. "Conscientious Consumerism Pushes Sales of Ethical Products to an All-Time High." ReportBuyer, May 23, 2007. http://www.reportbuyer.com/blog/conscientious-consumerism-pushes-sales-of-ethical-products-to-an-all-time-high.

Conservation Company. *Building the Capacity of Capacity Builders.* Philadelphia: Conservation Company, 2003.

Consultative Group to Assist the Poor. "About." http://www.cgap.org/about.

Consultative Group to Assist the Poor. *Financial Access 2009.* Washington DC: Consultative Group to Assist the Poor and World Bank, 2009.

Cooch, Sarah and Mark Kramer, with Fi Cheng, Adeeb Mahmud, Ben Marx, and Matthew Rehrig. "Compounding Impact: Mission Investing by U.S. Foundations." FSG Social Impact Advisors, March 2007. http://www.fsg-impact.org/ideas/pdf/Compounding%20Impact(5).pdf.

Co-operative Bank. "Ethical Consumerism Report 2008." Co-operative Bank, 2008. http://www.goodwithmoney.co.uk/assets/Uploads/Documents/ECR_2008_Web.pdf.

Co-operative Bank. *Ten Years of Ethical Consumerism: 1999–2008*. London: Co-operative Bank, 2009.

Corporate Register. "Corporate Register Webpage." http://www.corporateregister.com.

Corporation for National and Community Service. "Social Innovation Fund: Supporting Community Solutions." http://www.nationalservice.gov/about/serveamerica/innovation.asp.

Council of Foundations. "Donor Advised Funds Provide the Majority of Grant Funds Awarded by Community Foundations." Published January 13, 2009. http://www.cof.org/files/Documents/Research/08donoradvisedpaper.pdf.

Council on Foundations. "The Program-Related Investment Promotion Act of 2008: A Proposal for Encouraging Charitable Investments." http://www.cof.org/files/Documents/Conferences/LegislativeandRegulatory06.pdf.

Council on Foundations and Grantmakers for Effective Organizations. "Evaluation in Philanthropy: Perspectives from the Field." December 2009. http://www.geofunders.org/publications.aspx.

Cowe, Roger, and Simon Williams. *Who Are the Ethical Consumers?* London: Cooperative Bank, 2000.

Coydon, Marie-Amandine, and Véronique Molitor. *Commercial Insurers in Microinsurance*. Luxembourg: Microinsurance Network, 2011.

Crickett, John. "Enterprise Capital Funds: Are They Working?" Business Opportunities and Ideas Blog, November 30, 2007. http://www.businessopportunitiesandideas.com/508/enterprise-capital-funds-are-they-working.

Criterion Institute. "Women Effect Investments." http://criterioninstitute.org/womeneffectinvestments/.

Crouch, Colin. *The Strange Non-death of Neo-liberalism*. London: Polity Press, 2011.

Crutchfield, Leslie, John V. Kania, and Mark R. Kramer. *Do More Than Give: The Six Practices of Donors Who Change the World*. San Francisco: Jossey-Bass, 2011.

Cunningham, Katie, and Marc Ricks. "Why Measure? Nonprofits Use Metrics to Show That They Are Efficient. But What If Donors Don't Care?" *Stanford Social Innovation Review* 2.1 (Summer 2004): 44–51.

Cushnie, Lorraine. "SRI Funds Hit by Market Turmoil." *Investment Week*, November 13, 2009. http://www.investmentweek.co.uk/investment-week/news/1562065/sri-funds-hit-market-turmoil.

Dalal, Aparna, and Jonathan Morduch. "The Psychology of Microinsurance: Small Changes Can Make a Surprising Difference." In *Protecting the Poor: A Microinsurance Compendium*, vol. 2, ed. Craig Churchill and Michal Matul. Geneva: International Labour Organization and Munich Re Foundation, 2012.

Daley-Harris, Sam. "State of the Microcredit Summit Campaign Report." Microcredit Summit Campaign, 2009. https://promujer.org/empowerment/dynamic/our_publications_5_Pdf_EN_SOCR2009%20English.pdf.

Daniel-Echols, M., and Z. Xiang. "2000–2003 Follow-up Study of JumpStart Children." High Scope Educational Research Foundation, 2003.

Davis, Roger, and Alexandra Davis. *Nonprofit Corporations Borrowing with Tax Exempt Bonds*. San Francisco: Orrick, Herrington & Sutcliffe, 2001.

Deacon, Stefan, and Martina Kirchberger. *Literature Review on Microinsurance*. Geneva: Microinsurance Innovation Facility, International Labour Organization, 2008.

Deaton, Angus. "Instruments, Randomization and Learning about Development." Princeton University Program in Development Studies, Research Paper 269, 2010.

Deblon, Yvonne, and Markus Loewe. "The Potential of Microinsurance for Social Protection." In *Protecting the Poor: A Microinsurance Compendium*, vol. 2, ed. Craig

Churchill and Michal Matul. Geneva: International Labour Organization and Munich Re Foundation, 2012.

Defourny, Jacques, and Marthe Nyssens. "Social Enterprise in Europe: Recent Trends and Developments." EMES Working Paper No. 08/01, 2008. http://www.emes.net/what-we-do/publications/working-papers/social-enterprise-in-europe-recent-trends-and-developments/.

Dell and RGK Center for Philanthropy and Community Service. "Dell Social Innovation Challenge." http://www.dellchallenge.org/.

Deloitte and the Grocery Manufacturers Association. "Finding the Green in Today's Shoppers." http://www.deloitte.com/dtt/cda/doc/content/US_CP_GMADeloitteGreenShopperStudy_2009.pdf.

Deutsche Bank Research. "Microfinance: An Emerging Investment Opportunity." Published December 19, 2007. http://www.dbresearch.com/PROD/DBR_INTERNET_EN-PROD/PROD0000000000219174.pdf.

Dickinson, Roger A., and Mary L. Carsky. In *The Ethical Consumer*, ed. Rob Harrison, Terry Newholm, and Deirdre Shaw. London: Sage, 2005.

Dighe, Atul. "Demographic and Technological Imperatives." In *The State of Nonprofit America*, 2nd ed., ed. Lester M. Salamon. Washington, DC: Brookings Institution Press, 2012.

DiPasquale, Denise, and Jean L. Cummings. "Financing Multifamily Rental Housing: The Changing Role of Lenders and Investors." *Housing Policy Debate* 3.1 (1992): 22.

Domini Social Investments. "Domini—Home." http://domini.com.

Domini, Amy. *Socially Responsible Investment: Making a Difference and Making Money*. Chicago: Dearborn Trade, 2000.

Domini, Amy, Peter Kinder, and Steve Lydenberg, eds. *The Social Investment Almanac: A Comprehensive Guide to Socially Responsible Investing*. New York: Henry Holt, 1992.

DonorsChoose. "Impact to Date." http://www.donorschoose.org/about/impact.html.

Dorfman, Robert. *Measuring Benefits of Government Investments*. Washington, DC: Brookings Institution Press, 1965.

Dorfman, Robert, and Michael H. Rothkopf. "Why Benefit-Cost Analysis Is Widely Disregarded and What to Do about It." *Interfaces* 26.5 (1996): 1–6.

Down Jones with SAM. "Dow Jones Sustainability Indexes." http://www.sustainability-index.com.

Drexler, Michael, and Abigail Noble. Preface to "From the Margins to the Mainstream: Assessment of the Impact Investment Sector and Opportunities to Engage Mainstream Investors," by Michael Drexler et al. World Economic Forum, September 2013. http://www3.weforum.org/docs/WEF_II_FromMarginsMainstream_Report_2013.pdf.

Drexler, Michael, et al. "From the Margins to the Mainstream: Assessment of the Impact Investment Sector and Opportunities to Engage Mainstream Investors." World Economic Forum, September 2013. http://www3.weforum.org/docs/WEF_II_FromMarginsMainstream_Report_2013.pdf.

Dror, David, and Christian Jacquier. "Micro-insurance: Extending Health Insurance to the Excluded." *International Social Security Association Review* 52.1 (1999): 71–97.

Dror, Iddo, Aparna Dalal, and Michal Matul. *Emerging Practices in Consumer Education on Risk Management and Insurance*. Geneva: Microinsurance Innovation Facility, International Labour Organization, 2010.

Duncan, Allison, and Georgette Wong. "Social Metrics in Investing: The Future Depends on Financial Outperformance and Leadership." *Community Development Investment Review* 6.1 (2006): 60.

Dunn, Brittany. "Neighborhood Housing Services of America is Closing Shop." DSNews, June 11, 2010. http://www.dsnews.com/articles/neighborhood-housing-services-of-america-is-closing-shop-2010-06-11.

E.T. Jackson and Associates. "Accelerating Impact: Achievements, Challenges and What's Next in Building the Impact Investing Industry." Rockefeller Foundation, July 2012. http://www.rockefellerfoundation.org/uploads/images/fda23ba9-ab7e-4c83-9218-24fdd79289cc.pdf.

Easterly, William. *The Elusive Quest for Growth: Economists' Adventures and Misadventures in the Tropics.* Cambridge: MIT Press, 2001.

Ebrahim, Alnoor, and V. Kasturi Rangan. "The Limits of Nonprofit Impact: A Contingency Framework for Measuring Social Performance." Harvard Business School Working Paper 10-099, 2010.

Economic Innovation International. "Economic Innovation International Homepage." http://www.economic-innovation.com/.

Economist. "Ivory-Towering Infernos." *The Economist,* December 11, 2008. http://www.economist.com/node/12778077.

Economist. "Small Enough to Fail: The Sorry End to a Bold Banking Experiment." *The Economist,* August 28, 2010.

Edna McConnell Clark Foundation. "How We Work." http://www.emcf.org/how-we-work/.

Edwards, Michael. *Civil Society.* Cambridge: Polity Press, 2009.

Edwards, Michael. *Just Another Emperor? The Myths and Realities of Philanthrocapitalism.* New York: Demos, 2008.

Edwards, Michael. *Small Change: Why Business Won't Save the World.* San Francisco: Berrett-Koehler, 2010.

Eikenberry, Angela. "Fundraising in the New Philanthropy Environment: The Benefits and Challenges of Working with Giving Circles." *Nonprofit Management and Leadership* 19.2 (2008): 141–52.

Eikenberry, Angela. *Giving Circles: Philanthropy, Voluntary Association, and Democracy.* Bloomington: Indiana University Press, 2009.

Eikenberry, Angela, and Jessica E. Bearman. *The Impact of Giving Together: Giving Circles' Influence on Members' Philanthropic and Civic Behaviors, Knowledge, and Attitudes.* Washington, DC: Forum of Regional Associations of Grantmakers, 2009.

Elhauge, Einer. "Sacrificing Corporate Profits in the Public Interest." Prepared for Environmental Protection and the Social Responsibility of Firms. December 6, 2003. http://www.hks.harvard.edu/m-rcbg/Events/Papers/RPP_2-12-04_Elhauge.pdf.

Elson, D., L. Johns, and J. Petrie. "JumpStart's Service Learning Initiative: Enhanced Outcomes for At-Risk Children." In *From Passion to Objectivity: International and Cross-Disciplinary Perspectives on Service Learning Research,* ed. Shelly Billig and Sherril B. Gelmon. Charlotte, NC: Information Age Publishing, 2007.

Emerging Markets Committee of the International Organization of Securities. *Securitization and Securitized Debt Instruments in Emerging Markets Final Report.* IOSCO, 2010.

Emerson, Jed. "The Blended Value Proposition: Integrating Social and Financial Returns." *California Management Review* 45.4 (2003): 35–51.

Emerson, Jed, and Antony Bugg-Levine. *Impact investing: Transforming How We Make Money While Making a Difference.* New York: Jossey-Bass, 2011.

Emerson, Jed, Jay Wachowicz, and Suzi Chun. "Social Return on Investment (SROI): Exploring Aspects of Value Creation." Harvard Business School, Working Knowledge for Business Leaders, January 29, 2001. http://hbswk.hbs.edu/archive/1957.html.

Enterprise Capital Fund Guidance for Applicants, Third Round. April 2008. http://www.bis.gov.uk/files/file45483.pdf.

Erickson, David. "NeighborWorks America: Symposium Proceedings." San Francisco, Federal Reserve Bank of San Francisco. Forthcoming.

Erickson, David. "The Secondary Market for Community Development Loans: Conference Proceedings." *Community Development Investment Review* 2.2 (2006): 8–23. http://www.frbsf.org/community-development/files/investmentreview.pdf.

Erickson, David J. *The Housing Policy Revolution: Networks and Neighborhoods.* Washington, DC: Urban Institute, 2009.

Escobar, Arturo. *Encountering Development.* Princeton, NJ: Princeton University Press, 1995.

Ethical Property. "How to Invest." http://www.ethicalproperty.co.uk/howtoinvest.php.

European Venture Philanthropy Association. "About Us." http://evpa.eu.com/.

European Venture Philanthropy Association. *European Venture Philanthropy Directory 2010/11.* Brussels: European Venture Philanthropy Association, 2010.

European Venture Philanthropy Association. "European Venture Philanthropy Industry: Preliminary Results of First EVPA Survey." Published November 16, 2011. http://evpa.eu.com/wp-content/uploads/2010/08/VP-Industry-data_for-conference_FINAL.pdf.

European Venture Philanthropy Association. "EVPA—About Us." October 12, 2012. http://evpa.eu.com/about-us.

Eurosif. "European SRI Study 2010." Rev. ed. Eurosif, November 2010. http://www.eurosif.org/research/eurosif-sri-study/2010.

Eurosif. "European SRI Study: 2012." Eurosif, 2012. http://www.eurosif.org/research/eurosif-sri-study/sri-study-2012.

Evenett, Rupert, and Karl H. Richter. *Making Good in Social Impact Investment: Opportunities in an Emerging Asset Class.* London: Social Investment Business and The City UK, 2011.

F.B. Heron Foundation. "HFHI Write-up & Checklist." Unpublished internal document, 2008.

F.B. Heron Foundation. "Mission Investing at the F.B. Heron Foundation: Data Summary." Unpublished internal document, December 31, 2009.

F.B. Heron Foundation. *New Frontiers in Mission-Related Investing.* New York: F.B. Heron Foundation, 2004.

Fabozzi, Frank, Henry A. Davis, and Moorad Choudry. *Introduction to Structured Finance.* Hoboken, NJ: Wiley, 2006.

Fabozzi, Frank, Michael Ferri, and Steven Mann. "Overview of the Types and Features of Fixed Income Securities." In *The Handbook of Fixed Income Securities*, ed. Frank Fabozzi, 5. New York: McGraw-Hill, 2005.

Fabozzi, Frank, Richard Wilson, and Richard Todd. "Corporate Bonds." In *The Handbook of Fixed Income Securities*, ed. Frank Fabozzi, 320–22. New York: McGraw-Hill, 2005.

Fabrikant, Geraldine. "Yale's Endowment Drops 13.4%." *New York Times*, December 18, 2008. http://opa.yale.edu/news/article.aspx?id=6899#.

Fannie Mae. "About Fannie Mae." http://www.fanniemae.com/kb/index?page=home&c=aboutus.

Federal Financial Institutions Examination Council. "Community Reinvestment Act." Last modified August 21, 2012. http://www.ffiec.gov/cra/.

Federal Financial Institutions Examination Council. "Community Reinvestment Act, National Aggregate Reports." http://www.ffiec.gov/craadweb/national.aspx; $.

Federal Home Loan Bank of Atlanta. "Partnerships Online." Federal Home Loan Bank of Atlanta: Online Partnerships. "FlexCAP: Helping Finance: Habitat's Mission." Published Fall 2010. http://corp.fhlbatl.com/PartnershipsFall10.aspx?id=2489.

Federal Reserve Bank of New York. "Historical Changes of the Target Federal Funds and Discount Rates." http://www.newyorkfed.org/markets/statistics/dlyrates/fedrate.html.

Federal Reserve Bank of San Francisco. "Secondary Markets for Community Development Loans." *Community Development Investment Review*, Special Issue, 2.1 (June 2006). http://www.frbsf.org/community-development/publications/community-development-investment-review/2006/june/secondary-markets-community-development-loans.

Federal Street Advisors. "About Us." http://www.federalstreet.com/.

Feldstein, Sylvan, Frank Fabozzi, and Patrick Kennedy. "Municipal Bonds." In *The Handbook of Fixed Income Securities*, ed. Frank Fabozzi, 280–82. New York: McGraw-Hill, 2005.

Feltner, Tom. "Over Community Objections, the Federal Reserve Approves Capital One Acquisition of ING." Woodstock Institute Blog, published February 15, 2012. http://www.woodstockinst.org/blog/blog/over-community-objections,-the-federal-reserve-approves-capital-one-acquisition-of-ing/.

Ferguson, James. *The Anti-politics Machine*. Minneapolis: University of Minnesota Press, 1994.

Fidelity Charitable. "Learn about Charity." http://www.charitablegift.org/learn-about-charity/difference.shtml.

Fidelity Investments. "Inside Fidelity." http://content.members.fidelity.com/Inside_Fidelity/fullStory/1,,7799,00.html.

Field, Anne. "New Impact Investing Stock Exchange is Making Steady Progress." *Forbes*, August 30, 2012. http://www.forbes.com/sites/annefield/2012/08/30/new-impact-investing-stock-exchange-is-making-steady-progress.

Financial Markets Series. "Bond Markets 2011." London: TheCityUK, 2011. http://www.thecityuk.com/assets/Uploads/BondMarkets2011.pdf.

First Infrastructure. "Home." http://www.1stinfrastructure.com/.

Fitch Ratings. "Credit Analysis Report, International Finance Facility for Immunisation." September 2006.

Fleishman, Joel L. *The Foundation. A Great American Secret: How Private Wealth Is Changing the World*. New York: Public Affairs, 2007.

Ford Foundation. "About." http://www.fordfound.org/about.

Ford Foundation. *Investing in Social Change*. New York: Ford Foundation, 1968.

Ford Foundation. "Investing for Social Gain: Reflections on Two Decades of Program-Related Investments." 1991. http://www.fordfoundation.org/pdfs/library/Investing_For_Social_Gain.pdf.

Ford Foundation. *Investing for Social Gain; Reflections on Two Decades of Social Investments*. New York: Ford Foundation, 1991.

Forum for Sustainable and Responsible Investment. "Report on Sustainable and Responsible Investing Trends in the United States: 2012." US SIF, 2012.

Forum of Regional Associations of Grantmakers. "AsiaNextGen Giving Circle Profile." http://www.givingforum.org/s_forum/doc.asp?CID=4088&DID=8793.

Foster, William, and Gail Fine. "How Nonprofits Get Really Big." *Stanford Social Innovation Review* 5.1 (Spring 2007): 46–55. http://www.ssireview.org/articles/entry/how_nonprofits_get_really_big.

Foundation Center. "Change in Foundation Assets Adjusted for Inflation, 1975–2009." Published February 2011. http://foundationcenter.org/findfunders/statistics/pdf/02_found_growth/2009/06_09.pdf.

Foundation Center. *Foundation Yearbook: Facts and Figures on Private and Community Foundations.* 2008 ed. New York: Foundation Center, 2008.

Foundation Center. *Foundation Yearbook: Facts and Figures on Private and Community Foundations, 2010.* New York: Foundation Center, 2010.

Foundation Center. *Foundation Yearbook, 2007.* New York: Foundation Center 2008.

Foundation Center. *Foundation Yearbook, 2009.* New York: Foundation Center, 2010.

Foundation Center. "Highlights of Foundation Yearbook." Foundations Today Series (2011). http://foundationcenter.org/gainknowledge/research/pdf/fy2011_highlights.pdf.

Foundation Center. "Key Facts on Mission Investing." Published October 2011. http://foundationcenter.org/gainknowledge/research/pdf/keyfacts_missioninvesting2011.pdf.

Foundation Center. "Tools and Resources for Assessing Social Impact." http://trasi.foundationcenter.org/.

Freddie Mac. "About Freddie Mac." http://www.freddiemac.com/corporate/company_profile/.

Freeman, David F. *The Handbook on Private Foundations.* Published for the Council on Foundations. Cabin John, MD: Seven Locks Press, 1981.

Freireich, Jessica, and Katherine Fulton. "Investing for Social and Environmental Impact: A Design for Catalyzing an Emerging Industry." Monitor Group, 2009. http://www.monitorinstitute.com/downloads/what-we-think/impact-investing/Impact_Investing.pdf.

Friedman, Milton. "The Social Responsibility of Business Is to Increase its Profits." *New York Times Magazine*, September 13, 1970.

Frontier Economics. "Released Prisoner Support Programme Shown to Reduce Re-offending Rates." News release published March 15, 2010. http://www.frontier-economics.com/europe/en/news/894/.

Frumkin, Peter. "The Long Recoil from Regulation: Private Philanthropic Foundations and the Tax Reform Act of 1969." *American Review of Public Administration* 28.3 (1998): 266.

Frumkin, Peter. *Strategic Giving.* Chicago: University of Chicago Press, 2006.

Frumkin, Peter. *Strategic Philanthropy: The Art and Science of Giving.* Chicago: University of Chicago Press, 2006.

FTSE. "FTSE4Good Index Series." http://www.ftse.com/Indices/FTSE4Good_Index_Series/index.jsp.

Fulton, Katherine, and Jessica Freireich. *Investing for Social and Environmental Impact.* Boston: Monitor Institute, January 2009.

Funders' Network for Smart Growth and Livable Communities. "About Us." http://www.fundersnetwork.org/index.php/about/.

Fundraising123.org. "The Young and the Generous: A Study of $100 Million in Online Giving to 23,000 Charities." http://www.fundraising123.org/files/The%20Young%20and%20The%20Generous%20A%20Network%20for%20Good%20Study.pdf.

Gabriel, Yiannis, and Tim Lang. *The Unmanageable Consumer: Contemporary Consumption and Its Fragmentation.* London: Sage, 2006.

Gair, Cynthia. "A Report from the Good Ship SROI." REDF. http://www.socialreturns.org/docs/good_ship_sroi_gair.pdf.

Galloway, Ian. "Peer-to-Peer Lending and Community Development Finance." Federal Reserve Bank of San Francisco Working Paper 2009-06, 2009. http://www.frbsf.org/community-development/files/wp2009-06.pdf.

Garand, Denis, Clémence Tatin-Jaleran, Donna Swiderek, and Mary Yang. "Pricing of Microinsurance Products." In *Protecting the Poor: A Microinsurance Compendium*, vol. 2, ed. Craig Churchill and Michal Matul. Geneva: International Labour Organization and Munich Re Foundation, 2012.

Garand, Denis, and John Wipf. "Risk and Financial Management." In *Protecting the Poor: A Microinsurance Compendium*, ed. Craig Churchill. Geneva: International Labour Organization and Munich Re Foundation, 2006.

Garza, Cynthia. "Katrina Images Spark Record Pet Charity Giving." *Houston Chronicle*, November 11, 2005. http://www.chron.com/disp/story.mpl/special/05/katrina/3453906.html.

Ghosh, Monica. *Social Venture Partners 2005 Investee Feedback Survey: Summary Report*. Seattle: Social Venture Partners, 2005.

Gibson, Cynthia. *Funder Collaboratives: Why and How Funders Work Together*. New York: Grantcraft, 2009.

Gibson, Cynthia, and William Deitel. "What Do Donors Want?" *Nonprofit Quarterly*, September 2010. http://www.nonprofitquarterly.org/philanthropy/5866-what-do-donors-want.html.

Ginnie Mae. "About Ginnie Mae: History of Ginnie Mae." http://ginniemae.gov/about/history.asp?subTitle=About.

Global Alliance for Banking on Values. "Global Alliance for Banking on Values." http://www.gabv.org.

Global Envision. "The History of Microfinance." Published April 14, 2006. http://www.globalenvision.org/library/4/1051/.

Global Impact Investing Network (GIIN). "Impact Reporting & Investment Standards (IRIS)." http://iris.thegiin.org.

Global Impact Investing Rating Systems (GIIRS). "Pioneer Investors." http://giirs.org/for-investors/pioneer-investors.

GlobalRates.com. "3 Month US Dollar LIBOR Interest Rate." http://www.global-rates.com/interest-rates/libor/american-dollar/usd-libor-interest-rate-3-months.aspx.

Godeke, Steven, and Raúl Pomares, with Albert V. Bruno, Pat Guerra, Charly Kleissner, and Hersh Shefrin. "Solutions for Impact Investors: From Strategy to Implementation." New York: Rockefeller Philanthropy Advisors, November 2009. http://community-wealth.org/_pdfs/articles-publications/pris/book-godeke-pomares-et-al.pdf.

Godeke, Steven, and Doug Bauer. "Philanthropy's New Passing Gear: Mission-Related Investing, a Policy and Implementation Guide for Foundation Trustees." Rockefeller Philanthropy Advisors, 2008. http://rockpa.org/document.doc?id=16.

Goldman Sachs. "Goldman Sachs Philanthropy Fund Program Circular." https://gspf.goldman.com/gloria_static/DonorWebConfigs/gspf/1/forms/Program%20Circular.pdf.

Goodall, Emilie, and John Kingston. "Access to Capital: A Briefing Paper." CAF Venturesome, 2009. http://www.marmanie.com/cms/upload/file/CAF_Venturesome_Access_to_Capital_0909.pdf.

Government Accountability Office. "Tax Policy: New Markets Tax Credit Appears to Increase Investment by Investors in Low-Income Communities, but Opportunities Exist to Better Monitor Compliance." January 2007. http://www.community-wealth.org/_pdfs/articles-publications/cdfis/report-brostek-et-al.pdf.

Grameen Foundation. "Progress out of Poverty." http://progressoutofpoverty.org/.

Grantmakers in Health. "About GIH." http://www.gih.org/info-url_nocat2663/info-url_nocat.htm?requesttimeout=500.

Grantmakers in Health. "Home." http://www.gih.org/.

Grassroots Business Fund. "About Us." http://www.gbfund.org/about-us.

Grassroots Business Fund. "2011 Annual Report of the Grassroots Business Fund." 2011. http://gbfund.org/sites/default/files/GBF_AR_2011.pdf.

Grayghost Ventures. "First Light." http://www.grayghostventures.com/firstlight.htm.

Green Economy Initiative. "Enterprise Capital Fund—Sustainable Technology Growth Fund." http://greeneconomyinitiative.com/news/186/ARTICLE/1307/2009-01-02.html.

Greenpeace Foundation. "Dolphin-Safe Campaign." http://www.greenpeacefoundation.org/action/campInfo.cfm?campId=4.

Groh, Alexander P., Heinrich Liechtenstein, and Miguel A. Canela. "International Allocation Determinants of Institutional Investments in Venture Capital and Private Equity Limited Partnerships." IESE Business School, February 2009. http://www.iese.edu/research/pdfs/DI-0726-E.pdf.

Grossman, Allen, and Arthur McCaffrey. *JumpStart*. Cambridge: Harvard Business School Publishing, May 7, 2001.

Guthrie, Jonathan. "'Social Loan' for Cause-Based Groups." *Financial Times*, February 21, 2010. http://www.ft.com/intl/cms/s/0/41e6c628-1f11-11df-9584-00144feab49a.html#axzz2Xo4ZfNGe.

Habitat for Humanity. "Flexible Capital Program (FlexCAP): Information Memorandum." June 30, 2010.

Habitat for Humanity International. "Flexible Capital Access Program (FlexCap): Investment Summary." N.d. https://www.missioninvestors.org/system/files/tools/Habitat%20for%20Humanity%27s%20FlexCAP%20summary.pdf.

Hagerman, Lisa. *More Than a Profit? Measuring the Social and Green Outcomes of Urban Investments*. Cambridge, MA: Harvard Law School Labor and Worklife Program, July 2007.

Hagerman, Lisa, and Janneke Ratcliffe. "Increasing Access to Capital: Could Better Measurement of Social and Environmental Outcomes Entice More Institutional Investment Capital into Underserved Communities?" *Community Development Investment Review* 5.2 (2009): 46–64. http://www.frbsf.org/community-development/files/hagerman_ratcliffe.pdf.

Haiss, Peter, and Kjell Sümegi. "The Relationship between Insurance and Economic Growth in Europe: A Theoretical and Empirical Analysis." *Empirica* 35.4 (2008): 405–31.

Hall, Holly. "A Brave New World of Giving: Rapid Rise of On-line 'Portals' Raises Big Questions for Charities." *Chronicle of Philanthropy*, June 15, 2000. http://philanthropy.com/article/A-Brave-New-Worldof-Giving/50557/.

Hamilton, Ralph. "Moving Ideas and Money: Issues and Opportunities in Funder Funding Collaboration." Funders Network for Smart Growth and Livable Communities, February 27, 2002. http://www.fundersnetwork.org/files/Moving_Ideas_and_Money_Paper_2002.pdf.

Hammond, Allen L., William J. Kramer, Robert S. Katz, Julia T. Tran, and Courtland Walker. "The Next 4 Billion: Market Size and Business Strategy at the Base of the Pyramid." World Resources Institute and International Finance Corporation, 2007. http://pdf.wri.org/n4b_full_text_lowrez.pdf.

Haque, Umair. *The New Capitalist Manifesto*. Cambridge: Harvard Business Review Press, 2011.

Hart, Stuart L. *Capitalism at the Crossroads*. New York: Pearson Prentice Hall, 2007.

Hartzell, Jamie. "Creating an Ethical Stock Exchange." Skoll Center for Social Entrepreneurship Working Paper, Oxford University, August 2007.

Hattendorf, Laura. "The Trouble with Impact Investing: P2." *Stanford Social Innovation Review Blog*, April 18, 2012. http://www.ssireview.org/blog/entry/the_trouble_with_impact_investing_part_2.

Haufler, Virginia. *Public Role for the Private Sector: Industry Self-Regulation in a Global Economy*. Washington, DC: Carnegie Endowment for International Peace, 2001.

Hecht, Ben. "Revitalizing Struggling American Cities." *Stanford Social Innovation Review* 9.4 (Fall 2011): 27–29. http://www.ssireview.org/articles/entry/revitalizing_struggling_american_cities.

Hermes. "Homepage." http://www.hermes.co.uk.

Hill, Katie. "Investor Perspectives on Social Enterprise Financing." City of London, Big Lottery Fund, and ClearlySo, 2011. http://www.corpoflondon.com/NR/rdonlyres/1FC8B9A1-6DE2-495F-9284-C3CC1CFB706D/0/BC_RS_InvestorPerspectivesonSocialInvestment_forweb.pdf.

Hinkley, Robert. "How Corporate Law Inhibits Social Responsibility." Business Ethics Corporate Social Responsibility Report, January–February 2002. http://www.commondreams.org/views02/0119-04.htm.

Hirschman, Albert. *Exit, Voice and Loyalty: Responses to Decline in Firms, Organizations, and States*. Cambridge: Harvard University Press, 1970.

Hollis, Aidan. "Women and Microcredit in History: Gender in the Irish Loan Funds." In *Woman and Credit: Researching the Past, Reconfiguring the Future*, ed. Gail Campbell, Beverly Lemire, and Ruth Pearson, 73–89. Oxford: Berg, 2002.

Hope Consulting. "Money for Good: The US Market Opportunity for Impact Investments and Charitable Gifts from Individual Donor and Investors." May 2010. http://hopeconsulting.us/pdf/Money%20for%20Good_Final.pdf.

Hopkins, Bruce. *The Law of Tax-Exempt Organizations*, 9th ed. Hoboken, NJ: John Wiley & Sons, 2007.

Hopkins, Elwood. *Collaborative Philanthropies: What Groups of Foundations Can Do That Individual Funders Cannot*. Lanham, MD: Lexington Books, 2005.

Hougaard, Christine, and Doubell Chamberlain. "Funeral Insurance." In *Protecting the Poor: A Microinsurance Compendium*, vol. 2, ed. Craig Churchill and Michal Matul. Geneva: International Labour Organization and Munich Re Foundation, 2012.

Housing Partnership Network. "Enterprises: Charter School Financing: Business Approach." http://housingpartnership.net/enterprises/charter-school-financing/business-approach/.

Housing Partnership Network. "The Network." http://housingpartnership.net/network/.

HTC Group. "Welcome to HCT Group." http://www.hctgroup.org.

Hub, The. "About." http://www.the-hub.net/about.

Humphreys, Joshua. "Sustainability Trends in US Alternative Investment." US SIF Foundation: The Forum for Sustainable and Responsible Investment, 2011. http://www.investorscircle.net/accelsite/media/3195/Sustainability%20Trends%20in%20US%20Alternative%20Investments%20Report.pdf.

Hunziker-Ebneter, Antoinette, and Oliver Karius. "Sustainable Investment to Enhance the Sustainable Quality of Life." Presentation at the Oikos Anniversary Conference, St. Gallen, Switzerland, October 2007. http://www.oikos-international.org/fileadmin/oikos-International/Resources/071017_OIKOS_Presentation_Forma_Futura_long.pdf.

Hutton, Robert. "Cameron Opens $1 Billion Big Society Bank to Fund Charities." Bloomberg, April 4, 2012. http://www.bloomberg.com/news/2012-04-03/cameron-opens-1-billion-big-society-bank-to-fund-charities.html.

IDB Group. "The IDB Group: Your Partner for Impact Investing in Latin America and the Caribbean." http://idbdocs.iadb.org/wsdocs/getdocument.aspx?docnum=36886146.

IFFIm. "Bonds." http://www.iffim.org/bonds.

IFRS. "IFRS Resources." http://www.ifrs.com.

IGNIA. "Home." http://www.ignia.com.mx.

Impact Investment Shujog. "Impact Investors in Asia: Characteristics and Preferences for Investing in Social Enterprises in Asia-Pacific." Impact Investment Shujog and Asian Development Bank, 2011. http://evpa.eu.com/wp-content/uploads/2011/05/Impact-investors-in-Asia.pdf.

Imprint Capital. "Home." http://www.imprintcap.com/.

Inc.com. "How to Structure an Earn-out." http://www.inc.com/guides/earn-out-structuring.html.

InnoCentive. "About Innocentive." http://www.innocentive.com/about-innocentive.

Insight Center for Economic Community Development. "Starting a Regional Workforce Funders Collaborative." http://www.insightcced.org/index.php?page=starting-collaborative#Step_1.

Insurance Information Institute and Financial Services Roundtable. "2012 Financial Services Fact Book." http://www.fsround.org/fsr/publications_and_research/files/2012FinancialFactBook.pdf.

Interfaith Center on Corporate Responsibility. *Building Sustainable Communities through Multi-party Collaboration*. New York: Interfaith Center on Corporate Responsibility, 2011.

Internal Revenue Service. "Internal Revenue Manual—7.27.19 Taxable Expenditures of Private Foundations." http://www.irs.gov/irm/part7/irm_07027-019.html.

Internal Revenue Service. "IRS Announces the 'Dirty Dozen' Tax Scams for 2006." Published February 7, 2006. http://www.irs.gov/uac/IRS-Announces-%E2%80%9CDirty-Dozen%E2%80%9D-Tax-Scams-for-2006.

Internal Revenue Service. "Notice of Proposed Rulemaking:Examples of Program-Related Investments REG-144267-11." *Internal Revenue Bulletin*: 2012-21 (May 21, 2012). http://www.irs.gov/irb/2012-21_IRB/ar11.html.

International Association of Microfinance Investors. *Charting the Course: Best Practices and Tools for Voluntary Debt Restructurings in Microfinance*. New York: International Association of Microfinance Investors, 2011.

International Association of Microfinance Investors." Microfinance Investment." http://www.iamfi.com/microfinance_investment.html.

International Center for Research on Women. *Bridging the Gender Divide: How Technology Can Advance Women Economically*. Washington, DC: International Center for Research on Women, 2010.

International Cooperative Alliance. "Global 300 Report, 2010." London: ICA, 2010. http://ica.coop/sites/default/files/attachments/Global300%20Report%202011.pdf.

International Finance Corporation. "IFC's First Remittance-Secured Financing Enables Credit for El Salvador's Microenterprises, Lower-Income People." Press release issued on June 16, 2010. http://www.ifc.org/IFCExt/pressroom/IFCPressRoom.nsf/0/7703082F1497FBD385257744005CA5F8.

International Finance Corporation. "Interpretation Note on Small and Medium Enterprises and Environmental and Social Risk Management." International Finance Cooptation, World Bank Group, January 1, 2012. http://www.ifc.org/wps/wcm/connect/de7d92804a29ffe9ae04af8969adcc27/InterpretationNote_SME_2012.pdf?MOD=AJPERES.

International Finance Facility for Immunisation. "Bond Issuances." http://www.iff-immunisation.org/bond issuances.html.

International Finance Facility for Immunisation. "Bonds." http://www.iffim.org/bonds.

International Labour Organization. "Microinsurance Innovation Facility." www.ilo.org/microinsurance.

International Labour Organization. *Small Premiums, Long-term Benefit: Why Poor Women Need Microinsurance.* Geneva: Microinsurance Innovation Facility, ILO, 2010.

International Monetary Fund. "Restarting Securitization Markets: Policy Proposals and Pitfalls." Global Financial Stability Report, 2009. http://www.imf.org/External/Pubs/FT/GFSR/2009/02/pdf/chap2.pdf.

International Panel of Climate Change. *Fourth Assessment Report.* Geneva: IPCC, 2007.

Invest in Outcomes. "Home." http://investinoutcomes.org/.

Investment Company Institute. "2011 Investment Company Fact Book." http://www.ici.org/pdf/2011_factbook.pdf.

Investopedia. "Terms: Earnout." http://www.investopedia.com/terms/e/earnout.asp.

Investors' Circle. "Investor's Circle." http://www.investorscircle.net/.

Investors' Circle. "Our Role." http://www.investorscircle.net/about-us.

IRIS. "Frequently Asked Questions." http://iris-standards.org/faq.

Jacobs, Deborah L. "Charity Bankruptcy Leaves Many Donors in Distress." *New York Times,* November 11, 2009.

Jain, Ajit, and Caroline Norton. "Microfinance: Where Do We Stand Today?" *MicroBanking Bulletin* 18 (Spring 2009): 9–12. http://www.themix.org/sites/default/files/MBB%2018%20Spring%202009.pdf.

John, Rob. "Venture Philanthropy: The Evolution of High Engagement Philanthropy in Europe." Skoll Centre for Social Entrepreneurship Working Paper, June 2006. http://evpa.eu.com/wp-content/uploads/2010/10/Skoll-Centre-VP-Venture-Philanthropy-The-Evolution-of-High-Engagement-Philanthropy-in-Europe.pdf.

Jolly, David, and Jack Ewing. "Unemployment in Euro Zone Reaches New High." *New York Times,* November 30, 2012. http://www.nytimes.com/2012/12/01/business/global/daily-euro-zone-watch.html.

Joy, Iona, Lucy de Las Casas, and Benedict Rickey. "Understanding the Demand for and Supply of Social Finance: Research to Inform the Big Society Bank." New Philanthropy Capital and NESTA, 2011. http://www.nesta.org.uk/library/documents/BSFFUnderstandingthedemandprint.pdf.

JustGiving. "JustGiving, Our Story." http://www.justgiving.com/about-us/.

Jütting, Johannes P. "Do Community-Based Health Insurance Schemes Improve Poor People's Access to Health Care?" *World Development* 32.2 (2004): 273–88.

Kania, John, and Mark Kramer. "Collective Impact." *Stanford Social Innovation Review* 9.1 (Winter 2011): 36–41. http://www.ssireview.org/articles/entry/collective_impact.

Kansas Venture Capital. "Kansas Venture Capital, Inc. ("KVCI")." http://www.kvci.com/.

Kaplan, Robert S. "New Profit Inc: Governing the Nonprofit Enterprise." Harvard Business School Case Study 9-100-052, July 2001.

Kaplan, Robert S. *On Balance: The Balanced Scorecard and Nonprofit Organizations.* Boston: Harvard Business School Publishing, 2002.

Kauffman Foundation. "Angel Investors in Groups Achieve Investment Returns in Line with Other Types of Equity Deals." November 12, 2007. http://www.kauffman.org/Details.aspx%5C?id=1032.

Kazmin, Amy. "Microfinance: Small Loan, Big Snag." *Financial Times,* December 1, 2010. http://www.ft.com/cms/s/0/a3edfeba-fd85-11df-a049-00144feab49a.html.

Kelland, Kate. "Donors Asked for $4.3 Billion for Vaccines for Poor." Reuters, March 15, 2010. http://www.reuters.com/article/idUSTRE62E1CD20100315.

Kentucky Highlands Investment Corporation. "About KHIC." http://www.khic.org/about.html.

Kentucky Highlands Investment Corporation. "Equity Investments." http://www.khic.org/equity.html.

Ketkar, Suhas, and Dilip Ratha. "Securitization of Future Flow Receivables: A Useful Tool for Developing Countries." *Finance and Development* 38.1 (2001). http://www.imf.org/external/pubs/ft/fandd/2001/03/ketkar.htm.

Keystone Accountability. "Constituency Voice." http://www.keystoneaccountability.org/analysis/constituency.

Khanna, Tarun, and Jayant Sinha. "The Microfinance Catalyst." Project Syndicate, October 4, 2011. http:.//www.project-syndicate.org/commentary/the-microfinance-catalyst.

Kim, Tae Hyun. "Factors Associated with Financial Distress of Nonprofit Hospitals." *Health Care Manager* 29.1 (January–March 2010): 52–62.

Kiva Microfunds. "About Kiva, Statistics." http://www.kiva.org/about/stats.

Koh, Harvey, Ashish Karamchandani, and Robert Katz. "From Blueprint to Scale: The Case for Philanthropy in Impact Investing." Monitor Group, April 2012. http://www.mim.monitor.com/downloads/Blueprint_To_Scale/From%20Blueprint%20to%20Scale%20-%20Case%20for%20Philanthropy%20in%20Impact%20Investing_Full%20report.pdf.

Kohler, John, Thane Kreiner, and Jessica Sawhney. "Coordinating Impact Capital: A New Approach to Investing in Small and Growing Businesses." Aspen Network of Development Entrepreneurs, July 2011. http://www.scu.edu/socialbenefit/resources/upload/Coordinating-Impact-Capital.pdf.

Koken, David. "The Current State of Online Philanthropy." http://www.scribd.com/doc/24062122/Nonprofit-Marketplace-Report-D-Koken.

Kramer, Mark R., and Sarah E. Cooch. "The Power of Strategic Mission Investing." *Stanford Social Innovation Review* 5.4 (Fall 2007): 43–51.

Kramer, Mark, and Anne Stetson. "A Brief Guide to the Law of Mission Investing for U.S. Foundations." Boston: FSG Social Impact Advisors, 2008. http://www.fsg.org/Portals/0/Uploads/Documents/PDF/The_Law_and_Mission_Investing_Brief.pdf.

Kresge Foundation. "Social Investment Practice." http://www.kresge.org/sites/default/files/Brochure-socialinvestment.pdf.

Krishnaswamy, Karuna, and Rupalee Ruchismita. *Rashtriya Swasthya Bima Yojna— Performance Trends and Policy Recommendations*. Chennai: Centre for Insurance and Risk Management, 2011.

Kroll, Luisa. "Inside the 2013 Billionaires List: Facts and Figures." *Forbes*, March 25, 2013. http://www.forbes.com/sites/luisakroll/2013/03/04/inside-the-2013-billionaires-list-facts-and-figures/.

Kruk, Margaret E., Emily Goldmann, and Sandro Galea. "Borrowing and Selling to Pay for Health Care in Low- and Middle-Income Countries." *Health Affairs* 28.4 (2009): 1056–66.

LA County Maternal, Child, & Adolescent Health. "Nurse-Family Partnership Program." http://publichealth.lacounty.gov/mch/nfp/nfp.htm.

LaFrance, Steven, Andrew Robinson, Rick Green, and Nancy Latham. "Funder Networks in Action: Understanding Their Potential for Philanthropy." Grantmakers in Effective Organizations, 2004. http://www.socialimpactexchange.org/sites/www.socialimpactexchange.org/files/publications/Funder%20networks%20in%20action.pdf.

Lavalle, Marianne. "A U.S. Cap-and-Trade Experiment to End." *National Geographic*, November 3, 2012. http://news.nationalgeographic.com/news/news/energy/2010/11/101103-chicago-climate-exchange-cap-and-trade-election.pdf.

Lawrence, Steven. "Doing Good with Foundation Assets: An Updated Look at Program-Related Investments." In *The PRI Directory: Charitable Loans and Other*

Program-related Investments by Foundations, 3rd ed., ed. Jeffrey A. Falkenstein. New York: Foundation Center, 2010.

Lawrence, Steven. "Foundations' Year-End Outlook for Giving and the Sector." Foundation Center, November 2009. http://foundationcenter.org/gainknowledge/research/pdf/researchadvisory_economy_200911.pdf.

Lawrence, Steven, and Reina Mukai. "Key Facts on Mission Investing." Foundation Center, October 2011. http://foundationcenter.org/gainknowledge/research/pdf/keyfacts_missioninvesting2011.

LeapFrog Investments. "AllLife Portfolio." Last modified 2011. http://www.leapfrogInvest.com/PortfolioCompanyAllLife.

Leatherman, Shelia, Lisa Jones Christensen, and Jeanna Holtz. "Innovations and Barriers in Health Microinsurance." In *Protecting the Poor: A Microinsurance Compendium*, vol. 2, ed. Craig Churchill and Michal Matul. Geneva: International Labour Organization and Munich Re Foundation, 2012.

Lee, Ian B. "Corporate Law, Profit Maximization and the Responsible Shareholder." *Stanford Journal of Law, Business & Finance*, March 2005. http://ssrn.com/abstract=692862.

Lee, Yoolim, and Ruth David. "Suicides in India Revealing How Men Made a Mess of Microcredit." *Bloomberg Markets Magazine*, December 28, 2010.

Lee-St. John, Jeninne. "How Others Serve." *Time*, August 30, 2007.

Leftley, Richard. *An Overview of Insurance Product Design within the Opportunity International Network*. Oak Brook, IL: Technical Services Division, Opportunity International, 2002.

Leixner, Timothy C. "Securitization of Financial Assets." Washington, DC: Institute of Higher Education Policy, 2007. http://www.ihep.org/assets/files/gcfp-files/Securitization_of_Financial_Assets.pdf.

Lenkowsky, Leslie. "Nonprofit World Could Emerge Stronger from Economic Crisis." *Chronicle of Philanthropy*, October 30, 2008. http://philanthropy.com/article/article-content/57012/.

Lerner, John, and John Willinge. *A Note on Valuation in Private Equity Settings*. Boston: Harvard Business School Publishing, 2002.

Letts, Christine, William Ryan, and Allen Grossman. "Virtuous Capital: What Foundations Can Learn from Venture Capitalists." *Harvard Business Review* 75.2 (March–April 1997): 36–46.

Levy, Judd S., and Kenya Purnell. "Case Study: The Community Development Trust Taps Wall Street Investors." *Community Development Investment Review* 2.1 (2006): 57–63.

Lewin, Kurt. *Field Theory in Social Science: Selected Theoretical Papers*. Ed. Dorwin Cartwright. Westport, CT: Greenwood Press, 1976.

Lewis, Jonathan C., and Robert Wexler. "Mission Investing in Microfinance: A Program Related Investment (PRI) Primer and Toolkit." Microcredit Enterprises, July 2007. http://www.community-wealth.org/_pdfs/tools/pris/tool-microcredit-ent-pri.pdf.

Lewis, Michael. *The Big Short*. New York: Norton, 2010.

Liebman, Jeffrey. "Social Impact Bonds: A Promising New Financing Model to Accelerate Social Innovation and Improve Government Performance." Washington, DC: Center for American Progress. February 9, 2011. http://www.americanprogress.org/issues/open-government/report/2011/02/09/9050/social-impact-bonds/.

Light, Paul. *Sustaining Nonprofit Performance: The Case for Capacity Building and the Evidence to Support It*. Washington, DC: Brookings Institution, 2004.

Living Cities. "History." http://www.livingcities.org/about/history.

Lloyd's. "Insurance in Developing Countries: Exploring Opportunities in Microinsurance." Lloyd's 360 Risk Insight, 2010. http://www.microfinancegateway.org/gm/document-1.9.40798/Insurance%20in%20developing.pdf.

Lob-Levyt, Julian. "GAVI Celebrates 10th Anniversary, Welcomes New 'Decade of Vaccines.'" GAVI Alliance statement released January 29, 2010. http://www.gavialliance.org/library/news/statements/2010/gavi-celebrates-10th-anniversary,-welcomes-new-decade-of-vaccines.

Local Initiatives Support Corporation. *Charter School Bond Issuance: A Complete History*. New York: Local Initiatives Support Corporation, Educational Facilities Financing Center, 2011.

Loster, Thomas, and Dirk Reinhard. "Climate Change and Microinsurance." In *Protecting the Poor: A Microinsurance Compendium*, vol. 2, ed. Craig Churchill and Michal Matul. Geneva: International Labour Organization and Munich Re Foundation, 2012.

Lowell, Stephanie, Brian Trelstad, and William Meehan. "The Ratings Game: Evaluating the Three Groups That Rate the Charities." *Stanford Social Innovation Review* 3.2 (Summer 2005): 39–45.

Lower East Side People's Federal Credit Union. "About Us." https://lespeoples.org/about-us/25th-anniversary-gala.

Lucas, Jose A. "Using CAMELS Ratings to Monitor Bank Conditions." Federal Reserve Bank of San Francisco 19 (1990). Published July 11, 1999. http://www.frbsf.org/econrsrch/wklyltr/wklyltr99/el99-19.html.

MacArthur Foundation. "Frequently Asked Questions." http://www.macfound.org/fellows-faq.

Mair, Vibeka. "Peterborough Social Impact Bond Has Slashed Reoffending Rates Says MoJ." civilsociety.co.uk. http://www.civilsociety.co.uk/finance/news/content/15384/peterborough_social_impact_bond_has_slashed_reoffending_rates_says_moj.

Maloni, Michael J., and Michael E. Brown. "Corporate Social Responsibility in the Supply Chain: An Application in the Food Industry." *Journal of Business Ethics* 68.1 (2006): 35–52.

Manje, Lemmy, and Craig Churchill. "The Demand for Risk-Managing Financial Services in Low-Income Communities: Evidence from Zambia." Social Finance Programme Working Paper 31, International Labour Organization, 2002. http://www.ilo.org/wcmsp5/groups/public/—ed_emp/documents/publication/wcms_117979.pdf.

Margolis, Joshua David, and James Patrick Walsh. *People and Profits? The Search for a Link between a Company's Social and Financial Performance*. Hillsdale, NJ: Erlbaum 2001.

MarketsforGood. "Upgrading the Information Infrastructure for Social Change." Summer 2012. http://www.marketsforgood.org/wordpress/wp-content/uploads/2012/11/MarketsforGood_Information-Infrastructure_Fall-2012_.pdf.

Martin, Maximilian. "The Deconstruction of Development: A Critical Overview." *Entwicklungsethnologie* 7.1 (1998): 40–59. http://www.impacteconomy.com/node/178.

Martin, Maximilian. "F4F—Finance for Foundations." Social Sciences Research Network, June 25, 2007. http://ssrn.com/abstract=1322388.

Martin, Maximilian. "Managing philanthropy after the Downturn: What Is Ahead for Social Investment?" In Viewpoints (UBS Philanthropy Services) 2010, ed. Maximilian Martin and Andreas Ernst, 11–21. Geneva: IJ Partners, 2010. http://www.impacteconomy.com/node/91.

Martin, Maximilian. "Surveying Social Entrepreneurship." Viewpoints (UBS Philanthropy Services), 2004. http://www.impacteconomy.com/node/177.

Martin, Maximilian. "Surveying Social Entrepreneurship: Toward an Empirical Analysis of the Performance Revolution in the Social Sector." Working paper, Center for Public Leadership, University of St. Gallen, 2004. http://www.impacteconomy.com/node/175.

Massachusetts Capital Resource Company. "Mass Capital, Company." http://www.masscapital.com/company/.

Massachusetts Executive Office of Administration and Finance. "Massachusetts First State in the Nation to Announce Initial Successful Bidders for 'Pay for Success' Contracts." Published August 1, 2012. http://www.mass.gov/anf/press-releases/fy2013/massachusetts-first-state-in-the-nation-to-announce-ini.html.

Massachusetts Executive Office for Administration and Finance. "Request or Response: Social Innovation Financing for Youth—Intermediaries." Published January 18, 2012. http://hkssiblab.files.wordpress.com/2012/11/ma-rfr-youth-intermediaries.pdf.

Matul, Michal, Michael J. McCord, Caroline Phily, and Job Harms. *The Landscape of Microinsurance in Africa*. Geneva: Microinsurance Innovation Facility, International Labour Organization, 2010.

McCarthy, John. "Strategies for Selling Smaller Pools of Loans." *Community Development Investment Review* 2.1 (2006): 40.

McClaughlin, Steve. "Giving USA Report for 2008 and Online Fundraising Estimates." Connections: A Blog by Steve McGlaughlin. Blackbaud, published June 10, 2009. http://forums.blackbaud.com/blogs/connections/archive/2009/06/10/giving-usa-report-for-2008-and-online-fundraising-estimates.aspx.

McCord, Michael J., Felipe Botero, and Janet S. McCord. *AIG Uganda, a Member of the American International Group of Companies*. Geneva: Social Finance Programme, International Labour Organization, 2005.

McCord, Michael J., and Craig Churchill. *Delta Life, Bangladesh*. Geneva: Social Finance Programme, International Labour Organization, 2005.

McCord, Michael J., and Monique Cohen. *Microinsurance Disasters: Steps to Take to Mitigate Risks Next Time*. Washington, DC: Microfinance Opportunities, 2005.

McCord, Michael J., Gabriele Ramm, and Elizabeth McGuinness. *Microinsurance Demand and Market Prospects: Indonesia*. Geneva: United Nations Development Programme, Gesellschaft für Technische Zusammenarbeit, Allianz Group, 2005.

McCrudden, Christopher. *Buying Social Justice*. Oxford: Oxford University Press, 2007.

McGirt, Ellen. "A Charity of One's Own." CNN Money, December 6, 1006. http://money.cnn.com/magazines/fortune/fortune_archive/2006/12/25/8396761/index.htm.

McGuire, Michael. "Collaborative Public Management: Assessing What We Know and How We Know It." *Public Administration Review* 66.s1 (2006): 33–43.

MCII. "Munich Climate Insurance Initiative—Home." http://www.climate-insurance.org/front_content.php?idcat=858.

McKinsey and Company. "And the Winner is…Capturing the Promise of Philanthropic Prizes." McKinsey and Co., 2009.

Meehan, William F., Derek Kilmer, and Maisie O'Flanagan. "Investing in Society." *Stanford Social Innovation Review* 1.4 (Spring 2004). http://www.ssireview.org/articles/entry/investing_in_society.

Meier, Deborah. "Campbell's Law and testing." Bridging Differences (blog). *Education Week*, May 7, 2007. http://blogs.edweek.org/edweek/Bridging-Differences/2007/05/campbells_law_and_testing.html.

Mercer Consulting. "The Climate Change Report: The Impact Of climate Change on Strategic Asset Allocation." http://www.mercer.com/articles/1406410.

Metrick, Craig. "The Line in the Sand: ESG Integration vs. Screening and 'Economically Targeted Investments.'" Last modified July 11, 2012. http://www.mercer.com/articles/1407905.

Metz Cummings, Ashley, and Lisa Hehenberger. "Strategies for Foundations: When, Why and How to Use Venture Philanthropy." Alliance Publishing Trust, October 2010.   http://evpa.eu.com/wp-content/uploads/2011/06/EVPA-Knowledge-Centre_Strategies-for-Foundations.pdf.

Microfinance Africa. "Asian Development Bank Backs ShorCap II Fund with $10M." Published   December   10,   2012.   http://microfinanceafrica.net/tag/equator-capital-partners.

Microfinance Africa. "USAID and Impact Investors Capitalize New Equity Fund for East African   Agribusiness."   http://seedstock.com/2011/10/05/usaid-global-impact-investing-network-join-to-create-east-africa-agricultural-investment-fund/.

Microfinance Information Exchange. "2009, MFI Benchmarks." Published October 2010. http://www.themix.org/publications/mix-microfinance-world/2010/10/2 009-mfi-benchmarks.

Microfinance Information Exchange. "About MIX." http://www.themix.org/about-mix/about-mix#ixzz1IVbCKQei.

Microfinance Information Exchange. "Microfinance at a Glance–2010." http://www.mixmarket.org.

Microfinance Information Exchange. "Microfinance Information Exchange Brochure." http://www.themix.org/sites/default/files/MIX%20Brochure.pdf.

Microfinance Information Exchange. "Mix Market Homepage." http://www.mixmarket.org.

Microlinks, USAID. "J.P. Morgan, Omidyar-Tufts, TIAA-CREF: A Conversation with Prominent   Microfinance   Investors."   http://www.microlinks.org/events/jp-morgan-omidyar-tufts-tiaa-cref-conversation-prominent-microfinance-investors.

Miglietta, Angelo. "New Ideas and Experiences in Granting and Supporting Social Investment: The 'Strange' Case of Fondazione CRT and Its Network." Unpublished paper, 2010.

Miller, Clara. "The Equity Capital Gap." *Stanford Social Innovation Review*, Summer 2008,   41–45.   http://community-wealth.org/_pdfs/articles-publications/pris/article-miller.pdf.

Miller, Clara. "The Looking Glass World of Nonprofit Money." *Nonprofit Quarterly*, March 1, 2005. http://nonprofitfinancefund.org/files/docs/2010/NPQSpring05.pdf.

Miller, Clara. "The World Has Changed and So Must We." F.B. Heron Foundation, April 2012. http://www.missioninvestors.org/tools/world-has-changed-and-so-must-we.

Millinga, Altemius. *Assessing the Demand for Microinsurance in Tanzania.* Nairobi: MicroSave Africa, 2002.

Mirabella, Roseanne. "Nonprofit Management Education: Current Offerings in University-Based Programs." http://academic.shu.edu/npo/.

Mirabella, Roseanne. "University-Based Educational Programs in Nonprofit Management and Philanthropic Studies: A 10-Year Review and Projections of Future Trends." *Nonprofit and Voluntary Sector Quarterly* 36.4s (2007): 11S–27S. DOI:10.1177/0899764007305051.

Mission Investors Exchange. "About Mission Investors Exchange." http://www.missioninvestors.org/about-us/origins-mission-investors-exchange.

Mission Investors Exchange. "About Us: Mission Investors." http://www.missioninvestors.org/about-us.

Mission Investors Exchange. "The Origins of Mission Investors Exchange." http://www.missioninvestors.org/about-us/origins-mission-investors-exchange.

Mission Investors Exchange. "What's New in Mission Investing?" http://www. moreformission.org.

Monitor Institute. "Investing for Social & Environmental Impact: A Design for Catalyzing an Emerging Industry." http://www.monitorinstitute.com/impactinvesting/documents/InvestingforSocialandEnvImpact_FullReport_004.pdf.

Monserbraaten, Laurie. "Helping Youth Cycle Away from Poverty." *Toronto Star*, January 1, 2009. http://www.turnaroundcouriers.com/media/Jan_TorStar_09.pdf.

More for Mission. "About Us." More for Mission. http://www.moreformission.org/page/15/about-us.

More for Mission. "Consultants." http://www.moreformission.org/page/12/consultants.

More for Mission. "Home." http://www.moreformission.org.

More for Mission. "Mission Investing Policy." http://www.moreformission.org/page/11/mission-investing-policy.

More for Mission. "More for Mission: Current Practices and Trends in Mission Investing." Published October 2009. http://www.missioninvestors.org/system/files/tools/2009-survey-of-foundations-by-more-for-mission.pdf.

More for Mission. "What Is Mission Investing." http://www.moreformission.org/page/34/what-is-mission-investing.

Moyo, Dambisa. *Dead Aid*. New York: Farrar, Straus and Giroux, 2009.

Mulgan, Geoff. "After Capitalism." *Prospect Magazine*, April 26, 2009, 157–70. http://www.prospectmagazine.co.uk/magazine/aftercapitalism/.

Mulgan, Geoff. "Measuring Social Value." *Stanford Social Innovation Review* 8.3 (Summer 2010): 38–43.

Munich RE. "Munich Re Shares as a Sustainable Investment (2008)." http://www.munichre.com/sustainability/en/economy/munich_re_share/.

Murdoch, Jonathan. "The Microfinance Promise." *Journal of Economic Literature* 37 (December 1999): 1569–14. http://www.nyu.edu/projects/morduch/documents/.

Mutuo. *The Mutuals Yearbook 2009*. London: Mutuo, 2009.

Nairobi Women's Hospital. "Home." http://www.nwch.co.ke.

National Association of Development Companies. "504 Loan Approval Statistics." http://www.nadco.org/i4a/pages/index.cfm?pageid=3558.

National Charter School Resource Center. "Charter Schools and Qualified School Construction Bonds." http://www.charterschoolcenter.org/newsletter/march-2013-charter-schools-and-qualified-school-construction-bonds.

National Community Investment Fund. "NCIF Homepage." http://www.ncif.org.

National Community Investment Fund. "Too Important to Fail: The Impact of Community Development Banking Institutions: 2009 and Beyond." National Community Investment Fund, 2010. http://www.ncif.org/images/uploads/20101108_2009_ImpactReport_FINAL.pdf.

National Community Reinvestment Coalition. "Community Reinvestment Act." http://www.ncrc.org/programs-issues/community-reinvestment.

National Federation of Community Development Credit Unions. "Who We Are." http://www.natfed.org/.

National Philanthropic Trust. "2011 Donor Advised Fund Report." http://www.nptrust.org/images/uploads/2011%20Donor-Advised-Fund-Report%281%29.pdf.

National Philanthropic Trust. "Donor-Advised Fund Program Guide." http://www.nptrust.org/images/uploads/DAF-NPT-FOR-DAFPG-0311.pdf.

Nee, Eric. "Q&A with Jeff Raikes." *Stanford Social Innovation Review* 8.1 (Winter 2010): 13–15. http://www.ssireview.org/articles/entry/qa_jeff_raikes.

Neef, Dale. *The Supply Chain Imperative*. New York: AMACOM, 2004.

Nelson, Julia A. "Does Profit-Seeking Rule Out Love: Evidence (or Not) from Economics and the Law." Prepared for the Symposium "For Love or Money." September 2010. http://ase.tufts.edu/gdae/Pubs/wp/10-06ProfitSeekingAndLove.pdf.

NESTA. "About Us." www.nesta.org.uk/.

Net Impact. "Home Page." http://www.netimpact.org.

Network for Good. "Impulse on the Internet: How Crisis Compels Donors to Give Online." Published September 2006. http://www.networkforgood.org/downloads/pdf/Whitepaper/20061009_crisis_compels_donors.pdf.

Network for Good. "Internet, Nonprofit Leaders Launch 'Network for Good' to Support Local and National Charities." News release, November 19, 2001. http://www.networkforgood.org/npo/about/press/pressreleases/2001/11-19.aspx.

Network for Good. "The Online Giving Study: A Call to Reinvent Donor Relationships." Published December 2010. http://www.onlinegivingstudy.org/.

Network for Good. "Online Giving Study 2010." http://www.fundraising123.org/files/Community/Online_Giving_Study_2010R.pdf.

New Energy Finance. "Global Carbon Market Shrinks in Q3, but Activity in North America and in the International Credit Market Sees Continued Growth." New Energy Finance Press Release, 2009. http://about.bnef.com/press-releases/global-carbon-market-shrinks-in-q3-but-activity-in-north-america-and-in-the-international-credit-market-sees-continued-growth/.

New Energy Finance. *Global Trends in Clean Energy Finance Q4 2009 Fact Pack.* London: New Energy Finance, 2009.

New Profit. "About Us." http://newprofit.com/cgi-bin/iowa/about/9.html.

New York Community Trust. "The Fund for New Citizens." http://www.nycommunitytrust.org/AbouttheTrust/FundingCollaborativesandotherSpecialProjects/TheFundforNewCitizens/tabid/397/Default.aspx.

Nicholls, Alex. "The Institutionalization of Social Investment: The Interplay of Investment Logics and Investor Rationalities." *Journal of Social Entrepreneurship* 1.1 (2010): 70–100.

Nichols, Alex, ed. *Social Entrepreneurship: New Models of Sustainable Social Change.* Oxford: Oxford University Press, 2006.

Nicholls, Alex. "What Is the Future of Social Enterprise in Ethical Markets?" London: Office of the Third Sector, 2007. http://webarchive.nationalarchives.gov.uk/+/http:/www.cabinetoffice.gov.uk/media/cabinetoffice/third_sector/assets/future_social_enterprise_ethical_markets.pdf.

Nicholls, Alex, and Alex Murdock, eds. *Social Innovation: Blurring Boundaries to Reconfigure Markets.* New York: Palgrave Macmillan, 2012.

Nicholls, Alex, Rob Paton, and Jed Emerson, eds. *Social Finance.* New York: Oxford University Press, 2014.

Noonan, Kathleen, and Katharina Rosqueta. "'I'm not Rockefeller': 33 High Net Worth Philanthropists Discuss Their Approach to Giving." Center for High Impact Philanthropy, University of Pennsylvania. Published September 2008. http://www.impact.upenn.edu/images/uploads/UPenn_CHIP_HNWP_Study.pdf.

Nordan, Matthew M. "The State of Cleantech Venture Capital 2011." Whitepaper, ublished December 2011. http://mntempblog.files.wordpress.com/2011/12/the-state-of-cleantech-venture-capital-2011.pdf.

Novogradac & Co. "Resources: Reports and Research: CDFI Fund: NMTC Projects Finance through 2009." September 21, 2010. http://www.novoco.com/new_markets/resources/reports.php.

Novogradac & Co. "Resources: About LIHTC." http://www.novoco.com/low_income_housing/resources/program_summary.php.

Nyssens, Marthe. *Social Enterprise*. London: Palgrave Macmillan, 2006.

O'Donohoe, Nick, Christina Leijonhufvud, Yasemin Saltuk, Antony Bugg-Levine, and Margot Brandenburg. "Impact Investments: An Emerging Asset Class." J.P. Morgan. November 29, 2010. http://www.rockefellerfoundation.org/uploads/files/2b053b2b-8feb-46ea-adbd-f89068d59785-impact.pdf.

OASIS. "OASIS Seal—Home." http://www.oasisseal.org.

OECD. "Economic Survey of Mexico 2009: Achieving Higher Performance: Enhancing Spending Efficiency in Health and Education." July 30, 2009. http://www.oecd.org/document/48/0,3343,en_33873108_33873610_43394096_1_1_1_1,00.html.

Olson, John. "Foreword." *Community Development Investment Review* 2.1 (June 2006).

Opportunity Finance Network. "About." http://www.opportunityfinance.net/about.

Opportunity Finance Network. "CDFI Data Project, 2008." http://www.opportunityfinance.net/industry/default.aspx?id=236.

Opportunity Finance Network. "CDFI Federally Guaranteed Bond Summary of Terms." http://www.opportunityfinance.net/uploadedfiles/Policy/Bond/CDFI-Bond-Terms.pdf.

Opportunity Finance Network. *Inside the Membership: 2009 Statistical Highlights from the OFN Membership*. Philadelphia: Opportunity Finance Network, 2010.

Opportunity Finance Network. "Market Conditions." http://www.opportunityfinance.net/store/categories.asp?cID=29.

Opportunity Finance Network. "Overview of Opportunity Finance Network." http://www.opportunityfinance.net/about/.

Ostrander, Susan. *Money for Change*. Philadelphia: Temple University Press, 1997.

Oxford University. "Oxford Poverty and Human Development Initiative: Homepage." http://www.ophi.org.uk/.

Pacific Community Ventures. "About—PCV Fund." http://www.pcvfund.com/about.asp.

Pacific Community Ventures. "About Pacific Community Ventures." http://www.pacificcommunityventures.org/about.

Pacific Community Ventures. *Development Investment Capital*. Published May 2006. http://www.pacificcommunityventures.org/media/pdf/PCV-White-Paper-Development-Investment-Capital.pdf.

Pepsi Co. "Pepsi Refresh Project." http://www.refresheverything.com/.

Pernick, Ron, Clint Wilder, Trevor Winnie, and Sean Sosnovec. "Clean Energy Trends 2011." Clean Edge, March 2011. http://www.cleanedge.com/reports/pdf/Trends2011.pdf.

PGGM. "About PGGM." http://www.pggm.nl/about_pggm.

Philanthropic Initiative, The. "Donor Collaboration: Power in Numbers." April 13, 2009. http://www.tpi.org/resources/primer/donor_collaboration_power_in.aspx.

Phillips, Ronnie. "Benjamin Franklin and the Invention of Microfinance." Review of *Benjamin Franklin and the Invention of Microfinance* by Bruce Yenawine. Economic History Association Book Reviews, October 27, 2010. http://eh.net/book_reviews/benjamin-franklin-and-invention-microfinance.

Piper Jaffray & Co. "Pricing Final Curve for CRF-17." Unpublished work paper, November 2004.

Piper Jaffray & Co. "Private Placement Memorandum for CRF-17 LLC." October 19, 2004.

Pomares, Raúl. "KKF-MRI Evaluator, Beartooth Capital." http://www.klfelicitasfoundation.org/assets/finalpdfs/MRI_Evaluator/KFF_MRI_Evaluator_Beartooth_Capital_I_LP_V1.4_022108.pdf.

Porter, Michael E., and Mark R. Kramer. "Creating Shared Value." *Harvard Business Review Magazine*, January 2011. http://hbr.org/2011/01/the-big-idea-creating-shared-value.

Portney, Paul R. "Benefit-Cost Analysis." In *The Concise Encyclopedia of Economics 2008*. Indianapolis, IN: Library of Economics and Liberty. http://www.econlib.org/library/Enc/BenefitCostAnalysis.html.

Powell, Walter, Kenneth W. Koput, and Laurel Smith-Doerr. "Interorganizational Collaboration and the Locus of Innovation: Networks of Learning in Biotechnology." *Administrative Science Quarterly* 41.1 (1996): 116–45.

Prahalad, C. K. *The Fortune at the Bottom of the Pyramid: Eradicating Poverty through Profits*. Philadelphia: Wharton School Publishing, 2004.

Preston, Susan L. "Angel Investment Groups, Networks, and Funds: A Guidebook to Developing the Right Angel Organization for Your Community." Kansas City: Ewing Marion Kauffman Foundation, August 2004. http://www.kauffman.org/entrepreneurship/angel-investment-guidebook.aspx.

PRI Makers. "About Us." http://www.primakers.net/about.

Primary Care Development Corporation. "About Us." http://www.pcdc.org/about-us/.

Princeton Survey Research Associates, Independent Sector. "Wired, Willing and Ready: Nonprofit Human Service Organizations' Adoption of Information Technology." December 2001. http://www.independentsector.org/pdfs/wiredwillingready.pdf.

Promontory Interfinancial Network. "CDARS Homepage." http://www.cdars.com.

Proscio, Tony. "Common Effort, Uncommon Wealth: Lessons from Living Cities on the Challenges and Opportunities of Collaboration in Philanthropy." Living Cities. http://www.livingcities.org/knowledge/media/?id=42, p. 3.

Quercia, R., and Janneke Ratcliffe, with Michael A. Stegman. "The Community Reinvestment Act: Outstanding, and Needs to Improve." In *Revisiting the CRA: Perspectives on the Future of the Community Reinvestment Act*, ed. Prabal Chakrabarti, David Erickson, Ren S. Essene, Ian Galloway, and John Olson. San Francisco: Federal Reserve Banks of Boston and San Francisco, 2009.

Radermacher, Ralf, Iddo Dror, and Gerry Noble. "Challenges and Strategies to Extend Health Insurance to the Poor." In *Protecting the Poor: A Microinsurance Compendium*, ed. Craig Churchill. Geneva: International Labour Organization and Munich Re Foundation, 2006.

Radermacher, Ralf, Heidi McGowan, and Stefan Dercon. "What Is the Impact of Microinsurance?" In *Protecting the Poor: A Microinsurance Compendium*, vol. 2, ed. Craig Churchill and Michal Matul. Geneva: International Labour Organization and Munich Re Foundation, 2012.

Ragin, Luther M., Jr. "Program-Related Investments in Practice." *Vermont Law Review* 35 (2010): 53.

Ramdas, Kavita. "Philanthrocapitalism Is Not Social Change Philanthropy." Stanford Social Innovation Review blog, December 15, 2011, http://www.ssireview.org/point_counterpoint/philanthrocapitalism.

Ratliff, Gregory. "MacArthur PRI Portfolio Summary." Internal memorandum, January 23, 2000.

Ravitch, Diane. *The Death and Life of the Great American School System*. New York: Basic Books, 2010.

RBC Global Asset Management. "Access Capital Community Investment Fund." http://us.rbcgam.com/mutual-funds/fixed-income-funds/fg-4/fsg-7/fid-15/individual/overview/access-capital-community-investment-fund.fs.

REDF. "Rubicon Bakery SROI report." http://www.redf.org/system/files/%2820%29+SROI+Report+-+Rubicon+Bakery.pdf.

REDF. "Social Impact Report." http://www.redf.org/learn-from-redf/publications/122.

Redja, George E. *The Principles of Risk Management and Insurance*. Boston: Pearson, 1998.

Reed, Stanley, and Mark Scott. "In Europe, Paid Permits for Pollution Are Fizzling." *New York Times*, April 21, 2013. http://www.nytimes.com/2013/04/22/business/energy-environment/europes-carbon-market-is-sputtering-as-prices-dive.html.

Reichheld, Fred. *The Ultimate Question: For Opening the Door to Good Profits and True Growth*. Boston: Harvard Business School Publishing, 2006.

Reinvestment Fund, The. "Frequently-Asked Questions." http://www.trfund.com/about/faq.html.

Resource Generation. "Who We Are." http://www.resourcegeneration.org/Who/index.html.

Results for Development Institute. "Joint Learning Network for Universal Health Coverage. http://www.resultsfordevelopment.org/projects/joint-learning-network-universal-health-coverage.

Reynolds, Bruce. "Black Farmers in America, 1865–2000: The Pursuit of Independent Farming and the Role of Cooperatives." Rural Business-Cooperative Service, US Department of Agriculture, RBS Research Report 194, published October 2003. http://www.rurdev.usda.gov/rbs/pub/RR194.pdf;

Richter, Lisa. "Guide to Impact Investing." Grantmakers in Health, May 2011. http://www.gih.org/usr_doc/GIH_Guide_to_Impact_Investing_FINAL_May_2011.pdf.

Robeco and Booz & Co. "Responsible Investing: A Paradigm Shift." Published October 2008. http://www.booz.com/global/home/what-we-think/reports-white-papers/article-display/responsible-investing-paradigm-shift.

Roberts Enterprise Development Fund. "An Information OASIS." http://www.redf.org/learn-from-redf/publications/121.

ROC USA. "About Us—ROC USA." http://www.rocusa.org/about-us/background/default.aspx.

Rockefeller Philanthropy Advisors. *Diversity Funds Inventory*. New York: Rockefeller Philanthropy Advisors, August 2009.

Roddick, Anita. "A Dame of Big Ideas: The Sataya Interview with Anita Roddick." *Sataya Magazine*, January 2005. http://www.satyamag.com/jan05/roddick.html.

Rogers, Robin. "The Hidden Costs of Million-Dollar Donations." *Washington Post*, December 30, 2011. http://www.washingtonpost.com/opinions/the-hidden-costs-of-million-dollar-donations/2011/12/20/gIQAzpC1QP_story.html.

Rogner, H. H., Dadi Zhou, Rick Bradley. Philippe Crabbé, Ottmar Edenhofer, Bill Hare, Lambert Kuijpers, and Mitsutsune Yamaguchi. Introduction to *Climate Change 2007: Mitigation. Contribution of Working Group III to the Fourth Assessment Report of the Intergovernmental Panel on Climate Change*, ed. B. Metz, O.R. Davidson, P.R. Bosch, R. Dave, L.A. Meyer. New York: Cambridge University Press, 2007. http://www.ipcc-wg3.de/assessment-reports/fourth-assessment-report/.files-ar4/Chapter01.pdf.

Roob, Nancy. "$120 Million in Growth Capital Secured to Advance Opportunities for Low-Income Youth." Published June 2008. http://www.emcf.org/who/presidentspage/120millionsecured.htm.

Root Capital. "About Us." http://www.rootcapital.org/.

Rosenburg, Tina. "To Survive Famine, Will Work for Insurance." *New York Times*, May 12, 2011.

Ross, Stephen, Randolph Westerfield, and Jeffrey Jaffe. *Corporate Finance*. New York: McGraw-Hill/Irwin, 2006.

Roth, Jim, and Vijay Athreye. *TATA-AIG Life Insurance Company Ltd. India*. Geneva: Social Finance Programme, International Labour Organization, 2005.

Roth, Jim, Denis Garand, and Stuart Rutherford. "Long-term Savings and Insurance." In *Protecting the Poor: A Microinsurance Compendium*, ed. Craig Churchill. Geneva: International Labour Organization and Munich Re Foundation, 2006.

Roth, Jim, Michael J. McCord, and Dominic Liber. *The Landscape of Microinsurance In the World's 100 Poorest Countries.* Appleton, WI: Microinsurance Centre, 2007.

Roth, Lenny. "Social Impact Bonds." New South Wales Parliamentary Library Research Service, eBrief 17/2011, December 2011.

Rubin, Julia Sass, ed. *Financing Low Income Communities: Models, Obstacles, and Future Directions.* New York: Russell Sage Foundation, 2007.

Ruchismita, Rupalee, and Craig Churchill. "Microinsurance Development in India." In *Protecting the Poor: A Microinsurance Compendium*, vol. 2, ed. Craig Churchill and Michal Matul. Geneva: International Labour Organization and Munich Re Foundation, 2012.

Ruesga, Albert, and Dianne Puntenney. *Social Justice Philanthropy: An Initial Framework for Positioning This Work.* New York: Working Group on Philanthropy for Social Justice and Peace, 2010.

Rural Housing and Economic Development Gateway, U.S. Department of Housing and Urban Development. "Kentucky Highlands Investment Corporation." http://www.hud.gov/offices/cpd/economicdevelopment/programs/rhed/gateway/pdf/KentuckyHighlands.pdf.

Rutledge, Ann, and Sylvain Raynes. *Elements of Structured Finance.* Oxford: Oxford University Press, 2010.

Rutnik, Tracy A., and Jessica Bearman. *Giving Together: A National Scan of Giving Circles and Shared Giving.* Washington, DC: Forum of Regional Associations of Grantmakers, 2005.

Sack, Andy. "Godfather of Royalty-Based Finance." Interview by Arthur Fox. PE Hub, June 11, 2010. http://www.pehub.com/2010/06/11/arthur-fox-the-godfather-of-royalty-based-finance-on-what-vcs-are-missing.

Salamon, Lester M. *America's Nonprofit Sector: A Primer.* 3rd ed. New York: Foundation Center, 2012.

Salamon, Lester M. "Of Market Failure, Voluntary Failure, and Third-Party Government: Toward a Theory of Government-Nonprofit Relations in the Modern Welfare State." In Lester M. Salamon, *Partners in Public Service: Government-Nonprofit Relations in the Modern Welfare State.* Baltimore: Johns Hopkins University Press, 1995.

Salamon, Lester M. "Philanthropication thru Privatization: Building Permanent Assets for Social Progress." Il Mulino, 2014. http://ccss.jhu.edu/publications-findings?did=407.

Salamon, Lester M. "Privatization for the Social Good: A New Avenue for Global Foundation-Building." In *The Privatization Barometer Report: 2009*, ed. Privatization Barometer, July 2010.

Salamon, Lester M. *The Resilient Sector: The State of Nonprofit America.* Washington, DC: Brookings Institution Press, 2003.

Salamon, Lester M. *Rethinking Corporate Social Engagement: Lessons from Latin America.* Sterling, VA: Kumarian Press, 2010.

Salamon, Lester M. "The Rise of the Nonprofit Sector." *Foreign Affairs* 73.4 (July–August 1994): 109–22.

Salamon, Lester M., Editor. *The Tools of Government: A Guide to the New Governance.* New York: Oxford University Press, 2002.

Salamon, Lester M. "Tradable Tax Credits." *Chronicle of Philanthropy*, February 10, 2010. http://ccss.jhu.edu/tradeable-tax-credits-a-chronicle-of-philanthropy-op-ed-by-lester-salamon.

Salamon, Lester M. "What Would Google Do? Designing Appropriate Social Impact Measurement Systems." *Community Development Investment Review* 7.2 (December

2011): 43–47. http://www.frbsf.org/community-development/files/Investment-Review-Vol-7-Num-1.pdf.

Salamon, Lester M., and Stephanie L. Geller. "Investment Capital: The New Challenge for American Nonprofits." Listening Post Project Communiqué No. 5. Johns Hopkins Center for Civil Society Studies, 2006. http://ccss.jhu.edu/publications-findings?did=265.

Salamon, Lester M., Stephanie L. Geller, Kasey L. Spence, and S. Wojciech Sokolowski. "'Shovel-Ready' but Stalled: Nonprofit Infrastructure Projects Ready for Economic Recovery Support." Listening Post Project Communiqué No. 12. Johns Hopkins Center for Civil Society Studies, 2009. http://ccss.jhu.edu/publications-findings?did=257.

Saltuk, Yasemin. *A Portfolio Approach to Impact Investment: A Practical Guide to Building, Analyzing, and Managing a Portfolio of Impact Investments*. New York: J.P. Morgan Global Social Finance Research, October 2012.

Saltuk, Yasemin, Amit Bouri, and Giselle Leung. "Insight into the Impact Investment Market: An In-Depth Analysis of Investor Perspectives and Over 2,200 Transactions." J.P. Morgan Social Finance Research, December 14, 2011. http://www.thegiin.org/cgi-bin/iowa/download?row=334&field=gated_download_1.

Saltuk, Yasemin, Amit Bouri, Abhilash Mudaliar, and Min Pease. "Perspectives on Progress: The Impact Investor Survey." J.P. Morgan Global Social Finance, January 7, 2013. http://www.jpmorganchase.com/corporate/socialfinance/document/207350_JPM_Perspectives_on_Progress_2013-01-07_1018749_ada.pdf.

Saltzman, Sonia, and Darcy Salinger. "The Accion CAMEL, Technical Note." Published September 1998. http://www.mixmarket.org/sites/default/files/medialibrary/10011.150/CAMEL.pdf.

Santos, Filipe M. "A Positive Theory of Social Entrepreneurship" *Journal of Business Ethics* 111.3 (2012): 335–51.

Schmaedick, Gerald, ed. *Cost-Effectiveness in the Nonprofit Sector: Methods and Examples from Leading Organizations*. Westport, CT: Quorum Books, 1993.

Schneider, Pia, and François Diop. *Synopsis of Results on the Impact of Community-Based Health Insurance on Financial Accessibility to Health Care in Rwanda*. Washington, DC, World Bank, 2001.

Schwab Charitable Fund. "Schwab Charitable Treasury." http://www.schwabcharitable.org/pdf/Schwab_Charitable_Treasury.pdf.

Schwartz, Rodney. "Social Business." In *Sustainable Investing: The Art of Long Term Performance*, ed. Cary Krosinsky and Nick Robins, 137–48. London: Earthscan, 2008.

Schwartz, Rodney. *Social Investment*. London: ClearlySo, forthcoming.

Scott, Geri. *Funder Collaboratives: A Philanthropic Strategy for Supporting Workforce Intermediaries*. Boston: Jobs for the Future, March 2007.

Sebageni, Grace. *Assessing Demand for Microinsurance in Uganda*. Nairobi: MicroSave Africa, 2003.

Sebstad, Jennifer, and Monique Cohen. *Microinsurance: Risk Management and Poverty* Washington, DC: Consultative Group to Assist the Poor, 2001.

Securities Industry and Financial Markets Association. "U.S. Bond Market Outstanding." Published December 15, 2011. http://www.sifma.org/research/statistics.aspx.

SEEDCO Policy Center. *The Limits of Social Enterprise: A Field Study and Case Analysis*. New York: Seedco Policy Center, June 2007.

SeedStock. "USAID, Global Impact Investing Network Join to Create East Africa Agricultural Investment Fund." http://seedstock.com/2011/10/05/usaid-global-impact-investing-network-join-to-create-east-africa-agricultural-investment-fund/.

Seidman, Ellen. "Bridging the Information Gap between Capital Markets Investors and CDFIs." *Community Development Investment Review* 2.2 (2006): 36–39. http://www.frbsf.org/community-development/files/investmentreview.pdf.

Self-Help Credit Union. "Access to Capital." http://www.self-help.org/about-us/policy-initiatives/access-to-capital.

Self-Help Credit Union. "Our Mission." http://www.self-help.org/.

Self-Help Credit Union. "Self-Help Secondary Market." http://www.self-help.org/secondary-market.

Sepulveda, Leandro, Stephen Syrett, and Sara Calvo. "Social Enterprise and Ethnic Minorities." Third Sector Research Center Working Paper 48, 2010.

Shah, Anup. "Official Global Foreign Aid Shortfall: $4 Trillion." Global Issues, April 25, 2010. Last updated April 8, 2012. http://www.globalissues.org/article/593/official-global-foreign-aid-shortfall-over-4-trillion.

Shanmugalingam, Cynthia, Jack Graham, Simon Tucker, and Geoff Mulgan. "Growing Social Ventures." NESTA and Young Foundation, 2011. http://www.nesta.org.uk/library/documents/Growing_Social_Ventures_v10.pdf.

Sharma, Anupama, and Andrew Mude. "Livestock Insurance: Helping Vulnerable Livestock Keepers Manage their Risks." In *Protecting the Poor: A Microinsurance Compendium*, vol. 2, ed. Craig Churchill and Michal Matul. Geneva: International Labour Organization and Munich Re Foundation, 2012.

Sheehan, Sean. "Responsible Purchasing Network Trends 2009: The 'State' of Sustainable Procurement." Center for a New American Dream. http://www.responsiblepurchasing.org/publications/trends2009_naspo.pdf.

Shirky, Clay. *Here Comes Everybody: The Power of Organizing without Organizations*. London: Penguin, 2008.

Siegel, Dan, and Jenny Yancey. "Philanthropy's Forgotten Resource? Engaging the Individual Donor: The State of Donor Education Today and a Leadership Agenda for the Road Ahead." New Visions, 2003. http://www.hewlett.org/uploads/files/PhilanthropysForgottenResource.pdf, 16.

Siegel, Paul B., Jeffrey Alwang, and Sudharshan Canagarajah. *Viewing Microinsurance as a Social Risk Management Instrument*. Washington, DC: Social Protection Unit, World Bank, 2001.

SIFMA. "European Structured Finance Issuance." http://www.sifma.org/research/statistics.aspx.

SIFMA. "US ABS Issuance." http://www.sifma.org/research/statistics.aspx.

SIFMA. "US ABS Outstanding." http://www.sifma.org/research/statistics.aspx.

SIFMA. "US Mortgage-Related Issuance." http://www.sifma.org/research/statistics.aspx.

SIFMA. "US Mortgage-Related Outstanding." Published January 31, 2011. http://www.sifma.org/research/statistics.aspx.

Simkhada, Nav Raj, Sushila Guatam, Mira Mishra, Iswori Acharya, and Namrata Sharma. *Research on Risk and Vulnerability of Rural Women in Nepal*. Kathmandu: Center for Microfinance, 2000.

Simon, John, and Julia Barmeier. *More Than Money: Impact Investing for Development*. Washington, DC: Center for Global Development, 2010.

Sims, David, Katie Milway, and Carol Trager. "Finding New Leaders for America's Nonprofits." Bridgespan Group, 2009. http://www.bridgespan.org/Publications-and-Tools/Hiring-Nonprofit-Leaders/Hiring-Strategy/Finding-Leaders-for-America-s-Nonprofits.aspx#.UHg_n1FnAxE.

SJF Ventures. "Portfolio." http://www.sjfventures.com/portfolio.

Skipper, Harold. *Foreign Insurers in Emerging Markets: Issues and Concerns*. Washington, DC: International Insurance Foundation, 1997.

Skloot, Edward. "The Gated Community." *Alliance*, September 1, 2011. http://www.alliancemagazine.org/en/content/gated-community.

Skocpol, Theda. *Diminished Democracy: From Membership to Management in American Civic Life*. Oklahoma City: University of Oklahoma Press, 2003.

Sloss, Michael. "Aiding Resident Ownership in Manufactured-Home Communities: An Interview with ROC USA." Interview by Kim Martin. PRI Makers Network. http://primakers.net/files/Aiding%20resident%20ownership%20in%20manufactured-%20An%20interview%20with%20ROC%20USA%20%28edited%20ms%2012-17-2010%29.pdf.

Small Enterprise Education and Promotion Network. "About Us—SEEP." http://www.seepnetwork.org/Pages/AboutUS.aspx.

Smith, Ana, Eric Gerelle, Michiel Berende, and Grieve Chelwa. "The Technology Revolution in Microinsurance." In *Protecting the Poor: A Microinsurance Compendium*, vol. 2, ed. Craig Churchill and Michal Matul. Geneva: International Labour Organization and Munich Re Foundation, 2012.

Smith, Anja, Herman Smit, and Doubell Chamberlain. "Beyond Sales: New Frontiers in Microinsurance Distribution." In *Protecting the Poor: A Microinsurance Compendium*, vol. 2, ed. Craig Churchill and Michal Matul. Geneva: International Labour Organization and Munich Re Foundation, 2012.

Social Capital Partners. "Why SROI?" March 2009. http://socialcapitalpartners.ca/images/uploads/docs/Why_SROI_March_2009.ppt.

Social Enterprise UK. *Fightback Britain: A Report on the State of Social Enterprise Survey 2011*. London: Social Enterprise UK, 2011.

Social Finance. "Home." http://www.socialfinance.uk/print9.T.

Social Finance. "A New Tool for Scaling Impact: How Social Impact Bonds can Mobilize Private Capital to Advance Social Good." Social Finance, 2012. http://www.socialfinance.org.uk/resources/social-finance/new-tool-scaling-impact-how-social-impact-bonds-can-mobilize-private-capita.

Social Finance. "Social Finance Welcomes the Government's Initiative to Pilot Social Impact Bonds as Announced in Their Policy Paper 'Putting the Frontline First: Smarter Government' Launched Today by the Prime Minister." News release published December 7, 2009. http://www.socialfinance.org.uk/downloads/press_releases/Press%20Release%20SIB%20Dec%2009%20FINAL.pdf.

Social Finance. "Social Impact Bonds: Rethinking Finance for Social Outcomes." London: Social Finance, 2009. http://www.socialfinance.org.uk/sites/default/files/SIB_report_web.pdf.

Social Investment Forum. "About Us." http://www.socialinvest.org.

Social Stock Exchange. "Social Stock Exchange Home." http://www.socialstockexchange.com/sse/?page_id=11.

Somerville, Bill. *Grassroots Philanthropy: Field Notes of a Maverick Grant-maker*. San Francisco: Heyday Press, 2008.

Southern Bancorp. "Mission." https://banksouthern.com/mission/.

Starr, Kevin. "The Trouble with Impact Investing: P1." *Stanford Social Innovation Review* 23 (2011).

Statman, Meir. "Socially Responsible Mutual Funds." *Financial Analysts Journal* 56.3 (May–June 2000): 30–39.

Stegman, Michael, Roberto G. Quercia, and Walter R. Davis. "Sharing the Wealth through Homeownership: A Preliminary Exploration of the Price Appreciation Experiences of Low- and Moderate-Income Families Who Bought Homes under the Community Advantage Secondary Market Loan Program." Center for Community Capitalism, University of North Carolina, July 21, 2004, revised July 8, 2005. http://www.ccc.unc.edu/documents/ccc-sharethewealth.pdf.

Stein, Peer, Tony Goland, and Robert Schiff. "Two Trillion and Counting: Assessing the Credit Gap for Micro, Small, and Medium-Sized Enterprises in the Developing World." IFC and McKinsey and Company, 2010. http://www.mckinseyonsociety.com/downloads/reports/Economic-Development/Two_trillion_and_counting.pdf.

Strategic Development Solutions Group. "Strategic Development Solutions." http://www.sdsgroup.com/.

Strauss, William, and Neil Howe. *Millennials Rising: The Next Great Generation.* New York: Vantage, 2000.

Strom, Stephanie. "Confusion on Where Money Lent via Kiva Goes." *New York Times,* November 8, 2009.

SustainAbility. "Growing Opportunity." News release published March 28, 2007, http://www.sustainability.com/aboutsustainability/article_previous.asp?id=938.

Swack, Michael. "Expanding Philanthropy: Mission-Related Investing at the F.B. Heron Foundation." Carey Institute, University of New Hampshire, 2009. http://www.fbheron.org/documents/carsey_expanding_philanthropy_2009.pdf.

Sweat Free. "Policy List." http://www.sweatfree.org/policieslist.

Swiss Reinsurance Company Economic Research and Consulting. *Microinsurance: Risk Protection for 4 Billion People.* Zurich: Swiss Reinsurance Company, 2010.

Symbiotics. "Home." http://www.symbiotics.ch/en/index.asp.

Szubert, Dorata. *Understanding the Demand for Microinsurance in Albania: Results of Exploratory Qualitative Study.* Warsaw: Microfinance Centre, 2004.

Tactical Philanthropy. "All Donors Care about Impact." 2010. http://www.tacticalphilanthropy.com/2010/06/all-donors-care-about-impact.

Tansey, Charles, Michael Swack, Michael Tansey, and Vicky Stein. *Capital Markets, CDFIs, and Organizational Risk.* Durham, NH: Carsey Institute at the University of New Hampshire, 2010.

Taylor, Frederick W. *The Principles of Scientific Management.* New York: Norton, 1967.

TechSoupGlobal. "TechSoup Global by the Numbers, Quarterly Report, October 2010." http://www.techsoupglobal.org/press/selectcoverage.

Temkin, Kenneth, and Roger C. Kormendi. *An Exploration of a Secondary Market for Small Business Loans.* Washington, DC: Small Business Administration, 2003.

Teng, Shiree. *Packard Foundation Organizational Effectiveness.* Los Altos, CA: David and Lucile Packard Foundation, 2010.

Thomas, Landon, Jr. "As the Bailouts Continue in Europe, So Does the Flouting of Rules." *New York Times,* November 29, 2012.

Thornley, Ben, and Colby Dailey. "Building Scale in Community Impact Investing through Nonfinancial Performance Measurement." *Community Development Investment Review* 6.1 (2010): 1–46. http://www.frbsf.org/publications/community/review/vol6_issue1/Thornley_Dailey.pdf.

Thornley, Ben, and Colby Dailey. "Nonfinancial Performance Measurement." *Community Development Investment Review* 6.1 (2010).

Thornley, Ben, David Wood, Katie Grace, and Sarah Sullivant. "Impact Investing: A Framework for Policy Design and Analysis." Pacific Community Ventures and the Initiative for Responsible Investment at Harvard University. January 2011.

Tierney, Thomas J. "The Nonprofit Sector's Leadership Deficit." The Bridgespan Group. http://www.bridgespan.org/nonprofit-leadership-deficit.aspx?resource=Articles.

Tierney Thomas J., and Joel L. Fleishman. *Give Smart: Philanthropy That Gets Results.* New York: Public Affairs Press, 2011.

Timewell, Stephen. "Microfinance Gains Momentum." *The Banker,* February 2, 2005. http://www.thebanker.com/Banking/Retail-Banking/Microfinance-gains-momentum.

Tingerthal, Mary. "Turning Uncertainty into Risk: Why Data Are the Key to Greater Investment." *Community Development Investment Review* 2.2 (2006): 24–30.

TOMS. "Homepage." http://www.toms.com.

Toniic. "About: How It Works." http://toniic.com/about/how-it-works/.

Toniic. "About Toniic." http://toniic.com/index.php/about/.

Toniic. "Global Gathering." http://toniicglobalgathering.eventbrite.com/.

Toniic. "Home." http://toniic.com/index.php.

Toyama, Kentaro. "Lies, Hype, and Profit: The Truth about Microfinance." *The Atlantic,* January 28, 2011. http://www.theatlantic.com/business/archive/2011/01/lies-h ype-and-profit-the-truth-about-microfinance/70405/.

Toynbee, Polly. "Who's in the Market for Sub-prime Behaviour Bonds?" *The Guardian,* July 4, 2011, http://www.guardian.co.uk/commentisfree/2011/jul/04/sub-pr ime-behaviour-bonds-fools-gold.

Toyota. "Ideas for Good." http://www.toyota.com/ideas-for-good.

Transparencia Medica. "Home." http://www.transparenciamedica.com/.

Trelstad, Brian. "Simple Measures for Social Enterprises." *Innovations* 3.3 (Summer 2008). http://www.mitpressjournals.org/doi/pdfplus/10.1162/itgg.2008.3.3.105.

Triodos Bank. "Personal Savings Overview." http://www.triodos.co.uk/en/personal/ savings-overview/.

Tuan, Melinda. "Measuring and/or Estimating Social Value Creation: Insights into Eight Integrated Cost Approaches." Bill and Melinda Gates Foundation Impact Planning and Improvement Working Papers, December 2008. http://www.gatesfoundation.org/ learning/documents/wwl-report-measuring-estimating-social-value-creation.pdf.

Tuckman, Howard P., and Cyril F. Chang. "How Well Is Debt Managed by Nonprofits?" *Nonprofit Management & Leadership* 3 (Summer 1993): 347–61.

TurnAround Couriers. "About TurnAround Couriers." http://www.turnaroundcouriers. com/about/.

TurnAround Couriers. "TurnAround Couriers Social Return on Investment Report." 2004 to 2008 and the 6-year review 2002–2008. http://www.turnaroundcouriers.com/ about/social-audits.

Twersky, Fay, and Jed Emerson. "Webtrack and Beyond: Documenting the Impact of Social Purpose Enterprises: Profile of a Management Information System." In *REDF Box Set: Social Purpose Enterprises and Venture Philanthropy in the New Millennium.* San Francisco, CA: REDF, 1999. http://community-wealth.com/_pdfs/ articles-publications/social/report-redf99-2.pdf.

Tzetzes, John. *Book of Histories (Chiliades).* Trans. Francis R. Walton. Lipsiae, 1826.

UNEP Finance Initiative and UN Global Compact. "Principles for Responsible Investment." http://www.unpri.org.

United Kingdom, Cabinet Office, Office of the Third Sector. "Social Investment Wholesale Bank: A Consultation on the Functions and Design." July 2009.

United Nations. "Millennium Development Goals." http://www.un.org/millenniumgoals/.

United Nations Development Program. *Human Development Report.* New York: UN Development Program, 2011.

United Nations General Assembly, Twenty-Fifth Session, Official Records. "Resolutions Adopted by the General Assembly 1970." http://www.un.org/documents/ga/res/25/ ares25.htm.

United Nations Principles for Responsible Investment (UN PRI). "About Us." http://www. unpri.org.

United States Department of Agriculture Economic Research Service. "Global Food Markets: Global Food Industry Structure." http://www.ers.usda.gov/Briefing/ GlobalFoodMarkets/Industry.htm.

United States Department of Education. "Credit Enhancement for Charter School Facilities Program." http://www2.ed.gov/programs/charterfacilities/performance. html.

United States Department of Labor. "Interpretive Bulletin Relating to Investing in Economically Targeted Investments." EBSA Final Rules, published October 17, 2008. http://webapps.dol.gov/FederalRegister/HtmlDisplay.aspx?DocId=21631&AgencyId= 8&DocumentType=2.

United States Department of the Treasury. "Report to Congress on Supporting Organizations and Donor Advised Funds." Published December 2011. http://www. grassley.senate.gov/about/upload/Report-to-Congress-Sup-O rgs-and-DAF-FINAL-12-5-11-2.pdf.

United States Government Accountability Office. "Housing Finance: Expanding Housing Finance: Expanding Capital for Affordable Multifamily Housing." October 28, 1993. http://www.gao.gov/cgi-bin/getrpt?RCED-94-3.

United States Government Accountability Office. "Person-to-Person Lending: New Regulatory Challenges Could Emerge as the Industry Grows." July 2011.

United States General Accounting Office. "Community and Economic Development Loans: Securitization Faces Significant Barriers." October 2003.

United States Office of Management and Budget. "The President's Budget for Fiscal Year 2014." http://www.whitehouse.gov//omb/budget.

United States Patent and Trademark Office, Patent Technology and Monitoring Team. "U.S. Patent Statistics Chart Calendar Years 1963–2009." http://www.uspto.gov/web/ offices/ac/ido/oeip/taf/us_stat.htm.

United States Senate Committee on Finance, Charity Oversight and Reform. "Keeping Bad Things from Happening to Good Charities." Congressional hearing, June 22, 2004. http://www.finance.senate.gov/hearings/hearing/download/?id=066c0319-b 047-4bcb-b985-d7834070346e.

United States Small Business Administration. "7A Terms and Conditions." http://www. sba.gov/content/7a-terms-conditions.

United States Social Investment Forum Foundation. "Forum for Sustainable and Responsible Investment." http://www.socialinvest.org.

United States Social Investment Forum Foundation. "Report on Socially Responsible Investing Trends in the United States, 2010." http://ussif.org/resources/pubs/trends/ documents/2010TrendsES.pdf.

United States Social Investment Forum Foundation. "Sustainable and Responsible Investing Trends in the United States: 2012." US SIF Foundation, Forum for Sustainable and Responsible Investing, 2012.

University of North Carolina, Center for Community Capital. "Good Business and Good Policy: Finding the Right Ways to Serve the Affordable Housing Market." University of North Carolina, Center for Community Capital, July 2009. http://www.ccc.unc. edu/documents/CAP_Policy_Brief_July09.pdf.

Urban Institute. "Building a Common Outcome Framework to Measure Nonprofit Performance." September 2006. http://www.urban.org/UploadedPDF/411404_ Nonprofit_Performance.pdf.

Urban Partnership Bank. "Urban Partnership Bank—Foundations." https://www.upbnk. com/foundations.

Urschel, John C. "Coming out of the Green Closet: Wealth Discourse and the Construction of Social Change Philanthropies." In *Foundations for Social Change: Critical Perspectives on Philanthropy and Popular Movements*, eds. Daniel R. Faber and Deborah McCarthy, 245–70. Lanham, MD: Rowman & Littlefield, 2005.

USAID. *Assessment on How the Strengthening the Insurance Industry in Developing Countries Contributes to Economic Growth*. Washington, DC: USAID, 2006.

Vanguard Charitable. "Annual Report: Focus on Giving." Published June 30, 2009.

Vanguard Charitable Endowment Program. "Special Fund Allows Tax-Free IRA Gifts." https://www.vanguardcharitable.org/giving/news/news_specialfundallowstaxfreeiragifts_11072007.html.

Velasco, Carmen, and Andrea del Grando. "Resultados del Market Research para la Programa Financiera." ProMujer, June 2004.

Velasquez, Christa. Comments at Federal Reserve. "Advancing Social Impact Investment through Measurement." http://www.frbsf.org/cdinvestments/conferences/social-impact-investments/transcript/Velasquez_Panel_3.pdf .

Venture Philanthropy Partners. *Perception Matters: How VPP is Learning from Its Stakeholders: The Results of the Chatham Group Perception Study*. Washington, DC: VP Partners, 2009.

Venture Philanthropy Partners. "Social Outcomes: Missing the Forest for the Trees." http://www.vppartners.org/learning/papers-and-perspectives/chairmans-corner/social-outcomes-missing-forest-trees.

Venture Philanthropy Partners. "Venture Philanthropy 2002: Advancing Nonprofit Performance through High-Engagement Grantmaking." http://www.vppartners.org/sites/default/files/reports/full_rpt_0.pdf.

Venturesome. "Access to Capital: A Briefing Paper." CAF Venturesome, September 2009. http://evpa.eu.com/wp-content/uploads/2010/11/CAF-Venturesome-Access-to-Capital-20094.pdf.

Vera Institute of Justice. "Guardianship Practice: A Six Year Perspective." The Guardianship Project Issue Brief. Vera Institute of Justice, December 2011. http://www.vera.org/sites/default/files/resources/downloads/Guardianship-Practice-a-Six-Year-Perspective.pdf.

Vine, George. "Selling Affordable Housing Loans in the Secondary Market." *Community Development Investment Review* 2.1 (2006): 49–56. http://www.frbsf.org/community-development/files/cdireviewvol2issue12006.pdf.

Vogel, David. *The Market for Virtue: The Potential and Limits of Corporate Social Responsibility*. Washington, DC: Brookings Institution Press, 2005.

Volunteer Match. "Our 2011 Annual Report Infographic." http://blogs.volunteermatch.org/engagingvolunteers/2012/06/25/our-2011-annual-report-infographic-the-story-of-you/.

W.K. Kellogg Foundation. "Go: Investing for Impact—the Early Years." http://mdi.wkkf.org/Our-Process-and-Tools/Inside-the-MDI-Process.aspx.

Wade, Robert. *Governing the State: Economic Theory and the Role of Government in East Asian Industrialization*. Princeton: Princeton University Press, 2003.

Walsh, Mary Williams. "The Charitable Gift Fund Phenomenon: Is it a Boon for Nonprofits or a Ploy for Investors?" *New York Times*, 1999. http://www.tgci.com/magazine/The%20Charitable%20Gift%20Fund%20Phenomenon.pdf.

Warrell, Helen. "Bond Offers Return for Lower Offending." *Financial Times*, March 19, 2010. http://www.ft.com/cms/s/0/d9dca292-32f6-11df-bf5f-00144feabdc0.html.

Washington State Institute for Public Policy. "Benefits and Costs of Prevention and Early Intervention Programs for Youth." September 17, 2004. http://www.wsipp.wa.gov/rptfiles/04-07-3901.pdf.

Watson Wyatt Worldwide. "2008 Global Pension Assets Study." London: Watson Wyatt Worldwide, January 2008. http://www.watsonwyatt.com/research/pdfs/200801-GPAS08.pdf.

Weaver, Evan. "Marrying Cash and Change: Social 'Stock Markets' Spread Worldwide." *Christian Science Monitor*, August 30, 2012. http://www.csmonitor.com/World/Making-a-difference/Change-Agent/2012/0830/Marrying-cash-and-change-Social-stock-markets-spread-worldwide.

White, Allen. "Consumption, Commerce and Citizenship: Transforming Markets to Drive Sustainability." *People 4 Earth*, September 2009, 12–13.

White House Office of Management and Budget. "Paying for Success." http://www.whitehouse.gov/omb/factsheet/paying-for-success.

Wikipedia. "Venture Philanthropy." http://en.wikipedia.org/wiki/Philanthrocapitalism.

Wilkinson-Maposa, Susan, Alan Fowler, Ceri Oliver-Evans, and Chao F. N. Mulenga. *The Poor Philanthropist: How and Why the Poor Help Each Other*. Cape Town: University of Cape Town Graduate School of Business, 2009.

Willow Impact Investors. "About Us: Our Team." http://www.willowimpact.com/about-us/.

Willow Impact Investors. "Investment Policy." http://www.willowimpact.com/about-us/company/investment-policy.html.

Wilton, David. "Characteristics of Successful GPs in Emerging Markets." Emerging Market Private Equity Association, October 2010.

Wine, Elizabeth. "Helping the Poor Via the Capital Markets." Investment Dealers' Digest, February 28, 2005. http://www.highbeam.com/doc/1G1-129358437.html.

Winn, Doug. "Growing Pains." *Community Development Investment Review* 2.2 (2006) 29–33.

Wipf, John, and Denis Garand. "Performance Indicators for Microinsurance: A Handbook for Microinsurance Practitioners." 2nd ed. Ed. Bert Opdebeeck and Véronique Faber. ADA asbl, 2010. http://www.microinsurancenetwork.org/publication/fichier/KPI_MI_Handbook_v2_EN.pdf.

Wipf, John, Eamon Kelly, and Michael J. McCord. "Improving Credit Life Microinsurance." In *Protecting the Poor: A Microinsurance Compendium*, vol. 2, ed. Craig Churchill and Michal Matul. Geneva: International Labour Organization and Munich Re Foundation, 2012.

Wipf, John, Dominic Liber, and Craig Churchill. "Product Design and Insurance Risk Management." In *Protecting the Poor: A Microinsurance Compendium*, ed. Craig Churchill. Geneva: International Labour Organization and Munich Re Foundation, 2006.

Wolff, Henry W. *People's Banks: A Record of Social and Economic Success*. London: P.S. King & Son, 1910.

Wolk, Andrew. *Advancing Social Entrepreneurship, Recommendations for Policymakers and Government Agencies*. Cambridge, MA: Root Cause and the Aspen Institute, 2008.

Women's World Banking. "About WWB." http://www.swwb.org/.

Wood, Arthur. "Bottom-up and Top-down: A Sanitation Offer the Commercial Sector Cannot Resist?" Presentation during World Water Week, Stockholm, August 17, 2009, http://www.worldwaterweek.org/documents/WWW_PDF/2009/monday/K11/Presentation_2009_Stockholm_.pdf.

Wood, Arthur, and Maximilian Martin. "Market-Based Solutions for Financing Philanthropy." Viewpoints (UBS Philanthropy Services) 2006:58–63. http://www.impacteconomy.com/node/174.

Wood, William. "Role of the Financial Advisor." In *The Handbook of Fixed Income Securities*, ed. Frank Fabozzi, 47. New York: McGraw-Hill, 2005.

World Bank. "State and Trends of the Carbon Market 2010." World Bank, May 2010. http://siteresources.worldbank.org/INTCARBONFINANCE/Resources/State_and_Trends_of_the_Carbon_Market_2010_low_res.pdf.

World Bank. "State and Trends of the Carbon Market 2011." World Bank Group, 2011. http://siteresources.worldbank.org/intcarbonfinance/Resources.

World Bank, International Finance Corporation. "The Business of Health in Africa: Partnering with the Private Sector to Improve People's Lives." International Finance Corporation, 2007. http://www.unido.org/fileadmin/user_media/Services/PSD/BEP/IFC_HealthinAfrica_Final.pdf.

World Council of Credit Unions. *Statistical Report 2010*. London: World Council of Credit Unions, 2010.

World Health Organization. "Estimating Child Mortality Due to Diarrhea in Developing Countries." *Bulletin of the World Health Organization* 86.9 (September 2008). http://www.scielosp.org/scielo.php?script=sci_arttext&pid=S0042-96862008000900015&lng=en&nrm=iso.

World Health Organization. "Immunization against Diseases of Public Health Importance." Fact Sheet no. 288, March 2005. http://www.who.int/mediacentre/factsheets/fs288/.

World Health Organization, UNICEF, and World Bank. *State of the World's Vaccines and Immunization*. 3rd ed. Geneva: World Health Organization, 2009.

Wright, Graham. "The Power of Successful Market-Led Savings Mobilization." Published April 19, 2011. http://microfinance.cgap.org/2011/04/19/the-power-of-successful-market-led-savings-mobilisation.

WWF-UK. *Common Cause: The Case for Working with Our Values*. London: WWF-UK, 2010.

X PRIZE Foundation. "X PRIZE." http://www.xprize.org/.

Xu, Ke, David. B. Evans, Guido Carrin, Ana Mylena Aguilar-Rivera, Philip Musgrove, and Timothy Evans. "Protecting Households from Catastrophic Spending." *Health Affairs* 26.4 (2007): 972–98.

Yan, Wenli, Dwight V. Denison, and J. S. Butler. "Revenue Structure and Nonprofit Borrowing." *Public Finance Review* 37.1 (January 2009): 47–67.

Yetman, Robert J. "Borrowing and Debt." In *Financing Nonprofits: Putting Theory into Practice*, ed. Dennis R. Young, 243–70. Lanham, MD: AltaMira Press, 2007.

Young, Beth, Celine Suarez, and Kimberly Gladman. "Climate Risk Disclosure in SEC Filings." Ceres, June 2009. http://www.ceres.org/resources/repor.

Young, Dennis R., Lester M. Salamon, and Mary Clark Grinsfelder. "Commercialization, Social Ventures, and For-Profit Competition." In *The State of Nonprofit America*, 2nd ed., ed. Lester M. Salamon. Washington, DC: Urban Institute Press, 2012.

Yunus, Muhammad. "Letter from Nobel Laureate Professor Muhammad Yunus Addressed to Grameen Bank Members on his departure from Grameen Bank." http://www.grameen-info.org/index.php?option=com_content&task=view&id=1043&Itemid=0.

Žižek, Slavoj. "Nobody Has to Be Vile." *London Review of Books* 28.7 (2006): 10. http://www.lrb.co.uk/v28/n07/slavoj-zizek/nobody-has-to-be-vile.

INDEX